ENCYCLOPEDIA OF

URBAN STUDIES

Editorial Board

ENCYCLOPEDIA OF
URBAN STUDIES

edited by
RAY HUTCHISON
University of Wisconsin, Green Bay

volume
1

Los Angeles | London | New Delhi
Singapore | Washington DC

A SAGE Reference Publication

Copyright © 2010 by SAGE Publications, Inc.

For information:

SAGE Publications, Inc.
2455 Teller Road
Thousand Oaks, California 91320
E-mail: order@sagepub.com

SAGE Publications Ltd.
1 Oliver's Yard
55 City Road
London EC1Y 1SP
United Kingdom

SAGE Publications India Pvt. Ltd.
B 1/I 1 Mohan Cooperative Industrial Area
Mathura Road, New Delhi 110 044
India

SAGE Publications Asia-Pacific Pte. Ltd.
33 Pekin Street #02-01
Far East Square
Singapore 048763

Printed in the United States of America

Library of Congress Cataloging-in-Publication Data

Encyclopedia of urban studies/edited by Ray Hutchison.
    v. cm.
Includes bibliographical references and index.
ISBN 978-1-4129-1432-1 (cloth)
    1. Cities and towns—Encyclopedias. 2. Sociology, Urban—Encyclopedias. I. Hutchison, Ray.

HT108.5.E634 2010
307.76003—dc22   2009026609

This book is printed on acid-free paper.

10 11 12 13 10 9 8 7 6 5 4 3 2

Publisher:	Rolf A. Janke
Assistant to the Publisher:	Michele Thompson
Acquisitions Editor:	Robert Rojek
Developmental Editor:	Sara Tauber
Reference Systems Manager:	Leticia Gutierrez
Reference Systems Coordinator:	Laura Notton
Production Editor:	Tracy Buyan
Copy Editors:	Colleen Brennan, Jackie Tasch
Typesetter:	C&M Digitals (P) Ltd.
Proofreaders:	Kristin Bergstad, Rae-Ann Goodwin
Indexer:	David Luljak
Cover Designer:	Gail Buschman
Marketing Manager:	Amberlyn McKay

Contents

List of Entries

Reader's Guide

The *Encyclopedia of Urban Studies* is intended for a number of different audiences, ranging from high school students and teachers who require general information about topics that we have included here to advanced scholars who require an overview of topics not directly accessible in their area of study. This suggests that there are a number of ways to approach the encyclopedia—in other words, there are a number of ways to read the entries. In the following Reader's Guide, we suggest several ways to use this encyclopedia, whether you have picked up this volume to find information about a specific subject, or you are interested in a general overview of the field of urban studies.

At the beginning level, urban studies comprises a number of subfields within the more traditional disciplines that focus some part of their study of cities and urban life, as well as professional fields that deal with these topics. In addition to the entry on Urban Studies, there are entries on the following disciplines that contribute to urban studies:

Urban Anthropology
Urban Economics
Urban Geography
Urban History
Urban Planning
Urban Politics
Urban Psychology
Urban Sociology

Disciplinary Approaches in Urban Studies

The many urban disciplines have developed important concepts to explain both urban growth (urbanization) as well as characteristic features of urban life (urbanism). The encyclopedia includes entries on concepts in several of the disciplines:

Urban Economics
Affordable Housing
Deindustrialization
Developer
Downtown Revitalization
Ethnic Entrepreneur
Gentrification
Globalization
Growth Poles
Housing
Land Developer
Land Trust
Marxism and the City
Rent Control
Rent Theory
Tiebout Hypothesis
Uneven Development
Urban Agglomeration
Urban Planning

Urban Geography
City Map
Edge City
Exopolis
Fourth World

Racialization
Social Production of Space
Spaces of Difference
Spaces of Flows
Tourism
Urban Design
Urban Space

Sustainable Development
Community Planning
Developer
Downtown Revitalization
Environmental Justice
Environmental Policy
Growth Management
Housing
Neighborhood Revitalization
New Urbanism
Sprawl
Urban Planning
Urban Village
Waste

Urban Issues

Contemporary cities and urban regions confront a number of important issues, ranging from individual problems of poverty to societal problems of provision of adequate housing and social exclusion. While it is important not to problematize the city, the following entries discuss some of the important issues for urban studies in the twenty-first century.

Catastrophe
Crime
Deindstrialization
Disability and the City
Displacement
Drug Economy
Gentrification
Globalization
Healthy Cities
Homelessness
Marxism and the City
Nuclear War
Right to the City
Social Exclusion
Sprawl
Street Children

Suburbanization
Surveillance
Urban Crisis
Waste

Urban Planning

Urban planning represents a professional field that has long been associated with urban studies; a number of early urban planners, such as Patrick Geddes, were influential in the development of the field, and urban planning itself molds the urban environment where the subject matter of our field is found.

Advocacy Planning
Annexation
City Beautiful Movement
City Planning
Community Development
Convention Centers
Exclusionary Zoning
Garden City
Gender Equity Planning
General Plan
Growth Management
Housing
Planning Theory
Themed Environment
Tourism
Urban Design

Urban Theory

Cinematic Urbanism
Gemeinschaft and *Gesellschaft*
Globalization
Marxism and the City
Planning Theory
Stranger
Uneven Development
Urban
Urban Design
Urbanism
Urbanization
Urban Planning
Urban Semiotics
Urban System
Urban Theory
World-Systems Perspective

Urban Transportation

The study of transportation is an important subfield within urban studies; the entries included here reflect the fact that transportation systems have been important in the development of cities (Streetcars, Subway) and are an important part of planning for the urban future (Transit-Oriented Development):

Airports
Buses
Hotel, Motel
Journey to Work
New York World's Fair, 1939–1940
Railroad Station
SimCity
Streetcars
Subway
Transit-Oriented Development
Transportation Planning
Walking City

Urban Culture

Cities are said to represent the greatest achievement of human civilization, the place where culture and the great traditions are created and preserved. Entries in this category include those who create culture, varieties of urban culture, and urban life and lifestyles more generally.

Bohemian
Cinema (Movie House)
City Club
City Users
Creative Class
Flâneur
Graffiti
Hip Hop
Intellectuals
Landscapes of Power
Loft Living
Metropolis
Museums
Nightlife
Parks
Photography and the City
Placemaking
Public Art

Shopping
Simulacra
Skateboarding
Society of the Spectacle
Stranger
Urban
Urban Health
Urban Life
Urban Novel

Places

While metropolitan regions and individual cities often are the focus of study in urban studies, many other studies look at specific places within the urban environment, as seen in the following entries:

Airports
Banlieue
Barrio
Bazaar
Béguinage
Caravanserai
Convention Centers
Discotheque
Ethnic Enclave
Favela
Forum
Fourth World
Gated Community
Ghetto
Heterotopia
Metropolitan
Necropolis
Night Spaces
Piazza
Placemaking
Resort
Shopping Center
Sports Stadiums
Suburbanization
Technoburbs
Technopoles
Themed Environments
Toilets
Utopia
World Trade Center (9/11)
Zoöpolis

Cities

The encyclopedia includes entries on a number of cities. These entries include overview articles about cities in different historical periods (Renaissance City), regions of the world (Mediterranean City), and other categories that have been of importance in the development of urban studies (World City) There are also entries on specific cities (and their metropolitan regions) that are important because of their historical significance (Florence as the birthplace of the Renaissance and of Renaissance architecture and development of urban planning); examples of innovation in urban design and architecture (Bilbao); importance in the urban studies literature (London, New York City, and Tokyo are most frequently mention in the world city literature), and the like.

Historical Overviews
Allegory of Good Government
Capitalist City
Chinatowns
Colonial City
Divided Cities
Global City
Heritage City
Historic Cities
Ideal City
Informational City
Islamic City
Mediterranean City
Megalopolis
Multicultural Cities
Other Global Cities
Primate City
Progressive City
Renaissance City
Revanchist City
Situationist City
World City

Specific Cities
Amsterdam, the Netherlands
Berlin, Germany
Bilbao, Spain
Cairo, Egypt
Canberra, Australia
Chicago, Illinois
Damascus, Syria
Delhi, India
Florence, Italy
Hiroshima, Japan
Hong Kong, China
Istanbul, Turkey
Kolkata (Calcutta), India
Lagos, Nigeria
Las Vegas, Nevada
London, United Kingdom
Los Angeles, California
Manchester, United Kingdom
Manila, Philippines
Mexico City, Mexico
Moscow, Russian Federation
Mumbai (Bombay), India
New York City, New York
Paris, France
Rome, Italy
Santa Fe, New Mexico
Santiago de Compostela, Spain
São Paulo, Brazil
Savannah, Georgia
Shanghai, China
Singapore
Tokyo, Japan
Venice, Italy

Persons

The various urban disciplines have important figures that have influenced both the early development and current work in their field, and these persons are also listed in the urban disciplines (above). But a number of important figures in urban studies, such as Jane Jacobs and Lewis Mumford, were not trained in specific academic disciplines. The encyclopedia includes important scholars from many of the urban disciplines, as well as others who have had important influence on urban studies:

Alinsky, Saul
Alonso, William
Benjamin, Walter
Berry, Brian J. L.
Castells, Manuel
Childe, V. Gordon

About the Editors

General Editor

Ray Hutchison is Professor of Sociology and Chair of Urban and Regional Studies at the University of Wisconsin, Green Bay. He received his BA from the State University of New York at Binghamton, and his MA and PhD from the University of Chicago. Dr. Hutchison was Director of the HUD–Community Development Work Study Program at UW Green Bay and currently is Director of the Hmong Studies Center. His research has been funded by the U.S. Forest Service, National Institute of Mental Health, and the University of Wisconsin System Institute on Race and Ethnicity. He teaches Introduction to Urban Studies, Urban Sociology, The City through Time and Space, and Street Gangs in Urban America. He was a founding editor of *City & Community* and is a recipient of the International Award of Merit from the Fondazione Romualdo Del Bianco in Florence.

Dr. Hutchison is Series Editor of *Research in Urban Sociology* (the forthcoming tenth volume in the series, titled *Urban Life During Wartime,* is co-edited with Sonja Prodanovic from the Institute for Architecture and Town Planning, Belgrade). He is co-author (with Mark Gottdiener) of *The New Urban Sociology* (now in the fourth edition). He is the author of more than 40 articles, book reviews, chapters, and invited contributions to books and journals, including *Social Problems, City & Community, Journal of Marriage and the Family, Journal of Leisure Research,* and *Leisure Sciences,* and on topics ranging from street gangs and gang graffiti, Latino communities in Chicago and Asian American communities in Wisconsin and Minnesota, urban recreation, and leisure activities of ethnic populations. Dr. Hutchison organized sessions on *The Tourist City* as part of the 2008 Florence Festival sponsored by the Fondazione Romualdo Del Bianco, and serves as head of the planning committee for an international conference on *Everyday Life in the Segmented City* to be held in Florence in 2010.

Advisory Board

Manuel B. Aalbers, a human geographer, sociologist, and urban planner, is a researcher at the Amsterdam institute for Metropolitan and International Development Studies (AMIDSt), University of Amsterdam. From January 2007 until August 2008 he was a post-doctoral researcher at Columbia University, New York. He has been a guest researcher at the Center for Place, Culture and Politics at City University New York, the University of Milan–Bicocca, and the University of Urbino (Italy). Prior to working in academia, he was a researcher and consultant in housing and urban planning in the Netherlands and Belgium, and writer for an online music magazine.

Dr. Aalbers's main research interest is the intersection of finance, the built environment, and residents. He has published on redlining, social and financial exclusion, neighborhood decline, gentrification, the privatization of social housing, safety and security, public space, red-light districts, and the Anglo-American hegemony in academic research and writing. He is the author of a book on housing and community development in New York City and is preparing a manuscript for a book titled *Place, Exclusion and Mortgage Markets.* He is the guest editor of a special issue of the *International Journal of Urban and Regional Research* (volume 33, issue 2) on mortgage markets and the financial crisis, and the book review editor of *Rooilijn,* a Dutch urban studies/planning journal.

Robert A. Beauregard is a Professor of Urban Planning in the Graduate School of Architecture, Planning, and Preservation, Columbia University. He is director of the Urban Planning Program and chair of the Doctoral Program Subcommittee on Urban Planning. He teaches courses on planning theory, urban redevelopment policy, social theory, and research design. His PhD is in city and regional planning from Cornell University and he has a degree in architecture from Rhode Island School of Design. He previously taught at The New School, University of Pittsburgh, and Rutgers University and has been a visiting professor at University of California, Los Angeles and at the Helsinki University of Technology. In addition, Beauregard is a docent professor in the Department of Social Policy at the University of Helsinki and a part-time visiting professor in the Department of Geography, King's College, London.

Beauregard's research focuses mainly on urbanization in the United States with particular attention to industrial city decline after World War II—a story told in *Voices of Decline: The Postwar Fate of U.S. Cities* (2003)—and to current urban growth and decline with specific attention to resurgent and shrinking cities. He also writes on planning theory and urban theory. His most recent book is *When America Became Suburban* (2006). Currently, Beauregard is working on a comparative study of anti-urbanism, an interpretation of planning using actor–network theory, and an essay on truth and reality in urban theory. Future projects include a compilation of essays on urban epistemology titled *Writing Urban Theory* and an investigation of the reasons why some cities prosper while others do not, which will appear as a book titled *Why Cities Endure*.

Mike Crang is a Reader in Geography at Durham University. He has been at Durham since 1994 when he completed his PhD on the heritage industry at the University of Bristol, which had a concentration on urban pictorial and oral history. Since then his work has developed from looking at consumers of heritage to cultural tourism, to tourism more generally. He has written extensively on visual consumption and photography in tourism as well as other qualitative methods. He has edited two collections on tourism as well as coediting the journal *Tourist Studies*. He serves on the editorial board of *Environment and Planning A*, *Geography Compass* and for 10 years on that of *Social and Cultural Geography*.

His work on social memory has led to thinking through time and temporality in the city, and publication of *Thinking Space* (2000). He is also interested in more abstract issues regarding time–space, action, and temporality and coedited the journal *Time & Society* from 1997 to 2006. This focus on urban rhythms, spaces, and times led him to work on the transformations of space and time through electronic technologies, both theoretically and empirically, with Singapore's "Wired City" initiative and the "digital divide" in UK cities through an Economic and Social Research Council (ESRC) project on "Multi-speed Cities and the Logistics of Daily Life" and is now working on the notion of a "sentient city" and the politics of new forms of locative computing. Thinking through temporality and his work on urban ruins has led to work on wastescapes as part of a large ESRC project, "The Waste of the World." In total he has written and edited nine books and more than 50 articles and chapters.

Contributors

Manuel B. Aalbers
University of Amsterdam

Sheela Agarwal
University of Plymouth

Adrian Guillermo Aguilar
*Universidad Nacional
Autonoma de Mexico*

Gregory S. Aldrete
*University of Wisconsin,
Green Bay*

Nezar AlSayyad
*University of California,
Berkeley*

Harri Andersson
University of Turku

Alessandro Angelini
*The Graduate Center, City
University of New York*

John Armitage
University of Northumbria

G. J. Ashworth
University of Groningen

Blair Badcock
*Housing New Zealand
Corporation*

Carlos Balsas
Arizona State University

Tridib Banerjee
*University of Southern
California*

David W. Bartelt
Temple University

Murray Baumgarten
*University of California,
Santa Cruz*

Robert A. Beauregard
Columbia University

Harriot Beazley
University of Queensland

Barbara Becker
University of Arizona

Philip R. Berke
*University of North Carolina
at Chapel Hill*

Luca Bertolini
University of Amsterdam

Laurence Bherer
University of Montreal

Mike Biddulph
Cardiff University

David Bissell
University of Brighton

Iain Borden
University College London

Giacomo Bottà
University of Helsinki

Julie-Anne Boudreau
University of Quebec

Anna Maria Bounds
*Milano, the New School for
Management & Urban
Policy*

Alan Gerard Bourke
York University (Toronto)

Monique Bourque
Willamette University

David Boyce
Northwestern University

Bill Boyer
*Institute for the History
of the Production of
Knowledge*

Daniel Morgan Brooker
University of Durham

Gavin Brown
University of Leicester

Kyle D. Brown
*California State Polytechnic
University, Pomona*

Kath Browne
University of Brighton

Robert Buerglener
DePaul University

David Buisseret
The Newberry Library

Alessandro Busà
*Center for Metropolitan
Studies, Berlin*

Constance Carr
Humboldt University, Berlin

Andrew Thomas Carswell
University of Georgia

Ernesto Castañeda
Columbia University

Mary Ann Caws
*Graduate School, City
University of New York*

Sarah Chaplin
University of Greenwich

Igal Charney
University of Haifa

David Clapham
Cardiff University

Mark Clapson
University of Westminster

Matthew D. Cochran
University College London

Allan Cochrane
The Open University

Sarah Coffin
Saint Louis University

Claire Colomb
University College London

Mike Crang
Durham University

Laurence Crot
London School of Economics

Morten Daugaard
*Aarhus School of
Architecture*

Diane Davis
*Massachusetts Institute of
Technology*

Evelyne de Leeuw
Deakin University

Sabina Deitrick
University of Pittsburgh

Gerardo del Cerro Santamaría
*The Cooper Union for the
Advancement of Science an*

David Diaz
*California State University,
Northridge*

Edward Dimendberg
University of California, Irvine

Petra L. Doan
Florida State University

Bruce F. Donnelly
Independent Urban Planner

Michael Dudley
University of Winnipeg

Stephanie N. Duensing
University of Maryland

Len Duhl
*University of California,
Berkeley*

Claire Edwards
University College Cork

Bart Eeckhout
University of Antwerp

Paul Elliott
University of Nottingham

Graeme Evans
London Metropolitan University

David Victor-Harmen Evers
*Ministry of Housing, Planning
and Environment*

Paolo Favero
University College London

Marcia Marker Feld
University of Rhode Island

Barbara Ferman
Temple University

Maureen A. Flanagan
Michigan State University

William Flanagan
Coe College

Dean Forbes
Flinders University

Kathryn A. Foster
*State University of New York
at Buffalo*

Bridget Franklin
Cardiff University

Lance Freeman
Columbia University

Robert Freestone
University of New South Wales

Gerald E. Frug
Harvard University

Kuniko Fujita
Michigan State University

Gillian Fuller
University of New South Wales

Rolf Funck
University of Karlsruhe

Judith A. Garber
University of Alberta

Charles Gates
Bilkent University

Kristina E. Gibson
University of Connecticut

Graeme Gilloch
Lancaster University

Mary Gluck
Brown University

Greta Goldberg
Columbia University

Rubén Lois González
*University of Santiago de
Compostela*

Tracy M. Gordon
*University of Maryland,
College Park*

George Gorse
Pomona College

Aspa Gospodini
University of Thessaly

Kevin Fox Gotham
National Science Foundation

Mark M. Gray
Georgetown University

Clara Greed
University of the West of England

Rosalind Greenstein
Lincoln Institute of Land Policy

Jill Simone Gross
Hunter College of the City University of New York

Owen D. Gutfreund
Barnard College

Chris Hamnett
Kings College London

Keith N. Hampton
University of Pennsylvania

John Hannigan
University of Toronto

Ross Harley
University New South Wales

Hartmut *Häußermann*
Humboldt-Universität zu Berlin

Bruce D. Haynes
University of California, Davis

Jason Alexander Hayter
University of California, Berkeley

Sue Hendler
Queen's University

Stefan Höhne
Center for Metropolitan Studies

Adam Holden
Durham University

Meg Holden
Simon Fraser University

Eric Homberger
University of East Anglia, Norwich

Cynthia Horan
Yale University

Jyoti Hosagrahar
Columbia University

Phil Hubbard
Loughborough University

Edward H. Huijbens
Icelandic Tourism Research Centre

Ray Hutchison
University of Wisconsin, Green Bay

H. Patricia Hynes
Retired Professor of Environmental Health

Renee A. Irvin
University of Oregon

Michael D. Irwin
Duquesne University

Engin F. Isin
York University

Kurt Iveson
University of Sydney

Harvey M. Jacobs
University of Wisconsin, Madison

Jessica Jacobs
Open University

Robert A. Jacobs
Hiroshima Peace Institute

Johannes Jäger
University of Applied Sciences BFI Vienna

Russell Noel James
University of Georgia

Helen Jarvis
Newcastle University

Amy Elizabeth Johnson
Otterbein College

Janna Jones
Northern Arizona University

Paul Jones
University of Liverpool

Dennis R. Judd
University of Illinois at Chicago

Eun Jin Jung
Seoul National University

Akel Ismail Kahera
Prairie View A&M University

Paul Kantor
Fordham University

Judith T. Kenny
University of Wisconsin Milwaukee

Robert Kerstein
University of Tampa

Bart Keunen
Ghent University

Nikita A. Kharlamov
State University–Higher School of Economics

Chigon Kim
Wright State University

Yeong-Hyun Kim
Ohio University

Christopher Klemek
George Washington University

Robert C. Kloosterman
University of Amsterdam

James Kneale
University College London

Kenneth Kolson
Ohio State University

Constantine E. Kontokosta
Columbia University

Peter Kraftl
University of Leicester

Petra Kuppinger
Monmouth College

Michel S. Laguerre
*University of California,
    Berkeley*

Robert W. Lake
Rutgers University

Kimmo Lapintie
*Helsinki University of
    Technology*

Alan Latham
University College London

Alex Law
*University of Abertay at
    Dundee*

Ute Lehrer
York University

Panu Lehtovuori
Estonian Academy of Arts

Georg Leidenberger
*Universidad Autonoma
    Metropolitana–Azcapotzalco*

Charlotte Lemanski
University College London

Mark P. Leone
University of Maryland

Lila Leontidou
Hellenic Open University

Keith D. Lilley
Queen's University Belfast

Richard Lloyd
Vanderbilt University

Lyn H. Lofland
*University of California,
    Davis*

Dean MacCannell
University of California, Davis

Gordon MacLeod
Durham University

Katharina Manderscheid
Universität Basel

Maria-Jose Piñeira Mantiñan
*University of Santiago de
    Compostela*

Ann Markusen
*Humphrey Institute, University
    of Minnesota*

Eduardo Marques
University of São Paulo

Guido Martinotti
*SUM, Istituto Italiano di
    Scienze Umane, FI*

Margit Mayer
Freie Universität Berlin

David Mayernik
University of Notre Dame

Ruth McAreavey
Queens University Belfast

Keally McBride
University of San Francisco

Colin McFarlane
Durham University

Donald McNeill
University of Western Sydney

Gustavo S. Mesch
University of Haifa

Nadia A. Mian
The New School

Jennie Middleton
Cardiff University

Malcolm Miles
University of Plymouth

Don Mitchell
*Maxwell School, Syracuse
    University*

Circe Maria Gama Monteiro
*Universidade Federal de
    Pernambuco*

Terri Moreau
*Royal Holloway, University
    of London*

Richard Morrill
University of Washington

Eric Mumford
Washington University

David Murakami Wood
*University of Newcastle
    upon Tyne*

James M. Murray
Western Michigan University

Petter Naess
Aalborg University

Amos Nascimento
*University of Washington,
    Tacoma*

Zachary Neal
Michigan State University

Sionne Rameah Neely
*University of Southern
    California*

Arthur C. Nelson
University of Utah

Kathe Newman
Rutgers University

Walter J. Nicholls
*California State University,
    Long Beach*

Joshua Ben David Nichols
University of Toronto

Lars Nilsson
Stockholm University

Ayodeji Olukoju
University of Lagos

Michel O'Neill
Universite Laval

Nicole Oretsky
New School for Social Research

Itohan Osayimwese
*University of Washington,
Seattle*

Arthur O'Sullivan
Lewis & Clark College

Selma Akyazici Özkoçak
Bogazici University

Karina M. Pallagst
*University of California,
Berkeley*

Krista E. Paulsen
*University of
North Florida*

Deike Peters
Technical University Berlin

Edgar Pieterse
University of Cape Town

David Pinder
*Queen Mary, University of
London*

Elizabeth Plater-Zyberk
University of Miami

Patricia Baron Pollak
Cornell University

Jonathan Pratschke
University of Salerno

Milan Prodanovic
University of Novi Sad

Denise Pumain
University Paris I

Michael Punch
University College Dublin

Mrinalini Rajagopalan
*University of California,
Berkeley*

Xuefei Ren
Michigan State University

Jane Rendell
University College London

Ramon Ribera-Fumaz
*Universitat Oberta de
Catalunya*

Simon Richards
University of Leicester

Michael Ripmeester
Brock University

Eva Rosen
Harvard University

Ugo Rossi
University of Cagliari

Matthew Roth
Rutgers University

Tamar Y. Rothenberg
Bronx Community College

Ananya Roy
*University of California,
Berkeley*

Vincenzo Ruggiero
Middlesex University

Michael T. Ryan
*Dodge City Community
College*

Andrew Ryder
University of Portsmouth

Kim Rygiel
McMaster College

Susan Saegert
Vanderbilt University

Heywood Sanders
*University of Texas at San
Antonio*

H. V. Savitch
University of Louisville

Alex Schwartz
The New School

Amanda I. Seligman
*University of Wisconsin,
Milwaukee*

Gilles Sénécal
*Institut National de
Recherche Scientifique*

Mona Seymour
*University of
Southern California*

Robert Shaw
Durham University

Matti Siemiatycki
University of Glasgow

Michael Silk
University of Maryland

Walter Simons
Dartmouth College

William Sites
University of Chicago

Tom Slater
University of Edinburgh

Michael E. Smith
Arizona State University

Lydia M. Soo
University of Michigan

Geoff Stahl
*Victoria University of
Wellington*

Deborah Stevenson
*University of
Western Sydney*

Randy Stoecker
University of Wisconsin

Frederic Stout
Stanford University

Elizabeth L. Sweet
*University of Illinois at
Urbana-Champaign*

Malcolm Tait
University of Sheffield

Kian Tajbakhsh
Columbia University

Harold Takooshian
Fordham University

Serene K. Tan
York University

Nigel Taylor
University of the West of England

Jacques Thisse
Université Catholique de Louvain

Lorenzo Tripodi
Researcher in Urban Studies, Berlin

İpek Türeli
Brown University

Tracy Turner
Kansas State University

Zuhal Ulusoy
Izmir University of Economics

Anar Valiyev
Azerbaijan Diplomatic Academy

Joaquín Villanueva
Syracuse University

James Voogt
University of Western Ontario

Michiel Wagenaar
University of Amsterdam

David Wagner
University of Southern Maine

Allan D. Wallis
University of Colorado Downtown Denver Campus

Kevin Ward
Manchester University

Barney Warf
University of Kansas

Rachel Weber
University of Illinois at Chicago

Chris Webster
Cardiff University

Robert W. Williams
Bennett College

Robin Williams
Savannah College of Art and Design

David Wilson
University of Illinois at Urbana-Champaign

Ailsa Winton
National Autonomous University of Mexico (UNAM)

Robert Wojtowicz
Old Dominion University

Johan Woltjer
University of Groningen

Fulong Wu
Cardiff University

Brenda S. A. Yeoh
National University of Singapore

Tan Yigitcanlar
Griffith University

John Yinger
Syracuse University

Alford Young Jr.
University of Michigan

Douglas Young
York University

Belinda Yuen
National University of Singapore

Andrzej J. L. Zieleniec
Keele University

Doracie B. Zoleta-Nantes
University of the Philippines

Sharon Zukin
Brooklyn College and City University Graduate Center

Introduction

We live in an urban world. For the first time in human history, more than half of the world's population—some 3 billion persons—lives in urban areas. In the next two decades the number of persons living in urban areas will increase by another 2 billion persons—an amazing 60 percent increase—to 5 billion persons. The United Nations estimates that by 2030, more than two-thirds of total world population will live in urban areas. Most of this increase will take place not in Europe or in the United States, but in the megacities and newly emerging urban regions of countries in what used to be called the developing world.

These urban areas are linked in exciting and new ways that would have been unimaginable just a short time ago. We can text friends in other countries for a fraction of the cost of a long-distance telephone call, or SKYPE with family and colleagues on the other side of the world for even less. We are connected by a global economy where the life opportunities of persons in one country are dependent on capital flows of new investments from nations on the other side of the world. The mass media bring world music from Africa and the Middle East to balance the spread of hip hop and reggae. We use the Internet to make new friends in places we have never even heard of. At the beginning of the twenty-first century it is a global world, to be sure, but more than that, it is, for the very first time, an *urban world*.

The new urban world of the twenty-first century is the object of study for our field, urban Studies. There likely is no other more important area of study, for if we are to solve the very significant and growing problems of climate change and global inequality, among others, we must understand that these problems often are directly associated with the growing urban populations and cannot be solved without strategies that connect urban regions across international borders:

we know, for example, that the flow of undocumented workers from Africa to Europe is the consequence of economic disparities between these regions. Urban studies is the field of study that addresses both the growth and expansion of urban areas (urbanization) as well as the nature of and quality of urban life (urbanism)—the two most pressing areas of inquiry for the coming decades.

The specific areas of study in urban studies include subfields of the many disciplines that include the study of urban areas (such as urban anthropology, urban economics, urban geography, urban history, urban politics, urban psychology, and urban sociology), professional fields such as architecture and urban planning, and other fields such as art, literature, and photography that are situated within the built environment. Within each of these subfields and interdisciplinary areas, there are specific theories, key studies, and important figures that have influenced not just the individual discipline, but the field of urban studies more generally. Indeed, not only is the field of urban studies influenced by important work from the urban disciplines, but the disciplinary subfields themselves often share important bodies of work and even research traditions. To give but one example, the work of Henri Lefebvre has had profound influence not just in his home discipline of sociology, but in other disciplines including geography and political science—and across urban studies more generally.

In this encyclopedia, we have sought to include important work and traditions from each of the urban disciplines, but we also wanted to demonstrate the international and interdisciplinary nature of the field. To this end, we sought contributions from scholars in many different countries. Because certain areas of study have often been associated with particular countries (suburbanization in the

United States or gentrification in the United Kingdom, for example) we purposively sought authors from other countries to write these essays. And for each entry and we asked contributors to incorporate an international focus and to discuss the importance of the topic for urban studies more generally.

Rationale for Encyclopedia

Urban studies is an expansive and growing field, covering many disciplines and professional fields, each with its own schedule of conferences, journals, and publication series. While much of the important work in the field is published in the interdisciplinary urban studies journals, the volume of published work presents a challenge for researchers who wished to stay abreast of recent developments in the field. Add to this the many volumes of original research, and the increasing number of edited collections published each year, and it quickly becomes overwhelming for even advanced scholars to follow the many new lines of development. The *Encyclopedia of Urban Studies* is intended to present an overview of current work in the field and to serve as a guide for further reading in the field.

The encyclopedia will serve as an introduction to important topics in urban studies for an audience including undergraduate students, beginning graduate students of urban studies, and the related urban disciplines, a broader public that has an interest in the new urban world, and even established teachers and scholars who are exploring new areas of study. It should be noted that although the *Encyclopedia of Urban Studies* is intended to be comprehensive in its coverage of topics, it is not meant to provide comprehensive treatments of any single topic; we provide references for further reading on each topic and invite our audience to explore further the important work in our field.

Content and Organization

The encyclopedia is intended to provide comprehensive coverage of topics currently studied in urban studies. This is a difficult goal, and we recognize that there is not unanimous consensus on what such a list would look like. This is particularly the case with urban studies, a relatively new and rapidly evolving area of study that brings together scholars and research traditions from many different disciplines and professional fields.

Our approach has been to be as comprehensive as possible, and all entries include several associated topics and cross-references. In some cases, a topic that was covered in the context of larger topic may not receive its own entry; in those cases, the smaller topic is listed with a cross-reference to the entry in which it is discussed.

To help the reader navigate the encyclopedia, a Reader's Guide is provided, organizing the content into major areas of study (the urban disciplines) and topics (such as the city and film) as well as important figures in the field. There also is an alphabetical listing of all entries for both volumes.

The content of each entry is intended to be a concise summary of the major aspects of the topic. Authors were asked to present their entries in a nontechnical manner accessible not just to academics in the field but also to a wider audience of persons interested in learning more about urban studies. Finally, each entry is intended to give readers an overview of the topic, with suggested readings that will allow readers to learn more about the literature in the area and explore selected topics in greater depth.

We have included a number of entries for individual cities, some because of historical importance (Santiago de Compostela, a world heritage conservation site, was an important medieval pilgrimage site, and the Camino de Santiago was a major trade route connecting France with the Iberian peninsula), their connection with other entries (Venice is often discussed as the preeminent tourist city, while Las Vegas has long served as a topic of discussion for urban theory), others because of their importance within urban studies (London, Paris, and Tokyo have become the three cities most identified with the literature on world cities).

How This Encyclopedia Was Created

Development of the *Encyclopedia of Urban Studies* involved many steps, from beginning work done by a select group of scholars to writing of entries to editing the completed volumes:

Step 1—A select group of senior scholars worldwide was invited to serve on the editorial board; these individuals were selected to represent the breadth of study across disciplines and international focus of the field.

Step 2—A master list of topics for the book was created from multiple sources. First, a preliminary list of headwords was created from the indexed keywords from articles published the previous five years in major journals in the field, indexed entries in textbooks in the field, and a page-by-page search of indexed keywords from representative books in several urban studies disciplines. We also invited members on urban studies e-mail lists (including scholars in many disciplines and from many countries) to submit their suggestions for entries. The resulting list was then reviewed by the entire editorial board, and we then made a series of additions and subtractions. We also included topics that are not readily found in published sources to date but that we felt were just on the cusp of becoming mainstream, given their treatment in recent journal articles. Time will tell the extent to which we have accurately forecast the viability of these topics.

Step 3—We sought to recruit an international group of scholars from the many disciplines and professional fields that comprise urban studies. As we finalized our list of entries, members of the editorial board identified contributors for each entry, and invitations were sent to these persons. We invited authors from all career stages, ranging from established senior scholars to promising young doctoral students, as well as practitioners from many fields. In relatively few cases our invitations were declined (usually due to time commitments from senior scholars), but in these cases we often received suggestions of authors who were then invited to contribute to the encyclopedia.

Step 4—Contributors were provided with guidelines and instructions regarding the preparation of their entries.

Step 5—The editors reviewed each of the submitted draft entries in their area of study and requested revisions from the authors when necessary. Most entries were revised at least once prior to their acceptance for the encyclopedia.

Step 6—The senior editor reviewed the copyediting for all of the entries.

Ray Hutchison

Acknowledgments

The development of a project of the scale and scope of the *Encyclopedia of Urban Studies* requires the efforts of many persons over an extended period of time. The master list of entries and contributors was assembled by a group representing many fields of studies and several regions: Robert A. Beauregard (Columbia University); Mike Crang (Durham University); Nan Ellin (Arizona State University); Ray Hutchison (University of Wisconsin, Green Bay), and Carlos Reboratti (University of Buenos Aires). The actual contacts and invitations to contributors and the review of submissions for the main part of the project were handled by Robert A. Beauregard, Ray Hutchison, and Mike Crang. Manuel B. Aalbers (University of Amsterdam) joined us for the final half-year of the project to help finalize entries and contributors. Many colleagues from our wider urban studies family offered suggestions for entries and volunteered to contribute essays, although it was not possible to include all such topics and entries even in a two-volume encyclopedia.

The very experienced and talented publishing team at SAGE deserves special consideration, including Robert Rojek (who first contacted me about the project), Sara Tauber (who worked with the project from the very beginning), Colleen Brennan and Jackie Tasch (a team of very impressive copy editors), and Tracy Buyan (who oversaw the final project). And special consideration also to Rolf Janke, publisher of SAGE Reference, who provided support for the project at several critical junctures.

In the middle stage of the project I was unable to provide full attention to the encyclopedia because of a family emergency. Bob Beauregard made a continuing and sustained contribution to the project during this period, and I owe a special acknowledgement to him for his support before, during, and after this very difficult period.

And finally, a shout out to family and friends, at the University of Wisconsin, Green Bay, at the Del Bianco Foundation in Florence, in Buffalo and Glasgow and Bologna, and especially to Dulce Reyes Hutchison and to our daughters: Heather at Georgetown, Leilani at ASPIRO, and Jessica at Red Smith, who together will inhabit the new urban world of the twenty-first century.

Ray Hutchison

Acropolis

The term *acropolis* (Greek for "high city") denotes the hilltop citadel that dominated the topography of many ancient Greek cities. Thanks to the frequency of rugged landscapes, cities in the ancient Greek world, from Sicily to the Black Sea, often established themselves on high ground, later expanding down the slopes to areas below. However, not all cities were located on varied terrain; those on flat land, along coasts or in plains, could not have an acropolis.

Although an acropolis would be suited first and foremost for defense, fortification was not its sole function. Such a hilltop might have been used for a variety of purposes: as a settlement with houses, even palaces, and as a religious center. Indeed, as cities expanded, adding new fortification walls to enclose larger territory, the importance of the acropolis as a place of protection often declined. The rich history of the Acropolis of Athens from ancient to modern times illustrates different functions these urban hilltops have had over the centuries.

The Athenian Acropolis

In the Late Bronze Age, the Mycenaeans fortified the hilltop. The huge blocks of their defense walls survive in a few places. A royal palace is assumed to have existed, but evidence is scanty. Circa 1200 BC, a cleft in the rock of the north slope, a vertical cavity 30 meters (98 feet) deep, was turned into a protected water supply for those inside the citadel.

Erechtheum, Acropolis of Athens

Source: Vasilis Gavrilis.

1

Steps were installed from the top, and a deep well was dug at the bottom. After only 25 years the lower part of this "fountain house" collapsed; the shaft was then used as a garbage dump.

By the Classical period, the Acropolis had become the main religious center of Athens. The buildings of the mid- to late fifth century BC, the high point of Athenian power, are the best known: the Parthenon (the temple of Athena Parthenos), the Erechtheion (a temple-shrine sheltering several cults), the Temple of Athena Nike, and the Propylaia, the ingenious entrance gate. In between these and other buildings, statues and other offerings left by the pious filled the hilltop. The slopes of the Acropolis were utilized for theaters (the Theater of Dionysos and, added in Roman times, the Odeion of Herodes Atticus) and a variety of shrines and monuments.

In medieval and early modern times, as the population of Athens declined, the city retreated to the Acropolis and its north slope. A church was installed inside the Parthenon; in Ottoman times, the church was replaced with a mosque. The hilltop was fortified once again. Franks converted the Propylaia into a castle; Ottomans used the Parthenon for storage of gunpowder (exploded by Venetian artillery in 1687). Modest houses densely filled the spaces between the reused Classical buildings.

In the 1830s, when Athens became the capital of newly independent Greece, the Acropolis was radically altered. The hilltop promptly became an archaeological site. Postclassical constructions were stripped away in order to expose the buildings of the fifth century BC. The Acropolis, now turned into an expression of the glory of ancient Greece, would become a symbol of the new nation. This symbolism continues today. The Athenian Acropolis is Greece's premier tourist destination, and both by day and, floodlit, by night, the Parthenon dominates the skyline of central Athens.

Charles Gates

See also Agora; Ancient Cities; Athens, Greece; Mediterranean Cities

Further Readings

Camp, John M. 2001. *The Archaeology of Athens.* New Haven, CT: Yale University Press.
Hurwit, Jeffrey M. 1999. *The Athenian Acropolis.* Cambridge, UK: Cambridge University Press.
Wycherley, R. E. 1978. *The Stones of Athens.* Princeton, NJ: Princeton University Press.

ADVOCACY PLANNING

Advocacy planning represents a departure from scientific, objective, or rational planning, which was the dominant paradigm of the post–World War II era. It is premised upon the inclusion of the different interests involved in the planning process itself.

Advocacy planning was defined and promoted by planner and lawyer Paul Davidoff. The concept was first widely disseminated to other professional planners in Davidoff's 1965 article in the *Journal of the American Institute of Planners,* "Advocacy and Pluralism in Planning." Davidoff sought to provide an answer to a critical question that arose in urban planning in the late 1950s and early 1960s: "Who speaks for the poor, the disenfranchised, and the minorities?" He introduced the question "Who is the client?" into professional usage as well as "Who is the stakeholder or the constituent?" He was concerned that planning decisions significantly impacting urban neighborhoods were made with little or no representation from the residents. Because the residents of the target area of the planning process usually are neither skilled in nor knowledgeable about planning, they are unable to participate effectively in the planning decision process. They require professional representation equal to that of the official planners—those of the municipality or the land developer. Davidoff's view was that each of the interests in the planning process needed to be served and represented by a professional planner with equal knowledge and skill. The fundamental values of advocacy planning in the planning process are those of social justice and equity.

Advocacy Planning and Its Paradigm

The advocacy planning paradigm is predicated upon the concept of pluralism in planning. Davidoff argued that the goal of the planning process is to determine which of several alternative scenarios or vision-plans will be adopted and implemented. Each respective outcome has different benefits and costs to each of the groups involved in the planning decisions. Thus there would be no one single plan that would constitute the "right plan" for all.

The central aspect is the use of values as well as facts in making planning decisions. The process is explicitly not value neutral. The choices are driven by political and social issues rather than technical ones. Another significant point is the notion of pluralism in planning. For each planning situation a number of groups with different interests are involved. Given that situation, advocacy dictates that different planners represent competing visions of the future in the planning process. An advocate planner will represent one interest group, and other planners will represent different constituencies, including the municipal citywide perspective. This process, which joins together a geographic area, such as neighborhood, is the basis of understanding a pluralistic plan. The planner is, above all, an advocate planner serving the client groups who are unskilled and lack the appropriate knowledge for making planning decisions.

Davidoff answers his question in his article by designating as the client "the Negro and the impoverished individual." In this situation, one planner represents one special interest group. The advocacy paradigm asserts that a professional whose skills and political status are equal to those of the representatives of the municipality or the land developer will be present and identified as the planner for the neighborhood residents. Different planners, therefore, will represent different special interests in the planning process.

Davidoff led a small group of trained planners for whom advocacy planning was a normative commitment; these planners worked in a number of communities, preparing vision-plans. Davidoff was the leading spokesperson for these neighborhood residents in both his writing and his practice. A revered and respected activist–academic in the field of modern city planning, he was an unyielding force for justice and equity in planning. Davidoff viewed the city through a pluralistic lens, while he addressed a wide range of societal problems. He challenged academics and professionals alike to find ways to promote participatory, pluralistic planning and positive social change; to overcome poverty and racism; and to reduce the many-faceted disparities in society. He implemented major contributions to the planning field as an educator, practitioner, and intellectual, and

his influence on urban planning extends to this day. His work in advocacy planning constitutes a watershed in the theory and practice of American community planning.

Advocacy and Rational Comprehensive Planning

Davidoff contrasted advocacy planning with the rational comprehensive planning process that was the dominant paradigm in the 1960s and the 1970s. A significant distinction between the two models lies in the role of values as a key element of the planning process. The critical questions are "Where do values enter the planning process?" and "Is this a valid use of values clarification?" Another critical question is "Who is the client?" The differences in the two planning models (see Table 1) are found in the definition of *client* and the role of values in decision making. The central issue is whether the planning process is an objective, scientific, and technical endeavor or a normative question.

Critique of Advocacy Planning

Those critical of advocacy planning are traditional planners who are disturbed by the notion of pluralism and the consideration of multiple interests in the planning process. Some contend that many planning issues do not have an optimal solution; this is often reflected by the work of the municipal government, often resulting in inequitable solutions whereby clients are not equally served.

Pluralism and the identification of a client or special interest group are high on the advocate planner's list of important changes to be made rather than planning for the public as a whole. This approach is predicated on the notion of pluralism, whereby there is an acknowledgment of the number and kinds of social and political views available for inclusion into the neighborhood plan. More traditional planners find this a specious argument. Pluralism, they say, is a social myth created by those who would hide the growing economic concentration in cities and direct social and economic programs to the disadvantaged.

The advocate planner is one who is committed to the notion of pluralism in making planning decisions and does not represent central interests. He or she feels that there should be a plurality of

Table 1   Comparison of the Rational Comprehensive Planning and the Advocacy Planning Models

Processes	Rational Planning	Advocacy Planning
Assumptions	Perfect information Rational outcomes One solution is best City is a system of interrelated functions	Imperfect information Non–value-neutral decisions Pluralistic society Normative planning is rational Each group is entitled to its own planner Different outcomes benefit different interests
Client	Community as a whole Property owners	"The Negro and the impoverished" or poor, powerless, minority persons One or more interest groups
Public interest	Unitary public interest	Plural special interests
Role of planner	Advisor to political decision maker Technician	Expert advice
Locality of planning process	Municipality bureaucracy	Community-wide
Goals of paradigm	Hierarchy of goals Physical land use goals	Access, skills used for pluralistic clients Represent minority interests Citizen participation
Resource allocation	Through planning process	Redistribution of wealth and public power increases the choices for poor
Public participation	Public hearings	Coalition building
Planning methods	Comprehensive rational process Value-neutral Physical land use based	Policy techniques Rational model
Definition	Value-neutral, factual Procedural process Begin with goals Rationality and choice Decision making	Facts and values as decisions Procedural process and pluralistic society Normative planning is rational Each group has its own advocate Client centered and future oriented

Source: Marcia Feld.

plans than rather a single one in order to appropriately represent the neighborhood. The municipal government, when faced with a number of plans for one neighborhood, must select one of them. This kind of situation has led to issues of ethics and loyalty for the planners. When the municipal decision maker identifies with the one view representing the central public interest rather than select a plan from the several plans that have been developed specifically for the different groups in the neighborhood, this attitude can lead to inside-government divisions popularly known as "guerrillas" in the bureaucracy. Representing the public interest is the traditional view of the planner's role and has been the modus operandi of almost all planners in the United States. Some think that to change this approach by responding to the various interests rather than synthesizing them into one public interest would not suit the U.S. urban planning field.

The second issue presented by traditional planners argues that decisions in which values are utilized jointly with factual matters are unable to be substantiated in a technical or scientific mode. This approach, rational comprehensive planning, presupposes a series of steps developed by logical sequential thinking not open to the values and loyalties of the political context by which planning decisions are actually made. Unlike the mainstream U.S. planner, the advocate planner denies that planning decisions can be value free. As Davidoff said in his article, "Solutions to questions about the share of wealth…to go to different classes cannot be technically derived; they must arise from social attitudes."

Advocacy Planning in the United States

Planners for Equal Opportunity

In 1964, just prior to the publication of Davidoff's watershed article, the American Planning Association held their annual meeting in Newark, New Jersey. Walter Thabit, an advocate planner in New York, with strong commitments to Davidoff, attended the association meeting and met with various groups of students, young faculty, and practitioners. Together, under his tutelage, they founded Planners for Equal Opportunity, a national network of advocate planners. Chester Hartman, an academic and a political activist, chaired it for many years. Present and involved was the architect C. Richard Hatch, who organized the Architects' Renewal Committee in Harlem. These two groups operated primarily in New York City where Walter Thabit, as an advocate planner for the Peter Cooper Square community, led the fight against the Robert Moses urban renewal proposal to wipe out 11 blocks in the Lower East Side. The Cooper Square plan, developed by Thabit and others, was designed to hold 60 percent of all housing units for low-income housing. After many years, it was selected over the Robert Moses urban renewal plan.

Planners for Equal Opportunity formally ended in 1975. Its work has been extended and continued by two sustained efforts: the Planners Network and the equity planning movement. The Planners Network, a loosely held organization of progressive planners has membership throughout the United States and is chaired by Dr. Tom Angotti

of the Hunter College Planning School. The equity planning paradigm broadens the notion of client group to all interest groups in the community, broadening the scope of the most important social equity movement in the field, advocacy.

Equity Planning Movement

The equity planning movement was created and implemented by Norman Krumholz, the city planning director for Cleveland, Ohio. Fundamentally the movement is based on an expanded definition of the client for the redistributive resource process. It is the modern response to the racial crisis in urban areas, according to June Manning Thomas and others. It provides a location for all the people who have few if any choices. Pragmatic, not ideological, decisions shape the equity planning agenda. Equity planning is about working within the municipal planning structure to give special attention to the needs of poor and vulnerable populations, who also suffer from racial and sexual discrimination. However, the work need not be limited to the confines of the typical governmental structure nor need it follow past government decisions. Urban planners can break through the bonds of previous years and develop and implement new policies that reach out to the poor and minorities in the urban place.

Suburban Action Institute

As a professional planner, Davidoff put advocacy planning into practice. He founded the Suburban Action Institute, which challenged exclusionary zoning in New Jersey. A precedent-setting case involved the township of Mount Laurel. The case stemmed from an attempt by Mount Laurel to prevent the building of 36 apartments intended for working-class Black residents in the community. In 1975, the court ruled that the township's zoning ordinance was a form of economic discrimination that favored middle- and upper-income people. It was not until 1983, however, that the court issued Mount Laurel II, which served as a companion decision by establishing a formula for providing a fair share of affordable housing. In 1985, a Mount Laurel III (of sorts) took place as the New Jersey State Legislature, acting on Mount Laurel II, established the Council on Affordable Housing. The debate on this issue continues to this day.

Global Advocacy Planning

Advocacy at the global level is a method and process of influencing decision makers and the public perceptions of concerned persons; it mobilizes community action to achieve social change. The goal is to create an enabling environment—one where laws and public policy protect and promote rights and responsibilities. The strategies include an emphasis on partnerships with nonprofit organizations and on research case studies and policy areas. The content focuses on environmental justice, public health issues such as AIDS, and public housing. Advocacy strategies are emphasized primarily in the field of architecture as well as planning and other urban development professions.

Advocacy planning's global application differs from its application in the United States in several ways: First, the geographic unit treated in Europe and the United Kingdom usually targets national and international levels of government, whereas the United States focuses on neighborhoods and local municipalities. Second, different questions are raised by international advocate planners than by U.S. advocate planners; U.S. advocate planners raise such framing issues as "Who is the client?" and "Which or whose values are considered?" International planners reference the public interest broadly. Third, U.S. advocate planners interact primarily on the ground, whereas European planners shift their methodology to planning and policy analysis techniques. The international model focuses on conceptual distinctions, which differs from the U.S. emphasis on local issues and problems.

Marcia Marker Feld and
Patricia Baron Pollak

See also Citizen Participation; Planning Theory; Progressive City; Urban Planning

Further Readings

Angotti, Tom. 2007. "Advocacy and Community Planning: Past, Present and Future." Planners Network. Org/Publications. (Revised February 9, 2009.) Retrieved March 22, 2009 (http://www.planners network.org/publications/2007_spring/angotti.htm).

Checkaway, Barry. 1994. "Paul Davidoff and Advocacy Planning in Retrospect." *Journal of the American Planning Association* 60(2):139–61.

Clavel, Pierre. 1986. *Progressive City Planning and Participation, 1969–1984.* New Brunswick, NJ: Rutgers University Press.

Davidoff, Paul. 1965. "Advocacy and Pluralism in Planning." *Journal of the American Institute of Planners* 31(4):331–37.

Davidoff, Paul and Thomas Reiner. 1962. "A Choice Theory of Planning." *Journal of the American Institute of Planners* 28:103–31.

Feld, Marcia Marker. 1986. "Planners Guilty on Two Counts: The City of Yonkers Case." *Journal of the American Institute of Planners* 52:387–88.

———. 1989. "Paul Davidoff Memorial Symposium, Equity, Empowerment and Planning: Lessons from the Yonkers Case." *Journal of Planning Education and Research* 8:167–96.

Hartman, Chester. 2002. *Between Eminence and Notoriety.* New Brunswick, NJ: Center for Urban Policy Research.

Kennedy, Marie. 2007. "From Advocacy Planning to Transformative Community Planning." Planners Network.Org/Publications. (Revised February 9, 2009.) Retrieved March 22, 2009 (http://www .plannersnetwork.org/publications/2007_spring/ kennedy.html).

Krumholz, Norman and Pierre Clavel. 1994. *Reinventing Cities.* Philadelphia: Temple University Press.

Krumholz, Norman and John Forester. 1990. *Making Equity Planning Work: Leadership in the Public Sector.* Philadelphia: Temple University Press.

Legates, Richard L. 1996. *The City Reader.* Independence, KY: Routledge Press.

Levy, John. 1997. *Contemporary Urban Planning.* Upper Saddle River, NJ: Prentice Hall.

Mazziotti, Donald. 1974. "The Underlying Assumptions of Advocacy Planning: Pluralism and Reform." *Journal of the American Planning Association* 40(1):38–47.

Meyerson, Martin and Edward Banfield. 1955. *Politics, Planning and the Public Interest.* London: The London Free Press of Glencoe.

Piven, Frances Fox. 1970. "Whom Does the Advocate Planner Serve?" *Social Policy* 5:32–37.

AFFORDABLE HOUSING

The term *affordable housing* addresses the relationship between the cost of providing adequate housing and a household's ability to pay. Housing affordability is measured as a percentage of income:

Housing that consumes less than 30 to 40 percent of total household income is considered affordable. People at any income level can find affordable housing a problem, but it mostly afflicts poor and middle-class households since the private market rarely produces a sufficient amount of housing to meet their needs. As a result, governments often regulate housing and finance markets and provide subsidies to ensure that housing is affordable to households no matter their income.

In the United States, the U.S. Department of Housing and Urban Development has created a measure called the area median income (AMI) to determine who needs affordable housing. It is a relative measure of housing need and is calculated separately for metropolitan areas and families of different sizes. Most often, households with incomes less than 30 percent of the AMI are considered very low income, those with incomes 30 to 50 percent are low income, 50 to 80 percent are moderate income, and those above 80 percent are thought able to afford market rate housing. Because housing costs vary by locality, so also does affordability. In cities like New York City, it can reach 200 percent of the AMI.

The AMI has enabled governments to determine how many households need housing and to set guidelines for housing subsidies. Governments can provide subsidies to developers to produce additional housing units, or they can provide subsidies to individuals or building owners to make existing units affordable. Incentives for private developers include tax abatements, zoning changes, height allowances, infrastructure improvements, and financing assistance. Governments can also impose rent regulations that limit rental price increases.

In 1937 the federal government expanded its housing commitment by funding public housing construction, and in 1949 it established the goal of providing a "decent home and suitable living environment for every American family." Between the 1930s and the 1970s, the federal government produced public housing for very-low-income groups. In the 1970s, it shifted from public production and ownership to strategies that used subsidies to make existing private housing more affordable and spur the creation of new affordable housing in weak urban markets. In the 1980s the federal government withdrew from housing production almost entirely and left affordable housing construction and management to nonprofit, community-based organizations. New financial intermediaries—organizations that directed capital from financial markets to communities—such as the Local Initiatives Support Corporation and the Enterprise Foundation emerged to finance inner-city and rural housing construction. Federal efforts turned toward creating tax incentives. The 1986 Low Income Housing Tax Credit, which provides tax benefits to private investors, has created much of the affordable housing in the past 20 years. Little of this housing is affordable to very-low-income households without additional subsidies such as housing vouchers. Unlike the subsidies provided for public housing, which were largely permanent, the private subsidies from the 1970s and 1980s are time delimited; that is, they are designed to expire and thus significantly reduce the stock of affordable housing.

The debate about how best to provide affordable housing continues. Some argue that the increasing production of luxury housing will increase the availability of lower-income housing through a filtering process. Others argue that only vast production schemes will meet the needs of low-income communities. Who should provide the subsidies, who should be responsible for production and ownership, and who should receive these subsidies are questions that continue to be debated.

Kathe Newman

See also Fair Housing; Gentrification; Homeownership; Housing Policy; Right to the City

Further Readings

Bauman, John F., Roger Biles, and Kristin M. Szylvian, eds. 2000. *From Tenements to the Taylor Homes.* University Park: Pennsylvania State University Press.

Bratt, Rachel, Michael Stone, and Chester Hartman. 2006. *A Right to Housing: Foundation for a New Social Agenda.* Philadelphia: Temple University Press.

Schwartz, Alex. 2006. *Housing Policy in the United States: An Introduction.* New York: Routledge.

AGORA

Agora, a Greek word meaning, in early times, "a gathering place" (Homer), later "marketplace," is used in English particularly to denote the commercial and civic center of an ancient Greek city.

The Latin equivalent of agora is *forum*. The functions of the agora were much more varied than the English translations of the term might suggest. Typically located in the geographical heart of a city, on low-lying ground below the acropolis ("high city"), the agora was a place where people came together for a great range of activities: not only commercial, but also political, religious, and social. The overall layout of an agora followed no specific design. In cities of remote origins and long history, such as Athens, the agora developed gradually over centuries, its buildings and monuments placed according to the needs of a particular time. By the later Hellenistic and Roman periods, such city centers must have seemed like architectural jumbles. In newly founded cities, such as Priene (from the fourth century BC), the agora could be neatly planned, typically a rectangular plaza lined with stoas (porticoed buildings).

The ancient Greeks developed specific building types to house functions routine in the agora, such as the stoa and the *bouleuterion* (council chamber). One would also see such structures as fountain houses (where people obtained fresh water) and temples. In addition, certain activities might take place in buildings or areas that seem generic; that is, their features do not reveal any specific purpose. Identifying what uses such buildings or spaces were put to thus becomes an archaeological puzzle.

The best known of the ancient Greek agoras is that of Athens. The reasons for this are two. First, the great majority of Greek texts known to us were written by Athenians. Books, essays, speeches, poems, plays (tragedies, comedies), and inscriptions (documents carved on stone, for the attention of the public) contain a wealth of information about the life of Athens, including its agora. Second, the Athenian Agora has been explored continuously since 1931 (except for the years of World War II and immediately after), through archaeological excavations conducted by the American School of Classical Studies at Athens. These excavations have uncovered an enormous richness of buildings, monuments, inscriptions, and objects. In addition, the findings have been well published, both for a scholarly audience and for the interested public. So important is the Athenian Agora for understanding the ancient Greek city center that the rest of this entry is devoted to it.

Agora in Athens
Source: Vasilis Gavrilis.

The Athenian Agora

The Agora is located on low ground northwest of the Acropolis, a natural hill used in Greek and Roman times as the main religious center of the city. Agora and Acropolis together formed the central focus of Athens. The territory occupied by the Agora was further defined by a hill on the west (the Kolonos Agoraios) and a small river (the Eridanos) on the north, but was open to the east. Variously used in the Bronze Age and early Iron Age for housing and for burials, the Agora was first laid out as a public center in the early Archaic period, circa 600 BC. By 500 BC, vertical shafts of marble were set up at entrances to the open area to mark the space formally. These boundary stones were inscribed, "I am the boundary of the Agora." In addition, basins for holy water (*perirrhanteria*) were placed at the entrances, recalling the sacred character of certain functions. Indeed, those guilty of certain types of behavior were considered to have violated this sanctity and so could not enter the Agora: traitors, those who avoided military service or deserted, and those who mistreated their parents.

By 400 BC the character of the Agora as the civic center was well defined, thanks to the buildings erected during the previous 200 years. The Agora continued to serve as civic center through the Roman Empire, even with many changes to its buildings and monuments. During the Middle Ages, however, after devastating attacks on the city by such outsiders as Herulians (in 267) and Visigoths (395), and as political structures and socioeconomic needs veered away from Greco-Roman habits, the buildings of the Agora gradually fell into ruin. The area was transformed into a residential district, a character that would change only with the start of excavations in modern times.

Civic Buildings

During the period 600 to 400 BC, the west and south sides of the Agora were lined with major civic buildings. A look at their design and usage gives some insight into the nature of political and civic life in Athens.

The stoa was a favorite building type for public spaces such as an agora. Simple in concept, a stoa consisted of a roofed space, normally rectangular in plan, walled at the rear and on the sides, but with columns on the front. The stoa was thus a kind of portico. More complex designs might include shops at the rear, a second row of columns down the center, and even an upper story. This sheltered space could be used for many functions, official and informal. In the Athenian Agora, early stoas included the Royal Stoa (probably sixth century BC, rebuilt in the fifth century BC) and the Painted Stoa, or Stoa Poikile (475–450 BC), both located in the northwest sector. The former served as the seat of the king archon, the second-in-command of the city government. The Painted Stoa was so called after the paintings on wooden panels displayed inside, famous depictions of Athenian military prowess. Battles illustrated were both mythical, such as against Amazons, and real, notably the Battle of Marathon (490 BC), in which the Greeks defeated the Persians. The paintings survived until the late fourth century AD, emblems of Athenian greatness on permanent public view.

Government buildings located along the west side of the Agora at the base of the hill, the Kolonos Agoraios, included two bouleuterions (an "old" one, ca. 500 BC, later replaced by a "new" one, ca. 415–406 BC), the seat of the *boule,* the council of 500 men serving for one year that enacted legislation. Each structure must have looked like a small indoor theater, with seating on three sides. With the building of the New Bouleuterion, the Old Bouleuterion was transformed into the Metroon, a shrine to the Mother of the gods, but used also for the storing of archives. Next to these two was the Tholos (ca. 470–460 BC), a round building used as the dining hall of the *prytaneis,* the executive committee of 50 men that ran the daily affairs of the city, a rotating contingent of the council of 500. Nearby stood the Monument of the Eponymous Heroes (originally ca. 425 BC; rebuilt ca. 330 BC), a key center for disseminating information to the public. This monument consisted of a long, tall, narrow base with, on top, bronze statues of the mythical heroes representing the 10 tribes into which the Athenian citizenry had been divided during the political reforms of Kleisthenes, 508–507 BC. Below the statues, notices were posted, announcing legislation that would be introduced, military conscription, court hearings, and the like.

Other civic buildings included law courts, attested from written sources but not easily identifiable among the architectural remains; a prison; and a mint. This last, originally from the late fifth century BC, was a square building that contained evidence of bronze working: slag, water basins, and many bronze coin-blanks intended to be stamped as: coins.

Religious Buildings and Monuments

Religious practices in the Athenian Agora are reflected in numerous buildings and monuments. Crossing the Agora on the diagonal, from northwest to southeast, was the Panathenaic Way, the processional route used for the most important religious festival of the Athenians, the Panathenaia, a yearly festival in honor of Athena, the city's patron goddess. The route ran from the Dipylon Gate to the Acropolis, the center of Athena's cult. By this street, in the northwest corner of the Agora, stood the important Altar of the Twelve Gods, originally established in 521 BC, a square enclosure marked by a low wall, with an altar in the center. Here, suppliants were granted refuge. In addition, distances from Athens were measured from this point.

The grandest of the religious buildings was the Hephaisteion, a temple for both Hephaistos, god of the forge, and Athena, built on the Kolonos Agoraios. It continues to dominate the area, overlooking the Agora from the west. Built in the mid to late fifth century BC, this Doric order temple owes its excellent preservation largely to its long use as a Christian church.

Commercial Activities

A major commercial building was the South Stoa I, a long stoa that lined the south edge of the Agora. First erected in 430 to 420 BC, it was replaced in the second century BC by a complex of two stoas (Middle Stoa and South Stoa II) that together formed an enclosed rectangular space, the South Square. South Stoa I contained rooms at the rear that served as dining rooms, evidently necessary components of the businesses that operated here.

Just outside the formal boundaries of the Agora, numerous workshops were found. Trades attested include the manufacture of pottery and terracotta figurines, bronze and iron working, sculpture and other marble working, and shoemaking. Also in the area were wine shops and private houses.

Dedications by Foreign Rulers

Lastly, the interest of foreign rulers in Athens is worth noting. Although Athens lost its military and economic edge after its defeat in the Peloponnesian War in the late fifth century BC, the prestige of the city as an intellectual and cultural center continued undiminished. As a result, the city was granted handsome benefactions during Hellenistic and Roman times. One striking addition to the Agora was the Stoa of Attalos, a magnificent two-storied stoa placed along the east edge of the area, the donation of Attalos II, king of Pergamon (ruled 159–138 BC). Reconstructed in 1956, the stoa today serves as the museum for the Agora and the headquarters of the Agora excavations. Roman gifts

included a large Odeion, a covered concert hall, given by the emperor Augustus's son-in-law Agrippa in circa 16–12 BC, and a basilica (a three-aisled hall, for administrative and business matters) and a nymphaion (an elaborate fountain building), built during the reign of Hadrian (ruled AD 117–138).

Charles Gates

See also Acropolis; Ancient Cities; Athens, Greece

Further Readings

Camp, John M. 1992. *The Athenian Agora. Excavations in the Heart of Classical Athens.* Updated ed. London: Thames and Hudson.
———. 2001. *The Archaeology of Athens.* New Haven, CT: Yale University Press.
Camp, John M. and Craig Mauzy. 2007. *The Athenian Agora: A Guide to the Excavations and Museum.* 5th ed. Princeton, NJ: American School of Classical Studies at Athens.
Wycherley, R. E. 1978. *The Stones of Athens.* Princeton, NJ: Princeton University Press.

AIRPORTS

Airports are important transportation and communication nodes in the network age. As essential hubs in the global urban fabric, they show the extent to which the traffic of digital information, people, and things depends on high-speed logistical systems. The growth in world air travel relates directly to the major developments in globalization and demonstrates the extent to which the process of modernization is being rolled out across the first world and "developing" countries. To this extent, airports provide "early warning" signals or "laboratory conditions" for the study of global networks and information flows. This is particularly evident in the post–September 11, 2001, context, which has seen the intensification of data profiling, biometrics, and other intrusive security measure being trialed and tested throughout many international air terminals in the name of passenger safety and risk management. Although airports have always been important markers in the spectacularization of technology, it is important to consider the different ways in which technology has been implemented at the airport over the past 100 years.

The airport is one of the most significant sites of human–machine interaction in contemporary life. The airport is the site par excellence where multiple networks—both human and nonhuman, global and local—interact across multiple scales. In such a context, a new set of concerns needs to be taken into account when considering the human and cultural factors at play in everyday networks, not only those that are specifically concerned with aviation. This interaction of scale can be seen at the airport as increasingly mammoth: Airplanes interface with passengers, who are scanned and checked down to scales as minute as the irises of their eyes. Further, the ability of digital technologies to duplicate, distribute, and manipulate data has enabled networks to converge in an unprecedented fashion. "Hard" and "soft" networks (like technical infrastructure, code and information flows, the flesh of the passenger, and metal of the plane) can no longer be considered as discrete and separate.

The Birth of the Aerodrome

The modern airport evolved out of the converging operations of commercial, governmental, military, and private interests. The first structures built for air travel were largely produced in an ad hoc and unplanned manner. Runways, passenger terminals, and communication networks were constructed with little concern for logistical interconnection or future development. Initially aviation was not seen as suitable for mass transportation and was developed mainly for mail and small freight services. Due to the danger and discomfort of early planes, the transportation of human cargo was seen primarily as the preserve of a small and daring mobile elite. Passenger services were initially dependent on government policies that linked profitable mail contracts to the less profitable cargo of human passengers.

Moreover, government authorities were not keen to invest in the necessary infrastructure involved in this costly mode of transportation, and as a consequence, aviation regulation and planning was largely neglected. For this reason the growth of complex urban infrastructure around the early aerodromes quickly outstripped their original usage, and surrounding hinterland gradually became annexed as part of the growing regime of the airport. Many cities whose major airport developed out of the first aerodrome soon found their airport's physical capacity for expansion severely limited by the growth of suburban and exurban developments. This, coupled with a growing need for local, state, and national government regulation led to a number of crises that culminated during the immediate post–World War II period. Aided by the huge investments in aviation design and infrastructure made during war time, aviation as a mode of mass passenger transport began to boom.

As aircraft design and flight times improved, air travel became desirable and potentially profitable. In the years following World War II, urban planners and architects began envisaging a future in which air travel would facilitate new business opportunities on an international scale. Various design styles for both terminals and airports were trialed during this period. Large hall structures, satellite designs, and terminals encircling ring roads were all tried, each attempting to resolve logistical issues of getting passengers to terminal to plane, and plane to terminal to runway as seamlessly as possible.

The Airport as Mass Transportation Hub

Passenger services had always been one of the least stable sectors of aviation and remain secondary to military aviation in terms of profitability as well as research and development. Civil aviation, like telecommunications, has had vigorous competition on the profitable main routes, and airlines have had national obligations to service less-profitable regional routes. The introduction of jet aircraft such as the Boeing 707 (itself a spin-off of military aviation research) provided a major boost to the flagging civil aviation industry. Faster, quieter, more comfortable, and able to fly longer without refueling, jets began to make passenger services financially viable. The first full jet services in the early 1960s spawned a new popular vision of aviation as accessible to the "common person"—flight itself became a commodity.

Jet age airports staged this popular vision by way of their architecture, entwining capitalism and glamour in order to invoke a particularly optimistic vision of the future. Their individualistic shapes and vaulting interiors helped promote the idea that anyone could access the limitless horizons that had previously been the provenance of the rich and powerful. The age of the jet set popularized the practice of global travel and put it up for sale as a piece of the future, as part of progress.

Airports are extremely sensitive to global, cultural, and technological developments. They are constantly upgrading, adapting for bigger planes, more traffic, increased security measures, and for the frequent flying population (for whom perpetual transit is becoming a way of life). Few of the early airports remain, either being subsumed within larger structures, such as Heathrow in London or John F. Kennedy Airport in New York, or decommissioned entirely (e.g., Templehof in Berlin was decommissioned in 2008).

Hong Kong International Airport

The growth in world air travel relates directly to major developments in globalization, and is an essential part of the process of modernization that continues to advance (apparently unhindered by diminishing natural resources and associated problems of environmental degradation) across the first world and increasingly in so-called developing countries (Asia in particular). The huge amount of corresponding infrastructure required to manage the rapid movement of goods and people across large distances has led to innovations in the practice, procedure, and construction of airports and their related facilities. Many international airport terminals are built by well-known architects, such as Norman Foster, Paul Andreu, and Helmut Jahn, and are spectacular displays of a nation's ability to participate in the global economy.

Contemporary airports are a central part of the ubiquitous global networks that constitute contemporary spaces of flow. Due to their interconnected nature and the enormous loads of traffic that they process, recently built airports bear little resemblance to their jet age forebears. Modern airports—like cyberspatial networks—are designed according to a logic of procedures, exchanges, and traffic flows. Regardless of location they facilitate global procedures and follow standardized global signage using internationally agreed upon pictograms and typefaces.

Airports are first and foremost cultural nodes in a new form of global architecture based on networks. Like cyberspatial networks, airports defy traditional geography. Their architectures privilege connection, movement, and transience: They are highly procedural and operate across global and local institutions. The most recent iterations of airports resemble a convergence of shopping mall and glass tube, which regardless of the "brand name" architects (such as Paul Andreu's Dubai airport or Norman Foster's design for Hong Kong) all necessarily resemble each other. As modern air travelers traverse the globe, they move from one glass tube to another, taking in similar panoramic views of the tarmac procedures and airline livery while inside the terminal. With the exception of tourist shops selling local kitsch (windmill refrigerator magnets in Holland, stuffed kangaroos in Sydney, etc.), the traveler experiences a global shopping mall where Western commercial franchises sell identical electronic goods, fashions, cosmetics, and coffee. Contemporary airports render the experience of transit as a shopping experience that punctuates the intrusive surveillance systems that passengers must submit to in order to be able to fly.

New Direction in Mobility Research and Airports

In a world of constant mobility, information, and architecture convergence, bodies have quite significantly changed their relations to space. All modes of movement are increasingly subject to the same regimes of verification and control. At the airport, a complex series of discreet procedures (such as passenger and baggage processing by airline and government agencies, the turnaround of planes on the tarmac, and the management of ground and air traffic) are perfectly synchronized. Such precision is enabled by digital networks, systems of surveillance, and tracking techniques. Such synchronization and control is common in modern logistics companies, which can operate on some levels as "closed systems" within purpose-built informational networks that provide an integrated infrastructure across all operations. Such seamless integration is not possible at the airport where there is no one system that can manage and control all operations. The airport must remain for its own economic survival an open system. It necessarily needs to find ways to continually absorb new networks and their associated viral contaminations, such as monitoring people's temperature during a SARS (severe acute respiratory syndrome) outbreak or adapting to procedural changes stemming from the USA PATRIOT Act.

Contemporary airports are monumental structures designed to facilitate movement and are fully integrated into metropolitan infrastructures and global social panics. For this reason these spaces (airports, information networks, highways, and ports) are becoming crucial sites of political and technological activity as the global flow of information, people, and things intensifies.

Gillian Fuller and Ross Harley

See also Architecture; Transportation; Transportation Planning

Further Readings

Augé, Marc. 1995. *Non-places: An Introduction to an Anthropology of Supermodernity*. Translated by J. Howe. London: Verso.

Castells, Manuel. 1998. *The Rise of the Network Society*. Oxford, UK: Blackwell.

Cwerner, S., S. Kessering, and J. Urry, eds. 2009. *Aeromobilities: Theory and Research*. London: Routledge.

Edwards, Brian. 1998. *The Modern Terminal: New Approaches to Airport Architecture*. London: Spon.

Fuller, G. and R. Harley. 2004. *Aviopolis: A Book about Airports*. London: Blackdog.

Gordon, Alistair. 2008. *Naked Airport: A Cultural History of the World's Most Revolutionary Structure*. Chicago: University of Chicago Press.

Gottdiener, Mark. 2000. *Life in the Air*. Lanham, MD: Rowman and Littlefield.

Iyer, Pico. 2000. *The Global Soul: Jet Lag, Shopping Malls, and the Search for Home*. New York: Vintage Books.

Koolhaas, Rem, et al. 2001. *Mutations: Harvard Project on the City*. Barcelona, Spain: Actar.

Pascoe, David. 2001. *Airspaces*. London: Reaktion Books.

Pearman, Hugh. 2004. *Airports: A Century of Architecture*. London: Abrams.

Rossler, Martha. 1998. *In the Place of the Public: Observations of a Frequent Flyer*. Frankfurt, Germany: Cantz Verlag.

Salter, Mark B. 2008. *Politics at the Airport*. Minneapolis: University of Minnesota Press.

ALINSKY, SAUL

Saul Alinsky is often referred to as the father of American community organizing, though his influence was felt mostly in the United States rather than in the rest of "America." The civil rights movement was also important for generations of community organizers, but Alinsky was the strongest influence on neighborhood-based community organizing, which is the practice of bringing people together face to face to solve local problems and, sometimes, to change the distribution of power.

Alinsky was born in 1909 and grew up in Chicago, where the urban culture shaped his strategies of political action. As an undergraduate and then graduate student at the University of Chicago, he was greatly influenced by the criminologists there. He found himself impatient with the academics' emphasis on studying community change and became more interested in actually creating change.

Consequently, in the late 1930s when he was supposed to be studying juvenile delinquency in Chicago's notorious Back of the Yards neighborhood, he found himself fascinated by the struggle of the stockyards workers there to form a union. Socializing with union organizers and learning their craft, he imagined using a similar vehicle to help neighborhoods gain political power. He then set out to organize the Back of the Yards Neighborhood Council, which would go on to win important improvements in city services for the neighborhood and contribute to the success of the stockyards workers' unionization struggle.

Alinsky's career took off from there as he traveled the country building neighborhood-based community organizing groups. He also wrote about his efforts, producing two important books on how to do community organizing: *Reveille for Radicals* (1969) and *Rules for Radicals* (1971). Yet, he was hardly a radical in the normal sense. Alinsky was firmly rooted in the U.S. tradition of democracy and believed that poor people could have as much influence over policy as anyone else as long as they organized effectively. He did have a reputation for promoting confrontation and conflict. His reputation once led to his immediate arrest in 1940 when he arrived in Kansas City. After numerous conversations, though, the police chief agreed to provide security for a major event organized by the Alinsky-style group there. Although he was personally confrontational, few of the community organizing efforts he spawned engaged in disruptive protest. He did, though, use an approach based on the power of numbers that posed the threat of disruption. Perhaps the most famous example of the use of such a threat was in 1964 when The Woodlawn Organization (TWO), one of the Alinsky-organized groups in Chicago, threatened to occupy all the toilets at O'Hare airport, the first ever "shit-in." In response to the threat, Chicago's Mayor Richard J. Daley quickly called a meeting with TWO to reaffirm commitments on which he had previously reneged.

Alinsky had a rigidly anti-ideological approach to community organization. One of its weaknesses is that some of the organizations he built later turned undemocratic. In fact, when he died unexpectedly in 1972, on Alinsky's agenda was returning to the Back of the Yards neighborhood to start a new organization to overthrow the Back of the Yards Neighborhood Council, which had become racist and segregationist.

The Alinsky model of community organizing was unique. The secret to the strategy was building a neighborhood organization not one person at a time but with groups of people. He called his model an organization of organizations. When he went into a neighborhood, he looked for the churches, civic groups, garden clubs, veterans organizations, and every other entity through which people were already organized. Then he brought those organizations together, dramatically increasing the efficiency of the organizing effort.

The organization occupied a very important place in Alinsky's model. You did not organize people just to win on an issue or two and then disband. You organized in order to build an organization that could sustain itself and provide institutionalized power well into the future. The organization was the vehicle that allowed poor people to occupy a place in the political system.

The only way to build an organization of potentially ideologically diverse organizations was for the organizer to maintain a carefully honed, non-ideological stance. This produced one of the other hallmarks of the Alinsky model—"cutting" an issue. He did not go into neighborhoods with an issue already selected. Instead, he listened to what issues people cared about and then tried to organize around them. This did not stop him from stirring up people around an issue, but he was always careful to find an issue that excited them. Finding just the right issue that a group cared about, would work for, and could win was one of the geniuses of the approach. And, although Alinsky organizations had a reputation for being confrontational and conflict oriented, the goal was always for the organization to obtain a win or cut a deal with power holders. Alinsky-style organizations had a reputation to protect, so they avoided action that could be perceived as irresponsible or violent.

Perhaps the most important hallmark of the Alinsky-style organization was the development of the specialized role of community organizer. The organizer is not a leader in the Alinsky model; instead, the organizer's job is to identify potential leaders and build their skills, helping them identify issues and organize around them. A truly effective community organizer should be able to enter a community, build leadership and structure an organization, and then leave with the organization able to sustain itself.

Alinsky has influenced a long line of community organizers and the major national community organizing networks operating today. Perhaps the most important evidence of this is the faith-based community networks that emerged out of his ideas. Alinsky established the Industrial Areas Foundation, which still exists. The Industrial Areas Foundation has become a major faith-based community organizing network. Other networks influenced directly or indirectly by him include the PICO National Network, the Direct Action & Research Training Network, and the Gamaliel Foundation.

Alinsky's influence can also be found in the major secular national community organizing networks such as the Association of Community Organizations for Reform Now (ACORN) and National People's Action. These organizations, along with others, have been responsible for important neighborhood victories and astounding national policy victories such as the Community Reinvestment Act (1977) that thwarted the practice of redlining that prevented people in poor neighborhoods from obtaining conventional home loans. These organizations have been behind the push for living wage laws, antidiscrimination legislation, and citizen participation policies in many cities.

Alinsky's influence has extended even into areas one would not expect. One of Alinsky's original organizing staff members, Fred Ross, was working in Southern California in the 1950s when he was confronted by a young Latino man named César Chávez. The confrontation led to a strong working relationship and Chávez began organizing with Ross. Chávez, of course, went on to organize the United Farm Workers. Today there are thousands of Alinsky-style organizations. There are others, such as the Consensus Organizing Institute, that have created an organizing model in direct contrast to the Alinsky approach. Some organizing networks are building new political parties, such as the Working Families Party, rooted in ACORN's organizing efforts. Finally, they are empowering individuals who could never have imagined themselves leading any group or speaking in any public meeting and are now winning victories for their communities.

Randy Stoecker

See also Chicago, Illinois; Citizen Participation; Community Organizing; Right to the City

Further Readings

Alinsky, Saul. 1969. *Reveille for Radicals*. New York: Vintage Books.
———. 1971. *Rules for Radicals*. New York: Vintage Books.
The Democratic Promise: Saul Alinsky and His Legacy. 1999. Produced by Bob Hercules and Bruce Orenstein. Media Process Educational Films and Chicago Video Project.
Horwitt, Sanford D. 1989. *Let Them Call Me Rebel: Saul Alinsky, His Life and Legacy*. New York: Random House.

ALLEGORY OF GOOD GOVERNMENT

Ambrogio Lorenzetti's frescoes on three walls of the room known as either the *Sala della Pace* (Hall of Peace, after one of the allegorical figures in the frescoes) or the *Sala dei Nove* (Hall of the Nine, the elected rulers of the city) in Siena's Palazzo Pubblico are often called the first large-scale secular murals since antiquity. They both project an ideal political landscape and document aspects of contemporary daily life.

Before the Palazzo Pubblico became the home of Siena's elected officials and councils, town meetings had been taking place everywhere from the private palaces of influential citizens to the cathedral. Having a dedicated, imposing public building on a well-organized public space staked out Siena's claim to prominence as a powerful, wealthy commune (i.e., a town ruled by elected officials responsible for the common good).

The council of the Nine ruled Siena from 1287 to 1355. Following a period of government in which the city had won its greatest, and last, victory against the Florentines (at Montasperti, 1260) and completed building its cathedral, the Nine not only built the Palazzo Pubblico and the Piazza del Campo, they also began a vast project to enlarge the duomo in rivalry with that of Florence (aborted with the devastation of the black death in 1348). The Nine were proportionally related to the three districts of the city: The *Terzi* ("thirds") of *Città*, *San Martino*, and *Camollia* corresponded to the three legs of the Y, which defined the city's plan, spread across the

Ambrogio Lorenzetti's fourteenth-century fresco, The Allegory of Good Government, *at Palazzo Pubblico in Siena, Italy*

top of three intersecting ridges. Their intersection in a slightly depressed space would become the bowl-like Piazza del Campo when the decision was made in 1288 (work beginning in 1298) to shape it along with the new town hall; the fan-shaped plan of the piazza was reinforced by the brick paving (divided into nine triangular wedges), which slopes down toward the town hall. At the intersection of the two upper legs of the Y, the Palazzo was a hinge between the city center on the north side and the *contado*, or countryside, on the south; a top floor loggia on the south side looks out to the landscape below and beyond. The prominent bell tower, which rises vertiginously from the corner of the palazzo, was begun in the same year as Lorenzetti's frescoes. The cathedral, perched nearby on the highest point in town, had been effectively brought to completion 30 years before the piazza project was begun.

The frescoed allegories of Good and Bad Government were painted in 1338–1339. While the frescoes offer glimpses of what daily life looked like in Siena, they more tellingly convey the Sienese government's sense of itself, its mission, and its effects on town and country. As such they can be read as a visual treatise on the proper relationships of power, people, and environment in fourteenth-century Italy.

Content

The allegories of Good and Bad Government are found on the *piano nobile* (second floor) of the Palazzo Pubblico. Located on the south side of the building—that is, away from the Piazza del Campo and toward the countryside—the *Sala dei Nove* is accessed principally from the doorway on its east wall, which gives onto the main gathering space of the Palazzo, the *Sala del Mappamondo*. So called because of the large globe and circular map of the heavens that were displayed on the west wall, the *Sala del Mappamondo* was the chamber where the town council met and where its decisions were ratified. On the wall opposite the door to the *Sala dei Nove* Simone Martini had painted earlier in the century a large fresco of the *Maestà*, the Madonna and Child enthroned, surrounded by saints and wrapped by an admonitory inscription directing those in the room charged with governing to embrace Wisdom. This image looked toward the room with Lorenzetti's fresco cycle and provided a sacred corollary to his ostensibly secular allegories.

The allegories of Good and Bad Government wrap three walls of their room; the fourth wall, on the south side, is unfrescoed and has a window opening out to the landscape beyond (and the town market below). Good Government occupies the north and east walls, Bad Government the west, so that entering the *Sala dei Nove* the visitor is confronted with the image of Bad Government and Its Effects. This scene of decay and devastation presided over by a demonic image of the tyrannical ruler provides a stark contrast to Martini's Madonna.

Good Government and Its Effects

Lorenzetti's frescoes show the virtues and vices of two kinds of government and their effects: The message is that what makes a good or bad government ultimately depends on the society each creates and supports, and what we know about this society we can read in its public realm. It should be noted that there is a complex interweaving of secular and Christian iconography in the frescoes, just as the contemporary public realm was overlaid with a sacred reading and the church with a civic dimension.

On the north wall, Good Government presides over personifications of the moral and theological Virtues. The ruler of the good city in fact represents the Common Good (*Bene Comune*). While occupying a commanding position in the fresco and the room, *Bene Comune* actually draws his authority from the citizens of Siena. He is, in fact, off-center on his wall, balanced with one of two figures representing Justice. It is here—at the left side of the north wall—that the reading of the allegory begins (aided by the inscriptions that Lorenzetti provides over each figure).

Enthroned Justice is presided over by Wisdom (*Sapientia*), suspending a large balance whose scales Justice helps support; each scale contains an angelic figure who metes out two distinct kinds of justice: distributive and commutative. From the structure of the balance two ropes (or cords) also descend to the figure of Concord (*Concordia*) seated below Justice; she rests a musical instrument on her lap and grasps the two cords with her left hand, binding them together and passing them onto a group of 24 citizens arrayed in pairs in procession toward *Bene Comune*. They pass the cord up to this embodiment of Good Government, where it tethers the

base of the scepter he wields in his right hand. At his feet are the two mythical founders of Siena, infants suckling a she-wolf (like Rome's Romulus and Remus). Above his head are the three Theological Virtues: Faith, Charity, and Hope. Arrayed to his left and right, respectively, and on the same bench upon which he sits, are Peace, Fortitude, Prudence, and Magnanimity, Temperance, Justice (again). Below these last three on the right are soldiers in the colors of Siena (black and white, like *Bene Comune*'s robes) and their prisoners.

Justice guided by Wisdom creates Concord, who provides the authority for the Common Good to rule with Virtue. The proof would be available to us in both the persons of the Nine ruling this evidently well-governed city (which we would have seen outside in the Piazza del Campo and throughout the city), and in the adjacent fresco of Good Government's effects. Beginning in the northeast corner, the fresco of the effects shows a densely built hill town, where a striped marble campanile and a dome announces that the city depicted is Siena itself. The buildings of the town are varied in style and type; all are in good repair, and indeed builders are at work on the rooftop of one in the middle. Painted more than half a century before Brunelleschi's recovery of linear perspective, medieval conventions still obtain: Lacking a consistent horizon line and vanishing points, the apparent jumble of buildings suggests not disorder but healthy variety. A city wall near the middle of the fresco separates town from the rural countryside to the right. Inside the wall and below the buildings a wide variety of urban activity is taking place: From left to right, a noble wedding party processes on horseback toward the allegories on the north wall, bankers and jewelers ply their trades, a group of eight women dance, a cobbler tends a customer, a teacher teaches, and near the gate *contadini* bring fruits, vegetables, and livestock to sell at market. The dancing women are more allegorical than actual (dancing in the street was illegal in Siena at the time): They restate the theme of concord from the allegory, as they hand in hand weave a figure ∞, symbolizing eternity.

Over the gate *Securitas* flies toward the countryside holding a miniature gallows with a hanged criminal and bearing an inscription (in Tuscan) that declares in the just, well-governed city, people are also safe to travel in the countryside without fear. Communes like Siena often controlled large areas of the *contado,* which they depended on for agriculture, trade, and access to wider markets. All these functions are shown taking place in Lorenzetti's rural landscape. An actual window on the south wall looks out onto the cultivated fields beyond, linking the painted and the real.

Bad Government and Its Effects

If peace and justice are the operative conditions of the good city, violence and fear are the conditions in its opposite. In the fresco of *Bad Government and Its Effects* on the west wall, evil Tyranny presides over a collection of Vices (antipodes of the Virtues) and Fear, who are behind the disarray and decay of the buildings, the violence in the streets and incessant war in the countryside. Justice is bound at the feet of Tyranny; there is no figure of Concordia. Buildings decay or display wanton regard for the planning restrictions Siena had enacted. Swords and daggers are drawn, and disorderly mercenaries roam the streets and countryside, meaning no work is done in either. In these centuries of constant warfare, the images depicted here would have been familiar to the people of Siena.

David Mayernik

See also Florence, Italy; Medieval Town Design; Rome, Italy

Further Readings

Cunningham, Dolin. 1995. "For the Honour and Beauty of the City: The Design of Town Halls." Pp. 29–54 in *Siena, Florence, and Padua: Art, Society and Religion 1280-1400,* edited by D. Norman. New Haven, CT: Yale University Press.

Frugoni, Chiara. 1991. *A Distant City: Images of Urban Experience in the Medieval World.* Princeton, NJ: Princeton University Press.

Mayernik, David. 2003. *Timeless Cities: An Architect's Reflections on Renaissance Italy.* Boulder, CO: Westview Press.

Nevola, Fabrizio. 2008. *Siena: Constructing the Renaissance City.* New Haven, CT: Yale University Press.

Norman, Diana. 1995. "'Love Justice, You Who Judge the Earth': The Paintings of the Sala dei Nove in the Palazzo Pubblico, Siena." Pp. 145–68 in *Siena,*

Florence, and Padua: Art, Society and Religion 1280-1400, edited by D. Norman. New Haven, CT: Yale University Press.

Syson, Luke, ed. 2008. *Renaissance Siena: Art for a City.* London: National Gallery.

White, John. 1987. *Art and Architecture in Italy: 1250–1400.* New York: Penguin Books.

ALMSHOUSES

Boston (ca. 1685), Philadelphia, and New York (the 1730s) were the first cities in the United States to establish almshouses (also called poorhouses). Almshouses were initially supported with a combination of poor taxes and private donations and originally intended to temporarily house community members who were of good character but who were "unfortunate" and who had no family to support them: the poor, the elderly, abandoned or illegitimate children, the injured, or the insane or mentally defective. Almshouses supplemented, and occasionally replaced, the older "outdoor" relief system of payments in cash or goods to relatives of the afflicted or to community members who offered to take responsibility for paupers' support. In some areas (e.g., New York City's outlying counties, and in parts of New Jersey), overseers alternated between outdoor relief and housing the poor in rented or purchased residences, depending on how many folk were in need of care and how much money the town had to spend. Private aid from religious organizations or charitable organizations existed alongside institution-based aid, but focused on particular categories of need (e.g., their own congregations, widows, orphans, prostitutes).

Almshouses played a range of important roles in the social, economic, and political lives of both urban and rural communities. In addition to aiding the poor, poorhouses provided jobs for many of the working poor who would otherwise have been dependent on poor relief. The institutions worked to lower their operating costs by selling manufactured goods and by exchanging goods and produce with local residents. As public institutions, almshouses served as foci for debates over the use of public funds, the conduct of local elections, responses to crises such as epidemics, and other issues of concern to the public.

Urbanization and industrialization in eighteenth- and nineteenth-century Europe and North America were accompanied by universal problems of population dislocation, economic instability, and increasing tension between administrators, the public, and the poor over entitlement to relief. While the establishment of the British workhouse system in the 1830s was of considerable interest to administrators in the United States, and British manuals for providing residential institutions with adequate plumbing and ventilation were certainly consulted, U.S. poorhouses did not generally employ British or other non-American institutions as models. Instead, poor relief exhibited significant regional variation, and administrators adapted government regulations to local conditions and individual cases as they saw fit.

Between the mid-eighteenth century and the 1830s, most American cities adopted an institution-based system of poor relief in order to more efficiently spend and account for public funds (which now included regular appropriations for poor relief) and for more effective supervision of the poor. Poverty was a matter of increasing concern in both urban and rural areas as the numbers of applicants for relief grew and expenditures on relief increased in spite of local officials' efforts to take responsibility only for poor folk who lived in their communities. Real increases in poverty were accompanied by widespread public perception that the ranks of the poor were increasingly composed of the "vicious" poor, who did not deserve the support to which paupers of good character were entitled.

The first half of the nineteenth century saw a growing faith in institutions as solutions to a wide variety of social problems including mental illness, criminal behavior, and poverty; institutions set out to reform the characters and behaviors of their inmates by providing appropriate housing, constructive activity, and moral guidance. An institution-based system would remain the model for social welfare in the United States for the rest of the nineteenth century and into the twentieth, when by mid-century, poorhouses either closed or shifted to housing a variety of state-funded social service programs.

Monique Bourque

See also Homelessness; Housing

Further Readings

Crowther, M. A. 1981. *The Workhouse System, 1834–1929: The History of an English Social Institution.* Athens: University of Georgia Press.

Hoch, Charles and Robert A. Slayton. 1989. *New Homeless and Old: Community and the Skid Row Hotel.* Philadelphia: Temple University Press.

Katz, Michael B. 1996. *In the Shadow of the Poorhouse: A Social History of Welfare in America.* 10th anniversary ed. New York: Basic Books.

Mandler, Peter, ed. 1990. *The Uses of Charity: The Poor on Relief in the Nineteenth-century Metropolis.* Philadelphia: University of Pennsylvania Press.

Smith, Billy G., ed. 2004. *Down and out in Early America.* University Park: Pennsylvania State Press.

ALONSO, WILLIAM

William Alonso (1933–1999)—architect, regional scientist, urban planner, demographer, and regional policy analyst—developed the first and enduring model of metropolitan land use decision making and urban rent determination and went on to a distinguished career as an urban theorist, demographer, and policy advisor. Alonso came to the United States from Argentina in 1941 at the age of 14 when his distinguished philologist father fled the repression of the Perón regime to take up a position at Harvard University.

Early on, Alonso was a theorist relying upon deductive reasoning and empirical analysis to explore urban spatial form. He was the first PhD graduate of the University of Pennsylvania's pioneering regional science department and a founding member of the Regional Science Association. As a young professor in city and regional planning at University of California, Berkeley, he initiated, with others, the social science revolution in urban planning that addressed larger issues of urban evolution and policy with tools from economics, political science, and sociology. Alonso's interdisciplinary background was a tremendous strength, and he became a leading demographer in the 1970s as director of the Center for Population Studies at Harvard University, where he headed an extraordinary academic review of the U.S. Census that resulted in significant changes. He became a prominent theorist of European urban system change following the formation of the European Union and the dissolution of the Soviet Union.

Alonso's seminal work is *Location and Land Use,* in which he improved on Johann Heinrich von Thünen's early nineteenth-century zone theory of agricultural land use and rents, adapting it radically for a metropolitan setting. He sought to understand why higher-income households in twentieth-century United States chose to live farther from the city center, whereas in Europe and his native Argentina they favored the core. Part of his larger argument was a location model in which the household's utility is a positive function of land space consumed and dollars spent on a composite good (all goods other than land) and a negative function of commuting distance to work in the core. A budget constraint reflects the unit price of the composite good, a price for land that varies with distance to work, and the monetary cost of commuting, a function of commuting distance. He inferred that higher-income American families favored larger lots and housing size and were willing to incur greater time and money costs of commuting as a result. He predicted bid-rent curves (how much rent people will pay for residential land given its distance from a specified point) that decline with distance from the core. In his first foray into policy, he speculated on the implication of his and other historical and structural urban form theories for urban renewal.

Although he continued to use microeconomic and macroeconomic theories in influential intermetropolitan explorations of the economics of urban size, migration flows, urban disamenities, and longer-term development trajectories, Alonso pioneered the leavening of regional science with behavioral theory and methods in the social sciences. Two widely read collections that he coedited with John Friedmann showcased an eclectic approach that encompassed location theory and abstract urban modeling along with growth pole and other applied theories. His own elegant statement, "From Alfred Weber to Max: The Shifting Style of Regional Policy," did much to ensure that regional science would remain a field open to different disciplines and committed to policy analysis as well as theorizing.

As director of the Center for Population Studies at Harvard University from 1976 on, Alonso dramatically broadened the field of demography beyond mechanistic population forecasting by emphasizing the importance of social science theories of fertility behavior and interregional migration as important determinants of differential urban growth rates. More importantly, he launched a remarkable multiyear interdisciplinary study of the U.S. Population Census and its anachronisms, resulting in the book *The Politics of Numbers* (with Paul Starr) and prompting important improvements in future census content, process, and reporting.

Bitten by the policy bug at an early age, Alonso spent his final decade anticipating new pressures and changes in the European system of cities following the demise of the Soviet Union and the quickening pace of European economic integration. In several papers he predicted greater polarization in Europe as the largest cities jockeyed for position, with some specializing in trade, finance, and governance. He paid attention to the periphery and its problems, accurately predicting the key role that continued regional policy would play in building union-wide solidarity. Over his 40-year career, Alonso served on several panels of the National Academy of Sciences and as a consultant to the United Nations, the World Bank, the European Commission, the U.S. Departments of Commerce, Agriculture, and Housing and Urban Development, and 16 national governments beyond the United States. His many and diverse contributions were celebrated in a special issue of the *International Regional Science Review* in 2001.

Ann Markusen

See also Housing; Journey to Work; Location Theory; Urban Economics

Further Readings

Alonso, William. 1964. *Location and Land Use.* Cambridge, MA: Harvard University Press.
———. 1990. "From Alfred Weber to Max: The Shifting Style of Regional Policy." Pp. 25–41 in *Dynamics and Conflict in Regional Structural Change,* edited by M. Chatterji and R. E. Kuenne. London: Macmillan.
Alonso, William and Paul Starr, eds. 1987. *The Politics of Numbers.* New York: Russell Sage.
Friedmann, John and William Alonso, eds. 1964. *Regional Development and Planning: A Reader.* Cambridge: MIT Press.

AMSTERDAM, THE NETHERLANDS

Amsterdam is the capital of the Netherlands, and with 750,000 inhabitants it is also its largest city.

The city is part of the Randstad metropolitan area, which covers most of the west portion of the country and accommodates roughly half of the country's 16.5 million inhabitants. Randstad also includes the second- and third-largest cities, Rotterdam and The Hague.

The city of Amsterdam developed on a dam in the Amstel River at the end of the twelfth century. The period 1585 to 1672, the Golden Age, was the heyday of Amsterdam's commercial success. At the time Amsterdam was the staple market of the world. During this period the characteristic Amsterdam cityscape developed; the 1613 and 1663 urban expansions with concentric canals still determine the city's characteristic appearance. The year 1672 brought disaster for the Dutch Republic with the French and English attacking simultaneously: The Golden Age had come to an end. Nevertheless, Amsterdam managed to consolidate its prosperity during the period 1672 to 1795 (the Silver Age) in spite of the predicament the Republic found itself in. The city remained a major staple market and managed to retain its position as the financial center of Europe. The large number of dwellings built in the Golden and Silver Ages reflect the city's prosperity.

In 1795 the government of the patrician oligarchies was overthrown and the old Republic ceased to exist. Soon the French occupied the country. During the period 1795 to 1813, Amsterdam suffered badly from an economic recession. Many houses were vacant and some even collapsed for lack of maintenance. The period 1813 to 1920 is marked by economic recovery and, from 1870 onward, by expansion. The increasing wealth brought about a rapid population growth. This development was primarily the result of the Industrial Revolution, which triggered a New Golden Age. Large, often poorly built working-class neighborhoods were built. The period 1920 to 1940 was a time of economic recession. Therefore it is all the more remarkable that the so-called Ring 20–40 compares favorably to the nineteenth-century jerry-building. This was also the period of large-scale damage to the historical city center; canals were filled in and new traffic breakthroughs were realized. During the postwar period the population of the city proper grew only modestly, but the metropolitan area increased dramatically. Moreover, Amsterdam acquired an international reputation, both culturally and economically.

Many tourists are attracted by the museums that are now renowned far outside the Netherlands (such as the Van Gogh Museum, Rijksmuseum, and Stedelijk Museum), and because of its canals and architecture the city center is very popular—the historical wealth of this part of the city is still tangible. At least as important is the liberal image of Amsterdam, which, for tourists, is mainly connected to the city's red-light district and its policies on the use of soft drugs. These cultural features make tourism an important source of income. However, the main thrust of the city's income comes from commercial services (banking and insurance companies), trade, and

Modern Amsterdam demonstrating the merging of canals and traffic thoroughfares

Source: Karen Wiley.

distribution (the national airport Schiphol is located very close to Amsterdam, and the city also has a large seaport). The city has a highly educated workforce, partly due to the presence of two large research universities and various colleges. Amsterdam has never had a uniform industrial profile. To the contrary, the Dutch capital has always been characterized by a relatively strong financial sector, the presence of cultural industries, tourism, and other consumption-related sections of the economy. Amsterdam has a strong postindustrial economic and employment structure.

In this entry, two themes are highlighted: Amsterdam as a migrant city and the city's progressive potential.

A Migrant City

Amsterdam has seen immigration for centuries. When the city was a thriving center of global trade in the sixteenth and seventeenth centuries, it naturally received large flows of immigrants. In the years following World War II, Amsterdam's immigrant population has vastly grown. The share of people from ethnic minority groups is high (including the estimates for undocumented migrants, about 50 percent) and the ethnic variety is impressive: Amsterdam houses about 177 different nationalities, more than any other city in the world.

While Amsterdam is a city with poor immigrant groups, it is not a city where the spatial distribution of people and housing quality is simply a function of income and class. Amsterdam's ethnic groups are not extremely segregated, which is probably because Amsterdam is a mixed city with respect to housing types and because the social housing sector is not marginalized. This large social housing sector is highly regulated: The main criteria for housing allocation and residential differentiation in Amsterdam are income and household composition. The more-than-significant state intervention in the Amsterdam housing market has three major directions: a large amount of social housing; regulation in housing assignment by a variety of rules, until very recently even involving properties outside the social housing stock; and, quite significant, rent subsidies. The Moroccans are the only group showing a steady rise in concentrations in the least popular areas of the city. However, these concentrations are nowhere near ghettos; there is not even one area that consists of more than 50 percent Moroccans.

Many areas of the city are, however, minority–majority neighborhoods, but this is not very surprising, as the city itself is almost a minority–majority city.

Yet migration does pose some serious challenges to the city. Anti-migration and anti-Islam sentiments are becoming more and more common throughout the Netherlands. In many ways, some districts in the west of the city (collectively known as Westelijke Tuinsteden or "New West") have become not only the real battleground but even more so the symbolic battleground of the multicultural city and the discourse of failing immigrant integration. Ironically, the most ethnically diverse part of the city, De Bijlmer district, not long ago the most infamous housing estate in the country and formerly known as "the closest thing to a ghetto in the Netherlands," is now often cited as an example of successful integration. Ethnic diversity is often celebrated in De Bijlmer, not just by the communications bureau of the city district but also by many residents, and this is showcased by (multi)ethnic festivals. But discourse and reality are often two different things: For many people in De Bijlmer, in particular for a substantial group of undocumented immigrants, it remains an area full of insecurities and uncertainties; likewise, the western part of the city is not as problematic as many seem to suggest.

Progressive Policies

Amsterdam is known for its progressive policies and practices regarding squatting, drug use, prostitution, sexuality, housing, urban planning, and sustainable development. It is also known as one the world's "Gay Capitals." Three of these themes are discussed briefly in this entry.

1. *Housing, planning, and squatting.* Housing and urban planning in Amsterdam seem more progressive than in many other cities, although the city has clearly lost its edge over several other cities. Many policies are no longer radically different from those in many Nordic and German cities. And even though the city's share of social housing is still among the highest in the world, two large programs are contributing significantly to a decrease in the availability of social rented housing. One is a program to sell social-rented units to their tenants and is, in some ways, comparable to the United

Kingdom's "right to buy" program, although tenants can buy their home only *if* the landlord offers to sell it to them. The second is a program aimed at the renewal of postwar neighborhoods: Many dwellings are demolished and replaced by private-sector housing. In addition, squatting is also becoming less easy and less accepted than it once was. The national government is discussing a ban on squatting, and although the city of Amsterdam does not support such a ban, relations between squatters and authorities have become more and more hostile.

2. *Drugs*. The main aim of the drug policy in the Netherlands is to protect the health of individual users, the people around them, and society as a whole. Priority is given to vulnerable groups. Active policies on care and prevention are being pursued to reduce the demand for drugs. Regulations on drugs are laid down in the Opium Act. The Opium Act draws a distinction between hard drugs (e.g., heroin, cocaine, and ecstasy [also known as XTC or MDMA]), which are considered to pose an unacceptable hazard to health, and soft drugs (e.g., hashish and marijuana), which constitute a far less serious hazard. Importing and exporting drugs are the most serious offenses under the provisions of the Opium Act. The possession of drugs is an offense, but the possession of a small quantity of soft drugs for personal use is not criminalized. In addition, anyone found in possession of less than 0.5 gram of hard drugs will generally not be prosecuted, though the police will confiscate the drugs and consult a care agency. The city center of Amsterdam is dotted with so-called coffee shops, where soft drugs can be bought and consumed. National government recently forced the city to close a number of them because they are considered to be too close to schools. Surprisingly to many non-Dutch, drug use in the Netherlands, both soft and hard, is lower than in many other countries. For example, more than twice as many Americans regularly use marijuana or cocaine. Drug use is higher in Amsterdam than most other parts of the country, but this is probably true for most big cities.

3. *Prostitution*. As is the case with drugs, Amsterdam's lenient stance on prostitution seems to have risen as a special case at the intersection of national policies and local yet international tourism. In the Netherlands, prostitution was legalized in 2000. However, this does not mean prostitution is left completely to the free market; for example, brothel licensing is used to control illegal immigration. Registered prostitutes are taxed, which allows for legal action against nonlicensed prostitutes offering their services. Contrary to the impressions of many foreigners, Dutch citizens, in general, do not support or encourage prostitution and sexual commerce. Nonetheless, in the Netherlands, prostitution is much more accepted as a social fact than it is elsewhere. Chrisje Brants speaks of "regulated tolerance": Even before legislation, it involved "self-regulation, enforced if necessary through administrative rules, but always with the criminal law as a threat in the background," although "it is not an offence to make use of the services of a prostitute" or to offer services as a prostitute. Because of the unique situation in the Netherlands, Amsterdam's major red-light district, De Wallen, is not tied just to notions of danger, immorality, drugs, and crime but also to tolerance, excitement, and freedom—making De Wallen one of Amsterdam's major tourist attractions. The commodification of sex is not very hidden in the De Wallen. Unlike other red-light districts, De Wallen is not visited just by heterosexual men looking for sexual pleasure. The crowd on the streets includes locals passing through on a walk as well as by couples, women, homosexual men, business associates, and families with grandparents and children in tow. Both physically and socially, the area is not very strongly separated from its surroundings, and borders appear relatively porous: The occasional sex shop can be found on the adjacent streets among cultural institutions, respectable cafes, child care facilities, and residential housing (often located above the window brothels and the sex shops). Recently, the city of Amsterdam, and in particular the large social-democratic party, has started a campaign to significantly limit the red-light district in size. It could be argued that the city is undertaking a deliberate promotion of gentrification.

An Ordinary, Progressive City

Amsterdam is a significant place in urban studies, not just because of its historical significance and the resulting architectural heritage but also because it is often seen as an example of an almost utopian city with the most progressive policies in the world. Susan Fainstein, in her essay in the book *Understanding Amsterdam*, describes Amsterdam as "the just city." Although Amsterdam will still look more progressive than many of its counterparts on the other side of the Atlantic, Amsterdam is no longer the radically progressive city that it seemed in the 1970s. In fact, several other European cities now have as much progressive potential as Amsterdam. Nonetheless, Amsterdam remains significant as both an "ordinary city" and a "progressive city." Within Europe, Amsterdam is also a forerunner in becoming a minority–majority city with all its dynamics, opportunities, and tensions that brings about.

Manuel B. Aalbers

See also Gay Space; Gentrification; Historic Cities; Multicultural Cities; Red-Light District; Sex Industry; Social Housing; Squatter Movements; Tourism

Further Readings

Aalbers, M. B. 2005. "Big Sister Is Watching You! Gender Interaction and the Unwritten Rules of the Amsterdam Red-light District." *Journal of Sex Research* 42(1):54–62.

Aalbers, M. B. and M. C. Deurloo. 2003. "Concentrated and Condemned? Residential Patterns of Immigrants from Industrial and Non-industrial Countries in Amsterdam." *Housing Theory and Society* 20(4): 197–208.

Brants, C. 1998. "The Fine Art of Regulated Tolerance: Prostitution in Amsterdam." *Journal of Law and Society* 25(4):621–635.

Deben, L., W. Heinemeijer, and D. van der Vaart, eds. 2000. *Understanding Amsterdam. Essays on Economic Vitality, City Life and Urban Form.* 2nd ed. Amsterdam: Het Spinhuis.

Girouard, Mark. 1985. *Cities and People: A Social and Architectural History.* New Haven, CT: Yale University Press.

Mak, G. 1999. *Amsterdam. A Brief Life of the City.* London: Harvill Press.

Mamadouh, V. D. 1992. *De stad in eigen hand: Provos, kabouters en krakers as Stedelijke Sociale Bewegingen* (The State in Its Own Hands: Provos, Kabouters and Squatters as Urban Social Movements). Amsterdam: SUA.

Musterd, S. and W. Salet, eds. 2003. *Amsterdam Human Capital.* Amsterdam: Amsterdam University Press.

Terhorst, P. J. F. and J. C. K. Van de Ven. 1997. *Fragmented Brussels and Consolidated Amsterdam: A Comparative Study of the Spatial Organisation of Property Rights.* Amsterdam: Netherlands Geographical Society.

ANCIENT CITIES

The earliest cities developed within a broad transformation of human society called the "urban revolution." Simpler agricultural societies grew into complex, urban states independently in at least six parts of the world. The first large-scale complex societies, often referred to as "pristine states," developed in Mesopotamia, Egypt, the Indus Valley, North China, the Andes, and Mesoamerica. This entry covers ancient cities starting with the pristine states and ending prior to the Classical period in the Mediterranean and prior to European conquest in other parts of the world.

Early Urban Traditions

Cities within major world regions typically shared key principles of form and function, allowing them to be grouped into urban traditions. The following sections describe eight of the best documented early urban traditions.

Mesopotamia

The earliest large urban settlement was Tell Brak in the dry farming zone of northern Mesopotamia. During the Uruk period (3800–3100 BC) this city consisted of a central zone of public architecture surrounded by sprawling suburban settlement over 1 square kilometer in extent. At the end of this period, the site declined and the focus of urban development shifted to southern Mesopotamia. At the start of the Early Dynastic period (2900–2300 BC), the southern Mesopotamian site of Uruk grew explosively from a small town to a compact walled city of some 400 hectares (4 square kilometers). At the same time, nearby rural villages were abandoned, suggesting that people were moved forcibly into the city. This urban growth was part of a cultural explosion that saw the spread of cities and city-states across the Euphrates plain, the development of cuneiform writing, and a series of economic, religious, and cultural innovations.

Over the following millennia, the Near East witnessed several cycles in which periods of city-state organization (such as the Early Dynastic period) with numerous small interacting cities alternated with periods of political centralization dominated by large imperial capitals. Some of the most impressive cities of the ancient world were imperial capitals in the first and second millennia BC, such as Babylon, Nineveh, and Persepolis.

Egypt

Because archaeologists have failed to find large cities in Egypt prior to Akhenaten's capital at Amarna in the New Kingdom period (1350 BC), Egypt has sometimes been contrasted to Mesopotamia as a "civilization without cities." This label masks a distinctive form of urbanism, however. While it is possible that flooding by the Nile River destroyed earlier large capitals, it appears more likely that the Egyptians forged a form of dispersed urbanism characterized by smaller, more specialized urban settlements. Walled towns served as local administrative centers, large temples were built in religious compounds, and the temples were maintained by special settlements of workers and priests. Laborers for major construction projects were housed in walled villages. This pattern originated during the Old Kingdom period (2700–2100 BC) when the Egyptian state and associated institutions, such as kingship and hieroglyphic writing, were first consolidated. Egypt did not lack cities; rather its urban systems were structured differently from the more familiar form of Mesopotamian cities.

Indus Valley

A distinctive tradition of cities developed around 2300 BC in the valley of the Indus River in Pakistan and western India. The best known cities are Mohenjo-daro and Harappa. Each was composed of two parts: a large raised platform with public architecture on the west and dense residential zones on the east. Houses were serviced by a sophisticated system of drains, pipes, and ditches; this level of sanitary engineering was not matched until the Roman period two millennia later. Public architecture at these sites is enigmatic. The citadels support likely storage structures, but there are no obvious temples or royal palaces. A large open tank at Mohenjo-daro, known as the "Great Bath," was probably used for some kind of ritual bathing or purification rites. The basic patterns of urban architecture and layout are duplicated at a series of smaller sites, including walled towns and a port facility with a dock and warehouses. The

undeciphered script of the Indus Valley civilization may hold clues to this fascinating and enigmatic urban society.

North China

China was the home to the longest-lasting non-Western urban tradition. Urban settlements were first founded in the Erlitou period (2100–1800 BC) and expanded greatly in the following Shang period (1800–1100 BC). Many early cities were walled, but Anyang, the most extensively excavated city, lacked a wall. In spectacular royal tombs at Anyang, kings were accompanied by sacrificed retainers, whole chariots with oxen, and rich offerings. A tradition of bronze ritual vessels exhibits impressive technological and aesthetic sophistication. Unlike cities in most early urban traditions, Anyang presents no surviving large stone buildings; public buildings were constructed of timber on low earth platforms. Chinese writing was perfected in the Shang period, and numerous ritual texts survive on bronze vessels and on carved bones. Principles established in these early urban centers, such as city walls and orientation to the cardinal directions, were later incorporated into the long-lasting tradition of imperial capitals, an especially well documented form of non-Western urbanism.

The Andes

The Andean culture area included a variety of localized urban subtraditions. Impressive planned ceremonial complexes first appeared on the coast of Peru in the second millennium BC. These sites share key architectural features (e.g., a U-shaped form and sunken circular courtyards), but their residential areas have not been well studied. Specialists debate both their urban status and whether their builders were the rulers of states, or chiefs of smaller-scale societies. Polities based in the large and impressive highland cities of Wari and Tiwanaku dominated the Andes between AD 500 and 900. The most powerful polity to develop in the Andes was the Inka empire (AD 1400–1530). Inka kings used city-building as an imperial strategy, and cities with distinctive Inka masonry and urban forms were built across large parts of the Andes to administer the empire.

Mesoamerica

Like the Andes, Mesoamerica (central Mexico to Honduras) was the setting for a number of regional subtraditions of urbanism, starting around the time of Christ. Most spectacular are the Classic period (AD 200–900) Maya cities of the tropical lowland jungle; the best studied cities are Tikal, Copán, Palenque, and Caracol. These consisted of planned civic centers with impressive stone pyramids, palaces, and ballcourts, surrounded by sprawling, unplanned residential zones. Newly deciphered hieroglyphic texts on public stone monuments tell the stories of petty kings and their military and ceremonial deeds. Around AD 900, Maya civilization collapsed and the cities were overgrown by jungle vegetation. Other well studied Mesoamerican urban cultures include the Olmec, Zapotec, and Aztec, all of which built small cities that followed the Maya pattern of planned civic zones coupled with unplanned residential areas. The largest Mesoamerican cities were in central Mexico: Teotihuacan (AD 100–600) and the Aztec imperial capital Tenochtitlan (AD 1300–1519); each had over 100,000 inhabitants.

Southeast Asia

The largest city ever built—in areal extent—was the great Khmer imperial capital of Angkor (AD 800–1300), whose maximal extent was larger than 1,000 square kilometers. The temple compound of Angkor Wat (82 hectares in area) was only one of many monumental complexes, along with palaces and reservoirs, all carefully built and arranged following cosmological and mythological principles. Like the Maya cities, the ceremonial core was surrounded by low-density informal housing, and much of the city was devoted to intensive agricultural cultivation. The Khmer urban tradition began much earlier than Angkor, however, and over the centuries, kings and architects worked out distinctive canons of urban planning and architectural style that drew on both the Hindu and Buddhist religions. Southeast Asia was also home to a tradition of commerce-based coastal port cities.

Sub-Saharan Africa

Several urban subtraditions flourished in sub-Saharan Africa prior to European conquest. In West Africa, the city of Jenné-Jeno (AD 450–1100) combined extensive craft production and exchange systems with modest public architecture. The Yoruba cities (AD 1400–1900) were also busy commercial centers without large public buildings; warfare was rampant and these cities were surrounded by defensive walls. In eastern Africa, Great Zimbabwe was an impressive inland city (AD 1100–1400) with a large elliptical walled compound; its expansion resulted from an active system of inland–coastal commerce. At the coastal end of that relationship, Swahili settlements grew into busy port cities that maintained their independence until Portuguese conquest in AD 1500.

Conceptual Approaches

Two contrasting definitions of the terms *city* and *urban* are used by archaeologists. The demographic definition, based on the concepts of Louis Wirth, identifies cities as large, dense settlements with social heterogeneity. Many ancient cities had only modest populations, however (often under 5,000 persons), and thus are too small to qualify as "urban" from this perspective. The alternative functional approach defines a city as a settlement that contains activities and institutions that affect a wider hinterland. The most common of these "urban functions" existed in the realm of politics or administration, economics, and religion. The functional definition allows for different types of cities, both within and between urban traditions.

The concept of the "urban revolution," first identified by V. Gordon Childe (1892–1957), describes a series of social changes that brought about the development of the earliest cities and states in each of the six regions of pristine urbanism. These changes (such as the origin of social classes and the production of an agricultural surplus) provided the social context for the earliest cities. Once class-structured state societies took hold in a region, individual cities rose and fell in response to a variety of forces.

Patterns of Variation

Archaeologists in the eighteenth century began their programs of fieldwork in the Near East at urban sites because that was where they found the biggest monuments and the richest offerings. Today this approach continues in some areas, but most archaeologists take a more analytical approach to ancient urban sites. In this newer perspective, conceptual models are applied to the archaeological remains of early cities in order to learn about them as human settlements. The most common conceptual approach derives from political economy. Archaeologists look to agricultural production and demography as important factors in urban dynamics. Craft production and long-distance exchange are major topics of urban research today. Ancient state-level economies varied enormously, and economic processes and institutions affected urban form and dynamics. For example, cities under state-controlled noncommercial redistributive economies (e.g., Inka and Egypt) had more standardized plans and state storage facilities, whereas cities in areas with commercialized economies (e.g., Sumerian and Swahili) were typically smaller with less standardization in layout.

Political form and the dynamics of power are also major topics of archaeological research on ancient cities. Rulers used urban architecture to communicate messages about power, wealth, legitimacy, and other ideological themes. Accordingly, the capitals of city-states (e.g., Sumerian and Aztec) were small cities with relatively modest public architecture, whereas imperial capitals were larger in size and far more "monumental" in their cityscapes. The civic centers of ancient capitals were almost always carefully planned, following local rules and canons. Residential zones, on the other hand, were most commonly shaped by generative, bottom-up processes instead of central planning.

In the past two decades, the focus on economics and politics has been supplemented by a newer focus on the social characteristics of the urban population. Excavations of houses, workshops, and residential zones are now common, and urban households, neighborhoods, and social variation have become major topics of research. Archaeologists borrow models from urban geography to investigate the social dynamics of cities, including topics such as wealth and inequality, power and control, urban social identities, and spatial practices. Another tradition of research emphasizes the religious dimensions of early cities, including cosmological models of city layout and the symbolism of temples. It is known from historical documents that in some ancient traditions cities were highly sacred places and rulers deliberately aligned their capitals with the cosmos (e.g., China, India, and Southeast Asia), whereas cities in other traditions (e.g., Sumerian, Swahili) show far less evidence of such sacralization.

In comparison with modern cities, ancient cities were more strongly constrained by their environmental setting. Limitations in transport technology and organizational capacity required that food and other bulky resources come from close to the city. As a result, agricultural productivity and resource distribution played large roles in determining the locations and population levels of most ancient cities. Imperial Rome, with its seagoing fleets and advanced imperial and commercial grain procurement systems, was one of the first cities to outgrow the constraints of its local environmental context by importing food from North Africa.

Although most ancient cities had much smaller ecological footprints than Rome, many or perhaps most of them were responsible for serious environmental degradation. Archaeologists have documented agricultural overintensification and its ensuing negative effects on soils in the vicinity of many ancient cities. Nearly all ancient urban societies engaged in deforestation, often with disastrous consequences for soils and the water table. In temperate latitudes forests were cut down for firewood and construction materials. The most wood-hungry pyrotechnology-based industries were metallurgy and the production of cement and plaster from limestone. In tropical forest settings, forests were cleared for agricultural production.

Most ancient cities were ultimately destroyed or abandoned. Some, like Teotihuacan or Uruk, flourished for many centuries, whereas others, such as Akhenaten's capital Amarna and most Inka cities, were abandoned shortly after they were founded. These differences in longevity, which might be considered reflections of ancient urban sustainability, remain poorly understood. Because the dynamics of urban change typically require razing old buildings to construct new ones, cities with long lives are much more difficult for archaeologists to study. The most difficult ancient cities to excavate are those that have continued to thrive into modern times, such as Damascus, Beijing, Rome, London, and Mexico City. Although their archaeological resources present numerous problems for modern heritage conservation and planning, these cities do provide settings where large numbers of people can learn about ancient cities and urban lifeways.

In summary, the most striking result of archaeological fieldwork on ancient urban sites around the world is the recognition of a high level of variation among ancient cities. Each urban tradition exhibited its own distinctive forms and styles of architecture and layout, and cities in each tradition bore the marks of regional patterns of economy, politics, religion, and social organization. High levels of variation often existed within urban traditions as well. The two best documented ancient urban traditions—Mesopotamia and Mesoamerica—each included small city-state capitals, huge imperial capitals, port cities, industrial towns, and cultural centers. As archaeologists continue to excavate and analyze ancient cities, these patterns of variation are becoming clearer. It is increasingly possible to compare ancient, historical, and modern cities in order to uncover the broad patterning of similarities and differences in urban settlements across space and time.

Michael E. Smith

See also Acropolis; *Agora;* Athens, Greece; Childe, V. Gordon; Rome, Italy; Urban Archaeology

Further Readings

Chew, Sing C. 2000. *World Ecological Degradation: Accumulation, Urbanization, and Deforestation, 3000 BC–AD 2000.* Walnut Creek, CA: AltaMira.

Childe, V. Gordon. 1950. "The Urban Revolution." *Town Planning Review* 21:3–17.

Gates, Charles. 2003. *Ancient Cities: The Archaeology of Urban Life in the Ancient Near East and Egypt, Greece, and Rome.* New York: Routledge.

Hull, Richard. 1976. *African Cities and Towns before the European Conquest.* New York: Norton.

Marcus, Joyce and Jeremy Sabloff, eds. 2008. *The Ancient City: New Perspectives on Urbanism in the Old and New World.* Santa Fe, NM: SAR Press.

Smith, Michael E. 2008. *Aztec City-state Capitals.* Gainesville: University Press of Florida.

Steinhardt, Nancy S. 1990. *Chinese Imperial City Planning.* Honolulu: University of Hawaii Press.

Trigger, Bruce G. 2003. *Understanding Early Civilizations: A Comparative Study.* New York: Cambridge University Press.

Van De Mieroop, Marc. 1999. *The Ancient Mesopotamian City.* Oxford, UK: Oxford University Press.

ANNEXATION

Annexation is a procedure that enables a city to grow by expanding its boundaries to include neighboring territory. It is closely related to the idea of consolidation, a process that enables two or more cities to merge into one larger government. Virtually every major American city has grown either through annexation or consolidation.

Annexation has had a long history in the United States. In the nineteenth century, annexation and consolidation produced America's largest cities. New York, Chicago, Boston, and Philadelphia—along with many others—grew enormously. New York City expanded from approximately 44 to 300 square miles, and Chicago from 10 to 185 square miles. Boston grew to almost 30 times its original size. Philadelphia increased even more dramatically: from 2 to 130 square miles. Although suburbanization greatly enlarged the geographic reach of their metropolitan regions, annexation in major Eastern and Midwestern cities ended in the nineteenth century. But annexation continues elsewhere in the United States. Between 1950 and 1990, David Rusk reports, more than 80 percent of the nation's central cities grew by 10 percent or more. Important examples include Houston, Memphis, Oklahoma City, Jacksonville, Phoenix, and San Jose. And there are many others. The major cities of the twentieth century in the South and West, like the major Eastern and Midwestern cities of the nineteenth century, have thus grown by annexation.

There are two ways to understand why some cities in the United States continue to annex adjacent territory and others do not. One is that the arguments for and against annexation have a different impact in different parts of the country. The other is that the legal structure that empowers cities to annex neighboring territory differs from place to place.

Consider first the arguments for and against annexation. Many annexations have been fueled by the idea that size matters. Civic pride and boosterism have fostered expansion as cities have competed with each other to be one of America's largest cities. Often, this expansion has been supported by the business community. Land speculation and the desire to create an efficient geographic area for the delivery of city services have played a role as well. But the notion that size matters has also been embraced by opponents of annexation. Many residents of small communities like their connection to small city governments. Land speculators sometimes prefer working with smaller governments, and those interested in city services can also find advantages in them.

These traditional pro and con arguments now take place in the context of large-scale suburban sprawl. Opponents of suburban sprawl, and of the political fragmentation that generates it, frequently favor making annexation easy. Supporters of metropolitan fragmentation—or, as they are more likely to put it, people who favor offering potential residents a wide choice of communities to live in—oppose it. Current annexation debates also take place in metropolitan areas that are characterized by wide disparities between neighboring jurisdictions in terms of income, race, and ethnicity. The greater these disparities, the more likely it is that annexation will be fiercely contested.

The way in which these arguments for and against annexation are resolved is significantly affected by the different legal structures for annexation established by state law. Some states (such as Texas) have adopted rules that foster annexation and others (such as Massachusetts) have adopted rules that inhibit it. Many people assume that a territory cannot be annexed over the objection of its residents. But that is only one of the possible legal structures for annexation decisions. The state legislature can enlarge a city's territory on its own without a vote either of the expanding city or of the territory to be annexed. The state legislature can also authorize local elections. Yet these elections can be organized in different ways. Residents of both the annexing city and the annexed territory can be entitled to vote on the annexation proposal, but their votes can be counted either together, in one ballot box, or separately, with a majority required in each of the two jurisdictions. The dual ballot box option empowers the territory sought to be annexed to veto the annexation, whereas the single ballot box option (assuming that the annexing city has a larger population) makes annexation easier to accomplish. Some states organize annexation by empowering only the residents of the annexing city or its city council to approve annexation. Under this scheme, no vote at all takes place in the annexed territory. Other states do the opposite: They enable the residents of the annexed territory to vote but deny the vote to residents of the annexing city. Like the choice between a single and dual ballot box, these alternative structures can foster or inhibit annexation.

States clearly have the freedom to organize annexation in any of these ways. All of the voting procedures—along with the power of the state legislature to make the decision itself—have been upheld as constitutional. The leading U.S. Supreme Court case, decided in 1907, is *Hunter v. Pittsburgh*. That case upheld the single ballot box procedure. It allowed Pittsburgh to annex neighboring Allegheny over the objection made by Allegheny's residents that permitting the annexation, after a majority of Allegheny's residents voted against it, would deprive them of protected property rights.

The justification for such a combined ballot box is majority rule. A decision has to be made about how best to govern an expanding metropolitan region. If a majority of the combined territory favors an annexation, a minority, often a small minority, should not be able to stand in its way. The justification for the dual ballot box, however, can also be framed as a vindication of majority rule. In this case, the majorities of the two areas are considerably separately, not together. It is thought to be unfair, from this point of view, for a territory to be absorbed into another government structure over the objections of a majority of its residents.

The state government's selection from the list of possible legal structures can have a considerable effect on whether annexation takes place. It is easier to annex a territory if it cannot veto the proposal. Nevertheless, one should not assume that the choice of procedure always dictates the result. The initial annexation that enlarged Boston in the nineteenth century was a result simply of state legislation. Later, the law changed to require the consent of the annexed territory. Yet that consent was forthcoming from many suburbs, ending only with Brookline's rejection of annexation in 1874. Similarly, the annexations in Los Angeles from 1909 to 1915 took place after a majority in both the annexing and annexed territories supported the city's growth. Moreover, allowing the annexing city to decide the issue by itself also does not determine the result. The population of the annexing city can decide that the annexation is not in that city's best interest.

Determining whether a jurisdiction "consents" to an annexation is sometimes complex. Although the growth of Los Angeles was approved by its suburbs, their consent was generated by enormous pressure to get access to water. The consolidation of the city of New York in the late nineteenth century illustrates the opposite phenomenon. The decision to create the enlarged city of New York was made by the state legislature. But the legislature had previously sought to determine the attitudes of the affected jurisdictions by authorizing a nonbinding, advisory vote to be held in each area. All of the areas voted in favor of the consolidation, although the most important city, Brooklyn, did so only by the narrowest of margins (64,744 for, 64,467 against). Given the closeness of that vote, the state legislature did not immediately create the new city. Negotiations were undertaken to determine the appropriate process for writing the new city charter, and only after these negotiations had progressed did the state legislature, notwithstanding the objection of Brooklyn's mayor, approve the consolidation in 1898.

Many people concerned about the racial and class segregation of metropolitan areas support annexation as a solution. David Rusk made a forceful argument for this position in his book *Cities without Suburbs* by outlining the virtues of what he calls "elastic cities." These days, however, annexation will not solve the problems generated by metropolitan fragmentation. Metropolitan areas have simply grown too big. Indeed, the history of annexation demonstrates that city expansion has never adequately captured the entire regional population for long. Those concerned about metropolitan growth are thus exploring alternative solutions to metropolitan fragmentation ranging from regional government to urban growth boundaries to modifying the legal structure of school financing and exclusionary zoning.

Still, at least in some parts of the United States, annexation continues—as do the attempts to resist it. Sometimes annexation fights occur, pitting one possible annexing city against another, with each seeking to absorb a small but valuable portion of land into its borders. Even when annexations do not take place, the legal rules that make annexation easy or difficult can substantially affect interlocal relations. If central cities could annex their suburbs easily, the suburbs might well have an incentive to be more open to negotiations with the central city about issues such as revenue sharing. The suburbs might well think that revenue sharing is a better choice than annexation if both alternatives are

available; they might oppose revenue sharing, on the other hand, if annexation were not an option. The arguments for and against annexation, and the alternative legal structures that enable or restrict it, thus continue to affect the future of cities in the United States.

Gerald E. Frug

See also Local Government; Patchwork Urbanism; Regional Governance; Suburbanization

Further Readings

Jackson, Kenneth T. 1985. *Crabgrass Frontier: The Suburbanization of the United States*. New York: Oxford University Press.

Reynolds, Laurie. 1992. "Rethinking Municipal Annexation Powers." *Urban Lawyer* 24:247–303.

Rusk, David. 1993. *Cities without Suburbs*. Washington, DC: The Woodrow Wilson Center Press.

Teaford, Jon C. 1979. *City and Suburb: The Political Fragmentation of Metropolitan America, 1850–1970*. Baltimore: Johns Hopkins University Press.

APARTHEID

Apartheid refers to a formal, legally defined systematic attempt by a White supremacy government in the mid-twentieth century to organize all aspects of economic, social, cultural, and political life along racially defined lines with a view to promoting an ideology of separateness between race groups in South Africa. It had a particularly virulent expression in urban areas where the greatest likelihood of race mixing and "contamination" was likely to occur. In the contemporary era of rising intraurban and interurban inequality and segregation in many cities of the world as asymmetrical economic globalization impacts on city-building, the ideal and practice of urban apartheid in South Africa has become a powerful metaphor and precedent for understanding the dangers of unchecked urban inequality based on various forms of discrimination. This entry first explains the colonial origins of formal apartheid as introduced in 1948, in order to contextualize the key tenets of the system when it became enshrined in various pieces of legislation until its formal demise in 1994. Particular attention is devoted to the workings of urban apartheid.

Colonial Roots of Apartheid

From the outset of urbanization in South Africa, the colonial state engaged in deliberate policy interventions to establish residential segregation between indigenous Black Africans and Whites. After the abolishment of slavery in 1834, there was a considerable influx of Blacks into colonial towns. In response, the first form of separate settlement—a "location" for Blacks isolated from the town—was introduced in Port Elizabeth by the London Missionary Society. This would become the basic template for a "separate location" policy for the next 100 years, cementing racial segregation into the fabric of urban space from the outset of urbanization.

The Natives Land Act of 1913 was the first legislative attempt to give legal effect to divisions between White and Black groups. The Natives Land Act designated that Africans could own land only inside so-called Native Reserves, which amounted to 8.9 million hectares (less than 13 percent of the total land area of the Union). In terms of the act, Black Africans could not purchase land outside the designated reserves except for the Cape Province where their number was low, dating back to demographic patterns in precolonial times.

The most important legislative intervention in terms of urban segregation was the Native (Urban Areas) Act of 1923. It required municipalities to establish separate locations for Black Africans and to ensure the effective regulation of migration to towns. Even though there was some reluctance on the part of certain municipalities to establish separate locations because of the expense involved, urban historians agree that by 1948 when formal apartheid arrived on the scene, the system of physically separate African locations was firmly in place throughout much of the country. The blatant acts of segregation and movement regulation that stemmed from this act were further complemented by a range of covert urban reforms in the domains of public health, housing, and planning, which may have done even more to ensure thoroughgoing racial segregation in all domains of life. However, the system was not totally successful because the volumes of migration simply overwhelmed state capacity, which produced a patchwork of settlement in the ideal image of the segregationist ambition of the Union government of the time.

Apartheid Era

So it came to be that against this partially successful system of urban segregation, the National Party with its ideology and political program of apartheid (separateness), came to power in 1948, ushering in the era of the search for total racial segregation on the back of an overt agenda of White supremacy but couched in a pseudoegalitarian ideology that spoke of separate but "equal" development. These ambitions were spectacularly successful because the colonial era had thoroughly prepared the territory for racialized urban segregation. In other words, apartheid urban policies from 1948 to 1994 were spectacularly successful because it represented a *continuity* with what had gone before for.

The three central pillars of the apartheid government's urban segregation program were the Group Areas Act of 1950; the Reservation of Separate Amenities Act of 1953; and the regulation of African movement into cities and towns through "influx control" policies that stemmed from the Bantu Urban Areas Act of 1954. All three of these measures were premised on the Population Registration Act of 1950, which provided for the compulsory classification of everyone into distinct racial groups: White, African, and Colored (which initially included Indians).

The Group Areas Act aimed to achieve the *total* residential segregation of people on the basis of racial groups. Practically, urban areas would be zoned into residential and business areas but with an unambiguous racial label. Anyone who resided in the area from a different racial group would be forcibly removed to a "group area" where they ostensibly belonged. Significantly, planning and planners played a central role in the designation of areas into group areas to facilitate the race-based spatial grid that delineated residential and commercial areas. Planning was central because group areas had to be delimited and segregated through a panoply of urban land-use measures such as buffer strips, transport routes, access points, green field areas, and so forth. The Group Areas Act must be considered and understood in relation to the government's larger conception of the "place" of Africans in South Africa. In a sense there was no such place. Africans were deemed to belong to a number of ethnic "nations" that had their *own* territories (Homelands) inside the reserve areas designated by the Land Act of 1913.

The Separate Amenities Act was the pivotal instrument to ensure social segregation through the provision of separate and unequal municipal and public facilities—parks, swimming pools, restrooms, restaurants, and so on. Since different race groups had to use segregated schools and hospitals, the possibilities of chance encounters between groups grew fewer and fewer, counteracting the very essence of urban propinquity that normally underpins periods of urbanization and gives rise to cosmopolitanism. Of course, since Black labor was reserved for all the menial tasks of White economic and social reproduction, there was constant interrace interaction but always on a profoundly unequal footing.

Influx control regulations required all Africans in South African territories to carry a pass book, which was an identity document that proved the person had employment and a residential dwelling for the duration of the employment in the so-called White city. These had to be obtained at labor bureaus inside the Homeland territories. Africans anywhere in South African territories without this document were deemed illegal and could summarily be deported back to their so-called Homeland territory even if they were born and raised in urban areas. In other words, Africans were not meant to belong inside "South African" towns and cities but merely sojourned through them as temporary migrant laborers. Indeed, many Africans were displaced, giving rise to what Colin Murray has called "displaced urbanization" in his description of South Africa's rural slums. Nevertheless, influx control measures consistently failed to acknowledge the presence of large numbers of Africans who lived and worked in urban areas, invariably in horribly overcrowded conditions. This was because the state did not invest in housing provision since that would have represented an acknowledgment of their right to live and work in the city.

Furthermore, despite the engrained precursor of separatism that served as the foundation for formal apartheid, it took the apartheid government the better part of a decade to gear up its administrative capacity to implement the Group Areas Act. Thus, from the 1960s onward a wave of forced removals and rezoning set in, leading to massive and violent resettlement processes of Coloreds, Indians, and Africans. As a consequence, Coloreds and Indians were resettled on small and peripheral locations in urban areas, and Africans were relentlessly deported to Homelands or allowed to settle on overcrowded squatter settlements on the periphery of the towns and cities. Whites were granted access to the most profitable and convenient tracts of land along with extremely high levels of municipal services, which further enhanced the economic value of their properties. Municipal services for Whites were cross-subsidized by Blacks through property taxes and the rates account because all commercial and industrial areas were deemed as White group areas even if they were adjacent to or inside so-called Black group areas. In these senses, the apartheid system ensured that racial segregation was closely intertwined with the perpetuation of economic inequality.

In the post-apartheid era since 1994, urban apartheid has proven stubbornly resilient. In fact, because of the policy decision not to intervene in the functioning of land markets, the government's laudable investments to address the desperate living conditions of the Black majority have backfired. Specifically, formal urban segregation is now abolished but the public housing program of the government, which has delivered 2.5 million housing units between 1994 and 2008, has arguably made South African cities even more segregated because the only land available for this program is on the periphery of the city, far flung from economic, cultural, public, and mobility opportunities that urban living should offer. In other words, South Africa now confronts the problem of class-based, economic segregation, which happens to coincide with racial cleavages given the history of the country.

Edgar Pieterse

See also Divided Cities; Multicultural Cities; Social Exclusion

Further Readings

Beinhart, W. and S. Dubow, eds. 1995. *Segregation and Apartheid in Twentieth Century South Africa*. London: Routledge.

Christopher, A. J. 1998. "(De)Segregation and (Dis) Integration in South African Metropolises." In *Urban Segregation and the Welfare State*, edited by S. Musterd and W. Ostendork. London: Routledge.

Christopher, A. J. 2001. *The Atlas of Changing South Africa*. London: Routledge.

Hindson, D. 1987. *Pass Controls and the Urban Proletariat*. Johannesburg, South Africa: Wits University Press.

Mabin, A. 1991. "Origins of Segregatory Urban Planning in South Africa." *Planning History* 13(3):8–16.

Murray, C. 1995. "Displaced Urbanization: South Africa's Rural Slums." In *Segregation and Apartheid in Twentieth Century South Africa*, edited by W. Beinhart and S. Dubow. London: Routledge.

Posel, D. 1991. "Curbing African Urbanization in the 1950s and 1960s." In *Apartheid City in Transition*, edited by M. Swilling, R. Humphries, and K. Shubane. Cape Town, South Africa: Oxford University Press.

Robinson, J. 1996. *The Power of Apartheid. State, Power and Space in South African Cities*. Oxford, UK: Butterworth-Heinemann.

Subirós, P. 2008. "Racism and Apartheid Yesterday and Today: The White Man's Burden." In *Apartheid: The South African Mirror*, edited by P. Subirós. Barcelona, Spain: Centre for Contemporary Culture in Barcelona.

ARCADE

It is the arcades of early twentieth-century Paris that are the most familiar to scholars in urban studies because of the work of critical theorist Walter Benjamin and surrealist writers such as Louis Aragon and André Breton. This entry, however, focuses on the arcades of London.

Arcades arguably originated in London in the sixteenth century as the sites of financial exchange and trade. Adopting a spatial arrangement from Italian mercantile cities where the financial exchange of bankers took place in arcaded courtyards, the Royal Exchange, built in 1568, consisted of a two-story gallery around an open courtyard. In 1609 a rival, the New Exchange, was built farther west in the Strand, internalizing the courtyard and placing an arcaded walk around the outside, two rows of shops and a central corridor on the ground floor, and three rows of shops on the upper floor. The New Exchange and those that followed, such as the Exeter Change (1676) and the Middle Exchange, were located to the west of the city, their intended customers initially the nobility traveling west from their residences.

By siting trade internally and rationalizing the layout of booths, these commodity exchanges sanitized and regulated the market place, making it acceptable to a new bourgeois class, providing fancy goods—perfumes and clothes rather than the food products of traditional markets. The bazaar, a multistory building containing shopping stalls or counters, as well as picture galleries, indoor gardens, and menageries, by using a name that evoked the exotic qualities of the merchandise, took the process of commodification one stage further. Under the management of one proprietor, counters were rented out to retailers of different trades, attracting customers to a wider variety of commodities—dresses, accessories, millinery.

Precedents for English arcades also came from France, from the Jardins du Palais Royal (1781–1786), a quadrangle with an arcaded ground floor and shops along one side, described as the prototype of the prerevolutionary Parisian arcade, a meeting place for wealthy society prerevolution and postrevolution, converted into shops. The first arcades, places of transition as well as exchange, such as the Galleries du Bois, the Passage Feydeau (1791), and the Passage du Caire (1797–1799), followed shortly afterward. The first two arcades constructed during the early decades of the nineteenth century in London were the Royal Opera Arcade (1815–1817), designed by John Nash and G. S. Repton, and the Burlington Arcade (1818–1819), designed by Samuel Ware. A third London arcade, the Lowther Arcade, was also part of an urban improvement scheme around Trafalgar Square. The London arcades were part of plans to promote the fashionable and wealthy residential areas of the west around Piccadilly, Bond Street, Oxford Street, and Regent Street as a zone of luxury commodity consumption.

The Burlington Arcade was built for Lord Cavendish, the owner of Burlington House, to create a private realm, protected from the street, for an elite class of shopper. Arcades were represented as safe environments, usually under the management of one proprietor, physically secure with safety features, such as guards and lockable gates. Designed along strict and rational grids, with no hidden spaces or secret activities, these buildings promoted order and control. From the outset, entry to the arcade was moderated; members of Lord Cavendish's ex-military regiment were employed as beadles to guard entry to the arcade and to enforce certain regulations. These governed opening and closing times (the arcade closed at 8 p.m. and was locked at night); the kind of movement that could take place in the arcade (this excluded running, pushing a pram, and carrying bulky packages or open umbrellas); and the noise level in the arcade (there was to be no whistling, singing, or playing of musical instruments). In contrast to the surrounding unruly city, associated with danger and threat, emphasis was placed on order and control. The status of the arcade was clearly indicated to passersby at the point of entry, the threshold with the street, where the presence of the beadles and the colonnaded screens indicated a transition from the unruly and public to the ordered and private.

The district immediately surrounding the arcade at the beginning of the nineteenth century was described as a "morning lounge" for wealthy young men. The streets in the vicinity housed a large number of male venues, such as the clubs of St. James's Street and Pall Mall, and provided lodgings for single men of the nobility, gentry, and professional classes. As such, the location provided a concentration of wealthy male customers, and the district played an important part in the commerce of female prostitution. A number of high-class brothels were located in King's Place nearby, and at night the streets of St. James's, Pall Mall, Piccadilly, and the Haymarket formed a circuit notorious for streetwalkers.

As a consequence of this position, the Burlington Arcade was specifically mentioned in contemporary men's magazines as a pleasure resort and a place to pick up pretty women. It was at the threshold between street and arcade, where decisions were enacted by the beadles concerning who could and who could not enter the arcade. Men and women could be excluded on grounds of class, but prostitutes presented a particular threat, for they might "dress up" as respectable women and pass by the beadles or alternatively bribe them. The presence of prostitutes and possible confusion of them with respectable women meant that at certain times of day, specifically between 3 p.m. and 5 p.m., respectable women would not enter the Burlington Arcade.

The Burlington Arcade was described by various primary sources as an "agreeable promenade," "walk or piazza," "long and commodious archway," and "covered passage." As symmetrical streets and sky-lit spaces, arcades gave access to the interior of blocks, provided semipublic routes through private property, and allowed ways of organizing retail trade. The spatial layout of the arcades exploited possibilities opened up by divorcing the point of sale from the place of production. Shops could be smaller, allowing narrow strips of unusable urban land to be economically developed. The building of the Burlington Arcade utilized a narrow strip of land alongside Burlington House and made it commercially viable. Samuel Ware's early designs, based on the Exeter Change, described two entrances, four double rows of shops, and three open, intervening spaces. But as built, retail opportunities were increased by including unbroken rows of enclosed shops down each side, providing not only a space of static consumption, but also a space of transition, a place for a promenade.

The successful selling and buying of goods requires the right kind of environment, a seductive and convincing atmosphere, and a consistency between the type of goods on sale and the design of the shop. For the Burlington Arcade to succeed as a space for luxury consumption, the design of the shops required careful consideration. Shops selling high-class goods were distinguished by having workshops either off-site or located in distinct and separate areas. This separation of production and consumption allowed the shops in the arcade to be unusually shallow in their design.

The original purpose of the Burlington Arcade was to provide employment for women, and in the early- and mid-nineteenth century many of the shops of the arcade were occupied and owned by women. Each shop was designed as a discrete and self-contained unit, with a ground floor, a basement, and upper chambers, all accessed via a staircase. The upper chambers of the shops were considered sites of prostitution and featured in tales of early-nineteenth-century London, such as George Smeeton's *Doings in London*. While millinery shops were represented as fronts for brothels and scenes of seduction, the upper chambers of bonnet shops in the Burlington Arcade were described in fiction and by contemporary commentators such as Bracebridge Hemyng as the sites of sex and of prostitution.

The precise relation of the staircase, shop, and upper chamber remains unclear from existing accounts. It is likely these upper chambers were connected internally; certainly originally the architect favored renting out the upper floors to the shop tenants, and plans from 1818 show shops with internal staircases only. However, plans of 1815 also exist that show staircases positioned between the shop units, prioritizing the likelihood of external renting opportunities. The terminology used to describe the upper floor accommodation in Samuel Ware's design further confuses readers: The chambers are described variously as "sleeping apartments," "dormitories," and "suites of rooms." But given the separation of the upper chambers from the shops, it is certainly possible that these rooms were used for prostitution, either by the shopgirls themselves or hired out by prostitutes or clients.

Through their design and materials, shop fronts advertise business, represent social status, and attract customers. Luxury commodities require external display and so the shape of windows, as well as the type and amount of glass deployed, was a prime requirement in the Burlington Arcade. The design of the shops maximized display and enhanced viewing possibilities by adopting shallow depths, wide frontages, and bow windows. The use of large sheets of plate glass, a modern and very expensive material in the early nineteenth century, added to the perception of the arcade as a luxury zone. Its spatial qualities—reflective, transparent, and at times opaque—allowed a number of tensions to emerge between inside and outside.

As a transparent material, glass allowed an opportunity for presenting and protecting commodities. Close visual inspection of shop windows by passersby was enhanced by the arcade's narrow width, and the transparent glass created a close, though intangible, proximity between inside and outside: Commodities could be seen but not touched. As a reflecting material, as well as allowing a look through to the contents of the shop interior, the glass acted as a mirror for consumers to view themselves and other passersby.

The connection of arcades with the sexual availability of women, ornamentation, and deceit was reinforced through their origin as a foreign building type. Their precedent—the Galleries du Palais Royale in Paris—was the gathering place for libertines before and during the Revolution. The presence of prostitutes in the arcades was complemented by the commercial activities of gambling, drinking, and jewelry selling in the shops. The use of the Parisian precedent, providing flats above shops, in John Nash's designs for the arcaded Quadrant Colonnade section of Regent Street increased the association of arcades and colonnades with "foreign" and therefore suspicious attitudes. Some of these lodgings were rented out to performers at the Italian Opera House in the same district, who were often French, Italian, or German. The mixture of foreign building types and people at a time when France and England were political rivals was perceived as a sign of immorality. Prostitutes were considered to be French, while conversely, the French women living in the vicinity were thought to be prostitutes. The connection made between places selling ornamental luxury commodities and prostitution may be explained then by the French example of the Galleries du Palais Royale.

In the 1830s, arcades and colonnades were synonymous with prostitution. New plans for colonnades around the Italian Opera House in the urban vicinity of the Burlington Arcade were rejected on those grounds. It was the architectural form itself that was believed to be the sole determinant in establishing the use of colonnades or arcades by prostitutes. John Nash thought that some of the problems could be avoided by including minor adjustments to the overall design, such as making the columns round. By mid-century, as opposition to new proposals for arcades and colonnaded spaces was still made on the grounds of discouraging prostitution, a conscious attempt was made to promote arcades as sites of domesticity rather than adult pleasure zones. For example, by the 1860s the character of the shops in the Lowther Arcade, built in the early 1800s, had changed and the arcade became known as a place with a family atmosphere that specialized in children's toys.

Jane Rendell

See also Benjamin, Walter; *Flâneur;* London, United Kingdom; Sex Industry; Shopping

Further Readings

Benjamin, Walter. 1997. *Charles Baudelaire: A Lyric Poet in the Era of High Capitalism*. London: Verso.

Guiot, Johann Friedrich. 1983. *Arcades: The History of a Building Type.* Cambridge: MIT Press.

Hemyng, Bracebridge. 1967. "The Prostitution Class Generally." In *London Labour and the London Poor, London Morning Chronicle 1861–2,* Vol. 4, edited by H. Mayhew and B. Hemyng. London: Frank Cass.

MacKeith, Margaret. 1985. *Shopping Arcades: A Gazetteer of British Arcades 1817–1939.* London: Mansell.

Shepperd, F. H. W., ed. 1963. "The Parish of St. James's Westminster, Part 2, North of Piccadilly." *The Survey of London.* Vol. 32. London: Athlone Press.

Smeeton, George. 1828. *Doings in London; or Day and Night Scenes of the Frauds, Frolics, Manners and Depravities of the Metropolis.* London: Smeeton.

Tallis, John. 1851. *Tallis's Illustrated London: In Commemoration of the Great Exhibition.* London: J. Tallis.

Ware, Samuel. "A Proposal to Build Burlington Arcade" (16 March 1808) and "Schematic Plans for the Burlington Arcade and Burlington House" (1815, 1817 and 1818). Collection of Lord Christian, Royal Academy of Arts Drawing Collection, London.

ARCHITECTURE

Architecture refers both to those parts of the built environment that are designed by architects and the collective designation of the profession. This basic definition is complicated by a number of factors, not least of which is the fact that the types of buildings that can "properly" be considered architecture is of significant controversy and struggle, as is the right of designers to be recognized as architects. These significant questions are assessed in this entry against the backdrop of architecture's complex and contingent social production. Indeed, it is architecture's social foundation—rather than its existence either an object or as a formal practice—that leads social scientists to seek to reveal the many "external" social constraints that impinge on architectural production. Arguably urban studies scholars are uniquely well placed in this regard, as the frameworks that underpin urban studies research encourage those scholars to situate architecture relative to the broader urban process and to recognize the contested nature of the political economies of cities, of which architecture is an important component.

The Study of Architecture as Practice

One of the distinctive elements of architecture as a profession is the reliance on clients for the resources—including land and other capital—necessary for its practice. At one level this client dependency can be explained by the inherently expensive endeavor of the design and realization of buildings, but this connection must also be understood in light of the desire of the powerful to materialize their status in urban space. Studies of the architectural profession have frequently sought to develop this theme through revealing the extent to which architects' reliance on commissions from dominant political and economic actors conditions—and is subsequently legitimated through—their practice. This has been a particularly major concern in the urban studies tradition, where research on the political economy of architectural practice is among the most successful of social science contributions on the subject, not least because such studies can be situated in established "sociology of the professions" frameworks. By and large such research suggests that, in spite of the aforementioned dependence on capitalists and states for commissions and other resources, architects frequently reveal a highly ambiguous relationship with such social forces. In interviews and discussions of their practice, architects tend toward emphasis of their role in the production of socially meaningful buildings that connect to place, identities, and broader social values at the expense of a foregrounding of the interconnections between architecture and the states and capitalist enterprises that commission it. Commenting on this tension, the architectural theorist Diane Ghirardo suggests that positioning architecture within an aesthetic frame serves to divert attention away from the politics of architecture, including its symbiotic relationship with economic and political elites and their projects.

Research that situates architectural practice within particular urban contexts, political regimes, and capitalist models problematizes architecture's claims to autonomy from these processes; the profession's position somewhere between an art, primarily concerned with aesthetics and the creation of socially meaningful forms and spaces, and as a primarily functional response to material issues, such as shelter, is an important consideration in this regard. American sociologist Robert Gutman's classic study *Architectural Practice: A Critical View* is informed by the notion that architecture's unique "natural market" is for those landmark, monumental buildings that claim to reflect major civilizational values. Gutman claims that the struggle for such commissions—always limited in number and so creating competition between architects and a subsequent hierarchy of professionals—exists in the context of architects' attempts to retain distinction from other related design professionals, which is crucial to architecture's continued monopoly over this sphere of activity. Indeed, the question of architects' self-definition is significant here, with the emergence of the profession bound up with the capacity of renaissance architects to frame their work as a design practice separate from that of construction; the role of drawing is a significant part of this story, as it allows a form other than the finished building that can be understood as the intellectual property of architects. (Ongoing conceptions of the "architect as artist" must be understood against this backdrop.)

A related concern of studies on architecture has been to draw attention to the functions of social reproduction and social closure performed by the architectural field, understood in reference to both those internal struggles for symbolic capital (between architects and firms) and the desire for distinction (from other designers) that characterizes the architectural field, the very definition of which is a fundamental site of these conflicts. The partial, unrepresentative nature of the architectural profession in terms of class, gender, and ethnicity has also been a significant focus of social science attention and provides the context for ethnographic studies into the culture of architectural practice, which has made valuable contributions to the understanding of architects' socialization into particular offices and into the profession more generally, including their positioning of themselves relative to their colleagues and the profession's hierarchy more generally.

The Social Production of Architecture: Power and Form

Major architectural projects in cities the world over are testament to the widespread desire of socially dominant individuals and organizations to materialize their power in urban space. While the exact nature of architects' relationship with the politically and economically powerful varies as markedly across time and space as does the actual form that architecture takes, the durable nature of the relationship frames much critical inquiry on architecture. Revealing what Kim Dovey has called a "silent complicity" of architecture with dominant social groups has been a major preoccupation of urbanists, who largely have sought to challenge the aforementioned illusion of architecture as an autonomous, artistic practice concerned solely with form-making and disconnected from politics and the capitalist process. From this perspective architecture should not be considered as a neutral or free-floating cultural form but rather as a social practice that expresses the close relationship between architects and the agendas of the politically and economically powerful. From this perspective such "complicities" are reflected clearly in urban space, with architecture always and everywhere an inherently political—and thus contested—practice.

The eighteenth and nineteenth centuries, a period in which architects and their architecture were incorporated into state projects, illustrate something of the ways in which the built environment is positioned relative to political discourse. Architecture was one space in which emerging nation-states and the architects they commissioned sought to communicate a wide range of values and principles to mass publics. Major architectural projects were often commissioned explicitly to reflect the values and achievements of emerging states, which used cultural artifacts and space to emphasize their distinction from other nation-states and to develop a cultural association with some preceding national regimes. This context saw the emergence of national styles of architecture as an important part of a wider repertoire of cultural forms— including flags, currency, anthems, art, and national dress—which was developed and mobilized with the explicit aim of "inventing" national cultural traditions. In many national contexts there existed explicit architectural and political debates concerning the discovery of a "suitable" style for landmark public buildings. Architectural styles associated with previous regimes—such as Roman, Gothic, and Greek designs—had taken on stylized qualities and crucially had come to be read as cultural codes loaded with meaning, representing values that emerging states wanted to align themselves with. A contemporary example that mirrors these earlier strategies can be found in the European Union's (EU's) cultural construction of discourses of belonging around a European cultural identity, which draws heavily on architecture and space in an attempt to give form to the EU's often ambiguous postnational themes, such as "Unity in Diversity." The *Brussels, Capital of Europe* report is a clear expression of the contested project to identify existing, or construct new, buildings and spaces that can meaningfully be connected to the social and cultural components of the EU's political project.

From a broadly speaking social constructivist perspective, such social meanings are not derived from anything inherent in the aesthetic of the style, but rather they emerge through a range of contingent historical associations; it is not so much architecture's ability to reveal or capture identities accurately that is of concern but rather the role of architects and their designs in contributing to the social construction of discourses of belonging associated with cities, states, and other communities. Framing architecture as a politicized social process invites research into the capacity of the architect to manage the interpretation of their buildings in the face of any number of different interpretations from users, critics, or other publics. In *The Interpretation of Architecture,* Juan Pablo Bonta draws attention to the process of "collective plagiarism" between architects and critics that underpins the emergence of orthodoxies of aesthetic judgment on particular styles at any one time. Bonta's work reminds us that while the interpretation of architecture varies across time and space, and is always subject to challenges, certain individuals and institutions within the architectural field have greater capacity than others to shape the meanings attached to buildings and spaces. In doing so Bonta foregrounds power, in his analysis, into the social construction of architectural meaning; certainly a sense of who has the capacity to define the parameters of the architectural field, a boundary contested not only by architects, but also those commissioning buildings, influential critics, and other buildings professions, is crucial to understanding the social construction of the discourses that legitimate and consecrate both particular styles and buildings, and architects.

This is an especially interesting approach given that high-profile architects are increasingly active in disseminating interpretations of their own work in the public sphere. Such architects, operating at a rarefied level of a profession consistently revealed by studies to be socially unrepresentative in terms of gender, class, and ethnicity, must be highly reflexive when attempting to situate their work relative to social identities, as the danger of privileging one identity discourse—either in the form of the building through particular symbols and motifs or in what is said about the design—is a constant threat. The competition is crucial in this regard, as it is the stage at which drawings and models (increasingly computer-generated ones) and other representations of buildings are presented in response to a tender, or contract bid. Crucially, the competition requires architects to situate their design relative to social identities and values. Accordingly, the competition is an inherently normative endeavor in which architects are required to project a vision of possible futures onto particular social spaces.

Architecture, Iconicity, and Selling Places

Questioning architecture's social meaning relative to political–economic projects is crucial in understanding the role of the built environment in contemporary regeneration strategies. As well as being a prominent component of how urban spaces are used to generate surplus value, architecture is also a central component of the active construction of symbolic "brands" that position postindustrial urban centers as attractive places to visit and to invest. The incorporation of landmark architectural projects into regeneration strategies has been rejuvenated since the 1996 opening of the Bilbao Guggenheim Museum, a Frank Gehry–designed building that is by now an oft-cited reference point in research literature on the rebranding of cities. So-called iconic architecture has come to be viewed by boosterist agencies as a way of reviving the fortunes of cities, with architects commissioned to design bombastic, glassy buildings to serve as instantly recognizable symbols that will attract media and public attention sufficient to improve the image of urban centers. Such architecture is designed to offer both spectacular, distinctive façades and to house the "out-of-the ordinary"

The modern architecture of Vancouver: iconic high-rise glass condominiums

Source: Karen Wiley.

experiences that are attractive to an international class of tourists.

While maybe or maybe not physically dominating the surrounding landscape, icons are explicitly positioned relative to a visual consumer, considered either as the visitor standing in front of the building or, more likely, the viewer of an image of the architecture in the printed press, on television, or on film. Accordingly, a successful iconic building necessarily develops a strong association with place through an instantly recognizable form designed to be both distinctive and widely disseminated. It has also been observed that the emergence of a distinct aesthetic and language of "icons" reveals the aforementioned resonance between the architectural field and the desire of footloose globalized capitalist interests to give material form to their status and to extract surplus value from city spaces.

Recent research has sought to link the emergence of icons with the consolidation of a transnational elite of "starchitects," high-profile architects whose globally oriented business models and prominence in public discourse situate them as a mobile, global elite whose capacity to define transnational spaces—such as parliament buildings, airports, galleries, major shopping developments, and sports stadiums—makes them much in demand. As suggested earlier, close links to place

making are, in one reading at least, definitive of architecture's remit. Certainly how far architecture is, or is perceived to be, "rooted" in place has been one of the defining issues for architecture since its inception, and how meaningfully architect-designed buildings and spaces connect to local communities' visions of place is explored by a number of urbanists who call for a reforging of architecture's relationship to place.

Such calls echo the stance of critical regionalism, a popular refrain in architectural theory and, to a lesser extent, in practice in the 1980s and early 1990s. Critical regionalism was a reaction against the standardizing, "placeless" architecture associated with the high modernism of the international style, typified by skyscrapers in major financial centers. In seeking to defend the distinctive elements of place against the standardizing elements of capitalist process, this group of theorists was crucial to the emergence of vernacular architecture that sought to rejuvenate the relationship between the built environment and place through sensitivity to social and environment context, including for example a use of local material and styles, topographical integration of building, and the associated rejection of technocratic development and the domination of instrumentalized, profit-driven design and building technique. The potential of architecture as a resistant cultural form is an important question in this context. Critical region-alism's defense of cultural particularism and use of appropriate technology in the face of perceived homogenization was particularly resonant in the context of postmodernism.

The architectural discourse of postmodernism served to reinvigorate discussion of architecture's social meaning, not least by opening up the potential for multiple readings of buildings and spaces, and by celebrating a plurality of stylistic traditions and incorporating "nonpedigreed" architecture into existing canons. In general terms, postmodern perspectives were underpinned by a commitment that architecture should become a more "opened" discourse and practice, with the spaces created by architecture reflecting a plurality of social standpoints and supporting a range of different ways of being in the city, generally emphasizing democratic rights to public space. The notion of multiple readings, crucial for postmodernism in general terms, rendered the architects' reading of the symbolism in their building as just one among many, which opened the way for playful architecture that challenged the relationship between signifier and signified (and architect and user). Accordingly, postmodernism sought to challenge elitist conceptions of architecture—as profession and social practice—that had been dominant in modernism, including the capacity of the architect to offer definitive "truths" about the correct use and interpretation of urban spaces. Critical scholars engaged with the postmodern debate sought to demonstrate the superficial nature of much of postmodern architecture's promise for new "open" spaces by drawing attention to the synergies between postmodern discourse—albeit as one that unquestionably did disrupt previously deeply held values and practices within architecture—and the recasting of long-standing compliances with the economically powerful.

A major challenge for urban researchers is to both maintain a sense of architects' position as a cultural elite working in definite urban political economies, while at the same time engaging with architecture's status as a socially resonant form that is loaded with social meaning. In other words, although overwhelmingly conceived and funded by dominant political and economic actors, the built forms of architecture become meaningful to users and other citizens as markers of urban space and as reflections of a diverse range of social realities. At the same time, a primary focus on architecture's capacity to support diverse social meanings can often be at the expense of a deeper critique of the unequal power relations that underpin the social production of architecture. It is this ambiguous backdrop that means—far from being an unproblematic reflection of societal values—architecture reflects many of the tensions between elite and non-elite visions of urban space.

Paul Jones

See also Gendered Space; Landscapes of Power; Other Cities; Placemaking; Racialization; Urban Design; Urban Semiotics

Further Readings

Blau, J. 1984. *Architects and Firms: A Sociological Perspective on Architectural Practice.* Cambridge: MIT Press.

Bonta, J. P. 1979. *Architecture and Its Interpretation.* London: Lund Humphries.

"Brussels, Capital of Europe." 2001. Retrieved May 9, 2009 (http://ec.europa.eu/dgs/policy_advisers/archives/publications/docs/brussels_capital.pdf).

Cuff, D. 1992. *Architecture: The Study of Practice.* Cambridge: MIT Press.

Dovey, K. 1999. *Framing Places: Mediating Power in Built Form.* London: Routledge.

Frampton, K. 1983. "Towards Critical Regionalism: Seven Points for an Architecture of Resistance." In *Postmodern Culture: The Anti-aesthetic*, edited by H. Foster. London: Pluto.

Ghirardo, D. 1984. "Architecture of Deceit." *Perspecta* 21:110–15.

Gutman, R. 1988. *Architectural Practice: A Critical View.* Princeton, NJ: Princeton Architectural Press.

Jencks, C. 2005. *Iconic Buildings: The Power of Enigma.* London: Frances Lincoln.

Larson, M. S. 1993. *Behind the Postmodern Façade: Architectural Change in Late-Twentieth Century America.* Berkeley: University of California Press.

McNeill, D. 2009. *The Global Architect: Firms, Fame, and Urban Form.* London: Routledge.

Stevens, G. 1998. *The Favored Circle: The Social Foundations of Architectural Distinction.* Cambridge: MIT Press.

ASIAN CITIES

Asia extends from the Ural Mountains and Turkey eastward to the Pacific Ocean and includes the major island states along the western Pacific Rim. Asian cities are diverse in many major characteristics. The colonial era, particularly from the early nineteenth to the mid-twentieth century, produced a few common features among some larger cities. Decolonization, beginning in the 1940s, created new states and imprinted on the larger urban areas. The partition of the Indian subcontinent and the creation of Muslim Pakistan and Bangladesh had an impact on the cities. In Pacific Asia the emergence of socialist states in China, Vietnam, and elsewhere shaped distinctive urban land-use patterns. By the late twentieth century the escalating economic development of Asia had increased the recognizable international features of the majority of Asia's cities and accelerated the emergence of several giant megacities.

Asian Cities in History

Prior to World War II there was little analysis in the English language of Asian cities. However, throughout history, travelers regularly published descriptions of Asia's towns and cities. Marco Polo, the thirteenth-century Venetian trader, wrote of the Mongolian and Chinese towns he visited, though there is some dispute whether his story is told firsthand or is based on accounts by other travelers. He claimed to have visited Khanbaliq, present-day Beijing, the home of the Kublai Khan and capital of the Yuan Dynasty. Italo Cavalo has written a modern fictionalized account of Polo's journey.

Max Weber's writings in the first half of the twentieth century compared and contrasted the Occidental and the "Asiatic," or "Oriental," city, focusing mainly on China, India, and Japan. The sociologist Gideon Sjoberg drew extensively on Indian and Chinese urban histories in his conceptualization of the "preindustrial city." However, in general, Asian cities were marginal to the study of the evolving twentieth-century city.

The number of published analytical writings about Asian cities increased significantly in the mid-twentieth century. The demise of colonialism and the emergence of new independent nations, including India, Pakistan, Indonesia, and Vietnam, saw an expansion of Western interest in Asian cities. Independence coincided with an escalation in the pace of urbanization, especially through the migration of rural residents to the emerging capital cities and the centers of commerce and trade.

The Dutch sociologist William Wertheim edited nineteenth-century Dutch writings on the Indonesian town, revealing the poor conditions of the cities, with their wealthy colonial enclaves and the wretched village housing of the native Javanese. Another growing source of writings on Asian cities was Asian regional geography texts. Authors such as J. E. Spencer included descriptive chapters on the populations and economies of Asian cities.

Historians writing about the emergence of cities in Asia began to emphasize the deep historical roots of some of Asia's cities. Anthony Reid drew attention to the significant urban history of Asia, highlighting a long urban tradition in a region that was generally seen as agriculture oriented, because of the interest in the wet rice cultivation systems. A distinction existed between Asia's "sacred" cities and "market" cities. Sacred cities such as Kyoto and Yogyakarta were shaped by rulers and their cosmological beliefs. Market cities, including Singapore, Shanghai, and Kolkata, were a product of their locations on major trade routes and hosted a cosmopolitan population of merchants and traders.

Contemporary Asian Cities

Around two thirds of the world's population live in Asia, which encompasses the two most populous nations, China and India. Both have well in excess of 1 billion inhabitants. Four other countries, Indonesia, Pakistan, Bangladesh, and Japan, have populations of over 100 million.

Rapid decolonization and the establishment of independent states followed the end of World War II. Attention turned to the formation of new states trying to meet the challenges of recovering from the colonial experience and building new societies, economies, and political infrastructure. The process of urbanization and the challenges of the cities became an increasing focus. By the last quarter of the twentieth century, the escalating integration of many parts of Asia into the world economy meant that contemporary aspects of globalization became a dominant thread in urban scholarship. In parallel, postcolonial approaches and themes emerged as Asian writers became more prominent in exploring the features of Asian cities.

Urbanization

Urbanization is an outcome of rural–urban migration, fertility levels in cities, and boundary changes as cities grow and encroach upon the surrounding rural areas. Asian nations have urbanized at different rates. Singapore is an urban city-state, and the entire population of the Hong Kong Special Administrative Region is urban. In general, the more economically developed nations have over half their populations living in cities. These include the Pacific Asian countries of Japan, the Republic of Korea, the Democratic People's Republic of Korea, Mongolia, Brunei Darussalam, Indonesia, Malaysia, and the Philippines. Iran and Turkey also have more residents in urban than rural areas.

Less than half the people in China, Cambodia, Laos, Myanmar, Thailand, Timor Leste (East Timor), and Vietnam live in urban areas. Similarly, cities account for under half the populations of Afghanistan, Bangladesh, Bhutan, the Maldives, Nepal, Pakistan, Sri Lanka, Armenia, Azerbaijan, Georgia, Kazakhstan, Kyrgyzstan, Tajikistan, Turkmenistan, and Uzbekistan.

The emergence of the Communist regime in Russia in 1917 influenced the shape and functions of Russian cities. Communist and socialist ideas spread throughout the Asian region from the 1930s onward. Socialist regimes were established in China in 1949, and later in Vietnam, Cambodia, and Laos, and had a great impact on cities.

Asia's socialist regimes tried to slow the rates of urbanization in the period until economic reforms commenced in earnest in the early 1990s. By enforcing permit arrangements for moving to cities, such as the *hukou* in China, and controlling urban labor and housing markets and access to subsidized food, countries such as China and Vietnam slowed rural–urban migration to rates well below those of neighboring countries with market economies. However, the process was diluted when they embraced economic reform and entered into the

global economy, and the rate of rural–urban migration has increased in recent years.

Asia has hosted the growth of over half of the world's megacities, or cities with populations of 10 million or more. In 2005 Tokyo, Osaka-Kobe, Mumbai, Delhi, Kolkata, Shanghai, Beijing, Jakarta, Dhaka, Karachi, and Manila comprised over half of the world's 20 megacities. It is no coincidence that the megacities are located in countries with large populations: Japan, India, China, Indonesia, Bangladesh, Pakistan, and the Philippines.

There are several other large Asian cities that extend across formal urban boundaries and are, in effect, also of megacity size, including Istanbul, Bangkok, and Chongqing. Terry McGee has analyzed the growth of *desakota,* or extended metropolitan regions in which large cities effectively encompass and urbanize rural settlements around the periphery of the city, creating distinctive urban regions of considerable significance.

The Economy

Asian economies span a significant range. Japan, Singapore, and Brunei are in the high-income range. The two Koreas, Malaysia, Thailand, the Philippines, and a handful of western Asian countries (including Turkey, Iran, and Kazakhstan) are in the World Bank's middle-income band. The remainder, including the largest countries of China, India, Indonesia, Pakistan, and Bangladesh, are low-income countries. The major cities have overall higher levels of income than do the rural areas, and higher proportions of middle- and upper-income earners. This results in urban–rural disparities, such as striking contrasts between the thriving cosmopolitan center of modern Shanghai and the impoverished rural regions of western China.

With relatively few exceptions, Asian economies in the 1950s struggled to develop and bring benefits to people in both rural areas and the cities. Many countries sought to establish new industries, initially based on models intending to replace imports with home-produced goods. Industries were encouraged to establish themselves in the major cities where infrastructure and a potential labor force were located. This strategy of industrialization faltered, and countries such as Singapore shifted their orientation toward export-oriented industrialization. Contemporary industrial development has, in most instances, leapfrogged from inner-city locations to the areas around the major cities.

Industrialization absorbed only a small proportion of the available labor force in cities in Asia's less economically developed countries. The vast majority of migrants to the city work in the "informal sector," in microenterprises providing cheap goods and services. Metropolitan authorities frequently sought to suppress microenterprises, viewing them as inefficient and disruptive to the city. Others have pressed for more positive policy interventions, pointing out the need to provide employment for growing numbers of city workers and the low cost of the services microenterprises provide. At the instigation of the Bangladeshi economist Mohammad Yunus and the support of organizations such as the Grameen Bank, and more recently the Asian Development Bank, policies promoting the availability of low-cost finance for microenterprises have become more common.

A number of world cities are developing in Asia. High order services in finance, management, law, and architecture support the location of head offices of significant global companies, giving them an important role in the global economy. Tokyo, Hong Kong, and Singapore are prime examples of Asian world cities. Seoul is the next level down. The third tier of world cities includes Jakarta, Osaka, Taipei, Bangkok, Beijing, Kuala Lumpur, Manila, and Shanghai.

All of the Asian world cities are located in Pacific Asia. No south or west Asian city features in the list. The major cities of the Indian subcontinent have not yet acquired sufficient world city functions, because they are situated in economies with limited global links. The consistent rates of economic growth in India mean that Delhi, Mumbai, and possibly Bangalore will be the most likely to achieve world city status within a decade.

Asian cities are developing strategies to strengthen their engagement in information industries. With the slowdown in the information technology economy in the United States, many Indian information technology workers returned to India, and especially to Bangalore, where they played a key role in stimulating the industry. Bangalore is regarded as a center of high-tech industry in India and is diversifying into biotechnology and nanotechnology

industries. Kuala Lumpur is now connected to the "multimedia supercorridor," which extends south of the city to the Kuala Lumpur International Airport in Sepang.

Society and Environment

Islam is the main religion of many large Asian countries, including Turkey, Iran, Afghanistan, Kazakhstan, Pakistan, Bangladesh, Malaysia, and Indonesia. Some Middle East urbanists highlight the historical and contemporary influence of Islam on the evolution of the city and attribute the problems of contemporary Islamic cities to the negative impact of colonialism. Critics such as Yasser Elsheshtawy reject this "narrative of loss" and highlight the significance of globalization in shaping modern cities.

Assertive postcolonial voices on Asia's cities have become prominent. Turkish Nobel Prize winner Orhan Pamuk has written autobiographically about Istanbul, drawing inspiration from its long history as the center of the Ottoman Empire. Its pivotal location on the strategic Bosphorus Strait provides the backdrop for the juxtaposition within the contemporary city of evolving modernity and a fading past. His family history provides a framework around which Istanbul's story is told.

Suketu Mehta's outstanding writing on Mumbai, the giant Indian city, explores the city's history and its underbelly. Through extended biographical profiles of criminal "black-collar workers," poets, and makers of popular culture, he fashions an eclectic picture of this sprawling metropolis.

The social characteristics of Asian cities are varied. Most cities have high proportions of the young. Singaporean and Japanese cities, in contrast, have aging populations. Youth in the cities are increasingly free of traditional constraints. They are vulnerable to the scourge of Western cities, the pockets of youth-centered urban drug cultures. However, the opportunities for progression through school and into university study have increased at a faster rate than have populations. A small but significant proportion of students go abroad to the United States and Canada, the United Kingdom, and Australia to attend university and acquire the skills they hope will ensure them a place in the global knowledge economy. The Chinese and Korean governments have led the way by strengthening local universities. Singapore has also attracted significant foreign universities to establish small campuses and research centers in the city in order to build local skills and attract foreign students to Singapore.

Urban housing issues have attracted much attention. Migration-driven urbanization meant cities absorbed large numbers of rural workers and their families. Spontaneous shantytowns and squatter settlements appeared across many Asian cities. Residents generally built their own houses, often from secondhand or scavenged materials, and seldom had security over land. There has been some softening of attitudes toward settlements in the past few decades.

The escalating economic growth within Pacific Asia has seen the expansion of urban megaprojects that are transforming the cities in China, Japan, and Singapore. New middle- and high-income housing developments are generally intrinsic parts of new complexes of offices catering to the financial, services, and high-tech industries. Transport developments featuring extensive freeways and rail developments have become common. The magnetically levitating train that connects Pudong Airport with Shanghai at speeds of around 430 kilometers (267 miles) per hour is an eye-catching example of new forms of urban transport servicing Asian cities.

Environmental issues are a significant concern throughout most of the Asian region. The environmental risk transition spotlights the changing relationship between people and the environment as cities develop and incomes rise. "Traditional" environmental risks decline over time, but "modern" environmental risks increase. Asian cities cluster in three locations across the model. In the most disadvantaged Asian cities the problems center on water quality and management. The most significant risk to human well-being is the lack of access to clean water for human consumption. The low-lying delta cities of Bangladesh have the added risks of frequent flooding caused by either rainfall in the upper reaches of the Ganges River or tidal and storm surges through the Bay of Bengal.

Planning and Management

Building urban management and planning frameworks has been challenged by the size and rapid growth of Asia's principal cities, in addition to which so many are located in poor countries with limited financial and human resources. The problems being confronted range from the 2004 tsunami's devastation of cities in coastal regions of Sumatra and Sri Lanka, to the need to preserve Hanoi's architectural heritage in a period of rapid growth in urban investment. Looking forward, Asian urban planners will be at the cutting edge of urban change, as Shanghai's growth continues and the major cities along the Pacific Asian coast connect together into extensive mega urban regions. As Asia's urban population grows and the region's economies, particularly those of China and India, rapidly expand, the Asian city will attract greater world attention.

Dean Forbes

See also Hong Kong, China; Islamic City; Kolkata (Calcutta), India; Manila, Philippines; Megalopolis; Mumbai (Bombay), India; Delhi, India; Shanghai, China; Singapore; Squatter Movements; Tokyo, Japan; World City

Further Readings

Calvino, Italo. 1978. *Invisible Cities.* New York: Harvest Books.

Committee on Population, National Research Council. 2003. *Cities Transformed: Demographic Change and Its Implications in the Developing World.* Washington, DC: National Academies Press.

Elsheshtawry, Yasser, ed. 2004. *Planning Middle Eastern Cities: An Urban Kaleidoscope.* London: Routledge.

Forbes, Dean. 1996. *Asian Metropolis.* Melbourne, Australia: Oxford University Press.

Mehta, Suketu. 2004. *Maximum City: Bombay Lost and Found.* New Delhi: Penguin Books India.

Pahuk, Orhan. 2005. *Istanbul: Memories of a City.* Translated by M. Freely. New York: Knopf.

ATHENS, GREECE

Athens, the capital of modern Hellas (Greece), treaded a discontinuous itinerary reaching over six millennia, of which the classical period of the ancient city-state has time and again inspired the collective memory of Western cities. Athens stands

Parthenon at the Acropolis in Athens

Source: Vasilis Gavrilis.

between Occident and Orient and is considered a "theatre of memory," combining ancient and modern, original and copy, informal and postmodern, tourism and romantic traveling, and involving personalities from Gustav Flaubert and Sigmund Freud to Simone de Beauvoir and Jacques Derrida. However, between today's city of 3,187,734 inhabitants (Greater Athens 2001, 29 percent of the Greek population) or 3,761,810 if the broader Attica region is included, and the ancient city-state of the fourth century BC, there is a series of major discontinuities and interesting contrasts. As expected, there are certain constants in the landscape of cities in the same location: The multinucleated urban geography is centered on Athens and its port, Piraeus, and connected by Long Walls and then the railway, enclosed in the basin (*lekanopedio*) bounded by the Hymettus, Pendeli, Parnitha, and Aigaleo mountains and interspersed by seven hills, encircled by a multitude of other towns in the Attica region, *Demoi*, already since antiquity. These were all gradually connected and merged into one single agglomeration by the fast urbanization

waves of the twentieth century. Given the discontinuity of urban history, this entry uses a snapshot approach to the several metamorphoses of the city by "visiting" briefly four important periods during which Athens has become a prototype for urban geography: the ancient city-state, the artificial nineteenth-century capital city, the interwar prototype of Mediterranean fast urbanization, and the post-Olympic entrepreneurial city.

Classical Athens, Acropolis, and Agora

The first traces of life in Athens date from the fourth millennium BC, the late Neolithic period, but the cultural density of ancient or classical Athens has never been paralleled. The celebrated myth of the contest between the goddess Athena and god Poseidon for the patronage of the city, had Athena win and give the city-state her name and the sacred olive as a symbol. The Parthenon temple on the sacred rock of the Acropolis was dedicated to Athena, goddess of wisdom, with her large central statue inside and the evocative representations of myths and processions in her honor in the Parthenon marble friezes. It was the major monument of a city-state that rose to hegemony for a mere 100 years, but still, it became a model for European—and indeed global—culture: language, political institutions, philosophy, drama, art, and architecture. This eternal "city of memory" inspired European geographical imaginations and reproduced global prototypes not only in archaeology or philosophy or cultural studies but in several fields, including urban studies.

After the sixth century BC, following a first wave of flowering of Greek culture in Ionian cities and especially Melitus in Asia Minor, classical Athens rose from a sea of tyranny, first defeating the Assyrians and then expelling its tyrant, Hippias, in 510 BC. Its short-lived civilization (510–404 BC) offered many of the advances and concepts of today's European culture and global institutional discourse: Citizenship from "city" (*politis* from *polis*), the person participating in public life, in contradistinction from *idiotis*, the private person and the etymology for idiot, as in Marx's "rural idiocy"; *polis*, policy, politics, *politismos*, that is, civilization; *theatron*, with "view" as its etymology; tragedy, comedy, philosophy, history; *geography* is a Greek word, too, though a later one, of the Hellenistic period (second century BC). The main thrust of classical culture was not commerce and material production but the quest for knowledge, advances in sexuality and politics—generally, reason, culture, and investigation rather than religion.

In the realm of politics, Athens offered the word, the theory, and the practice of *democratia*, "democracy." The etymology comes from *demos/ demoi*, local communities surrounding the city-state. According to Aristotle, the union or community (*koinonia*) of *Demoi* was the full *polis*—a society, a community, and a state. The words *polis/ politeia/politis* (i.e., city/citizenship/citizen) have a common root and denote urbanism in a positive light. This legitimizes the introduction of "citizenship" on multiple spatial levels, as we do today, using it in connection with the urban, the national, and now the European level—despite its etymology based on the *city*. Planning also centered on the city by definition—*polis/poleodomia* (i.e., city/ town planning)—and classical architecture contributed the Doric and Ionian orders, while later

the Corinthian order emerged in Corinth. The harmonic rules for building were perfected in the Acropolis temples, especially the Parthenon, built by Ictinos and Callicrates in the age of Pericles and inaugurated in 432 BC. Hippodamus from Miletus introduced the "hippodamian system" of urban design there and also in Piraeus and Rhodes: A checkerboard of equality engraved on the urban landscape represented democracy on the ground and in effect introduced modern urban design.

The ancient city-state was centered on the *agora,* the *forum,* the urban public space where direct democracy and citizenship were concretized (*civitas, politeia*). Ideas and policies were debated here in the citizens' assembly without any censorship. Decisions were made by all eligible "citizens" rather than just their representatives, and every man (but no women) participated, irrespective of income, property, or rank. Leaders were elected to office only to carry out the people's will. Pericles was not a ruler but the city's leading citizen, who was elected annually. The *agora* was much more than physical space (*urbs*: Latin) or a "speakers' corner" or an open space for strolling. It literally meant "marketplace," where commerce was centered, but it was actually a complex space of mixed uses and intense social interaction. In the *agora,* the Acropolis, and the city at large, the interpenetration of nature and culture was harmonized in classical architecture by the in-between space of the colonnade, the *stoa,* a pathway of columns open to the outside but also connected with the inside through the roof of the relevant building bordered by the *stoa.*

This was the landscape in which classical civilizations developed. Citizenship and participation in a real, natural city were considered as a precondition of civilization and the essence of democracy. However, among the three claims of citizenship in modernity, the city-states of antiquity respected two: the right to voice, to express (democratization); and the right to human flourishing; but *not* the right to difference. In this, classical Athens was a weak democracy in many senses. Citizenship was bounded by gender, territoriality, and social exclusion—of women, slaves, and "barbarians," or noncitizens. It was actually this exclusion of the "others" from citizenship and the army that constituted the main weakness of the Athenian democracy and its difference from both the Macedonian period and the Roman Empire. Rome established a decentralized administrative mechanism and a multicultural army and respected local cultures. Emperor Hadrian lived in Athens occasionally and constructed Hadrian's gate, the library by the Roman Forum in the city center, and an admirable aqueduct, which was revived in the nineteenth century and relieved water shortages in Athens for a while. In classical Athens, by contrast, the social exclusion of noncitizens would soon backfire, as citizens became vulnerable to attacks by noncitizens during the Peloponnesian wars. After flowering for a mere century, Athens surrendered to the Spartans by 404 BC, the Long Walls to Piraeus were demolished, and democracy was shattered by the regime of the 30 tyrants.

Neoclassical Athens

Athens followed Aegina and Nafplion as the capital of Hellas after independence from Ottoman rule (according to the 1830 London Protocol) and has been one of the most successful experiments of creation of an artificial capital on a global scale. In 1834 it was declared the capital of the new Greek Kingdom, was rebuilt with modern urban design and neoclassical architecture, and metamorphosed from a deserted village of 12,000 inhabitants during the last years of Ottoman rule, into a bustling city of 242,000 inhabitants at the turn of the twentieth century (1907). The creation of the new capital was successful, despite negative forecasts and an interesting debate about the rivalry between Athens—then a village—and cosmopolitan Constantinople as symbols of Hellenism.

Urban colonization of the Greek territory via urban planning started in Athens through Bavarian planning by royalty, their architects, and planning teams. The physical process of building a capital with neoclassical architecture was also an intellectual itinerary in the fragments of history that would constitute a coherent narrative, or perhaps rather iconography, forging national identity by connecting the present with antiquity and its material manifestation in classical architecture. The core of the city obtained its celebrated iconic neoclassical "Athenian trilogy"—university, academy, library—as well as other monumental buildings, generously funded by the "great national donors." These were affluent diaspora Greeks located throughout places of "unredeemed" Hellenism, who sponsored conspicuous monuments and public buildings.

One main reason for legitimation of Bavarian design on the level of the local societies was the echo of classical Hellas. Neoclassical architecture returned to the birthplace of classicism via European cities and became crucial in the process of construction of a new national Greek identity. Athens was mostly built by Bavarians, but the buildings were "naturalized" by the inhabitants and the modern Greek nation, because of their familiar classical forms. This has facilitated the reception of European design trends imported especially by Bavarians and, even more important, has undermined colonial domination, despite the character of nineteenth-century Athens as a colonial city.

A second reason for legitimation of Bavarian planning was its departure from irregular Ottoman or Mediterranean models. An interesting aspiration was the recovery of Hellenism through the "de-turkization" of Greek towns via regular plans in the tradition of the "hippodamian" system, yet another classical heritage. However, orthogonal grids, straight streets, and regular town squares were rarely realized. The Athens plan has been revised more than 3,000 times, due to pressures from local landowners. Citizens have objected to the methods of implementation of the plans they themselves had asked for and criticized planners who constructed a virtual city, the unreal landscape represented on blueprints, which has been exciting and at times menacing—as, for example, in the momentary risk of having the Acropolis incorporated in the royal palace as a *décor,* in accordance with Schinkel's plan drawn by a man who never visited Athens.

Neoclassicism, "de-turkization," and cosmopolitanism were all aspects of an underlying Greek "dualism," wherein modernity was underplayed in urban cultural discourse, overshadowed by debates over cosmopolitanism versus tradition or nationalism, which also cut through language, creating bilingualism. Alternating acceptance of, and resistance to, Westernization has been the main contradiction in the past—at present, Europeanization has put all this to rest. Power plays were stirred by the "protective powers," who intervened in several spheres, from political life to archaeological excavations and the plundering of Hellas's past. The Acropolis remained a contested monument of collective memory with unceasing conflicts over "property" and appropriation. The Parthenon marbles—all pediments, friezes, metopes, and even more—were smuggled to England in 1805 by Lord Elgin and are now standing at the British Museum.

Conspicuous neoclassical monuments and civic architecture in the midst of unpaved streets and rudimentary infrastructure revealed the contradictions of urban development. The monumentalization of Athens and the revival of the Olympic Games in 1896 came up three years after the national bankruptcy in 1893 and just before a humiliating defeat in 1897 by the Ottoman Empire. As in other nineteenth-century cities, pomp and monumentalization in Athens in the midst of decline counteracted it on the symbolic level.

Interwar Athens

Interwar Athens during the 1920s and the 1930s became a prototype of Mediterranean rapid urbanization after the arrival of refugees from Asia Minor in 1922, and since then it has been restructured to a major agglomeration and a typical Mediterranean metropolitan center growing by urbanization without industrialization. Informal work and informal housing, *afthereta,* built on the urban periphery by migrants and the poor on land where it was illegal to build, became one of the major issues (if not the dominant one) in public policy (non)responses and urban social movements. From 1922 until the 1970s, urban poverty went in parallel with precarious owner-occupation in illegal self-built shacks, which improved as the family income grew. These were finally controlled by the dictatorial government (1967–1974) by force (demolitions) and consent (legalizations). Meanwhile, it had solved the housing problem for many internal migrants, workers, and the poor.

First the refugee arrival and then rural–urban migrants to Athens have established the basic axes of spatial segregation since the 1920s: Inside/outside the official city plan was a duality also echoed in inner city/outskirts, but also east/west of the agglomeration, concentrating middle/working classes, respectively. Spontaneous urban development and social segregation created a cityscape antithetical to the Anglo-American one, that is, an inverse-Burgess model. Already in the 1920s a southwest–northeast axis emerged in the Athens agglomeration, defining the contrast between the elegant architecture of bourgeois buildings proliferating around the center and the sector to the northeast, on the one hand, and the shacks and lack of adequate urban infrastructure, especially along the western ring of the city, on the other.

A central feature of the mode of housing production in bourgeois and popular suburbs was "self-building" (*aftostegasi*), under the responsibility and the supervision of each family. The inner city, by contrast, was built to be very compact by middle- and upper-class land plot owners and entrepreneurs in a piecemeal manner: Multistory apartment buildings, *polykatoikies,* were produced by a system of exchange arrangements (*antiparochi*) on land provided by the landowning family in exchange for some flats. The overheated construction sector and speculation on land demolished pieces of neoclassical architecture and urban heritage and erased several layers of urban history. Only the "Athenian trilogy" stood in the center, and of course the sacred rock of the Acropolis remained a focal point for the city in the midst of increasing urban densities.

In 1933 Athens became the cradle of modernism, hosting the pioneers of modernity in architecture and town planning, which was discursively established with the Congrès International d'Architecture Moderne ([CIAM]; International Congress of Modern Architecture) manifesto: The *Charter of Athens,* written by Le Corbusier and his colleagues, was drafted during the CIAM conference in Athens. Modern architects also admired the Acropolis and the archaeological sites. These were landscaped after the war and remained the object of clashing narratives and power conflicts over property and appropriation, as in the nineteenth century. The Acropolis has been as much a European, or rather global, construction as a Greek monument, and it became the symbol of appropriation and conquest of the city itself. The Germans flew the Swastika flag on the Acropolis when they occupied Athens, and the same flag was taken down and destroyed in a notorious act of resistance by Manolis Glezos and Apostolos Santas on May 31, 1941.

Independence from German occupation followed three years later, on October 12, 1944. A bloody civil war followed, starting with the bloody Sunday of December 3, 1944, in Athens, when a large popular demonstration faced governmental and allied forces' assault and gunfire. The civil war then raged in the mountains, and urban guerilla clashes went on in the narrow city streets of Athens and Piraeus refugee quarters, where in the 1930s an important labor movement had emerged and in the 1940s an underground resistance movement erupted. Since the period of German occupation, Athens had become a refuge from retaliations in rural Hellas, and politically induced internal migration formed the first postwar wave of massive urbanization toward Athens. In the years that followed, rural-to-urban migration escalated and increased the Greater Athens population from 453,042 in 1920 to 1,124,109 in 1940, 1,852,709 in 1961 and as high as 3,016,457 in 1981, when the capital concentrated about one third of the Greek population. After Greece's accession to the European Union in 1981, internal migration to Athens slowed, and by the 1990s it had stabilized.

Post-Olympic Entrepreneurial Athens

Post-Olympic and entrepreneurial Athens for the last decade at the turn of the new millennium—a decade starting around the 1996 unsuccessful bid for the "Golden Olympics" and culminating during the 2004 Olympics—belongs to an era of European urban development where neoliberal governance and globalization stir and reproduce urban competition. Athens has remained a tourist city recovering from a major slump during the 1990s. The postmodern collage in its landscape and society predominated long before there was such a label, until the present when the city has seen several foreign migrant quarters while adopting entrepreneurial city marketing (on occasion of mega-events) and postmodern iconic architecture. Its sprawling landscape stretched to an ecological footprint, reaching up to the Evinos River in Fokida, as far as 500 kilometers (310 miles) to the northwest of Athens. Before this conduit for the transportation of water to Athens was completed in 2001, there was a succession of infrastructural works: the Marathon dam, built 1926

to 1931 in Attica; the Yliki Lake pumping station, built 1957 to 1958 in Beotia; and the dam and reservoir constructed in the Mornos Lake in Fokida, in the 1980s. The commodification of nature created by a thirsty growing city is well illustrated by the enormous expansion of its ecological footprint.

The inner city prides itself of iconic architecture built on occasions of major international events, especially the 2004 Olympics. Calatrava's stadium faces the Acropolis with the audacity of postmodernism, following the much-criticized volume of the modernist Hilton Hotel, built in the 1960s. The literature on mega-events now includes Athens as the host of the Olympics "returning to their birthplace" just over a century after their revival in the same city. The dual focus of cities in similar occasions—planned revival of local heritage for visibility on the one hand, and global references in cosmopolitan architecture and innovative design, on the other—has gravitated toward the latter in the case of Athens. The city was "glocalized" by structures built by celebrity architects in various locations, as well as new transport infrastructure: the international airport, the ring motorway of *Attiki odos,* the Athens metro, and an extended suburban railway system expanding to Corinth and later to Kiato. This infrastructure has been constructed in the context of a new model of urban governance in the entrepreneurial city, which is now Athens, through public–private partnerships.

The mega-event created a new set of urban dynamics and a new wave of urban sprawl. Illegal urban sprawl continued in Attica, though by different social classes. Increasing population and industry followed new infrastructure created in anticipation of the 2004 Olympics. Attica has been gradually merged with the Athens basin into one major agglomeration, bustling with businesses in mixed-use areas around the new international airport, as well as socially segregated communities, second residences turned to main ones, and leapfrog developments. Many urbanized areas, however, lacked water runoff and sewage systems. Illegal building continued in a new speculative—rather than popular—guise, cooperatives created settlements, and highways leading out of the compact city were surrounded by sprawling activities and created surface sealing at the expense of traditional vineyards in Attica, that have been there since antiquity. Changes in the landscape are thus destroying a lot of "nature," wherever the ecological footprint of Athens reaches.

Culture, by contrast, has been protected—though not that of all epochs, as Athens grew by construction through destruction of its neoclassical heritage. In European imaginations, or even global ones, Athens is the standard of civilization in the abstract sense, but only on the basis of antiquity. The Acropolis has remained a global symbol, perceived in different ways through space-time. The overwhelming presence of the Parthenon as an icon of European civilization and American republicanism, has lasted since the Renaissance in Europe and since Thomas Jefferson's cities, built in classical and Hellenistic styles and accompanied by the discourse for democracy and equality in the United States. Today's city, by contrast, is not considered up to the standards of European modernity. And indeed Athens has destroyed many layers of history that rendered it a "theatre of memory," according to Mike Crang and Penny Travlou, or in effect a "city," but has been living its own history, retaining a postmodern collage in its landscape of spontaneous urbanization and informality, which solved problems of homelessness and unemployment, even if temporarily, before new foreign migrant waves transformed the city of the new millennium.

Lila Leontidou

See also Acropolis; *Agora*; Mediterranean Cities; Other Cities

Further Readings

Beriatos, E. and A. Gospodini. 2004. "'Glocalising' Urban Landscapes: Athens and the 2004 Olympics." *Cities* 21(3):187–202.

Boyer, M. C. 1996. *The City of Collective Memory: The Historical Imagery and Architectural Entertainments.* Cambridge: MIT Press.

Crang, M. and P. S. Travlou. 2001. "The City and Topologies of Memory." *Society and Space* 19:161–77.

Kaika, M. 2005. *City of Flows: Modernity, Nature and the City.* Abingdon, UK: Routledge.

Leontidou, L. [1990] 2006. *The Mediterranean City in Transition: Social Change and Urban Development.* Reprint, Cambridge, UK: Cambridge University Press.

———. 1993. "Postmodernism and the City: Mediterranean Versions." *Urban Studies* 30(6):949–65.

———. 1996. "Athens: Inter-subjective Facets of Urban Performance." Pp. 244–73 in *European Cities in Competition,* edited by C. Jensen-Butler, A. Shakhar, and J. van den Weesep. Aldershot, UK: Avebury.

Leontidou, L., A. Afouxenidis, E. Kourliouros, and E. Marmaras. 2007. "Infrastructure-related Urban Sprawl: Mega-events and Hybrid Peri-urban Landscapes in Southern Europe." In *Urban Sprawl in Europe: Land Use Change, Landscapes and Policy,* edited by G. Petchel-Held, C. Couch, and L. Leontidou. Oxford, UK: Blackwell.

Loukaki, A. 1997. "Whose *genius loci?* Interpretations of the 'Sacred Rock of the Athenian Acropolis.'" *Annals of the Association of American Geographers* 87(2):306–29.

Williams, A. and G. Shaw, eds. 1998. *Tourism and Economic Development: European Experiences.* 3rd rev. ed. London: Wiley.

B

BACK-TO-THE-CITY MOVEMENT

Popularized in academia by Shirley Bradway Laska and Daphne Spain in the title of their widely referenced book *Back to the City: Issues in Neighborhood Renovation* (1980), the term *back to the city* became one of the keywords of the 1980s and 1990s literature on neighborhood revitalization and gentrification in the United States. It refers to households moving back to urban neighborhoods after many years of suburban life. The term focuses more on people and their preferences rather than on neighborhoods or the housing market. Of particular interest are newly formed families or young couples, many of whose parents had left cities decades earlier, returning to the city from the suburbs.

In many instances, though, rather than people literally returning, what occurred was that urban neighborhoods became viable alternatives to the suburbs and places of choice for certain types of households. More and more people seemingly preferred to live close to work, spend time outside the home, have easy access to cultural amenities and events, acknowledge the character of urban neighborhoods by investing in old buildings, and live in socially mixed communities. Promoters of this trend argued, in effect, that the assets of urban living outweighed the conveniences of suburban living. Moreover, they pointed to the costs of suburban life, including commuting to the city for work but also low-density development and social isolation.

The overall extent and significance of the back-to-the-city movement in the residential decisions of households have been points of controversy in the literature. Furthermore, the argument is criticized on the basis that the underlying explanation relies mainly on empirical findings based on demographic changes and preference patterns; that is, it focuses too much on the consumption side of urban neighborhood revitalization. Such an approach is criticized for ignoring the economic and political dynamics that led to the production of those neighborhoods as well as the role played by various actors, such as developers and local government. The counterargument has been that the emergence of these new consumers of urban life represents a profound change in the labor market and the lifestyle trends of young professionals. Thus, the back-to-the-city movement is a spatial reflection of new residential choices that people make in response to emerging social, political, and economic conditions and, thus, an indicator of future urban prosperity.

Zuhal Ulusoy

See also Downtown Revitalization; Gentrification

Further Readings

Journal of the American Planning Association. 1979. Special supplement with papers presented at the Symposium on Neighborhood Revitalization, 45(4).
Laska, Shirley Bradway and Daphne Spain, eds. 1980. *Back to the City: Issues in Neighborhood Renovation.* Elmsford, NY: Pergamon Press.

BANLIEUE

The *banlieue* refers to the area surrounding a French city, commonly used in reference to Paris. The word *faubourg* also means "lying outside the city," but now it commonly refers to areas in central Paris that were incorporated early into the city. There is an implicit tendency to compare the banlieues with the American suburbs, but there are important differences. In the United States the word *suburb* carries a positive connotation associated with private property, middle-class ease, low-density population, and an overall high quality of life. In contrast, the immediate connotation of the French *banlieue* and its inhabitants, the *banlieue-sards*, is one of overcrowded public housing, people of color, new immigrants, and crime. It is something closer to the stereotype of the ghetto in the United States; what is common to the French banlieue and the American ghetto are the aspects of categorical inequality, exclusion from the labor market, and social boundaries resulting in residential segregation. Today, the word *banlieue* carries a negative connotation; yet this hardly approximates the complex history and social reality of these spaces.

History of the Banlieue

The importance of the banlieue can be fully understood only in a historical perspective and in relation to the city to which it is a periphery. Like many medieval cities, Paris was a walled city for defensive purposes. As the city grew, new walls were constructed, totaling six. In the years preceding the French Revolution a new wall was built, but this time it was built mainly for taxation purposes. The wall demarcated Paris proper. Its doors included custom posts, and everyone entering or leaving with commercial goods had to pay a tax or right of passage called the *octroi*. This physical barrier to free trade and mobility—*mur d'octroi*—created a real boundary between those living inside (*intra-muros*) and those living outside (*extra-muros*), which had economic consequences for trade and production. Consequently the cost of living was lower outside Paris than inside, resulting in an early division between a large fraction of the labor force settling in the banlieue and consumers, visitors, financiers, and administrators living inside the city walls.

In the ancient regime, the Parisian banlieue contained vast open areas where the nobility of Paris and Versailles went to spend time surrounded by nature. This taste was acquired by many *arrivistes* of the French bourgeoisie and the petite bourgeoisie, who would go to the green banlieue during the weekends as a sign of distinction, as told in short stories by Guy de Maupassant and depicted by Jean Renoir in his celebrated film *Une Partie de Campagne* (1936). But as more people built houses in these idyllic lands, the banlieues were quickly transformed from forests into suburban and then urban areas. The remaining forests of Vincennes and the Bois de Boulogne are protected and have been annexed by the city.

After the French Revolution of 1789, the Constitutional Assembly decreed the limits of Paris to be a circle with a circumference determined by a radius of three leagues (*lieues*) around the center, which was set at Notre Dame Cathedral. In 1841, the politician Adolphe Thiers ordered the construction of a new set of walls and custom tower to be surrounded by a zone where it was forbidden to build. In 1860 the city was expanded by Baron Georges-Eugène Haussmann, and taxes continued to be levied. In this expansion Paris officially engulfed *l'ancienne banlieue*, which included the communes of Batignolle, Belleville, Bercy, Passy, la Villette, and other neighboring areas. The Paris octroi was instituted in these communes. This forced many industries to move out of the new city borders for fiscal reasons; many workers followed. The most developed and industrialized external communes also charged octroi to raise funds for local infrastructure and spending, whereas poorer banlieues did not in order to give tax incentives to attract industry and population. The octroi of Paris and its surrounding metropolitan area was not abolished until 1943, during the German occupation, when it was substituted with a sales tax.

As the density of Paris increased, the city looked to the banlieue to locate its new cemeteries and public parks. In 1887 a large building was constructed—a *dépôt de mendicité*—to house Parisian mental patients, homeless, vagabonds, and aged people and to imprison women in the exterior commune of Nanterre. In 1897 this building was turned into a hospital. Today this building offers shelter to the very poor of the region and to newly arrived immigrants.

Continuous Need for Housing

The Paris region has always been the destiny of many internal and international migrants. Female workers from the provinces, Spain, and then Africa would live in servant apartments, *chambres de bonnes,* atop bourgeois buildings in western Paris, while the high cost of living and the limited housing in Paris forced members of the working class to move to the eastern end of the city (formerly the industrial area) and to its banlieues. Industrialization led to a large rural-to-urban migration.

The painter, architect, and urbanist Charles-Édouard Jeanneret, also called Le Corbusier (1887–1965), published the influential books *Towards a New Architecture* (1923) and *The Radiant City* (1935), in which he sketched and proposed planned, rational, and utopian residential complexes formed by many large housing projects. His work would influence the construction of public housing and large public works in Brasília, the new capital of Brazil; Co-op City in New York; the Robert Taylor Homes in Chicago; and the many cities built in banlieues throughout France that house thousands of people in areas that offer very little employment and industry, in contrast to the area of La Defense, in a banlieue west of Paris, which in 2008 provided 150,000 jobs but housed only 20,000 residents. The project of La Defense was launched in 1958 in order to make Paris the capital of Europe and to attract transnational corporations. The plan succeeded in the latter, but it failed to reproduce the mixed use and busy public areas that are found in downtown Paris.

Following a public scandal about the *mal lotis*—people who had acquired and built in new lots in the banlieue that lacked any public services like water, roads, electricity, or gas—in 1914 the socialist politician Henri Sellier (1883–1943) pushed for the creation of *habitations à bon marché* (HBM), affordable housing. A number of HBMs are built around the city in the area where the Thiers wall was laid. Between 1921 and 1939 the HBM administration built garden-cities (*cités-jardin*) inspired by the British urbanist Ebenezer Howard. In 1935 the architect and urbanist Maurice Rotival introduced the term *grandes ensembles,* which corresponds to

"the projects" in the United States, to refer to a set of large public housing buildings to house multiple families that share common areas. Among the most famous HBMs is *La Cité de la Muette* in Drancy, built between 1931 and 1935, which was used as a Jewish internment camp during the German occupation, leading to the death of over 67,000 deportees.

At the end of World War II, *îlots insalubres,* slums in the construction-free zone around the Thiers wall, were replaced with modernist housing projects. After Algeria's independence in 1962 and the migration to France of *pied noirs* (White colonists), Jewish people formerly living in Algeria, and *harkis* (Muslims who had fought on the French side), the French state decided to house the new arrivals in projects in remote banlieues of Paris, Marseille, and Lyon.

In 1964 there was a public scandal surrounding the *bidonville de Champigny,* a slum that housed more than 10,000 Portuguese in conditions of extreme poverty an hour away from the luxuries of Paris. Many Algerians lived in similar conditions. To appease public opinion the Debré law was passed to improve the conditions of the migrant workers explicitly to prevent them from leaving and thus hindering the reconstruction and growth of France from 1945 to 1975, a period that came to be known as *Les Trente Glorieuses* or "The Glorious Thirty." Provisional housing was provided for Maghrebi workers. The SONACOTRA was created in 1956 in order to provide more formal housing to these new immigrants from Algeria and their families.

Although the state opposed the creation of ghettos, the political opposition from the richest quarters inside and outside Paris pushed for the concentration of immigrants in certain distant and poor banlieues. This has resulted in a durable inequality due to the lack of access to quality education and good jobs. This is why many inhabitants of these stereotypical areas of the banlieues live off unemployment and other social benefits. In order to address these inequities, special education zones (*zones d'éducation prioritaire*) were created in 1981 to dedicate more funds to education in certain "sensitive areas."

The rise of the welfare state along with the increasing cost of living in Paris led to the construction of subsidized public housing (*habitations à loyer modéré*). French workers from Paris and the province lived there first, but there was an eventual involuntary conversion to relative majorities of immigrant workers, many from former colonies, despite the fact that laws stand against the concentration of more than 15 percent of a given group in order to explicitly prevent the creation of urban ghettos such as those in the United States, something deeply feared and disdained by the French. Originally, the heavy concentration of the French working class, many coming from other regions of France and Europe, led to the appearance in certain banlieues of the so-called red banlieue, where the communist and socialist mayors were often elected. According to some hypotheses this hegemony changed after the Communist Party failed to incorporate the large arrival of new immigrants into its local agenda and thus lacked their complete support. What the French failed to see is that social networks, unemployment, and solidarity bring underrepresented groups together to survive strong labor market discrimination, spatial segregation, and social exclusion.

Borders of Distinction and Exclusion

In 1943 the idea of the *boulevard périphérique,* an expressway around the city, was conceived with the explicit purpose of making sure than the boundary between Paris and the growing banlieue would be clearly drawn. In 1954 the project was launched and built along HBMs in the zone formerly reserved for the Thiers wall.

Many French banlieues still give testimony to their past as old provincial villages that have been engulfed by the growing metropolitan area and thus share many a common element: train station, public square, church, city hall, stores, restaurants, private houses, and *cités* close by, with buses going farther inside into the banlieue and with green areas not far from reach. Day-to-day experiences of the banlieuesards often contrast sharply with the stereotypes held by many Parisians. The movie *La Haine* (Hatred), directed by Mathieu Kassovitz, presents a powerful metaphor but an exaggerated representation life in the banlieue. It draws attention to the issue of police violence and broad discrimination, but it helps to reproduce the negative stereotype. *L'Esquive* (in its English version, *Games of Love and Chance*) of Abdellatif Kechiche does a much better job of portraying the everyday life of young banlieuesards.

In 1947 Jean-François Gravier published *Paris et le désert français* (*Paris and the French Desert*), in which he blamed Paris for devouring all the resources, talent, and wealth from the whole country and, one could add, the French colonies. This centralization of power, influence, and resources will end in the symbolic desertification of the whole of France unless something is done to build industry in the provinces and to decentralize public functions and priorities. Even Haussmann was concerned about a luxuries center surrounded by a proletariat ring of workers that it could not house. Thus, more than talking about the poverty and lack of the banlieue, one has to talk about the overconcentration of wealth in western Paris and the continuous gentrification of the city. As many French thinkers have warned, France in the twenty-first century risks becoming a city museum for 2 million of its richest inhabitants and to the millions of tourists who visit it every year, oblivious to the backstage that is the banlieue, which they perhaps see only as they pass through it from the airport to their hotels.

Among other things, the work of sociologist Loïc Wacquant stresses the diversity among the different French banlieues. This is something important to keep in mind given the differences between western banlieues, which include areas like La Defense, Bois Colombes, or Neuilly (where current French President Nicolas Sarkozy was mayor for many years), and stigmatized and heavily populated cités, such as La Courneuve or Sarcelles.

The lived space and experiences of the *franciliens* (Parisians and banlieuesards, inhabiting the *Île de France*) goes beyond obsolete political and administrative boundaries. In the end the banlieues are an integral part of Paris because much of its work and daily life are done in the backstage of the banlieue without which the Parisian front-stage could not hold. Thus one cannot talk about the Parisian banlieue without talking about Paris, and in the same way one cannot talk seriously about Paris without taking its banlieues into account; the same holds for other major Francophone cities.

Ernesto Castañeda

See also *Favela;* Ghetto; Paris, France

Further Readings

Fourcaut, A., E. Bellanger, and M. Flonneau. 2007. *Paris/Banlieues—Conflits et solidarités*. Paris: Creaphis.

Pinçon, M. and M. Pinçon-Charlot. 2004. *Sociologie de Paris*. Paris: Découverte.

Sayad, A. 2006. *L'immigration ou les paradoxes de l'altérité: L'illusion du provisoire*. Montreal, QC: Editions Liber.

Wacquant, L. J. D. 2008. *Urban Outcasts: A Comparative Sociology of Advanced Marginality*. Cambridge, MA: Polity.

BARCELONA, SPAIN

Located in the region of Catalonia in northeast Spain, Barcelona is the second largest city in Spain, with a population of around 1,600,000 in 100 square kilometers. Largely as a result of the regeneration processes of the 1980s that culminated in the 1992 Olympic Games, Barcelona has become renowned internationally for its postindustrial urban restructuring planning. Indeed, the "Barcelona model" of regeneration is often held to be exemplary in repositioning the city in the global economy and balancing economic outputs with sociocultural goals.

Industrialization and Expansion

The actual urban morphology of Barcelona is based strongly on its transformation and expansion toward a modern city in the mid-nineteenth century. In this period, Barcelona suffered from three basic problems. First, though industrialization and demographic growth were already taking place in the first half of the century, the city was constrained within its medieval walls until 1860. Second, despite becoming the industrial center of Spain, it lacked any political influence on state politics. And third, industrialization and growth were accomplished through local capital, but there was not a strong and consolidated financial industry. These problems reflected directly on how the city developed. Almost any attempt to improve the city and create the conditions for fixing capital flows in town has necessarily implied resorting to attracting nation-state government support and

capital through events. Thus, the evolution of the city is linked to big events (e.g., the Universal Exposition of 1888 or the International Exposition of 1929) or aborted ones (Popular Olympics of 1936, Expo of 1982). These events were usually catalyzers for developing broader planning projects (e.g., Cerdà, 1860; Macià, 1932; General Metropolitan Plan, 1976). In this sense, it is no wonder that contemporary city councils have been using events such as the Olympics and the Forum 2004 for the same purposes.

Modern Urban Development

Barcelona's urban development has been characterized primarily by three moments: (1) the approval in 1860 of the Cerdà Plan to guide the expansion of the city outside its medieval walls, (2) the chaotic urban and economic growth during the years of Spanish dictatorship, and (3) the Olympic-led regeneration once democracy had returned.

The Cerdà Plan

The first stages of Barcelona's modern development began with the implementation of the Cerdà Plan, beginning in 1860. This was a plan that conceived the city as a reticular grid based on three modern, functional, and pioneering principles: hygienism, circulation, and planning growth outside the city borders. Although the plan contained many progressive ideas for the time it was envisioned, some of them disappeared in the construction of *l'Eixample* (the neighborhood around Barcelona's Old Town) as a result of the pressures of speculative real estate. Yet, this grid and the Cerdà Plan are the bases of Barcelona's twentieth-century urbanism.

Franco Dictatorship and *Porciolismo*

The second key moment for Barcelona's urbanism came with the arrival of a fascist regime in 1939. After a long postwar and international isolation that ended in the 1950s, the collapse of the Spanish state was avoided by the first and possibly last successful International Monetary Fund structural adjustment plan (1957–1959). This adjustment was followed by years of disordered growth for Spain, where Barcelona was one of the main

Las Ramblas—a pedestrian mall—and surrounding Barcelona

Source: Ralf Roletschek.

industrial poles. Industrialization, immigration (from other parts of Spain), and automobiles become the cornerstones of Barcelona development and policy. This model of urbanization was called *Porciolismo,* after José María Porcioles, the mayor of Barcelona from 1957 to 1973. Porcioles's reign gave shape to three basic characteristics: First, the growth pattern of the city matched the anarchic capitalism of that period, which was based on the rapid industrialization. The new factories were producing low-quality manufactured goods for the domestic market through labor-intensive processes. The city was transformed through chaotic sprawl and destruction, high-rise housing, and expressways to accommodate the factories and the labor force and to allow the flow of commodities and commuters. Second, this constructionist fervor characterized the city elites, property developers who became wealthy through

a combination of land purchasing and high-density building. The final characteristic was its metropolitan conception. These processes started in the city but quickly spread to the goal of building *la Gran Barcelona.*

Franco Opposition and Neighborhood Movements

However, the particular form of urbanism that represented *Porciolismo* sowed the seeds for change. The speculative construction of Barcelona was critical in creating and being the instrument of opposition to the fascist regime at the local level. The opposition to the Franco government was mainly urban and consolidated during the 1960s, first in the universities and then in the workplace and neighborhoods. The opposition was formed by different clandestine organizations that included political parties (left wing, nationalistic, or both), unionism, and neighborhood movements. From this mix, contestation took several forms and produced what would be the future democratic leaders of Barcelona and Catalonia. Though these leaders were mostly but not exclusively university academics and middle-class men, there were strong working-class movements as well.

Neighborhood associations have been important players in Barcelona's urban politics since the 1970s. They began forming in the late 1960s and eventually connected with labor and political movements, which included the help of critical urbanists and architects. During the early 1970s, opposition to the Franco regime and neighborhood associations wisely used the opportunities and forms of the reform of the planning tools of the city to set a more rational and less speculation-friendly spatial ordering. Yet, the crucial moment was with the presentation of the General Metropolitan Plan (GMP) in 1974. Its inception was a response to the anarchic growth model of *Porciolismo:* the saturation and collapse of greater Barcelona. Opposition movements, mostly neighborhood associations, and a new generation of urbanists and activists recently graduated from university were involved in the planning effort, as some became civil servants. Financial capital holders and developers in the city interpreted the first draft of the GMP as a socialist plan completely against their interests. For two years they attempted to change it, using direct influence on the political system (in fact, the key political figures were among them), media lobbying, and legal procedures. However, their lobby clashed with the FAVB (Federació d'Associacions de Veïns i Veïnes de Barcelona), who used nonviolent means to fight speculation, private transport, and breaches by developers. The final approbation came in 1976 (after Franco's death). It was the first partial victory for changing the layout of the city. The final GMP put, if not a stop, then a break to high-density speculation in the city, opened spaces for the construction of infrastructure in the neighborhoods built during the 1960s, and rationalized the industrial space in the metropolitan area

Post-Franco Years

Two years after the death of Franco in 1975, the first democratic elections were held and a commission was created to write a new Spanish constitution, which was approved in 1978. Spain was attempting to relocate itself in Europe, both economically and politically, and to consolidate democracy. Democracy was threatened on February 23, 1981, with a failed coup d'état. Integration into the European Economic Community came in 1986. In sum, the central administration had to modernize the country and show it internationally. In this context, the 1980s were a period of intensive devolution of the nation-state. If Barcelona and Catalonia had historically difficult relations with Spain and its central government, this antagonistic relationship was renewed with nation-state devolution to regional governments. On the one hand, the regional government was dominated from the first elections in 1980 until 2003 by a Right-nationalistic coalition. On the other hand, the city council had been dominated since the first elections by a coalition of left-wing parties. Tensions were apparent in 1987, when the Catalan regional government abolished the left-dominated Metropolitan Corporation of Barcelona (in a move similar to Thatcher's dismantling of the Greater London Authority). Thus, to implement any major project, the city council had to deal with both administrations, which had different agendas and were suspicious of the city for different reasons.

Olympic Games: A Strategy for Urban Renewal

In these circumstances, Barcelona not only has had to handle the transformation from an industrial to a postindustrial city, but importantly to fit itself into this conflictive scenario. A first step taken in the late 1970s and early 1980s was also characterized by small-scale (relatively inexpensive) interventions in the city, including demolition of old dwellings, "sponged" reurbanization (small public spaces in high-density areas), and social housing. But that was not enough to redefine the city in better terms, and the city council's strategy led as well to a particular politics of engagement in the city. Hosting the Olympic Games was a strategy for regenerating Barcelona through the support of the central and regional government. It is within this framework of interscalar conflict and with the aim of implementing and improving the GMP that the Olympics took form. Nevertheless, the Olympic Games were not a new idea. The first attempt to bring the Olympic Games to Barcelona was during the Second Republic, when the city lost its bid against Berlin. Before launching the second bid, the support of the International Olympic Committee president, Juan Antonio Samaranch, was obtained, and the strategy fit with other interests, such as the willingness of the Spanish socialist government to show how modern Spain had become and the aim of the nationalist regional government to promote the Catalan identity internationally. Its primary goal was different from the 1980s Olympic Games: neither national promotion (Moscow 1980 and Seoul 1988) nor private profit (Los Angeles 1984). It was an investment tool to change the city, a strategy later claimed by other cities organizing bids for mega-events.

From this framework, the strategy can be considered entrepreneurial: branding the city internationally, attracting investment and tourism, and relocating the city in the European hierarchy of cities. The strategy was also successful in engaging with different levels of government, the private sector, and the citizens, but with important qualitative differences from the entrepreneurialism that predominated the 1980s in Europe and North America. First, it not only "built to boost," but there was a clear idea of what the city wanted, taking into account social issues, the long-term perspective, and even development in the city, with the spread of Olympic projects all over the city. Second, there was a partnership structure, but with strong public leadership, controlling the private sector. And last, the city council led the whole project, imposing its criteria on the other administrations. The outcomes were mostly positive, bringing a more social democratic approach to entrepreneurialism.

In sum, after the Olympics, Barcelona became an international model for urban regeneration, and the post-Olympic scenario in Barcelona was shaped by the successful repositioning of Barcelona as one of the most admired and visited cities in Europe. This success resulted in the return of local, national, and foreign capital back into the city, making corporate interests a major force in pressing and shaping the city council's agenda. Furthermore, the early 1990s corresponded with the locking in of neoliberalism in Spanish politics through the application of the Maastricht Treaty

and its stability pact. This, together with the financialization of the economy, the liberalization of labor markets, the privatization of public enterprises, and the return of centralized planning and spending centered in Madrid, have all added pressure for rethinking a new strategy for Barcelona.

The outcome of these processes has been to enhance the competitive position of Barcelona through supply-side economic policies, market competition, and the abandonment of redistributive concerns. In this context, Barcelona has relied on new strategies and discourses that attempt to reposition Barcelona within the flow of the global economy. These are organized along a threefold strategy involving a cultural strategic plan, a cultural mega-event, and the creation of digital neighborhoods in order to insert the city into the upper levels of the international division of labor and the hierarchy of global cities (or at least not to lose its position) and to produce a new consensus over the Barcelona model able to construct a territorial alliance involving public and private actors engaging with supralocal sources of investment and support. The mega-event in mind was the Universal Forum of Cultures 2004, an event "to promote the global consciousness and the exchange of theories, opinions, experiences and feelings around globalization," organized around three axes: cultural diversity, sustainable development, and conditions for peace. The city's long-term goal is to redevelop the northern part of the waterfront, renamed Diagonal Mar and located between Poblenou and the River Besós. Complementing this event, the city council has been replanning several working-class and former manufacturing areas such as la Maquinista, Zona Franca, and Poblenou as new digital quarters. At the moment, the only consolidated area is in Poblenou, between Diagonal Mar and the Olympic Village; the strategy of regeneration has taken the form of a digital quarter. The aim of the project, named 22@bcn, is to transform Poblenou into the industrial district of the new economy, with special relevance for the informational and communication technologies, and cultural (mainly audiovisual) and research and development activities as well.

However, this later stage of Barcelona regeneration has increasingly been put into question, as a change of direction from the trajectory set from the Cerdà Plan to the Olympic regeneration, fragmenting the modernist grid of Barcelona. On the one hand, in the past decade, economic, cultural, and migratory changes have substantially altered the life and identity of the city (e.g., the percentage of foreign residents rose from 1.9 percent in 1996 to 15.6 percent of the total population in 2007), presenting new challenges to planning institutions. On the other hand, more local and foreign voices, of urban social movements and academics, have been more focused on branding the city, attracting investment, and dealing with the effects of gentrification.

Ramon Ribera-Fumaz

See also Mediterranean Cities; Urban Planning

Further Readings

Busquets, J. 2005. *Barcelona. The Urban Evolution of a Compact City*. Rovereto, Italy: Nicolodi and Actar, in association with Harvard University Graduate School of Design.

Calavita, N. and A. Ferrer. 2000. "Behind Barcelona's Success Story: Citizens Movements and Planners' Power." *Journal of Urban History* 26:793–807.

Degen, M. and M. García, eds. 2008. *La metaciudad: Barcelona. Transformación de una metrópolis* (The Metacity: Barcelona. Transformation of a Metropolis). Barcelona, Spain: Anthropos.

Ferrer, A. 1997. "El plan general metropolità. La versió de 1976." *Papers regió metropolitana de Barcelona* 28:43–53.

Marshall, T., ed. 2004. *Transforming Barcelona*. London: Routledge.

McNeill, D. 1999. *Urban Change and the European Left: Tales from the New Barcelona*. London: Routledge.

BARRIO

Barrio is a conventional term for Latina/o communities. They have been fundamental to cities since the mid-1800s and were influenced by racism and segregation in relation to residential patterns in U.S. cities. Barrios are also significant in relation to Latina/o culture and identity.

Important physical characteristics of barrios are related to sustainable environmental features, including mixed density, mixed uses (especially commercial uses in residential areas), live–work spaces, public transportation, walking, and recycling. Barrios are also noted for being a cultural community that exhibits the importance of social networks.

Prior to the late twentieth century, key urban problems in relation to structural underdevelopment were a lack of affordable housing, local economic development, and the acute failure of government to address urban amenities, including streets, sewers, gas, and lighting.

Barrios are also a zone of conflict with planning and urban policy elites. These problems include a lack of inclusionary planning, racism and elitism within urban policy, neighborhood destruction related to highway corridors, redevelopment and private sector development, gentrification, and land speculation.

Barrio formation is an example of how cultural transformations within working-class constituencies help them to recapture space in their own vision; it is also an example of the essential role of cultural practices in defining places and the importance of their symbolic representations irrespective of ownership patterns or attempts at social control.

Initial Era of Barrio Formation

Barrios during the initial period of urbanism in the early twentieth century were generally located in ethnically specified, segregated sections of towns and cities. *Colonias* were characterized by declining housing conditions; poor internal roads (in reality, dirt streets); and limited or no basic infrastructure in relation to water, sanitation, and flood control. Ethnic spatial separation was impacted by natural barriers or features of the built environment, including rivers, railroad tracks, and agricultural buffer zones. Latinas/os also resided in small agricultural encampments on the periphery of cities and towns. They constituted a renter class, with limited land ownership patterns through the mid-twentieth century.

Numerous colonias developed adjacent to local employment centers, railroad yards, manufacturing districts, and in agriculture zones, on the urban fringe. These "livable spaces" ranged from substandard homes, to tents, to shantytowns constructed from a potpourri of local materials. The conditions of these urban residential zones established the negative characterizations of Latinas/os in urban space. Locked into substandard, deteriorating conditions, the barrio was viewed as a repository of marginalized families with limited desire for improving their lifestyle. Regressive ethnic stereotypes reinforced situating Latina/o culture as a legitimation for the evolution of systemic residential apartheid and social repression.

Two typologies of barrios evolved during this period. Barrios in close proximity to civic centers, which were enclosed by rapid urbanization, experienced improvements in basic infrastructure associated with the conventional extension of urban systems. San Antonio, Denver, Phoenix, and El Paso typify this type of barrio–city relationship. Streets, sewers, water, and electricity were generally provided in these barrios. Although the quality and maintenance suffered from disparity in the allocation of government resources, the provision of these services was necessary in relation to the economy of the city.

Conversely, barrios located on the periphery of urban zones or in outlying semirural areas lacked most basic urban amenities. While labor was essential to the local economy, segregated residential zones governed spatial patterns. Many barrios exhibited dirt streets well into the 1960s. Cities in the South Rio Grande Valley, and other cities along the *frontera*, are prominent examples of this type of neglect. Colonias in these areas relied on remedial septic systems, water delivery, wood and propane for cooking and heating, haphazard electrical service, and informal trash collection. Flood control, street curbs, and connections with local sewer systems did not occur until well after World War II. This acute lack of urban infrastructure was especially problematic in mid-size and small cities in which the structural condition of the barrio was not deemed essential. This legacy of deficient infrastructure continued to characterize numerous barrios into the 1990s, especially in Texas. In numerous barrios, even in major cities, there are some residential streets without curbs and sidewalks. This is a legacy of discrimination in public works policy that began during the initial era of urban growth.

East Los Angeles, California

During the late 1910s and early 1920s, the increasing demand for industrial labor changed the urban character of cities. For example, one of Los Angeles's earliest urban barrios was centered along Mateo and Seventh Streets, which is currently in a major manufacturing zone east of the civic center. This demand for manufacturing space resulted in the eventual deconstruction of numerous barrios in the Southwest.

In this instance, the evolution of the most significant urban barrio in the United States, East Los Angeles, provides a perspective on this type of urban transition. The initial Chicana/o households migrating east of the Los Angeles River was related to being forced out of Sonora Town (now Chinatown) and the industrial center, into the Belvedere barrio. Another barrio, Joyo Maravilla, was established farther east. This community was east of Boyle Heights, which during the early 1920s exhibited a resistance to Chicana/o mobility. Demands for improved housing opportunities led to increased Latina/o migration into this area. Thus, the initial cultural transition of the East Los Angeles barrio was followed by a tradition of urban ethnic ascendancy that characterizes urban expansion in this society. By the early 1930s, the influx of Chicanas/os had a significant impact on the cultural dynamics of this community. Within 20 years (1920–1940) East Los Angeles became the largest barrio in the United States. Since that period it has evolved into the most substantial minority urban enclave in U.S. history: a conurban zone that Valle and Torres label as the "Greater Eastside." This zone of cultural influence extends over 20 miles east of downtown and is approximately 1,000 square miles.

Post-1970s and the Evolution of the Modern Barrio

The spatial limitations of barrios historically turned them into dense, overcrowded social and physical environments. Prior to 1960, population growth rates severely tested the geographic confines of barrio space. However, social sanctions reinforced by racism in real estate practices could not be sustained during the rapid population expansion related to Latina/o household growth rates. The initial working-class suburban migration, not distant in historic terms from the traditional barrio, was a response to this demographic transformation. Older neighborhoods directly adjacent to barrios were the first zones that Latina/os pioneered.

East Los Angeles, due to its immense size, was the precursor for the dynamic urbanization occurring in other cities. Adjacent neighborhoods were merged into significant zones of Latina/o cultural dominance. The reach of the barrio surged throughout regions of the Southwest, creating a new period of barrio urbanism.

By the late 1970s, three types of patterns emerged: (1) traditional barrios surging into adjacent neighborhoods; (2) cities and regions that evolved into a system of intermittent Latina/o dominated zones, working-class suburbs, and inner city; and (3) the duality of a traditional barrio disjointed from middle-class Latinas/os migrating suburbia, older or new locations. This often resulted in the acceleration of economic decline in traditional barrios. Whereas the Los Angeles basin exhibits all three typologies, other cities formed dissimilar spatial relationships. El Paso is an example of the first scenario: El Segundo Barrio continued to expand into adjacent zones, creating a totally controlled Chicana/o urban zone. Phoenix, Denver, and Sacramento have evolved into the second topology in which selected suburban communities have experienced significant multiethnic integration, while other adjacent zones have remained predominately European American. Tucson, San Jose, and San Diego exhibit the third type of relationship in which suburban migration has created a spatial and social distance from the traditional barrio. Logan Heights in San Diego is isolated from suburban patterns north of the central city, and Tucson, mainly because Viejo Barrio was destroyed, led to a pattern of distinct barrio zones.

The Twenty-First-Century Barrio

Barrios remain in crisis. Affordable housing is a Latina/o urban crisis in the Southwest. Environmental pollution and land use conflicts increasingly place barrios at risk in relation to public health. Economic revitalization, job generation, and small business stability are problematic in urban barrios. This is a legacy in which barrios were systemically denied capital reinvestment. Uneven development has left barrios in a permanent status of deterioration, social dysfunction, limited economic opportunity, and political marginalization. Planning is now confronted with an era of bilingualism and bicultural practices to ensure active minority participation in land use policy. In particular, demands for bilingualism and inclusion have forced urban elites to increase public information in relation to urban policy. Exclusionary practices such as censorship of information, sequestering Housing and Urban Development regulations, ignoring environmental issues, and blatant racism are gradually subsiding. Barrio residents have begun to demand a quality of life for lower-income residents. Simultaneously, barrio urbanism has expanded into virtually all major urban centers in the United States.

David Diaz

See also *Favela*; Ghetto; Los Angeles, California

Further Readings

Davis, Mike. 2000. *Magical Urbanism*. London: Verso.

Diaz, David. 2005. *Barrio Urbanism*. New York: Routledge.

Rodriguez, Nestor. 1993. "Economic Restructuring and Latino Growth in Houston." In *In the Barrios*, edited by J. Moore and R. Pinderhughes. New York: Russell Sage.

Valle, Victor M. and Rodolfo D. Torres. 2000. *Latino Metropolis*. Minneapolis: University of Minnesota Press.

BAZAAR

Originally referring to a vaguely defined "oriental" market, the bazaar, as an institution and a space, has for many centuries exercised its attraction upon observers from all over the world. A sensorially and semiotically overloaded space and a point of encounter of various influences, actors, artefacts, and symbols, the bazaar is commonly presented in most travel guides, novels, and reportages (and often in scholarly work too) as the epitome of Middle Eastern (and Asian) societies; as the arena where visitors can capture the most picturesque and "authentic" impressions of the "culture" of such areas. An originally localized space and notion, the bazaar has therefore become a constitutive part of translocal fantasies as well as an example of Western exoticizing and orientalistic representations of the world.

Hats on display at a bazaar outside of Topkapi, Turkey

Source: Jill Buyan.

Among scholars, the bazaar has captured the attention of individuals from different disciplinary environments. In earlier scholarship it was approached primarily in terms of economic behavior, hence becoming a field of encounter primarily between economists, historians, and anthropologists. Later on, however, it was identified as a key arena for understanding societal issues at large. In scholarly work, thus, the bazaar has two main connotations. On the one hand, it signifies a particular space and place of exchange (that some authors have proposed as the ideal precursor of the fairs, the world exhibition, and the contemporary department stores); on the other hand, it refers to an economic system (originally denoting the peasant markets) opposed to the competitive "Western" markets. In the past few decades the bazaar has also become a popular metaphor for addressing various aspects of late modern societies. Carrying along its original orientalistic connotations, the bazaar is today a recurrent term and notion (in scholarly as well as public discourse) for addressing the contemporary hybrid, multifaceted, globally interconnected, and digitalized world.

After a brief introduction presenting the origins of the term, this entry will outline a number of passages and notions that have characterized research on the bazaar. Divided in three sections focusing first on the bazaar as an economic system, second as a space of convergence, and finally as a metaphor, the entry does not, however, aim at offering a thorough chronological account of the history of scientific research in this field. Rather, it suggests some critical insights into the main visions, interpretations, and turns that have characterized its presence within the social and humanistic sciences.

The Term

A term of Persian origins connoting a market or a marketplace, the term *bazaar* has, across the centuries, spread to different parts of the world. Eastward it has been adopted in south and southeast Asia (in India, in particular, it came to connote also a single shop or stall). Westward, it has reached Arabic, Turkish, and European languages alike. Whereas some of these languages have adopted it literally, in many European countries the term *bazaar* has become synonymous with the "oriental marketplace" at large and been used to indicate chaotic, disorderly, and irrational places of exchange, where an array of objects and ideas could be found. Generically, however, the bazaar is also often used to address marketplaces (often open aired and indigenous) in most areas of the world.

The Bazaar as an Economic System

In the past 50 years, two main approaches have dominated the work of scholars interested in the study of the bazaar as an economic system. Whereas older accounts presented the bazaar almost as the precursor or prototype of the modern capitalist competitive market, more recent ones have addressed it as an arena so deeply entrenched in its own sociocultural context as to appear totally outside of modern economic analysis. Among the most influential scholars representing the latter (and more recent) approach to the bazaar is anthropologist Richard G. Fox. In his work on a market town in North India, Fox presented the bazaar as a place of the irrational. Describing it as an activity and a system based on the simultaneous presence of lack of specialization and overspecialization, and on the disorderly overlapping of services and products, Fox promoted a vision of the bazaar as the prototypical counterexample of Western capitalist markets. In a similar manner, anthropologist Clifford Geertz looked upon the bazaar as a bizarre milieu and phenomenon. Its defining traits as a system were, according to him, the heterogeneity of products, the continuous price bargaining, and the stable ties of clientship. Clearly challenging the logic of the Western market, the bazaar was for Geertz characterized by poor and maldistributed information (about the products and their production) and thus by a form of "known" ignorance. The constant search for, and protection of, knowledge and information (i.e., attempts at reducing this ignorance) were, according to him, the leading social activities taking place within the bazaar. Neither a simple mirror of nonmarket economies nor of industrial markets, the bazaar was a distinctive system of social relationships.

While being later on accused of having produced, as Fanselow has suggested, yet another exoticizing account of a non-Western phenomenon, Geertz contributed to the enlargement of the scientific approaches on the bazaar. Focusing on the social act of being in that particular space, and linking this aspect with his main theoretical concerns about anthropology as an interpretative enterprise, Geertz, in his article on bazaar economy, presented the act of being in the bazaar as an advanced art centered around individuals' capacity for combining the signs that filled the space surrounding them. Geertz's work on the Moroccan bazaar of Sefrou marked a shift in the approaches to the bazaar. No longer just an arena for economic exchange, the bazaar was also a place to capture the spirit of a society; the ideal locus for studying heterogeneous social relations.

The Bazaar as a Space of Convergence

In tune with Geertz, much scholarly work in the social sciences has approached the bazaar as a space from which to gather insights about wider social, cultural, and historical issues. Not just the delimitated locus of economic exchanges, the bazaar has been addressed as a microcosm in which economics merge with other aspects of social life,

such as ritual, religiosity, and politics. The bazaar, scholars such as Anand Yang have suggested, is an ideal setting for approaching the merging of individuals' lived experiences and larger narratives defined by contexts such as the market and the state. Historians devoted to the study of colonial India, among others, have approached the bazaar as a privileged scene of contention and a site of production of communal identities. Defined by the encounter of opposed categories, such as center and periphery, public and private, foreign and local, the bazaar, it has been suggested, has represented for India (and the parallel could be drawn for other countries as well) a vivid expression of the larger processes investing the nation.

Such an approach, focusing on the bazaar as a space of confluence for various influences, interests, and agendas, characterizes also much work on the contemporary bazaars. The bazaar has in fact recently been looked upon as the ideal arena to approach questions relating to the staging and creation of ethnic identities; to gender and class positionings; to questions of visuality and aesthetics; and to social actors' interpretations of the "public." It has attracted the attention of those scholars working on the public display and commoditization of culture and on the cultural politics of representation (an area in which the contributions of geographers and tourism researchers have been extensive) as well as those interested in the relation between subjectivity, identity, and space, that is, in the modalities through which individuals shape their lives through the space surrounding them.

The bazaar, however, is also a valid location for approaching questions of travel, movement, and flows of meanings and signs across territorial borders. Similar to Marc Augé's "non-places," the bazaar is, in a sense, a passage; a (spatially and temporally) suspended "heterotopic" arena witnessing to the fast overlapping of messages, people, and artefacts. With its overload of sensorial (in particular visual) stimuli, the bazaar highlights also the pivotal role played by imagination and fantasy in everyday life. An expression of a translocal public sphere defined by encounter, exchange, and merging, the bazaar blurs the borders between local and global, tradition and modernity, past and present, thus interrogating the conventionally oversimplified correspondence between culture and space. Moreover, it also contributes in questioning conventional assumptions about the novelty of globalization. The most historically renowned bazaars have, in fact, been touched by major trade routes for centuries and have always grown under the influence of a translocal scenario. Hence, the latest globalizing trends may have simply added new artefacts, messages, people, and a new speed of movement but not qualitatively generated a new phenomenon altogether. Looking upon the bazaar in the contemporary world as a space of convergence thus raises central issues regarding globalization and the cultural logics of late modernity.

The Bazaar as a Metaphor for the Contemporary World

Already in the 1970s Clifford Geertz noted how, from being a purely descriptive term, the bazaar had also turned into an analytic concept. Recently, within the social sciences (and within public discourse too), another turn has taken place whereby the bazaar has been translated into a metaphor for addressing a variety of phenomena belonging to the contemporary world. A perspective informed by orientalistic and exoticizing notions as well as by postmodern theoretical insights, the bazaar has become a symbol for the disorderly, hybrid, fragmented, multifaceted, and commercialized organization of social life in late modernity.

One connotation of such metaphorical usage presents the bazaar as a term and a notion useful for addressing the late modern city. Intended as an arena of multiplicity, trade, and movement, the bazaar has been used for epitomizing the border-zone, undefined, and at times dangerous and illegal character of the urban world. As the ultimate space of Otherness, the bazaar sums up, in such approaches, the notions of a universe made up of unstable roles (of part-time work, semi-illegal occupations, etc.) that runs parallel to the open official market.

On a more abstract level the bazaar has also recently been used to address the spaces of digitalized, virtual reality. In his analysis of the developments of the open source software model, Eric Raymond, inspired by poststructuralist thinkers such as Michel Foucault and Gilles Deleuze, opts for the bazaar as the key metaphor for addressing the new, open, nonlinear, flexible models of software developments able to host differing agendas and approaches. Stretching Raymond's approach farther, Benoît Demil and Xavier Lecocq have chosen the same metaphor for describing new models of (bazaar) governance inspired by the open licenses model. It is with no surprise that the bazaar is also one of the most used terms in commercial and noncommercial web spaces (such as Internet shops and data banks).

The metaphorical presence of the "bazaar" in the discourse surrounding digital networks and virtual spaces once again reminds us of the evocative potential of such a notion. It also highlights its associations to notions of anarchic freedom, deterritorialization, and individualism expressed in a number of works (coming mainly form the field of cultural studies) devoted to issues of identity and subjectivity in late modernity. In tune with the postmodern interest for the deterritorialized subject, the bazaar represents here a creative enterprise. A liminal zone of subject creation, it provides the individual with an interstitial (and hence uncontrolled) space for the negotiation of identity.

Given these latter metaphorical dimensions, the bazaar, as a term and a notion, could be approached alongside that chain of terms (*hybridity*, *nomadism*, etc.) that, since postcolonial times, have gone through an inversion of connotation. Once terms of discrimination and oppression, such words and notions have become positive symbols of renewal. Adopted by several scholars, public administrators, artists, and commentators, these terms express (and perhaps help celebrate) the openness and fluidity of the contemporary (Western but not exclusively) world. It may be worth adding that, in fact, the bazaar is a much deployed metaphor and inspiration for many public events and festivals devoted to promote integration and intercultural dialogue in contemporary Europe.

Hence, from being a place of decay (as in E. M. Forster's novel *Passage to India*), the bazaar, in contemporary industrialized societies, has become synonymous with encounter and dialogue across borders and with openness, individuality, and freedom. Informed by orientalistic fantasies identifying it with an exotic, prototypical space of Otherness, the bazaar stands, in the contemporary West in particular, as one of the charming epitomes of cultural diversity. And, from being a counterexample of the organized and rational Western markets, it has today become an often uncritically approached hymn to creativity. Parallel to such celebratory tones, in fact, in many regions of the world today, the bazaar (as a proper physical space) has become a security issue. Due to its uncontrollable and chaotic character, the bazaar is today the selected location for acts of terrorism and dissidence, a phenomenon that should make scholars reflect upon the varying and context-specific associations that this term may give rise to.

A traveling term, the bazaar, in its metaphorical usage, brings to the surface wider questions of cultural politics of representation. Offering precious insights into wider social and cultural changes, a critical analysis of its "metaphorical history" within Western academia can open the field also for considerations about the potential reproduction of popular orientalistic and exoticizing notions (with their annexed power gaps) within academic work and discourse.

Paolo Favero

See also Islamic City; Public Realm; Shopping

Further Readings

Augé, Marc. 1995. *Non places: Introduction to an Anthropology of Supermodernity*. London: Verso.

Bhabha, Homi K. 1998. "On the Irremovable Strangeness of Being Different." In *PMLA* 113(1):34–39.

Demil, Benoît and Xavier Lecocq. 2006. "Neither Market nor Hierarchy nor Network: The Emergence of Bazaar Governance." *Organization Studies* 27(10):1447–66.

Fanselow, Frank S. 1990. "The Bazaar Economy or How Bizarre Is the Bazaar Really?" *Man, New Series* 25(2):250–265.

Fox, Richard G. 1969. *From Zamindar to Ballot Box: Community Change in a North Indian Market Town*. Ithaca, NY: Cornell University Press.

Geertz, Clifford. 1978. "The Bazaar Economy: Information and Search in Peasant Marketing." *American Economic Review* 68(2):28–32.

———. 1979. "Suq: The Bazaar Economy in Sefrou." In *Meaning and Order in Moroccan Society*, edited by C. Geertz, H. Geertz, and L. Rosen. Cambridge, UK: Cambridge University Press.

Hetherington, Kevin. 1997. *Badlands of Modernity: Heterotopia and Social Ordering*. London: Routledge.

Raymond, Eric S. 2001. *The Cathedral and the Bazaar*. Rev. ed. Sebastopol, CA: O'Reilly.

Ruggiero, Vincenzo and Nigel South. 1997. "The Late-modern City as a Bazaar: Drug Markets, Illegal Enterprise and the 'Barricades.'" *British Journal of Sociology* 48(1):54–70.

Yang, Anand A. 1998. *Bazaar India: Markets, Society, and the Colonial State in Bihar*. Berkeley: University of California Press.

BÉGUINAGE

A *béguinage* denotes a community of béguines (French: *béguines,* from Latin: *beguinae*), or lay Catholic women living together religiously without taking permanent monastic vows; the term may also refer to the physical and social space that the community occupied in a city or town, usually marked by a wall, a moat, or both, and comprising a chapel, several residences where béguines lived alone or with few companions, a few larger buildings for common life, a hospital for poor and elderly members of the community, and various service buildings like a bakery or farm. Originating in the high Middle Ages, some of the larger béguinages survived well into the modern age, leaving their mark on the cityscape of various Belgian and Dutch cities. Thirteen béguinages that have been preserved in Flanders, the northern part of Belgium, were placed on UNESCO's World Heritage List of sites "of worldwide significance" in 1998. After a brief introduction to the historical origins of the béguine movement, this entry examines two types of béguinages ("convent" and "court") and their divergent history; it will also discuss current research on béguinages in urban studies.

Béguines

Béguines are first mentioned as "religious women" (*mulieres religiosae* in the original Latin) in early thirteenth-century sources of the Low Countries, the Rhineland, and northern France. They lived alone or in small informal groups and were devoted to the care of the poor and the sick (including lepers), to teaching, and to the promotion of a penitential lifestyle, without, however, joining a recognized monastic order. Despite the multiple legends surrounding their origins—some of which were taken as historical fact in the scholarly literature until recently—the movement did not have a single founder but arose from a variety of similar local initiatives in cities of Liège and Brabant, now eastern and central Belgium. These initiatives were led by women, usually single but in rare cases living in

Beguinage Amsterdam in its renovated state

of friars, for their religious services. In Belgium and the Netherlands, however, the béguinage often took the form of a walled compound for several hundreds of women in which béguine church, hospital, and residences were laid out in a grid or arranged around a central open square. These became de facto single-sex neighborhoods governed by béguines, supervised by the local clergy for their religious observances, and supervised by the secular, urban authorities for their charitable work. St. Catherine's of Mechelen, Belgium, possibly the largest of these "court beguinages" (Dutch: *begijnhoven*; Latin: *curtes beguinarum*), counted more than 1,500 béguines in the early sixteenth century.

"Court" béguinages, more influential and of lasting importance to many cities in the Low Countries, grew through a combination of push and pull factors that reflect the ambivalent position of such women in medieval urban society. Unlike nuns, who took solemn religious vows governing their life until death and were strictly cloistered and could not hold property individually, béguines were required only to promise obedience to their superior ("the grand mistress") and chastity for the duration of their stay in the béguinage, which they could leave at will; in most cases they were expected to provide for their own living, either through their labor or on the basis of rent income. Under these circumstances it was imperative that béguines freely exercised a profession within the béguinage or outside it, unhindered by strict rules of enclosure. Béguines are mentioned in the sources as nurses, teachers, merchants, but most often as workers in the textile industry, as spinsters or carders of wool, as weavers of linen and sometimes of woolen cloth. Many if not all of these tasks demanded a relatively free flow of people and goods between béguinages and the city. It was precisely because of their economic services that city authorities in the Low Countries collaborated with béguines to acquire large expanses of urban territory on the city's outskirts for the establishment of a béguinage. Evidently béguines delivered the right kind of inexpensive

a "chaste marriage." They received help from a few male clerics who were inspired by new thought on pastoral theology developed around the turn of the century at the University of Paris and who publicized their efforts, ultimately securing Church backing in the form of episcopal charters of protection and occasional papal support. Béguines never formed a single religious order but congregated locally to form independent béguinages that acquired and rented out property to individual women, elected their own superiors, and by the end of the thirteenth century also adopted local rules or statutes to regulate internal life. At that time, the movement had spread to a large area of continental northern Europe, from Marseilles in southern France to the Baltic coast. The *beatae* of Spain and the *pinzochere* or *bizzoche* of Italy were comparable to béguines but usually formed smaller communities more closely associated with recognized religious orders such as the Third Order of St. Francis.

Types and History of Béguine Communities

In most parts of northwestern Europe, béguines lived in single-residence communities known as "convents," each headed by its own "mistress" and dependent on parish clergy or monasteries, especially those labor force crucial to the burgeoning textile industries of these cities, providing help for elderly female workers and other social services as well. It is no accident that many béguinages were founded on low-lying, infertile lands, which in earlier times might have garnered marginal agricultural use but served no real function in the expanding urban economies of the high Middle Ages. Converting that land into a large béguinage giving shelter to numerous female workers, always paid less than males, made economic sense, not only in the early thirteenth century, when the textile industry was booming in the large urban centers of Bruges and Ghent, but sometimes in later centuries too. Béguinages indeed proved to be powerful devices to attract young women from the countryside eager to make a living in the city but in need of support and protection, as medieval cities were dangerous places for them.

The informal religious life "in the world" therefore offered opportunities for single women but also presented challenges. From the very beginning, the more conservative elements in the church and society regarded béguines with suspicion, expressed by the name given to these women, *beguina*, a pejorative term derived from the root *begg-*, which means "to mumble or pray indistinctly"; hence, *beguina* stood for a lay woman whose devotion was uncertain. Gathering such women in the single, quasi-monastic enclosures of court béguinages helped allay these misgivings. While it surely coincided with the women's own desire for greater seclusion to practice their penitential life and attend services in privacy, it also facilitated monitoring of béguine behavior and detecting possible heretical activity, which seemed all the more pressing after the 1230s, when intellectually gifted béguines developed an interest in mystical approaches to religious enlightenment, began to interpret scripture, and expressed their opinions in writing. Tensions increased around 1300, at a time when an economic downturn threatened employment for many béguines and weakened public support. Marguerite Porete, a béguine from Valenciennes who, in her *Mirror of Simple Souls*, advanced forms of mysticism that appeared to bypass ecclesiastical mediation, was condemned by a Parisian Inquisition and died at the stake in 1310. In the next few decades, bishops and other church authorities carefully investigated the orthodoxy of béguines in their lands. Many small "convents," lacking powerful patrons, were closed or died out because they lost financial support. The great court béguinages survived only through making concessions. Greater limits were placed on the women's ability to leave their béguinage, even for work in town. They were to adopt a suitable, nun-like habit that clearly distinguished them from ordinary citizens. In this form, the movement gained a second efflorescence during the Counterreformation (1575–1700). It lost its appeal in the second half of the twentieth century; the last béguine died in Belgium in 2008.

Béguines and Urban Studies

Béguines occupied a unique place in medieval and early modern urban society, straddling the divide between the secular and the religious. Historical research has long concentrated on their charitable institutions, well documented, and on their spirituality, dominated by major writers like Hadewijch (thirteenth century), Marguerite Porete (d. 1310), and Mechtild of Magdeburg (ca. 1208–1282). The study of the social, cultural, and economic integration of béguinages in the urban environment is now under way, informed by modern scholarship on gender, art, and urban space. They suggest a socially diverse membership, with lower- and middle-class groups in the majority and a significant contribution of rural women. By all accounts, gender factored strongly in both the support that the movement gained from city populations—for the economic reasons outlined earlier—and the skepticism displayed by church authorities. Current research now investigates, among other issues, if and how the religious art produced by and for béguinages reflects their unique position, to what extent béguinages may be called religious spaces, and indeed the concept of semi-religiosity (a term coined by historians to describe the béguines' halfway status) itself. Since the closure of court béguinages in the late twentieth century, local city governments in Belgium and the Netherlands have stimulated projects to renovate their buildings and properly reincorporate them into the urban fabric. These have sometimes included extensive archaeological and art historical study of the monumental remains, for instance at the béguinage of Sint-Truiden, Belgium, where the church from the late thirteenth and fourteenth centuries has preserved a remarkable program of wall paintings.

Walter Simons

See also Bruges, Belgium; Gendered Space; Historic Cities; Women and the City

Further Readings

Coomans, Thomas and Anna Bergmans, eds. 2008. *In zuiverheid leven. Het Sint-Agnesbegijnhof van Sint-Truiden. Het hof, de kerk, de muurschilderingen* (To Live in Purity: The Béguinage of St. Agnes in Sint-Truiden: The Court, the Church, the Wall Paintings). Brussels, Belgium: Vlaams Instituut voor het Onroerend Erfgoed; Provincie Limburg.

Koorn, Florence. 1981. *Begijnhoven in Holland en Zeeland gedurende de middeleeuwen.* (Béguinages in Holland and Zeeland in the Middle Ages). Assen, Netherlands: Van Gorcum.

Majérus, Pascal. 1997. *Ces femmes qu'on dit béguines. Guide des béguinages de Belgique. Bibliographie et sources d'archives* (Those Women Who Are Called Béguines. Guide to Béguinages in Belgium: Bibliography and Archival Records). Brussels, Belgium: Archives générales du Royaume/ Algemeen Rijksarchief.

McDonnell, Ernest. 1954. *The Beguines and Beghards in Medieval Culture: With Special Emphasis on the Belgian Scene.* New Brunswick, NJ: Rutgers University Press.

Reichstein, Frank-Michael. 2001. *Das Beginenwesen in Deutschland. Studien und Katalog* (Béguines in Germany: Studies and Catalogue). Berlin, Germany: Köster.

Simons, Walter. 2001. *Cities of Ladies: Beguine Communities in the Medieval Low Countries, 1200–1565.* Philadelphia: University of Pennsylvania Press.

Wilts, Andreas. 1994. *Beginen im Bodenseeraum* (Béguines in the Lake Constance Region). Sigmaringen, Germany: Jan Thorbecke.

Ziegler, Joanna E. 1992. *Sculpture of Compassion: The Pietà and the Beguines in the Southern Low Countries c. 1300–c. 1600.* Rome: Institut historique belge de Rome.

BENJAMIN, WALTER

The German–Jewish writer Walter Benjamin (1892–1940) is now widely regarded as one of the most original and insightful cultural theorists of the twentieth century. An associate of the Frankfurt Institute for Social Research (the Frankfurt School), and close friend of the critical theorist Theodor Adorno, the Judaic scholar Gershom Scholem, and the playwright Bertolt Brecht, Benjamin developed a highly idiosyncratic critical and redemptive theoretical approach to cultural phenomena drawn from, and interweaving in complex and enigmatic ways, Marxism, Judaic mysticism and messianism, and modernism (in particular, surrealism). Principally a literary theorist, his attention was nevertheless drawn to an extremely diverse range of cultural forms, media, and practices: film and photography; architecture, monuments, and urban space; commodities and fashions; and children's toys and fairytales. The significance of his characteristically fragmentary and disparate writings on the theme of the city is now increasingly recognized by urban theorists and scholars. Although they articulated no systematic or totalizing theory of the modern metropolis as such, Benjamin's texts nevertheless provide a rich and suggestive series of concepts and insights for the critical analysis of metropolitan architecture and consumer capitalism in the nineteenth century; of urban experience and memory; and of the cinematic, photographic, and literary representation of the cityscape.

Essays on the Urban Experience

During the mid- to late 1920s Benjamin wrote a series of impressionistic essays under the rubric of "thought images" (*Denkbilder*), sketching the cities he visited and explored: Naples (1924–1925), Moscow (1926–1927), Weimar (1928), Marseilles (1928–1929), San Gimignano (1929), and a piece on Bergen titled "North Sea" (1930). Deliberately eschewing theoretical specification and elaboration, these journalistic pen portraits were intended to capture and juxtapose vivid images of the concrete lived reality of these contrasting urban settings, foregrounding in this way their colorful street scenes (markets, vendors, swindlers, milling crowds, traffic and tramcars); their differing architectural and spatial configurations (buildings, stalls, streets, squares, interiors); and their myriad experiences (sensory inundation, disorientation, shock, eroticism, intoxication).

Published in 1928, Benjamin's *One-Way Street* (*Einbahnstrasse*) is a collection of aphorisms and witticisms influenced by the surrealist vision of the contemporary city as an intoxicating and seductive dreamscape of secret potentialities. Taking the architecture and nomenclature of the city as an organizing principle, the book comprises a series of penetrating observations about the possibilities of personal, individual, and collective experience in contemporary Berlin, Paris, and elsewhere (Riga, for instance, home of his then-lover). Benjamin's own intensely contradictory responses to the contemporary metropolis and urban culture find expression in these fragments: On the one hand, the city is a site of fascination and stimulation, of sexual encounters and intrigue, of inspiration, creativity, and cosmopolitanism; on the other, it is a locus of ruthless capitalist exploitation, of alienation and the diminution of human faculties, of bourgeois snobbery, egoism, and narrow self-interest.

Two cities preoccupied Benjamin: Berlin, the city of his birth and his home until the Nazi seizure of power; and Paris, the city for which he had a particular predilection and where he was to live in exile from 1933 until his suicide in 1940 when attempts to escape from occupied France failed.

Berlin Writings

Appropriately, Benjamin's various Berlin writings are bound up with the theme of childhood, albeit in rather different ways. Between 1927 and 1933 Benjamin wrote and delivered some 84 radio broadcasts for Berliner Rundfunk and Südwestdeutsche Rundfunk in Frankfurt am Main. Mainly written for children's programs, these narratives, stories, and histories frequently took as their theme particular places or settings in Berlin, or aspects of the capital's life and literature. Factories, tenement buildings, toy shops, old marketplaces, and the distinctive Berlin accent—all these became subject matter for Benjamin's scripts. In 1932, the imminent prospect of exile led Benjamin to compose two series of reflections upon his native city: *Berlin Chronicle* and *A Berlin Childhood around 1900*. Benjamin was at pains to deny the purely autobiographical character of these two texts, emphasizing instead the elusive, Proustian character of memory itself and, above all, the status of his recollections as memories both of and in the metropolis. Hence, he claimed, the Berlin essays were less concerned with tracing and narrating the life of an individual than with recalling particular spaces and moments of a city one was about to leave for the last time, with redeeming images of the Berlin cityscape seen at "last sight."

Paris Writings and the Arcades Project

Benjamin understood his *One-way Street* collection as his first genuine engagement with Paris. From 1927 onward, and once again inspired and informed by the surrealism of Louis Aragon and André Breton, Benjamin began work on a study of the city's shopping arcades, glass and iron constructions from the early nineteenth century, which had fallen into neglect and disrepair by Benjamin's time. Originally conceived in collaboration with his friend Franz Hessel as a short essay on the remaining ruinous Parisian arcades in the present, the "Arcades Project" (*Passagenarbeit*) expanded in terms of material gathered and scope to become a panoramic critical historical exploration of the structural and experiential transformation of Paris occurring principally, but not exclusively, during the Second Empire.

Benjamin regarded nineteenth-century Paris as the capital of capital, as the preeminent site of new forms of spectacle, enchantment, and phantasmagoria, phenomena that he understood as modern manifestations and reactivation of mythic domination. Benjamin's attempt to unmask capitalist ideology and mystification came to focus on two key material aspects: the commodity form as fetish and the ostentatious new architecture of the city (boulevards, railway stations, world exhibitions, as well as the arcades) as fantastical "dream-houses." In exposing both the utopian and illusory character of these, Benjamin hoped to "disenchant" the cityscape, to stimulate a revolutionary collective awakening from the complacent dream-sleep of the recent past.

Although the Arcades Project came to be Benjamin's central preoccupation during the 1930s, it remained unfinished, indeed unwritten, at the time of his tragic death. First published in German as volume five of Benjamin's collected writings in 1982, and first translated into English in 1999, Benjamin's magnum opus, and his most sustained and substantial piece of writing on the city, comprises numerous sketches and drafts and hundreds of pages of notes and quotations, grouped into folders or convoluted under headings and identified by a complex system of numbers and color codes. In this incomplete, incompletable form, the Arcades Project remains today as one of the most enigmatic and provocative studies of the modern city.

Writings on Film and Baudelaire

During the 1930s, the ill-fated Arcades Project formed the sun that gave life to, and around which circulated, a plethora of much shorter studies. Two of these are of particular relevance for urban theory: Benjamin's famous 1935–1936 essay "The Work of Art in the Age of Its Technological Reproducibility" and his essays (1938–1940) on the nineteenth-century Parisian poet Charles Baudelaire.

The "Work of Art" essay constitutes Benjamin's most sustained and coherent discussion of the new medium of film, and as such, articulated most explicitly an idea that finds more indistinct and undeveloped expression in a number of Benjamin's writings: the "elective affinity" between film as the quintessential new mass medium and the city as the definitive modern environment. For Benjamin, film was a privileged medium for capturing the flux and dynamism of the cityscape, for penetrating deeply into its obscure crevices, for illuminating its dark and hidden secrets, and, above all, for bringing the city's own revolutionary energies and tendencies to the point of critical tension and explosion.

Benjamin's studies of Baudelaire emerged from, and were intended to provide a model in miniature of, the wider Arcades Project. For Benjamin, Baudelaire was the first true poet of the modern metropolis, a melancholy figure who sought to give voice to the novel and traumatic urban experiences of his time. Baudelaire demanded a new aesthetic of the fleeting present, *modernité,* one that insisted upon the representation of the contemporary as the vital subject matter of the genuine modern artist. His own poetry drew upon the vernacular of Paris to evoke the shock encounter with the milling urban crowd, the bohemian life of the boulevards, the fate of the artwork turned commodity, the destitution of the outcasts of the city—heroic figures like *flâneurs,* prostitutes, ragpickers, and, of course, poets. Of these, the figure of the flâneur, the aloof and aimless stroller in the city, and a self-image not only of Baudelaire but also of Benjamin, has become a key motif for writers and urban theorists today.

Indeed, Benjamin's critical studies in metropolitan experience and representation are now essential reading for scholars and students of the modern city.

Graeme Gilloch

See also Arcade; Berlin, Germany; Paris, France

Further Readings

Benjamin, Walter. 1973. *Charles Baudelaire. A Lyric Poet in the Era of High Capitalism.* London: Fontana.

———. 1985. *One-way Street and Other Writings* London: Verso.

———. 1999. *The Arcades Project.* Cambridge, MA: Harvard University Press.

Buck-Morss, Susan. 1989. *The Dialectics of Seeing: Walter Benjamin and the Arcades Project.* Cambridge: MIT Press.

Frisby, David. 1988. *Fragments of Modernity: Theories of Modernity in the Work of Simmel, Kracauer and Benjamin.* Cambridge: MIT Press.

Gilloch, Graeme. 1996. *Myth and Metropolis: Walter Benjamin and the City.* Cambridge, UK: Polity.

BERLIN, GERMANY

Berlin today is the "capital of memory." Six different political systems have left their imprints in public spaces: the kingdom of Prussia from the eighteenth century, the imperial German Reich (1871–1918), the first democratic system (1918–1933), the Nazi period (1933–1945), the communist period in East Berlin (comprising the old city center), and the most recent democratic period after 1990 (often referred to as the Berlin Republic).

Divided Berlin

In all these diverse contexts, Berlin was assigned the central position of state capital. During the so-called Third Reich, the Nazi regime made far-reaching plans for transforming Berlin into a city that would match their vision of a "world capital Germania." Keys to these urban development plans were the monumental buildings planned by the architect Albert Speer of whose work few traces remain. At the end of World War II and the beginning of the cold war, Berlin was divided into four sectors, each of which was under the control of one of the four Allied powers (the United States, France, Great Britain, and the Soviet Union), corresponding to the Allied control of Germany as a whole. Due to Berlin's geographical location within Germany, it became a space of shared Allied control surrounded by Soviet-controlled territory. When the United States,

France, and Great Britain joined the administration of the parts under their control in 1948, the Soviet Union responded with the blocking of ground access to West Berlin. This situation led to the famous airlift that provided West Berlin with basic supplies between June 1948 and May 1949. While ground access was reestablished afterward, the rift between the Western Allies and the Soviet Union continued to deepen and led to the building of the Berlin wall in 1961, which was dismantled in 1989.

Due to its unique post–World War II history, Berlin holds a position that is quite unlike that of any other city within the Federal Republic of Germany. Until 1990, the city was divided into two parts that were governed by two opposed political systems: the West, belonging to the Federal Republic of Germany; and the East, serving as the capital of the German Democratic Republic (GDR). In 1990, Berlin became the capital of a reunited Germany. Many streets in the former East have been renamed, and many new monuments devoted to the victims of National Socialism have been erected in order to both bear witness to the terrorist regimes and commemorate instances of resistance against them. It is this constant presence of history that makes the city unique.

Postreunification Effects

Housing and Land Redevelopment

Since reunification, not only have the economic and political spheres undergone tremendous changes, but also the housing situation of various districts has changed dramatically. Furthermore, the social composition of many neighborhoods has been transformed as a result of recent migratory movements into and out of the city.

As of 2008, the city of Berlin has 3.4 million inhabitants living in an area of approximately 889 square kilometers (552 square miles). Sixty-three percent of the population lives in the former western part of the city. Following the radical political collapse of the GDR in 1989 and the reunification of both parts of the city in 1990, far-reaching economic, social, and spatial transformation processes have affected the city as a whole.

The former eastern part has faced particular challenges: Here, virtually all conditions for urban development changed in the early 1990s.

These changes encompass the redistribution of property, new planning laws, new players, new investors (private investors, the federal government, the federal state, the borough administrations, and citizen interest groups), and new planning concepts. Those city quarters that had formerly been situated in the vicinity of the wall and had therefore either been neglected or cleared during GDR times now found themselves at the very heart of Berlin's reconstruction and modernization efforts. Furthermore, the center of former East Berlin is partly under redevelopment according to a master plan (*Planwerk Innenstadt*) that aims at reconstructing the spatial structure of a European city. This structure is posited as a contrast to the modernist concepts underlying communist planning, which had led to the removal of much of the old housing stock and to a fundamental redesign of spatial patterns. Wide streets are determined to be narrowed again, and new buildings should be constructed along the further vanishing line.

The present transformation of East Berlin can be captured by the label "marketization." It is therefore diametrically opposed to the development it underwent between 1949 and 1989. This development was characterized by a process of "demarketization" or "decommodification," which was triggered by the transition from capitalism to socialism. Starting in 1989, the reintroduction of a market economy, including private ownership, manifested itself in the reconstitution of private property, achieved either through property restitution to former owners or by means of land and property sales to new investors. This radically changed control structures and led to new sociospatial patterns.

Land prices as well as rents under newly formulated rent agreements increased significantly immediately after unification took place. The political decision to move the seat of the federal government of Germany back to Berlin in 1991 led to a boom in real estate investment in West Berlin. However, by the year 2000 it had become clear that Berlin was not on track to regain its dominant position in the German urban system and that the expected strong growth of population would not come into effect. Accordingly, rents stagnated and land prices declined. The overall level of rents in Berlin today remains lower than that of economically vibrant German cities like Munich and much lower than levels in London or Paris. As a result, both young people and "creatives" (two groups that often overlap) are attracted to the supply of cheap space and the low cost of living in a city that is rapidly establishing its position as a cultural metropolis.

Economics and Employment

The economic changes that took place between 1992 and 1997 are particularly noticeable in the manufacturing industries, where more than one third of the 270,000 jobs have disappeared. It was not until 2006 that an increase could be observed. As a consequence of this dramatic reduction in jobs, there was a continuous rise in unemployment during the 1990s. In East Berlin, unemployment rose from 12.2 percent in 1991 to 16.5 percent in 1997 while the unemployment rate for Berlin as a whole exceeded 15 percent. This is considerably higher than the average rate for Germany and the rates for most of the cities in western Germany.

The decreasing number of jobs made access to the labor market ever more difficult both for the unemployed and for new migrant groups from abroad, leading to a constant increase in long-term unemployment. Migrants who were recruited in the 1960s to work specifically in the manufacturing sector (a sector that has been in rapid decline since the early 1990s) constitute one of the groups who suffer most from this development.

The relocation of the national government from Bonn to Berlin did not fundamentally alter the situation on the labor market. Due to contracts between the national and the state governments, there are still more civil servants working with national institutions in Bonn than in Berlin. However, the demand for both high-skilled and low-skilled service workers has been growing rapidly since then, while the middle segment is declining. Far away from positioning itself as a global hub in the global economy, Berlin is today characterized by a polarizing employment structure.

Sociospatial Patterns

This is further reflected in changing sociospatial patterns. Two different types of hot spots for poverty and unemployment exist within Berlin's urban structure: on the one hand the former working-class neighborhoods north and south of the city center (i.e., Wedding, Kreuzberg, and Neukölln), and on the other hand the big housing estates at the periphery of both East and West Berlin. Measuring changes in neighborhoods according to their share of unemployment and poverty exposes a process of polarization of sociospatial segregation. The most privileged areas are those that held a similarly privileged position in prewar times: the low density areas in the southwestern and southeastern parts of the city and the upper-class neighborhoods in central locations of West Berlin (Charlottenburg, Wilmersdorf).

Although city planners under the communist regime tried to forge socially diverse living quarters in the newly constructed prefabricated housing estates (*Plattenbauten*), social segregation still occurred: The neglected old housing stock in inner-city areas was predominantly inhabited by citizens whom the political authorities viewed as disloyal and who were thus marginalized. These areas, however, were attractive to artists and young people who exercised political dissent and at times succeeded in creating an alternative milieu. Immediately after unification, when freedom of movement across the former border to West Germany had been restored, many students and creative youth filled these vacant structures with new types of activities. Furthermore, many families, especially those with higher education, moved from the periphery to the newly renovated old housing stock. They served as pioneers in a classical cycle of gentrification in neighborhoods in Mitte, Prenzlauer Berg, and Friedrichshain, which today host the "creative class." As long as the Berlin government could control the renewal process by means of restrictions and sponsorship, the demands of modernization and the needs of old tenants were both taken into account and balanced. However, the post-Fordist withdrawal of state intervention, which was at least partially due to the financial crisis of the city, led to a situation in which the process of renovation and modernization is now controlled by market powers. As a result, low-income households are increasingly forced to leave popular living quarters and move to disadvantaged parts of the city.

Whereas the small remaining parts of the famous Berlin wall have become popular tourist destinations, most of the wall has been torn down;

thus opening up space in central urban locations that have been reconstructed and now feature office buildings and prestigious hotels. In contrast to this, the previously mentioned rapid and fundamental process of deindustrialization that went hand in hand with the development of a new service economy has left many sites and buildings in other locations underused or even vacant. This provides space for low-budget initiatives that manifest in an abundance of galleries, bars, theaters, and small start-ups, which in turn give rise to the widely shared perception of Berlin as an open, vital, and innovative place. Many stakeholders hope that this creative milieu, together with Berlin's increasingly multicultural identity, will eventually be transformed into new economic growth. To what extent the diverse groups inhabiting Berlin will be included in this new development remains an open question. At this point in time, the formerly divided city has become a fragmented one—administratively unified but socially divided along new border lines.

Hartmut Häußermann

See also Benjamin, Walter; Capital City; Other Cities; Simmel, Georg

Further Readings

Bernt, Matthias and Andrej Holm. 2005. "Exploring the Substance and Style of Gentrification. Berlin's 'Prenzlberg.'" Pp. 106–20 in *Gentrification in a Global Context: The New Urban Colonialism*, edited by R. Atkinson and G. Bridge. London: Routledge.

Häußermann, Hartmut. 2003. "Berlin." Pp. 113–24 in *Metropolitan Governance and Spatial Planning: Comparative Case Studies of European City-Regions*, edited by W. G. M. Salet, A. Thornley, and A. Kreukels. London: Routledge/Spon.

———. 2006. "Public Space in Five Social Systems." Pp. 157–70 in *Toward a New Metropolitanism: Reconstituting Public Culture, Urban Citizenship, and the Multicultural Imaginary in New York and Berlin*, edited by G. H. Lenz, F. Ulfers, and A. Dallmann. Heidelberg, Germany: Universitätsverlag Winter.

Häußermann, Hartmut, Andrej Holm, and Daniela Zunzer. 2002. *Stadterneuerung in der Berliner Republik. Modernisierung in Berlin—Prenzlauer Berg* (City Renewal in the Berlin Republic. Modernization in Berlin—Prenzlauer Berg). Opladen, Germany: Leske + Budrich.

Häußermann, Hartmut and Andreas Kapphan. 2005. "Berlin: From Divided to Fragmented City." Pp. 189–222 in *Transformation of Cities in Central and Eastern Europe towards Globalization*, edited by F. E. I. Hamilton, K. D. Andrews, and N. Pichler-Milanović. Tokyo: United Nations University Press.

Strom, Elizabeth A. 2001. *Building the New Berlin: The Politics of Urban Development in Germany's Capital City*. Lanham, MD: Lexington Books.

BERRY, BRIAN J. L.

One of geography's most productive scholars, Brian Berry has played an enormously influential role in urban and economic geography, primarily as the steadfast defender of traditional quantitative modeling. Not without reason, Gordon Clark argues that "Brian Berry is perhaps the most important of a handful of people who transformed human geography over the second half of the twentieth century."

Born in 1934 to working-class parents in England (both of whom left school at age 14), Berry defied the confines of the British class system to rise to the top-most tiers of academia. He completed a BS in economics at the London School of Economics in 1955, where he was exposed to historical geography and introduced to the quantitative modeling of spatial phenomena. Immediately thereafter, he traveled to the University of Washington in Seattle just as the geography program there initiated the quantitative revolution in American geography. Berry thus formed both part of the "British invasion" of influential geographers in the 1960s and one of the famous "space cadets," along with Duane Marble, William Bunge, Michael Dacey, Arthur Getis, Richard Morrill, John Nystuen, and Walter Tobler, arguably the discipline's most successful and famous single cohort of students.

Three years later, armed with a PhD—at age 22—he began the first of a long list of academic positions at prestigious institutions, including the University of Chicago (1958–1976), where he was the Irving Harris Professor of Urban Geography, chair of the Department of Geography, and director of the Center for Urban Studies. From 1976 to

1981, he taught at Harvard University, where he served as the Frank Backus Williams Professor of City and Regional Planning, chair of the PhD program in urban planning, director of the Laboratory for Computer Graphics and Spatial Analysis, professor of sociology, and as a faculty fellow of the Harvard Institute for International Development. From 1981 to 1986 he served as Dean of the School of Urban Public Affairs at Carnegie Mellon University in Pittsburgh. Beginning in 1986 he taught at the University of Texas, Dallas, where, in 1991, he became the Lloyd Viel Berkner Regental Professor of Political Economy and, in 2006, dean of the School of Social Sciences. He is the recipient of numerous awards and medals. In 1968, he received the Association of American Geographers' Meritorious Contributions Award. In 1975, he became the first geographer and youngest social scientist ever elected to the National Academy of Sciences. In 1977–1978, he served as president of the Association of American Geographers. He was elected a fellow of the American Association for the Advancement of Science in 1987, awarded the Victoria Medal from the Royal Geographical Society in 1988, and made a fellow of the British Academy in 1989. He also served as a founding coeditor and editor in chief of the journal *Urban Geography* from 1980 to 2006.

Berry's publication record—including in toto more than 500 books, articles, and other publications—has earned him enormous recognition as one of geography's most fecund scholars. He followed Fred K. Schaefer's famous critique of "exceptionalist" geography in advocating for a discipline that was self-consciously nomothetic in outlook and positivist in epistemology, thus emphasizing the need for general laws of explanation, quantitative methods, and rigorous empirical testing of hypotheses. Throughout his long career, he subscribed to a paradigm that privileged the abstract over the concrete, deduction over induction, and the universal over the specific. Drawing on a Cartesian view of space, Berry emphasized the use of models as a means to simplify and shed light on the bewildering complexity of the world. He was instrumental in the adoption of multivariate statistics in the discipline. His early papers stressed the applicability of central place models of urban systems and detailed studies of retail shopping patterns. Subsequent work on market centers and

retailing was very influential in geography and business and economics. He also delved into the rank-size distributions of cities, hierarchal diffusion processes, and the impacts of transportation systems. In addition, Berry had a long-standing interest in urban morphology and urban problems such as inner-city poverty. Over time, Berry's works came to be characterized by increasing conceptual sophistication and a sustained concern for the role of public policy. In doing so, he abandoned much of the earlier emphasis on simplified models in exchange for rigorous empirical and statistical analyses.

Berry's later career focused on the dynamics of regional development in different national contexts. He conducted extensive work in India, Australia, Indonesia, and other countries. Comparative analyses of urbanization bridged these national contexts. Urban trends in the United States received considerable attention as well, including the question of counterurbanization and the specific development patterns of Chicago. A persistent theme was the relation of demographic shifts and migration to regional change. This phase of his career was characterized by a mounting interest in issues of globalization, particularly the ways in which multinational corporations intersected with state policies to shape urban growth around the world. In the 1990s, Berry turned his focus to the role of long wave cycles, or Kondratief waves, and their relation to regional development and political relations. Subsequent work viewed utopian communities as attempts to escape the maelstrom of change and turmoil associated with the periodic restructuring brought about by long waves.

As the embodiment of positivism and the quantitative revolution, Berry's intellectual position came under mounting criticism from the 1980s onward. A newer generation of geographers attuned to political economy and social theory began increasingly to question the relevance of abstract, ahistorical models and the unrealistic neoclassical logic of utility maximization. This schism was exemplified in a famous debate between Brian Berry and the Marxist geographer David Harvey. As a result of academic geography's shift to political economy, Berry appeared, to many observers, as increasingly conservative and disconnected from the field. Never one to give up, Berry is known to this day for the enthusiasm and commitment with which he advocates his views, and whatever philosophical differences some geographers may have with him, he remains widely respected.

Barney Warf

See also Urban Geography; Urban System; Urban Theory

Further Readings

Berry, Brian. 1967. *Geography of Market Centers and Retail Distribution.* Englewood Cliffs, NJ: Prentice Hall.

———. 1973. *The Human Consequences of Urbanization: Divergent Paths in the Urban Experience of the Twentieth Century.* New York: St. Martin's.

———. 1976. *Urbanisation and Counter-urbanisation.* London: Sage.

———. 1980. "Creating Future Geographies." *Annals of the Association of American Geographers* 70:449–58.

———. 1991. *Long-wave Rhythms in Economic Development and Political Behavior.* Baltimore: Johns Hopkins University Press.

———. 2002. "Clara Voce Cognito." In *Geographical Voices: Fourteen Autobiographical Essays,* edited by P. Gould and F. Pitts. Syracuse, NY: Syracuse University Press.

Clarke, Gordon. 2004. "Brian Berry." In *Key Thinkers on Space and Place,* edited by P. Hubbard, R. Kitchin, and G. Valentine. London: Sage.

Schaefer, Fred K. 1953. "Exceptionalism in Geography: A Methodological Examination." *Annals of the Association of American Geographers* 43:226-49.

Warf, Barney. 2004. "Troubled Leviathan: The Contemporary U.S. versus Brian Berry's U.S." *Professional Geographer* 56:85–90.

BILBAO, SPAIN

Bilbao seems to have gone global overnight. A peripheral city in Western Europe with an old industrial tradition but largely unknown to most people outside Spain, Bilbao came to the attention of commentators worldwide thanks to the opening of a branch of the Guggenheim Museum in 1997—a project widely acclaimed as a resounding success, turning the city into a destination for global pilgrimage. Millions have visited the city to contemplate the art and admire the titanium building that wraps the museum, a work hailed as architect Frank O. Gehry's masterpiece. According to outsiders, the museum triggered the city's revitalization. After 20 years of decline, Bilbao's good economic performance since 1994 was attributed uncritically to the Guggenheim "miracle." New claims were made about the role of spectacular architecture and the arts in urban renewal and globalization, with urban officials worldwide seriously considering bidding for a Guggenheim for their own cities. Bilbao became synonymous with the Guggenheim, and many cities around the world wanted to imitate the Basque capital's success and become instantly "global."

Historical Development

A city's fortunes, however, go beyond the reach of a cultural artifact, regardless of how successful and "global" it may be. Bilbao was already a globalizing city shortly after its foundation in 1300—the King of Castile chartered the city as a node in the networks of trade between Castile and the world. As the place from which Castilian wool and Basque iron were exported to Europe, the city played a key role in the European subsystem of trade. Basque merchants were present and active in the major world cities at the time. Bilbao's development during the following centuries shows an expanding city struggling to preserve its commercial freedoms vis-à-vis the Spanish state. For much of its history, the city has been a frontier town between Spain, Europe, and America, adapting its commercial relations to the ebb and flow of world markets and the success or failure of centralizing efforts from Madrid. Whereas for most of the Fordist period Bilbao was gradually integrated into the Spanish economy, the current phase of globalization, together with the high degree of political autonomy for the Basque Country, is again taking the city on a path to globalization.

Bilbao's industrialization in the late nineteenth century gave rise to its modern business elite, which grew out of the mining business and diversified investments in other sectors and other regions in Spain, exemplifying the *Spanishness* of Basque capitalism. At the same time, foreign economic relations continued at a good pace in Bilbao. Exports of local iron, in particular, reached unprecedented levels as the city became the main supplier for Great Britain during the latter's imperial apogee prior to World War I. Structural adjustments in the Basque industry and the consolidation of liberalization and centralization policies undertaken by the various Spanish governments during the nineteenth and twentieth centuries, however, meant that Bilbao's industry was much more geared to producing and selling in a protected Spanish market than competing in foreign arenas. Following the abolition of the Basque privilege to import goods duty-free, the city became fully integrated into the Spanish economy. In historical terms, Fordist Bilbao was an era of deglobalization for the city, especially the period from 1936 to 1973. Through its port, Bilbao continued to serve as a node in trade between Spain and the world, but uneven development within Spain helped Basque industrialists to execute a strategy of industrial expansion, which strengthened the structural ties between the city and the nation-state. These were the times when Bilbao's per capita income was the highest of all Spanish cities.

The decades of 1970 and 1980 represented the crisis of the Fordist model and the transformation of Bilbao into a "postindustrial" economy through restructuring and tertiarization. The political atmosphere in the Basque Country (marked by attempts by local nationalist elites to gain power quotas during the Spanish transition to democracy and by Basque nationalist ETA's violent fight for independence) and the overall industrial policy implemented by the then socialist government in Madrid greatly influenced the fate of Bilbao's steel manufacturing and shipbuilding industries. Because local plants were not adapted to the environment of lower industrial demand and had to be downsized or closed, the global restructuring of these sectors also contributed to Bilbao's decay. The specific ways in which restructuring took place, however, were matters of political choice at the national and regional levels. Ironically, Bilbao's strengths—Fordist industrial power, entrepreneurship, and linkages to the world system—made the city particularly vulnerable to world trends.

Local and regional authorities were slow to react to the changing economic framework and circumstances, and Bilbao essentially became a Rustbelt city, but one with great autonomous power and state support that—unlike most Rustbelt cities elsewhere—would give it the resources and control to overcome a crisis situation. Starting in the late 1980s, and determined to reposition Bilbao as a rising metropolis among global cities, the local authorities developed an ambitious revitalization plan similar to other struggling urban economies in the United States and Europe. The critical, most visible piece of this plan became the Guggenheim Museum, projected to be built in an area called Abandoibarra, which became the urban megaproject in post-Fordist Bilbao.

Abandoibarra: The Urban Megaproject

Abandoibarra—a piece of industrial land in downtown Bilbao being transformed into a new central business district—exemplifies the global aspirations of the *new* Bilbao. Abandoibarra shows the contrast between the city's globalization via revitalization plans and the "selling the city" strategy reflected in the planners' global rhetoric, on the one hand, and the organizational and political obstacles present in local urban planning development and implementation on the other. The potential of the project to become Bilbao's territorial link to the global economy has not yet been realized. Abandoibarra remains a global project in its aims but, in practice, is one of only local reach and impact, with foreign investment playing little significant role in the redevelopment of this downtown waterfront area. The role of Bilbao Ría 2000 (an urban development corporation) in the development of Abandoibarra as manager of the project was significant, and the many project modifications implemented over time demonstrate that the global ambitions of the local elites often have to face internal strife and obstacles that might ultimately slow down or immobilize global megaprojects. In view of Abandoibarra's fate, one is led to think that, because it has influenced contemporary urban planning's organizational and managerial tools, globalization has acquired a relatively new dimension in recent times, with megaprojects representing the physical manifestation of urban elites' entrepreneurialism and global aspirations.

The Guggenheim Museum Bilbao

All in all, however, it is the Guggenheim project that has put Bilbao on the map and the enterprise that represents the latest of Bilbao's globalization efforts. The motives of Basque political leaders in bringing the museum to Bilbao, after a negotiation process in

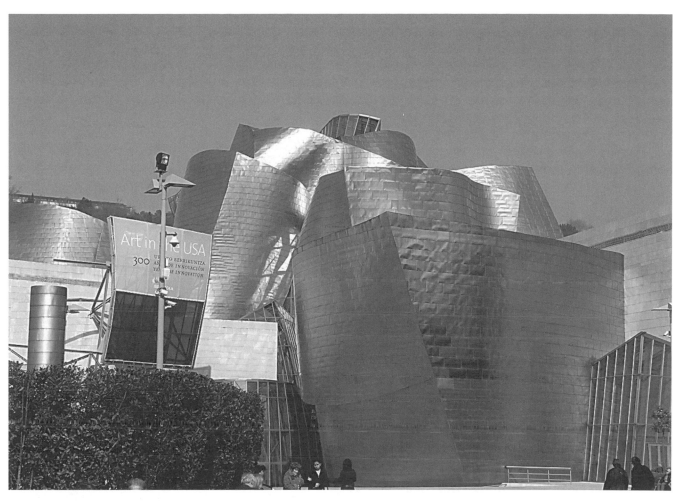

Frank Gehry's Guggenheim Museum Bilbao in Spain

Source: Andreas Praefcke.

which coincidences played an important role, were not shaped primarily by "cultural" concerns, but, instead, are better explained by two factors, one global and one domestic: (1) recognition of the need for regional image change and urban regeneration in Bilbao under conditions of contemporary globalization—which in practice meant participating in a global venture for spectacular architecture, and (2) the long historical desire on the part of the Basque Nationalist Party leaders for political emancipation from Spain, reflected in this case in the realm of cultural politics. In this way, the Guggenheim project was not an isolated case of urban boosterism. Instead it is the latest and most successful example of how Basque leaders, in the only subnational government in Europe with exclusive powers to levy taxes, have managed to bypass Madrid and conduct their own independent international affairs. The project's political overtones are clear, but its economic dimension is also important. Although

the museum has been hailed by the international press as the icon that has turned Bilbao's economy around, the evidence leads us to question the strategy's long-term feasibility and shows that an urban economy the size of Bilbao's cannot rely simply on a museum for economic development. Nonetheless, as a state project fully funded with public money, the Bilbao Guggenheim will remain an urban icon independent of financial pressures. One of the lessons of Bilbao's Guggenheim Museum is that, because it has the power of *rescaling* the significance of specific buildings and the cities where they are built, iconic, spectacular architecture—driven, in this case, by the ambitions of entrepreneurial politicians and cultural managers rather than transnational corporations—plays a fundamental role in the worldwide deployment of contemporary globalization and the creation of large-scale social spaces representing capitalism's transnational strategies.

In Bilbao, the museum became a spectacular worldwide image campaign due not only to a possibly irreplicable building, but also to local, contextual economic and political conditions. Far from being the trigger for and prime mover of revitalization, the museum postdated it. So far it has not generated substantial foreign investment in the Basque city, let alone had sizable positive consequences in the job market. Bilbao's relatively good economic performance in recent years, which so many in the media attribute to the Guggenheim, began prior to its opening and was due to both a reasonable regional economic policy developed by the Basque government and the positive phase of a long economic cycle, which came to an end in 2001 and seemed to rebound by 2004. Continued media attention preserves the Bilbao effect, but if tourist attendance to Bilbao starts to decrease (no one can guarantee that it will keep its current levels) and the architecture world begins to privilege alternative aesthetics in design and building, the star of Bilbao might begin to dim. The real consequences for the Basque city, however, would be relatively limited, just as the impact of the Guggenheim success was in the first place. Cities are complexly determined formations, and a spectacular media event, even projected on a worldwide scale, is not enough to shift their fortunes.

If spectacular architecture does not suffice in turning a struggling urban economy around, how can cities and regions successfully implement globalization policies that bring economic benefit to citizens? Here is where the recent economic globalization of the city-region in the Basque Country, as it is clearly seen in patterns of transnational finance and foreign trade, plays a prominent role. The pillars of this recent Basque move toward globalization show themes that were already present in the golden years of industrial Bilbao: industrialization based on exports and the reach of the local financial bourgeoisie and its banks. This recent globalization, therefore, is hardly a new phenomenon in Bilbao (except, perhaps, for its scale, scope, and complexity), but rather a new cycle in a centuries-old tendency by the city to join global circuits in the world system.

Contemporary Economic Globalization

Bilbao's contemporary international role and the city-region's new economic globalization are based on the power of its regional foreign trade, which has found a main partner in the European Union, with export figures tripling between 1994 and 2004. Part of this foreign trade, which, inter alia, reveals the Basque Country's strength as a high-tech manufacturing region, is channeled through the port of Bilbao—a port managed by the Spanish government's agencies and one that continues to serve its ancient function of linking large segments of the Spanish economy with the world. Bilbao's international role is also based on the flow of transnational banking deployed by the city's global bank, Banco Bilbao Vizcaya Argentaria, mainly in Latin America. These three important dimensions of contemporary Basque economic power (trade globalization, global connectivity via Bilbao's port, and financial globalization) demonstrate that present-day Basque globalization is based on traditional regional strengths that fostered local links with global circuits in past historical periods, thus questioning the alleged radical newness of globalization's current phase. Thus, as evidence of historical continuity and a reminder that globalization is but a partial factor in a city's development, Bilbao's international role is a product of both the region's dependency on global trade and financial networks and the intricate relationships of the region with the nation-state.

Gerardo del Cerro Santamaría

See also Architecture

Further Readings

Abadie, A. and J. Gardeazabal. 2001. "The Economic Costs of Conflict: A Case-Control Study for the Basque Country." Working Paper No. 8478, National Bureau of Economic Research, Cambridge, MA.

del Cerro Santamaría, Gerardo. 2007. *Bilbao: Basque Pathways to Globalization.* London: Elsevier.

Díez Medrano, J. 1995. *Divided Nations.* Ithaca, NY: Cornell University Press.

Douglass, W., C. Urza, L. White, and J. Zulaika, eds. 1999. *Basque Politics and Nationalism on the Eve of the Millennium.* Reno: University of Nevada, Center for Basque Studies.

González Ceballos, S. 2005. "The Politics of the Economic Crisis and Restructuring in the Basque Country and Spain during the 1980s." *Space and Polity* 9(2):93–112.

Guasch, A. M. and J. Zulaika, eds. 2005. *Learning from the Bilbao Guggenheim.* Reno: University of Nevada, Center for Basque Studies.

McNeill, D. 2000. "McGuggenisation? National Identity and Globalisation in the Basque Country." *Political Geography* 19(4):473–94.

Plaza, B. 2000. "Evaluating the Influence of a Large Cultural Artifact in the Attraction of Tourism: The Guggenheim Museum Bilbao Case." *Urban Affairs Review* 36(2):264–74.

Rodríguez, A. and E. Martínez. 2003. "Restructuring Cities: Miracles and Mirages in Urban Revitalization in Bilbao." Pp. 181–209 in *The Globalized City: Economic Restructuring and Social Polarization in European Cities,* edited by F. Moulaert, A. Rodríguez, and E. Swyngedouw. Oxford, UK: Oxford University Press.

Zulaika, J. 2001. "Krens's Taj Mahal: The Guggenheim's Global Love Museum." *Discourse* 23(1):100–18.

BOHEMIAN

In Europe, the term *bohemian* began as an ethnic designation and evolved into a general epithet meaning gypsy or beggar. During the middle decades of the nineteenth century in Paris, the term was adopted as a way to describe the growing class of disaffected young artists and intellectuals populating the garrets and cafés of the burgeoning metropolis. This usage retained some of the pejorative connotations left over from earlier applications, with many condemning these new bohemians as a morally dubious and parasitic bunch, though the mantle was soon adopted by many adherents as a point of pride. Since then the term has proven both durable and portable and is used to refer to the spaces and lifestyles of artists, intellectuals, and aesthetes in a host of European and North American cities. Bohemian, then, describes both a distinctive set of cultural affectations and also the distinctive urban districts in which adherents congregate. As both a historical phenomenon and in its present-day incarnations, bohemia has become an important topic in urban studies.

The Parisian Prototype

While cities throughout history have played a role as incubators of cultural innovation, in the nineteenth century new ideas about the nature of the artist and his or her relation to the city began to be elaborated. This was particularly true in Paris, a city that Walter Benjamin calls "the capital of the nineteenth century" and a central site of the cultural innovations that would constitute European modernism. Drawing on the freshly minted example of the Romantic poets, artists began to be thought of not as skilled crafts people, integrated into the social system, but as exalted and often tortured geniuses, liable to be alienated from a society unable to grasp the contents of their sensitive souls. What Parisians such as the poet Charles Baudelaire and the painter Édouard Manet added to the Romantic paradigm was a distinctively urban vision, both in terms of the works of art they produced and the lifestyles that they adopted.

By the mid-nineteenth century, Paris was flooded with adherents to this design for urban living. This overabundance of intellectual and creative fervor in Paris can be attributed to the general tumult of the period—the spatial revolution spurring the spectacular growth of the great city and the political and economic upheavals transforming the nature of social class relations. Bohemians blurred the boundaries in an emergent society, evincing the commitment to cultural distinction of the fading aristocracy, the individualism of the ascendant bourgeoisie, and the hedonism and licentiousness of the urban demimonde. Perhaps because so many were frustrated applicants to the professions, overeducated and undernourished within the new urban economy, bohemians became known for their fierce antipathy toward the bourgeoisie (which in this case refers to both the entrepreneurial and the professional class in Paris) and ethics of instrumental labor.

In *Un Prince de la Bohème* (*A Prince of Bohemia*), Honore de Balzac used the term to refer to "the vagrant students of the Latin Quarter," describing bohemia as a way-station through which talented youth pass on the way to more legitimate and remunerative occupational pursuits. The notion of bohemia as the "El Dorado of youth" has remained durable since then, although subsequent observers have tended to reject its depiction as merely a rite of passage preceding bourgeois respectability. In the latter 1840s, Henri Murger, himself an exemplary practitioner of the lifestyle, produced a collection of vignettes concerning a cenacle of Latin Quarter artists that would be collected as *Scènes de la Vie de Bohème* (Scenes from the Bohemian Life, 1848). His accounts were extremely popular, resulting in a well-received stage adaptation and eventually serving as the source material for Giacomo Puccini's opera *La Bohème*. From these romanticized works one may glean many enduring ideals of the bohemian lifestyle: the vaunted bonhomie, the balance of hedonism and self-sacrifice, the rejection of bourgeois values of instrumentality and security, and the primacy of *art pour l'art* (art for art's sake).

By the end of the nineteenth century, the hillside village of Montmartre began to displace the Latin Quarter as Paris's bohemian center of gravity. Montmartre was particularly notable for the lively café and cabaret nightlife found there, frequented by both bohemian participants and slumming members of the bourgeoisie. The presence of such exotic nocturnal diversions, serving as platforms upon which bohemians would enact their often spectacular lifestyle innovations, has become an especially important feature of the bohemian district in subsequent iterations.

The American Bohemian

In the early decades of the twentieth century, New York's Greenwich Village would emerge as the United States' own bohemian center, drawing on the European example and incorporating European expatriates such as Marcel Duchamp and Mina Loy. In Greenwich Village, an ethnic working-class section of lower Manhattan, avant-garde artists and writers mingled with political radicals, including John Reed, Max Eastman, and Emma Goldman. Among the distinguishing features of the Greenwich Village bohemia was the new attention to feminist politics and the expansive role played by women such as Edna St. Vincent Millay, Djuna Barnes, and Margaret Anderson within the milieu. Uptown, the segregated African American district of Harlem was simultaneously experiencing a cultural flowering, demonstrating that bohemia was not solely the property of Whites.

After World War II, a new bohemian style known as "beat" came to the fore. The term is credited to Jack Kerouac, whose novel *On the Road* is the most prominent example of beat literature, in which he described himself and his friends as a "beat generation," similar to the "lost generation" of post–World War I writers such as F. Scott Fitzgerald, Ernest Hemingway, and Gertrude Stein. Other prominent beat writers include Allen Ginsberg, Lawrence Lipton, and William S. Burroughs. As

with prior bohemian movements, these artists and affiliated lifestyle adherents favored particular urban districts, including North Beach in San Francisco, Venice Beach in Los Angeles, and Greenwich Village in New York.

While Parisian bohemians rejected the emergent conventions of bourgeois utilitarianism, members of the beat generation pitched themselves against the blandness of postwar consumer society, especially as represented by the middle-class suburbs and their presumed conformism. The beats were inspired by cultural innovations that they gleaned as coming from the African American community, especially jazz. In 1959, Norman Mailer penned a manifesto of beat bohemianism that he titled "The White Negro," advocating that White hipsters take their cultural cues from urban Blacks, whose experience he viewed as an authentic alternative to that of the suburban White square, "trapped in the totalitarian tissues of American life, doomed willy nilly to conform if one is to succeed."

Though beat is mainly regarded as a literary movement, in an account of the Greenwich Village beat scene in 1960, the sociologist Ned Polsky noted that the scene was crowded with participants who lacked literary ambition and were best distinguished by fondness for jazz and deep antipathy to gainful employment. These adherents came to be known by the generally pejorative designation *beatniks* and were identified by a presumed affinity for goatees, berets, and bongo drums.

Bohemia Since the 1960s

An examination of the Parisian prototype, the Greenwich Village bohemia, and the beat movement of the postwar decades reveals both evident continuity in the bohemian lifestyle and the ways in which it takes particular forms depending on distinctive historical periods and urban locales. Trends in the last half of the twentieth century further illustrate this point.

The explosion of the youth counterculture during the 1960s marked a new turn in the articulation of bohemian lifestyles. The 1960s hippies continued to be associated with the urban milieu, most particularly San Francisco in the United States. There were clear lines of descent connecting the new counterculture with their beat predecessors; *On the Road* was required reading for countercultural youth, beat icon Neal Cassidy served as the driver of Ken Kesey's famous day-glo bus, and Ginsberg was a sort of elder statesmen for the movement. What was new in the 1960s was the evident increase in the scale of new bohemian movements and the connections between these subcultures and a new left politics organized around sexual and gender identities, race, and opposition to the Vietnam War. Also evident in the 1960s was the growing link between the bohemian counterculture and commercialized popular culture, especially music, despite the antimaterialist rhetoric adopted by many hippies.

Since the 1960s, bohemian enclaves have become more frequent features of both large and mid-sized cities throughout the United States and Europe, even as urban economies have undergone dramatic changes. From the 1970s to the present, new bohemian districts have sprung up in cities and districts such as New York's East Village, Los Angeles's Silver Lake, Chicago's Wicker Park, Atlanta's Five Points, and many others. The lifestyles articulated in these districts evince qualities recognizably of a piece with their bohemian predecessors, though they have also come to play a new and expanded role in the cultural, and especially the economic, lives of the cities that host them.

Led by the pioneering work of the sociologist Sharon Zukin, scholars have paid increasing attention to the role of the arts and bohemianism in the urban economy. While manufacturing declines as a core component of urban economies, the "symbolic economy" of knowledge work and cultural production has become vital to urban fortunes. Under these circumstances bohemian districts become seedbeds of residential gentrification, amenities for highly educated workers who favor funky and offbeat entertainment scenes, incubators of enterprise in media and marketing, and sources of input for culture industries like music, film, and television. Particularly influenced by the contributions of Richard Florida, an enthusiastic promoter of the "creative class" and its essential role in urban prosperity, policymakers have begun to actively seek out and nurture bohemian scenes, increasingly seen not just as quirky bits of local color but as hard economic assets.

Richard Lloyd

See also New York City, New York; Paris, France

Further Readings

Crane, D. 1987. *The Transformation of the Avant-garde: The New York Art World, 1940–1985.* Chicago: University of Chicago Press.

Gluck, Mary. 2008. *Popular Bohemia: Modernism and Urban Culture in Nineteenth-century Paris.* Cambridge, MA: Harvard University Press.

Lloyd, Richard. 2006. *Neo-Bohemia: Art and Culture in the Postindustrial City.* New York: Routledge.

McFarland, Gerald W. 2005. *Inside Greenwich Village: A New York City Neighborhood, 1898-1918.* Amherst: University of Massachusetts Press.

Seigel, Jerrold. 1967. *Bohemian Paris: Culture, Politics, and the Boundaries of Bourgeois Life, 1830-1930.* London: Penguin.

Wilhide, Elizabeth. 1999. *Bohemian Style.* London: Pavilion Books.

BOMBAY, INDIA

See Mumbai (Bombay), India

BRASÍLIA, BRAZIL

Brasília, the capital of Brazil, was founded on April 21, 1960. The city is considered a symbol of architectural modernism for its aesthetic qualities, functionality, centralized urban planning, landscaping with regional flora, autochthonous culture, and economic organization. Inspired by the ideas of Le Corbusier, Brasília represents an attempt at erecting a new "modern" city disconnected from Latin American colonialism, slavery, underdevelopment, and dictatorships. However, Brasília also experiences tensions between strict planning and creative initiatives, militarism and democracy, open space and public manifestations, political representation and corruption, as well as social injustice and the emergence of new urban cultures.

Epic History

In official accounts the history of Brasília begins on April 21, 1960. However, its epic origins go back to the alleged "discovery" of Brazil by the Portuguese on April 21, 1500. Salvador had been the capital city of Brazil since the sixteenth century, but in 1789 a group of rebels planned the independence of Brazil and envisioned moving the Brazilian capital to Ouro Preto. This attempt failed. However, when Napoleon invaded Portugal the Portuguese king fled to Brazil with the support of the British Empire, and Rio de Janeiro became the capital of the United Kingdom of Brazil and Portugal in 1808. Soon after, in 1809, British Prime Minister William Pitt announced that a new capital would be built in the center of Brazil and be called Nova Lisboa.

With the Brazilian independence from Portugal on September 7, 1822, the idea of a capital cleansed of colonialism remained, but with a new name: Brasília. Already in 1823, a document titled "Memoir on the Need and Means of Building a New Capital in the Interior of Brazil" was presented in Parliament. In 1834, the viscount of Porto Seguro indicated the Amazon River Basin as the most appropriate location for such an enterprise. This proposal was disregarded for decades until rumors circulated in 1883 about a dream by the Catholic priest Dom Bosco in which a site between parallels 15 and 20 would become the "promised land of milk and honey, of unconceivable wealth."

In 1889, exactly 100 years after the failed rebellion of 1789, a military-supported revolution transformed Brazil from a monarchy to a republic. Older plans were renewed and a commission was established by the Constitutional Assembly in 1892 to define the future location of Brasília. After a series of studies, the cornerstone was erected on September 7, 1922, marking the centenary of independence from Portugal. In 1953, a federal commission was created by President Getúlio Vargas to study the technical aspects involved in the building of the new capital. In 1956 the newly elected president, Juscelino Kubitschek, promised to build the new city in five years and name it Brasília. The plan gained support and on April 21, 1960, Kubitschek was installed in the new capital city.

The Modernist City

Brasília was seen as a latent dream made possible by its politicians, intellectuals, artists, and engineers, who shared the ideals of modernism.

Many intellectuals, such as Caio Prado Jr. and Sergio Buarque de Hollanda, provided the discourse that fit facts neatly into a nation-building process. While Mario de Andrade and Oswald de Andrade led the artistic front of the Brazilian modernist movement, which declared the need for cultural independence, Mario Pedrosa criticized the mere repetition of European models and saw Brasília as an authentic political and cultural monument that should reorient history.

President Juscelino Kubitschek became a political national hero who promised to create 50 years of development in just five years. Brasília was the symbol of his achievement. Lucio Costa, Oscar Niemeyer, and Burle Marx brought together their expertise in urban planning, architecture, and landscaping and became internationally recognized for their planning of Brasília according to Le Corbusier's modernism. Lucio Costa had worked with Le Corbusier in Rio de Janeiro in the planning of federal buildings. Oscar Niemeyer had worked with Kubitschek in the city of Belo Horizonte (planned in 1897, it is the capital of the state of Minas Gerais). Burle Marx used Brazilian plants in landscaping, based on species he had found in the Botanical Garden of Berlin in the 1920s.

Urban Reality

The Lucio Costa pilot plan proposed for Brasília was based on the intersection of two main axes in the form of an airplane, with two lines cutting across the city and intersecting at the center of power in Brazil. At the intersection are the government buildings, public services, the cathedral, and the "Square of the Three Powers," with its famous two towers and two inverted bowls at their center. Along the north–south axis, residential complexes, parks, and shopping areas were built. Streets and avenues follow a precise grid with "super-blocks" (*superquadras*).

Such a strict approach to urban planning was later related to militarism. The city was de facto built only after the military coup d'état in 1964. Under military dictatorship, construction provided room for a new political bureaucracy, attracting a new population of workers who were segregated in "satellite" areas and settling landless people who had been invading federal lands.

From a sociological point of view, this strict urban organization brought about not only new social actors and economic development but also corruption, lack of sensitivity to the needs of the people, segregation, and an aura of military security. All these elements gave the impression that politicians in Brasília were detached from reality, abstracted from the real problems of other Brazilian regions. However, oppositional groups formed despite censorship and persecution. The process toward democracy turned Brasília into a center for many political manifestations. The military regime finally lost its power after 1984.

With time, Brasília became less a dream and more of a real city with a variety of social and urban issues. Researchers noticed that social life had disappeared in its residential areas, which were separated from commercial areas, while parks were lacking trees, and pedestrians found it difficult to walk—especially because of the hot weather, the distance between buildings, and the primacy given to cars. Different linguistic, cultural, and social patterns became stratified, thus creating a social structure that was supposed to have been overcome by modernist urban planning.

City Life

Brasília, was planned as something unique, representing the eruption of a new "modern" time and space disconnected from older events. In its modernity, Brasília was supposed to mark a definitive break from previous historical moments in Brazil and Latin America. However, it remained embedded in the political climate of the region. It became a symbol of totalitarianism during the times of militarism in Latin America, and then a center for democratic activity as different groups used its open spaces for public demonstrations and their struggle for democracy.

New public and democratic initiatives shaped Brasília at the end of the twentieth century. The central city spaces were used by both activist groups, such as the Central Worker's Union and the Landless Movement in their efforts toward better wages and agrarian reform, and traditional lobbyists, such as the Union of Rural Landowners. Traditional, conservative, progressive, and postmodern religious groups gained more visibility, including not only the Liberation Theology movement, but also the Charismatic Movement within the Catholic Church, the powerful political coalition of Evangelicals, as well as New Age groups that chose Brasília as their center. Moreover, with these changes an active underground city life emerged. Women's groups, workers, students, and environmental activists, as well as young artists, musicians, and followers of new religions began to use public spaces and urban niches for their expressions.

These groups also shaped Brazilian democracy, bringing people from the periphery to the center stage of national politics. With the founding of the Worker's Party in 1980, a new movement in Brazilian politics was inaugurated, which reached its peak with the election of Luis Inácio "Lula" da Silva as president in 2002, thus bringing to Brasília a former steelworker to occupy the center of political power.

Brasília in the Twenty-First Century

Brasília was originally seen as establishing a new time and space in Latin America. It became a symbol of modern architecture, urban planning, radicalized centralism, and militarism. Then, with democracy, alternative cultures and forms of living began to emerge and change the urban landscape. Thus, in the twenty-first century Brasília looks more like a real city, more diverse and less centralized, still a symbol of modernism, but now conscious of its internal tensions.

Amos Nascimento

See also Le Corbusier; São Paulo, Brazil; Urban Planning

Further Readings

El-Dahdah, Farès, ed. 2005. *Lucio Costa: Brasília's Superquadra.* Cambridge, MA: Harvard University Graduate School of Design.

Epstein, David. 1973. *Brasília, Plan and Reality: A Study of Planned and Spontaneous Urban Development.* Berkeley: University of California Press.

Holston, James. 1989. *The Modernist City: An Anthropological Critique of Brasília.* Chicago: University of Chicago Press.

Paviani, Aldo. 1996. *Brasília: Moradia e exclusão* (Brasília: Living Condition and Social Exclusion). Brasília, Brazil: Editora UNB.

Telles, Edward. 1995. "Structural Sources of Socioeconomic Segregation in Brazilian Metropolitan Areas." *American Journal of Sociology* 100(5): 1199–1223.

BROADACRE CITY

In April 1935, at an industrial arts exposition held in Rockefeller Center, New York City, Frank Lloyd Wright unveiled a detailed scale model of his ideal community: Broadacre City. As a critic of centralized urban development that characterized pre–World War II urban America, Wright believed that the large cities of his time dehumanized values, robbed people of their individuality, and jeopardized their democratic yearning. People would reap the full benefits of the machine age only by returning to the land.

This entry starts with a review of Wright's philosophy of Broadacre City, continues with an outline of its central design features, identifies some limitations of the concept and how Broadacre City compares to other utopian forms of the times, and offers a prospective role for Broadacre City in shaping the American exurban landscape.

Philosophical Foundations

Through Broadacre City, Wright expressed his principles of urban decentralization, economic self-sufficiency, and individualism. The traditional city, with its masses of buildings, was replaced by small houses dotting the rural landscape. In Broadacre City, the built environment would be distributed over open countryside and would be organically constructed to harmonize with natural surroundings. Each lot would be inwardly oriented, thereby promoting a domestic, family-oriented lifestyle where every person would be at least a part-time farmer. Indeed, the notion of individualism was a crucial element of Wright's vision of Broadacre City. He owed much of this vision to the Jeffersonian ideal of rural self-reliance.

Broadacre City would provide for the universal ownership of land and a society of individual proprietors. There would be no rent, landlords, or tenants, and no private ownership of land. Everyone would have the skills and knowledge to be a part-time farmer, mechanic, and intellectual—much as Jefferson was. Goods would flow directly from the producer to the consumer with no intermediary. Industry in Broadacre City would be privately or cooperatively owned. Local government would be the only local public administrative group within the city. Like modern conservative economists, the sole purpose of national government would be the regulation of natural resources, the provision of national defense, and the compilation of information.

Despite Wright's penchant for communal ownership, however, his "democratic decentralization" would allow every person to own at least one acre of land in Broadacre City. The resulting urban pattern would greatly decentralize population and replace the city's concentration of wealth and power with a society where the means of production would be widely held.

Design Features

Broadacre City was publicly displayed in print media and in a showing of a model from 1934 to 1935. The version of his plan published in *Architectural Record* in 1935 is conceptualized in Figure 1.

Broadacre City would cover an area of 4 square miles or 2,560 acres and would support a population of approximately 5,000 people living in 1,400 homes. Each person regardless of age would be provided at least 1 acre of land. The typical residential lot configuration would be 165 feet by 264 feet, or precisely 1 acre. The lot would allow for a garden or small farm next to the house. Families would also live in small apartments, single-family cottages, worker quarters above shops, or larger hillside houses. Scattered throughout would be a dozen or so 15-floor towers, each with 33 apartments. Everyone would be within walking distance of work, and vehicular transportation would be used primarily to travel between cities.

Among the small farms would be factories, schools, stores, professional buildings, hospital, cultural centers, and other institutions. The local government buildings would be in a single high-rise building by a lake, but it would not be the focus of the community. A single freeway and railroad system would provide access to other Broadacre Cities.

Using the modern rule of thumb for a family-oriented household size of three, the population base of Broadacre City would be about 4,200 people. The density is slightly more than 1,000 people per square mile, which is comparable to that of the nation's most densely populated state, New Jersey, or roughly equivalent to the population density of Kansas City, Missouri. Broadacre City would clearly qualify as an urban place according to the U.S. Census. In effect, Broadacre City would be an oasis of settlement set in a rural landscape.

Limitations and Relation to Garden Cities and the Neighborhood Unit

The population base of Wright's Broadacre City is the same as Clarence Perry's Neighborhood Unit

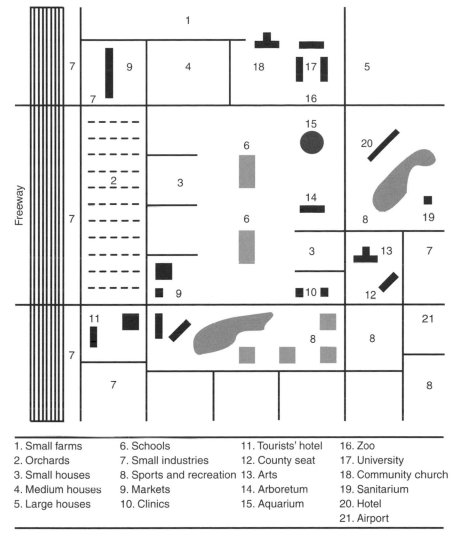

1. Small farms
2. Orchards
3. Small houses
4. Medium houses
5. Large houses
6. Schools
7. Small industries
8. Sports and recreation
9. Markets
10. Clinics
11. Tourists' hotel
12. County seat
13. Arts
14. Arboretum
15. Aquarium
16. Zoo
17. University
18. Community church
19. Sanitarium
20. Hotel
21. Airport

Figure I   Stylized Adaptation of Frank Lloyd Wright's Planning Scheme for Broadacre City

Source: Adapted by Arthur C. Nelson. Figure by Nicole Sitko. Used with permission.

To function, Broadacre City must be connected economically, socially, and, to some extent, physically to urban centers. It follows that Broadacre City must be planned and designed to play a definitive role in a metropolitan region while serving its principal function of an exurban neighborhood.

Some if not many of the limitations of Broadacre City can be overcome by allowing for a larger population base but holding to its planning and design themes. One is Ebenezer Howard's "Garden City" in which about 90 percent of the 32,000 residents would live on slightly less than 2 square miles but itself be part of a master planned community of about 10 square miles of land. Fast-forward a century, however, and we find that with smaller families than during Howard's time, the Garden City population falls to about 16,000, assuming no more homes than Howard envisioned—a reasonable assumption since house sizes have also increased in the meantime. Garden City is thus about four times more populous but only about two-thirds more densely developed than Broadacre City.

and, later, Clarence Stein's designs for Radburn, New Jersey. Perry and Stein viewed their communities as building blocks within a larger urban framework.

In contrast, Broadacre City is an isolated community; this is its principal shortcoming. With such a small population base, most residential services such as shopping, medical care, specialized repair, higher education, and vocational training cannot be supported. The modern "neighborhood" scale shopping center cannot survive. The threshold required to support a general medical practitioner is not achieved. Residents of such an isolated community would resort to mail-order shopping, commuting to urban centers, or doing without.

Following Howard, a network of Broadacre Cities within a metropolitan region could create the critical mass of population and employment to function in modern times. Howard's Garden City concept envisioned six garden cities of 32,000, each, surrounding a Social City of 58,000 for a total population base of 250,000. Of course the actual population is reduced by about half. Great Britain's largest new town, Milton Keynes, is based loosely on this model, but it is designed to attain the larger population base assuming smaller household sizes. Similar to Howard's scheme, all communities within Milton Keynes are connected by roads (but not rail) to each other and to its center. With 250,000 residents, virtually all economic, social, political, and personal service functions of a city are available. A Broadacre City version of Social City would look vastly different, however, taking on Wright's characteristics of low-density development dominated by single-family detached homes instead of pockets of higher-density modules.

Application to the American Twenty-First-Century Landscape

Since Wright's death in 1959, many of his Broadacre City ideas have come to be realized but not in the form he advanced. Extensive freeway networks crisscross the countryside, and expansive suburbanization consumes vast areas of land at low densities. Much of the built environment is now characterized more as "exurban" sprawl than suburban sprawl. Such community services such as fire and police protection, new road construction, water and sewer, and garbage collection are much more expensive to provide in exurbia than in alternative development patterns, such as Broadacre City. Could the continued exurbanization of America be managed better through Broadacre City?

Perhaps up to a quarter of American households live in exurban areas. These are areas where population density (less than 1,000 persons per square mile) falls below that able to support important public utilities. Providing transportation and urban services across large areas of low-density development is very costly. Uncoordinated exurban sprawl may weaken the economic efficiencies associated with urban agglomeration and undermine the socioeconomic well-being of both the city and country. Broadacre City may be a solution to the management of exurban development in America.

Arthur C. Nelson

See also Suburbanization; Urban Planning

Further Readings

Collins, George R. 1963. "Broadacre City: Wright's Utopia Reconsidered." In *Four Great Makers of Modern Architecture*. New York: Columbia University Press.

Fishman, Robert. 1977. *Urban Utopias in the Twentieth Century*. New York: Basic Books.

Johnson, Donald Leslie. 1990. *Frank Lloyd Wright versus America: The 1930s*. Cambridge: MIT Press.

Nelson, Arthur C. 1992. "Characterizing Exurbia." *Journal of Planning Literature* 6(4):350–68.

———. 1995. "The Planning of Exurban America: Lessons from Frank Lloyd Wright's Broadacre City." *Journal of Architecture and Planning Research* 12(4):337–56.

Nelson, Arthur C. and Kenneth J. Dueker. 1990. "The Exurbanization of America and Its Planning Policy Implications." *Journal of Planning Education and Research* 9(2):91–100.

Twombly, Robert C. 1972. "Undoing the City: Frank Lloyd Wright's Planned Communities." *American Quarterly* 24(4):538–49.

BRUGES, BELGIUM

Now a small provincial capital of the federal state of Belgium, Bruges is significant for urban history both for its status as a medieval commercial center and for its rebirth as a destination for modern tourists. From the tenth century, Bruges emerged first as the residence and governmental center of the counts of Flanders, then as a seaport and trading center for materials that supplied the Flemish cloth industry, and then for the finished product itself. By the fourteenth century, the city succeeded in making itself the sine qua non of northern trade for nearly two centuries before reverting to a secondary market and production center thereafter. Bruges reached its economic nadir in the nineteenth century, with little industry and a chronically impoverished populace. Bruges was discovered by devotees of European romanticism, whose fondness for all things medieval transformed the rundown city of neglected old buildings into an outdoor museum visited by multitudes of tourists.

The powerful counts of Flanders of the central Middle Ages established Bruges as a part of their economic and political development of the *pagus Flandrensis,* the heart of a realm that at its greatest extent stretched as far south as Picardy and west to Boulogne and Dunkirk. An important network of fairs was one of their initiatives, as was an ambitious program of land reclamation along the coasts near Bruges. Bruges thus became a significant center of transportation and exchange before 1200, as well as a minor center of cloth production. But nothing could have predicted Bruges's rise to the status of the first commercial center of northern Europe, which it achieved around 1300. This was due in part to the decline of the Champagne fairs and a shift to seaborne freight. This trend accelerated during the near-continuous war conditions that prevailed across France after 1337 (Hundred Years' War), which expanded the resident merchant communities in Bruges, especially the English, Italians, Spaniards, and Hanseatics. With committal grants of extensive legal privileges and efficient means of legal redress guaranteed by the local Bruges government, the city became a good place to do business.

At the intersection of important industries and flourishing trade, Bruges became the first northern capital of banking and finance, which gave the city considerable importance even as its trade declined after 1480. Based upon a payment and credit system developed by native money changers and hostellers, Bruges integrated the various communities of foreign merchants into a far-reaching network of foreign and domestic exchange through bills of exchange, book transfers, commission sales, and credit operations. In the course of the fifteenth century, this financial community acquired a formal meeting place around a public square named for a prominent commercial hostel, and the "place de la Bourse" was born. Until supplanted by its near neighbor and erstwhile commercial satellite, Antwerp, which built its own bourse in 1531, Bruges was a more important commercial center than either Paris or London.

From the sixteenth to eighteenth century, Bruges declined but did not cease being an important urban center of the southern Low Countries. A significant Spanish merchant colony remained through the sixteenth century, and in the seventeenth century there was a modest Renaissance in the city's importance as a shipping center with the construction of new canals and the development of Ostend as a major port with frequent ferry service to England. But it was not until Bruges had endured the waves of adversity stemming from the French Revolution and Napoleonic era, the brief incorporation into the Dutch state, and the Belgian revolution of 1830 that a new direction for the city was developed.

While some Belgian cities, notably Ghent, industrialized, the Bruges economy slowly reoriented itself toward attracting foreign visitors and residents in search of an authentic experience of the Middle Ages. Despite many changes through the years, Bruges had maintained its "medieval" appearance, largely avoiding the massive destruction of old neighborhoods so common in other European cities. Attracted by the city's architecture, as well as its nearness to home and relative cheapness, a significant English colony developed. Numbering as many as 1,200 permanent residents by around 1870 and hundreds more summer and occasional visitors, the English established schools and orphanages and drew many converts to Roman Catholicism from among their compatriots, who came to Flanders in search of the medieval roots of their religion. Simultaneously, Bruges's canals and quaint squares and neighborhoods attracted artists who sought to capture the city's Romantic allure on canvas. The literary expression of this was Georges Rodenbach's 1892 novel, *Bruges-la-morte,* the story of a grief-stricken widower who takes refuge in Bruges, only to become obsessed with a ballet dancer who resembles his late wife.

The efforts of artists, visitors, and long-term English residents, especially art historian W. H. James Weale and art collector John Steinmetz, contributed to a movement to preserve Bruges's medieval patrimony while constructing new buildings in harmony with the medieval past of the city. Thus "neogothic" became the sometimes controversial answer to all new construction in the city, leading to, among many examples, the present post office building on the central square, which replaced an eighteenth-century classical style building on the same site. Much like London with its arts and crafts movement, Bruges became a center of architecture, design, and crafts that sought to restore the aesthetic and craftsmanship of the Middle Ages to modern construction. Efforts at historic preservation, meanwhile, led to the establishment of an important historical society (Société d'Emulation), a society for the preservation of Christian art (Guild of St. Thomas and St. Luke), and many others.

The international exposition of 1902 dedicated to the fifteenth-century artists known collectively as the Flemish Primitives marks the high point of this new direction for Bruges as both tourist and artistic city. Bringing together works from such artists as Jan van Eyck, Rogier van der Weyden, Hugo van der Goes, Hans Memling, Dirk Bouts, and Gerard David—many of them little known at the time—the

Bruges is well known for its historic architecture and canals that comprise the heart of the city.

Source: Karen Wiley.

exposition was a sensation. There were tens of thousands of visitors to Bruges, with other exhibits following in Paris, Düsseldorf, and London. Thereafter, Bruges has sought to construct a string of notable museums, as well as to resurrect and refurbish medieval costumed processions and reenactments, and to sponsor an annual festival of early music. The success of this cultural program was sealed by the European Union's declaration of Bruges as one of the two cultural capitals for the year 2002.

James M. Murray

See also Medieval Town Design; Tourism

Further Readings

Girouard, Mark. 1985. *Cities and People: A Social and Architectural History*. New Haven, CT: Yale University Press.

Houtte, J. A. van. 1977. *An Economic History of the Low Countries, 800–1800*. London: Weidenfeld and Nicolson.

———. 1982. *De Geschiedenis van Brugge*. Tielt, Belgium: Lannoo.

Munro, John H. A. 1972. *Wool, Cloth, and Gold: The Struggle for Bullion in Anglo-Burgundian Trade, 1340–1478*. Toronto, ON, Canada: University of Toronto Press.

Nicholas, David. 1992. *Medieval Flanders*. London: Routledge.

BUENOS AIRES, ARGENTINA

The city of Buenos Aires, capital of the Republic of Argentina, was founded in 1580 by Spanish conquistador Juan de Garay, following a failed attempt by earlier colonizers to create a settlement on the same grounds in 1536. The city is seated on the banks of the River Plate estuary, a strategic gateway location that profoundly contributed to its demographic and economic expansion. At the beginning of the twenty-first century, the Greater Buenos Aires metropolitan area, host to a population of more than 13 million, was among the world's 10 largest urban agglomerations. The metropolitan region, however, is made up of separate politico-administrative units. The central area, known as the Autonomous City of Buenos Aires and populated by almost 3 million inhabitants, is governed by an autonomous city government whose prerogatives and responsibilities are analogous to those of an Argentine province. This central district is encircled by two metropolitan rings composed of 24 municipalities with limited administrative powers and placed under the authority of the Buenos Aires provincial government. Mirroring most of its Latin American counterparts, the Argentine capital's urban area commands a disproportionate share of the country's human resources and economic activity, with one third of the national population concentrated on just 8 percent of the territory and a contribution to national gross domestic product of almost 50 percent.

A European City in Latin America

Buenos Aires does not resemble Latin American megacities on all counts. Its particular socioeconomic profile, combined with the specific route followed by Argentina's national politics, has crafted a complex and singular urban development path that set Buenos Aires apart from the region's other capital cities. The promotion of Buenos Aires as the country's capital in 1881 stimulated the modernization of its port facilities and the development of the railway network, connecting the city with its resource-rich hinterland. The remarkable commercial expansion that ensued contributed to the acceleration of national economic growth, propelling Argentina at the beginning of the twentieth century to the status of a rich and developed nation. Economic expansion was also fueled by successive waves of European migration to Buenos Aires, most notably between 1880 and 1910. By the mid-1940s, the population of the city's central area had already reached its current size of 3 million residents, and the inner

metropolitan ring had started to swell with a population approaching 2 million.

In contrast to other Latin American nations, the indigenous population was wiped out to such an extent during the colonization era that there remained virtually no natives in Argentina, except for a few enclaves in the northern territories. The European origins of Buenos Aires's demographic profile thus exerted a strong influence on the city's territorial development, providing it with a physical landscape notably different from that found in other Latin America cities. Even the Spanish colonial architecture originally found in the central neighborhoods was quickly replaced by higher-rise and modernist buildings modeled after the European architectural precepts of French and Italian urbanists.

Urban Development Without Plans

Buenos Aires's European architectural principles were never accompanied or underpinned by comprehensive planning practices. The capital's development always suffered from a chronic lack of urban planning, the absence of which induced symptoms that were to become more manifest as the city expanded. Broad urban master plans for Buenos Aires—including one formulated by Le Corbusier in 1929—were never implemented. The failure of urban planning efforts is explained by Buenos Aires's uncomfortable status within Argentina's political system. The economic primacy of the city over the rest of the country and the attendant territorial disequilibria were permanently perceived as a threat by national authoritarian and democratic regimes alike. The federal state was thus careful to keep the city under control by denying it all forms of political and administrative autonomy. As a result, public policies aimed at shaping and ordering Buenos Aires's future never developed, leaving the city without a proper urban agenda. Within the overall context of decentralization reforms implemented by most Latin American countries in the 1990s, the revision of Argentina's National Constitution in 1994 marked a significant turn in the city's history. For the first time, Buenos Aires was granted political autonomy and the right to democratically elect its mayor, who was previously handpicked by the president. In 1996 the city was accordingly renamed *Ciudad*

Autónoma de Buenos Aires (Autonomous City of Buenos Aires) and was henceforth governed under the auspices of a city constitution.

A Widening Socioterritorial Divide

The city's newfound capacity to preside over its own urban future is particularly significant in light of the socioterritorial transformations provoked by the neoliberal policy formulation embraced by Argentina since the early 1990s. Along with institutional deregulation and financial liberalization, economic globalization has provided a framework amenable to large capital investments whose locational selectivity has created territorial imbalances between different parts of the urban map. Throughout the twentieth century, Argentina's comparatively advanced level of economic development combined with Peronist redistributive policies have ensured a relatively homogeneous pattern of socioterritorial development in Buenos Aires. This pattern was reminiscent of the European compact city rather than the North American model of diffusion and fragmentation observed in other Latin American metropolises. Yet since the early 1990s, deindustrialization and rising unemployment, generally sensed as by-products of structural adjustment policies, have entailed the pauperization and shrinking of Buenos Aires's large urban middle class, which had until then constituted the city's most distinctive feature among its regional peers.

These trends have found their spatial echo in territorial fragmentation and segregation. Fragmentation characterizes the central area in which privileged islands of luxury housing, shopping, and entertainment have emerged, whereas segregation refers to the spectacular expansion of gated communities in the metropolitan region. Previously existing territorial imbalances, most conspicuously between the city's affluent northern neighborhoods and deprived southern areas, have sharpened with the social polarization flowing from the new economic conditions. To make matters worse, Argentina's economic crisis in December 2001 threw countless city households into unemployment and poverty.

With respect to urban infrastructure and public services, in the first half of the twentieth century their quality in Buenos Aires compared favorably with those of the world's most advanced metropolises. Following Argentina's economic decline during the second half of the century, the construction and maintenance of urban facilities ceased to keep pace with territorial expansion, leading to infrastructural breakdown and a crisis in the provision of urban services in the 1980s. The absence of an interjurisdictional entity capable of overseeing and coordinating policies at the metropolitan level, together with the lack of economic resources for public investment, paralyzed any action that might have been taken in this domain in the years following Argentina's return to democracy in 1983. In the early 1990s, the new government of President Carlos Menem embarked on a policy of privatization of selected basic public services as part of the package of neoliberal reforms advocated by multilateral financial institutions. The quality and coverage of urban services now operated by foreign multinationals improved, although at a consumer cost that has become ever more prohibitive for an increasingly impoverished population.

Buenos Aires in the Twenty-First Century

In parallel with the global trend toward megaprojects of urban regeneration and rehabilitation of old industrial districts, the 1990s witnessed important physical transformations in the central district. The revival of the old Puerto Madero riverfront and the derelict Abasto neighborhood provide spectacular examples of such grand schemes. Yet these targeted interventions on selected portions of the city, for all their underlying symbolic power, offer very little by way of an answer to the city's most pressing problems. Traffic congestion, high levels of noise and air pollution, as well as an inefficient water drainage infrastructure are among the many issues that need to be addressed. Finally, the growth of the city's slum settlements has accelerated considerably since the early 1990s, most markedly within the city center, where it was previously believed that numbers had stabilized and would even start decreasing.

Whereas the Autonomous City's new institutional framework provides grounds for hope, solving Buenos Aires's urban problems will require more than a mere change in formal institutions. If the Argentine capital is to acquire the capacity to guide and craft its own future in the twenty-first century, a new mind-set with regard to the planning and management of urban matters is to emerge and be nurtured. The municipality has consequently chosen to open policy-making processes to greater public participation, for instance, through the creation of popular platforms of strategic planning and participatory budgeting. It is expected that these mechanisms will help pave the way toward more inclusive and balanced urban development in Buenos Aires.

Laurence Crot

See also Globalization; Urban Crisis; Urban Policy

Further Readings

Ciccolella, Pablo and Iliana Mignaqui. 2002. "Buenos Aires: Sociospatial Impacts and the Development of Global City Functions." Pp. 309–25 in *Global Networks, Linked Cities,* edited by S. Sassen. New York: Routledge.

Keeling, David J. 1996. *Buenos Aires: Global Dreams, Local Crises.* New York: Wiley.

Pírez, Pedro. 2002. "Buenos Aires: Fragmentation and Privatization of the Metropolitan City." *Environment and Urbanization* 14(1):145–58.

BUNGALOW

The bungalow has been described as the single form of residential architecture common to all continents. It is a single-story building with a moderately sloped roof, set in a landscaped, spacious urban or peri-urban plot, and occupied by a nuclear family. It is generally interpreted in relation to modern capitalist industrial expansion and its effect on settlement patterns and built forms, as expressed originally in British India. Discussions of the bungalow have therefore focused on tracing its origins, evolution, and sociospatial impact.

Etymology

Bungalow derives from the Hindi, Mahrati, or Gujurati *bangla*, meaning "of or belonging to Bengal." The term was used by Indians and Europeans in India during the seventeenth century. It was anglicized during the eighteenth century, with the standard English spelling first recorded in 1784. The term was documented in England in 1788, but it was still identified as linguistically Indian. By the mid-nineteenth century, it was fully incorporated into the English language. "Bungalow" is found in at least 10 European languages. It was first recorded in Australia in 1876 and in North America in 1880. Scholars argue that the bungalow was popularized in West Africa in the 1890s. Thus, the etymology of *bungalow* suggests a timeline and geography of cultural diffusion. Yet, most scholars agree that the term *built form* and associations have not always been coterminous. Proposing a single origin and course of development for the bungalow might therefore be unproductive.

The Bungalow in India

According to Anthony King, a tropical dwelling type for European use emerged in British India by the late eighteenth century. It incorporated features from four sources: a local Bengali house form, the non-Bengali Indian appellation "bungalow," the adaptation of said form and nomenclature by European settlers, and the further development of the veranda under Portuguese influence. A desire to separate British and Indian bodies and modes of living lay at the core of the bungalow's development. The resulting form, a large central room surrounded by smaller rooms and a veranda, translated colonial ideology into the fabric of home life. Deep verandas protected an inner sanctum from excessive heat and allowed for greater control of interactions with "natives." Its efficacy was enhanced by placing the building at the center of a large garden segregated from Indian settlements. Thus the Anglo-Indian bungalow-compound was associated with protosuburban settings like military cantonments, "civil lines," and hill stations. Two overlapping architectural expressions of the bungalow were in place in the nineteenth century: a sprawling single-story structure under a pitched roof that referred directly to Bengali prototypes and a one- to two-story flat-roofed villa influenced by neoclassical architecture in England. For a few lucky Indians, inhabiting a bungalow was a sign of assimilation into the colonial order. By the twentieth century, the colonial bungalow was reintegrated into Indian culture, where it described any detached single-family dwelling.

William J. Glover and Swati Chattopadhyay have complicated this view of the bungalow-compound. Glover shows that the bungalow was an idealized site for the enactment of upper-middle-class British values, whose attainability was compromised by the building's unfamiliar materiality. As Chattopadhyay has shown for Calcutta (Kolkata), the boundaries between the "White town" of Europeans and the "Black town" of Indians were blurry, with various classes of Europeans living in Indian-built bungalows in close proximity to locals. Indeed, the bungalow was so unstable discursively that a countermetropolitan femininity flourished under its auspices. In a sense then, the bungalow served as a prop for British colonial authority.

Bungalows, Leisure, and Suburbanization

India was part of the global system of capitalist expansion whose most important node was Britain. By the mid-nineteenth century, a surplus of capital had accumulated in Britain. Railways and their associated urban developments were an important outlet for this surplus, as was the growing market for leisure activities and products. The image of leisurely colonial life disseminated through publications coincided with the desires of wealthy classes and produced the physically isolated seaside bungalow. From the seaside bungalow emerged the suburban bungalow, a permanent and populist form made possible through the popularization of automobiles. The bungalow in Britain was eventually demonized because of its effects on the pristine countryside.

Bungalows in Britain, North America, and Australia owe their existence to similar forces. From the 1880s, a globally mobile network of architects and builders ensured that the "bungalow idea" was adopted for bourgeois seaside houses in the eastern United States. Though they incorporated some of the stereotypical elements of the Anglo-Indian type, these bungalows adhered more closely to the bungalow's social function than to its form. Bungalows became more popular at the end of the century when the middle class adopted an Arcadian ideology whose ultimate expression was the craftsman bungalow.

A smaller, permanent, developer-built version of the bungalow became standard first in American streetcar suburbs and then in automobile suburbs. California, with its seemingly infinite supply of cheap land, available private capital, prevailing anticommunitarian ideology, and willingness to experiment with new transportation technologies, offered an ideal setting for the full development of the suburban bungalow between 1905 and 1930. The California bungalow formed the basis of a national type repeated with minor variations throughout the country alongside its large-scale complement, the suburb. Bungalow-led suburbanization, however, consolidated the segregation of racial and ethnic minorities in the inner city in ways that recall the bungalow's colonial origins.

In Australia, fewer social, cultural, and political constraints allowed for the widespread adoption of the bungalow by British settlers, many of whom had experience from other parts of the empire. A free market economy, relatively homogenous population, and even greater access to land meant that the single-family, detached dwelling was viable for a large proportion of the European population. Since the colony was integrated into the global capitalist system, fluctuations in capital and subsequent shifts in social preoccupations led to the construction of vacation bungalows in the 1870s and California-style bungalow suburbs in the 1910s.

Previous analyses of the bungalow in Africa have relied on incomplete knowledge of the continent's material and social histories. Anthony King, for example, explains the bungalow as a European residential form imported from India at the end of the nineteenth century to provide shelter for a new crop of British colonial administrators. By stimulating urbanization, the bungalow became a tool and later a symptom of Westernization.

Advances in Africanist archaeology, however, confirm that urban living was not anomalous in Africa before the nineteenth century. Tarikhu Farrar and others have shown that complex, dense, organized settlements were typical of precolonial West Africa. Furthermore, elements of the bungalow existed both independently and in combination. European presence on the West African coast from the fifteenth century offered ample opportunity for a two-way cultural exchange that included these forms, as Jay Edwards has shown.

The specific social, cultural, and economic functions of the Anglo-Indian bungalow imported to the British African colonies, and their subsequent appropriation by postcolonial elites, arguably distinguished it from existing African "house and veranda" types. However, some of these functions, like the use of verandas as a social space and as a means to control interior building temperatures, were common to both West African and Anglo-Indian examples.

Other colonial authorities in Africa also used the bungalow. From the 1820s, the Swiss-German Basel Missionary Society used a similar building type in the Gold Coast as part of a comprehensive proselytization policy. In 1895 German colonial administrators identified the Anglo-Indian bungalow as the building type best suited for European use in East Africa.

Theories of the development of the bungalow in colonial contexts share a common disregard for the continued development of the "original" bungalow form, arguing that the postcolonial elite's use of the building type owes more to European influence than anything else. Future work on the topic might investigate the coexistence of "original" and "imposed" forms in order to achieve a more holistic understanding.

Itohan Osayimwese

See also Colonial City; Suburbanization; Veranda

Further Readings

Chattopadhyay, Swati. 2000. "'Blurring Boundaries: The Limits of White Town in Colonial Calcutta." *Journal of the Society of Architectural Historians* 59(2):154–79.

———. 2002. "Goods, Chattels & Sundry Items: Constructing 19th-century Anglo-Indian Domestic Life." *Journal of Material Culture* 7(3):243–71.

Farrar, Tarikhu. 1996. *Building Technology and Settlement Planning in a West African Civilization: Precolonial Akan Cities and Towns*. Lewiston, NY: Edwin Mellen Press.

Fishman, Robert. 1987. *Bourgeois Utopias: The Rise and Fall of Suburbia*. New York: Basic Books.

Glover, Williman J. 2004. "'An Absence of Old England': The Anxious English Bungalow." *Home Cultures* 1(1):61–81.

King, Anthony. 1984. *The Bungalow: The Production of a Global Culture*. London: Routledge.

Lancaster, Clay. 1985. *The American Bungalow, 1880–1930*. New York: Abbeville Press.

Osayimwese, Itohan. 2008. "Colonialism at the Center: German Colonial Architecture and the Design Reform Movement." PhD Dissertation, University of Michigan, Ann Arbor.

BUNKERS

There is an increasing interest, in urban studies, sociology, and archaeology, in military bunkers. The concept informed Paul Virilio's *Bunker Archaeology* (1994), for instance, and has been significant for the Brutalist tradition of European architects, including Le Corbusier. European cultural sociology has also expanded its themes and theorizing within particular militarized landscapes and bunkered urban locations, as has contemporary British archaeology.

Military bunkers, then, are a key component of the urban condition, if not always consciously acknowledged as such. Nevertheless, the concept has been reframed regarding the increasingly synchronized themes of postmodernity, war, and the emerging interests of the new subject of combat archaeology. The well-known characteristics of postmodern war—the worldwide scope of militarism, information warfare, unmanned aerial vehicles, compulsory or intentional urban mobility and confinement, nomadic terrorists, unstable patterns of military deployment, and so on—have fundamentally changed the everyday experience and symbolic associations of military bunkers. Consequently, the supposed certainties of modern urban identity, confidently situated beyond the particularities of military bunkers, which typically house an underground shelter of reinforced concrete with an incline and embrasures for artillery above ground, are increasingly disturbed and relocated. A useful approach is to conceive of military bunkers as military spaces, for military spaces such as military bunkers are fields of military action. Military bunkers, accordingly, are military spaces to which the potentiality for military action has been assigned. Hence, military bunkers establish a sense of militarized and civilianized urban identities through various communicative and physically destructive relationships, such as what is meant by the "home front" or where the home front is located.

Postmodern critics argue that the link between military spaces and military bunkers—which, in the modern period, physically positioned military–urban affairs, social behavior, cultural rites, and archaeological customs—has disappeared in contemporary societies. Virilio, for example, discussing the currently prevailing "orbitalization" of militarization and information, suggests that urban meaning has vanished from military bunkers, and thus from the city, which has itself disappeared and dispersed in the postmodernized logic of militarized spaces of orbitalization. This corroborates Mike Gane's belief that Virilio's allegiance to the concept of military bunkers as involving genuine inertia and a feeling of imprisonment adds up to little more than an unresolved dilemma or a plea for a new kind of resistance that has no means. Alternatively, Gane proposes a model of urban living influenced by Jean Baudrillard's analyses of simulation founded on spaces subject to reversibility.

Yet John Schofield asserts that sensitivity to military bunkers can offer an essential anchor in material culture and a stable approach to modern warfare. He perceives military bunkers as archaeological sites and theoretical objects that can extend the methodologies of contemporary archaeology. Challenging established archaeological principles, Schofield travels beyond recent conflict to an accelerated field of research that deals simultaneously with historical events, material remains, heritage, and human catastrophe. Such an intense combination evokes a global awareness of political events, military actions, and military bunkers. Schofield's investigation into these issues in theoretical terms and in essays on military culture and archaeological literatures, history, and anthropology gracefully combine sociological discussion and concrete case studies of military bunkers as heritage management practice.

John Armitage

See also Urban Archaeology; Urban Semiotics

Further Readings

Gane, Mike. 2000. "Paul Virilio's Bunker Theorizing." Pp. 85–102 in *Paul Virilio: From Modernism to Hypermodernism and Beyond*, edited by J. Armitage. London: Sage.

Schofield, John. 2005. *Combat Archaeology: Material Culture and Modern Conflict*. London: Duckworth.

Virilio, Paul. 1994. *Bunker Archaeology*. Princeton, NJ: Princeton Architectural Press.

BUSES

Buses are often seen as a cheap, dirty, inconvenient, and unreliable mode of transport, used only by those who have no other option. Yet Transport for London estimates that around 6 million bus journeys are made in London every day, with buses the fastest-growing mode of transport in the city. While light rail or metro systems typically exist only in the largest cities or in cities that have experienced extended periods of socialist government, bus riding is a feature of urban life globally and has been for some time: Early bus services were horse drawn, with the first proliferation of "omnibuses" occurring in European cities in the 1830s. Bus links remain important to residents in marginal communities, *banlieues*, suburbs, or slums, representing connections to city centers and providing opportunities for employment. Their very banality, however, as a taken-for-granted aspect of everyday life, has meant that they have often escaped the attention of urban researchers. Despite this, buses are vital parts of urban infrastructure, can expose inequalities in urban governance, and can reveal the practices involved in everyday urban mobilities.

Buses as Urban Infrastructure

Buses represent the cheapest form of urban transport infrastructure development for cities. They cost the least to instigate and maintain, and they are able to collect fares from a far greater number of locations than is their major current competitor, light rail. Despite this, they tend to be less popular than larger infrastructural projects among city governments. This is partially due to their disadvantages: They tend to have lower capacities, can be more uncomfortable, and are more susceptible to disruption from roadwork and traffic problems than are other forms of public transportation. They also have a negative image that contributes to their avoidance by some city governments, who find that flagship metro or light rail projects bring greater external capital investment. In some cities, however, bus rapid transport systems (BRTSs) have been developed as a central part of transport infrastructure. These BRTSs integrate services, amenities, computing and information technologies, and dedicated roadways to produce a fast and frequent service. Due to the comparatively low up-front costs, these are most extensive in, but not limited to, the Global South. The BRTS in Curitiba, Brazil, is viewed as one of the biggest successes, being used by around 70 percent of commuters. It makes use of local minibuses to connect passengers to larger-capacity, high-speed central routes with dedicated road lanes. Bus companies operate independently but are regulated and supported by the city. Stops are fully wheelchair accessible and contain facilities to allow passengers to purchase tickets, as well as public telephones and conveniences. BRTSs, however, require extensive planning, meaning that transposing certain examples of best practice without regard to contextual issues can result in poorly implemented schemes in some cities. The BRTS currently under development in Delhi has been heavily criticized during its trial period because of the ecological damage involved in its construction, as well as poor planning, which has reduced road space for car users and which has placed bus stops between busy lanes of traffic. Broadly, it seems that city governments often require the autonomy of those in South America to produce successful bus rapid transit schemes, something unavailable to many Asian cities.

The ownership of buses can be indicative of local government attitudes toward public control of urban amenities. Bus company ownership varies from state monopolies to privately owned but publically regulated services to privately owned enterprises. Although private ownership might provide more efficient and effective bus services as loss-making routes are dropped, government operation of buses can reflect the belief that social welfare requires certain services irrespective of their ability to make profit and that markets are not always adequately robust to ensure that suitable bus services are provided. In a review of the liberalization of bus services in various cities in the Global North and South, D. A. C. Manuder and T. C. Mbara found no overall pattern of better performance between private and state-owned bus services,

suggesting that contextual influences are more important than ownership. In many Western cities, buses are privately operated but publicly regulated, leading to struggles over planning and service integration that can reveal the power relations between private and state parties in cities.

Buses and Social Inequalities

Due to their relatively low cost, bus services are typically used by the urban poor and can often act as indicators of the inequalities of a city. In many cities in the United States, passengers are drawn mainly from the poorer Black communities and are also predominantly female, typically using buses for daily shopping or to travel to employment in central urban areas. Where bus provision is inadequate, inequalities along gender, ethnic, and class lines can be increased. This creates a politics of mobility in which access to and provision of bus services alter the life opportunities of city residents. Sikivu Hutchinson explores these issues in Los Angeles with one of the few extended analyses of the experiences of bus travel in a Western city. Los Angeles is famous as a city built around automobility, with infrastructure developed around freeways and light rail. As with other cities with such street design, this lends itself to one-way trips between central and suburban areas, rather than the triangular mobility patterns that bus services cater to. Buses are run by private companies whose services are not integrated, with return or transfer tickets not available. This has reduced the mobility of the urban poor, aiding the decline of downtown in favor of urban sprawl. Activist groups such as the Bus Riders Union have argued that this amounts to racial discrimination, favoring the transport of the White majority over that of the Latina/o and Black populations. These divisions in transport provision have contributed to the fragmentized nature of postmodern Los Angeles.

Buses in Urban Studies Research

Despite these various roles in urban life, buses have generally remained absent from urban researchers' work, outside of the specialized field of transport studies. Research into urban transport has traditionally looked at large infrastructural projects, such as the development of freeways, suburban road systems, and light rail networks, rather than at the more mundane and less visible networks of bus travel. Indeed, it is only in recent years as part of a wider trend in social science toward studies of "mobilities" that urban studies has taken people's daily transport practices seriously. Mobilities research focuses on the embodied practices of movement, from practices of car use to the challenges faced by transnational migrants. This is inspired both by theoretical engagement with poststructuralist philosophers such as Giles Deleuze and Michel de Certeau and by an understanding of the empirical increase in global mobility in recent times. Even within this literature, however, there has been a focus toward driving or walking practices over bus journeys.

The mobilities research that has focused on bus routes has emphasized that buses rarely form a visible part of the urban spaces through which they travel. Rather, they pass through unnoticed, traveling along the pavement as cars speed by. Whereas some researchers define the internal space of the bus as a "non-place" that fills the time traveling between places, Renee Human describes the variety of practices that are involved in the production of the space of the bus. She discusses, for example, the very regular patterns that passengers follow when positioning themselves on the bus, spreading themselves out as much as possible. Human also identifies differing practices of communication between passengers on the bus, varying from discussions of travel logistics to more in-depth conversations between regular riders. In this understanding of bus-riding mobilities, riding the bus involves a series of learned practices that may be indicative both of community formation and, when less-experienced passengers use the bus, of the social divisions within a city.

Buses, then, play a series of roles in cities, from high-speed BRTSs, which can move commuters around a city efficiently, to low-cost transport options for the urban poor. They often indicate the attitude of city governments toward the structural inequalities of urban space and infrastructure, whether this is through the level of state support and regulation of bus companies or through the patterns of transportation investment. Their negative image can make buses less attractive to cities than metro or light rail links, but they can provide better value for the money. The practices of bus riding can reveal some of the microsociologies of urban navigation and the embodiment of social divisions and inequalities within a city.

Robert Shaw

See also Journey to Work; Local Government; Streetcars; Subway; Transportation; Transportation Planning

Further Readings

Flyvbjerg, Bent. 1998. *Rationality and Power: Democracy in Practice.* Chicago: University of Chicago Press.

Human, Renee. 2008. "Flowing through the City." *Liminalities* 4(1). Retrieved January 28, 2009 (http://liminalities.net/4-1/bus/index.htm).

Hutchinson, Sikivu. 2000. "Waiting for the Bus." *Social Text* 18(2):107–20.

Larsen, Jonas, John Urry, and Kay Axhausen. 2006. *Mobilities, Networks, Geographies.* Aldershot, UK: Ashgate.

Levinson, Herbert S., Samuel Zimmerman, Jennifer Clinger, and Scott C. Rutherford. 2002. "Bus Rapid Transit: An Overview." *Journal of Public Transportation* 5(2):1–30.

Maunder, D. A. C. and T. C. Mbara. 1996. "Liberalisation of Urban Public Transport Services: What Are the Implications?" *Indian Journal of Transport Management* 20(2):16–23.

C

CAIRO, EGYPT

Cairo, or Al-Qahira (the Victorious), the Egyptian capital, is the core of a vast metropolitan area (Greater Cairo). In 2004, the city of Cairo, colloquially also referred to as Misr (as is the country), or lovingly as Um Al Dunya (mother of the world), was estimated to have about 7.6 million inhabitants. The Greater Cairo region, one of the world's most densely populated urban regions, has almost 17 million residents. Greater Cairo includes the city of Cairo (on the east bank of the Nile) with its historic quarters around Fatimid Cairo and Old/Coptic Cairo; older popular quarters like Husainiyah, Shoubra, and Bulaq; colonial quarters like Heliopolis (Misr El Gedida), Zamalek, and Maadi; and postcolonial modernist developments like Medinet Nasr. In between are numerous newer low-income neighborhoods like Zawiya Al-Hamra, Sharabiya, and Manshiet Nasr. Greater Cairo includes the city of Giza on the west bank of the Nile. The last available population estimate (1996) lists Giza's population as 2.2 million. Considering Giza's recent phenomenal growth, the current figure is likely to be over 3 million. Giza includes its old core on the Nile, colonial neighborhoods (Doqqi, Sharia Al-Haram), older middle- to low-income quarters (Al-Agouza, Doqqi Al-Balad), postcolonial modernist middle-class developments (Muhandessin), and areas of low-income public housing (Munib). Interspersed in this cityscape are several older villages that were engulfed by the city (Mit Oqba, Huttiya).

Surrounding this core cityscape is a vast and dense expanse of newer neighborhoods that have been built by their residents largely without official permits. Millions of residents live in these neighborhoods (e.g., Embaba, Dar As-Salaam, Matariya), often built around former villages. Greater Cairo also includes the cities of Shourbra Al-Khayma (Qalubiya Governorate) to the north and Helwan (Giza Governorate) to the south.

Long History

Over the millennia, Cairo's urban development followed a vague layering or mosaic pattern, where new additions were constructed not at the expense of existing quarters but adjacent to them. This pattern still underlies much of Cairo's cityscape, which is a mosaic of elements from different historical eras displaying vastly varying styles and spatial conceptualizations that produced a multitude of spatial forms and social and cultural practices.

On the Nile, where Giza and Misr Al-Qadimah are today, there has been, for millennia, a river crossing point. A small settlement developed by this small port on the east bank. Under Roman occupation, this settlement ("Babylon") was fortified. With the rise of Christianity in Egypt, Babylon was slowly surrounded by churches and developed into today's Misr Al-Qadimah (Old/Coptic Cairo). Some of its old churches still exist. Cairo's oldest synagogue, built in AD 882 (site of the Cairo Geniza), is located on the eastern edge of this quarter. When the Muslim forces under Amr Ibn Al-Aas conquered and settled in Egypt in AD 641, they built their first mosque (the first in Africa), the Amr Ibn Al-Aas Mosque, immediately north of Misr Al-Qadimah. Muslim troops then built the city of Fustat as an expansion to the existing town. Fustat became the capital of the province of Egypt. Arab rulers and dynasties that followed continued the city's northward expansion. The Tulinids under Ahmad Ibn Tulun built the splendid Ibn Tulun Mosque (AD 879), which once more moved the town center north. In AD 969, the Fatimid rulers started building the walled city of Al-Qahirah north of the existing city. The Fatimid mosque and university of Al-Azhar (AD 972) came to be the oldest university in the world and remains a central institution of Muslim learning. The Ayyubids under Salah al-Din added the citadel above the city (AD 1182) to the east and further fortified the city. Under the Fatimids, Ayyubids, and the Mamluks (1250–1517), Cairo was a vibrant merchant city and the site of magnificent palaces, mosques, and large trading yards. In the fourteenth century Cairo had around 500,000 residents and was one of the largest cities in the world, larger than its European contemporaries.

The discovery of the sea route around the Cape of Good Hope to India in 1498 harmed Cairo's role as a trading city, when goods started to bypass the eastern Mediterranean. Cairo's expansion slowed down as it became a more regional center. Nonetheless, the city slowly started to spill over the Fatimid walls and the older quarters. By the eighteenth century, many craftsmen had left the increasingly crowded city and had moved their shops north, beyond the gate of Bab El-Futuh, to the quarter of Husainiyah. Others moved south to Sayida Zeinab. Similarly, the area around a small lake immediately west of the walled city, which had been used for summer homes, turned into a permanent quarter, Ezbekiya. By the late eighteenth century, the lake's waterfront was lined with splendid mansions of wealthy merchants. Finally, the small port town of Bulaq west of the city on the Nile was a thriving merchants and crafts town.

European Conquest, Modernity, Colonialism

In 1798, Napoleon Bonaparte invaded Egypt. Bombing its way into Alexandria, his army defeated the Egyptian forces by the village of Embaba, then crossed the Nile at Giza and conquered Cairo. The French army confiscated the lakefront mansions in Ezbekiya to set up their quarters. Although the French occupation lasted for only three years and as such was fairly inconsequential, it ushered in some transformations. After some years of local strife, Muhammad Ali, an Albanian officer who had been fighting for the Ottoman forces sent to defeat the French, was successful in gaining control over the country in 1805. To prevent further European attacks in a political climate of aggressive imperialism, he designed projects of forceful modernization to make Egypt an equal to the European powers. Muhammad Ali (ruled 1805–1848) did not use an urban master plan but changed specific elements of Cairo's physical and political structure. Cutting main thoroughfares through dense urban quarters (Sharia Muhammad Ali), setting up new institutions (governmental printing press in Bulaq, hospital and medical school of Qasr Al-Aini), and introducing new styles (using European architects), he implanted vague seeds of a modern city while keeping much of the existing cityscape intact.

In later decades of the nineteenth century, Muhammad Ali's descendants, in particular Khedive Ismail (ruled 1863–1879), intensified Cairo's modernization. Inspired by the architecture of Paris, Ismail set out to create his "Paris on the Nile." Using the time-honored method of expansion just outside the city, he designed the tract of land between Ezbekiya and the Nile front south of Bulaq to become "Ismailiyah," his modern city. A street grid was laid out and regulations formulated that all construction there had to be modern. The Qasr El-Nil Bridge across the Nile was opened in 1872, initiating Giza's integration into Cairo's cityscape. European powers deposed Ismail in 1879, and only three years later, in 1882, Egypt was invaded by the British. The British long-term high commissioner in Egypt, Lord Cromer (1883–1907), who ruled Egypt with an iron fist, had no comprehensive urban vision but acted solely with a view to increasing political power and economic profits. For Cairo this meant that developers and speculators were free to do as they pleased. Within a larger context of global economic boom and colonial speculation, Cairo witnessed an unprecedented economic and construction boom.

Infrastructural projects like bridges across the Nile and a new tramway (1896, Ataba to Abassiya) accommodated the construction frenzy as more distant lands were opened up for construction. Heliopolis, Garden City (guided by Ebenezer Howard's model), and Maadi were created as suburbs for the colonial elite. Lower-class foreign residents (craftsmen, shopkeepers) swelled the population of the neighborhood of Shoubra, north of Cairo's main train station. Middle-level colonial bureaucrats moved to new apartment buildings on the Nile island of Zamalek. The new national university (today's Cairo University), planned and constructed by the emerging anticolonial nationalist movement, settled on agricultural land in Giza in 1914. Many members of the emerging Egyptian professional elite settled in the 1920s and 1930s in the new neighborhoods north of the university.

In the first decades of the twentieth century, Cairo's modern infrastructure was rapidly extended to serve the colonial quarters and the outposts of an emerging global touristscape. The nascent tramway system was extended in 1900 to connect downtown Cairo to the Pyramids to allow for a comfortable ride for the local elite and tourists, and yet older quarters and villages (on the west bank) had no water, electricity, or phone lines. The Mena House Hotel, located at the foot of the Cheops pyramids, had a swimming pool in 1906, but there were still some households in 2006 in older Giza quarters without their own water tap.

Postcolonial Metropolis

After Egypt's full independence from British rule in 1955 to 1956, the government under Gamal Abdel Nasser (1954–1970) embarked on a course of rapid modernization and industrialization. His populist politics included the construction of vast tracts of public housing in Cairo and Giza. The quarter of Muhandessin was designed for bureaucrats and functionaries. Medinat Nasr was similarly designed for army officers and private construction. The downtown Mugamma, a megasize administration and public service building located at the southern end of the central square of Midan Al-Tahrir, and the TV building on the Nile in Bulaq best symbolize Nasserist popular architecture and projects. Political (1967 Six Day War) and economic problems and the sudden death of Nasser in 1970 ended this populist phase. President Anwar Al-Sadat quickly ushered in a new era of economic liberalization and capitalist global integration. Cairo's face changed. Tourism increased, and the number of international five-star hotels increased along with it. Import and export businesses started to flourish, many of whose proceeds were invested in local real estate and construction. These developments are best symbolized in the dramatic changes in Muhandessin. Many Nasserist villas or small apartment buildings were replaced by apartment towers that were 20 or more stories high. Sadat's assassination in 1981 brought Hosni Mubarak to power; Mubarak continued Sadat's policies. Real estate speculation boomed, yet little housing was built for low-income groups. The economic liberalization of the 1970s had allowed growing numbers of Egyptians to migrate to the oil-rich countries of the Arab Gulf. When they returned with their remittances, many started to construct "informal" housing on the city's outskirts on agricultural land. Since the late 1970s, older quarters and villages, like Dar As-Salaam or Bulaq Al-Dakrour, have thus grown into densely populated urban quarters that today house millions of residents. Built without permits, these quarters were provided with public services only after they filled up. These quarters continue to grow.

In the early 1990s the government put considerable tracts of desert land surrounding the metropolitan area up for sale. This triggered a speculation and construction frenzy in the process of which the area of Greater Cairo (or the area to be built up) quintupled. Gated communities and other upscale developments started mushrooming, in particular around the planned desert city of 6th of October west of Giza, but also in the Muqattam area east of the city. Lower-middle-class condominiums were built in the quarter of Sheikh Zayed west of the Pyramids. Private clubs, amusements parks, and ever more glitzy malls were built at a rapid rate. Cairo's neoliberal face of the early twenty-first century is a new one: a high-density core (34,000 square kilometers in the city of Cairo) interspersed with fortresses of leisure and consumption (malls, hotels) and a lower-density "suburban" ring where the elite and new middle class enjoy larger spaces, greenery, malls, less-polluted air, and the relative absence of the poor. However, 6th of October

City already includes a growing number of lower-class residential areas.

Urban Spaces

Urban lives and cultures in Cairo, like elsewhere, take on many forms and expressions, which are constituted by dynamics of historical context, class, gender, age, urban regions, and religion or religiosity. The following illustrates four spatial, social, and cultural contexts to provide impressions of this vast cultural cityscape.

Midan Tahrir (Liberation Square), the former Midan Ismailiyah, the heart of Khedive Ismail's modern Cairo, still marks the core of Cairo. The recent history of this square represents many transformations in the larger cityscape. In the early 1980 Midan Tahrir was an immensely busy traffic node that included Cairo's central bus station. A small bridges system allowed pedestrians to traverse parts of the square above the busy streets and intersections. Bordered by the Egyptian Museum to the north, the Nile Hilton to the west, and the ubiquitous Mugamma building to the south, the square symbolized the political and economic complexity of Cairo, indeed Egypt, while simultaneously it was in the firm grip of the masses who maneuvered the square to ride buses, conduct bureaucratic works, and shop. Starting from the late 1980s the square saw a frenzy of construction, spatial change, and experiments done largely with the aim of getting the masses off the streets and indeed ultimately off the square. For most of the 1980s, Midan Tahrir was an ever-shifting construction site as the long-awaited Cairo subway was built. Simultaneously, the bus station was moved and removed, split up and resplit. The final solution was that several smaller terminals were set up in the vicinity of the square that now require passengers to walk longer distances for connecting buses. As Islamic militants in the early 1990s started to attack tourist locations, the parking lot in front of the Egyptian Museum became a security issue. In this context, lower-class citizens no longer were simply a crowded mass but a security issue; their spatiality became politicized. The experience of Midan Tahrir symbolizes two dynamics: the city's attempt to organize and control transportation and the lesson that ultimately it is impossible to control large public spaces and the masses that

inhabit them. Along with other factors, this lesson triggered the government's decision to relocate the museum, a central element in Cairo's touristscape, to the more controllable outskirts of Cairo, where the Grand Egyptian Museum is currently under construction for $350 million.

El Tayibin (an ethnographic pseudonym) is a small, low-income enclave in the middle of a centrally located upper-middle-class neighborhood. Once an agricultural village, El Tayibin was engulfed by the colonial city decades ago. The community consists of an assortment of older village-style housing and newer, very small apartment buildings located on alleys too narrow for vehicular traffic. The residents, many of whom are descendants of the earlier peasant residents, are part of Cairo's vast lower class. Men engage in a variety of jobs, including car mechanics, itinerant vendors, lower-level civil servants, janitors, taxi drivers, newspaper vendors, and public sector workers. Many younger, unmarried women work low-paid industrial or sales jobs to assemble costly dowries that include refrigerators, semiautomatic washers, and stoves, among other items. Once married, most women stop working, as their meager salaries do not add much to the family budget, considering the expenses of transportation, clothes, and child care. Yet many women contribute much to the household's finances, or they stretch resources by providing services to others (sewing, haircutting, beauty services, child care). Some women keep chickens, ducks, geese, or goats. For some this is a way to provide meat for their families; for others this is a source of extra income if they sell eggs or animals for meat. The alleys of El Tayibin from early in the morning to late at night are full of people and activities as residents, like in similar communities, negotiate their lives and needs in the context of limited resources and space.

The CityStars Mall, located in the supersized Stars Centre entertainment complex, is a recent addition (2005) to Cairo's glamorous mall scene. Located in Medinat Nasr, the mall includes 550 stores of local, regional, and global brands, an indoor theme park, and a 16-screen movie theater. For those weary of the crowd, dust, and noise of the city, the mall even includes a bazaar (Khan el-Khalili) section, which offers high-price arts, kitsch, and Egyptiana. Numerous food courts include local ("Fuul Tank"), regional (Fattoush, Lebanese), and global (McDonald's, Monchow Wok) fare. Beano's Coffee Shop serves coffee in beautifully designed local, "Fathi Mahmoud," porcelain and provides a globalized coffee shop flair, replete with newspapers and laptops. The mall's inner court, which at the ground floor boasts a huge round fountain with a large palm tree, is held up by stylized pharaonic columns that reach to the sixth floor. As one showcase of new Middle Eastern or Muslim consumerism, CityStars offers a wide variety of fashions, including upscale modest Islamic women's fashions such as local dresses (gallabiya), Gulf-style abayahs, and South Asian shalwar-qameez outfits.

Suq El-Talat, or the Tuesday market, takes place every Tuesday, starting early in the morning in the midst of public housing in Giza. The market is very old and indeed predates the public housing. Located south of the hospital of Um Al-Masriyyin, Suq El-Talat offers a large variety of affordable food and household goods. One can enter the market from different sides as it literally spills from its center around the apartment blocks into neighboring streets. Entering from Salah Salim Street, one encounters sellers of plates and other kitchen ware made from crude recycled plastic. Farther down is a seller with manually manufactured sieves and strainers. There are vendors with cart loads of industrially produced cheap kitchen ware. Farther down are female vendors, some of whom come at dawn from surrounding agricultural areas. They sell rice, eggs, vegetables, or homemade cheeses. One woman who has been shopping here for decades noted: "I always buy my rice from one woman from the Fayoum, her rice and the prices are good and I have known her for a long time." Taking a left turn at one point gets the shopper to an area where women sell live chickens, ducks, geese, and pigeons. One can carry one's merchandise home alive, or sellers will slaughter the animal on the spot. Turning back (south) farther along the apartment blocks, there are fabric stands (for clothes, furniture, curtains). There is nothing that one needs to start and maintain a household that is not available at reasonable rates at this market.

Global Metropolis

Over the millennia, the (Greater) Cairo region has always been part of various, often overlapping political, economic, cultural, and social networks. Whether as part of the extensive medieval trade network that linked the entire Old World, as a colonial capital, or as an emerging global city, Cairo has always been a center with multiple, often far-reaching connections. Over the millennia, ties intensified at times and faded at other times. Situated as an important crossroad between Europe, Africa, and Asia, and in another context between Islam, Christianity, and Judaism, Cairo has long played an important role as a center for Arabs and Muslims, and because of its cosmopolitan nature it has also been a point of economic, cultural, and religious exchange and tolerance. For the past 200 years, in the context of colonialism, modernization, and globalization, Cairo has entered yet another phase of intense links and ties—this time, however, not as a central power but starting from the nineteenth century as a colonial capital and in the postcolonial era as a regional center. In recent years, as political and economic dynamics are in dramatic flux, Cairo's regional and global roles are once more threatened, this time by a regional newcomer and urban novice: Dubai.

Petra Kuppinger

See also Colonial City; Islamic City; Shopping Center

Further Readings

Abu-Lughod, J. 1971. *Cairo. 1001 Years of the City Victorious.* Princeton, NJ: Princeton University Press.

Al Aswany, Alaa. 2004. *The Yacoubian Building.* Cairo, Egypt: American University in Cairo Press.

Ayoub-Geday, Paul, ed. 2002. *The Egypt Almanac.* Cairo, Egypt: American University in Cairo Press.

Ghannam, Farha. 2002. *Remaking the Modern: Space, Relocation and the Politics of Identity in a Global Cairo.* Berkeley: University of California Press.

Mahfouz, Naguib. 2001. *The Cairo Trilogy: Palace Walk, Palace of Desire, Sugar Street.* New York: Everyman's Library.

Raafat, Samir. 1994. *Maadi 1904–1962 Society and History in a Cairo Suburb.* Cairo, Egypt: Palm Press.

Raymond, Andre. 2002. *Cairo.* Cambridge, MA: Harvard University Press.

Scharabi, Mohamed. 1989. *Kairo: Stadt und Architektur im Zeitalter des europäischen Kolonialismus.* Tübingen, Germany: Verlag Ernst Wasmuth.

Singerman, D. and P. Amar, eds. 2006. *Cairo Cosmopolitan*. Cairo, Egypt: American University in Cairo Press.

CALCUTTA, INDIA

See Kolkata (Calcutta), India

CANBERRA, AUSTRALIA

Canberra is Australia's only inland capital city and the seat of its national government. The city celebrates its centenary in 2013. It is one of the major planned cities of the twentieth century and represents an exceptional open air museum of modernist planning, architecture, and landscape architecture ideas. It is the product less of one plan than of many plans, which have shaped its physical growth through distinctive phases of development. Canberra has grown from scratch to a planned suburban city of 330,000 with a diversified economy, major cultural institutions, and a high quality of life. While Canberra is still a place apart to many average Australians, the reality is an increasing convergence with other Australian cities in economic, social, and planning terms.

Site of the Australian National Government

The federation of the six former British colonies in 1901 demanded a seat of government. To reconcile the ambitions of the two largest cities, Sydney and Melbourne, a compromise was written into the Australian Constitution providing for a commonwealth territory, not less than 100 square miles (258 square kilometers) but at least 100 miles (160 kilometers) from Sydney. In the interim, Melbourne would provide a temporary home for the new federal government. In 1908 the site of Canberra was chosen, and three years later the government reoccupied an area of nearly 2,400 square kilometers in southern New South Wales to be retained in public ownership. The leasehold administration of the Australian Capital Territory has facilitated overall control of city planning and development. Derived from a local Aboriginal word meaning "meeting place," the new city's name was made official on March 12, 1913—now celebrated as Canberra Day.

The Griffins' Winning Design

The Congress of Engineers, Architects, Surveyors, and Members of Allied Professions, held during the commonwealth celebrations in May 1901, was the first major opportunity for professionals to discuss design issues. The idea of an international city design competition emerged as the ideal way to attract the best plan in the world. The competition, announced by the commonwealth government in April 1911, was nonetheless dogged by controversy. A total of 137 plans submitted for judging by early 1912 provided a kaleidoscopic overview of best-practice global planning cultures on the eve of World War I. The winning entry was Design No. 29 by Walter Burley Griffin and Marion Mahony Griffin. Both were former protégés of Frank Lloyd Wright, based in Chicago.

The brilliantly presented axial-polycentric design of the Griffins mixed City Beautiful and Garden City influences with more exotic eastern and ancient inspirations in a highly original landscape composition for a low-rise streetcar city of 75,000 organized around central ornamental waters. Unlike fortified ancient cities, the hilltops were largely kept free of development. After winning the competition, Walter Griffin was invited to Australia, but the government substituted a plan concocted from various competition entries before sanity prevailed and Griffin returned in 1914 as Federal Capital Director of Design and Construction. He endured an unhappy tenure, with progress stymied by the financial stringencies of World War I and the opposition of public servants. A major government inquiry exonerated Griffin, but he left the project in 1921 and spent the rest of his time in Australia in private practice as an architect and town planner.

City Planning Post-Griffin

After Griffin's departure, the Federal Capital Advisory Committee consolidated his start but retreated to a cost-saving strategy of "utilitarian development and economy." Canberra was reconceptualized through extensive tree planting and suburban style planning into a "garden town" while some departures from Griffin's recommendations for the allocation of land uses and placement of buildings were set in motion. With less than 100 houses by 1924, the pace of development had to quicken if the federal parliament was to meet in the national capital within the three years stipulated by the government. The gazettal of Griffin's scheme as a road plan in 1925 paid lip service to the richness of his planning vision but nonetheless established the geometric framework for later planning—notably the central "parliamentary triangle." The same year a new Federal Capital Commission was appointed. This was a powerful body with ample financing, a large number of staff, and full corporate control over planning, construction, maintenance, and general administration. It achieved the goal of opening the first (albeit temporary) parliament house in 1927. The wider nation was still skeptical about the concept of a remote but indulged "bush capital" for privileged politicians and elite public servants, an antagonism that remains.

After the job was done, the commission was disbanded and Canberra's population declined with the onset of the Great Depression. From 1930 until the late 1950s the planning and administration of Canberra was divided among several federal ministries including Home Affairs and Works. A city administrator provided a semblance of coordination alongside the National Capital Planning and Development Committee. Critics still complained about "a good sheep station spoiled." There were few new major public buildings, the Australian War Memorial (1941) being a notable exception; it is now one of Australia's major domestic tourist attractions. The city had a diffuse garden suburb character, but even this was threatened by severe housing shortages as it became established as a national center for military operations during World War II.

The National Capital Development Commission

Political embarrassment at the state of the city led to a crucial 1955 inquiry by a Senate committee. The major recommendation was to create a single central authority with sufficient finance and power to carry out a balanced, long-term program of urban development. The resultant National Capital Development Commission (NCDC), guided initially by advice from British planning authority William Holford, transformed Canberra from a small garden town into Australia's largest noncoastal city and a planned metropolis of international significance. Population growth was fueled by a major relocation program of public servants from Melbourne in the 1960s, Canberra's so-called golden era.

The NCDC was effectively a new town corporation with extraordinary powers buttressed by public land ownership. For the first time since the early Griffin period, Canberra again became a national center for planning innovation. By the 1970s the city was also the exemplar of a national policy of planned urban decentralization. Planning was dominated by a technocratic physical approach that worked efficiently while the NCDC's major brief was the production of a standardized urban environment. The key strategic document was *Tomorrow's Canberra* (1970), whose analytical rationale came from a major land use and transportation study undertaken by American consultants Alan Vorhees and Associates. The desired urban structure of metropolitan Canberra was a Y-plan articulated as a series of discrete communities of 50,000 to 100,000 residents with nodal town centers and linked by an internal public transportation spine and peripheral freeways. This schema laid the blueprint for the new suburban towns of Woden, Belconnen, Tuggeranong, and Gungahlin and remains evident today.

Since the 1960s, landmark elements in the planned landscape came to fruition, from major national buildings such as the National Library, the High Court, and the National (Art) Gallery, to a metropolitan hierarchy of commercial retail nodes to the damming of the Molonglo River to create the centerpiece, Lake Burley Griffin. The high point was the new Parliament House designed by Mitchell, Giurgola, and Thorp and opened to celebrate the Australian bicentennial of European settlement in 1988.

By then winds of change were evident. The NCDC's corporate planning approach was seen at odds with moves toward greater community participation, with a Legislative Assembly already having been established in 1974. Pursuing an economically rationalist ideology, the federal government was keen to divest itself further of massive investment responsibilities. A series of administrative and efficiency reviews laid the foundations for self-government, and the NCDC was disbanded in 1989. Associated with the thrust toward smaller government was a climate of deregulation, which, in Canberra's case, saw greater discretion accorded market forces in the development process, a trend that has intensified. Planning and development control was split between the small National Capital Authority responsible for the main parliamentary and other designated national areas, and a territory planning authority, a cross between a state and local government agency. The National Capital Plan (which first came into effect in 1990) provides the overarching legal framework for planning and development, complemented by the Territory Plan providing for "the people of the Territory."

Contemporary Canberra

Since the late 1980s, when the city headed past the quarter million population mark, it has begun to confront many of the same housing, land use, transport, and environmental management problems faced by the established cities: car dependency and traffic congestion; demands for more multiunit dwellings and urban infill; accommodating and caring for an aging population; redevelopment of brownfields precincts; coping with environmental hazards, including bush fires; climate change; and historic preservation. Strategic planning emphasizes archetypal sustainable city planning objectives such as full employment, a healthy community, compactness, a responsive transport system, and respect for the natural environment. A federally funded "Griffin Legacy" study (2004) identified urban design opportunities in the spirit of historic planning proposals, but concerns have been raised by the private sector at prospects for overdevelopment and lack of community consultation by a vigilant and well-informed electorate.

Canberra has a highly mobile population, predicted to grow to 400,000 by 2050. Its dual planning systems endure, but under increasing scrutiny within a political climate geared to planning deregulation and following a change of government at the federal level in late 2007. A 2008 commonwealth government inquiry into the National Capital

Authority made a series of recommendations aimed at securing more integrated and holistic governance but reaffirmed the national commitment to the city. Although development pressures and the process of "normalization" evident since the 1980s have eroded the city's iconic status as a product of enlightened public planning, Canberra remains unique for historical, political, and geographic reasons and well deserving of consideration for UNESCO World Heritage listing.

Robert Freestone

See also Capital City; City Beautiful Movement; Urban Planning

Further Readings

Fischer, K. 1984. *Canberra: Myths and Models.* Hamburg, Germany: Institute of Asian Affairs.

Headon, D. 2003. *Symbolic Role of the National Capital.* Canberra, Australia: National Capital Authority.

Overall, J. 1995. *Canberra: Yesterday, Today and Tomorrow.* Canberra, Australia: Federal Capital Press.

Reid, P. 2002. *Canberra following Griffin.* Canberra, Australia: National Archives of Australia.

Reps, J. W. 1997. *Canberra 1912: Plans and Planners of the Australian Capital Competition.* Melbourne, Australia: Melbourne University Press.

Taylor, K. 2006. *Canberra: City in a Landscape.* Sydney, Australia: Halstead Press.

Vernon, C. 2006. "Canberra: Where Landscape Is Preeminent." Pp. 130–49 in *Planning Twentieth Century Capital Cities,* edited by D. A. L. Gordon. London: Routledge.

CAPITAL CITY

From ancient Athens and Rome to Beijing and Tenochtitlan, the capital city was a national or imperial command center. Face-to-face contacts were essential in consultation and decision making or as sources of history where written texts were nonexistent, as in the realms of the Incas and Aztecs. The capital city also offered an overwhelming demonstration of the superiority of the gods. Athens focused on the Parthenon, Rome on its Forum, and the pre-Columbian capitals boasted enormous temples and pyramids in their city centers. Thus, the capital city provided legitimacy to worldly rulers and their expansionist policies.

It is remarkable to notice that all four capital cities (Athens, Rome, Beijing, and Tenochtitlan) have continued their role until this very day, although the last one is now better known as Mexico City, the world's second largest agglomeration. Obviously they were flexible enough to adapt to the requirements of the modern state.

Premodern Capital Cityscapes

The two functions of the premodern seats of government were revived in Europe's seventeenth century when power was sanctioned by the Christian churches, added to which came the role of the capital as the visible demonstration of national grandeur. Absolutist regimes dominated the continent, with the capital as the visible apex of the urban hierarchy. Both its size and splendor depended on the national tax-extracting capacity. The consuming power of the court, nobility, and clergy entertained a vast army of service providers, from luxury craftsmen to porters and servants. Thus, 8 out of Europe's 10 largest cities were parasitic court capitals. They filled no economic function remotely consistent with their size.

These court capitals were rivals in ostentatious display. Their urban design made abundant use of the discovery of the perspective. Streets were not conceived primarily as traffic arteries but as a

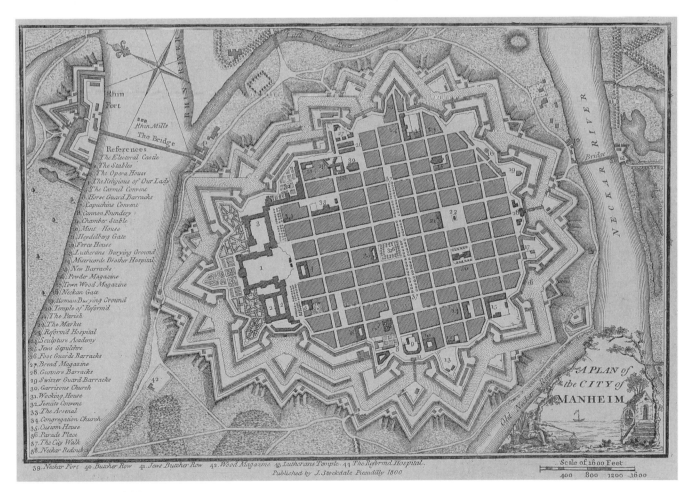

Mannheim around 1800

Source: Andrews, J. Ca. 1776. "A Plan of the City of Manheim [Mannheim]." In *Plans of the Principal Cities in the World.* London: John Stockdale. Copper engraved Plate XXII with decorative title. Sheet size 255 mm × 350 mm, plate size 185 mm × 275 mm.

Table 1   Europe's 10 Largest Cities in 1750
             (population × 1,000)

1.	London	676
2.	Paris	560
3.	Naples	324
4.	Amsterdam	219
5.	Lisbon	213
6.	Vienna	169
7.	Moscow	161
8.	Venice	158
9.	Rome	157
10.	St. Petersburg	138

scenography offering broad vistas on statues, noble palaces, or impressive art galleries. Their flanks were kept sober and stern so as to not distract the eyes of the visitor from the monument in the distance. Classicist architecture, with its emphasis on symmetry and proportion, was ideally suited for that aim. The resulting cityscape impressed people as truly monumental. The orthogonal layout testified to the ruler's will imposed on what previously was an irregular agrarian parcellation. The land was brought into his hands by expropriation and extortion.

Saint Petersburg

No other capital demonstrated its ruler's superiority as newly founded Saint Petersburg in Russia did. But opposite to Versailles or Caserta, the royal alternatives to Paris and Naples that were also created ex nihilo, Czar Peter the Great founded a veritable capital. Although its location was extremely peripheral and its marshy soil and harsh climate were serious disadvantages, all these things were secondary to the czar's wish to open a window to the West, and thus to progress and civilization. Enormous squares and parade grounds in its center testified to his disdain for the costs of urban land reclaimed at great expense. The volume and design of his palaces, built in natural stone that had to be hauled over hundreds of miles, were unmatched elsewhere in Europe. But even miniature capitals like Mannheim or Nancy developed the language of urban display and grandeur that became the almost universal vocabulary of power in following ages.

Amsterdam and Venice

Two cities did not fit the absolutist trend. The size of Amsterdam and Venice was consistent with their economic function. Politics hardly played a role. Venice was a city-state, whereas Amsterdam dominated the Dutch Republic (1648–1795) commercially and financially, without, however, claiming the title of capital, which would have been of little value in this extremely federalist state with its weak central government.

Both cities had to be drained constantly by a network of canals. This required urban planning, resulting in the unique system of waterways that is typical of them. But individual building patrons were left free to display their design preferences. Opposite to the court capitals, top-down aesthetic control was unthought of. It resulted in townscapes that were valued as *picturesque*, in which residences were conceived as individual statements of the owners, differing from the neighbors in building materials, volume, and design, and yet not producing a chaotic environment.

Paris

However much admired, no one in the nineteenth century saw the picturesque as a suitable carrier for a capital city. For this, one needed the elaboration of the proven techniques of the baroque era adapted to the needs of the age. Nowhere was such exercise more convincing than in the *grands travaux* of Baron Haussmann in Paris (1853–1870). He transformed the *goût du roi* into the *goût bourgeois* and thus brought the taste of absolutism to the broader public.

The visual impact of Paris's new townscape was considerable. The many new states founded in nineteenth-century Europe were eager to impress foreign visitors and their own citizens alike as worthy members of the European community. One way to gain respect was to develop the national capital into the icon and the showcase of the nation, highlighting statues of the heroes of science, industry, culture, and the battlefield. The "special effects" to manipulate the eyes of the visitor to these carriers of national pride were copied from Paris. Haussmann's influence was also felt outside Europe. From Buenos Aires to Cairo we find the traces of this townscape of power, but it was certainly not universal.

Berlin

Federal states did not offer favorable conditions for emulating such townscapes. Its members resisted contributing to the grandeur of the capital, always suspected of usurping more power to the detriment of local states. This was the case in Germany, indisputably continental Europe's most powerful state since its unification in 1871. However successful, the country was a federation of kings, princes, and citizens of the free cities. They were brought together under the banner of the Second Reich but jealously guarded their local prerogatives. They refused spending their taxpayers' money on the embellishment of its new *Reichshauptstadt* Berlin. What splendor the city offered dated back to its role as the capital of absolutist Prussia. Even authoritarian Emperor Wilhelm II did not succeed in harnessing parliament into generous funding of its new capital.

What further added to Berlin's unimpressive image was dominant laissez-faire rule. Political liberalism emphasized a thin state, providing barriers against arbitrary spending. Embellishment schemes should be funded by local, not national, taxes. Compulsory purchase was rare and circumscribed by detailed procedures. Thus, laissez-faire liberalism was just as powerful an obstacle to massive urban intervention and embellishment as London illustrated. Foreigners visiting the capital of the world's wealthiest and most powerful nation were perplexed by the chaotic free market townscape of its central areas, with its cacophony of styles, each building trying to shout down its neighbor. Commerce, not the state, ruled supreme in the city.

Washington, D.C.

But the twin forces of federalism and laissez-faire did not prevent the young American republic from creating an impressive capital. Its grid plan was devised by L'Enfant (1791), an enlightened French architect, but it attained true glory in 1902 with the upgrading of the Washington, D.C., National Mall under supervision of Daniel Burnham, who had just returned from a study trip to the leading capitals of Europe. Funding was a minor problem now that the United States was beginning its ascendancy as an international power that required a truly awe-inspiring capital. It became one of the more convincing statements of the City Beautiful, in which Old World precedents were domesticated by a less assertive indigenous monumentalism.

Totalitarianism and the Capital City

The World War I experience muted enthusiasm for the capital as a carrier of national superiority. But not for long. The triumph of totalitarian rule in Europe became manifest in the reshaping of the capital into an overwhelming demonstration of power. Mussolini's interventions in Rome had no other motive than to point Italians to the continuity between the Roman Empire and the fascist state. He carefully excavated the Via dei Fori Imperiali so as to confront his countrymen with the remnants of Roman triumph. In the near distance they stood eye to eye with modern translations of *Romanità* (the Roman world) as conceived by Mussolini's court architect Marcello Piacentini, with their stern, uncompromising facades clad in marble, the undisputed symbol of beauty and durity. In his plans for the transformation of Berlin into *Germania*, the new capital of the Third Reich, Hitler's favorite architect, Albert Speer, stretched axiality and symmetry to oversized dimensions to accommodate mass manifestations in which millions of uniformed Germans paraded for their Führer. Joseph Stalin's proposals for the radical restructuration of Moscow served similar aims, although here a major concern was to eliminate as many cathedrals and churches as possible, eradicating the memory of what, until 1917, had been the capital of the Russian Orthodox Church. Here, Boris Iofán developed an eclecticist rhetoric that suited Stalin's preference for socialist realism.

Triumphant urbanism continued its fatal attraction on totalitarian rulers well after 1945, as is illustrated by Ceauşescu's presidential palace in Bucharest and Mao's Tiananmen Square in Peking. In both cases, planning by clearance provided the space needed for these megalomaniacal projects.

The Modern Developing Capital City

Many postcolonial, nontotalitarian states considered such vocabulary of the Grand Manner old-fashioned and no longer capable of expressing their nation's orientation on the future. Thus, India's president Jawaharlal Nehru rejected both triumphalist monumentalism and a return to "indigenous" vernacular as suitable architectural carriers for the Punjab's new capital, Chandigarh. Modernist architecture, with its rejection of the past and a functionalist town plan in which aesthetics ceased to play a role, brought the message home of a progressive young nation that identified with looking ahead, not back. In 1950 Nehru offered Le Corbusier the chance of a lifetime to finally demonstrate what his paper plans meant in reality.

The results were stunning. Chandigarh became the Mecca of modernism, where functionalism reigned triumphant. Le Corbusier removed the dependence of urban form on natural features. Despite the almost complete absence of car ownership, work and residential spaces were rigidly separated over great distances. Marginal markets and bazaars were zoned out. Huge concrete volumes such as the assembly hall and other public buildings stood isolated in the low-density Punjabi capital.

The example of Chandigarh proved particularly attractive to developing countries. In 1956, Oscar Niemeijer and Lúcio Costa, who both had worked with Le Corbusier, set out to design Brasília, which was to replace overcrowded Rio de Janeiro as the capital of the largest nation-state of Latin America. They produced a dazzling collage of futuristic structures in a scattered townscape that once again negated past styles or a genius loci. As a mission statement of Brazil's orientation on times to come, widely publicized Brasília was a success. As a city, however, it suffered from the same problems as the new capitals implanted in Africa and Asia. It was far removed from the everyday needs of the majority of the people. Shantytowns and *favelas* continued to spring back up each time they were bulldozed away. Illegal street markets, hawkers, and beggars disturbed sanitized utopia.

The Changing Role of the Capital City

In the 1990s many felt that the role of the nation-state and thus of its capital was diminishing in an increasingly globalizing world. The main exceptions were emerging states, such as Bosnia, for whom the capital was the icon of newly gained independence. But in long-established, stable states, the symbolic value of the capital as solidified national pride no longer played a role. The broad boulevards and magnificent panoramas that were part of the nineteenth-century special effects to highlight statues and monuments have lost their political and educational meaning. Generally speaking, the symmetrical layout correlates with "despotism," German sociologist Georg Simmel wrote around 1900. Such associations are lost on the contemporary tourist. He cherishes monumental Saint Petersburg for its sheer urban beauty. That ancient Rome was unearthed and displayed as a tool to imbue Mussolini's subjects with a profound feeling of *Romanità* is irrelevant for the visitor who is overwhelmed by the "capital of antiquity." And whether he interprets London's chaotic townscape as the logical outcome of a liberal laissez-faire order, as Simmel suggested, is doubtful. Washington, D.C., may occasionally serve as the patriotic shrine of the nation, but it just as often serves as a metaphor for fat government. To arouse feelings of national pride and to create a collective national identity, two major goals in the recent past, other techniques are used that are considered more powerful. Film, television, and the Internet create special effects that are more convincing than the built environment.

If size is an indicator of a city's significance, the European capital still dominates all other urban settlements in that continent, with one exception, Saint Petersburg, which was a capital until 1918.

Table 2 Europe's 10 Largest Cities in 2008

Rank	City	Country	Population
1	Moskva (Moscow)	Russia	8,297,000
2	London	UK	7,074,000
3	St. Petersburg	Russia	4,678,000
4	Berlin	Germany	3,387,000
5	Madrid	Spain	2,824,000
6	Roma	Italy	2,649,000
7	Kiev	Ukraine	2,590,000
8	Paris	France	2,152,000
9	Bucuresti (Bucharest)	Romania	2,016,000
10	Budapest	Hungary	1,825,000

Even on a global scale, 5 of the 10 world's largest cities are national capitals (see Table 2). But as in Europe, whether their current size is a reflection of their political function is doubtful. What these megacities share is a heavy emphasis on financial and commercial services, be they informal or not, followed by the media industries.

Michiel Wagenaar

See also Berlin, Germany; Haussmann, Baron Georges-Eugène; Le Corbusier; Paris, France; Simmel, Georg; Urban Planning

Further Readings

Almandoz, Arturo. 2002. *Planning Latin America's Capital Cities.* London: Routledge.

Gordon, David L. A., ed. 2006. *Planning Twentieth Century Capital Cities.* London: Routledge.

Lortie, André, ed. 1995. *Paris s'exporte. Le modèle parisien á travers le monde.* Exhibition catalogue 1995. Paris: Picard Editeur/Pavillon de l'Arsenal.

Noever, Peter, ed. 1994. *Tyrannei des Schönen, Architektur der Stalin-Zeit.* Munich, Germany: Prestel.

Schneider, Romana and Wilfried Wang, eds. 1998. *Moderne Architektur in Deutschland 1900 bis 2000. Macht und Monument.* Stuttgart, Germany: Hatje.

Vale, Lawrence. 1992. *Architecture, Power, and National Identity.* New Haven, CT: Yale University Press.

Wagenaar, Michiel. 2000. "Townscapes of Power." *GeoJournal* 51(1–2):3–13.

CAPITALIST CITY

The historical development of the capitalist city is a key theme in urban studies and, in many respects, also in the broader social sciences. Capitalism and urbanization are indeed among the leading forces in the evolution of contemporary societies. Although cities existed well before the advent of industrial capitalism, this latter and its subsequent postindustrial (or post-Fordist) version have provided the basic framework for the development of contemporary forms of urbanization. This entry illustrates how the relationship between capitalism and urbanization has evolved over time through the lens of the ways in which urban scholars have theorized and analyzed this relationship. It does so as follows: The first section is dedicated to the discovery of industrializing cities as a laboratory of nascent manufacturing capitalism and related social phenomena and behaviors; the second section reviews the main passages of the theoretical elaboration that was produced in the 1970s around the capitalism–urbanization nexus; and the third section refers to the legacy of this theoretical work in light of the more recent reshaping of a neoliberal and globalized capitalist city.

The Nascent Capitalist City: The Urban Space as a Living Laboratory of Capitalism

Since the publication of *The Condition of the Working Class in England* in 1844 by Friedrich Engels, the modern urban phenomenon has been intimately linked to capitalism as a mode of production and social reproduction. In that book the young Engels famously described industrializing English cities such as Manchester, London, and Sheffield as unique laboratories of nascent manufacturing capitalism. The newly built working-class neighborhoods showed conditions of social alienation and deprivation that were typical of developing capitalist societies. In first-generation capitalist cities, the social divisions of capitalism were paradigmatically translated on a spatial level: The advent of capitalist urbanization had led to a simultaneous process of decomposition of the old city center and of sociospatial segregation between the lower classes and the upper classes. The making of the capitalist city was characterized, on the whole, by the coexistence of antinomic phenomena of order and disorder, of dissolution of the previous forms of spatial organization, and of creation of a fragmented urban environment.

Engels's pioneering work has been a crucial source of inspiration in subsequent streams of research on the capitalist city: most notably, the sociobehavioralist literature investigating the capitalist city as a laboratory of social hardship that gave rise to the so-called Chicago School from the 1920s onward; more recently, in the 1970s, the scholarship that theorized and widely discussed the relationship between capitalism and the urban process, inaugurating the influential tradition of Marxist urban studies. Similar to what

Manchester meant for Engels, Chicago was approached by twentieth-century urban sociologists as a paradigmatic example of the contemporary capitalist city. The rapid and massive population growth that had taken place in the city of Chicago during the last decades of the nineteenth century had shed light on a number of social problems and related deviant behaviors such as deprivation, poor living conditions, alcoholism, and homicides, which were associated with the rise of capitalism. The members of the Chicago School empirically investigated these phenomena and linked their rise and characteristics to the specific environmental conditions of the urban areas in which they appeared and developed. Urban social problems were thus described by Chicago urban scholars in terms of environment and human ecology rather than social structure and the capitalist mode of production. In this context, not only the crucial relationship between capitalism and the city but also related issues such as the role played by the state and other political agencies in the evolutionary paths of capitalist urbanization remained overlooked and undertheorized. The capitalist city was approached merely as a spatial context in which social problems had to be investigated and analyzed (starting from the assumption that the environment of large industrial cities intensifies such problems) rather than as an object of study itself and thus as an ontologically autonomous social entity.

Albeit strongly questioned in more recent times, as shown later in this entry, the empiricist orientation in urban studies has survived over the years, in part as a reaction to the critiques of the more theoretically engaged urban scholars and in part as a consequence of a specific demand for applied research coming from the social policy sphere. In the 1980s the "empiricist" position was explicitly defended by sociologist Peter Saunders, who contended that investigation of urban social issues ought not to entail approaching the capitalist city as an independent social entity. In more recent times, the tradition of more conventional social inquiry on the capitalist city has been continued by those (not only sociologists but also epidemiologists and other public health scholars) concerned with issues relating to the capitalist urban environment but not necessarily interested in providing a critical interpretation of the capitalist city as such.

The Mature Capitalist City: Theorizing the Capitalism–Urbanization Nexus

The Marxist interpretation and critique of the capitalist city gained ground since the early 1970s when a rising generation of radical urban scholars based particularly in France and other western European countries (in contrast to the predominantly Anglo-American origin of classical urban sociology), led by Manuel Castells and the other founders of the so-called new urban sociology, spelled out their dissatisfaction with the empiricist approach of the existing urban scholarship.

The historical context in which emerging ideas and research directions about the capitalist city appeared and took shape is particularly relevant. At the time, capitalist cities in the West and beyond were experiencing the formation of new urban social movements and related urban struggles along with, particularly in the United States, the surge of ethnoracial riots in the deprived and segregated neighborhoods of the larger cities. This exceptional sociohistorical context provided emerging Marxist urban scholars with the moral and political justification for the advocacy of a more politically engaged and theoretically informed urban social science. In his now classic book on the "urban question," Manuel Castells was the first scholar to systematically engage with a theoretical explanation of the urban-capitalist process. Drawing on Althusserian structuralist Marxism, Castells suggested looking at the urbanization process in terms of relationship between society and space, whose form is determined by the contingent organization of the means of production and the reproduction of the labor force. Elaborating on this conceptual framework, Castells identified four basic elements of a capitalist urban structure: (1) production, which takes the form of the spatial outcomes deriving from the social process of reproduction of the fixed capital; (2) consumption, represented by the spatial outcomes arising from the social process of reproduction of the labor force; (3) exchange, which appears as a spatial manifestation of the transfers between production and consumption; and finally (4) management, that is, the institutional process (in the form of urban planning schemes and regulations) coordinating the relationships among the former three elements of the urban structure. In the subsequent years, while coming to terms with the dogmatism of his previous structuralist-Marxist approach, Castells completed his theoretical trajectory by interpreting urban social change in the capitalist city as the result of the mobilization of grassroots movements demanding access to social services in times in which the fiscal base of the city government was eroded by the shrinkage of the welfare state.

Whereas Castells understood the capitalist city primarily as a site of social reproduction, the other major contributor to the theorization of the capitalist city, geographer David Harvey, laid the greatest emphasis on the role of finance and particularly of land rent as engines of urban growth and sociospatial transformation. As in the work of Castells and the other French urban Marxists of the 1970s, the work of Harvey on the capitalist city was deeply influenced by the specific sociohistorical context in which his theories were grounded. The highly segregated city of Baltimore and, more generally, the socially and racially unequal access to housing markets and finance in the United States drew the attention of Harvey and his colleagues and students since the early 1970s. In his theoretical endeavor, Harvey applied the Marxian theory of accumulation to the study of the urban process under capitalism. In his view, the capitalist city grows as a consequence of investment in the built environment, which follows the rhythms of capitalist accumulation (given by the periodic devaluations of fixed capital) and at the same time is limited by the physical and economic lifetime of the elements within the built environment itself. Uneven sociospatial development is the result of this cyclical evolution of capitalist societies at varying geographical scales, including that of the city. Within the urban spatiality the housing sector is managed and exploited by the ruling classes as a "contracyclical" regulator of the wider accumulation process, as happened during the golden age of postwar capitalism or in recent times with the more ephemeral flourishing of global financial capitalism.

The Globalized Capitalist City: Urban Development as a Politics of Scale

The work of the first neo-Marxist urban scholars produced a number of important strands of research on the capitalist city: most notably, the Marxian literature on gentrification, which shares with Harvey's work a fundamental concern with the structural dynamics of capitalist urbanization; then the more recent theoretical reevaluation of geographical scale within the context of globalization for which Castells's classic book has represented a "lightning rod," as an important contributor to this literature has written; finally the studies on the politics of urban development in an era of neoliberalism. These interrelated strands of research and their subfields, albeit variously accused of spatial fetishism, theoreticism, and economic determinism, have widely occupied the mind of scholars concerned with the formulation of a critical stance on the capitalist city in the past two decades, reviving the tradition and the influence of Marxian urban studies.

Whereas the rise of Marxian urbanism took place in times of insurgent social struggles and the crisis of Fordist capitalism and related fiscal crises at the urban level, the shaping of an increasingly globalized world has strongly influenced this more recent body of work on the capitalist city. Previous theorization of "rent gap" as a dynamic of capitalist exploitation of the changing value of urban space, while tracing back to the late 1970s, has been actualized and reconnected to the forces of globalization and neoliberalism that in recent years have triggered processes of gentrification, "social mix," and selective neighborhood change in a number of cities worldwide. More generally, the whole Marxist framework of urban analysis, centered on notions of residential differentiation and segmented class structure, has proven to be a fertile repertoire of theoretical tools for the understanding of the crucial role played by capitalist cities in the contemporary remaking of economic-political space under conditions of globalization.

Similarly, critical scholars of the city have revitalized Marxist theorizations, particularly of philosopher Henry Lefebvre, of geographical scales as strategic though long-neglected dimensions of capitalist accumulation. Geographical scales are not understood as pregiven spatial entities but as heterogeneous social formations produced through a complex set of discursive processes, sociopolitical struggles, and economic strategies. In this context the influential work on global and world cities has highlighted the strategic role of the urban spatiality in the development of capitalist globalization and in the mobilizing of different sources and sites of economic regulation.

The attention devoted to the shifting forms of regulation and governance of the globalized capitalist city reconnects the literatures on the spatialities of neoliberalism and globalization to the studies exploring the evolution of urban politics in post-Fordist societies. The "new urban politics" literature that developed since the early 1980s with reference to the U.S. city was concerned primarily with strategies and dynamics of local economic development on the urban level, including those related to the revitalization of downtowns, to the pursuit of large-scale projects, and to the confrontation between opposing coalitions struggling over the entrepreneurialization of urban governance. This literature made a fundamental contribution to the formulation of a political economy of place and helped to explain the novel forms of multiscalar intercapitalist competition for which the global capitalist city represents a crucial arena of investigation. The ongoing credit crunch and the structural crisis of global financial capitalism in which the housing sector and finance have played a central role provide further evidence of the long-term and strategic interconnectedness of capitalist accumulation and the urban process.

Ugo Rossi

See also Castells, Manuel; Chicago, Illinois; Chicago School of Urban Sociology; Gentrification; Global City; Harvey, David; Manchester, United Kingdom; Marxism and the City; New Urban Sociology; Revanchist City

Further Readings

Brenner, Neil. 1998. "Between Fixity and Motion: Accumulation, Territorial Organization and the Historical Geography of Spatial Scales." *Environment and Planning D: Society and Space* 16:459–81.

Brenner, Neil and Nick Theodore. 2002. "Cities and the Geographies of 'Actually Existing Neoliberalism.'" *Antipode* 34:349–79.

Castells, Manuel. 1972. *La Question urbaine*. Paris: Maspero.

———. 1983. *The City and the Grassroots. A Cross-cultural Theory of Urban Social Movements*. London: Arnold.

Cox, Kevin R. 1993. "The Local and the Global in the New Urban Politics: A Critical View." *Environment and Planning D: Society and Space* 11:433–48.

Engels, Friedrich. 1999. *The Condition of the Working Class in England*. Oxford, UK: Oxford University Press.

Harvey, David. 1989. *The Urban Experience*. Oxford, UK: Blackwell.

Logan, John R. and Harvey L. Molotch. 1987. *Urban Fortunes: The Political Economy of Place*. Berkeley: University of California Press.

Park, Robert E. and Ernest W. Burgess. 1984. *The City: Suggestions for Investigation of Human Behavior in the Urban Environment*. Chicago: University of Chicago Press.

Sassen, Saskia. 1994. *Cities in a World Economy*. Thousand Oaks, CA: Pine Forge Press.

Saunders, Peter. 1981. *Social Theory and the Urban Question*. New York: Routledge.

Smith, Neil. 1996. *The New Urban Frontier: Gentrification and the Revanchist City*. New York: Routledge.

Zukin, Sharon. 1980. "A Decade of the New Urban Sociology." *Theory and Society* 9:575–601.

CARAVANSERAI

The Persian word *karawan* refers to a group of merchants, pilgrims, soldiers, or other persons traveling together, often over extended distances; the animal most often used for the caravan routes across the Middle East and Arabian desert was the camel, whereas donkeys and horses were used for caravans through the mountains along the Silk Road. The size of the caravan depended upon many factors, including the availability of pack animals, relative security of the route traveled, and volume of trade and commerce. The largest recorded caravans for the pilgrimage from Cairo and Damascus to Mecca numbered more than 10,000 camels. Other important caravan routes flourished through the 1800s, when railroad and road transport led to their decline. The great salt caravans from the Saharan desert to Timbuktu included 20,000 camels as late as 1908, and some pilgrim caravans continued even later because of the status accorded to travel to the religious shrine by traditional method and route.

The *caravanserai* (combining the Persian *karawan* and *sarayi*, meaning dwelling or enclosed court; in Turkish, *kervansaray*, or *caravanserai*) were the public shelters for merchants, pilgrims, and other travelers in the Middle East. The caravanserai served as the traditional road inns of the Muslim world, providing shelter and protection for the traveler and for the merchant's goods. A distinction is made between the highway khan (with short-term lodging for both commercial travelers and their transport animals, thus the caravanserai) and the urban khan (a lodging house, warehouse, and trading center). A substantial gateway, large enough to allow passage of a camel with loaded bags on each side, provides access to the central court, an open area large enough to contain 300 to 400 camels. Two-story buildings surrounded the rectangular courtyard, with an arcaded corridor creating a permeable space between the courtyard and the interior. The introverted spatial conception corresponds to the protective nature of the institution and its sheltering function, which is achieved by arranging the rooms along the second floor for travelers facing the open courtyard, while the windowless walls facing the outside space create a protected fortress-like appearance. After the mosque, the caravanserai is the most common building type dated to the medieval Moslem world, and in the present day they include world heritage sites as well as examples of adaptive reuse: Several are now modern hotels.

The caravanserai were spread along the major land routes in the Muslim world at regular intervals with the intervening distances ordered by the speed of caravan travel by camels, donkeys, mules, and loaded horses. Because this speed and distance did not change for millennia, the caravanserai may be linked to the routes of the advancement of armies of Alexander the Great, then to the Romans and Byzantines, and even more so to Seljuk Turks following their conquest of Byzantium. The Ottoman Empire (ruled in direct lineage 1077–1407) stretched from the Mediterranean to the Black Sea, crossed by overland roads. The famous Silk Road from China to Europe and related legends of Venetian Marco Polo's travel were also part of the caravanserai.

Located one day's travel time (about every 30 kilometers) along the major trade routes, the caravanserai completed the communication network of the Ottoman economy and gave shelter to persons on pilgrimages across the empire. It was considered a pious duty to provide for the endowment of caravanserai for pilgrims. Over time the caravanserai acted as growth poles, and market towns would develop adjacent to them. In places where the regional conditions and population gravitation were suitable, permanent trade bazaars would develop, and charitable institutions—the *vaquf*, an essential element of urbanity for the Muslim town—were established. In addition to the bazaar, or market center, the vaquf would

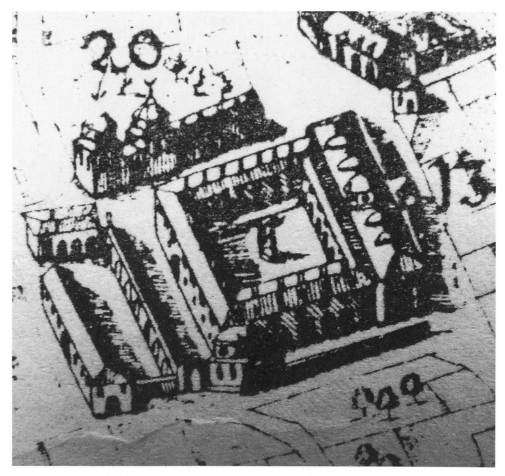

Caravanseri of Mehmed Pasa Sokolovic in Belgrade. Detail of the map of Belgrade by Gump, end of the seventeenth/early eighteenth century.

Source: Serbian National Library.

normally include buildings with specific religious (mosque), education (madrasah), and charitable functions such as the public kitchen (imaret).

Ibu Batutah, the famous Arab traveler of the fourteenth century who journeyed from his home in Morocco to India and China and back, noted caravanserai along the route from Baghdad to Mecca, founded in the eighth century by the wife of Hārūn al-Rashīd, the fifth Abbasid caliph. The Seljik sultan 'Alā' al-Dīn Kayqubād (1220–1237), renowned for the rich architectural legacy and court culture that flourished under his reign, constructed many caravanserai along roads linking the Anatolian capital to important trade routes. At the peak advance of the Ottoman Empire under Süleyman the Magnificent (1520–1566), a number of subcapitals emerged, including Bursa in Asia and Edirne in Europe. Both cities had remarkable vaqufs with mosques, bazaars, madrasahs, imarets, and the caravanserai to accommodate traders, pilgrims, and an increasing number of visitors. The Sokollu Mehmed Pasha Complex on the main highway between the two Ottoman capitals of Istanbul and Edirne included a caravanserai, bathhouse, mosque, madrasah, and market streets built in 1549 by the architect Sinan (and extended as a palace with private apartments for the sultan's use in 1569).

Whereas some of these caravanserai remain protected in full architectural grandeur, many in the Balkans and in the East were destroyed, and memory of these urban institutions remains only in old documents, maps, and contemporary records. Many surviving caravanserai have important architectural merit, with construction following the Saracenic style, and elaborate decoration on the gateway structures. Some historic caravanserai have been preserved as tourist sites (such as the caravanserai of Sa'd al-Saltaneh in Qazvin [Iran] and Khan al-Umdan in Acre) while others have been converted into hotels for the contemporary traveler (including the caravanserai of Shah Abbas in Sfahan). The Rustem Pasa caravanserai in Edirne, partially destroyed in an earthquake, was reconstructed for modern use as a tourist hotel, although this adaptive reuse was judged unsuccessful due to limitations in the earlier design. In 2007 the director of the Cultural Heritage, Handcrafts, and Tourism department in Kerman Province (Iran) announced plans to convert the historic Vakil caravanserai, built by Mohammad Ismaeil Kahn Vakil-ol Molk, ruler of Kerman in the seventeenth century, to a

five-star hotel featuring rooms decorated to represent different historical periods in Iranian history. Modern hotels across the Middle East sometimes replicate the basic design features of the original, as have resort hotels in other regions of the world.

Milan Prodanovic

See also Bazaar; Islamic City

Further Readings

Ciolek, T. Matthew. 2006. "Old World Trade Routes Project (OWTRAD): A Catalogue of Georeferenced Caravanserais/Khans." Retrieved April 9, 2009 (http://www.ciolek.com/OWTRAD/caravanserais-catalogue-00.html).

Erdmann, Kurt and Hanna Erdmann. 1961. *Das anatolische Karavansary des 13. Jahrhunderts*. 3 vols. Berlin, Germany: Mann.

Hillebrand, Robert. 1994. *Islamic Architecture: Form, Function, and Meaning*. New York: Columbia University Press.

Sims, Eleanor. 1978. "Trade and Travel: Markets and Caravanserais." In *Architecture of the Islamic World: Its History and Social Meaning*, edited by G. Mitchell. London: Thames and Hudson.

CASTELLS, MANUEL

Manuel Castells, born in 1942, is a distinguished representative of the late-twentieth-century progressive European intellectual. Of Catalan origin, having fled the Franco dictatorship, he was trained as a professional sociologist in France and taught for more than a decade at the University of Paris (Nanterre) between the 1960s and the 1970s, with more short-term academic appointments in pre-Pinochet Chile and in Montreal, Quebec. In the late 1970s, Castells moved to the United States, where he is still a professor of communication, technology, and sociology at the University of Southern California, after having taught city and regional planning at the University of California at Berkeley from 1979 to 1993, where he is now professor emeritus. In recent years he also obtained a research professorship in his native country at the Open University of Catalonia.

What is typical of Manuel Castells, as a late-twentieth-century intellectual whose perspectives were influenced by the political upheaval of 1968, is his active engagement in progressive politics and his fascination with the then-rising urban–social movements. At the same time, a specific feature of Castells's intellectual pathway lies in his characteristic cosmopolitan profile, a trait that has deeply influenced his vantage point and that at the time was not common among European academics. Castells is thus simultaneously a typically progressive European intellectual and a precursor of the cosmopolitan academic that nowadays has become increasingly widespread within the context of the globalization of academic labor markets.

Likewise, Manuel Castells's contribution to the field of urban studies has been path-breaking as well as temporally ephemeral. In fact, on the one hand, he is generally recognized in the field as one of the founders of what came to be known the "new urban sociology" from the 1970s onward. On the other hand, his belonging and concrete affiliation to the scholarly and institutional field of urban studies, with its set of specialized publications, conferences, and organized academic communities, has vanished in the years of his professional and scientific maturity, when Castells engaged in his most challenging intellectual endeavor: the trilogy on the network society and the age of information. In these more recent years, while occasionally applying his ideas and empirical findings on the network society to urban issues and problems (mainly on the occasion of invited lectures and papers), Castells has abandoned the field of urban studies, which gave him early notoriety and intellectual fame albeit within more limited audiences and readerships compared to those that have become acquainted with his subsequent work on the information age.

This entry explores the stages of Manuel Castells's intellectual trajectory in which his main field of investigation and concern was the urban phenomenon: particularly, his initial attempt to provide a systematic theory of the urban process under capitalism; then, his subsequent revision of his own departing theoretical hypotheses, with a consideration of social movements and technology as fundamental agents of urban and societal change.

The Encounter Between Structuralist Marxism and Urban Theory

At the beginning of his career Manuel Castells dedicated himself to the elaboration of a Marxist approach to the study of urban and social issues, which was deeply influenced by the rereading of Marxian thought offered by the Althusserian school in the late 1960s and beyond. The debt to Althusserian philosophy was evident in Castells's influential book on the "urban question," originally written in French and then translated into English and many other languages, and was later repeatedly acknowledged in interviews and personal memories. French philosopher Louis Althusser famously theorized the ways in which the complex social whole is overdetermined by specific "structures in dominance," namely, by economic practice under capitalism. The dominant instance represented by the economic sphere determines the way in which capitalist society is ultimately organized within all its spheres and aspects and the way in which contradictions between forces and relations of production are arranged in time and space.

Castells applied Althusserian philosophy of society and capitalism to the urban realm, which he theorized in terms of structure whose shape and organization are determined by the combination of different "systems of practice"; the economic, the political-institutional (or juridical), and the ideological. In light of this conceptual framework, Castells argued that in the capitalist city the economic system is organized around relations between the labor force, the means of production, and non-labor, and of related relations of property (the appropriation of the product) and of "real appropriation" (the technological working process), whose combination is shaped by the dialectic among (a) *production* (resulting in goods and information generated by industries and offices), (b) *consumption* (measuring the individual and collective appropriation of the product), and the derived element of (c) *exchange* (notably commerce and other spatialized transferences such as interurban circulation and what he called the sociological problematic of transportation). In Castells's view, only consumption is functionally specific to the urban phenomenon, as he demonstrated in his explanation of urban crisis. On the whole, the three elements of the economic system are regulated by the politico-institutional instance through the double movement of integration–repression at an urban and suburban level and through that of "domination-regulation," both enacted by the state apparatus. This latter was an important aspect in Castells's theorization of urban capitalism. Castells, indeed, viewed the state as a strategic actor and a crucial source of power, exercised through urban planning on a spatial level and through the institutionalization of social conflict on a political–societal level.

Castells's structuralism was thus an interpretation that, while recognizing the primacy of the economic instance, attributed an important role to the state as a guarantor of the capitalist process of development and social reproduction. Unlike another influential urban-Marxist line of interpretation in the 1970s and beyond such as that of David Harvey, who explained the crisis of urban capitalism as a crisis of capital accumulation, Castells argued that the decline of the postwar pattern of urban development arose out of the increasing difficulty of keeping the basic mechanisms for accomplishing the provision of urban services functioning efficiently in such basic realms as housing, transportation, education, and health care. Put briefly, Castells understood the urban crisis of the mid- and late 1970s as a failure of the state in managing a crisis of collective consumption, that is, of the distinctive element of the urban process. The state, indeed, received pressure both from the grassroots, in the form of social movements and from the business sector, and this twofold demand ultimately induced a fiscal crisis for local governments in large inner cities in the United States: According to Castells, this happened because, on the one hand, corporate capital needed to build directional centers requiring service workers and facilities downtown; on the other hand, the state had to provide welfare and public services to the large underemployed and unemployed populations in the inner cities. The "urban question" in the mid-1970s was particularly epitomized in the United States by this crucial contradiction between corporate needs, rising social demands, and the budget constraints of the state in a market-led economy.

Beyond Structuralism: Grassroots Movements and Technology as Agents of Urban and Social Change

After the large theoretical endeavor of *The Urban Question*, in 1983 Castells published a book on urban social movements that reported the findings of urban research conducted internationally since the early 1970s. The last chapter of *The Urban Question* had concluded by noting the scarce attention paid by social scientists, including Marxists, to research on urban social movements

and, in doing so, underlined the explanatory power of everyday social struggles to disrupt the rationality of the technocratic city. *The City and the Grassroots* was conceived, therefore, as an ambitious attempt at filling that void by entering the real world of urban grassroots movements in capitalist cities. Although researched in the same years as the previous book, *The City and the Grassroots* came out in times of growing disillusionment over the need for a comprehensive theory of social processes, most notably one centered on the primacy of the economic over the social and the spatial, and was announced by the author as an intellectual project sharply departing from the theoretical hypotheses spelled out in *The Urban Question*. The final result was a book presenting mainly empirical material in the form of powerfully narrated case studies, anticipated by a short conceptual introduction and supported by a long concluding section dedicated to the research design. The book aimed at providing a comparative account of urban social movements in different geographical and historical contexts, showing the simultaneous concern for the expansion of collective consumption, the assertion and defense of cultural identity, and the search for political organization that drives urban protest movements in capitalist societies. Although the book disappointed those who expected another major contribution to Marxist urban theory (and probably the book's subtitle "a cross-cultural *theory*" was largely responsible for these frustrated expectations), its influence has been, in many respects, even stronger than that of the *The Urban Question*. Indeed, the book contributed fundamentally to the development of the lively and still expanding field of research on urban social movements, while also clearly inspiring subsequent work of Castells on identity-based social movements in the information age.

The abandonment of structuralism, therefore, entailed a new relationship between theory and empirical analysis that has since accompanied Castells in the remainder of his career: Theory was now intimately blended with the observation and discussion of social phenomena, rather than the other way around as it was in *The Urban Question*. This way of proceeding—a typical case-study research methodology in many ways—informed also his last contribution to urban scholarship: that on the informational and technological city in the 1980s and the early 1990s.

When Castells started to conduct research on this subject in the early 1980s, human history had not yet been revolutionized by the advent of the Internet and the related electronic means of communication, cultural exchange, and trading. Even so, in the 1980s Castells, like a growing number of social scientists at that time, was already aware of the fundamental importance of the new information technologies in shaping the evolution of human societies and particularly that of cities and regions. In fact, cities and especially large metropolitan areas were in the front line of the "service economy" process of expansion: Even the booming computer industry in the so-called American Sunbelt appeared to be persistently dependent on the old established base of headquarters and corporate services in major U.S. cities such as New York, Chicago, San Francisco, and Los Angeles. At the same time, however, while noticing how the cores of the dominant metropolitan areas preserved their function as location for most of the command and control centers of the economy, Castells also emphasized the process of regional decentralization and suburbanization of information and office activities linked to second-rank business services and to producer services of what he called the "new industrial space." The lower land prices and office rents and the linkage with residential suburbanization were the most important factors lying behind the preferences for a suburban site over the traditional downtown location in the service sector.

In his account of the process of technoeconomic restructuring and its related spatial manifestations, consistent with his persistent commitment to a critical urban sociology, Castells was particularly concerned with the changes in the urban social structure, proposing an interpretation of urban and social change centered on notions of social polarization and economic dualism, which, a few years later, became popular and widely discussed in the early debate over the globalizing city. Drawing also on a large research program on the informal economy conducted in collaboration with economic sociologist Alejandro Portes, Castells described the occupational structure of large cities in the United States as a "complex pattern" combining the creation of new, highly paid jobs in advanced services and high-technology sectors; the destruction of mid-level jobs in old manufacturing; the gradual shrinkage of protected jobs in the public sector; and the proliferation of new, low-paid jobs in services, in downgraded manufacturing, and, most particularly, within the expanding informal and criminal economies. The increasing polarization and segmentation of the local labor markets, Castells argued, produced a highly differentiated labor force displaying distinct lifestyles in terms of household structures, intergender family relationships, and uses of the urban space. Far from aiming at providing a schematic representation of the urban realm, Castells's dual city thesis intended to make sense of the multifaceted social realities that took shape from the overlapping of structural dualism and sociospatial polarization in postmanufacturing capitalist cities.

In these early studies dealing with the informational city that inspired Castells's subsequent major research effort on the network society, the structuralist mode of thinking that still informed his interpretation of urban and social issues was mitigated by an increasing awareness of the complex character of human societies, irreducible to dialectical relations of cause–effect and to a purely rationalist understanding of social change. The overcoming of structuralism became even clearer in his subsequent work on world technopoles, coauthored with geographer Peter Hall. Cities and regions were described in this book not only as sites of economic restructuring and technological innovation, but also as emerging "economic actors" whose strength lies in their ability to adapt to the changing conditions of the global economy and in their response capacity to promote development projects, negotiate with multinational firms, and foster the growth of medium and small-sized firms, as well as in their long-term attitude to compete with each other in becoming places of greater innovation and efficiency. What is noteworthy in the work on technopoles is the cross-national research approach that Castells and Hall developed. While other authors at that time were publishing single-case study research on successful technological cities, this remarkable book provided a truly global picture of the rise of technopoles located in different regions of the world: from the celebrated cases of endogenous entrepreneurial spin-off in Silicon Valley, California, and in greater Boston, Massachusetts, to less known examples of planned science cities in Siberia, Japan, and Korea, where the state played a major role in the development trajectory.

Conclusion

According to Castells, in an essay written in 2000 as his own contribution to *The Castells Reader on Cities and Social Theory*, the advent of an information age has radically changed the "urban question," as this was dealt with both by Chicago sociologists and by the new urban sociologists of the 1970s, including himself. While the former gave prominence to the building of a unified urban culture through a process of social integration and the latter investigated the ways in which the state responds to urban struggles over collective consumption, the urban question is now articulated—in Castells's view—around the fundamental tension between the city as a "space of flows" and as a "space of places." The space of flows links up immaterially separate locations in an interactive network that connects activities and people in distinct geographical entities. The space of places, on the other hand, organizes experience and agency around the confines of locality. The issue of social integration, which was at the core of the foundational reflections on urban societies at the time of the Chicago School, should be now approached—Castells suggests—by urban scholars so as to understand the multiple ways in which the spaces of flows are folded into the spaces of places through material infrastructures, technical devices, and everyday practices of communication and exchange, the latter either at a distance or in the form of face-to-face interactions.

These reflections powerfully resonate with contemporary key debates over the resurgence or dismissal of scalar approaches, the meaning of sociospatial relations in an age of globalization, and the values of territoriality and positionality in a persistently socially and spatially uneven world, which have animated the intersected disciplines of urban sociology, critical geography, and urban and regional studies in recent years. Even though Castells has not directly taken part in these more recent debates, he is still widely recognized as a leading intellectual authority by contemporary urban and regional scholars and other sociospatial scientists, well beyond the judgment about the present relevance of his "classic" theorization of the urban question. Despite the "specters" of structuralism in urban theory that Castells inevitably evokes, he is one of the most influential scholars and public intellectuals to have emerged in the field of critical urban studies over the past four decades or so.

Ugo Rossi

See also Capitalist City; Citizen Participation; City Planning; Global City; Globalization; Harvey, David; Informational City; Local Government; Marxism and the City; New Urban Sociology; Social Movements; Technopoles; Urban Sociology; Urban Theory

Further Readings

Brenner, Neil. 2000. "The Urban Question as a Scale Question: Reflections on Henri Lefebvre, Urban Theory and the Politics of Scale." *International Journal of Urban and Regional Research* 24:361–78.

Castells, Manuel. 1972. *La Question urbaine*. Paris: Maspero.

———. 1983. *The City and the Grassroots. A Cross-cultural Theory of Urban Social Movements*. London: Arnold.

———. 1983. "Crisis, Planning, and the Quality of Life: Managing the New Historical Relationships between Space and Society." *Environment and Planning D: Society and Space* 1:3–21.

———. 1989. *The Informational City*. Oxford, UK: Blackwell.

———. 2002. "Conclusion: Urban Sociology in the Twenty-first Century." Pp. 390–406 in *The Castells Reader on Cities and Social Theory*, edited by I. Susser. Oxford, UK: Blackwell.

Castells, Manuel and Peter Hall. 1994. *Technopoles of the World: The Making of Twenty-first Century Industrial Complexes*. London: Routledge.

Castells, Manuel and Alejandro Portes. 1989. "World Underneath: The Origins, Dynamics, and Effects of the Informal Economy." Pp. 11–37 in *The Informal Economy: Studies in Advanced and Less Developed Countries*, edited by A. Portes, M. Castells, and L. Benton. Baltimore: Johns Hopkins University Press.

Pflieger, Géraldine. 2006. *De la ville aux réseaux: Dialogues avec Manuel Castells*. Lausanne, Switzerland: Presses Polytechniques et Universitaires Romandes.

Ward, Neil and Eugene J. McCann. 2006. "'The New Path to a New City'? Introduction to a Debate on Urban Politics, Social Movements and the Legacies of Manuel Castells' *The City and the Grassroots*." *International Journal of Urban and Regional Research* 30:189–93.

Zukin, Sharon. 1980. "A Decade of the New Urban Sociology." *Theory and Society* 9:575–601.

CATASTROPHE

Worldwide, cities face increasing risk of catastrophes. The Indian Ocean tsunami of 2004, with more than 240,000 deaths, and Hurricane Katrina of 2005, considered the most costly disaster in U.S. history at over $200 billion, captured world attention. Most of these losses were sustained in urban areas with high concentrations of people and property located in extremely low-lying hazardous areas. These devastating events are likely precursors to more frequent and severe catastrophes to strike cities in the foreseeable future.

Catastrophic events can be conceptualized according to their source. Some events result from largely uncontrollable forces of nature such as earthquakes, hurricanes, and tsunamis. Other events are caused by combinations of natural forces and human action. For example, dredging and filling in wetlands for urban development often results in loss of the capacity of watersheds to store stormwater runoff, which increases the risk of flooding for downstream communities. Still other catastrophes result from deliberate human will like terrorism, arson, and armed conflicts.

Catastrophic events can be slow-onset, multi-episodic events or rapid-onset, single episodic events. Slow-onset catastrophes result from clusters of traumatic episodes (e.g., protracted drought due to long-term absence of precipitation, large-scale abandonment of inner cities due to prolonged divestment in built environments or recurring crime). Rapid-onset events include terrorist attack, hurricane landfall, and earthquakes.

Catastrophes need to be distinguished from disasters when considering the rising global environmental risk to cities. Both *catastrophe* and *disaster* refer to crisis events of sufficient enormity to cause disruption to infrastructure (sewer, water, electricity, and roads), local economies, housing, and everyday functioning of cities. Yet, a clear distinction exists between them that must be understood when assessing the risk to cities. Several dimensions of these crises help us to make the distinction. First, there is the scale of destruction.

Most or all of a city's built environment is heavily impacted in a catastrophe, but only partial destruction occurs in a disaster. The damage in New Orleans from Hurricane Katrina was catastrophic, as 80 percent of the city was flooded. The 1902 volcanic eruption of Mount Pelée buried the entire city of St. Pierre on the island of Martinique in the Caribbean. Nearly 30,000 residents perished, and only one man survived: a prisoner in solitary confinement. In contrast, disasters strike only parts of a city. The Mexico City earthquake of 1985, considered a major disaster, caused destruction of only 2 percent of the residential housing stock. The damage caused by the attack on the World Trade Center on September 11, 2001, was confined to only a few city blocks in lower Manhattan.

Second, there is the degree of accessibility of aid. Aid for emergency response and recovery is much more problematic in a catastrophe compared to a disaster. An entire region of communities is devastated and unable to contribute to the need for personnel, supplies, and communication. In a disaster there is usually only one major target for the convergence of assistance, but in a catastrophe many nearby localities are targets and often compete to gain the attention of external aid donors. After Katrina, the devastated cities in southern Mississippi (Biloxi, Gulfport, Pass Christian) could have anticipated a flow of assistance from the major metropolitan city, New Orleans, but the catastrophic conditions throughout the region precluded this possibility.

Third, there is the severity of disruption of everyday lives. Daily activities of a city are severely affected in a catastrophe but not in a disaster. Most if not all places of work, recreation, worship, and education are completely shut down, and lifeline infrastructure systems that supply electricity, water, communication and transportation services are severely disrupted for months or even years. Even in major disasters, no such massive disruption of community life occurs even if particular neighborhoods are devastated. In the 1985 Mexico City earthquake, life in many contiguous areas went on almost normally. This was also the case following the Loma Prieta earthquake of 1989 when the San Francisco Bay region experienced the collapse of the Oakland expressway and the closure of the San Francisco Bay Bridge. These incidents did not cause a major disruption of the regional transportation system, as commuters were able to commute to work as usual because most of the system remained intact. Most cities can cope with disaster events through emergency response systems, but they are ill prepared to deal with the sheer scale of devastation associated with catastrophes.

Risk to Cities

Rather than originating from unexpected events, catastrophes are a predictable result of interactions among several major global forces: (1) rapid urbanization, (2) growth in extremely hazardous locations, (3) growing inequities in social vulnerability, and (4) global climate change. The accelerating rate of urbanization has caused greater concentrations of people and property that can increase risk if hazards are not anticipated and addressed. Global statistics for urban growth indicate that in 2000 more than 50 percent of the world's population lived in urban settlements. By 2020, 90 percent of the population growth in developing countries will be urban. Although cities comprise only 1 percent of the earth's land area, they concentrate more than half of the world's population and the majority of its physical capital, including buildings and infrastructure. Frequently, growth occurs too rapidly to allow cities to keep pace in expanding the capacity of their hazard mitigation programs. These programs include proactive land use planning to steer new development away from hazard areas, building codes to strengthen new and existing buildings to withstand hazardous forces (wind, floods, and seismic shaking), and resilient infrastructure systems that serve as critical lifelines for stricken populations. Istanbul, Turkey, which is highly vulnerable to earthquakes, exemplifies a city in which the rate of growth far exceeds its ability to effectively mitigate the risks. This city grew from 1 million people in the 1950s to about 10 million today, a tenfold increase in half a century. Yet, by 1999 only 20 schools out of 1,783 schools and 2 hospitals out of 308 hospitals in Istanbul have been retrofitted.

Second, cities are growing in perilous geographic locations such as gently sloping floodplains, coastal shorelines, and uplifted precipices along seismic faults. These places confer benefits that attract development (e.g., buildable lands, strategic sites for transportation, scenic amenities).

In the United States, the number of people residing in earthquake- and hurricane-prone regions is growing rapidly. Over the past several decades, the population growth rate along the hurricane- and storm-prone U.S. coast is more than double the national growth rate. Worldwide, 11 of the 15 largest cities in 2000 were highly exposed to one or more natural hazards, including coastal storms, earthquakes, and volcanoes. Beijing, Los Angeles, Mexico City, and Tokyo sit astride active seismic faults, while Bombay (Mumbai), New York, and Shanghai are vulnerable to coastal storms, and Jakarta and Tokyo are in close proximity to active volcanoes.

Third, deep inequities in social vulnerability result in wide variations in how catastrophes affect different populations. Whereas physical vulnerability emphasizes the location, frequency, and magnitude of hazardous forces and the resiliency of the built environment to withstand such forces, social vulnerability centers on characteristics of social groups that affect their ability to cope with and rebound from a catastrophe or disaster. Several factors comprise the social vulnerability of populations including socioeconomic status, gender, race/ethnicity, and age. Differences in these factors result in a system of stratification of wealth, power, and status. In the United States, this has caused social inequities in fiscal and human resources between older core areas of cities and wealthier suburban areas. Spatial differences, in turn, result in uneven distribution of exposure and vulnerability to catastrophic events and access to aid for planning and recovery. The Hurricane Katrina catastrophe in New Orleans laid bare these inequities. Inner-city New Orleans had the highest social vulnerability of all the impacted coastal jurisdictions along the Gulf Coast. Displaced low-income minority populations were left behind at the New Orleans convention center and elsewhere because they did not have access to vehicles to evacuate, while suburban residents with automobiles were able to flee the destruction.

Dissimilarities in social vulnerability can also be observed between cities in developed and developing countries. Inhabitants and businesses in cities of developed countries can afford new construction and the retrofitting of existing structures to disaster-resistant building standards, mapping of hazard locations, widespread insurance to cover losses, and investment in structurally strengthened lifelines (i.e., roadways for evacuation; water, sewer, and electrical utilities; and communication systems). In developing countries, poverty makes many people more vulnerable to hazards and less able to recover from them. Impoverished city governments lack the resources to plan for future disasters, while most, if not all, of their capacity is directed at providing basic services. Waves of migrants crowd into existing houses, often substandard, or put up cheap shelters wherever they can, frequently on land left empty because it is extremely hazardous. In Quito, the capital of Ecuador, many flimsy houses perch on the sides of hills, where they are vulnerable to landslides caused by earthquakes or volcanic eruptions. Substandard construction puts impoverished neighborhoods at extreme risk to tropical storms in Bombay, floods in São Paulo, and earthquakes in Guatemala City.

Lastly, global warming has increased the prospects for catastrophes in cities. Although the connection between global climate change and gaseous emissions from urban-industrial regions is a controversial topic, there is no question that global warming is occurring. Global warming raises the temperature of sea water, which acts like fuel for hurricanes and typhoons. The strike range of these tropical storms could increasingly extend into nontropical coastal cities. New York City, the most populous city in the United States, is now the American city at second highest risk for potential total economic loss from a major hurricane, preceded only by the Miami–Fort Lauderdale area in Florida. Global warming is causing sea level rise along coastlines to increase 1 to 1½ feet or more per century. The numerous consequences of sea level rise, including higher storm surge and tsunami wave heights, increased beach erosion, and ultimately the loss of low-lying coastal areas and coastal wetlands, increase the vulnerability of many coastal cities. Global warming also raises the chances of tipping many cities and metropolitan regions into drought and full-blown water shortage crises. Warmer, dryer land and vegetation caused by higher climate temperatures also increase the likelihood of wildfires that threaten urban areas.

Resilient Cities

In light of the available evidence, the threat of catastrophic events to cities is apparent and rising. Cities often contain all the ingredients for catastrophic losses: growth of concentrated settlement patterns in hazardous locations, urban poverty and increased vulnerability of disadvantaged groups, and heightened exposure to the forces associated with global warming.

The creation of resilient cities has become a prominent goal. Resiliency is the ability of a city to anticipate and mitigate hazards, contain the effects of a crisis event, and recover in ways that minimize social disruption and mitigate risks from future events. Four challenges establish a framework for action to enable cities to move from response and recovery to proactively enhancing their resiliency.

First, cities should develop hazard mitigation plans. A well conceived plan identifies hazard areas where new development should not take place and potential sites free of hazards that can serve as relocation zones for existing development when hazardous areas sustain damage. Where hazard areas have significant cultural or economic advantages for redevelopment that cannot be forgone, a mitigation plan should include provisions that guide development (or redevelopment after disasters) to the least hazardous parts of building sites and modify construction and site design practices so that vulnerability is minimized.

Second, cities should support meaningful citizen participation in planning for resiliency. When citizens are exposed to the more resilient alternatives for dealing with catastrophes, they are more likely to mobilize and insist that elected officials attend to the impending threat. Active citizens who are deeply involved in planning and understand the forces that increase risk are more likely to be committed to seeing a mitigation plan through to implementation.

Third, external aid delivery organizations (both public and private) treat disaster-stricken people as participants in the recovery process, rather than helpless, poor victims. Specific approaches need to be employed in which those with a stake in recovery planning can develop a bottom-up ability to take collective action. External aid delivery programs that take a bottom-up approach enable local people to have greater access to extra-community institutions that expand resources potentially available to the community. Moreover, issues of local concern have a greater chance of being communicated to external authorities. In contrast, top-down aid delivery denies grassroots-level involvement in response to local needs, disconnects and weakens bonding social capital, and thus degrades local resilience.

Fourth, hazard mitigation plans should include "moralistic possibilities" and not solely "actuarial probabilities" in anticipation of catastrophes. Public officials and engineers in charge of mitigation planning reason like actuaries, building to a standard designed to protect only most of the people most of the time. However, given the heightened risk of catastrophes, officials must start from the premise that there are some harms that all citizens must be protected from, whatever the cost. Any anticipatory action must defend a foundational moral intuition: All lives are worthy of protection at the highest standard. That is how the British reasoned when they built the River Thames barrier and how the Dutch reasoned when they built their flood control and land use planning system.

In sum, creation of a resilient city requires proactive planning for protecting and restoring a city's physical fabric. Just as critical are efforts to build a city's social fabric—a process that fundamentally entails connecting and strengthening social networks often on a grassroots level, neighborhood by neighborhood.

Philip R. Berke

See also Citizen Participation; Hiroshima, Japan; Istanbul, Turkey

Further Readings

Godschalk, David, Timothy Beatley, Philip Berke, David Brower, and Edward Kaiser. 1999. *Natural Hazard Mitigation: Recasting Disaster Policy and Planning.* Washington, DC: Island Press.

Mitchell, James K., ed. 1999. *Crucible of Hazards: Mega-cities and Disasters in Transition.* Tokyo: United Nations University Press.

Pelling, Mark. 2003. *The Vulnerability of Cities: Natural Disasters and Social Resilience.* London: Earthscan.

Perry, Ron and E. L. Quarantelli, eds. 2005. *What Is a Disaster? New Answers to Old Questions.* Philadelphia: Xlibris Books.

Vale, Lawrence and Thomas J. Campanella. 2005. *The Resilient City: How Modern Cities Recover from Disaster.* London: Oxford University Press.

CHICAGO, ILLINOIS

Within half a century of its founding in 1833, Chicago, Illinois, became the second largest city in the United States, thanks to its location at the hub of the nation's growing railroad network. A center of manufacturing and commerce, Chicago attracted millions of transnational and American migrants during the nineteenth and twentieth centuries. As an exporter of products and ideas, Chicago influenced how Americans lived, and it served as an exemplar for those who thought about what a city was. Toward the end of the twentieth century, however, Los Angeles's automobile-oriented population outstripped Chicago's, dropped the "second city" to third in rank, and replaced it as the paradigm of urban form.

Chicago's Origins

Modern Chicago originated at the mouth of the Chicago River. The flat and marshy site was periodically occupied in the seventeenth and eighteenth centuries by Miami, Potawatomi, Ottowa, and Ojibwa people. The Potawatomi who dominated the region in the late eighteenth century used the local waterways as transportation routes for French fur trade. The possibilities of commerce attracted American settlers to the north bank of the river in the 1780s. Amid a series of treaties, through which the federal government ultimately secured the region for American settlement and expelled the native population, the U.S. Army established Fort Dearborn on the river's south bank in 1803. The last Potawatomi moved west after the 1833 Treaty of Chicago left the region open to permanent White settlement. Chicago incorporated as a town that year, becoming a city four years later. The city's first residents quickly became enmeshed in a frenzied real estate trade. The possibility of easy wealth lured fortune seekers, who increased the city's 1840 population to 4,470 people.

Growth and Conflict

Many midwestern U.S. cities in the nineteenth century experienced dramatic real estate speculation that caused swift growth until the bubble burst. But Chicago became the largest city in the nation's interior because it served as the center point for shipping between the East and the West. The initial promise of Chicago's central location was suggested by the construction of the Illinois and Michigan Canal (1848). The canal linked the Mississippi River and the Great Lakes, enabling goods to move from New Orleans to the Atlantic Ocean entirely by water routes. Entrepreneurs responded by founding the Chicago Board of Trade, which made the city a major commodities and futures clearinghouse. The significance of the canal's opening, however, was immediately dwarfed by the first trip of the Galena and Chicago Union Railroad later that year. The continent's newly built rail lines from the East and the West soon converged in Chicago, making the city indispensible to international commerce.

The chance to find work and get rich through Chicago's real estate, commercial, and employment opportunities drew tens of thousands of northeastern U.S. and European migrants, especially from Germany and Ireland. Cyrus McCormick, for example, decided that Chicago was the right place from which to manufacture and market his reaper; he established a company that eventually became the world's largest maker of grain harvesting equipment. As Chicago's population swelled, city government moved to provide infrastructure and services to secure local health and welfare. The construction of an elaborate water and sewer system enabled the city to annex surrounding communities that could not afford to provide these services independently, dramatically increasing Chicago's size. The park system, developed over the course of the nineteenth century, helped direct settlement patterns and boost local real estate values. By the time the Great Fire of October 8–9, 1871, devastated the city's downtown and North Side and drew international aid, Chicago's population had reached approximately 300,000.

Although the fire left a third of the city temporarily homeless, it left intact the essentials of Chicago's industrial base. Chicagoans immediately began rebuilding the city, and undeterred migrants continued to arrive over the next several decades. Immigrants from southern and eastern Europe—notably but not exclusively Italians, Poles, and Jews—joined Chicago's already heterogeneous population mix. Almost every nationality group migrating to the United States had representatives

in Chicago. Although Chicago is often seen as a series of distinct ethnic enclaves, most immigrants lived side by side with neighbors with whom they did not share immediate language or cultural roots. By 1890, Chicago's population of more than a million surpassed Philadelphia's, making it the second largest city in the United States; 10 years later, Chicago had almost 1.7 million residents.

Most new Chicagoans were members of the working class, toiling in small homes or one of the growing numbers of large industrial concerns. In addition to continuing to serve as a transshipment point for Midwestern products such as grain and lumber around the continent, Chicago increasingly became home to enterprises that produced, packaged, or otherwise transformed goods before selling them elsewhere, taking advantage of the city's location in the railroad network. The 1865 opening of the Union Stock Yard signaled Chicago's ascension over Cincinnati as the leading meatpacking city in the nation. Montgomery Ward and Sears, Roebuck and Company, the nation's two largest mail-order catalog companies, established their headquarters in Chicago. George Pullman established the Pullman Palace Car Company—and a much-vaunted model town for his employees to live in—in a southern suburb later annexed into Chicago. Manufacturers of iron and steel built enormous factory complexes on the city's far South Side and in neighboring suburbs. In 1916, poet Carl Sandburg memorialized Chicago as the "city of the big shoulders," a tribute to the muscularity of its denizens' labor.

The breadth of opportunities for work did not mean that laboring Chicagoans were comfortably employed. Poor wages, dangerous work conditions, and fierce competition for jobs fostered an active labor movement; between the end of the Civil War and 1919, Chicago's workers participated in at least six waves of strikes. Business owners resisted union organizing, helping turn the Pinkerton National Detective Agency into the nation's leading private strikebreaker. Labor disputes frequently turned violent. On May 4, 1886, a rally advocating for the eight-hour work day turned the Haymarket site into an international icon. An unknown bomb-thrower killed a police officer, drawing a violent response from police. Ultimately, eight anarchists were convicted of murder on flimsy evidence. In the "Memorial Day Massacre" of May 1937, ten participants in a strike on Republic

Steel were killed by police. One response to the plight of working-class Chicagoans was Hull House, the most famous of the nation's settlement houses. Established in 1889 by Jane Addams and Ellen Gates Starr, it served the cultural and material needs of the poor, particularly immigrants.

Not all of Chicago's conflicts were based in work. Beginning in the 1910s, large numbers of southern African Americans began the "Great Migration" to northern urban centers; Chicago was a prime destination. White Chicagoans saw Black migrants as unwelcome neighbors and competitors for scarce jobs. Although prior to the twentieth century the city's small Black population lived intermingled among Whites, soon African Americans found few housing opportunities outside the jealously guarded boundaries of the South Side ghetto. Blacks who violated the strict segregation of housing, such as banker Jesse Binga, were threatened with violence and sometimes attacked. In July 1919, hostilities between Whites and Blacks exploded into a race riot that killed 38 Chicagoans.

Despite its internal conflicts, Chicago's boosters marketed the city to the world as a paragon. Most famously, in 1893 the city hosted the World's Columbian Exposition, a celebration of American progress, in the South Side's Jackson Park. Daniel Burnham, the fair's director, divided the grounds into two parts: the ornate, neoclassically styled "White City" and the Midway. The temporary structures of the White City displayed the achievements of American civilization, while the exotic and seedy Midway showcased the world's indigenous people and the Ferris Wheel, invented as the fair's answer to the Eiffel Tower. Through planning the fair, Burnham developed the foundation of the City Beautiful movement and the modern profession of city planning. Burnham went on to write plans for several American and international cities, including Chicago in 1909. The Burnham Plan, while never fully executed, remains the cornerstone of the city's redevelopment efforts in the twenty-first century.

The Chicago Schools

Chicago's contributions to the world extended beyond manufactured goods. It also exported ideas and practices developed locally. Many of Chicago's contributions to American intellectual life, particularly in the analysis of cities, were based at the University of Chicago, founded in Hyde Park in 1892. Under the leadership of Robert Park and Ernest Burgess, the university's sociology department pioneered what came to be called the "Chicago School of Sociology." Treating the city as their personal research laboratory, the department's faculty and graduate students developed an ecological model of urban life. Cities could be divided into distinct "natural areas" with characteristics that sustained themselves over time, even as their populations shifted. Especially influential was Burgess's schematic of the city as a series of concentric circles, with the downtown "Loop" at the center, and surrounding zones differentiated by class and function. For much of the twentieth century, American urbanists could not untangle themselves from the Chicago School's basic assumptions. The Chicago School of Economics, although focused on the free market rather than cities, was similarly significant.

Chicago's built environment is testimony to the innovative practices and designs of the first and second Chicago Schools of Architecture. From the late nineteenth century onward, Chicago architects experimented with skyscraper design. The downtown Loop is dotted with dozens of their landmark buildings. The structure of Dankmar Adler's Auditorium Building (1888), for example, stands upon a raft that allows it to float on the Loop's marshy ground. William LeBaron Jenney pushed Chicago architects away from designing load-bearing walls toward using iron and steel construction. Their post–World War II successors designed buildings that derived their beauty from structure rather than ornament. The Prairie School of architecture, with its emphasis on residential building, originated in Chicago with Louis Sullivan and Frank Lloyd Wright and radiated around the world.

World War II and the Postwar Period

Chicago's demographics held steady through the Great Depression, but significant changes occurred during and after World War II. Hundreds of thousands of Americans, many of them southern African Americans, migrated to the city, drawn by manufacturing jobs created by the war effort. The city's housing supply was grossly inadequate for the needs of the new residents, forcing people to live in makeshift cubicles or subdivided apartments, or to double and triple up with family and strangers. When the end of war production made building materials available again, population concentrations in the metropolitan area shifted dramatically. New single-family houses, constructed on the mostly undeveloped northwest and southwest sides, made it possible for the city's White population to spread out. White Chicagoans also moved outward to newly incorporated and developing suburbs. Some men used automobiles to commute to jobs that remained within the city, but increasingly commercial and manufacturing enterprises kept suburbanites outside the city for work as well.

African Americans, however, continued to live and work within Chicago's boundaries. Neither the South Side's Bronzeville area nor the small West Side settlement could contain the sheer numbers of new migrants. As African Americans sought new housing opportunities in blocks adjacent to ones already established as areas of Black residence, Whites responded first by resisting their arrival— sometimes violently—and then by leaving. In addition, public authorities used federal urban renewal monies to clear out dilapidated Black neighborhoods and build high-rise public housing. Although Chicago Housing Authority staff aspired to use public housing to promote racial integration, city officials and White citizens blocked these attempts, leaving Chicago as racially segregated as it had been prior to the Second Great Migration. Chicago's segregation was much studied by social scientists, who used it as a model for explaining racial settlement patterns around the nation.

Like other northern cities, Chicago suffered from postwar deindustrialization, as steel, meatpacking, catalog, and other companies closed their plants, changed the character of their operations, and suburbanized. Nonetheless, the city's downtown remained a center of commercial activity embodied by the increasing numbers of skyscrapers constructed after 1955. Modernist architects led by Ludwig Mies van der Rohe and the firm of Skidmore, Owings and Merrill contributed designs such as the John Hancock Center (1969) and Sears Tower (1974)—which was the world's tallest building until the completion of the Petronas Towers in Kuala Lumpur in 1998. Mayor Richard J. Daley (1955–1976) carefully managed the postwar redevelopment process, brokering some land deals personally. Daley, operating on the theory that revitalization would spread outward from a strong center, focused on preserving the vitality of the downtown. By contrast, Mayor Harold Washington (1983–1987), the city's first African American mayor, spared some money and attention for renewing infrastructure and services to the city's residential neighborhoods.

A huge steel sculpture of a Puerto Rican flag stands at the gateway to Chicago's primary Puerto Rican barrio, which is part of the Humboldt Park neighborhood.

Source: Eric Mathiasen.

Chicago in the Twenty-First Century

Between 1960 and 2000, Chicago suffered a population loss of some 600,000 people, suggesting that it was in decline like other Rustbelt cities. In 1990, Los Angeles surpassed Chicago's falling population, displacing Chicago from its century-old status as the nation's second largest city. The Los Angeles School of Sociology, which emphasized a multinodal view of metropolitan areas, also challenged the supremacy of the Chicago School's downtown-centered approach to understanding urban space.

Nonetheless, Chicago remained a vital part of the metropolitan region and the United States in the twenty-first century. Mayor Richard M. Daley (1989–) paid special attention to maintaining Chicago as an international tourist destination, consolidating the lakefront park and museum campus and launching a bid for the city to host the 2016 Olympics. Large numbers of Latina/o and Asian migrants revitalized commerce in older neighborhoods on the city's North and West Sides. The city finally sent its first president to the White House in 2009, when former community organizer Barack Obama was inaugurated the country's first African American president. Although Chicago is no longer growing as it had in the boom years of the late nineteenth century, it continues to muscle its "big shoulders" around the world.

Amanda I. Seligman

See also Alinsky, Saul; Chicago School of Urban Sociology; City Beautiful Movement; City Planning; Community Organizing; Ghetto; Housing Policy; Local Government; Multicultural Cities; Neighborhood Revitalization; Parks; Political Machine; Racialization; Redlining; Restrictive Covenant; Sewer; Shopping; Suburbanization; Subway; Tenement; Tourism; Transportation; Urban Crisis; Urban Ecology (Chicago School); Urban History; Urban Planning

Further Readings

Condit, Carl W. 1973. *Chicago, 1910–1929: Building, Planning and Urban Technology*. Chicago: University of Chicago Press.
———. 1974. *Chicago, 1930–70: Building, Planning, and Urban Technology*. Chicago: University of Chicago Press.
Cronon, William. 1991. *Nature's Metropolis: Chicago and the Great West*. New York: Norton.
Drake, St. Clair and Horace R. Cayton. 1945. *Black Metropolis: A Study of Negro Life in a Northern City*. Chicago: University of Chicago Press.
Grossman, James R., Ann Durkin Keating, and Janice L. Reiff. 2004. *The Encyclopedia of Chicago*. Chicago: University of Chicago Press.
Hirsch, Arnold R. 1983. *Making the Second Ghetto: Race & Housing in Chicago, 1940–1960*. Cambridge, UK: Cambridge University Press.
Keating, Ann Durkin. 2005. *Chicagoland: City and Suburbs in the Railroad Age*. Chicago: University of Chicago Press.
Mayer, Harold M. and Richard C. Wade. 1969. *Chicago: Growth of a Metropolis*. Chicago: University of Chicago Press.
Pierce, Bessie Louise. 1937–1957. *A History of Chicago*. 3 vols. New York: Knopf.
Royko, Mike. 1971. *Boss: Richard J. Daley of Chicago*. New York: Signet.

CHICAGO SCHOOL OF URBAN SOCIOLOGY

The Chicago School of Urban Sociology refers to work of faculty and graduate students from the University of Chicago during the period 1915 to 1945 and, more directly, to the work of students who studied under Robert Park and Ernest Burgess during those years. This small group of scholars— the full-time faculty in the department of sociology never numbered more than six persons—developed a new theoretical model and research methodology using the city of Chicago as a social laboratory in a conscious effort to create a distinctive field of study within the social sciences (the title of Park and Burgess's 1921 textbook was *Introduction to the Science of Sociology*). The Chicago School defined the contours of urban sociology for much of the twentieth century, most clearly in the contributions of urban ecology and applied research within the urban environment, and continues to influence urban studies in the United States and beyond (note the many references to the Chicago School and to individual scholars associated with the Chicago School in many entries in this encyclopedia).

Origins and Founders

The origin of the Chicago School of Urban Sociology—the first such department in the United

States—is intimately associated with that of the university itself, which was founded in 1890 as a research university modeled after Johns Hopkins University and Clark University. The Chicago School of the period discussed here is represented by three generations of faculty. Albion Small (founder of the department), W. I. Thomas, Charles R. Henderson, Graham Taylor, and George E. Vincent comprised the founding generation. The second included Small, Thomas, Burgess, Ellsworth Faris, and Park. It was this group that trained the graduate students who would write what Mary Jo Deegan has called the "Chicago School Studies." The third generation included Park, Burgess, Louis Wirth, and William Ogburn. This group of faculty would remain intact until Park retired from the university in 1934.

Although it is common to date the origin of urban sociology at Chicago with Park's arrival in 1914 and his subsequent work with Burgess, the idea of the city as a laboratory for social research came much earlier. Henderson applied for research funds for a systematic study of the city in the first decade of the twentieth century, and a 1902 description of the graduate program published in the *American Journal of Sociology* stated that

> the city of Chicago is one of the most complete social laboratories in the world. While the elements of sociology may be studied in smaller communities . . . the most serious problems of modern society are presented by the great cities, and must be studied as they are encountered in concrete form in large populations. No city in the world presents a wider variety of typical social problems than Chicago.

The overlooked figure in the founding of the Chicago School is Thomas, whom Small recruited from the University of Tennessee. Trained in anthropology, Thomas arrived at Chicago with an extensive publication record. In 1912 Thomas was invited to attend the International Conference on the Negro at Tuskegee Institute, organized by Park in his capacity as personal secretary to Booker T. Washington. Park and Thomas corresponded regularly over the next year, and Thomas invited Park to come to the University of Chicago to teach (although there was no guarantee of a full-time teaching position). Burgess, Park, and Wirth shared a common intellectual approach influenced by William James, John Dewey, and George Herbert

Mead (Park and Thomas studied with James, Burgess and Thomas with Mead, and Park with Dewey). Thomas was dismissed from the university in 1918 following a scandal over his involvement with the pacifist groups opposing U.S. involvement in World War I. The classic study of immigration, *Old World Traits Transplanted*, published in 1921 with Park as first author, was largely written by Thomas; Park later wrote that Thomas's work formed the foundation for the department.

Research Methods and Topics

The sociology faculty pioneered empirical research using a variety of methods, ranging from ethnography (Park) to the use of the personal document (Thomas). Park's observations of the city were borrowed from the natural sciences: Competition and segregation led to formation of *natural areas*, each with separate and distinct *moral order*. The city was "a mosaic of little worlds that touch but do not interpenetrate." Burgess's model for the growth of the city showed a central business district surrounded by concentric zones labeled the zone in transition, the zone of workingmen's homes, the residential zone, and the commuter zone. Roderick McKenzie expanded the basic model of human ecology in his later study of the metropolitan community.

The extensive research and publication program of the Chicago School was supported by more than $600,000 from the Laura Spellman Rockefeller Memorial Fund from 1924 to 1934. The research was carried out under the auspices of Local Community Research Committee, an interdisciplinary group that included faculty and graduate students from sociology, political science (Charles Merriam), and anthropology (Robert Redfield). Graduate students mapped local community areas and studied the spatial organization of juvenile delinquency, family disorganization, and cultural life in the city. The resulting studies represent a diverse array of studies broadly organized around the themes of urban institutions (the hotel, taxi dance hall), social disorganization (juvenile delinquency, the homeless man), and natural areas themselves. Among the notable Chicago School studies are Frederick Thrasher, *The Gang* (1926); Louis Wirth, *The Ghetto* (1928); Harvey W. Zorbaugh, *The Gold Coast and the Slum* (1929); Clifford S. Shaw, *The Jackroller* (1930); E. Franklin Frazier, *The Negro Family in Chicago* (1932); Paul

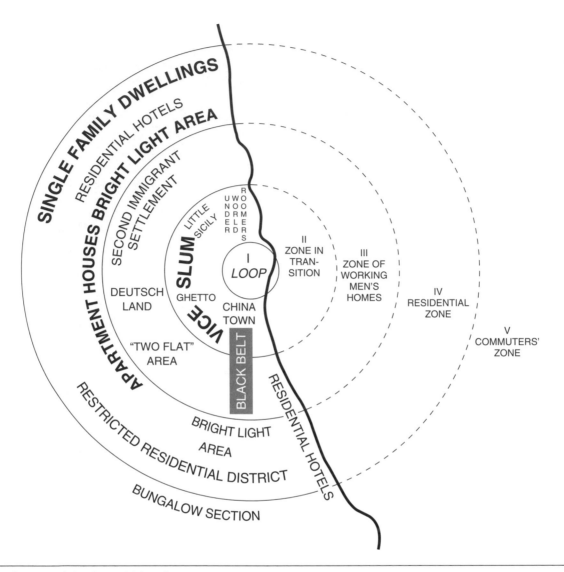

Figure I   Growth of the City—Urban Areas

Source: Adapted from Ernest W. Burgess. 1925. "The Growth of the City: An Introduction to a Research Project." In Robert E. Park and Ernest W. Burgess, *The City*, page 55. Chicago: University of Chicago Press.

G. Cressey, *The Taxi-Dance Hall* (1932); and Walter C. Reckless, *Vice in Chicago* (1933).

The Chicago School dominated urban sociology and sociology more generally in the first half of the twentieth century. By 1950 some 200 students had completed graduate study at the University of Chicago. Many were instrumental in establishing graduate programs in sociology across the country, and more than half of the presidents of the American Sociological Association were faculty or students at Chicago. The *American Journal of Sociology*, started by Small in 1895, was the official journal of the American Sociological Association from 1906 to 1935. The dominance of the Chicago School also generated antagonism,

and a "minor rebellion" at the annual conference in 1935 would result in the founding of a new journal, the *American Sociological Review*, which published its first volume in 1936.

Critical Opposition

Early critiques of the Chicago School included Missa Alihan's (1938) extensive critique of human ecology (Park wrote that "on the whole" the criticisms were correct), and Maurice Davie (1938) reanalyzed data from Clifford Shaw's *Delinquency Areas* (1929) and showed that delinquency was associated with areas of physical deterioration and high immigrant populations—and not in the concentric zone model used in the Chicago studies. Burgess's concentric zones were soon replaced by a variety of models showing multiple nuclei and eventually the decentralized, polycentered city. Still, urban ecology remains the dominant model and method among urban sociologists in the United States, in no small part because of the extensive funding opportunities for demographic and census research.

Chicago sociology, and the Chicago sociologists, was also criticized for the lack of critical engagement with contemporary social and political issues, and it is striking that labor history, housing conditions, and the like did not figure more importantly in their work. But Thomas and Wirth were involved in the pacifist movement that arose during World War I, and Wirth would later serve as host of the University of Chicago roundtable discussions broadcast on NBC radio network from 1938 until his death. Charles S. Johnson, Park's student and later president of Fisk University, was the author of the report by the Chicago Race Commission on the deadly race riots in 1919. Another of Park's students, Ernest T. Hiller, completed a dissertation that was published as *The Strike* in 1928. But the Chicago School focus on the natural history of urban neighborhoods left out an institutional analysis of the possible causes of these problems, all the more striking because of the involvement of many students and faculty in social movements and struggles of the day.

Deegan has argued that the contribution of women associated with the Hull House settlement was marginalized by Park and other male faculty. Jane Addams's Hull House had conducted early community studies, including the influential *Hull House Maps and Papers: A Presentation of Nationalities and Wages in a Congested District of Chicago* (1895). Edith Abbott was a part-time instructor in the department, and Addams had been offered a part-time position. Many of the Chicago faculty were involved with Hull House and other social reform movements: Graham Taylor was one of the early members of the department. Burgess noted that systematic urban research at Chicago began with the Hull House, and many of the early graduate students used the settlement houses to assist their research (several, including Thrasher and Wirth, had early training as social workers). In 1908 the School of Civics and Philanthropy (later the School of Social Service Administration) was started at the Chicago Commons under the leadership of Graham Taylor, and in 1920 the school was moved to the University of Chicago.

Legacy

Some have argued for a second (or even third) Chicago School, although there has not been the systematic and ongoing study of urban neighborhoods that characterize the earlier work. Still, the influence of the classic studies may be seen in several community studies directed by Morris Janowitz and Gerald Suttles in the 1970s and 1980s, and in the continuing urban ethnographies of Elijah Anderson and Mitch Duneier. William Julius Wilson's work on poverty neighborhoods in 1980–1995 once again made use of the city as a social laboratory, including a sustained program of training for graduate students, but Wilson would leave for Harvard University before this research agenda was completed. The Chicago School of Urban Sociology has not had lasting influence of work of the department.

Although the focus here is on the Chicago School of Urban Sociology, there are claims to various other Chicago schools in architecture, crime and delinquency, ethnic studies, political science, symbolic interaction, and other fields. The more general use of the city as a social laboratory across the disciplines in summarized in *The University and the City: A Centennial View of the University of Chicago: The Urban Laboratory* (1992).

The Chicago School would seem not to have stood up well against the claim of the Los Angeles School that whereas Chicago was the model for the industrial city of the twentieth century, Los Angeles is the model for the postindustrial city of the twenty-first century. First presented in the introduction to a 1986 special issue of the journal *Society and Space,* in which Allen Scott and Edward Soja referred to Los Angeles as the "capital of the twentieth century," edited volumes titled *The City: Los Angeles and Urban Theory at the End of the Twentieth City* (1996) and *From Chicago to LA: Making Sense of Urban Theory* (2001) directly challenged the work of the Chicago School (*The City* is the title of a volume edited by Burgess, Park, and McKenzie in 1925). This has largely been a one-sided fight, as the subjects of the attack are long gone from the scene, and few have stepped up to defend the Chicago School. It is worth noting that while the recent scholarship has been self-styled as the Los Angeles School of Urban Studies, the Chicago School of Urban Sociology was just one of many such research programs that used the city as a laboratory.

Ray Hutchison

See also Chicago, Illinois; Human Ecology; Los Angeles School of Urban Studies; New Urban Sociology; Urban Sociology; Urban Theory

Further Readings

Abbott, A. 1999. *Department and Discipline: Chicago Sociology at One Hundred.* Chicago: University of Chicago Press.

Becker, H. S. 1999. "The Chicago School, So-Called." *Qualitative Sociology* 22(1):3–12.

Blumer, M. 1984. *The Chicago School of Sociology: Institutionalization, Diversity, and the Rise of Sociological Research.* Chicago: University of Chicago Press.

Deegan, M. J. 1986. *Jane Addams and the Men of the Chicago School, 1892–1918.* New Brunswick NJ: Transaction Books.

———. 2007. "The Chicago School of Ethnography." Pp. 11–25 in *Handbook of Ethnography*, edited by P. A. Atkinson, S. Delamont, A. Coffey, J. Lofland, and L. Lofland. Thousand Oaks, CA: Sage.

Faris, R. E. L. 1970. *Chicago Sociology, 1920–32.* Chicago: University of Chicago Press.

Kurtz, L. R. 1984. *Evaluating Chicago Sociology: A Guide to the Literature, with an Annotated Bibliography.* Chicago: University of Chicago Press.

Manella, Gabriele. 2008. *Nuovi scenari urbani: La sociologia del territorio negli USA oggi.* Milan: Franco Angeli.

Matthews, F. H. 1977. *Quest for an American Sociology: Robert E. Park and the Chicago School.* Montreal, Quebec, Canada: McGill-Queen's University Press.

Short, J. F., ed. 1971. *The Social Fabric of the Metropolis: Contributions of the Chicago School of Urban Sociology.* Chicago: University of Chicago Press.

The University of Chicago Centennial Catalogues. n.d. *The University and the City: A Centennial View of the University of Chicago. The Urban Laboratory.* Retrieved April 9, 2009 (http://www.lib.uchicago.edu/projects/centcat/centcats/city/citych3_01.html).

CHILDE, V. GORDON

V. Gordon Childe (1892–1957) was the most influential archaeologist of the twentieth century. His model of "the urban revolution" was a major contribution to scholarly understanding of the earliest cities. Childe's career began with excavations and publications on European prehistory in the 1920s. In the 1930s he turned to synthesis on a larger scale. Until this time, the conceptual approach of archaeologists was focused rather narrowly on chronology and technology. Childe was the first to apply explicit and theoretically grounded social interpretations to archaeological data, producing novel (and influential) syntheses of prehistory. Using a Marxist approach, Childe identified two fundamental social transformations in the human past: the neolithic revolution and the urban revolution. The first signaled the initial adoption of agriculture and a sedentary lifestyle, and the second the appearance of the earliest class-structured state societies. These two transitions occurred independently in several parts of the world, but Childe's publications emphasized the Near East, the scene of their earliest manifestations.

Childe initially described the neolithic and urban revolutions in his 1936 book, *Man Makes Himself.* He went on to discuss the two models in other books for the public and in technical archaeological articles. They were quickly adopted, debated, and expanded by other archaeologists, and they formed the basis for most subsequent archaeological thinking on these transformations. Although contemporary models are quite different from Childe's original formulations, there is general agreement that he correctly identified the most far-reaching social transformations prior to the Industrial Revolution, as well as some of the major processes involved in those changes.

V. Gordon Childe's model of the urban revolution was presented in its clearest form as a 10-point scheme in an influential article in *Town Planning Review* in 1950. It is important to note that "urban revolution" was a label for the broad transformation or evolution of nonhierarchical societies into state-level societies. The appearance of cities was an important part of the model, but this was not a model of urban origins narrowly conceived. Childe's presentation of the urban revolution model in the 1950 paper took the form of a list of 10 characteristics that set the earliest states apart from their earlier ancestors. They can be paraphrased as follows:

1. Large population and large settlements (cities)
2. Full-time specialization and advanced division of labor
3. Production of an agricultural surplus to fund government and a differentiated society

4. Monumental public architecture
5. A ruling class
6. Writing
7. Exact and predictive sciences (arithmetic, geometry, astronomy, calendars)
8. Sophisticated art styles
9. Long-distance trade
10. The state

Some writers have called this is a simple checklist that lacks consideration of social and historical processes. Most archaeologists, however, see the dynamic and functional aspects of the model as implicit in Childe's discussion, and they are treated more fully in his other works. In fact, Childe's model forms the basis for virtually all subsequent theorizing of the rise of the earliest states and cities. In today's complex systems models of state origins, Childe's factor numbers 1, 2, 3, 5, and 10 are still regarded as crucial processes involved in the urban revolution.

Michael E. Smith

See also Ancient Cities; Mumford, Lewis

Further Readings

Childe, V. Gordon. 1936. *Man Makes Himself.* London: Watts.
———. 1950. "The Urban Revolution." *Town Planning Review* 21:3–17.
Smith, Michael E. Forthcoming. "V. Gordon Childe and the Urban Revolution: A Historical Perspective on a Revolution in Urban Studies." *Town Planning Review.*

CHINATOWNS

Chinatowns are spaces within a city that represent a culture distinct from the majority culture of the host society. They are a global phenomenon historically founded in major urban areas, conceived of as housing large communities of overseas Chinese immigrants. Although popularly known in many North American and European cities, they are as common in cities in every region, particularly in Southeast Asia, Australia, and South America.

Kay Anderson has described Chinatown as a concept that, like race, belongs to "White" European cultural traditions. As such, Chinatown is seen as a social construction that reflects the perceptions of White Europeans based on racial classification of the Chinese. This classification system serves to differentiate self and other, and creates insiders and outsiders. The resulting categories further create different kinds of places and imaginations within the urban landscape. While the creation of this classification of a single Chinese identity, or "Chineseness," is not solely the result of Western imperialism, there is a sense of a shared characterization put forth by both the Chinese community and the European society. According to Rey Chow, Chinatowns are also landscapes produced through Chinese diasporas, which tend to reproduce upon themselves imaginations and identities created by the effects of Western imperialism and cultural hegemony. The creation of "Chineseness" and prevalent images in the landscapes of Chinatown that appear in the West are mutually created by both the Chinese and the Europeans, oriental and occidental, insider and outsider.

The significance of these joint insider–outsider productions of essentialized identities of people and places is that Chinatowns are geographical imaginations. While these imaginations are often based on imaginary concepts of what China is like, it is more often a representation—and, arguably, a homogenization, of migrant Chinese culture.

In the mid-nineteenth century, cities like Vancouver, British Columbia, and San Francisco, California, attracted a massive immigration of cheap Chinese labor due to railway building and mining developments. The large Chinese communities eventually settled in discrete parts of the cities, creating Chinatowns. In many parts of Southeast Asia, Chinese immigration occurred as early as the seventeenth century, as merchants and traders dominated the economic landscape of growing maritime cities such as Bangkok, Manila, and Singapore. This would eventually burgeon into large migrant working communities with the advent of European colonization in the region. The rapidly developing cities attracted unskilled laborers from the southern regions of China. Initially, the overseas Chinese were commonly thought of as sojourners, transient labor with the intention of returning to China. However, most of the migrant workers settled at their destinations and carved out sections of the cities for themselves.

Chinatowns are imagined to be reproductions of the same place all over the world. In spite of a

Chinatown in London's West End

Source: Karen Wiley.

created an image of the Chinese as wealthy and of Chinatown as an expensive neighborhood. This is not the case in North America, where the overwhelming majority of the original Chinese settlers were hired as cheap labor, who would contribute to the resulting image of Chinatown as run-down parts of the city with low rent.

Differing interactions with host societies can be seen in the assimilation of the Chinese into the local communities. This has happened at a high rate, for many different reasons, in many of the Southeast Asian cities like Singapore, Ho Chi Minh City, and Bangkok. The Chinese in Bangkok are deeply involved in Thai politics. In the case of Singapore, the ethnic Chinese make up the majority population, prompting state-led claims of "racial harmony." However, in the cities of North America, Australia, and the United Kingdom, the Chinese were seen as "unassimilable foreigners." Chinatown developed as a defensive strategy as the host society endeavored to separate "us" from "them," and the Chinese insulated themselves out of unfamiliarity and fear. This has created a tension that still exists, but in Canadian and Australian cities today, the presence of the Chinese is a marker of "multiculturalism." Although this appears to bring similarity to separate and distinct Chinatowns, the underlying power and social relations between the Chinese and host communities demonstrate very localized and regional differences.

Location

Although initially located in the inner city as a result of age and urban history, Chinatowns are undergoing a process of suburbanization. The increasing occurrence of Chinese enclaves outside

common cultural background and source nationality, Chinatowns are predicated upon similar identities and reactions to the other, but have essential differences, based on their geographical localities. The major factors of these differences are the communities' initial migration motives and their interactions with their host societies. Differing migration motives have resulted in the divergent natures of the Chinatowns in Southeast Asia compared with those in North America. Many of the Chinese settlers in Southeast Asia set up and ran businesses, forming a large upper-middle class. The effect of this in cities like Rangoon and Kuala Lumpur has of downtown cores is indicative of the growing social mobility of the ethnic Chinese population. In Toronto, large Chinese communities in the suburbs of Markham and Richmond Hill have paved the way for "new" Chinatowns. These are centered on large shopping malls that provide culturally specific goods and services and serve a largely Asian audience. The goods and services are not only Chinese in nature, source, or manufacture, but also include Japanese, Korean, and Thai, among others.

Sites of Difference

The movement of Chinese communities to the outskirts of cities indicates the changing nature of Chinatowns in general. Their internal demographics also are changing: Chinatowns are increasingly populated by other East and Southeast Asian immigrants as many of the older ethnic Chinese have moved away to wealthier sections of the city. Chinatowns are sites of difference. Ethnic enclaves represent difference in the nature of race, ethnicity, nationality, and social and migrant status. The development of Chinatown is markedly different from that of other ethnic enclaves given the nature of the communities' initial migration and settlement. Particular to the Chinese is the male-dominated society of the early migrant force, caused by the nature of their work: railway building and mining. The great imbalance in sex ratio in the cities of particularly Canada and the United States resulted in a greatly differing social structure.

The marked difference between the suburban and downtown Chinatowns is in their representation of socioeconomic difference. As downtown Chinatowns are associated with perceptions of poverty, marginalization, and the earlier ethnic community, suburban Chinatowns are disassociated from this image and usually represent communities that have achieved not only a higher economic status but also a certain level of residency and citizenship. Related to this, downtown Chinatowns are further typified as the receiving locales for new immigrants. In many North American cities now, the new immigrants to Chinatown are not only Chinese, but encompass other East and Southeast Asian nationalities in growing proportion.

As racial and ethnic sites of difference within the city, Chinatowns are often delineated by a markedly different demographic in comparison with the rest of their urban settings. However, the idea that only Chinese people live in Chinatown is a contrived one. Cities are intrinsically places of intense diversity, and even enclaves like Chinatowns can be no different. The movement of Chinese communities to the outskirts of cities indicates the changing nature of Chinatowns. Internal demographics are changing; Chinatowns are increasingly populated by other East and Southeast Asian immigrants as many of the older ethnic Chinese have moved away to wealthier sections of the city.

Common Imagery

The image of Chinatown is commonly likened to a "combat zone," "red-light district," or African American "ghetto"—districts of crime and social problems. Another common perception is the image of an exotic foreign enclave. Chinatowns are often imagined as places of vice, owing to the concentration of gambling dens and opium parlors in the early days. The rundown, ghetto imagery of the Chinese neighborhoods is also related to the low levels of hygiene and high incidences of illness. This was, in many cases, due to the development of the enclaves on undesirable land, usually on low-lying, flood-prone, marshy sections of the city. Further, the close conditions that many of the Chinese lived in contributed to the transmission of many sicknesses. These imaginations are reinforced by fictitious re-creations in the media, for example, in the film noir *Chinatown* with its psychological mystery plot, despite the fact the film is about public corruption in Los Angeles, and not about Chinatown at all.

These popular imaginations are often overlooked in occurrences of Chinatowns outside of the West—in major cities like Bangkok in Thailand and Nagasaki in Japan, for example; as well as in the reality that such Chinatowns are often simply places of businesses dominated by the Chinese. Further examples include Vancouver's Chinatown, managed by a Business Improvement Association, and the Singapore Tourism Board, which oversees the development of Chinatown with the Chinatown Business Association. The contrast between the oft-imagined seedy underworld and the actuality of business- and tourism-oriented Chinatowns is due largely to the lingering effects of the sensationalized journalistic reporting that burgeoned in the late nineteenth century.

In many places, the forms, formats, and functions of Chinatowns are changing. Chinatowns have developed in stages. From the early days of low-priced immigrant housing and cultural-specific business, to the abandonment and incorporation of other ethnic groups, many Chinatowns are now experiencing gentrification, as cities—realizing the value inherent in heritage and cultural tourism—rebuild, enhance, and preserve the Chinese cultures that once dominated the place. While the culturally and nationally specific placename of "Chinatown" remains, the particular character of overseas Chinese culture has decreased. In cities such as Singapore, this reduction has been rectified through heritage preservation, gentrification, and, some would argue, Disneyfication. This has resulted in a sterile parody of what was once a complex and multilayered cultural landscape.

Main Texts and Existing Literature

Research on Chinatowns was brought into the forefront with both David Chuenyan Lai's book *Chinatowns: Towns Within Cities in Canada* (1988) and Kay Anderson's *Vancouver's Chinatown: Racial Discourse in Canada, 1875–1980* (1991). Peter Kwong's *The New Chinatown* (1988); Min Zhou's *Chinatown: The Socioeconomic Potential of an Urban Enclave* (1992); Jan Lin's *Reconstructing Chinatown: Ethnic Enclave, Global Change* (1998)—all three use New York's Chinatown as case studies. Gregor Benton and Frank Pieke's edited book *The Chinese in Europe* (1998) and Flemming Christiansen's *Chinatown, Europe* (2003) are also fundamental texts about Chinatowns. The situation of these studies in North America and Europe indicates conspicuously the lack of Chinatown-related studies outside of the western hemisphere.

Studies of Chinatown are commonly contextualized within the cultural, the urban, and the economic. There are two pertinent trends in the existing literature. The first is that much of the literature approaches Chinatowns from a racial and/or ethnic perspective, frequently in the context of migration, and the second is that almost all of it focuses on Chinatowns in Europe or in North America. Little has been written about Chinatowns beyond their appearance in the western hemisphere, particularly in Asia. There are also a few studies on the urban development (often in terms of gentrification or tourism) and economics of Chinatown (generally concerning business relations and Sino-global networks). Much has been written about ethnic enclaves in general, and Chinatowns in particular, in Western cities, from the point of view of racial discourse, issues of transnationalism and Chinese diaspora, urban spaces and city planning, and as economic networks facilitating the social mobility of immigrants in a foreign society.

Much less has been said about Chinatown as an ethnic enclave in the "Orient," in the form of left-over bordered racial communities in once colonized, postcolonial cities such as those in Southeast Asia, for example, in Singapore or Manila. Much of the existing literature in the Asian context focuses on the Chinese diaspora (e.g., Michael Charney et al. and Elizabeth Sinn); and Brenda Yeoh and Lily Kong have situated studies on Chinatown in Singapore on the topic of landscape and landscape meanings, demonstrating that spaces of difference in Asian societies are uniquely constructed and maintained. From a cultural approach, Katharyne Mitchell has explained that much of the research on "ethnictowns" like Chinatown, Koreatown, and Japantown have studied either the development of the ethnic community itself or the structural forces of racism and European hegemony that shaped these communities. The existing research has focused on the factors and histories leading to the creation and growth of the enclave and grappled with transnational effects on culture and how urban centers deal with the beginnings of multiethnicity.

Serene K. Tan

See also Ethnic Enclave; Ethnic Entrepreneurship; Global City; Racialization

Further Readings

Anderson, K. J. 1991. *Vancouver's Chinatown: Racial Discourse in Canada, 1875–1980.* Montreal, Quebec, Canada: McGill-Queen's University Press.

Benton, G. and F. N. Pieke, eds. 1998. *The Chinese in Europe.* New York: St. Martin's.

Charney, Michael W., Tong Chee Kiong, and Brenda S. A. Yeoh, eds. 2003. *Chinese Migrants Abroad.* Singapore: Singapore University Press.

Christiansen, F. 2003. *Chinatown, Europe: An Exploration of the European Chinese towards the Beginning of the Twenty-first Century.* London: RoutledgeCurzon.

Kincaid, G. 1992. *Chinatown: Portrait of a Closed Society.* New York: HarperCollins.

Kwong, P. 1996. *The New Chinatown.* New York: Hill and Wang.

Lin, J. 1998. *Reconstructing Chinatown: Ethnic Enclave, Global Change.* Minneapolis: University of Minnesota Press.

Ma, L. J. C. and C. Cartier, eds. 2003. *The Chinese Diaspora: Space, Place, Mobility, and Identity.* Lanham, MD: Rowman and Littlefield.

Sinn, E., ed. 1998. *The Last Half Century of Chinese Overseas.* Hong Kong, China: Hong Kong University Press.

Yeoh, B. S. A. and L. Kong. 1996. "The Notion of Place in the Construction of History, Nostalgia and Heritage in Singapore." *Singapore Journal of Tropical Geography* 17(1):52–56.

Zhou, M. 1992. *Chinatown: The Socioeconomic Potential of an Urban Enclave.* Philadelphia: Temple University Press.

CHRISTOPHER WREN, PLAN OF LONDON

Sir Christopher Wren's plan for London after the Great Fire of 1666 (Figure 1), preserved in two drawings (All Souls I. 7 and 101), constitutes his only, and never implemented, work of urban design. Presented to the king just five days after the fire had ended, Wren's design was to solve the deplorable problems, recognized for decades, that had developed within the medieval city as the result of drastic social changes. Furthermore, he proposed to do so in a new way. Disasters had occurred in cities before, wiping clean large areas—in the case of the Great Fire, it destroyed two thirds of the city's rundown, crowded, and unsanitary fabric. But instead of rebuilding the city as it had been before, Wren presented a new idea—to create a completely new design of streets and buildings on the original site.

At least six new plans for London were produced during the weeks following the fire: first by Wren, then by his close friends John Evelyn and Robert Hooke, followed by the city surveyor Robert Mills (now lost), the surveyor and map-maker Richard Newcourt, and Captain Valentine Knight. Hooke's and Newcourt's proposals for a grid of straight streets creating uniform blocks over the destroyed area, with no regard to what had been lost or what had survived, were derived from ideal city designs found in Italian architectural treatises and from new towns recently constructed on the continent. Wren's and Evelyn's proposals for wide diagonal and radiating avenues coming together as *triviums* or *rond-points,* where major urban spaces or buildings are placed, were inspired by the Rome of Sixtus V (1580s), by the new *places* of Paris created under Henry IV (1605–1610), and the gardens of André Le Nôtre (1650s–1660s). Rather than ideal, as shown by the discourse titled *Londinium Redivivum* attached by Evelyn to his plan, he and Wren were very much concerned about the earlier conditions. Using the available but inaccurate maps of the city as base plans—Newcourt's of 1658 (Wren) and Hollar's of 1666 (Evelyn)—they generally maintained the location of major streets, joining them into surviving streets and gates. Major monuments, including St. Paul's, the Exchange, the Custom House, as well as many of the churches remained in their original locations.

Wren's plan, a sensitive adaptation of continental ideas to the original pattern of the destroyed city, was seriously considered at the House of Commons soon after the fire and as late as February 1667. To make the plan feasible, it proposed that all the ground be purchased by the city and placed in trust while the new streets were laid out. Then individual sites would be sold, giving preference to former owners. In the end, however, many factors stood in the way—lack of money, the cumbersome legislative process, and suspicious property owners. The lack of an accurate and detailed survey and map meant that Wren's design could not be finalized and implemented immediately—haste was essential to prevent the migration of inhabitants and their business. In fact, it took more than five years after the Rebuilding Act was passed in late March 1667 for Hooke to complete the survey of the ruins and properties, as well as the negotiations with owners over "lost ground." This slow and difficult process made reconstructing the original fabric the only option. There were, however, a few

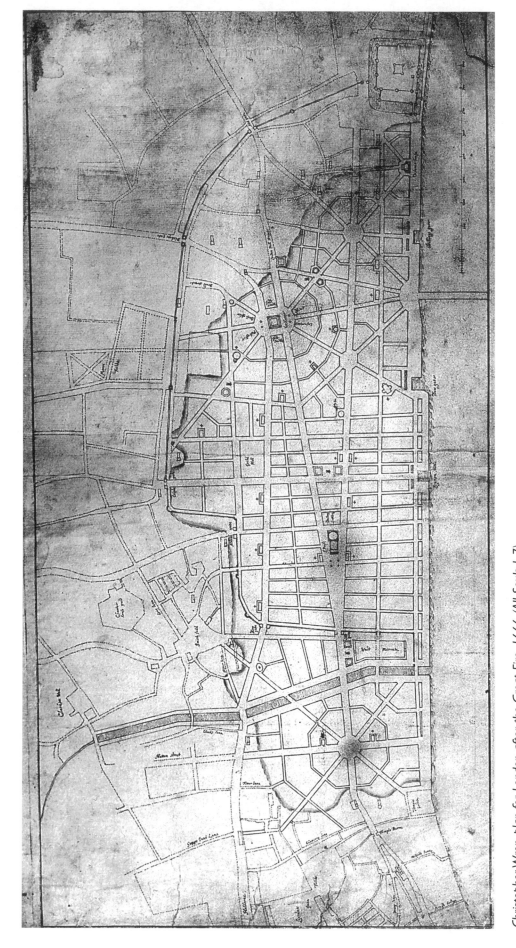

Christopher Wren, plan for London after the Great Fire, 1666 (All Souls I.7).

Source: Warden and Fellows of All Souls College, Oxford. Used with permission.

major changes—the widening of major streets; the creation of two new north–south streets, King and Queen; and the establishing of new, off-street market spaces—all ideas initially proposed by Wren and Evelyn.

Although Wren's plan for London was never implemented, it was disseminated through numerous engravings beginning in 1724 and continuing through the eighteenth century, including a French version in 1758. Thus, as a visionary project, Wren's 1666 plan for London may have had an important influence on the designs of capital cities, including L'Enfant's Washington, D.C. (1791), and Haussmann's Paris (1853–1870).

Lydia M. Soo

See also Haussmann, Baron Georges-Eugène; London, United Kingdom; Paris, France; Urban Planning; Wren, Sir Christopher

Further Readings

Cooper, Michael. 2003. *"A More Beautiful City": Robert Hooke and the Rebuilding of London after the Great Fire.* Thrupp, UK: Sutton.

Evelyn, John. 1938. *London Revived: Considerations for Its Rebuilding in 1666,* edited by E. S. de Beer. Oxford, UK: Clarendon.

Reddaway, Thomas F. 1940. *The Rebuilding of London after the Great Fire.* London: Jonathan Cape.

Soo, Lydia M. Forthcoming. "A Baroque City? London after the Great Fire of 1666." In *Giambattista Nolli, Rome and Mapping: Before and after the Pianta Grande,* edited by I. Verstegen and A. Ceen. Rome: Gangemi.

CINEMA (MOVIE HOUSE)

A cinema or movie house is a public site where motion pictures are exhibited to a paying public. Movie house architecture, audience composition, and filmic entertainment have changed dramatically since the first storefront theaters were opened in the earliest years of the twentieth century. However, in almost all of its manifestations, the cinema has been a vital element of urban life. The cinema can be viewed as a portal for understanding the various developmental cadences of urban

centers, as well as the pursuits of leisure for working- and middle-class city dwellers during the twentieth century.

Film was the first mediated popular entertainment. From a local perspective, the development of the motion picture projector enabled films to be exhibited to large groups of people who were often strangers to one another. They sat together in one room or hall and watched either a portion of a film or an entire motion picture simultaneously. From a national perspective, the mass distribution of motion pictures created the conditions for audiences across a large geographic region, or even an entire country, to view the same motion picture nearly simultaneously. These conditions helped to create an urban identity, constructed around the pursuit of leisure and visual entertainment.

As both cities and the movie industry changed and grew, so did the movie houses that projected motion pictures. During the first few years of the twentieth century, for example, when the motion picture industry was still in its infancy, motion pictures were not projected in movie houses at all. They were exhibited in vaudeville theaters, as only part of the evening's entertainment, or they were exhibited in storefronts; entrepreneurs purchased motion picture projectors, chairs, and makeshift screens and opened for business. As the motion picture industry matured and as films grew more sophisticated and longer in length, the movie house in its earliest manifestation was born.

Nickelodeon

The nickelodeon was a gathering place for urban immigrants and the working class and the first successful expression of the movie house. It was the predominant movie house form from approximately 1905 to 1917. Generally situated in working-class neighborhoods, on side streets where rent was cheap, but in close proximity to popular shopping areas, the nickelodeon served as a gathering place for the working class. On the way home from work, factory workers would congregate at the nickelodeon, and women, children, and entire families used the nickelodeon as a way to enjoy public life. The humble conditions of the inexpensive movie house frequently paralleled the realities of working-class life. While the quality of both the films and the movie houses was generally poor, the movies were well enjoyed by patrons. The nickelodeon provided an inexpensive public space for newly arrived immigrants and other working-class urban dwellers. The burgeoning urban middle class, particularly in the United States, found both the films and the nickelodeons to be unacceptably vulgar and crude.

The Movie Palace

The movie palace (picture palace) is an urban phenomenon. Its development and popularity coincided with the maturity of both the motion picture industry and the twentieth-century city. While various expressions of the nickelodeon appeared in rural areas and small towns, movie palaces were so large in scale that only populated urban areas could accommodate them. Although in general, picture palaces were built only during the second decade of the twentieth century, they were the predominant movie theater form until the mid-twentieth century.

The construction and opening of a picture palace, often the most expensive and opulent structure in a city center, marked the moment when a city and its inhabitants had "arrived." Representing the pinnacle of urban development during the boom years of the 1920s, the movie palace was a symbol of cosmopolitanism and sophistication.

Located in prime downtown locations, the theaters were generally situated next to a trolley or streetcar stop and were close to restaurants and department stores, enabling city dwellers to spend their leisure hours and their disposable income in high-traffic commercial areas.

With the arrival in 1915 of multireel films that told compelling narratives using cinematic language, the middle class began to accept film as a form of pleasurable and appropriate public entertainment. The picture palace design was meant to impress and dazzle the middle class, as well as to assure them they were in a reputable public space. Usually built with 2,000 to 5,000 seats or more, the theaters were designed to sell thousands of tickets each day. The picture palace was consciously designed to assure cinema's new audience that motion picture entertainment was held to the highest standards. All working-class signifiers were eliminated, and a brigade of ushers assured audiences that appropriate behavior was enforced.

Elaborate architectural details often simulated designs of European palaces, Far East temples, and castles from other exotic locales, fostering an atmosphere of high culture. Most movie palaces in the United States were segregated spaces with upper balconies reserved primarily for African Americans.

Picture palaces lost their audiences due to desegregation, the decline of the urban center, suburbanization, the popularity of television, and the rise of the suburban and drive-in theaters during the late 1950s and 1960s. The theaters fell into disrepair, and many were demolished, as a result of feverish urban renewal. Some survived by showing pornographic and exploitation films. During the 1970s, when the historic preservation movement began to burgeon, picture palaces remaining in city centers were often the first buildings to be considered for restoration.

Neighborhood Movie Houses

Neighborhood movie houses were built for suburbanites who moved away from city centers during the 1950s and 1960s. Dramatically different in scale from the picture palace, the neighborhood theater seated several hundred patrons, had minimal décor, and frequently had two screens. The grandeur of the movie palace was no longer necessary or appropriate: Architectural elements featuring streamlined modern designs were de rigueur and middle-class suburbanites needed no assurances that cinema was an appropriate form of entertainment. The development of the academic study of cinema in the 1970s coincided with some neighborhood theaters being transformed into art houses and exhibiting non-Hollywood and foreign films, particularly in large cities and university towns. The neighborhood theater had to compete with the drive-in theater, which was situated in or near the suburbs and was usually located on a huge parcel of undeveloped land.

Mall Cinema

The neighborhood movie house moved into the suburban mall when mall development proliferated in the 1960s and 1970s. Malls helped further shift the purchasing power and the awareness of the middle class away from the city center. Mall cinemas shared characteristics with the neighborhood movies houses; they were architecturally uninspired and seemed to be designed only to move large amounts of people through them. Yet, in one way they resembled the movie palace; they were situated in high-traffic areas designed to accommodate middle-class consumers. As malls grew, so too did their theaters. Multiple-screen movie theaters offered patrons more cinematic choices and generated more ticket sales for theater owners. The blockbuster film born in the mid-1970s (e.g., *The Exorcist* and *Jaws*) found its home in the mall cinema.

The Multiplex

The multiplex (cineplex) is a cinema with many screens, often as many as 20. The movie industry began to suffer in the 1990s as a result of shifting patterns of middle-class leisure, a multitude of choices for in-home entertainment, and a lull in dynamic movie making. So to improve ticket sales, theater owners looked back to the tactics of picture palace designers and built theaters designed to impress consumers. Although most multiplex designs are not nearly as extravagant as the picture palace, they do incorporate massive murals, architectural designs that suggest a sense of the past, eye-catching lighting, IMAX, entertainment areas for children, cafés with gourmet foods, and places for repose. As urban centers were renovated, lessened of crime, and commercialized in the 1990s, multiplexes became a standard feature of city life once again. However, the multiplex is at home in suburbia as well.

The Boutique

The most recent manifestation of the movie house is the cinema boutique. It is usually a one- or two-screen theater located in a dense urban center. The boutique is part of a movement of new urban living in which creative professionals (who can afford it) live and play near where they work. Often in a renovated building, the boutique first appeared in the late 1990s and early 2000s. Its popularity is, in part, a response to the mass appeal of the cineplex and the blockbuster film. The boutique suggests a sense of refinement, exclusion, and high culture by way of its exhibition of independent and foreign films, small environs, stylish design, and gourmet offerings.

Janna Jones

See also Cinematic Urbanism; City and Film; Shopping Center

Further Readings

Jones, Janna. 2003. *The Southern Movie Palace: Rise, Fall, and Resurrection*. Gainesville: University Press of Florida.
Nasaw, David. 1993. *Going Out: The Rise and Fall of Public Amusements*. New York: Basic Books.
Rosenzweig, Roy. 1977. *Eight Hours for What We Will*. New York: Cambridge University Press.
Valentine, Maggie. 1994. *The Show Starts on the Sidewalk: An Architectural History of the Movie Theater, Starring S. Charles Lee*. New Haven, CT: Yale University Press.
Wilinsky, Barbara. 2001. *Sure Seaters: The Emergence of Art House Cinema*. Minneapolis: University of Minnesota Press.

CINEMATIC URBANISM

Cinematic urbanism reflects the increasing interdependence of the processes of image and spatial production in the general frame of the symbolic economy. It is an emerging field of study capturing—in the relation among movement, image, and the city—one essential aspect of modernity, as well as epitomizing the present shift toward any possible postmodernity. There are more ways to understand this term in the current critical discourse, which represent, however, different vantage points from which to observe general processes affecting the urban world. In the main view, cinematic urbanism is a way to analyze the urban environment through the cinematic sphere and to assess how films contribute to the formation of the urban identity. It also can be seen as a way to explore the "imaginary" of emotional geographies, as if to travel toward an urban world plastered with images. From another perspective, cinematic urbanism can be understood as a way to look at the structural transformation of the urban environment endorsed by the pervasiveness of cinematic devices in the information age, analyzing how moving images are increasingly populating spaces and surfaces of contemporary cities and how urban design is increasingly turning into a logistics of perception.

The etymology of the word cinematic is in the Greek verb *kinein,* to move. The essence of the cinematic urbanism is indeed in such relations as movement/image and space/velocity. In this sense, if the premodern urban condition has been one characterized by settlement, intimacy, and a sense of belonging to place and community, modernity has represented a shift toward mobility, crossing, anonymity, and otherness. Modern city, from being the walled, defended site of staying, becomes an attractor of flows, a node in a dynamic system of trajectories, characterized by complex codification of access procedures and sensorial overstimulation. Far before the invention of cinema, it has been the experience of traveling, the view from the train passing through, to modify the perception of landscape and the relation with places. It prefigures annihilation of distance and time compression, along with dominance of the visual perception as the ultimate urban experience. Perhaps the first to clearly capture this passage was Charles Baudelaire, singing the "transitory, the fleeting and the contingent" of urban life, praising the experience of the anonymity in the crowd, picturing the urban café as the screen through which to look at the spectacle of the city. In the same era, Georges-Eugène Baron Haussmann was opening up—through demolition—the visual domination of the urban space as an essential means of managing power. Since then, modernity and visuality have been concepts developing parallel with one another.

"Just as water, gas and electricity are brought into our houses from far off to satisfy our needs in response to a minimal effort, so we shall be supplied with visual or auditory images, which will appear and disappear at a simple movements of the hand, hardly more than a sign," said Paul Valéry, quoted by Walter Benjamin in "The Work of Art in the Age of Mechanical Reproduction"; the view of Benjamin is probably the most influential in anticipating the figures of a cinematic urbanism, with his monumental project about Parisian passages, its theorization of the *flânerie* as a lens to capture modernity, and its capacity to preview the effects of cinema in changing the perceived space of citizens. "The film corresponds to profound changes in the apperceptive apparatus—changes that are experienced on an individual scale by the man in the street in big-city traffic, on a historical scale by every present-day citizen," states Benjamin in the same piece.

More recent is the work of such thinkers as Jean Baudrillard and Paul Virilio. In a frequently quoted passage of *America,* Baudrillard notes, "The American city seems to have stepped right out of the movies" and "[t]o grasp its secrets, you should not, then, begin with the city and move inwards towards the screen; you should begin with the screen and move outwards towards the city." If Baudrillard's intention is to depict the inherently cinematic nature of the American city, in opposition to the nature of the historical European city, globalization processes are in a way making this observation appropriate in every context. But it is probably Virilio, with his attention to phenomena as time compression, the diffusion of visual technologies and interest in *dromology* (the science of velocity), who has developed one of the most influential sets of analytical tools for the emerging cinematic urbanism. In Virilio's work, the development of visualizing technologies produces visibility without confrontation, in which the traditional vis-à-vis streets disappears, giving way to the single temporality of an instantaneous diffusion. "With the interfaçade of monitors and control screens, *elsewhere* begins here, and vice versa," he wrote in *L'espace critique,* describing the incoming *overexposed* contemporary city. The idea of cinematic urbanism as a product of postmodernity can be retraced as well in the classical and controversial work *Learning from Las Vegas,* by Robert Venturi, Denise Scott Brown, and Steven Izenour. Here, the Las Vegas strip is interpreted as a new paradigm for the urban, where billboards, signs, and buildings act as signs, are designed according to the aim of capturing the attention of the driver, stressing the relation between visuality and velocity.

A Cinematic Epistemology of the City

The profound, constitutive relationship between cinema and city is the topic of a range of recent studies, as in Nezer AlSayyad's attempt to retrace a history of urban modernity "from reel to real." In this kind of analysis, film studies are employed as significant contributions to the knowledge of the urban world. Paris, Berlin, and New York are among the most exemplary cinematic cities, cities whose role stands out from being merely frequent backgrounds of film action, whose identities have been continuously molded by cinematic narratives. If Paris has assumed such a role even before the advent of cinema as a mass medium, Berlin is probably the first metropolis to become the sole protagonist, as in Walter Ruttmann's *Symphonie der Großstadt* (1927), a film wherein the modern rhythm of the city is captured as a harmonic choreography, producing mixed feelings of fascination, disquiet, and uncanniness. Similarly inspired by the urban rhythm, but with a peculiar attention to the gaze of the camera itself, at its social and political reflex on the production of place, is the almost contemporary Dziga Vertov's *The Man with the Movie Camera* (1929), set in Odessa. With a similar gaze on the urban as a fascinating, unceasing, harmonic process, with either critical or empathic, dubious or enchanted participation, films such as Charlie Chaplin's *Modern Times,* Fritz Lang's *Metropolis, or* Jacques Tati's *Playtime* are essential to the general understanding of modernism, urbanization, and their consequences for the everyday. Ridley Scott's *Blade Runner* or Terry Gilliam's *Brazil,* Jean-Luc Godard's *Alphaville,* or John Carpenter's *Escape From New York* represent essential views on possible urban dystopias and a critique of the urban future.

Screenscapes

If the role that more and more cities have in cinema is unquestionable, not enough has been stressed about the symmetrical undergoing process: that is, that moving images are increasingly becoming a constitutive element of the urban landscape. It is a colonization operated by the cinematic realm on the lived space of the everyday but as well, vice versa, as production and consumption increasingly merge in the postmodern condition, and everybody incessantly contributes, consciously or not, to the proliferation of images. Such a process is fostering a relationship with the environment, as well as among individuals, intensively mediated through moving images and managed by digital devices. Pictures, projections, *movies* multiply in public as well as in private space: a process rendering the difference

between the public and private realms a biased and ineffectual one, redefining, in the meantime, the concept of public space itself.

The cinematic experience is no longer a sacral moment, separated from the ordinary and daily life; rather, it is liberated from the constraints of dedicated space, extracted from the *camera obscura* of theatrical venues or from domestic living rooms dedicated to television rituals; it pops up in the urban fabric through all possible surfaces. Parallel to the exponential evolution of information technologies, fostering communication tools and practices to permeate all sectors of human activity, the representational world of images is gaining a hegemonic role in the everyday realm of citizens. Carried both inside and on the external frame of public transports, broadcast through myriad constantly smaller, more mobile, and connectible personal devices, in the personal screens of computers, cell phones, and consoles, set in the programmable surfaces of new architectures, images pervasively inhabit the city: Images build up a parallel meta-urbanity, engendering what is alternatively referred to as augmented reality.

From this standpoint, the cinematic city is eventually the result of three intertwined processes, affecting urbanization at a global scale:

1. The progressive fluidization and mobilization of human behavior in connection to the increased mobility of goods, people, and money
2. The overwhelming production of images and data constituting the dominant form of production in the urban contemporary landscape
3. The increasing mediation of interpersonal relationships through technological devices and institutional protocols

Such processes engender epistemological spaces that can be alternatively analyzed as space of flows, space of exposure, or mediated space. Furthermore, they represent the three constitutive dimensions of contemporary public space:

1. The inherently horizontal dimension of mobility, producing an interpretation of public space specifically as transport infrastructure, articulated as a system of roads, squares, open spaces, airports, and railways

2. The essentially vertical articulation of semantic surfaces, that is, the representational space where symbolic productions are displayed, distributed, and exposed to the public, including not only shop windows and billboards, signage and architectural facades, galleries, and cultural centers but also, and increasingly so, screens of computers, televisions, and PDAs (personal digital assistants)

3. A networked dimension, that is, the mediated space of information communication technologies; linking together both the former dimensions, it has the extensivity of the first combined with the parametric temporality of the second. In this last perspective, public space becomes essentially *interface*. It has no inherently spatial nature, but instead is strictly dependent on the material presence and performativity of wires, cables, antennas, chips, encoders and decoders, magnetic supports, and data storage devices.

The urban production process in the global system is increasingly distributed in delocalized networks, but it emerges from production to consumption through the vertical articulation of surfaces that represent the predominant aspect of the contemporary global city, determining an urban palimpsest experienced as a succession of frames. Programmed flows of images represent the core of the urban experience. The screen becomes the main morphological element in a city where to be visible is as important as what is actually done inside architecture, if not more. Persistence succeeds existence in the essential urban ontology.

Such conditions are determining the emergence of what can be analyzed as a vertical urbanism, urbanism in which the semantic use of vertical urban surfaces is overcoming the horizontal logistic use of spaces in engendering value and rent. Urban design moves from fields to frames: Land's logistic use of horizontal surfaces loses relevance with respect to the semantic use of vertical surfaces. If, in the past, the design of the city has been basically drawing plans from an aerial point of view, distributing functions through the physical space in a primarily horizontal articulation, now we face the emergence of a discipline aimed at organizing the visual perception of the citizen. Citizenship tends to be understood as spectatorship flattened into audience, a vision that in

many respects recalls not only Guy Debord's arguments in *The Society of Spectacle* (1967) but also a phenomenon recognized by David Harvey as an effect of the flexible accumulation regime.

Spatial transformation processes are increasingly influenced by the necessity to capture the potential attention of citizens/spectators, determining what has also been depicted as an attention economy, connected more and more with the distribution of information through digital networks. It is not a coincidence if, among the most important players in the urban new economies, we find today corporations of the entertainment and media sectors, which deploy an aggressive attitude toward monopolizing control of urban surfaces and exploiting their communication potential, and that often extend their interests to sectors such as mobility, retail, urban furniture. Their strategies are easily inscribed in the entrepreneurial transformation of urban government, significantly contributing to a neoliberalist urbanism focused on private–public partnership and remarkably unbalanced toward speculative attitudes.

Image Production

As a matter of fact, the process of image production assumes a fundamental role in the urban economies, redirecting capital toward specific spatial transformation, redefining the architectural consistency of the city, or reshaping citizens' everyday experience through intensive mediation of personal interchanges. It is a form of production that implies a massive use of tools and techniques derived from media and the entertainment industry, redirected to engender and exploit value from the urban location. Image production stands out as the complex production–consumption chain reshaping the urban experience of citizens as an essentially visual one; engendering a metropolis where the space of exposure becomes the structured embodiment of public space, designed to optimize the exposition of city users to the spectacle of goods, being impressed, entertained, directed by flows of commodified images. The management of imagery is therefore more or less evident at the core of the main phenomena affecting the contemporary urban world and in many terms inhabiting current disciplinary discourse. *Urban* renewal programs, urban marketing, gentrification, Disneyfication, festivalization, mass tourism, cultural heritage, cultural economy, and creative city are all current locutions describing social phenomena, structural adjustments, or transformations of the urban economy strictly related to image production forms. They speak of building, changing, or preserving the image of the city. To renew the image of a place is the first step toward financial investment and physical transformation. The new creative class, invoked as a panacea for revitalizing declining cities, is one composed mainly of image professionals. This brings tools and techniques initially refined by visual arts and media industries to assume a relevant role in the design and management of urban space, in combination with the traditional tools of disciplines as planning, architecture, marketing, and policy making. The entertainment industry and spatial production increasingly share a similar attitude. Film production in itself becomes a model for spatial production, where the development of fictional narratives is the framework for the realization and consolidation of actual processes of urban restructuring. Set and light design, graphic design, digital rendering, and script writing are contributing to the redefinition of urban design as a discipline dedicated to managing the visual perception of the city.

Urban landscape is no longer divisible from its mediascape.

Lorenzo Tripodi

See also Benjamin, Walter; City and Film; Harvey, David; Las Vegas, Nevada; Urban Semiotics

Further Readings

AlSayyad, Nezar, ed. 2006. *Cinematic Urbanism: A History of the Modern from Reel to Real.* New York: Routledge.

Baudrillard, Jean. 1988. *America.* London: Verso.

Benjamin, Walter. 1969. "The Work of Art in the Age of Mechanical Reproduction." Pp. 217–51 in *Illuminations,* edited by H. Arendt and translated by H. Zohn. New York: Schocken.

Clarke, David, ed. 1997. *The Cinematic City.* London: Routledge.

Denzin, Norman. 1995. *The Cinematic Society: The Voyeur's Gaze.* Thousand Oaks, CA: Sage.

Harvey David. 1989. *The Condition of Postmodernity: An Enquiry into the Origins of Cultural Change.* Oxford, UK: Basil Blackwell.

———. 1990. "Flexible Accumulation through Urbanization Reflections on 'Post-modernism' in the American City." *Perspecta* 26:251–72.

Lash, S. and J. Urry. 1994. *Economies of Sign and Space.* London: Sage.

Shiel, Mark and Tony Fitzmaurice, eds. 2003. *Screening the City.* London: Verso.

Soja, Edward. 1989. *Postmodern Geographies: The Reassertion of Space in Critical Social Theory.* London: Verso.

Tripodi, Lorenzo. 2008. "Space of Exposure: Notes for a Vertical Urbanism." In *Die Realität des Imaginären,* edited by J. Gleiter, N. Korrek, and G. Zimmermann. Weimar, Germany: Verlag der Bauhaus-Universität.

Venturi, Robert, Denise Scott Brown, and Steven Izenour. 1977. *Learning from Las Vegas.* Cambridge: MIT Press.

Virilio, P. 1984. *L'espace critique: Essai sur l'urbanisme et les nouvelles technologies.* Paris: Christian Bourgois.

———. 2000. *Information Bomb.* London: Sage.

CITIZEN PARTICIPATION

Citizen participation encompasses efforts to engage the citizenry in a community's decision making. Starting with the voting process in a representative democracy, government administrators expand the citizen involvement by using public hearings and debates, referenda, collaborative forums, and electronic media. The widespread enthusiasm for more citizen participation rests on the belief that an engaged citizenry will produce government policy that is closer to the preferences of the public.

Over three decades of academic theory have focused on the superiority of decision making that engages citizens. A participatory process can educate the public and, conversely, the process can assist government decision makers in determining when policies are unpopular with the public. In addition, participatory forums and other processes enable citizens to build their skills at civic leadership as well as gain access to government officials. This gives them an empowering "voice" beyond the ballot box.

Table 1   Advantages of Citizen Participation in Government Decision Making

	Advantages to Citizen Participants	*Advantages to Government*
Decision process	Education (learn from and inform government representatives) Persuade and enlighten government Gain skills for activist citizenship	Education (learn from and inform citizens) Persuade citizens; build trust and allay anxiety or hostility Build strategic alliances Gain legitimacy of decisions
Outcomes	Break gridlock; achieve outcomes Gain some control over policy process Better policy and implementation decisions	Break gridlock; achieve outcomes Avoid litigation costs Better policy and implementation decisions

Source: Irvin, Renee, and John Stansbury. "Citizen Participation in Decision Making: Is It Worth the Effort?" *Public Administration Review* 64 (January/February 2004): 55–65. Reprinted with permission of Wiley-Blackwell.

Sherry Arnstein described a ladder of participation that illustrates the ascending forms of engagement, from nonparticipation (manipulation and therapy) to tokenism (informing, consultation, placation), and finally citizen power (partnership, delegated power, and citizen control). Many participatory strategies utilized by governments, such as public hearings, fall in the "consultation" or "informing" range of the participation ladder. Working groups such as watershed councils and other citizen advisory forums can achieve results beyond "placation," to a true shaping of government initiatives.

The gains from a more participatory process need to be weighed against potential costs. First, a participatory process will be time consuming for government representatives and citizens alike. Second, individuals taking part in a participatory process may not be representative of the public. In fact, they tend to come from the highest socioeconomic groups in a community. Consequently, interest groups or engaged individuals may mold the decision making in their interest rather than in the public interest.

At the very least, government decision making requires a keen awareness of public sentiment on current issues and proposed policy issues. Participatory processes must be carefully designed to solicit and act upon citizen recommendations for improvements in policy making.

Renee A. Irvin

See also Advocacy Planning; Community Organizing; Governance; Urban Planning; Urban Politics

Further Readings

Arnstein, Sherry R. 1969. "A Ladder of Citizen Participation." *Journal of the American Institute of Planners* 35(3):903–57.

Irvin, Renee A. and John Stansbury. 2004. "Citizen Participation in Decision Making: Is It Worth the Effort?" *Public Administration Review* 64(1):55–65.

Pateman, Carole. 1970. *Participation and Democratic Theory.* Cambridge, UK: Cambridge University Press.

CITIZENSHIP

Citizenship is a complex (political, legal, social, and cultural but perhaps also sexual, aesthetic, and ethical) institution of domination *and* empowerment that governs both *who* citizens (insiders), subjects (strangers, outsiders), and abjects (aliens) are and *how* these figures are to govern themselves and each other in a given body politic. The essential difference between citizenship and membership is that whereas the latter governs conduct *within* social groups, citizenship is about conduct *across* social groups that constitute a body politic. Being a citizen almost always means not only being an insider but also one who has mastered appropriate modes and forms of conduct of being an insider. This creates a figure in the sense of both a *person* (law) and an *image* (norm). For subjects and abjects, becoming a citizen means either adopting modes and forms of being an insider (assimilation, integration, incorporation) or challenging these modes and forms and thereby transforming them (identification, differentiation, recognition). Just what constitutes citizenship and its appropriate modes and forms of conduct are always objects of struggle among citizens, subjects, and abjects with claims to citizenship as justice. It is through these claims to citizenship as justice that it becomes a site of rights and obligations. These claims and the combination of rights and obligations that define it work themselves out differently in different sites and produce different figures. Thus, *sites* (cities, empires, nations, states), *figures* (citizens, subjects, abjects), and *substances* (rights, obligations, duties) can be said to be the elements of citizenship that constitute a body politic.

Sites of Citizenship

The ancient Greeks have been given the distinction of inventing citizenship roughly around the eighth century BC by producing a new image of the city: *polis*. Until then, the city was governed by god-kings and after that, the citizens. It appears that cities in ancient kingdoms, states, and empires did not develop citizenship precisely because they were "despotic" regimes of government. But the ancient Greeks did not see much conflict between despotic regimes of government and citizenship. The three forms of governing the city as identified by Greek thought—oligarchy, aristocracy, and democracy—already assumed the existence of the citizen. Nonetheless, what happened in that originary moment? The answer, ironically, has much to do with what we are struggling over right now. At that originary moment, it seems that a new figure entered onto the stage of history, who was male and a warrior and owned property (not the least of which were the means of warfare). That figure became the dominant image. Those who were not male and did not own property—such as women, slaves, peasants, merchants, craftsmen, and sailors—found themselves thrown into being, or had become, the others of that figure as subjects and abjects. The figure of the citizen involved the

right to govern his city (belonging) and bequeath that right to his son (blood). By governing himself by the laws of his city, he also governed the strangers, outsiders, and aliens of the city. We already recognize in this figure attributes (property, warriorship, masculinity) that were reproduced time and again as conditions of citizenship and yet worked themselves out differently in different sites. The site of polis would remain as the originary site through which citizenship has been reinvented through the centuries. The issues that polis articulated, such as the relationship between citizenship and forms of government, subjects, and abjects and rights and responsibilities of citizenship would, time and again, be repeated, albeit producing different sites, figures, and substances of citizenship. It is now impossible to conceive citizenship without orienting ourselves to that original site of history, polis, and its figure of the citizen.

The Roman figure of the citizen worked itself out through different sites. When fully articulated, being a Roman citizen was above all being a member of an empire that was beyond the city. The site of citizenship, it seems, extended beyond the city. Yet, it is clear that while Romans invented a new site for citizenship, it was articulated through the city. "Being Roman" nicely captures that duality: being of Rome and its empire. What that meant is that while being male, warrior, and property owner were still the elements that constituted a Roman citizen, dominating its other figures—such as strangers (women, plebeians, clients, slaves), outsiders (merchants, foreigners), and aliens (barbarians)—he was still essentially Roman precisely because he was of Rome. Being Roman was simultaneously an imperial and civic identity, but it eventually became an imperial identity by the famous declaration in AD 212. The empire as the site of citizenship and its graded characteristics were the contested claims upon which citizenship developed. We will perhaps always debate whether the fall of the empire was because of that aspiration to, or necessity of, universal citizenship.

The emergence of new sites of citizenship after the disintegration of the Roman Empire is among the most fascinating episodes. Much has been written about the rebirth of the city during the eleventh and twelfth centuries in Europe. The invention of the charter as the founding instrument of the city as a body politic (and corporate) and the emergence of the new figure of the citizen who embodies not a warrior but a peaceable merchant or artisan of the medieval commune, has given us a new originary moment, not disconnected from Athens and Rome yet with a new inflection. Perhaps the new site of citizenship was now best represented by Florence, though, of course, there were regional differences throughout Europe. Between the twelfth and fifteenth centuries thousands of cities were founded as bodies politic and corporate with varied relationships of autonomy and autocephaly (administrative independence) from the "surrounding" lordships, kingships, and incipient states. For the emerging European citizenship, its site was definitely the city but more through belonging than blood. The famous residency requirement of a year and one day before one could become a citizen (a burgher) is one of the telling clauses of the charter that founded the city. Just how these scattered and heterogeneous patchwork worlds of contested sovereignties, autonomies, and class of burghers (hence the origin of the word *bourgeois*) were transformed into the world of states will always remain debatable. But the city was undeniably still at the center of the development of the state rather than the state being the city writ large. The transformation from the fifteenth to the eighteenth century was, if you like, from Florence to Paris. If Florence represented that world of contested sovereignties, Paris embodied a new figure, a new scale of citizenship. Though its self-image aspired to become even wider, behind that aspiration stood the figure of a dominant group: the bourgeois, male, and Christian citizen.

Then there is the episode of what Hannah Arendt called the conquest of the state by the nation when the state was defined as the territory of a people constituted along not just bourgeois, Christian, and male properties but cultural and ethnic properties. What Arendt meant by this conquest is that if the state was a body politic (Arendt called it an artifact) that enabled negotiation of differences among various social groups as their claims to citizenship, nationality instituted the domination of a group over others as immutable. It was then that citizenship was reconfigured as nationality. While the difference between citizenship and nationality ought to be as profound as

that between citizen and subject or abject, it rapidly became and remains still an accepted, if not given, association or synonymy.

The three attributes of citizenship (masculinity, warriorship, property) persisted well into the scales of the state and nation-state. The medieval commune was perhaps a departure during the twelfth to fifteenth centuries in Europe when being a warrior was not associated with being a citizen, but of being of the city (even if a citizen did not dwell in the city). Yet, being a citizen still involved owning property and being male. Perhaps then the most significant divergence occurred in the late eighteenth and early nineteenth centuries when citizenship became associated with nationality and was understood as belonging to the state rather than the city. The state was seen as the city, and nation as the citizen, writ large. It was then that the principles of jus sanguinis (by blood) and jus soli (by territory) were rearticulated through the state and reinscribed in the nation.

Figures of Citizenship

If each site articulated the figure of the citizen rather differently, and if the state constituted a qualitatively different scale of citizenship, what explains the ostensible unity of "citizenship" to the point that we talk about it rather than different institutions or designations? The answer, in part, lies in the fact that every dominant group in the occident reinscribed and reinvested itself in that originary figure of the citizen as the foundation of its symbolic and imaginary occidentality. It also lies in the fact that the originary attributes of citizenship—property, war, and masculinity—remained foundational and differentiated citizens from subjects (strangers, outsiders) and abjects (aliens).

But the future may well interpret the twentieth century as having recast the foundational elements of citizenship: It was in that century that property was no longer tied to citizenship, women became at least formal if not substantive claimants upon it, and the nature of war and warriorship were fundamentally altered by being fought by special kinds of mercenaries and technological weaponry. Moreover, it was in that century that the universal figure of the citizen was shown to have represented the attributes of a particular occidental social group:

147

Christian, heterosexual, male, White, and adult. Does this mean the end of citizenship? Judging by the seemingly inexorable rise of another figure of being—the consumer—in the second half of the twentieth century, it certainly appears as though citizenship had come to some kind of an end. Perhaps, just as Roman citizenship ceased to be a functional institution at the moment of its declaration of universality in AD 212, the twentieth century had consummated the gradual expansion of civil rights in the eighteenth, political rights in the nineteenth, and social rights in the twentieth century, as suggested by T. H. Marshall.

Yet, while we have witnessed the recasting of the fundamental elements of citizenship (property, warriorship, masculinity) and the emergence of a counter figure, we have also observed the emergence of a new figure of the citizen that was much less constituted by what it possessed than by what it ostensibly lacked: strangers, outsiders, and aliens had become claimants to citizenship. Perhaps those new historical narratives that are now being told about citizenship indicate this transformation. They make citizenship appear less a bastion of property, warriorship, and masculinity, let alone occidentality, and more about the struggles of redistribution and recognition by those who had been its strangers, outsiders, and aliens.

Substances of Citizenship

The substance of citizenship is the relationship between rights and responsibilities and the virtues that constitute that relationship. Each site (and scale) and figure of citizenship configures a series of rights and responsibilities appropriate to their relational strengths. If the figure of citizenship is dominant in a given site for landed property, warriorship, and masculinity, then those who "lack" these properties will become dominated. Their claims to citizenship will address injustices to which their dominated status gives rise. While not a zero-sum game, substances of citizenship are relationships that reflect dominant sites and figures of citizenship. It would have been inconceivable to imagine claiming rights for disabled subjects or refugee abjects in either the Greek polis or the Roman civitas. Similarly, it would be inconceivable today to institute a parliament of

warriors. The relationships between and among sites, scales, and figures of citizenship are not zero-sum games either. It is flawed to think that citizenship was once a city phenomenon and that it was eclipsed by the state and then the nation, and then perhaps the world. These sites articulate through each other rather than eclipse each other. They also stretch and permeate each other. Rather than being nestled and concatenated, the sites of citizenship are tentacular and amorphous and bleed into each other. It is these intersections between different sites (and scales) that produce different figures and substances of citizenship.

Engin F. Isin

See also Athens, Greece; Social Exclusion; Stranger; Urban Politics

Further Readings

Arendt, H. 1951. *The Origins of Totalitarianism*. New York: Harcourt Brace Jovanovich.

Black, A. 1984. *Guilds and Civil Society in European Political Thought from the Twelfth Century to the Present*. Ithaca, NY: Cornell University Press.

Gardner, J. F. 1993. *Being a Roman Citizen*. London: Routledge.

Heather, P. J. 2006. *The Fall of the Roman Empire: A New History of Rome and the Barbarians*. New York: Oxford University Press.

Isin, E. F. 2002. *Being Political: Genealogies of Citizenship*. Minneapolis: University of Minnesota Press.

Isin, E. F. and P. K. Wood. 1999. *Citizenship and Identity*. London: Sage.

Manville, P. B. 1990. *The Origins of Citizenship in Ancient Athens*. Princeton, NJ: Princeton University Press.

Marshall, T. H. [1949] 1992. *Citizenship and Social Class*. London: Pluto Press.

Poggi, G. 1990. *The State: Its Nature, Development, and Prospects*. Cambridge, UK: Polity Press.

Smith, R. M. 1997. *Civic Ideals: Conflicting Visions of Citizenship in U.S. History*. New Haven, CT: Yale University Press.

Weber, M. [1921] 1958. *The City*. New York: The Free Press.

Young, I. M. 1989. "Polity and Group Difference: A Critique of the Ideal of Universal Citizenship." *Ethics* 99(January), 250–74.

CITY AND FILM

The invention of motion pictures in the final decade of the nineteenth century is a milestone in the development of modern urban society and culture. Arguably the most significant cultural form of the twentieth century, film introduced new representations of the urban environment. Its images and narratives of the metropolis joined the productions of the visual arts and literature to generate many of the century's most significant ideologies and cultural myths. Yet if the metropolis was prominent in film, the reverse was equally the case. Cinema sparked new urban social behaviors, especially practices of leisure and consumption, that led women, young people, and members of varied ethnic and racial communities to reconceive their identities. Film exhibition transformed urban neighborhoods as cinema theaters appeared, disappeared, and relocated across metropolitan regions and mimicked more general processes of urbanization, decline, and redevelopment.

Drawing upon the medium of photography popularized after the invention of the Daguerreotype process in 1839, as well as older media such as painting, line engraving, literature, music, and theater, the cinema was the most successful of the many nineteenth-century popular entertainments, such as the diorama and the panorama, which sought to create a realistic image of the external world. Like other contemporaneous technologies such as photography, the railroad, the sewing machine, and the wind-up pocket watch, it introduced industrialization into the everyday lives of city dwellers and decisively altered their experiences of space and time.

By bringing distant objects nearer, magnifying the invisible, slowing down or speeding up actions, juxtaposing images through editing, or being able to endlessly repeat a single process, the cinema generated new possibilities of urban perception that in turn promoted new physical forms of the built environment, new social relations, and new aesthetic ideals. Trading upon the popularity of newspapers, mass-produced books, and photographic images in the nineteenth century, the silent cinema was quickly heralded as a "universal language" capable of fostering a world community. Film genres such as the melodrama, newsreels depicting topical events, and images of urban landmarks traveled rapidly across national boundaries and established film as the first true cultural form of globalization. Cinema made the planet seem smaller, more akin to a single global city, as heterogeneous audiences in far flung locations now felt that they were visiting the same places, consuming the same stories, and pining for the same movie idols.

Representing motion far more effectively and realistically than earlier devices, such as the zoetrope, film excelled at depicting the passage of time and seemed uniquely suited to represent the temporal dimension of city life, as in *The Crazy Ray* by René Clair in 1925, which suggested what would happen if all movement in Paris were to be stopped. Poet Charles Baudelaire's nineteenth-century aesthetic credo of preserving the fleeting and the evanescent found in it an ideal vehicle. Whether depicting the latest clothing fashions or urban neighborhoods on the verge of destruction, the cinema has fascinated most serious commentators, since its invention, for its remarkable ability to record—and hence preserve for future viewers— the urban here and now.

Thoroughly aligned with the rationalization of labor, the body, and cultural production understood as defining traits of modernity, the film medium nonetheless belies generalizations about its supposedly monolithic identity and effects. Decried for allegedly instilling homogeneous behavior and attitudes, cinema simultaneously created possibilities for local receptions and interpretations, oppositional public cultures and varied subcultures, that challenge conformism. Assertions about its effects upon public morality, mental and physical health, political consciousness, social identity, and urban violence therefore must be examined within specific contexts rather than accepted as universally valid truisms.

Silent Film and Its Audience

From the moment of the first public film exhibitions in 1895, more or less simultaneously in Paris, Berlin, and New York, film coincided with rapid population growth and increasing core density in most world metropolises. The first widely trumpeted public film projection by Auguste Lumière of his Cinématographe took place on December 28, 1895, in the Salon Indien of the Grand Café in

Paris. Throughout much of its early history, film was exhibited in music halls, cafés, vaudeville theaters, and fairs that were often socially off limits to middle-class audiences.

Early films recorded public spaces such as streets, train stations, and world exhibitions and consequently remain key sources of visual information about the nineteenth-century metropolis. A significant early film genre was the so-called actualité that presented current events such as parades, visits by heads of state, and inaugurations and became the basis for later newsreels. Filmmakers such as the magician Georges Méliès opted for a controlled interior environment over the street or the workplace (epitomized in the Lumière short, *Workers Leaving the Factory*) and initiated the studio filmmaking still dominant today. Many studios created fastidiously designed artificial streets, and even today relatively few narrative fiction films utilize actual cities as locations for more than a few scenes filmed by second-unit crews.

The lack of reliable evidence necessitates that film historians proceed with caution when making claims about the social composition of early cinema audiences. Nonetheless, most scholars of early film agree that women, children, and recent immigrants to the metropolis were disproportionately present at early film screenings, especially those held at storefront "nickelodeons," which sprang up in the United States around 1905. Film proved a significant means of inculcating the responsibilities of citizenship and what, for many recent emigrants from rural settings, must have appeared often bewildering urban codes of behavior. Movie houses became an inviting environment accessible to viewers on the bottom rungs of the social ladder whose subversive potential did not escape notice by the guardians of public virtue. Feared as breeding grounds for licentiousness, political contestation, and the spread of disease, they were heavily policed and the films shown within them were subject to censorship.

The introduction of the sound film in 1927, associated with Al Jolson's performance in *The Jazz Singer* (Alan Crosland), connected cinema with both the spoken language and music of varied ethnic and social groups in the city. Gangster films such as *The Public Enemy* (William Wellman, 1931) and *Little Caesar* (Mervyn Leroy, 1931) proved especially popular in the 1930s and presented the conflicting attitudes toward legal authority and property in Depression-era cities such as Chicago. Musicals of the 1940s and 1950s frequently appropriated urban subject matter, perhaps most famously in *42nd Street* (Lloyd Bacon, 1933), a celebration of the New York neighborhood whose characters walked up walls but provided little insight into the urban area's real problems and challenges.

Film and the Early Modern Metropolis

Filmmakers explored the vitality of the metropolis from the earliest days of the cinematic medium. D. W. Griffith's *The Musketeers of Pig Alley* (1912) took urban criminal gangs as its theme. Harold Lloyd's performance in *Safety Last* (Fred C. Newmeyer and Sam Taylor, 1923) and King Vidor's *The Crowd* (1921) explored the implications of leisure in the city and suggest how the logic of Fordism, the dynamic cycle of industrial production and consumption, had thoroughly permeated silent cinema, by then a respectable form of middle-class entertainment. In the early 1920s the genre of the city symphony emerged, taking the dynamism of the large city as its explicit theme. Films such as *Manhatta* (Charles Sheeler and Paul Strand, 1921) and *Berlin: Symphony of a Great City* (Walther Ruttman, 1927) presented a cross-section of the speed mechanization and the social heterogeneity of the city. Generally avoiding staged action and filming people without their conscious awareness, these films, exemplified by the Russian experimental *The Man with a Movie Camera* (Dziga Vertov, 1929), critically engaged with political and economic realities of life in an industrialized city. They count among the earliest examples of urban documentary cinema, later developed by filmmakers such as Jean Rouch (*Chronicle of a Summer,* 1961). This documentary aesthetic proved especially influential for filmmakers in the developing world concerned with documenting life in the colonial metropolis, such as Senegal's Ousmane Sembene's *Black Girl* (1967) and Brazil's Glauber Rocha's *Land in Anguish* (1967).

Cultural critics such as Walter Benjamin and Siegfried Kracauer, writing in Europe in the 1920s and 1930s, were struck by the affinities between film and the metropolis. Benjamin compared film to the impact of assembly lines on the consciousness of workers and understood its representation of urban shock as a decisive element in training modern sense perception. Kracauer praised the female white-collar workers who attended film screenings for their ability to glean practical wisdom about urban life from the cinema. Both writers deeply admired the films of Charlie Chaplin, such as *Modern Times* (1936), for their comic yet ultimately deadly serious portrait of the human body at the mercy of urban technological society. In Kracauer's *Theory of Film: Redemption of Physical Reality* (1960), he developed an account of film as uniquely suited to recording quotidian urban realities.

Cinema also played a significant role in the promotion of new urban schemes by municipal authorities and planning organizations. In films such as *Die Stadt von Morgen—Ein Film vom Städtebau* (Maximilian von Goldbeck and Erich Kotzer) and *Architecture Today* (Pierre Chenal, 1931), proponents of the modern movement in architecture criticized the density and unhealthful conditions of traditional cities and proposed alternatives ranging from apartment towers to greenbelt towns. Shown to much acclaim at the 1939 World's Fair, *The City* (Ralph Steiner and Willard Van Dyke, 1939) epitomized this tendency. Its evocation of the values of a small New England town and depiction of the modern metropolis as chaotic and unhealthy suggests a transformation in the cinematic image of the city, now tinged with anxiety, indicative of a shift from early to late modernity.

Film and the Late Modern Metropolis

The American film noir cycle of the 1940s and 1950s is the most noticeable expression of the trend away from earlier optimistic treatments of the metropolis. At once a reworking of earlier depictions of urban violence and perversion associated with Weimar German films such as *The Cabinet of Dr. Caligari* (Robert Wine, 1919), *The Street* (Karl Grune, 1923), *Dr. Mabuse, the Gambler* (Fritz Lang, 1922), and *M* (Fritz Lang, 1931), the film noir presented a conspicuously downbeat vision of the American city, populated by losers and innocent bystanders trapped in deadening routines in a dark and treacherous environment.

Classic examples of film noir include *Double Indemnity* (Billy Wilder, 1944), *The Naked City* (Jules Dassin, 1948), and *The Asphalt Jungle* (John Huston, 1949). Produced as urban renewal initiatives were eradicating many downtown neighborhoods, film noir evinced a nostalgia for older urban forms, elevated subway tracks, and decrepit industrial districts whose impending demise rendered them fascinating. The neo-noir movement of the 1970s and 1980s presented an idealized version of a mythical 1930s Los Angeles in *Chinatown* (Roman Polanski, 1974) and a dystopian pastiche of earlier cultural styles and ethnicities in *Blade Runner* (Ridley Scott, 1982).

Negotiating the eradication of older urban forms and the arrival of new forms of the built environment, as well as the anxieties accompanying these changes, became a defining issue for the postwar cinema in a way it had not been for earlier film. Fear of communism and the hostility of many Americans during cold war America of the late 1940s and 1950s to any form of public housing found its most vociferous expression in the adaptation of Ayn Rand's *The Fountainhead* (King Vidor, 1949), a defense of the skyscraper as a symbol of masculine individualism. A rejection of studio filmmaking and the recent fascist past, the film movement Italian neorealism featured actual urban locations in *Rome, Open City* (Roberto Rossellini, 1945) to convey a democratic humanism.

French New Wave filmmakers investigated the impact of urbanization on the young in films such as *Paris Belongs to Us* (Jacques Rivette, 1960) and *Les bonnes femmes* (Claude Chabrol, 1960). The modern postwar urban cityscape was explored by Jean-Luc Godard in *Alphaville* (1965) and *Two or Three Things I Know about Her* (1966) and later taken up by German Wim Wenders in *The American Friend* (1977). American cities appeared ambivalently portrayed in films such as *Taxi Driver* (Martin Scorsese, 1976) and *The Conversation* (Francis Coppola, 1974), and *Death Wish* (Michael Winner, 1974), which gave voice to anxieties about crime, police ineffectiveness, surveillance, and corporate corruption during the post-Watergate era.

Beginning in the 1960s a new generation of urban filmmakers emerged. Their work treated racial and ethnic groups largely denied access to filmmaking in the past. Shirley Clarke directed *The Cool World* (1964) and Melvin van Peebles made his notorious *Sweet Sweetback's Baadasssss Song* (1971), the first blacksploitation film, that commenced its run in Detroit and soon took other inner-city theaters by storm. Later filmmakers such as Chantal Akerman, Spike Lee, Charles Burnett, Wayne Wang, and Hanif Kureishi presented new and original visions of cities such as New York, London, San Francisco, and Los Angeles, inflected by the perspectives and experiences of women, African Americans, Asian Americans, and Pakistanis. Iranian director Abbas Kiarostami explored the cityscape of Tehran in the film *A Taste of Cherry* (1997), and Hong Kong–based filmmaker Wong Kar Wai presented his city's unique urban environment in *Chung King Express* (1994). Suburban settings in films by Todd Haynes (*Far from Heaven,* 2002) and Todd Solondz (*Storytelling,* 2001) suggested that the conflicts of social identity in modern life could develop away from the concentrated metropolis.

Film Exhibition and the City

The flowering of the feature-length narrative film following the success of D. W. Griffith's *The Birth of a Nation* (1914) led to the proliferation of movie theaters and entertainment districts such as New York's Times Square, London's Piccadilly, and Berlin's Kurfurstendamm. Unlike early nickelodeon screenings, which were shown in a continuous loop, feature films had specific show times that required spectators to coordinate their viewing with theater schedules. A centrifugal movement of the American population to the suburbs after 1945 shifted the locus of first-run exhibition away from the urban center. Competition from television further siphoned away ticket sales from movie houses located in the metropolitan core, as drive-in theaters and theaters located in malls prospered. Many once-lucrative downtown movie theaters shut their doors or became exhibitors of pornography, now increasingly regulated by zoning laws and redevelopment guidelines that regulated where the sex industry could operate. Before the introduction of the VCR and the home video revolution of the 1970s, the promise of erotic content, whether in art films such as *I Am Curious Yellow* (Vilgot Sjöman, 1967) or more explicit sex films such as *Deep Throat* (Gerard Damiano, 1972), generated ticket sales for many urban cinemas.

The tension between film as a mass cultural form and a medium for artistic expression became evident in postwar exhibition practices and locations. Art films, especially those from Europe, captured the attention of American audiences in the 1950s and 1960s and were exhibited in neighborhoods such as New York's Upper East Side and Boston's Cambridge, to the detriment of districts such as Times Square. Avant-garde films or those with controversial political content, long exhibited in small film societies and on university campuses, attained their own alternative venues, such as New York's Anthology Film Archives, or were shown as midnight movies in commercial cinemas. Teenage cults such as the late-night screenings of *The Rocky Horror Picture Show* (Jim Sharman, 1975), whose fans dress as characters in the campy spectacle, issue a reminder that urban film spectatorship often was more about participating in a ritual and a sense of belonging than about actually watching a film.

Cinema and Its Urban Future

In the early twenty-first century, the urban future of cinema appears uncertain. The proliferation of the DVD and home entertainment systems, satellite and cable delivery of films, and suburban multiplexes has attenuated the traditional connection between cinema viewing and the metropolitan movie theater. While no contemporary urban redevelopment scheme appears complete without a multiplex cinema, these are typically located in shopping malls, which have eclipsed the conventional public space of the street and transformed the film-viewing experience into a privatized cultural transaction, increasingly indistinguishable from shopping.

The near extinction of the small independent cinema and its replacement by a multiplex, more likely than not to employ digital projection in lieu of actual 35-millimeter film prints, has homogenized the theatrical exhibition audience, typically at the expense of attracting older film viewers. Today, urban multiplexes have become key sites of leisure and consumption for young people, a fact long recognized by the Hollywood studios. In an age of films often dominated by action and special effects, scholars debate whether the notion of a national cinema is still coherent, or if in fact films have lost such specificity by becoming ever more attuned to a generic global audience. Yet the recent international success of *Crash* (Paul Haggis, 2004) and *Caché* (Michael Haneke, 2005), both of which prominently treat ethnic and racial conflict, suggests that audiences still respond to films that explore topical urban themes.

Despite the overwhelming dominance of Hollywood films in the global market, smaller national cinemas continue to flourish and to produce films that treat local urban cultures.

As nations such as China, Russia, and Turkey develop further economically and create larger domestic audiences, their cinemas will likely realize more films treating the city and metropolitan life and receive greater notice by foreign viewers. Although some mode of theatrical exhibition will likely survive in large cities, it may well become the exception rather than the rule for film viewing that it was for most of the twentieth century. Yet continued technological developments and the often homogenizing tendencies of globalization seem unlikely to eradicate the prominence of the city in cinema and cinema in the city as hallmarks of a still incomplete modernity.

Edward Dimendberg

See also Benjamin, Walter; Cinema (Movie House); Cinematic Urbanism; Kracauer, Siegfried; *Metropolis*; Urban Semiotics

Further Readings

Dimendberg, Edward. 2004. *Film Noir and the Spaces of Modernity.* Cambridge, MA: Harvard University Press.

Friedberg, Anne. 1995. *Window Shopping: Cinema and the Postmodern.* Berkeley: University of California Press.

Gomery, Douglas. 2002. *Shared Pleasures: A History of Movie Presentation in the United States.* Madison: University of Wisconsin Press.

Hansen, Miriam. 1991. *Babel & Babylon: Spectatorship in American Silent Film.* Cambridge, MA: Harvard University Press.

Jancovich, Mark and Lucy Faire, with Sarah Stubbings. 2003. *The Place of the Audience: Cultural Geographies of Film Consumption.* London: British Film Institute.

Jousse, Thierry and Thierry Paquot. 2005. *La ville au cinéma.* Paris: Cahiers du cinéma.

Schwartz, Vanessa and Leo Charney. 1995. *Cinema and the Invention of Modern Life.* Berkeley: University of California Press.

Shiel, Mark and Tony Fitzmaurice, eds. 2003. *Screening the City.* London: Verso.

Vogt, Guntram. 2001. *Die Stadt im Kino. Deutsche Spielfilme 1900–2000.* Marburg, Germany: Schueren.

CITY BEAUTIFUL MOVEMENT

The City Beautiful movement rose in late nineteenth-century America as a reformist attempt by the ruling elites to solve the urban crisis that was plaguing big cities across the country during the Industrial Revolution of the late nineteenth century and particularly during the economic depression of 1893 to 1897. With its emphasis on comprehensive, large-scale planning, the City Beautiful movement would set the standards for modern city planning.

The vanishing of the agrarian society, coupled with the increasing processes of immigration and urbanization, had led to a drastic rise of the population in urban areas across the country. From 1860 to 1910 the American population as a whole had increased from 31.4 million to 91.9 million, and 46 percent of Americans lived in urban areas, as manufacturing jobs in the city industry replaced agriculture jobs in the countryside. In the same time period, the number of American cities with over 100,000 residents rose from 8 to 50, while in 1910 several cities had a population exceeding the 1 million mark.

The striking concentration of poverty in core urban areas created dangerous sanitary conditions, phenomena of congestion and overcrowding in tenements, while at the same time the improvement of transportation systems spurred the unrelenting outmigration of the upper classes to the suburbs and the countryside. The massive migration of families to the city in search of opportunity in the rising industry led to a climate of social unrest, labor struggles, and ethnic conflicts.

Overcrowding, blight, and crime became major concerns for the elite classes, who lived in fear for their own safety. In 1890 Jacob Riis reported about the living conditions in the tenements of New York City:

[T]hree-fourths of its [New York's] people live in the tenements, and the nineteenth-century drift of the population to the cities is sending ever-increasing multitudes to crowd them. We know now that there is no way out; that the system that was the evil offspring of public neglect and private greed has come to stay, a storm-center forever of our civilization.

Riis's writings, a dramatic documentation of poverty and disenfranchisement in dense urban settlements, were interpreted as a strong call for social reform.

The City Beautiful movement rose as a response by the ruling elites to these concerns. The reformist and paternalistic goal of the movement (which mobilized architects, planners, and social reformers) was to bring social order and control to the city through an improved, orderly, and beautified urban environment: A new city would lead to a new harmonious sense of community and belonging for all citizens, thus removing the causes of social conflicts. According to Julie K. Rose, the underlying assumption of the movement was "the idea that beauty could act as an effective social control device."

In major industrial cities, the growing phenomenon of labor upheaval had resulted in legislatures damping down labor movements, systematic state repression, and violent confrontations between police and labor protesters. The Haymarket Affair in Chicago (May 1886), which had begun as a peaceful rally in support of striking workers, resulted in the death of several protesters, police officers, and civilians. The highly controversial trial that followed brought the capital executions of four, presumably innocent, anarchists. Following the example of the 1851 Universal Exhibition in London's Crystal Palace—which was strongly encouraged by the British government to counter the spread of political radicalism and to celebrate the global expansion of the British Empire—Chicago's Columbian Exposition of 1893 was championed by the city's political and economic elites with the aim of cementing a badly divided society and of rescuing the city's reputation after the worldwide publicity and outcry over the Haymarket trial.

The World's Columbian Exposition in Chicago (also known as the Chicago World's Fair) was the first large-scale display of the principles of the City Beautiful movement. The "White City," under head planner Daniel Burnham, was a model for an idealized, utopian, harmonious urban environment unknown to most American city dwellers of the time: It featured monumental buildings (all of uniform cornice height, all painted white, all generously decorated) orderly articulated among green spaces, wide canals, and reflective pools, and a picturesque lagoon designed by Frederick Law Olmsted, Sr. Its stylistic vocabulary was the neoclassicism of the Parisian École de Beaux-Arts, the leading international school of architecture that, from the 1870s to the 1930s, instructed artists and architects from all over the world in the teachings of harmony through the use of a historicist repertoire, and in the art of large-scale planning—as in Baron Georges Eugène Haussmann's redesign of Paris during the reign of Napoleon III. Several American architects who studied at the École des Beaux-Arts, such as Richard Morris Hunt, George Post, and Daniel Burnham, imported these aesthetic ideals to America for the occasion of the Chicago World's Fair.

The Columbian Exposition was the first materialization of a utopian city, unknown to most Americans. According to historian Roy Lubove, the fair "created new ideals and standards by which to measure the quality of urban life." In this ideal city, the more than 27 million visitors could see what their lives could be like in a crime- and poverty-free, orderly and magnificent urban setting. The popular reaction of the time was overwhelmingly positive, and the grandeur of the White City set the standards for several City Beautiful plans across the country and abroad.

In the following years, the leading proponent of the movement, Daniel Burnham, flanked by leading planners, architects, and designers of the time, directed the general plans for Washington, D.C. (in 1902), for Cleveland (in 1903), for San Francisco (in 1905), and finally for Chicago (in 1909); the Chicago plan is still considered one of the most consistent and magnificent endeavors of the City Beautiful movement.

The Built Legacy of the City Beautiful Movement

Burnham was quoted as saying, "Make no little plans, they have no magic to stir men's blood. . . . Make big plans . . . remembering that a noble, logical diagram once recorded will never die, but long after we are gone will be a living thing asserting itself with ever growing consistency." All of his plans were indeed the materialization of his own philosophy.

Even if not all City Beautiful plans were consistently brought to completion, their built legacy of grand parks, public squares, panoramic boulevards, and prominent civic buildings would forever change the shape of major American cities. The arrangements and transformations adopted by Burnham, and the legacy of grandeur and order these plans impressed on the urban fabric, are still widely appreciated by the public.

Burnham, together with Frederick Law Olmsted, Jr. and Frederick Law Olmsted, Sr., was also a major advocate of parks and green spaces integrated in the urban fabric. According to Burnham, public parks would provide a healthy outlet for those citizens stuck in the misery and congestion of the tenements; the parks would enrich their lives through recreation and entertainment and through a salutary contact with nature: "Fifty years ago," Burnham explained, "before population had become dense in certain parts of the city, people could live without parks, but we of today cannot." Parks and public spaces would thereby contribute to cementing together different social strata of the population.

Following in the footsteps of his father, Frederick Law Olmsted, Jr.'s work massively contributed to advancing landscape architecture to an honorable status in city planning. His work was directly inspired by what he saw as the harmonious integration of parks, avenues, and residential areas typical of European cities. In his view, replicating the European model would provide American cities, severely lacking in recreational and public space, with a much needed antidote to their congestion and density and, in his own words, to "the restraining and confining conditions of the town, which compel us to walk circumspectly, watchfully, jealously, which compel us to look closely upon others without sympathy." In 1902 he joined the McMillan Commission (together with Burnham, architect Charles F. McKim, and sculptor Augustus St. Gaudens) and redesigned the Mall area of the Capitol in Washington, D.C., in a successful attempt to bring to completion what had remained unfinished in the 1791 plan of Pierre L'Enfant.

The movement's built legacy is still universally appreciated and enjoyed by citizens and visitors alike. Monumental squares and parks, as well as grand boulevards, prominent civic centers, museums, and most university campuses are a product of this movement.

The emphasis on intra- or extra-urban transportation planning was also a distinctive feature of City Beautiful endeavors. Grand public boulevards, malls, and parkways were designed as scenic corridors, while rail stations connecting urban areas with outer villages (such as Union Station in Washington, D.C., by Burnham) were designed in magnificent proportions as monumental gates to the city.

The Burnham plan for Chicago, although uncompleted, created an impressive network of grand parks, boulevards, bridges, and civic buildings and fully redesigned the lakefront area as a public space. The recent landscaping of the lakefront and the design of Millennium Park embody the spirit of the unfinished plan by Burnham.

In Washington, D.C., the McMillan plan sought to emulate the grandeur of European capitals such as Paris and Rome and brought to completion the vision of L'Enfant. It insulated the federal government area from the rest of the city, creating a monumental core featuring white marble federal buildings designed in the Beaux Arts style, a vast public mall, and a series of public gardens.

Downtown Cleveland, Ohio, has inherited an impressive array of City Beautiful buildings and public space: Massive prominent buildings of similar height, scale, and proportion, each featuring slightly different historicist revival vocabularies, were placed around a central mall area. The mall and civic center, the University Circle buildings, the Cleveland Museum of Art, and Case Western Reserve University are still widely appreciated.

The Columbia University campus in New York City, built between 1891 and 1913 by McKim, William Rutherford Mead, and Stanford White, was conceived as a miniature version of the World's Columbian Exposition of Chicago. John Russell Pope's 1919 plan for Yale University in New Haven, Connecticut, was another distinctive endeavor of the movement.

However, City Beautiful plans reached far beyond the U.S. borders: After American troops had invaded Manila in 1898 and waged war with the Spaniards and Filipinos, the new colonial government planned to transform the city of Manila into a grand capital on the model of Washington, D.C. In 1904 it was again Burnham who conceived a plan for Manila, which he envisioned as a garden city featuring a blend of tropical landscapes, grand panoramic axes, and eclectic colonial architecture. The plan called for a linear mall, bordered by monumental government buildings, which was to connect the Bay of Manila with a capitol building; a series of panoramic roads was to radiate from the national mall. Although the Burnham plan of Manila was never fully implemented, the city's underlying road network still follows the directions set forth by Burnham.

The utopian city envisioned by the architects of the Chicago Columbian Exposition was also a major inspiration for Walter Burley Griffin's plan for Canberra, the Australian capital founded in 1908. The 1911 to 1912 international competition for Canberra gave architects and reformist planners the opportunity to design a brand-new city from scratch. Most competition entries displayed their commitment to the teachings of the City Beautiful movement. The winning entry by Griffin bore the hallmarks of the movement, calling for a harmonious blend between natural landscape and grand architectural design, with residential settlements sporting a mix of Georgian and Mediterranean stylistic repertoire (arches, balconies, tile roofs, and terracotta decorations) and pleasant gardens articulated around lakes and water. The plan for Canberra remained largely unaccomplished: After construction eventually got under way in the 1920s, later the Great Depression and World War II halted building.

The Cultural Legacy of the City Beautiful Movement

By the early 1920s the popularity of the movement declined as the new international style of modernism imposed a focus on pragmatism over aesthetic and on technological innovation and functionality over beauty and decoration.

Yet, with its emphasis on comprehensive, large-scale planning, the City Beautiful movement has left a long lasting mark in the urban fabric of major American cities and has set the standards for modern and rational city planning. According to historian Lubove, its most valuable legacy was the ideal it embodied of the "city as a work of art."

Especially in recent times, elements of the City Beautiful movement's idea have been reappraised and brought back to center stage in the planning debates about car-free cities, smart growth, transit-oriented development, and new towns—attempts to counteract the shapelessness of modernist urban planning and to restore human scale, livability, and pedestrian friendliness in the urban fabric. The historicism and neotraditionalism of planning movements such as the new urbanism are particularly indebted to the legacy of the City Beautiful. New urbanism owes its formal roots to the City Beautiful, adopting its emphasis on the arrangement of civic architecture, plazas, landscaped parks, and public spaces around carefully designed axes and grids. The City Beautiful's long-lasting cultural legacy is also evident in the popular favor that classicist repertoires, vernacular architecture, and historic revivals have encountered in recent times, as the success of neotraditionalist design movements has shown.

The City Beautiful movement has moreover deeply influenced the planning of spaces of leisure and entertainment: the Coney Island of the early 1930s (with its magnificent revivals of vernacular architecture) and the theme parks of today (with their carefully designed sceneries and their historicist revivals) are strongly indebted to the City Beautiful movement and particularly to Burnham's White City. Stephen Mills has argued that today's Disneyland originated from the earliest Victorian world's fairs, in particular the Chicago Fair and the Centennial Exposition of 1876 in Philadelphia. Again with regard to the Columbian Exposition, Pierre De Angelis has contended that contemporary theme parks continue the tradition of a large-scale "urban control zone" by adhering to two key strategies developed at the White City: "embracing a uniform and harmonious architectural style which suggests consensus and contentment, and crafting a simulation of the world which is idealized and stripped bare of any significant risk, conflict or controversy."

The emphasis on order over vitality and on rigid aesthetic rules over the spontaneity and authenticity of the urban setting is probably one of the less convincing elements of City Beautiful ideals. Yet, what City Beautiful architects and planners have accomplished in their grand plans—the built legacy of civic buildings and public spaces, of parks and boulevards—has proven largely beneficial to entire communities up to our day and is still universally appreciated.

Alessandro Busà

See also Architecture; Chicago, Illinois; General Plan; Haussmann, Baron Georges-Eugène; Historic Cities; Ideal City; New Urbanism; Paris, France; Riis, Jacob; Urban Planning; Utopia

Further Readings

Beveridge, Charles E. 1995. *Frederick Law Olmsted: Designing the American Landscape*. New York: Rizzoli.

Boyer, Paul S. 1978. *Urban Masses and Moral Order in America, 1820–1920*. Cambridge, MA: Harvard University Press.

Burnham, Daniel H. and Edward H. Bennett. 1909. *Plan of Chicago*. Edited by C. Moore. Chicago: Commercial Club.

De Angelis, Pierre. 2008. "Beautiful Urbanism: How a Short Lived, Feeble Movement Continues to Shape the Contemporary American City." *Mudot—Magazine on Urbanism* 6:69–72.

Hines, Thomas S. 1979. *Burnham of Chicago: Architect and Planner*. Chicago: University of Chicago Press.

———. 2004. "Architecture: The City Beautiful Movement." In *The Electronic Encyclopedia of Chicago*, edited by J. L. Reiff, A. D. Keating, and J. R. Grossman. Chicago: Newberry Library. Retrieved May 10, 2009 (http://www.encyclopedia .chicagohistory.org/pages/61.html).

Muschamp, Herbert. 1992. "The Nina, the Pinta and the Fate of the White City." *New York Times Architecture View*, November 8.

Reps, John W. 1992. *The Making of Urban America*. Princeton, NJ: Princeton University Press.

Riis, Jacob. 1890. *How the Other Half Lives: Studies among the Tenements of New York*. New York: Scribner.

Rose, Julie K. 1996. "The World's Columbian Exposition: Idea, Experience, Aftermath." MA Thesis, University of Virginia, Charlottesville. Retrieved May 10, 2009 (http://xroads.virginia.edu/~ma96/WCE/ title.html).

———. 1997. "City Beautiful. The 1901 Plan for Washington D.C." Department of American Studies, University of Virginia, Charlottesville. Retrieved May 10, 2009 (http://xroads.virginia.edu/~cap/ CITYBEAUTIFUL/dchome.html).

Smith, Carl. 2007. *The Plan of Chicago: Daniel Burnham and the Remaking of the American City*. Chicago: University of Chicago Press.

Wilson, William H. 1994. *The City Beautiful Movement*. Baltimore: Johns Hopkins University Press.

CITY CLUB

Men seeking to reform city governments in the late nineteenth and early twentieth centuries in the United States founded organizations they called city clubs. These clubs were typical Progressive-era reform organizations that were seeking to diminish the influence of party politics in municipal governments. City club members generally believed that the personal corruption and fiscal irresponsibility of many party politicians and their followers had fostered serious economic, political, and social problems. The stated purpose of these organizations was to foster a sense of civic engagement that would promote honest and efficient administration of city affairs through nonpartisan political action. City clubs originated in eastern and midwestern cities, including Philadelphia, New York City, Chicago, Boston, and Cleveland. Western cities such as Portland and Denver followed this practice. Many of these clubs, espousing the same goals, still exist. Newer clubs, such as the one founded in Seattle in 1981, have kept the tradition alive.

Early in their history, membership in city clubs was all male, with women often not even allowed to participate as guest speakers. Membership was also largely comprised of middle-class, White businessmen and professionals. Clubs enforced their exclusivity through membership rules that carefully controlled admission even though the clubs publicized themselves as open to men from every walk of life. The rigid gender segregation of city clubs was relaxed over time, but by the second decade of the century, women had responded to their exclusion by organizing their own women's city clubs. A key difference between the male and female clubs was in how they perceived their purposes. The women's city clubs generally stressed the fostering of a collective social responsibility for solving municipal issues, whereas clubs of men spoke about wanting more civic engagement among men who were otherwise disaffected from municipal affairs.

City clubs worked through civic committees that investigated specific urban issues such as tax reform, public education, transportation, parks and playgrounds, municipal services such as police, fire, and garbage collection, city planning, and labor. These committees made monthly and annual reports to the club at large. Regularly scheduled luncheon meetings featured invited speakers who addressed the members on pressing urban issues. City clubs generally published bulletins and newsletters in which they publicized their meetings and discussions and presented the club's position on important municipal concerns. City clubs of this type described themselves as dedicated as much to informing city residents of the state of municipal affairs as to effecting actual reforms or recommending particular candidates for municipal offices. While obviously class and gender bound, the early city clubs expressed optimism that once urban residents were better informed of city affairs, they would elect honest and efficient municipal officials who would serve the best interests of the community rather than the interests of political parties. Dedication to fostering civic engagement and political responsibility distinguishes these city clubs from other clubs that may use the name but are actually businessmen's private social clubs.

Maureen A. Flanagan

See also Gendered Space; Progressive City; Public–Private Partnerships; Women and the City

Further Readings

Flanagan, Maureen A. 1990. "Gender and Urban Political Reform: The City Club and the Woman's City Club of Chicago in the Progressive Era." *American Historical Review* 95:1032–50.
Schiesl, Martin J. 1977. *The Politics of Efficiency: Municipal Administration and Reform in America: 1880–1920.* Berkeley: University of California Press.

CITY MAP

Cities began to be mapped almost as soon as they appeared. We have stone city maps from ancient Babylon and many such maps on paper from an early period in China and Japan. The classical Greeks were chiefly known for their maps of the whole world. But the Romans produced remarkable stone plans of such cities as Orange and Rome itself, often setting them up in public places.

All of these ancient plans were more or less planimetric, showing the city as if from directly overhead. In early modern Europe, inspired to some degree by the city plans found in some versions of the *Geography* of Claudius Ptolemy, town plans began to multiply, offering three main types. Particularly in Italy, plans of the classical type became common in the sixteenth century. They were joined, then, by two new types: the "profile" and the bird's-eye view. The profile, analogous to the marine "landfall," showed the city as it would appear to a person approaching it on the ground, while the bird's-eye view showed it from a high oblique angle (and involved some ingenious imaginary constructions).

Many such plans were produced in the first great age of copper-engraving, in the sixteenth century, and at the end of that century many city plans were collected together into the *Civitates Orbis Terrarum* (Cities of the World), published by Georg Braun and Franz Hogenberg in Cologne between 1595 and 1617. Like the contemporary atlas of Abraham Ortelius, the work of Braun and Hogenberg relied on a large number of contributors to provide images drawn, eventually, from much of the world.

These images might adopt any of the three types described earlier. As time went by, the profile became less common, as did the bird's-eye view. Clearly, from the point of view of city planning, a planimetric view offered the greatest possibility for precision. However, profiles and bird's-eye views have never fallen completely out of use. Modern skyscraper cities are often shown as profiles, and bird's-eye views, often with the main buildings shown in an exaggerated way, have proved one of the best ways of introducing a city to tourists.

In the age of computer mapping, city images are of course generally planimetric. The possibility of overlaying a great many variables—streets, electrical conduits, schools, sewers, crime sites, and so on—offers the modern city planner possibilities of analysis that are full of potential.

David Buisseret

See also Urban Geography; Urban Planning; Urban Semiotics

Further Readings

Buisseret, David, ed. 1998. *Envisioning the City: Six Studies in Urban Cartography.* Chicago: University of Chicago Press.
Elliott, James. n.d. *The City in Maps: Urban Mapping to 1900.* London: British Library.
Harley, J. B. and David Woodward, eds. 1987, 1994. *The History of Cartography.* 2 vols. Chicago: University of Chicago Press.

CITY OF MEMORY

Cities and their relationship to memory have been the subject of analysis by authors and scholars in psychology, history, critical theory, philosophy, and architectural theory. This rich body of work has elaborated on several relevant issues, here briefly summarized: the persistence of the past in the city of the present, the metaphor of the city as a palimpsest, and the dialectic of cities and memory—that is, their relationship of dependence, denial, selection, or manipulation of memory.

The persistence of traces of the past in the city of the present is investigated in fragments of Walter Benjamin's work on the Parisian arcades; in these writings he codifies an aesthetic of the City of Memory through the metaphor of archaeological layering: "Each street is a vertiginous experience. The street conducts the *flâneur* into a vanished time"; thus the city is "an epic book through and through, a process of memorizing while strolling around." The city is described as a labyrinthine archaeological landscape in which traces of lives, customs, and events already extinguished still survive. Walking through the streets of Paris, he contends, the multiple layers of history unfold before our very eyes.

In the introduction to *The Architecture of the City*, Aldo Rossi poetically describes the city as an open-air archive of collective and personal memories:

Architecture, attesting to the tastes and attitudes of generations, to public events and private tragedies, to new and old facts, is the fixed stage for human events [. . . .] One need only look at the layers of the city that archaeologists show us; they appear as a primordial and eternal fabric of life, an immutable pattern.

Recalling the images of disemboweled houses of European cities after the bombings of World War II, he too compares the city of the present to an archaeological landscape marked by the traces of past events, by personal memories as well as epic events.

The metaphor of the palimpsest has been paramount in the literature about cities and memory. According to its Greek etymology, the term *palimpsest* refers to papyruses or parchments whose ink was scraped off and written on again, with the earlier writing incompletely erased and still visible beneath the surface. Freud was the first to use the metaphor of the Roman palimpsest to describe the structure of the human unconscious in his psychoanalytic research. In *Civilization and Its Discontents*, Freud recognized a similarity between the layered construction of cities, made of gradual additions and erasures, and the human psyche: "Suppose that Rome is not a human habitation but a psychical entity with a similarly long and copious past—an entity, that is to say, in which nothing that has once come into existence will have passed away and all the earlier phases of development continue to exist alongside the latest one."

Also José Munoz Millanes compares the city to a palimpsest on which time leaves its indelible mark. Its built environment "comes to be the testimony *par excellence* of daily life, because in its fixity the vicissitudes of humankind are registered throughout time."

Freud's metaphor of the Roman palimpsest has proven particularly useful in the analysis of a city's relationship to memory. Classical Rome, medieval Rome, renaissance Rome, baroque Rome, eighteenth-century Rome, postunification Rome, fascist Rome, and reconstruction Rome are all present in today's Rome, overlapped together in a multilayered urban ensemble.

An aesthetic of contrasts and overlapping is the paradigm of the City of Memory. Its multilayered character, made of centuries of additions and subtractions, allows for a reading of the city as a composite of innumerable stories. As the permanence of the past in the present form of the city may manifest itself through sharp contrasts and a disorienting chaos, the urban fabric of Rome shows how these contrasts can be reconciled as parts of a harmonious picture.

An important account of the relationship between time and urban space is Lewis Mumford's conception of the city as both a spatial and temporal container. In *The Culture of Cities,* he writes: "Cities are a product of time. They are the molds in which men's lifetimes have cooled and congealed." He contends that not only monuments and buildings but also fragments of long-gone social behaviors, customs, and traditions may survive in the urban environment of the contemporary city.

The Dialectic of City and Memory

The way cities dialogue with their memory casts a light on the way they relate to their other temporal dimensions: One city's interpretation of its past is inextricably connected to the city's way of envisioning its future, because memory is not a mere transcript of past events but rather a mechanism of interpretation and selection.

Kevin Lynch analyzes the way in which the past is able to influence present and future meanings. According to Lynch, the urban space contains not only physical traces of old morphologies of the city but also crystallizations of meanings that will influence its future. The dialogue that a city establishes with its past is essential to the construction of the city's own identity. As Lynch observes, the city constructs its urban identity through the use of memory: that is, by manipulating its past through a process of selection.

In urban politics, strategies of identity making through a manipulation of the city's collective memory (in city marketing, placemaking, spectacularization, and festivalization efforts) are paramount; such strategies focus on highlighting chosen moments of the history of the city while removing less marketable or unfavored ones. The erasure of memory can be accomplished by means of mere neglect or, in some cases, by physically removing its apparent signs. This has been the case in most east European cities after the fall of the communist regimes, where buildings have been demolished, streets renamed, and monuments removed. Yet, politics of manipulation of memory can also be

carried forward by means of new developments or reconstruction of long-gone buildings and structures: In many cases around the world, buildings whose former existence carried a positive symbolic meaning or embodied a particularly marketable time of the history of the city have been rebuilt *ex novo.*

This issue has been brought up by several authors, including Brian Ladd in his study of Berlin. Pointing to the mistreatment that the Berlin municipality has granted to the built legacy of the communist era after the fall of the Berlin wall, Ladd observes that the way in which urban politics negotiate the physical legacy of their past casts a light on a collective identity. In Berlin the reinvention of a manipulated, purified past goes alongside the idealization of a wishful future. And the way Berlin has negotiated its haunted past and its painful memories is through a double strategy of removal and reinvention of memory.

By privileging selected elements of the past while disregarding unwelcome ones, most postmodern redevelopments of historical sites (from the festival marketplaces to the theme parks, from the renovated historic downtowns to the so-called theaters of memory) deliver a sugarcoated and stereotyped version of history whose objectivity is highly questionable and whose main purpose is to reinvent the image of the city as a more marketable one, thus catering to the lust for nostalgia of citizens and tourists alike.

In his work on the "politics of memory," Andreas Huyssen analyzes the key role of memory in current urban politics. By focusing on the different ways of monumentalizing the past in three cities that have undergone major shocks (Berlin, New York, and Buenos Aires), he concludes that in contemporary societies the celebration of memory has become a global obsession.

A similar conclusion is drawn by Mark Crinson. In his *Urban Memory: History and Amnesia in the Modern City,* he reflects on cities in the postindustrial era and on their frantic search for identity through a pervasive engagement with the past. The same cities that, a few decades ago, were sites of futurist experimentation and centers of forward-looking modernist culture are now reinventing their images as theaters of memory. The spread of movements for historic preservation, the monumentalization of the past, the burgeoning of strategies of commemoration, musealization, and festivalization, all indicate a revolution in a city's approach to memory.

More on "City of Memory"

"City and Memory" is one of 11 categories of cities illustrated in Italo Calvino's book *The Invisible Cities*. In Calvino's book, each of the five imaginary Cities of Memory (Diomira, Isidora, Zaira, Zora, Maurilia) has established a different relationship with its past. Calvino focuses on the massive influence of the past in shaping the present city, explaining the different degrees in which the past may influence the present city: Whereas the city of Maurilia isn't capable of any connection to its memories, Zora is doomed to extinction because it isn't able to leave its past behind. In Zora, the past is a trap that prevents the city from evolving and from being alive.

"City of Memory" is the name of an online narrative cartography created by City Lore, Inc. (a New York City–based organization sponsored by the National Endowment for the Arts and the Rockefeller Foundation), devoted to the documentation and representation of urban folk culture in the city of New York. The website showcases an interactive geographical map of New York City on which New Yorkers' personal stories and memories come to life through open contributions.

"Città della Memoria" (City of Memory) is the title of a cycle of discussions organized by Cesare De Seta, Guido Martinotti, and Massimo Morisi, which took place in Florence in June 2008. The main topics of the debates were the relationship of dependence of great historical cities to their past and memories, the commodification of memory, and the phenomenon of festivalization of the public space in historic downtowns.

The City of Collective Memory is a book by Christine Boyer that describes the ways cities represent themselves and their relationship to their past and future. Boyer analyzes models of self-representation used to construct a selective reading of the city.

Alexandria: City of Memory is the title of a book that revives what author Michael Haag calls "the heydays of cosmopolitan Alexandria" between World Wars I and II. He investigates the complex history of the city through anecdotes and biographies of three great writers in whose work the city figured prominently: Constantine Cavafy, E. M. Forster, and Lawrence Durrell. Haag describes a city filled with memories and secrets, a multilayered, labyrinthine, and fascinating palimpsest whose rich multiethnic texture would later be destroyed by what the author calls former Egyptian President Gamal Abdel Nasser's "puritanical socialism."

Alessandro Busà

See also Architecture; Benjamin, Walter; Berlin, Germany; Lynch, Kevin; Mumford, Lewis; Rome, Italy; Urban Archaeology; Urban Politics; Urban Semiotics

Further Readings

Benjamin, Walter. 1999. *The Arcades Project*. Cambridge, MA: Belknap Press.

———. 1999. *Selected Writings*. Vol. 2, *1927–1934*. Cambridge, MA: Belknap Press.

Boyer, Christine. 1996. *The City of Collective Memory: Its Historical Imagery and Architectural Entertainments*. Cambridge: MIT Press.

Busà, Alessandro. 2008. "Palimpseststadt—The City of Layers." *Mudot, Magazine for Urban Documentation, Opinion, Theory* 1:26–29.

Calvino, Italo. 1978. *Invisible Cities*. Fort Washington, PA: Harvest Books.

Crinson, Mark. 2005. *Urban Memory: History and Amnesia in the Modern City*. New York: Routledge.

Freud, Sigmund. [1930] 1989. *Civilization and Its Discontents*. Translated by P. Gay. New York: Norton.

Haag, Michael. 2005. *Alexandria: City of Memory*. New Haven, CT: Yale University Press.

Huyssen, Andreas. 2003. *Present Pasts: Urban Palimpsests and the Politics of Memory*. Palo Alto, CA: Stanford University Press.

Ladd, Brian. 1997. *The Ghosts of Berlin: Confronting German History in the Urban Landscape*. Chicago: University of Chicago Press.

Lynch, Kevin. 1960. *The Image of the City*. Cambridge: MIT Press.

———. 1976. *What Time Is This Place?* Cambridge: MIT Press.

Mumford, Lewis. 1981. *The Culture of Cities*. Westport, CT: Greenwood Press.

Muñoz Millanes, José. 2003. "The City as Palimpsest." Lehman College and Graduate Center, City University of New York. Retrieved April 5, 2009 (http://www.lehman.cuny.edu/ciberletras/v03/Munoz.html).

Rossi, Aldo. 1984. *The Architecture of the City.* Cambridge: MIT Press.

CITY PLANNING

City planning is a continuous, public process that guides how complex issues such as the provision of infrastructure and the maintenance of an affordable housing stock are balanced with limited community resources. It is the means of creating and maintaining a desirable environment that promotes the health, safety, and well-being of community residents. Using professional planners as guides, communities identify a common vision and collective set of goals for their future. Citizens, with the assistance of planners, decide how their community can be improved today and in the future. Once a community's vision and goals have been determined, city planning provides overall guidance and direction for growth, development, and redevelopment, frequently over a 20-year time period.

American cities have always had some form of planning, dating back to colonial settlements. By the mid-1800s, with rapid growth due to industrialization, cities had evolved into places of severe pollution, filthy streets, and epidemic diseases. A reform movement focused on the improvement of sanitary conditions and housing and ultimately led the U.S. Supreme Court to establish the validity of "police power," allowing communities to legally safeguard the public health, safety, and welfare. Today, city planning deals not only with the physical but also with the social and economic development of metropolitan regions, small towns, and neighborhoods.

The comprehensive or master plan is the document that guides overall growth and development within a community based on a commonly held vision for the future. It is anchored in a planning process that involves several key steps. First, planners gather background data for analysis and interpretation in order to project current and future trends and solicit input from residents and business owners. This leads to alternative scenarios for future growth and development and, eventually, to a plan. Once the plan is formulated and accepted by the governing body, planners work with public agencies and the private sector to carry out the recommended courses of action outlined in the planning document. Planners use implementation tools such as zoning, subdivision regulations, and capital improvements plans that guide how public improvements can be financed. The timing and financing of public improvements ensure the wise and efficient use of public funds for future development and redevelopment.

City planning often involves creating plans for specific geographic areas within the city, such as a neighborhood, district, or transportation or retail corridors. Particularly in large cities, it is easier to create a plan for a portion of the city than for the city as a whole. These area plans differ from a comprehensive plan because of the limited geographic area, the narrower focus, and the greater level of detail. The most typical area plans are for neighborhoods, downtowns, industrial or commercial areas, airports, historic districts, and sensitive environmental sites. Whereas the role of the planner remains the same, typically these area plans have much greater public input because citizens can understand the direct correlation between the planning process and what they will be living with in the near and distant future.

Cities typically have agencies and departments—economic development, housing, transportation, recreation, and open space—that deal directly with different elements of a plan. These elements are directly affected by emerging opportunities. For example, the national as well as local economies have changed from economies based on natural resource extraction and manufacturing to those in which services and information providers are dominant. This shift has created new employment opportunities and business location decisions. Industries were once located near natural resources used in production in order to save on transportation costs. Today, firms are attracted to cities where there is a skilled labor force and a perceived quality of urban life that attracts future qualified employees.

A typical element addressed in the comprehensive plan is housing, the largest consumer of land in communities and a major contributor to overall economic activity. Some of the earliest planning efforts of the late nineteenth and twentieth centuries addressed housing through regulations to ensure direct access to light and air for housing units. Today planners are concerned with such issues as housing affordability and whether or not there is an adequate supply to meet demand. Just as in the comprehensive planning process, planners start by gathering and analyzing data in detail specific to housing. Beyond looking at population and projected population, planners also concern themselves with housing condition, costs, projected new housing starts, household size and income, and vacancy rates. While typically government does not provide housing, zoning and subdivision regulations can directly affect housing supply, including the availability of multifamily housing. Government provision of streets, sewers, water delivery and treatment, and other public facilities and services is planned to encourage development in areas where growth is desired.

Because of the current complexity of cities, planners must deal with land use codes, review development plans, evaluate annexation proposals, encourage infill and sustainable development, set development guidelines and standards, and carry out numerous other tasks that guide development. There are a number of legal means of implementing plans. Based on comprehensive plans, zoning ordinances and subdivision regulations are tools for encouraging growth in some areas and not others. Zoning ordinances divide land uses into zones and regulate land use activity specific to each zone. Subdivision regulations deal with the division of land and the location, design, and installation of infrastructure to service the activities located there. Site reviews done by planners on a site-by-site basis ensure that development conforms to zoning and subdivision regulations and that there is adequate parking, buffering, and landscaping on the site for the particular use. As cities have evolved, the legal tools have become increasingly sophisticated to meet the demands of different land uses. If special environmental or historic sites need protection, overlay zones with greater restrictions may be put into place. Today, cities are seeking more and varied means of controlling growth through such legal tools as infill incentives, transfer of development rights, planned area development, and impact fees.

Another key aspect of city planning is protection of the environment. As cities and towns have expanded into the urban fringe, planners and residents alike are committed to saving open space, protecting wildlife and watersheds, and promoting rural trails and pedestrian and bicycle pathways. Under "smart growth" practices, the comprehensive planning process identifies natural areas and open space, recognizing the importance of balance between the natural and the built environment. A related tool is that of "sustainable" development, which recognizes the need to promote conservation in building practice, including green building, urban water–harvesting techniques, and compact development to encourage use of alternative modes of transportation such as bus, light rail, and bicycle travel.

City planning is vital to ensure that communities make rational choices for their future. The roles that residents and business owners take in the process are key to making decisions that enhance the quality of life for all. Public decision makers are guided by planning and the use of legal tools to obtain the growth, development, and redevelopment desired by community members. As Paul Farmer, executive director and chief executive officer of the American Planning Association, stated in 2005 to the U.S. Government's House Transportation and Infrastructure Subcommittees on Water Resources and Environment, and Economic Development, Public Buildings and Emergency Management, "Planning is, at its core, about managing change in a way that engages citizens, reflects their vision, and results in increased value. . . . Planners have historically been at the forefront of designing places and standards that ensure safety while bolstering vitality and a sense of community."

Barbara Becker

See also General Plan; Planning Theory; Urban Planning; Urban Policy

Further Readings

Dalton, Linda C., Charles J. Hoch, and Frank S. So, eds. 2000. *The Practice of Local Government*. 3rd ed. Washington, DC: International City/County Management Association.

Kelly, Eric Damian and Barbara Becker. 2000. *Community Planning: An Introduction to the Comprehensive Plan*. Washington, DC: Island Press.

Levy, John M. 2003. *Contemporary Urban Planning.* 6th ed. Upper Saddle River, NJ: Prentice Hall.

"A Vision and Strategy for Rebuilding New Orleans." Testimony of Paul Farmer speaking for the American Planning Association before the House Transportation and Infrastructure Subcommittees on Water Resources and Environment, and Economic Development, Public Buildings and Emergency Management, October 18, 2005. Retrieved April 20, 2009 (http://www.planning.org/katrina/pdf/farmerwrittentestimony.pdf).

CITY USERS

City user is a fancy label applied to an analytically based concept, elaborated for two reasons: (1) The inadequacy of the traditional urban analysis, largely based on resident populations, to cope with the accrued mobility of urban areas, and (2) the increased difficulty in explaining urban dynamics based on concepts requiring strong assumptions of collective rationality like all class-based analyses. Thus in 1993 I proposed to reintroduce the concept of populations in urban analysis.

Populations and Collective Rationality

Urban structures, in which we walk or ride every day, are already deeply different from the urban images we have in our mind and in our hearts. Thus there is urgency for a profound reconceptualization of the intellectual and empirical tools we need for the study of urban social facts and processes. It would be naive to pretend to lay down a new theory of urban development, and I do not propose to offer one. But I would like to suggest an effort to analyze urban change, evading the straightjacket of strict social ecological thinking and class analysis, based on the simple concept of population—namely, an aggregate of individuals defined by one or more simple traits—without any strong assumption about their rational collective behavior. This is contrary to the kind of theoretical assumptions we need in order to analyze classes, movements, groups, or organizations. To give an example of both the simplicity of definition and

empirical power of the concept of population, it is sufficient to look at current patterns of urban migration from the third worlds to the developed ones. Migration flows are composed of individuals and households responding to personal circumstance; the effects of these aggregate decisions are far reaching precisely because they are a loose sum of individual actions.

Four Urban Populations

Based on these cursory considerations I propose to represent schematically various types of urban morphologies by using a simple combination of *four populations* differentiating out in successive phases; measurement of these variables is conceptually neat, and labels are needed only for discursive purposes.

		Live	*Work*	*Consume*
A.	Inhabitants	Y	Y/N	Y
B.	Commuters	N	Y	(Y)
C.	City users	N	N	Y
D.	Metropolitan business persons	N	Y	Y

From the Traditional City to the First-Generation Metropolis

In the traditional town, on which all the current thinking about urban life is still largely molded, the inhabitants, or the population living in the city, coincided with the population working in the city. The Industrial Revolution did not greatly affect this situation, because production of goods in the secondary sector requires mostly the shifting of raw materials, manufactured goods, and financial assets, while workers and entrepreneurs remain largely concentrated in urban areas.

The early metropolitan development that took place in the United States from the 1920s, and after World War II in Europe, can be essentially seen as a growing differentiation of two populations: the inhabitants and the workers. One can think of this early metropolitan development as two circles progressively separating one from the other while they both grow in diameter, as in a Venn diagram. While a sizeable portion of the diagram remains overlapping, the two circles come increasingly apart. Commuting is the consequence of this process. All in all, however, early metropolization coexisted with the traditional urban structure to a fair degree.

City Users and the Second-Generation Metropolis

Some of the same factors that contributed to the first-generation metropolis, however, contributed to a further differentiation. The increased mobility of people, combined with the availability of greater income and leisure, allowed the differentiation of a third population in our diagram, the city users, namely, a population composed of persons moving to a city in order to use its private and public services: from shopping, to movies, to museums, to restaurants. This is a swelling population that has increasing effects on the structure of cities and actually uses them in a rather uncontrolled way. There are cities that have a very small population of inhabitants, a slightly larger population of commuters, but a vast population of city users. Venice, Italy, is the extreme case, but many other cities of the world experience phenomena of this kind. Contrary to commuters, city users make use of the public areas of the city, more often than not in a rather barbaric way. It is not surprising that at the beginning of 1990 the mayor of West Berlin declared that he was not worried about disposing of *Der Mauer* "because tourists will take it away." East Berliners seem more organized: They have apparently created a corporation to sell chunks of the Berlin wall, but whether by sale or by theft, the result is the same: A dramatically important piece of the built environment is being used. In practical fact, city users have given body to the famous prophecy of Marx and Engels that the Chinese wall would be destroyed by "the heavy artillery of the soft prices of merchandise."

The size of this city user population is growing, but it is difficult to assess precisely because all collective cognitive apparatus is geared to a traditional city that is undergoing a profound mutation, and statistics still deal mainly with inhabitants, to a smaller degree with commuters, but practically in no way with users. If we want to perceive these

new trends systematically, we have to look to entirely new sources of information. Every year large airport systems handle a transient population numerically equivalent not to the inhabitants of any of the world metropolises, but to entire nations like Italy or the United Kingdom.

Huge traffic clogs in central cities occur not only in the regular commuting hours—to a degree foreseeable and resolvable with public transportation systems—but also during shopping sprees, and in coincidence with great symbolic leisure moments. In Italy by far the most consistent boost to urban development in recent years came from the world soccer championship of 1990. And competition for the hosting the Olympic games or the EXPOs witnesses the increasing crucial importance attached to the city user population by local elites. Sociologically the population of users is difficult to define, for the very lack of statistics just deprecated. An educated guess would assess it as being fairly differentiated, from hinterlands kids roaming and cruising on evenings and weekends, to middle-class tourists and shoppers of all ages, to special groups like soccer fans or concert and exhibition goers. It is very different from the city we are accustomed to deal with in popular and scientific terms and could be defined as the second-generation (or mature) metropolis.

Metropolitan Businesspersons and Global Cities

A fourth metropolitan population is differentiating out. This is a small but very specialized population of metropolitan businesspersons. These are persons who go into central cities to do business and establish professional contacts: businesspeople and professionals visiting their customers, convention goers, consultants, and international managers. This fourth population, relatively small but growing, is characterized by having a considerable availability of both private and corporate money. They typically stay for a few days and sometimes for more extended periods, but they are not a permanent population. They spend part of the time doing business and part of the time using the city, at relatively high levels of consumption. This is a population of expert urbanites; these individuals tend to know their way around, be selective in their shopping and hotel and restaurant use, as well as in the use of top cultural amenities, such as concerts, exhibitions, museums, but also saunas and gyms. Increasingly business and top-level tourism go together. Both the city users and the metropolitan businesspersons are a product of the service industry; whereas secondary-type industries shift goods, services in large part require the shifting of people.

Positing of these four populations does not imply that more traditional class relations and conflicts have disappeared, but there is little doubt that they are undergoing deep transformations that undermine some of the classical socioecological factors of urban class conflict. The strength of the industrial urban proletariat was to a large degree, as it has been noted repeatedly since Marx, a function of its territorial organization. Working-class districts reinforced and projected on the urban plane, so to speak, the class solidarity created in the factory, while the organization of traditional working-class parties and movements relied heavily on the urban ecological niches in which subcultural factors created an extraordinary synergy of economic, social, and political interactions. Much of the lore about industrial cities and early metropolitan areas is centered on these essential components of the urban landscape that tend to wane in the present-day metropolis. In purely numerical terms, the inhabitants are probably the most disfavored of the four populations by the overall dynamic. All in all, then, the traditional class cleavages and solidarities, while by all means still existing and perceivable, give way to new cleavages and group realignments. This analysis receives additional insights in the frame of Anthony Giddens's concept of disembedding as a trait constituent of what he calls "radical modernity." One of the leads suggested by the concept of disembedding points to the analysis of the social consequences of the information and communication technologies.

Guido Martinotti

See also Shopping; Tourism

Further Readings

Giddens, A. 1990. *The Consequences of Modernity.* Stanford, CA: Stanford University Press.

Martinotti, G. 1993. *Metropoli la nuova morfologia sociale delle città.* Bologna, Italy: Il Mulino.

———. 2005. Social Morphology and Governance in the New Metropolis. In *Cities of Europe: Changing Contexts, Local Arrangements, and the Challenge to Urban Cohesion,* edited by Y. Kazepov. Oxford, UK: Blackwell.

COLONIAL CITY

The human appropriation of resources—whether they be land, raw materials, or labor—is by nature a colonial act and, in this respect, urban settlement may be considered inherently colonial. However, here, the colonial city is defined by two parameters: the city as a nucleus of human settlement dependent on, yet separated from, the agricultural hinterland; and the colonial, which is the domination of a minority population over indigenous peoples (who are usually ethnically, racially, or religiously distinct from their colonizers). Whereas many colonial cities were products of nineteenth-century European domination over non-Western lands, the phenomenon of colonial urbanism has a longer trajectory.

Definitions and Features

The words *colony* and *culture* share a common Latin stem—*colere*—that is, to cultivate. *Colonia* was the term used to indicate a public settlement of Roman citizens in a hostile or newly conquered country where settlers, while retaining their Roman citizenship, received land and acted as a garrison for the Roman Empire. The words *colony* and *plantation* were sometimes used interchangeably. Indeed, the Colonial Office of the British Empire was originally called the Board of Plantations. In its early usage in the sixteenth century, the word *plantation* simply referred to settling people; however, it later came to denote a New World mode of production based on the exploitation of slave labor for the production of agricultural staples for a metropolitan market. The cities that grew out of colonization were based on social segregation and political dominance. Colonial cities served as physical expressions of dominance in which the relationships between the dominator and the dominated were clear, and are often characterized by the physical segregation of their ethnic, social, religious, and cultural constituencies. The terms *periphery* (referring to the territory that is colonized) and *metropole* (referring to the imperial center of power) indicate the geographically separate but ideologically related components of colonial urbanism.

Due to the asymmetry of power between the colonized and the colonizers, the colonial project may be defined as a power struggle oscillating between dominance and dependence, and often the morphological layout of the cities reflected this equation. For example, many colonial cities followed a dual-city model with sharp segregation between the urban realms of the colonizer and the colonized. French colonial cities of Morocco such as Fez, Rabat, and Casablanca were marked by the distinction between a European town and "traditional" or native city.

Colonial cities often served as the very apparatus through which domination was maintained over this subject population. Motivated by religious, cultural, or economic ideologies, colonial cities functioned as the environments through which religious or cultural conversion and economic exploitation occurred. For example, colonial cities such as Bombay, Singapore, Kingston, and Rio de Janeiro grew around the ports that serviced the surplus extraction of resources and labor from the colonies to the metropole.

Colonial cities often displayed social diversity, with various racial, cultural, and religious groups organized into a rigid stratification system. This social hierarchy was composed of a ruling elite (colonial settlers), the colonized indigenous population, and an intervening group intermediate in status and power. For example, in Calcutta, British colonists deliberately cultivated a segment of the indigenous elite, who served as intermediaries between the colonizers and the colonized. These elites often lived in grand spaces that were comparable to those of the dominant population and exercised considerable control over their urban environment.

History and Geography

The task of identifying the earliest colonial city is complicated by the limits of archaeology. Therefore, while we know that the sea-based Minoan empire (3000–2200 BC) with its capital at Knossos colonized large tracts of Egypt and Mesopotamia, little evidence regarding the colonies themselves remains from which to glean their colonial nature.

Archaeology, however, has provided some evidence regarding the urbanizing tendencies of the ancient and classical empires such as Egypt and Greece. For example, between 1500 and 1100 BC, the Egyptian Empire established a vast network of colonial cities in the Nubian Nile Valley. The design of these colonial towns was fairly uniform, with a square or rectangular layout enclosed with thick mud-brick walls. Excavations at New Kingdom towns such as Amara West and Sesebi have shown that streets, at least initially, were laid out along the lines of a grid. At the center of each town was a large stone temple, surrounded by storerooms for goods and domestic residences. The Grecian Empire emerged in the late fifth century as an alliance between 300 tribute-paying cities along the Aegean coast. Miletus (in modern Turkey) stands out as the most famous of these and followed Hippodamus's plan for an "ideal" city, where the citizenry would be divided into three classes: artisans, farmers, and soldiers. Urban land would be demarcated as sacred, public, or private and at the center of the city were replicas of the agora (public commons) and the stoa (marketplace) of Athens.

In the postclassical era the Roman Empire provided paradigmatic colonial cities whose grid form evoked the formal organization of the metropole. Following the Roman conquest of Damascus (first century BC) the city was reorganized around an east–west axis (decamanus) and a north–south axis (castrum). Colonnaded streets and a forum further consolidated it as a city of the Roman Empire. Colonial cities also emerged from the Islamic Empire in various parts of North Africa, the Middle East, and the Fertile Crescent. Starting in the late seventh century, Arab invaders to the Nile valley set up garrison towns for their troops. These temporary military camps became the urban kernels around which mosques, commercial markets, and residential quarters grew, eventually turning into a permanent city. Early towns settled by the Arab invaders such as Kufah were arranged around a system of gridded streets that demarcated specific areas for the various tribes that served the colonial army. Colonial cities appear in the Americas around AD 1200, when the Aztecs established the city of Tenochtitlán (present-day Mexico City). By the fifteenth century, owing mainly to the military prowess of the Aztecs, Tenochtitlán served as the center of the Aztec alliance—a confederation of towns from which it received tribute. On the eve of the Spanish conquest, the city was so densely populated (approximately 9 million persons) that the Aztec ruler tried to pressure the "colonies" to increase their tributes to Tenochtitlán, which in turn caused several rebellions. The fourteenth century also saw the rise of the Inca Empire, with its capital at Cuzco (in modern-day Peru). This empire was renowned for its large public works, such as road networks, irrigation systems, and so on. Incan towns such as Chan-Chan and Huanuco Pampa were organized around large plazas from where the Inca himself presided over state ceremonies.

The sixteenth to the late nineteenth century, or the early modern period, was marked by the rise of European powers such as Spain, Portugal, and the Netherlands. The Iberian colonization of the Americas has been understood through the motivation of the colonizers to convert the indigenous population in a religious and cultural sense in an attempt to wipe out existing native cultures. Thus the North American cities of San Francisco and San Diego grew around the religious institution of a Catholic mission that provided the first change from a largely agrarian economy to an urban one. The Dutch colonial city of Zeelandia off the southwest coast of China, established as a trading port in 1624, proved to be one of the most profitable and strategic ports for the Dutch East India Company.

Modern imperialism of the late nineteenth and early twentieth centuries was marked by the rise of empires such as France, Britain, and Italy. The rise of modern industrial capitalism was the primary catalyst for this phase of colonialism, and the success of the Industrial Revolution in Europe was entrenched in the surplus extraction of resources from the peripheries of North Africa, South Asia, and Southeast Asia. During this period colonial administrators and planners used the colonized peripheries for various sociospatial experiments. Colonial urban planners saw the colonies as a tabula rasa (blank slate) onto which they were free to impose their utopian urban ideals—visions that would have been impossible to implement in the metropoles of Paris or London. Thus, the professionalization of urban planning in Europe should be viewed as deeply rooted in the colonial experience.

Theoretical Frameworks

Contemporary understanding of the colonial city owes much to Edward Said's path-breaking book *Orientalism,* which argued that colonialism was based on the epistemological and ontological production of difference between the colonizer and the colonized. Thus, a key element of the process of colonialism was the representation of the native population as powerless, organizationally backward, traditionally rooted (and therefore stagnant), and culturally inferior to the dominant population. Inspired by Said's argument, urban historians and theorists began to look upon colonial cities as the laboratories where this difference was produced and the primary apparatus through which control and domination over the colonized was ensured. These scholars theorized the colonial city through various approaches.

The paradigm of modernization (Rostow) claims that colonial cities were divided into two types of spaces: modern (representative of the dominant population of colonizers) and a preindustrial or traditional city (representative of the native subject population). The space of the modern city is arranged around an industrialized economy and therefore has components such as ports, post offices, and commercial centers, whereas the native space continues to be organized around traditional bazaars based on a workshop system of production. Based on a linear notion of urban development, this paradigm proposes the colonial city as gradually shedding its traditional modes of production and growing into a Western-style capitalist economy.

The colonial city has also been understood as contact between distinct cultures (King) and the physical form that arose out of the imposition of a nonindigenous cultural system on the colonized landscape. This framework of understanding the colonial city assumes that the cultures of the colonizer and colonized were mutually exclusive, and the colonial city is predominantly the result of the contact between these two distinct cultures. In other words, this theoretical framework argues that the form of the colonial city was a direct result of the culture of colonial domination.

A political economy approach (Wallerstein) situates the colonial city within larger economic systems of production and consumption where the urbanization of the third world periphery was based on an unequal exchange of goods and labor with the first world core, and colonial cities were deliberately created to facilitate European capitalist expansion. This theoretical framework was expanded upon by dependency theorists (Frank) who further argued that the core–periphery model of development also replicated itself within the third world, where, once established, colonial cities then developed a dominant relation with the agricultural hinterland, which in turn led to uneven development within the colonies themselves. As it drew labor, raw materials, and agricultural resources from the hinterland, the development of the colonial city went hand in hand with the underdevelopment of the city (through slums, squatters, and tenements) as well as of the rural countryside.

In recent years, urban historians and theorists have looked more closely at colonial cities as the site of indigenous agency (Yeoh), suggesting that the colonized population was more than simply passive recipients of the visions and schemes of the colonizers, but rather exercised agency in the construction of colonial cities through everyday use and negotiations with the dominant population. The end result of the colonial city was thus a compromised version of the ideal schemes as imagined by the colonizer and incorporated a whole host of elements that catered to the indigenous population.

Form and Function

The primary motivations of the colonial project often manifested themselves in the physical formal arrangements of the colonial city. The following paragraphs list some examples of nineteenth- and twentieth-century colonial urbanism.

Racial segregation was a primary preoccupation of colonial planners and administrators. Cities such as Fez (Morocco) and Algiers (Algeria) were designed with distinct quarters for the indigenous population and European colonizers. The two sections of these dual cities were separated by a *cordon sanitaire*—an open green zone—that served as a hygienic as well as symbolic division between the racially distinct areas. Motivated by the medical profession's racial explanation of epidemics and contagious disease, European colonizers justified the cordon sanitaire as vital to the protection of their own health and lives. Colonial racial anxieties were thus manifested as urban apartheid.

Colonial cities were also used as the symbolic devices through which imperial power was represented and displayed. In 1911, when Delhi was proclaimed as the capital of the British Empire in India, a new city was built to house the administrative center of the empire. New Delhi was built adjacent to Shahjahanabad—a city that had been the seat of the Mughal Empire for over 200 years. In building New Delhi, British administrators sought, through visual elements and architectural styles, to represent the British Empire as the rightful successors to the Mughal Empire that they had recently abrogated. Similarly Addis Ababa (in modern-day Ethiopia) became a capital of the Italian empire in 1936. The new capital city, as envisioned by Benito Mussolini, would achieve two interrelated goals: (1) It would establish strict segregation between Black natives and White colonizers, and (2) it would represent the Italian empire as comparable in strength and domination to its French and British counterparts.

A crucial element in the culture of colonialism was the notion of the colonizers as the rightful "proprietors" or "guardians" of the colonized. This paternalistic attitude often manifested itself in the management of indigenous heritage by the colonial authorities. For example, during the late phase of French colonization of North Africa, the colonial authorities took on the mandate of preserving the "native" city in its traditional, picturesque, urban form. In cities like Casablanca and Marrakesh, modern urban amenities such as plumbing, sewage, and street lighting were restricted to the European sections of the town. This strategy denied the indigenous population access to modernity by freezing them into the role of tradition as defined by the colonizers.

The colonial project entailed the movement of large populations of human labor and the subsequent need for housing them in cities. In the late nineteenth century the British colony of Trinidad received 144,000 indentured laborers (mostly Indian males) who were housed in barracks.

Constructed from the cheapest materials, the barracks were essentially warehouses with several rooms (often beds) in a row with shared facilities, which offered very little in the way of privacy for the individuals. Barrack housing was also common in South Africa and was most famously used by the De Beers diamond company in their mining towns (such as Kimberly) to house their convict labor. Here the barracks were arranged around a courtyard and functioned as a closed compound, where the activities of the inmates were monitored as in a prison camp.

Continuing Legacies and New Empires

Does a colonial city stop being colonial when the colonizers leave? The processes and apparatuses put into place during the colonial era did not simply disappear at the moment of decolonization, and several cities continue to be shaped by the legacies of colonialism. The vacuum of power left behind by the departing colonizers was quickly filled by local elites while the urban poor filled the same roles and occupied the shantytowns that were once the realm of the colonized indigene. Urban segregation continues to define many cities with a colonial legacy—albeit along the lines of class and wealth as opposed to race. The legacy of colonialism is also complicated by the fact that there comes a point at which the formerly colonized people cease to perceive their history as colonial and begin to absorb colonial heritage into their postcolonial narratives of national identity. This is apparent in a case like Mexico, where Spanish colonial architecture has now been co-opted as Mexican vernacular heritage.

Globalization has radically altered the form of empire, and as imperial technologies change so do colonial urban forms. A good example is that of Guantánamo Bay: A piece of land occupied by the Americans following the Cuban Spanish American War of 1898, it is a self-sufficient U.S. naval base that is a geographic, legal, and political state of exception. A place where neither the U.S. Constitution nor international law holds sway, Guantánamo has been the site of incarceration for over 700 men from 40 countries starting in early 2002. Labeled as enemy combatants by the U.S. government (rather than prisoners of war), the inmates are neither protected by the Geneva Conventions nor have

access to legal representation that alien prisoners on U.S. soil would normally receive. The inhumane conditions of shackled inmates trapped in small isolated cells and under constant surveillance are reminiscent of early penal colonies of the British Empire in the Caribbean or internment camps built by the United States during World War II to segregate Japanese Americans from the general population.

If indeed the colonial city is defined by the urban manifestation of dominance by a minority population over indigenes, then closer attention must be paid to contemporary imperialism, which manifests itself not in the normative spaces of urbanism but rather in the spaces of exclusion, incarceration, and torture. These may well be the colonial cities of the present as well as the future.

Nezar AlSayyad and
Mrinalini Rajagopalan

See also Capital City; New Delhi, India; Social Exclusion; Urban Planning; World-Systems Perspective

Further Readings

Abu-Lughod, Janet. 1991. *Before European Hegemony: The World System A.D. 1250–1350.* Oxford, UK: Oxford University Press.

Agamben, Giorgio. 2005. *State of Exception.* Chicago: University of Chicago Press.

AlSayyad, Nezar. 1992. *Forms of Dominance: On the Architecture and Urbanism of the Colonial Enterprise.* Brookfield, VT: Avebury.

Frank, Andre Gunder. 1969. *Capitalism and Underdevelopment in Latin America: Historical Studies of Chile and Brazil.* New York: Monthly Review Press.

Home, Robert. 1997. *Of Planting and Planning: The Making of British Colonial Cities.* London: Spon.

Kaplan, Amy. 2003. "Homeland Insecurities: Reflections on Language and Space." *Radical History Review* 85:82–93.

King, Anthony. 1976. *Colonial Urban Development, Culture, Social Power and Environment.* London: Routledge & Kegan Paul.

Ross, Robert and Gerard J. Telkamp, eds. 1985. *Colonial Cities: Essays on Urbanism in a Colonial Context.* Dordrecht, the Netherlands: Martinus Nijhoff.

Rostow, Walter. 1990. *The Stages of Economic Growth: A Non-communist Manifesto.* Cambridge, UK: Cambridge University Press.

Said, Edward. 1978. *Orientalism.* New York: Vintage Books.

Ucko, Peter, Ruth Tringham, and G. W. Dimbleby. 1972. *Man, Settlement, and Urbanism.* London: Duckworth.

Wallerstein, Immanuel. 1974. *The Modern World System.* London: Academic Press.

Wright, Gwendolyn. 1991. *The Politics of Design in French Colonial Urbanism.* Chicago: University of Chicago Press.

Yeoh, Brenda. 1996. *Contesting Space: Power Relations and the Urban Built Environment in Colonial Singapore.* Oxford, UK: Oxford University Press.

COMMON INTEREST DEVELOPMENT

Common interest developments (CIDs) go by several names, including residential community associations and common interest communities. They can include many types of housing ranging from detached single-family homes or townhouses in a planned unit development to apartment units in a condominium or cooperative. They may be gated—that is, surrounded by walls or fences restricting access—or not gated.

The distinguishing feature of a CID is common property ownership. In addition to an individual interest in a house or an apartment, each property owner holds a shared interest in a common asset such as the streets, parks, or recreational facilities of a large, master-planned community or the stairways and hallways of a high-rise apartment building.

Each homeowner is automatically a member of a homeowners association that manages the common areas and enforces community-wide deed restrictions known as conditions, covenants, and restrictions (CCRs). Drafted by the land developer, CCRs are servitudes or contracts that "run with the land" and bind all future homebuyers. Amendments to CCRs typically require a two-thirds vote of homeowners. The association's elected board of directors can adopt operating rules on its own or by a simple majority vote.

As private membership organizations, homeowners associations can exercise greater control than municipalities over resident land use and behavior. Common restrictions include limits on exterior paint colors, lawn maintenance, and architectural design as well as "lifestyle" constraints on pet ownership and sign posting. CCRs also authorize the homeowners association to levy assessments for collective services such as snow removal, garbage collection, street cleaning and lighting, and security. Assessments are backed by the power to place liens on delinquent properties and, ultimately, to foreclose without judicial approval. Because their activities resemble those of traditional local government, CIDs are often called "private governments."

Over the past 40 years, these private governments have proliferated. In the early 1960s, there were fewer than 500 CIDs in the United States. In 2006, there were an estimated 286,000 of them representing 17 percent of the housing stock. Although some of the largest and best-known CIDs are in the East (e.g., Columbia, Maryland, and Reston, Virginia), their growth has been concentrated in the Sunbelt region. In California, for example, CIDs include roughly one quarter of the housing stock and 60 percent of current housing starts. Planned developments alone represent more than 40 percent of new single-family home sales.

Several commentators have referred to the growth of CIDs as a "quiet revolution." Viewpoints differ on whether this is positive or negative. Proponents argue that CIDs protect homeowners from declining neighborhood quality and promote efficiency in the delivery of local public goods. Critics argue that CIDs overly restrict individual freedoms and harm nonmembers by exacerbating residential segregation and undermining public support for local taxes and spending.

Tracy M. Gordon

See also Condominium; Gated Community; Homeowners Associations; Tiebout Hypothesis

Further Readings

McKenzie, Evan. 1994. *Privatopia.* New Haven, CT: Yale University Press.

Nelson, Robert H. 2005. *Private Neighborhoods and the Transformation of Local Government.* Washington, DC: Urban Institute Press.

COMMUNITY

The concept of community has appeared regularly throughout urban studies and is generally employed in reference to all aspects of the social life of cities, including population size, demographic distribution, and neighborhood composition. Traditionally used by anthropologists, sociologists, geographers, and urban planners to signify a set of social relationships operating within a specific boundary, location, or territory, community is arguably one of the most contested concepts used in the study of the city and society. Many of these usages are either actual or ideal in description, and it is often difficult to separate analytical from normative usages of the term.

Although conventionally evoked to describe the characteristics of a specific locality or area, the idea of community has also been used in far more ideological terms as a means by which to substantiate a particular identity (e.g., lesbian community) or to further a specific political project (e.g., community-based grassroots activism). Recent definitions of community have tended to depict it more in social and political terms rather than as a distinctly spatial structure.

Defining Community

Notwithstanding the fact that community has been notoriously difficult to define in any concise and uncontested manner, four broad approaches can be identified. The first approach conceives of community as a set of social relations occurring within a distinctly spatialized and geographical setting. Within the disciplinary fields of anthropology, sociology, geography, rural studies, and community studies more generally, there exists a rich body of work that has focused upon the form and function of specific communities in this sense of the term.

A second approach conceptualizes community as the outcome of a particular mode of social interaction among individuals or social groups. Premised upon varying degrees of consensus and conflict, this more sociological approach essentially views community to be the product of ongoing negotiation between social actors.

Community has been used in a third sense to describe a particular type of social relationship between the individual and society. This perspective is perhaps closest to a commonsense interpretation of community, as it evokes the notion of community as a search for belonging and desire for group membership.

The fourth approach looks at how the foundational nature of community has been decisively altered by innovations in the use of communications and computer technology. According to this view, developments in communicative and virtual technology have fundamentally undermined more traditional conceptualizations of community and radically altered the means by which individuals and social groups generate bonds of attachment. Rather than defining community in terms of geographical or spatial proximity, communities in this sense are virtual and cyber-based.

Classical Formulations of Community

Variously conceptualized throughout classical social theory as threatened with dissolution by the advent of modernity, the concept of community has proven to be a resilient and recurrent trope in both theoretical and practical analysis. Writing in the late nineteenth and early twentieth centuries, European classical sociologists such as Ferdinand Tönnies and Émile Durkheim expressed concern regarding the breakdown of traditional social bonds and sources of moral cohesion. The dynamic effects of industrialism, demographic growth, immigration, and rapid urbanization were seen as combining to produce a fundamental rupture between the traditional social formations of folk society and those of modern urban society. In this view, the obligatory ties of duty and responsibility toward the community that were characteristic of premodern society were being replaced by social formations based on mutual differentiation and contractually based social relations.

Tönnies suggested that forms of communal association based upon family, kinship group, and spatial proximity (*Gemeinschaft*) were yielding to forms of societal association premised upon impersonal and contractual relationships (*Gesellschaft*). This view essentially suggested the realization of community to be incompatible within the institutional complexity of modern society. According to Tönnies, the transition from Gemeinschaft to Gesellschaft entailed a fundamental sociopsychological shift in human consciousness. Whereas traditional forms of human association had produced organic communities of social and moral cohesion, the sheer complexity of modern society has led to the irreparable fragmentation of communal and social bonds. The transition from relatively close-knit and proximal spatial configurations to the large-scale dispersal of population aggregates within urban settings was seen by Tönnies to fundamentally challenge the very existence of community as traditionally conceived.

Although sharing a concern with Tönnies regarding the disintegrative effects of social change, Durkheim argued that the type of group solidarity produced in complex urbanized societies could also form the basis for the emergence of new forms of communal life. A key question in this regard was how a sense of collective morality could be maintained amid the increasing differentiation and complexity of modern society. The answer proposed by Durkheim initially seems contradictory. On the one hand, an increase in occupational specialization and the development of complex social arrangements has meant that traditional ways of life have declined, thereby creating pervasive feelings of social and moral disintegration. Durkheim referred to this condition of social discord as "anomie." Conditions of anomie arise when sudden and disruptive changes occur in social structure. Rather than lament this state of affairs, however, Durkheim suggested that new forms of solidarity and community could grow from the institutional bases of modern society. Although Durkheim remains vague as to what precise shape these communal forms may take, his emphasis upon the nature of collective morality, social cohesion, and the differentiation of modern life was to exercise a significant influence upon subsequent theories of community.

Such conceptualizations of community often held it to be synonymous with an attachment to locality. In this view, urbanization was gradually transforming the Gemeinschaft of intimate communal relations into the Gesellschaft of instrumentally conceived and bureaucratized mass society. If society is conceived as the locus of the lifeworld, situated between the twin institutional pillars of state and economy, community represented a bounded spatiality in which cohesive social mores could be embedded. This suggests community to be, in essence, a value term. Despite the many ways in which community has been defined, attention should be directed to the fact that many such descriptions posit a certain type of community as the normative ideal. In this sense, debates on community have been bedeviled by conceptual and methodological disagreement as to where the boundaries of community could or should be drawn. Although differing in terms of theoretical analysis, the classical theorists held the decline of community to be of the most profound consequence with regard to the effects on collective morality and social life.

More recent discussions in social theory have reformulated these dynamics in terms of the interconnections between the local and the global. Given the extent to which the forces of globalization have intruded upon the lifeworld of the local context, the study of community as a bounded entity has undoubtedly lost much of the legitimacy it once held. A prominent example of this has been the decline of community studies as a clearly recognizable field of study. Traditionally a strength of Anglo-American anthropology and sociology, the transformation of industrial and workforce relations has revealed how the study of any particular community must now by necessity take account of an encompassing context of globalization. Indeed, even to assume the existence of community is to risk the accusation of adhering to a reactionary and conservative interpretation of contemporary social and political relations.

Although classical social theory presented the decline of community as a critique of Western industrialism and urbanization, such appraisals have been of less salient concern in the global South. Indeed, if the transformative dynamism of industrialism in Western society was implicitly juxtaposed with the perceived stasis of the non-Western world, such considerations are indicative of an ethnocentric bias informing classical theories of community. Critiques of industrialism and urbanization outside of the Western tradition, thus, often eschew discussion on the decline of community in favor of critical engagement with the effects of global and economic growth. Ranging from South Africa to Manila to Sydney, community-based grassroots activism and resistance to globalization and capitalist expansion have been of more urgent concern. Typically focusing on determinants of employment, health, poverty, and demographic change, theorizations of community outside of the Anglo-American tradition have been far more applied in nature.

Community and the City

A concern with the effects of urbanization and demographic change in the city has been central to urban studies throughout the twentieth century. The Chicago School of Urban Sociology proposed a vision of urban study in which the city was revealed as a composite "mosaic of little worlds." While inheriting from the European theorists a concern with the disintegrative effects of modern society, Chicago School research also emphasized the means by which community found expression in large urbanized settings. Ethnographic explorations of everything from particular social groups, neighborhood locales, and occupational niches (e.g., gangs, street corners, taxi-cab drivers, and many others) revealed distinct sociocultural enclaves of communal sentiment worthy of further investigation.

Central to the Chicago School analysis of urban growth and development was the employment of a human ecology perspective in which the city was seen to develop and expand organically due to ongoing waves of immigrant invasion and succession. Although much criticized by subsequent scholars for making vast generalizations regarding processes of urban development deemed specific to northeastern U.S. cities, the ecological framework nonetheless remained a dominant paradigm in U.S. urban studies of urban planning and development until the 1960s. A key insight of Chicago School scholarship was the recognition that dynamics occurring at the local and community level had significant impact upon the overall structure of the city.

Arising out of the Chicago School approach, the study of subcultures in the city challenged the prevailing determinism in urban sociology by advocating that the heterogeneity of city life, and associated dynamics of urban growth, led to the development of recognizable subcultural enclaves characterized by the presence of distinct class and ethnic communities. Emphasizing the means by which community was realized in complex urban settings, this perspective fundamentally challenged the theory of social anomie as proposed by the European social theorists. Furthermore, the emergence of such thriving ethnic and immigrant neighborhoods seemed to directly contradict the guiding thesis of Chicago School sociologists that such groups would eventually assimilate and blend with their host society.

Notwithstanding the legacy and influence of the Chicago School, urban scholars have continued to contest the form and function of community in city life. Signaling a shift from anthropologically inclined studies of urban life to political economy perspectives, many critically and Marxist oriented scholars have argued that the rise of global capitalism has proven detrimental to the realization of community in contemporary urban settings. Arguing that the hegemony of global capitalism has led to the displacement of community in city life, such perspectives suggest community to be antithetical to the logic of a capitalist and neoliberal world order.

Many such discussions have been conducted within the context of debates on gentrification and urban regeneration. Indeed, visions of urban planning and renewal often evoke the semantics of community as being of central importance to the revival and rejuvenation of dilapidated urban areas. In this regard, renewal initiatives are seen as breeding new life into stagnant and dilapidated urban areas that would otherwise fall into a state of even greater disrepair. Often described as involving the relocation of middle-class professionals from suburban neighborhoods back into central urban areas, practices of gentrification are thereby seen as displacing working-class populations, ethnic minority residents, bohemian lifestyles, and economically stagnant business enterprises from their long-standing communities. In addition, the declining analytical salience of the Chicago School approach has been further undermined by its lack of applicability to the developmental logic of cities in the global South.

The growing strength of critical perspectives on community and urban life has been paralleled by an emphasis upon the intensification of ethnoracial practices of marginalization. For example, sociologist Loïc Wacquant has argued that an institutionalized system of urban exclusion has led to the American ghetto becoming an "impossible community" within the contemporary civic order. Accordingly, racialized segregation, systemic discrimination, declining social capital networks, the withdrawal of social services, and pervasive stigmatization have all combined to prevent the emergence of community in poverty stricken areas of the city. The rise of gated communities and fortified urban enclaves (ranging from São Paulo to Los Angeles) has only served to exacerbate this discrepancy in social-economic and psychological division through the production of mere simulacra of community. Indeed, the idea of community as a gated or defensive enclosure intuitively contradicts the positive connotations that often accompany the inclusion of the notion of community in planning and policy discourse.

International migration has also fundamentally altered the constitution of community in the contemporary global city. Characterized by the maintenance of transnational personal and economic networks, contemporary immigrant communities avail of the communicative and technological innovations of globalization to forge links between homeland and host country. In a study of West African street vendors in New York, Paul Stoller and Jasmin McConatha demonstrate how religious and ethnic affiliation form the basis of the maintenance of the transnational spaces that increasingly typify community diasporas in the contemporary city. Furthermore, revitalized "ethnic enclaves" (e.g., Chinese and Korean communities) have adapted to the morphology of cultural and economic globalization to become dynamic transnational communities and catalysts of urban growth.

The Revival of Community

Three broad trends can be discerned when considering the utility of the concept of community in contemporary urban studies. A first trend is contained in communitarian debates regarding civic engagement. If identification with a particular community is dependent upon the cultivation of a sense of belonging, the revival of civic associations and local community networks are deemed essential. Such imperatives as the maintenance of social capital networks, public participation in decision making, the ongoing provision of goods and services, and the facilitation of economic activity and growth all resonate with the emphasis placed upon community in communitarian thought.

Combining an emphasis on the importance of community with a stress on citizenship, the communitarian position is most clearly understood when conceived of as a position that challenges the liberal emphasis placed upon individual autonomy and achievement of personal fulfillment. The perceived decline of a culture of volunteerism, coupled with an increasingly atomized urban order, has led many communitarian scholars to lament the passing of a strong sense of civic engagement. Influential political scientist Robert Putnam has suggested that the decline in the strength of social capital networks can be reversed by investment in community building civic initiatives and increased levels of democratic participation. Such community building imperatives, however, often posit an idealized rather than actualized model of civic cooperation and thereby fail to empower marginalized social groups. As a result, the communitarian position has been subject to considerable criticism with regard to what is perceived as a limited, nostalgic, and somewhat retrogressive interpretation of what constitutes community. It is in this sense that critics of the concept have cited its frequently ideological usage and tendency to depict the changing nature of community in modern urban life in strictly pathological terms. Notwithstanding these criticisms, communitarian thought continues to exercise significant influence upon government policy and community development initiatives.

A second trend suggests that the nature of community has become a far more voluntaristic means of social engagement as individuals come together on the basis of similarity of ideas, taste, lifestyle, and niche interest. In this view, community is heavily circumscribed by the nature of the particular identity or interest pursuit, and characterized by relatively fluid and transient criteria of membership. Accordingly, community members come and go as levels of commitment wane and differ. The political implications of this can be seen in social movements that evoke the semantics of community as a rallying call. Although such social movements can be either liberatory or conservative in their stated aim, the sheer abstractness and complexity of contemporary society often compels individuals and groups to seek solidarity and membership in such voluntaristic collectivities. When considering that these new forms of communities are certainly not as cohesive or obligatory as those formed by kin and clan, the question remains of whether employing the term *community* is even applicable in these instances.

Thirdly, the dis-embedding of community from local sites of social interaction, due to developments in media and communicative technology, has decisively altered the means by which community is constituted. In this view, community has become less dependent upon face-to-face forms of social interaction and more upon virtual networks of connectivity. Accordingly, the emergence of new communicative technologies, such as the proliferation of personal and professional social networking sites on the Internet, offer immense potential with regard to the fostering of social bonds across lines of both distance and difference. Although debates continue as to the actual rather than potential degree of democratization such innovations facilitate, the growing predominance of virtual networking supports the thesis that spatial and residential proximity are no longer defining prerequisites for the constitution of community.

Undoubtedly, innovations in virtual technology have greatly facilitated the expression of new forms of community and group membership. Although care is needed to avoid the conflation of the idea of connectivity with that of community, the type of attachments formed in virtual networks can, if they are not communities in themselves, certainly provide the basis for them. In this regard, the claim that virtual communities exist in parallel expression with grounded communities is a highly plausible one. While such a claim collapses the distinction between real and imagined communities, a key point of contention involves a questioning of the degree of obligation and commitment such communities seemingly require. If face-to-face interaction and residential location are no longer the primary determinants of community belonging, the episodic nature of virtual communities is indicative of their highly personalized and compartmentalized nature.

Rather than being rendered obsolete by the transformative impact of the effects of globalization, the importance of community in urban studies today arguably lies in the achievement of newly emergent forms of belonging. Sociologist Zygmunt Bauman has suggested that much contemporary scholarship has demonstrated a veritable "lust" for community in this regard. As the global economy becomes increasingly dependent upon the transnational flow of people, capital, goods, and services, the changing face of international mobilities and virtual technologies continues to fundamentally reconfigure the form and function of community in everyday life.

Alan Gerard Bourke

See also Chicago School of Urban Sociology; Community Development; Community Studies; Gated Community; *Gemeinschaft* and *Gesellschaft*; Human Ecology

Further Readings

Bauman, Zygmunt. 2001. *Community: Seeking Safety in an Insecure World.* Cambridge, UK: Polity Press.

Caldeira, Teresa P. R. 1996. "Fortified Enclaves: The New Urban Segregation." *Public Culture* 8(2):303–28.

Calhoun, Craig. 1998. "Community without Propinquity Revisited: Communications Technology and the Transformation of the Urban Public Sphere." *Sociological Inquiry* 68(3):373–97.

Desai, Ashwin. 2002. *We Are the Poors: Community Struggles in Post-apartheid South Africa.* New York: Monthly Review Press.

Durkheim, Émile. 1984. *The Division of Labour in Society.* London: Macmillan.

Hampton, Keith and Barry Wellman. 2003. "Neighboring in Netville: How the Internet Supports Community and Social Capital in a Wired Suburb." *City and Community* 2(3):277–311.

Park, Robert. 1952. *Human Communities: The City and Human Ecology.* Glencoe, IL: The Free Press.

Putnam, Robert. 2000. *Bowling Alone: The Collapse and Revival of American Community.* New York: Simon & Schuster.

Shatkin, Gavin. 2007. *Collective Action and Urban Poverty Alleviation: Community Organizations and the Struggle for Shelter in Manila.* Aldershot, UK: Ashgate.

Stoller, Paul and Jasmin T. McConatha. 2001. "City Life: West African Communities in New York." *Journal of Contemporary Ethnography* 30(6):651–77.

Tönnies, Ferdinand. 1963. *Community and Society.* New York: Harper.

Vromen, Ariadne. 2003. "Community-based Activism and Change: The Cases of Sydney and Toronto." *City and Community* 2(1):47–69.

Wacquant, Loïc. 1993. "Urban Outcasts: Stigma and Division in the Black American Ghetto and the French Urban Periphery." *International Journal of Urban and Regional Research* 17(3):366–83.

COMMUNITY DEVELOPMENT

Community development refers to a wide variety of practices that enable communities to rebuild their housing, local economies, and social fabric. It can be conducted in poor rural communities to improve agricultural practices and poor urban communities to rebuild deteriorated housing. It can also occur in small towns around downtown revitalization. Community development can even provide residents with access to computer technology and is frequently used in crime-ridden communities to reestablish social relationships.

Community development is sometimes confused with economic development. Economic development, though, is not necessarily community based and may be controlled by large corporations or governments. A government- or corporation-imposed development plan is not considered community development. Both the United Nations 50 years ago and the Community Development Society today specify that involvement of community members in diagnosing problems and developing solutions to them is crucial to successful community development.

There is also international variation in the use of the term. Whereas in the United States, community development has been referred to as "sticks and bricks"—the practice of refurbishing decayed central city properties—in the rest of the world it can easily refer to rebuilding social relationships among neighbors or even advocating for social change through the practice of community organizing.

International History

Much of the international emphasis of community development has been on communities in the third world. Large international organizations such as the World Health Organization or the World Bank are often considered community development organizations. But they do not meet the requirement of community participation and control. However, a number of practitioners working for large governmental or nongovernmental organizations did practice community development in the post–World War II era. Community development was integrally connected to the green revolution of the time, which attempted to establish new forms of high-yield agriculture in third world nations.

Community workers of the time promoted the practice of involving and empowering grassroots community members. Some worked against the official policies of their government or organization to conduct community development. These practitioners left behind new attitudes and hope and provided the groundwork for the modern sustainable development movement in the third world. Upon returning to the United States or Europe, they ushered in a new emphasis on grassroots participation at home.

Perhaps because of the variety of conditions that community workers found across the third world, the multiplicity of needs and issues in any one place, and the presence of community workers from nations that provided a stronger social safety net than the United States, community development in the third world focused on housing, rural agricultural development, urban commercial and human-scale industrial development, and community organizing, often together. In the United States, community work is compartmentalized into separate and specialized organizations.

Community Development in the United States

The historical origins of community development in the United States are uncertain. The early 1900s settlement house movement is one starting point, in which upper-class women established agencies in central city immigrant communities to combat a lack of city services, discrimination, and unhygienic conditions. The most famous of such settlement houses was Hull House, established by Jane Addams and Ellen Gates Starr. Another trend of about the same time was the Extension Service of the U.S. Department of Agriculture, often connected to land-grant colleges and universities, which helped farm families to be more successful and achieve a higher quality of life.

Community development experienced its greatest transition in the 1960s and 1970s with the rise of the community development corporation (CDC). From its origins in the Bedford-Stuyvesant neighborhood of New York City in 1967, the CDC movement has grown to the point that nearly all medium and large U.S. cities now have at least one CDC. In many cases, CDC growth was fueled by the philanthropic funders' increasing distaste for the more political community organizing groups and their desire to fund organizations that had more of a social service mission. The original CDCs addressed a wide range of problems in neighborhoods, but most CDCs found their greatest successes later in building housing and redeveloping commercial buildings. CDCs today are primarily specialized nonprofit organizations governed by a board of directors who may or may not represent the neighborhood in which the CDC operates.

Methods of Community Development

The community development process often starts with the diagnosis of an undesirable community condition. Where factories, middle-class residents, and the commercial base have departed, this is often difficult. The diagnosis needs to fully incorporate the conditions of the community and offer some hope that improvements can be made. A variety of methods are used in the diagnostic process, ranging under the headings of SWOT (strengths, weaknesses, opportunities, threats) analysis, rapid rural appraisal (and a variant called participatory rural appraisal), needs assessments, and asset assessments. Although varying in focus, all concentrate on helping residents identify what is happening in their community so that they can develop plans for changing those conditions that are deemed undesirable.

Once the diagnosis has been completed, a strategy for change is developed. This involves community planning and can range from broad-based "visioning" of what a community might look like in the future to concrete planning around a specific issue or place. The challenge is to identify and bring together stakeholders such as landlords and tenants, workers and business owners, or government officials and members of excluded communities who may have antagonistic goals.

The next step is to implement the program that has been developed through the first two stages. Gaining community participation and involvement is part of the program. Doing so prevents the further disempowerment of disinvested communities through intervention programs that are top-down and treat community members as clients rather than as people with talents and wisdom.

The final step in effective community development is evaluation, though it is misleading to think of evaluation as occurring at the end of a program. Good evaluation actually begins at the diagnostic stage, as people define an issue, work to understand the issue, and then design an intervention. A good intervention plan will include methods for determining how well the intervention is working. Such evaluation can improve the success of the intervention.

Community Development Intermediaries

Although the emphasis is on grassroots involvement and control, many community development efforts require a high level of skill and a large amount of capital. A large number of CDCs are small, nonprofit organizations with only a few staff and have boards made up partly or wholly of residents from the neighborhoods they serve. Such organizations often lack expertise in real estate, insurance, contracting, finance, and the other technical areas crucial to successful community development.

This is where community development intermediaries play a role. Intermediaries provide technical assistance and capital for community development organizations to undertake complex and comprehensive community development tasks. Organizations such as the Development Training Institute and the Local Initiatives Support Corporation have been created to improve the success of community-level community development organizations in the United States, though they are sometimes seen as controlling rather than facilitating community processes. Internationally there are numerous organizations providing technical assistance within nations and international organizations, such as the Institute of Development Studies in Sussex, England.

Major Trends

One of the trends in community development has been a shift from "deficits" to "assets." Promoted by the Asset-Based Community Development Institute, this emphasis is controversial. Supporters argue that focusing on community needs makes poor communities appear helpless and incompetent. Opponents argue that a focus on assets mystifies or ignores processes of exploitation and oppression that keep down communities. Another recent trend is the refocusing of CDCs on community organizing. After being criticized for becoming overly professionalized and separated from the communities they were charged with redeveloping, CDCs in the 1990s looked for new ways to involve residents in developing their own communities. While they called this practice "community organizing," it was more often a form of resident participation rather than a process of forming an independent, resident-led community organization. The most developed of these programs is the Ricanne Hadrian Initiative for Community Organizing sponsored by the Massachusetts Association of CDCs.

The comprehensive community initiative is another innovation. The idea of solving multiple community problems simultaneously has never left the field of community development, even when it became clear that the CDC was not an effective vehicle for dealing with crime, housing, jobs, education, and all the other issues affecting marginalized communities. In its most recent form, comprehensive community development now involves a coalition of community organizations coordinating their efforts on a single neighborhood.

Faith-based community development is another recently popular approach. Church-sponsored community development organizations, most commonly CDCs, have long been a part of the community development scene in the urban United States. But they became politically significant with the establishment of a special funding stream under the George W. Bush administration. Their community development strategies are similar to those of secular CDCs.

The final trend worthy of note is the community informatics movement. As computers and the Internet have become more and more important in daily life, the recognition of the consequences of not having access to such technology has grown. The field of community informatics focuses on information and communication technology as a form of community development.

Through these different trends, community development is broadening its perspective and diversity of practices in the United States and the world. More U.S.-style community organizing is being incorporated into community development practices in developing countries, and more grassroots participation in "bricks and sticks" community development is happening in the United States. In the coming decades, as the world grows yet smaller, we will likely see a more globalized community development practice where successes and tools are more readily shared and adapted across borders and cultures.

Randy Stoecker

See also Community Organizing; Housing Policy; Neighborhood Revitalization; Public–Private Partnerships

Further Readings

Green, G. and A. Haines. 2001. *Asset Building and Community Development*. Thousand Oaks: CA: Sage.

Journal of Urban Affairs. 2004. Special Issue on Community Development, 26(2).

Kenny, S. 1999. *Developing Communities for the Future: Community Development in Australia*. South Melbourne, Australia: Nelson.

Rubin, H. 2000. *Renewing Hope within Neighborhoods of Despair: The Community-based Development Model*. Albany: State University of New York Press.

Stoecker, R. 1997. "The CDC Model of Urban Redevelopment: A Critique and an Alternative." *Journal of Urban Affairs* 19:1–22.

Yin, J. 1998. "The Community Development Industry System: A Case Study of Politics and Institutions in Cleveland, 1967–1997." *Journal of Urban Affairs* 20:137–57.

COMMUNITY GARDEN

Community gardening is an urban social phenomenon that arose in the United States and Canada in the 1970s as a form of grassroots reinvestment by local communities. A series of fiscal depressions in the 1960s and 1970s led to widespread disinvestment in many inner-city neighborhoods. City services such as garbage collection, street repair, and maintenance of public spaces were often nonexistent in poverty-stricken areas. Landlords found it increasingly profitable to let buildings deteriorate or to actively burn structures down for insurance monies, leaving many neighborhoods with numerous vacant lots. Coupled with national trends of middle-class flight to suburban developments and broad shifts in the economy away from a manufacturing-based workforce, the resulting social landscape was of high unemployment rates in rapidly depopulating neighborhoods already blighted with derelict buildings and rubble-strewn vacant lots. Urban decay left communities feeling isolated and powerless in physical and social ghettos. The first community gardens were planted when local residents began cleaning up vacant lots for community use.

Gardens varied widely based on local needs. Gardens were used to educate schoolchildren, run voter registration drives, feed the homeless, and rehabilitate drug addicts. Larger gardens were often divided into sections containing everything from ornamental ponds and vegetable boxes to performance stages and basketball courts. In general, gardens provided sites of community solidarity, multigenerational cooperation, safe play spaces for children, environmental education, food production, cultural heritage, and informal public gathering spaces. The resulting proliferation of community gardens closely paralleled a national trend toward grassroots urban activism. Cities began promoting community gardening efforts by legalizing existing gardens and issuing temporary leases to new gardens sited on city-owned land.

A community garden in Portland, Oregon

Source: Teresa Herlinger.

Beginning in the 1980s, large numbers of community gardens sited on public land were cleared to make way for new development. In part due to increasing land values, municipal governments began selling off community garden lots for housing and business projects. Gardeners responded through public protests, petitions to city governments, and pleas through the popular media. A politicized community gardening movement coalesced through calls for local solidarity and empowerment in many cities, aided inpart by support from environmental and antigentrification groups. Recent academic work on community gardens has focused heavily on the discourse and meaning of contested public space, the right to the city of marginalized social groups, and the strategies used by both local communities and the state to define and control community-run public spaces.

Kristina E. Gibson

See also Community Organizing; Gentrification; Neighborhood Revitalization; Right to the City

Further Readings

Schmelzkoph, Karen. 1995. "Urban Community Gardens as Contested Space." *Geographical Review* 85(3):364–81.

———. 2002. "Incommensurability, Land Use, and the Right to Space: Community Gardens in New York City." *Urban Geography* 23(4):323–43.

Staeheli, Lynn, Don Mitchell, and Kristina Gibson. 2002. "Conflicting Rights to the City in New York's Community Gardens." *GeoJournal* 58: 197–205.

Warner, Sam. 1987. *To Dwell Is to Garden: A History of Boston's Community Gardens.* Boston: Northeastern University Press.

COMMUNITY ORGANIZING

Community organizing is the practice of bringing people together, face to face, to solve local problems and, sometimes, change the distribution of power. The practice is associated mostly with Saul Alinsky, but the civil rights movement of the 1950s and 1960s in the United States also organized people on a local basis.

Community organizing usually begins with a trained community organizer entering a community that has been excluded from power, from which investment has been withdrawn, or both. The organizer talks to residents, often by utilizing a practice called door-knocking, where he or she literally goes door to door asking about residents' concerns. Once the organizer has identified the concerns about which people feel strongly, he or she will call meetings so that residents can develop actions to address their problems. The early meetings often involve just a few people and are of the scale of a block or house meeting. In other cases, the organizer works not just with individuals but also with existing community organizations to build an "organization of organizations."

Once the residents' group decides on an issue to address, the organizer helps them to form an organization and develop strategies. The strategies may involve doing a "quick hit" to achieve an "easy win," for example, engaging in a public action to obtain a minor concession from business or government. Historically, the easy win was for a poor community to have a stop sign placed at a dangerous street intersection. Today, there are many kinds of easy wins, such as convincing the city to clean up a vacant lot or putting speed bumps on a busy residential street. Sometimes the strategies include larger confrontations and protest, though many community organizations successfully solve problems with negotiation alone. Along with winning on issues, a major goal of community organizing is to help residents build a stable community organization that will allow them ongoing influence over the government and corporate policies that affect them.

In contrast to social action, one of the distinguishing features of community organizing is that it brings residents together to choose an issue, rather than having someone choose an issue and then organize residents around it. Effective community organizations thereby maintain flexibility for tackling any community issue, whether it be a dispute between two neighbors or a campaign against a global corporation. The drawback of this approach is that some community organizations, because they are not based in a strong political ideology, can become racist, homophobic, or otherwise antidemocratic.

From the early days of Saul Alinsky's community organizing in the 1930s and the civil rights movement in the 1950s, thousands of small community-based organizations and a number of important national community organizing networks have evolved. The original national community organizing network was Alinsky's Industrial Areas Foundation. It has become a major faith-based entity focused on organizing church congregations. Others include the PICO National Network, the Direct Action and Research Training network, and the Gamaliel Foundation. Secular national community organizing networks include the Association of Community Organizations for Reform Now and National People's Action. Community organizing has also gone global with community organizing networks and training centers now in existence on every continent.

Community organizing has permeated the culture to the point that thousands of rural and community organizations have sprung up without a trained community organizer starting them. Perhaps one of the most famous was the Love Canal Homeowners Association, which brought Lois Gibbs to prominence as she went from being "just a housewife" to a leader in the environmental justice movement. She and her neighbors successfully struggled to have the state government acknowledge that they were living on a toxic dump. Most of these groups go unrecognized except in their local settings. There, they build community identity, empower their members, and impact local policies.

Randy Stoecker

See also Alinsky, Saul; Citizen Participation; Urban Politics

Further Readings

Bobo, K., J. Kendall, and S. Max. 2000. *Organizing for Social Change*. Cabin John, MD: Seven Locks Press.

Brown, M. J. 2006. *Building Powerful Community Organizations*. Arlington, MA: Long Haul Press.

Chambers, E. T. and M. A. Cowan. 2003. *Roots for Radicals: Organizing for Power, Action, and Justice*. New York: Continuum.

COMM-ORG: The On-line Conference on Community Organizing and Development (http://comm-org.wisc.edu).

Rivera, F. and J. Erlich. 1995. *Community Organizing in a Diverse Society*. 2nd ed. Boston: Allyn & Bacon.

COMMUNITY STUDIES

Community studies is an academic field concerned with the study of community and the characteristics of particular localities. A key focus of many programs of community study is the effects of social change upon the form and function of social life within such specific settings. Unlike more theoretically oriented research on the concept of community, the field of community studies employs the methodological tools of the social sciences as a means by which to describe, contextualize, and investigate the sociocultural and psychological dynamics that affect everyday life in the community.

Research conducted on community in this sense is often directly concerned with the effects on social and economic life of such variables as family, youth, health, leisure, gender, employment, immigration, education, crime, poverty, and inequality. As such, community studies is often closely linked with policy implementation and analysis.

The Origins and Development of Community Studies

The predominately Anglo-American tradition of community studies has been primarily concerned with the holistic analysis of the social organization and institutional structure of three distinct settings: small towns, rural areas, and working-class districts. Although definitional tensions continue to plague the precise meaning of the term *community*, the interdisciplinary field of community studies has generally assumed the mandate of investigating patterns of social groupings or population aggregates contained within a particular setting. The field has its origins in three complementary approaches.

First, the study of population growth and demographic change by social surveyors, statisticians, and social reformists working in the late nineteenth and early twentieth centuries was a notable precursor of what later became known as the community study. Although focusing largely upon issues of health and sanitation in overcrowded and impoverished urban conglomerates, implicit within such investigations was an emphasis on the effects of social change and modernization upon the social and moral order of community life.

Second, many of the investigative and methodological approaches utilized within community studies have also been influenced by the classificatory schemas of cultural anthropology, particularly in regard to how such variables as employment, family, kinship, political structure, and patterns of religious belief contribute to the stability of the social order and the maintenance of a functionally integrated society. Although later criticism sought to reveal the complicity of anthropological theory and method with colonialism, the fundamental focus placed upon the everyday dynamics of community life served as a point of commonality between classical anthropological studies, traditionally conducted in distant locales, and the application of such approaches in Western societies.

Third, the founding fathers of sociology were concerned with the decline of traditional social relations amid the transformation from folk society to urban society. Fearing that traditional ways of life and communal relations were being threatened with dissolution by the increasing heterogeneity and sheer social complexity resulting from the combined forces of industrialism and urbanization, classical social theory sought to explore the effects of social change upon community life and mechanisms of social integration. Building upon the legacy of these three traditions, community studies subsequently emerged as an independent focus of study in its own right to occupy a central role in sociology, anthropology, social geography, urban studies, and social policy programs.

Although primarily concerned with empirically demonstrating the transition from a rural to a predominantly urban society, early work on community exhibited a strong continuity with the concerns of classical social theory: namely, the transition from an agrarian to an industrial-based urban economy, the shift from folk to mass society, and the general tendency to dichotomize the nature of community and society in terms of tradition and modernity, respectively. Whereas traditional society was seen as the repository of the bounded, harmonious, and homogenous community, modern society was seen in far more heterogeneous and differentiated terms. It is in this sense that critics of community studies have suggested that the notion of community employed at the heart of community studies is an outmoded one and unsuited to the often antagonistic nature of community life in its contemporary manifestations. Despite this discrediting, the semantics of community continue to be regularly evoked in a wide range of disciplinary fields.

Engagement with the community study was perceived as being all the more difficult by urban scholars when considering the growth of individualism, the decline of traditional social bonds of attachment, an increasingly specialized and migratory occupational structure, and the socially debilitating effects of urban sprawl and suburbanization. It was largely due to these reasons that the institutional strength of community studies began to decline significantly during the 1970s. The popularity of Marxist approaches to social organization, coupled with an increased recognition of the often conflict-ridden nature of community life, entailed that any approach that centered upon the functional differentiation of social roles and institutions was perceived as methodologically and conceptually suspect.

Community studies thus lost much of the scientific legitimacy it had previously held and became relegated to the investigation of subcultures conducted within the subdisciplinary areas of social anthropology, cultural studies, and human geography. Although the concept of community continued to be regularly evoked in academic, popular, and policy discourse, considerable skepticism was directed toward any research endeavor that aimed at rendering an account of community in any holistic sense. Rather than focusing upon the types of attachments that bind the individual to a community in a strictly localized sense, analysis had shifted to address the nature of transnational and global attachments. In this view, the community study as traditionally conceived came to be seen as inherently limited and parochial with regard to its analytical scope and interpretative potential.

Two useful introductions to the field of community studies are Colin Bell and Howard Newby's *Community Studies: An Introduction to the Study of the Local Community,* and Maurice Stein's *Eclipse of Community: An Interpretation of American Studies.* Abandoning efforts to pin down the meaning of community with any degree of definitional precision, Bell and Newby suggested that attempts to define community should rather be decided upon by practitioners working in the field. Critical of whether the tradition of community studies could offer any systematic and cumulative knowledge of the nature of social life in human communities, their analysis nevertheless offered a useful and comparative overview of the terrain of community studies in the American and European traditions. Focusing specifically upon the American tradition, Stein presents a similar disciplinary overview in the form of a methodological primer on how to analyze and conduct a community study. Although the implicit aim of both texts was to reinvigorate the increasing analytical sterility of the tradition, many scholars have deemed the wide-ranging effects of social and economic transformation as having dealt a fatal blow to the very existence of community studies as a viable field of study. In this sense, community studies as an autonomous field of study no longer exercises the same degree of influence and appeal it once had. Remaining predominately interdisciplinary in tone, and continuing to focus on specific areas of practical concern, community studies in both British and American contexts has become integrally linked with planning, policy, and local government initiatives.

Community Studies in the American Tradition

From its origins in the ethos of social reformism in the early twentieth century, the community studies tradition in the American context has its origins in the Chicago School of Urban Sociology. Influenced by the methods and techniques of anthropological inquiry, central to the investigations of the Chicago School scholars was an exploration of the means by which the territorial expansion of the city was affected by the forces of industrialization and urbanization. Dramatic increases in the rate of immigration and of the ethnic composition of the city were seen as fundamentally altering the social and moral order of the city. Although predominately concerned with explicating the disintegrative effects of metropolitan growth upon social life, the Chicago School scholars also explored the means by which community was maintained in the context of the city.

In contrast to prevailing views on the alienating effects of large-scale urbanization, increased population growth, and the rise of suburbia, the research mandate of the Chicago School became focused upon how the emergence of distinct subcultural milieus served as a means by which social groups could adapt to metropolitan life. What the Chicago School scholars found was that the city was composed of a multitude of lifeworlds based upon a range of class, ethnic, and identity attachments. In this sense, the pioneering work of the Chicago School paved the way for a thriving field of community studies in the American social sciences.

Building upon the influence of the Chicago School, a classic work of community study in American scholarship is *Middletown: A Study in American Culture* by Robert Lynd and Helen Lynd. Initially setting out to investigate patterns of religious belief in an unnamed American city given the pseudonym of Middletown (later identified as Muncie, Indiana), the Lynds found that their focus inevitably led to a much wider exploration of the means by which community life was sustained. Although the Lynds did not begin their study with any highly developed hypothesis or with the aim of substantiating any particular thesis, their work is typical of its time in that it focused upon how social institutions contributed to the functioning of the wider community.

Studies such as Middletown presented small town America as a relatively homogenous entity with a clearly defined pattern of social organization and cultural outlook. Many subsequent studies adopted a similarly holistic perspective in focusing upon how the nature and workings of family and community operated as self-functioning social systems. Although such studies presented a view of small town America as a relatively stable and culturally homogenous environment, later criticism sought to reveal the implicit downplaying of conflicting and oppositional voices in the community. For example, a subsequent follow-up to the Middletown study found it to be a far from unified community and riddled with social divisions obscured by the methodological approach adopted in the original analysis. In this sense, the archetypical American community study of the mid-twentieth century often stood accused of utilizing a conservative and analytically limited approach to the study of community life.

Although the growing utilization of critical perspectives signaled a decline in the influence of community studies as a field of institutional strength, the publication of notable studies continued to periodically reaffirm the tradition. Gerald Suttles's *The Social Order of the Slum: Ethnicity and Territory in the Inner City* and Carol Stack's *All Our Kin: Strategies for Survival in a Black Community* are two such exemplars. Evoking the spirit of the Chicago School tradition, such studies sought to illustrate the means by which disadvantaged populations constituted community-based forms of reciprocation and mutual dependency.

Working-Class Communities in Britain

Early investigations on the importance of public hygiene and health among working-class communities in Britain led to the development of programs of community study in which systematic knowledge of towns and cities was sought as a means to understand and alleviate problems associated with urbanization. A particularly strong tradition of community studies emerged during the era of economic change that followed World War II and what was perceived to be a widening gap between government policy and the concerns of the working classes.

Whereas community studies of the mid-twentieth-century American context focused upon factors related to immigration and the diffusion of population aggregates toward suburban and regional areas, the orientation of the British social sciences ensured that social class came to be seen as a key determinant of many programs of community study. These studies were focused predominately upon practical rather than theoretical issues, and research findings were often closely linked with policy analysis. Central to such studies were investigations of the distinct social, economic, and political conditions among people who shared a similar experience within a given locality. Commensurate with the approach taken by the community studies tradition in the American context, working-class communities were seen as homogenous and close-knit embodiments of the spirit of community due to the perceived similarity of lifestyle and standard of living.

Founded in 1954, the pioneering Institute of Community Studies was a research center specifically focused upon the investigation of life in British communities. A study of the London working-class district of Bethnal Green was perhaps the most famous work that emerged from this era. Blending a social anthropological perspective with a sociocultural analysis, the publication of *Family and Kinship in East London* signaled a decisive move away from more statistic-laden studies in favor of more ethnographically minded descriptions of community life.

A primary aim of the Bethnal Green study was a focus upon how patterns of working-class family and community organization became transformed by the interventions of urban planners and welfare agencies engaged with the revitalization of what was perceived as a dilapidated area in East London.

Although the Bethnal Green area was depicted as the epitome of working-class life and as embodying the ethos of communal solidarity, such working-class community studies were later subjected to significant criticism for the extent to which neighborhood antagonisms and internal community conflict were obscured from the analysis. Focusing upon the coalescence of community and employment, many studies of working-class areas tended to emphasize how certain industries became the fulcrum point for the development of a local community. Critics accused such studies of perpetuating an inherently romanticized depiction of working-class life and as containing an implicit legitimation of the class system. Indeed, it is perhaps a significant irony of the community studies tradition that the field achieved its greatest degree of prominence at precisely that time when many such working-class communities were beginning to fragment as a result of the wider effects of socioeconomic and industrial change.

In addition to the study of community life in metropolitan settings, a number of investigations were also conducted outside of the major metropolitan regions. A classic study of this era is Norman Dennis's *Coal Is Our Life: An Analysis of a Yorkshire Mining Community.* Offering an exploration of family and labor relations in coal mining communities, such studies investigated the effects of industrial and economic change upon community life in British rural areas. Presenting a view of family and community life as predominately mediated by the centrality of the mining industry, these studies were later criticized for presenting a world hermetically sealed against the wider effects of Western industrial economies.

Indeed, the decline of the coal mining industry in Britain came to epitomize the loss of the type of foundational occupational identity that was seen as holding such working-class communities together. Without the protective framework of an integrated community and occupational structure, community life came to be seen as increasingly episodic and fragmented. In place of the communal solidarity,

traditionalism, and spirit of collectivism deemed central to the constitution of working-class life, the effects of industrial change, coupled with initiatives of urban renewal and population relocation, did much to challenge and undermine the disciplinary strength of community studies. It is largely in these terms that the field of community studies encountered significant criticism for its conceptual and methodological limitations with regard to its failure in accounting for the global ramifications of social and industrial change. Notwithstanding these criticisms, such studies arguably offer valuable insight into a unique period of social history in British rural areas.

Other investigations of community life in rural areas tended to present the nature of community as an unchanging repository of tradition and custom. For example, Conrad M. Arensberg and S. T. Kimball's *Family and Community in Ireland,* an influential study conducted in western Ireland, presented rural life as unchanging and seemingly resistant to social change. Although such works inspired a substantial body of similar work by social geographers and social anthropologists, they also encountered significant criticism due to the emphasis placed upon community depicted as a functioning totality to the exclusion of conflicting and repressive elements of community life. In place of the emphasis upon homogeneity, continuity, and tradition, community life was revealed to be a far more kaleidoscopic entity and one mediated by a wide variety of external factors.

The Future of Community Studies

Notwithstanding the cumulative strength of the criticisms directed toward community studies, many scholars have continued to defend the field against accusations of redundancy by emphasizing how such study provides detailed analysis of the social, cultural, and psychological effects of embedded social relations. Often employing an ethnographic perspective augmented by statistical data, many such works focus substantively upon the effects of health, employment, youth, crime, racism, immigration, ethnicity, gender, identity, sexuality, environment, urban planning, and the effects of policy initiatives upon life in particular areas. In this sense, the community studies tradition remains an active and engaging field.

Furthermore, research conducted by theorists more accepting of the argument regarding the declining significance of place and locality has led to an exploration of the inherently socially constructed nature of community. Accordingly, community is seen as something that is symbolically constituted around particular beliefs and forms of social practice such as festivals, identity parades, and neighborhood gatherings. In this view, community becomes something that is interpreted in many different ways and subject to an ongoing process of redefinition and negotiation.

Notwithstanding the definitional and methodological dilemmas surrounding the employment of the concept of community, the frequency and salience of its habitual usage has ensured its continual relevance to urban and community studies.

Alan Gerard Bourke

See also Chicago School of Urban Sociology; Community; Gans, Herbert; Urban Anthropology; Urban Sociology

Further Readings

Arensberg, Conrad M. and S. T. Kimball. 1968. *Family and Community in Ireland*. Cambridge, MA: Harvard University Press.

Bell, Colin and Howard Newby. 1971. *Community Studies: An Introduction to the Sociology of the Local Community*. London: Unwin.

Dennis, Norman. 1969. *Coal Is Our Life: An Analysis of a Yorkshire Mining Community*. London: Travistock.

Gans, Herbert. J. 1967. *The Levittowners: A Way of Life and Politics in a New Suburban Community*. London: Allen Lane.

Lynd, Robert S. and Helen M. Lynd. 1929. *Middletown: A Study in American Culture*. New York: Harcourt Brace.

———. 1937. *Middletown in Transition: A Study in Cultural Conflicts*. New York: Harcourt Brace.

Park, Robert E., Ernest W. Burgess, and Roderick D. McKenzie. 1967. *The City*. Chicago: University of Chicago Press.

Stack, Carol. 1974. *All Our Kin: Strategies for Survival in a Black Community*. New York: Harper & Row.

Stein, Maurice. 1960. *Eclipse of Community: An Interpretation of American Studies*. Princeton, NJ: Princeton University Press.

Suttles, Gerald. D. 1968. *The Social Order of the Slum: Ethnicity and Territory in the Inner City*. Chicago: University of Chicago Press.

Young, Michael D. and Peter Willmott. 1957. *Family and Kinship in East London*. Harmondsworth, UK: Penguin.

CONDOMINIUM

A condominium is a form of housing in which property is both owned in common and individually owned. It can take various forms, from apartment-style structures, townhouses, and even fully detached housing communities. Apartment units or flats within the structure are individually owned, whereas other areas such as hallways, stairs, and lobbies, and amenities like swimming pools and tennis courts are common property shared by those who reside in the building complex. Community members, generally in a homeowners association, elect a board of directors who manage the common areas of the property.

Purchasing a condominium is similar to buying a house. A mortgage is paid to the bank, and a deed is signed. The difference lies with the space that is being bought. The owner of a condominium is purchasing only the space within the unit, not the structure itself or the property surrounding the structure.

There are advantages and disadvantages to owning a condominium. For retired individuals and the younger generation who are unable to afford a starter home, condominiums offer affordability and stability. A condominium can be less expensive than a single-family (detached) house, while the owner is still able to build equity and has ownership rights. There is also less responsibility in owning a condominium than owning a freestanding home. Households are provided with the same maintenance and repair services that one would find with a rental unit. Owners do not have to worry about shoveling snow, raking leaves, or making repairs outside the home.

There are also disadvantages. In addition to paying a mortgage, owners must pay monthly maintenance fees, which are used to manage the building and its public spaces. Condominium owners also face restrictions. Because space that exists outside the unit is shared, an individual owner cannot alter the appearance of those spaces. Moreover, the individual owner cannot paint hallways or plant flowers that are inconsistent with the appearance of the property.

Many condominiums are former apartment buildings that have been converted by developers or building owners. In cities where rent stabilization and rent control laws protect rental apartments, landlords cannot increase rents except as mandated by law. Owners who feel restricted by rent stabilization and control laws often convert apartments to condominiums in order to increase profits. The conversion of apartments to condominiums is indicative of a trend that further segregates the rich from the poor. With more and more apartments being converted, there is less affordable rental housing available for low-income families.

Cooperative housing or co-ops are not the same as condominium housing. Co-op units are not owned; they are corporations with a board of directors and with tenants acting as shareholders. Tenants do not sign a deed but rather purchase shares of the corporation, which includes the lease of a unit. There is no real estate mortgage involved with a co-op building. A loan from the bank is used to purchase shares and the number of shares owned is based on the size of unit. Like condominium owners, co-op tenants pay monthly maintenance fees and cannot make any changes to common areas. As a form of housing, condominiums are a compromise between renting an apartment and owning a house.

Nadia A. Mian

See also Common Interest Development; Housing

Further Readings

Friedman, J. P. 2000. *Keys to Purchasing a Condo or Co-op.* Hauppage, NY: Barron's Educational Series.

Schill, M. H., I. Voicu, and J. Miller. 2006. "The Condominium v. Cooperative Puzzle: An Empirical Analysis of Housing in New York City." Working Paper, Furman Center for Real Estate and Urban Policy, New York University.

Siegler, R. and H. J. Levy. 1986. "Brief History of Cooperative Housing." *Cooperative Housing Journal of the National Association of Housing Cooperatives,* 12–19.

CONSTANTINOPLE

See Istanbul, Turkey

CONVENTION CENTERS

Places for large-scale public assembly have long been a part of cities—from public halls and fairgrounds to stadia and opera houses. Although private venues such as Chicago's International Amphitheater (home to five national political conventions through 1968) often housed major conventions, the twentieth century saw a substantial expansion of new public convention facilities. The City Beautiful movement and the promotion of large civic centers provided a locus for the development of buildings such as San Francisco's Civic Auditorium, Kansas City's Municipal Auditorium, St. Louis's Kiel Auditorium and Cleveland's Public Auditorium.

The great burst of convention center development came after World War II, with the advent of the federal urban renewal program and the local initiatives aimed at downtown revitalization and development. Cities sought to revive downtowns surrounded by slum neighborhoods and respond to competition from outlying suburban retail development. A new convention center was viewed as a veritable lifesaver that promised to lure hundreds of thousands of visitors to fill hotel rooms and spur the development of new hotels and retail development with the ready availability of inexpensive land cleared under the urban renewal program's aegis.

Chicago's privately owned amphitheater was effectively replaced in 1960 by the McCormick Place convention center on the lakefront south of the downtown "Loop." Other major cities sought their own share of the national and regional convention trade with new public structures. New York City's Coliseum was developed by Robert Moses in 1956 on a Columbus Circle site cleared under urban renewal. Cleveland's new convention center was finally approved by the city's voters in 1960, after two failed attempts, and constructed in part under the civic center mall. Boston's Hynes Auditorium was developed adjacent to the new mixed use Prudential Center on a former rail yard, and St. Louis acquired a site on the northern end of the downtown core, long mapped for slum clearance, for the development of its new Cervantes Convention Center, which opened in 1976.

From the 1970s, convention center construction was often linked to larger local efforts to implement tourism and visitor-based economic development efforts. Cities like Atlanta, Baltimore, Cleveland, Milwaukee, and St. Louis often paired convention facilities with new hotels, downtown retail malls, festival marketplaces, aquariums, stadiums, and entertainment districts. These projects, many built with federal government grant funds, sought to both bolster downtown core areas and spur new tourist oriented private investment through the creation of tourist zones.

The convention center development boom has expanded in recent years, propelled by a combination of political, economic, and fiscal forces. One national count found 193 major exhibit halls in 1986 with a total of 32.5 million square feet of exhibit hall space. At the top of the list stood Chicago's McCormick Place, expanded to a total of 1.87 million square feet. By 1996, the number of major halls stood at 254 with a total of 49.1 million square feet of space.

Convention center exhibit space in the United States reached 66.8 million square feet in 2006—a 106 percent increase from 1986—at 313 centers. The growth reflects two parallel trends. The largest centers have consistently expanded, with the argument that ever-growing events demand more space. Chicago's latest McCormick Place expansion would bring it to 2.7 million square feet in 2007 at a cost of $850 million while New York City is undertaking a massive expansion of its Jacob K. Javits Convention Center, and the Las Vegas Convention Center, with 2 million square feet of space, is being expanded and revamped.

Small and medium-sized communities have also sought to gain the purported economic benefits of convention visitors by developing new or expanded facilities. Communities such as Hartford, Connecticut; Springfield, Massachusetts; Virginia Beach, Virginia; Raleigh, North Carolina; Columbia, South Carolina; Shreveport, Louisiana; McAllen, Texas; Schaumburg, Illinois; Fort Wayne, Indiana; Erie, Pennsylvania; St. Charles, Missouri; Branson, Missouri; Santa Fe, New Mexico; Omaha, Nebraska; Spokane, Washington; Tacoma, Washington; and

Anchorage, Alaska, have all built new convention facilities.

The contemporary convention center development reflects a substantive change in the politics and finance of public investment. Most of the convention venues built during the 1950s, 1960s, and 1970s were funded by city governments using general obligation bonds. New convention centers have commonly been financed with debt backed by taxes on visitors and tourists, such as hotel, rental car, and restaurant meal taxes. The Washington Convention Center, in the nation's capital, was developed in 2003 by the Washington Convention Center Authority and financed by dedicated taxes on hotel rooms and restaurant meals in the District of Columbia. Revenues from taxes on all local hotel rooms, car rentals, and visitor attractions now provide places like Las Vegas, Orlando, New Orleans, and Boston with substantial streams of funding for regular investment in additional center expansions and improvement.

The boom in convention center development has also been sustained by the notion of a consistently expanding convention and tradeshow market. This image of growing demand has sustained the argument that communities must expand their convention facilities or lose out to competitors. In a 1994 study of a potential expansion of San Francisco's Moscone Center, Economics Research Associates examined the performance of the Tradeshow Week 200—the 200 largest conventions and trade shows—in terms of exhibit space used each year. The firm found that these events showed consistent and strong growth over the years and forecast that large events would continue to grow for the foreseeable future, requiring ever more space.

The actual attendance of the 200 major convention and tradeshow events has not grown in accord with the historical observations of the consulting firms, or in line with the growth in convention centers and exhibit space. Average event attendance did grow by some 20 percent from 1985 to 1994, but there was no consistent growth during the 1990s, and convention attendance was dampened by the recession of 2000 and the terrorist events of September 11, 2001. Average attendance at major events fell to 20,753 in 2002 with some recovery to 21,670 for 2005—equal to the 1995 average.

The development of major convention centers in new markets such as Las Vegas and Orlando has also resulted in a dramatic shift in the location of major events. In 1991, Chicago's McCormick Place hosted 28 of the Tradeshow Week 200 meetings, but by 2005 that figure had dropped to 15 events with 532,000. New York has seen its count of 200 events fall from 30 in 1991 to 16 for 2005. Las Vegas won out over competing cities, increasing from 22 major events in 1991 to 44 events in 2005, encompassing 34 percent of the total exhibit space used by all Tradeshow Week 200 events.

The combination of no real growth in convention attendance, major supply expansion, and a shift to newer communities has made convention centers far less consistently productive public investments than often assumed, yielding quite modest actual economic impact. Feasibility studies for New York City's Jacob Javits Convention Center had forecast that it would house about 1 million convention attendees per year, each of whom would stay and spend money in the city for three to four days.

Actual delegate attendance at the Javits Center at first exceeded those forecasts, with a peak of 1.9 million in 1990. In the face of the competitive market, delegate attendance fell to 962,000 for 2004. A recent consultant study found that the Javits Center yielded just 660,000 annual hotel room nights from out-of-town visitors—a fraction of the 2 to 3 million annual hotel room nights forecast by the studies in the 1970s, or about 3 percent of the city's total annual hotel room demand recently.

Convention facilities in other nations have developed in a different manner from those in the United States. In Europe and Asia, large exhibition halls or trade fairs, often privately owned, are typically located at the edge of the urban area. These exhibition halls, such as Germany's Messe Hanover (5.3 million square feet) and Messe Munich (4.7 million) or Italy's Fiero Milan, dwarf the largest American counterparts. Within historic urban core areas, specialized congress or conference centers of far smaller size, such as the Palais de Congrès in Paris or London's Queen Elizabeth II Conference Centre, provide auditoriums and rooms to accommodate traditional meetings.

Heywood Sanders

See also Growth Machine; Sports Stadiums; Tourism; Urban Design; Urban Planning

Further Readings

Judd, Dennis and Susan Fainstein, eds. 1999. *The Tourist City*. New Haven, CT: Yale University Press.
Nelson, Robert, ed. 2004. *Current Issues in Convention and Exhibition Facility Development*. Binghamton, NY: Haworth Press.
Petersen, David C. 2001. *Developing Sports, Convention, and Performing Arts Centers*. 3rd ed. Washington, DC: Urban Land Institute.
Sanders, Heywood. 2005. *Space Available: The Realities of Convention Centers as Economic Development Strategy*. Research Brief, Brookings Institution, Washington, DC.

CREATIVE CLASS

The *creative class* refers to people who share a common interest in, and ability to create, meaningful new forms of economic activity. It is comprised of two groups: the supercreative core and creative professionals. The supercreative core group consists of those employed in fields such as science and engineering, high technology, research, the arts, and design. Its members produce innovations that can be readily applied and broadly used, such as designing a piece of software or writing a musical composition. The second group, creative professionals, includes workers in knowledge-based professions such as financial services, health care, law, and business management. By relying on extensive knowledge, these professionals engage in creative problem solving and seek innovative solutions.

Creative workers generate economic growth through developing technological innovations, advancing scientific thinking, and increasing knowledge. Therefore, a high concentration of the creative class is thought to be linked to the economic growth of a city. One estimate is that the creative class accounts for roughly 30 percent of the U.S. workforce, or about 40 million workers. Only one third of the workforce, they earn roughly 50 percent of all the wages and salaries. The creative class also possesses nearly 70 percent of all discretionary income, more than double that of workers in manufacturing and services combined.

In 1998, the term *creative class* was developed by social scientist Richard Florida in a study that found that high-technology professionals—typically young and mobile—make location decisions based on lifestyle interests rather than employment. Florida claimed that members of the creative class are drawn to vibrant cities that possess a variety of cultural and recreational experiences. His conclusions were mirrored by work on the location patterns of gays. High-technology workers and gays seemed to be attracted to the same locales. In subsequent research, Florida created the Bohemian Index, which measures the density of artists, writers, and performers in a region. His Creative Class Index attests to a city's concentration of creative workers.

Although the creative class is primarily influenced by an area's quality of life, the availability of employment still remains an important factor in choosing a place to live. More important, though, are community assets such as lifestyle diversity, entertainment, and environmental quality. A diverse cultural and demographic population reflects an open and tolerant community, and an active and informal street life provides for new experiences. A nightlife that offers a wide array of options is also important. As a result, cultural amenities and professional sports complexes are perceived to be less of a draw than vibrant entertainment and nightlife destinations. The promotion of environmental sustainability and access to outdoor recreational activities such as bike paths and public parks are additional attractions. To entice the creative class to relocate, city and regional economic development strategies focus on improving the local quality of life and, in some cases, passing progressive social and environmental legislation.

The values of creative class members signal a shift away from economic security toward ideals that reflect individual expression. Individuality and self-statement are prized over actions that reinforce group identity. Demonstrating merit, exhibited by ambition and hard work, is another important value. Diversity is also an ideal but seems to be interpreted as seeking an environment that accepts nonconformity rather than one that addresses racial and gender inequalities.

Consequently, the creative class is viewed as being indifferent to the economic and social disparities between them and the working poor. In fact, income disparities between the creative class and those employed in the manufacturing and service sectors often lead to issues of housing affordability, uneven development, and sprawl. Class division may also be reinforced as the number of low-wage workers in the retail and entertainment sectors increases to meet the leisure needs of the creative class. As a result, political polarization may occur as these groups become divided over economic rewards and social status.

To attract the creative class, cities are encouraged to implement initiatives to strengthen the three T's of economic growth: technology, talent, and tolerance. Technology plays a vital role by providing opportunities to further knowledge. Talent reflects the number of people who actually have creative occupations as opposed to educational levels. Tolerance is also critical. Cities should strive to be open and diverse in terms of ethnicity, race, and sexual orientation. Universities are also an inducement through their ability to advance and distribute knowledge. Based on these elements, creative cities in the United States include San Francisco, Boston, Seattle, Washington, D.C., and Dallas. Members of the creative class are attracted to them because they promote creative thinking and the expression of identity.

Critics have argued that there is no causal link between the presence of the creative class and economic growth. Instead, high technology, high human capital, and increased immigration are better predictors of growth. Moreover, a creative class approach to economic growth focuses the urban development agenda on the lifestyle interests of an elite class rather than addressing the city's social problems. Yet, city governments continue to pursue the creative class. Channeling creativity and changing culture, though, are daunting goals. And, although the creative class may be attracted to cultural amenities and a rich social life, they still require employment to remain in place.

Anna Maria Bounds

See also Bohemian; Gay Space; Technopoles; Tourism

Further Readings

Florida, Richard. 2002. *The Rise of the Creative Class.* New York: Basic Books.

Peck, Jamie. 2005. "Struggling with the Creative Class." *International Journal of Urban and Regional Research* 29(4):740–70.

Rausch, Stephen and Cynthia Negrey. 2006. "Does the Creative Engine Run? A Consideration of the Effect of Creative Class on Economic Strength and Growth." *Journal of Urban Affairs* 28(5):473–89.

Scott, Allen J. 2006. "Creative Cities: Conceptual Issues and Policy Questions." *Journal of Urban Affairs* 28(1):1–17.

CRIME

The concept of crime is used to refer to patterns of behaviors that violate the values, norms, and laws of the society in which they take place. The study of the definition, correlates, and consequences of crime has a long tradition in social sciences, and in this entry, consistent with the aim of the encyclopedia, the focus is on the understanding of the link between urbanism and crime, looking at the central perspectives that explain crime rates and victimization, as well as the consequences of crime in globalized urban society.

Definition

The definition of crime implies that unlawful behavior is socially defined, and there is variation between societies (e.g., in Korea adultery is a crime, whereas in most Western countries it is not; in some countries gambling is legal, and in others it is a crime). In addition, criminal behavior should come to the notice of, and be processed through, an administrative system or enforcement agency. Law enforcement is dependent on social resources that are allocated and on political priorities of each society; accordingly, enforcement is directed to certain activities and not to others. Thus, crime rates are affected more by law enforcement and less by the true figures of crime.

How do researchers learn about criminal behavior? Criminologists use three principal sources to study criminal behavior. The first is official police reports, data that are regularly collected by police agencies as part of their daily activities, recorded according to standard definitions of crime based on the criminal law, and include information about the crime that was reported to the police or was discovered by the police. Official police reports are available through time and location, facilitating the comparison of trends through the years and the increases or declines of crime and its different types at the city, county, and state levels. One major disadvantage of this data source is that crimes are not always reported to the police, resulting in an underestimation of the real crime figures. A second source is victimization surveys that inquire from a large representative sample of the population the extent that respondents have been a victim of a crime during a fixed period of time. Victimization surveys provide more information than official reports, as crimes that have not been reported to the police are more likely to appear in the victimization survey. In addition, the survey gathers information on the social and demographic characteristics of the victim, thus facilitating the understanding of the nature of the crime, the characteristics of the place in which it took place, and the characteristics of the interaction between offender and victim. The third method of studying crime is conducting self-report studies. In surveys, individuals report on their involvement in the perpetration of a crime. This method allows for the collection of data on the characteristics of offenders and their social surroundings.

History of Scholarship Linking Urbanism and Crime

One of the early arguments that raised the possibility for a link between urban life and crime can be found in the writings of Émile Durkheim (1951), who argued that rapid social change was associated with a breakdown of informal and formal social control, an increase in nonnormative behavior, and crime. At the beginning of the twentieth century, populations of cities started growing rapidly in Western countries; people moved to the city, attracted by rapid industrialization and lack of employment in agricultural areas. Cities were going through rapid social change from relatively small settlements to growing urban landscapes with increases in population size, ethnic heterogeneity, and density.

In the 1920s Clifford R. Shaw conducted one of the first studies on the spatial distribution of police data on juvenile delinquency in the city of Chicago and found that the distribution is not random. The central findings of the study were that (1) delinquency was more likely to be concentrated in old neighborhoods that were located close to the commercial and industrial center; (2) the lower the median income, the median rental, and the percentage of homeownership were in an area, the higher was the rate of juvenile delinquency; and (3) the rate of juvenile delinquency was associated with higher concentrations of immigrants and African Americans.

In 1969, Shaw and Henry McKay concluded that delinquency is closely associated with the process of urban change. In areas going through a process of population change, when a low-income population is replacing more established groups, social control declines, a subculture of crime develops, and urban crime is more concentrated.

Over the years a number of critiques on this work were raised. They relied on official police records that may be biased to overreporting crime in low-income neighborhoods, and it was unclear whether the disruption of social control, called social disorganization, was the result of social heterogeneity or of a delinquent subculture that takes advantage of crime opportunities in the city center located nearby.

In the late 1980s Robert Sampson and Casey Groves developed a research agenda to further investigate the process of social disorganization. Their reformulation of social disorganization theory focused on ethnic heterogeneity, low level of homeownership, and percentage of single-headed families. The aforementioned negative community features are perceived as having deleterious consequences for community social organization, increasing the likelihood that neighbors will be strangers and diminishing and restricting the development of informal community ties. Form this work, a new concept—collective efficacy—has been used to describe the differential ability of neighborhoods to realize common values.

Victimization and Fear of Crime

A second line of study was directed to the understanding of crime victimization in the urban context. According to the routine activities approach, crimes occur when motivated offenders encounter suitable targets in the absence of capable guardianship. Changes in the social organization of society decreased capable guardianship and increased target suitability. Nowadays, people spend less and

less time at home; thus their households and the goods contained therein are subjected to less and less guardianship. Robert F. Meier and Terance D. Miethe have attempted to make more explicit the concept of opportunity and maintain that two factors, in addition to capable guardianship and target attractiveness, can be identified. The first is proximity to crime or the physical distance between the areas where potential targets reside and areas where large populations of potential offenders reside. The second is exposure to crime and is indicative of the visibility or accessibility to crime. This model suggests a "structural choice theory of victimization," as proximity and exposure should be considered as structural factors because they predispose households and individuals to different levels of risk. Each of these models suggests that certain areas within cities may be more susceptible to crime—and also accepts the general idea that crime is more prevalent in urban areas.

Urban dwellers are aware of crime risks and tend to express fear of crime. Fear of crime has been defined as a negative emotional reaction to crime or the symbols associated with crime, and studies have been directed to explain the genesis of this emotional reaction. Albert Hunter and Terry Baumer had proposed in 1982 that community decline gives rise to social and physical incivilities and crime. Social incivilities are signs of lack of adherence to norms of public behavior and include public drinking, drunkenness, or drug use. Physical incivilities include graffiti, litter, vacant houses, and abandoned cars. Residents perceiving more clues to the underlying level of disorder in their immediate environment feel more vulnerable and thus more fearful.

A salient effect of fear of crime is the development of exclusionary mechanisms that aim to support trust and personal security by excluding the other, whose behavior is perceived as a public concern. *Urban surveillance* refers to the use of technological tools to monitor and record the regular movement of populations and individuals in the city. As individuals go about their daily routines (driving to work, shopping, walking the streets, etc.), their movements are being recorded and stored. Originally, closed caption television cameras (CCTVs) and electronic cards were installed in cities as part of the technological infrastructure to monitor and regulate traffic. With time, an increasing reason for the expansion in their installation from street corners to additional public spaces such as shopping strips and entertainment areas is urbanites' uneasiness and fear of crime. The city is characterized by high-mobility, social and cultural diversity that increases the likelihood of encountering strangers who differ in their behavior from ours. Meeting the different other is perceived as a risk, and many cities are managing potential risks through the installation of CCTVs. Urban surveillance influences our public behaviors: Knowing that our presence, behaviors, and faces are being recorded is an inducement to self-control. Surveillance devices installed originally to improve transportation systems are also being used for coercive purposes, becoming more and more part of the crime-fighting equation. Police departments are using these data to identify suspects and track their movements, thereby supporting crime-solving efforts.

The fear of crime has led to the development of gated communities in many countries. *Gated communities* are residential areas with restricted access designed to privatize normally public spaces. Containing controlled entrances and walls and fences, gated communities create a border for in-group members, excluding access to out-group members. These residential areas are spreading in different countries and are reported in increasing numbers in the United States, Argentina, Brazil, Bahrain, and Saudi Arabia. In each country they are slightly different, but the common theme is to exclude other ethnic, national, and cultural groups from certain residential areas. In the literature, four different types of gated communities have been described:

1. *Lifestyle communities* provide separation for leisure activities and the amenities that are part of community life. This type includes retirement and leisure communities that are designed for residents who engage in a wide variety of activities close to their own homes.

2. *Elite and upper-middle-class communities* are primarily occupied by the rich and wealthy. These communities focus on exclusion according to social status and on image and security. They are becoming common not only in developed countries like the United States and the United Kingdom, but also in less-developed countries like Mexico, Brazil, and Argentina.

3. *Security zone communities* differ from the other types in that they are not the result of urban planning but of the activities of their residents. Residents mark the neighborhood boundaries and restrict access to traffic and individuals that are perceived as bringing crime to the community.

4. *Foreign gated communities* are a new type of gated community that is associated with economic globalization that has created a demand for foreign workers in culturally homogenous and traditional countries. These are communities that are built to allow foreign workers to continue their lifestyle and at the same time separate them from the host society. These are common in Saudi Arabia, Bahrain, and recently in China.

Urban crime and the perception of urban insecurity have been reflected in attempts to formulate exclusionary policies, increasing urban surveillance and the separation of the wealthy from other urban residents.

Consequences of Globalization

Global processes have facilitated human trafficking. Since the fall of the former Soviet Union, women from impoverished countries of the eastern block have joined the sex industry in Western Europe, the Middle East, and North America. It is estimated that women from these countries are in prostitution in more than 50 countries. In cities in these countries, street prostitution has increased, sex districts have developed, and land use has changed from residential to sex-related commercial activities (sex shops, massage parlors, and bars). In Southeast Asia the development of the tourist industry combined with rural impoverishment and rapid migration to the cities led to the development of a sex tourist industry and the development of urban sex districts. Street prostitution takes over the street and turns urban communities into unsafe places as women are harassed, drug trafficking increases, and health problems abound.

Crime and enforcement have other impacts upon urban neighborhoods. Enforcement of various drug laws as part of the War on Drugs has led to massive increase in the prison system in the United States, such that the country has the highest rates of incarceration in the world. A majority of persons serving prison time for drug offenses are from minority communities, and the expansion of the War on Drugs has led to an absence of young men from these neighborhoods and the disenfranchisement of many adults (in most U.S. states, persons convicted of a felony are not entitled to vote). Incarceration reduces the employability of ex-offender young males, contributing to high rates of unemployment in disadvantaged communities. High incarceration rates have effects on families and family structure. The disproportionate incarceration of males compared to females leads to a reduction in the number of males available for marriage, contributing to higher rates of female-headed families and welfare dependency in disadvantaged neighborhoods, reinforcing a cycle of poverty.

City and crime are closely linked and often mutually reinforcing. Some of the sources of crime rates are the result of neighborhoods' social disorganization and lack of collective efficacy. At the same time the perception of crime has urban implications, increasing the perception of fear and uneasiness and the willingness of the middle and upper classes to close themselves inside gated neighborhoods. Global trade of drugs and individuals reinforce social disorganization at the local level.

Gustavo S. Mesch

See also Chicago School of Urban Sociology; Gated Community; Sex and the City; Sex Industry

Further Readings

Cohen, Lawrence E. and Marcus Felson. 1979. "Social Change and Crime Rate Trends: A Routine Activity Approach." *American Sociological Review* 44:588–607.

Durkheim, Émile. [1897] 1951. *Suicide: A Study in Sociology*. Translated by J. A. Spaulding and G. Simpson. New York: The Free Press.

Hunter, Albert, and Terry L. Baumer. 1982. "Street Traffic, Social Integration, and Fear of Crime." *Sociological Inquiry* 52:122–31.

Meier, Robert F. and Terance D. Miethe. 1993. "Understanding Theories of Criminal Victimization. *Crime and Justice* 17:459–99.

Ross, Catherine E., John R. Reynolds, and Karlyn J. Geis. 2000. "The Contingent Meaning of Neighborhood Stability for Residents' Psychological Well-being." *American Sociological Review* 65:581–97.

Sampson, Robert J. and W. Byron Groves. 1989. "Community Structure and Crime: Testing Social Disorganization Theory." *American Journal of Sociology* 94:774–802.

Sampson, Robert J., Jeffrey D. Morenoff, and Felton Earls. 1999. "Beyond Social Capital: Spatial Dynamics of Collective Efficacy for Children." *American Sociological Review* 64:633–60.

Shaw, Clifford and Henry D. McKay. 1969. *Juvenile Delinquency and Urban Areas*. Chicago: University of Chicago Press.

CULTURAL HERITAGE

Heritage is that which is handed down from the past; it is what a people have inherited from their ancestors. Particular to a time and a place, cultural heritage expresses the cumulative knowledge and experience of generations, affirming and enriching cultural identities. As a repository of human knowledge, and a record of human achievement, cultural heritage is often considered to be the legacy not only of a community or a nation but of humankind.

Cultural heritage is commonly comprised of historic monuments, museums, archaeological sites, and masterpieces of art and architecture. More broadly conceived, it includes the natural environment, flora and fauna, and natural features and water systems specific to a place and a time, as well as a broad variety of material things and immaterial practices such as inherited physical artifacts, monuments, buildings, and places. Tangible heritage can be moveable as in small objects and artifacts, or immovable such as buildings, streets, and settlements. Intangible heritage refers to traditions, myths, religion, beliefs, practices, knowledge, and language. Heritage transmits the memory of human societies through forms of expression and thereby binds material objects to the immaterial dimensions that lend them meaning.

What survives from the past is irreplaceable. As a legacy, a storehouse of knowledge, and an identity of a time, a place, and a people, heritage should be respected and maintained and passed to future generations. Modern interest in heritage was founded on a sense of history as a narrative of progress and a romantic nostalgia for the past. Other motivations for conservation included a respect for past achievements and a desire to learn from the past.

Value of Cultural Heritage

Cultural heritage was once defined as the structures or artifacts (such as the Parthenon in Athens) that expressed the highest attainment of a civilization. Increasingly, groups of buildings and parts of the city in which the site is located and the beliefs and practices that give meaning to the place are considered part of a cultural landscape and thus valuable heritage as, for instance, with the palaces and temples of Lhasa in Tibet. From single monuments, protection for cultural heritage has expanded to include historic districts and territories. In addition, preservation efforts have moved from concentrating solely on the structures of the powerful and wealthy to an appreciation of their interconnectedness to the vernacular fabric in which they are situated. Gardens, open spaces, streets, festivals, folk music and dance, and religious and artistic practices are the connective tissue that binds the built world into an organic whole. Even the remains of mines and mining settlements have achieved heritage status in recent years in the United Kingdom and in Japan. Of course, not everything that has been or should be inherited from the past can be preserved. A society faced with the burden of caretaking heritage has to decide what heritage is to be retained.

The value of cultural heritage is in the significance that society attaches to it. Hence, the worth of cultural heritage is socially constructed. People imbue the physical structures or spaces with cultural meanings, and religious traditions are often at the root of these meanings. The Richtersveld cultural landscape in South Africa, home of the semi-nomadic Nama people, is significant not for any grand monuments but for reflecting seasonal patterns that may have persisted for over two millennia. The Nama oral traditions mark places and the attributes of their landscape rich with spiritual meanings. Heritage structures and sites mean different things to different people, and their interpretation is often contested by different ethnic, religious, or national groups. The old city of Jerusalem is a striking example of the disputes among several meanings and groups.

Cultural heritage can become an icon for a community, a city, or a nation and, as such, can be a tool for political or ethnic assertion. War-time crimes have historically focused on the destruction of targeted cultural property. In recent years, the bombing of the fourth-century statues of Buddha by the Taliban in Bamiyan, Afghanistan, or the devastation of significant parts of Dubrovnik in Croatia during the Balkan wars demonstrate the symbolic power of cultural heritage. Preservation then becomes an effort at preserving cultural uniqueness as well as cultural identity.

Histories of war and contestation, such as the heritage of European colonial rule in Asia and Africa, are often problematic in the celebration of nationhood and national narratives. The cultural heritage of apartheid, the holocaust, and genocide cannot be ignored because they are distasteful reminders of conflict and aggression, nor can they be represented only from the perspective of the rulers or the perpetrators. The Genbaku Dome in Hiroshima in Japan, the site of the first atomic bomb explosion in a city, is also an expression of hope for world peace.

Rise of Institutionalized Protection

The modern conservation movement found its first expression in eighteenth-century Europe with an emphasis on Greek and Roman antiquities. It collected historical works of art and artifacts and placed them in museums. Gradually, this led to government control of designated sites and the establishment of norms and legislation for the care and administration of selected heritage properties. The idea of protecting cultural heritage came to the forefront during the nineteenth century with the rise of the nation-state, the losses due to frequent wars, and rapid industrialization. Eugène Viollet-le-Duc, John Ruskin, and William Morris were among the intellectuals who influenced the preservation of heritage. In North America, historic preservation began as a philanthropic effort by elite groups such as the Mt. Vernon Ladies Association, which in 1859 consisted of well-to-do, Anglo-Saxon women. Since then, in North America and in Western Europe, preservation has grown from being the effort of a few upper-class antiquarians to a broad movement with community support to preserve urban districts and streets as well as historic cities and towns. In the United States, community-led efforts for preservation (such as the National Trust for Historic Preservation's program for rejuvenating Main Streets) have focused on self-reliance and economic revitalization of traditional commercial districts rather than large-scale rebuilding by corporate commercial interests.

Generally, heritage preservation has been the responsibility of the state. The Athens Charter of 1931 for the Restoration of Historic Monuments, adopted by the first International Congress of Architects and Technicians of Historic Monuments, institutionalized this notion. Placing the responsibility of cultural heritage on the government has led to the privileging of national narratives of culture and history that support the government's legitimacy.

Bound up with cultural heritage and its conservation are notions of loss and destruction. The second half of the twentieth century saw a massive destruction of heritage. Wars, urban development, large-scale agriculture, mining, natural and environmental disasters, looting, unsustainable tourism, and poor tourism management have all been responsible for the destruction of cultural heritage. The extensive loss of heritage in many Western European cities at the end of World War II created a keen awareness of safeguarding what remained. As newly emergent nations gained independence from European colonial rule, the idea of preserving cultural heritage took on new significance and demanded new fiscal, legal, and administrative instruments and partnerships.

One of these new instruments is the United Nations Educational, Scientific and Cultural Organization (UNESCO), established as an intergovernmental organization in 1945. Although its initial objective was to protect cultural property during conflict and war, UNESCO developed international charters and conventions for the preservation of world heritage with the idea of preserving cultural heritage that expressed the achievement of humankind globally. The Convention Concerning the Protection of World Cultural and Natural Heritage was adopted in 1972. It provides a global mechanism for identifying and protecting important

sites. Today there are 878 World Heritage sites in 185 countries. Of these, more than 250 are towns or historic centers and many more are monuments located in urban contexts. In the past few decades, other international organizations such as International Council on Monuments and Sites, International Center for the Study of Preservation and Restoration of Cultural Property, the Getty Foundation, and UN Development Program have contributed significantly to the recognition of cultural heritage.

Heritage, Tourism, and Development

Protecting cultural heritage has generally been pitted against development and change. A central dilemma has been to preserve what is valuable while contending with, or even encouraging, modernization and development in the face of globalization. London's changing skyline and commitment to make room for new commercial towers while retaining significant heritage structures is evidence of this struggle to make London a global city while keeping key historical elements as identifiers of place and history. This brings into focus questions about the costs and benefits of preservation efforts. First, whose heritage is being preserved? Second, what are the short- and long-term economic and social costs and benefits of preservation and who bears them? Third, what are the consequences of protecting cultural heritage for urban development? These questions are of paramount importance in countries with high rates of urbanization. Faced with the pressures of rapid urban growth (as, e.g., in the Kathmandu Valley in Nepal), inadequate infrastructure, and debilitating social inequities, governments ignore the neglect and destruction of cultural heritage or are unable to control it. This problem is especially sharp where local development needs have conflicted with the global good of heritage conservation. Along these lines, UNESCO and other international organizations, as well as national and local governments and nongovernmental organizations, recognize the potential of cultural heritage to be a tool for poverty reduction and local economic development. The strategy for the sustainable redevelopment of both the historic city of Zamość in Poland and the twelfth-century towns of the Hoysala heritage region in India have emphasized the importance of sustainable local economic development.

Global tourism to heritage sites and cities, at times excessive and insensitive, has exacerbated the conflicts between global cultures and local beliefs and practices. Venice, one of the most popular destinations, attracts more than 20 million tourists a year from around the world, but has lost its own culture and local population. The flow of capital, the demands of tourists for familiar modern amenities, and the environmental externalities of tourism have distorted the value of heritage and destroyed the fragile systems that nurtured it. In Siem Reap in Cambodia, seat of the Angkor Vat, hotels are said to have depleted the groundwater reserves while the dominance of a few large multinational companies operating with imported staff or exploiting the labor of local women and youth has reduced economic benefits for residents. Tourism can introduce or accelerate social change and revive folk arts but also exacerbate commodification. The pressure to retain every aspect of its heritage has stymied development and marginalized the needs of local residents in many places.

Cultural Politics of Heritage

Where cities are competing globally for investments and tourism, cultural richness can become a significant selling point. Cultural heritage has become a way of branding cities and making them interesting and significant. Whereas cities such as Vienna, Prague, and Barcelona have long been known as cultural centers, others such as Rio de Janeiro, Buenos Aires, and Singapore have made efforts in recent years to reconnect with their histories. Uniqueness and character command attention; cities with heritage have what some scholars call designer quality. Such market pressures have led cities to invent cultural practices and exaggerate or essentialize heritage.

The conflicts between contemporary cultures and historical authenticity are everywhere. The debate ranges between those who would like to protect heritage sites in their entirety, wishing to recreate their original context, and those who see change as reflecting multiple layers of history and culture. Furthermore, the concern for an imageable and consumable identity has resulted in the creation of structures, settings, and rituals that mimic a sanitized and aesthetic past. In cities such as Santa Fe in New Mexico, Annapolis in Maryland, and Charleston in South Carolina, critics regard efforts to capture only the delectable and delightful in heritage settings as caricatures of cultural heritage, not as repositories of knowledge.

Global politics is reflected in institutional mechanisms for managing cultural heritage. Colonial powers once assumed stewardship of cultural heritage, as for instance, the French in Morocco or the British in India. In so doing, they imposed historical narratives and national identities on the colonized nations. The views of local people were entirely disregarded. In the postcolonial era, although many nations have made efforts to redress the colonial prejudices and reinscribe nationalist histories, political imbalance has persisted in the global selection of cultural heritage and the charters and conventions that govern them as well as in the relationships between the state and local community over the ownership, interpretation, and management of heritage. Although philanthropists and the wealthy elite pioneered the protection of heritage in Europe and North America, since the late nineteenth century the responsibility for protecting historic buildings and works of art has been placed on public institutions. This has raised questions of ownership and access to heritage. The idea that the inheritors and local communities have a stewardship of the sites and a voice in their management is gradually becoming more current.

Inclusiveness, Equity, and Sustainability

Social and economic change and the inclusion of private property under heritage have resulted in multiple stakeholders and shared responsibility. The inclusion of stakeholder participation ranges from encouraging private investments in the revitalization and adaptive reuse of historic neighborhoods and buildings such as the industrial neighborhoods and waterfront warehouses of many North American cities, to the strengthening of heritage values and identification of meaningful roles for marginalized people. Inherent in these partnerships with stakeholders is the idea of balancing the value of preserving heritage with the needs of current use or finding a value for heritage within contemporary economic, social, and political frameworks. Many of the historic centers of Latin American towns, such as Salvador in Brazil, struggle to balance the present

A plaza near the Teatro Nacional in the Casco Antiguo World Heritage Site in Panama City. The main building in the photo is beautifully restored and has a popular restaurant on the ground floor. The trees are located in the plaza, while to the left of the main building the walls of an unrestored building are visible. To the left of the scene in the photo are buildings in various states of disrepair. The area contains stark contrasts between the homes of those wealthy enough to fully restore the historic buildings and those who occupy buildings that, until the Heritage designation, were cheap and often undesirable buildings that were poorly maintained.

Source: Eric Mathiasen.

Large-scale development, real-estate interests, and tourism-led aestheticization of culture have threatened to erode the fragile and intangible heritage of indigenous peoples. Ambiguities about authenticity are further complicated by histories of aggression. In recent years, many see a need to make reparations for past aggressions and respect the spirit of plurality and diversity that cultural heritage represents. A bottom-up approach in contrast to the top-down one of the past has created a heightened awareness of the importance of community and stakeholder participation. Various governmental agencies, private investors, nongovernmental organizations, local citizens, and international aid agencies have a stake in the management of cultural heritage. The policies that emerge from such a participatory process are cooperative rather than hierarchical. Emphasizing diversity in culture and inclusiveness in access and management of heritage enables the voices of local and indigenous peoples to be heard.

Today, there is a greater awareness of the value of sites sacred to indigenous peoples. Although international conventions and many national policies have addressed gender biases and recognized the heritage of marginalized peoples, new inequities have emerged. Cultural heritage has increasingly become part of culture-led redevelopment of urban areas for improved economic returns and increased competitiveness between cities. Consequently a bias exists for the aspects of inheritance that are easily commodified. Critics have faulted places such as South

needs of their poor and marginalized residents with the colonial identity of the town and the demands of a tourist destination.

Street Seaport in New York and Penang in Malaysia for redeveloping in a way that markets the most consumable aspects of heritage with a view to improving economic returns.

There is a growing awareness of the need to judiciously use and protect resources with a view to sustainability. Inherent in the idea of sustainability is development and change: the idea of making careful use of resources and finding ways to replenish and enrich in protecting for the future. In similar ways, conservation of heritage does not mean a return to a premodern past but negotiation of identities and forms of the past with the future through sustainable development.

Jyoti Hosagrahar

See also Heritage City; Historic Cities; Public Realm; Santa Fe, New Mexico; Urban Culture

Further Readings

Fitch, James Marston. 1982. *Historic Preservation: Curatorial Management of the Built World.* Charlottesville: University Press of Virginia.

International Council on Monuments and Sites (ICOMOS) (http://www.international.icomos.org/home.htm).

Jokilehto, Jukka. 1999. *A History of Architectural Conservation.* Oxford, UK: Butterworth-Heinemann.

National Trust for Historic Preservation (http://www.nationaltrust.org).

Price, N. Stanley, M. Kirby, and A. Melucco Vaccaro, eds. 1996. *Historical and Philosophical Issues in the Conservation of Cultural Heritage.* Los Angeles: John Paul Getty Trust.

UNESCO World Heritage Center (http://whc.unesco.org).

CYBURBIA

Cyburbia broadly refers to the study of how new information and communication technologies (ICT), also called new media and computer-mediated communication, such as the Internet and mobile phones, influence community and social interactions at the neighborhood level. This approach is distinct from traditional urban studies, which privilege face-to-face relationships, and studies of virtual community, which distinguish between the virtual and the real. Instead, this approach recognizes that the physical and the virtual geographies of community overlap and are intertwined in the maintenance and formation of everyday social relations in the urban setting.

Urban Studies and Technological Change

Interest in how technological change influences everyday urban interactions has its origins at least as early as the Chicago School of Urban Sociology. This early work was a reaction to the ways in which changes in urban transportation and communication technology, such as public transportation, the automobile, and the telephone, transformed the social and physical organization of the city. Researchers such as Robert Park and Ernest Burgess noted that while new communication technologies expanded opportunities for social interaction, the increased mobility offered by technologies like the telephone was argued to be responsible for the deterioration of local community and social relationships. Concerns over the impact of new technologies on social relationships endured through the twentieth century, focusing primarily on the introduction of the telephone and the television, and have extended into the twenty-first century with the growth of the Internet and related technologies.

ICTs and Social Networks

The study of how new ICTs influence social relationships in the urban environment has been explored as part of a larger debate related to how, or if, social networks have been transformed as a result of the Internet. This research has broadly focused on the question: Is the Internet replacing social contact, either in person or through other forms of communication? The conclusion of this body of research is that the Internet, in particular e-mail use, has become an important and integrated part of people's everyday life. It supports interaction with preexisting strong social ties as well as more extensive social ties. There is little indication that Internet use substitutes for other forms of contact, such as telephone calls or face-to-face encounters. Instead, the evidence suggests that those who are in frequent contact with members of their personal network by e-mail are also in frequent contact in person and through other media. Similarly, e-mail users tend to have more social ties than nonusers. Although some have argued that e-mail communication, or any form of computer-mediated communication, is inferior to in-person contact, there is only a slight difference in how people rate the quality of online interactions in comparison with face-to-face and telephone conversations. There is little doubt that new media can be used in the exchange of aid and support. However, despite the ubiquity of Internet use, in-person and telephone contact remain the dominant modes of connectivity when people communicate with their closest ties.

While Internet use does not appear to reduce the number of contacts or frequency of communication, it is less clear how it influences the composition of personal networks and where people maintain their networks. Related to the question of whether the Internet substitutes for other means of social contact is the question of whether new media shift the maintenance of personal networks out of the public and into private spheres of interaction.

Robert Putnam documented extensive evidence demonstrating that, starting in the 1970s, Americans have gradually spent less and less time with members of their social networks. A similar pattern of declining social capital has been found in other countries, such as Australia and Britain. These studies suggest that people have been exchanging public participation for private interactions; people are increasingly likely to socialize in small groups in private homes rather than with large groups in public spaces. Although the Internet and other new media originated too recently to be responsible for the trends observed by Putnam and others, there is some evidence that new media facilitate privatism. Research by Miller McPherson, Lynn Smith-Lovin, and Matthew Brashears on the size and composition of people's core "discussion networks," identified a decline in the number of people with whom the average person discusses important matters, as well as a shift away from public participation toward networks found in the private sphere of the home. Although McPherson and his colleagues do not directly link Internet use to changes in social networks, the time period they studied overlaps with the rise of the Internet. This finding is also consistent with existing observations that link home-based media use, including television and the telephone, to increased privatism. Increased home centeredness comes at the expense of interaction in traditional public and neighborhood spaces, spaces that have traditionally provided exposure to diverse people as well as new cultural

and political information. If opportunities for interaction with those beyond the private sphere decline, so do opportunities for exposure to diverse social networks and resources.

In an attempt to directly examine the circumstances under which the Internet does or does not encourage privatism, a number of studies have examined the role of Internet use in different urban settings, such as neighborhoods.

ICTs and Neighborhoods

Netville

The Netville study was one of the first studies to specifically test the impact of new information and communication technologies on social relationships at the neighborhood level. The Netville experiment was an attempt to provide future levels of Internet connectivity and services to a typical middle-class suburban neighborhood that was located outside of Toronto, Ontario, Canada. Residents who moved to the community were promised free broadband Internet access, online music services, online health services, and a variety of communication tools, such as a videophone, instant messaging, multimedia chat rooms, and a neighborhood e-mail discussion list. However, unanticipated problems in the deployment of the technology left almost half of the community residents without any kind of Internet connectivity at all. A researcher, Keith Hampton, moved into the community and spent two years interviewing community residents and conducting an ethnography that compared "wired" and "nonwired" residents.

The results of the Netville study suggested that despite the common characterization of the Internet as a global media that facilitates distant connections, it can also afford very local interactions. When wired residents were compared with non-wired neighbors, those who received access to Netville's technology were more involved with their community: They recognized three times as many neighbors, talked to twice as many, visited 50 percent more in person, and called them on the telephone four times as often. Although those with the technology had more ties and more frequent interactions in person and over the telephone, it was relatively weak, not strong, intimate ties that were formed as a result of the services. Consistent with Mark Granovetter's theory of weak ties, the large number of weak neighborhood-based ties was found to support residents' ability to organize collectively when dealing with local issues and concerns. Counter to concerns that the Internet encouraged privatism, the Netville study found that Internet use facilitated greater involvement within the parochial realm. However, the Netville study was one case study, and at its conclusion, the generalizability of the findings was not clear.

e-Neighbors

The e-Neighbors study attempted to clarify the contexts under which Internet technologies facilitate interaction at the neighborhood level. Data for the e-Neighbors project were collected by Hampton through a series of three annual surveys administered to the adult residents of four Boston, Massachusetts, neighborhoods. The neighborhoods were selected to be socioeconomically similar: They were all middle class but contrasted in terms of housing type. Each neighborhood consisted of 100 to 200 homes. Two of the four neighborhoods were suburban communities, one was an apartment building, and the fourth was a gated community. Three of the four neighborhoods were given access to a series of simple Internet services: a neighborhood e-mail discussion list and a neighborhood website. The fourth neighborhood, the second suburban site, served as a control group. To maintain the ideal of a natural research setting, participants were not given a computer, Internet access, or any training.

Of the three experimental neighborhoods in the e-Neighbors study, only the suburban neighborhood widely adopted the e-mail list intervention, and none of the communities extensively used a neighborhood website. The apartment building had the lowest use of the provided services. Even though the apartment building had the youngest and most technologically savvy population of the four field sites, it was also the least conducive to social tie formation; it had the lowest levels of residential stability, fewest cohabitating couples, fewest children, lowest home ownership, little preexisting sense of community, and a low sense of community obligation. This contrasted strongly with the suburban neighborhood, where residents frequently used the neighborhood e-mail list to discuss local services, local politics, local issues, and for collective action. Unlike the residents of the apartment building, the residents of the suburban community were residentially stable, most were married or cohabitating, and they were in the midst of their child-rearing years. Most suburban residents actively wanted more contact with their neighbors. When the residents of the suburban experimental community were compared with the control group, those residents who actively participated in the neighborhood e-mail list experienced an average increase in the size of their neighborhood networks of four new ties per year. As with the Netville study, the new neighborhood ties formed as a result of the intervention were relatively weak.

The e-Neighbors study also found that Internet use, in general, was increasingly embedded into neighborhood networks. In particular, those who were early adopters of the Internet were found to know more neighbors over time, whereas those with less experience using the Internet were found to have local networks that shrank over time. In addition, the longer a person had been using the Internet, the more neighbors he or she was in contact with by e-mail.

The e-Neighbors study concluded that those who live in neighborhoods with a preexisting context that supports the formation of local social ties (such as low residential mobility and the presence of children), and those with high levels of Internet penetration, are the most likely to benefit from the Internet. In these situations the Internet does not privatize. Instead, as the Internet becomes increasingly pervasive, it may be an antidote to privatism, affording the formation of networks at the neighborhood level. In addition, evidence that e-mail exchanged between neighbors often includes ordinary political discussion, debates about civic duties, and collective action suggested that use of the Internet in the parochial realm may lead to broader political participation and more deliberative democracy. However, the finding that only those neighborhoods that are already well positioned, in terms of Internet access and existing social capital, benefit from the Internet, suggests that there is the potential for a widening of a social capital divide between the haves and the have-nots.

i-Neighbors

Case studies from Australia, Canada, Israel, the United Kingdom, and the United States have explored the influence of everyday Internet use on social relations at the neighborhood level. However, there have been few studies of how ICTs are used locally at a more generalizable level.

In contrast to the experimental nature of Netville and e-Neighbors, where communities were chosen ahead of time and given the technology by researchers, the i-Neighbors project run by Hampton examines how the Internet is adopted and used in the maintenance of neighborhood relationships across thousands of neighborhoods within a number of countries.

Findings from the i-Neighbors project are consistent with the results of the experimental Netville and e-Neighbors studies. The Internet is most likely to facilitate the formation and maintenance of local social ties in neighborhood contexts that are already conducive to local tie formation, such as new neighborhoods, suburban areas, and areas with higher income and low residential mobility. However, unlike previous studies, the i-Neighbors study also found that the Internet undermines contextual influences that inhibit tie formation and collective action in neighborhoods with concentrated disadvantage. The i-Neighbors study found that a disproportionately high number of "truly disadvantaged" neighborhoods, low-income neighborhoods high in racial segregation and unemployment, were successfully using the Internet to build local social ties, discuss local issues, and act collectively to address local problems. This suggests that the Internet not only reduces privatism through engagement at the neighborhood level but provides new opportunities for social and political involvement that were previously inaccessible to those embedded in an ecological context of concentrated disadvantage.

Keith N. Hampton

See also Chicago School of Urban Sociology; Community Studies; Urban Studies

Further Readings

Arnold, Michael, Martin R. Gibbs, and Philippa Wright. 2003. "Intranets and Local Community: 'Yes, an intranet is all very well, but do we still get free beer and a barbeque?'" In *Communities and Technologies,* edited by M. Huysman, E. Wenger, and V. Wulf. Norwell, MA: Kluwer Academic.

Baym, Nancy, Yan Bing Zhang, and Mei-Chen Lin. 2004. "Social Interactions across Media: Interpersonal Communication on the Internet, Telephone and Face-to-Face." *New Media & Society* 6(3):299–318.

Boase, Jeffrey, John Horrigan, Barry Wellman, and Lee Rainie. 2006. *The Strength of Internet Ties.* Washington, DC: Pew Internet & American Life Project.

Crang, Michael, Tracey Crosbie, and Stephen Graham. 2006. "Variable Geometries of Connection." *Urban Studies* 43(13):2551–70.

Fischer, Claude. 1992. *America Calling: A Social History of the Telephone to 1940.* Berkeley: University of California Press.

Granovetter, Mark. 1973. "The Strength of Weak Ties." *American Journal of Sociology* 78:1360–80.

Halpern, David. 2005. *Social Capital.* Malden, MA: Polity Press.

Hampton, Keith. 2003. "Grieving for a Lost Network: Collective Action in a Wired Suburb." *The Information Society* 19(5):417–28.

———. 2007. "Neighborhoods in the Network Society: The e-Neighbors Study." *Information, Communication and Society* 10(5):714–48.

Hampton, Keith and Barry Wellman. 2003. "Neighboring in Netville: How the Internet Supports Community and Social Capital in a Wired Suburb." *City and Community* 2(3):277–311.

i-Neighbors (http://www.i-neighbors.org).

McPherson, Miller, Lynn Smith-Lovin, and Matthew E. Brashears. 2006. "Social Isolation in America: Changes in Core Discussion Networks over Two Decades." *American Sociological Review* 71:353–75.

Mesch, Gustavo S. and Yael Levanon. 2003. "Community Networking and Locally-Based Social Ties in Two Suburban Localities." *City & Community* 2(4):335–51.

Park, Robert and Ernest Burgess. 1925. *The City.* Chicago: University of Chicago Press.

Putnam, Robert. 2000. *Bowling Alone.* New York: Simon & Schuster.

Sennett, Richard. 1977. *The Fall of Public Man.* New York: Knopf.

Zhao, Shanyang. 2006. "Do Internet Users Have More Social Ties? A Call for Differentiated Analyses of Internet Use." *Journal of Computer Mediated Communication* 11(3): article 8.

D

DAMASCUS, SYRIA

Capital of the Arab Republic of Syria, Damascus claims to be the oldest continuously inhabited city in the world (although recent excavations in Aleppo, Syria's other major city, might shift this claim). In its long history it has been the center of the Aramaean region, one of the 10 cities of the Roman Decapolis and the capital of the first (and vast) Islamic empire created by the Umayyads (between 661 and 750) as well as the center of Greater Syria (Bilād ash-Shām دالب الشام, made up of present-day Syria, Lebanon, Israel, Palestine, and Jordan). The city still has an incredible architectural heritage, including remains from antiquity, one of the oldest mosques in the Islamic world (the Umayyad mosque built 706–715), and over 8,000 intact commercial buildings and private houses dating from the Ottoman period (1516–1918). In 1979 UNESCO made Damascus a site of World Cultural Heritage, a heritage that a 2001 UN report believes to be at risk.

As Mark Twain extolled in *The Innocents Abroad,*

> To Damascus, years are only moments, decades are only flitting trifles of time. She measures time, not by days and months and years, but by the empires she has seen rise, and prosper and crumble to ruin. She is a type of immortality. . . . Damascus has seen all that has ever occurred on earth, and still she lives. She has looked upon the dry bones of a thousand empires, and will see the tombs of a thousand more before she dies. Although another claims the name, old Damascus is by right the Eternal City.

In Arabic دمشق الشام (Dimashq ash-Shām) is usually shortened to either Dimashq دمشق or ash-Shām الشام (also the colloquial term for the whole of Syria and/or the "north"). The English name Damascus is thought to come from the Greek Δαμασκός, via Latin, which in turn originated from the Aramaic קשמרד Darmeśeq, (a well-watered place), although it is likely the name predates the Aramaic era.

Damascus is located about 80 kilometers inland from the eastern Mediterranean coast and 680 meters above sea level in the fertile Ghouta (الغوطة al-ġūta) oasis sheltered by the Anti-Lebanon mountain range. The temperate climate and abundant supply of water from the nearby Barada River certainly would have encouraged early settlement; Aram Damascus was established there in 1100 BC by the Aramaeans, Semitic nomads from Arabia, who built a complex water distribution system of canals and tunnels (later improved by the Romans and the Umayyads). The settlement became a sought-after prize among the region's empire builders until the Roman ruler Pompey incorporated Damascus into the 10 cities of the Decapolis in 64 BC, fusing the Greek and Aramaean foundations into a new city layout measuring approximately 1500 by 750 meters, surrounded by a city wall. Roman Damascus was an important city in early Christian history—the "road to Damascus" is the site of St. Paul's conversion to Christianity in the New Testament (Acts 9:11). The street called Straight (referred to in the story of his conversion), also known as the Via Recta, was the *cardo* (main street) of Roman Damascus.

In 661 Damascus became the capital of the Umayyad Empire, the first Muslim dynasty, which at its height stretched from India to Spain. One of the greatest buildings remaining from this period of history is the Umayyad Mosque, built between 709 and 715 on the site of a Byzantine church dedicated to John the Baptist (itself built on a Roman temple to Jupiter that had previously been an Aramaean temple to the storm and rain god Hadad). The mosque, often described as the first monumental work of architecture in Islamic history, was designed to resemble the organizational spaces of the house of the Prophet in Medina and is also a reinterpretation of late antique tradition.

Damascus's strategic location—on the growing trade route between Europe and China and the hajj pilgrimage route to Mecca—has undoubtedly shaped its focus on both the mercantile and spiritual. The city gradually changed from a Greco-Roman city with a grid of straight streets to an Islamic city with narrow, winding streets where most residents lived inside *harat* closed off at night by heavy wooden gates. During Salah al-Din's rule in the twelfth century, Damascus acquired its reputation as a city for seekers of academic excellence. While returning from his pilgrimage to Mecca in 1184, Islamic scholar, poet, geographer, and traveler Ibn Jubayr is credited with saying, "If there is paradise on Earth, it is without a doubt Damascus. If it is in the heavens, Damascus is such that it rivals it in glory."

It was also during the twelfth and thirteenth centuries that Damascus began to attract more attention in Europe, particularly for its manufacturing skills and high-quality products. Damascus became synonymous with high-quality steel (patterned steel is still referred to as damascened) and luxurious fabric (damask refers to the patterned Byzantine and Chinese silks that started to become more widely available in Europe).

In 1516, after a period of relative obscurity as a Mamluk provincial capital, Damascus entered a period of 400 years as an Ottoman city (except for a brief occupation by Ibrahim Pasha of Egypt from 1832 to 1840). Architecture flourished, in particular *bayt arabis,* a Syrian strain of Ottoman grand merchant houses built around open courtyards, as well as mosques (Damascus is said to have over 1,000 mosques) and madrasahs (Islamic schools). In the late nineteenth and early twentieth centuries, the Ottoman state and society adopted European ideas, and a "Europeanized" residential quarter appeared on the road between al-Merjeh (the meadow) and Salihiyye (a district that grew around the shrine of Sheikh Muhi al-Din ibn Arabi). Ideas of nationalism also began to flourish, but a brief period of independence during the Arab Revolt in 1918 was quickly replaced by French mandate rule in 1920. In 1925 the Druze revolt in the Hauran spread to Damascus, and the French responded by bombing and shelling a whole quarter of the Old City, which was later fenced off with barbed wire. A new road was built outside the walls and the city's commercial and administrative center also shifted northward toward this area, so that Salihiyye began to merge with other villages on the slopes of Mount Qasioun to form new districts often named after their first refugee residents such as al-Akrad (Kurdish soldiers) and al-Muhajirin (the migrants).

Syria gained independence in 1946 and Damascus is now the capital of the Syrian Arab Republic, a parliamentary state dominated by the secular Ba'ath Party and currently headed by Bashar al-Assad (the son of Hafez al-Assad, who was its previous president for more than 30 years). The city's estimated population of 4.5 million people is still expanding as a result of the influx of migrants and refugees. (In 1955 thousands of Palestinian refugees moved into the new district of Yarmouk, and in the early twenty-first century it is estimated that more than 3 million Iraqis are now in Syria, many in Damascus.) In general the northern end of the city is more affluent (in particular the western Mezze district, the Barada valley in Dumar, and on the slopes of the mountains at Berze), while poorer areas (often built without official approval) have developed mostly in the south. The shrunken Ghouta oasis is now heavily polluted because of the city's traffic, industry, and sewage.

Two thirds of the city's population is Sunni with the rest made up of Shi'ites, Ismailis, and Alawites, some Druze (though most live to the southwest of the city), and a significant Christian minority (about 11 percent) of Maronites, Catholics, Greeks, Armenians, and Assyrian Orthodox. A very small Jewish community remains in the Old City.

While Damascus is still rich in Classical and Islamic monuments, it is the amount of surviving domestic Islamic architecture (in particular the *bayt arabis*) that makes Damascus (and Aleppo) so unique. Approximately half of the 16,832 houses listed in the Ottoman 1900 yearbook were still remaining in 2001, according to the UN report by Stefan Weber of the Aga Khan University in the United Kingdom. However, Weber warns that Syrian administrations and others assume the city's status as a World Cultural Heritage site covers only the area within the city walls, when it refers to the whole city. This oversight has led to minimal (or nonexistent) protection for extramural areas, where twelfth-century homes are being replaced with multistory concrete buildings.

Continued strained relations with the United States (including accusations by the Bush administration in 2005 that Syria is part of the "axis of evil") have led to limited Western investment in the city. However, the Old City, at least, has no shortage of willing investors from Syria itself and elsewhere in the Arab world, in particular the Gulf and newly resident Iraqis.

Applications for restoration licenses have increased tenfold in recent years, and the number of "renovated" cafes and restaurants had risen from approximately 5 in 1998 to more than 100 by April 2007. Luxury boutique hotels and nightclubs (now about 10) soon followed. The Old City's famous markets have also been the focus of speculation. In 2006, Kuwaiti prince Majed Al Sabah proclaimed the street called Straight to be the next Bond Street when he opened his luxury designer store Villa Moda in a restored house there amid a flurry of attention from the world's fashion media.

Although this development is mostly welcomed, there is concern about the general quality of the work carried out, and Weber's report calls for a training and planning center to help investors in this work.

Jessica Jacobs

See also Historic Cities; Islamic City

Further Readings

Damascus Online (http://www.damascus-online.com).

Flood, Finbarr Barry. 2000. *The Great Mosque of Damascus: Studies on the Meanings of an Umayyad Visual Culture*. Leiden, the Netherlands: Brill.

Old Damascus (http://www.oldamascus.com).

Rihawi, Abdul Qader. 1979. *Arabic Islamic Architecture in Syria*. Damascus, Syria: Ministry of Culture and National Heritage.

Salamandra, Christa. 2004. *A New Old Damascus: Authenticity and Distinction in Urban Syria*. Bloomington: Indiana University Press.

Umayyad Mosque of Damascus (http://archnet.org/library/sites/one-site.tcl?site_id=7161).

Weber, Stefan. 2002. "Damascus—A Major Eastern Mediterranean Site at Risk." Pp. 186–88 in *Heritage at Risk: Report of the International Council of Monuments and Sites*. Retrieved March 25, 2009 (http://www.international.icomos.org/risk/2001/syri2001.htm).

———. 2007. "Damascus 1900: Urban Transformation, Architectural Innovation and Cultural Change in a Late Ottoman City (1808–1918)." In *Proceedings of the Danish Institute Damascus*. Aarhus, Denmark: Aarhus University Press.

DAVIS, MIKE

Mike Davis (1946–) is a prolific Marxist labor historian whose renown stems from a memorably trenchant, provocative mix of scholarship and reportage on urban issues, especially those concerning Los Angeles. Davis labels himself a "writer-activist," "former meat cutter and long-distance truck driver," and "Marxist-environmentalist"; his perspective on American cities is consciously that of someone who grew up in a southern California marked by deindustrialization, suburbanization, and racism. Alongside these working-class credentials stand prestigious MacArthur and Getty fellowships, two books—*City of Quartz* (1990) and *Ecology of Fear* (1998)—on the *Los Angeles Times* bestsellers list simultaneously, and celebrity status within and outside of academia.

Davis has directed much of his analysis and critique of urban conditions toward the detrimental effects of economic restructuring and welfare state shrinkage for the urban working class. Nevertheless, he has an expansive understanding of the forces affecting cities. Davis tackles such core urban issues as land uses, crime control, and ethnic politics, but also less obvious topics that range from pandemics to avocado farming. Throughout, Davis insists on the class-based, materialist core of Marxist analysis, although a non-orthodox version that replaces the proletarian revolution with pessimistic scenarios for workers and the poor and grants spatial relations some independence from the economy. Although Davis was among the academics who conceived of the Los Angeles School of Urban Studies (and reportedly was the first to use that name, in *City of Quartz*), his attachment to economic structure and uneasy relationship with postmodernism leaves him somewhat outside the school as it has evolved.

Davis began a PhD at the University of California at Los Angeles, then left for Britain and worked during the 1980s for the socialist journal *New Left Review*. His intellectual influences include key thinkers such as the Marxist historian Perry Anderson and the critical theorist Herbert Marcuse. While in Britain, Davis published his most theoretical book, *Prisoners of the American Dream* (1986). It is an account of the party system's abandonment of the working class in light of a White, suburban, middle-class electoral majority—ultimately, the Ronald Reagan coalition—along with organized labor's hostility to African Americans, women, and immigrants.

In the late 1980s, Davis returned to the United States and turned his attention to the ills of Los Angeles and the widespread erosion of central cities. Davis's best-known and academically most celebrated book is *City of Quartz* (1990), now an urban studies "classic." Davis makes a scathing, sweeping, and historically grounded indictment of the control of Los Angeles by business and political leaders, property developers foremost among them. He highlights the mobilization of the police state against, especially, young minority males, homeless people, and illegal immigrants—among the compelling images in *City of Quartz* is that of "Fortress L.A." Although affluent White homeowners and international investors increasingly competed for power with the traditional local elites, all shared an interest in fortifying Los Angeles against perceived threats coming from lower-class "others."

City of Quartz appeared in paperback in 1992, the year of the Rodney King rebellion in Los Angeles. Among Davis's most angry and captivating works is an informal coda to *City of Quartz* (and to *Prisoners of the American Dream*), "Who Killed Los Angeles?" There, Davis detailed the "federalized and federally driven"—heavily militarized—strategies that were already used in antidrug, antigang, and anti-immigrant efforts but that were perfected in reaction to the breakdown of law and order. At the same time, the bipartisan consensus in California and in Washington against spending for public employment and services "figuratively burned down the city a second time."

In several pieces collected in *In Praise of Barbarians* (2007), Davis shows that this governing experiment was both employed and abandoned in federal, state, and local responses to New Orleans after Hurricane Katrina. New Orleans, like Los Angeles, has been denied the resources sufficient even to address its predisaster needs, let alone to rebuild its economic, social, and physical infrastructure. Ironically, however, in New Orleans, the federal government and military were glaringly passive, to tragic effect. And unlike Los Angeles, which epitomizes the cities being recreated through Latina/o (and Asian) immigration, as Davis argues in *Magical Urbanism* (2000), an evacuated New Orleans is being "deliberately murdered" by public- and private-sector efforts to remake it as a wealthier, Whiter city.

Davis is fascinated with the disjunction between the "sunshine" image of Los Angeles purveyed by the recording, film, and tourism industries and the "*noir*" reality of its social and environmental conditions elaborated in grimmer, yet popular, genres of film and literature. This theme unifies *Ecology of Fear* (1998), the beginning of a continuing exploration into why and how capitalist-inspired human settlement patterns have intervened in natural phenomena. Davis views southern California as defined by fear of the wild, whether in nature or society. His core, most contentious argument is that much of the real danger—filtered as it is by popular culture, political discourse, and the news—has resulted from development patterns that are ignorant of the workings of the ecosystem. Critically, "malice towards the landscape" includes animus toward cities and city dwellers. Davis's characterization of the areas affected by the 2007 wildfires as "pink stucco death valleys full of bored teenagers and desperate housewives" typifies his assessment of southern California's class and spatial structure.

Ecology of Fear contributes to Davis's overall argument about the global and historical relationships among capitalism, urbanization, and epic human disasters. His shift in focus beyond North America came with *Late Victorian Holocausts* (2001), a mammoth examination of the "making of the Third World" in the last half of the nineteenth century. Using scientific studies for evidence, Davis charges colonial forces with exploiting El Niño–caused droughts and famines for economic and political expansion (much as contemporary developers in southern California enjoy the opportunities presented by natural disasters). *The Monster at Our Door* (2005) traces the avian influenza threat to globalization and the "superurbanization" of poverty, while *Buda's Wagon* (2007) identifies the car bomb—"the hot rod of the apocalypse"—as the first indigenously urban form of guerilla warfare. In *Planet of Slums* (2006), Davis returns specifically to cities, tying the late twentieth-century explosion in the size and expanse of slums to the structural adjustment regime of marketization and privatization. The importance of these five books lies in Davis's argument that two eras of economic and geographic restructuring serving the interests of capital have not only wrought social and ecological havoc in the third world, but inadvertently brought political and biological terror to the West.

Davis's best work often appears as topical pieces in left and mainstream periodicals, and he publishes and is interviewed widely online. He excels as a commentator on contemporary events: elections and labor politics as well as natural disasters and terrorist attacks. Davis's writing contains strong narrative elements, and his appeal to academic and public audiences rests, in large part, on his ability to tell absorbing tales of cities, people, and events even while employing sometimes-impenetrable turns of phrase. He uses photographs to communicate wit and anger.

One result of the entrance of Davis's work into the public sphere is controversy. From the Right, he has been excoriated as hysterical, given to concocting facts, and an academic elite in working-class garb. *Ecology of Fear* instigated furious responses and denunciations from conservative commentators nationally, the Los Angeles business community, and some California scholars. At issue were the tone of the book—that is, Davis's diagnosis of the cause of California natural disasters and his apocalyptic predictions for the future—and the veracity of his evidence. From the Left, Davis is treated as a hero and defended from what are considered smear campaigns. He is portrayed as prophetic and a meticulous chronicler of the havoc wrought by capitalism. Nonetheless, even some urban scholars who are disposed toward Davis's general point of view regarding the vast problems of cities have objected that he is unnecessarily apocalyptic and insufficiently attentive to the importance of culture and gender.

In sum, Mike Davis's appeal lies in his ability to cross the boundary between the academy and the world of what he calls "the honest working class." He has energized the field of urban studies and, by fashioning a complex explanation of urban conditions in California and globally, has made himself an object of both praise and condemnation.

Judith A. Garber

See also Los Angeles, California; Los Angeles School of Urban Studies; Urban Theory

Further Readings

Bearman, Joshuah. 2004. "Mike Davis." *The Believer* 2(February). Retrieved March 25, 2009 (http://www.believermag.com/issues/200402/?read=interview_davis).

Davis, Mike. 1986. *Prisoners of the American Dream: Politics and Economy in the History of the U.S. Working Class.* London: Verso.

———. 1990. *City of Quartz: Excavating the Future of Los Angeles.* London: Verso.

———. 1998. *Ecology of Fear: Los Angeles and the Imagination of Disaster.* New York: Metropolitan Books.

———. 2001. *Late Victorian Holocausts: El Niño Famines and the Making of the Third World.* London: Verso.

———. 2006. *Planet of Slums.* London: Verso.

———. 2007. *In Praise of Barbarians: Essays against Empire.* Chicago: Haymarket Books.

DE CERTEAU, MICHEL

Michel de Certeau (1925–1986) has become one of the oft-cited theorists of everyday urban life. This entry gives a brief outline of his work, his theoretical background, and the key concepts taken from his work into urban studies and sets those concepts in the context of some of the limits created by this appropriation. The key theoretical tradition is one of a theory of practice that stresses how objects and happenings exceed people's conceptualizations of them. With this, his work has been picked up for, first, how it points to a critique of urban ideologies, and especially those of planning and rationalism; second, as offering an account of life that exceeds notions of planned space in terms of a model active practice transforming spaces through, third, a sense of local "tactics" that, fourth, form part of urban consumption practices.

Theoretical Background

Michel de Certeau's background as an ordained Jesuit priest working on their archives and a member of Jacques Lacan's *l'école Freudienne* from its start to finish, whose most sustained work was on the spiritual possessions of medieval Loudun and popular religious mysticism, hardly seems like obvious origins for theorizing urban affairs. De Certeau underwent something of a personal revelation through the events in Paris in 1968 and moved his later scholarship onto more topical urban matters. Through his work on urban matters, he became known as the champion of the common folk, of a street-level social theory. It is in this guise that de Certeau has become a darling to some, as a counterpoint to stratospheric theory, and villain for others, as an example of taking micro theory too far.

His most cited essay, "Walking in the City," opens with what is now an anachronistic evocation of urban theory and its desire for an orderly view of what he calls the "concept city":

Seeing Manhattan from the 110th floor of the World Trade centre. Beneath the haze stirred up by the winds, the urban island, a sea in the middle of the sea, lifts up the skyscrapers. . . . A wave of verticals. Its agitation momentarily arrested by vision. The gigantic mass is immobilized before the eyes. It is transformed into a texturology. . . . To what erotics of knowledge does the ecstasy of reading such a cosmos belong? Having taken voluptuous pleasure in it, I wonder what is the source of this pleasure of "seeing the whole," of looking down on, totalizing the most immoderate of human texts. (de Certeau 1984:91–2)

This has keyed into a whole series of critiques of urban theory that question the subject position and viewpoint of planners, the panoptic disciplining of space, and the pretensions of social theory. Here he asks us to think about the enjoyment mobilized by theoretical and management accounts that offer us a privileged and "powerful" view of urban process—there is no innocent viewpoint, and the gaze of theory offers to satisfy desires for knowledge and order. In other words, the popularity of these approaches is not just about their better insights but also how they position us as powerful knowing subjects. As such, de Certeau is critical of visual metaphors for knowledge and practices of visualizing society, arguing, "Our society is characterized by a cancerous growth of vision, measuring everything by its ability to show or be shown and transmuting communication into a visual journey. It is a sort of epic of the eye and the impulse to read." His caution is that this converts the world into a "texturology" that we can read, but in so doing it freezes urban life and thus occludes a great many urban practices. Thus he argues that representational art and science immobilize the city's "opaque mobility" into a transparent text that offers only the "empire of the evident," where practices are often treated as inert contents or as cultural attributes to be measured. This leaves theory "mourning at the tomb of the absent," speaking about the laws or structures but not the actions themselves.

de Certeau's Urban Theory

De Certeau suggests that urban theory often replicates the epistemological vision of the powerful. Thus even if its purpose is critical or oppositional, it too tends to believe in plans, regularities, and structures, as though they were the limits of urban life. Instead he looks to a "scattered polytheism" of different systems of thought. The dispersed knowledges of practices elude the gaze of theory. He does not see an aggregate sum of practices but an innumerable mass of singularities—not too numerous to count, but ontologically uncountable. In this he sees tactics transforming the *places* designed by hegemonic powers and envisioned as the neat and orderly realm of the concept city, into unruly *spaces*. That is, he sees practices as spatializing places. Here, then, he looks to the control of space as a matter of strategy that is oriented through the construction of powerful knowledges. In contrast, there are tactics—the arts of making do, like reading or cooking—that use what they find there in multiple permutations. This practical knowledge of the city transforms and crosses spaces, creates new links, comprising mobile geographies of looks and glances as people walk through and walk by these given places. Strategy claims territory and defines places, whereas tactics use and subvert those places.

The strategic vision of power and theory are thus transformed by small-scale tactics. De Certeau sees strategy as the imposition of power through the disciplining and organization of space—zoning activities, prescribing some activities in some places and proscribing them in others. Tactics are the "ruses" that take the predisposition of the world and make it over, that convert it to the purposes of ordinary people. The giant order of urban planning and the concept city is thus both vast yet also strangely tenuous when set against the "maritime immensity" of scattered practices—the city is an "order-sieve." The gaze of power transfixes objects but also thus becomes blind to a vast array of things that do not fit its categories. Thus empirically we might look at different modes of knowing the city—what de Certeau called the "wordless histories" of things such as ways of walking, modes of dress, cooking, or childhood memories. These create absences and ghosts in the machine that render the city truly "habitable" and inhabited. Thus he is skeptical of knowledges that "map" cities from a God's-eye view and more concerned with "stories" as epistemologies of actually getting by in cities, and in spatial terms he saw walking as a form of practical narration. The city is known by walking rather than looking down at a static plan.

His work looks at the use of objects and places rather than their ownership and production. So he turns our attention to how tactics appropriate what has been created by hegemonic knowledge systems. Thus children make jungles and castles out of apparent wasteland or "spaces left over in planning"; street signs become associated with social memories that may reject their formal significance (instead of commemorating generals, for instance, they may be associated with a first kiss, a riot, or something different entirely); and monuments become refigured into popular culture (statues of reclining women in fountains in both Birmingham and Dublin have earned the local epithets of "the floozy in the Jacuzzi"). The city for de Certeau is as much about dreams as things. It is through taking what is there and reusing it that cities become meaningful and inhabited. But if we were to look for conventional indicators of production or use, then we would see nothing of this urban life. He has thus become associated with seeing consumption not as an end point or an afterthought to producing urban spaces and service, but as an active process. Although here he points to the overall framing of hegemonic power, he sees the Brownian movements of myriad practices within that system.

Nor can we map different uses into discrete urban cultures and neighborhoods of practice. The plurality of urban practices means we do not see a mosaic of discrete subcultures located in separated places but, according to de Certeau, a "piling up of heterogeneous places. Each one, like the deteriorating page of a book, refers to a different mode of territorial unity, of socioeconomic distribution, of political conflicts and of identifying symbolism." That is, multiple practices, some of which may be powerful and others residues of former systems of knowledge, overlap. Thus, for example, gentrified neighborhoods may have been built to service factories that have disappeared, with streets named after forgotten heroes of empires that have fallen. "The whole [is] made up of pieces that are not contemporary and still linked to totalities that have fallen into ruins," de Certeau observes.

Limitations of de Certeau's Theory

Finally, it is worth pausing to think about the limits of the adoption of de Certeau into urban theory. He has perhaps been too easily co-opted as the champion of the common man. One might build three sets of critiques of how he has been used and his urban thinking. First, his conceptualization of power tends to see a totalizing and powerful form of knowledge pitted against the ordinary citizen. This lacks a more sociological sense of the mediation of power by different institutions and actors within those institutions, all of whom have their own agendas (or tactics) about their work. Second, the opposition of tactic and strategy is thus rather more like a series of gaps or misalignments in a dance than how it is often portrayed as resistance or transgression. De Certeau's tactics are not politically oppositional; they are evasive of the orders and plans of the dominant knowledge rather than forming a coherent, and equally limited, resistance. Third, his empirical connection to practices of neighborhood life and walking the streets connects him to an imaginary of urbane life that is located in a European intellectual culture that may not reflect all urban lifestyles. Finally, these are linked in the sense that de Certeau had a coherent overall philosophical view and project, with its own language and terminology. The over-quick use of his terms and ideas in urban studies can often sound like invocation rather than analysis and risks losing the subtleties of his work.

Mike Crang

See also Architecture; Graffiti; Heterotopia; Urban Theory; Walking City

Further Readings

Buchanan, I. 2000. *Michel de Certeau: Cultural Theorist.* London: Sage.

Crang, M. 2000. "Spaces of Practice: The Work of Michel de Certeau." Pp. 126–40 in *Thinking Space,* edited by M. Crang and N. Thrift. London: Routledge.

de Certeau, M. 1984. *The Practice of Everyday Life.* Translated by S. Rendall. Berkeley: University of California Press.

de Certeau, M., L. Giard, and P. Mayol. 1998. *The Practice of Everyday Life: Living and Cooking.* Translated by T. Tomasik. Minneapolis: University of Minnesota Press.

DEINDUSTRIALIZATION

In the 1970s, a new word, *deindustrialization*, was invented to refer to the rapid restructuring of national, regional, and urban economies. Technological advances in production processes, such as the use of robots for assembly, made it possible to produce goods with far fewer workers than in the past. In the 1970s and 1980s, although the volume of production increased, the number of manufacturing jobs fell in many places. Deindustrialization also occurred because factories left urban regions. The exodus of firms occurred more rapidly in the United States than elsewhere because companies reaped tax advantages for doing so. Firms began to move from older metropolitan areas to such places as the Caribbean, Latin America, and Asia, where wages were much lower and environmental regulations were lax. This process was somewhat slower in some countries because of regulations imposed by national governments. In Germany, for example, companies were required to give workers advance notice if they planned to leave, and they were required to meet other regulations as well.

Having absorbed one blow after another, and now facing this final disaster, workers in older urban regions wondered if they would weather the storm. The Pittsburgh, Pennsylvania, region experienced a 44 percent loss in manufacturing jobs from 1979 to 1988, three quarters of them related to steel. Unemployment levels reached as high as 20 percent. In Glasgow, Scotland, shipbuilding and metal manufacturing experienced dramatic decline in employment from the mid-1960s through the 1980s, resulting in unemployment levels as high as 22 percent. The miles of docklands that had once been teeming with shipyard workers stood empty. Hamburg, Germany, lost 46 percent of its manufacturing jobs from 1970 to 1987. This experience was duplicated in older port and industrial cities throughout the United States and Europe.

But there were glimmers of hope. The number of service jobs began to rise, though regions and cities differed in the speed with which this process unfolded. Over the past decades this historic development has utterly transformed national, regional, and urban economies. In seven northeastern and midwestern metropolitan areas in the United States, the percentage of jobs in manufacturing fell from 32 to 12 percent in the 40 years from 1960 to 2000. The largest gains came in services, which grew from 15 percent of local employment to

36 percent over the same period. These changes closely paralleled the U.S. national profile.

In European countries, the human impact of deindustrialization was moderated somewhat by large public-sector employment and by housing and income support programs. Nevertheless, the dislocations stemming from high unemployment rates were extreme in older manufacturing and port cities throughout the advanced nations. In Europe, national governments and cities undertook aggressive programs to restructure local economies. Liverpool, for example, received massive amounts of aid from the U.K. government to renovate the abandoned Albert docks into a mixed development containing housing, a museum, shops, and bars and restaurants. By contrast, under the leadership of President Ronald Reagan, the U.S. federal government advised people to move to more prosperous regions. Urban leaders responded by launching efforts to regenerate their own economies, a process that continues to the present day.

Dennis R. Judd

See also Disinvestment; Gentrification; Revanchist City; Uneven Development; Urban Crisis

Further Readings

Altena, Bert and Marcel van der Linden. 2002. *De-industrialization: Social, Cultural, and Political Aspects.* Cambridge, UK: Cambridge University Press.

Bluestone, Barry and Bennett Harrison. 1982. *Deindustrialization of America: Plant Closings, Community Abandonment, and the Dismantling of Basic Industry.* New York: Basic Books.

Cowie, Jefferson and Joseph Heathcott, eds. 2003. *Beyond the Ruins: The Meanings of Deindustrialization.* Ithaca, NY: Cornell University Press.

Dandaneau, Steven P. 1992. *A Town Abandoned: Flint, Michigan, Confronts Deindustrialization.* Albany: State University of New York Press.

Edensor, Ted. 2005. *Industrial Ruins: Space, Aesthetics, and Materiality.* Oxford, UK: Berg.

High, Steven and David W. Lewis. 2007. *Corporate Wasteland: The Landscape and Memory of Deindustrialization.* Ithaca, NY: Cornell University Press.

Jakle, John A. and David Wilson. 1992. *Derelict Landscapes: The Wasting of America's Built Environment.* Lanham, MD: Rowman & Littlefield.

DELHI, INDIA

Contemporary Delhi is the crystallization of a long history of absorption of different epochs and rulers, a place of convergence of influences from all over the world. A city conventionally divided into an old and a new part (roughly corresponding to the center/north and the south of the city), Delhi offers a precious window onto the political and cultural changes that have taken place in India. This entry introduces the city by summing up its history and by offering a few perspectives onto how its developments can be interpreted.

Before Independence

Historically, Delhi is composed of seven cities; all have functioned as centers for their respective kingdoms. First known as Indraprashta (home of the dynasty of the Pandava in the epic Mahabharata), Delhi became known as a capital during the reign of the Hindu dynasty of Tomar (around the year AD 1060) and through a succession of kingdoms lasting until the arrival of the Muslim conquerors. The Islamic Mughal period (which started at the end of the twelfth century and ended with the arrival of the British) was a flourishing period for Delhi. Best known is the phase from the Lodhi dynasty (early sixteenth century) to that of Shahjahan (1627–1658). The latter ruler brought the capital back to Delhi in 1638, after a long period of shifts, and founded Shahjahanabad, which today is the heart of Old Delhi.

When the British Crown took over Delhi from the East India Company in 1858, a new period was inaugurated. In 1911, King George V moved the capital from Calcutta back to Delhi and laid the foundation for the expansion of the city. The construction of New Delhi (located south of the old city) was a grandiose undertaking aimed at producing the ultimate symbol of the empire. Clearly detached from the old city, New Delhi was to develop as an area of low population density and open green spaces. Edwin Lutyens, the creator of the imperial Delhi plan, also created a new square (named after Admiral Connaught) south of the wall of the old city to demarcate even more clearly the distance between New and Old Delhi. Connaught Place was conceived as a natural divide between old/north and new/south Delhi. A topographical buffer zone between the Indian and the British, the colonizers and the colonized, Connaught Place helped the British, who inhabited what was south of Connaught Place, to keep a safe distance from the old city with its high population density, bad planning, lack of hygienic structures, poverty, and congestion.

After Independence

After partition, the economic, infrastructural, and social gaps between different areas of the city Delhi widened even further. By the beginning of 1948, after the exodus of Muslims from India to Pakistan and of Hindus in the opposite direction, roughly 16 million people had lost their homes, and at least 1 million people (according to unofficial estimates) had lost their lives. These years were central to the construction of modern Delhi. Within two months, the population doubled, and the planning of the city experienced a drastic break. New colonies (the local term for *block*) were created to host the thousands of refugees coming from what had just become Pakistan.

In the 1960s, 1970s, and 1980s, Delhi would continue to attract people from all over northern India, and the city's growth would prove to go far beyond the expectations of the planners. During these decades, the pattern of Delhi's growth would be the continuous expansion toward the suburbs and the forcible displacements of poor people and migrants. The construction of new industries and infrastructures and the 1982 Asian Games, in particular, contributed to the creation of this pattern. Because of the need for cheap labor, migrant workers were welcomed to settle in the city, next to the construction sites, only to be moved away into the periphery on completion of the work.

The sanctioning of India's entry into the free market in 1991 did indeed boost this process even further. During this period, Delhi fully emerged as the epicenter of India's economic modernization. From being a purely political center, the city became an attractive business and industrial center. More than half of the multinational companies that entered India in that decade chose Delhi as their base. According to statistics, Delhi had, in the late nineties, the fastest rate of job creation in India and the country's most affluent market. The population of the city grew by 43 percent between 1991 and 1999, and according to unofficial estimates, it turned into a city of 15 million inhabitants. This period entailed the definitive enlargement of Delhi across the border with those surrounding satellite cities (Gurgaon, Noida, etc.) that were once built to absorb the stream of migrants heading for the city. The construction of the new metro (a grand project connecting the city with its suburbs) has sanctioned this new redefinition of the city's map.

City of Divides

Delhi's development as a globalizing hub has, evidently, also generated social and infrastructural problems. The differences in access to electricity, water supply, and sanitation are great between different colonies. Moreover, illegal settlements and slums have grown, as an answer to immigration, in the most diverse parts of the city. Several architects suggest that since the Delhi Master Plan of 1962, the authorities in charge of the city's development have shown a lack of capacity to interpret the needs of its inhabitants. According to them, this plan promoted an ideal of urban development detached from indigenous patterns. It gave the authorities the right to acquire almost all land within the boundaries of the city capable of being urbanized and led to the implementation of large-scale projects that reproduced the monumental aura of Delhi as a capital city but did not respond to the city's needs.

Indeed, the strong divisions in areas with different lifestyles, incomes, and ethnic profiles were present before that. In the immediate postindependence period, Delhi presented itself as already clearly divided. The areas with the most evident special character were the relatively rich West Delhi, South Delhi, Civil Lines, and Delhi University (in the north), and, at the other end, an increasingly commercial, polluted, and congested Shajahanabad. In the middle of the city was the imperial area, flagged by its completely unique and detached character.

Throughout the years, however, the divide between Old and New Delhi has become the most distinguishing trait of the city. Whereas the inhabitants of new/south Delhi consider themselves the most successful and modern inhabitants of the city, the Old Delhi *wallas* present themselves as the more authentic and genuine ones. According to the Delhi master plan, Old Delhi is indeed full of the fragrances of the past, but it is also a planner's nightmare with

Modern-day Delhi

Source: Steven K. Martin.

its congestion, unsanitary conditions, and narrow lanes. South Delhi, on the other hand, is regarded as the modern, middle-class part of the city, evoking the colonial and modern era with its structured streets, its overpasses, and its spectacle of architecture ranging from the modernism of the 1960s and 1970s to Punjabi Baroque (see below) and to the most recent (post)modernist styles echoing also ancient pan-Indian mythologies. Today, the booming suburbs of Noida and Gurgaon are problematizing such a division, emerging as symbols of the new, young, upcoming, successful, and globally oriented India.

The Aesthetics of the City

Another way to understand Delhi is to approach it as a living art installation displaying the cultural trends at play in the city. The architectural development of modern Delhi can be roughly divided into two different stages. While the first period began with the colonial creation of Lutyens's Delhi, independence entailed a conscious attempt at forging a new Indian architecture able to represent the nation and its inhabitants.

In the 1950s and 1960s, architecture was mainly influenced by the logic of austerity promoted by Nehru's government to modernize quickly while administering its scarce resources. The construction inspired by this utilitarian modernism presented Delhi as a city with long lines of flat buildings with flat roofs and lime-washed façades. These buildings were intercalated by the impressive nationalistic monuments of modernity built to represent the government. This epoch also witnessed, however, the birth of a popular trend favoring opposite ideals. The extravagant Punjabi Baroque became the favorite style adopted by members of the elites to represent their ambitions. Offering a continuity with the colonial past while also displaying the cosmopolitan desires of the middle and upper classes, such new designs also expressed the changing notions of home (which now became a symbol of the owner's identity and a refuge from the frightening outside world) and of the public and the private. A trend whose traces are easily detected in the most recent buildings, Punjabi Baroque epitomizes the image of a new India, globally oriented while at the same time firmly rooted in a sense of national pride.

Delhi's urban growth is, therefore, a window onto the political and cultural changes that have touched on the Indian subcontinent. Containing a story of successes, expansions, and transformations, today's Delhi also offers a precious window onto the delicate balances of the country.

Paolo Favero

See also Colonial City; Divided Cities; Urban Planning

Further Readings

Bhatia, G. 1994. *Punjabi Baroque and Other Memories of Architecture*. New York: Penguin.

Chaudhuri, D. N. 2005. *Delhi: Light, Shades, Shadows*. Delhi: Niyogi Offset Books.

Dupont, V., E. Tarlo, and D. Vidal, eds. *Delhi: Urban Space and Human Destinies*. Delhi: Manohar.

Favero, P. 2005. *India Dreams: Cultural Identity among Young Middle Class Men in New Delhi*. Stockholm Studies in Social Anthropology, 56. Stockholm: Socialantropologiska Institutionen.

Jain, A. K. 1990. *The Making of a Metropolis: Planning and Growth of Delhi*. Delhi: National Book Organisation.

Jain, A. K. 1996. *The Indian Megacity and Economic Reforms*. New Delhi: Management Publishing.

Khanna, R. and M. Parhawk. 2008. *The Modern Architecture of New Delhi: 1928–2007*. Delhi: Random House India.

Miller, S. 2008. *Delhi: Adventures in a Megacity*. Delhi: Penguin.

Sengupta, R. 2008. *Delhi Metropolitan: The Making of an Unlikely City*. Delhi: Penguin Books.

Singh, K. 1990. *Delhi: A Novel*. New Delhi: Penguin.

DEVELOPER

Real estate developers allocate land, capital, material, and labor to the production of the built environment. Their goal is the highest and best use of a site—that is, the use that will yield the maximum return on investment—given various legal and regulatory parameters. Although often considered a homogeneous group, developers vary considerably with respect to organization type and size, geographic focus, market specialization, and sector (private, public, or nonprofit). The developer provides the entrepreneurial initiative, management skills, and professional expertise needed to coordinate resources and interests within established institutional structures in order to transform the built environment. Developers, for example, were responsible for building the renovated Faneuil Hall marketplace in Boston, the office complex on Canary Wharf in London, the famous suburb of Levittown (New York), the Mall of America outside Minneapolis, and the entertainment complex known as Staples Center/L.A. Live in Los Angeles.

History

The history of modern real estate development in the United States has been shaped by the ideological dominance of property rights, free markets, and entrepreneurial spirit. Developers in the late nineteenth century were predominantly corporations that built their headquarters within the central business districts of cities. By the 1900s, speculative developers emerged to capture new demand for office space. As the pace of development accelerated and competition among developers increased, municipalities began to use zoning, land use, and building regulations to protect public health, stabilize property markets, and enhance land values. Residential developers turned their attention to the expanding opportunities in the urban periphery, purchasing and subdividing land to sell to builders. By the mid-1920s, land use regulations had spread to the suburbs in the form of subdivision guidelines. The 1920s also witnessed the professionalization of real estate as an industry, as developers began to form trade associations, advance their standards of practice, and engage the public sector. The end of the Great

Depression brought with it new capital markets and institutional structures for real estate, but development languished until after World War II.

The postwar years provided developers with demand and capital for substantial residential, retail, hospitality, and industrial growth outside of central cities, while urban renewal programs created new opportunities in the urban core. Suburban residential development firms grew in size and sophistication as family organizations such as Durst, Rudin, and Tishman—all based in New York City—dominated the urban office market. The volatility of market cycles and shifting spatial demand that defined the late 1960s to the late 1990s resulted in the ebb and flow of development in urban and suburban markets. The increasing complexity and internationalization of regulatory and institutional structures and capital markets led to the growth of national and international real estate developers, including such firms as Trammell Crow and Olympia & York.

Purpose and Organization

Developers are both entrepreneurs and managers. Real estate development requires the ability to create a conceptual plan and the capability to see a project to completion while managing interactions among a diverse and extensive range of actors, including consultants, municipal planners, citizen groups, nonprofit organizations, elected and appointed officials, and contractors. In addition, developers coordinate, and in many cases contribute to, the capital necessary to advance a project from concept to fruition.

Developers are a diverse group and include firms that subdivide land for sale, purchase individual parcels and construct buildings, consult for or partner with landowners and investors, or provide both equity and expertise while controlling the entire development process. Each type has different organizational structures and capacities, access to resources, and levels of control over the completion of a project. There is also significant variation in the scale of development organizations; they range from large consulting firms and publicly traded investment entities (such as real estate investment trusts [REITs]) to small entrepreneurs and family-owned businesses. Developers, particularly large firms with substantial project volume such as Toll Brothers—a major suburban residential developer—can also provide in-house design, mortgage, and construction services.

Geographic Focus

The geographic focus of development firms can be international, national, regional, or local. Given the complexities of urban land markets and regulatory schemes—as well as the range of actors that must be managed, coordinated, and appeased—most developers specialize geographically. This allows developers to acquire knowledge about local real estate markets and the community and political actors who might influence project approval and completion. These networks facilitate development plans as relationships forged with consultants, contractors, and other local groups can often lead to lower costs, reduced risk, and new opportunities.

Large development firms, acting as consultants or equity partners in joint ventures, are often able to operate at the international scale using local branch offices and contacts to implement development plans in unfamiliar markets. One such development firm is Texas-based Hines Interests, which maintains offices and develops property in more than 16 countries. The number of multinational development firms has increased dramatically since the early 1980s, as greater access to capital and the convergence of international investment in real estate has created a higher degree of uniformity across countries in terms of financing structures, product amenities, and consumer preference. For example, shopping malls and new urbanist projects in England, South Africa, and Singapore look strikingly similar as they are designed and located according to common principles.

Market and Sector Specialization

Real estate developers typically specialize in specific market segments, or products, of real estate, such as residential, office, hospitality, industrial, or retail. This specialization is necessary given the unique regulations and market dynamics that affect different product types. As with geographic specialization, larger firms are best able to engage in development activities in a range of products as economies of scale provide greater opportunities to retain expertise within the organization or to hire consultants as needed. Smaller development firms often focus on only one or two products—residential or retail, for example—in an effort to maximize the limited capacity of the firm and gain competitive advantage through experience.

Developers can be found in the for-profit, nonprofit, and public sectors, although real estate development as an industry is typically associated with the private sector, where for-profit developers seek to maximize financial returns. In the 1970s and 1980s, nonprofit developers, such as community development corporations, entered the development industry in response to the dwindling availability of public funds for neighborhood revitalization and low-income housing. In fact, community development corporations have become central to the building of affordable housing in many cities. During the same time period, local governments began to emphasize economic development activities that would enhance their municipality's ability to attract and maintain a constant flow of private investment. These shifting motivations and changing institutional structures have expanded the opportunities for collaboration among sectors. Public–private partnerships, for instance, have become a common method of leveraging public funds with private investment and expertise. Metrotech Center in Brooklyn, New York, offers an early example of a large-scale project developed using such a partnership. When the government acts as a developer or development partner through public or quasi-public agencies, it can provide regulatory relief, tax abatements, and other incentives to stimulate and shape private development schemes.

Real Estate Markets and Planning

Developers are sensitive to market fluctuations, demand, and risk. In an effort to minimize risk and respond to demand, development firms perform extensive market and feasibility analyses that are used to determine and verify conceptual plans. The availability of debt financing or equity investment also heavily influences the nature, pace, and location of real estate development activities, as do the risk management efforts of lending institutions. When capital is abundant and markets are relatively unfettered, speculative development—building without specific tenants—is often the result. The overbuilding associated with speculative development has historically precipitated downturns in real estate market cycles.

Real estate developers operate in a highly regulated environment where local zoning laws and planning requirements determine allowable uses, densities, and the scale of individual site development. State and federal regulations, particularly in the form of environmental laws, also affect most development projects by increasing potential cost and uncertainty during the project approval process. This regulatory landscape has created an often contentious relationship between real estate developers and government officials and planners. Interestingly, it was developers, in an effort to minimize competition from speculators and reduce risk, who were a significant force in the creation of zoning laws and subdivision regulations in the early twentieth century.

The role of the developer varies significantly from country to country, based on differing political and economic systems. While the institutional structure of development in the United Kingdom, for example, is similar to that of the United States, national governments in continental Europe, and in many parts of Asia, play a more substantial and direct role in the development of land. Public officials and government agencies often limit the discretion of private firms by determining the location, type, timing, and scale of new projects.

Emerging Trends

For developers, the future may require significant changes in business activities and organizational structures. Increased scrutiny of real estate development projects and evolving measures of success will necessitate greater collaboration between sectors to achieve outcomes that are economically efficient, socially equitable, and environmentally sustainable. However, conflicts arising from the homogeneity encouraged by increasing standardization within capital markets and the contextual development demanded by local communities may serve to exacerbate the tension between developers, community groups, and planning agencies. In addition, tighter regulatory environments, sophisticated alternative sources of capital, and economies of scale will change the complexion of the real estate industry. This could force smaller organizations out of the market or into joint ventures with other developers. Finally, the convergence of real estate asset markets across countries, supported by globalizing capital and demographic trends, might lead to new opportunities in developing countries experiencing rapid urbanization.

Constantine E. Kontokosta

See also Real Estate; Suburbanization; Urban Economics; Urban Planning

Further Readings

Fainstein, Susan S. 2001. *The City Builders: Property Development in New York and London, 1980–2000.* Lawrence: University Press of Kansas.

Miles, Mike E., Gayle Berens, and Marc A. Weiss. 2002. *Real Estate Development: Principles and Process.* 3rd ed. Washington, DC: Urban Land Institute.

Peiser, Richard B. and Anne B. Frej. 2003. *Professional Real Estate Development: The ULI Guide to the Business.* 2nd ed. Washington, DC: Urban Land Institute.

Rybczynski, Witold. 2007. *Last Harvest: How a Cornfield Became New Daleville: Real Estate Development in America from George Washington to the Builders of the Twenty-first Century, and Why We Live in Houses Anyway.* New York: Scribner.

Weiss, Marc A. 1987. *The Rise of the Community Builders: The American Real Estate Industry and Urban Land Planning.* New York: Columbia University Press.

DICKENS, CHARLES

London is the protagonist of Dickens's fiction, as it defined his popular success. Even as a mature writer Dickens continued to draw on the experience of the young newspaper reporter who had written *Sketches by Boz* (1836) in his spare time, capitalizing on his walks through the city to outline the different neighborhoods and their distinctive inhabitants. "What inexhaustible food for speculation, do the streets of London afford!" he comments. We "have not the slightest commiseration for the man who can take up his hat and stick, and walk from Covent Garden to St. Paul's Churchyard, and back into the bargain, without deriving some amusement—we had almost said instruction—from his perambulation." Throughout his career as a novelist, journalist, editor,

actor, and theatrical impresario, Dickens found in London an inexhaustible source for the instruction and amusement of his readers, including Queen Victoria. Throughout his life he was a walker in the city, a vagabond of the streets.

His close friend, John Forster, notes that for the young Dickens to walk "anywhere about Covent Garden or the Strand, perfectly entranced him with pleasure. But, most of all, he had a profound attraction of repulsion to St Giles's." Focusing on the cognitive dissonance generated by the city, this attraction of repulsion became his characteristic London signature. "'Good Heaven!' he would exclaim, 'what wild visions of prodigies of wickedness, and beggary, rose in my mind out of that place.'" This part of the city always evoked his childhood, and all those places in the neighborhood of Warren's Blacking Factory and Hungerford Stairs are central to his writing: Covent Garden, the Temple, St. Giles, Waterloo Bridge, the Strand, and Temple Bar.

Like the *Sketches*, the humor of *Pickwick Papers* (1838) illuminates the dark corners of the city's urban labyrinth and would continue to inform his fiction. Published in serial form, either in monthly or weekly installments, the 15 novels he wrote map the city and its characteristic inhabitants. Realism in Dickens's time was magical, for the city was a fairytale come to life: grim, exhilarating, and transformative. To describe this urban world was to create a new Bible, encompassing heaven and earth, and all that lies between.

The first great practitioner of the detective novel, Dickens created a linguistic universe that in the energy, deftness, and surprise of its syntax simulates the theatrical experience of life in the modern city. As we read his writing we participate in the modern theatrical project of urban life: Modern identity has become staged identity.

Like the detectives of the London Metropolitan Police, founded in 1844, whom he admired and wrote about in *Household Words*, Dickens teaches us how to decode that city world and navigate its darker streets. His fiction trains us in keen and swift observation, careful judgment, and wide-ranging sympathy.

When Dickens was born, on February 7, 1812, London was a city of horse-drawn carts and carriages, which entered through city gates like Charing Gate, NewGate (with its formidable prison), and

Kennington Toll Gate. When Dickens died 58 years later in 1870, the gates and city wall had been pulled down and built on, and London turned into a sprawling monumental city, transformed by the Industrial Revolution, especially the railroad and entrepreneurial capitalism as well as the British imperial venture, into the first world-city.

During Dickens's lifetime, London was more excavated, more cut about, more rebuilt, and more extended than at any time in its previous history. A huge sewer system had been built by 1853, when *Bleak House* was published, and a viaduct had been completed that brought clean drinking water to all parts of the city, thus ridding it of the fear of cholera and typhus, which had plagued it for centuries. Victoria Station and Euston Station had become the termini of the railroad, effectively bringing the commerce of the world and its people into the city. The underground was under construction by 1864 when Dickens completed *Our Mutual Friend*, and the Thames, relieved now of carrying the city's waste to the sea, had been organized into a pleasing promenade via the great Embankment projects. Spacious boulevards now graced the city, among them Victoria Street, Garrick Street, and the newly extended Oxford Street. Now there were four times as many streets and roads in London as when Dickens had arrived in the city with his parents at the age of 11. The remaining fragments of the city gates were now surrounded by universes of urban activity rather than the rural countryside.

Dickens was acclaimed in his time as an accurate recorder of economic, social, and cultural conditions. He was also a social reformer who explored the impact of past conditions on the present. His evocation of the workhouse, for example, in *Oliver Twist,* recorded the misery of the poor and outcast at a moment when reform had already changed some of the worst conditions. But the emotional impact of the novel led to further efforts at remediation. And the workhouse as the place where the poor and destitute were warehoused remained as a central theme in the last novel he completed, *Our Mutual Friend,* which was published in 1864, six years before his death. Yet his vision of Victorian England always implied the possibility of social, economic, and culture improvement, and of change directed toward greater sympathy and understanding.

In his fiction Dickens records and responds to an era of unprecedented rapid and radical social change, which he sought to influence and shape.

According to F. S. Schwarzbach, for Dickens, this magical place evoked the "attraction of repulsion" for it was "such a gritty city; such a hopeless city . . . ; such a beleaguered city" as Bleak House renders it a waste and wasteland, and yet also a celebration "of the city as the most impressive embodiment of change," increasingly the dominant fact of modern life.

Murray Baumgarten

See also London, United Kingdom; Manchester, United Kingdom; Tenement

Further Readings

Forster, John. 1872. *The Life of Charles Dickens*. Vol. 1. Philadelphia: Lippincott.
Schwarzbach, F. S. 1979. *Dickens and the City*. London: Athlone Press.

DISABILITY AND THE CITY

Disability is a diverse lived experience that is frequently shaped by barriers and exclusions in the context of the city. Definitions of disability that stress the way in which the organization of society serves to disadvantage people by a devaluation of the disabled body shed particular light on the barriers that shape disabled people's access to urban spaces and participation in city life. Inaccessible buildings and transport, or unclear signage, are some of the more obvious manifestations of these barriers. Disabled people and disability groups are, however, increasingly challenging and influencing urban policy processes and decisions about urban space. The experience of disability therefore illuminates processes of social division, exclusion, and resistance which are manifest in, and shape, the urban environment.

Definitions of Disability

Definitions of disability have tended to revolve around two different conceptual starting points, expressed as the medical and social models of disability. The former equates disability with a biological impairment or condition that needs to be treated or cured if the individual is to function normally in everyday life. Hence, disability is located in the individual and understood in terms of the limitations of a "less than normal" body. This medicalized definition has arguably dominated understandings of disability in Western society. However, since the 1970s this definition has been challenged by disabled people, who have critiqued its representation of disability as a personal tragedy and disabled people as dependent and worthy of charity. In setting out a social model of disability, an emergent disability movement has located the "problem" of disability within the structures and social relations of a society that systematically ignores the needs of people with impairments.

Proponents of the social model draw a distinction between the terms *impairment*, as the actual bodily limitation or physiological state, and *disability*, as the construction of a society that devalues impaired bodies, thereby leading to disabled people's economic, political, social, and cultural marginalization. According to the social model, it is within the structures and organization of society rather than in disabled people's physiology or impairment that we are to find the answers to questions about disabled people's unequal status. The model has become the basis for the development of a disability movement that stresses disabled people's rights as citizens and calls for their equal participation in society. However, this model has been criticized for underplaying the bodily pain that many disabled people experience, as well as for more readily explaining the experiences of people with physical or mobility impairments, rather than those with learning disabilities or mental illness. It has thereby been accused of failing to address the heterogeneity of disability.

Barriers in the Disabling City

The insights of the social model nevertheless open up an understanding of the ways in which the contemporary city serves to disable individuals through its social, political, and economic organization. A key locus of debates about disabled people's access to the city lies in the built environment, whether this be understood as public thoroughfares, private and public buildings (including places of consumption, workplaces, civic amenities, and housing), or indeed transport systems. The barriers that render the city environment inaccessible are often clear to

see: For example, for people with mobility impairments or wheelchair users, the absence of ramps into buildings, doorways that are too narrow, or broken paving stones are huge impediments. For others, they are less visible: A lack of clear and simple signage for people with learning difficulties, or the absence of induction loops for people with hearing impairments, mediate the experience of access. The presence of these barriers in the built environment hinders disabled people's ability to move around unaided and limits their participation in city life, whether as consumers, workers, or as members of local groups or communities. The physical fabric of the city has therefore been seen as a spatial manifestation of disabled people's oppression in society, reflecting a historical legacy in which many disabled people were sequestered away from society and thus came to be seen as "out of place" in urban environments and public space.

These barriers point to the need to explore the broader political, economic, and institutional processes that give rise to the creation of disabling urban spaces. The policies and practices of urban planning and development systems form an important institutional context here. Within these systems, professionals—architects, property developers, and local planning officials—have been shown to play a key role in creating the built environment and influencing outcomes in terms of access. Frequently, these outcomes are shaped by the imperatives of architectural aesthetics, economic efficiency, or both, rather than accessibility for disabled people. Such recognition has led the United States and many European countries to address the issue of access through the introduction of planning regulations and policies, and in some cases, antidiscrimination legislation. The U.K. Disability Discrimination Act 1995, for example, suggests that providers of goods and services and employers should make "reasonable adjustments" for disabled people, including, where appropriate, access to workplaces or other premises. However, although such regulations are seen to offer some form of safeguard against discrimination, they have been criticized for their voluntaristic nature and a reliance on technical solutions to disabled people's exclusion.

Many disability scholars have stressed that the barriers disabled people experience in the city cannot be explained by the institutional context of urban planning and development alone, but are rooted in the broader structural dynamics shaping the city and urban space. Through the commodification of land and labor power, cities have been shown to be sites and spaces of capitalist accumulation. Under neoliberal regimes of governance, maximizing land rents and privatizing public space have become key trends in the cities of advanced industrialized nations. In this climate, it has been suggested that the interests of private property developers and maximizing profitability from urban space frequently take precedence over creating inclusive environments that accommodate difference and promote access by minority groups in the city, including disabled people. Meanwhile, in linking disabled people's exclusion in the city to a historical–materialist analysis, others have stressed how the emergence of the industrial (capitalist) city served to separate out the productive (able-bodied) worker from the unproductive (disabled) worker. The spatiality of workplaces based on urban factory production and work routines were inaccessible to many disabled people, who thus became devalued in terms of their labor power, and marginalized on the basis of economic inactivity. For many, the inaccessibility of the contemporary city—and disabled people's continuing exclusion—has to be located within the legacy of these changing economic structures and the environments they created.

Contesting Urban Space: Disabled People's Organizations

More recently, the city has become the site of contests by disabled people over access, and organizations have emerged that seek to politicize and transform the structures and relations that lead to the creation of disabling environments. The past 20 years have witnessed a growing number of groups *of* disabled people (often distinguished from groups *for*, which are run by able-bodied people). Some of these are impairment specific, whereas others cut across impairment type. What many of these groups have in common is the projection of a positive disability identity and the assertion of a politics that draws on the social model of disability, in stressing disabled people's independence and self-determination. Whereas some have grown out of national networks, others have their roots in the communities and interests of (urban) localities. For example, the emergence of ethnic minority disability groups has become a feature of some areas of cities in the United Kingdom.

Many of these groups have directly sought to challenge and influence urban policy processes and the role of professionals in determining decisions about urban space, arguably with varying levels of success. Specific sites in the city—buildings, civic amenities, public transport systems—have often become a focus for negotiation and struggle around issues of access. Thus, some groups have used direct action approaches, highlighting the inaccessibility of public transport or particular buildings by literally occupying urban spaces (blocking roads with wheelchairs, for example, or chaining themselves to buses). In other cases, disabled people have sought to participate in, and influence, planning policies and practices at the local level. Within the United Kingdom, for example, local access groups have been established in many localities to assess planning applications and meet with planning officers. However, questions remain about how far disabled people are able to access and influence key decision makers. The impact of disabled people's organizations appears to be contingent on a number of factors, including the size and resources of the group and how far local officials and institutions understand disability and are facilitative of engagement with disabled people. The disability movement itself has often been accused of being fragmentary, based as it is on so many different impairment groups with different interests. Developing effective political strategies that assert disabled people's rights to access the city therefore remains an ongoing challenge for many disability organizations.

Claire Edwards

See also Public Realm; Transportation; Urban Planning

Further Readings

Hahn, Harlan. 1986. "Disability and the Urban Environment: A Perspective on Los Angeles." *Environment and Planning D: Society and Space* 4:273–88.

Imrie, Rob. 1996. *Disability and the City*. London: Chapman.

Oliver, Michael. 1990. *The Politics of Disablement*. Basingstoke, UK: Macmillan.

Parr, Hester. 1997. "Mental Health, Public Space and the City: Questions of Individual and Collective Access." *Environment and Planning D: Society and Space* 15:435–54.

DISCOTHEQUE

Discotheque is a word built by the combination of δίσκος *dískos* (disk) and θήκη—*théke* (box, chest, tomb), both of ancient Greek origin. The *-théke* suffix has been used in a variety of contexts and languages to signify the physical place in the city, where one particular function is performed or where one kind of object is stored: for example, *Apotheke* (German for pharmacy), *bibliothèque* (French for library), *emeroteca* (Italian for printed media archive), *videoteca* (Italian for video rental shop). Discotheque is the physical place "where disks (i.e., records) are."

Definition

Currently the word is not so commonly used, and the abbreviation *disco* or the term *club* is preferred to refer to the same kind of physical place.

The word was first coined in France and it is connected to a historical era: During the Nazi occupation of Paris in World War II, the live performance of jazz ("degenerate" music) was banned from all clubs. Parisian youth were able to get around the prohibition by setting up illegal dancing places in cellars on the left bank of the river Seine, where people danced to music from record players. People began referring to this kind of place as *discothèque*.

From this short semantic and historical introduction to the term, it is possible to underline certain features of the discotheque:

- Urban
- Based on the storage and use of a certain kind of music support (record) and on the performance of a certain kind of practice (dancing to recorded music)

- Located in a closed, secluded physical space, usually apt to contain a certain number of people and limiting the emission of noise to the surroundings
- Connected to the expression of a political dissent, alternative, or resistance

The discotheque as a physical space reproduces some of the traits of city life: anonymity and density, social distance, and spatial closeness are all urban features that are brought to the excess on a dance floor. Simultaneously, the discotheque offers also a subversion of these same urban traits, first of all through an "excess of sociability" (e.g., dancing, touching, hugging), which contests the notion of urban *Blasiertheit* and indifference described by Georg Simmel, and celebrates unity, love, and community. Second, the discotheque challenges the people's daytime identity based on their professional, economic, social, and cultural status and destroys social boundaries, typical of the regulated and controlled daytime urban life. It allows the creation of a temporary alternative nighttime identity, which can be later maintained or not, in a manner similar to the carnivalesque as described by Mikhail Bakhtin.

The discotheque also redefines the way a city functions, shifting centers and peripheries, modifying social and spatial boundaries, and turning the emphasis on production to an emphasis on consumption.

Sometimes illegalities, ranging from squatting to drug dealing, may concentrate in and around discotheques, in connection to the habits of certain scenes and subcultures. This has brought up issues of social control involving door selection, bouncers, the use of security cameras, and even dedicated legislation (concerning, for instance, age limits, opening hours, licensing, and freedom of assembly).

Dance Music

Music played in discotheques is determined on one side by the music industry and on the other by the choices and practices of local subcultures and scenes. In this regard, it shares with many other urban cultural expressions an intrinsic tension between a mainstream and an underground.

Many more or less lasting music styles (with their corollary of dance moves, performing artists, films, clothes, and merchandise) have been marketed and played in discotheques. The first is probably the Twist, brought to success by Chubby Checker. The Twist became the first dance craze to achieve a global success. In the late 1960s, North American disc jockeys (DJs) started experimenting with various dance music styles such as soul, Latino, electro, and funk, to achieve a musical flow able to last uninterrupted for the whole party-night in the disco. This was happening especially within African American and Latin American communities in New York City, in connection to the rising hip hop culture. At the same time, gay males began attending and organizing discos, and these locations became central for the self-identification of queer communities in cities like Chicago and New York. At the end of the 1970s, discos were taken over by the multinational corporate music industry. The legendary Studio 54 opened in Manhattan, New York City, in 1977. In the same year the film *Saturday Night Fever* (directed by John Badham) popularized practices and conventions of New York City disco dancing all over the world.

Discotheque and the Industrial City

The industrial outskirts of cities have had an important role for the consumption of music in discotheques. The adoption of secluded industrial outskirts for the opening of discotheques is connected to the noise, which increased thanks to the technological development of more sophisticated public address systems; to the rent, which was cheaper than in entertainment areas of the city; and to the need for bigger empty spaces to fit more people. Most important, it mirrors a topography of urban exclusion, in connection to the Latino and African American gay scenes in the United States.

This is particularly true of the dance music scenes, which originated at the end of the 1970s, in contrast to the commercial normalization of disco music. For instance, The Warehouse, a discotheque in Chicago West Loop, recruited Frankie Knuckles as DJ in 1977. Knuckles's style in mixing and re-editing was tagged "house" as in "Warehouse," the physical place where this kind of music was first created and danced to.

In the 1980s, discotheques around the world, especially in the United States and in Europe,

located in liminal and industrial areas, started playing house. The Haçienda opened in May 1982 in Manchester, United Kingdom, in a former yacht showroom. It started as a live music venue, but in 1986 changed its weekly program because of the increasing demand for house music. In Berlin, in 1991, soon after the fall of the wall, Dimitri Hegemann, previously involved in the West Berlin techno scene, and Johnnie Stieler from East Berlin, opened a club called Tresor. The club was located in a building on the former death strip (the empty area left by the disappearance of the wall) in the Leipziger Strasse. House music changed within the European context and was soon renamed *acid* house, because of the involvement of a new synthetic drug: ecstasy.

Discotheque and Real Estate

Discotheques play an unusual role within the shift from industrial to postindustrial cities. On one hand, they foresaw the chances given by abandoned industrial architecture and usually pioneered dilapidated downtown (in the United States) or peripheral (in Europe) areas that would later regain real estate value. In some cases, it could be stated that discotheques actively collaborated in the process, boosting the symbolic value of certain areas within cities. This effect was created by the sense of community and excess of sociability linked to the bustling house scene.

On the other hand, discotheques were the first to be excluded, within the final accomplishments of the urban renewal process in the 1990s, because of the increasing value of the built properties and to the retransformation of scene-related entertainment districts into residential ones. For instance, the previously mentioned Haçienda closed definitely in 1997. A private company, Crosby Homes, bought and demolished it. Between 2002 and 2004 on the site, an apartment and office complex was completed. The project maintained the same name of the club. Tresor in Berlin closed in 2005, because of its proximity to the renewed Potsdamer Platz.

The shift from industrial to postindustrial urban economy brought tourism and city attractiveness in general to the forefront. Discotheques of the past or present have sometimes achieved an important status in city-branding campaigns.

Discotheque and Resort Architecture

Discotheques have also been one of the ingredients in the homogenization and standardization of holiday resort architecture, together with souvenir shops, hotels at walking distance from the sea, shops, and cruising and pub-crawling "miles." Places like Ibiza (Spain) or Goa (India) became world capitals of dance music, and clubbing is a major element of their tourist attractiveness. Discotheques in these locations often acquire hybrid features responding to a desire for both escapism (sometimes related to orientalism) and a vague supranational "urban" style, just like in the case of theme parks.

Discotheque and Technology

Technology affected the development of discotheques on three levels: the music support, the sound diffusion, and the lighting. From the point of view of the support, discotheques adopted, from their historical beginning, the vinyl record. The vinyl started as 78 rpm (revolutions per minute) and soon developed into the $33\frac{1}{3}$ rpm, which is still used for domestic listening. In the 1950s, the 45 rpm (7-inch single), which contained two to four songs (available on two sides), became the most popular format and the most used in discotheques. In the 1970s, the 12-inch record, a single with the size of an LP (i.e., the $33\frac{1}{3}$ rpm), but with just one or two tracks per side, began to replace the 7-inch record. The 12-inch resisted the heavy duty of mixing, scratching, and repetitive playing. Dedicated mixing desks (which included a mixer and two record players) were also produced in this period for specific use in the discotheque. Record labels and often DJs themselves started pressing "white label" 12-inch records in limited editions. Nowadays the 12-inch record is still the most used support by DJs, although the digitalization of music with the MP3 has given DJs the opportunity to store, play, and elaborate on an enormous number of tracks. The availability of sequencers and drum machines from the 1970s and of music software from the 1980s enabled DJs to become producers.

Technology is also responsible for the development of dedicated sound amplification systems for discotheques, able to diffuse the sound in its entire range and evenly within the dance floor, limiting the emission in the so-called chill-out zones or in proximity to the bar. Lighting also developed, and the professional figure of the VJ (visual jockeys) is, in certain contexts, as important as the DJ for the success of a dancing event.

Giacomo Bottà

See also Gay Space; Hip Hop; Manchester, United Kingdom; Nightlife

Further Readings

Cohen, Sara. 2007. *Decline, Renewal and the City in Popular Music Culture: Beyond the Beatles.* Aldershot, UK: Ashgate.

Fikentscher, Kai. 2000. *"You Better Work!" Underground Dance Music in New York City.* Hanover, CT: Wesleyan University Press.

Jones, Alan and Jussi Kantonen. 1999. *Saturday Night Forever: The Story of Disco.* Edinburgh, UK: Mainstream.

Poschardt, Ulf. 1998. *DJ Culture.* London: Quartet Books.

Rehead, Steve, Derek Wynne, and Justin O'Connor, eds. 1998. *The Clubcultures Reader: Readings in Popular Cultural Studies.* Oxford, UK: Blackwell.

Thornton, Sarah. 1996. *Club Cultures: Music, Media and Subcultural Capital.* Hanover, CT: Wesleyan University Press.

DISINVESTMENT

Most real estate development is investment driven, meaning that private financiers expect to make an adequate profit in return for providing funds for building construction and operations. When investors do not think they can make enough money from a particular kind of property or location, they often sell their holdings, taking money out of real estate and switching it to other assets (e.g., stocks and bonds), other types of property, or other locations. This withdrawal of capital from office buildings, apartment towers, schools, shopping malls, vacant land, and other types of real estate is what is meant by disinvestment.

Different kinds of investors engage in different types of disinvestment. Landlords, for example, may withhold money for crucial renovations, maintenance, and repairs if they do not perceive an adequate return on their investment. "Redlining" is a type of disinvestment initiated by lenders: Banks and other financial institutions turn down mortgage applications in specific areas because they believe that the growing presence of racial and ethnic minorities increases the chances of borrowers defaulting on their loans. Individual homeowners make similar decisions when they sell their homes in response to a real or perceived decline in housing and land values. This is known as "panic selling." Disinvestment in isolated properties in otherwise stable or appreciating areas is rare; most disinvested properties are located in places where neighboring properties have received a similar treatment.

The physical signs of disinvestment may include construction projects that have not been completed and buildings that have fallen into disrepair because money for maintenance and upgrading is withheld. Disinvestment can repel existing and potential tenants, suppressing rental revenues and leading, in some cases, to abandonment and demolition. It can also have potentially negative social and political consequences, including arson, crime, property tax delinquency, public service reductions, and health hazards.

The active withdrawal of capital from real estate may be distinguished from a decline in investment. All real estate investment occurs in boom–slump cycles, and investment might drop off in relative terms after a phase of overinvestment and overbuilding within an individual market. In the office building market in the early 1990s, for example, floor space exceeded demand in most North American cities, which caused vacancies to increase, prices to fall, and investors to expend less money on such projects than they did in prior years. However, the subsequent decline in investment did not last long, and most urban office markets recovered within the decade.

In many instances suburbanization, with the promise of fewer risks and more profit, has drawn capital outside city limits. The lure of the suburbs—made more accessible by cheap credit and public infrastructure—along with deeply embedded racial discrimination turned urban areas into relatively less attractive investments.

Disinvested locations, however, provide fertile grounds for the process of neighborhood change known as gentrification, which is essentially sustained local reinvestment. Most disinvested areas and properties can reverse direction with the right amount of public and private assistance. Indeed, investors often take advantage of previous rounds of disinvestment to buy up properties cheaply, renovate, and sell them for a handsome profit when consumer demand rebounds.

Rachel Weber

See also Deindustrialization; Real Estate; Redlining; Uneven Development

Further Readings

Beauregard, Robert A. 1993. *Voices of Decline: The Postwar Fate of US Cities.* New York: Blackwell.
Scafidi, Benjamin, Michael Schill, Susan Wachter, and Dennis Culhane. 1998. "An Economic Analysis of Housing Abandonment." *Journal of Housing Economics* 7:287–303.
Smith, Neil. 1996. *The New Urban Frontier: Gentrification and the Revanchist City.* New York: Routledge.

DISPLACEMENT

For as long as humans have congregated in urban centers, people have been forced to move for various reasons. Scholars, though, have struggled to define this displacement. Grier and Grier developed a definition in the 1970s that encapsulates people's general understanding. They defined displacement as occurring when a household is compelled to leave its residence because of conditions that affect the dwelling or its immediate surroundings and (1) are beyond the household's control, (2) occur despite the household's adherence to previously imposed conditions of occupancy, and (3) cause continued occupancy to be impossible, hazardous, or unaffordable.

Natural disasters and human conflict are perhaps responsible for the largest amount of displacement. Hurricane Katrina in 2005 is an example of widespread displacement caused by a natural disaster. Some 50 percent of the population of New Orleans was initially displaced and the total number of displacees in the various areas hit by Hurricane Katrina is estimated to be as high as 1 million. The Asian tsunami of 2004 displaced upwards of 5 million people.

Wars, too, can create widespread displacement, reconfiguring the settlement patterns of entire nations. United Nations estimates of the number displaced by the Iraq War (2003–present) range as high as 50,000 per month. World War II is estimated to have displaced tens of millions of people. Indeed, the boundaries of many central European nations (e.g., Germany, Poland) were redrawn as a result of the displacement of millions.

While natural disasters and wars offer the most dramatic examples of displacement, many households are displaced by the normal workings of housing markets or government policy. Some households have to move when the cost of their current unit becomes unaffordable. Gentrification, a process whereby relatively low-income neighborhoods experience an influx of investment and affluent households, has been thought to cause widespread displacement. Recent research suggests, however, that normal turnover rather than displacement is responsible for much of the demographic shift associated with it. Nonetheless, a number of individuals are forced out of their homes because of gentrification, even if the number is not as high as previously thought.

Governments exercising the powers of eminent domain have also contributed to displacement. Although painful to displacees, a need exists for public goods such as highways or military bases, whose construction often requires displacement of households. When the government is viewed as abusing this power or defining the public good too broadly, the resultant displacement can be controversial. City residents opposed the urban renewal program of the 1950s and 1960s, which provided government funds to condemn properties and assemble sites for redevelopment, when it caused too much displacement, particularly among low-income Blacks, without producing substantial benefits. The *Kelo v. City of New London* Supreme Court decision of 2005 generated concern because of the rather elastic way the Court interpreted "public use." The benefits stemming from economic development were construed as a public use, as opposed to narrower definitions that focus on specific public facilities and uses like parks or roads.

The impact of displacement on the lives of displacees depends largely on postdisplacement conditions. The more similar conditions are to what life was like prior to displacement, the less traumatic the experience will be. When one can relocate nearby and maintain employment, routines, and social networks, the experience is unlikely to be disconcerting. At the other extreme, if an entire community is uprooted and unable to reestablish itself, the experience is likely to be traumatic. In fact, research shows that displacees from gentrification often achieve higher levels of residential satisfaction. In contrast, refugees from war often find it impossible to create any semblance of normalcy.

Lance Freeman

See also Catastrophe; Gentrification; Housing Policy; Neighborhood Revitalization; Rent Control

Further Readings

Freeman, Lance and Frank Braconi. 2004. "Gentrification and Displacement in New York City." *Journal of the American Planning Association* 70(1):39–52.

Grier, G. and E. E. Grier. (1978). *Urban Displacement: A Reconnaissance*. Washington, DC: U.S. Department of Housing and Urban Development.

Schill, Michael H. and Richard P. Nathan. 1983. *Revitalizing America's Cities: Neighborhood Reinvestment and Displacement*. Albany: State University of New York Press.

DIVIDED CITIES

Divided cities are urban regions in which social, political, or economic barriers have segregated the residents, affected the distribution of infrastructure and services, and generated parallel jurisdictions. The globe is full of cities, big and small, that were either divided but are now reunited or were divided and remain so. As divided cities are not uncommon, and the problems they have are manifold, they are an important issue in urban studies. There are several causes of divided cities. Most often, divisions occur as a result of shifts in national boundaries brought about by war and conflict. Europe's landscape is dotted with such cities. There are also some in China and in North America. Internal processes can also cause urban divisions. A particular form of ghettoization—which was once found throughout Europe in the form of Jewish ghettoes and today is more common in the United States in the form of African American ghettos and American barrios—is one such process. Another internal process of socio-spatial urban division are those cities that contain gated communities. These are enclosed and protected territories designed to house a certain social stratum of the urban population. The following paragraphs describe some of these examples of cities divided by external and internal factors. Jerusalem as a divided city is discussed separately, as it belongs in a category of its own.

Cities Divided by External Causes

Shifting national boundaries as a result of war is the most common cause of urban divisions. There are many cities in Europe that have been divided in this manner. In the early nineteenth century, Napoleon divided Laufenburg across Switzerland and Germany. Later, after World War I and the collapse of the Austro-Hungarian Empire, conflicts between Slavic and German-speaking populations resulted in the creation of Bad Radkersburg as a border city. It was split by the Mura River into Bad Radkersburg, Austria, and Gornja, Radgona (which is now called Slovenia). Also in this time, the Lainsitz River formed the new border between Austria and what is now the Czech Republic. The city of Gmuend, on this river, was divided into Gmuend and České Velenice. Similarly, the city of Komarom of the Austro-Hungarian Empire was divided across the jurisdictions of Hungary and what is now Slovakia along the Danube River. Fighting over the Gorizia also began in World War I. It was not until after World War II, however, that the city became divided across the jurisdictions of Italy and what is now Slovenia.

After World War II, the reformation of Germany's northeastern border caused the division of cities sitting along the Oder and Neisse rivers. Muskau was divided into Bad Muhskau and Łęknica, Görlitz was divided into Görlitz and Zgorzelec, Guben was divided into Guben and Gubin, Forst was divided into Forst and Zasieki, Frankfurt (Oder) was divided into Frankfurt (Oder) and Słubice, and Küstrin was divided into Küstrin-Kietz and Kostrzyn and Odrą. Since the fall of the Berlin wall the restrictions in mobility have been greatly relaxed, but the fragmented parts remain under the corresponding political jurisdictions of either Germany or Poland. The division of Germany into the eastern German Democratic Republic and the western Federal Republic of Germany, following the discussions at Potsdam, also created the famous divide of the city of Berlin (now reunified).

Cities divided as a result of changing national borders can also be found elsewhere on the globe. In the eastern hemisphere, the annexing of Hong Kong to the British Empire after the Opium Wars also generated some divided cities. In 1997, as Hong Kong was handed to China, the cities of Lo Wu (Hong Kong) and Luohu (China) were reunited under one jurisdiction. Similarly, Sha Tau Kok (China) and Shatoujiao (Hong Kong) were also reunited. Upon reconciliation, the parts that were previously governed by British Hong Kong came under the jurisdiction of the Hong Kong Special Administrative Region, while the other halves would be administered by Guangdong Province. In the western hemisphere, the dissension and separation of the United States from Britain led to the creation of the Canadian–American border that divided Derby Line in Vermont from Rock Island in Quebec, Canada. This border also split several North American Indian nations. The annexing of Sault Ste. Marie south of St. Mary's River from Ontario, Canada, to Michigan, United States, divided not only the city but also the Chippewa communities. Between New York and Ontario, the St. Regis Mohawk Reservation was also divided.

One of the most spectacular twentieth-century examples of a divided and reunited city is Berlin. Because it is a large metropolitan area, it showcases how extreme the problems associated with division can be. After World War II, Berlin was divided among the Allies, and the separate neighborhoods were occupied by the respective military powers. However, the allied cooperation broke down, and the city was divided into administrative areas, with the Soviets occupying the eastern half, and the French, British, and Americans occupying the western half. In 1961, the Soviet Union began building the "anti-fascist wall of protection"

(*Antifaschistische Schutzmauer*). At first, the barrier consisted of merely a guarded barbed wire fence. Later, as this was not enough to halt migrations, a concrete wall with 24-hour surveillance was constructed in its place. As the City of Berlin was located geographically in the middle of the Soviet-controlled German Democratic Republic, the barrier fully encircled the western sector. These years were marked by the cold war, and Berlin was a place where it played out at a local level, as the two sides of the wall became showcases of socialism and capitalism. At the Museum of Check Point Charlie in Berlin, numerous stories of attempts (sometimes successful, sometimes deadly) at crossing this barrier over the following 28 years are told.

The fall of the wall in 1989 was celebrated around the world. Today, sections of the wall that have been preserved as memorial can be viewed at Bernauer Street, as well as at the East Side Gallery near East Station (*Ost Bahnhof*). The reconnection of the city, however, was a sizable planning undertaking. A good introduction to the complexities of this task are articles from Hartmut Häußermann, Elizabeth Strom, Dieter Frick, and Karin Baumert, who discussed the geographic, political, sociological, and economic implications of reunification. The newly reconnected city had two of everything (e.g., two city halls, two opera houses, two subway systems). To physically reconnect East and West Berlin, roads, bridges, subways, and bus lines had to be built. The dismantling of the peripheral borders of West Berlin also meant that expansion of the built environment into the surrounding state of Brandenburg was possible for the first time in 30 years. Although many celebrated the collapse of Soviet control in the region, and families were reunited, the fall also presented some dilemmas. The characteristics that defined East Berlin between 1945 and 1989 were those that reflected socialist thought: (1) The "artistic" urban design of the city centers reflected the success of the socialist regime; (2) there was no suburbanization; (3) presocialist structures were neglected and left as reminders of the pitfalls of capitalism; (4) there was no segregation based on economic status but rather on political status and the capacity to participate in the socialist regime; and (5) an extreme centralization of power and decision making resulted in token municipal

participation. The ramifications of this transition from socialism to capitalism posed many problems, and many felt that the west had simply expanded eastward without assessing the merits of the former system—there was, for example, no homelessness or unemployment, and women were fully educated and occupied high-level positions of employment. And indeed, after the wall fell, there were huge expectations over a reunified Berlin as a city well situated for eastern markets. Developers from around the globe scurried to Berlin and began rebuilding. In the 1990s, Berlin became famous for its construction cranes, and tourists flocked to Berlin to see them.

Cities Divided by Internal Causes

Internal divisions can be identified throughout urban regions. Divided cities, however, should be differentiated from what might otherwise be referred to as fragmented cities. Cities, today, are riddled with spaces that are not accessible to everyone. The béguinages in the Netherlands, Belgium, and northern Germany were communities for women. There are also housing cooperatives in Canada that house members of specific groups with specific needs: lesbian and gays; or people of a specific language; or seniors. Cities governed by Islamic law also have spatial divisions according to gender and social status. Yet, these spaces are part and parcel of the city as a whole, because the people who live in these spaces often tap into the same infrastructural resources, participate in the same overarching political and economic milieus, and their membership is neither instituted nor protected by force. On the contrary, differentiated spaces of a fragmented city are said to provide spaces of empowerment for their users. Nancy Fraser, one famous proponent of this position, for example, refuted Jürgen Habermas's concept of a single and open public sphere where everyone participated equally. Fraser argued that alternative discourses are not guaranteed in such models of democratic discourse. Rather, alternate discursive spaces are required—such as women-only spaces—where dialogues and ideas can emerge that might otherwise be drowned out in democratic forums such as Habermas's model. In this way, the number and scope of topics that can be addressed in wider inclusive democratic forums is expanded.

Thus, as Fraser argues, such spaces that might seem exclusive at first glance are actually contributing to, and broadening, wider democratic discourse.

Cities that are internally divided, however, reveal a much higher degree of separation than spaces of fragmented cities. For example, cities that contain ghettos or barrios constitute divided cities. Loïc Wacquant had done extensive research on ghettos and had arrived at a specific definition of the term for the purposes of social scientific investigation and for the purposes of distinguishing ghettos from enclaves, disadvantaged neighborhoods, or alternate spaces. In his view, ghettoes exhibit four characteristics: stigma, constraint, spatial confinement, and institutional encasement. The ghetto is a place in which the greater society singles out a particular segment of the population and sections them off, either through force or through systematic institutional exclusion. The result, according to Wacquant, is the growth of an extreme form of parallel institutionalism. According to Wacquant, this urban form existed in Europe as Jewish ghettos. Throughout the last millennium—fifteenth-century Rome, fifteenth- and sixteenth-century Venice, seventeenth-century Vienna and Prague, nineteenth-century Frankfurt, to name a few—many cities across Europe contained Jewish ghettos as regions where persons of Jewish faith were permitted to reside and work. In the twentieth century, myriad Jewish ghettos were established under the rule of Adolf Hitler, the most famous and largest being the Warsaw Ghetto. In the United States, Wacquant focused much attention on Chicago and the ghetto of Woodlawn, whose residents (1) lacked basic public services such as adequate schooling, health care, transit services, advocacy, and security—even the police stayed away; (2) endured a high degree of stigma and suffered substandard living conditions and life expectancies; (3) were dominated by a booming underground economy in weapons and narcotics trafficking; and (4) identified the world outside the neighborhood as inaccessible and foreign. Chicago is therefore a divided city because life inside and life outside of the ghetto represent two separate and independent urban systems. Similarly, it has been argued that American barrios, such as East Los Angeles, exhibit, although not as severely, structural and systemic segregation similar to African American ghettoes. High rates of unemployment and poverty and low investment in infrastructure and services lead to patterns of social and spatial segregation that resemble urban enclaves at best and ghettoes at worst.

Perhaps the ghetto's opposite are urban gated communities that have been emerging throughout South America over the past 30 years as a result of socioeconomic changes around the region. Effectively, these become urban spaces for the rich, whose lifestyle expectations concerning comfort and security needed to be met. They are known as "gated communities" (*barrios cerrados*), "private urbanizations" (*urbanizaciones privadas*), or "gated condominiums" (*condomínios fechados*), and are found in Santiago de Chile, Buenos Aires, Mexico City, São Paulo, and Rio de Janeiro. The AlphaVille community of São Paulo is the oldest such development. It is home to 30,000 residents, it has an infrastructure that employs 150,000 workers, and it boasts its own private university and health care system. Utilities are provided without public assistance by the AlphaVille Urbanismo corporation. The community is outfitted with 24-hour surveillance by armed security personnel, and this is claimed to protect residents from the urban ills of São Paulo and its high homicide rates. The cost of living in AlphaVille is beyond the reach of the average Brazilian family. Thus, these communities may be seen as deepening and reinforcing the socioeconomic divides among the respective urban populations.

Segregation of elites is by no means a new phenomenon. The middle-class flight to the suburbs in North American cities is a twentieth-century example of this and is said to have exacerbated ghetto formation inside cities. In earlier times, religion often played a key role in separating the wealthy, educated, and powerful from what was viewed as the profanity of daily urban life. Monasteries, abbey complexes, and cloistered communities in the Middle Ages were home to servants of the Christian faith as custodians and guardians of the church's social, political, and economic capital. In China, the Forbidden City (*Zijin Cheng*), built to house the emperor—the earthly counterpart of the celestial emperor—was also a place that segregated the wealthy and the powerful from their subjects. Its construction occupied over a million workers, and upon completion during the Ming Dynasty, its interior was vast. Its 8-meter wall and 6-meter-deep moat enclosed 7 hectares with 90 palaces with gardens and courtyards, 980 buildings, and 8,704 rooms. For 500 years it was entirely off bounds to the public. In both of these cases, these segregated communities of elites were backed with armies, ready to exert force over possible dissidents.

Jerusalem

Probably the most controversial divided city that exists today, at the beginning of the twenty-first century, is Jerusalem—a city whose religious significance is shared by members of many denominations and whose political situation reaches into wider global and historical political economics. Ever since the arrival of Jewish populations in the late nineteenth century—arrivals that came in waves referred to as immigrations (*aliyahs*)—there has been conflict with the Palestinian population. The conflict intensified to such a degree that in 2000 the prime minister of Israel, Ehud Barak, approved plans to erect a physical barrier. A neutral account of the humanitarian consequences of this barrier can be found in a document written in 2005 by the UN Office for Coordination of Humanitarian Affairs in cooperation with the UN Relief and Works Agency for Palestine Refugees. Israel began building the 8-meter-high and 670-kilometer concrete barrier, which is reminiscent of the Berlin wall, in 2002 as a temporary measure to protect against Palestinian attacks. Because the barrier extends into the West Bank, the length will be almost twice that of the West Bank Armistice Line (the Green Line)—the border between Israel and the West Bank. Palestinians living in lands located between the barrier and the Green Line have, as a result, hindered access to markets located on the western side of the barrier (the remainder of the West Bank). Along the barrier, various communities are severed from their agricultural lands and water wells, as well as services such as schools and hospitals. To ease movement, various gates will be built. There are agricultural gates for those needing to access their land on the opposite side. There are general access checkpoints manned by the Israeli Border Police, and military gates (not for civilian Palestinian use). Road gates are placed to ease the flow of traffic, school gates are for Palestinian schoolchildren,

seasonal gates are provided during harvest times, and settlement gates are designed for the Israeli settlers living in gated communities in the West Bank. To use any of the gates, the required permit must be shown. Generally, Palestinians must show either a permit to enter Israel or a Green permit to enter a closed zone. Palestinians who reside inside a closed zone receive a Green permit automatically that is valid for two years.

The barrier is not scheduled to cross through the middle of the city as one might expect were it to follow the Green Line. Instead, the wall will reach around the western districts of the city, encompass the Arab neighborhoods, and divide them from the West Bank. As is planned throughout the rest of the barrier along the Israeli–West Bank border, the barrier around Jerusalem will also be dotted with various gates. The *Qalandiya* checkpoint, for example, is designed to act as the gateway into Jerusalem for West Bank commuters and schoolchildren who are educated within the city limits but live in the West Bank countryside. To move through the gates, Palestinian civilians must retain the respective permit, which is granted for limited amounts of time.

The City of Jerusalem will not be divided in the same way that other cities mentioned earlier in this entry have. It will not be a city with a part of it sectioned off. Instead the division results as Palestinians are encompassed inside a closed zone and divided from the rest of the West Bank, forcing a degree of parallel institutionalism among their communities. Jerusalem is also not a city being divided by external forces per se, as the Israeli government is building the barrier for itself as a means of protection. It might be argued, however, that the Arab communities are being divided by external forces—namely, the Israeli government—because Israeli sovereignty over Arab lands is in dispute. Moreover, movement of Palestinians across the gates will be sharply surveilled.

There are cities all around the globe that are, or once were, divided, and there are varying degrees of separation. Some have been divided for so long that two separate and independent cities have emerged that peacefully coexist, such as Laufenburg (in Germany and Switzerland) and the cities along the German–Polish border. Some are divided or being divided and tensions are negative or hostile, such as is the case in Jerusalem and possibly barrios and African American ghettos. Some are reunited and are rebuilding relations, such as Berlin. The forms of divisions also vary. Sometimes the division is formed by a national border, such as all the German examples. Sometimes it is administrative—such as the divided cities in Hong Kong. Sometimes the division is social and economic, as ghettos, barrios, and gated communities are. Divisions of all forms, because of their characteristic of permanency, are often a result, but also a further source, of deep-seated social, political, and economic problems and are thus an important lesson in the study of urban systems.

Constance Carr

See also Barrio; Berlin, Germany; Capitalist City; Chicago, Illinois; Gated Community; Ghetto; Hong Kong, China; São Paulo, Brazil; Social Exclusion

Further Readings

Baumert, Karin. 2003. "Social Movement and the Present Challenges of Global Competitive Cities." *Bulletin of the International Network of Research and Action* 25:18–20.

Fraser, N. 1993. "Rethinking the Public Sphere: A Contribution to the Critique of Actually Existing Democracy." In *The Phantom Public Sphere*, edited by B. Robbins. Minneapolis: University of Minnesota Press.

Frick, Diether. 1991. "City Development and Planning in the Berlin Conurbation." *Town Planning Review* 62(1):37–49.

Häußermann, Hartmut. 1996. "From the Socialist to the Capitalist City: Experiences from Germany." Pp. 214–31 in *Cities after Socialism*, edited by G. Andrusz, M. Harloe, and I. Szelenyi. Oxford, UK: Blackwell.

Häußermann, Hartmut and Elizabeth Strom. 1994. "Berlin: The Once and Future Capital." *International Journal for Urban Regional Research* 18(2):335–46.

UN Office for Coordination of Humanitarian Affairs and the United Nations Relief and Works Agency for Palestine Refugees. 2005. "The Humanitarian Impact of the West Bank Barrier on Palestinian Communities." East Jerusalem, Israel: United Nations OCHA.

Wacquant, Loïc. 2004. "Roter Gürtel, Schwarzer Gürtel: Rassentrennung, Klassenungleicheit und der Staat in der französischen städtischen Peripherie und im amerikanischen Ghetto" (Red Belt, Black Belt: Racial Segregation, Class Inequality and the State in the French Urban Periphery and in American Ghettos). Pp. 148–202 in *An den Rändern der Städte* (On the Edge of the City), edited by H. Häußermann and W. Siebel. Frankfurt am Main, Germany: Suhrkam.

DOWNS, ANTHONY

From fluctuations in the U.S. real estate market to the causes and consequences of traffic congestion and suburban sprawl to the workings of a two-party democratic political system, Anthony Downs's career as an economist has been grounded in the principles of choice, rationality, and market forces. His work has been important to a broad spectrum of audiences, including academics, public policy makers, and corporate decision makers. Rooted in economic assumptions, Downs has hypothesized how and why people and institutions make decisions about property, development, politics, and transportation and has pointed to the likely consequences of these decisions.

Downs, born in 1936, received a PhD in economics from Stanford University in 1956. The following year he published his dissertation, *An Economic Theory of Democracy* (1957) and, a decade later, he penned *Inside Bureaucracy* (1966). These books are widely cited by social scientists studying elections, political participation, political parties, and government. Their popularity has grown over time. Since 1980, they have been cited nearly 4,500 times in social science journals. *An Economic Theory of Democracy*, in particular, contributed to the understanding of how parties compete for voters in a two-party system by moving toward the center and why voters choose to vote or abstain in these elections. Political scientists have used these theories to explain changes in voter behavior when institutional changes shift the costs and benefits of participation. This work has led to a long-standing paradox as the costs of voting almost always outweigh the benefits for each individual voter, yet many individuals still vote in national, two-party, winner-take-all elections.

Downs's work has highlighted how micro-level decisions often lead to unintended and unfortunate macro outcomes. He has advocated implementation policies that would shift costs and benefits—such as changes to tax policy or the use of vouchers, quotas, or tolls—that in turn might produce more desirable social outcomes, such as the development of more affordable housing or an easing of racial tensions. At times, Downs views what is widely considered to be a problem, such as traffic congestion at peak hours, as an important consequence of local economic vibrancy rather than insufficient planning or infrastructure. His work on issue-attention cycles has provided insight into how the public perceives crisis and reacts to social and political issues over time.

Reviewers of Downs's work have sometimes noted that his policy prescriptions are very difficult or impractical to achieve given political realities. Yet, certain recommendations, such as the use of high-occupancy toll lanes in congested areas that have been implemented locally have resulted in outcomes consistent with Downs's predictions. Some of Downs's reviewers have found his underlying economic assumptions to be too abstract or too simple. Others note that Downs's predictions regarding the availability and pricing of housing and rents in the 1980s did not meet his expectations. Downs's advocacy for policies to break up disadvantaged urban communities in the late 1960s have been seen as both an important impetus to urban renewal efforts as well as a step that disempowered many in poor communities by diluting geographic concentrations.

Since 1977, Downs has been a fellow at the Brookings Institution in Washington, D.C. He has also worked in government for both Republican and Democratic administrations and has frequently consulted for and served on the boards of corporations, nonprofits, and other organizations related to real estate, public planning, insurance, and finance. His father, James Downs, founded one of the nation's first real estate research endeavors, the Real Estate Research Council, in 1931. Anthony Downs later went on to work at the Real Estate Research Council and served as its chairman for four years.

Mark M. Gray

See also Governance; Local Government; Real Estate; Rent Control; Suburbanization; Urban Economics

Further Readings

Downs, Anthony. 1973. *Opening Up the Suburbs: An Urban Strategy for America.* New Haven, CT: Yale University Press.
———. 1981. *Neighborhoods and Urban Development.* Washington, DC: Brookings Institution Press.
———. 1996. *A Reevaluation of Residential Rent Controls.* Washington, DC: Urban Land Institute.
———. 1998. *Political Theory and Public Choice: The Selected Essays of Anthony Downs.* Vol. 1. Cheltenham, UK: Edward Elgar.
———. 1998. *Urban Affairs and Urban Policy: The Selected Essays of Anthony Downs.* Vol. 2. Cheltenham, UK: Edward Elgar.
———. 2004. *Still Stuck in Traffic: Coping with Peak-hour Traffic Congestion.* Washington, DC: Brookings Institution Press.

DOWNTOWN REVITALIZATION

Public efforts to remake downtowns long predated their decline. By the turn of the twentieth century, high-rise central business districts surrounded by low-rise residential neighborhoods were a distinctive feature of American cities, unlike European cities that typically intermingled commerce and housing.

Reform: 1900–1930

Functionally and visually distinguished, downtown became the iconic heart of the city: the engine of economic growth, the embodiment of civic pride, the "100-percent district" of peak real estate values, the showcase of cultural sophistication, and the meeting ground of diverse populations. Business and civic leaders worried, however, that downtowns were confronting the physical limits of growth. This was represented most vividly by inharmonious downtown traffic, a chaotic and hazardous mix of pedestrians, bicyclists, streetcars, carriages, and a small number of cars.

Two broad approaches arose to address this problem. One, rooted in the accomplishments of nineteenth-century civic engineering, sought to continually modernize infrastructure to accommodate growth. The next logical step in transit, for example, was to replace streetcars and elevated trains with higher-capacity subways. Boston (1898) and New York City (1904) led the way, but soon subway plans were proposed even in smaller cities such as Cincinnati and Detroit in anticipation of what municipal leaders argued was inevitable future growth. Modernization signaled a city's aspirations.

The second approach originated in the "urban housekeeping" of women's clubs. Devoted to physical cleanliness, esthetic unity, and social surveillance, urban housekeeping had less success on city streets than in the more easily controlled environments of downtown office buildings and department stores (and later in suburban malls and theme parks). Subsequently, City Beautiful planners such as Chicago's Daniel Burnham argued that order and beauty could be achieved only by fundamentally rethinking downtown geography. In particular, they fought for height limits on buildings so that downtowns would be forced to expand outward, beyond their constraining borders, rather than upward. This would create space for parks and plazas, relieve traffic congestion, and generally humanize the scale of downtown. The battle over height limits in New York City resulted in the nation's first zoning laws (1916).

Renewal: 1945–1965

The presumption of a harmony between downtown and the rest of the city began to break down in the 1920s when plans for subways failed, in part because of neighborhood resistance. The first civic associations devoted exclusively to downtown development emerged in cities like Oakland (1931), Chicago (1939), and Pittsburgh (1943)—and nationally in the Urban Land Institute (1940). These groups faced the fact of decentralization. With the growing popularity of cars, accommodated only with difficulty by compact downtowns, both residents and retailers began moving beyond city borders and between the radial spokes of rail transit, while industry bought cheap land on the outskirts for its sprawling assembly lines.

The Depression and war masked some of the effects of decentralization, however, allowing some planners to maintain their faith in downtown hegemony. Modernizers shelved subway plans in favor of more up-to-date technologies: hub-and-spoke automobile highways that would funnel traffic downtown, from suburbs as well as city neighborhoods, into multilevel parking facilities. With the dispersal of industry, planners envisioned downtown to be the center of the highest, if no longer all, of an area's economic functions. In its bid for renaissance, Pittsburgh replaced industrial blight with the acclaimed Gateway Center office complex (1949) at the same time that its ordinance against industrial smoke (1945) became a model for others to emulate.

Retailers perceived the need to compete with outlying business districts and suburban chain stores. They began with promotions ("Saturday Downtown Value Day"), but soon pushed for renewal along City Beautiful lines: a more attractive downtown that, in spreading outward, had the additional advantage of displacing "blighted" residential neighborhoods that deterred visits from suburbanites. They were aided by Title I of the Housing Act of 1949. Originally created to rebuild the nation's poorest slums by utilizing eminent domain, the act failed to mandate the replacement of condemned housing while empowering city agencies to choose which neighborhoods to renew first.

Before 1955, much of the funding for these transformations was local. Federal grants authorized in the 1949 Housing Act—which would pay up to two thirds of renewal projects—spent years in the pipeline. But the Highway Act of 1956 and a 1954 amendment to the Housing Act, allowing federal funding for nonresidential projects, led to massive expenditures to transform downtowns and nearby neighborhoods. Between 1955 and 1965, urban renewal surged in cities such as New Haven, Connecticut, which successfully lobbied Washington, D.C. Public officials pursued a vision of a downtown integrated into a regional transportation system, relieved of traffic congestion, and cleared of both residential and industrial blight. It was a distinctly American vision, as Europeans rebuilt their city centers along prewar lines, reserving more radical redevelopment for the outskirts.

An attempt to revitalize the 65-block business district that is downtown Los Angeles with upscale lofts and condominiums, chic restaurants, vibrant nightlife, and cultural and entertainment experiences has improved the look and feel of the once-dilapidated and -neglected area.

Source: Tracy Buyan.

Revival: 1965–Present

By 1965, there was a backlash against both the failures and successes of urban renewal. At its worst, it resulted in vacant lots in the heart of downtown—St. Paul's "Superhole" or St. Louis' "Hiroshima Flats"—and destroyed neighborhoods along its edge, whose residents painfully relocated to poorer areas or into high-rise public housing. On the other hand, renewal often succeeded in its goal of creating more office space. Easily stacked into tall buildings and benefiting from the proximity to professional and government services, offices continued to be viable in compact downtowns at the same time that American occupations shifted toward white-collar work. Some cities for the first time gained impressive skylines. The result, however, was often a monotony of International Style megaliths that paradoxically deadened downtowns even further.

In response, a new beautification movement, following the lead of critics such as Jane Jacobs and Kevin Lynch, conceived of cities as delicate ecologies of interlocking functional zones. Opposing the grand plans of renewal, they thought small. A new downtown residential population—artists, bohemians, gays, young professionals—reclaimed warehouse districts block by block. Historical preservationists retrofitted old industrial spaces for new commercial uses, often following the example of San Francisco's Ghirardelli Square (1964). As a grassroots phenomenon, similar efforts would continue for decades not only in large downtowns, but in satellite business districts and Main Streets: Mansfield, Ohio, sparked renewal with a refurbished carousel (1991).

In the early 1970s, a recession joined decentralization, rising crime, and municipal insolvency to bring downtowns to a postwar low. With shrinking federal support for neighborhood programs, a new generation of enterprising, deal-making mayors—often from ethnic or racial minorities—focused again on the downtown economy. They subsidized development using tax-increment financing, which earmarked future gains in tax revenue for bond payments, and federal Urban Development Action Grants, authorized in 1977 following the end of urban renewal (1974).

As suburban growth slowed, developers viewed downtowns as fresh territory—but not as blank slates. Because the charm of premodernist buildings was a draw, rehabilitation became the basis for commercial revival. James Rouse created Boston's Quincy Market (1976) by transforming a decaying downtown warehouse into an attractive setting for specialty shopping. Quincy Market inspired numerous imitations, including Baltimore's Harborplace (1980) and New York's South Street Seaport (1983). These "festival marketplaces" addressed new desires for rootedness while hewing to exacting standards of urban housekeeping. Developers also adapted more conventional malls to downtown, notably Chicago's vertical Water Tower Place (1976) and Philadelphia's Gallery at Market East (1977).

Grassroots and commercial beautification often emerged in tandem with big-ticket modernization projects. With revived public spending for public transportation, beginning with the Mass Transit Act of 1964, some cities improved commuter and intracity rail, including direct lines from airports. But much of the new infrastructure has been, like the festival marketplaces, "spectacular"—that is, created to attract and entertain visitors. Cities scrambled to build convention centers, hotels, sports stadiums, and (more recently) casinos with the aim of again connecting downtowns to a vital periphery, which now encompassed a global population of tourists and businesspeople.

The success or failure of revitalization has depended on a mix of factors. Larger downtowns with existing commuter rail and safer images garnered reliable daytime populations of office workers and increasing numbers of residents, who in turn made festival marketplaces feasible. Downtowns that could best capitalize on an aura of excitement and sophistication became tourist and business destinations. Born in the age of industrialism, the downtowns that have revived the most are the ones that have adapted to a postindustrial economy.

Matthew Roth

See also Developer; Gentrification; Public–Private
    Partnerships; Shopping; Urban Crisis; Urban Policy

Further Readings

Abbott, Carl. 1993. "Five Downtown Strategies: Policy Discourse and Downtown Planning since 1945." *Journal of Policy History* 5:5–27.

Fogelson, Robert M. 2001. *Downtown: Its Rise and Fall, 1880–1950*. New Haven, CT: Yale University Press.

Frieden, Bernard J. and Lynne B. Sagalyn. 1989. *Downtown, Inc.: How America Rebuilds Cities*. Cambridge: MIT Press.

Isenberg, Alison. 2004. *Downtown America: A History of the Place and the People Who Made It*. Chicago: University of Chicago Press.

Teaford, Jon C. 1990. *The Rough Road to Renaissance: Urban Revitalization in America, 1940–1985*. Baltimore: Johns Hopkins University Press.

DRUG ECONOMY

Some 200 million people, or 5 percent of the world's population aged 15 to 64, use drugs at least once a year. The number of opiate users is estimated at around 16 million (11 million of which abuse heroin), while the number of cocaine users is said to be close to 14 million. Confining our overview to heroin and cocaine: Following strong increases in the 1980s, opium production has been basically stable at around 4,000 to 5,000 metric tons per year since the early 1990s. It is also estimated that 87 percent of opium destined for the illicit market is now produced in Afghanistan. As for cocaine, after the peak reached during the second half of the 1990s, production is now estimated at 674 metric tons per year, a 29 percent decrease when compared to the late 1990s. According to a 2005 United Nations report, most of the world's cocaine is produced in three countries: Colombia (50 percent), Peru (32 percent), and Bolivia (15 percent).

Although some commentators tend to focus on the profits generated within heroin- and cocaine-producing countries, many authors would concur that it is at the level of international trafficking, wholesale and retail distribution, namely in consuming countries, that the bulk of the proceeds of the drug economy is found. Descriptions of the drug economy devote specific attention to these three levels, and despite slight definitional differences, it is normally accepted that the organizational structure of the groups involved in this economy varies according to the function or task: manufacturing, international trafficking, or wholesale, medium level, and retail distribution. Large, formally organized groups are said to prevail at the international trafficking level, namely, groups that manage to establish steady partnerships with producers. Trafficking routes, however, shift according to the groups involved, political circumstances, law enforcement efforts, and, finally, legitimate trade routes. The latter aspect is deemed crucial, as illicit drugs would normally follow the same commercial conduits carrying legitimate goods. Countries that are positioned on the traditional trade routes of the main source countries of heroin and cocaine, or are historically engaged in imperial and postimperial relationships with these countries, may therefore be major importers. In such countries, communities of residents whose background is in producing areas are said to play a central importing role.

Upper and Medium Markets

Drug trafficking, however, does not necessarily require access to producing countries, as transactions may take place in major distribution hubs, for example, in Pakistan or, as far as Europe is concerned, the Netherlands. Distribution in individual countries is not as structured as one may assume. Dorn, Murji, and South (1992), for example, found that domestic supply systems were not characterized by neat, top-down hierarchies controlled by a Mr. Big. Rather they painted a picture of a fragmented and fluid system populated by a range of opportunistic entrepreneurs from a variety of backgrounds, including licit businesses with an illicit sideline. These entrepreneurs were described as career criminals who turn to the drug business from other "project crimes," such as bank robbery or major fraud. Upper- and medium-level distribution, therefore, is carried out by a variety of actors, including flexible groups engaged in the supply of other illicit goods and services, affinity groups based on family ties, small organizations formed through ethnicity links, and freelancers, namely, ephemeral entrepreneurial groups operating in a variety of areas in a contingent manner.

Other authors differentiate between middle- and upper-level markets but are aware that such differentiation obscures the fact that many "layers" of distribution can be found within both levels. The fragmentation of drug markets, the mobility of distributors between levels, and the overlapping "layers" at which transactions take place may further complicate attempts to precisely classify the different market levels.

In brief, it would appear that the chaotic traits normally attributed to local markets increasingly characterize also the middle level of the drug economy. However, this chaotic and competitive climate does not always translate into violence, as groups seem to tolerate each other. At times violence may instead connote the bottom of the market.

Local Markets

Different types of users tend to be serviced by different types of supply systems. Recreational users, for example, may not engage in proper economic transactions, as they might receive drugs through friends and acquaintances. Problem users, on the other hand, are forced to maintain stable relationships with networks of suppliers and sources of legal or illegal income. At the local level, there are "place-specific markets," such as street-level or indoor markets supplying regular users, and so-called open markets, which supply any buyer, with no need for prior introduction to the seller by known reliable buyers. More vulnerable to policing, open markets tend to slowly disappear and turn into closed ones, with the result that occasional, recreational users are forced to establish connections with problem users and professional suppliers.

Research conducted at the local level suggests that involvement in the drug economy does not necessarily imply embracing a specific drug subculture. Buying and distributing illicit substances appears to be increasingly determined by the profit prospect and perceived as a one-off remunerative enterprise or as a regular occupational choice. This is a relatively new phenomenon, as previous research found widespread use of "techniques of neutralization," whereby dealers justified their activity by claiming that they were users as well, and by arguing that they provided a "service" to needy people similar to them. The different actors involved in local markets do not share motivations, values, or lifestyles, thereby inhabiting an economy based on fragmented roles and cultures rather than a homogenous social setting. Each actor, in other words, might participate in that economy while ignoring the rationale guiding other people's participation. Often users and small suppliers know and work with only one or two other people in the distribution network, thus confining their activity to a single segment of the drug economy. It is at this level that the majority of individuals involved may acquire from this economy what amounts to a criminal "minimum wage."

Many young users and dealers supplement this illicit minimum wage with income derived from the hidden, or informal, economy. Here they perform unregistered work, and it is often here, in the informal economy itself, that their first encounter with illicit drugs takes place. This mainly applies to the vulnerable sectors of the drug economy, namely, individuals who are more exposed to detection and arrest. In brief, drug-dealing networks develop, first, as a result of mere occupational choices, and second, through involvement in the hidden economy in which many make a living. In this economy, marginalized youths may start using drugs on an occasional basis, but as barriers between recreational and problematic use are being eroded, "poverty drugs" become increasingly available.

Ethnicity and Drugs

Research, such as that conducted by Pearson and Hobbs, has previously suggested that drug-dealing networks are often organized along lines of kinship and ethnic identity. It is also suggested that this may be changing, as new market conditions increasingly encourage alliances between dealing networks and partnerships among different ethnic groups, according to the National Crime Intelligence Service.

At the international trafficking level, organized groups appear to be multiethnic, as business entails contact with a variety of countries and operators. The United Nations' research, in this respect, suggests that in the majority of cases criminal groups are not tied together by ethnic linkages. Studies have also identified mobile groups of international traffickers, often from marginalized communities, acting as independent operators, who offer their trafficking services to a variety of large national distributors. These groups may be culturally homogeneous and consist of members of extended families, but the transactions in which they engage are multiethnic in character. In most cases, therefore, risky international operations are covered by less-powerful groups and networks.

The development of drug-supplying networks might be understood through what are known as ethnic succession arguments. These have posited that crime can serve as a path of socioeconomic mobility for minorities, who eventually gain access to the formal economy. However, mobility can be constrained within criminal economies, and law enforcement efforts toward certain minority crime groups may have the unintended effect of creating opportunities for the upward mobility of other minority groups. Attention to certain criminal groups may create "vacancies," which are being increasingly filled by new ones.

While the ethnic element is important, market dynamics may overshadow such an element. Mono-ethnic markets appear to be limited to small-scale supply, while partnerships are inevitable at upper supply level. This is not surprising, if one bears in mind that drug economies mirror some aspects of legitimate economies. Big businesses and large-scale financial operators are not discriminatory on the basis of their customers' or partners' ethnic background or skin coloration, whereas those who occupy the more disadvantaged positions in the labor market may very well be. It is ironic to note that, while users and small dealers are often engaged in the strenuous affirmation of ethnic identity, those above them conduct business in total multiethnic harmony.

Vincenzo Ruggiero

See also Crime; Urban Crisis

Further Readings

Bourgois, P. 1995. *In Search of Respect: Selling Crack in El Barrio*. Cambridge, UK: Cambridge University Press.

Centre for International Crime Prevention. 2002. *Towards a Monitoring System for Transnational Organised Crime Trends*. Vienna: United Nations.

Dorn, N., M. Levi, and L. King. 2005. *Literature Review on Upper Level Drug Trafficking*. London: Home Office.

Dorn, N., K. Murji, and N. South. 1992. *Traffickers: Drug Markets and Law Enforcement*. London: Routledge.

Natarajan, M. and M. Hough, eds. 2000. *Illegal Drug Markets: From Research to Prevention Policy*. New York: Criminal Justice Press.

Naval Criminal Investigative Service. 2003, January 21. "Trafficking and Supply of Heroin and Cocaine by South Asian Groups" Press release. Washington, DC: Naval Criminal Investigative Service.

O'Kane, J. M. 2003. *The Crooked Ladder: Gangsters, Ethnicity, and the American Dream*. New Brunswick, NJ: Transaction.

Pearson, G. and D. Hobbs. 2001. *Middle Market Drug Distribution*. London: Home Office.

Ruggiero, V. 2000. *Crime and Markets*. Oxford, UK: Oxford University Press.

———. 2000. "Criminal Franchising: Albanians and Illicit Drugs in Italy." In *Illegal Drug Markets: From Research to Prevention Policy*, edited by M. Natarajan and M. Hough. New York: Criminal Justice Press.

Ruggiero, V. and K. Khan. 2006. "British South Asian Communities and Drug Supply Networks in the UK." *International Journal of Drug Policy* 17:473–83.

Ruggiero, V. and N. South. 1995. *Eurodrugs*. London: UCL Press.

United Nations. 2005. *World Drug Report*. Vienna: Office on Drugs and Crime.

Du Bois, W. E. B.

William Edward Burghardt (W. E. B.) Du Bois (1868–1963) was an African American sociologist, historian, author, editor, and political activist whose contributions to the discipline of urban studies can be found primarily in his groundbreaking socioeconomic study of Black Americans in Philadelphia, *The Philadelphia Negro* (1899).

Education, Academic Career, and Research Goals

Born in 1868, W. E. B. Du Bois was educated at Fisk University, the University of Berlin, and Harvard University. In 1895 he became the first African American to receive a PhD in the social sciences at Harvard University. Du Bois's academic career began at Wilburforce University (the older African American University), moved to Philadelphia in the mid-1890s (where he conducted research for his classic study *The Philadelphia Negro*), and then moved to Atlanta University from 1897 until 1910 (where he sought to establish a program for the study of African Americans, including their transition from rural to urban living). Over the course of this time, which circumscribed his formal academic career, Du Bois aimed to design and implement a series of systematic studies on African American social organization and culture. A significant part of his agenda concerned the status and fate of African Americans in urban America. The emergence of the industrial order in the United States, coupled with the end of slavery and the beginning of the migration of African Americans to urban areas, allowed Du Bois to consider the city to be the central geographic terrain for assessing the status of, and future prospects for African Americans.

Ultimately, Du Bois's early scholarly mission was to transcend the still-developing formal academic disciplines in order to create a supradisciplinary understanding of the social character, cultural status, and policy needs of African Americans, especially as they began the process of cementing themselves into the urban sphere of early twentieth-century American life. A major point of emphasis in these analyses was framing an orientation to interpreting, defining, and measuring social problems for this constituency. A core part of his objective was to document the barriers and obstacles inhibiting the social advancement of African Americans, to define some strategies and ideas for resolving them, and to illustrate how historical analysis, demographic data, fieldwork, and survey research can be employed to help achieve those ends.

The Philadelphia Negro

The strength of Du Bois's empirical contributions is best found in his most regarded study, *The Philadelphia Negro* (1899). Du Bois's approach to this work was influenced by his reading of Charles Booth's *Life and Labour of the People of London* (1891–1897) and the *Hull House Maps and Papers* (1895), authored by the Residents of Hull House. In his own work, Du Bois observed and documented the life experiences and social conditions affecting African Americans in Philadelphia's Seventh Ward, which housed one fifth of the city's African American population. He set out to document and interpret a range of social issues pertinent to the Black experience in Philadelphia, including northern migration, social conditioning, the social institutions and lifestyles of the Black community, and the enduring effects of slavery. Du Bois employed a questionnaire on family structure, income and wealth, and qualities of residential life. He also observed public interaction in the community. Finally he acquired or created diagrams and blueprints of the physical structures throughout the Seventh Ward in order to offer a comprehensive account of unemployment, family decay, and social hierarchies in the ward.

Du Bois's commitment to empirical research emerged during his studies in Germany, where under Gustav von Schmoller he was exposed to empiricism. The multiple method approach to data collection, unparalleled in social research for years afterward, blended structural analysis with micro-level depictions of public interaction and behavior in private settings. In *The Philadelphia Negro,* Du Bois provided a masterful weaving of class and racial effects in documenting the conditions of the Seventh Ward in Philadelphia. Through such an effort, he was able to argue that the urban slum was a symptom, and not a cause, of the economic, social, cultural, and political condition of African American urban life. In the chapters where he presented his agenda for Whites and Blacks, he divided his discussion of what Black Americans must do for racial advance into specific charges for the different class segments of the African American community. This effort reflected Du Bois's reformist inclinations. He aimed to produce not only a scholarly contribution but an illustration of how scholarship connects to a policy platform for redressing problems, as in Philadelphia's Seventh Ward.

His efforts here helped him to argue that slavery, prejudice, and environmental factors were the three principal causal factors affecting African American life in Philadelphia. Moreover, he promoted a nonhomogeneous depiction of African Americans by elucidating the class distinctions along the behavioral and organizational dimensions of social life. *The Philadelphia Negro* was the first comprehensive community study in American sociology. This work reflected precisely the kind of community-centered sociology that appeared on the American landscape in the following two decades (in large part because its proponent, and one of the early leaders of the University of Chicago school of sociology, Robert Ezra Park, also studied under the empiricists in Germany). *The Philadelphia Negro* remains a pathbreaking community study that helped establish a vernacular for writing about the social conditions of Black Americans, despite its moralistic claims and an elitist disposition taken toward lower-income Black Americans.

Essentially, Du Bois regarded the city as the site of great promise and opportunity for African Americans as they escaped the ravages of slavery and as an incubator of disease, filth, crime, vice, and moral decay for its inhabitants who were not yet following a path toward socioeconomic mobility and stability. The city became Du Bois's sociogeographical backdrop for the processes of African Americans' adaptation to modernity. Accordingly, for him any cultural advance for African Americans would be reflected by the degrees to which they turned away from vice, criminal activity, and folk mores and moved toward the staples of American modernity, which included securing employment and cultivating stable families. The proliferation of wage labor in the city's emerging industrial sphere and commitments to community-level organizing for social betterment were two of the mechanisms that Du Bois believed would firmly position African Americans in modernity.

Critical Reactions

There was some critical reaction to Du Bois's theories of cultural advance for African Americans. Some argued that he too aggressively embraced White American standards for social conduct and cultural inclinations in making his case for what African Americans should strive for, both in and beyond the confines of the city. Others, like Ross Posnock, have argued that Du Bois did not equate Whiteness, per se, with being culturally advanced but that, instead, Du Bois was asserting that without having suffered the burdens of being African Americans, White Americans generally achieved a level of cultural advancement that most Black Americans had yet to acquire. Du Bois's high regard for cultural advancement, together with his conviction that most socioeconomically disadvantaged African Americans lacked his sense of cultural sophistication, is what has led some observers to consider him a cultural elitist.

Contributions to Urban Studies

Du Bois's importance to urban studies may be seen in his pioneering social-scientific investigation of the African American urban community in multiple ways. First, he gave credence to the idea that African Americans were capable of surviving and contributing to American life and culture. Second, he documented how the city served as a geographical arena of increasing significance for assessing how that outcome could be achieved. He explored and explained how cities bring individuals and social groups into close and consistent contact such that opportunities for socioeconomic advancement, but also for conflict and tension, might unfold. Furthermore, he explained how different interactive styles and the various ways in which people represented themselves in public lead to perceptions of social status and significance and how that shaped the means by which strangers engaged and maneuvered with each other in city life. Finally, he introduced how a range of methodological techniques, including observational studies, interviews, census data, and reviews of historical documents, could lead to different as well as complementary portraits of the social experiences of city dwellers and the social flavor of city life.

Alford Young Jr.

See also Ghetto; Social Exclusion

Further Readings

Booth, Charles. [1891] 1897. *Life and Labour of the People of London.* Reprint, London: Macmillan.

Du Bois, W. E. B. 1896. *The Suppression of the African Slave Trade to the United States of America, 1683–1870.* New York: Longmans, Green.

———. 1897. "The Striving of the Negro People." *Atlantic Monthly* 80(Aug):194–98.

———. 1898. "The Study of Negro Problems." *Annals of the American Academy of Political and Social Science* 11(Jan):1–23.

———. 1903. "The Laboratory in Sociology at Atlanta University." *Annals of the American Academy of Political and Social Science* 21(May):16–63.

———. 1910. "Reconstruction and Its Benefits." *American Historical Review* 15(July):781–99.

———. [1899] 1996. *The Philadelphia Negro: A Social Study.* Reprint, Philadelphia: University of Pennsylvania Press.

Lewis, David Levering. 1993. *W. E. B. Du Bois: Biography of a Race.* New York: Henry Holt.

Residents of Hull House. 1895. *Hull House Maps and Papers.* New York: Crowell.

E

EDGE CITY

Edge city is a term used to refer to the edge of an urban area, an area dense with businesses, entertainment, shopping, and recreation. Some argue it has become the major form of urban growth worldwide, pushing residential suburbs even farther aware from the urban core.

Edge City in Popular Culture

Edge city is everywhere. The *Edge City Review* is billed as the "world's only conservative literary magazine, featuring New Formalist Poetry, fiction, and book reviews." *Edge City View* is a website that features articles on "Waco, Vince Foster, and the Secret War" and a review of the Mexican foto-novela genre *Mascaras en Accion*. Edge City is a cyberpunk game in which characters battle it out for control of Edge City: "Enter Edge City as the ultimate hacker, a Data Ripper, and jack into an exciting future. Battle Body Rippers in the apocalyptic Sprawl." *Goodbye to the Edge City* is a 2001 recording by indie rock band Preston School of Industry, described as similar to early-period alternative or post-pop bands in a review of Laconic's *Funhouse* compact disc. The Edge Cities Network is a business resource website including links to municipalities on the suburban fringe of European cities (e.g., Croydon–London, Espoo–Helsinki, Fingal–Dublin, Kifissia–Athens, Loures–Lisbon, Nacka–Stockholm, and Horth Down–Belfast) and

notes that "the Edge Cities forums are in place to encourage discussion and interaction between the various Edge Cities' partners and businesses."

The Edge City Collective in Philadelphia—offering improvisational music from beyond the new frontier—pays direct homage to Joel Garreau:

> It's an ironic reference to Joel Garreau's compellingly written, but ultimately disturbing book, *Edge City—Life on the New Frontier*, which details the seemingly unstoppable trend in our society toward a homogenized quasi-suburban culture. In this world, every place could be anyplace. Minds are numbed by fast food, television, and countless hours spent driving between shopping malls and office parks. And music is shaped primarily by the profit motive and a resulting desire to please the masses. We seek out a different "frontier."

Garreau's *Edge City*

Most urbanists are familiar with the ideas presented in Garreau's *Edge City* (1991). The edge city represents the third wave of urban history, pushing us into new frontiers at the edge of the metropolis. Garreau analyzed urban development across the United States and identified 123 places as true edge cities and another 83 up-and-coming or planned edge cities across the country. This first list included some two dozen edge cities in Los Angeles, 23 in Washington, D.C., and 21 in the greater New York City region. The edge city is distinguished by a number of features, including the following:

1. The area must have more than 5 million square feet of office space (about the space of a good-sized downtown).

2. The place must include over 600,000 square feet of retail space (the size of a large regional shopping mall).

3. The population increases every morning and decreases every afternoon (i.e., there are more jobs than homes).

4. The place is known as a single end destination (the place "has it all": entertainment, shopping, recreation, etc.).

5. The area must not have been anything like a "city" 30 years ago (cow pastures would have been nice).

Garreau goes on to identify three distinct varieties of edge city: boomers (the most common type, which develop around a shopping mall or highway interchange); greenfields (master-planned new towns on the suburban fringe); and uptowns (activity centers that have been built over an older city or town). The last two types are in opposition to the five distinguishing features in the previous list: Greenfields that are master-planned new towns include residential areas as well as entertainment and shopping and will not suffer the morning increase and afternoon decrease in population; uptowns that have developed from earlier satellite cities were, in fact, suburban cities at some earlier point in time.

Garreau notes that the actual boundaries of the edge city may be difficult to define, because they do not have the same look, political organization, or visual cues as older cities (they are less concentrated, do not have elected officials, and the semiotics of space and design are different). But Garreau asserts that edge cities are "the most purposive attempt Americans have made since the days of the founding fathers . . . to create something like a new Eden."

Moving beyond the classification of place based on physical structure and economic function, the edge city is also described as beyond the political boundaries of both the central city and suburban municipalities: "The reasons these places are tricky to define is that they rarely have a mayor or a city council." Although this definition may sound similar to the "interstitial areas" that figured prominently in the Chicago School studies, Garreau's definition of the edge city contradicts the definition of *city* in political science and in sociology.

Other Definitions of the Edge City

Sociologists have many definitions of cities and urban areas, and it is common for books in urban sociology to contrast definitions of "cities" and "urban areas" based upon the numbers of persons and population densities required for places to be considered urban. But these are administrative and legal definitions that go beyond sociology and social theory. Perhaps the best-known sociological definition of urbanization is that of size, density, and heterogeneity from Louis Wirth's essay "Urbanism as a Way of Life," but this is presented not as a definition of a city per se but rather as a means of distinguishing between urban and rural places.

The lasting theoretical definition of the city is provided by Max Weber. In the first chapter of *The City*, Weber explains how cities developed from market centers that had gained political independence from earlier patriarchal and patrimonial regimes. The argument is presented in some detail, and it is clear from his description that the city is the result of the administrative regulation of economic markets.

Weber's definition of the city is constructed as an ideal type, allowing for a comparison of cities across time and space, and it remains the starting point for the sociological study of the city and the modern metropolis. Crucial to Weber's understanding of the rise of the modern city as a distinct form of social organization is the ability of the city to regulate economic activity and guarantee rights and privileges to the citizens. Garreau's definition of the edge city specifically limits the edge city to areas that are outside the political boundaries of contemporary cities and suburbs. They cannot, therefore, be cities, because they do not have political boundaries and therefore do not have political authority or the ability to regulate activity or guarantee rights and privileges.

Edge City Studies

Discussion of edge cities has become almost ubiquitous in the many disciplines that comprise urban studies. John Macionis and Vincent Parillo include an extensive discussion of edge cities at the end of their chapter on urban ecology ("Edge Cities: The Latest Growth Pattern"). In this presentation, the edge city follows concentric zones, sector theory, multiple nuclei theory, social area analysis, and factorial ecology to emerge as the new model for explaining the ecology of urban areas. Garreau's claim to having information about 200 edge cities is comparable to Homer Hoyt's analysis of growth patterns in 142 cities. "New patterns of urban growth since 1975 demand some fresh insights. . . . What Joel Garreau (1991) calls *edge cities* have become the dominant form." The text presents Garreau's definitions of the common characteristics of the edge city, and the type of edge city, followed by a discussion of evolving middle-class urban centers in the edge city and a note that edge cities are now appearing worldwide, on the fringes of Bangkok, Beijing, London, Paris, and Sydney. In this scenario, the edge city is placed alongside other models in urban sociology and then presented to students as the dominant form of urban development in the contemporary city.

William Flanagan's *Urban Sociology: Images and Structure* presents a more tentative view of edge cities and relates Garreau's work to other discussions of segmented development and multiple urban centers. Flanagan notes without comment that "edge cities rarely have a governing body nor do their dimensions respond to official municipal boundaries. More of the residents live outside the city proper than within it." Much of his summary focuses upon the aesthetics of edge city development and popular taste and of the role of real estate developers in translating consumer behavior and preferences into collective special representations (edge cities) and profits. He then suggests that the negative views of edge city development may be similar to the "anti-urbanism" of the past: "As we consider the new sprawling urban annexes, some of us may find ourselves in a position of making nostalgic comparisons between the old, preferred urban form and the new, alien one. But as students of social science, we have to remind ourselves that a large part of our job is to discover and explain the authenticity that these new forms represent as an urban way of life." In this manner the concept of edge city is unchallenged and indeed is presented as an authenticized model of urban

growth that sociologists must incorporate into their work.

The edge city appears in numerous studies in the United States and, increasingly, in European research as well. But in most cases "edge city" has become a generalized label that no longer follows the definition outlined in Garreau's original statement. For example, Richard Greene's *New Immigrants, Indigenous Poor, and Edge Cities* argues that the "modern-day edge-city landscape of Chicago stands in dark contrast to the nineteenth-century industrial landscape depicted in the Chicago School's classic model," yet the study is based upon an analysis of percentage change in employment for incorporated places in the metropolitan region, areas that would not be edge cities according to Garreau's definition. The edge city also figures prominently in discussions of urban growth in the Los Angeles region by Edward Soja and others, but once again the edge city is the same as the satellite city of an earlier era, the technopole of the postwar period.

Edge cities also appear in recent studies of European cities. Gordon MacLeod and Kevin Ward, for example, describe Joel Garreau as the preeminent thinker on the urban/suburban/exurban form and suggest that the edge city represents a "self-contained employment, shopping, and entertainment mode permitting millions of contemporary Americans to live, work and consume in the same place," although Garreau's definition of the edge city specifically states that these are not residential areas (the population during the day is greater than the population during the evening hours—the edge city is a place for people to work and to shop, but it is not a residential suburb). Nigel Phelps has studied political governance and economic development in edge cities in five European countries; in each case, these are "edge urban municipalities" that are part of a "self-styled network of European edge cities." This is quite different from Garreau's note that edge cities may be difficult to define in part because they do not have the same political organization as older cities and do not have elected officials.

Los Angeles School adherents argue that the growth of the postmodern city creates emergent suburban landscapes that require new models and new methods of study. Edge city is used extensively in this literature (although alongside older labels such as the satellite city, outer city, technopole, and suburban fringe). While the edge city may have a more direct application to geography—it is after all the result of the concentration of business, commercial, office, and retail space—in current usage, edge city has lost the original meaning, and use of the concept challenges conventional understandings in political science and sociological analysis. Although urban scholars seek new models as well as new labels to better describe the continued expansion of metropolitan regions, there is recognition that models developed in the United States may not transfer to other countries because of differences in political governance. Contemporary research in the United States, United Kingdom, and beyond will allow scholars to better evaluate whether models, such as the edge city and growth machine, are applicable across cultures and regions.

Ray Hutchison

See also Exopolis; Suburbanization; Technopoles

Further Readings

Bontje, Marco and Joachim Burdack. 2005. "Edge Cities, European-style: Examples from Paris and the Randstad." *Cities* 22(4):317-30.
Edge City Collective (http://www.edgecitymusic.com).
Flanagan, William. 2001. *Urban Sociology: Images and Structures*. 4th ed. New York: Allyn & Bacon.
Freestone, R. and P. Murphy. 1993. "Edge City: Review of a Debate." *Urban Policy Research* 11:184-90.
Garreau, Joel. 1991. *Edge City: Life on the New Frontier*. New York: Doubleday.

ENVIRONMENTAL JUSTICE

Environmental justice is both a normative principle describing the equitable distribution of environmental benefits and burdens and a political and legal movement that seeks to realize that goal. A closely related term, *environmental equity*, represents the state, achievement, or outcome of environmental justice, and *environmental racism* is the practice of contravening environmental justice along racial or ethnic lines.

Beginning in the United States in the early 1980s, advocates advanced environmental justice claims within the logic of racial equality of the civil rights movement and did so by following a legal strategy seeking change through litigation in the courts. Movement organizers also saw environmental justice as a means to move mainstream environmental organizations from their traditional focus on conserving and protecting nature to an anthropocentric concern with protecting people, especially those burdened by low income and racial and ethnic segregation or discrimination, from inequitable exposure to the harmful effects of environmental pollution.

More recently, the scope of environmental justice has expanded beyond the original focus on the inequitable spatial distribution of environmental burdens. This expansion has entailed the reconceptualization of justice beyond distributional considerations to consider procedural, systemic, and structural dimensions, and the reconceptualization of environment beyond the siting of noxious activities to include the economic and political construction of the geographic landscape within a broad political ecology framework. The conceptual evolution of environmental justice has prompted, in turn, a redirection of method and practice beyond the original, narrowly construed legal strategy to encompass a broader and potentially more far-reaching challenge to underlying sociospatial processes.

Historical Roots

The pivotal moments in the introduction, diffusion, and popularization of environmental justice have been memorialized in frequently rehearsed histories of the movement. Although local protests in the United States over noxious environmental conditions date back to colonial-era objections to rendering plants and mill ponds, the rubric of environmental justice emerged with the conjunction of the civil rights and environmental movements in the late 1960s and 1970s. The first organized protest to explicitly invoke themes of environmental racism and environmental justice is widely acknowledged to be the opposition mounted in 1982 by residents of rural Warren County, North Carolina, to the proposed construction of a landfill for disposal of contaminated soil containing highly toxic polychlorinated biphenyl. Prolonged protests, the arrest of more than 500 demonstrators, and support from national civil rights and environmental groups captured widespread national attention to protesters' claims that siting the proposed landfill in the African American community constituted a violation of residents' civil rights.

A report released the following year by the U.S. General Accounting Office found that three of the four commercially operated hazardous waste disposal sites in the southeastern United States were located in predominantly African American communities. Prompted by the Warren County protest and the General Accounting Office report, the United Church of Christ established a Commission for Racial Justice, whose landmark report titled "Toxic Wastes and Race in the United States," published in 1987, found a strong statistical correlation between the racial and ethnic (i.e., non-White) proportion of the population in an area and the presence of both commercial hazardous waste disposal facilities and uncontrolled (unregulated or abandoned) toxic waste sites. The concept of environmental justice became popularized with the publication in 1990 of sociologist Robert Bullard's widely read textbook, *Dumping in Dixie: Race, Class, and Environmental Quality.*

The movement demonstrated its national stature by convening more than a thousand participants in the First National People of Color Leadership Summit in Washington, D.C., in 1991 (a second National Leadership Summit met in 2002) and releasing a 17-point statement, Principles of Environmental Justice. Among other claims, these principles asserted a fundamental right to environmental self-determination for all people. Environmental justice attained federal recognition with the 1992 establishment of the Office of Environmental Justice within the Environmental Protection Agency and with President William Clinton's signing in 1994 of Executive Order 12898 requiring federal agencies to consider the effect of their actions on the environmental conditions of people of color.

The origins of environmental justice in the civil rights movement account for the initial impetus among activists to pursue their aims through litigation. The strategy challenged individual instances of the proposed siting of environmentally noxious activities such as toxic landfills or hazardous waste disposal facilities in low-income communities of color. In most instances, remedies were pursued under Title VI or Title VIII of the Civil Rights Act of 1964 or as violations of equal protection under the Fourteenth Amendment.

The case-by-case litigation strategy, however, faced difficult legal and methodological hurdles and rarely prevailed in court. Cases brought on either statutory or constitutional grounds required plaintiffs to show discriminatory intent, which proved difficult to do when facility proponents defended siting choices on economic or technical grounds. Where the presence of the noxious facility predated the arrival of communities of color, discriminatory intent was rendered moot even as the resulting spatial juxtaposition violated the normative principle of environmental justice. Demonstrating a spatial correlation between environmental harm and communities of color encountered methodological obstacles when opposing expert witnesses produced differing statistical results depending on the geographic units—block groups, census tracts, zip code areas, municipalities, counties—employed in the analysis. Because a strong statistical correlation observed at one geographic scale might disappear when calculated using a different spatial unit, advocates were hard-pressed to prove that an observed relationship was real and not simply a statistical artifact.

The litigation strategy was more successful in cases challenging government administrative procedures rather than statutory or constitutional violations, but these successes were still unable to transcend the inherent limitations of the case-by-case approach. Successful opposition to an undesirable facility might simply relocate the problem to an equally marginalized but less-well-organized community elsewhere, displacing rather than attenuating the environmental injustice. Pursuing environmental justice based on the spatial distribution of environmental burdens took production of those burdens as given without challenging the mechanisms—from private investment decisions to land use controls and environmental regulations—that produced the environmental burdens. And the distributional understanding of environmental justice was unable to resolve the apparent paradox of impoverished communities seeking economic survival by "volunteering" for noxious facilities they would otherwise oppose on grounds of distributive justice, as when a jobs-starved community agreed to a chemical plant in its midst.

Reconceptualizations

Growing awareness of the limited scope for case-by-case solutions, combined with theoretical advancements in the broader social sciences, prompted a reconsideration of the conceptual and theoretical underpinnings of environmental justice. Expanded conceptualizations of justice, rights, environment, and race have redirected the scope and approach of environmental justice from a legal strategy based on individual rights to a social and political movement seeking broad structural change.

Recognition of the limitations inherent in focusing exclusively on the spatial patterns of environmental burdens increasingly directed attention from distributional outcomes to causal processes and from distributive to procedural justice. Within a procedural justice approach, claims asserting a right of communities of color to participate in distributional decisions quickly gave way to more vigorous demands for participation in decisions affecting the production of environmental burdens to be distributed and for pollution reduction rather than mere redistribution.

Procedural justice demands in turn focused attention on the constraining effects on participation of entrenched social and economic inequality, prompting a debate between structuralists calling for the elimination of class, income, and racial disparities as a necessary precondition for equal participation, and proceduralists urging participation, however initially imperfect, as a means for exposing and thus challenging structural inequity. Political theorists pointed to an underlying shift within the environmental justice debate from a Rawlsian liberal framework of individual rights granted by the state to a structural understanding of the social and political construction of nature and the environment.

In practical terms, these reconceptualizations shifted attention from seeking distributional equity in the siting and location of individual noxious facilities to pursuing environmental justice in the large-scale structural processes through which both people and environments are distributed across the geographic landscape. A parallel conceptual expansion broadened the theorization of race in the attainment of environmental justice from a concern with individual racist acts to a focus on institutional and systemic racism pervasive throughout society. In place of the traditional understanding of race as a characteristic of individuals differentiating people into preexisting categories, environmental justice theorists advanced the concept of White privilege as a diffuse social practice that works through racial categories such that privilege—including, in this case, access to privileged environments—is differentially distributed. The shift from individual noxious facilities to the structural production of large-scale environments, from individual rights to social justice, and from the racial categorization of individuals to systemic racist practices all cohere in a conceptualization of environmental justice as a responsibility shared not only by individuals held liable for transgressing principles of equity but by all those who benefit from membership in a political community. Environmental justice, on this account, is a responsibility of all.

Robert W. Lake

See also Environmental Policy; Landscapes of Power; Racialization; Social Production of Space

Further Readings

Bullard, Robert D. 1990. *Dumping in Dixie: Race, Class, and Environmental Quality*. Boulder, CO: Westview Press.

Dukic, Mustafa. 2001. "Justice and the Spatial Imagination." *Environment and Planning-A* 33: 1785–1805.

Kurtz, Hilda E. 2003. "Scale Frames and Counter-Scale Frames: Constructing the Problem of Environmental Injustice." *Political Geography* 22:887–916.

Lake, Robert W. 1996. "Volunteers, NIMBYs, and Environmental Justice: Dilemmas of Democratic Practice." *Antipode* 28:160–74.

Pulido, Laura. 2000. "Rethinking Environmental Racism: White Privilege and Urban Development in Southern California." *Annals of the Association of American Geographers* 90:12–40.

Swyngedouw, Erik and Nikolas C. Heynen. 2003. "Urban Political Ecology, Justice and the Politics of Scale." *Antipode* 35:898–918.

Young, Iris M. 2004. "Responsibility and Global Labor Justice." *The Journal of Political Philosophy* 12:365–88.

ENVIRONMENTAL POLICY

Environmental policy is the framework and means by which public decisions take into account the natural, nonhuman environment. The origins of environmental policy in modern cities can be traced to efforts at comprehensive planning. Early examples include John Claudius Loudon's Breathing Places plan for London in 1829, Frederick Law Olmstead's work on Boston's Emerald Necklace beginning in about 1878, and Daniel Burnham's 1909 Plan for Chicago. Such plans incorporated the felt need for green spaces that would improve the physical beauty of cities, living conditions, and public access to nature. In the early stages of industrialization, cities turned to environmental policy to mitigate air and water pollution from industry and inadequate sanitation infrastructure and thus to prevent damage to human health.

Urban Environmental Policy and Regulation

Increased scientific evidence and public consciousness of the ill effects of industrial toxins on ecosystems and human health in the 1960s drove the development of regulations to monitor toxic waste in North America and Europe. Following this, environmental impact assessment protocols were legislated as part of national, and sometimes state or subnational, development requirements. Today, urban environmental policy packages encompass these historical concerns for green space, air and water pollution abatement, sanitation, and the regulation of toxins in the environment, but they also contain a new suite of policy approaches related to emerging concerns for urban sustainable development. The latter include policies to reduce energy use and greenhouse gas emissions to a per capita "fair earth share" in order to achieve distributional equity and mitigate climate change. As a means to reduce global economic insecurity, sustainable development policies may also encourage farmland preservation and food production for bioregional

resilience and close and localize production loops. Building industry and preservation activities include improving environmental construction practices and protecting ecology and biodiversity.

The starting point for urban environmental policy has been the need for a dependable and high-quality supply of the basic inputs to life like water and air and more effective "waste sinks"— means and mechanisms to externalize waste from urban production and consumption cycles—in order to reduce resource- and technology-driven limits to growth. Thus cities have developed lead paint abatement programs, air pollution reduction strategies, and recycling systems. Over time, environmental policy has become more broad-based and cross-sectoral, addressing environmental dimensions of citywide issues in urban management. Land use and strategic planning, transportation planning, site and building design, waste management, environmental impact assessment, environmental audit procedures, and state-of-the-environment reporting are some of the economic tools and regulatory systems pursued in the name of environmental policy.

Impact of Urbanization on the Environment

Despite the city's long-standing promise of a new, liberated set of human–nature relationships through scale efficiencies, technological modernization, and social, political, and economic innovations, the net impact of cities on the nonhuman environment is still grossly negative. Moreover, these negative impacts and hazards are a reality of urban life for all but the wealthiest citizens and are the result of rational and conscious trade-offs as well as neglect and oversight. The city provides a view to the consequences of environmental degradation that are impossible to ignore and that thus play an important role in shaping and rationalizing environmental policy.

Urbanization can bring about irreversible changes in water patterns and availability and other natural ecosystem functions. Urbanization also increases energy consumption along with expectations for complex humanmade infrastructural standards and systems. The concentration of industrial emissions and increased use of private automobiles severely erodes air quality and other key elements of quality of life. Acute respiratory illness associated with poor air quality and poor housing conditions impact human and economic productivity. These are highly regionalized phenomena that track closely with rapid rates and volume of urban population growth.

Sprawling patterns of urban growth, evident in developed and developing countries alike, have consequences for the potential of cities to be resilient to external environmental shocks and to accommodate continued population growth without sacrificing quality of life. Environmental land use and growth management policies recommend, to varying degrees, high-density urban development as a means to decrease residents' need to travel via private automobile, increase transportation alternatives, reduce energy consumption, improve health, increase sociability and social capital, and create other scale efficiencies.

Responses to Environmental Policy

Individuals and groups in the city are affected differently by, and have different responses to, environmental policies based on socioeconomic status, job category, gender, and race. In particular, environmental policies are often charged with being discriminatory toward the poor, in spite of the persuasive argument of the World Commission on Environment and Development in 1987 that environmental degradation and poverty often coexist. Poverty generates environmental degradation; this increases the vulnerability of the poor. Basic infrastructure is missing from many poor households in cities in the developing world, as these households are confined to slum settlements. Lack of access to clean water and sanitation in slums leads to contamination of water and land and is a cause of many prevalent waterborne illnesses. Slum dwellers also suffer disproportionately from the risk of natural and human disasters. They lack access to green spaces and functioning ecosystems. Living in areas with depleted natural resources and a lack of public services, slum dwellers also suffer disproportionately from environmentally caused illnesses.

International Environmental Policy

Environmental policy has been advocated at the city scale in the international arena since the 1972 UN Conference on the Human Environment was held in Stockholm, Sweden. There, the importance of developing patterns of urbanization that are compatible with the limits of the natural environment was first discussed. The result was a number of recommendations emphasizing the importance of planning and managing human settlements, including cities, with sensitivity to local and global environmental quality.

Twenty years later, the 1992 UN Conference on Environment and Development in Rio de Janeiro, Brazil, expanded upon these recommendations via Local Agenda 21, a document that ties environmental and development policies together with local authorities, along with civil society groups initiating processes for the design of context-dependent policies. Local Agenda 21 also emphasizes the long-term nature of this work and the need for democratic involvement of civil society and local institutions for implementation and follow-through. Local Agenda 21 has been pursued primarily in Europe and Latin America. In North America, city-scale policies and programs for reduction of greenhouse gas emissions and other climate change mitigation and adaptation strategies provide good examples in the spirit of Local Agenda 21, as these interpret 1997 Kyoto Protocol national commitments down to the local scale. Voluntary commitments made under such policy packages include, as a means to greenhouse gas emissions reduction, higher environmental building standards, development of transportation alternatives and alternative fuels, and educational and behavioral challenges for households and institutions.

The Rio Conference also resulted in the popularization of a new organizing concept for environmental and development policy: sustainable development. As applied to cities, sustainable development expands the concerns of environmental policy to explicitly consider the integration of the "three pillars" of environmental, social, and economic priorities in urban development and management. Sustainable city policies attempt such integration with a consideration for intergenerational impacts. The framework of the sustainable city also raises the specter of environmental policies that address not just the human need for natural resources, systems, and services but also the intrinsic needs of nature as it adapts to growing cities. Examples of such policies include ecological restoration, biodiversity recovery strategies, bird migration policies, and stream daylighting policies. This approach to urban environmental policy is seen to have strong potential for the long-term mitigation of environmental hazards that put cities at increasing risk under climate change, perhaps the clearest example of nature's adaptation to urban development worldwide.

The decision to take action against environmental degradation is socially constructed. The point at which waste becomes pollution, risk becomes unacceptable, or consumption goes beyond basic needs is a matter of context-specific interpretation. Even environmental policies that seem to be uncompromising attempts to dematerialize cities or separate cities from their dependence on increasing resource throughput, such as Canberra, Australia's "No Waste by 2010" policy, are implemented through public education about waste, waste valuation, and marketization programs.

Future of Environmental Policy

Urban environmental policy relies on sound science, access to resources, and political dialogue and decisions. The extent and severity of environmental problems in contemporary cities continue to be objects of much debate and conjecture. The holistic and forward-looking stance of sustainable urban development is appealing for its promise of coherence and balance, as demonstrated by "triple bottom line accounting" whereby the economic benefit–cost ratio of a given project must be balanced against both social and environmental benefit–cost ratios. Despite coherence in theory, practices of environmental policymaking in cities derive from a wide range of motivations—recreational, educational, ecological, economic, equity, health, reputation—and these can conflict. For example, providing for the basic needs of all people in the context of resource scarcity implicitly requires decreasing excessive consumption by some people. Also, activities that are environmentally harmful to cities in the aggregate and over the long term often make individuals' lives more convenient and immediately enjoyable. Dissent about the drivers of, and best policy responses to, urban environmental problems may be considered a sign of progress, as more diverse actors become engaged with the issues and challenge existing and proposed policies and positions.

Urban environmental policy has an uneasy relationship with urban governance, as it is usually quite separate from the core functions of urban government and as arguments persist about the utility of "command and control" compared to voluntary approaches to improving environmental performance. Considerable advances in environmental policy have made urban lives tolerable and often rewarding for billions of people through a range of legislative, voluntary, and partnership-based approaches. Most preferred by private sector interests are voluntary associations and agreements, often pursued at the international scale. Two prominent examples are the International Standards Organization's ISO 14,001, which offers an extensive list of environmental performance standards for signatories, and, specific to the construction industry, the Leadership in Energy and Environmental Design points-based accreditation system for green buildings. City governments and nongovernment organizations also engage in international networks for environmental policy research, dialogue, and action, such as the International Council for Local Environmental Initiatives and the UN-HABITAT World Urban Forum, proving that cities are capable and prepared to play active roles in international environmental improvement.

Meg Holden

See also Environmental Policy; Sustainable Development

Further Readings

Bulkeley, Harriet and Michelle Betsill. 2003. *Cities and Climate Change: Urban Sustainability and Global Environmental Governance.* New York: Routledge.

Daly, Herman E. and J. B. Cobb. 1994. *For the Common Good: Redirecting the Economy toward Community, the Environment, and a Sustainable Future.* 2nd ed. Boston: Beacon.

Hardoy, J. E., D. Mitlin, and D. Satterthwaite. 2001. *Environmental Problems in an Urbanizing World.* London: Earthscan.

Meadows, D. H., D. L. Meadows, and J. Randers. 1972. *Limits to Growth.* New York: Universe Books.

Tarr, Joel. 1996. *The Search for the Ultimate Sink.* Akron, OH: University of Akron Press.

World Commission on Environment and Development. 1987. *Our Common Future.* Oxford, UK: Oxford University Press.

ENVIRONMENTAL PSYCHOLOGY

The interdisciplinary field of environmental psychology began in the 1960s in the United States with the founding of the Environmental Design Research Association, the journal *Environment and Behavior,* and the first PhD program in environmental psychology at the City University of New York Graduate Center. Institutionally different but parallel efforts occurred in Europe, Scandinavia, and Asia about the same time. Environmental psychology focused on the important role of the physical environment in shaping human behavior and development. It offered an alternative to accounts based on internal psychological processes and social relations devoid of a physical context. There was also widespread agreement that environmental design, urban planning, and environmental conservation would benefit from a better understanding of people's perceptions, understandings, and behaviors.

Most founders of environmental psychology also believed that a valid account of psychological processes must start from the unit of "person in environment" rather than viewing psychological processes as internal to the person or to some particular region like the brain or function such as cognition. From this perspective, environmental psychology is a new interdisciplinary area of inquiry engaging not only psychology but also the multiple disciplines that account for human behavior and experience in terms of more macroscopic spatial, social, and cultural processes and structures, as well as the physical sciences that contribute to knowledge of the material nature of the environment and of human beings.

Kurt Lewin's field-theoretic orientation in social and developmental psychology, his student Roger Barker's development of ecological psychology, and the pragmatic psychology of William James and John Dewey each offer analytic tools to study "person in environment" units. Environmental psychologists also draw on existing mainstream psychological theories through, for example, applications of behaviorist paradigms to shaping proenvironmental behaviors or cognitive psychological approaches to wayfinding.

Not all of the founders of environmental psychology were themselves psychologists. Urban planner Kevin Lynch's book *Image of the City* in 1960, anthropologist Edward T. Hall's book *The Hidden Dimension* in 1966, architect Christopher Alexander's book *A Pattern Language,* the Chicago School of Urban Sociology and the fields of human ecology, and systems theory, as well as the social upheavals of the times, all strongly contributed to the birth of environmental psychology. These ideas and disciplines remain important for environmental psychology, as does the problem- and action-centered, "real world" orientation that arose from the sense of the urgency of social and environmental problems facing the world.

Major Conceptual and Methodological Contributions

By starting with the question of how individuals engage with the world around them, environmental psychologists formed new concepts that place human experience in a dynamic relationship to the material and social world. In this regard environmental psychology shares many perspectives with geographical, sociological, and anthropological conceptions of how human experience is shaped. However, interest in the individual level of analysis prompted a focus on the experiential, face-to-face, everyday aspects of life rather than starting with more societal or cultural levels of analysis. Environmental psychology studies human experience and behavior at multiple levels of analysis. Environmental psychologists struggle, not always successfully, to avoid environmental determinism as well as the reductionism of all experience and behavior to individual-level processes. The focus on "individual in environment" led to new approaches to understanding human behavior. The concepts that follow constitute some major contributions of the field.

Affordances

James Gibson, a perception psychologist, defined *affordances* as the behavioral potential of the properties of the physical environment relevant to the particular perceptual and behavioral capacities of the organism. For example, a ledge one foot off the ground affords sitting comfortably for a three-year-old but not for a six-foot-tall adult. The concept has been extended to include socially organized capacities for behavior and the social-historical nature of the material environment. For culturally competent members of the United States, a mailbox affords posting a letter. Gibson rejects the idea that there is a little man in the head who must take in information about the environment, represent it or process it, and then act. He places perception in a continuous process of moving, looking, seeking, correcting errors in which learning is not a matter of internalizing contingencies in the environment but rather of increasingly skilled pickup of information that resides in the environment.

Behavior Mapping

Numerous standardized methods have been developed to record human behavior in environments ranging from systematic observation of target individuals across environments through multiple approaches to recording the range of people and activities in a particular environment over time. This method has been useful in assessing the efficacy of interventions to increase variety and frequency of use of environments ranging from urban playgrounds and plazas through dayrooms in big city mental hospitals. In one well-known study, *The Social Life of Small Urban Spaces*, William H. Whyte used time-lapse photography to study how people use the sidewalks, plazas, and parks of New York City.

Behavior Setting Theory

Roger Barker developed the theory of behavior settings through naturalistic observation of children in their daily lives. He concluded that the behavior of one child in different settings varied more than the behavior of different children in the same setting. This led to the theory that there were "quasi-stable" person–environment units organized temporally and spatially (such as classes, bridge clubs, and coffee shops) that regulated the behavior of inhabitants in predictable ways through "programs" that organize the behavior of participants in coordination with the temporal and physical environment. These programs also enforce goals and norms. Alan Wicker, Barker's student, later modified the theory to (1) contextualize behavior in relationships within broader institutional and societal systems; (2) elaborate the role

of specific individuals over the life course of behavior settings, especially during founding of the settings; and (3) use multiple methods. Behavior setting studies often reveal that the settings and programs actually existing within an organization are at odds with the ostensible mission of the organization, as when hospitals organize spaces and operating procedures to facilitate staff coping with the volume of patients in ways that interfere with patient care.

Cognitive Mapping

Cognitive maps are psychological representations of environments that guide way finding and affect the quality of experience in them. Urban planner Kevin Lynch and psychologist Edward Tolman both developed this concept though they viewed it very differently. For Lynch, the "image of the city" was conveyed by the legibility of its paths, edges, districts, nodes, and landmarks. For Tolman, cognitive maps arose in the brain through learning about how desires and needs could be satisfied in different places. Both approaches continue to be employed in efforts to make environments easier to navigate and more satisfying to inhabit. Later researchers differentiated the cognitive maps formed by social groups: people with different levels of visual, auditory, and cognitive capacities and developmental ages. Some study cognitive maps as products of cultural and media representations and socioeconomic and political regulation.

Environmental Meaning and Perception

Environmental psychologists use theories ranging from perception psychology to discourse theory, and Pierre Bourdieu's concept of "habitus" to understand the behavioral, affective, and symbolic meaning of environments for people using a range of methods, including physiological measurement, behavioral and cognitive mapping, interviews, psychoanalytic techniques, visual recording, narratives, and ethnographies. Thus they have described the multiplicity of meanings and perceptions of urban plazas, community gardens, playgrounds, and inner-city neighborhoods that guide use of space, reinforce or challenge group identities, and promote conflict or tolerance among inhabitants located differently in structures of power and resources as well as differently spatially situated in the physical environment.

Environmental Stressors

Environmental stressors have preoccupied the field since its inception. For all organisms, environments can provoke a physiological stress response when the adaptive capacity of the organism is challenged by environmental conditions, for example, extreme heat or cold. Environmental psychologists study human responses to high levels of noise, crowding, heat, cold, and air pollution, as well as more complex stressors such as environmental chaos. Some research includes studies of the physiological concomitants of stress, but much of it examines the effects of exposure to stressors on cognitive performance, affect, motivation, mental health, and environmental evaluation. The presence of many of these stressors in cities, along with conditions that often contribute to human stress (presence of strangers, fast pace, diversity of populations, unpredictability, and poverty), has been an important topic of study for environmental psychologists. In general, all of these conditions are found to increase negative responses after a certain threshold, but the findings are not uniform and are often subject to qualifications about the types of situations in which the effects will be more negative and the populations most at risk for stress. Chronic stress and exposure to multiple stressors are particularly problematic. People who are already depressed or coping with other life problems are often more sensitive to the negative effects of environmental stressors. Efforts to cope with stressors and psychological reactions to stress often increase social withdrawal and interfere with effective parenting.

Gary Evans and his colleagues' successful intervention to decrease stress among urban bus drivers exemplifies the commitment of environmental psychology to taking seriously environmental and not only psychological causality and intervening at both levels. For example, Evans et al., in cooperation with the Stockholm Transit Authority, demonstrated lower blood pressure and heart rate as well as lower perceived stress among bus drivers on routes redesigned to reduce congestion and job hassles that in prior research had been shown to create psychological pressures on drivers associated with not only greater psychological stress and less job satisfaction but also higher incidences of cardiovascular, muscular–skeletal, and gastrointestinal problems.

Participatory Research, Planning, and Design

Among environmental psychologists, the focus on people's goals, needs, and capacities as criteria for good place design has led to the steady growth of interdisciplinary participatory research, planning, and design internationally. Environmental psychologists adopt these approaches out of the practical desire for better environments but also as a political response to power inequities and exclusion from decision making of some groups and individuals and a philosophical position on the nature of truth and knowledge. For example, residents of a squatter settlement in Caracas, Venezuela, demanded participation in a large-scale urban development project to increase access to clean water. Environmental and community psychologists engaged in participatory research with the residents in an organized information-gathering and problem-solving strategy that promoted critical reflection among residents. This process led to clear demands for specific components to the project (such as employment opportunities for residents) and to urban design changes.

Habermas's theories about communicative action; Paulo Freire's ideas about pedagogy, power, and knowledge; the American Pragmatic tradition; discourse theory; critical social theory, in general; and feminist theory, Black social thought, and queer theory all contribute to the rationale for participatory approaches and to particular methodological approaches.

Participatory methods involve researchers in engaging those who will be or are affected by an aspect of the physical environment in defining and analyzing the problems they face and the hopes they have for the environment and then conducting collaborative research, data analysis, and development of action plans to achieve goals as well as working on concrete design or environmental use programs. Participatory methods have been used to design schools, urban parks, multifamily residences, and even sections of cities as ways of creating environments that promote the goals and satisfactions of those who use them and also promote democratic decision making and citizens', residents', or students' active engagement with the physical environment.

Person–Environment Fit

This concept captures the match between the affordances of an environment and people's personalities, goals, and capacities. Many disciplines use the concept to assess the suitability of the social environment to particular personalities. For environmental psychologists, the physical design, layout, other people, and anything that promotes or denies certain possibilities for behavior or experience are on the environmental side of the equation. For example, a crowd at a football game is likely to be congruent with the goal of cheering your team to victory but troublesome if you lose your child. Introverts may be less comfortable in such a setting than extroverts; a lone supporter of the opposing team may be less comfortable than the hometown fans. People who develop an attachment and identification with cities are likely to find it harder to satisfy their desires for aesthetic experiences, activities, and social interactions in nonurban settings.

Place Attachment and Place Identity

The concepts of place attachment and place identity have been used to study the bonds people have with particular places. Place attachment describes the extent to which a person finds it difficult to leave a particular place. This attachment is not always a positive experience and may arise from lack of resources, burdensome obligations, or exclusion from other environments. But more often it describes a positive affective bond to a place in its multiple social and physical aspects. Place identity signifies a deep, in many ways unconscious, relationship to place, for example, comfort on a city street for a native urbanite, or aesthetic appreciation of the flora and fauna associated with particular places. The smoothness of the way a person moves and the sequencing of habitual acts in particular places can be markers of place identity. In both concepts, places can be the repository for memories and evoke particular social identifications. Research has begun to suggest that manifestations of social capital are sometimes tied to place attachment and place identity.

Preoccupancy and Postoccupancy Evaluation

Environmental psychologists attempt to improve person–environment fit by developing tools to understand what makes environments more satisfying and useful. Preoccupancy evaluation combines place-specific needs assessments with many of the activities common to architectural programming, such as determining the number of users in a particular space, the tasks they must accomplish, and the equipment, furnishings, technology, and spatial organization that would facilitate their effective functioning. Postoccupancy evaluations assess the extent to which built environments serve the needs, desires, and required activities of inhabitants. Postoccupancy evaluations also allow designers and researchers to learn about the implications of their design decisions for building users and how design influences psychological and social processes.

Privacy and Territoriality

The human regulation of interaction through the organization of space has been a core area of study. The ability to have privacy has been linked to a greater willingness to engage with others voluntarily and to allow people to regulate their emotions and restore coping and cognitive capacities. For example, both college students in crowded dorm rooms and parents in extremely dense urban housing in India interact less with those they share their space with than people in similar households in less crowded residences. Notions of territoriality from ethology have been expanded to explain the social and cultural functions of human territories, including the role of "defensible" space in discouraging crime and incivilities.

Restorative Environments

Natural or "green" environments have been shown to have positive restorative effects leading to recovery from stress, positive psychological states, and enhanced cognitive capacities. Even views of nature from the windows of hospitals have been related to reduced pain and quicker healing. In public housing, views of nature have been associated with greater attention capacity and more effective life problem solving. "Nearby nature" in the form of gardens, street trees, and urban parks appears to increase environmental satisfaction and residential attachment. Urban green spaces also seem to attract social interaction, children's play, and use for physical activity. Hospitals and other health care settings sometimes incorporate "healing gardens" to calm both patients and health care professionals as well as to improve moods and increase perspective on problems. Despite these encouraging findings, the evidence base in the area of restorative environments is relatively thin and the theoretical explanation of restorative environments leaves many gaps.

Significant Areas of Study

Environmental psychologists have made particular contributions to the study of child development and child-friendly environments and environments for the elderly and those with disabilities. Environmental psychologists help design and evaluate schools, playgrounds, residential facilities for the elderly and disabled, health care facilities, workplaces, and jails. They work with urban designers and planners, as well as landscape designers, to apply their concepts and interventions to neighborhoods and whole cities. For example, environmental psychologists in many countries participate in the Healthy Cities movement.

Research and interventions on environmental sustainability runs a wide gamut from behavior modification interventions to participatory community research and action. Some of the most sophisticated contributions have been around the issue of how the meaning and social organization of places change during disasters and their aftermath, and in the face of toxic hazards. These analyses are used to develop policies and practices that facilitate greater cooperation and trust in programs to manage hazards and recovery and to make these programs more responsive to the experiences of residents.

The interdisciplinary fields of urban studies and environmental psychology overlap in that both study neighborhoods and cities. Environmental psychologists have made important contributions in the area of community development, urban housing, assessments of the quality of the built environment, the relationship between the condition and uses of urban environments and crime, and the meanings of urban environments to residents. Both areas grapple with how spaces are produced, used, and understood. The theoretical debates common to all disciplines concerned with space and society occur in environmental psychology as well. As in urban planning, these debates have implications for practice as well as for research. Important journals that publish articles advancing knowledge in areas of shared interest include *Environment and Behavior* and the *Journal of Environmental Psychology*.

Susan Saegert

See also Simmel, Georg; Urban Design; Urban Psychology

Further Readings

Altman, Irwin and Setha M. Low. 1992. *Place Attachment*. New York: Plenum Press.

Bartlett, Sherrie, Roger Hart, David Satterthwaite, Xemena de la Barra, and Alfredo Missair. 1999. *Cities for Children: Children's Rights, Poverty and Urban Management*. New York: UNICEF, and London: Earthscan.

Bechtel, Robert B. and Arza Churchman. 2002. *Handbook of Environmental Psychology*. New York: Wiley.

Cooper-Marcus, Clare and Marnie Barnes. 1999. *Healing Gardens: Therapeutic Benefits and Design Recommendations*. New York: Wiley.

Evans, Gary W. 2006. "Child Development and the Physical Environment." *Annual Review of Psychology* 57:423–51.

Evans, Gary W., Gunn Johansson, and Leif Rystedt. 1999. "Hassles on the Job: A Study of a Job Intervention with Urban Bus Drivers." *Journal of Organizational Behavior* 20(2):199–209.

Gibson, James J. 1979. *The Ecology of Visual Perception*. Boston: Houghton Mifflin.

Heft, Harry. 2001. *Ecological Psychology in Context: James Gibson, Roger Barker, and the Legacy of William James's Radical Empiricism*. Mahwah, NJ: Erlbaum.

Saegert, Susan and Gary H. Winkel. 1990. "Environmental Psychology." *Annual Review of Psychology* 41:441–77.

Stokols, Daniel and Irwin Altman. 1987. *Handbook of Environmental Psychology*. New York: Wiley.

ETHNIC ENCLAVE

Ethnic enclaves are singular demographic and spatial fixtures that contribute to the multicultural makeup, restructuring, and revitalization of urban metropolitan centers throughout the world. Some, like the Jewish *mellah* of North Africa or the Armenian quarter in Jerusalem, date back to the premedieval era, whereas others, like the Fujianese enclave of Hong Kong, the Slavic neighborhood in Kansas City, the Japanese area in São Paulo, or the Surinamese district in Amsterdam, are of a more recent origin. These *neighborhoods of globalization*, because they are multicultural sites and engaged in various forms of transnational relations, are diasporic communities with an ancestral homeland, were politically incorporated into the new country when the territory they shared with other groups became a nation-state, or both. They are *ethnic or diasporic* because they are the offshoots of a larger group located elsewhere and *enclave* because they are enclosed inside a legally recognized social formation. Some are integrated in the upper echelon of society, like the British in Hong Kong, whereas the majority of ethnic enclaves, like the old Chinatowns or the recent Little Indias, are located in the lower stratum in their city of residence.

Formation of Ethnic Enclaves

Three prominent factors have contributed to the formation of ethnic enclaves. They have come into being either through immigration, the changing legal status of the territory, or the redesigning of territorial boundaries. Ethnic enclaves occupy contiguous space based on linguistic affinity (Spanish Harlem as a barrio), religious tradition (the Jewish Quarter in Paris), or ethnicity (the Italian neighborhood in Montreal). In contrast, other urban enclaves are based on proximity to employment (African Americans in Harlem), same social class status (Russian Hill in San Francisco), same profession (Soho or the artists' quarter in Lower East Manhattan), or same sexual orientation (the Castro district in San Francisco).

The social standing of ethnic enclaves is reflected in their portrayal by the mainstream community, which places them in a hierarchical axis. Some are considered to be a miniature town, a duplicate, or a pole of a continent (Little Africa), of a country (Chinatown, Little Italy), or of the capital city of the homeland (Manilatown, Little Havana). In contrast, the mainstream refers to its site not as a town but as a "new" city ("New" York, "New" Orleans, "New" Jersey) to inscribe in space the superiority of its status vis-à-vis the others. To draw a line and distinguish itself from the non-Anglo Europeans in the United States, it also refers to their ethnic enclaves as "Hill" such as Russian "Hill" in San Francisco.

Jewish quarters, Spanish barrios, Black ghettos, and Chinatowns have been the focus of most of the historical, political, sociological, and geographical studies of ethnic enclaves. Since World War II, because of mass migration, other groups have joined the fray and established their diasporic neighborhoods in North America, the European Union, and elsewhere: the Bangladeshi neighborhood in East London, the Korean neighborhood in Tokyo, the Turkish neighborhood in Berlin, the Caribbean neighborhood in Toronto, and the Brazilian neighborhood in New York.

Interpretations of Ethnic Enclaves

Interpretive approaches to ethnic enclaves see them in binary but complementary terms. On the one hand, they are singled out as "communities," with their own institutions (churches, schools, newspapers, businesses) and their distinct cultural practices that glue the members together; and on the other hand, they are seen as "administrative units" that have their own needs in terms of housing, street electrification, water supply, and employment but are capable of influencing wider election results because of their ability to vote for candidates of their preference. The community approach privileges the culture and ethnicity of the group, whereas the administrative perspective prioritizes the integration factor that needs to be managed in its various facets.

The study of ethnic enclaves has had identifying features such as the reliance on assimilation theory to explain their integration in a given locale (political participation, voting behaviors, and participation in civic organization). The dubious assumption here is that with time they will mingle and mix with the mainstream and will thereby contribute to the harmony of society. Such a vision projects the nation-state and diasporic communities as entities that must be understood inside the territorial space they are enclosed in and tends to ignore the diversity of their political inscription, as different state policies affect ethnic enclaves in different ways. Assimilation was supposed to lead to some kind of a "melting pot" that unites the various components of the nation, Americanizes foreign diasporic cultures, and harmonizes them with the hegemonic practices of the mainstream community. This way of interpreting integration is now challenged by globalization theorists who propose a new way of understanding ethnic enclaves more in tune with daily observations of the behaviors of residents in the digital age.

As a result of previous studies in the assimilation mode, much is known about the role of race in enhancing or undermining social integration of these groups, the impact of poverty on family life, criminality, overcrowding, the strengths of the informal economy and ethnic enterprises, and ethnic institutions such as language schools, media (newspapers, radio, television), and churches. In these studies, residents of these ethnic enclaves are seen as a "reserve army of the unemployed" that provides cheap labor and services, or they are portrayed as a problem that is a source of crime, disease, territorial disorganization, and a welfare clientele.

The newest interpretation of the social and political integration of ethnic enclaves uses globalization theory to redefine the local place not as a self-contained niche but rather as a node in a transnational circuit to which it contributes and that also influences its daily activities. This new approach forces us to relocate the unit inside of a much larger universe and to explain its relations with other units. Early typologies that emphasize ethnicity, religion, profession, and sexual orientation were developed to meet the assumptions of assimilation theory; therefore a new typology that concords with globalization theory is badly needed.

Types of Global Ethnic Enclaves

Ethnic enclaves in this global age can be divided into six types that reflect both their modus vivendi and modus operandi. The global connections that sustain their daily practices are the criteria used to develop this new typology. The *global asylopolis* is a community of refugees that seeks either to gain legal immigrant status in the receiving country or to return to their homeland; it is a community whose status is in limbo and who hopes to resolve the problem one way or another. As a group of asylum seekers consumed by their transition status, they need to be differentiated from other types of immigrants because of the acuteness of the problem of transitory settlement they confront and because of their high level of emotions concerning the country they had just left or were forced to leave. The Somalian neighborhood in Cairo is an example of a global asylopolis.

The *global ethnopolis* characterizes the typical ethnic enclave that relies on ethnicity as the underlying principle of its organization. These are legal immigrant residents who maintain their homeland language and develop institutions to ensure the survival and reproduction of their cultural practices. They maintain ongoing relations with the homeland through occasional visits, e-mail, radio and television programs, and homeland newspapers, and some return to vote on election day or financially contribute to the campaign of candidates. The Congolese neighborhood in Brussels is an example of a global ethnopolis.

The *global panethnopolis* is a neighborhood made up of more than one ethnic group; they may be grouped there because of religion, as in the case of the Christian Quarter in Jerusalem; language and culture, as in the case of the Mission District in San Francisco; or race, as in the case of Harlem, which houses Blacks from the United States, Africa, and the Caribbean. Residents of a panethnopolis occupy the same contiguous space but maintain ongoing transnational relations with their country of birth. The Mission District in San Francisco, with its Mexican Americans, Cuban Americans, Chilean Americans, and Peruvian Americans, is an example of a global panethnopolis.

The *global chronopolis* operates as a community on the basis of a temporality different from that of the mainstream. Whereas the dominant society uses the Gregorian calendar, the chronopolis uses the calendar of its homeland (lunar or lunar–solar) in which the peak day of the week is either Friday (Muslims) or Saturday (Jews) and the New Year day falls on a different date than January first. The rhythm of the community in reference to holidays, festivals, and days of work and rest is in disharmony with mainstream society, and that negatively affects the schooling of their children, their employment availability, and their business practices. The situation is reverse in places like Israel or Saudi Arabia, where the native calendar prevails over the Western calendar. The Jewish quarter of Scheunenviertel in early twentieth-century Berlin-Mitte is an example of a global chronopolis.

The *global technopolis* is a community constituted by high-tech technicians that feed by their labor and expertise the need of a regional high-tech economic sector. They are recruited for this kind of work, and the migration to such a neighborhood is influenced by their skills, labor demand, and family reunification schedules. The Indians of Fremont in Silicon Valley form a global technopolis, whereas elsewhere in the United States, Indian communities can justly be identified as ethnopolises.

Anglo-American neighborhoods are also presented here as ethnic enclaves. They can be called *global Creolopolises* because they are immigrant communities who maintain symbolic relations with their homeland or ancestral region and, in times of crisis, their ethnic consciousness comes to the fore. In daily life, they are unlike the other ethnic communities that more forcefully express their relations with their homeland.

These ethnic enclaves operate on the basis of their participation in a web of transnational relations that daily link them to their homeland and the other diasporic sites in the circuit. They are engaged in transglobal diasporic urban practices that explain the logic of their local interventions. *Transglobal diasporic urbanism* implies that each node is influenced by, and influences, the rest of the global network of sites. For example, products are purchased in a node and sold in another; events in a node may have a ripple effect on the others; and in case of persecution, members of a node may emigrate to resettle in another. This newer form of diasporic urbanism is transglobal and cannot be understood simply by focusing on one single nation-state or one single neighborhood without seeing its connections to other locales in other countries. Therefore the logic of action of a node must be seen within the context of the larger logic of the global network of sites.

Michel S. Laguerre

See also Banlieue; Chinatowns; Divided Cities; Ethnic Entrepreneurship; Ghetto; Global City

Further Readings

Abrahamson, Mark. 1996. *Urban Enclaves: Identity and Place in America.* New York: St. Martin's.

Bell, David and Mark Jayne. 2004. *City of Quarters: Urban Villages in the Contemporary City.* London: Ashgate.

Laguerre, Michel S. 2000. *The Global Ethnopolis: Chinatown, Japantown and Manilatown in American Society.* New York: Macmillan.

———. 2007. "Diasporic Globalization: Reframing the Local/Global Question." *Research in Urban Sociology* 8:15–40.

———. 2007. *Global Neighborhoods: Jewish Quarters in Paris, Berlin and London.* Albany: State University of New York Press.

Logan, John R., Richard Alba, and Wenquan Zhang. 2002. "Immigrant Enclaves and Ethnic Communities in New York and Los Angeles." *American Sociological Review* 67:299–322.

Mumford, Lewis. 1954. "The Neighborhood Unit." *Town Planning Review* 24:256–70.

ETHNIC ENTREPRENEURSHIP

Ethnic entrepreneurship is, by definition, located at the intersection of one sociocultural category, ethnicity, and one socioeconomic category, the status of self-employment. Although a useful concept to examine contemporary and historical urban societies from various perspectives, ethnic entrepreneurship is by no means clear-cut. Self-employment—operating a business as a sole proprietor, a partner, or a consultant—seems fairly straightforward. However, people can be part-time self-employed, or they can run their business without being officially registered. Who has to be labeled as self-employed or entrepreneur then becomes arbitrary. Since the demise of Fordism, nonstandard forms of employment have been increasing, and more people now have a portfolio of economic activities, often including some kind of self-employment. Ethnicity is even more problematic, as it results from the interaction between complex processes of labeling of others, on the one hand, and self-identification by different social groups on the other. The outcomes of such processes, defining borders between insiders and outsiders, are contingent. Ethnic entrepreneurship, then, can be delineated only within a concrete context, and this dependence makes cross-border comparison difficult.

History

Ethnic entrepreneurship is anything but a new phenomenon. In preindustrial times, "ethnic" entrepreneurs already played a pivotal role in long-distance trade networks. As members of relatively tight-knit groups dispersed over a number of important trade cities, they were able to create far-flung networks in a world where contracts and their enforcement were rare or even absent. Notably, Armenian, Jewish, and Chinese diasporas facilitated flows of trade and finance and thus formed the backbone of the emerging "global linkages" in the Mediterranean basin, northwestern Europe, Southeast Asia, and other parts of the world. The extension of the international rule of law has eroded much of the necessity for these ethnic trade networks, but in specific trades (e.g., diamonds) they are still significant.

Ethnic entrepreneurs have also been conspicuous in another way. Mainstream entrepreneurs, tapping into the same pool of knowledge and routines, tend to share a more or less circumscribed outlook on the world. This collective view, inevitably, sheds light on some aspects but obscures or ignores others. Newcomers, Joseph Schumpeter's "new men," may be more sensitive to new opportunities for businesses than are established entrepreneurs. By exploiting these opportunities, they may become drivers of innovation. Ethnicity but also religion and coming from elsewhere can constitute grounds for "otherness." Ethnic entrepreneurs have at times been crucial in introducing new ways of production, new products, and new ways of marketing and distributing. More recent examples of this can notably be found in food (e.g., Turkish entrepreneurs introducing *döner kebab* to the German mainstream) and in music (e.g., the almost continuous stream of innovations in popular music from *ragtime* to *rap* generated by African Americans in the twentieth century), and nowadays also in software development with Chinese and Indian entrepreneurs in the forefront.

Relevancy

Notwithstanding the conceptual ambiguity surrounding it, ethnic entrepreneurship is an important and useful tool to describe and analyze contemporary economic activities. It rose to prominence after the widespread deindustrialization and economic restructuring of the 1980s, when small businesses made a comeback in advanced economic societies. On both sides of the Atlantic, migrant or "ethnic" entrepreneurs seemed especially eager to set up shop. Many of them had become unemployed when factories closed and, as jobs were scarce, opted for self-employment. "Ethnic" businesses then became a familiar element in many urban landscapes, mainly to be found in low-value-added economic activities in markets with low thresholds in terms of educational qualifications (human capital) and start-up costs (financial capital). These businesses were mainly, but not exclusively, to be found in the poorer neighborhoods of cities.

Anthropologists and urban sociologists were among the first to look closer at this phenomenon, and they focused on the issue of how much these businesses differed from their mainstream counterparts. This "ethnic" dimension has been associated on a micro level with resources but also with markets. More recently, the broader context has also been drawn in to explain patterns of ethnic entrepreneurship.

Ethnic Resources

When research on ethnic entrepreneurship took off in the 1980s, first in the United States with Ivan Light and Roger Waldinger as pioneers, this type of self-employment was strongly associated with the lower end of markets in retailing, restaurants, and small-scale manufacturing (sweatshops). Migrants and ethnic minorities were funneled and pushed into these activities as other opportunities were blocked by their lack of human capital, financial capital, access to indigenous networks, and, in cases, by sheer discrimination. They seemed to be able to survive the cut-throat competition in these saturated, low-threshold markets partly by deploying their "ethnic" resources. These ethnic resources were understood to consist of a specific kind of social capital, namely, "ethnic" capital: the resources (e.g., financial capital, knowledge, production inputs) that can be accessed by making use of networks of coethnics. To some extent, other sets of resources (notably financial and human capital) can be substituted by ethnic capital. Even more than "common" social capital, coethnic networks are seen as generators of trust—as was the case in the historic diasporic trade networks. Trust lowers transaction costs as formal contracts can be much shorter and even be done away with, making dealings between coethnics cheaper. This also holds especially true for the production inputs, as lending money and employing workers without the red tape can cut costs significantly. These strategies based on trust, more generally, facilitate informal economic activities that can be crucial for a business to survive in these markets.

Ethnic Markets

Ethnicity may also bestow advantages on businesses in another way. Members of a particular ethnic group typically have the knowledge and the trappings that are necessary to sell products strongly associated with their culture (e.g., foodstuffs, music, books, and magazines) to a clientele of coethnics. These so-called captive markets are usually too small for large firms and constitute attractive niches for ethnic entrepreneurs. A captive market may give a head start to a business, but it also entails the risk of eventually getting trapped in a stagnant market as coethnics may leave or assimilate, or as large firms may enter the scene and adapt to these consumer tastes.

Opportunity Structure

The first studies were focused on single cases of ethnic entrepreneurship. Some of them were liable to suffer from a myopic view tracing all kinds of behavior back to some essentialist interpretation of "ethnicity." In the second wave, more comparative studies were undertaken and the approach that puts the entrepreneur and his or her resources at the center of the ethnic market proved to be insufficient to grasp differences in patterns of ethnic entrepreneurship. Similar ethnic groups showed rather divergent patterns of entrepreneurship in different places. The local and national context had to be brought in, because the kind of business

an immigrant starts and its subsequent role in the immigrant's process of incorporation are not determined just by the resources this aspiring entrepreneur can mobilize but are also decided by time- and place-specific opportunity structures. Not just the supply side but also the other part of the equation, the demand side—or in other words, the set of opportunities that can be discovered and exploited by individual entrepreneurs—have to be taken into account to explain entrepreneurship.

In capitalist societies, opportunities are related to markets for goods and services. The opportunities in these markets have to be, first, legally accessible (e.g., no discriminatory formal rules or informal practices banning certain groups from starting a business in general or in a particular line of business) and, second, they should match the resources of the aspiring ethnic entrepreneurs. If, as in many cases, ethnic entrepreneurs are on average less well endowed in terms of human and financial capital, they are dependent on opportunities with low thresholds with respect to educational qualifications and start-up capital.

On the national level, institutional frameworks generate, along path-dependent ways, different opportunity structures with diverging sets of openings for small businesses. Different welfare regimes can create different economic opportunity structures (types and sizes of economic sectors) by creating or hampering markets. If, for instance, (full-time) female labor participation is relatively low due to institutional obstacles (e.g., as in Italy), the potential openings for new firms in personal services that could substitute household production (e.g., child care, catering, cleaning) are concomitantly small. Opportunities may also be relatively modest if the state is strongly present (e.g., Sweden) and is crowding out chances for small businesses. In the United States, by contrast, outsourcing by households has created a sizeable demand for low-end services (e.g., housecleaning, catering, dog-walking services). Other components of the institutional framework, such as the tax system and the labor relations, may also impinge on the opportunity structure and either foster or impede business start-ups.

On the level of individual cities, the specific trajectory of the local economy (orientation and dynamics) is important in determining the set of opportunities. A city struggling with its legacy of an industrial past dominated by a few large firms will offer a rather different set of opportunities for small businesses compared to a booming, diverse postindustrial city. Ethnic entrepreneurs in New York face a very different opportunity structure compared to those in Detroit, or in London compared to Coventry.

The matching between resources of ethnic entrepreneurs and concrete local institutional opportunity structures is not a mechanistic, predetermined process. Entrepreneurs can be highly reflexive actors seeking and even creating opportunities while changing their set of resources. Nevertheless, opportunity structures imply almost palpable constraints to starting businesses.

The Emergence of a New Ethnic Entrepreneur

Recently, a relatively new phenomenon has surfaced as highly skilled migrants from emerging economies start businesses at the high end of markets in, for instance, software development, advertising, or fashion design. The concept of ethnic entrepreneurship, which once seemed so apt to describe poor and unskilled members of ethnic groups *pushed* toward self-employment, now appears to be less suitable to include these high-flying entrepreneurs as well. These new ethnic entrepreneurs bring with them a different set of resources, and this enables them to target a completely different part of the opportunity structure. Their emergence in many advanced urban economies in different parts of the world seems to have more in common with their preindustrial diasporic counterparts than the archetypal ethnic entrepreneur running a small grocery or café.

Robert C. Kloosterman

See also Chinatowns; Ethnic Enclave; Shopping

Further Readings

Barrett, G. A., T. P. Jones, and D. McEvoy. 2001. "Socio-economic and Policy Dimensions of the Mixed Embeddedness of Ethnic Minority Business in Britain." *Journal of Ethnic and Migration Studies* 27(2):241–58.

Haller, William J. 2004. *Immigrant Entrepreneurship in Comparative Perspective: Rates, Human Capital Profiles, and Implications of Immigrant Self-employment in Advanced Industrialized Societies.* Princeton, NJ: Princeton University, Center for Migration and Development.

Kloosterman, R. and J. Rath. 2003. *Immigrant Entrepreneurs: Venturing Abroad in the Age of Globalization.* Oxford, UK: Berg.

Light, I. and E. Bonacich. 1988. *Immigrant Entrepreneurs: Koreans in Los Angeles 1965–1982.* Berkeley: University of California Press.

Light, I. and C. Rosenstein. 1995. *Race, Ethnicity, and Entrepreneurs in Urban America.* New York: Aldine de Gruyter.

Panayiotopoulos, P. 2006. *Immigrant Enterprise in Europe and the USA.* London: Routledge.

Rath, J. 2001. "Sewing up Seven Cities." Pp. 169–193 in *Unravelling the Rag Trade: Immigrant Entrepreneurship in Seven World Cities,* edited by J. Rath. Oxford, UK: Berg.

Saxenian, A. L. 2006. *The New Argonauts: Regional Advantage in a Global Economy.* Cambridge, MA: Harvard University Press.

Waldinger, R., H. Aldrich, and R. Ward. 1990. "Opportunities, Group Characteristics, and Strategies." Pp. 13–48 in *Ethnic Entrepreneurs,* edited by R. Waldinger, H. Aldrich, and R. Ward. London: Sage.

Zhou, M. 2004. "Revisiting Ethnic Entrepreneurship: Convergencies, Controversies, and Concepts and Advancements." *International Migration Review* 38(3):1040–74.

EXCLUSIONARY ZONING

Exclusionary zoning refers to land use regulations that discriminate against some types of people, especially those with low incomes. Whereas all zoning exists to exclude specified land uses from certain areas, exclusionary zoning separates particular people from certain areas. Exclusionary zoning works to limit the amount and pace of residential development, thereby rendering housing in a local jurisdiction unaffordable for low-income residents (and even municipal workers such as teachers and firefighters). Zoning codes might also place outright bans on apartment complexes or other types of affordable housing. In the United States, where numerous suburban localities have used exclusionary zoning to stabilize community character and curtail demand for government services, excluding lower-income residents segregates racial and ethnic minorities within metropolitan areas. Whether such class and race effects are intentional or merely the logical result of regulations that control the housing supply is debated.

Exclusionary zoning includes requirements and prohibitions regarding residential development. Typical requirements are for minimum lot sizes, house sizes, or set-backs from the street; rigorous landscaping or building code standards; complex development approval processes; and provision of extensive infrastructure and public amenities. Common prohibitions involve moratoria or caps on multifamily housing, mobile homes, accessory apartments, subsidized housing, or group homes; limits on the number of bedrooms or children in a residence; and growth controls applying citywide or to undeveloped land.

Studies of exclusionary zoning report mixed findings regarding its consequences—local situations differ, and the influence of provisions like large-lot zoning may be inseparable from other factors. However, evidence suggests that exclusion fuels certain problems: first, hampering African Americans, Latinas/os, or Asian Americans who seek denser, less costly housing than is available; second, creating a "spatial mismatch" between the low-skilled service-sector jobs located in suburbs (and exurbs) and the workers tied by housing markets to central cities and older suburbs; and, third, contributing to urban sprawl, traffic congestion, and environmental damage linked to low-density development.

Affordable housing and civil rights advocates have challenged exclusionary practices. Courts and legislatures usually defer to the land use choices of local citizens and their representatives, but New Jersey's Supreme Court ruled in landmark 1975 and 1983 cases that the Township of Mount Laurel and other suburbs were illegally zoning out low-income residents. Controversially, the court ordered offending localities to facilitate production of their "fair share" of affordable housing. This "inclusionary zoning" remedy, also used throughout California, depends on developers agreeing to produce low- and moderate-price housing, which is also controversial. Other models of anti-exclusionary policies are Oregon's comprehensive

planning, which encourages land conservation along with affordable housing; "anti-snob zoning" in Massachusetts, which allows developers of affordable housing to appeal denial of development permission; and the Fair Housing Act, which outlaws various types of housing discrimination nationally.

Judith A. Garber

See also Housing Policy; Social Exclusion; Suburbanization

Further Readings

Haar, Charles M. 1996. *Suburbs under Siege: Race, Space, and Audacious Judges.* Princeton, NJ: Princeton University Press.
Pendall, Rolf. 2000. "Local Land Use Regulation and the Chain of Exclusion." *Journal of the American Planning Association* 66:125–42.

EXOPOLIS

Exopolis (from the Greek *exo* "outside" and *polis* "city") is one of many surnames given by the ancient Greeks to the goddess Athena because of the location of a statue in her honor outside the city walls of Athens. In urban studies, Edward Soja has used *exopolis* to refer to the edge city and other developments taking place outside of the city in what used to be called the suburban fringe, but it also refers to what comes after the city (thus *ex* "after" and *polis* "city"). Exopolis is the city without, but also the noncity, the city without a center, "a kaleidoscopic social-spatial structure of geometric fragmentation, increasingly discontinuous, orbiting beyond the old agglomerative nodes." Exopolis is a *simulacrum*—an exact copy of a city that never existed—where image and reality are "spectacularly confused."

Exopolis has had an interesting history in the Soja canon. It has not yet been born in "Los Angeles: Capital of the 21st Century," the programmatic essay introducing the Los Angeles School, in which Soja and Scott describe the new peripheral agglomerations around Los Angeles as "the nodes of the new technopolis." And in *Postmodern Geographies*

Soja describes decentralized urban and suburban growth in the Los Angeles region as peripheral urbanization for the suburbs (producing technopoles in the "outer city") and as peripheralization of the urban core of the city (following the increased internationalization of the regional labor market). Soja first introduces us to exopolis in "Inside Orange County" (published in Michael Sorkin's influential *Variations on a Theme Park,* in which he describes "improbable cities where centrality is nearly ubiquitous and the solid familiarity of the urban melts into the air." The new urban spaces—based upon what elsewhere are described as edge cities—require new methods of observation to "take apart those deceptively embracing similarities and reconstruct a different topography of power mapped out inside exopolis." Yet by the time this article was revised for inclusion in *Thirdspace,* exopolis had become simply another label for "the anonymous implosion of archaic suburbia"—the outer cities, edge cities, technopoles, technoburbs, postsuburbia, and metroplexes of urban disciplines.

In *Thirdspace* Soja is celebrating Baudrillard, and so exopolis has become "infinitely enchanting; at its worst it transforms our cities and our lives into spin-doctored 'scamscapes,' places where the real and the imagined, fact and fiction, become spectacularly confused, impossible to tell apart." Soja argues that exopolis "stretches our imaginations and critical sensibilities in much the same way that it has stretched the tissues of the modern metropolis: beyond the older tolerances, past the point of being able to spring back to its earlier shape" and that we must acquire a new language to capture the multidimensional urbanscape. But exopolis—the city and the noncity, and the city in-between—has been relegated to a minor place in this interrogation, becoming yet another name for standard discussions of inner city and outer city, theme parks and Disneylands, edge cities on the suburban fringe. Indeed, in his essay on Amsterdam, Soja notes that "Greater Amsterdam" corresponds to the Randstad and may be seen as Europe's largest exopolis—or edge city.

Exopolis also refers to those areas in between the city and the suburb, a meaning that bears close resemblance to the interstitial areas of the Chicago School (this appears to be Soja's most original use of the term, and one that should have

a longer life than the exopolis of edge cities and technopolis). While exopolis has been widely used as a catch-all label for suburban growth, this more specific usage has been followed by others, such as Del Castillo and Valenzuela Arce, who articulate the transborder exopolis as the pedestrian spheres and ideological zones of the transborder area shared by San Diego and Tijuana, an area where urban life is indeed in between cultural and economic spheres represented by the two border cities.

Exopolis appears in the recent *manga* (graphic novel) titled *Metro Survive,* created by Yuki Fujisawa. The series follows Mishima, a repairman working in the Exopolis Tower, a new high-rise business and entertainment complex that includes its own subway station and luxury stores on the galleria level. But the Exopolis Tower was built from substandard materials and rushed into service, and it collapses during a massive earthquake, trapping Mishima and others in an elevator. The survivors must make their way to the ruined subway station and escape through the underground tunnels. Ultimately, *Metro Survive* is part of the postdisaster story genre (similar to movies such as *Poseidon Adventure*), and exopolis is a label for a skyscraper rather than a definition of a new architectural form or process of urbanization. While Soja's exopolis invites us to explore the expanding metropolitan spaces of the postmodern landscape, and in the original version challenged us to think of new ways to describe developments in an ever-changing urbanscape transformed by global capital, Mishima's escape from the Exopolis Tower offers a cautionary tale of rapid urbanization in the global city of the twenty-first century.

Ray Hutchison

See also Edge City; Suburbanization; Technopoles

Further Readings

Del Castillo, Adelaida R. and José Manuel Valenzuela Arce. 2004. "The Transborder Exopolis and Transculturation of Chican@ Studies." *Aztlán* 29(1):121–24.

Fujisawa, Yuki. 2008. *Metro Survive.* 2 vols. San Jose, CA: Dr. Master Publications.

Soja, Edward. 1989. "It All Comes Together in Los Angeles." Pp. 190–221 in *Postmodern Geographies: The Reassertion of Space in Critical Social Theory.* New York: Verso.

———. 1992. "Inside Orange County: Scenes from Orange County." Pp. 94–122 in *Variations on a Theme Park: The New American City and the End of Public Space,* edited by M. Sorkin. New York: Noonday Press.

———. 1996. *Thirdspace: Journeys to Los Angeles and Other Real-and-Imagined Places.* Cambridge, UK: Blackwell.

———. 2000. "Exopolis: The Restructuring of Urban Form." Pp. 233–63 in *Postmetropolis: Critical Studies of Cities and Regions.* Oxford, UK: Blackwell.

Soja, Edward and Allen J. Scott. 1986. "Los Angeles: Capital of the 21st Century." *Society and Space* 4:249–54.

F

FACTORIAL ECOLOGY

Factorial ecology uses factor analysis to analyze social aspects of spatial units that are of theoretical importance to urban ecologists. Factor analysis is a statistical technique that assesses a large number of variables to find a few common underlying dimensions (factors). In the 1960s, with new computing technology and the dissemination of computerized census data, urban ecologists found this technique uniquely suited for statistical assessment of intra- and interurban spatial differentiation. Generally, any research of the 1960s through 1980s that applies factor analysis to the study of sociospatial units is termed factorial ecology.

Beginning with F. L. Sweetser in 1965, early factorial ecology tested theoretical propositions about natural areas of the city. A decade earlier, social area analysis hypothesized that the formation of neighborhood social homogeneity, a concept central to ecology in the Chicago School, is created by three unique social dimensions of an area: socioeconomic status, family status, and race/ethnic status. Factor analytic techniques allowed rigorous statistical evaluation of these dimensions with hundreds of indicators. Factorial ecology ultimately provided partial support for this theory. The method quickly expanded to related areas of substantive interest to urban ecologists.

From the late 1960s through the 1980s, factorial ecology research, especially the work of Brian J. L. Berry and collaborators, provided systematic evaluation of sociospatial differentiation and identification of socioeconomic functional differentiation across cities and regions. Notably, Berry and Rees in 1969 used a factorial approach for evidence that contending theories of land use patterns—concentric zone, sector, multinucleation, and ethnic enclave theories—were based on separate factors that exist alongside one another in many cities. This work led to a theoretical synthesis of land use perspectives. Berry in 1972 used a factorial ecology approach to elucidate latent functional dimensions of the U.S. urban system. Comparative urban analysts adapted factorial ecology to create new classificatory schemes for the study of international urbanization.

Criticisms of factorial ecology studies were numerous but generally part of a larger critique of human ecology, aggregate analysis, and quantitative methods, not critiques of factorial ecology per se. Criticisms included the failure of factorial ecology to incorporate individual volition and subjective interpretation into the modeling process as well as lack of attention to the role of capitalism and cultural context.

Since the 1980s, studies that are explicitly labeled factorial ecology have been rare. However, factor analysis continues to be a widely used method in quantitative spatial analysis, and the identification of underlying social dimensions in space remains a central research issue in urban ecology.

Michael D. Irwin

See also Berry, Brian J. L.; Chicago School of Urban Sociology; Human Ecology

Further Readings

Berry, Brian J. L., ed. 1971. "Comparative Factorial Ecology." *Economic Geography* 47(Supplement).

———. 1972. "Latent Structure of the American Urban System." Pp. 1–60 in *City Classification Handbook*, edited by B. J. L. Berry. New York: Wiley.

Berry, Brian J. L. and Philip H. Rees. 1969. "The Factorial Ecology of Calcutta." *American Journal of Sociology* 74(5):445–91.

Sweetser, F. L. 1965. "Factorial Ecology: Helsinki, 1960." *Demography* 2:372–85.

FAIR HOUSING

Fair housing policy is a product of the American civil rights movement. Prior to the 1960s, American laws promoted segregation and discrimination in the housing market. Although the Fourteenth Amendment of the U.S. Constitution granted equal protection of the laws to Anglos and African Americans, segregationists argued that these provisions did not prevent the government from separating the races, hence "separate but equal." In response, civil rights proponents noted that access to resources, such as adequate housing, was not distributed equally, and, in turn, the races were separate but not equal, rendering the laws unconstitutional.

Anglo communities populated good neighborhoods, and minorities inhabited bad neighborhoods. Moreover, with the expansion of Anglo suburbanization and urban decline after World War II, the polarization of housing opportunity grew. Predominately African American and Latino communities were left behind in the urban centers, where the built environment suffered from public and private disinvestment. Consequently, removing discriminatory barriers to minority movement into good neighborhoods became a central objective of fair housing advocacy.

Federal Action

In 1962, President John F. Kennedy issued Executive Order 11063, barring racial discrimination in federally assisted housing. Congress followed in 1964 with the U.S. Civil Rights Code. However, civil rights advocates argued that the central problems of segregation and unequal access to housing remained unaddressed. After extended debate, one week after the assassination of Dr. Martin Luther King, Jr., and one year following the civil riots of 1967, Congress amended the code with Title VIII, known as the Fair Housing Act (FHA) of 1968. The act declared that "it is the policy of the United States to provide, within constitutional limitations, for fair housing throughout the United States." To do so, it prohibited discrimination in the sale or rental of housing based on race, color, country of origin, and religion. The law abolished exclusionary zoning and mandated equal access to housing tenure, mortgage credit, and good neighborhoods through integration.

Twenty years later, the Fair Housing Amendments Act (FHAA) of 1988 expanded the categories of protected groups to include disability and familial status. Problems of enforcement of the act, however, have been endemic. In 1988, various amendments addressed enforcement issues and many other practical limitations of the legislation. New enforcement measures were created to address U.S. Department of Housing and Urban Development (HUD) administrative complaints. As a result, HUD was authorized to initiate discrimination cases; punitive damages and attorneys fees applicable to private lawsuits were liberalized; and Congress authorized the Justice Department to award civil penalties to injured parties. In addition, the amendments created administrative law judges within HUD.

As stipulated by the FHA, and as amended, property owners, real estate and insurance agents, and residents are sanctioned from engaging in practices that exclude protected groups from housing access and/or impose increased costs relative to nonprotected clients. Notwithstanding legislation, however, discrimination continues to be prevalent in U.S. housing markets. Significant practices addressed by fair housing laws include steering, exclusion, harassment, poor service quality, exploitation, and blockbusting.

Steering occurs when real estate agents guide clients to vacancies in neighborhoods where there is a significant population of similar people. If clients are interested in renting or purchasing housing in an area where their race or ethnicity is relatively underrepresented, the agent may discourage pursuit of the property. This practice complicates processes of supply and demand by creating submarkets based on segregation.

Exclusion occurs when information about housing vacancies, financial conditions, prices, rents, or security deposits is either concealed or distorted. *Harassment* involves intimidation or psychological abuse aimed at convincing households to move, while *poor service quality* results when minority clients do not receive the same services enjoyed by nonminority clients. By encouraging White homeowners to panic and sell based on suggestions that minorities are going to move into the area, agents engage in *blockbusting*. Documented cases exist where minority agents have been sent into Anglo-dominated neighborhoods to solicit homes, thereby reinforcing panic.

Mechanisms of Discrimination

Housing discrimination is said to occur for the following reasons. First is agent, broker, and landlord prejudice, which treats individuals poorly because they are from a particular minority group, even if it means losing revenue. Second, customer prejudice leads an agent to steer clients to a neighborhood where people like them live or steer them away from areas where residents discriminate against the client's racial or ethnic group. Third, potential customer prejudice influences landlords and agents not to offer housing to someone who may be seen as unacceptable to existing residents, fearing loss of business as a form of retaliation. Fourth, landlords may exclude people based on statistical discrimination, where their ethnic or racial group identification signals them to be inferior tenants. Fifth, and most important, pure-profit maximizing occurs when a particular group is viewed as having a low elasticity of demand and thus is denied access. A group with a higher elasticity of demand is able to generate higher sales prices, rents, or insurance premiums.

Many states and municipalities have adopted fair housing laws that reinforce provisions of the federal law. Some have expanded the number of protected groups to include marital status, military service, and sexual orientation. Municipalities have also attempted to regulate the activities of real estate agents. Prohibitions include the use of "for sale" signs to promote blockbusting practices and broker solicitation activities that maintain do-not-call lists for potential home sellers. Realty firms might also be required to register with the city government and agree to abide by fair housing policies.

In addition to the FHA, the 1975 Home Mortgage Disclosure Act (HMDA) and the Community Reinvestment Act (CRA) (1977) provide antidiscrimination legislation. They focus on discriminatory practices in mortgage lending. Congress passed the HMDA in response to community organizing against the practice of redlining, the collective disinvestment from select neighborhoods by lending institutions. The legislation requires lenders to disclose the number, amount, and location of mortgages. The CRA requires most lenders to meet the credit needs of their local communities, including financing for low- and moderate-income housing. More specifically, the law requires depository institutions (above a minimum size) to offer credit opportunity to all individuals in the communities from which they take deposits. Section 109 of Title I of the CRA also prohibits discrimination based on race, color, national origin, sex, or religion when implementing infrastructural projects using the federal Community Development Block Grant.

Fair housing laws have been criticized by housing scholars for being limited to the litigation of individual acts of discrimination. The housing problem is thus cast as idiosyncratic wrongdoing by agents and organizations and not systemic and institutionalized racism. Fair housing advocates call for laws that challenge the systematic structural arrangements that reproduce segregation and predominately minority, low-income communities.

Nicole Oretsky

See also Exclusionary Zoning; Ghetto; Housing; Housing Policy; Redlining; Social Housing: Suburbanization

Further Readings

Bratt, Rachel G. et al. 2006. *A Right to Housing: Foundation for a New Social Agenda*. Philadelphia: Temple University Press.

Schwartz, Alex. 2006. *Housing Policy in the United States: An Introduction*. New York: Routledge.

Schwemm, Robert G. 1998. "Fair Housing Amendments Act of 1988." In *Encyclopedia of Housing*, edited by William Van Vliet. Thousand Oaks, CA: Sage.

FAVELA

The term *favela,* or *favella,* designates spontaneous settlements, all types of informal, illegal occupations, invasions, slums, and squatter settlements in Brazil. The Portuguese word *favela* characterizes different urban settlements inhabited by the poor population. They are also called *barriadas* in Peru, *villas miserias* in Argentina, *tugúrius* in San Salvador, *colonias* in México, *vilas de lata* in Portugal, *callampas* in Chile, *geçekondu* in Turkey, *ranchos* in Venezuela, *bidonvilles* in Morocco, *bustee* in India, *cantegriles* in Uruguay, *chabolas* in Spain, in addition to many other local epithets.

Urban slums are self-organized systems that are commonly portrayed as complex and apparently disorganized space built by the poor. This universal trait is recurrent, as are many others. All around the world, slums emerge from similar necessities: to find shelter and to survive amid the lack of resources, scarcity of land, and the external threats. All these settlements present similar spatial morphology because of their dynamic of growth. However, this spatial resemblance could be misleading; slums evolving from different social and cultural backgrounds present great diversity, which could be better understood regarding dwellers' socialization patterns, political organizations, and their beliefs about the future.

The Emergence of Favelas

The name *favella* (an old form of the spelling) was initially given to a hillside settlement in Rio de Janeiro, which, by the end of the nineteenth century was occupied by soldiers who had become homeless after a regional war. Soon after, shacks on other hills were informally built and occupied by a new incoming urban population of freed slaves and workers excluded from rural areas and now seeking opportunities in the city. The inhabitants were named *favelados* and from early on were stigmatized as poor and unskilled people living at the edge of society. They were also depicted as lazy people, scoundrels, and prone to criminal activities.

The twentieth century witnessed the growth of the favelas in the state capitals of Brazil. The first wave of rural–urban migration was mainly caused by drought in the rural areas, land expropriations arising from conflicts, or extensive farming. In cities, the favelas usually occupied unwanted land, such as the steep hills in Rio de Janeiro and the mangrove swamps in Recife. Given the nature of the illegal occupation of urban space, other locations were also favored: river banks, public land alongside railways or near electricity power lines, vacant public lands; later, there was also squatting on privately owned land.

A Local Denomination for a Global Phenomenon

Favelas are an urban phenomenon present in most developing countries and for nearly a century have presented challenges for which solutions have been sought. The United Nations estimates that 837 million people were living in favelas in 2002, and this has been increasing at the rate of 25 million people a year. If this pace of growth is maintained, 1,500 million people will be living in spontaneous settlements by 2020. Most of these numbers are raw estimates because there is great variance in the definition of what a favela is. This definition is the object of much debate because the traits that can be said to comprise the concept are very wide ranging: illegal occupation of land, poor housing conditions, absence of or disputed land tenure, and level of residents' income; the definition also depends on the level of urbanization, the extent of the infrastructure, and the consolidation of the areas. According to other viewpoints, these places can also be called subnormal settlements, informal neighborhoods, or zones of social interest; after some degree of consolidation, they may be considered as popular (i.e., upper working-class) neighborhoods.

The favelas used to be a special feature of the landscape of large cities only in poor regions; but again, this is no longer the case. In countries like Brazil, medium-size towns have been displaying a major increase of population living in favelas. The favelas are growing and spreading into the wealthiest and most industrialized regions under a new mode of occupying the peripheral areas of towns and cities. This new pattern is seen as a result of the country enduring social inequality associated with urban growth and the inefficiency of economic and urban policies aiming at reducing poverty.

Favelas' Spatial and Social Features

Favelas have, in the main, been described as areas that have been illegally and densely occupied with poor-quality housing. They lack infrastructure and urban services, and yet all sorts of poor people with no qualifications find shelter there. Having thrived for nearly a century, today's favelas differ from this original state of being. Nowadays, they are complex places that may well have different physical and social features depending on their location, level of consolidation, and internal organization; consequently, they are also inhabited by people with diverse social and economic profiles.

Favelas are places of both great poverty and opportunity; this marks a change from the time when they were regarded as places of despair or little hope. In any case, favelas are lively and dynamic social environments. The morphology is of dense occupation, narrow alleys and patios entwined with domestic spaces. Windows, doors, steps, and front gardens are always open, thus leading to a highly interactive social pattern. Everywhere, men are talking or playing board games, women are chatting while doing their domestic tasks, and children are running free wherever they like. In this context, spatial proximity plays a fundamental role in the establishment of social ties and reciprocal relationships. Life in favelas is marked by informality: the few rules of behavior are loose; there are few moral judgments and great acceptance of the so-called facts of life. The inhabitants praise their lifestyle and usually say they are satisfied with their residential arrangements.

Despite the presence of strong ties between neighbors, in most cases this is not enough to conform to the definition of a community. Residents may act as a community when the situation demands, but usually they report that the daily struggle to survive in the city means individuals set goals for themselves rather than joining in collective goals. Favela inhabitants report they are discriminated against because of where they live and the conditions under which they live, and they complain about the prejudice that society shows toward poor people, in particular because they are regarded as marginal.

In the favelas, most of the households are headed by women, who generally play an important role in local organizations. Reports from favelas commonly describe brave working women, bringing up children as single-parent mothers and fighting against all odds to sustain the family. Their households expand incrementally and generally consist of members from different age ranges and thus in different life cycles: grandmothers, single mothers, children, nieces and nephews, and other relatives. Joint family income is fundamental to maintain families economically.

Favelas' Cultural Relevance

These poor areas, wherever the location, are places of cultural effervescence. In Rio de Janeiro, the favelas were the cradle of samba, carnival schools, and other important artistic movements. On the hills and mangroves, folkloric manifestations of music and dance that give and symbolize the identity of the country are nurtured and kept alive. From these same environments, new movements spring up and flourish, such as hip hop, funk, and recently an amalgam of rock and folk music from the peripheries that expresses residents' roots, and the fact that while their feet are in the favela, their minds are on the world.

Different Views and Policies Toward Favelas

Favelas were initially seen as the cause of health and aesthetic problems, a case for public concern in view of the precariousness of the environment shaped and characterized by open sewage channels, no running water, and shacks made of wood, tin, and cardboard boxes. From this perspective, the favelas were regarded as dangerous places for general public health, and the authorities feared outbreaks of contagious diseases and were concerned about the risk of fire. With this outlook, the first official notion about favelas considered them as a social scourge that should be removed from cities by any means.

Early last century, cities witnessed the occupation of land by a migrating population and the proliferation of favelas; at the same time, new ideals of urban renovations and innovative projects for their transformation were arising. The example of the renovation of Paris inspired projects for modernization and urban reforms all over the world and aimed to order and civilize the cities and to shape their landscape with modern and progressive features. In this context, the favelas were seen as an evil, a "cancer to be extirpated from the city."

In Brazil, most of the policies at the time sought to remove them from central areas. The first interventions intended to remove the shacks by force and to relocate inhabitants in temporary residential sites until they could be rehoused in the periphery. Most of these earlier experiences failed. First of all, this was because forced removal was usually accompanied by great violence, which had a negative impact on the lives of the residents.

In the middle of last century, abjectly poor housing areas—that is, favelas—were part of the scenery of major cities. The cities grew and spread out beyond their original boundaries. This meant that many favelas stood on land that once had no other use but now became very attractive for expanding commercial activities or even new residential areas.

The state's policies allied to pressures from the property market engendered eviction projects: road works and urban improvement projects invariably passed through the favelas and required expropriations. The high value given to the lands adjacent to favelas put the population under pressure from real estate agents. The market strategies for acquiring land were subtle but efficient and led to a so-called White expulsion.

Favelas as the Outcome of Structural Poverty

The 1970s brought a new way of looking at favelas: The theory of marginality was proposed as a model to explain urban poverty and the persistence of favelas in many cities. The theory considered that poor people's inability to be included in the formal industrial circuit explained who this mass of urban residents were. The favela was no longer seen as a problem in isolation but as the consequence of structural forces leading to social exclusion and consequently poverty. The structural situation of developing countries was also explored by theories on dependency or imperialism and was used to explicate enduring poverty in these contexts.

Sociologists began to look at favelas as phenomena worthy of attention. In Brazil, the American sociologist Anthony Leeds devoted much time to an extensive and in-depth study of favelas. He dedicated himself to understanding the diversity of these spaces by living in the favelas of Rio de Janeiro. The first Brazilianists consolidated a local view that contradicted the theory of marginality and the culture of poverty, which considered the presence of a subculture of the poor as responsible for their neither being suited for, nor able to adapt to, the urban environment.

The Consolidation of Favelas Within the City

Urban policies in the 1970s saw the issue of the favela as one of housing shortage, and a most ambitious program was set up to build large housing estates on the outskirts of cities. The solution was again to remove people from shanty homes in the central areas to apartments and houses on the periphery. The results of this policy were well reported by social researchers, who demonstrated the inadequacy of the solution. When people who mostly lived on income from informal jobs were removed to a place where they had to bear the regular costs of running a home and paying for urban services, they often abandoned the housing projects. The favelados sold their homes to people with formal jobs, who were able to absorb this type of commitment, while they themselves returned to other favelas in the city.

Several types of housing were proposed as housing solutions for the poor. The general model adopted was low-rise apartment buildings. This modern typology was shown to be very unpopular with favela residents. Apartments did not offer flexible solutions for family growth, and this type of condominium living demanded an internal organization that did not exist among the rehoused residents.

Pieces of evidence from other Latin American countries showed the need for new perspectives that considered the inhabitants as assets and had respect for their achievements. A new approach advocated that favelas must remain in the cities and that governments should seek solutions to improve housing and to supply settlements with a basic set of infrastructures.

Architects such as John Turner offered an original framework of analysis. In 1972, Turner, who worked to understand the favelas or barriadas in Peru, criticized the proposed solution of housing estates and, from a point of view that borders on premonition, considered them a major problem. He pointed out that favelas should be regarded as concrete solutions built up by an extremely resourceful population to tackle the lack of adequate housing. In other words, the favela is a solution that itself provides its residents with the means for survival in the city.

Given the great chasm between the increase in the housing deficit and the inability of governments to respond to the expansion in the demand for housing, policies have emerged aimed at increasing the access of very-low-income groups to the full range of basic infrastructure services. The premises of the proposals for sites and services put forward in the 1970s and 1980s had the intention of offering and advertising infrastructure services at low cost. The projects also relied on people's own resources to build and improve their homes. These experiments led to bolstering experiments in self-help housing throughout all of Latin America.

The Urbanization of Favelas

The 1980s saw a major shift in policies toward the favelas; for the first time, the urbanization of these areas was considered a viable policy. The official policies sought therefore to integrate these informal areas within the city, and solutions for urbanization, in general, aimed to transform the favela into something more like the orthodox city. In areas of flat-lying land, the urbanization projects endeavored to lay out straight streets and clearly defined blocks, with public areas separated from privately owned land. In other words, urbanizing was about molding the favela to the formal city. The notion of urbanization also brought the understanding that access to income and services such as education and health, besides sanitation, were fundamental to combat poverty.

Some of the solutions for providing infrastructure in poor areas use new technological proposals deemed as alternatives. Thus began a period of applying alternative technologies to sanitation, cheap drainage systems, and the use of various materials for paving the streets. Solutions for cheaper homes used prefabricated panels, walls of soil or cement, and hybrid building systems. Most were purely technological solutions without fitting into the cultural reality of the various sites and many areas refused alternative technologies as solutions.

The Regularization of Favelas and the Movement for Land Tenure Rights

Urbanization unaccompanied by regularizing land tenure prompted the perverse effect of great pressure from the real estate market, which sought out the lands of the favelas with the best locations in cities. The consolidation of studies on poverty and the already extensive empirical data on favelas made it possible to understand why some previous policies were equivocal or limited.

The residents of favelas demonstrated they were well integrated into city life and able to get jobs in the formal and informal sectors of the economy. They also demonstrated they were important agents in social movements, fighting for land tenure rights and demanding participation in the planning processes of cities.

It became clear that the issue of favelas was also a political issue. Successful solutions stemmed from strengthening the residents not only in economic terms but also politically, through fostering citizenship and encouraging them to fight for their rights to participate in city life. The 1980s saw the emergence of social movements with demands for housing improvement, access to education and health services, income-earning opportunities, and physical safety.

The onset of the new century witnessed a new approach to reducing poverty and new perspectives on dealing with favelas in cities. The first important shift was the recognition of favela residents' rights to be in and remain in their places in the city. The second aspect considered the need to foster community organization to promote a sense of citizenship as a means of achieving social and economic inclusion and access to urban services. Several countries enacted innovative legal instruments and urban laws aimed at consolidating and making improvements to favelas.

The New Generations of Favelas

After a century, the new generation of favelas presents complex and diverse features. There are good examples of favelas having been improved and integrated with cities, as well as cases where poverty has persisted and proved impervious to change. In cities like Rio de Janeiro, some favelas are associated with drug trafficking dominated by warring criminal organizations that establish rules from the gang-dominated hills to the Town Hall asphalt. These favelas threaten the formal city by disputing power with the police and keeping nearby city inhabitants under siege. Other favelas, deemed as neofavelas, are consolidated and organized places with good infrastructure, Internet access, and globalized patterns of consumption, housing a population that can no longer be regarded as poor. The generation of consolidated favelas demands new policies for renovation, while the evolving peripheral favelas are still wanting effective economic, social, and urban policies to deal with their increasing poverty and isolation in the cities, these being more fragmented and less inclusive than ever before.

Circe Maria Gama Monteiro

See also Banlieue; Ghetto; Housing; São Paulo, Brazil; Social Exclusion; Squatter Movements

Further Readings

Davis, Mike. 2006. *Planet of Slums*. London: Verso.

Leeds, Antony. 1969. "The Significant Variables Determining the Character of Squatter Settlements." *America Latina* 12(3):44–86.

Perlman, Janice. 1977. *The Myth of Marginality: Urban Politics and Poverty in Rio de Janeiro*. Berkeley: University of California Press.

Turner, John. 1976. *Housing for the People: Towards Autonomy in Building Environment*. London: Marion Boyars.

UN-Habitat. 2005. *Sounding the Alarm on Forced Evictions*. Nairobi: UN-Habitat.

Valadares, Licia P. 2006. *La Favela d'un siècle à la autre: Mithe d'origine, discours scientific* (The Favela from One Century to Another: Myth of Origin and Scientific Discourse). Paris: Maison de Sciences de L'Homme, ETEditions.

Ward, Peter, ed. 1982. *Self-help Housing: A Critique*. Oxford, UK: Mansell.

FLÂNEUR

During the past two centuries, the figure of the *flâneur* has metamorphosed from a literary type associated with the public places of Paris into a protean cultural myth used to represent the fragmented experiences of modernity. This paradoxical figure came into existence within an increasingly democratized and commercialized cultural marketplace that emerged in Paris during the early nineteenth century. He was both the product and the producer of popular literary texts such as guide books, illustrated essays, *feuilletons,* and cheap pocket-size booklets called *physiologies* that were devoted to the classification of urban types. This entry looks at the character, his impact, and his evolution.

Characteristics

Invariably depicted as a man of leisure, meticulously dressed in black frock coat and top hat and carrying a walking stick or umbrella, the flâneur was both a familiar and yet an ambiguous figure. He was the consummate urban stroller at home on the boulevards and in the shopping arcades, restaurants, and art galleries of the city. As an observer of the everyday occurrences of the city, the flâneur was explicitly contrasted to the busy professional, who was oblivious to the fleeting nuances of modern life. As a recorder of these events, however, the flâneur was implicitly understood to be the modern journalist or popular artist, whose task it was to represent the unprecedented experiences of the modern metropolis.

How can one explain the cultural resonance of this seemingly ordinary figure? How did he transcend his relatively humble origins in popular literature to become an icon of modernist culture? The answer has to be sought in the flâneur's radical sensibility and innovative visual practices, which made him distinct from all other social types of his age. The flâneur's unique achievement was to pioneer a new way of seeing, experiencing, and representing urban modernity that privileged the everyday perspective of the man of the street over the bird's eye view of the rationalist or the moralist. At a time when the city was increasingly perceived as a dangerous labyrinth that escaped the control of elites, the flâneur valorized the dynamic and democratic possibilities of the modern scene. He had no interest in stabilizing the flux of the new environment, and he distinguished himself from political reformers and middle-class philanthropists who attempted to impose control over the city by eliminating poverty, inequality, crime, immorality, and aesthetic squalor. Neither critical nor celebratory of the city, the flâneur was contemplative and reflexive. He resembled a "moving panorama," wrote Walter Benjamin, who mirrored the fluid realities of the urban scene. He aspired to provide a synthetic representation of the contemporary world, without, however, imposing stable moral, ideological, or aesthetic formulae on it.

The flâneur's simultaneous commitment to mobile experience and panoramic vision explains his profound ambiguity as a cultural symbol. Inscribed within his figure was a fundamental duality that was invariably represented by two distinct images: the idle *badaud,* who passively abandoned himself to the crowd and gave in to the seductions of the city; and the discriminating observer, who retained his personal autonomy and was capable of privileged insights into modernity. As a characteristic text of the 1840s by de Lacroix summarized it: "The *badaud* does not think; he perceives objects only externally," while the flâneur is the "most elevated and most eminently useful example of the observer." Oscillating between irreconcilable opposites, the modern flâneur lacked a stable representational formula. Creators of the type occasionally splintered the flâneur into two distinct figures, but just as frequently, they fused them together in unexpected combinations.

Historical Evolution

While there is no single "historical flâneur," it is possible to trace a genealogy of *flânerie* on the basis of the changing historical relationship between badaud and flâneur that was articulated in the course of the nineteenth and twentieth centuries. The flâneur of the early nineteenth century, exemplified by the anonymous pamphlet of 1806, *Le Flâneur au Salon ou M. Bonhomme* (The Flâneur in the Salon, or M. Bonhomme), was a mock-heroic figure in whom the traits of badaud and flâneur were not yet separated. Ironically presented as the potential founder of an illustrious lineage of future flâneurs, he remained a slightly ridiculous figure with no visible source of income or family connections. This early flâneur's participation in the public life of the city was at the expense of useful occupations or tangible accomplishments.

The flâneur's transformation from an ineffectual idler into a keen observer of modern life took place in the 1830s and early 1840s, when the mass circulation newspaper and popular literary genres such as the feuilleton, the physiology, and the serial novel provided new opportunities and a public role for the journalist. This was the golden age of the flâneur, who was, for the first time, sharply distinguished from his inferior half, the badaud. Whereas the badaud was dismissed as a frivolous creature, satisfied with a superficial impression of the city, the true flâneur was presented as an astute observer capable of penetrating the hidden aspects of urban life and exercising control over the seductions of an emerging commodity culture. Lifted to the status of an intellectual aristocrat, the flâneur of the July Monarchy embodied the heroic, utopian aspirations of his age.

During the 1850s, in the wake of failed revolution and Baron Georges-Eugène Haussmann's massive urban renewal projects, the figure of the flâneur underwent yet another transformation. The flâneur of the Second Empire, anticipated by Edgar Allan Poe's famous short story "The Man of the Crowd," merged once again the passive qualities of the badaud with the active attributes of the flâneur and became the prototype of the modernist artist. Baudelaire's pivotal essay of 1859, "The Painter of Modern Life," provided perhaps the best-known definition of this *artiste-flâneur.* Through the exemplary figure of the popular lithographer, Constantin Guys, Baudelaire created a subtle amalgam of the badaud and the flâneur, a man who had the capacity to merge with the crowd but also to separate himself for brief moments when he dashed down the impressions he gathered during the day.

Although Baudelaire's artiste–flâneur lived on into the latter half of the nineteenth century, finding fictional incarnation in such works as Zola's *Le Ventre de Paris* and *L'Oeuvre,* the figure rapidly lost relevance by the early twentieth century. It was reinvented once again in the 1920s and 1930s, primarily through the fragmented but influential writings of the German émigré philosopher, Walter Benjamin. Benjamin reframed Baudelaire's artiste–flâneur through the lenses of Marxism and surrealism and created a powerful new vision of the flâneur that remained paradigmatic for much of the twentieth century.

Although still connected to the modern city, Benjamin's flâneur became the universal symbol of commodity culture as embodied by the modern intellectual who was forced to sell himself in the capitalist market. The commodified flâneur assumed the attributes of the nineteenth-century badaud, who had also been characterized by passivity and self-loss. In Benjamin's tragic reformulation of flânerie, the passive and active sides of the flâneur were once again splintered off from each other, with the commodified flâneur assuming the role of the badaud and the modernist artist that of the creative flâneur.

The acceleration of social and cultural transformations in the late twentieth century has given rise to an even more multifaceted image of the flâneur. Linked to an ever-widening range of phenomena, from the cinema and cyberspace to global tourism and the themed environments of Las Vegas and Disneyland, the postmodern flâneur has sometimes been accused of losing all coherence as a meaningful cultural symbol. According to some critics, this figure bears few traces of the historical flâneur who flourished in the Parisian arcades of the early nineteenth century. A symbol of a commodified and aestheticized culture, he has become "a pure sign, a signifier freed from, bereft of, any special signified," according to Gilloch.

While such observations are undeniable, it is important to stress that the postmodern flâneur's continuity with the past lies precisely in his instability as a cultural image. For the flâneur was, from his inception, characterized by mobility and resistance to stable definitions and essentialized identities. Compared to the reassuring promises of scientific objectivity and political analysis, the flâneur undoubtedly offers only a mobile and contingent image of the social world. Yet, he also provides an invaluable corrective to the objectivist perspective of the traditional social sciences. The flâneur's intimate association with the world of popular culture opens up new possibilities for conceptualizing the shifting constellations of modern experience. More important still, his affirmation of the discursive world of culture legitimates the individual's freedom to create meaning within the destabilized environment of modernity.

Mary Gluck

See also Benjamin, Walter; Cinematic Urbanism; Photography and the City; Paris, France

Further Readings

Baudelaire, Charles. 1965. *The Painter of Modern Life and Other Essays.* Translated and edited by Jonathan Mayne. London: Phaidon.

Benjamin, Walter. 1973. *Charles Baudelaire: A Lyric Poet in the Era of High Capitalism.* Translated by Harry Zohn. London; New York: Verso.

———. 1999. *The Arcades Project.* Cambridge, MA: Harvard University Press.

Buck-Morss, Susan. 1986. "The Flâneur, the Sandwichman, and the Whore: The Politics of Loitering." *New German Critique* 39(Fall):99–140.

Cohen, Margaret. 1995. "Panoramic Literature and the Invention of Everyday Genres." Pp. 227–52 in *Cinema and the Invention of Modern Life,* edited by Leo Charney and Vanessa Schwartz. Berkeley: University of California Press.

De Lacroix, Auguste. 1841. "Le Flâneur." Pp. 66–72 in *Les Français peints par eux-mêmes: Encyclopédie morale du dix-neuvième siècle* (The French Painted Themselves: Moral Encyclopedia of the Nineteenth Century), Vol. 4, edited by Léon Curmer.

Friedberg, Ann. 1993. *Window Shopping: Cinema and the Postmodern.* Berkeley: University of California Press.

Gilloch, Graeme. 1997. "'The Figure That Fascinates': Seductive Strangers in Benjamin and Baudrillard." *Renaissance and Modern Studies,* 40:17–29.

Gluck, Mary. 2003. "The Flâneur and the Aesthetic Appropriation of Urban Culture in Mid-nineteenth-century Paris." *Theory, Culture, and Society* 20(5):53–80.

Hartman, Maren. 2004. *Technologies and Utopias: The Cyberflaneur and the Experience of "Being Online."* Munich: Fischer.

Hollevoet, Christel. 2001. "The Flaneur: Genealogy of a Modernist Icon." PhD dissertation, City University of New York.

Prendergast, Christopher. 1992. *Paris and the Nineteenth Century.* Oxford, UK: Blackwell.

Tester, Keith, ed. 1994. *The Flaneur.* London; New York: Routledge.

FLORENCE, ITALY

Florence is as much a complex cultural phenomenon as a physical place, and it is this culture that the city projects to the world. Founded by the Romans, the city recovered from the collapse of the empire to become a leading commercial and banking center in the Middle Ages and an important cultural center at the dawn of the Renaissance. Following two centuries of relative stagnation, the city emerged temporarily as the capital of Italy in 1865 and underwent substantial urban redevelopment. In the twentieth century and beyond, while confronting industrialization, sprawl, the devastation of World War II, and lately mass tourism, the historic center continues to be an urban model.

History

The Ancient City and the Collapse of the Roman Empire

The city the Romans called Florentia was founded in 59 BC by Julius Caesar on a plain near the banks of the Arno River, at a narrow spot where crossing was easiest (the Etruscans had founded a town much earlier on the hillside to the north on the site of modern day Fiesole). The new town was laid out as a *castrum*: proceeding from a central *umbilicus*, the surveyor (*agrimensor*) established the principal east–west and north–south streets (the *decumanus* and *cardo*, respectively), defined the limits of the town, and laid out the gridded network of streets; the forum was located near the *umbilicus*. Its position near the wider Roman road network (especially the Via Cassia) helped the town to flourish. The leisure components missing from the original foundation—a theater, amphitheater, baths, and so on—were established beyond the original wall circuit in the first and second centuries AD.

Set out on the cardinal axes, Florentia only approximately responded to the course of the river and was removed from it by the equivalent of a few blocks; a wooden bridge extended from the southern end of the cardo to span the Arno toward a small suburb pinched between the riverbanks and the hills rising to the south. This original Roman urban framework—cardo and decumanus, grid, walls, and to a certain extent bridge—is still evident when looking at a map or aerial photograph of the modern city.

Florence, like Rome itself, achieved a degree of stability after the collapse of the western empire and its replacement by the Byzantines, albeit at a much reduced scale—first under the Ostragoths and later

the Lombards. New walls were introduced well inside the original Roman circuit, corresponding to the shrunken population (from 20,000 under the Romans to perhaps as few as 1,000). By AD 500, however, the foundation of the city's two principal churches, San Lorenzo (the first cathedral) and Santa Reparata (the future site of the Duomo), indicates a degree of modest recovery, in part because these structures were located outside the reduced mural circuit. These vulnerable centers of devotion are precursors of later ecclesiastical foundations that would push the city's growth outward from the twelfth through the fourteenth centuries. Near the end of Lombard rule, perhaps during the seventh century, the Baptistery was built facing Santa Reparata; its role as the site of baptism for every Florentine citizen made it an urban focus on par with the Duomo.

Carolingian Recovery and Medieval Consolidation

A late-ninth-century circuit of walls marks the beginning of Florence's growth in the Carolingian era; larger than the Byzantine circuit but still smaller than the Roman enclosure, these walls protected a population of perhaps 5,000. Monastic communities began to settle in the outskirts of the city; the Benedictines founded San Miniato on a hill south of the Arno in 1018; its façade and that of the Baptistery were sheathed in polychrome marble in the next century. Another circuit of walls was built under Countess Matilda in 1078, extending beyond the most ancient walls to the north and south to the river. By this time, the city's population equaled that of the Roman city.

The second to-last circuit of walls was built between 1173 and 1175, enclosing an area almost five times the size of the original Roman enceinte. These walls crossed the Arno to capture the burgeoning district known as the Oltrarno—they also, therefore, protected the oldest bridge across the river, the Ponte Vecchio (originally on the site of the Roman bridge, it was eventually relocated slightly and rebuilt in its final form in 1345). Three new bridges followed in the next century.

The Florence of Dante and the Black Death

The new bridges built beyond the twelfth-century walls, the Ponte alla Carraia (1218–1220), the Ponte Rubaconte (1237, now alle Grazie), and

A view of Florence, as well as the Ponte Vecchio—the oldest of the city's six bridges—seen in the foreground

Source: David Ferrell.

the Ponte Santa Trinità (1258), indicate the growth of the city, the scale of traffic in people and goods, and the increasing importance of the Oltrarno.

The city's last circuit of walls was designed by Arnolfo di Cambio and begun in 1284, enclosing an area 24 times the size of the Roman castrum; they protected not only the urban fabric—the old gridded core and the streets extending from it in all directions to the regional road network— but also large areas of semirural land. The mendicant orders (Franciscans, Dominicans, Servites, Carmelites) settled during the middle of the 1200s in the loosely organized zone outside the twelfth-century circuit of walls. The Dominicans and Franciscans in particular—at their centers of Santa Maria Novella on the west and Santa Croce on the east sides of town, respectively—also offered large piazzas that served the crowds who came to hear popular itinerant preachers.

Their ambitious building enterprises attracted artisans and tradespeople to their neighborhoods, while their theological schools (*studium generale*) made them internationally known centers of scholarship. The monastic complexes, not responsible to the local bishop but instead to their own order's hierarchy and ultimately to Rome, were physically and politically independent of their urban context; they had extensive land with gardens and livestock, making them effectively self-sufficient.

Numerous hospitals were also scattered throughout the zone between the twelfth- and early-fourteenth-century circuits of walls. These served pilgrims, the rural poor who filtered into the city looking for work, and the urban poor; essentially caretaking hospices, they mediated the effects of the population growth of the burgeoning late medieval city. Like the monastic complexes, they could be large and self-sufficient; estimates are that they provided roughly one bed per hundred citizens. They would be stretched to capacity and beyond by the plague, the Black Death, which struck in 1348 and reduced the population by nearly 40 percent.

The Palazzo del Podestà (now Bargello), begun in 1255, was the first permanent home of the communal government; it was soon replaced by the Palazzo del Popolo (begun 1299; now Palazzo Vecchio) on the site of the old Roman theater. Wrapped by the Piazza della Signoria, it occupied a hinge point between the edge of the Roman grid and the network of streets oriented toward the river. Its large bell tower established the civic pole of authority on the skyline, counterbalanced by the cathedral and its campanile: Santa Maria del Fiore was begun in 1296; designed by Arnolfo di Cambio to hold 30,000 worshippers (the city's population was then about 100,000), it dwarfed rival Siena's cathedral. The freestanding campanile was designed by Giotto in 1334. The encircling Piazza del Duomo, loosely following the shape of the cathedral and baptistery, was created by progressive clearing of the surrounding urban fabric.

Early humanists of the late fourteenth and early fifteenth centuries believed they had found evidence of Florence's Roman past in buildings like the Baptistery (thought to have been a temple of Mars); the architectural and urban Renaissance in Florence was just as likely to be influenced by local Roman-looking Romanesque buildings as the actual remains of antiquity in Rome. Florentine humanists were active in civic affairs, and the city's chancellors, such as Leonardo Bruni, were often eminent scholars (Bruni was the author of a comprehensive history of the city): They both defined Florence to the world and helped shape it.

The Medici and Florence

In this century of the Medici's rise to power, the conservative pretenses of ostensibly republican rule precluded drastic urban planning interventions; it is, rather, the building of massive, prismatic private palaces like the Palazzos Strozzi and Medici that impacted their local fabric (in the former case by creating an adjacent piazza, in the latter by encouraging development around the Via Larga and toward the north). Brunelleschi's cathedral dome (begun in 1420), an engineering achievement on par with antiquity, continues to define the city's skyline; it is an orientation point both within the urban fabric and from the landscape beyond. His plans for the Foundling Hospital (the *Ospedale degli Innocenti*, on Piazza Santissima Annunziata) created the first regular piazza-defining building of the century (imitated later in Venice at the Procuratie Vecchie and at the Piazza Ducale in Vigevano by Bramante) under the patronage of Florence's renowned charitable guilds. Lorenzo (Il Magnifico) de Medici's de facto reign did not impact the city fabric in any substantial way. His

death coincided with Savonarola's ascent; but with the burning of Savonarola at the stake in the Piazza della Signoria in 1498, a complex century ended and an even more tumultuous one began.

If the first decades of the sixteenth century were tumultuous, the century ended with several decades of pomp, stability, and relative prosperity under the Medici dukes. This is the century of the Medici: No less than three popes (the first, Leo X, a boon to the city; the second, Clement VII, a disaster in the balance; and the final, Leo XI, largely irrelevant in part due to a brief reign), the establishment in midcentury of ducal rule under Cosimo I (made duke in 1537 and grand duke in 1569) over most of what is now Tuscany, the Tuscan language ubiquitous in Italy as the language of humanism in part thanks to Medici sponsorship, building and art patronage on a grand scale sponsored by popes and dukes. The Medici returned to definitive control of the city after a long siege (whose resistance Michelangelo had aided) in 1530. During the brief reign of the ruthless Alessandro de' Medici (1530–1537), his principal urban intervention was the Fortezza da Basso, a modern bastion meant as much to protect the city toward the west as subdue it.

Cosimo I's interventions herald a change from the last vestiges of republicanism to totalitarian rule with its attendant bureaucracy (the Uffizi complex); they also introduce the definitive symbols of private power (the Corridoio Vasariano, the Pitti palace and gardens, the Fortezza Belvedere). By moving his place of residence from the Palazzo Vecchio (from whence it was known as "old") to the suburban Pitti Palace across the river, he symbolically initiated an autocratic process that would culminate in the next century with Louis XIV's transference of the center of power from the Louvre to Versailles. Linking the old palace with the new by a raised, completely internal corridor designed by his court artist Giorgio Vasari, Cosimo articulated the transformation of the city and its civic focus.

Seventeenth and Eighteenth Centuries

While some significant buildings were built during this period, little substantial changed in the urban fabric (indeed, the map of Florence would look much the same until 1860). New or remodeled churches like San Gaetano and San Frediano, religious complexes like the Oratorian's San Firenze and the house of the Canons Regular of San Jacopo, and palaces like Palazzo Capponi and the vast Palazzo Corsini along the Arno enlivened the skyline and the streetscape, but they didn't make of Florence a Baroque city as the building boom of the same period did in Rome.

Firenze Capitale: The Nineteenth Century

The nineteenth century began as a period of dormancy that transformed by mid-century—with Florence's brief role as capital for the new nation of Italy—into decades of major building and rebuilding. Giuseppe Poggi's plans for the city (after the capital moved there briefly from Turin in 1865) both facilitated growth into the periphery and transformed the historic center. In the first case, Poggi proposed taking down the outmoded mural circuit and replacing it with wide boulevards. These *viale* facilitated transportation around the historic center, and the destruction of the walls allowed expansion of the urban fabric into undeveloped outlying areas. The viale were continued across the Arno to form a necklace of picturesque boulevards.

Today, only a small stretch of wall in the Oltrarno remains. The urban fabric filled out Arnolfo di Cambio's mural circuit, and beyond; this outlying residential development is characterized by a knowledgeable respect for Florence's Renaissance architecture. In the center, Poggi made a drastic proposal to demolish the market district centered on the site of the old Roman forum; Vasari's fish market loggia was relocated to another part of town, while whole blocks (much of it the Jewish ghetto) were replaced by large *palazzos* for commercial (hotels and cafes) and civic (post office) uses, defining the present Piazza della Repubblica. The scale of the demolitions mobilized the substantial British expatriate community to work for the preservation of medieval buildings and artifacts elsewhere in the city.

Futurism and Fascism

Belated futurism and growing fascism collaborated in Florence between the two world wars to build the infrastructure of the modern city: The train station and its support buildings, factories, a sports stadium, and an Air Warfare School marked a building boom of the 1930s. Deliberately contrasting with the historic city fabric, these modern buildings define a relatively brief period in which discontinuity with the past was the norm in central Florence. Rapid expansion along the Arno (mostly to the west) of industry and working-class neighborhoods changed forever the historic relationship of city and countryside; only to the south—San Miniato and the old mural circuit—and the north—toward Fiesole—were vestiges of monastic holdings and villas retained. Real estate development on a large scale also characterizes this era, when the bones of Poggi's plan were more densely fleshed out and extended. The scope of the growth east and west established the geographic extent of the city even after the war.

Postwar Florence: Rebuilding and Conservation

Florence suffered from both Allied bombing and the German retreat in the waning months of World War II in Italy. Most notably, the German commander was ordered to blow up the city's six bridges, of which five were demolished while the sixth, the Ponte Vecchio, was saved by demolishing buildings at either end to block it. In the aftermath of the war debate centered on the nature of reconstruction: replicating what had been destroyed or building new. A compromise resulted: The buildings bracketing the Ponte Vecchio were rebuilt in a modern character with traditional materials, whereas the bridges were mostly rebuilt in their original form with modern reinforced concrete structures. Preservation, important in Florence since the later nineteenth century, fostered a half-century of "repristination" of the historic fabric (accelerated by the devastating flood of 1966) that is still ongoing.

Postwar public housing has been as problematic here as elsewhere in Italy, but efforts to redress it (e.g., Léon Krier's plan for Novoli) continue, if only on paper. Pressures of the mass tourism industry have taken their toll on the demographics of the historic center, now largely absent full-time Florentine residents. Unlikely to experience future population growth as it did in the century after the unification of Italy, the city's challenges today have more to do with managing its resources and fixing past mistakes.

David Mayernik

See also Allegory of Good Government; Medieval Town Design; Renaissance City; Rome, Italy; Venice, Italy

Further Readings

Dameron, George W. 2004. *Florence and Its Church in the Age of Dante*. State College: University of Pennsylvania Press.

Fei, Silvano, Grazia Gobbi Sica, and Paolo Sica. 1995. *Firenze: Profilo di Storia Urbana*. Firenze: Alinea Editrice.

Girouard, Mark. 1985. *Cities and People: A Social and Architectural History*. New Haven, CT: Yale University Press.

Goy, Richard. 2002. *Florence: The City and Its Architecture*. London: Phaidon.

Mayernik, David. 2003. *Timeless Cities: An Architect's Reflections on Renaissance Italy*. Boulder, CO: Westview Press.

Norman, Diana. 1995. *Siena, Florence, and Padua: Art, Society, and Religious Life 1280–1400*. Vol. 1, *Interpretative Essays*. New Haven, CT: Yale University Press.

Turner, Richard N. 1997. *Renaissance Florence: The Invention of a New Art*. New York: Prentice Hall.

Wirtz, Rolfe C. 2000. *Florence: Art and Architecture*. Cologne, Germany: Konemann.

FORUM

In a Roman city, the forum was a large, rectangular, centrally located, open space, usually surrounded by monumental public structures. These buildings typically included many of the principal political, religious, and commercial centers of the city. The forum was often the site of local markets, although as towns grew, this function was sometimes transferred to secondary fora, as at Rome. The forum was also the setting for a variety of spectacular urban rituals, such as aristocratic funerals, court trials, religious ceremonies, public assemblies, and popular entertainments. Due to the concentration of these essential structures and functions in and around the forum, to the Romans, this space was imbued with potent symbolic meaning as the core of the city and the repository of its most Roman qualities.

The main forum at Rome (the Forum Romanum), which subsequently became the model for all later fora in other Roman cities, was originally a seasonally swampy depression located at the foot of the Capitoline and Palatine Hills and close to a key ford of the Tiber River. Despite its marshy nature, this space was a natural crossroads, and the first major construction project in the history of the city of Rome was the digging of a drainage ditch from the Forum to the Tiber, accompanied by the dumping of many thousands of cubic meters of fill in the Forum to raise the ground level and render the area dry and habitable year-round. These transformations, which were accomplished by the kings of Rome during the seventh and sixth centuries BC, paved the way for the rapid development of the Forum in the centuries that followed.

By the middle of the Roman Republic (509–31 BC), the key structures that would define the space of the Forum were in place. Among these were the Temple of Vesta (where the sacred flame of the city was kept), the Curia (the usual meeting place of the Roman senate), the rostra (speakers' platform), and the temples of Castor, Saturn, and Concord. The Forum at this point was a rectangular open space roughly 150 meters long and 75 meters wide, with its long axis stretching out in a southeasterly direction from the slopes of the Capitoline Hill. The two long sides of the Forum were originally lined by shops and businesses, especially those involving financial transactions, but these were displaced over time by two enormous multistory colonnades, the Basilica Aemilia along the north side and the Basilica Julia along the south.

The open space of the Forum was the setting for many of the most dramatic public events of Roman history, including Cicero's fiery orations and Mark Antony's funeral speech for Julius Caesar, which ended in violent rioting and the impromptu cremation of Caesar's body in the Forum itself. Prior to the construction of the Flavian Amphitheater (Colosseum) in the first century AD, many public entertainments such as wild beast hunts and gladiator games were held in the Forum.

During the empire (31 BC–AD 476), the Forum became progressively more crowded with shrines, statues, and other monuments. The emperors also constructed a series of new, huge, lavishly decorated imperial fora to the north of the old Forum, which assumed many of the day-to-day juridical and political functions of the original Forum. Even as its official roles declined, however, throughout the Roman period, the Forum Romanum retained its symbolic identity as the heart of both the city and the empire. It was imitated in all other Roman towns, so that throughout the empire, the urban life of all Roman cities focused around a central forum and its attendant monumental buildings.

Gregory S. Aldrete

See also *Agora;* Piazza; Public Realm; Rome, Italy

Further Readings

Aldrete, Gregory. 2004. *Daily Life in the Roman City: Rome, Pompeii, and Ostia.* Westport, CT: Greenwood.

Coarelli, F. 1983 and 1985. *Il Foro Romano,* 2 vols. Rome: Quasar.

Favro, Diane. 1988. "The Roman Forum and Roman Memory." *Places* 5(1):17–23.

Frischer, Bernard. 2004. "The Digital Roman Forum Project of the Cultural Virtual Reality Laboratory: Remediating the Traditions of Roman Topography." Berkeley: University of California, Los Angeles, CulturaVirtual Reality Laboratory. Retrieved May 15, 2009 (http://www.cvrlab.org/research/images/ FrischerWorkshopPaperIllustratedWeb.htm).

Machado, Carlos. 2006. "Building the Past: Monuments and Memory in the Roman Forum." Pp. 157–92 in *Social and Political Life in Late Antiquity,* edited by W. Bowden, C. Macaho, and A. Gutteridge. Leiden, the Netherlands: Brill.

Steinby, E., ed. 1995. "Forum Romanum." In *Lexicon Topographicum Urbis Romae,* Vol. 2. Rome: Quasar.

Thomas, Edmund. 2007. *Monumentality and the Roman Empire: Architecture in the Antonine Age.* Oxford, UK: Oxford University Press.

FOURTH WORLD

Fourth world refers to those persons, groups, and places left behind in the process of globalization and resulting changes in urban and regional systems—including urban and nonurban spaces in both developed countries and the developing world. The term has an interesting history, emerging from an earlier discourse that highlighted the social exclusion of indigenous and minority populations, then highlighting increased poverty and social exclusion in third world nations, and now finding its place within urban studies with new and significant meanings.

The generic label *fourth world* begins in the development literature that described different regions of the world according to the geopolitics of the postwar twentieth century: The first world included Europe and the United States, and the second world included the Soviet Union and satellite countries in Eastern Europe. The Third World included all other countries, a diverse collection of countries with high levels of industrial development as well as less developed economies, including nations in Africa, South America, and Asia that are commonly thought of as the developing world. Immanuel Wallerstein's world systems theory placed countries within a three-tier system of core, semiperiphery, and periphery based on their level of incorporation within the global capitalist economy; nations might move upward or downward within this system as resources and obstacles within the world capitalist system change.

While fourth world refers to concepts from and thereby fits within the general development literature, it has substantially different meanings. In North America, the fourth world emerged from the growing Native American activism over environmental issues and the development of American Indian Studies programs in North America. George Manuel and Michael Poslum's *The Fourth World: An Indian Reality* argued that the fourth world contains "many different cultures and lifeways, some highly tribal and traditional, some highly urban and individual" and included aboriginal populations across the globe, including Native Americans as well as aboriginal groups in Australia and New Zealand and the Sami in Scandinavia. The Dene Declaration, signed by some 300 delegates to the Indian Brotherhood at Fort Simpson (Northwest Territories) in 1975, stated, "We the Dene are part of the Fourth World. And as the peoples and nations of the world have come to recognize the existence and rights of those peoples who make up the Third World the day must come and will come when the nations of the Fourth World will come to be recognized and respected." A contemporaneous United Nations study of fourth-world populations highlighted the social exclusion of included ethnic and religious minorities around the globe, including aborigines in Australia, ethnic minorities in Africa, and religious minorities in the Soviet Union. Within this framework, in other words, the people of the fourth world may share common status of social exclusion and denial of basic rights due to their condition of statelessness. The 2007 Declaration on the Rights of Indigenous Peoples recognized the struggle of indigenous peoples and has led to increased communications and organizing among fourth-world peoples as well as international treaties between aboriginal nations for the purposes of trade, travel, and security. The Center for World Indigenous Studies, founded in Canada in 1984, gives voice to the shared concerns of these stateless and marginalized nations across the globe through the *Fourth World Journal*, which includes articles on globalization, land rights, climate change, and other issues.

Manuel Castells has offered important revisions to Wallerstein's schema of a stable core, semiperiphery, and peripheral countries. The information revolution has lessened the importance of manufacturing and trade on which the world system was based for much of the twentieth century, replacing it with wealth accumulation based on networks and flows of information. Within this new international division of labor, there is an emerging fourth world that Castells describes as "the poorest of the poor," where increasing inequality and social exclusion has produced conditions of life characterized by polarization, poverty, and misery throughout the world. In the new network society, areas that are nonvaluable from the narrow perspective of informational capitalism are systematically excluded from opportunities that would allow them to engage with the emerging informational economy; they do not have access to or control of significant economic or political interests. The exclusion of both people and territory from participation in the network society means that entire countries, regions, cities, and neighborhoods are left behind, denied the social rights of citizens for participation in the major economic, occupational, and social opportunities that might enable them to pursue an acceptable standard of living within their society. People living in these areas are relegated to the fourth world, a position below that of citizens in the (former) third world countries.

The use of labels such as third world has faded from academic discourse with the end of the Cold War, the cascading effects of globalization, and actual changes within the global economy, as many developing nations (such as the Asian Tigers) have achieved ever greater levels of urbanization and industrial production. Globalization has also produced important changes affecting the fortunes of urban places, where cities that occupied important positions within an earlier colonial world system have become less central to the global economy, and other metropolitan regions have emerged as new and important sites of economic development and political control. World systems theory is better able to capture these changes, as countries move from the semiperiphery to the core, and as urban regions move from the periphery to the semiperiphery within developing nations.

The new vision of the fourth world that emerges from these earlier traditions emphasizes the impact of global capitalism and informational technologies on individuals, groups, urban areas, regions, and countries within the world system of the twenty-first century. One's position relative to the world system, and thus one's opportunity to participate fully as a citizen of that system, no longer depends on residence within a specific nation-state but instead is defined by the position that the region and urban area occupy within the world system. Cities that occupied important positions within an earlier colonial world system, such as Manila, capital of the Spanish colonial system in Asia and later the hub of U.S. activities in the region, have become less central to the world economy and less important in global politics; with a poverty rate of more than 50 percent and nearly half of the population of the capital city living in slums, many people now find themselves in the fourth world. The old mechanisms of social integration have lost their currency and exhausted their effectiveness, and a new urban underclass has emerged with no hope for homeownership or formal employment, a new dangerous class. The increased commodification of land and housing within cities in the developing world results in increased polarization and an environment where immigrants are unlikely to be incorporated into the formal sector.

But globalization produces the fourth world within developed nations as well, whether this be the extensive *banlieues* of the French city, the inner-city ghettos of the American city, or, with the collapse of the global manufacturing economy, entire cities that evolved within the Fordist mode of production that resulted in the concentration of automobile manufacturing in the urban regions around the Great Lakes of the United States.

Indeed, many of the industrialized nations of the former periphery and semiperiphery countries have seen a decline of rural and small-town populations, leaving behind a fourth world in the urban fringe that is similar to the fourth world of the inner city: All of these areas share a common fate because they have become structurally irrelevant to global capital accumulation.

Some have cautioned against the assumption that economic restructuring within the less developed countries produces a fourth world that is excluded from the global capitalist system. While these countries may be characterized by economic stagnation, increasing marginality, and potential for social upheaval, such a model does not recognize the important ways that these countries remain integrated within the global system. Gavin Shatkin suggests that these countries are linked by the diffusion of new technologies, regional economic change, and changes in the flow of information and people. Indeed, in many of the less developed countries, we see an urban region that is linked to the world system through information networks, financial investment, population flows, and the like. It is the asymmetric nature of these flows that reminds us of the former colonial world system (flows of labor from the Philippines to developed nations, flows of capital from developmental agencies to Phnom Penh, and the like) and results in the expansion of the fourth world to what Mike Davis has called a world of slums. Often these people are linked by cell phone technologies and the World Wide Web to others around the globe, complicating our models of a new informational society just as the fourth world (places left behind in the new global economy) becomes more noticeable in metropolitan regions around the world.

Ray Hutchison

See also Castells, Manuel; Globalization; Urban Theory; World-Systems Perspective

Further Readings

Castells, Manuel. 1998. *The Information Age: Economy, Society, and Culture.* Vol. 3, *End of the Millenium.* Oxford, UK: Blackwell.

———. 2000. "The Rise of the Fourth World." Pp. 348–54 in *The Global Transformations Reader: An Introduction to the Globalization Debate,* edited by David Held and Anthony McGraw. Cambridge, UK: Polity Press.

Davis, Mike. 2007. *Planet of Slums.* London: Verso.

Hall, Sam. 1975. *The Fourth World: The Heritage of the Arctic and its Destruction.* New York: Alfred A. Knopf.

Keyder, Cagler. 2005. "Globalization and Social Exclusion in Istanbul." *International Journal of Urban and Regional Research* 29(1):124–34.

Manuel, George and Michael Posluns. 1974. *The Fourth World: An Indian Reality.* Don Mills, ON: Collier-Macmillan Canada.

Neuwirth, Robert. 2006. *Shadow Cities: A Billion Squatters, a New Urban World.* New York: Routledge.

Shatkin, Gavin. 1998. "'Fourth World' Cities in the Global Economy: The Case of Phnom Penh, Cambodia." *International Journal of Urban and Regional Research* 22(3):378–93.

Whitaker, Ben, ed. 1973. *The Fourth World: Victims of Group Oppression.* New York: Schocken Books.

FUJITA, MASAHISA

Born in Yamaguchi prefecture (Japan) in 1943, Masahisa Fujita completed a BS in civil engineering at Kyoto University in 1966. Soon after, he went to the Department of Regional Science of the University of Pennsylvania, where he graduated with his PhD in 1972. He then became a professor of regional science there. After two decades, he joined the faculty of the Institute of Economic Research of Kyoto University, where he remained until 2006. Fujita is the recipient of the 1983 Tord Palander Prize, the 1998 Walter Isard Award in Regional Science, and the First Alonso Prize awarded with Paul Krugman.

Out of more than 100 scientific books and articles, some major contributions emerge. The core of urban economics is the monocentric city model of which Fujita's urban economic theory provides the definitive exposition. The main weakness of this model was the lack of explanation for the existence of a central business district. Fujita argued that cities are concentrations of agents of different types (mainly, firms and households). The centripetal force is communications among firms, which permit the exchange of information:

Other things being equal, each firm has an incentive to establish itself close to the others, thus fostering the agglomeration of firms. The centrifugal force is less straightforward and involves land and labor markets. The clustering of many firms in a single area increases the average commuting distance for workers, which in turn increases the wage rate and land rent in the area surrounding the cluster. Such high wages and land rents discourage further agglomeration of firms in the same area. The equilibrium distributions of firms and households are thus a balance between these opposite forces. In two seminal papers published in the early 1980s, Fujita identified the conditions to be imposed on communication fields and commuting costs for a monocentric, polycentric, or integrated urban pattern to emerge as the market outcome.

The dominant view through about 1990 was that agglomeration was a condition produced by spatial externalities of various types, including knowledge spillovers, matching externalities in labor markets, and the provision of local public goods. The more recent approach, with roots in general equilibrium models of monopolistic competition, focuses on demand side advantages arising from clustering when agents have a preference for variety and local competition is limited by product differentiation. In 1988, Fujita developed the monopolistic competition foundations of the economics of agglomeration, which makes him one of the founders of the new economic geography. In *The Spatial Economy*, coauthored with Paul Krugman and Anthony Venables, Fujita provided a synthetic application of nonlinear dynamics to regional economics and international trade, as well as to urban economics. This book is a landmark in spatial economics and has established new economic geography as an economic field proper.

Jacques Thisse

See also Journey to Work; Urban Economics

Further Readings

Fujita, M. 1989. *Urban Economic Theory. Land Use and City Size.* Cambridge, UK: Cambridge University Press.

———. 1988. "A Monopolistic Competition Model of Spatial Agglomeration: A Differentiated Product Approach." *Regional Science and Urban Economics* 18:87–124.

Fujita, Masahisa and Tomava Mori. 1996. "The Role of Ports in the Making of Major Cities: Self-agglomeration and Hub-effect. *Journal of Development Economics* 49(1):93–120.

Fujita M., P. Krugman, and A. J. Venables. 1999. *The Spatial Economy. Cities, Regions, and International Trade.* Cambridge: MIT Press.

Ottaviano, Gianmarco I. P. and Diego Puga. 1998. "Agglomeration in the Global Economy: A Survey of the 'New Economic Geography.'" *World Economy* 21:707–31.

Parr, John B. 2002. "Agglomeration Economies: Ambiguities and Confusions." *Environment and Planning A* 34:717–31.

G

GANS, HERBERT

The sociologist Herbert J. Gans was born in 1927 in Cologne, Germany, and was naturalized as an American citizen in 1945. His work has informed social science and public opinion for almost half a century, ranging from publications in prestigious academic journals, to award-winning books, to widely read articles in the popular media. In particular, he has made an enormous contribution to the field of urban studies. Gans is a true public intellectual, tackling polemic social problems whose relevance is widely recognized, defying stereotypes, and uncovering new perspectives.

Gans's biography reveals the trajectory of a scholar who has contributed to a wide range of fields in social science including urban studies, urban planning, poverty, race and ethnic studies, and American studies, as well as the media and popular culture, liberal democratic theory, and public policy. Gans received his PhD in planning from the University of Pennsylvania and went on to work at various municipal and federal agencies. In 1971, he was appointed to Columbia University's Department of Sociology, holding the title of Robert S. Lynd Professor from 1985 until he retired in 2008. Gans served as president of the American Sociological Association (ASA) in 1989. He was honored in 1999 with the ASA's Award for Contributions to the Public Understanding of Sociology, and in 2005, he was recognized by the association for his career of distinguished scholarship.

Gans's urban ethnographic work was rooted in the tradition of urban community studies, in the footsteps of Louis Wirth's 1927 *The Ghetto* and William Foote Whyte's 1943 *Street Corner Society*. This tradition, born of the Chicago School, focused on the importance of place and highlighted the rich social ties that were a fundamental part of social life in the city. Gans firmly advocated that participant observation must be part of the methodological tool kit in analyzing urban and suburban life. *The Urban Villagers*, published in 1962, was an ethnography of Boston's West End neighborhood, which was slated for demolition and replacement with modern high-rise apartments. His criticism of urban renewal and its effects on communities remains salient today. Gans's well-known academic correspondence with Mark Granovetter, concerning the failure of West End residents to effectively mobilize to prevent the demolition, highlighted the limitations of network analysis for uncovering complex social processes. Gans's work repeatedly advocated the importance of highly contextualized ethnographic data—gleaned from extended field immersion—to generate social scientific claims.

In *The Levittowners*, published in 1967, Gans challenged the prevailing postwar stereotype of suburbs as spaces promoting social conformity, isolation, and moral bankruptcy. He argued that individual agency plays a strong role in shaping social outcomes; physical environment does not automatically produce social, moral, and cultural outcomes. Gans's *Middle American Individualism: Political Participation and Liberal Democracy* is a subtle analysis of middle- and working-class

Americans. Gans showed both the fears and aspirations of these newly arrived suburbanites and argued for the need to understand the residents as individuals struggling to achieve the American Dream.

Gans's criticism of the term *underclass* in his book, *The War against the Poor* (1995), highlights his propensity to take on hotly contested subjects, often changing the trajectory of the debate. The term underclass was commonly used by both journalists and social scientists in an effort to highlight a social group seemingly isolated geographically and apparently outside the bounds of normative American conduct. But Gans argued that, in the tradition of the controversial report by Daniel Patrick Moynihan in 1965, "The Negro Family: The Case for National Action," the term perpetuated an essentialist understanding of the ghetto poor as culturally deficient and undeserving of aid. In dialogue with William Julius Wilson, author of *The Truly Disadvantaged: The Inner City, the Underclass, and Public Policy,* he abandoned the term underclass. They proposed that through ethnographic work, the overly simplistic and often derogatory understanding of the poor as an underclass should be challenged by portraying the complexity and diversity of the ghetto poor and the context in which they are embedded.

Eva Rosen

See also Ethnic Enclave; Gentrification; Ghetto; Neighborhood Revitalization; Suburbanization

Further Readings

Gans, Herbert. 1962. *Urban Villagers: Group and Class in the Life of Italian-Americans.* New York: The Free Press.

———. 1967. *The Levittowners: Ways of Life and Politics in a New Suburban Community.* New York: Pantheon Books.

———. 1988. *Middle American Individualism: The Future of Liberal Democracy.* New York: The Free Press.

———. 1996. *The War against the Poor: The Underclass and Anti-poverty Policy.* New York: Basic Books.

Whyte, William Foote. 1943. *Street Corner Society: The Social Structure of an Italian Slum.* Chicago: University of Chicago Press.

Wilson, William J. 1987. *The Truly Disadvantaged: The Inner City, the Underclass, and Public Policy.* Chicago: University of Chicago Press.

Wirth, Louis. 1928. *The Ghetto.* Chicago: University of Chicago Press.

GARDEN CITY

The Garden City is a planning concept and model developed by Ebenezer Howard, who founded the Garden City Association in 1899. Howard's writing strongly influenced an early generation of urban planners, as well as the City Beautiful movement in the United States. Two garden cities were built in England in the early 1900s, and urban planners and architects in Europe and South America followed with garden cities in their countries. In the United States, garden cities were promoted by the Regional Planning Association, resulting in the construction of three communities in the 1930s. The Garden City has served as a model for urban development and an inspiration for other planning models to the present day.

History

In 1899, Ebenezer Howard founded the Garden City Association, a group formed to promote his ideas for planned communities, which would be include balanced areas of residential, industrial, and commercial spaces, surrounded by greenbelt and agricultural areas, to produce a healthy living environment—smokeless, slumless communities—for the urban dweller. Howard was influenced by his reading of Edward Bellamy's socialist utopian novels, *Looking Backward* (1888) and *Equality* (1897), although elements of the Garden City could be found in earlier planning efforts (Benjamin Ward Richardson, for example, published *Hygeia: A City of Health*, his plan for a model city to alleviate the unhealthy conditions of the industrial city, in 1876). Howard's plan for the Garden City was first published in 1899 as *Tomorrow: A Peaceful Path to Real Reform,* but the book did not generate much attention; a revised version titled *Garden Cities of Tomorrow,* published in 1904, became a cornerstone in urban planning.

The Garden City was designed to house some 32,000 people on a site of 6,000 acres. Six radial boulevards 120 feet wide extended from the center,

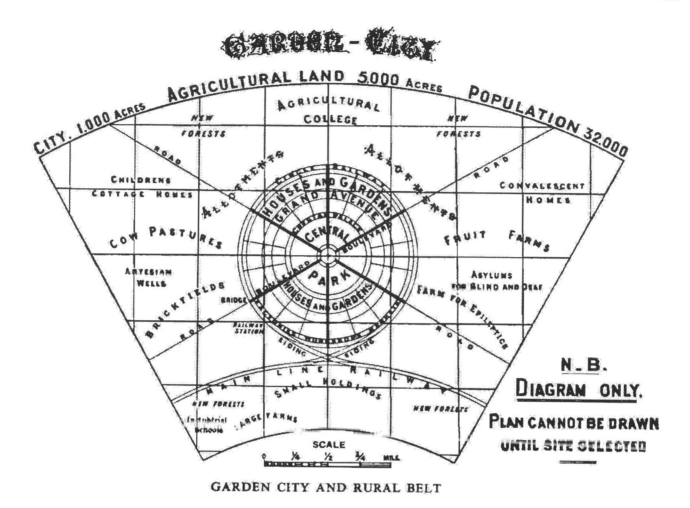

Ebenezer Howard's design for the Garden City

Source: Howard, Ebenezer. 1902. *Garden Cities of Tomorrow*, p. 22. London: Swan Sonnenschein & Co.

creating a radial pattern, with open spaces and parks separating areas for residential, industrial, institutional, and other uses. The Garden City was intended to be self-sufficient, to include a mix of employment as well as sufficient agricultural land to feed the local population. The Garden City was bordered by a greenbelt to separate it from other cities. In one mapping included in the original publication but not in *Garden Cities*, a ring of planned communities surrounds a larger, central city; the communities are connected to the central city and to the other suburban centers by rail transport. The Garden City was a blend of the city and nature, but without the problems of pollution and overcrowding found in the large industrial city.

With financial support from William Hesketh Lever, the first Garden City, Letchworth, was built in Hertfordshire, north of London (Lever was in the midst of construction of Port Sunlight, a planned industrial community outside of Liverpool, during this period). Letchworth was viewed as a successful implementation of the Garden City, with new homes and ample open space, a wide range of industries to provide employment for town residents, and an agricultural greenbelt to control further expansion. After World War I, the British government provided support for the second Garden City, in Welwyn, also in Hertfordshire. The Garden City would also serve as a more general model for smaller developments, including the Hampstead garden suburb and Gidea Park in London, and for garden cities in other countries as well, including Hellerau (a suburb of Dresden) in 1909 and Bromma (in Stockholm) beginning in 1910.

In 1909 the Garden City Association changed its name to the Garden Cities and Town Planning

Association (in 1941 the name would be changed once again, to the Town and Country Planning Association). By this time, there was a worldwide Garden Cities movement, as Howard's ideas served as a model for urban development in other countries. In 1908, the Australian government selected the site for a new national capital (present-day Canberra) and commissioned an international competition to design the new city. The winning design, by two Chicago architects, is derived in part from the comprehensive regional mapping for central city and surrounding garden cities published in *Tomorrow: A Peaceful Path to Real Reform*. New Delhi, in northern India, was similarly designed (in the 1910s) as the new capital city for the British colonial rule of the Indian subcontinent, and the broad axial boulevards and clustering of functional areas within the city (built in the 1920s) are derived from Howard's Garden City model.

In the United States, the Regional Planning Association of America (RPAA), a group of architects, planners, and economists, including Lewis Mumford, was formed in 1923. Influenced by Patrick Geddes, Ebenezer Howard, and the British Garden City, the RPAA lobbied for regional planning to replace the haphazard growth of urban centers in the United States. Inspired by the success of the British garden cities, two members of the group (the architects Henry Wright and Clarence Stone) designed two new suburban communities, Sunnyside (in Queens) and Radburn (in New Jersey). During the Depression, the Roosevelt administration planned for the development of 19 suburban garden cities as part of New Deal legislation and Work Progress Administration (construction of the new homes would provide jobs for unemployed workers). But Congress provided funding for just nine of the greenbelt towns, and only three were actually built (Greendale in Milwaukee, Green Hills in Cincinnati, and Greenbelt in Maryland). From the beginning the towns were attacked by the real estate and builders lobbies as socialistic enterprises, and Congress later required the government to sell the housing.

Postwar New Towns

In post–World War II Great Britain, with London and other cities suffering extensive damage from aerial bombing, Peter Abercrombie's *Greater London Plan* of 1944 proposed the relocation of up to 500,000 people in of 8 to 10 satellite towns separated from London by greenbelts. In 1946, Parliament passed the New Towns Act, authorizing the construction of 20 new towns across Great Britain, including eight in the greater London area and five in Scotland. In the 1960s, a second group of new towns was authorized to further control urban expansion of Greater London, and the last (and largest at more than 200,000 residents), Milton Keynes, was begun in 1967. In the United States as well, the legacy of the Garden City influenced later urban development in the form of new towns built in Reston, Virginia, and Columbia, Maryland (both in the Washington, D.C., area). In France, nine *villes nouvelles* were built in the 1960s to control the expansion of older urban centers, and other European countries have followed this model in later decades.

A Continuing Legacy

Howard's plan for the Garden City was influential among urban planners in the first decades of the twentieth century, influencing the design not just of new garden cities but of new national capitals as well. Howard was president of International Garden City Association, which later became the International Housing and Town Planning Federation. Although the Garden City was opposed by powerful business interests in the United States (which effectively halted the Roosevelt administration's plan for more extensive development of the cooperative communities), the planning model was influential in the design of new towns in both the pre- and postwar period. In recent decades, the continuing legacy of the Garden City movement can be seen in urban planning around the world, most directly in the new urbanism and sustainable development initiatives that have become part of urban development in almost every country.

Ray Hutchison

See also City Beautiful Movement; City Planning; Ideal City; New Urbanism; Sustainable Development; Urban Planning

Further Readings

Beevers, Robert. 1988. *The Garden City Utopia: A Critical Biography of Ebenezer Howard*. New York: Macmillan.

Buder, Stanley. 1990. *Visionaries and Planners: The Garden City Movement and the Modern Community.* Oxford, UK: Oxford University Press.

Christensen, Carol Ann. 1986. *The American Garden City and the New Towns Movement.* Ann Arbor: University of Michigan Press.

Hall, Peter. 2002. *Cities of Tomorrow: An Intellectual History of Urban Planning and Design in the Twentieth Century.* 3rd ed. New York: Wiley-Hall.

Hertzen, Heikki von and Paul D. Spreiregen. 1973. *Building a New Town: Finland's New Garden City, Tapiola.* Rev. ed. Cambridge: MIT Press.

Howard, Ebenezer. 1898. *Tomorrow: A Peaceful Path to Real Reform.* London: Swan Sonnenschein & Co.

———. 1902. *Garden Cities of Tomorrow.* London: Swan Sonnenschein & Co.

Meachem, Standish. 1999. *Regaining Paradise: Englishness and the Early Garden City Movement.* New Haven, CT: Yale University Press.

Miller, Mervyn. 1989. *Letchworth: The First Garden City.* Chichester, UK: Phillimore.

Parsons, Kermit Carlyle and David Schuyler. 2002. *From Garden City to Green City: The Legacy of Ebenezer Howard.* Baltimore: Johns Hopkins University Press.

Ward, Stephen V., ed. 1992. *Garden City: Past, Present, Future.* London: Taylor and Francis.

GATED COMMUNITY

Privatized spaces have become an increasingly dominant urban trend over the past 30 years, radically altering the use of space in the city as well as the nature of urban society. From Los Angeles to Rio de Janeiro and Johannesburg, an archetype of militarized space, with electrified fences, impenetrable walls, and armed security guards, has developed, protecting and securing residential, commercial, and corporate zones from the dangerous outside world. Concurrently, the label *gated community* has gained popularity in academic, policy, and popular discourse, employed to describe and critique this urban trend, although the historical roots and regional variations of the phenomenon are far older and broader than the American label suggests.

Definitions

Gated communities are traditionally defined by their physical attributes: a perimeter enclosure (e.g., electrified fence, wall), surveillance (e.g., CCTV, security patrols), and access control (e.g., boomgate, security gatehouse). In other words, gated communities inhabit spaces that are closely restricted, monitored, and controlled; they are reserved exclusively for residents and their appointed guests, with no access for uninvited outsiders. In reality, the term is applied to a wide range of territorial strategies, from total security estates (residential or commercial) with electrified high walls and permanently patrolling security guards, sometimes including schools, shops, and social clubs within the walls, to sectional title developments, apartment blocks with a keypad entry system, and everything in between. In addition, recent analyses of gated communities emphasize definitions based on the private and/or collective governance mechanisms that control these spaces, rather than the physical presence of gates or walls per se. However, the form of gated community predominantly imagined and implied by commentators is that of a cluster of residential homes, surrounded by walls and protected by private security of some form (although these inevitably also rely on communal governance mechanisms, such as homeowner associations, the latter are not a primary defining feature).

The Global Rise of Gated Communities

Explanations for the rise of gated communities differ significantly according to local and regional contexts, but factors such as rising violent crime and decreased confidence in public security are common rationalizations. The global rise of gated communities is often understood as a distinctly American trend, spreading from U.S. middle-class suburban enclaves and urban ethnic securitized ghettos to cities throughout the world. However, the concept and practice of urban gating has a much longer and wider history and is subject to regional variations.

For example, in the medieval era, entire cities were walled off; in the context of nineteenth-century European industrialization, the wealthy elite increasingly deserted run-down city centers in favor of private residential zones on the urban edge; and historical examples of the sixteenth-century Venetian ghetto and thirteenth-century *béguinages* in European cities demonstrate gated community principles of social exclusion via physical barriers. While the contemporary trend toward gated communities has spread fastest in the United States and Latin America, gated communities are not merely

A gated community in a suburb of Los Angeles.

Source: Steven K. Martin.

an American export but also a response to local specificities (e.g., high crime and inequality in South Africa and Brazil), and they exist in regions and countries with diverse cultures and urban histories such as the Arab world, Australia, the Caribbean, Eastern and Western Europe, China, New Zealand, Russia, South Africa, and Southeast Asia.

This explosion in the number of gated communities worldwide is matched by the growth in literature explaining and analyzing them. Edward J. Blakely and Mary Gail Snyder's book *Fortress America* is widely considered the classic text, charting the modern rise of gated communities in the United States, which brought the issue of gated communities to the forefront of academic and policy agendas in the late 1990s. Building on this work, anthropologists Setha Low and Teresa Caldeira, focusing on America and Brazil respectively, have more recently explored the reality of life "inside the gates," as well as the implications for those excluded.

The global spread of gated communities is partly driven by the construction and security industries, promoting a public discourse of fear related to the risks of urban life, which they allege can be ameliorated through the secure environment of a gated community. In addition, such communities are often promoted by local municipalities eager to attract high-rate taxpayers, particularly those who consume so few public services. Residents of gated communities themselves explain their decision to move to a gated community as predominantly couched in the desire for increased security that, in the context of neoliberal state withdrawal, is not reliant on a government or its associated public security enforcement, often perceived as ineffective (and in some contexts, corrupt). This desire for security is not an exclusively physical need for protection from crime but is equally financial, as gated communities offer a secure investment that is lifestyle based. For example, residents describe their way of life in a gated community in terms of a rural idyll—harking back to a bygone era in which children could play outside and doors were left unlocked—a lifestyle no longer possible in the contemporary metropolis but one that can be successfully re-created inside a gated community, albeit reliant on walls and private security. In other words, families can remain in proximity to the services of the city (such as good schools, shopping centers, and employment opportunities) but detach themselves from its less desirable realities such as crime and general insecurity, without moving to a rural backwater. It is therefore ironic that Teresa Caldeira's "insider/outsider" discourse based on research in São Paulo found that residence in a gated community actually serves to increase fear of crime among those inside the gates, as the dual effects of everyday "talk of crime," in which insecurity "beyond the gate" is magnified, combines with insular movement patterns to produce amplified panic and fear related to life outside. Despite broad recognition that residents favor gated communities to meet household desires for privatized physical, financial, and lifestyle security, it is important to stress the absence of a singular or uniform experience of gating throughout the world.

Implications for the City and Society

Although gated communities are eulogized by residents, developers, and real estate agents for providing safe family spaces and secure financial investments, they have received a largely negative press from academics and the media, who perceive them as private fortresses that destroy the vibrancy of the city through their exclusivity. A minority of researchers endorse gated communities, highlighting their role in protecting threatened groups from ethnic conflict, providing employment and services for nearby poor communities, demonstrating economic efficiency in service provision, and ensuring the retention of financial capital in weak states. In the main, however, gated communities are understood as problematic urban domains.

To summarize the argument: Although moving to a gated community can be a rational individual decision, especially in the context of severe violent crime and weak state capacity, the collective consequences for the rest of society and the city are considered destructive. Two major negative outcomes are stressed in the literature: the exclusion of individuals and the fragmentation of the city. Although middle- and low-income gated communities exist in some contexts (notably the United States), most gated communities (in the United States and elsewhere) are populated by high-income

residents and thus effectively incarcerate the wealthy in highly exclusive spaces. Because these spaces are consequently accessible only to the minority with financial means, spaces (which often were previously public) become privatized, thus restricting freedom of movement in the city and deepening social polarization by excluding the unknown mass of "others" or "them" from "our" safe spaces. As gated community residents tend to be socioeconomically similar (a consequence of house prices and restrictive covenants), often functioning with limited interaction outside their walls, spatial separation is inevitably entangled with social exclusion. In addition, gated communities are criticized for physically fragmenting the city into a series of elite private citadels that ultimately lead to an urban future of increased exclusion and segregation. This imminent urban dystopia is visualized as a series of secure forts, in which the wealthy maneuver from private space to private space, functioning without physical, social, or civic engagement with the dangerous outside world, which is populated by the excluded factions of society. Less exaggerated accounts of this spatial distortion emphasize the influence of gated communities on disrupting traffic flows and their inevitable role in displacing crime into nongated zones.

A further implication, which receives less direct attention in the literature, is the political withdrawal of gated community residents. Gated communities represent an extreme form of citizen retreat in the global era of neoliberal state withdrawal. In this context, the private sector has emerged as the dominant service provider, alongside the growing privatization of space in contemporary cities. Gated community residents demonstrate an augmented version of this trend because they are in some cases wholly dependent on private services and governance, and thus their reliance on the state is further depleted, and consequently, they exhibit reduced willingness to submit to the state in other aspects of everyday life. Thus, at a larger scale, gated communities contribute to challenging the very basis of modern society, that of the state as sovereign.

Indeed, research in South Africa indicates that preference for living in a gated community is not solely a residential or security-based decision; it also reflects a desire to disconnect from civic engagement and abstain from the responsibilities of civil society. In other words, gating is about much more than the physical fragmentation of the city or the social exclusion of citizens; it can also be understood as representing the absolute secession of some dwellers from civil society. Gated community residents essentially wield their market-oriented power as private property owners and consequently reject citizenship-based interaction with the state as part of civil society. As an extreme interpretation, gated communities thus provide an alternative reality for residents, one that is detached and sheltered from the physical, social, economic, and political attributes of wider society. However, as indicated, the implications for the city and society can be highly destructive.

Charlotte Lemanski

See also Common Interest Development; Crime; Divided Cities; Suburbanization

Further Readings

Blakely, Edward J. and Mary G. Snyder. 1997. *Fortress America: Gated Communities in the United States*. Washington, DC: Brookings Institution Press.

Caldeira, Teresa P. R. 2000. *City of Walls: Crime, Segregation, and Citizenship in São Paulo*. Berkeley: University of California Press.

Davis, Mike. 1990. *City of Quartz: Excavating the Future in Los Angeles*. London: Verso.

Glasze, Georg, Chris J. Webster, and Klaus Frantz. 2006. *Private Cities: Global and Local Perspectives*. London: Routledge.

Le Goix, Renaud and Chris Webster. 2008. "Gated Communities." *Geography Compass* 2(4):1189–1214.

Low, Setha. 2003. *Behind the Gates: Life, Security, and the Pursuit of Happiness and Fortress America*. London: Routledge.

GAY SPACE

Gay space, particularly urban clusters of leisure venues serving a male homosexual clientele, first attracted the attention of urban geographers and sociologists in the late 1970s. As historians have demonstrated, there were vital (and often overt) urban homosexual subcultures in many major cities from at least the eighteenth century onward. However, it was not until the 1970s, with the growth of the modern gay liberation movement, that concentrations of gay venues were consolidated in the landscape of major North American and European cities and became the subject of academic and popular attention. The title of this entry consciously highlights the uneven gendering of the geographies that have examined these spaces.

Early studies of gay space centered on the experience of major metropolitan centers in the United States. In a much cited study, Castells and Murphy focused on the development of the Castro district in San Francisco as gay territory. Their study mapped concentrations of visible bars, clubs, and retail outlets patronized by gay men; it also attempted to map residential clustering by gay men and examined the spread of votes cast in municipal elections for pro-gay candidates. In the 1980s, this work was extended to examine the role of gay men in the gentrification of inner-city neighborhoods.

Initially, (male) researchers could not find similar territorial concentrations of lesbians and theorized that women had been socialized not to claim space in the same way and furthermore were materially disadvantaged by the systemic inequalities in women's income. Subsequent research has identified districts (such as Park Slope in Brooklyn) where lesbians have been primary agents of gentrification; of course, lesbian bars also exist, but they have frequently been more precarious and short-lived than male-oriented venues. However, lesbian and feminist scholars have contended that most analysis of urban space is overinvested in reading for public visibility and, consequently, overlooks women's use of the city. In contrast they advocate expanding analyses to include women's social networks, domestic spaces, and quotidian routines to offer a more comprehensive understanding of the spatiality of lesbian lives. Such an approach also offers further insights into bisexual space, as bisexuals operate in both gay and heterosexual space as well as creating bisexual spaces, and yet are seldom visible (as bisexuals) in either.

Early studies of gay space tended to stress how these were liminal spaces occupying marginalized areas of the inner city. During the 1990s, many clusters of gay space became recentered within their cities, being integrated into urban regeneration schemes and place marketing initiatives. This, in turn, led many users of these sites to complain that they were becoming systematically "de-gayed" as they attracted heterosexual consumers keen to demonstrate their cosmopolitan cultural capital. For some critical queer theorists, the incorporation of gay space into urban planning regimes is indicative of how it has become colonized by the market and also has become a privileged site that is complicit in the reproduction of normative masculinities, class prejudice, and White supremacy.

For most of the last three decades, theories of gay space have centered on the experience of inner-city neighborhoods in the metropolitan centers of the global North. Increasingly, geographers of sexualities have highlighted how the predominance of these theorizations may obscure far more than it reveals; they have embarked on the spatiality of gay urban life in other contexts, such as the suburbs, small towns, and cities in the global South, where gay identities (as they are understood in Europe and North America) may be the preserve of a privileged, transnational elite and coexist with indigenous homosexualities that have their own distinct spatialities.

Gavin Brown and Kath Browne

See also Castells, Manuel; Discotheque; Gendered Space; Gentrification; Non-Sexist City; Sex and the City; Social Exclusion; Social Movements; Spaces of Difference

Further Readings

Brown, G. 2008. "Urban (Homo)sexualities: Ordinary Cities, Ordinary Sexualities." *Geography Compass* 2(4):1215–31.

Browne, K., J. Lim, and G. Brown, eds. 2007. *Geographies of Sexualities: Theory, Practices, and Politics.* Aldershot, UK: Ashgate.

Castells, M. and K. Murphy. 1982. "Cultural Identity and Urban Structure: The Spatial Organization of San Francisco's Gay Community." Pp. 237–59 in *Urban Policy under Capitalism*, edited by N. I. Fainstein and S. S. Fainstein. London: Sage.

Chauncey, G. 1994. *Gay New York: Gender, Urban Culture, and the Making of the Gay Male World 1890–1940.* New York: Basic Books.

Hemmings, C. 2002. *Bisexual Spaces: A Geography of Sexuality and Gender.* London: Routledge.

Knopp, L. 1992. "Sexuality and the Spatial Dynamics of Capitalism." *Environment & Planning D: Society & Space* 10:651–69.

Podmore, J. A. 2001. "Lesbians in the Crowd: Gender, Sexuality, and Visibility along Montreal's Boul. St-Laurent." *Gender, Place, and Culture* 8(4):333–55.

Rothenburg, T. 1995. "'And She Told Two Friends': Lesbians Creating Urban Social Space." In *Mapping Desire: Geographies of Sexualities*, edited by D. Bell and G. Valentine. London: Routledge.

GEDDES, PATRICK

Patrick Geddes (1854–1932) was a polymath who covered a remarkable number of disciplines and subjects. He was a biologist and a sociologist, an educationalist and an aesthete. Geddes is perhaps best known for making important contributions to the development of town planning, especially the Regional Planning Association of America, although his influence extended in many directions. Lewis Mumford acknowledged Patrick Geddes as "my master" and claimed that Geddes "was one of the outstanding thinkers of his generation, not alone in Great Britain, but in the world." In Britain, Geddes's ideas were amplified further by his close collaborator, Victor Branford. Although Geddes's ideas were championed in the United States by thinkers like Mumford, until recently, Geddes merited no more than a footnote in urban studies. In the past decade, scholarly interest has revived Geddes's legacy for urban studies.

Career

Geddes gave up on a career as a professional biologist after being blinded temporarily in Mexico in 1879. He settled in Edinburgh's Old Town in 1886 and helped renovate the tenements of the Ramsay Garden set of buildings and Short's observatory on Edinburgh's Royal Mile. This became the renowned Outlook Tower and has been called the "world's first sociological laboratory." An educational museum, the Outlook Tower provided a gradually ascending overview of, and commentary on, the evolution of the city in history, from its roots in the world on the ground floor, through continental, national, and regional levels, before arriving at the top floor, where the contemporary vista of Edinburgh's topography was contextualized in the

Forth Valley region through the lens of a *camera obscura*.

Around the same time, Geddes was appointed to a personal chair in botany at University College Dundee (1889–1914), and he was later professor of civics and sociology at Bombay University (1919–1923). Geddes was in no way a conventional academic. He never completed a formal degree and failed to be appointed to a number of academic positions, until the Dundee textile magnate James Martin White founded the Dundee College post especially for Geddes. The generous terms of the Dundee chair allowed Geddes nine months of the year away from the college to pursue his other passions. Geddes also helped found the Sociological Society in 1903 and presented his seminal statement, "Civics: As Applied Sociology," to the first Sociological Society conference. Later, he was awarded the international gold medal for his applied sociology exhibition at the 1913 International Exposition at Ghent. He accepted a knighthood in the last year of his life (although only after earlier refusing one).

Thought

Geddes has been situated by Volker Welter as part of the pre-1914 mainstream of European utopian thought, a "larger modernism" where scientific rationality was mixed with aesthetics, myth, and religion. In his home country of Scotland, Geddes was deeply attracted to neoromanticism and Celtic revivalism. He also absorbed intellectual influences from around the world. Geddes studied and worked in Paris, Montpellier (where he designed the College des Ecossais), Mexico, Palestine, and Bombay, as well as in Dublin, Edinburgh, London, and Dundee. Geddes's civic modernism placed great stress on developing a national and regional environmental consciousness within an internationalist ethics and placed a special emphasis on the evolution of place as historically constituted.

Geddes was committed to an evolutionary model of social development. He studied Darwinian evolution under Thomas Huxley in the mid-1870s and attended the Positivist Church in London, where he embraced the teachings of Spencer and Comte before warming to Ruskin's social and aesthetic critique of contemporary social conditions. But his unique form of civic modernism took firmer shape in Paris where, under the influence of Le Play and Demoulins, he was inspired by the progressive possibilities of fusing evolutionary science with social science. Geddes centered his civic modernism on the city because it alone represents nature's drive to balance free individuals with the propagation of the species. Complex social formations like the city evolved from more basic and simpler units. For Geddes, the earlier development causally determines the form of the later one under changed social conditions by being inscribed into concrete spatial relations. Cities are structured by unconscious survivals from past epochs. Geddes typically exaggerated this unconscious inheritance, for instance, that Haussmann's boulevards in Paris unconsciously echoed wide medieval hunting passages through the forests that once covered the region.

In 1904, Geddes published one of the seminal documents in civic modernism, *City Development: A Study of Parks, Gardens, and Culture Institutes*. This represented a full-scale (and never realized) plan for the civic restoration of the ancient Scottish capital of Dunfermline. *City Development* was financed by a local trust founded by Andrew Carnegie, who was born and raised in the town, and it can be viewed retrospectively as a bridging document between twentieth-century civic modernism and nineteenth-century Garden City planning.

At the same time, Geddes tried to stimulate interest in applied sociology by advocating the value of civic exhibitions as instructive tools for engendering civic action. Later city-region studies were carried out under Geddes's supervision in India and Palestine. In India, Geddes looked to preserve the historic traces of the 30 or so towns he surveyed, even as rapid urbanization began to take hold. Geddes's reverence for indigenous culture informed his plans for civic reconstruction of urban India. He did not share the Eurocentric contempt for the temple cities of South India but viewed them as the most complete integration of culture, history, and urban form.

Geddes published few major works, and his writing style was often elusive and digressive. Notable, however, was his sociobiological history, *The Evolution of Sex* (1889), written with John Arthur Thomson, a provocative study of gender and sex that was thought shocking in Victorian society. His *Cities in Evolution* (1915) was an attempt to summarize his brand of evolutionary urbanism in a popular and accessible style. It must be judged an unsatisfactory statement of Geddes's intellectual ambition for the study of the city. The excessive recourse by Geddes to specialized concepts derived from biology and the many neologisms that he constructed could seem obscure and bewildering. For instance, to better express the development of vast city-regions devouring small towns and boroughs Geddes minted a term that would become part of the lexicon of urban studies, *conurbation*. Geddes's other neologisms included *megalopolis*, *geotechnic*, *paleotechnic*, *neotechnic*, and *Kakotopia*. Nevertheless, *Cities in Evolution* contains insightful clues into urban modernity, especially with regard to physical environment, culture, spatial form, community, evolutionary history, and civics that, with more careful elaboration and illustration, continue to resonate.

Influenced by his own semirural childhood and the regional perspective of the French geographer and anarchist Élisée Reclus, Geddes came to favor regionalism as a way to extend the heterogeneity of cities to a broader, more diverse, and self-regulating unit. In the image of a river flowing through a valley, Geddes was attracted to Reclus's idea of the "regional valley section" as a coherent unit for research-informed action. His favored example was Glasgow. For Geddes, the incipient "buds" of the future society based on the city-region model were already emerging in Glasgow because its river, the Clyde, combined the various facets of advanced industrial and social organization, which other cities like London dispersed onto geographically specialized quarters of the city. For this reason, Geddes claimed, Glasgow was also preeminent intellectually in the applied sciences and political economy.

Civic Modernism

Unlike many contemporary environmentalists, Geddes's civic modernism was far from hostile to urban life and technological innovation. For Geddes, the early modern centralization of industry and government represented a Paleotechnic age while the modern evolution toward more decentralized economy and government could evolve into the Neotechnic age. In its blind drive toward industrialization and accumulation for its own sake, the Paleotechnic age wasted natural resources, material, and energy on a huge scale, only to create mass physical and cultural impoverishment as well as a catastrophic relationship to the environment. Geddes called this situation a Kakotopia, in contrast to the emerging utopia that was being made possible by electric energy. Geddes positioned his image of the utopian city at a point "like the mathematician's zero," somewhere between the grim reality of the industrial city as Dante's inferno and the wholly abstract conception of the utopian city. The civic modernism of utopian cities like Glasgow was rooted in social, technological, and natural conditions, but its realization was dependent on social action through the many-sided flourishing of environmentally sensitized action.

Despite being identified with large-scale public planning schemes, Geddes opposed the neat orderliness of anti-urban town planning and urged an active, reciprocal interaction with the natural and built environment. Practical intervention should be modest, small scale, and localized, a process he called conservative surgery. Urban improvement ought to develop along the grain of local traditions. Only careful study, sensitive to the environmental distinctiveness of city-regions, would reveal which evolutionary buds could be self-consciously nurtured for the utopian future.

Alex Law

See also City Beautiful Movement; City Planning; Mumford, Lewis; Urban Planning; Utopia

Further Readings

Geddes, P. 1904. *A Study in City Development: Parks, Gardens, and Culture Institutes.* Dunfermline, UK: Carnegie Dunfermline Trust.

———. [1915] 1968. *Cities in Evolution: An Introduction to the Town Planning Movement and to the Study of Civics.* London: Benn.

———. 1979. "Civics: As Applied Sociology." In *The Ideal City*, edited by H. E. Meller. Leicester, UK: Leicester University Press.

Meller, H. 1990. *Patrick Geddes: Social Evolutionist and City Planner.* London: Routledge.

Welter, V. M. 2002. *Biopolis: Patrick Geddes and the City of Light.* Cambridge: MIT Press.

GEMEINSCHAFT AND GESELLSCHAFT

Gemeinschaft and *Gesselschaft* are two abstract concepts developed by Ferdinand Tönnies to encapsulate the characteristics of society as it shifted from a rural base and reliance on agriculture to dependence on commerce within an urban setting. Gemeinschaft highlights community relations based on kinship in a preindustrial, agrarian society; many of these associations are extolled. Conversely, Gesellschaft is presented on the whole as a critique to modernity, with relationships based on economic transactions.

The concept is highly significant to urban studies as it warns against some of the threats of modernity that are more typically found in an urban setting. Gemeinschaft and Gesellschaft denote relations between individuals within social structures while paying attention to the importance of human will. The ascent of Gesellschaft-type relations denotes an enhanced role for the state in representing the interests of society. Social entities and norms and the shifting role of the nation-state are therefore embedded within the analysis. This entry begins with a discussion of Tönnies and then provides a more extended analysis of his influential ideas.

Biographical Background

Ferdinand Tönnies, along with Max Weber and Georg Simmel, is described as one of the fathers of classical German sociology. Like them, he sought to learn from the past in order to understand the future, and in so doing, he considered the characteristics of societies both traditional and modern. In his works he was heavily influenced by Hobbes and his theory of the human will. Today, and together with Simmel, he is credited with providing a leading contribution to urban sociology.

Tönnies grew up on a farm in Germany and witnessed the impact of both commercialization and mechanization on daily life. The historical context for ideas has relevance because they were promoted at a time when European society was experiencing a transition from an agrarian base to one that was increasingly reliant on commerce and trade. There was a fascination across the continent with the implications of modernity for traditional society; as evidenced in the works of Émile Durkheim and Weber.

At the end of the nineteenth century, Tönnies published the book *Gemeinschaft und Gesellschaft*. This first edition (1887) gained a very limited readership, allegedly because of the old Germanic style of writing. Tönnies was ultimately a prolific writer in his native language, but it is often claimed that his work has been somewhat neglected. While seven German language editions were published between 1912 and 1940, an English language publication of the original book did not appear until the latter half of the twentieth century.

Tönnies had no advocate within Europe and beyond Germany. The impact of his work is therefore much less apparent. But closer scrutiny of twentieth-century sociology reveals a less than wholesale disregard of his work within a European context. Clearly, we see evidence of Tönnies's central ideas within theories of urbanization and associated dichotomies of urban and rural ways of life. His thinking is further implied in many of the community studies debates that emanated from the United Kingdom during the 1970s. Indeed, his influence is sometimes considered so hidden and inferred so that while the basic theory is well known, it is not widely read and as a result it is not fully understood.

The book was written in the positivist tradition, meaning that it is descriptive. But it also offers opinion and ultimately seeks to provide an archetype for the ideal society. Broadly, Gemeinschaft and Gesellschaft provide a mechanism for understanding relations of community and society. Even though Tönnies was a progressive, the book provides an explanation of the major elements of the conservative style of thought that represented the German intellectual thought of the time. He tapped into a European fascination with modernity: Just as Durkheim expressed concern for the emergent modern society with the loss of social integration and the rise in suicide, Tönnies sought to understand the perils of modernity using social relationships. Although the theory is often approximated to relations within rural (Gemeinschaft) and urban (Gesellschaft) societies, the two are not mutually exclusive. In other words, the dual concept intermingles within many social relations and a steady progression from one to the other is not necessarily evident within society. Gemeinschaft and Gesellschaft continue to have resonance for modern urban societies so that in a modern Gesellschaft world, Gemeinschaft-like relations persist, *but with diminishing strength,* to remain a reality of social life. In Tönnies's pursuit of the ideal type, he was concerned with retaining stronger Gemeinschaft relations in the new world order.

Pre- and Postindustrial Society

The desire for the profitable use of money prevailed during seventeenth- and eighteenth-century Europe in the mercantile age. Major social change was brought about by the development of large-scale trade, technological changes, and the advent of capitalism. Further major changes were occurring within society in relation to science, religion, and the role of the nation-state in an era that is known today as the Age of Enlightenment. During this time, reason and scientific inquiry took precedence over irrationality and superstition.

These transformations had a direct impact on rural areas, which faced decline as people left the land and moved to industrial centers. In parallel with this shift, the supremacy of the ruling aristocracy was eroded due to the declining role of land within society. Consequently, the old ideologies of agrarian society were gradually swept away with the dawn of the capitalist age. Meanwhile, industrial society witnessed the rise of city and metropolitan areas. Central to this change was the shift from a predominantly closed community, where common interests are pursued for the greater good, to a more heterogeneous society, where individuals pursue their own interests. In the new world order, society is governed by a remote state rather than one that is structured around the locale. Protection of individuals and their physical and intellectual property and freedom form key roles for the state. The centrality of these issues (of individual freedoms, social relations, and state governance) implies that the original theory is germane to studies of society today.

Relations Within Society

Ties through blood and marriage comprise Gemeinschaft relations so that kinship bonds form the central unit, but friendships and neighborly connections are also important. Relations are perceived to be personal, familiar, strong, and close-knit. Levels of trust and reciprocity are high. These relations prevail within rural settlements, be they towns or villages. Moreover, society is intimately connected to the land. Those who work the land earn a living and derive pleasure from this task. Traditional values and customary practices abound within social relations, which as a result are described as organic and natural. In other words, they are genuine inasmuch as they are instinctive and have emerged from within the community, rather than resulting from enforced relations. These are manifest in relations within the family; among man, woman, and child.

By contrast, in the Gesellschaft of the capitalist society there is no shared set of social norms or collective history. Set in a city environment, individuals develop relations as a result of economic transactions; they seek to exchange merchandise or services to further their own self-interest. Relations are impersonal, artificial, perfunctory, loose, and superficial. As a result, individuals are cut off from nature, and they experience isolation from one another and from their community.

In the Gemeinschaft, it is proposed that women are driven by conscience and sentiment, whereas men are driven by calculation and effort. Although Tönnies contends that these merely represent different types of individuals within a society, the gendered nature of the analysis is apparent. It suggests that women tend to develop natural relations, such as the deep, instinctive mother–child connection. These relations are superior to those of their male counterparts, which are artificial and authoritarian. In the utopian society, relations would be more akin to those found among women in the Gemeinschaft.

Government and Individual Will

Society is underpinned by the human will, specifically *Wesenwille* and *Kurwille*. Although intellect and reason pervade both, the former is associated with Gemeinschaft and refers to the will that is natural and innate within the individual. It represents the traditional and unchanging essence of the community. Choices are made instinctively on the basis of habit and custom, for the greater good of the community. Relationships are formed for their intrinsic value.

These are upheld by a higher authority, typically with input from religious bodies, through common law. Peace prevails because individual interests overlap with those of the community. Moreover, these traditional communities are distinct, with powerful social norms and bonds, and they share common enemies.

In contrast to the prevailing community interests of the Gemeinschaft, the Kurwille is the modern individual's will. It is arbitrary and is based on the notion of choice, rational judgment, the pursuit of self-interest and pleasure, and the attainment of power. Although the transition from natural to rational will signifies freedom for the individual, the gains are considered temporary. As free agents, individuals form associations as a means to achieving particular ends. Individuals have distinctive personal property, and altruistic deeds are viewed with suspicion.

Random choices may be made, but they are deemed to be preferable for the individual making those choices, with little attention paid to the common good. Such motivation is found within the industrial society with an accompanying fragmentation of the close-knit Gemeinschaft community. In this society, the metropolis and the super-/supra-nation state have a central role in creating and enforcing positive law; this central role of the state alone signifies the advent of modern society. Peace is maintained through convention by a legitimate nation-state; it does not emerge from within the community.

As society matures and citizens experience a shift from Gemeinshchaft to Gesellschaft relations, their character changes and kinship ties, community bonds, superstitious beliefs, and connections to nature are all eroded. The rise in commerce brings a more rational, detached, and diverse society.

Although critics would contend that the theory of Gemeinschaft und Gesellschaft is naive and romantic, the concepts are abstract. They represent ideal types that were devised to assist with understanding modern social structures. The classification of the different relations, of human will, and of the role of the state are necessarily abstract to provide a deeper understanding of social relations. In reality, the theory maintains that society will progress from a period where Gemeinschaft relations predominate, to one that is epitomized by the Gesellschaft, before evolving into a new society. It was this society that Tönnies was interested in

influencing. Ultimately, the theory is not pessimistic; it contends that the prevalence of Gesellschaft is a temporary condition, with new social relations emerging in the modern world. A critical question for urban studies must be: How can urban areas overcome the seemingly negative aspects of Gesellschaft relations and simultaneously reinvent Gemeinschaft links from a bygone era?

Ruth McAreavey

See also Capitalist City; Community; *Metropolis;* Simmel, Georg; Urban Sociology; Urban Theory

Further reading

Adair-Toteff, Christopher. 1995. "Ferdinand Tönnies: Utopian Visionary." *Sociological Theory* 13(1):58–65.

Roth, Guenther. 1971. "Sociological Typology and Historical Explanation." In *Scholarship and Partisanship: Essays on Max Weber,* edited by Reinhart Bendix and Guenther Roth. Berkeley: University of California Press.

Tönnies, Ferdinand. [1887] 2002. *Community and Society: Gemeinschaft und Gesellschaft.* Translated and edited by Charles Price Loomis. New York: Courier Dover.

Truzzi, Marcello. 1971. *Sociology: The Classic Statements.* New York: Oxford University Press.

GENDERED SPACE

Gendered space is a central concept for feminist scholars working in urban studies, geography, and planning. Gendered space is not absolute but is shaped by the dominant social and cultural institutions that reinforce traditional gender roles. For many years, gender as a subject was largely ignored by academics and policymakers concerned with urban spaces. In the late 1970s and early 1980s, feminist geographers and planners began critiquing the situation of women in cities and focusing on the various ways that women and men experience these spaces differently. In particular, scholars analyzed the spatial expectations about women and their ability to move through urban spaces, to engage in labor outside the home, and to participate fully in the social and political system created and dominated by men.

The genesis of this approach to space can be traced to Henri Lefebvre, who argued in *The Production of Space* that spatial patterns are not absolute but are shaped by the social and economic systems dominated by institutions and individuals who wield political power. In Western society, men traditionally have exerted the greatest social and economic power and have influenced the spaces around them to meet their needs. Some locations benefit, and others are disadvantaged as a result of these dominant forces. Similarly those individuals without power are restricted from using the favored spaces, causing spatial inequality.

Gendered Nature of Public and Private Spaces

In medieval Europe, women in rural villages worked in the fields and in village markets; other opportunities for women to live and work outside the home were quite limited. Some women sought the protection of the cloistered life in monastic orders that accepted them as sisters. Others found safety among the *beguines,* whose communities enabled women to live apart from men under semi-monastic conditions without formal religious vows and to be active in charitable works in the community. The Industrial Revolution accentuated the spatial separation of men and women. Linda McDowell argues that, for many years, the field of urban studies ignored gender in tracking social changes associated with the rapid urbanization of the Industrial Revolution. She suggests that the spaces of rapidly industrializing cities were considered unsafe for women, and this perception led to the Victorian era division of space into public and private arenas, which constrained women to the private space of the home and allowed men free rein to move through the public streets and seek out employment and entertainment in the city.

This understanding persisted during the first half of the twentieth century and established a pervasive basis for discrimination against women, which constrained them to private domestic spaces while allowing men to dominate the public workplace settings. Men were free to ramble through the Victorian city, but women who ventured into public spaces in cities were considered to be either lower-class or "fallen" women.

In some situations, women were permitted to join the labor force, although the effects of this varied considerably. Doreen Massey argues that differences in employment regimes in mining areas, cotton towns, and inner London resulted in different spatial employment relations and differences in women's spatial empowerment. In mining regions, men worked in the mines, and women kept the home fires burning. In cotton mill towns, women were allowed to do the weaving tasks, which created new possibilities for them to organize and improve their lives. In London, women worked in various trades but mostly undertook home-based piecework, which was less threatening to the male patriarchy in the clothing industry. In the United States, groups like the Women's Christian Temperance Union (WTCU) and the settlement house movement worked to establish safe spaces for women and immigrants within urban areas and raised social awareness of issues like suffrage, temperance, and the need to protect working women from men's advances.

The form of the newly developing cities was also shaped by many of these long-standing gender biases. Delores Hayden critiques influence of the male-dominated field of architecture on the physical form of cities. She argues that this control over the built environment enabled the sexist nature of urban spaces. Houses were built in suburban locations that provided a tranquil home for men returning from work in the city, but at the same time, such spaces kept women isolated from each other. One solution to this bias was to reconfigure the urban fabric, especially in residential locations, to alleviate the isolation of women and create a more equitable society.

Daphne Spain provides a seminal treatment of this topic in her book, *Gendered Spaces,* in which she explicitly recognizes the status differential between men and women creates specific urban spatial configurations linked to the patriarchal spatial institutions that reinforce the dominance of men. In particular, she examines the spatial institutions of the family, the educational system, and the labor force, which operate through a variety of physical locations including dwellings, schools, and workplaces. In each of these settings, Spain argues, the social systems in place provided advantages to men that were denied to women. She also extends her analysis with a useful description of the nature of gendered space in non-Western cultures. She argues that women's status is lower when domestic spaces are sex segregated, when men have separate initiation rituals, and when there is a highly differentiated division of labor. When spatial institutions are controlled by men, then the space within which they operate can be said to be biased in their favor and against women, making them effectively gendered spaces.

Shifting Understanding of Space as a Binary

To focus attention on the gendered nature of urban spaces, some scholars have critiqued the dichotomous nature of public and private spaces. Nancy Duncan suggests that the spatial binary is used to legitimate the oppression of women, and she deconstructs the binary of public–private space, suggesting that quasi-private space provides a richer description. Other writers have discussed the nature of urban spaces that are neither fully public nor entirely private, including shopping malls, bars, restaurants, and suburban lawns. The less rigid gendering of these intermediate spaces allows both women and men greater freedom to move between locations and to express a wider range of behaviors. Susan Gal even suggests that such division of public and private might be best conceptualized using a kind of fractal analysis that breaks down the subcategories of space into geometric fragments. There is a need to move beyond this public–private duality and reconceptualize gendered space along a continuum.

Kristine Miranne and Alma Young have produced an influential edited volume, *Gendering the City,* in which they note that women's lives in urban spaces are shaped by the visible and invisible boundaries created by the social structures that gender the city. Violence toward women is one of the mechanisms for perpetuating this dichotomy so that women who do transgress the spatial binary and enter public spaces must contend with an internalized fear of male violence. Women who enter male-dominated public spaces may be subject to a wide range of verbal and physical harassment for transgressing the accepted boundaries. In addition, other individuals whose identities reflect marginalized categories, such as race or sexual identity, also encounter this highly gendered spatial system and may feel especially constrained in the ways

that they may express themselves in public spaces controlled by the largely White and heterosexual regime.

Other scholars have used a different strategy to critique the dichotomous nature of sex and gender as well as the public/private dichotomy. Feminist scholars have long argued that not all males are or need to be masculine and not all females are or need to be feminine. This recognition has required gender theorists to develop more complex theories of what gender is and how it is constructed and whether the gender binary continues to be a useful construct for looking at space. Judith Butler has challenged the traditional gender binary and argued that gender is not located just in people's physical bodies; rather, it is constructed through everyday performances of gender, which can challenge dichotomous conceptualizations and add fluidity to the range of possible gendered identities.

In the Western world, when people express gender variance in public spaces, they are often faced with significant discrimination and harassment. People may assume that a woman who is a little too masculine or a man who is a little too feminine is lesbian or gay, but gender identity and sexual orientation are quite different phenomena. In any case, the response to visible public gender variance is often violent and quite personal. Transgender political activists argue that the perpetrators of hate crimes against gays and lesbians frequently select their victims because of their visible gender variance, not because they have direct evidence of their sexual orientation. Thus, the performance of gender at odds with social expectations can be unsettling for some and for others can trigger an outpouring of rage. This is an extreme example of the way that space is gendered.

Non-Western Conceptions of Space

European and North American scholars have sometimes failed to recognize the cultural dimensions of gender and the ways that the colonial enterprise exported Western conceptions of gendered space. Sara Mills suggests that colonial town planning was used to separate "native" peoples from the colonists and reinforced a distancing based on race and gender. However, when either party moved across this artificial spatial boundary, the highly sexualized contacts that often resulted had a profound influence on both the colonizer and the colonized. Yet, Western observers continue to perpetuate colonialist discourses that marginalize women of the third world by situating them in spaces that have limited relevance to third world cultures.

In the Islamic world, there are strong cultural and religious restrictions on women's ability to move unaccompanied through public spaces. Visitors to Muslim countries are struck by the strongly gendered distinctions in both public and private spaces. Male visitors to a Muslim household are typically welcomed into a formal sitting area with a nearby dining space. Drinks and food are brought by the male head of household or one of his sons. The interior space of the dwelling is set up so that the women of the household can move through the rest of the space without being seen by anyone in the public rooms. This separation extends into the public sphere because women in public spaces must be covered or veiled. Similarly, in the public spaces of the mosque, there are separate areas for men and women to pray. Yet, within the culture, some women consider veiling an enabling device that frees them to enter public spaces that would otherwise be inaccessible to them. Other crossings into public space can occur in what Amy Mills describes as *Mahalle* space in Istanbul. These neighborhood spaces shift when men are at work, permitting the space outside the houses to become a semiprivate space shared by women in neighboring houses and that reverts to its fully public nature when the men return and becomes off limits to women.

In other parts of the world, the nature of domestic space is quite variable. Louise Johnson has edited a special series of ten articles in the feminist geography journal, *Gender, Place, and Culture,* that examined the varied understandings of kitchen space across cultures. Although in the West kitchens are usually within a private dwelling place, contributors to this issue note that many kitchens in developing nations are shared spaces located in a courtyard or other communal space.

In some cultures, land is inherited solely by men, but in parts of West Africa, land is inherited via the maternal lineage. Accordingly, in the case of the wife's death or divorce, the land reverts to the wife's family, leaving the husband without a home or producing crops. There is great variability in the gendered nature of public commercial activity. For example, in the West African nation of Togo, women known as the Mama Benzs are the dominant force in commerce, especially for cloth and household goods, and because of their influence have also begun to exert political influence on the government. However, in other parts of West Africa, commercial activity is the sole province of men.

Many non-Western cultures show greater tolerance of gender diversity, and the resulting array of possible gender categories also undermines binary understanding of gendered space. These different cultural situations provide useful insights into the spatial implications of more fluid gender possibilities. Anthropologist Gilbert Herdt, in *Third Sex, Third Gender: Beyond Sexual Dimorphism in Culture and History,* has provided a rich collection of perspectives from around the globe demonstrating variations in gender categories. Some of these variations also have direct spatial implications. Sometimes, sacred spaces are protected or otherwise associated with nonbinary genders. For instance, traditionally, the guardians of the holy places of Islam were special eunuchs known as *mukhanath,* who were considered a kind of third gender, which enabled them to be present while both men and women approached the holy sites. In India, third-gender people known as *hijra* play important public roles during religious ceremonies marking births and weddings.

The gendering of urban spaces is a result of specific sociocultural processes, including religion, social structure, and economic class. As societies evolve, the social forces that create the gendered spaces may also change. For example, although some view religion as a conservative force in terms of gender, in fact, the spread of religion is dynamic and rises and falls with global expansion. In Turkey, for instance, in the 1920s, Ataturk led a revolutionary change toward a more secularized interpretation of Islam that decreed that veils would no longer be worn in "modern" society. More than half a century later, some of those secular changes are under considerable pressure with the rise of Islamist parties in Turkey, and the nature of gendered space is in flux.

In 1996, South Africa adopted its first postapartheid constitution, which includes some of the most progressive constitutional protections against discrimination on the basis of race, gender, sex, pregnancy, marital status, ethnic or social origin, color, sexual orientation, age, disability, religion, conscience, belief, culture, language, and birth. It remains to be seen how such legal changes are reshaping the nature of gendered spaces in this country. In 2005, after many years of civil war in Liberia, a woman was elected president, the first female head of state in an African country. Once again, a gendered change in political leadership is likely to lead to a shift in the basic understanding of the gendered nature of government and its associated spaces.

These processes of social change are dynamic and nonlinear, reflecting changes in the social, economic, and cultural institutions of power. When sociocultural processes no longer demonize gender and gender variance, a broad array of gendered behaviors in public spaces may be possible and the gendered nature of urban spaces may be reduced.

Petra L. Doan

See also *Beguinage*; Gender Equity Planning; Urban Theory

Further Readings

Butler, Judith. 1990. *Gender Trouble: Feminism and the Subversion of Identity*. New York: Routledge.

Hayden, Delores. 1984. *Redesigning the American Dream: The Future of Housing, Work, and Family*. New York: W. W. Norton.

Herdt, Gilbert, ed. 1994. *Third Sex, Third Gender: Beyond Sexual Dimorphism in Culture and History*. New York: Zone Books.

Johnson, Louse. 2006. "Browsing the Modern Kitchen—A Feast of Gender, Place, and Culture (Part 1)." *Gender, Place, and Culture* 13(2): 123–32.

Lefebvre, Henri. 1991. *The Production of Space*. Oxford, UK: Blackwell.

Massey, Doreen. 1994. *Space, Place, and Gender*. Oxford, UK: Blackwell.

McDowell, Linda. 1983. "Towards an Understanding of the Gender Division of Urban Space." *Environment and Planning, D: Society and Space* 1:59–72.

Mills, Amy. 2007. "Gender and Mahalle (Neighborhood) Space in Istanbul." *Gender, Place, and Culture* 14(3):335–54.

Mills, Sara. 1996. "Gender and Colonial Space." *Gender, Place, and Culture* 3(2):125–47.

Miranne, Kristine B. and Alma H. Young, eds. 2000. *Gendering the City: Women, Boundaries, and Visions of Urban Life*. Lanham, MD: Rowman & Littlefield.

Spain, Daphne. 1992. *Gendered Spaces*. Chapel Hill: University of North Carolina Press.

GENDER EQUITY PLANNING

Gender equity planning highlights the effects of planning on males and females, as well as the impacts of men and women on planning itself. Gender refers to the subjective, dichotomous characterization of individuals as being male/masculine or female/feminine whereas sex refers to the categorization as males and females based purely on biological characteristics (chromosomes, genitalia, etc.). The two terms, gender and sex, are often confused in discussions of gender equity planning, and the idea that the latter is about more than biology is important to remember.

Masculine and feminine characteristics are often thought to be socially constructed; what counts as meaningful gendered traits changes with the times. Jobs that were once seen as appropriate only for men, such as planning, are now available as acceptable choices for women. Physical traits, such as hair length and musculature, vary, too, according to their perceived relevance in classifying an individual as being feminine or masculine. In this way, practices such as gender equity planning become increasingly complex the more carefully one explores the concept and the more finely key distinctions are made.

If gender pertains to societal notions of what it means to be female or male, equity is concerned with fairness in terms of how those who are labeled as male or female are treated. Fairness may mean being treated equally, or it may mean that unequal practices are called for to create a more equitable situation. An interest in equity also implies an interest in, and commitment to, correcting injustices. Thus, gender equity planning is about preventing or remedying existing or potential injustices in cities and regions. Like gender categories, ideas about what counts as an injustice are not static, and so whether something (e.g., females not being able to own property or sign a contract) is an injustice varies across time and cultures. Even if an injustice seems relatively unequivocal, its perceived severity or intensity may change, thus affecting the priority it receives by planners and policymakers.

Gender equity planning has arisen because of a perceived bias on the part of planning and planners to adhere to a gender-neutral approach. This bias is a consequence of a society in which males have the most power and public presence as well as, more specifically, dominating the planning profession in both numbers and prestige. Developed as a response to this bias, gender equity planning turns the attention of planners and publics to issues such as personal safety, child care, diverse and affordable housing, transportation, and public space to address many of the issues that women and girls, especially, face in their environments. In developing countries, gender equity planning is often particularly concerned with economic development and the provision of services that make life easier and more equitable for women.

For example, a gender equity approach to planning in a developing country might highlight the provision of small loans to women to support their business endeavors. Such loans might traditionally be given to men; these sorts of programs capitalize on the fact that women have been found to have a relatively high rate of loan repayment and accompanying economic success. Moreover, this success can also permeate an entire family or household, thus multiplying the benefits potentially derived from the program.

Analogous examples in Europe, Australia, and North America include safe-city projects in numerous communities, women's housing cooperative developments, gender mainstreaming projects in organizations such as the Royal Town Planning Institute, and purposeful input on planning decisions from the point of view of women's groups, such as Women Plan Toronto in Ontario, Canada.

Beyond instances of policies, plans, and programs are the impacts of a gender equity perspective on more fundamental aspects of planning. Leonie Sandercock and Ann Forsyth, for example, discuss a new gender agenda for planning and planning theory; this agenda includes different ways of knowing in planning (i.e., how we understand what planning is and how we go about doing planning). Thus, a new focus on treating men and women, as well as masculine and feminine attributes, fairly in

planning means that new planning methods, epistemologies, and modes of communication must be incorporated into planning theory and practice. Emphasizing participatory approaches, the involvement of marginalized individuals and groups, and more discursive ways of conducting planning exercises is consistent with these methods and epistemologies. Even new ethical guidelines are appropriate, given that women often think differently about ethical issues than men. This might mean that ethical codes could include norms other than those they do now: principles of doing no harm, a focus on interdependencies and relationships, and positive visions of a well-planned community, for example.

Equity here does not refer necessarily to equality. When one starts with an uneven playing field, as it were, equality is insufficient for making the situation fairer. For example, if a city caters to transportation patterns that are connected more to men's needs than those of women, fairness requires more than equal use of that system. It might mean that public transportation should actually favor routes and stops that address the particular, multifaceted needs of women. Similarly, professional planning practice that was focused almost exclusively on particular sorts of technical information might have to undergo a considerable shift to encompass other ways of knowing.

Furthermore, and as suggested earlier, as societies change, the gender roles of men and women change. Child care, for example, once almost always the purview of women, is slowly becoming also a male responsibility. Nevertheless, women continue to do the majority of child care and household chores, despite also working outside their homes. Thus, even in changing times, some gender stereotypes remain relevant, and these are at the heart of planning that has gender equity as a guiding principle. If these stereotypes and accompanying societal practices became obsolete, so too would gender equity planning.

However, some would argue that planning itself is a masculinist endeavor that emphasizes built form instead of people, for example. Histories of planning suggest that the social strands of the field split from a more physical orientation relatively early in the development of the profession. While those who were more interested in social relationships, including many women, went on to work in fields such as social work, those who were more inclined toward the physical form of the city went on to become planners. In the early days, these were almost all men. Again, however, as it has become more acceptable for women to pursue professional education in fields such as planning, the proportions of them in practice have increased. Gender equity in professional planning organizations continues to encourage women to join the profession, but it is also concerned with the status of these women in the profession as well as their diversity with regard to such defining characteristics as race.

Although the effects of gender equity planning are difficult to discern or measure, it is clear that there are more women in the profession than there once were. It is also clear that so-called women's issues have received greater attention than they once did. However, gender gaps remain in terms of the salaries received by male and female planners in North America, with planning education still seen as focusing on masculinist approaches to planning and professional socialization. This inhibits female planners from asserting feminist perspectives in their work.

Thus, challenges to implementing gender equity planning principles include the continued domination of the field by men who may or may not perceive the need for this approach; professionalization of women who are often taught that their chosen careers are, or should be, neutral or unbiased (and thus not amenable to feminist or gendered concerns); and a postfeminist environment in which questions arise about the need for a continued focus on sex- and gender-based equity considerations. Other challenges—such as the increased voice and visibility of transgendered people, which further complicates notions of sex and gender; the enhanced integration of various aspects of identity (class, race, sexuality, etc.); and uncertainty regarding the validity or nature of the category woman or female—all point to the need for gender equity planning to advocate for sex- and gender-based fairness and to consider other aspects of people that contribute to inequities in cities and regions.

Sue Hendler

See also City Planning; Gendered Space; Sex and the City; Urban Planning; Women and the City

Further Readings

Fainstein, S. and L. Servon, eds. 2006. *Gender and Planning: A Reader.* New Brunswick, NJ: Rutgers University Press.

Greed, C. 1994. *Women and Planning: Creating Gendered Realities.* New York: Routledge.

Sandercock, L. and A. Forsyth. 1992. "Feminist Theory and Planning Theory: The Epistemological Linkages." *Planning Theory Newsletter* 7/8:45–49.

Sandercock, L. and A. Forsyth. 1992. "A Gender Agenda: New Directions for Planning Theory. *Journal of the American Planning Association* 58(1):49–60.

GENERAL PLAN

A general plan is a legal document that states the goals, principles, policies, and strategies to regulate the growth and development of a particular community. In the literature, general plan, comprehensive plan, and master plan are synonymous. The main characteristics of general plans are their comprehensiveness, long-range time frame, and holistic territorial coverage. General plans include elements on land use, economic development, housing, circulation and transportation infrastructures, recreation and open space, community facilities, and community design, among many other possible elements. After approval, the general plan is an expression of what the community wants for a certain time horizon, usually 15 to 20 years into the future. A general plan covers all territory within a jurisdiction.

Historical Evolution

The first plans in the United States were devised as ways of bringing order to the turn-of-the-century industrial city. Examples of initial plans are the 1907 plan by Henry Wright for St. Louis and the 1909 plan by Daniel Burnham for Chicago. The general plan was formally defined in the Standard City Planning Enabling Act of 1928 with the

purpose of guiding and accomplishing a coordinated, adjusted, and harmonious development of the municipality and its environs which will, in accordance with present and future needs, best promote health, safety, morals, order, convenience, prosperity, and general welfare, as well as efficiency and economy in the process of development. (Section 6)

General plans evolved over time. Initially, they were seen as means to achieve an urban order in a democratic society, whereas, after World War II, plans were perceived more as expressions of control over growing municipal territories and devices of technical and scientific planning expertise. In the late 1960s and early 1970s, the general plan instrument was greatly criticized for being too strict and for its inability to adapt expeditiously to changing circumstances and market forces.

Nowadays, general plans are still very much in use but allow for more public participation during the making of the plan and for more flexibility in terms of their principles and in terms of the time frames for incorporating revisions. General plans are useful documents to establish the means for moving toward the desired long-term goals and to help guide decision-making processes.

How They Work

Typically, the general plan represents the fulfillment of a governmental legal requirement. For instance, in Arizona, the state statutes characterize a general plan as a municipal statement of land development policies, which may include maps, charts, graphs, and text in the form of objectives, principles, and standards for local growth and redevelopment. The most common goals today are public health and safety, effective circulation, provision of municipal services and facilities, balanced fiscal health, economic opportunities, and environmental conservation.

A general plan goes through five phases: a research phase, a period to articulate and clarify goals and objectives, a phase of plan formulation, an implementation phase, and finally a revision phase. One of the main challenges of the general plan approach to municipal development is its need for both comprehensiveness and relevance in rapidly growing urban areas.

Carlos Balsas

See also City Planning; Urban Planning

Further Readings

Abbott, M. 1985. "The Master Plan: A History of an Idea." PhD dissertation, Purdue University, West Lafayette, IN.

Kelly, E. and B. Becker. 2000. *Community Planning: An Introduction to the Comprehensive Plan.* Washington, DC: Island Press.

Ken, T. 1964. *The Urban General Plan.* San Francisco: Chandler.

GENTRIFICATION

In the mid-1960s, as middle-class households began to purchase and renovate rundown, tenanted Georgian and Victorian terraces in the West End of London, the British sociologist Ruth Glass coined the term *gentrification* to describe a process of working-class displacement that changes the district's prevailing social character. Initially, the defining features of gentrification included an influx of middle-class households and the renovation of working-class housing, invariably resulting in the displacement of tenants from gentrifying neighborhoods. Eventually, these processes are capable of completely changing the class composition and dominant tenure of inner area communities. Hence, in usage, gentrification has always referred to both the physical and social transformation of neighborhoods.

These days, given the large-scale residential redevelopment that is occurring in inner cities around the world, it is difficult to justify restricting the study of gentrification and displacement processes to what began as essentially home renovation. Gentrification studies have expanded to embrace all forms of residential investment and redevelopment in declining inner area neighborhoods; and now, although the context is quite different, in many postindustrial economies affluent newcomers and second-home owners are driving up house prices and destabilizing local housing markets for long-time residents in rural villages and coastal communities, producing effects akin to gentrification.

The effects of what is now characterized as urban revitalization were simply inconceivable to urban theorists confronted with suburbanization after World War II. Urban rent models predicted the decentralization of employment and housing, never envisaging that gentrification would become one of the key signifiers of late-twentieth-century urban restructuring. Besides providing a visible expression of forces at work in the finance, labor, and housing markets of global cities, by the 1990s, gentrification had been seized on by politicians and urban managers in Europe, North America, and Australasia as a strategy for bringing the inner city "back to life" and as a catalyst for urban renaissance.

Urban revitalization has reached the stage in numerous cities where residential property investors and middle- and upper-class home buyers can choose between the inner city's renovation, building conversion, townhouse, condominium, or apartment submarkets. Significantly, the much higher levels of investment required for multiunit redevelopment can quickly push up house prices and rents in old neighborhoods. So much has been written about gentrification that it is possible in this entry to point to only some key touchstones.

Seminal Studies of Gentrification

In the United States, the first commentaries on "central city revival" and a "back to the city" movement date from the mid-1970s. Isolated studies of neighborhood renewal and middle-class resettlement in older American neighborhoods were also beginning to appear. Yet, two decades of White flight had accentuated inner-city decline, making conditions so unpromising that, in the mid-1980s, Brian Berry went so far as to dismiss the phenomenon in North America as "islands of renewal in seas of decay."

In the case of Australian cities, although the population decline, depletion of the housing stock, and job losses resembled trends at the heart of Anglo-American cities, race was not an issue, nor was abandonment as widespread. In that regard, the Australian experience more closely resembled the inner area conditions of Canadian cities. Early Australian studies documented housing conflict arising from gentrification in inner Melbourne—by the Centre for Urban Research and Action—and the contribution of displacement to the decline of boarding and lodging in inner Adelaide. Hal Kendig's *New Life for Old Suburbs,* an analysis

of postwar land use and housing change in the Australian inner city, established that as well as middle-class incursion, displacement was being caused by freeway building and the expansion of large public institutions.

One of the best studies of class and tenure transformation actually follows up on the early observations of Ruth Glass. Flat break-up in Inner London was recorded by Chris Hamnett and Bill Randolph over a 15-year period (1966 to 1981): While the number of unfurnished flats fell by over half, the number of owner-occupied units doubled. Much of this was due to the sale of flats by property trusts, with a government home improvement grant acting as an incentive to remodel and convert them for homebuyers. As a result, extensive tracts of low-rent accommodation were lost within the heart of London.

Causes of Gentrification

It's unlikely that Ruth Glass could have imagined the spirited debate that would occur about the causes of gentrification. Because of gentrification's significance as a harbinger of urban restructuring in the 1970s and 1980s, it has served as something of a theoretical and ideological standard bearer within urban studies. Indeed, the evolving literature on gentrification has been shaped by opposing epistemology (structuralism vs. postmodernism; totalizing theory vs. eclecticism) and ideology (neo-Marxist vs. neo-Weberian analysis), as well as by the challenge posed to class analysis by the rise of influential social movements in civil society, for example, feminism, sexual liberation, and identity politics based on the celebration of cultural difference.

The Rent-Gap Hypothesis

The most fully developed theories of gentrification originally drew on quite different intellectual traditions but after a lot of dispute have come to be recognized as essentially two sides of the same coin; after all, housing is at once a consumption and an investment good. On the one hand, in the late 1970s, Neil Smith applied Marxist analysis to argue that gentrification was initiated by capital, rather than people, moving back to the inner city to exploit investment opportunities opened up by a developing rent gap in run-down neighborhoods. This rent-gap hypothesis, which was tested in Malmo and Adelaide, recognizes that as housing disinvestment sets in, land becomes undercapitalized relative to its redevelopment potential.

By bringing together Marxian concepts such as uneven development, capital switching, and class conflict, Smith presents a theoretically coherent account of gentrification as an urban output of the capitalist mode of production. But the rent-gap hypothesis does not properly accommodate the role of the state: As part of urban revitalization, public development agencies actively underwrite neighborhood improvement to lower the risk for institutional investors and gentrifiers. Nor does the rent-gap hypothesis admit to how much of the emerging demand from gentrifiers is due to noneconomic processes such as demographic change, social restructuring, and shifts in culture and consumption preferences.

The rudiments of the competing hypothesis were originally outlined in a 1980 paper by David Ley on liberal ideology and the postindustrial city. Significantly, Ley's narrative directs attention away from the economic forces driving reinvestment in gentrifying neighborhoods to concentrate on the gentrifiers, the formation of a distinctive mode of consumption, and the demographic, social, and ideological influences acting on them. He begins by sketching the implications for gentrification of the shift from an economy dominated by the manufacturing sector to one with rapidly growing services. He postulated that a new middle class was forming as a consequence of the growth of financial, professional, administrative, and other advanced services in postindustrial economies.

A New Middle Class

A fraction of this new middle class—most still prefer the suburbs—gravitated to the central city, along with the rapid growth in employment opportunities for college-educated and therefore well-paid workers. In turn, some city workers sought out housing opportunities in the inner area. But note that this demand-side explanation makes no mention of how dependent gentrifiers ultimately are on the appraisal of risk by institutional finance, especially mortgage lenders. Progressively, the new middle class went about remaking the central city and in the process challenged the balance of power in urban politics.

In a similar vein, Saskia Sassen argues that in genuinely global cities like New York and Los Angeles, with their huge immigrant populations, and London or Tokyo, the production of gentrifiers is directly explicable in terms of the *socioeconomic polarization* caused by economic restructuring. Dual labor markets are forming in the service economy and concentrating jobs at both ends of occupational and pay scales. But according to Chris Hamnett, compared with New York or Los Angeles, the process in London has been closer to one of professionalization because more high-end jobs have been created in business and government relative to the numbers jobs available to lower-paid service workers.

As well as leading to a more critical examination of the gentrifiers, this focus broadened out into a consideration of the contribution to gentrification of the feminization of work, the winning of sexual freedom by gays and lesbians, and the postmodern refashioning of mass consumption. With this has come a deeper appreciation that the new middle class doing the gentrifying is also fragmented to varying degrees according to gender, race, sexuality, and culture.

Gender and Sexual Identity

Feminist theorists like Damaris Rose and Liz Bondi argue that the focus on economic class ignores an important gender dimension of gentrification. With the pursuit of career and more women postponing marriage and childbearing, many partnered and young single professionals find that working and living in the inner city is more supportive of their lifestyle than living in family-oriented suburbs. In fact, after analyzing longitudinal data on London gentrifiers, Michal Lyons concluded that young and single professional women probably played a greater role in transforming inner London's housing market through the 1980s than households with two high-status workers. In this way, women are solving problems of access to work and home, as well as the challenge of combining paid and unpaid work, where they choose to, with parenting.

The assertion of sexual identity by a growing number of gays and lesbians in the second half of the twentieth century gave rise to a number of reasonably self-contained communities such as San Francisco's Castro and Mission districts or Sydney's Darlinghurst, Paddington, and Surrey Hills. Manuel Castells was the first to note the similarities between Castro and Mission, with their affluent gay communities and local "pink" economies, and other gentrifying neighborhoods in the United States. But what sets neighborhoods like Castro and Mission apart is their reputation for inclusiveness, tolerance of difference, and comparative security. Many other large cities have equally well-defined enclaves, and the presence of gay and lesbian couples and singles has lent added impetus more generally to gentrification processes.

Accordingly, these greater opportunities for congenial social interaction, self-expression and personal safety that gentrifying neighborhoods offer to women and homosexuals led Jon Caulfield to regard such enclaves in inner Toronto as emancipatory by comparison with the sameness and lack of inclusiveness that typify suburban social and cultural life.

A further perspective emphasizes the underlying importance of consumption to the lifestyle choices of the new middle class and where they can best access fashion goods and leisure activities. The inner city offers well-paid workers with disposable income greater scope for shopping, eating out, visiting galleries and museums, taking in music and theater, or attending festive events. Thus, gentrifiers are often found at the vanguard of trends in postmodern consumption.

Arts and Culture

Even as the debate on the causes of gentrification was warming up, the sociologist Sharon Zukin had decided that to explain how derelict Manhattan lofts came to be gentrified, she had to give as much credit to the search for space by people working in the creative arts (culture) as to those capitalizing on investment opportunities (capital). She coined the term *cultural capital* to describe how artists first reclaimed the loft district of SoHo for work and residence, thus paving the way for the much greater capital investment in housing that accompanied the rise of financial and business services in lower Manhattan.

Since then, by relaxing the insistence on one or other of the predominantly economic or cultural perspectives, it has been possible to reach a good deal of agreement about the fundamental causes of gentrification. Findings from numerous comparative studies have shown that gentrification processes are bound to reflect strikingly different urban histories and public policy settings in European and New World cities, not to mention non-Western cities. For example, disinvestment and neighborhood decline has seldom been part of the gentrification process at the center of many European cities, where gentrifiers have gravitated to long-established enclaves for the wealthy.

Eventually, in 2006, Tom Slater declaimed, in what was both a postmortem and a rallying cry, that for too long the theoretical and ideological squabbles over the causes of gentrification had diverted attention from critically examining the contribution of gentrification to displacement as well as the consequences of neoliberal urban strategy for neighborhoods earmarked for revitalization.

Contribution of Gentrification to Displacement

Researchers, policymakers, and commentators remain divided over the effects of gentrification. Where urban managers see it as the antidote to inner-city decline, their critics point to unacceptable social costs. Indeed, the mid-winter eviction in 1990 and 1991 of about 300 homeless people on Manhattan's Lower East Side—from a tent city in a local park surrounded by gentrified housing—prompted Neil Smith to liken the middle-class takeover of the American city to the revenge meted out on workers by bourgeois *revanchists* following the uprising of the Paris commune. According to Smith, the revanchist city marks a postrecession hardening in middle-class sentiment toward the urban poor in the United States, especially those made homeless by inner-city revitalization and gentrification.

Hence, the effects of gentrification are evident as much in the struggle to save the neighborhood as in well-documented research. Displacement is notoriously hard to measure because of the difficulty of tracing movers, especially if they are poor. In a systematic, rather than comprehensive review of the evidence on gentrification, Rowland Atkinson finds that displacement is the dominant research theme in more than half the 114 books, papers, and items of gray literature examined.

A U.S. Department of Housing and Urban Development survey prompted by widespread protest over condominium conversion in the 1970s remains one of the most thorough of its kind. Households in 12 major cities with high levels of conversion activity were surveyed. Between 1977 and 1980, 58 percent of the original households were displaced. Of the incoming residents, 70 percent were new owners.

Similarly, the combined results from two separate analyses of the New York City Housing and Vacancy Survey, which is conducted by the U.S. Bureau of the Census every three years, revealed that estimates of displacement rates for the years 1991 to 1993, 1996 to 1999, and 1999 to 2001 were 5.47 percent, 6.2 percent, and 9.9 percent, respectively, reflecting a tightening housing market; however, rents are either controlled or regulated for more than half of all housing units in New York City.

On the other hand, a larger study for the National Bureau of Economic Research of 15,000 U.S. Census tracts, representing gentrifying neighborhoods in 64 metropolitan areas, concludes that there is no evidence of displacement of low-income non-White households over the decade 1990 to 2000. Rather, the bulk of the increase in average family income in gentrifying neighborhoods can be attributed, first, to the retention of Black high school graduates (33 percent of the income gain) and, second, to the disproportionate in-migration of college-educated Whites (20 percent of the income gain). The out-migration rates of Black residents who never finished high school proved not to be significantly different between gentrifying and nongentrifying neighborhoods.

In conclusion, the weight of gentrification research points to the adverse effects of neoliberal urban policies designed to revitalize the inner city. Also, as the first years of the new century have shown, booming housing markets intensify displacement pressures. In these circumstances, the only sure way to preserve class shares of space is to permanently take housing in gentrifying neighborhoods out of the market. One of the boldest attempts occurred in the mid-1970s when the Australian government purchased three historic neighborhoods in inner Sydney and Melbourne to demonstrate the efficacy of community preservation. With affordable housing at a premium in many inner cities, more governments are subsidizing not-for-profits with a presence in vulnerable neighborhoods and are requiring contributions from developers where new investment threatens low-rent accommodations. But this is costly intervention and can hope to secure only a modicum of affordable housing in gentrifying communities.

Blair Badcock

See also Creative Class; Global City; Neighborhood Revitalization; Revanchist City; Social Movements; Urban Culture

Further Readings

Atkinson, Rowland and Gary Bridge, eds. 2007. *Gentrification in a Global Perspective*. London; New York: Routledge.

Hamnett, Chris and Bill Randolph. 1988. *Cities, Housing, and Profits: Flat Break-up and the Decline of Private Renting*. London: Hutchinson.

Kendig, Hal. 1979. *New Life for Old Suburbs. Post war Land Use and Housing in the Australian Inner City*. Sydney: Allen & Unwin.

Ley, David. 1996. *The New Middle Class and the Remaking of the Central City*. Oxford, UK: Oxford University Press.

Smith, Neil and Peter Williams, eds. 1986. *Gentrification of the City*. London: Unwin Hyman.

Van Weesep, Jan and S. Musterd, eds. 1991. *Urban Housing for the Better-off: Gentrification in Europe*. Utrecht, the Netherlands: Stedelijke Netwerken.

Zukin, Sharon. 1982. *Loft Living: Culture and Capital in Urban Change*. Baltimore; Johns Hopkins University Press.

GHETTO

Ghetto has a specific historical reference to the segregation of Jews within the Ghetto Nuovo in Venice of the 1400s, from which the name is derived, and to the segregated residential quarters that developed in European cities in the following century. The ethnic communities of Jewish immigrants in American cities were also called ghettos. In more recent times, ghetto has been used to describe

African American communities in the inner city, often characterized by high rates of poverty, crime, and social dislocation. Current discussions about the ghetto have raised concerns about the use of the term to define other ethnic communities and about the connections drawn to low-income communities in other countries—the Brazilian *favela*, French *banlieue*, South American shantytown, and Asian slum. This entry looks at the original Venice ghetto and the subsequent usage of the term in the United States.

The Venice Ghetto

The Jewish community in Venice dates to AD 1382, when the Venetian government authorized Jews to live in the city; the first residents were money lenders and businessmen. The enclosure of the Jews came after an outbreak of syphilis—a disease introduced from the New World that had no certain name, diagnosis, or treatment; it was said to be linked to the arrival of the Marrani Jews fleeing the Spanish Inquisition. By act of the Venetian senate on March 29, 1516, some 700 Jewish households were required to move into the Ghetto Nuovo, an island in the *cannaregio sestieri* on the northwest edge of the city, with entry controlled by two gates that were locked at sundown (the term refers to the original use of the island as a foundry and is from the Italian verb *gettare*, which means "to pour").

The Jewish ghetto would eventually include the Ghetto Nuovo, Ghetto Vecchio (1541), and Ghetto Nuovissimo (1633). Jews emerged from the world of the ghetto each morning to work or to shop, their clothing marked with a yellow circle (for men) or yellow scarf (for women) and spent the workday among gentiles, returning to the ghetto each evening before sundown. Within the ghetto, Jews were free to wear jewelry and other clothing prohibited on the streets of Venice following the Decree of 1512, and, in 1589, a charter of Jewish rights guaranteed the right to practice their religion. There eventually would be five synagogues for the separate groups of French, German, Italian, Levantine, and Spanish Jews.

Although the Ghetto was intended to isolate the Jews from the Venetian world outside its gates, physical segregation provided the community with some measure of protection. When groups of angry Catholics tried to attack the ghetto in 1534 during Lent, the bridges were drawn up and windows closed, and those inside were safe from the outside threat. Bernard Dov Cooperman notes that residents saw the ghetto as a biblical "camp of the Hebrews" rather than as a jail, a holy place en route to the Promised Land. The establishment of a ghetto in Verona was an occasion of celebration.

Segregation from the outside world would also turn the community inward, leading to the development of a religious culture different from other Jewish communities. By the end of the sixteenth century, fear of assimilation and intermarriage led rabbinic courts to forbid dancing between Jewish women and Christian men.

The example of the Jewish ghetto in Venice connects with the racialization of urban space across many dimensions. The process of racialization in this instance begins with the forced relocation of a group of people identified by a particular ethnic characteristic—their religion—to a physical space isolated from other areas of the city. People living outside of the ghetto view the behavior and beliefs of those inside with suspicion, and their bodies are seen as dangerous; as Richard Sennett comments that outsiders saw the ghetto as a place cut off from sun and water, supporting their beliefs that the Jews who lived there were prone to crime and idolatry.

The Venetian ghetto early on became a tourist destination as part of the grand tour of the 1600s and 1700s. Rail travel in the 1800s would directly link Venice with cities across Europe—although by this time there were travel narratives from many visitors from Europe and the United States. The Venetian ghetto is associated in the popular imagination with *The Merchant of Venice* (performed 1597, folio in 1600). The play likely has its origins in Edward de Vere's visit to Venice in 1575 and 1576, at a time when it was fashionable for young aristocrats to complete their classical education in Greek and Latin literature with visits to Italy. Although the ghetto is not referenced in the play, and none of the scenes are set in the ghetto, popular culture still associates Shylock as *The Merchant of Venice* and situates the play within the ghetto. In Julia Pascal's 2008 production of the play at the Arcola Theatre in London, a survivor of the Nazi Holocaust confronts a group of actors in the ghetto.

Today, the Museo Communita Ebraica in Campo Ghetto Nuevo offers tours of the ghetto, with visits to three of the historic synagogues. There is a guided tour in the footsteps of Shylock (to connect us back to *The Merchant of Venice*). The ghetto remains a tourist destination, somewhat off the beaten path even though it is very near the train station; and there is an official tourist map available in English, Japanese, and other languages at the Venetian tourist offices.

The Ghetto in the United States

Given the usual narrative concerning the influence of the Chicago School of Urban Sociology, one might expect that the beginning point for discussion of the ghetto in American cities would be the publication of Louis Wirth's classic study, *The Ghetto*. But although *ghetto* was used by African American scholars to describe segregated neighborhoods as far back as the 1890s, it was not commonly used in the social sciences to refer to black settlement patterns for another quarter century.

Early References

References to the ghetto were commonplace in Jewish popular culture from the late nineteenth century onward. *Children of the Ghetto* (1892) by the British journalist Israel Zangwell (1864–1926) was dramatized and performed in England and America (he also published a series of biographical studies titled *Dreamers of the Ghetto*, 1898). Abraham Cahan (1860–1951), the Russian American journalist, immigrated to New York in 1882 and published *Yekl: A Tale of the New York Ghetto* (1898). This work presents the ghetto both as a historic entity and contemporary place and refers to the continuity of "ghetto culture" from the old world in New York's Lower East Side.

During the same period, African American scholars used ghetto to describe urban neighborhoods with significant Black populations. In *The Black North: A Social Study*, W. E. B. Du Bois describes the growth of the Black population in Philadelphia's Seventh Ward, which he says was a residential area for 50 years before African Americans were forced into "a ghetto bordering the Delaware River." The ghetto here refers to an area of first settlement.

Louis Wirth's classic study of the Chicago ghetto, completed under the direction of Robert Park, was published first as an article in the *American Journal of Sociology* (this was common for the Chicago School studies) and appeared as a book a year later in 1928. Wirth gives a historical overview of the Jewish ghetto in Frankfurt and other European cities before describing the Chicago ghetto, where he traces the movement of the Chicago ghetto from the Maxwell Street neighborhood (the area of first settlement known as the ghetto) into North Lawndale (called "Deutschland" because this was the area of second settlement for German Jews) and notes that already there was a movement out of this area into the north side neighborhoods. (This was not the first discussion of the Maxwell Street ghetto, as the area is described by Manuel Zeublin in *The Chicago Ghetto,* published in 1895.)

Robert Park's race relations cycle provided the theoretical narrative; according to Park, the first stage of contact would be followed by competition, then accommodation, and finally assimilation. For Wirth, the Chicago ghetto was similar to other ethnic enclaves, an area where first-generation immigrants live and over time become assimilated to the mores of the larger society. Wirth's description of the assimilation of Jewish immigrants in *The Ghetto* would serve as a model for the acculturation of other ethnic—and later racial—groups. Although his work is cited in many of the Chicago School studies, it is important to note that in these studies the *ghetto* is used strictly to refer to the Jewish ghetto, not to other poverty neighborhoods (these remain slums), not to other ethnic neighborhoods (these remain Little Italy and the like), and not to African American areas (this will remain the Black Belt in the Chicago School literature). St. Clair Drake and Horace Cayton's classic work *Black Metropolis* (1945) presents a study of Bronzeville, as the south side Chicago had become known. The term *ghetto* is used in only one section (it does not appear in the index), and it is used as a geographical reference to describe the poorest area of Bronzeville. Clearly, the ghetto was located within Bronzeville, but Bronzeville itself was not a ghetto.

Denoting African American Communities

Gilbert Osofsky's landmark study *Harlem: The Making of a Ghetto* (1963) marks the common usage of ghetto to refer to African American communities (the second edition of the book was published in 1971 with a concluding chapter titled "The Enduring Ghetto," which argues that the essential nature and structure of the ghetto have remained in the north since the end of slavery). Osofsky's work was followed by many other studies of the history of Black settlement in the urban north, including Allan Spear's *Black Chicago* (1968), Kenneth Kusner's *The Making of a Negro Ghetto* (1976), and Thomas Philpott's *The Making of the Second Ghetto*. In geography of the same period, Harold Rose would describe the African American ghetto as a new urban subsystem and refer to suburban Black communities as *minighettos*. By the 1970s, the use of *ghetto* to describe not just specific areas within the city, but African American communities as a whole, had become solidified.

By the end of the century, the ghetto migrated from popular culture to scholarly research and then back into popular culture—with a vengeance. Indeed, the ghetto is ever present: in popular music, in the cinema, in consumer products (boom boxes became known as ghetto blasters), and of course, in the ever-present labeling of speech, behavior, and dress: *that's so ghetto!*

The ghetto remains a central concept in sociological research and in urban studies more generally. William Julius Wilson has published important books based on two decades of study in Chicago (*The Truly Disadvantaged, When Work Disappears*), and Loïc Wacquant reprised his own research from the same inner-city Chicago neighborhoods and the Paris banlieues in *Urban Outcasts*. Mary Pattillo has suggested that the boundaries of the Chicago ghetto (roughly the area encompassed by Drake and Cayton's *Black Metropolis*—although they did not consider all of Bronzeville to be a ghetto) should be expanded to include segregated neighborhoods for Blacks even if they are not poor, arguing that this would be more comparable to the original use to define Jewish communities. In 2007, *City* magazine published "Banlieues, the Hyperghetto, and Advanced Marginality: A Symposium on Loïc Wacquant's

Urban Outcast," a 60-plus-page collection of essays focusing on the work of Wacquant. And a recent symposium on the ghetto in *City and Community* invited scholars from several disciplines (and three continents) to discuss the usefulness of the term *ghetto* in the study of urban communities. This symposium notes that the gentrification of former ghettos such as Harlem and the Fillmore District in San Francisco, depopulation and gentrification on Chicago's south side (the area studied by Wilson and Wacquant), dispersal of African American populations from inner-city neighborhoods in other cities, and the like suggest that it is time to evaluate the conceptual merits and usefulness of the ghetto for understanding emergent patterns of social exclusion across the metropolitan region. In Chicago and Harlem, the visitor may take guided tours of the ghetto, and the earlier zones of exclusion now appear in the official city websites for tourists. With the commercialization of ghetto spaces, important questions emerge as to the usefulness of the ghetto to understanding the social exclusion of ethnic and racial minorities in the United States and other countries.

Ray Hutchison

See also Banlieue; Chicago, Illinois; Ethnic Enclave; *Favela*

Further Readings

Chatterton, Paul, ed. 2007. "Banlieues, the Hyperghetto, and Advanced Marginality: A Symposium on Loïc Wacquant's Urban Outcast." *City* 11(3):357–421.

Curiel, Roberta and Bernard-Dov Cooperman. 1990. *The Ghetto of Venice*. London: Tauris Parke.

Davis, Robert C. and Benjamin Ravid, eds. 2001. *The Jews of Early Modern Venice*. Baltimore: Johns Hopkins University Press.

Drake, St. Clair and Horace Cayton. 1945. *Black Metropolis*. Chicago: University of Chicago Press.

Hutchison, Ray and Bruce Haynes, eds. 2008. "Symposium on the Ghetto." *City and Community* 7(4):347–98.

Pattillo, Mary. 2003. "Expanding the Boundaries and Definitions of the Ghetto." *Ethnic and Racial Studies* 26(6):1046–57.

Sennett, Richard. 1995. *Flesh and Stone: The Body and the City in Western Civilization*. New York: W. W. Norton.

Wacquant, Loïc. 2008. *Urban Outcasts: A Comparative Sociology of Advanced Marginality*. Cambridge, UK: Polity Press.

Wirth, Louis. 1928. *The Ghetto*. Chicago: University of Chicago Press.

GLOBAL CITY

Global cities are key urban nodes that concentrate command and control functions in the global economy. They are mechanisms through which global economic integration takes root because they play a generative economic role not just within their national borders but also within increasingly global networks of production and consumption. In addition, they usually exhibit a high degree of ethnic diversity and are marked by social and spatial fragmentation.

Evolution of the Concept

Building on Peter Hall's *The World Cities* (1966), the most recent popularization of the term derives from a series of seminal articles of the 1980s and 1990s. John Friedmann and Anthony King developed their concepts of world or global cities through empirically grounded research and engagement with the third world; King examined both the developed and developing world, and Friedmann mostly the latter. Starting in the 1990s, attention turned to the advanced capitalist world, driven largely by the work of Saskia Sassen. Her 1991 book, *The Global City: New York, London, Tokyo*, set forth a major research agenda on issues like the nature and workings of economic globalization, the role of cross-border finance in urban development, and social or class polarization, thereby shifting the focus toward rich and prosperous cities in democratic nations and inviting a larger debate.

Sassen's view of the global city as exemplified by a particular class of economic activities increasingly tied to high finance and advanced services is contested. Similarly, her explanation of social polarization in global cities has been qualified by proponents of dualization and fragmentation, while her initial marginalization and even disregard for the role of the state in shaping global cities

has invited sustained criticism. Nevertheless, Sassen's research program propelled cities into a global context and onto the social science and policy agenda. It also contributed to a rising and heated debate over the nature and features of globalization and its impact on the urban realm. With the growing popularity of the global city paradigm, even the most conventional topics long studied by urbanists, ranging from suburbs and midtowns to real estate, architecture, and urban governance, are now examined in a global context.

Global cities are considered good cases for exploring the workings of economic globalization. The globalization of capital and labor affects both urban employment patterns and shifts in the sectoral character of the urban economy in many European and American cities. Global cities are those whose growth and character are determined by the generative economic role they play within their national borders and within global networks of production and consumption. Consequently, global cities are no longer to be seen as fetters on the national development of their host countries, as in the past with the dependent urbanization literature, but more likely to be conceptualized as the mechanisms through which global economic integration takes root and greater prosperity is achieved.

Emerging Analytical Perspectives

At least four main themes have emerged in this rapidly changing field: (1) a nuanced appreciation of scale as a means for overcoming relatively schematic accounts of the local–global relationship, (2) more detailed examination of the links between world networks and global cities as a strategy for describing both cities' embeddedness and the multiscalar nature of globalization, (3) increased attention to the continuing relevance of the state and levels of development in analyzing global cities, and (4) efforts to describe and explain the role of historical trajectories, pathways, and path-dependence in global city formation.

Scaling the Global in Global Cities

Early approaches to the global city implicitly or explicitly adhered to a strong globalization thesis; namely, the *unmediated* and *unilinear* impact of global forces over particular territories worldwide. The global city became as much a process as a place, and similarities between global cities were highlighted to the detriment of their specificities and differences. Many studies treated social and spatial polarization as a universal consequence of globalization and as a prominent feature of all global cities. Few scholars considered the multiplicity of interacting and changing spatial scales of globalization, and most worked under the assumption that globalization processes intertwined two clearly delineated conceptual categories—the "local" and the "global." This framing posited the global as active and powerful and the local as passive and weak; it also omitted possible covariations with places larger than the city (or the city-region) yet smaller than the global level.

This schematic characterization of local against global has been overcome by integrating multiple spatial scales (local, regional, national) in the analysis. The new assumption is that regional and national states play a significant role in the reconfiguration of local processes, not only because they react to processes occurring at the global level but because they mobilize resources to actively link cities and nations with the global economy. The problem with the earlier local–global duality was that it confined cities to a politically irrelevant role in the face of globalization and reified spatial scales as self-contained units.

Networks and Global Cities

One approach to world cities focuses on the transnational networks in which cities are embedded and then analyzes the composition and character of these networks in a global context. This is quite compatible with the growing interest in the changing locations and economic roles that cities play in regional, national, or international hierarchies of urban places. It is also used to historically study cities embedded in colonial and imperial networks. With this approach, as much attention is paid to the transnational network itself as to the institutions or practices linking particular cities and mediating the development of the network.

A second, equally popular approach shares a concern with global networks but focuses on territorially bounded locations in these global networks.

To use Manuel Castells's terminology, the concern is as much the "spaces of places" as the "spaces of flows." Scholars who employ this perspective would argue that the globalization of capital and labor fuels the growth and economic successes of some cities (e.g., New York) while constraining others (e.g., Detroit), thereby exacerbating regional economic polarization.

A third approach is the regional approach but understood in transnational as much as intranational terms. This is a conceptual departure from the past when the notion of region referred to a spatial territory within a single nation-state. Scholars of Europe (and slightly less so East Asia) now study the urban effects of globally integrated (transnational) regionalism, perhaps because their home nations are caught up in these dynamics. Their concern is how globalization increases transnational economic integration so as to form megaregions with their own supranational governing institutions; whether locales on the receiving end of global investments and labor flows assume greater political and economic significance; and the conditions under which globally integrated cities will bypass the nation-state and negotiate directly with each other in larger regional pacts.

These lines of research have implications for understanding the dynamics of cities as well as the global context in which they operate, if only because they underscore the ways that, in an increasingly globalized world, the nation-state or other subnational or supranational jurisdictions are challenged or remain the most politically relevant unit for mediating among cities, addressing intranational regional disparities, or coordinating new practices and institutions. Instead of having to choose between the local and the global view, the network approach posits a global entity that is continuously local, even as it builds on relational thinking.

Nation-State in the Production of Global Cities

Although the nation-state was a significant factor in the early literature on global cities, it fell to the sidelines in the initial heyday of global cities discourse, partly owing to the claims of globalization theorists that national governments had increasingly less control over flows of capital passing through their borders. Efforts to remove this blind spot are under way, even among those initially responsible for the oversight. Saskia Sassen now argues that the declining significance of the state in the global economy has been over-emphasized and that it would be more accurate to say that globalization is transforming the state.

The unanswered question is whether the nation-state plays a different role in different cities/nations around the globe and whether and how time has changed that role. For example, do global cities in democratic, authoritarian, and communist societies develop similarly? How might established democracies differ from newer ones or from non-democracies? Such issues were once the source of critical debate in the third-world urban literature, and recent trends suggest they are relevant again, partly because postnational discourses are increasingly being questioned in the face of evidence that states continue to have the capacity to mold globalization processes and affect how global cities link to the world economy. Studies of the role of national financial institutions and how they implement new global rules are central in sustaining such propositions.

Despite the renewed emphasis on the state, particularly from scholars who study financial regulations and institutions, efforts to bring politics into the literature on global cities are still limited. Indeed, there is surprisingly little writing on social movements, civil society, and popular politics, especially in the advanced capitalist context. These points of entry are still more likely to be found in the general literature on economic globalization in the form of studies of antiglobalization protests. With very few exceptions, writings that focus on antiglobalization or transnational social movements have not been situated in the context of the city, and when they are, they appear as antiliberalization or antiglobalization movements rather than as urban movements. What remains to be studied is the extent to which globalization-fueled social movements emerge in opposition to formal urban politics or urban dynamics—global "city-ness," as opposed to globalization itself.

Pathways and Path-Dependence in Global City Formation

A final line of research concerns pathways to global city formation and the interrelationship among path-dependence, multiscalar networks, and globalization. Much of the debate revolves around the asserted newness of globalization and whether patterns in the contemporary world build or depart from patterns of the past. Scholars who claim that globalization is a radically new process rarely examine past developments, while analysts who turn to history claim there is nothing new to current global processes. In an attempt to bridge this divide, scholars are bringing together historical macrosociology, world systems analysis, and global city research, and turning their attention to the path-dependence of current developments.

In addressing such concerns, a key point of departure is contemporary capitalism and its dynamics. So far, the hegemonic view holds that global cities concentrate most of the economic processes that are significantly changing the landscape of capitalism because certain cities are key nodes that remain centers of command and control for the main agents of global capital accumulation. This returns the field to the original claims of Saskia Sassen. Yet, it is still unclear as to whether contemporary global cities constitute a unique social formation in late capitalism because of their interactions with the global economy or whether they simply concentrate in a few critical locales the general and enduring processes that occur in many other cities.

Among those who are tackling this set of issues is British geographer Peter Taylor, director of the Globalization and World Cities (GaWC) Research Network. He acknowledges the fact that cities as international financial centers have steered the capitalist world economy for centuries; but he also builds on four overlapping and systematic accumulation cycles—globalization cycles—in the capitalist world economy, ranging from the Genoese/Iberian cycle from the late fifteenth century through the Dutch and British cycles of the interim centuries and up to the American cycle of the late nineteenth century to the present. This leads Taylor to claim that current descriptions of recent, world economy restructuring are not unique, a proposition that is consistent with David Harvey's view of the historical transition from Fordism–Keynesianism to flexible accumulation, understood as the latest capital accumulation phase, another epoch of financial expansion, and the latest rebirth of capital. Taylor then concludes that because economic globalization has provided new outlets for capital, competitive intercity relations have given way to cooperation. The outcome is "a contemporary world city network" linked to global capitalist prosperity.

In short, the global city paradigm has evolved and matured since the 1980s. What started as an attempt to give shape to a concept and emergent field of study led to a the proliferation of new research questions and is now preoccupied with overcoming premature generalizations expressed in the initial formulations while also replacing them with more nuanced accounts of the spatial, temporal, and scalar contexts that influence the formation of global cities and urban outcomes worldwide.

Questions still remain. One is whether there is some implicit or unexplored assumption that global cities can exist only in economically vigorous nations or in those in transition to such status. This pivots on whether global cities generate national prosperity or national prosperity generates global cities. The evidence suggests, for already poor countries at least, that it might be the absence of global linkages that thwarts urban prosperity or another mediating factor independent of the linkage. There also are methodological concerns. Is it possible to pursue reliable theory building (let alone testing) about global cities if most research is focused on "like" or developed cases? How much of the shift in emphasis to the generative economic impact of the global city is owed to timing, including the fact that more scholars now are examining major cities in a post-Fordist period when the global economy itself may have transformed considerably, at least in comparison to the post–World War II period when cities were first examined in a global context?

Diane Davis and
Gerardo del Cerro Santamaría

See also Globalization; Sassen, Saskia; Urban System; World City

Further Readings

Borja, J. and M. Castells. 1997. *Local y global. La gestión de las ciudades en la era de la información* (Local and Global: The Management of Cities in the Information Era). Madrid: Taurus.

Davis, Diane E. 2005. "Cities in a Global Context: A Brief Intellectual History." *International Journal of Urban and Regional Research* 29(1):92–109.

King, A. 1990. *Global Cities: Post-imperialism and the Internationalization of London.* New York: Routledge.

Lo, F.-C. and Y. Yeung. 1998. *Globalization and the World of Large Cities.* New York: UN University Press.

Sassen, S. 2002. *The Global City: New York, London, and Tokyo,* Princeton, NJ: Princeton University Press.

Scott, A. J., ed. 2002. *Global City-Regions: Trends, Theory, Policy.* Oxford, UK: Oxford University Press.

Short, J. R. and Y.-H. Kim. 1999. *Globalization and the City.* Harlow, UK: Longman.

Taylor, P. J. 2004. *World City Network: A Global Urban Analysis.* New York: Routledge.

GLOBALIZATION

Globalization entails a growing economic, social, political, and cultural interdependence between different nations and localities. It is a process made possible by advanced technology, which drives both the speed and volume of cross-border transactions. These transactions cover a wide range of goods and services, capital flows, and information. Since the 1970s, globalization has become a powerful force in almost all aspects of our lives, with hardly a place in the world untouched by this phenomenon. From business corporations located in New York City to street vendors in Mumbai (Bombay), all have found themselves part of a worldwide, seamless, and indivisible web of interconnected parts.

Politics plays a pivotal role in globalization. Globalization has magnified interactions among states, localities, and social movements throughout the world. Signs of this are visible in the rise of multilateral organizations, regional pacts, and talk of a borderless world. States, localities, nongovernmental organizations, and labor unions increasingly ignore old boundaries and are driven by the seemingly contradictory stimuli of cooperation and competition. For some, this has opened new worlds of opportunity where masses of people can be mobilized for democratic ends. This interaction, both in place and across cyberspace, makes government more accountable and also more replaceable. For others, it signifies a concentration of wealth and power and the threat of lower living standards. This has led to perilous instability and thunderous reaction from both left- and right-wing protestors.

In addition, globalization shifts economic power from governments to transnational organizations and corporations. With the active role of the World Trade Organization (WTO), World Bank, and International Monetary Fund (IMF), trade, tariff and investment barriers have been lowered, sharply reducing the role of national government. A succession of crises in the 1990s—Mexico, Thailand, Indonesia, Argentina, Turkey, and Brazil—vividly demonstrated the importance of global financial institutions for redressing fiscal imbalances.

Accompanying the shift in economic power is increased interdependence facilitated by standardization. Defined as the international acceptance of uniform criteria for producing goods and services, standardization has promoted globalization. Once goods and information become alike, they become recognizable and interchangeable and thus more easily traded. Common standards of measurement, universal criteria, interchangeable parts, and identical symbols are essential. Just as the grid system of streets enabled land development, so too does standardization facilitate globalization. Products sold at Sony, Nike, and McDonald's can be found across the globe and are easily recognized by consumers. Licenses and professional certifications have also become standardized to allow human resources to flow across regulatory boundaries. International free trade, championed by the WTO, has become an instrument of standardization. Complying with the WTO's regulations, member countries have developed common criteria for their products and opened new markets.

A number of developing countries have also embarked on the road toward global integration. China, India, Malaysia, Brazil, Mexico, South Korea, and Thailand no longer export only raw materials but also finished products and services. In India, for example, software exports accounted for about 10.5 percent of India's total exports in 1999 and 2000. Meanwhile, free trade and the competitive advantages stemming from it have made industry there more efficient and increased wealth.

Globalization has brought opportunities as well as problems. It has facilitated the proliferation of innovative technologies and medical advances that have significantly decreased mortality rates, especially in developing countries, as well as promoted liberal democracy, human rights, and good governance. During the last 25 years, for example, life expectancy rose by over a decade in industrialized countries and by over 20 years on average in developing countries. Moreover, although globalization has created prosperity, it has not created comparable mechanisms for redistribution of benefits among and within countries. Conditions in some countries have improved, but in others, they have stagnated. Problems include deeper disparities between social classes, increased levels of poverty, and large-scale demographic displacement. As one UN report stated, "Homeless people are living in cardboard boxes on sidewalks of gleaming corporate skyscrapers, whose budgets exceed those of many countries."

How do cities fit into this overall picture? Although the noted urbanist Henri Lefebvre wrote before the onset of globalization, he was quite prescient in foreseeing a world in which over half of the human population would live in cities. Lefebvre also argued that as society developed the language of cities, its identities, forms of capital, and organization of social reproduction would become dominant. As Lefebvre saw it, cities mediate between the person and the rest of the world, with city life a prism through which the world is viewed.

For centuries, urban areas have been the centers of production, distribution, services, finance, and banking. As globalization weakens national borders and intensifies competition, cities have become the main driving forces of globalization, its agents of change. In cities, global operations are centralized and manifested in changes in the structure of employment, the formation of public/private partnerships, the development of mega-projects, and the spatial exclusion of certain population groups. Cities have quickly transformed their economies to accommodate multinational corporations, international media, and foreign tourism. World trade centers, international festivals, and immigrant communities saturate the urban landscape.

Cities also have taken the initiative in competing for Olympic Games, courting multinational corporations, and selling their products abroad.

Some cities have appointed representatives to foreign nations to pursue inward investment or market local products. Other cities have declared themselves to be "nuclear free zones"; while still others have taken steps to welcome immigrants. The term *glocalization* has come to denote the growing impact of global forces on local decision making.

Cities now operate in a borderless world in which they search for capital markets, political influence, or wider recognition. These "glocal cities" have drifted from their national moorings. London, Tokyo, Mumbai, and New York are already larger than some nation-states and play a role on the world stage. London's economy would rank as the ninth-largest in all of Europe, surpassing entire national economies of countries like Austria, Greece, and Portugal.

The advent of globalization has brought increased foreign immigration and international tourism to many cities. Most of the immigration moves from the underdeveloped world to cities with the most advanced economies. By 2000, more than 50 percent of the population in New York and Toronto were classified as ethnic minorities or foreign born. In London, the percentage of foreign residents has risen to 29 percent, while in Paris, the percentage is above 15 percent. Many immigrants take lower-paying jobs cleaning offices and hotel rooms or working as day laborers in construction. At times, the presence of large immigrant populations has bred violence, xenophobia, and social tensions. Youth whose parents were born in North Africa rioted in the Paris suburbs; cultural tensions have erupted between immigrants and native residents in Amsterdam and Brussels; and attacks against immigrants from the Caucasus mountains are common in Moscow and St. Petersburg.

Another aspect of globalization involves a substantial increase in international tourism. More than 6 million international tourists on average visit New York annually, and the figures for Paris and London are even higher, reaching 15 million and more than 11 million, respectively. Tourism is a major urban industry involving massive flows of people across continents. It has become a major agent of change and one of the most visible expressions of globalization. Cities have become centers of consumption, entertainment, culture, and services to accommodate this industry by investing in infrastructure, construction of airports, mass transportation systems, and urban amenities.

While cities such as New York, London, and Tokyo have large financial resources, global connections, and substantial opportunities, other cities located in less developed economies have been unable to establish diversified economies or generate a substantial tertiary sector. For leading cities (New York, London, Tokyo) or those quick to adapt (Singapore, Bangkok, and Shanghai), globalization has been a blessing and a key for transforming their industrial base. For less fortunate regions, the capacity for converting local resources into an export sector has limited their interaction with the global economy. Cities like Lagos, Dar es Salaam, and Cairo have increased in population but have not been able to boost their economies to supply their swelling populations. In many other cities, a paucity of affordable housing and discriminatory practices force newcomer immigrants to live in spatially segregated ghettos. Growth without development continues to hinder cities in many parts of the world.

One might suppose that globalization makes cities less important or more alike as they are swept into a common world of economic competition and social interchange. Presumably, people could be located anywhere and conduct business via the Internet from a mountaintop retreat. In fact, the opposite is true—at least for some cities. A knowledge-based economy has accelerated face-to-face and informal contacts. In addition, businesses search for that extra advantage that comes from personal contact.

Cities in strategic locations, such as Singapore, have successfully used international opportunities to shed heavy industries and switch their economies to accommodate financial centers, corporate directorships, and other professional services. Less fortunate cities, mostly in Africa, have lost industries and been unable to attract emerging economic sectors. Globalization has had differential impacts on cities, and not all cities share the same fate. Thanks to globalization, cities like New York, London, and Paris have become switching stations where many global transactions take place. London, for instance, has emerged as a banking center where capital is concentrated, New York as a producer of financial instruments where loans and mergers are consummated, and Paris as a seat for corporate headquarters and professional services where deals are made. Each of these cities has carved out a niche for itself as a command post in a larger world economy. Other cities, like Detroit, Liverpool, and Essen, have been hit with devastating losses in jobs, trade, and population.

The differences can be palpable in the built environments of cities. A booming central business district, sleek office towers, and chic hotels arise in one city and are contrasted with boarded-up storefronts and vacant factories in another. Despite the ascendance of digital technology, geographic location or place continues to matter. Neat suburban residential enclaves, edge cities, busy commercial downtowns, urban ghettos, vacated industrial areas, and campus-like office parks are all part of a complex urban fabric that differentiates opportunities. Some cities have taken advantage of those opportunities and the enormous wealth that springs from global trade.

Moreover, the absence of internal and international redistributive mechanisms has made poor areas extremely vulnerable. For some cities, hypermobile capital and free-floating money eroded economic bases because businesses rapidly shifted from one location to another in search of the highest return on investment. Cities in less developed economies have been reduced to a secondary status as suppliers of primary products or cheap labor. This leaves countries vulnerable to fluctuations in the world price of their main products.

Other negative spillovers attributed to globalization include increasing disparities in income, threats to traditional ways of life, and allegations that power is increasingly concentrated in advanced economies. These consequences have been the main reason for abuse of labor and human rights, air pollution, and global warming.

As technological innovations and free trade advance, globalization appears to be gaining strength. This process is likely to continue and even accelerate within the next decades. Much as the Industrial Revolution changed the course of history, globalization will bring tremendous transformations. Some cities will take advantage of its opportunities and emerge as global centers, while others will be bogged down in economic and social problems.

Anar Valiyev and H. V. Savitch

See also Castells, Manuel; Global City; Sassen, Saskia; Urban System; Urban Theory; World City

Further Readings

Lefebvre, H. 2003. *The Urban Revolution*. Minneapolis: University of Minnesota Press.
Sassen, S. 1994. *Cities in World Economy*. Thousand Oaks, CA: Pine Forge.
Savitch, H. V. and P. Kantor. 2002. *Cities in the International Marketplace: The Political Economy of Urban Development in North America and Western Europe*. Princeton, NJ: Princeton University Press.
United Nations. 2001. *Cities in a Globalizing World: Global Report on Human Settlements 2001*. London: Earthscan.

GOTTDIENER, MARK

Mark Gottdiener has been a leading proponent of the new urban sociology, a paradigm of urban analysis that has challenged human ecology since the 1970s. Emphasizing academic dialogue and work ranging across disciplinary boundaries, he has developed ideas of European critical and social theory to serve urban analysis. Notably, he was the first person to systematically introduce in the Anglophone world Henri Lefebvre's theory of the social production of space.

Active in the 1960s student movements, Mark Gottdiener started his career as a transport analyst and consultant. He studied mathematics, economics, and sociology and defended his PhD (sociology) in 1973. Gottdiener has been full professor at several universities, including University of California, Riverside (long periods in 1980s and 1990s) and Hunter College, part of City College of New York (1991–1992). He has been invited as a visiting professor to University of Colorado, Boulder, and Helsinki University of Technology, Finland. Since 1994, Gottdiener is the professor of sociology at State University of New York at Buffalo.

In his 16 books and numerous journal articles, Gottdiener has analyzed the real estate industry, metropolitan development, themed consumption environments, and urban and suburban lifestyles, to take some examples. Although most of his research focuses on the United States, its explicit discussion of the ways to explain urban patterns and processes facilitates comparisons with other contexts. This entry explores Gottdiener's influences, research themes, and new theoretical formulations, emphasizing the linkages between ostensibly separate topics and the coherence of his oeuvre.

The Social Production of Urban Space as the Center of Analysis: Henri Lefebvre

In the 1970s, Gottdiener was already aware of the philosophical and sociological ideas of Henri Lefebvre. When preparing his first book, *Planned Sprawl* (1977), he realized the weakness of the dominant urban ecology in explaining metropolitan growth patterns. However, Marxian political economy, as developed by Manuel Castells and David Harvey among others, also had limitations. To achieve a better theoretical frame, Gottdiener took the task of introducing into the Anglophone debate Henri Lefebvre's work on Marxism, everyday life, and conception of space, a project that culminated in *The Social Production of Urban Space* (1985).

For Gottdiener, Lefebvre's value as an urban thinker lies in four areas. First, Lefebvre showed that economic categories such as rent, profit, or uneven development, which Marx and Engels used in the study of industrial urban capitalism, can also be applied in analyzing cities. Second, Lefebvre valorized real estate investment as a "second circuit of capital," a partly independent area to make profit and acquire wealth. Third, Lefebvre maintained that space never is neutral background for social activities but both the condition and product of those activities, reproducing social relations and the very relations of production. Fourth, Lefebvre discussed the importance of government and state actions in space.

Gottdiener develops Lefebvre's theory, showing how both the real estate industry and the state conceptualize space through its abstract qualities, such as size, distance, monetary value, and profit. For people, however, space is the milieu of everyday life. The uses and meanings of this appropriated social space, for example, home and neighborhood, may be undermined by real estate projects and public plans, causing conflicts.

According to Lefebvre, the conflict between abstract and social space is fundamental, ranking with the separate and different conflict among classes. Gottdiener notes that, with this view, Lefebvre departed from the Marxian perspective, which holds that class conflict is the basic force in the history of capitalism.

In his engagement with Lefebvre's thinking, Gottdiener goes beyond a mere introduction: He successfully operationalizes Lefebvre's theory in the field of urban analysis. By introducing Anthony Giddens's scheme of social structuration, where the structures, institutions, and agency all play a role, Gottdiener makes Lefebvre's theory more applicable. He maintains that space—its social production and struggle about it—is an indispensable element of contemporary urban analysis. In *The Social Production of Urban Space,* he states that "the contingent process in the production of space must always be at the centre of analysis, rather than focusing on the political economy of capitalist development per se."

This epistemological position has informed Gottdiener's work from 1970s till the present. From the realist and materialist angle, he has mounted a systematic critique of several contemporary currencies in urban studies, especially ideas of Edward Soja and the postmodern geographers. Gottdiener rejects their "structurationist formulations which deploy an abstract and nominalist account of space circumscribed around a disembodied signifier such as 'spatiality.'" Gottdiener claims that, on the one hand, every level of urban social analysis has to be spatially embedded, and, on the other, the underlying structures always have to be analyzed as political, economic, and cultural.

Understanding Signification as Culturally Conditioned: Sociosemiotics

Like Lefebvre, Gottdiener is keenly interested in the symbolic aspect of space. To complement the new methodological frame needed to understand contemporary metropolitan areas, Gottdiener, with Alexandros Lagopoulos, tailored in the 1980s a new version of semiotics. The approach is called *sociosemiotics*. It draws together ideas from Ferdinand Saussure, Algirdas Greimas, and Louis Hjelmslev.

The foundation of all semiotics is the concept of sign. According to Saussure's well-known definition, a sign is composed of the signifier and the signified. In urban semiotics, material objects and forms of settlement space are studied as vehicles of signification. In these studies, the symbolic act always involves a physical object and social discourse on it. The objects of analysis can be streets and facades or planning texts and real estate advertising. As a subfield of urban semiotics, sociosemiotics focuses on the study of culturally constructed connotations, the deeper meanings or conception people attach to spaces (in distinction to denotations that work on the level of perception), or the ideological conditioning of the individual experience. Sociosemiotics is thus explicitly linked to critical theory, avoiding the individualist bias of much of cultural studies. In *The City and the Sign,* Gottdiener defined it as "materialist inquiry into the role of ideology in everyday life" (p. 14).

Applied in urban analysis, sociosemiotics questions the epistemological legitimacy of cognitive geography and mental mapping as being limited to perceptions only and stressing psychobiological adaptation to the environment. As Gottdiener sees it, urban practitioners create connotative codes as social products. If this is true, both social affiliations and spatial practices shape the meanings and emotions each individual invests in a particular material object. Indeed, red lights, McDonald's logo, or a modern glass façade are interpreted and experienced differently, depending on the individual's income, age, ethnicity, education, and gender.

The actual sociosemiotic method decomposes spatial signs. Both the *expression* and *content* (signifier and signified) are broken down to form and substance. Instead of two terms, the analysis deals with four. Data gathering requires both visual methods and cultural research. Once researchers have a good command of the subject, they can produce rich studies of the relations between conditioning ideology, immediate perception, objects, and their wider urban context. In *Postmodern Semiotics* (1995) and *The Theming of America* (1997) Gottdiener presents sociosemiotic analyses of environments for consumption, leisure, and tourism. Sociosemiotics can also be applied to gang graffiti, visual demarcation of ethnic areas, and many other elements, which together compose the contemporary settlement space.

Bringing the Threads Together: Sociospatial Approach

The theoretical frame Gottdiener has developed can best be called the sociospatial approach to urban analysis. It is a synthetic perspective, which takes what is best in the new ideas while avoiding the endemic reductionism characteristic of both traditional human ecology and recent Marxian political economy. It does not seek explanation by emphasizing a single principal cause such as transportation technology, capital circulation, or production processes. Rather, it takes an integrated view of growth as the linked outcome of economic, political, and cultural factors.

When elaborating on Anthony Giddens's analysis of urban process, Gottdiener lists three main structural changes working behind the emerging new regional settlement space: (1) the emergence of the global corporation, (2) the interventionist state (since the 1930s Depression), and (3) knowledge and technology as forces of production. In the other end of the process, the real-estate sector receives an important agency. Gottdiener views it as the partly voluntaristic power that can influence the outcome of societal structures as actual built environments and urban systems.

These considerations are elements of the sociospatial approach described in *The New Urban Sociology*, which Gottdiener summarizes in the following six points:

1. The unit of analysis is not the city, but the multicentered metropolitan region (MMR), which is seen as the new, qualitatively different form of settlement space.

2. Settlement spaces are considered not only in their local and national contexts but also as part of the global system of capitalism.

3. Settlement spaces are affected by government policies and by the actions of developers and other actors of the real-estate industry, creating definite "pull factors" that partly explain urban patterns and growth directions.

4. Analysis should not overlook everyday life, human signification, and meaningful places. Symbols and objects are likely to have different meanings to different individuals or groups, which the sociosemiotic perspective helps to explain.

5. Both social classes and different social groups are essential elements of industrial and postindustrial societies.

6. The sociospatial approach emphasizes the interaction between society and space. To class, gender, race, and other social characteristics that define the difference among groups in contemporary society, the element of space itself needs to be added.

The importance of space as an independent category of analysis reflects Henri Lefebvre's notion of space as product and condition of production. In *The New Urban Sociology,* Gottdiener further elaborates the dynamism of space and the interdependence of actors producing space, saying that

the spatial arrangements found in urban and suburban settlement space have both manifest and latent consequences: They influence human behaviour and interaction in predictable ways, but also in ways the original planner or developer may not have been anticipated. But individuals, through their behaviour and interaction with others, constantly alter existing spatial arrangements and construct new spaces to express their needs and desires. (p. 19)

Multicentered Metropolitan Region: The New Form of Settlement Space

For Gottdiener, the emergence of the multicentered metropolitan region is a qualitative change that ranks in importance with invention of the city itself as a separate social form. When analyzing this new form, Gottdiener argues against technological determinism. He shows that the long process of suburbanization since the nineteenth century can be understood through real-estate investment and speculation, government housing programs and tax subsidies to homeowners, and the big demographic and social changes after World War II. Automobiles and highways are not the cause of urban change, but one of its means.

The distinguishing characteristic of the MMR is the way downtown has spun off its functions to other centers so that each is more functionally specialized, including the old city center. A twin process of overall decentralization and local

recentralization of functions and a parallel deconcentration and local reconcentration of population characterizes the MMR. Decentralization involves the dispersal not only of actions but also of social organization. Although there are differences between the speculation-led U.S. process and more planned urban regions in Europe and Asia, the general effects of sprawl and clustering do play a role across the contexts.

In the field of urban studies, the sociospatial approach, with the MMR as the unit of analysis, is unique in its ability to provide a rigorous theoretical framework for the study of a broad range of empirical issues. Examples of subjects that can be better understood include urbanization and suburbanization, immigration and ethnicity, urban problems such as racism and housing shortage, and issues of third world urbanization such as shanty towns, planning, and social policy.

Conclusion

Throughout his career, Gottdiener has developed the unifying sociospatial framework. In *The New Urban Sociology,* he confesses that "Lefebvre is responsible for many of the ideas that inform the sociospatial perspective" (p. 71). Gottdiener's relation to Lefebvre recalls Lefebvre's relation to Marx. Both Gottdiener and Lefebvre took a certain critical orientation and key concepts from the preceding thinker and developed them to serve the situation and intellectual climate of their own time. Marx (and Engels) theorized about capitalism when its spatial product, the industrial city, was just emerging. Lefebvre used Marxian concepts to study the city at a time when the centrality of the industrial city was challenged by the new regional settlement form, MMR. Building on Lefebvre's conception of space, Gottdiener has achieved a mature theory about the political, economic, and cultural aspects of that form. In his oeuvre, several topics not discussed in this entry's concise introduction further valorize the condition of the new settlement space. Those include urban crises and uneven metropolitan development, sociology of air travel, postmodern lifestyles, and global tourist attractions.

Panu Lehtovuori

See also Castells, Manuel; Chicago School of Urban Sociology; Harvey, David; Human Ecology; Lefebvre, Henri; Sprawl; Suburbanization

Further Readings

Giddens, Anthony. 1984. *The Constitution of Society: Outline of the Theory of Structuration.* Cambridge, UK: Polity Press.

Gottdiener, Mark. 1977. *Planned Sprawl: Public and Private Interests in Suburbia.* Beverly Hills, CA: Sage.

———. 1985. *The Social Production of Urban Space.* Austin: University of Texas Press.

———. 1994. *The New Urban Sociology.* Boulder, CO: Westview Press.

———. 1995. *Postmodern Semiotics: Material Culture and the Forms of Postmodern Life.* Oxford, UK: Blackwell.

———. 1997. *The Theming of America: Dreams, Visions, and Commercial Spaces.* Boulder, CO: Westview.

———. 2001. *Life in the Air: The New Culture of Air Travel.* Lanham, MD: Rowman & Littlefield.

Gottdiener, Mark and Leslie Budd. 2005. *Key Concepts in Urban Studies.* London: Sage.

Gottdiener, Mark and Ray Hutchison. 2006. *The New Urban Sociology.* 3rd ed. Boulder, CO: Westview Press.

Gottdiener, Mark and Alexandros Ph. Lagopoulos, eds. 1986. *The City and the Sign: Introduction to Urban Semiotics.* New York: Columbia University Press.

GOVERNANCE

Governance is a term referring to the nexus among states, civil society, and market actors who collaborate to achieve public purposes. Over the past three decades, urban studies scholars and practitioners have given significant attention to the question of how governments can more effectively provide public services and be receptive to rapidly changing urban populations in resource-poor, local environments. In the context of globalization, cities must respond to the pressures of growth, economic restructuring, service needs, and the demands for representation of an increasingly transnational and multiethnic population. They must do so in a context of rising labor costs and capital mobility and declining public resources. The response has been a shift away from purely state- or market-led approaches to service provision and toward "multiple actor" or "partnership" models of serving the urban public.

In the United States, the focus of these discussions has revolved around the concept of regime theory, whereby urban coalitions have been formed to govern in the economically competitive metropolitan environment. Across the rest of the world, a different framework focuses on the network of actors who work collaboratively across public and private boundaries to respond jointly to public needs. The divergence in approach reflects tangible differences in the role and power of state actors and in the governing networks forming among and within state, civil society, and market sectors, as well as a difference in the conceptualization of power, instrumentality, and capacity.

Origins of the Term

The term *governance* has been widely used by social scientists but often in divergent ways. Historically, the concept was derived from its roots in two other words—*government* and *governing*. Government (the noun) has been traditionally understood as a structural entity with the authority to make and enforce laws and, more generally, to allocate public goods. To govern (the verb) reflects the actions taken by governments, described loosely in relationship to their ability to direct, control, or to regulate the public sphere. Governance (the noun) has historically referred to the system or manner in which governments govern. Governance therefore is reflective of a political process shaped by a dynamic and changing institutional environment. Not surprisingly, the term is often used in a generic sense to refer to the governing process.

The term *governance* is not the exclusive domain of urban studies. One can find references to governance in business (e.g., corporate governance) and in international relations, where a growing discourse exists around global governance. For the most part, these disciplines use governance to describe processes through which outcomes are achieved—be they the tangible goods of a business or the less tangible outputs of international organizations such as treaties and regulations.

Understanding this systemic or process-oriented interpretation reveals the historic usage of the term governance, its cross-disciplinary application, and its fluid and changing conceptual orientation. Given both its generic origins and the multifaceted contemporary context of globalization, governance has become a complex and at times contested term. Despite its complexity, agreement exists among urban scholars as to its principal elements.

Principal Elements

Urban governance is understood as a way of describing new combinations of actors and power flows involved in public decision making in the city. Traditionally, local governments, as arms of the state, held primary responsibility for the allocation of local public goods. Power was hierarchical, flowing from the top down. The power of the state was, of course, limited and, in democratic societies, subject to popular will and the rule of law (authority). During the late 1970s, in the aftermath of recessions, oil shocks, and economic restructuring, a shift ensued. Private-sector actors were increasingly enlisted as partners with local state actors in urban policy and politics. Public goods were allocated competitively and distributed through the "invisible hand" of the market. Urban governance theory emerged more recently in the context of a retracting state and a growing civil society. Governance is premised on the existence of a wide group of actors united by shared needs, working collaboratively through networks and using different types of power than those of either states or markets.

Power in urban governance is cast as being primarily instrumental. In turn, the goals of governance networks are defined by network members and structured around their ability to achieve ends. Effective governance is based on the capacity to achieve goals. By virtue of the underlying interdependency of actors in governance, one finds networks operating through collaboration. By contrast, market power is competitive. Ideal markets are generally viewed as those operating under no regulations, where individuals exert choices premised on calculations of costs and benefits. Governmental power most commonly involves regulation or control through the rule of law. The underlying view is that the complexity of the urban arena and the challenges of responding to the needs of urban publics lead to the realization that no actor has the capacity to effectively govern alone and that neither states, markets, nor civil society can amass the needed power or resources to administer unilaterally.

Governance theories point to the emergence of new mechanisms (specifically, networks) through which decisions are made and goods allocated. Decision-making processes in governance networks operate both horizontally (across state, civil society, and market sectors) and vertically (across local, regional, national, and supranational governmental levels). Researchers also suggest that governance is undergirded by different motivations, that is, collaboration rather than competition or control. This is not to suggest that conflict has disappeared, nor that state control is absent, but rather that conflict and stringent control can be damaging to the outputs of governance.

What Does Governance Add?

Governance theory, to some degree, is a corrective to American regime theory. Regimes represent enduring coalitions of actors who are united for the purpose of governing. Unity is maintained by selective incentives, and the actions of regimes are shaped by a competitive political economy. Critics argue that regime theory has a normative bias that accepts the competitive external environment as a given and then focuses on internal dynamics and resource constraints. Governance, in contrast, considers institutions and the structures of government, looking at how they connect with external environments, norms, and value systems.

In addition, critics also suggest that regime theory is incompatible with the strong states common across Western Europe and Pacific Asia. Regime theory is thus positioned as an abstraction of the U.S. political economy.

Cross-National Variation

While most urban political scholars agree on the core elements of urban governance and on its utility as an advance on regime theory, a great deal of cross-national variation appears when normative questions of effectiveness and equity are considered.

These differences are most evident when contrasting the governance literature emerging from cities in the northern hemisphere as compared with cities in the south.

Because governance theorists seek to incorporate contextual knowledge in our understanding of networks, power, and collaboration, one finds great variation in how scholars evaluate governance. These normative views are often shaped by national context; that is, strong versus weak states, empowered versus disempowered civil societies, open versus closed decision-making systems. Differences also relate to the institutional origins of governance. In some localities, governance is the result of a highly formalistic top-down arrangement while in other places governance emerges out of a highly informal bottom-up process. The way governance networks function is also conditioned by the urban economy, for example, whether it is embedded in strong and developed markets, operating at the core of the global system, or existing in weak and emerging markets that operate on the periphery of the capitalist economy.

Normative discourses on urban governance are most common in the United Kingdom where government has seemingly been eclipsed by governance. Governance is viewed as "governing without government." This normative interpretation leads to the emergence of two rival camps: those who see governance as a more creative process for solving societal problems and those who viewed governance as a mechanism for allowing the state to abdicate its responsibility for providing social care and support. Underlying this normative discourse is the question of where power should rest.

For those who view governance as an abdication by states, a parallel debate concerns the democratic dangers in such a shift. Particularly in democratic governments in which power bases derive from the rule of law, power is limited, and leaders are subject to controls. Governance, in contrast, takes decisions beyond elected officials and, at times, outside the electoral arena, which can result in corruption. Several scholars remind us that governance, while enhancing capacities (instrumental power), may at the same time undermine democratic accountability. The growing fear is that the new partners are not subject to the same controls. Governance networks may be vulnerable to the machinelike tendencies of particularism and parochialism. Unlike democratic governments, governance is only tenuously and indirectly subject to democratic control.

In Latin America and Africa, urban governance has been viewed as an opening up to a wider set of actors, often in the absence of a democratically legitimate state. Governance becomes an opportunity to provide a more influential voice for civil society actors who have historically been relegated to the informal periphery of decisions made by strong autocratic states. Thus, in the global South, the governance literature is viewed optimistically as enhancing urban political systems and processes. The debate broadens the urban challenges in developing countries away from the technical confines of urban management and local government. This is considered a useful move because it focuses attention on issues of governmental legitimacy, citizen empowerment, and the vibrancy of civil society.

Conclusion

Theories of urban governance are filled with conceptual complexity. One response is a hybrid north/south view of governance as a process that brings state and nonstate actors together in networks (vertical and horizontal) to generate, manage, and implement public policy, or in other words a group of interdependent actors negotiating around public purposes. Governance in and of itself might best be viewed as the contemporary scaffolding supporting public decision making in a global era. How that scaffolding is built and the types of poles and planks that one uses to construct it will depend on the ground on which it is built, the actors who build it, and the reasons for its construction.

Thus, there are agreed-on trends in governance theory, such as the changing role of the state, the emergence of a range of new partners in civil society, and the promotion of more collaborative mechanisms for public decision making. At the same time, the way governance networks ultimately operate will be conditioned by the breadth and vision of the actors participating in them and the institutional environments in which they are embedded.

Jill Simone Gross

See also Citizenship; Regime Theory; Urban Politics

Further Readings

Davies, J. 2002. "The Governance of Urban Regeneration: A Critique of the 'Governing without Government' Thesis." *Public Administration* 80(2):301–22.

Gross, J. S. and R. Hambleton. 2007. "Global Trends, Diversity, and Local Democracy." Pp. 1–12 in *Governing Cities in a Global Era: Competition, Innovation, and Democratic Reform*, edited by R. Hambleton and J. S. Gross. New York: Palgrave Macmillan.

Jordan, A., R. Wurzel, and A. Zito. 2005. "The Rise of 'New' Policy Instruments in Comparative Perspective: Has Governance Eclipsed Government?" *Political Studies* 53:477–96.

Pierre, Jon. 2005. "Comparative Urban Governance: Uncovering Complex Causalities." *Urban Affairs Review* 40(4):446–62.

Rhodes, R. A. W. 1997. *Understanding Governance*. Buckingham, UK: Open University Press.

Sørensen, E. and J. Torfing. 2005. "The Democratic Anchorage of Governance Networks." *Scandinavian Political Studies* 28(3):195–218.

Stoker, G. and K. Mossberger. 2000. "Urban Political Science and the Challenge of Urban Governance." Pp. 91–109 in *Debating Governance*, edited by Jon Pierre. Basingstoke, UK: Palgrave Macmillan.

Stone, Cl. N. 1989. *Regime Politics: Governing Atlanta 1946–1988*. Lawrence: University Press of Kansas.

GRAFFITI

Urban surfaces have always carried unauthorized messages and images—famously, graffiti has been found among the ruins of ancient Pompeii. These graffiti messages and images have taken all sorts of forms. Some are political, some are humorous and witty, some are expressions of individual or collective identity, some are claims of territorial ownership, and others are elaborate forms of artistic expression. The emergence of new graffiti styles and techniques in recent decades has provoked sustained debate among policymakers and scholars. After briefly outlining these changes in graffiti, this entry discusses different perspectives on the nature of the so-called graffiti problem in contemporary cities.

Historical Evolution

Graffiti is certainly not a new phenomenon, but in the late 1960s and early 1970s, new forms of graffiti began appearing on the streets and public transportation systems of Philadelphia and New York City in the United States. Young people in these cities started writing their tag names with ink markers and aerosol paint. Gradually, as these graffiti writers sought to maximize the exposure of their tag identities, both the quantity and the quality of their productions increased. By the late 1970s, elaborate artistic productions (or "pieces") by writers like Dondi, Futura 2000, and others covered whole subway cars in New York City.

These new graffiti styles gradually gained wider exposure through books like 1984's *Subway Art* by photographers Martha Cooper and Henry Chalfant, and through early films such as the Public Broadcasting Service documentary *Style Wars* and the film *Wild Style*. This media circulation of graffiti subsequently helped facilitate its global diffusion and proliferation. Thriving graffiti scenes exist in hundreds of cities around the world, with every populated continent boasting its own hot spots and styles. These scenes and styles are by now exhaustively documented in glossy books published by major commercial publishing houses and in graffiti-related magazines and websites.

Graffiti might be viewed as an example par excellence of Michel de Certeau's tactics—an appropriation of space that insinuates into and against the dominant normative values inscribed in the urban environment. Graffiti writers see urban surfaces not as sanctified private property but as a medium for circulating their identities, artistic ambitions, and messages for each other and the wider public.

An Urban "Problem"

Not surprisingly, then, the global diffusion and proliferation of these new forms of graffiti have typically been viewed as a problem by urban authorities. Graffiti is frequently described as a kind of antisocial behavior that undermines urban quality of life. Indeed, critiques of graffiti played a formative role in the development of current approaches to law and order, which place emphasis on the need to curb antisocial behavior in the name of quality of life, such as the "broken windows"

Examples of urban graffiti

Source: Erin Monacelli.

crime control thesis advanced by Wilson and Kelling, which claimed that signs of physical decay would lead to neighborhood decline. As a variety of scholars have emphasized, such a reading of graffiti was not uncontested and has been privileged over other possible readings in the service of quite particular political and economic interests. And, just like graffiti itself, this particular reading of graffiti as antisocial has spread from its epicenter in New York City to other cities where graffiti scenes have emerged.

Prevention Approaches

With the spread of this discourse of graffiti as a quality of life offense, a variety of measures designed to prevent and eradicate graffiti have been developed and deployed in cities where the existence of graffiti is defined as a problem for urban policy. Antigraffiti measures include: new forms of urban fortification intended to deny graffiti writers access to strategic spaces; new forms of urban design and graffiti-proof materials designed to deny opportunities for graffiti; electronic surveillance to deter and catch writers; the formation of specialist graffiti squads by policing agencies; increased penalties for graffiti writing, including custodial sentence for repeat offenders in many jurisdictions; bans on the sale of aerosol paints to minors, and restrictions on the display of aerosol paints in shops; rapid removal of graffiti to deter writers seeking fame (now frequently contracted out to specialist graffiti removal companies by public and private urban authorities); and censorship of graffiti publications and websites. In many cities, vast resources are devoted to various combinations of these graffiti prevention measures.

When the effectiveness of these measures is assessed at the local scale, there may be some evidence of success in reducing or eliminating graffiti. However, if we measure efforts to prevent graffiti on a wider metropolitan or even global scale, they have certainly failed to stem the widespread growth of graffiti. Considered at this wider scale, it would appear that the waging of wars on graffiti has led to the mutation, rather than eradication, of graffiti writing practices. Writers have developed new styles and techniques designed to evade or outmaneuver the efforts of urban authorities. The rapid growth of sticker and stencil graffiti toward the end of the 1990s, for instance, was in part a response to antigraffiti measures—both stickers and stencils can be designed and executed in advance of their application to a surface, thus reducing the risks associated with graffiti by markedly reducing the time it takes to "get up." Similarly, new forms of graffiti-proof glass resistant to ink and paint, which is used on trains and bus stops, are now frequently adorned with etched tags cut into the glass itself. Indeed, some graffiti observers and scholars have pointed out that one irony of the currently dominant approach to graffiti prevention is that it has tended to lower the quality of graffiti by pushing writers toward styles that can be quickly executed.

Graffiti as Art

Efforts to curb graffiti are limited in their success by the capacity of graffiti writers to evade them. In addition, certain styles of graffiti have been embraced in both the marketplace and the art world. Established graffiti writers are often commissioned to do work to lend street credibility to advertising campaigns or to lend an urban edginess to film and television sets. Contemporary art galleries in many cities have sponsored exhibitions of work by graffiti writers. And, of course, paint manufacturers stand to gain from the ongoing proliferation of graffiti, and many have developed products specifically designed for graffiti writing.

Furthermore, there has been substantial (if uneven) support for the provision of legal graffiti spaces in many cities, and often, this support comes from state or state-funded agencies who work closely with young people. Here, however, there is an important distinction to be made between those who support the provision of legal graffiti spaces as a different means to address the graffiti problem (i.e., as a way to reduce graffiti), and those who argue that the way graffiti is framed as a problem is itself problematic (e.g., where legal graffiti spaces are provided as a means to improve the quality of graffiti).

Different positions in political debates over the construction and solution of the "graffiti problem" are informed by different understandings of graffiti writers and their motivations. Are writers simply antisocial vandals, as some would have it, or are their motivations more complicated? Sociologists and others tend to disagree. Richard Sennett, for instance, sees no more in graffiti than a "smear of the self"—a narcissistic concern with displays of individual identity that seek no genuine engagement with a wider public on issues of substance. Others like Nancy Macdonald and Kevin McDonald, who have undertaken ethnographic research with graffiti writers, see more complex negotiations of age, class, and gender in the graffiti scenes they have studied.

Yet others have sought to understand graffiti scenes as *counterpublic spheres* through which different ways of inhabiting and mobilizing urban space have been constructed. These latter perspectives present a picture of graffiti writing as a fundamentally *social,* rather than *antisocial,* practice. That is to say, they portray graffiti scenes as collectives engaged in their own discussions over the aesthetic and ethical values of different graffiti styles and practices. This is not necessarily to position the graffiti writer as some kind of folk hero but rather to assert that the writing of graffiti is not simply a form of mindless vandalism attributable to dysfunctional individuals.

The Writers Speak

Of course, graffiti writers themselves are not passive spectators in such debates. In particular, they continue to debate whether or not there can be any such thing as legal graffiti. These debates tend to hinge on whether the essence of graffiti lies in its legal status, or its style, or its placement. Some graffiti writers take sides in such debates, whereas others work across these different realms, putting on gallery shows and doing legal commissions (sometimes under the label of street art) in the public realm while maintaining an active profile on the streets through uncommissioned and illegal graffiti work.

More work remains to be done to bring the insights of graffiti writers into dialogue with scholarly discussions in sociology, criminology, and urban geography about the urban public realm. In particular, there is certainly more scope for research that asks what graffiti writers themselves tell us about the city. As they inhabit the city in different ways and mobilize urban space for different purposes in the face of significant normative and legal regulation, have graffiti writers developed new insights into the nature of the cities in which they write? Criminologist Jeff Ferrell's work on graffiti begins to address such questions. Ferrell has firsthand experience to draw on, having himself been an active graffiti writer and arrested for graffiti writing. He situates graffiti among a range of urban practices that point toward alternative and more anarchic ways of inhabiting the city and negotiating urban life.

Kurt Iveson

See also Crime; Hip Hop; Urban Semiotics

Further References

Austin, Jon. 2001. *Taking the Train: How Graffiti Became an Urban Crisis in New York City.* New York: Columbia University Press.
Cooper, Martha and Henry Chalfant. 1984 *Subway Art.* London: Thames and Hudson Ltd.
Cresswell, Tim. 1996. *In Place/Out of Place: Geography, Ideology, and Transgression.* Minneapolis: University of Minnesota Press.
de Certeau, Michel. 1984. *The Practice of Everyday Life.* Berkeley: University of California Press.
Ferrell, Jeff. 1993. *Crimes of Style: Urban Graffiti and the Politics of Criminality.* New York: Garland.
———. 2002. *Tearing Down the Streets: Adventures in Urban Anarchy.* Basingstoke, UK: Palgrave.
Iveson, Kurt. 2007. *Publics and the City.* Oxford, UK: Blackwell.
Macdonald, Nancy. 2001. *The Graffiti Subculture: Youth, Masculinity, and Identity in London and New York.* Basingstoke, UK: Palgrave.
McDonald, Kevin. 1999. *Struggles for Subjectivity: Identity, Action, and Youth Experience.* Melbourne, Australia: Cambridge University Press.
Sennett, Richard. 1994. *Flesh and Stone: The Body and the City in Western Civilization.* London: Faber and Faber.
Wilson, James Q. and George L. Kelling. 1982. "Broken Windows: The Police and Neighborhood Safety." *The Atlantic Monthly*, March.

GROWTH MACHINE

The growth machine concept appears most systematically developed in John Logan's and Harvey Molotch's *Urban Fortunes,* published in 1987. The book follows a series of research papers by the authors and develops the ideas crafted by Molotch in his 1976 classic paper, "The City as a Growth Machine." In these pieces, Logan and Molotch proposed a distinct approach to urban theory. This entry looks at the idea's evolution, its current application, and cross-national contrasts.

Conceptual Background

In the 1970s, the field of urban sociology—and other fields focusing on urban research such as economics, urban geography, and planning—were proponents of the idea that cities could be understood as mere containers of human action. According to this idea—which echoes the original proposals of the Chicago School—a competition among actors takes place in the city for land and other resources. City form, distribution of land uses, and central place theory can be explained by this seemingly impersonal competition. By opposing this approach, the growth machine idea placed social action in the urban realm at the forefront of analysis.

Emerging to explain the political economy of the city, the growth machine idea countered the structuralist overtones present in urban theory since the publication in 1972 of Harvey's *Social Justice and the City* and Castells's *The Urban Question* by focusing on urban actors rather than forces. Explicit in the concept is the claim that land parcels are linked to specific interests, especially commercial, sentimental, and psychological interests. Prominent among the city shapers are the land interests of those whose properties gain value when growth occurs. These social actors make up *the local growth machine*—a term that has become standard in urban studies. The growth machine approach suggests that human action, especially urban action by specific actors, carries causal power when it comes to explaining the organization, shape, and distribution of people and jobs in the city. Interpersonal market forces are not enough to explain these mechanisms. Rather, social action, including manipulations and dealings guided by interest, becomes a key explanatory force in urban studies.

Cities and towns in the United States have traditionally welcomed capital investment, with little regard to the social or fiscal costs involved. Under tensions generated by the growing international concentration of capital, however, communities are realizing that the costs of such investments have risen. Some localities resist the usual growth agenda, and both the property-oriented *rentier* elite and the middle and working classes sometimes try to substitute other local goals. Capital responds with new efforts to penetrate localities by activating their branch managers, increasing political campaign contributions, and directly participating in the property development business. National politics and policies such as Ronald Reagan's New Federalism—help capital by manipulating urban policy to provide advantageous sites.

Contemporary Applications

The growth machine concept has generated substantial research in the United States and abroad. Comprehensive literature reviews were published in 1997 and 1999. A twentieth anniversary edition of *Urban Fortunes* was issued by the University of California Press in 2007. International surveys of contemporary U.S. urban sociology identify growth machine research as one of the four main themes in the field.

Urban research studies focusing on renewal and redevelopment show the wide influence that the growth machine concept has had since the 1980s, especially in the United States. What seems to be missing in many analyses, however, is a careful examination of the role of urban politicians and officials, political opportunity structures, and state

actors in explaining the genesis, development, and impact of growth coalitions.

The concept has been enriched with the use of narratives of path dependency, historical accounts, and policy feedback to argue that past events, structures, and actions, as well as key decisions and conflicts, have the potential to alter or narrow the field of action of growth coalitions and policy strategies. Growth policies can be affected by shifting alliances between the growth machine and urban development agencies over time. As a result, investigations into path dependency in redevelopment schemes and institutional alliances may be helpful to understand how exactly growth and development agendas emerge and change as a result of new socioeconomic frameworks and circumstances as well as past agendas and projects. Such investigations may also reveal linkages between local growth machine arrangements and political and economic macro processes.

Further refinements of the concept also include discussions of the changing composition of pro-growth coalitions and, specifically, the importance of immigrant place entrepreneurs in revitalizing growth machines. Immigrant entrepreneurs may play a role in regional property development. One researcher has argued that they can seriously restructure a city's morphology by developing residential and business clusters for immigrants. Immigrant communities, having an origin in the arrangements by immigrant property developers, expand and coexist with already established ones. Immigrant property developers operate as a typical growth machine by buying land cheaply, promoting it within ethnic communities, and then selling it. This process may have consequences for the perception of immigration processes (as it enhances their appeal), as well as the reality of immigration (because it eases it). Ethnic residential clustering, thus, does not necessarily arise from leaderless social processes. Deliberate dealings and plans requiring political and economic knowledge and experience are at the root of the creation of residential clusters. As this process develops, place entrepreneurs of immigrant origin join the local growth machine.

Cross-National Applications

Growth machine-type coalitions are to be found both in the United States and abroad, but one can argue that one interesting thing about the model is its variations and specificities across time and space. For example, it is becoming increasingly clear that pro-growth coalitions in many cities now aim at gaining global visibility to attract flows of money and people so that growth can take place, but one of the keys is to identify the specific local outcomes produced by the articulation of local, regional, national, and global forces as they develop over time. Rather than becoming a meta-narrative, the model gets enriched by accounting for multiple scales of social and political action, and especially so if one deals with cities and regions showing contentious political relationships with their nation-states.

Global visibility is sometimes achieved by the organization of mega-events, and thus another cross-national application of the concept has been in studies of urban development and more specifically the impact of mega-events on urban development. Mega-events such as the Olympics and world fairs are typically short-term and high-profile events aimed at having a significant impact on the urban realm. They have an impact on policy priorities and discussions about best uses of facilities. In addition, they tend to enhance redevelopment strategies and serve as catalysts for urban ideologies and plans aiming at maximizing economic growth. Cities in emerging regions and nations have been joining the trend of urban mega-events usually organized in Western cities. In studying mega-events in connection with growth coalitions, one can pose the question as to whether the form of development represented by mega-events just legitimizes growth machines and business interests or whether this phenomenon may be analyzed in conjunction with the role that state actors and agencies play in urban restructuring. Growth machine coalitions may represent a form of urban/national boosterism repositioning cities in the global economy. Mega-events, as pro-growth strategies advocated by political and economic elites, may be less important as events at the grass roots than as symbols or catalysts of economic improvement and potential prosperity.

Contemporary problems such as urban environmental challenges have been studied from a growth machine perspective and framed within the entrepreneurial city debate. Urban officials and elites increasingly need to approach the politics of local economic development with effective policies and tools to manage environmental expectations and demands, as well as economic impacts. Obviously, interurban competition and pressure from the grass roots foster debates about quality of life in cities, but the increasing significance of ecological concerns is also a reflection of larger forces working to change the relationship between nature, the environment, and the urban realm. As a result, there is evidence that adopting and implementing green ecological policies may have a significant impact on the social regulation of urban governance, as it may represent a shift away from neoliberal approaches. This may lead to a redefinition of the growth machine concept by suggesting that evolving urban economy–environment relations can be understood as a set of practices of government designed to manage and ideally resolve shifting and conflicting demands (economic, political, sociocultural) at various spatial scales.

Criticism

There is considerable debate as to whether the growth machine idea can be fruitfully applied in empirical research beyond the United States. One approach to this question is that the concept can be used for the study of cities abroad insofar as it is appropriately applied. According to proponents of this view, the limitations of the growth machine idea in transnational settings simply originate in misunderstandings and misapplications of the concept. In his review of research about business interest mobilization in Britain, Wood critically examines this argument and reaches the opposite conclusion. Wood's central claim is that, even when focused on the right issues and questions, U.S. frameworks quickly exhaust their explanatory capacity. The author suggests that one needs to acknowledge the narrowness of the growth coalition approach and leave it behind for an appropriate understanding of disparate urban contexts in different national settings.

In addition, one can argue that the growth machine concept needs to be used carefully, considering how its geographic emphasis changes over time, from suburban to city core growth, as has been happening in U.S. and European cities for the past 20 years. Authors proposing this criticism argue that, rather than being value free (as is suggested in

Urban Fortunes), the geographical constraints of growth are value laden; that is, the matter is about how exchange values can be used to achieve a new and improved set of use values, as it occurs in gentrificative processes. Typically, gentrification (regardless of whether it is triggered by supply or demand) represents the replacement of old-use values by the exchange values established by growth coalitions, which market displacement of the poor as positive and necessary to overcome concentrated poverty and other social problems.

Another set of criticisms suggests that changes in state policies relative to the private sector render the effective use of the growth machine concept problematic. As the private sector gained importance in the management and governing of society, the state semiabandoned some of its traditional responsibilities in health care, education, and welfare. Whether the cause is the changing character of state policies or neoliberalism's latest turn, the result is that the private sector has become almost intertwined with local state forces, agencies, and actors in the entrepreneurial city. Thus, rather than speaking of growth machines, it is more appropriate to refer to local/regional states in the case of American cities.

Growth Machine and Global Forces

Contemporary uses of the growth machine concept are increasingly embedded in the variable geometry and specific trajectories or pathways of global forces' urban impact and the mediation of developmental states. According to one author, these pathways consist of (1) economic and political strategies developed at the regional level to establish flows and transnational connections with the world economy (such as state-led export-oriented growth strategies), (2) local developments to cope with changes triggered at the global level (such as industrial restructuring), and (3) structural and territorial adjustments to position the city in the context of world cities (such as megaproject development).

Pro-growth coalitions usually identify with the aims of developmental states, especially (although not only) in emerging economies. Local growth machines may be presented as seeking national or regional competitiveness globally, in a comparative

framework that provides local elites and actors with external models to emulate. This context intensifies, although it does not essentially modify, the thrust and aims of state policies because growth and productivity were national priorities for many countries and regions even before the current global era. In fact, local growth machines and commercial–state alliances seeking the retention of local commercial privileges are visible in many European regions during the shaping of modern capitalism in the sixteenth century. In some cases, the focus on growth and development had a reflection in the local legal code.

Late industrializers seem to require a strong state that prioritizes growth to overcome the drawbacks of comparative disadvantage. In this context, the role of local growth machines may be viewed as addressing (and benefiting from) state priorities concerning industrialization and development; the matter of effectiveness typically replaces debates of state intervention in the economy. The common goal of both the state and pro-growth coalitions is that of maximizing gains from global trade and export-led development, as well as strategically deploying the local reserves of capital, information, and labor.

Global market efficiency and economic advantage may not be the only strategic goal pursued by aligned state and pro-growth actors in nations, cities, and regions. Expanding the local economic reach may also be related to gaining global visibility to better preserve local political autonomy and identity. Such preservation strategies about autonomy and identity are carried out by local elites in reterritorialized national states and local/regional governments. Together with the expansion of foreign direct-investment flows, the corporate goals of foreign trade and investment become a policy priority for regional governments in multinational states with the aim of increasing the ability to maneuver politically vis-á-vis nation-states. This process may have a direct influence in the particular articulation of the local growth machine.

Gerardo del Cerro Santamaría

See also Growth Management; Urban Politics; Urban Sociology; Urban Theory

Further Readings

del Cerro Santamaría, G. 2007. *Bilbao: Basque Pathways to Globalization*. London: Elsevier.

Gotham, K. F. 2000. "Growth Machine Up-links: Urban Renewal and the Rise and Fall of a Pro-growth Coalition in a U.S. City." *Critical Sociology* 26(3):268–300.

Hiller, H. H. 2000. "Mega-events, Urban Boosterism, and Growth Strategies: An Analysis of the Objectives and Legitimations of the Cape Town 2004 Olympic Bid." *International Journal of Urban and Regional Research* 24(2):449–58.

Jonas, A. E. G. and D. Wilson. 1999. *The Urban Growth Machine: Critical Perspectives, Two Decades Later*. Albany: State University of New York Press.

Light, I. 2002. "Immigrant Place Entrepreneurs in Los Angeles, 1970–99." *International Journal of Urban and Regional Research* 26(2):215–28.

Logan J. R. and H. Molotch. 1987. *Urban Fortunes: The Political Economy of Place*. Berkeley: University of California Press.

Logan, J. R., Rachel Bridges Whaley, and Kyle Crowder. 1997. "The Character and Consequences of Growth Regimes. An Assessment of Twenty Years of Research." *Urban Affairs Review* 32:603–30.

Manella, G. 2007. *Nuovi scenari urbani: La sociologia del territorio negli USA oggi* (New Urban Sceneries: The Sociology of the Territory in the USA Today). Rome: Franco Angeli.

Molotch, Harvey. 1976. "The City as a Growth Machine: Toward a Political Economy of Place." *American Journal of Sociology* 82:309–18.

While, A., Andrew E. G. Jonas, and David Gibbs. 2004. "The Environment and the Entrepreneurial City: Searching for the Urban 'Sustainability Fix' in Manchester and Leeds." *International Journal of Urban and Regional Research* 28(3):549–69.

Wood, A. 2004. "Domesticating Urban Theory? U.S. Concepts, British Cities, and the Limits of Cross-national Applications." *Urban Studies* 41(11):2103–18.

GROWTH MANAGEMENT

Beginning in the 1960s in the United States, dissatisfaction with the negative effects of urban sprawl led to an interest in growth management. Starting with the land use initiatives of a few local U.S. jurisdictions, today growth management has attained the status of a mainstream planning tool.

Definitions of growth management have changed over time, with each definition representing a different epoch and planning philosophy. The early definitions were related to emerging growth policies of the 1970s. Growth management was defined as a more effective means to time, regulate, or even halt an increase in population. During the 1990s, growth management definitions added governance, institutions, and incentives, as growth management imposed an ideological obligation on governments to establish institutional arrangements for using taxes, expenditures, and regulatory powers to influence the distribution of land use activities in a community. At the same time, more emphasis was put on collaboration and regional initiatives. Under growth management, local governments would aspire to contain a community's development in ways that balance competing land uses and coordinate interlocal benefits.

The various definitions make clear that growth management is about regulating and steering land use with policy tools. However, as planning has shifted over time, growth management has evolved from a singular focus on regulation to a more complex set of activities that reach beyond a single community and take various stakeholder interests into consideration.

Development of Growth Management

Growth management emerged as a movement in U.S. planning in the 1960s. Given the problems related to urban sprawl, such as environmental degradation and overstretched infrastructure, citizens grew more conscious of their urban and natural environment. Preserving environmental resources was the overriding concern of many of the first-generation growth management programs.

Following regulative and quantitative planning modes fashionable at the time, tools such as boundaries, staging, and growth caps were applied. These first-generation regulations were generally implemented in conjunction with existing planning and zoning regulations.

The development of growth management can be divided into programs driven by the initiatives of single municipalities and those driven by individual state governments. Prominent examples on the local level include Ramapo, New York, where in 1969 the community was divided into land use segments to be realized in a certain order (tiers; staging). In Boulder, Colorado (1972), and Boca Raton, Florida (1972), population growth was limited to 40,000 additional housing units. Petaluma, California, established a growth rate (cap) of 500 housing units per year in 1972.

State growth management programs grew out of land use reform meant to fulfill environmental protection goals. State and local governments would share authority to protect designated areas from growth.

Oregon's innovative growth management system has been a role model for other states. It was the first to empower the state government to control land use by partially shifting growth control power from local governments to the state and by combining different land use approaches. Of especial importance in the development of the Portland metropolitan area is the Metropolitan Service District, a regional government. One of the prime responsibilities of this elected regional government is to manage a growth boundary that curtails development around Portland.

By the 1980s, growth management had become an established tool of mainstream planning. In that decade, the public became more involved. Collaborative approaches engaged task forces, and advisory committees were integrated into the growth management strategy. Unlike the regulative strategies of the 1970s, these approaches were embedded in a comprehensive framework that melded economic, environmental, infrastructure, and quality of life concerns.

Other states formulated comparable legislative frameworks to control and steer development locally and regionally and to ensure that it was consistent with local and state planning goals. In addition, states instituted incentives for collaborative approaches, adjustment between state agencies, regional control mechanisms, the use of geographic information systems, and bodies for conflict resolution.

Smart Growth

Another policy shift took place in the 1990s, with the move toward the newly and highly celebrated trend of smart growth. The term is grounded in participation in planning and an emphasis on the rediscovery of small-scale development. The approach is similar to "growing smart," a registered term of the American Planning Association, and the "livable communities" movement.

Both sustainable development and smart growth rely on the three principles of economy, environment, and social equity. Compared to previous growth management approaches, the social equity component is new. Unlike sustainability, however, smart growth does not explicitly consider the requirements of future generations, and growth is still the primary concern. Other definitions of smart growth include diversity, density, and design as subgoals. They point to a quality of urban development that reaches beyond a focus on regulating growth, as was done by the earlier growth management approaches with growth caps, staging, and urban growth boundaries. One important example is Maryland's state legislation for smart growth. The legislation targets resource conservation, infill development, and infrastructure costs in a comprehensive approach.

Growth Management Today

On the local level, the application of regulations, in particular urban growth boundaries, has increased steadily over time. At the state level, Tennessee and Virginia have developed or adapted existing growth policies according to smart-growth principles. However, by the end of the 1990s, only 12 states had established growth management systems: Hawaii (1961), Vermont (1970), Florida (1972), Oregon (1973), Georgia (1989), New Jersey (1986), Maine (1988), Rhode Island (1988), Washington (1990), Maryland (1997), Tennessee (1998), and Virginia (1998). The regional scale has become increasingly important, and smart-growth advocates have sought to incorporate both regulations and aspects related to the quality of urban development. Smart growth has yet to be proven to be a solution to the cities' growth problems.

Growth Management in Europe

The multifaceted planning systems of European countries, often driven by national land use and planning regulations, offer an insight into a different growth management realm. Europe has a much denser settlement pattern than the United States such that, in most countries, national land use planning law mandates that cities set up growth boundaries distinguishing the settlement area from the urban fringe. Switzerland, the Netherlands, and Germany are good examples.

Switzerland has quite strict regulations. As in the United States, the 1970s marked a shift in planning toward stronger environmental consciousness and landscape protection. Switzerland's response was mainly on the cantonal (regional) level, with regional plans that reduced the growth plans of many cities. Despite growing tensions between the cantons and the cities over the new regulations, a reverse-zoning policy that cut back land use areas previously designated for further urban growth was widely implemented. This normative approach was considered successful. Newer policy approaches of Swiss growth management include denser settlement structures. This is achieved with incentives provided by the cities such as higher-density allowances when a developer provides better quality and better design, and the shifting of zoning regulations between lots, a process monitored by a land management system.

Being a small country with a high population density, the Netherlands has generated nationwide growth management principles steered by national-level directives. This policy establishes the basic regulations and locations for housing, employment, public transportation, and other land uses. The aim of the Dutch policy is to enhance the development of the Randstad, a metropolitan area consisting of the agglomerations of Amsterdam, The Hague, Utrecht, and Rotterdam, while at the same time protecting a large territory within the Randstad—the Green Heart—from further settlement. Whereas the central government usually outlines the planning vision, implementation is dependent on other planning bodies. For this reason, there is a close collaboration between the national government, the provinces (regions), and the cities as to the future allocation of housing. The Fourth Report on Physical Planning, "Extra" from 1990, continued this policy approach and placed more emphasis on implementation at a city–regional level. Development directives indicated that development should take place at the outer fringes of the Randstad, keeping the Green Heart free from settlement.

The German approach to growth management is similar to the Swiss regulations. It has a relatively detailed national planning code and is based on the consensus that effective growth management should include legal, regulatory, economic, and organization-oriented tools. Economic or market-oriented tools became of interest during the 1990s when planners claimed that normative tools were too strict and ineffective to react to land use changes. The market-oriented tools include taxes, soil sealing fees, density or infrastructure incentives, and road pricing. Some of these approaches have found their way into national planning law, paving the way for more flexibility in growth management.

Criticism

When the growth management movement in city and regional planning started, developers and property owners opposed it. For most of them, growth management represented a challenge to their property rights. One popular argument of the time (and which is still raised) is that growth management raises land prices and housing values.

Moreover, contemporary growth management approaches, like the smart-growth movement, are criticized for being ineffective at steering land use expansion. Smart growth has not been sustainable, with citizens using smart-growth initiatives to disguise a NIMBY agenda.

Karina M. Pallagst

See also Environmental Policy; Growth Machine; New Urbanism; Suburbanization; Sustainable Development; Urban Planning; Urban Village

Further Readings

Evers, David with Efraim Ben-Zadek and Andreas Faludi. 2000. "The Netherlands and Florida: Two Growth Management Strategies." *International Planning Studies* 5(1):7–23.

Pallagst, Karina. 2007. *Growth Management in the U.S.: between Theory and Practice*. Aldershot, UK: Ashgate.

Porter, Douglas, R. 1997. *Managing Growth in America's Communities*. Washington, DC: Island Press.

Stein, Jay M., ed. 1993. *Growth Management: The Planning Challenge of the 1990s*. Newbury Park, CA: Sage.

Szold, Terry S. and Armando Carbonell, eds. 2002. *Smart Growth: Form and Consequences*. Cambridge, MA: Lincoln Institute of Land Policy.

GROWTH POLES

Growth poles refer to a grouping of firms or an industry that generates expansion in an economy. Economic growth from a lead or propulsive firm or industry induces growth in other firms or sectors of an economy through agglomeration—or positive external—economies. Growth poles are at once a theory of development and a regional development strategy or policy application.

As many in the development planning literature have noted, the origin of the growth pole had little to do with geography per se and certainly not with regional development. Nonetheless, growth poles—and its related term, growth centers—played a major role in regional development policies in the 1950s and 1960s. Across developing countries, growth poles or growth centers were targeted as places to concentrate public investment to promote development and spread it to outlying areas. The principal and most commonly used means was through industrialization strategies. Growth poles were not limited to developing and industrializing countries, however. They were also used to promote development in lagging, or backward, regions in countries such as the United States, France, Japan, and the United Kingdom.

The notion of growth poles originated with the French economist Francois Perroux and the French School of Spatial Economics. In the 1950s, Perroux developed his theory of growth poles—or what he called the pole of development. Perroux built on the work of economists Joseph Schumpeter and John Maynard Keynes and proposed growth poles as *nonspatial* propulsive forces of economic growth. The propulsive enterprise generated growth in other parts of an economy through its own growth and innovation. The driver was what he called a propulsive unit in the economy—the growth pole. The growth pole could be firms in an industry, such as steel or electronics, or a set of related firms. The growth pole generated rapid growth through innovation and advanced technology applications. This occurred as growth and development spread to related sectors, creating multiplier effects of development through linkages.

Multiplier effects are achieved through increasing scale economies, which lower the costs of production to firms. Linkages can be upstream to suppliers—backward linkages—or downstream to customers—forward linkages. Growth poles develop new linkages with the rest of the economy over time, as well as with other poles. Thus, as the growth pole grows, so do other related firms, and the economy expands. As in the work of Schumpeter, who analyzed the role of entrepreneurship and innovation in capitalist development, innovation was key for Perroux in the development process.

Perroux was part of a group of regional development theorists writing at the time who understood that economic growth was unbalanced and thus development was an unequal, rather than equilibrating, process. Along with Albert Hirschmann and Gunnar Myrdal, Perroux challenged national equilibrium growth models by observing and attempting to operationalize uneven growth. Myrdal termed this cumulative causation. Growing regions would generate more growth over time, while backward regions would lag further and further over time. John Friedmann developed a further extension of unbalanced regional growth through his core–periphery model, a dualistic model of growth and decline. Here, Friedmann promoted the need for regional policy and planning in those parts of developing countries that were declining or not growing, or what he called the peripheral regions to the country's growing core.

Although Perroux's initial conception of a growth pole was aspatial, the term and theory quickly took on territorial dimensions and entered into the regional development literature. Economists and geographers placed Perroux's growth pole in geographic space. Governments and policymakers soon followed, developing subsidy and incentive programs with a decidedly spatial orientation to expand and induce regional growth. French economist Jacques Boudeville, among others, used the growth pole as a central tenet of regional development planning and a focal point for regional investment decisions. The pole became an urban center in a less developed or lagging region, with the policy goal to induce growth throughout the region.

Policies based on growth pole theory expanded during the 1960s. Support for growth pole policies extended from advanced industrial nations to the developing world and through the communist bloc. In practice, growth center policies spanned a wide range of investment decisions of nations and regions, from creations of large industrial complexes to subsidies to industrial plants to rural growth centers in developing nations. Academics debated topics such as what size growth centers should be. Policymakers across the world, meanwhile, focused investments in growth centers as small as rural villages and as large as major metropolitan areas. Goals usually included reducing regional disparities, reducing unemployment, increasing income, and modernizing "backward" sectors and regions.

Growth pole policies in advanced economies centered on lagging regions. Traditional macroeconomic policies to reduce unemployment were deemed inadequate to deal with regional inequalities. In the United Kingdom, for example, growth center policies promoted regional regeneration through manufacturing modernization in older industrial regions. In the United States, the Appalachian Regional Commission (ARC), established to promote development in rural Appalachia, created growth centers more as service provision locations based on central place theory rather than on industrialization and propulsive industries. In the case of the ARC, the desire to spread funds politically created other goals for growth centers. The work of Andrew Isserman, among others, shows that growth pole policies can be based on political determinations as well as regional development strategies.

By the 1970s, growth center policy began to be evaluated. Evaluations of planned growth poles in rural areas of developing nations and lagging areas of advanced industrial nations were showing few spread effects from the development investments. Reasons for failure included time horizons too short for development to occur; inadequate resources from the state sector to induce agglomerative effects of planned development; unsuitable implementation of policies; inaccurate assumptions about how growth diffuses spatially; and preoccupation with manufacturing sectors to the neglect of growing information and service sectors.

Nonetheless, the theories underlying growth poles and growth centers have continued to be important in regional development and regional planning. By the 1980s and 1990s, the importance of innovative firms driving regional economic development was evident in places from new high-technology centers such as Silicon Valley in California to older industries clustered in the Emilia-Romagna region in Italy. Industrial clusters became one of the main means to examine the agglomerative effects of firm colocation, rather than growth poles, although the underlying forces of innovation on generating growth through agglomeration economies remained at the root.

Sabina Deitrick

See also Technopoles; Urban Economics; Urban Planning; Urban System

Further Readings

Chapman, Keith. 2005. "From 'Growth Centre' to 'Cluster': Restructuring, Regional Development, and the Teesside Chemical Industry." *Environment and Planning A* 37:597–615.

Darwent, David F. 1975. "Growth Poles and Growth Centers in Regional Planning: A Review." In *Regional Policy: Readings in Theory and Applications*, edited by John Friedmann and William Alonso. Cambridge: MIT Press.

Higgins, Benjamin and Donald J. Savoie, eds. 1988. *Regional Economic Development: Essays in Honor of François Perroux*. Boston: Unwin Hyman.

Isserman, Andrew. 1995. "The Economic Effects of the Appalachian Regional Commission." *Journal of the American Planning Association* 61:345–64.

Perroux, Francois. 1988. "The Pole of Development's New Place in a General Theory of Economic Activity." In *Regional Economic Development: Essays in Honor of François Perroux*, edited by Benjamin Higgins and Donald J. Savoie. Boston: Unwin Hyman.

Pred, Allan. 1976. "The Interurban Transmission of Growth in Advanced Economies: Empirical Findings versus Regional-planning Assumptions." *Regional Studies* 10:151–71.

H

HALFWAY HOUSE

A halfway house is an intermediate residential facility for people who are making the transition from an institutional to an independent living situation. Halfway houses are known by several names, including community-based residential facilities, community-based residential centers, community residential centers, and community residential facilities. The majority of residents have moved from regulated settings, such as prisons or mental institutions, to places with greater independence and freedom.

Halfway houses allow residents to maintain relationships with friends and family and reestablish connections to the labor market while providing support and services during the transition period. Thus, while residents work, attend school, or undertake employment training, they also, for example, receive counseling or treatment for substance abuse. The programs are delivered in informal settings under less supervision than residents would receive in a regulated institution. Residents, however, are provided with structure to facilitate their readmission into the larger community. That structure might include required curfews, abstinence from alcohol or other substances, restricted visits to certain people or neighborhoods, and attendance at drug treatment.

In addition to basic needs, such as food and shelter, halfway houses provide services themselves or coordinate with outside service providers who can assist the resident while living at the halfway house and after the resident moves to independent living. The services vary but may include employment counseling, vocational testing and training, education counseling, financial literacy classes, leisure and recreation activities, community service projects, medical and services, personal appearance assistance, and housing counseling and assistance. Counseling is an important component of many halfway houses. Individual and group counseling may be offered to address several issues, including family or marital problems and drug and alcohol abuse.

One of the largest issues that halfway houses face is their location within residential communities. The needs of residents must be balanced with community opposition. To serve residents, some locations are more desirable for halfway houses; for example, they should be close to public transportation, employment opportunities, educational institutions, medical facilities, and other community resources.

Many neighborhood residents do not want halfway houses in or near their neighborhood because of concerns that such facilities will decrease real estate values and bring crime and drugs to the neighborhood. Although a common belief is that a halfway house devalues a neighborhood, empirical evidence shows otherwise. The concerns about crime are also unfounded; rates of recidivism decrease significantly for people who make a gradual transition into the community through stays in a halfway house. To overcome community opposition, research suggests that working closely with neighborhood groups in the planning process facilitates the acceptance of halfway houses.

Greta Goldberg

See also Homelessness; Housing Policy; Neighborhood Revitalization

Further Readings

Keller, O. J. and B. S. Alper. 1970. *Halfway Houses: Community-centered Correction and Treatment.* Lexington, MA: Heath Lexington Books.
Rausch, H. L. with C. L. Rausch. 1968. *The Halfway House Movement: A Search for Sanity.* New York: Appleton Century Crofts.

HALL, PETER

Sir Peter G. Hall (1932–) is the author and editor of 40 books on the influence of technological and economic change on metropolitan development, the cultural and planning history of cities, and the urban structure and planning systems of the United Kingdom and the United States. He has been professor of planning at the Bartlett School, University College London, since 1992, after being chair in city and regional planning at the University of California at Berkeley (1980–1992).

In the 1950s, Hall focused on the economic geography of London before broadening his inquiry to the development problems of world metropolitan areas in *The World Cities* (1966). Hall then focused on planning systems: In *The Containment of Urban England* (1973), he analyzed the postwar British town and country planning system in terms of urban sprawl, arguing that it led to suburbanization, the growing separation of home and work, and shortages in the supply of building land. *Planning and Urban Growth* (1975), a follow-up to *Containment,* compared English and U.S. planning systems.

Throughout the 1970s, Hall became increasingly frustrated with the rejection of the social–scientific comprehensive planning of the 1960s with which he was associated, as well as with the structuralist Marxism that came to dominate urban and regional planning studies. Although

Hall recognized the causal link between social evolution, economic development, and technical change; he believed in the creative power of capitalist enterprise to generate growth and well-being, albeit in alternative forms mediated by historical, geographical, and political circumstances.

In 1980, Hall moved to the University of California at Berkeley. His fascination with nearby Silicon Valley led him to focus on the nature of innovation in successful metropolitan regions in the United States and the United Kingdom. Four books resulted: *Silicon Landscapes* (1985), *High-Tech America* (1986), *Western Sunrise* (1987), and *The Carrier Wave* (1988). Hall then worked with Manuel Castells on a study of the *Technopoles of the World* (1994), which investigated innovation in planned science parks and cities. In parallel, Hall prepared a major study of urban planning ideas in the twentieth century: *Cities of Tomorrow: An Intellectual History of Urban Planning and Design in the Twentieth Century* (1988). In that book, he critiqued the influence of Le Corbusier on planning; in *Sociable Cities* (1988), he highlighted the value and legacy of Ebenezer Howard's Garden Cities.

By the early 1990s, Hall had returned to London and published his most important book, synthesizing a decade of research on innovation and planning: *Cities in Civilization: Culture, Technology, and Urban Order* (1998). This comparative cultural history explores the nature and geography of cultural creativity in the world's great cities, from ancient Athens to late twentieth-century London. Hall analyzes the emergence of urban creative milieus leading to industrial innovation, artistic creativity, and urban planning innovation, and he investigates how cities like London, Paris, and New York have successfully renewed themselves over time. In the last decade, he has worked collaboratively on London's economic competitiveness and on the development of polycentric mega-city regions in northwest Europe (*The Polycentric Metropolis,* 2006).

Since the 1960s, Hall has been an influential policy adviser to U.K. governments. He has often been credited with being the father of the concept of enterprise zones—designated areas in which planning and tax constraints are relaxed to encourage inward investment—introduced in 1980 in the United Kingdom by the Margaret Thatcher government.

In 2005, Hall won the "Balzan Award for the Social and Cultural History of Cities since 1500" for his "unique contribution to the history of ideas about urban planning, his acute analysis of the physical, social, and economic problems of modern cities, and his powerful historical investigations into the cultural creativity of city life."

Claire Colomb

See also City Planning; Growth Poles; Informational City; Technopoles; World City

Further Readings

Hall, Peter G. 1966. *The World Cities*. London: Weidenfeld.

———. 1988. *Cities of Tomorrow: An Intellectual History of Urban Planning and Design in the Twentieth Century*. Oxford, UK: Blackwell.

———. 1996. "It All Came Together in California: Values and Role Models in the Making of a Planner." *City* 1–2:4–12.

———. 1998. *Cities in Civilization: Culture, Technology, and Urban Order*. London: Weidenfeld and Nicolson.

Hall, Peter G., Michael Breheny, Ronald McQuaid, and Douglas Hart. 1987. *Western Sunrise: Genesis and Growth of Britain's High Tech Corridor*. London: Allen and Unwin.

Hall, Peter G. and Manuel Castells. 1994. *Technopoles of the World: The Making of 21st-century Industrial Complexes*. London: Routledge.

Hall, Peter G. and Marion Clawson. 1973. *Planning and Urban Growth: An Anglo-American Comparison*. Baltimore: Johns Hopkins University Press.

Hall, Peter G. and Ann Markusen, eds. 1985. *Silicon Landscapes*. Boston: Allen and Unwin.

Hall, Peter G., Ann Markusen, and Amy Glasmeier. 1986. *High Tech America: The What, How, Where, and Why of the Sunrise Industries*. Boston: Allen and Unwin.

Hall, Peter G. and Kathryn Pain. 2006. *The Polycentric Metropolis: Learning from Mega-city Regions in Europe*. London: Earthscan.

Hall, Peter G. and Paschal Preston. 1988. *The Carrier Wave: New Information Technology and the Geography of Innovation, 1846–2003*. London: Unwin Hyman.

Hall, Peter G., Ray Thomas, Harry Gracey, and Roy Drewett. 1973. *The Containment of Urban England*. London: Allen & Unwin.

Hall, Peter G. and Colin Ward. 1988. *Sociable Cities: The Legacy of Ebenezer Howard*. Chichester, UK: Wiley.

HARVEY, DAVID

Few scholars have affected our understanding of cities in North America and Western Europe more incisively than David Harvey (1935–). Long affiliated with Johns Hopkins University, briefly at Oxford University, and currently at the City College of New York, where he holds a distinguished chair in anthropology and the Center for Place and Culture, Harvey has written prodigiously and to wide acclaim. At the core of his vision has always been a commitment to seeing and understanding cities as the expression of generalizable principles and forces that permeate capitalist societies. Above all else, Harvey has been a modeler of city dynamics, explaining their evolving character by emphasizing regularity and generalization rather than contingency and place-specificity. His "multiple facets" of cities—neighborhoods, districts, downtowns, social relations, restructuring projects—have continuously been rooted in locally sustained but society-wide forces. Unleashing a powerful understanding of cities, to Harvey, requires a thorough understanding of the "inner laws" of societal realities.

Early Works

Before his arrival at Johns Hopkins University in 1973, Harvey embraced the utility of logical empiricism. The centerpiece of this research, *Explanation in Geography* (1969), emphasized quantitative methods, spatial science, and a positivist philosophy. In this landmark study of the methodology and philosophy of geography, Harvey argued for the logic of a robust empiricism and rigorous testability to advance understanding of a spatialized world. Chapters on systems, models, deductive and inductive reasoning, the role of mathematics and geometry, and the philosophy of science codified a "science of geography," which had recently ascended in the discipline but which lacked a unifying theoretic exposition. As Anglo-geography moved from a descriptive–regional to a positivist–scientific paradigm, it drew heavily on Harvey's *Explanation in Geography*.

In the early 1970s, Harvey abruptly broke from positivist science to begin a lifelong expedition into understanding the Western European and U.S. city from a Marxist perspective. Harvey now presented the city as a complex human-made space set in capitalist economic realities. His seminal contribution to this project, *Social Justice and the City* (1973) argued, first, that geography and urban studies were deeply political enterprises that could never produce value-free understandings. Harvey sought to smash the myth of value-free research to position Marxist analysis as one among many competing analytic perspectives with political designs and content. He proposed that explanations for and policy directives about urban issues and problems (e.g., poverty, deprivation, homelessness) always contain a bundle of values that reflect existing power relations as well as the need for social change. The book argues, second, for a new focus in urban studies: on the explanatory power embedded in the societal structures of capitalist societies. Set against the power of such structures (e.g., the drive to accumulate, the necessity to reproduce labor power, the impulse to legitimate existing capitalist social relations), Harvey asserts that other kinds of explanation are superficial.

Harvey's subsequent work has laid out a distinctive Marxian frame that has become more nuanced and multitextured over time. The city, a whirlwind of complexity, is a place that both reflects and generates crisis, in his view. Its dynamic is one of a deep and pervasive struggle between competing and opposing classes whose turbulent relations must be managed and controlled. Crisis follows from antagonisms between capital and labor over the extraction and distribution of surplus value, labor-exploitive practices, and repressive political strategies rooted in the social relations of production. The never-ending concentration and centralization of capital and the tendency for the rate of profit to plummet thereby create periodic bouts of overconcentration and less profitable investment. The key crisis, to Harvey, is the tendency for investment to overaccumulate in economic circuits and thus to force a collision of classes from which new economic and political forces emerge. Cities are ultimately instruments for capital accumulation, engines of economic growth whose everyday rhythms depend on capital exploiting labor to create surplus.

On Capitalist Cities

In *Limits to Capital* (1982), Harvey offered his first extended analysis of space and time in capitalist cities. His analysis is organized around three dimensions of capitalist crisis. The first dimension stresses how the cycle of overaccumulation and devalorization are ritualistic in national and urban economies. Investors rhythmically follow each other and concentrate capital in production, thus establishing the basis for overaccumulation and lower rates of profit. The second part of the crisis involves attempts to fix the problem of overaccumulation. Here investors unwisely create fictitious capital to manage the fluctuating and long time lags between investment and payoffs. The third part of the general crisis entails a spatial fix, which involves finding new terrains as outlets for profitable investment. Harvey views all responses as merely temporarily ameliorative; investment inevitably concentrates in a particular economic circuit and overaccumulates to produce falling rates of profit.

Harvey applied this theoretical perspective to Paris in his *Consciousness and the Urban Experience* (1985). (See also *Paris, Capital of Modernity*, 2003.) There, he explores, through a Marxist lens, the massive 1850s and 1860s restructuring of Paris. Baron Haussmann's initiative—constructing massive boulevards and physical infrastructure, clearing slums, building bourgeois neighborhoods—is dissected as a complex government response to the instability of profitable accumulation. Crisis, never far from the surface, drives intense rounds of physical restructuring. Peeling away any hint of an innocent or crisis-free redevelopment under Haussmann, Harvey reveals how real-estate capital and the local state seek to both thwart falling profit and benefit themselves. Thus, capital switching from the primary (industry) to the secondary (built environment) circuit drives the building of roads, highways, and railways that "bourgeoisied" a massive population and enriched financiers and manufacturers. A property boom, manipulated by bankers and the state, filled the coffers of local government with revenue to sustain the frenetic restructuring. New patterns of industrial location and social class segregation followed and collectively imposed new social and physical spaces that renewed Paris as a built form for extracting real-estate and industry profits.

Response to Postmodernism

By the late 1980s, Harvey found it necessary to defend the intellectual rigor of Marxian political economy from a dramatic post-1985 emergence of "the postmodern turn." His forceful *Condition of Postmodernity* (1989) critically examines the ascendant postmodern movement in academia and urban studies and its proclamation of something new: a postmodern world and postmodern city. Harvey argues that the many supposed manifestations of postmodernity—a new culture, a new city form, a new set of societal spaces and temporal realities—flow from a continued powerful force: the operation of a capitalist political economy. To Harvey, capital's operation is a constant that persists to produce new spatialities, temporalities, and cultural forms. What is new, and what propels these new appearances, is the rapid supplanting of a modern, relatively fixed system of production (Fordism) by an unparalleled flexible form of production (post-Fordism). This ascendant reality, particularly visible in how humans experience space and time on a daily basis, follows most fundamentally from a capital-inducing time–space compression. So-called postmodern cities and society, it follows, have not broken with the trajectory of history but merely reflect a continuation of capitalism where capital seeks to harness space, cultural forms, and time in the service of class interests and profit accumulation.

The theme of alternative geographical imaginings, increasingly important to Harvey in recent years, is most forcefully taken up in *Spaces of Hope* (2000). Harvey argues that capitalism and its entanglement with cities should be seen as open and rife with alternative political possibilities. The challenge issued to readers and others is never to lapse into a deterministic conception of capitalism. Identifying a new punishing and demeaning capitalism ("new neoliberal times"—see *The New Imperialism*, 2003) the socialist possibility is offered as a fruitful source of contemplation and a potential humanly made reality. Capital's hold on power, Harvey argues, is always tenuous and an ongoing human endeavor that requires guile and dexterity. The source of the tenuousness is a city and world that grow more impoverished, despoiled, and in need of a constant set of rhetorical infusions to be viewed as normal. In his conclusion, Harvey speaks of a utopia that came to him in a dream—Edilia, a postrevolutionary world of tranquility. This image, Harvey concludes, can become a reality, given the instability of current class and military–theocratic authority.

Harvey's structural Marxism has proved a compelling force in urban studies. His perspective deepens our understanding of urban ills and quandaries that have eluded more contingent, place-specific visions. Current conditions and processes in these cities—deepening minority poverty, growing economic segregation, the intensified splintering of city morphology, the upgrading and increased policing of downtowns—verify Harvey's rendition of city dynamics written more than 25 years ago. As Sharon Zukin notes, contemporary newspaper headlines are spot-on with Harvey's prognostications about city conflict, social relations, the kinds of spaces that are being created, and how government operates. Harvey's perspective provides us with something vital, a rendition of restless, humanly made structural forces in cities that continues to challenge and provoke.

David Wilson

See also Capitalist City; Marxism and the City; Urban Geography; Urban Theory

Further Readings

Harvey, David, 1969. *Explanation in Geography.* London: Edward Arnold.

———. 1973. *Social Justice and the City.* London: Edward Arnold.

———. 1982. *The Limits to Capital.* Oxford, UK: Blackwell.

———. 1985. *Consciousness and the Urban Experience.* Oxford, UK: Blackwell.

———. 1989. *The Condition of Postmodernity.* Oxford, UK: Blackwell.

———. 2000. *Spaces of Hope.* Edinburgh: University of Edinburgh.

———. 2003. *The New Imperialism.* Oxford: Oxford University Press.

———. 2003. *Paris, Capital of Modernity*. New York: Routledge.

Zukin, Sharon, 2006. "David Harvey on Cities." Pp. 102–21 in *David Harvey: A Critical Reader*, edited by N. Castree and D. Gregory. Oxford, UK: Blackwell.

HAUSSMANN, BARON GEORGES-EUGÈNE

Baron Georges-Eugène Haussmann (1809–1891) was charged by Emperor Napoléon III with turning Paris into a capital worthy of an empire. Creating broad boulevards that connected the city and highlighted its greatest monuments, Haussmann used the principles of axiality and symmetry to build a city that was a showcase not only for France but for all of Europe. His model was widely admired, and it had many imitators. The power of the imperial government was required, however, to pay the enormous costs and to summarily eliminate large neighborhoods whose shabbiness did not suit the plan. This entry looks at the context of Haussmann's project, summarizes its principal features, and contrasts it with other European cities.

Historical Context

After the coup of 1851 that established the Second Empire in France, the complete lack of *grandeur* that its capital displayed proved unbearable for its Emperor, Napoléon III. Its sanitary conditions were appalling, demanding a heavy toll from epidemic diseases. Its road infrastructure was incapable of handling traffic, which had increased dramatically since 1842, when Paris became the national railway hub. Its townscape was more reminiscent of the late Middle Ages than of a modern representative capital.

The city government was slow to react to Napoleon's growing pressure to intervene. After two years, the Emperor lost patience. He sacked aldermen and council. By appointing Georges-Eugène Haussmann as prefect of the Seine, he initiated the largest urban renewal project Europe had ever witnessed.

Although not trained as an architect, Haussmann had demonstrated his skills as a ruthless manager as a Prefect of various *départments*. In Paris, he immediately set out to reorganize the public works department. He replaced its staff with talented engineers, architects, and surveyors, who produced Paris's first reliable and detailed city map. On it, Haussmann drew his first major intervention, the *Grande Croisée*.

The First Initiative

Starting from the northern and eastern railway stations, he projected a major street cutting right through the city's core, the Boulevard Sébastopol, crossing the Seine at the Ile de la Cité, and continuing its devastating course on the South Bank as the Boulevard Saint Michel until it reached Montparnasse. The Ile de la Cité was almost completely razed, providing room for impressive new administrative buildings and isolating Notre Dame de Paris from its decrepit surroundings, showing the cathedral in all its splendor.

This major new artery met with the Rue de Rivoli, a street dating back to Napoléon I, at Châtelet, turning this square close to city hall into the focus of Paris. Its eastern extension, although never fully realized, found its pinnacle at today's Place de la Bastille, mirroring its western counterpart, the Place d'Étoile.

Unlike his predecessors, Haussmann did not see the Great Crossing as an isolated intervention. Rather, he linked it to a number of secondary streets, thus demonstrating that he conceived of the city as a whole. Until 1850, Paris had been a collection of rather isolated quarters. In 1870, the year of Haussmann's abdication, the city's infrastructure had become a veritable network.

Improving Lifestyle and Appearance

The surgical operations in the dense urban fabric served more purposes. Most new arteries were planned to destroy as many slums as possible, ridding Paris of its vast army of beggars, rag pickers, and marginal craftsmen. Under the surface of the new boulevards, Haussmann created a subterranean infrastructure for the provision of gas, sewage, and drinking water, thus adding substantially to residential hygiene and comfort.

Until then, foul water was carried through open gutters to the river Seine, the main source for drinking water. Haussmann gave orders to tap two unpolluted rivers several hundred miles east of the capital. The construction of aqueducts and canals to bring clean water to Paris cost a fortune, but it improved sanitary conditions dramatically. Finally, Haussmann created 24 public squares and parks, offering urbanites artfully designed excerpts of French natural geography.

Both scale and speed of the *transformation de Paris* were dazzling. But what impressed visitors to the capital most was that all these improvements were inextricably linked to *embellishment*. Few new arteries demonstrated Haussmann's aesthetical preferences more convincingly than the Avenue de l'Opéra.

This artery was destined to become one of the most prestigious avenues due to the construction of the New Opera. Begun in 1861, it was clear that Charles Garnier's masterpiece would become the ultimate temple of bourgeois opulence. Thus, it deserved to be highlighted by a monumental axis. To further visual drama, every obstacle was removed. Haussmann destroyed recently built apartment blocks and ordered the clearing of a natural elevation, the Butte des Moulins as well. Much more land was obtained than was needed for the new road. Its flanks were reserved as building sites for monumental new apartments. Haussmann made sure that developers strictly obeyed his architects' supervision. Façades should be stately, uniform, and symmetrical, not distracting the eye of the pedestrian from the main objective, the Opéra.

A National Showcase

Paris was to become the showcase of the nation. By combining massive expropriation with the twin techniques of axialiaty and symmetry, the special effects of urban design, Haussmann drew the visitor's attention to icons of French glory such as the Arc de Triomphe. Older monuments such as the Gothic Tour St. Jacques were disengaged to bear witness to the city's venerable past. Indeed, the prefect created the city as a work of art.

The human toll, however, was considerable. With the destruction of an estimated 27,000 premises, some 350,000 slum dwellers were removed from the central areas. At first, they took for the *petite banlieue,* still within the walls of Paris. But

after its annexation in 1860, Haussmann continued his social cleansing. By raising excises on raw materials, he forced industry, rail depots, and other undesirable land users outside city limits. They took their workforce with them. Thus, he created the grim *grande banlieue.* Its social stigma haunts French governments to this day. No foreign visitor set foot in this urban wilderness that ringed the city. They came for the splendor of New Paris, the city that continued slum clearance and embellishment well after Haussmann's abdication in 1870, creating an almost exclusively bourgeois residential domain of unprecedented size.

International Impact

Haussmann was admired no more in France than in other countries. For the many new states in Europe, Paris became the design standard for a capital that would be instrumental in forging a collective national identity and convincing foreign visitors that here was a modern and prestigious nation state. Brussels, Budapest, and Rome testified to the impact of Paris.

To emulate Haussmann's *grands travaux,* a first requirement was a strongly centralized national administration, capable of taxing the nation to the benefit of the capital. This was no easy task, given the predominantly rural outlook of both France and its emulators. To suppress the widespread protest from rural communities, an authoritarian implementation of such a centralist structure was a second prerequisite. It also provided Haussmann with the legal instruments to proceed energetically. During his reign no less than 80 Imperial Decrees, issued in a matter of days, ordered the compulsory purchase of all the property that stood in the way of his plans. The mounting debts of the compensation costs were carried by the state.

Such preferential treatment of the capital was unthought of in a country like Great Britain. Dominated by liberal laissez-faire politics, it had a decentralized administration that denied special privileges to *any* city. Each expropriation of private property required a separate Act of Parliament.

Thus, despite widespread admiration for Haussmann's work, nothing much happened in London as a result. Legal and political obstacles were not the only barriers. The dominant residential culture in

Britain was not favorable to urbanism of the Grand Manner either.

French residential culture was decidedly urban. It enabled the prefect to complete his *grand projet*. For all his might, he was dependent on market forces for the building of the flanks of his new arteries. That private developers were willing to pay high prices for the cleared sites and accept strict architectural supervision means they felt that wealthy tenants were willing to pay high rents for these apartments. From a land rent perspective, building in the city's periphery would have been more advantageous. But no developer would even consider building luxury dwellings there.

Although most Frenchmen lived in the countryside, residential culture was oriented on the city. Rural France was considered an underdeveloped backwater. This paradox was equally prevalent in countries like Italy, Hungary, and the new Balkan states, where the Haussmann strategy was enthusiastically embraced.

Great Britain offers an opposite image. Residents preferred the suburban alternative to living in the congested city. No British developer would have considered building the inner-city luxury apartments that their French counterparts did. They focused their attention on suburbia, where they provided single-family homes ranging from terraced housing to detached villas.

As a result, visitors from continental Europe were astonished to see that the world's leading economic and colonial power was accommodated in such an unimpressive capital. Although France was a more modest power, Paris had become the role model for the representation of national grandeur.

Michiel Wagenaar

See also Capital City; City Beautiful Movement; City Planning; London, United Kingdom; Paris, France; Rome, Italy; Urban Planning

Further Readings

Olsen, Donald. 1986. *The City as a Work of Art: London, Paris, Vienna.* New Haven, CT: Yale University Press.

Pinon, Pierre. 2002. *Atlas du Paris haussmannien : La ville en héritage du Second Empire à nos jours* (Atlas of Haussmann Paris: The City Inherited from the Second Empire to Today). Paris: Parigramme.

Wagenaar, Michiel. 2001. "The Capital as a Representation of the Nation." Pp. 339–58 in *The Territorial Factor: Political Geography in a Globalising World,* edited by Gertjan Dijkink and Hans Knippenberg. Amsterdam: Vossiuspers.

HAWLEY, AMOS

Amos Henry Hawley (1910–) is the founder of neo-orthodox human ecology and a prominent scholar in population analysis, urban sociology, and population policy. He is currently professor emeritus at the University of North Carolina at Chapel Hill, fellow of the American Academy of Arts and Sciences, and Kenan Professor at the University of North Carolina. He has served as president of the Population Association of America and of the American Sociological Association; as demographic adviser to the governments of the Philippines, the Netherlands Antilles, Thailand, and Malaysia; as adviser to the director of Selective Services during World War II and to the Michigan State Planning Commission. He has assisted the National Academy of Sciences and the U.S. Senate in population projects. He is a recipient of the Lynd Award from the Urban and Community Sociological Section of the American Sociological Association (ASA) and of the Award for Human Ecology Contributions from Cornell University. The Amos H. Hawley Distinguished Professorship at UNC is named in his honor. The author of 150 papers and books, his work redefines human ecological study as a general theory of social organization, which has become the primary theoretical perspective in contemporary human ecology.

Born in 1910 in St. Louis, Missouri, Amos Hawley received his AB degree from the University of Cincinnati in 1936. Here Hawley was exposed to sociology and human ecology by James A. Quinn who, like Hawley, would later figure prominently in the neo-orthodox movement in human ecology. Taken with the macrosocial approach aspects of society, Hawley pursued his graduate work at the University of Michigan under one of the best-known human ecologists of his day, Roderick D. McKenzie. In his first year, Hawley worked closely with McKenzie on a comprehensive treatise on human ecology. This collaborative manuscript was lost in a fire, and McKenzie, then suffering from a debilitating illness, turned over restoration of the work to Hawley.

Early Works

Hawley received his PhD in 1941 and joined the faculty at the University of Michigan in the same year, taking over the position left open by the death of his mentor a year earlier. His dissertation research, published as *An Ecological Study of Urban Services,* is notable in that it departs from the Chicago School's stress on space as an object of study. Instead, his work focuses on urban institutional arrangements and their relationship to nonspatial elements of cities. This emphasis on the structure of social organization underlying spatial patterns and of the organizational units constituting this structure would come to characterize his approach to human ecology.

Throughout the 1940s, Hawley reconstructed the notes from the lost collaboration with McKenzie, largely from memory, adding his own theoretical perspective as he went. In particular, Hawley turned to new concepts emerging in animal ecology, especially the idea that all populations are engaged in collective adaptation to the environment. In a seminal article (1944), Hawley applied this notion to human population and highlighted the role macrosocial organization plays in the process of human adaptation. These ideas are honed and expanded in his final manuscript based on the collaboration, *Human Ecology: A Theory of Community Structure* (1950). This work retains McKenzie's influences, especially in its emphasis on the effect of transportation systems on land use and on the metropolis as an analytic unit. However, this work departs from traditional human ecology in ways that came to define neo-orthodox human ecology.

Holding to the traditional ecologist's notion that adaptation refers to the struggle for existence in its creative form, Hawley's 1950 work reorients ecology from the study of spatial regularities to the study of organization of collective action to adapt to resources. Where traditional ecology stressed competition as the mechanism of adaptation in human systems, Hawley asserts that ecological relationships reflect an interactive process of competition and interdependence. Organized around basic sustenance activities, human social systems move toward integrated organizational interdependence.

In this, social systems are seen as adaptive collectivities that supersede individual action. Humans better themselves by expanding the number of interdependencies and increasing the complexity of social structure. This holistic, macrosocial, and material reconception of human ecology reinfused human ecological theory and launched the neo-orthodox movement in the field. Furthermore, Hawley's 1950 reformulation places the organization of society as the main point of focus for human ecology, moving it from a limited theory of city patterns and development to a general theory of social organization.

Hawley remained at the University of Michigan until 1966, serving as chair from 1951 through 1961. During this period, Hawley engaged in a number of empirical studies with students and colleagues, on subjects ranging from fertility and migration to suburbanization and metropolitan reorganization. Many of these projects explicitly tested his theoretical propositions whereas others expanded on his earlier work. This interaction between empiricism and theoretical development is a distinguishing characteristic of Hawley's sociology. Emblematic of this synthesis is his 1963 article, "Community Power and Urban Renewal Success," which builds an ecological notion of social power as a property of ecological structure, a notion missing in the 1950 work but figuring prominently in further theoretical and empirical development.

Moving Forward

Hawley joined the Department of Sociology at the University of North Carolina at Chapel Hill in 1966. Here he produced a series of theoretical and empirical works that solidified human ecology as a prominent approach to the study of society. His 1968 article, "Human Ecology," both summarizes ecological principles and provides the outlines for his subsequent development of an ecological theory of change. This codified theoretical approach can be seen applied in *Urban Society: An Ecological Approach* (1971). Hawley situates the analysis of the city, as an organizational aspect of larger society, through a careful historical exegesis from an ecological perspective.

This concern with cities as a theoretical and real object of study is found in his presidential address for the Population Association of America, "Population Density and the City" (1972). Here Hawley makes the point that social density and spatial density are increasingly separated, with emphasis on the increasing importance of social density. This emphasis keeps with the theme of the primacy of organizational over spatial aspects.

This work also suggests Hawley's increasing interest in the study of change itself, which culminates in his 1978 Presidential Address at the ASA, "Cumulative Change in Theory and in History." Here Hawley carefully explicates types of change and argues that the study of change in social systems should focus on patterns that are nonrecurring and irreversible because these two patterns lead to accumulation of further change.

Although retiring in 1976, Hawley continued to serve actively as mentor and adviser on theses, dissertations, and independent study, shaping several generations of students. His scholarship continued, unabated, resulting in additional explorations of human ecological theory (see "Human Ecological and Marxian Theories," 1984) and a number of influential edited volumes. These volumes brought together macrosocial researchers to encourage, shape, and expand ecological approaches on such topics as the analysis of social change, nonmetropolitan change, metropolitan trends, and environmental issues.

During this time period, Hawley pursued his final sociological book, a culminating work of the essence of his approach to ecological theory: *Human Ecology: A Theoretical Essay* (1986). In his more recent reflective essay, "The Logic of Macrosociology" (1992), Hawley notes the completion of his neo-orthodox revolution in human ecology shifted interest from spatial patterns to the change, functioning, and structure of the social system in environmental context and as a result, "Human ecology takes its place as one of several paradigms in the inclusive field of sociology."

Michael D. Irwin

See also Factorial Ecology; Human Ecology; Urban Sociology

Further Readings

Hawley, Amos H. 1941. "An Ecological Study of Urban Service Institutions." *American Sociological Review* 6(5):629–39.

———. 1944. "Ecology and Human Ecology." *Social Forces* 22(4):398–405.

———. 1950. *Human Ecology: A Theory of Community Structure*. New York: The Ronald Press.

———. 1963. "Community Power and Urban Renewal Success." *The American Journal of Sociology* 68(4):422–31.

———. 1968. "Human Ecology." In *International Encyclopedia of Social Sciences*, edited by David L. Sills. New York: Crowell, Collier and Macmillan.

———. 1971. *Urban Sociology: An Ecological Approach*. New York: The Ronald Press.

———. 1972. "Population Density and the City." *Demography* 9(4): 521–29.

———. 1978. "Cumulative Change in Theory and History." *American Sociological Review* 43(6):787–96.

———. 1984. "Human Ecological and Marxian Theories." *The American Journal of Sociology* 89(4):904–17.

———. 1986. *Human Ecology: A Theoretical Essay*. Chicago: University of Chicago Press.

———. 1992. "The Logic of Macrosociology." *Annual Review of Sociology* 18:1–14.

HEALTHY CITIES

Healthy Cities is a worldwide movement developed by the European office of the World Health Organization. It has been implemented formally through WHO in many cities, and others have adopted the model. Grounded in 11 qualities that range from housing to economy and social characteristics such as a supportive community, Healthy Cities goes well beyond the definition of health as an absence of disease. This entry looks at its development and implementation around the world.

Historical Context

Population health and urbanization have been inseparable twins since the dawn of humankind. Cohen, in his 1989 masterpiece of paleo-epidemiology, demonstrates that the shift from nomadic to sedentary and eventually urban lifestyles impacts on occurrence of disease. Still, rural etiology and population pathology differ considerably from urban patterns. Urban organization, on the other hand, allows for different types of interventions, and it is no surprise that the emergence of modern public health can be traced back to urbanization (from public toilets in ancient Rome to sewage systems in industrializing Britain, and from city-state "Health Police" in medieval Germany to surveillance systems in contemporary megacities). In the late 1990s, Porter and Hall even maintained that the shape of twenty first century cities is dictated by health considerations.

Clearly, they find that modern public health is a direct result of sanitarian programs emerging in mid-nineteenth-century industrializing nations. The Health of Towns movement in Britain (established in 1844) is a direct precursor to Healthy Cities. Modern cities, however, seem to have failed to recognize the most recent shifts in health and disease patterns and their unique potential urban assets to address these.

The etiological shift has moved from predominantly parasitic to microbial infectious and currently chronic diseases; public health interventions have moved from surveillance (such as quarantine) via high-tech pharmaceutical and other clinical interventions to addressing social determinants of health (e.g., inequity and community development). Urban environments are uniquely impacted by such social determinants but are also in a historically unparalleled position to deal with them.

This was recognized as early as 1963 by Duhl and colleagues. In describing what would later become the Healthy Cities movement, they laid down the tenets for analysis and intervention in, for, on, and with social, natural, economic, and built urban environments for the promotion of human and ecosystemic health.

Foundations

The first city to truly adopt these principles became Toronto, more than two decades later (1984). In a serendipitous confluence of global and local developments, the city celebrated emergent emancipatory

health promotion approaches by the World Health Organization (WHO) and a decade of innovation in Canadian health policy (the Lalonde Report); its leaders had the ambition to take a radical stance on the health of city dwellers.

The model was quickly taken up by the European Office of WHO, engaging Duhl and Toronto health entrepreneur Hancock to launch an urban health demonstration project. In collaboration with a small group of European cities, they developed 11 qualities a healthy city should attempt to achieve:

1. a clean, safe physical environment of high quality (including housing quality)
2. an ecosystem that is stable now and sustainable in the long term
3. a strong, mutually supportive, and nonexploitive community
4. a high degree of participation and control by the public over decisions affecting their lives
5. the meeting of basic needs (food, water, shelter, income, safety and work) for all people
6. access to a wide variety of experiences and resources, for a wide variety of interaction
7. a diverse, vital, and innovative city economy
8. the encouragement of connectedness with the past and heritage of city dwellers and others
9. a form that is compatible with and enhances the preceding characteristics
10. an optimum level of appropriate public health and sick care services accessible to all
11. high health status (high levels of positive health and low levels of disease)

The original ambition of WHO to run a small-scale demonstration project exemplifying the potential of urban administrations to deal with late twentieth-century health and disease demands was quickly challenged by its enormous popularity. Within the first five years, hundreds of European cities had expressed an interest in joining the project, and cities outside Europe used guidelines to establish their own. This put a demand on WHO at a global level. In Europe, a small group of WHO-designated cities (meeting strict entry requirements into the project) were to be hubs for national, language-, or topic-based networks of Healthy Cities.

International Exemplars

The initiative continued to be popular in Australia and Canada; in Central and South America, it easily linked with WHO policy on SILOS (Sistemas Locales para la Salud—Local Health Systems) and the Healthy Cities equivalent in the Americas became Healthy Communities. Japan has had a long-standing relation with Healthy Cities, with Tokyo taking an early lead in the 1980s. A broad range of groups, agencies, and communities associates itself with Healthy Cities, from national networks and Agenda 21 initiatives mostly in Europe, the Civic League in the United States, a global International Healthy Cities Foundation (www.healthycities.org) providing a clearing house function, and the Asian–Pacific Alliance for Healthy Cities (www.alliance-healthycities.com). In some counts, there are close to 10,000 Healthy Cities worldwide, the smallest reputedly being l'Isle Aux Grues (Canada, population around 160) and the largest metropolitan Shanghai (China, population in excess of 20 million).

Ever since the initiative was formally launched in 1986, it has been subjected to an evidence-based health paradigm, asking whether Healthy Cities actually deliver health. This is a highly contentious issue, as a core tenet of the paradigm that embeds the movement is that health is not the absence of disease but a resource for everyday life. It is created by individuals and communities and heavily determined by public and corporate policy. It is therefore no surprise that the 11 qualities listed above have been translated by Healthy Cities into an enormous range of actions, themes, and interventions. Sofia (the Bulgarian capital) was a member of the movement for a short while in the late 1980s and used its designation to upgrade the public transport system. Liège (Belgium) addresses the high prevalence of antidepressant use by tackling general practitioners' prescription behavior while at the same time running programs in community-driven neighborhood cleanups. Kuressaare (Estonia) uses the Healthy City label to restore its tsarist-era reputation as a great spa town on the Baltic. Accra (Ghana) aims to coordinate the international aid industry's attempts to clean up its heavily polluted Korle Lagoon under the Healthy Cities banner. Curitiba (Brazil), positioning itself as an ecological city, is highly successful in generating synergy between enhanced (public) mobility, poverty reduction, and primary education. Wonju City (Korea) has established innovative programs in health promotion financing, just as Recife (Brazil) has. Noarlunga (South Australia), one of the longest running Healthy City projects in the world, has effectively addressed health inequity, multiculturalism, severe environmental degradation, and sustainability issues. Several cities around the world are involved in approaches such as community gardening, walkability, urban design, safety, and the informal economy. Virtually all cities look at equitable access to services reaching far beyond the health sector alone. An additional illustration of the range of activities that can be undertaken by a Healthy Cities initiative can be found in the directory of projects of the 199 members of the "Réseau québécois des villes et villages en santé," one of the oldest networks of such initiatives in the world situated in the province of Québec, Canada (see www.rqvvs.qc.ca/membres/realisations.asp).

Healthy Cities also has become the vanguard of other settings-based health initiatives with which the project connects locally: Healthy Marketplaces, Prisons, Workplaces, and Islands; Health Promoting Universities, Hospitals, and Schools. In itself, this is an important proxy of the effectiveness of the approach, inspiring actors and communities at many different levels and domains to be engaged with a social model of health.

Quite apart from the formal Healthy Cities movement, there is increasing attention to the impact of urban planning and design on parameters for health. This increase could be attributed to Healthy Cities, but more important, it will provide new impetus to the movement: The evidence that physical activity is directly affected by urban design parameters has become a high political priority in the early twenty-first century, when the obesity epidemic is predicted to *decrease* future population life expectancy for the first time in history. There is general agreement that the belief that the epidemic can be tackled in behaviorist manners is untenable now and that community-based, integrated, institutional, systemic, and hardware solutions must be sought—precisely the Healthy Cities tenets launched over 40 years ago.

Evelyne de Leeuw, Len Duhl, and Michel O'Neill

See also Sustainable Development; Urban Climate; Urban Planning

Further Readings

Cohen, M. N. 1989. *Health and the Rise of Civilization.* New Haven, CT: Yale University Press.

de Leeuw, E. 2001. "Global and Local (Glocal) Health: The WHO Healthy Cities Programme." *Global Change and Human Health* 2(1):34–53.

Dooris, M. (2006). "Healthy Settings: Challenges to Generating Evidence of Effectiveness." *Health Promotion International* 21(1):55–65.

Duhl, L., ed. 1963. *The Urban Condition: People and Policy in the Metropolis.* New York: Simon & Schuster.

Hall, P. 1998. *Cities in Civilization: Culture, Innovation, and Urban Order.* London: Weidenfeld & Nicolson.

Marmot, M. and R. Wilkinson. 2005. *Social Determinants of Health.* Oxford, UK: Oxford University Press.

O'Neill, Michel and Paule Simard. 2006. "Choosing Indicators to Evaluate Healthy Cities Projects: A Political Task?" *Health Promotion International* 21(2):145–52.

Porter, R. 1999. *The Greatest Benefit to Mankind: A Medical History of Humanity from Antiquity to the Present.* London: Fontana Press.

HERITAGE CITY

The notion and designation of the Heritage City conflates two distinct concepts: city and heritage. City status involves not just size but symbolic importance as well, with the latter a function of history and institutional and political processes. Royal charters, cathedral cities, provincial and administrative cities, and capital cities are all examples. Heritage, on the other hand, is a more recent and fluid concept open to contestation. It involves interpretation of a legacy from the past and therefore requires the identification and valorization of an authentic provenance. This is commonly manifested in terms of buildings, monuments, the physical environment, and artifacts and occurs through individual and group collective memory. Heritage, therefore, is sometimes passed down from previous generations and is of special value and thought worthy of preservation. Who controls this preservation and valuation process and what relationship such heritage has to the city—spatially, culturally, and symbolically—are of increasing concern and debate. The commodification of heritage assets creates economic benefits that accrue to property interests and the heritage tourism industry. Heritage has, therefore, moved from a benign, specialist concern to a central role in city branding and the promotion of the city to its citizenry and to the outside world.

Selectivity is key to heritage planning. A dichotomy exists between the original positivist *preservation* and the normative *heritage,* which implies a process of selection and conservation of history, memory, and relics, as well as their interpretation for contemporary consumption. The concept of *heritage,* which encompasses all historic and style periods without exception, is different from *tradition,* which is only a component of the former and requires a choice be made by (or more often, on behalf of) the public and by certain social classes. Heritage in both of these senses is socially produced.

Heritage as represented in art and architecture is also subject to assessment and valuation by the scholarly canons of art history and through codification and curation and the symbolic importance attached by heritage experts. Although such designation has been dominated by classical and iconic styles represented by historic monuments, castles, churches, cathedrals, palaces, museum quarters, and their collections—*grand projets* of the past—more recent heritage has begun to appear in designation and preservation movements. The importance of visible clues that anchor the development of cities to the past typifies the current desire to reconcile modern development and change with remnants of the city's past. This also reflects the wider democratization of social history or urban archaeology; that is, the heritage of ordinary citizens and the everyday, for example, houses, workplaces, and leisure pursuits. Industrial and twentieth-century heritage is now subject to the preservation and value judgments applied previously to the historic. Consequently, the heritage question and heritage city branding have been applied to a wider range of sites and typologies.

World Heritage

World Heritage site inscription was introduced following the UNESCO Convention on World Heritage in 1972. The Convention responded to the growing conservation and preservation movement and a rising concern about the deleterious encroachment of modernization and modern construction that, directly and indirectly, was responsible for the destruction of historic buildings, structures, and views. Listing and preservation of buildings and historic sites had been practiced in Europe since the late nineteenth century, and from the mid-twentieth century, national and city conservation legislation was created specifically to protect buildings and heritage quarters from modern development, for example, in London (Civic Amenities Act, 1967), Paris (*Plan de Sauvegarde,* 1970), and Montreal (*Héritage Montréal,* 1975). World Heritage Site designation was thus an international recognition of the universal value and importance of a site. It brought both international branding (through the use of the UNESCO logo) and the installation of heritage management and interpretation measures to protect and control access to these sites. In 2007, there were 830 inscribed sites, of which 644 are cultural (manmade), located across 138 countries. The over 200 cities that host World Heritage Sites are members of the Organization of World Heritage Cities (OWHC). More than half of them are based in Europe (with 25 in Italy); 38 are in Latin America, 25 in Arab states, and 20 in Asia. Heritage city sites include the Stone Town (Zanzibar); Alhambra, Granada (Spain); Jerusalem (proposed by Jordan in 1981); Kyoto (Japan); Oaxaca (Mexico); Bath and Edinburgh (UK). Heritage sites from past city civilizations are not included because they are no longer populated or functioning cities (e.g., the pre-Colombian Mayan cities of Central America).

The dominance of the Western European cultural hegemony in heritage designation has effectively exported this preservation ethic and system to other countries, mostly under the auspices of international heritage agencies such as UNESCO and ICOMOS (Paris). The preservation of heritage in towns and cities in non-European countries is a reflection of this movement and also of the imperative for heritage tourism and development aid from the West. Conversely, the belated recognition of "oriental culture" as seen from the perspective of Western cities now forms part of cosmopolitan city heritage in designated ethnic quarters, festivals, and institutions; for example, *Arab Monde,* Paris, and Native American museums in New York City and Washington, D.C.

Who owns this heritage, culturally as well as legally, is contested when political and cultural power shifts. For example, Québec City, the administrative and political capital of francophone Québec Province (and Canada), was founded by Samuel de Champlain in 1608. Its historic quarter, fortifications, and battlefield sites were designated a World Heritage Site in 1985 and have been a national monument since 1952. However, the site is actually the British garrison, which replaced the French garrison in the 1750s with the support of Native Americans, earlier explorers, traders, and migrants. This particular heritage city, therefore, represents local (residents), provincial, separatist, national (Canadian), First Nations, migrant, and colonial (English, French, Irish) interests and histories, but not on equal terms.

Modern Heritage

Recent modern heritage listings include Gaudi's works in Barcelona, Oscar Neimeyer's Brasilia, Bauhaus sites in Germany, The White City of Tel Aviv, the Maritime Merchant City (Liverpool), and Le Havre, France, and proposed additions of modern and industrial heritage include Chatham Dockyard in England and the Art Deco buildings of Miami. These listings reflect the growing intervention of architectural movements (e.g., DOCUMOMO) and the recognition of modern architecture as worthy of preservation.

Few cities actually use the designation *heritage city* because this generally applies to specific buildings, sites, or areas as in Lyon and Bath within the larger city. The label can also refer to a collection of cultural and historic elements such as museums and galleries, monuments, historic buildings, and palaces or to a sociocultural legacy as represented by living culture, language, food, fashion, and festivals. Different aspects of heritage serve resident, visitor, and tourist markets, particularly in terms of the historic, culture,

The historic center of Bruges, Belgium, and the city's medieval architecture, are protected under the UNESCO World Heritage site convention.

Source: Karen Wiley.

nightlife, and shopping attractions of the tourist destination.

The Heritage City is one example of competitive city place-making, along with designations such as City or Capital of Culture, Knowledge City, Creative City, Science City, and Sport City, among others. These are not exclusive, as cities strive to maintain multiple images and brands. The absence of heritage in a city implies a lack of a past legacy of value and a dearth of opportunities for heritage tourism and self-identity, which only the most insular and autocratic city-state could risk.

Old-world cities have had longer to reconcile the largely incremental pressures from growth and new building with preservation and heritage, whereas in new and resurgent cities such as Shanghai, Beijing, Dubai, and Kuala Lumpur, the heritage protection and value system is weaker—the new is reified over the old. In cities of renewed national and political freedom, legacies from the past can sit uncomfortably with both painful memories and new directions, as in former Eastern bloc capitals, where communist monuments (e.g., of Marx or Lenin) are dismantled; this is also the case in places where despotic leaders are deposed as in Saddam City (Baghdad), first renamed Al Thawra "Revolution City," then "Sadr City" after the late Imam. The dismantling of the *Palast der Republik* (People's Palace) in the former East Berlin, along with the re-creation of the historic castle that predated it, is an example of city heritage rejection and reversion. The redevelopment of the Museum Quartier from the Imperial Stables in Vienna into a "Shopping Mall for Culture" is another approach. Here, contemporary culture (museums, galleries, theater spaces) was created within the walls of an historic structure.

Heritage City Tourism

The globalization of tourist space has fueled the exploitation of city heritage sites as places of internal and external consumption. This latter phenomenon has become common to major cities and urban heritage sites and is not a recent development but an expansion of inscribing power through the materialization of bourgeois ideologies that has occurred since the nineteenth century. Historic City quarters, along with medieval, old town areas, have been rediscovered and zoned as heritage assets, necessitating the displacement of poorer, often working-class and migrant communities. These now serve as locations for culture-led regeneration, with the siting of contemporary cultural facilities such as Pompidou (Paris) and MACBA (Barcelona) and the associated gentrification through residential, office, and retail property use.

Entire cities can adopt the heritage tag where built environment and heritage legacy is of sufficient scale and homogeneity, notably in heritage cities such as Venice and Florence. The use of heritage designation for industrial sites and cities has also helped repair postindustrial decline in places such as Lowell, Massachusetts, and Bradford, Yorkshire (UK). Former industrial complexes in ports and docklands, mines, mills, and manufacturing plants have also been recognized by heritage listing, such as Essen, Germany (coal mining), and the open museum at Ironbridge, Shropshire (UK). Redundant industrial buildings increasingly serve as atmospheric sites for cultural facilities, whether celebrating industrial heritage itself (e.g., brewery buildings: Heineken, Amsterdam; Guinness, Dublin) or, more often, undergoing conversion to modern galleries and museums, such as the Tate Modern (a former turbine station in London); Salts Mill, in Bradford, Yorkshire; Musée D'Orsay (a former railway station in Paris); and Parc de La Villette (a former slaughterhouse, market in Paris).

As perhaps the location for the ultimate accumulation of artifacts and architecture and subject to continuous interpretation, the city defies a single heritage branding such as "Gaudi Barcelona" or "Macintosh Glasgow." Moreover, the imperative for heritage policies and selection can be counterproductive, when the drive for being different and unique indicates how much cities have become the same. As postindustrial cosmopolitan cities multiply in number and in the range and layers of their heritage, they become both invisible and self-consciously visible through the official narratives and interpretation of heritage. As a consequence, cities become more and more alike.

Graeme Evans

See also Cultural Heritage; Historic Cities; Tourism

Further Readings

Ashworth, Greg J. 2003. "Conservation as Preservation or as Heritage: Two Paradigms and Two Answers." Pp. 20–30 in *Designing Cities: Critical Readings in Urban Design,* edited by A. R. Cuthbert. Oxford, UK: Blackwell.

City Mayors. 2008. *Historic Cities—Living Cities.* Paris: World Heritage Centre. Retrieved March 24, 2009 (http://www.citymayors.com/culture/historic_intro .html).

Evans, Graeme L. 2002. "Living in a World Heritage City: Stakeholders in the Dialectic of the Universal and the Particular." *International Journal of Heritage Studies* 8(2):117–35.

Evans, Graeme L. 2003. "Hard Branding the Culture City—From Prado to Prada." *International Journal of Urban and Regional Research* 27(2):417–40.

Larkham, Peter J. 1996. *Conservation and the City.* London: Routledge.

UNESCO. 2003. *World Heritage Papers 5, Identification and Documentation of Modern Heritage.* Paris: UNESCO World Heritage Center.

HETEROTOPIA

The term *heterotopia* was first used in a social–theoretical context by the French philosopher Michel Foucault. It refers in one sense to a place that is socially different from the (implicitly normal) spaces surrounding it. However, the difference presented by heterotopia is not essential to that place. Instead, heterotopia is foremost an ambiguous, variable, and dynamic site that incites (re-)consideration and (re-)negotiation of sociospatial norms. The concept has therefore been deployed by critical theorists, architects, and geographers to interrogate the ways in which social norms and differences are built into particular places. Most important, the concept of heterotopia has been interpreted creatively to theorize new forms of thinking and living differently grounded in ordinary everyday spaces (rather than in utopian plans).

The variable usage of the term *heterotopia* should initially be considered with reference to Foucault's theoretical corpus. First, Foucault's direct treatment of heterotopia was inconsistent and unfinished, represented by merely one book chapter and a short lecture. The preliminary nature of Foucault's discussion means that its usage varies, as does the degree to which his original texts are read literally rather than metaphorically. Second, although Foucault's influence on geography and urban studies is widespread, his theorization of space remained underdeveloped. Hence, critics have warned against a literal and simplistic reading of heterotopias as physical, locatable sites (Foucault offers examples such as asylums and cemeteries), which can be compared with other "normal" sites. Third, in overcoming this danger, heterotopia can be more usefully aligned with Foucault's writings on power, difference, and discourse. Foucault was concerned with ways in which normative political power was exercised (and resisted) through small-scale social practices and structures. More complex deployments have thus asserted that heterotopia provides a space or rupture—conceptual–discursive as well as literal—that can unsettle expected conventions. Heterotopia provide(s) a methodological tool, therefore, to effect contestations of normative political power.

Since the 1990s, heterotopia has figured relatively prominently in Anglo-American urban studies. Conceptually, it has been related to contemporaneous writings on otherness and marginality (e.g., those of Henri Lefebvre and the Situationists). Much empirical research on heterotopia has aligned the concept with postmodern urbanism and in particular with the place-specific emergence of new spatial expressions of power in Los Angeles. Elsewhere, the concept has enabled sophisticated readings of the idealistic, aesthetic, and commercial imperatives that inform new urban developments as diverse as the Las Vegas Strip and gated communities in postapartheid South Africa. Finally, the term has been used to identify alternate and unpredictable forms of (largely urban) utopian experimentation that shed new light on the historical processes inherent to the emergence of modernity. Heterotopia remains contested—indeed, its boundaries with both nonheterotopian and utopian spaces are still blurry. Yet, this ambiguity is its greatest strength: the power of spatial practice and discourse to unsettle convention and to evoke alternative forms of living.

Peter Kraftl

See also Lefebvre, Henri; Los Angeles School of Urban Studies; Situationist City; Soja, Edward W.; Urban Theory

Further Readings

Hetherington, K. 1997. *The Badlands of Modernity: Heterotopia and Social Ordering*. London: Routledge.
Soja, E. 1996. *Thirdspace*. Oxford, UK: Blackwell.

Hip Hop

Hip hop, like any historical process, has shifting meanings over time. At one scale, it is the global transmission of the localized cultural practices of urban Black and Latino youth in the United States. At another, it is the persistent reconfiguration of these gestures by global participants in locally situated contexts. At another scale, hip hop is a kind of diaspora, a condition of the dispossessed and dislocated. As Alex Weheliye points out, hip hop links those excluded from the nation-state to a global citizenship where alternative belonging, desire, and imagination can be expressed. At yet another scale, hip hop is an effect of unbalanced power relations. Like other U.S. forms of material and ideological culture, hip hop is mediated across the globe, creating varying degrees of friction and synergy with indigenous cultural traditions. Last, hip hop is how bodies, technologies, and built environments are continually remade to produce locally relevant meanings in music, speech, dance, and public art.

A Brief History

Hip hop includes at least four elements: MCing, DJing, B-girling/B-boying, and graffiti. Additional elements of hip hop include fashion, slang, beatboxing—an improvisational exercise of the mouth—and R&B music. Hip hop is a polyrhythmic practice that merges the percussive instruments and chant circles of West African traditional folk music, the call and response of Black gospel sermons, the improvisation of blues and jazz, and the cadence of Black arts movement poetry.

The origin of hip hop is heavily contested as it combines many aesthetics of West African and West Indian cultural performance. Hip hop's genesis is largely accredited to Jamaican-born DJ Kool Herc, who began throwing block parties in the South Bronx in 1973. Jeff Chang writes that the 1970s was a time of social upheaval as the dreams of the civil rights movement fell flat in the South Bronx with the relocation of Yankee Stadium, massive deindustrialization, White and Black middle class flight to the suburbs as houses were razed for an expressway, and the construction of urban renewal public housing projects. The music reflected these harsh social conditions as "good times" disco died out. Known for his Hercules sound system, Herc would loop and mix the bridge between verses repeatedly ("the breaks"), switching between two records. To keep the momentum, MCs would chant over records in a style similar to the toasting of Jamaican DJs.

Hip hop, in its earliest form, was a live improvisational event inspired by the interaction between performers and the crowd. Hip hop sprouted from a culture of idleness due to rampant unemployment, social program cuts, and overcrowded housing. As Robin D. G. Kelley suggests, the bodies of Black and Latino youth were used as sites of competitive labor to advertise their distinct, individualized work and create financial and social networking opportunities. Crews divided by neighborhoods would battle, on benign and hostile terms, for bragging rights on the dance floor.

"We on Award Tour!" Hip Hop Across the Globe

Hip hop has always been a global process. Mixtape cassettes, magazines, music videos, and hip hop films have been circulating throughout parts of Africa, Europe, and the Caribbean since the early 1980s. Historically, forms of popular culture are exchanged along migration routes between the United States and other countries as people travel for work, military/government service, education, health care, and leisure. Hip hop's global presence has intensified with advancement in technologies of travel, communication, and immediate access to worldwide information. Digital media have transformed sound production and the recording process. Consumers can now become producers and manipulate sound into an infinite composition of remixes. Hip hop aficionados identify, engage, and collaborate with one another across geographical distance through free profile sites, blogs, chat rooms, and podcasts, along with Web sites such as Nomadic Wax, AfricanHipHop.com, okayplayer.com, flight808.com and cell phone text messaging and ringtones. For instance, North Carolina–based rapper Phonté, half of the group Little Brother, recorded and released 2004's *The Foreign Exchange: Connected* album with Dutch producer, Nicolay, entirely over instant messaging and e-mail.

Although digital media access is not distributed equally across place, youth cultural politics have been critically reconfigured through hip hop in many countries. Unfortunately, hip hop artists, particularly in differently developed countries, experience great difficulty securing record contracts and confront issues like payola and a lack of copyright protection for their work. Hip hop outside the United States is not pure mimesis but rather an intricate web of local and global dialects, cultural histories, gestures, and capital. In Senegal, Positive Black Soul revolutionized youth participation in electoral politics with lyrics about government corruption and AIDS. In Ghana, rappers Reggie Rockstone and Talking Drum created hiplife, a mix of U.S. hip hop and Ghanaian high life music. Hiplife combines the beats of hip hop, soukous, and dancehall with traditional folk instruments and rapping/singing in the local dialects of Twi, Ga, Ewe, Fante, pidgin, and English. In fact, highlife artist Gyedu-Blay Ambolley's simigwa music featured rapping as early as 1973.

In Brazil, *favela* life is the cornerstone of hip hop. Popular artists such as Racionais MCs and MV Bill fuse together hip hop, funk, manguebeat, and samba. Artists, breakers, capoeira players, and cinema often challenge police brutality, domestic abuse, political corruption, and the drug economy. Hip hop's entrance into Japan and Germany began about 1983 with the film release of *Wild Style*. B-boy competitions are regularly held in Japan with RockSteady Crew Japan member Crazy A's annual "B-Boy Park" and Germany's "Battle of the Year." U.K. grime music mixes diasporic memory with garage, dancehall, and hip hop music by popular artists Dizzy Rascal and Sway (Ghanaian descent) and M.I.A. (Sri Lankan descent). Hip hop in Cuba was imported from Miami in the 1990s. The government formed the Agencia Cubana de Rap, which houses a record label and magazine and supports the annual Havana Hip Hop Festival organized by the Black August Collective, a group of progressive U.S. hip hop artists.

Hip hop has become an interchangeable term for *urban* and *ghetto* in popular discourses, often in ways that circumscribe Black and Latino subjectivities. However, hip hop music and cultures are important for considering how local practices of urban identity are made global and then relocalized as innovative capacities. Hip hop, as an overlapping series of Black expressions that are not bound by race, is an ongoing articulation of political identity for and by the youthful of the world

Sionne Rameah Neely

See also *Favela*; Ghetto; Graffiti; Racialization

Further Readings

Chang, Jeff. 2005. *Can't Stop, Won't Stop: A History of the Hip Hop Generation*. New York: St. Martin's.

Kelley, Robin D. G. 1998. *Yo Mama's Disfunktional! Fighting the Culture Wars in Urban America*. Boston: Beacon.

Weheliye, Alex. 2006. *Phonographies: Grooves in Sonic Modernity*. Durham, NC: Duke University Press.

HIROSHIMA, JAPAN

Hiroshima, the tenth-largest city in Japan, is located on the Seto Inland Sea and is the capital of Hiroshima Prefecture. With a 2007 population of 1.16 million people, Hiroshima is the largest city in the Chugoku region of western Honshu Island and is the commercial and cultural hub of western Japan. The automobile manufacturer Mazda is headquartered in Hiroshima and accounts for roughly one third of the city's economic base. In 1945, Hiroshima became the first city in the world to be attacked with nuclear weapons. Hiroshima is today known worldwide as a Peace Memorial City. Its municipal government and civic groups, especially those begun by *Hibakusha* (atomic bomb survivors), have historically been at the forefront of global efforts to abolish nuclear weapons.

Hiroshima is of particular importance in Urban Studies for two reasons: Hiroshima demonstrates the temporality of existing city centers because the destruction of the nuclear attack was more absolute than that of the fire bombing inflicted on most Japanese cities in World War II and because hilly Nagasaki, which was also hit with an atomic bomb, retained some previous structures. In addition, said to be uninhabitable for decades after the attack, the city nevertheless survived and rebuilt, offering a blank slate to city planners. It provides an example of an urban area sustaining and recovering from unique challenges presented by modern warfare.

Hiroshima is a river delta town, located at the mouth of the Ota River, built on land reclaimed from the Seto Inland Sea. In 1589, the local *daimyo* (feudal lord) Mori Terumoto changed the name of the town to Hiroshima ("wide island") and began construction of Hiroshima castle, which would anchor urban development for generations. In 1871, during the Meiji period, feudal domains were abolished and Hiroshima Prefecture was established, and in 1889, the city of Hiroshima formally gained municipality status.

On August 6, 1945, Hiroshima was attacked by the United States, which dropped a single atomic bomb on the city. It was the first city in the world to have been attacked with a nuclear weapon. This single bomb unleashed destructive power equivalent to 15,000 tons of TNT, destroying 69 percent of the city's buildings and killing or injuring more than 300,000 people. During the war, Hiroshima was among a small number of towns removed from U.S. conventional and fire bombing target lists to provide undamaged targets that would facilitate later atomic bomb damage assessments. The important military facilities located in Hiroshima during the time of the bombing were not targeted (and largely survived), but rather, the bomb was aimed at the city center. On August 9, 1945, the world's first plutonium bomb, nicknamed the "Fat Man," was dropped on Nagasaki, the second and last city to be attacked with a nuclear weapon. There is widespread disagreement about the extent to which the bombings of Hiroshima and Nagasaki led to the end of World War II.

After the end of the war, Hiroshima moved fairly rapidly from a population low of 137,000 in late 1945 to the vibrant city that it is today. In 1949, first the city government and then national government declared Hiroshima a Peace Memorial City, and construction was begun on the Peace Memorial Park to honor the victims of the bombing. In 1996, the Atomic Bomb Dome, a former industrial promotion center near the hypocenter of the blast, whose mangled shell was preserved after the war, was declared a UNESCO World Heritage Site.

Among the challenges facing modern Hiroshima is how to keep the memory of the experiences of the Hibakusha salient for future generations. Toward this end, the newly built Hiroshima City University in 1998 established the Hiroshima Peace Institute, an academic research institute focused on global peace research so that the name Hiroshima would always be associated with work toward a peaceful planet for generations to come.

Robert A. Jacobs

See also Catastrophe; Heritage City

Further Readings

Hachiya, Michihiko. [1955] 1995. *Hiroshima Diary: The Journal of a Japanese Physician, August 6–September 30, 1945*. Rev. ed. Chapel Hill: University of North Carolina Press.

Hogan, Michael, ed. 1996. *Hiroshima in History and Memory*. Cambridge, UK: Cambridge University Press.

Kamada, Nanao. 2005. *One Day in Hiroshima: An Oral History*. Translated and edited by Richard C. Parker and Rick Nelson. Hiroshima: Japanese Physicians for the Prevention of Nuclear War.

Kort, Michael, ed. 2007. *The Columbia Guide to Hiroshima and the Bomb*. New York: Columbia University Press.

Ogura, Toyofumi. 2001. *Letters from the End of the World: A Firsthand Account of the Bombing of Hiroshima*. Tokyo: Kodansha International.

Weller, George. 2007. *First into Nagasaki: The Censored Eyewitness Dispatches on Post-atomic Japan and Its Prisoners of War*. New York: Three Rivers Press.

HISTORIC CITIES

The historic city is a concept; a creation of the human imagination. The raw materials from which the imagination shapes it, however, may be, and usually are, composed of tangible physical structures, forms, and shapes as well as nontangible memories and associations with past events and personalities: all of which can be related to actual physical locations on the Earth's surface. The adjective *historic* modifies the noun *city*, separating historic from nonhistoric, assuming the existence of two categories of cities. The answers to two questions are sought here. What is a historic city? Why and how have historic cities been created?

What Is a Historic City?

We can distinguish three approaches to time, their expression in urban environments, and their relationship with place management philosophies. There are old cities, historic cities, and heritage cities.

The past is the totality of whatever has happened being continuously augmented by the passage of time. Logically, cities are new only at the instant of their creation and subsequently vary in the degree of their antiquity. However, some arbitrary comparative division could separate old from new cities, raising the question how old is old. Also, does an old city, in this sense, need to be characterized by a dominance of old buildings or morphologies? Old cities are not necessarily the same as cities composed of old buildings. There are many cities in the world that conceive of themselves as old, in the sense of being conscious of having had a lengthy or even distinguished history, even though little physical record of this remains in the urban fabric. Hamburg, Germany, for example, thinks of itself as old and stresses in its promotion its antiquity and historic associations, expressed especially through its historically significant citizens and its former role in the Hanseatic League. It is, however, uncompromisingly modern in its postwar rebuilt city center. The reverse situation could conceivably occur, although the globalization of the heritage industry renders this increasingly unlikely, namely that a city composed of old buildings and structures would be unaware of its antiquity and its potential historicity.

History is the attempt of the present to describe, necessarily highly selectively, aspects of the past. As, by definition, the past does not exist any longer in the present, a city of history, in this sense, can exist only in the descriptions of historians. However, relict structures, street patterns, and sites that have associations with historical events and personalities may survive and be acknowledged in the present. Old cities become historic cities through the application of the strategy of preservation. Preservation is the action of preserving from harm but involves first recognizing that the object to be preserved has value through its antiquity or beauty and then imposing physical and legal protective measures. Such official designations of historic city may be local, national, or even international, through organizations such as UNESCO, and there are officially sanctioned leagues or networks of such historic cities nationally and internationally. A conclusion might be that a historic city is a city declared to be so by a competent authority.

However, differences in the criteria for inclusion as historic are wide. China, for example, lists 62 officially designated historic cities based on their absolute historic values, thus including all the major cities. The Council of Europe, on the other hand, lists historic cities based on proportional values, thus ignoring London, Rome, and Vienna as nonhistoric in favor of more completely historic Bath, Florence, and Salzburg.

Preservation rarely remains a purely defensive strategy. There is a spectrum of increasing intervention through preservation activities. This proceeds from protection of what remains from further harm, maintenance so that it remains in the current state, repair of damage, replacement of what is missing, renovation to return it to an original condition, reconstruction of what once was but is now not, facsimile building in the spirit of what once might have been, ultimately to the creative invention of what should have been but never was. Cities cannot be left as ruined relicts if they are to continue to function as cities, although individual buildings may be, if like the Kaiser Wilhelm Gedächtniskirke in Berlin, they are deliberately endowed with a new meaning as a ruin. The functional demands of cities on space predispose management to intervene beyond protective maintenance and repair to facilitate adaptive reuse for modern functions.

The difference between history and heritage is that the former attempts, however imperfectly and selectively, to describe or re-create a past believed to have once existed, whereas the latter is the contemporary uses of pasts that are products of the imagination in the present designed to satisfy present needs. Although both are contemporary creations, the motives and criteria of the creators are different. In preservation planning, the focus is on the maintenance of the forms and morphologies for their own sake. Although there is inevitably some consideration of function, this will always be a secondary and usually subsequent concern. Conservation, however, is preserving purposefully, with the contemporary and future function being a crucial criterion for selection. The conservation planning of historic cities concerns function as well as form and thus urban planners and managers as much as historians and architects.

Heritage makes no assumptions about a fixed endowment of intrinsically valued artifacts from a past but views the past solely from the standpoint of the present, using the past as an almost infinite resource to be quarried for the creation of contemporary products through the process of commodification. The resulting cities reflect how the present sees the past, or even wishes it to have been. The postwar Polish reconstruction of the nation's destroyed cities, especially Warsaw, in a detail so meticulous as to produce a cityscape too perfect to have ever been, was considered a necessary cultural assertion of a Polish identity and the political legitimacy of a reborn Polish state. Violett-le-duc's renovation of Carcassonne owed more to his imagined medieval city than to the actual historical experience of the place.

Dual Definitions of the Historic City

Historic cities can be defined in two significantly different ways, which, while not mutually exclusive as both meanings can coexist in the same city, are not describing the same phenomenon.

First, the term can refer to the city as a whole, its essence or *genius loci*. The city conceives of itself as historic or projects an image of being historic for internal or external consumption. This place identity does not necessarily imply that all or even most of the existing physical structures are themselves historic, in the sense of possessing an ascribed historicity. It can be little more than a state of mind, whether felt by insiders or imposed by outsiders.

Second, the term *historic city* may relate to a specific district of the city and may be used to differentiate it from other districts that compose the modern city. The second sense of historic may contribute to, or be the justification of, the first sense, but equally is not a condition of its existence. This may be no more than a reflection of the evolution of the urban form through time as the older city is physically expanded by the addition of later newer districts. However, it normally means more. The older part of the city may serve a significantly different function and be treated in a different way. The historic city in this sense is a functionally specialized district within the city in which historicity is expressed through both the built environment and by the uses to which the district is put. History becomes a function that can be regionalized in much the same way as other such districts, such as the shopping city, the administrative city, or the residential city. The creation, evolution, and management of historic districts within cities have been modeled in the tourist–historic city, a concept that has been applied globally to many different types of city, within many different cultural and political environments.

Why Have We Created Historic Cities?

The reasons why historic cities are created and the criteria used for selecting appropriate elements in their creation can be divided into two categories, intrinsic and extrinsic.

Intrinsic values are those that are purported to be intrinsic to the object, whether the structures or the site itself. These values are regarded as existing independently of the observer and thus waiting to be discovered. The three most commonly used intrinsic criteria, which have often been inscribed into the protective legislation in most countries, are age, aesthetic beauty, and place associations with historic personalities or events. These criteria are assumed to be capable of objective determination and verification, usually by dispassionate experts. The concept of authenticity becomes central to these decisions and the benchmark against which the objects and sites are judged. There is a quite fundamental distinction between the authenticity of the object, building, or site and the authenticity of the historical record as a whole. The first would question the authenticity of the buildings, ensembles, associations, and location itself. The second argues that the total of what is preserved together represents an authentic reflection of what has occurred.

Extrinsic values by contrast are ascribed to the structures and areas of the city for a wide variety of contemporary reasons, which are neither inevitable nor immutable. The benchmark for assessment is not the intrinsic qualities but the extent to which extrinsic needs are satisfied. These needs may be sociopsychological, relating to the identification of individuals and social groups with a heritage; political–ideological, legitimating a jurisdiction or dominant ideology; or economic, in which heritage becomes a resource to be commodified for sale on many economic markets, of which tourism is only one. Few heritage cities have been created to serve a single purpose. Most are as multifunctional in their heritage component as in their other functions, serving many different heritage markets, internally and externally, for a variety of motives, political and social as well as economic. Even "epitome historic cities," that is, those that are selected to represent and symbolize wider, often national cultures and their values, such as Rothenburg ob der Tauber (Germany), Eger (Hungary), or Telč (Czech Republic), have major tourism functions as well as their symbolic cultural–political roles. Historic cities performing multiple heritage functions are more typical than aberrant, but this condition of serving multiple markets raises the possibility of conflict and thus the necessity for continuous heritage management.

Historic Cities Are Also Cities

Most of the above discussion has focused on the meaning and importance of the adjective *historic* rather than the noun, *city,* to which it is applied. However, it needs to be simply stated that historic cities must also be cities. The danger is that the process of "heritage-ization," that is, creating historicity for contemporary purposes, can threaten the existence of the city itself. Historicity may be a threat to urbanicity. The conceptual problem is that the conferring of historic status turns what was a functional building, ensemble, or city into a monument. The very act of preservation, through its interference with the process of change and decay, replaces what was with something new. The related planning problem is that of fossilization, that is, the denial of the right and capacity of the city to change. This raises the question: Can a preserved city remain a city rather than an extended museum exhibit?

It is easy to distinguish in theory between historic cities that are functioning cities with an historic component and heritage theme parks that have been created solely as a vehicle for the transmission and selling of heritage. Few would confuse a Disneyland creation of a streetscape with a settlement. However, the line between the two can become very blurred indeed. There are many reconstructed and usually relocated open-air museums (following the Hazelius archetype of the Skansen), some of which are urban, being not just located in cities but endeavoring to express urban life. These may be animated by a costumed population engaged in activities suitable to the period being reenacted. *Den Gamle By* near Aarhus (Denmark), begun in 1909, is one of the oldest, but other well-known cases would be Williamsburg (Virginia, United States), Louisbourg (Nova Scotia, Canada), or even the Blist's Hill Victorian Town in the Ironbridge Gorge museum complex (Shropshire, United Kingdom). Although these heritage theme parks try to represent cities of the past, they clearly are not cities, having no permanent population or modern urban functions: They are theatrical stage sets.

However, in the town of Shelburne (Nova Scotia, Canada), the older central part of the town has been fenced off to become a museum experience with the inhabitants remaining in situ and behaving, at least within the defined heritage area, in costume and in period while the rest of the town functions normally. Then there are the fossilized "gem cities," usually small and compact historic towns, whose historic fabric has survived more or less intact and whose subsequent preservation has been total. These are often fortress towns, such as Willemstad or Naarden (Netherlands), Cittadella (Italy), and Mont St. Michel or Neuf-Brisach (France). The strict and complete preservation of the historic town expels modern facilities from the city. The dilemma is clearly that such functions are disruptive to or discordant with the historic town but necessary for its continuing functioning, including those serving the needs of the heritage industry itself.

The management of historic districts within multifunctional cities poses similar dilemmas and necessitates similar compromises. Many cities contain heritage action spaces that are little more than open-air museums mono-functionally serving heritage industries. Elm Hill (Norwich, United Kingdom), for example, is a historic street renovated, substantially rebuilt, and enhanced with period paving and street furniture in the early 1960s. It functions as a heritage tourism experience and is dominated by tourism shopping and catering businesses. It became an archetype for the reconstruction of the medieval streetscape, as expected by the tourism industry, and has been globally replicated, from Vancouver's Gastown to Sydney's Rocks, all of which both house specific heritage-related functions and help designate the city concerned as historic.

Thus the historic city is not the totality of its preserved artifacts from the past nor the spatial setting in which remembered events and personalities acted. It is a phenomenon created by the present, which like the study of history itself, will be re-created anew by each generation according to the needs and attitudes that then prevail. The historic city may often freely make use of the preserved architectural forms, morphological patterns, and promoted historical associations, but it remains a creation of the present in the service of contemporary needs. Authenticity, defined as the accurate representation of the past through the conservation of its relict features, has little relevance to this creation. Between the archaeological site and the heritage theme park there are many intermediate points, and a series of short steps links preserving what is, restoring what was, re-creating what was but somewhere else, and building what was not but could or should have been. Similarly, there is a clear difference between a museum of urban history and a modern functioning city, with historic cities occupying a sometimes uncomfortable middle ground. Therein lies the role of urban heritage planning and management.

G. J. Ashworth

See also Heritage City; Tourism; Venice, Italy

Further Readings

Ashworth, G. J. 1991. *Heritage Planning: The Management of Urban Change.* Groningen, the Netherlands: Geopers.

Ashworth, G. J. and J. E. Tunbridge. 1990. *The Tourist-Historic City.* London: Belhaven.

———. 2000. *The Tourist-Historic City: Retrospect and Prospect of Managing the Heritage City.* Oxford, UK: Elsevier.

Burke, G. 1976. *Townscapes.* Harmondsworth, UK: Penguin.

Tiesdell, S., T. Heath, and T. Oc. 1996. *Revitalising Historic Urban Quarters.* Oxford, UK: Architectural Press.

HOMELESSNESS

While no doubt there have always been people who lived outside of regular abodes, as defined by a customary four-walled home or dwelling, it took the development of Western notions of civilization, modernity, and capitalism for homelessness, along with associated terms such as *vagrancy*, *transience*, and *vagabondage*, to be defined as a social problem. Scholars note that in medieval times, there was little stigma to begging or living on the streets, and social groups such as students and religious travelers were frequently associated with street living. The rise of modernity stigmatized those who lacked homes and linked those who had no "regular settlement" with being "savages," such as those encountered in the forests of the New World.

While the history of homelessness is long and complex, its nature as a social problem depends on both its scale and the level of threat it appears to pose to the social order. Such threats may be political or criminal, and most often these fears overlap. As urban America developed, three historical periods have led to particular concerns among the public about homelessness: the period between the Civil War and the close of the nineteenth century; the Great Depression period; and the late 1970s to the present. Following the Civil War, a combination of the demobilization of troops along with changing economic conditions gave rise to a large number of men who were labeled tramps. Although most men traveling along the roads and railroads were no doubt migratory workers (or, in the argot of late nineteenth century, would be better labeled hoboes than tramps), cultural rebellion in the form of petty crimes, riding the rails without paying fares, and the tendency of the very poor to be associated with social protests such as the Great Railroad Strike of 1877 and Coxey's Army of 1894 gave tramps a radicalized and feared reputation. By the 1880s, most states had strengthened their tramp and vagrancy laws to develop draconian punishments for begging or even standing in or walking on the roads without an established settlement or a job. While most victims of these laws were thrown into houses of corrections or workhouses, there were instances of tramps being killed or severely injured by mobs or special police hired by railroads and other companies.

Depressions, however, particularly the Great Depression of the 1930s, lessened some of the stigma of poverty and evoked sympathy. The late nineteenth-century depressions led to the creation of soup kitchens and municipal lodging houses to serve the poor, and in the 1930s, the first New Deal program, the Federal Emergency Relief Agency (FERA), actively aided homeless encampments. At times, homeless people of the 1930s joined the ranks of what was seen as the "deserving poor." They participated in public works programs and were pictured by famous New Deal artists and photographers as desolate migrants searching for jobs. Such empathy should not be overstated. Often,

A homeless youth on the streets of New York City

Source: Steven K. Martin.

homeless people were treated harshly, evicted from trains and makeshift accommodations, and removed from towns and cities as they did not hold legal settlements there. Only with World War II did the number of homeless people begin to fall.

Although homelessness never totally vanished, the word virtually disappeared in the 1950s and 1960s, to be replaced by the association of severe poverty with the skid rows of urban areas. No matter how harsh life was in the single-room occupancy apartments, hotels, and boarding houses of American cities, where the "bums" and hoboes lived, the occupants had roofs over their heads. Suddenly, around the late 1970s, residents of large cities noticed something new, people without any apparent homes at all. Advocates in Washington, D.C., led by the charismatic Mitch Snyder and his Coalition for Creative Non-Violence (CCNV) and the New York–based Coalition for the Homeless led by attorney Robert Hayes, defined the "new

homelessness" and demanded that government provide emergency assistance as well as economic and housing aid. The more structural or socioeconomic proposals of advocates (and later homeless people themselves) for jobs, permanent housing, and income were lost amid both the public perception and political leaders' desire to stress charity or public emergency measures of amelioration such as soup kitchens and shelters.

In the 1980s, homelessness emerged as a public issue for the first time since the 1930s. On the one hand, a furious debate raged, with liberals and radicals condemning the massive social welfare cutbacks of the Reagan administration, as well as blaming housing gentrification, deindustrialization, and other systemic problems (lack of jobs and income, for example). On the other side, conservatives, led by a president who commented that many people chose to live out on the streets, emphasized alcohol, drugs, laziness, and mental illness to different degrees to account for the sudden appearance of homelessness.

Moreover, the very definition of homelessness became contested. Advocates argued with much justification that a true measure of homelessness would include not only those literally on the streets or in shelters but those who were "crashing" or "doubled up" with relatives or friends and those living in group homes and prisons. In spite of the seemingly vast differences between liberals and conservatives, homeless shelters and similar palliative strategies from soup kitchens to clothes pantries to case management to increasingly specialized casework services dominated the response of almost all governmental levels. These solutions crossed the mainstream political spectrum.

The federal government's first response came with the passage of the Stuart A. McKinney Act of 1987, which provided reimbursement for a growing number of palliative measures (shelters, case management services, emergency food provision). Like other periods in which reformers spoke for the poor, it was hardly clear if the answer of shelters and services was what homeless people and those at risk for homelessness most wanted. By the later 1980s to the mid-1990s, new groups of indigenous organizations of the poor emerged, including some national efforts such as "Up and Out of Poverty" and the National Union of the Homeless, and many more localized efforts consisting of homeless encampments and tent cities spread throughout the nation. Despite some radicalism reminiscent of the earlier periods of high homelessness, these efforts also seemed to have led to palliative remedies, and even to repressive measures rather than any major social structural changes.

As homelessness entered the 1990s and the new century, a central paradox was the growing national recognition and acceptance of homelessness along with an increased "compassion fatigue" among the middle class and deepening repression of the very poor at the local level. These responses are perhaps not as contradictory as they seem. The election of a national administration (President Bill Clinton) that had little investment in denying homelessness led to a rhetorical acceptance that there were many people who were homeless and/or in poverty. However, with neither the Clinton nor George W. Bush administrations supporting major social welfare or employment initiatives, not

surprisingly the optimism of the big charitable events of the 1980s—such as the "Hands Across America" rallies (the large corporate and government sponsored event in the 1980s to hold hands and help the homeless)—quickly faded. As the middle classes pulled away from the optimistic voluntarism of the early 1980s, cities and towns moved by economic competition and a new criminal justice approach of "broken windows" (i.e., the belief that prosecuting minor and status crimes would make for a better overall economic, social, and civic environment) cracked down on the homeless. Typified by New York City's former Mayor Rudolph Giuliani, but copied in nearly all major cities, loitering, begging, congregating in public spaces, and various sorts of "shadow work" ("off the books" work such as New York's famous "squeegee men") have been banned or repressed. Increasingly, homeless people have been pushed out of view to suburban or less central urban areas. These changes are well documented by the National Coalition for the Homeless.

As the new homelessness reaches its third decade, it is clear that what was once seen as a temporary crisis is fairly consistent with American history's long tolerance of extreme poverty. While economic upswings and more jobs have had little effect on the wages of working-class people, there is even less reason to believe that those most poor will benefit. At this time, it does not appear that either political party or major figures in the national debate endorse any major strategies to end homelessness.

David Wagner

See also Affordable Housing; Housing; Housing Policy; Social Housing; Squatter Movements

Further Readings

Baxter, E. and K. Hopper. 1984. *Private Lives/Public Spaces: Homeless Adults on the Streets of New York*. New York: Community Service Society.

Duneier, Mitchell. 2000. *Sidewalk*. New York: Farrar, Straus, and Giroux.

Geremek, B. 1997. *Poverty: A History*. London: Blackwell.

Hopper, Kim. 2003. *Reckoning with Homelessness*. Ithaca, NY: Cornell University Press.

Kusmer, K. 2002. "Down and Out." In *On the Road: Homelessness in American History.* New York: Oxford University Press.

National Coalition for the Homeless & National Law Center on Homelessness and Poverty. 2006. *A Dream Denied: The Criminalization of Homelessness in U.S. Cities.* Washington, DC: Authors.

Rossi, Peter. 1991. *Down and out in America: The Origins of Homelessness.* Chicago: University of Chicago Press.

Snow, David A. and Leon Anderson. 1993. *Down on Their Luck: A Study of Homeless Street People.* Berkeley: University of California Press.

Wagner, D. 1993. *Checkerboard Square: Culture and Resistance in a Homeless Community.* Boulder, CO: Westview Press.

Wright, Talmadge. 1998. *Out of Place: Homeless Mobilizations, Subcities, and Contested Landscapes.* Albany: State University of New York Press.

HOMEOWNERS ASSOCIATIONS

Homeowners association (HOA) is a specific term used in the United States and some other countries for incorporated associations of homeowners who have formed an organization to govern common property. Common property might include shared parts of buildings, parking lots, streets, recreational facilities, and, in larger developments, schools and private town halls. Homeowners associations collect monthly fees from homeowners (assessments) and organize a contractual version of local government, delivering services and enforcing private land use restrictions. Decisions are made by an elected executive board and are governed by an annual homeowners' meeting. The board employs a property management company to execute its day-to-day estate management responsibilities.

Homeowners associations are set up variously as companies, trusts, and other entities, depending on the legal instruments a country has at its disposal. In the United States, homeowners associations govern landed properties, usually in master planned developments, and are distinguished from condominium associations, which govern shared property in apartment developments. *Community association* is the more general term used to describe private organizations that govern neighborhoods and may include condominium associations, homeowners associations, cooperatives, and their variants.

The idea of a legal entity governing shared private territory has a long history. In France, the first modern joint-ownership (condominium) law was created in 1804. For 200 years, every new land subdivision in France has been required to establish restrictive covenants and, in the case of private streets, a homeowners association. Condominium law was exported from France to the United States in the 1960s; subsequently, there was a veritable explosion of private local governments. In 1964, the United States had 500 community associations. This grew to 274,000 by 2005, providing housing for 54.6 million Americans (18.5 percent of the population). The economist Robert Nelson views the rise of homeowners and condominium associations as the greatest innovation in ownership since the birth of the modern joint stock company in the late nineteenth century. He argues that it redistributes ownership of urban infrastructure stock from the few to the many, decentralizes control, and radically changes the incentive structure and the politics of investment and stock management.

Not surprisingly, a great many controversies are associated with the phenomenon. Privately governed neighborhoods are alleged to reduce political participation and change voting behavior. They are said to exacerbate social–spatial segregation, fuel the fear of others, displace crime and traffic problems, and pose a long-term risk to social cohesion. On the other hand, they clearly offer something of value to homeowners, including reduced investment risk, a greater sense of community, a better quality of local services, and more clearly packaged neighborhood choice. The balance between costs and benefits is an empirical matter and currently subject to much scrutiny.

As important as the alleged social and systemic costs are the private costs of contractual government (the legal costs of setting up a well-founded administration and the cost of settling disputes). There is a growing body of research on the coevolution of private and public urban governance and a variety of institutional models are emerging in different economic and cultural contexts.

Chris Webster

See also Common Interest Development; Condominium; Governance; Housing

Further Readings

Glasze, G., C. J. Webster, and K. Frantz, eds. 2006. *Private Cities: Local and Global Perspectives.* London: Routledge.

McKenzie, E. 1994. *Privatopia: Homeowner Associations and the Rise of Private Residential Government.* New Haven, CT: Yale University Press.

Nelson, R. 2005. *Private Neighborhoods and the Transformation of Local Government.* Washington, DC: Urban Institute Press.

HOMEOWNERSHIP

Homeownership refers to the possession of certain rights as regards the housing unit in which one lives. This may involve control and use of both the dwelling and the property on which the dwelling is built, a popular form of homeownership in the United States. Alternatively, homeownership may take the form of condominium or apartment ownership, whereby an individual has rights regarding a housing unit that is one of many units, each sharing a common property area. In this instance, an individual has sole ownership of the dwelling unit and collective ownership of the property on which the unit is built as well as any other common areas associated with the dwelling unit. Condominium or apartment ownership tends to be popular in urban areas where land is scarce, particularly in European cities. In the case where the property comes with garden amenities, as is common with condominium ownership in the United States, maintenance of the land tends to be contracted out, allowing individuals to own their dwelling units without laboring to maintain the common property areas.

Homeownership rates vary by world region and tend to be highest in low-income countries and nonurban areas of higher-income countries. Dwelling ownership takes many forms, and in many of the countries, owner-occupied housing units frequently lack basic amenities such as potable water and indoor cooking facilities. High-income countries tend to have well developed mortgage markets and, as a result, a relatively high-quality housing stock as well as widespread homeownership. After exploring those topics, this entry summarizes the extensive research on homeownership issues: Wealth and family composition are important determinants of dwelling ownership, homeownership generates private as well as social benefits, and although homeowners tend to be more politically conservative, political beliefs are determined by factors associated with homeownership rather than homeownership per se. Finally, in the United States, federal policy initiatives have played a role in boosting the homeownership rates of households in general and, more recently, for historically underrepresented groups.

Characteristics of Ownership

In most countries, homeownership is the dominant form of housing tenure, with homeownership rates varying by world region. Asian and sub-Saharan African countries have among the highest rates of dwelling ownership, at roughly 75 percent, and Western European countries have among the lowest, with a country-average rate of slightly less than 60 percent. In some Western European countries, such as Austria, Germany, and the Netherlands, the majority of households are tenants. The United States has one of the highest homeownership rates of the industrialized countries. Homeownership also tends to be lower in urban than rural areas.

The predominant form of homeownership in the United States is a single-family detached unit, whereas individual ownership of apartments in multifamily buildings is common in European countries. In developing nations, self-built housing, often lacking piped water and other basic amenities such as indoor cooking and bath facilities, makes up a significant portion of the owned housing stock. For example, although the estimated rate of owner occupancy is roughly 85 percent in Mali, the percentage of occupied dwelling units estimated to have piped-in water is only 4 percent.

One of the most common ways to purchase a home is through mortgage financing. This involves the home buyer contributing a lump sum toward the purchase of the house, known as a down payment, and a lending institution providing the funds for the remainder of the home price. The buyer then makes payments to the lending institution over a fixed time period, known as the mortgage maturity, until the loan is repaid. The down payment serves as collateral on the loan. Should the borrower fail to make loan payments, the bank may take possession of the home, and the borrower loses his or her funds in the house.

The availability of mortgage financing, low down-payment requirements, and long-term loans plays an important role in determining the quality of the housing stock, homeownership rate, and age profile of homeownership. Countries such as the United States, Australia, Canada, and the United Kingdom have well-developed mortgage markets, relatively high-quality housing stock, and relatively high homeownership rates as well as high ownership rates among young families. In other industrialized countries with less extensive mortgage markets, such as Spain, Italy, and Germany, homes are purchased later in life, with the average age of first purchase in the late thirties or forties. Only a small fraction of the owned housing stock in developing countries tends to be financed. In Mexico, for example, although the homeownership rate is at 77 percent, only 13 percent of the housing stock is mortgaged, and self-built housing lacking basic amenities accounts for roughly half of all dwellings.

Related Research

There has been extensive research on homeownership issues. Three areas of importance include the determinants of homeownership, benefits of homeownership, and the impact of homeownership on political activity and beliefs.

Determinants of Ownership

First, consider the determinants of homeownership, particularly as they operate in the United States. At nearly 70 percent, the homeownership rate in the United States is at an all-time high. The national average, however, masks important differences in homeownership rates across groups. The rate for White, non-Hispanic households is 76 percent, whereas rates for Asian, Black, and Hispanic households are 60 percent, 49 percent, and 48 percent, respectively.

The lower ownership rates of non-White households reflect, in part, past discriminatory practices in U.S. mortgage and real estate markets and differences in household characteristics. The extensive research on U.S. housing markets finds that the cost of homeownership relative to renting, wealth, permanent and transitory income, income uncertainty, price uncertainty, and family composition are important in explaining housing decisions. Many of these homeownership determinants vary by race and ethnicity. Recent work suggests that the primary constraint to homeownership in the United States is having adequate wealth to meet down payment requirements, and the current Black–White gap in homeownership rates in the United States is largely explained by differences in wealth.

Low homeownership rates of certain groups may come about because few households enter into homeownership or those who enter have high exit rates. Households may exit homeownership due to crisis events such as family instability or financial distress. Recent research suggests that Black and Hispanic households sustain homeownership at rates similar to those of White households, suggesting that gaps in homeownership rates are due to differences in entry rather than exit rates.

Benefits of Ownership

Second, homeownership yields both private and social benefits. The private benefits include pride of ownership and increased social status, greater selection of housing attributes through owning, and declining real housing expenditures over time for households with fixed mortgage payments. Homeownership has also been associated with improved quality of life through positive impacts on children and greater life satisfaction. Through mortgage financing, moreover, homeownership may serve as a means for households with little wealth to acquire wealth, as the monthly mortgage payment serves as a form of forced saving for households that would have difficulty saving otherwise.

Another private benefit of homeownership is the potential for wealth creation as property values rise. The evidence for U.S. markets suggests that homeownership is an important means for households to accumulate wealth. The median net wealth of U.S. homeowners is higher than that of renters when compared across age groups, race, ethnicity, and annual income. Home equity is the primary source of wealth for most households. In the late 1990s, despite strong stock market gains, home equity was a dominant investment for most U.S. households. Whereas roughly two thirds owned their homes, less than half of all households held stock. Of those households owning both stocks and homes, 60 percent had more wealth in home equity than in stocks. Recent research suggests that even low-income homeowners acquire wealth through homeownership. In addition, among low- and moderate-income households, wealth accumulation is associated with homeownership stability, and even households that are only temporary homeowners appear to achieve greater wealth holdings than persistent renters.

Homeownership also generates social benefits. It is said that homeownership gives people a stake in society, inducing them to care about their communities. Becoming a homeowner is thought to motivate the individual to better maintain his or her property, be more vigilant in preventing crime in the neighborhood, and vote for policies that improve the community. Such activities by a homeowner increase the quality and stability of the community, thereby raising property values. Research on these topics finds that homeowners are more civically involved, while increasing rates of homeownership in a community tend to improve community quality. Undoubtedly, the recent collapse of housing markets in the United States (and around the world) will be an important topic of research in the coming years, with a reevaluation of earlier findings concerning benefits of homeownership and related issues.

Link to Political Beliefs

Third, several studies indicate that homeowners are more likely to be politically active, with some researchers believing that homeownership causes people to become more conservative in their political beliefs. Since the writings of Friedrich Engels, it has been argued that owning property makes one part of the system of capitalism and thus gives one a stake in preserving the status quo. A broad system of homeownership ostensibly creates a group of people with common housing interests that transcend class differences and weaken the political focus of the worker class. Others maintain that

housing tenure might have been important in shaping political beliefs in early industrial Great Britain or currently in countries in the early stages of economic development, but not so in countries like the United States, where the capitalistic system is firmly established and a high homeownership rate, quality of housing stock, and standard of living exist.

At first glance, U.S. data seem consistent with the idea that homeownership is associated with a more conservative political persuasion. Homeowners are far more likely to identify themselves as conservative and far less likely to identify themselves as liberal than renters. However, as a group, homeowners are evenly split by political party. Evidence suggests that wealth has a greater effect on political affiliation than homeownership per se. Age and education (factors associated with greater wealth holdings) as well as religiosity also seem to have more of an impact on political beliefs than the act of owning one's dwelling.

Government Role

In regard to the political implications, the U.S. government has played a role in encouraging homeownership since the Great Depression. With passage of the Federal Home Loan Bank Act of 1932 and the Homeowners Loan Act of 1933, funds were targeted to help homeowners pay mortgages, undertake maintenance, and pay taxes. The National Housing Act of 1934 created the Federal Housing Administration (FHA), which changed the way in which homes were financed. The FHA initiated the long-term, fixed-payment loan covering a large portion of the appraised value of the property. The Federal National Mortgage Association, known as Fannie Mae, was created in 1938 to expand the U.S. mortgage market and homeownership opportunities. Mortgage interest has been deductible from federal taxable income since the inception of the income tax. Currently at roughly $70 billion, the deductibility of mortgage interest is the second-largest revenue loss to the U.S. federal government.

In response to persistent gaps in homeownership and because of the belief that homeownership creates social benefits, boosting the homeownership rates of low-income and minority households has been a federal priority since the early 1990s. Successive presidential administrations have launched policy initiatives, largely using front-end programs that help households attain homeownership, such as homebuyer training programs, down payment assistance, and housing rehabilitation. Furthermore, financial institutions have expanded their commitment to lending to low-income and minority households in response to the passage of what are known in the United States as fair-lending laws, an example of which is the Community Reinvestment Act of 1977, which requires lending institutions to demonstrate they are meeting the credit needs of all households in the communities they serve. These policies have been successful in boosting the homeownership rate of low-income and minority households.

Tracy Turner

See also Common Interest Development; Condominium; Homeowners Associations; Housing; Housing Tenure; Social Housing; Suburbanization

Further Readings

Chiuri, Maria Concetta and Tullio Jappelli. 2001. "Financial Market Imperfections and Home Ownership: A Comparative Study." Discussion Paper No. 2717, Centre for Economic Policy Research, London.

Colton, Kent W. 2003. *Housing in the Twenty-First Century.* Cambridge, MA: Harvard University, Wertheim Publications Committee.

Gilderbloom, John I. and John P. Markham. 1995. "The Impact of Homeownership on Political Beliefs." *Social Forces* 73(4):1589–1607.

Turner, Tracy M. 2003. "Does Investment Risk Affect the Housing Decisions of Families?" *Economic Inquiry* 41(4):675–91.

United Nations. 2005. *Financing Urban Shelter: Global Report on Human Settlements 2005.* United Nations Human Settlements Program (UN-HABITAT). London: Earthscan.

HONG KONG, CHINA

Hong Kong, meaning "fragrant harbor" in Chinese and officially called Hong Kong Special Administrative Region (Hong Kong SAR) since 1997, is located on the Pearl River Delta, south China. Hong Kong SAR is made up of Hong Kong Island, Kowloon Peninsula, New Kowloon, and New Territories. It borders Guangdong province in the north and faces the South China Sea in the east, west, and south. It has a land area of 1,068 square kilometers and a population of 6.9 million (as of 2006), giving an overall population density of 5,385 people per square kilometer.

Hong Kong is among the world's most compact and densely populated cities. Whereas average population density in the New Territories is 2,560 people per square kilometer, on Hong Kong Island, Kowloon Peninsula, and New Kowloon, population density increases to 26,950 people per square kilometer. Within the urban area, for example, the Mongkok district, population density can be as high as 116,531 people per square kilometer. Hong Kong's population is predominantly Chinese (95 percent); the rest are non-Chinese residents and expatriates. Hong Kong is one of the world's leading financial centers, a major business hub where East meets West.

Historical Evolution

Its modern history started when Hong Kong Island became a British entrepot for China trade in 1842 following China's defeat in the first Anglo–Chinese Opium War (1839–1842). Britain ceded the Kowloon Peninsula in 1860 during the Second Opium War (1858–1860). In 1898, the New Territories was leased to Britain for 99 years. British colonization transformed the onetime village into a town and introduced planned settlement through urban planning, as practiced under British town planning legislation. For much of the colonial period, the administration's attitude was largely laissez-faire, as concern was with trade development. The British administered Hong Kong through a governor appointed by the Colonial Office in London, aided by the executive and legislative councils. No Chinese officially sat on either council until 1880.

Hong Kong's early development was driven by the growth of international trade between Europe and Asia. Its free market enterprise society soon became the center of immigration for Chinese from mainland China and a refuge for reformers and revolutionaries, including Sun Yat Sen (1866–1925), who had significant roles in shaping China's modern history.

Following the establishment of the People's Republic of China in 1949, more migrants fled to Hong Kong in fear of persecution by the communist regime. They further swelled the population, adding pressure to its housing. Acute housing shortage and overcrowding prevailed. By the end of 1949, an estimated 300,000 people lived in squatter homes built on hillsides, on rooftops, and in street alleys. Most of these squatter huts were dark; badly ventilated; without water, plumbing, and other facilities; and under constant threat of termites, typhoon, and fire. Many private companies in Shanghai and Guangzhou also shifted their operations to Hong Kong. Prior to China's present open door policy in 1978, Hong Kong was the only contact place between mainland China and the rest of the world. After China's open door policy, Hong Kong remains an important source of foreign direct investment to China. Its dynamic growth offers a model for other Chinese cities.

In recent decades, Hong Kong's economy has grown rapidly with industrialization, especially in textile and manufacturing industries where labor costs are low. By the 1980s, Hong Kong had become one of Asia's economic "tigers" or newly industrializing economies. Since the 1990s, it has restructured its manufacturing base and shifted to business services, emphasizing financial services, tourism, trading and logistics, professional services, and other product services. Manufacturing plants have been relocated to the Pearl River Delta, promoting the development of regional economy and formation of a metropolitan region from Hong Kong to Guangzhou, south China. China's economic policy innovation of special economic zones in Shenzhen and Zhuhai in the late 1970s further augmented Hong Kong's hinterland.

In 1997, Hong Kong entered a historical phase of development. The city returned to Chinese sovereignty under the 1984 Sino–British Joint Declaration. Hong Kong is granted a high degree of autonomy in all areas except defense and foreign affairs under the "One Country, Two Systems" policy, at least up to 2047, allowing Hong Kong's capitalist system and lifestyle to continue for a further 50 years. The chief executive and Executive Council govern Hong Kong as a unitary authority or special administrative region. Its legal system continues to follow the English Common Law tradition established by the British colonial administration. Although presenting challenges as it is an untried formula, the One Country, Two Systems policy also yields opportunities for policy coordination such as in trans-border issues, regional infrastructure, tourism, technology policy, financial markets, and coordination to stabilize exchange rates. Many of those who emigrated ahead of the 1997 handover have since returned to Hong Kong. Hong Kong's vision for the twenty-first century is to develop as Asia's world city.

High-Density Vertical City

What makes Hong Kong unique is its high-density vertical urbanization. Its high-density development is a result of geography, historical development, and land policy. Much of Hong Kong is hilly to mountainous; more than 75 percent of the land is on a hill slope. The average distance from the harbor front to the steep hills of Hong Kong Island is only 1.3 kilometers. Only 25 percent of Hong Kong's land area is developed. About 40 percent of the remaining land is reserved as country parks and nature reserves. Most of its urban development exists on Kowloon Peninsula, along the northern coast of Hong Kong Island, where most of the flat land was created by government-sponsored hill levelling and land reclamation, and in scattered areas throughout the New Territories.

Government Role

The government owns all the land in Hong Kong. The sale of land leases for terms of 75, 99, or 999 years is one of the major sources of government revenue. Land is amalgamated before leasing to private developers through auction and tender. The government has full control over the timing, location, and amount of land to be leased, in part a factor behind the city's high land prices. The lack of horizontal space combined with high land prices have led to vertical city development; 38 of the world's 100 tallest residential buildings are located in Hong Kong. There are more than 7,600 tall buildings, rising from 50 to 88 floors and heights of above 200 meters; the tallest is 415 meters. Hong Kong has more people living or working above the 14th floor than anywhere else on Earth, making it the world's most vertical city. The inevitable consequence of vertical urban development is that few older low-rise buildings remain. The city has become a showcase for modern, high-rise architecture.

A distinctive feature of Hong Kong's vertical urbanity is its large-scale, high-rise public housing. As with Singapore, about half of Hong Kong's population live in high-rise public housing. In the initial years, these were built to resettle fire victims and squatters. The construction of the Shek Kip Mei Estate following the Shek Kip Mei fire, which left 53,000 people homeless in 1953, marked the beginning of Hong Kong's public housing program and the government's role as financier, contractor, and landlord of housing. Designed and built as emergency housing, each apartment block could house 2,000 people, 340 people including children per floor. These early buildings were generally seven stories tall with an average space allocation of 3.25 square meters per person (the lowest is 0.85 square meter). Cooking was done outdoors along the common corridor, immediately in front of residents' apartment doors. Residents shared communal bathing and toilet facilities, and there were no elevators.

Over time, public-housing space standards and facilities have improved in response to consumers' needs and demands for better quality housing. With technology advancements, taller buildings were constructed. Residents are increasingly consulted to find out what they want and what works for them best before a new design is introduced. There is consideration beyond the utilitarian approach to domestic comfort and lifestyle. New estates are planned as neighborhoods, with such urban amenities as kindergartens, playgrounds, wet markets, sports facilities, clinics, and shopping malls. Old estates are upgraded. In 1997, the government introduced its aim to increase home ownership to 70 percent, giving further impetus to public housing improvement.

A Green Environment

Although Hong Kong is intensely urbanized, in recent years it has made much effort to promote a green environment. Since 2004, the government has started to develop greening master plans for its urban districts. Community forums are held to gather public feedback on the contents of these master plans, which are due for completion by 2009. The government has also started a green Hong Kong campaign to promote and enhance public awareness of greening in the community, including greening activities among school children.

Hong Kong suffers from increasing pollution, compounded by its geography, proximity to the Pearl River Delta, and high-density urbanization. About 80 percent of the city's smog originates from nearby industrial areas in south China. On the transportation front, Hong Kong introduced strong car-restraint and bus-priority measures early in its development. Hong Kong has a well-developed transportation network that encompasses bus, tram, rail, and ferry, both public and private. More than 90 percent of daily trips (11 million) are on public transport, one of the highest usages in the world. The development of Hong Kong provides important lessons in planning creative solutions for a number of urban challenges, including urban expansion, economic development, housing redevelopment, and participatory planning at the city level.

Belinda Yuen

See also Social Housing; Urban Planning

Further readings

Ngo, Tak-Wing, ed. 1999. *Hong Kong's History: State and Society under Colonial Rule.* London: Routledge.

Tsang, Steve. 2007. *A Modern History of Hong Kong.* London: I. B. Tauris.

Yeung, Y. M., ed. 2007. *The First Decade: The Hong Kong SAR in Retrospective and Introspective Perspectives.* Hong Kong: The Chinese University Press.

Yeung, Y. M. and T. K. Y. Wong, eds. 2003. *Fifty Years of Public Housing in Hong Kong.* Hong Kong: The Chinese University Press.

HOTEL, MOTEL

Contemporary urban theorists have explored how cities are profoundly defined by the nature of their circulation, whether of cars, goods, or people. If we accept this, then we have to look for sites that coordinate, stage, or enable that circulation. Hotels and motels are a key articulating mechanism for such flows, a central element of modern practices such as driving, rationalized work routines, architectural design, and new building technologies. This entry looks at their history and role in urban life.

Historical Evolution

At their essence, hotels emerged to replace older forms of hospitality shown to travelers (from the inns of medieval England to the *caravanserai* of traditional Arab cultures), with a systematized, modern equivalent. As historians such as Cynthia Cocks and Andrew Sandoval-Strausz have described, the modern hotel offered a controlled, commodified way of dealing with strangers, a challenge posed by the vast explosion in city populations experienced in the booming commercial economies of the nineteenth century.

Many of the earlier urban hotels were designed to cater to a rural elite visiting the city for social functions such as weddings or dinners, or else to meet with the distributors and purchasers of their farm products. However, the growing sophistication of modern consumer economies increased the demand for basic hotel space by agents pursuing all manner of commercial services, from traveling salespeople to touring entertainers featuring in adjacent music halls and theaters. With the growth of international trade relations, hotels became important way stations in the maintenance of colonial economies.

Luxury Hotels

Within some of the key commercial cities of major nation-states or imperial economies, luxury hotels became important features of central business districts. Through the provision of a full suite of services—restaurants presenting international (and hence familiar) cuisine, laundry services, and telex, telephone, and then fax and Internet systems—the large hotel often boasted that it was a city in miniature. Annabel Wharton,

in *Building the Cold War,* showed how, from the 1950s, the Hilton Corporation fused modern techniques of hotel management with innovation in modernist design (including the use steel, glass, modern plumbing, telephony, and ventilation systems) as part of a strategy of international expansion that mirrored the economic expansionism of American firms. Five-star hotels were, in these cases, designed to insulate the traveler from the unpredictability of a foreign culture (or else, back in the United States, from the mean streets of the inner city, in the context of the perceived dangers of the postwar American downtown).

Of course, it is important to note that alongside the large, full-service hotels, many cities and towns have sustained an ecology of hostels, boarding houses, single-room occupancy hotels, and cheap hotels with basic facilities, all crucial institutions in the provision of affordable options for migrant workers, pilgrims, budget travelers, and the homeless. This can often be an expression of social polarization in developing economies. As David Gladstone has shown, Indian cities such as Delhi display a stark contrast between gated luxury hotels and the multitude of *dharamshalas* (pilgrims' rest houses), dormitories, guest houses, and small hotels tucked into the densely packed older city quarters, with intermittent water supply and no air conditioning.

Basic Products

Such privations underline the fact that the hotel product can be fairly basic. Hotels can specialize in the provision of a bedroom, but with minimal services, given the preponderance of options—be it dry cleaners or cafés—in the bright lights of big cities. Most recently, the rise of the boutique hotel (a reaction to the studied homogeneity of the chain hotel), pioneered by the likes of Ian Schrager in Manhattan, has leveraged the excitement of its urban location, allowing carefully designed, but typically small hotel rooms to be charged at relatively high prices. This is underpinned by a typical guest who seeks the buzz of cultural life in Shanghai or New York, rather than the bland and the predictable.

This contemporary hotel in Beijing, China, offers a taste of Eastern decor along with the basic comforts that Westerners seek when traveling far from home.

Source: Blake Buyan.

While big-city hotels became key institutions within central cities, the rapid expansion of road networks in the first decades of the twentieth century brought a new architectural form to the fore. The motel was an important aspect not just of the city but also of the development of nation-states into an urbanized system of communications and markets. Motels were emblematic of a major tension within American cultural life: Main Street versus Wall Street. As described in Jakle et al.'s *The Motel in America,* motels were an early embodiment of popular American culture as seen in the "mom and pop" form of hands-on, independent motel management, where families converted their roadside properties into spartan lodgings (an important economic activity during the Depression).

By the early 1950s, these were being increasingly challenged by the corporate power of chains such as Holiday Inn or Days Inn, which emerged as harbingers of standardized, homogenized landscapes based around franchise models. They signified modular construction and a minimum of decoration and the standardized, bulk purchasing and supply of towels, toilet rolls, and soap; they usually guaranteed the guest a television, serviceable bed, and modern plumbing. Motels have continued to play important roles in automobile-centered economies, yet are examples of the cultural homogenization of American landscapes.

So, motels and hotels have always existed for a very functional reason: to meet the leisure or business demands of travelers. This can be as simple as a room and bed (and parking space) for the night, with a single staff member on duty, or as elaborate as a fully provisioned, meticulously designed, and heavily staffed luxury hotel. In the contemporary context, the growing sophistication of information technology and mobile communications has required that hotels upgrade their communications infrastructure. In the extreme, this allows the wired-up, hypermobile executive traveler to remain constantly in contact with business associates with a strong degree of predictability and trust, a central element for businesses in undertaking the risk (in terms of lost time traveling and time spent away from the base office) of travel.

Social and Cultural Roles

It is worth dwelling on the role that luxury hotels have always played in the gendered cultures of display and social identity that are such an important part of advanced urban economies. From the nineteenth century onward, hotels provided an opportunity for women to appear in public in a male-dominated public realm. As Carolyn Brucken has noted, single-sex "Ladies' Parlors"—often located in prominent positions on the street fronts of hotels, yet segregated from the clublike surroundings of male society—played an important role in allowing middle-class women to be both literally and metaphorically in the public eye as never before, certainly in the context of polite American society, offering them an unprecedented opportunity to enjoy forms of self-expression in public space. A century later, it is worth noting that hotel chains still stand accused of neglecting the specific needs of female travelers, from specific demands in terms of room design and layout to a desire for privacy and security in the public areas of hotels. In strict Muslim societies, such as Saudi Arabia, hotel design is still governed by careful segregation of men and women. In 2008, the country saw the opening of its first women-only hotel, seen by some as an important step forward (given existing practices of requiring male permission to check in), but by others as a retrograde step, one that further institutionalizes male–female segregation.

Finally, hotels are important, although often neglected spaces of labor relations. Economic development agencies often support large-scale hotel construction because of the sizeable number of jobs they create (many requiring little formal prior training). As such, they have been promoted as important contributors to local economies where unemployment is high. However, this often means that their wages are low and conditions harsh, particularly given the demanding physical nature of the work tasks performed by room-service staff, cleaners, and kitchen staff. As Jane Wills has demonstrated in a study of London's Dorchester Hotel, many of the most luxurious hotels possess a glittering front of house design, while hiding a backstage of nonunionized labor, often drawn from recent immigrants and ethnic minorities. In many ways this is a metaphor for the city, where debates over public and private space, luxury and poverty, and the gendered nature of city life can be illuminated.

Donald McNeill

See also *Caravanserai*; Las Vegas, Nevada; Railroad Station

Further Readings

Bell, D. 2007. "The Hospitable City: Social Relations in Commercial Spaces." *Progress in Human Geography* 31(1):7–22.

Brucken, C. 1996. "In the Public Eye: Women and the American Luxury Hotel." *Winterthur Portfolio* 31(4):203–20.

Cocks, C. 2001. *Doing the Town: The Rise of Urban Tourism in the United States, 1850–1915*. Berkeley: University of California Press.

Crang, M. 2001. "Rhythms of the City: Temporalised Space and Motion." Pp. 187–205 in *TimeSpace: Geographies of Temporality*, edited by J. May and N. Thrift. London: Routledge.

Gladstone, D. L. 2005. *From Pilgrimage to Package Tour: Travel and Tourism in the Third World*. New York: Routledge.

Groth, P. 1994. *Living Downtown: The History of Residential Hotels in the United States*. Berkeley: University of California Press.

Jakle, J. A., K. A. Sculle, and J. S. Rogers. 1996. *The Motel in America.* Baltimore: Johns Hopkins University Press.

Katz, M. 1999. "The Hotel Kracauer." *Differences: A Journal of Feminist Cultural Studies* 11(2):134–52.

McNeill, D. 2008. "The Hotel and the City." *Progress in Human Geography* 32(3):383–98.

Sandoval-Strausz, A. K. 2007. *Hotel: An American History.* New Haven, CT: Yale University Press.

Tufts, S. 2006. "'We Make It Work': The Cultural Transformation of Hotel Workers in the City." *Antipode* 38(2):350–73.

Wharton, A. J. 2001. *Building the Cold War: Hilton International Hotels and Modern Architecture.* Chicago: University of Chicago Press.

Wills, J. 2005. "The Geography of Union Organizing in Low-Paid Service Industries in the U.K.: Lessons from the T & G's Campaign to Unionise the Dorchester Hotel, London." *Antipode* 37(1):139–59.

HOUSING

The urban character is shaped through its residential neighborhoods, some of which have been intact for centuries. Scholars and public policy officials recognize housing as a critical element of community development. Thus, efforts to rejuvenate communities within metropolitan areas are often accompanied by a strategy to rejuvenate housing as well. Because of the multidimensional nature of housing, it is both an important element of an urban area's macrolevel character and a primary determinant of individual living experiences through its interaction with the physical and natural environment. In addition, social policy is often concerned with issues of homeownership, commonly seen in cities' attempts to move families and households along a continuum of housing, in hopes of improving both consumer welfare and socially desirable outcomes. Improving social well-being through housing choice also requires policies directed toward improving the physical quality of the housing unit itself, the degree of choice in housing selection, and the variety of housing that is made available across urban areas and cultures.

The Importance of Housing to Community

Over the past century, there has been an attempt throughout the developed and the developing worlds to recognize a universal right to housing. During the Great Depression of the 1930s in the United States, the Roosevelt administration legitimized the role of the federal government in creating and providing housing through the formation of large-scale public housing. This was followed shortly thereafter by the National Housing Act of 1949, which went further than any national government had previously gone in legitimizing a standard of housing for citizens by stating the need for "a decent home and a suitable living environment for every American family," without necessarily codifying the terms of such a standard.

On the international stage, the United Nations created its own standardization of a basic level of housing quality through the passage of its Universal Declaration of Human Rights in 1948, which stated that "everyone has the right to a standard of living adequate for the health and well-being of himself and his family, including . . . housing." In addition, housing's importance as a driver of economic growth cannot be underestimated. In the developed world, residential transactions directly create a variety of job categories, including home builders, real estate agents, mortgage lenders, and appraisers, just to name a few. Beyond these direct employees, such activity generates enormous multiplier effects on the general economy.

In many areas, a distinct architectural quality of housing helps define the urban area's character. For example, Baltimore's historic row-house model is uniquely identified with the city as a housing form unlike any other. In other cultures, there is an emphasis on vernacular housing, in which locally available resources and production methods are employed, as a way of maintaining local tradition rather than being influenced by a particular architect or designer. By emphasizing purpose over aesthetic appeal, such an approach allows neighborhoods and cityscapes to be created and maintained in a consistent manner and for habitants to feel a sense of connectedness as a result.

The Integration of Housing Within Existing Sociological Theoretical Frameworks

Housing serves an important role within the context of one's physical and natural surroundings. The human ecology model, popularized by Bubolz and Sontag in 1993, emphasizes that the built environment serves as a conduit between the self and both the social–cultural environment and the natural environment. Similarly, housing also has a connection with each stage along the pyramid structure of Maslow's hierarchy of needs, first popularized in the 1940s. The most basic need is physiological. Housing serves this role by providing shelter and protection from the natural elements. Housing also serves the second stage of Maslow's pyramid by providing safety and security to its inhabitants, as a form of protection from potential harm. In the subsequent level, a sense of belonging, the home environment serves as a place in which families are raised and nurtured and where people interact with friends and other community members. The final two stages of the hierarchy, self-esteem and self-actualization, address the important roles that housing plays in people's identity and social status and in satisfying their creative side and allowing them to reach their full potential.

Housing Continuum

Morris and Winter, in *Housing, Family, and Society*, put forward a housing adjustment theory, which shows that housing consumption can be analyzed along a continuum. Just as it is important from a community standpoint to plan for area growth through the adequate construction and provision of housing and housing infrastructure, it is also important from a household perspective to prepare for different levels of housing consumption along a household's life course. As a result, at each stage of a household's development, there will be a shift in the types of housing norms or housing expectations. The need for housing space, and hence, housing consumption, tends to increase along with increased family size and economic resources during the early years of a household. As household size stabilizes, housing consumption may also stabilize. Later, as children leave the home and household size shrinks, space needs will tend to decrease. Finally, as age brings functional decline, more accessible and supportive housing characteristics become critical.

However, this ideal of housing consumption across the life course is often unavailable. At the most extreme end of this continuum, families experience homelessness. Homelessness typically means an individual has no access to a conventional residence. This can result in sleeping in homeless shelters or nonresidential public or private spaces, such as abandoned buildings, cars, streets, subways, bus terminals, or parks. Although statistics on world homelessness are not consistently available, it is safe to say that homelessness is a concern in both developing and developed countries throughout the world. The reasons behind homelessness are myriad, ranging from displacement of people after natural disasters, the failure of cities and metropolitan areas to adequately provide enough low-income housing stock for their populations, and the individual lack of available income due to unemployment, drug and alcohol abuse, mental disorder, or expenses associated with children.

Government Support

Affordable housing is often developed through government support of private development or direct government construction and management of housing. In the United States, there has been a shift away from concentrating government-managed affordable housing in large, centralized public housing projects in one location (normally in mostly low-income neighborhoods) within each urban area. Instead, newer strategies encourage diffusion of poverty through construction of smaller, scattered-site public housing and subsidization through housing vouchers that allow low- and moderate-income recipients to choose from many private-market dwellings, often in less economically disadvantaged neighborhoods.

From an international perspective, several developed and developing countries also offer varying degrees of public assistance to low-income households, often with the intention of having these households eventually transition to nonsubsidized housing. Such a transition is rarely an easy one, however, in that the ability of these households to afford housing has been hampered by years of rapid house price appreciation in many urban areas.

Beyond the transition to nonsubsidized market rent housing, a common policy objective is to encourage homeownership. Several city governments encourage such a move along the housing continuum through offering such incentives as down payment and closing cost assistance, a phenomenon that accelerated during the 1990s. Despite the recent housing downturn, such home buyer assistance programs are still widely offered by many states and large municipalities.

The concept of the housing continuum, of course, also allows for movement away from, as well as toward, homeownership. For example, in the event of a mortgage default, owners may be forced back into renting. In addition, life cycle changes may cause older homeowners to voluntarily forgo the effort and expense of home maintenance by selling and returning to renting.

Housing Quality and Residential Satisfaction

Many urban areas attempt to ensure the quality of their housing stock through the implementation of zoning laws and building codes. Zoning, which became widespread during the early twentieth century, was intended to subdivide land parcels throughout a metropolitan area and to limit the uses of land for particular purposes within particular zones. This usually meant separating commercial and industrial land uses from those intended for residential purposes. In major industrial areas, these types of laws helped to create more value within a city's built environment and drastically reduce public health concerns by separating residential areas from factory areas.

Building codes are city or county regulations that mandate the quality of the built residential structure, rather than the location of residential homes. Building codes can improve building safety and quality, as well as force the incorporation of modern building and construction techniques. However, in some areas, building codes may also add excessive requirements designed to keep the construction costs of new housing high and limit the entry of low-income residents into wealthier enclaves.

Housing quality concerns can come from the aging of the current housing stock as well as a lack of affordable housing. In many nations, the lack of habitable housing stock, coupled with the large number of urban dwellers in extreme poverty, forces many city residents to occupy high-density slums. As housing ages, the need for capital repairs begins to mount. Historically, repair needs for low-income apartment units in major cities have been ignored, causing housing quality to suffer as a result. Within U.S. cities, there is a demonstrated pattern of housing "filtering" occurring, in which housing is gradually passed down to lower-income populations as it gets older. Such a situation helps to create an imbalance in the quality of housing among income groups. As construction techniques and processes improve, the potential increases for even wider disparities in housing expenses related to housing quality. For example, the move toward more environmentally sensitive and energy-efficient housing, sometimes referred to as "green" housing, dramatically reduces energy expenses, but it is generally available only to higher-income households.

Aside from the residential structure itself, many cities are currently experiencing difficulties in their supportive infrastructure systems as well. Such inadequate services can lead higher-income residents to leave the cities for suburban or exurban locations, where newer housing stock with adequate road networks, utilities, and other services are offered. To counter some of these forces of inequality in housing, urban planners have advocated, and in many cases implemented, mandatory mixed-income housing within urban areas.

Housing quality and residential satisfaction can also have indirect effects for families and societies. Low residential satisfaction is a key predictor of residential mobility. Excessive residential mobility prevents individuals from rationally investing in community and neighborhood well-being. People who are not planning to stay in a neighborhood generally do not invest their time or resources in improving the neighborhood. This lack of investment in neighborhood social capital in turn produces socially undesirable neighborhoods. Poor neighborhood quality, especially in issues of safety and security, can be a key driver of residential dissatisfaction. Such dissatisfaction leads to increased mobility for those with opportunities to move, which can exacerbate the downward spiral of some communities.

Differences in Housing Across Cultures and Countries

Across regions and across time, the very character of housing may change dramatically. In the United States, the average square footage of a new house rose from about 1,000 square feet in the 1950s to more than 2,600 square feet in the beginning of 2008. Such changes correspond with increases in the average American household's housing norms over time. This trend is occurring despite a concomitant drop in household size. Meanwhile, in other countries, average square footage per living area is much lower. In some international urban cities, housing size may be limited by the lack of developable land, when compared to a country such as the United States. The joint effect of the two trends on the built environment has been an increasing stress on the natural environment.

Housing Tenure

The difference in housing tenure trends across countries is also notable. Since the mid-1990s, the United States has heavily advocated a homeownership strategy, culminating in a homeownership rate approaching 70 percent by the mid-2000s. Such a high homeownership rate is unusual in many other countries. For example, Germany has a homeownership rate just over 40 percent, suggesting a difference in housing norms across the two countries. However, tenant rights also vary dramatically across nations, which makes it difficult to compare tenure categories. The disparities in homeownership rates across different ethnic and racial groups in the United States is also dramatic, with African American and Hispanic homeownership rates consistently more than 25 percentage points below non-Hispanic White homeownership in recent census surveys.

The age of the housing stock can also differ dramatically across urban cities. In the case of Paris, nearly two thirds of its housing stock was erected before 1949, while about half was constructed before 1915. The age of New York City's housing stock is slightly lower by comparison. Those American cities incorporating more land mass and sprawling housing developments, such as Los Angeles and Houston, meanwhile, have much younger housing stock. Across the international landscape, the age of the housing stock may not necessarily be negatively associated with quality. Several cities, such as Florence, Italy, boast of centuries-old housing that is among the highest priced within the metropolitan area. In several other cities where older neighborhoods are protected by historic preservation policies, housing is both well preserved and highly valued.

Throughout much of the world, a nascent movement is gaining strength toward implementing adaptive reuse as a redevelopment strategy. Such a strategy seeks to recycle older commercial buildings for residential purposes, allowing such things as old factories and schools (among other building types) to become apartments and condominiums. Housing can also be shaped by cultural differences such as religion. In some Muslim countries, for example, housing is placed in an environment built for promoting Muslim societal behavior. Such architecture blends basic spatial/policy parameters with existing religious tenets and local conditions.

The persistent drive for greater and greater residential size may have peaked in the United States and elsewhere. Average new home sizes have actually began to fall recently in the United States, driven by economic change and possibly growing concern for green living and limiting one's ecological footprint. The ever-expanding American suburbs have led to an increased realization of the ecological impact of housing choices. Dramatically increased commuting time and fuel consumption accompany these suburban and exurban expansions. Ironically, it is often the desire for green space, in the form of one's own private large yard or garden, that drives suburbanization.

Return to the City

In the United States and elsewhere, the limits of suburbanization and commuting have led to a reemergence of urban residential living as an appropriate and desirable solution. Here, however, the amenities are of a quite different character than suburban developments. Rather than the focus being on individual yards and perhaps a neighborhood pool, urban residential developments are large multifamily buildings where amenities include retail and cultural opportunities conveniently located within walking distance or available by mass transit. Such urban residential amenities may differ substantially by climate and culture. For example, the shared open courtyards of the Mediterranean may be less functional in the colder climates of Scandinavia.

While various cultural and climactic circumstances can impact the design and function of housing, many characteristics are consistently important for housing satisfaction across regions, nations, and cultures. In studies of residential satisfaction in Japan, Western Europe, and the United States, the presence of noise from traffic or neighbors has a dramatically negative effect on residential satisfaction. Although greater size is typically associated with higher residential satisfaction, the characteristics of the space, especially the inclusion of areas such as multiple bathrooms that allow for zones of privacy, are more important in determining residential satisfaction. However, many of the factors that drive residential satisfaction do not relate to the physical structure of the home itself. For example, a variety of studies have shown that perceived neighborhood safety and security is a driving characteristic of residential satisfaction.

Individual housing choice may be driven by specific characteristics, but almost inevitably, broad location choices are based on available employment. In nations where public school availability is based on housing location, such extra-housing characteristics can also drive housing choice for families with children. As with many issues within urban studies, the goal of residential satisfaction can be achieved only with a combination of successes at the individual, neighborhood, community, city, and regional levels.

*Andrew Thomas Carswell
and Russell Noel James*

See also Affordable Housing; Housing Policy; Housing Tenure; Social Housing; Suburbanization

Further Readings

Bratt, Rachel, Michael E. Stone, and Chester Hartman. 2006. *A Right to Housing: Foundation for a New Social Agenda*. Philadelphia: Temple University Press.

Bubolz, M. M. and M. S. Sontag. 1993. "Human Ecology Theory." In *Sourcebook of Family Theories and Methods: A Contextual Approach*, edited by P. Boss, W. J. Doherty, R. LaRossa, W. R. Schumm, and S. K. Steinmetz. New York: Plenum Press.

Glaeser, Edward and Joseph Gyourko. 2002, March. *The Impact of Zoning on Housing Affordability*. Working Paper No. 8835, National Bureau of Economic Research, Cambridge, MA.

Housing Education and Research Association. 2006. *Introduction to Housing*. Upper Saddle River, NJ: Pearson Education.

James, Russell N., III. 2007. "Multifamily Housing Characteristics and Tenant Satisfaction." *Journal of Performance of Constructed Facilities* 21(6):472–80.

Kemp, Peter. 2007. *Housing Allowances in Comparative Perspective*. London: Policy Press.

Lim, Gill-Chin. 1987. "Housing Policies for the Urban Poor in Developing Countries." *Journal of the American Planning Association* 53:2176–85.

Maslow, Abraham H. 1943. "A Theory of Human Motivation." *Psychological Review* 50(4):370–96.

Morris, Earl and Mary Winter. 1978. *Housing, Family, and Society*. New York: Wiley.

Ohls, James C. 1975. "Public Policy toward Low-income Housing and Filtering in Housing Markets." *Journal of Urban Economics* 2(2):144–71.

Housing Policy

Housing policy may be defined as government action to achieve housing objectives. These objectives could include the improvement of the quality of the housing stock of dwellings or dealing with homelessness. Another definition of housing policy would be government intervention in the housing field. The difference is that some interventions in the housing field may be directed at objectives outside the field. Examples could be the regulation of housing finance markets to influence activity in the national economy or restrictions on the amount paid in subsidy to low-income households to encourage incentives to work. Research shows that increasingly more housing policy is directed at economic objectives of efficiency in the national economy with the result that housing policy is increasingly becoming intervention in the housing field to achieve economic objectives.

This entry seeks to examine the objectives and mechanisms that are used by governments in their housing policies; look at categorizations of countries constructed according to their housing policy; consider the forces that shape the similarities and differences in housing policy in individual countries; and examine the scope of individual governments to define their own national policy.

Government Objectives

Governments may have a number of objectives in the housing field. One set may relate to the supply and condition of the housing stock. For example, many countries have policies to ensure that new housing is built to stipulated standards. Also, many countries will intervene to improve the condition of existing housing, such as through slum clearance or upgrading. Policy may also be directed at the quantity or location of new production.

Another set of objectives may relate to the consumption of housing. Intervention may be directed at the legal structures of tenure that determine the rights and obligations of the parties involved. Another area of intervention is access to housing, usually for low-income groups. Thus housing finance and subsidy systems may be designed to enable households with low incomes to access housing that otherwise they could not afford and may be related to policies on income distribution and the alleviation of poverty.

Policies may also be aimed at the functioning of housing markets. Governments set the framework within which markets operate and may intervene to stabilize or change the level of activity.

To achieve these aims governments may use a variety of forms of intervention. One may be the direct provision of housing, as in forms of state housing such as council housing in the United Kingdom. Regulation is another form where the state will influence the actions of other parties by setting standards or frameworks. An example would be building codes or regulations. Another

common form is a system for the regulation of new development through a land use planning system. Subsidies may be used to influence the behavior of either housing developers or consumers. Intervention may take the form of the provision of information or guidance to the relevant parties. An example could be the provision of information on the legal rights of tenants. Government also sets the framework of accountability that can make parties respond to the needs of particular groups. An example may be the institutional structure of public housing, which may be run by local councils with tenants having rights to be consulted.

Categorizing Housing Policy

Individual countries will vary in their mix of housing objectives and forms of interventions. There is a substantial literature on the categorization of these differences and the factors that explain them.

Much work has followed the welfare state regimes approach of Esping-Anderson. He was not specifically concerned with housing but with the identification of three categories or regimes of welfare state as a whole. The first category is the liberal regime in which can be included Britain, Ireland, and the United States. The second category is the conservative regime—and the examples used are Germany and France. His third category is social democratic, and examples are Sweden and Denmark. Housing researchers have used his categorization and have sought to identify the housing models that relate to each type.

For example, in the liberal regime, housing is dominated by market provision, primarily owner occupation but also private rental. Direct government provision is usually small scale and limited to the poorest of the population, which means it is usually stigmatized and unpopular. State help for the poorest is often directed through housing elements of income support programs such as housing allowances or vouchers. The emphasis is on choice through participation in markets. Help for the poorest may also be reflected in support for homeless people, either through the state or voluntary organizations. Further state intervention is in the form of regulation of the market, for example by setting frameworks for financial institutions or for land use planning.

In contrast, the social democratic regime is characterized by substantial direct state provision of housing aimed not just at the poorest. Housing is viewed as a right for citizens, and state responsibility for homeless people may reflect this. Housing finance mechanisms may be designed not only to help the poorest but to achieve egalitarian aims. State intervention in the housing market may be extensive and designed to change market outcomes to reflect social aims.

The conservative regime is characterized as corporatist in nature with partnerships between government and long-standing social institutions such as churches or professional or trade groups. Provision of housing is often through these institutions and vehicles such as housing associations that serve the interests of their members. The state may protect these institutions from market competition. The access of households to housing may depend on their relationship to these institutions rather than on market participation or state conferred rights.

Other categories of housing regime have been considered. For example, there was been much debate in the 1990s about whether or not there is an Eastern European model. Clapham and others have argued for the existence of an East European model based on state ownership and distribution, centrally planned production; housing was all but free at the point of use, and market mechanisms were excluded. It is argued that this model never really existed in a pure form because of a shortage of resources and the costs and difficulties of achieving state control. Political changes in the late 1990s meant that democratically elected governments pursued policies of privatization and market freedom and most moved quickly to a liberal regime.

Others have argued for a separate category for southern Europe, where there is generally a reliance on extended family structures for the provision of housing through self-build. Housing policy in many of these countries is undeveloped compared to northern European countries. Eastern countries such as Japan or China also have very different housing systems and policies that do not seem to fit the three regimes.

Convergence or Divergence

The second major area of debate and academic research has been on the movement over time of these models and the scope for individual countries to vary their systems. The major schools of thought have been divided into the convergence and divergence approaches.

Convergence Approaches

The convergence approach stresses the similarities in the movement of housing policies over time, usually based on the economic sphere. This is sometimes called the "logic of industrialism" approach and is associated with "end of ideology" theories. There are a number of different examples of this approach. One idea is that welfare states change as the rights of citizenship develop, and one author suggested a move from a focus on civil rights to political rights and then social rights. Donnison adopted this perspective on the development of housing policy identifying embryonic, social, and comprehensive models, which bear more than a passing resemblance to Esping-Anderson's later classification.

Examples of embryonic states were given as southern European countries such as Portugal or Greece, which have more recently become industrialized states with the concomitant urbanization. In these countries, the states had only just begun to intervene in the housing system, partly because housing is seen as a consumption good and the priority has been given to economic development.

The second category of social states included countries such as United Kingdom and the United States, where the primary aim of government is to come to the aid of people who cannot secure housing for themselves through the market. Interventions are designed to rectify particular problems or deficiencies in the market and do not reflect a government responsibility for the housing of the whole population, which is the defining element of the third category—the comprehensive model. Examples given are Sweden and the former West Germany where governments have taken a long-term view of their involvement in housing. Donnison argued that states moved along the continuum from embryonic to comprehensive as they developed economically. However, the credibility of this analysis has been hit in recent years by the retrenchment of many welfare states despite increasing affluence.

A very different example of a convergence approach is that used by Ball, Harloe, and Martens. They argued that common economic forces move housing policies in broadly similar directions, although the uneven spread and speed of economic development means that countries start from different places and move at different speeds. They highlighted the common trend across many countries of commodification that involves a reduction and restructuring of state involvement in housing and the growth of market provision. These common trends do not necessarily result in similar housing policies or systems because of what the authors term the *structures of provision* in each country. By this they mean the institutions and cultures that structure the housing field and through which policy is perceived and policy decisions made.

More recently, focus has been on the impact of globalizing economic trends. For example, Clapham has shown how the discourse of globalization has been adopted in the United Kingdom and has lead to constraints on the state that impact on the housing sector. For example, the perceived need to support entrepreneurship has resulted in constraints on the ability to fund government action through taxation on high earners. Also the deregulation of financial markets has reduced the ability of governments to intervene in housing markets by making ineffective traditional policy instruments such as credit controls. At the same time, the perceived need to increase the flexibility of labor markets to increase economic efficiency has changed the focus of housing policies. Geographic mobility is seen as being important in enabling people to follow employment opportunities, and so flexibility in housing with new-house production in growing areas and low mobility and transactions costs are given prominence in policy. Another key policy area is the need to design policy to avoid or minimize income disincentives and poverty and employment traps to reinforce incentives to work. Acceptance of the discourses of globalization and flexible labor markets seems to be associated with neoliberal housing policies that emphasize market processes and outcomes.

Divergence Approaches

The second major approach is the divergence approach. This sees countries as differing substantially in their housing systems despite similar levels of economic development and does not see them as necessarily converging. It is argued that political ideologies and cultural norms differ and profoundly influence the shape of housing structures. Kemeny and Lowe use the work of Esping-Anderson on different kinds of state welfare to point to the influence of political ideology in shaping state policy. In his own work, Kemeny examines the nature of cultures of homeownership in different societies, arguing that these are related to different political philosophies of individualism or collectivism. In homeowner societies, Kemeny argues, government housing policy is related to socially constructed ideologies and cultural myths that vary between different societies. These are used to justify special support for owner occupation and measures to prevent cost-renting from becoming too large and a competitive tenure.

Common measures are the stigmatization of tenants of cost-rental landlords or the forced sales of housing stock. In cost-rental societies, the state-subsidized sector dominates private rental provision, and government may intervene to create a unitary system in which the rights and obligations of tenants are similar and state institutions regulate access and conditions in the private sector. In these societies, cost-renting can compete with owner occupation for middle-class households and so will not be stigmatized.

The distinction between convergence and divergence approaches is increasingly questioned because it does not uncover the underlying bases of the different approaches but concentrates on and overemphasizes one of the outcomes of their application. In other words, the key issue is not whether different countries are converging or diverging. Rather, it is which factors are the key influences on policy. The approach of Ball and Harloe is loosely based on what may be termed a realist position, whereas Kemeny's approach is built on social constructionism. Clearly, this leads to different emphases and conclusions on the factors to be taken into account in examining housing policy. However, the two approaches have more in common than is immediately apparent. Convergence approaches reduce to a residual important factors that explain the evident differences between countries. Furthermore, convergence approaches do not develop a theoretical position that can explain divergence or any differences in the direction or speed of social change. For example, Ball and Harloe identify structures of provision in each country, which they argue are at the core of differences between countries. However, this is seen as a sensitizing concept to alert researchers to recognize differences. The concept lacks a theoretical underpinning that would allow an analysis of why differences exist and why they may change over time.

The areas of agreement of the different approaches are great. Some common trends are driven by the globalizing forces of advanced capitalism. Globalization may be seen as a socially constructed discourse accepted and promulgated by governments and economic agents or as a real economic force. But, this difference of view does not necessarily hinder agreement on the impact of globalization on housing policy in different countries. General trends can be identified, such as marketization, liberalization, and the restructuring of state intervention from direct provision and subsidy toward forms of regulation. In addition, there has been a move by governments away from social objectives in housing policy and toward economic objectives.

However, there is not a clear and direct relationship between this level of change and institutional housing structures and state housing policy in particular countries. Some of the differences may be due to the position of different countries in the globalized economic world. Also, governments may differ in their acceptance of the globalization discourse or their openness to global economic forces. The scope for political choice in responding to globalizing trends is an important matter of debate. The degree of freedom of maneuver may be influenced by many factors including existing institutional structures and political discourses and ideologies.

The need for an effective housing policy is felt by governments in many different contexts. The problem may be the failure of housing markets in the declining parts of older cities in Western countries or the counterpart of the rapidly expanding need for new housing construction in economically thriving areas. In rapidly developing and urbanizing countries such as India or China, there is a need to ensure that housing standards are high and

that cities expand in efficient and sustainable ways. An effective housing policy is a major instrument of urban policy, and the successes and failures of housing policies can explain the developing features of cities across the world.

David Clapham

See also Affordable Housing; Homeownership; Housing; Housing Tenure; Social Housing

Further Readings

Ball, M. and M. Harloe 1992. "Rhetorical Barriers to Understanding Housing Provision: What the Provision Thesis Is and Is Not." *Housing Studies* 17(1):3–15.

Ball, M., M. Harloe, and M. Martens. 1988. *Housing and Social Change in Europe and the USA*. London: Routledge.

Clapham, D. 1995. "Privatization and the East European Housing Model." *Urban Studies* 32(4–5): 679–94.

———. 2006. "Housing Policy and the Discourse of Globalisation." *European Journal of Housing Policy* 6(1):55–76.

Doling, J. 1997. *Comparative Housing Policy*. Basingstoke, UK: Macmillan.

Donnison, D. 1967. *The Government of Housing*. Harmondsworth, UK: Penguin.

Esping-Anderson, G. 1990. *The Three Worlds of Welfare Capitalism*. Cambridge: Polity Press.

Kemeny, J. 1992. *Housing and Social Theory*. London: Routledge.

Kemeny, J. and S. Lowe. 1998. "Schools of Comparative Housing Research: From Convergence to Divergence." *Housing Studies* 13(2):161–76.

Housing Tenure

Housing tenure refers to the possession of residential real estate. The term tenure stems from the Latin *tenere,* meaning "to hold." *Homeowner* and *renter* distinguish individuals with permanent or temporary possession of property. About 70 percent of Americans own their home, and 30 percent rent. Homeownership is the cornerstone of American conceptions of prosperity. High numbers of homeowners are equated with economic and social well-being. Increased numbers of renters are viewed as a sign of diminishing prosperity.

Basic Characteristics

Between 1940 and 1960, the United States changed from a country of renters in cities to one of suburban homeowners. During the Great Depression, a decline in homeownership led to government loan programs and changes in the housing finance system. As a result, and during a time of improved economic conditions, homeownership increased from 44 percent to 62 percent. Homeownership increased by 2.5 percent in the following two decades. In years prior to 2007, low interest rates, an increased number of mortgage products, and government support translated into a rate closer to 70 percent.

Housing tenure of a single residential property can be complex. Six primary property rights can be owned or rented by different parties. They include the right to exclude others, to profit from the sale of a property, to improve or demolish structures, to develop the land beneath structures, and to access air and light. Some forms of tenure combine elements of renting and owning. Examples include cooperatively owned housing, where multiple residents retain equity in the property, and the leasing of land by mobile homeowners.

The choice to rent or own is subject to constraints differentially distributed along class and often racial lines. Constraints include: household financial resources and prospects, relative costs between purchasing and renting, discrimination in housing and mortgage markets, and employment opportunities.

Tenure Sectors

Housing can be held through legal arrangements that are classified within three tenure sectors, delineating who owns and resides in the house and how it is priced and allocated. Policymakers are often asked to endorse or oppose housing polices according to tenure sector. Private-sector housing is privately owned, priced, and allocated by the free market. Single- and multifamily properties retain exchange value (their value in the housing market) above use value (their value to the homeowner). There are owner-occupied and rental properties. About 90 percent of U.S. housing is privately held, and public policy favors this sector.

Public-sector housing is owned by the state or a quasi-public corporation. Units are priced and allocated by nonmarket methods. Price controls are established by public policy and through means testing to meet low-income demand. Third-sector housing is privately owned but priced and allocated by nonmarket methods. Price controls limit rental and sales assessments and are based on predetermined contractual limits. Units are produced for use value rather than exchange value. Among industrialized countries, the third sector is comparatively small in the United States.

Nicole Oretsky

See also Affordable Housing; Fair Housing; Housing; Social Housing

Further Readings

Davis, John Emmeus. 1998. "Tenure Sectors." Pp. 587–89 in *Encyclopedia of Housing*, edited by William van Vliet. Thousand Oaks, CA: Sage.

Schwartz, Alex. 2006. *Housing Policy in the United States: An Introduction*. New York: Routledge.

HUMAN ECOLOGY

Human ecology is a theory of human population adaptation to the environment in time, space, and social structure. Initially associated with theories of the spatial and social organization of cities, contemporary human ecology is considered a general theory of social organization that encompasses earlier urban ecological approaches. The history of human ecology is divided between the traditional period, often associated with the Chicago School, and the contemporary period, associated with sociocultural human ecology and neo-orthodox human ecology.

All approaches share common characteristics: a concern with macrosocial structure, the centrality of community as a theoretical object of study, and a holistic conception of macrosocial community structure. This holistic approach is often summarized as an interaction among four major analytic components: population, organization, environment, and technology, termed the *ecological complex*. In its various forms, human ecology is a definitive theoretical approach that has substantial impact on sociology and geography.

Traditional Approaches

Associated with Robert Ezra Park, Ernest W. Burgess, and Roderick D. McKenzie as a perspective overlapping but not encompassed by sociology, the main focus of traditional ecology was on the city as an object of study. These Chicago School ecologists drew on an eclectic milieu of social theory (Durkheim, Simmel, Comte, Spencer, Tönnies), on Charles Darwin's notions of competitions and the "web of life," and on the writings of plant bioecologists who were developing a biologic economics of plant and animal communities. Blending these conceptions created a materialist approach that viewed the city as an interdependent system that could be analyzed by spatial structure and function.

Traditional ecology argues that the social organization of human populations, like plant and animal populations, is distributed in time and space. The human community is organization divided into the biotic (natural) and societal (cultural) levels. Traditional human ecology takes as its object of study the biotic processes: competition, succession, and dominance. The city is conceived as a territory delimited by the scope of economic and residential competition among individuals. As with biotic communities, this competition gives rise to spatial differentiation. Different activities take place in specific areas within the city. Cultural elements of social organization are assumed to be constrained by these ecological forces. Yet all are linked as a single ecological system functioning as an interdependent unit.

This conception generated three complementary lines of research for Park and his colleagues. The first focused on socioeconomic regularities in the distributions of people and activities. These natural areas are exemplified by Burgess's 1925 model of concentric zones. The second line of research evaluated effects of these areas on populations. This work focused on aspects of social disorganization such as crime rates and mental illness. Finally, the assumption that these natural areas shaped the cultural conditions for individuals gave rise to a rich tradition of urban ethnography. Works by Harvey Zorbaugh (*The Gold Coast and the Slum,* 1929) and Louis Wirth (*The Ghetto,* 1928) exemplify this approach, using natural ecological areas to delimit close analysis of individual behaviors and attitudes.

Despite commonalities in these three areas, the integration of cultural and material (biotic) conditions proved contentious in theoretical development. The main thrust of theory was toward the externally imposed constraints of space and environment while incorporation of culture introduced volition and an internal source of change. Cutting across these issues was an increasing awareness among critics that community was treated as both an analytic construct and as an empirical unit of analysis (the city). This was most problematic to the early ecologists' inductive methodology, where the conceptual division between biotic and cultural elements could not be distinctly operationalized and was often tautological.

These intrinsic problems gave rise to a number of substantive and theoretical criticisms leveled at traditional ecology. Furthermore, during the 1930s and 1940s, empirical findings of ecologists on spatial configurations of social organization studied by the Chicago School were contradicted by other studies. Critics argued that because ecologists denied the presence of culture and symbols, essentially they were presenting an economic/technologically determinist view of communities. Most important for scholars working within the ecological tradition was the criticism that the analysis of spatial units did not fit the theoretical tenets of ecology.

Responding to Critiques

In response to these criticisms, human ecologists reconceived human ecology along two distinct lines. Sociocultural ecologists retained traditional ecology's inductive foundations but rejected attempts to theorize the underlying forces determining the mode of human organization. This approach, first presented by Walter Firey in "Sentiment and Symbolism as Ecological Variables" in 1945, incorporated inductive study to explicate the role of culture and attitudes in creating sociospatial organization.

Neo-orthodox human ecology rejected both an individualist and cultural approach. This approach sought to develop the concept of the ecological community as an abstraction, then verify theoretical propositions deductively through empirical analysis. Amos H. Hawley's *Human Ecology: A Theory of Community Structure* (1950) stands as the foundation of the neo-orthodox approach.

Hawley's reconception of human ecology moved it into mainstream sociology by orienting the discipline away from the study of spatial regularities to the study of collective action of a population in adaptation. Hawley's conception of human ecology differed from the traditional in a number of ways: the assumption that general and human ecology address the same central problem, the recognition that ecological relationships reflect a combination and interaction of competition and interdependence, the view that the adaptation of human population is a collective rather than individual accomplishment, and the identification of sustenance activities as the principal component of social organization.

Furthermore, Hawley's 1950 work directly addresses both the cultural and methodological criticisms of the 1940s. Hawley explicitly defines an ecological community as the smallest unit in which a full range of ecological interactions takes place, building further theoretical postulates on this concept. The question of whether the city is coterminous with an ecological community is left as an empirical question. By making explicit that the smallest effective unit in the ecosystem is an organization, Hawley excises theoretical problems associated with the volitional and ideological elements in ecology.

The Neo-Orthodox Movement

This holistic, macrosocial, and material reconception of human ecology reinfused human ecological theory and launched the neo-orthodox movement in the field. Furthermore, Hawley's 1950 reformulation places the organization of society as the main point of focus for human ecology, moving it from a limited theory of city patterns and development to a general theory of social organization. Hawley has clearly and completely enunciated the major principles of ecological organization elsewhere. A brief summary of principles is given below.

Hawley argues that human ecology may be stated as three propositions on population level: (1) adaptation proceeds through the formation of interdependencies; (2) system development continues to the maximum size and complexity afforded by social organization. Once the limits of technology and organization are reached, system growth stops, that is, it reaches equilibrium, and (3) system development is resumed when new information

increases organizational and technological capacity. This ecosystem can be abstracted into four broad components: population, organization, environment, and technology.

These four components are conceptually, not necessarily analytically, separate. Population refers to any collectivity of units that has a clear boundary and that interacts. As a common denominator of ecological analysis, the population exhibits a number of properties not shared by individual members. Organization is synonymous with social system structure. It refers to the entire network of interdependencies that a population uses to sustain and maximize survival. Environment is defined by the potential resources for any social system. In this, it is both the physical environment and other social systems external to the population in study. Technology refers to the set of artifacts, tools, and techniques employed by a population to organize sustenance. Together, these four components comprise an ecological community: any bounded area where the full range of ecological interactions takes place. Given that social systems arrange themselves to maximize external environmental conditions, there is an explicit causal arrangement among these four analytic components. The environment is the primary causal mechanism of system change.

From these basic premises, contemporary human ecology has generated a variety of supporting concepts regarding community adaptation to environment, explored through deductive empirical analysis from the 1950s through the 1980s. Ecological research explored and evaluated the role key functions play in ecological structure, showing that they exert disproportionate control of community power. Implications for basic types of interdependence—symbiotic (based on specialization) and commensalistic (based on aggregation)—were evaluated at societal, community, and organizational levels. The formation of fundamental types of units is typified by these types of association; corporate (symbiotic) and categoric (commensalistic) have been evaluated, and the implications of alternative sustenance structures were studied. Prominent in these theoretically driven empirical studies were the works of John D. Kasarda, Dudley Poston, Miller McPherson, and Parker Frisbie.

Michael D. Irwin

See also Chicago School of Urban Sociology; Factorial Ecology; Hawley, Amos; Urban Sociology; Urban Theory

Further Readings

Berry, Brian J. L. and John D. Kasarda. 1977. *Contemporary Urban Ecology*. New York: Macmillan.

Burgess, Ernest W. 1925. "The Growth of the City: An Introduction to a Research Project." Pp. 47–62 in *The City*, edited by Robert Park, Ernest Burgess, and R. D. McKenzie. Chicago: University of Chicago Press.

Faris, Robert E. L. and H. Warren Dunham. 1939. *Mental Disorders in the Urban Areas*. Chicago: University of Chicago Press.

Firey, Walter. 1945. "Sentiment and Symbolism as Ecological Variables." *American Sociological Review* 10(2):140–48.

Hawley, Amos H. 1944. "Ecology and Human Ecology." *Social Forces* 22(4):398–405.

Hawley, Amos H. 1950. *Human Ecology: A Theory of Community Structure*. New York: Ronald Press.

———. 1986. *Human Ecology: A Theoretical Essay*. Chicago: University of Chicago Press.

Micklin, Michael and Harvey M. Choldin, eds. 1984. *Sociological Human Ecology: Contemporary Issues and Applications*. Boulder, CO: Westview Press.

Quinn, James A. 1939. "The Nature of Human Ecology: Reexamination and Redefinition." *Social Forces* 18:161–68.

Shaw, Clifford, F. M. Zorbaugh, Henry McKay, and Leonard Cottrell. 1929. *Delinquency Areas*. Chicago: University of Chicago Press.

Theordorson, George A., ed. 1961. *Studies in Human Ecology*. New York: Harper and Row.

Wirth, Louis 1928. *The Ghetto*. Chicago: University of Chicago Press.

Zorbaugh, Harvey W. 1929. *The Gold Coast and the Slum*. Chicago: University of Chicago Press.

I

IDEAL CITY

Sharp straight lines create linear perspective dominated by a rotunda in the painting *Ideal City* (c. 1470), attributed to Italian Renaissance painter Piero della Francesca. Symmetrical blocks of buildings border the frame of the painting. Patterned pavement in the foreground augments the perspective. Rare vines are seen on several facades. No person is seen.

Francesca's *Ideal City* was praised for its perfect linearity and orderliness and shunned for its perfect sterility and emptiness. The apparent contradiction between Francesca's idealized orderly vision and the common image of the city as a bustling, lively, messy entity reveals the crucial problem embedded in the notion of ideal city: What is ideal according to a set of standards and logical statements may turn out to be not at all acceptable in terms of real life.

"Ideal city" is a trope found throughout the history of human habitation. As a systematic description of the vision of how the city, its form, and content should be, it originates in classical Greek thought. This vision may also be revealed as underlying city building practice before and after that. Its varieties include ideal cities in the Western utopian tradition, visions of ideal city in planning practice, and anti-utopian and dystopian antipodes of ideal city. All these visions have important consequences as they are actualized in human practice.

The Phenomenon of Ideal City

An ideal city is a religious or secular vision of the city in which the portrayed urban environment reflect a complex of conceptions about what is deemed good, desires for something better, and imaginations about what should be. Behind this vision is the intention to best satisfy the needs of the population while subjecting it to an idealized order. This is a normative ideal of the city. It is a product of the desire to represent and actualize those features and properties of cities and societies that are perceived to be absent in real life.

A range of traits may be found, to varying degrees, in most visions of ideal cities. Ideal city reflects the values of harmony and order. It encompasses the eternal desire of humankind to succeed in creating a balanced social fabric where the anthropogenic environment serves the needs of the people and overcomes the age-old ills of urban living—density, congestion, dirt, crime, poverty, inequality. Ideal city offers its residents comfort, justice, happiness, cleanliness, beauty, health, and well-being. Ideal city is a fundamental entity: planned and developed by an intentional subject such as a visionary architect. It implies a totalizing vision whereby every facet of ideal order is included and accounted for in the design.

The residents are assumed to voluntarily comply with the rules and conditions imposed on them by the designer and by the environment. The power of nature in the ideal city is implicitly considered destructive and is effectively eliminated by imposing the same seamless orderly pattern on urban nature. Grass, trees, and animals often find their way into ideal conceptions only in the form of parks and gardens.

The core assumption behind the ideal city is spatial determinism: the belief that the people's happiness may be achieved by putting them into the correct environment, which will guide their behavior and channel it in acceptable directions, thus ensuring smoothness and seamlessness (and even rigidity) of imposed urban social organization.

Although there is a narrow class of representations that are explicitly labeled ideal city, such as Francesca's painting and a number of similar artworks, to an extent city plans, design conceptions, and urban utopias, as well as imaginations and projects of architects, planners, rulers, and administrators, are all ideal cities. Ideal city differs between cultures and times. It need not necessarily be explicitly described in artistic form or planning conceptions: As Lewis Mumford once suggested, ideal city is implicit and may be inductively grasped by examining the actual practice of planning and building cities. Ideal city may have different degrees of relation to the actual human practice. The ideal city of utopia has, perhaps, the farthest relation.

The Ideal City of the Western Utopian Tradition

The origins of the Western utopian tradition, as Krishan Kumar has shown, are found in the classical Greek thought and in Judeo–Christian religious thinking. Utopian thinking throughout its history has produced ideal cities as forms of utopias. The very conception of utopia as city may be traced to the Hellenic utopias of Plato, who in his *The Republic* and particularly in *Laws* has portrayed his utopia as an urban form. Aristotle's *Politics* continued this focus. Among the best-known Western urban utopian visions are those found in literature after *Utopia* of Thomas More and *The City of the Sun* of Tommaso Campanella. All these ideal cities share the properties of orderliness, cleanliness, and rationality as well as clear-cut governmentality.

However, utopian thought does not necessarily take the form of ideal city. Rather, description of an ideal city gives utopian visions a very tangible and demonstrable form that conveys the properties of utopia. Ideal city is a powerful spatial imagination of utopian thought. In his explorations of ideal urban geometries, Spiro Kostof stresses the connection between the "diagram" of the ideal city and, on the one hand, the idea of power and government embodied in the ruler who uses the urban diagram to organize and govern the population, and on the other hand, the aura of divinity and sanctity of political order. Utopian ideal cities typically share this kind of clear-cut power, which may be sanctified by the belief in rationality and possibility of rational social organization as well as by religious beliefs. Yet utopian ideal cities are but imaginations conveyed through artistic media. Ideal cities in urban planning are species having more direct impact on human practice.

Ideal Visions in Architecture and Urban Planning

Although modern theoretical urban planning was invented in the second half of the nineteenth century, urban planning as practice may be said to have existed since the earliest human settlements. Designs and plans of architecture and urban planning bear many features of ideal cities. They are created on purpose with the idea of managing human settlement and ordering the urban process. They often aim at alleviating what their creators perceive as the ailments of existing settlements. Yet the crucial distinction from utopian visions is that urban planning is a practice that entails human agency in actually changing the material environment. The Renaissance tradition of architecture (Filarete, Leon Battista Alberti) and architectural painting (Piero Della Francesca school) clearly reveals the close connection of architecture and planning and ideal visions of the city.

Kevin Lynch, discussing sets of ideas about proper city form that he calls "normative theories of good city form," has outlined three such conceptions: the cosmic city, understood as a reflection of the universe and divine order (seen in ancient temple cities); the machine city, seen as a rational design for fulfillment of certain social goals (evident in modernist planning); and the organism model, invoking the analogy of living body (present in planning influenced by ecology). Essentially, these are varieties of understandings of ideal cities actually found in the history of city planning and building.

Very often, ideal cities of architecture and planning leave the minds and drawings of their creators and enter the actual process of constructing and altering urban environment. One of the model examples of an ideal city plan actually built in Renaissance Europe is Palmanova (commenced in 1593), a military outpost town in the Friuli region of northeastern Italy. Palmanova was constructed in the form of a nine-pointed star and employed state-of-the-art military defense design. St. Petersburg in Russia is an example of a city that was built from scratch according to a preconceived plan in 1703. The Russian Tsar Peter I the Great wanted the new city to correspond to his vision of European cities of the time and devised the original city plan accordingly. Baron Georges-Eugène Haussmann's reconstruction of Paris in the 1850s is a well-known occasion of reconstructing an existing city according to an idealized vision. Brasilia, the new capital of Brazil, is one of the most striking moments in the history of twentieth-century urban planning. Designed by Lucio Costa (the principal planner) and Oscar Niemeyer (the principal architect), its airplane-shaped city plan first brought to life in 1956 embodied the modernist planning principles of Le Corbusier.

On a lesser scale, many urban designs and planning projects—such as community development programs, planned communities, urban revitalization projects, historic city center reconstructions—all imply an idealized vision of the city or its part, whether conceived as reinstating a past that has once been or realizing a conception of how things should be. Even the shopping mall evokes the ideal-city design principles implemented at the scale of consumer facility.

Anti-Utopian and Dystopian Visions

The last species of ideal city to be discussed here is the anti-utopian portrayal of anti-ideal cities. Anti-utopia is a genre dedicated to depicting imagined societies where utopian ideals lead to terror, abandonment of humanity, violence, totalitarian repression, and excessive control. The genre of dystopia is sometimes distinguished from anti-utopia. In dystopia, catastrophe, war, disaster, or just the continuing "business as usual" of a flawed society result in desolation, poverty, and terror.

Anti-utopian and dystopian literature, such as Yevgeny Zamyatin's *We* (1921) or Aldous Huxley's *Brave New World* (1932), often portrays cities and urban living. But these are the imaginations of what the principles of utopia and ideal city may lead to if actually implemented. Even dystopian cities of devastation may be considered instances where "ideal city" is portrayed as a warning or foreboding. This kind of vision has grown particularly vivid with manifold cinematic anti-utopias, such as Fritz Lang's *Metropolis* (1927), Jean-Luc Godard's *Alphaville* (1965), and Terry Gilliam's *Brazil* (1985) and dystopias, such as Ridley Scott's *Blade Runner* (1982) and *The Matrix* (1999–2003) series.

Ideal Cities and Real Cities

The phenomenon of ideal city reflects the grounding of human practice in conceptions, ideas, and designs. However, it is a double-edged sword: Ideal cities of the utopian tradition serve as hallmarks of imagination and hopes for progress and yet may also signify the possible unintended consequences of striving for the good. Even the classical utopian cities of Plato and More may be viewed as negative examples of unjust and freedom-less worlds.

Although they are often designed with the best intentions, ideal cities realized in planning practice may lead to unfavorable outcomes, as is seen in many failures of modernist architecture and planning. Brasilia is arguably a case of such failure to provide true comfort and satisfaction to its inhabitants. The Pruitt-Igoe housing project in St. Louis, Missouri, stands as a model of failure of design, which also was guided by the vision of "good city" form. Furthermore, what has been seen as good at the outset may later come to be seen as an opposite. Early communist urban design and planning was done in accordance with the conception of ideal living in a new society and yet came to be seen as unfit for habitation. In the 1950s, the Soviet Union solved its housing crisis with massive construction of cheap prefab concrete five-story buildings. Seen as a miracle and a long-awaited rescue at their time, "Khrushchevkas" (after the USSR First Secretary Nikita Khrushchev) now stand for all the misery of Soviet architecture and construction, as they still form the decaying backbone of housing stock in much of the contemporary former Soviet Union.

Nevertheless, ideal city is the principal challenge for planning, design, and management of urban landscape. It embodies the fundamental questions of how to create better cities and to alleviate the ills of existing ones. It also embodies the fundamental problem that the ideal city for some people may not at all be the ideal city for other people, and furthermore, what is believed ideal now may be a disaster tomorrow. Another challenge of ideal cities is that many traits of actual cities throughout the history of civilization—diversity, multitude, crowds, pollution, dense habitation, opportunities for different groups of people to mingle and conflict—are part of what the very notion of city entails, and therefore, ideal cities may in fact be something different from cities altogether.

Finally, the ideal city is also a legitimate object for research. The important fields of interest include history of idealized artistic depictions of the urban and ideal cities in the history of architecture; the way conceptions of an ideal city guide the actual practice of planning and design; and the way the outcomes of attempts to realize the ideal city are coming to be successful or unsuccessful.

Nikita A. Kharlamov

See also Architecture; Brasilia, Brazil; Lynch, Kevin; Medieval Town Design; Mumford, Lewis; Renaissance City; Urban Planning; Utopia

Further Readings

Kostof, Spiro. 1999. *The City Shaped: Urban Patterns and Meanings through History.* London: Thames & Hudson.

Kumar, Krishan. 2003. "Aspects of the Western Utopian Tradition." *History of the Human Sciences* 16(1):63–77.

Lynch, Kevin. 1984. *Good City Form.* Cambridge: MIT Press.

Mumford, Lewis. 1965. "Utopia, the City, and the Machine." *Daedalus* 94(2):271–92.

———. 1989. *The City in History: Its Origins, Its Transformations, and Its Prospects.* New York: Harcourt.

Rosenau, Helen. 1983. *The Ideal City: Its Architectural Evolution in Europe.* London: Methuen.

Solinís, Germán. 2006. "Utopia, the Origins and Invention of Western Urban Design." *Diogenes* 53(1):79–87.

Informational City

Many cities worldwide face the prospect of major transformation as the world moves toward a global information order. In this new era, urban economies are being radically altered by dynamic processes of economic and spatial restructuring. The result is the creation of informational cities, or their new and more popular name, knowledge cities.

For the last two centuries, social production had been primarily understood and shaped by neoclassical economic thought, which recognized only three factors of production: land, labor, and capital. Knowledge, education, and intellectual capacity were secondary, if not incidental, factors. Human capital was assumed to be either embedded in labor or just one of numerous categories of capital. In the last decades, it has become apparent that knowledge is sufficiently important to deserve recognition as a fourth factor of production. Knowledge and information and the social and technological settings for their production and communication are now seen as keys to development and economic prosperity.

The rise of knowledge-based opportunity has, in many cases, been accompanied by a concomitant decline in traditional industrial activity. The replacement of physical commodity production by more abstract forms of production (e.g., information, ideas, and knowledge) has, however paradoxically, reinforced the importance of central places and led to the formation of knowledge cities.

Knowledge is produced, marketed, and exchanged mainly in cities. Therefore, knowledge cities aim to assist decision makers in making their cities compatible with the knowledge economy and thus able to compete with other cities. Knowledge cities enable their citizens to foster knowledge creation, knowledge exchange, and innovation. They also encourage the continuous creation, sharing, evaluation, renewal, and update of knowledge.

To compete nationally and internationally, cities need knowledge infrastructures (e.g., universities, research and development institutes); a concentration of well-educated people; technological, mainly electronic, infrastructure; and connections to the global economy (e.g., international companies and finance institutions for trade and investment). Moreover, they must possess the people and things necessary for the production of knowledge and, as important, function as breeding grounds for talent and innovation.

The economy of a knowledge city creates high value-added products using research, technology, and brainpower. Private and public sectors value knowledge, spend money on its discovery and dissemination, and, ultimately, harness it to create goods and services. Although many cities call themselves knowledge cities, currently, only a few cities around the world (e.g., Barcelona, Delft, Dublin, Montreal, Munich, and Stockholm) have earned that label. Many other cities aspire to the status of knowledge city through urban development programs that target knowledge-based urban development. Examples include Copenhagen, Dubai, Manchester, Melbourne, Monterrey, Singapore, and Shanghai.

Knowledge-Based Urban Development

To date, the development of most knowledge cities has proceeded organically as a dependent and derivative effect of global market forces. Urban and regional planning has responded slowly, and sometimes not at all, to the challenges and the opportunities of the knowledge city. That is changing, however. Knowledge-based urban development potentially brings both economic prosperity and a sustainable sociospatial order. Its goal is to produce and circulate abstract work.

The globalization of the world in the last decades of the twentieth century was a dialectical process. On one hand, as the tyranny of distance was eroded, economic networks of production and consumption were constituted at a global scale. At the same time, spatial proximity remained as important as ever, if not more so, for knowledge-based urban development. Mediated by information and communication technology, personal contact, and the medium of tacit knowledge, organizational and institutional interactions are still closely associated with spatial proximity. The clustering of knowledge production is essential for fostering innovation and wealth creation.

The social benefits of knowledge-based urban development extend beyond aggregate economic growth. On the one hand is the possibility of a particularly resilient form of urban development secured in a network of connections anchored at local, national, and global coordinates. On the other hand, quality of place and life, defined by the level of public service (e.g., health and education) and by the conservation and development of cultural, aesthetic, and ecological values, gives cities their character and attracts or repels the creative class of knowledge workers; this is a prerequisite for successful knowledge-based urban development. The goal is a secure economy in a human setting: in short, smart growth or sustainable urban development.

Creative Class of Knowledge Workers

One of the greatest challenges of the knowledge city is its social and environmental setting. In the production of places of knowledge, image is as important as reality. The presence of knowledge professionals and creative talent attracts innovative, knowledge- and technology-based industries. When a place is home to a creative class of knowledge workers, social interactions drive value creation and further concentrate creative knowledge workers (e.g., computer and mathematical occupations; architecture and engineering; life, physical, and social science occupations; education, training, and library occupations; and arts, design, entertainment, sports, and media occupations).

A key determinant in attracting and retaining these people is the quality of life of a place. Knowledge workers do not select their residence simply to maximize their salary. They are also concerned with consumption opportunities. Typically, knowledge workers value a whole series of place-based characteristics, not the least being cultural activities and amenities. Consequently, quality of place and life is a factor of growing importance for knowledge-based cities. Besides that, the city's heritage—the meanings attached to the past and present from the foundations of social, political, and cultural knowledge—can attract additional talented workers.

One of the goals of knowledge-based urban development is a virtuous circle of attraction that retains skilled and creative people, who, in turn, attract smart industries and businesses that need their labor and investors looking to invest in high-value production. With a strong sense of community and a pool of skilled and talented people, a knowledge city will enjoy robust growth at way above average rates.

Technology Parks as Essential Knowledge Clusters

The ongoing transformation of advanced economies from manufacturing to services and knowledge-based activities has important implications for the formation of knowledge cities. Firms increasingly use technology as their prime source of competitive advantage, and the economic wealth of nations is increasingly tied to their technological competence.

The increasing interconnectedness of the world economy as part of the ongoing process of globalization depends on technologies such as information and communication technology. These are the keys to corporate success and national growth. Such technologies impose an almost irresistible drive to be part of international growth. Similarly, since the end of the 1980s, the development of the knowledge-based economy, globalization, and international competitive pressure has increased the importance of innovation. Simultaneously, globalization increases local differences arising from local capabilities and environments.

New developments in globalization and communications technology have prompted countries and cities to focus their competitive strategies on improving innovation. This shift has increased the value of knowledge-based activity. Knowledge-based production, however, generally clusters in areas with a rich base of scientific knowledge tied to specific industries. This spatial imperative has polarized high-growth activity in a limited number of areas of the world.

Proximity generates and transfers knowledge. Thus, new knowledge-based activities cluster in specific geographic localities. Proximity is essential to stimulate company learning, create compatible knowledge spillover effects, and establish positive feedback among various local agents. Such clusters are built around advanced technological infrastructure and mature networks of innovation.

Knowledge clusters are not all equal but have differing dynamics. Among the forms already identified are the knowledge (or technology) park, the knowledge village, the knowledge corridor, the knowledge hub, the knowledge district, and, beyond the knowledge city, the knowledge region. Tacit knowledge embedded in a city is also critical. The most successful cities are those able to combine the structural or spillover effects of a rich local knowledge base with international best practice.

For example, the successful development of Silicon Valley in the United States was based on a knowledge network that encompassed both regional learning institutions (i.e., the universities of northern California) and for-profit industry research teams. Innovations produced in the knowledge network were adopted and developed economically by proximate industries operating in an environment of flexible development. Silicon Valley has inspired knowledge-based urban development around the world. Since the 1970s, the establishment of technology parks and precincts in both developed and developing countries has become widespread.

Technology park, knowledge park, research park, business park, industrial park, and innovation park are descriptors that have been used interchangeably to refer to knowledge clusters—the high-growth technology industry. The term technology park distinguishes the functional activity in an area and refers to an area where agglomeration of knowledge and technological activities has positive externalities for individual firms located there.

Technology parks are generally established with two primary objectives in mind. The first objective is to be a seed bed and an enclave for knowledge and technology and to play an incubator role nurturing the development and growth of new small high-technology firms, facilitating the transfer of university know-how to tenant companies, encouraging faculty-based spin-offs, and stimulating innovative products and processes. The second objective is to act as a catalyst for regional economic development, which promotes economic growth and contributes to the development of a knowledge city.

While there are many different models of technology parks, a technology park generally provides both support and an environment of technology transfer that nurtures the start-up, incubation, and development of innovation-led, high-growth, knowledge-based businesses. Although technology parks strive to focus research and development

(R&D) and innovation in their area, the types of R&D and the sectors they focus can vary widely. Overall, by attracting new firms, technology parks can create substantial agglomerative effects for the regional economy.

Despite their differences, contemporary technology-park initiatives have the following aspects in common. They have knowledge and technology-based enterprises (e.g., Nokia in Helsinki Digital Village), knowledge workers, and R&D and educational institutions; provide living facilities that promote creativity, cater to emerging lifestyle choices, and celebrate the experience of place; and are guided and managed by partnerships between governments, real estate developers, educational or research institutions, and information and new media companies.

Strategies for Building Successful Knowledge Cities

Attempts to transform cities into knowledge cities will likely fail if they are not guided by sound strategic visions. These strategic visions should incorporate policies for attracting and retaining knowledge workers and industries and also for empowering citizens as knowledge creators and innovators. The top-tier knowledge cities specialize in a few sectors only and set ambitious goals for each; they develop their knowledge-based policies carefully.

The common strategies include political and societal will; strategic vision and development plans; financial support and strong investments; agencies to promote knowledge-based urban development; an international, multicultural character of the city; metropolitan Web portals; value creation for citizens; creation of urban innovative engines; assurance of knowledge society rights; low-cost access to advanced communication networks; research excellence; and robust public library networks.

Implementation of the above-mentioned strategies and policies requires a broad intellectual team with expertise in urban development, urban studies and planning, socioeconomic development, models of intellectual capital, and knowledge management. It also requires understanding of the diverse spatial forms of the knowledge city, where a large number of knowledge clusters are particularly

important in promoting the spillover effects vital for long-term economic prosperity.

Tan Yigitcanlar

See also Castells, Manuel; Creative Class; Cyburbia; Technopoles; Urban Planning

Further Readings

Carrillo, F., ed. 2006. *Knowledge Cities: Approaches, Experiences, and Perspectives.* Oxford, UK: Butterworth-Heinemann.

Corey, K. and M. Wilson. 2006. *Urban and Regional Technology Planning: Planning Practice in the Global Knowledge Economy.* New York: Routledge.

Florida, R. 2004. *Cities and the Creative Class.* New York: Routledge.

ISoCaRP. 2005. *Making Spaces for the Creative Economy.* Madrid: Author.

Landry, C. 2006. *The Art of City Making.* London: Earthscan.

Yigitcanlar, T., K. Velibeyoglu, and S. Baum, eds. 2007. *Knowledge-based Urban Development: Planning and Applications in the Information Era.* New York: Idea.

INTELLECTUALS

There has been much heated debate among journalists, academics, and others recently on the question of who is an intellectual and whether there has been a decline in intellectual life. The trend now is toward a less prescriptive definition than the one previously accepted. The label *intellectual* now tends to be applied to individuals who employ their mind to learn, understand, think abstractly, or apply knowledge rather than allowing their emotions to dominate behavior, although modern psychology recognizes a more complex interrelationship between emotions and intellect, for instance, with respect to creativity. Those labeled as intellectuals are not necessarily associated with any particular field of endeavor, but they usually make some effort to communicate ideas to an audience either verbally, in writing, or artistically. Although there is no hard and fast division between intellectual and artistic life, intellectuals have usually been regarded as a separate group from artists.

The concept of intellectuals, therefore, usually includes philosophers and writers inspired by the archetypal model of the classical philosopher exemplified by the life and especially the death of Socrates. The inclusion of scientists, academics, and professionals is regarded as more problematic. It is important to note that although the term intellectual is used for convenience here, it was not employed as a noun until the late nineteenth century, by which time the concept of intellectuals as omnivorous polymaths was being seriously challenged by the specialization, institutionalization, and commensurate fragmentation of scholarly endeavor.

In the eighteenth and nineteenth centuries, designations such as man of letters, *philosophe*, philosopher, savant, and scholar were used to denote some of the characteristics we now associate with the noun *intellectual*. Intellectuals are sometimes combined together as a social class or grouping known as intelligentsia and held to comprise professionals such as teachers, artists, and academics, especially in France, Russia, and Central and Eastern Europe, where they have played a public role as political commentators. However, the concept of intelligentsia and the label intellectual are regarded much less favorably in Britain, the United States, and the English-speaking world, especially by right-wing commentators.

In the present context, we are primarily interested in public intellectuals as a social group rather than lone private figures as, in this form, intellectuals have had the greatest impact on urban society and urban studies. At least since the Enlightenment, intellectuals and intellectual communities have become primarily regarded as an urban-centered phenomenon, although this has not precluded, of course, residence in—nor inspiration from—the countryside. In fact it is ironic that many intellectuals, including William Wordsworth, Mathew Arnold, and John Ruskin, while making considerable use of urban networks, audiences, and experiences, made strong criticisms of modern urban society. In the rich and dense cultural interstices of urban-centered living, intellectuals have had a major impact in the modern world.

Some modern commentators have argued variously that there has been a decline in the quality of intellectual life, the number of intellectuals, or the opportunities for intellectuals to thrive in modern institutions such as universities. Developments in information technology have, to some extent, severed the link between intellectuals and urbanity, and it is now possible for remote or roving thinkers to remain part of a virtual global intellectual community with the aid of the World Wide Web. It has been argued that government institutions and other bodies can intervene to nurture the development of intellectual or creative communities in urban areas to further economic regeneration. This has encouraged renewed analysis of the cultural geography and urban contexts in which intellectual communities have thrived in the past. This entry begins with a look at history, then examines current issues.

The Enlightenment Intellectual

Although a period of striking modernity, the Enlightenment was steeped in reverence for antiquity, and the principal model for the intellectual in society was the classical philosopher. The Enlightenment has traditionally been associated with French philosophes and autocratic rulers, but recent work has tended to emphasize the differences between Enlightenment cultures. Although some intellectuals such as Jean-Jacques Rousseau remained suspicious of urban living, the city was idealized in the Enlightenment as a polite, refined, cultural, and intellectual center that embodied rationality in its ordered neoclassical buildings, squares, circuses, public walks, and piazzas, where a lively public intellectual culture thrived.

Enlightenment citizens were idealized for their urbanity, civic humanism, and rationality, whereas the intellectual was idealized as a trenchant, independent-minded, public—usually male—philosopher such as Francois Voltaire, Rousseau, David Hume, Benjamin Franklin, Erasmus Darwin, and Johann Wolfgang von Goethe. Enlightenment ideas were generated and experienced in a variety of public and semipublic places including coffeehouses, public houses, salons, Masonic lodges, theaters, clubs, and knowledge-based societies as part of a broad urban civility that offered opportunities for women as well as men.

In England, for example, the Royal Society tended to be superseded by metropolitan coffeehouse clubs and provincial intellectual associations such as the Lunar Society of Birmingham,

Manchester Literary and Philosophical Society, and the Derby Philosophical Society. In France, the academies that came to dominate provincial organized intellectual life such as those at Bourdeaux, Lyon, and Toulouse, were closer to states and monarchies than their British counterparts. Likewise in the German states, the Berlin Academy fostered by Frederick II (the Great) was intended to rival Italian, French, and British institutions and nurtured the international scientific careers of philosophers such as Leonard Euler and Pierre Louis Maupertuis.

The broad concerns of all these European philosophical associations reflected the Enlightenment ideal of interdependent fields of intellectual endeavor and practical activity from meteorology, electricity, and botany to medicine, architecture, and antiquities.

Nineteenth- and Twentieth-Century Intellectuals

The importance of intellectuals in modern urban industrial and industrializing society is demonstrated by their diverse role in public aesthetic culture and political activity. Major urban centers produced intellectual cultures with their own distinctive characteristics, and there is a complex cultural geography of urban savant culture over the nineteenth and twentieth centuries. As during the Enlightenment, this intellectual life was often centered on formal or public institutions, but webs of informal social networks and semiprivate associations were often equally important.

In postwar Parisian cafés such as Les Deux Magots and the Café de Flore, for instance, during the 1950s and 1960s, existentialists and poststructuralists such as Jean-Paul Sartre and Simone de Beauvoir held court for their philosophical and political discussions. Urban intellectual culture frequently thrived in centers of mixed populations or international entrepots, reflecting the characteristics of immigrants and established cultures. While the intellectual culture of *fin-de-siecle* Vienna, for instance, reflected general contemporary European cultural concerns, its special qualities stemmed from the importance of Jewish culture, the decline of liberalism, and the flight toward late-Romantic escapism variously embodied in different mediums in the works of Gustav Mahler, Sigmund Freud,

Ludwig Wittgenstein, Arthur Schnitzler, and Hugo von Hofmannstahl.

Similarly, New York was the polycentric gateway between the old and new worlds, and this was reflected in the distinctive intellectual life of a complicated and contentious city where diverse European ideas and cultural ideals combined with developing U.S. culture to create rich cultural complexity. In the milieu of 1920s and 1930s New York, for instance, Edmund Wilson strove to embrace European Marxism and modernism, demonstrating how the Europeanization of American intellectual life was encouraged by the city's growing international political and cultural status.

The importance of intellectual interventions in political campaigns is evident throughout the nineteenth century from the French Revolution (actually eighteenth century) to the Paris commune of 1871 and the St. Petersburg uprising of 1905. These interventions are most evident where intellectuals act together as an intelligentsia consisting of teachers, academics, artists, writers, and other educated or self-taught individuals, forming powerful groups that had a major impact on political developments. Although some, of course, sided with aristocratic elites, many social thinkers, as Karl Marx and Friedrich Engels hoped, formed centers of opposition to aristocratic, monarchical, and reactionary regimes, especially in the Austro-Hungarian, Turkish, and Romanov empires of Central and Eastern Europe. Working-class intellectual movements also emerged strongly in the period, and there was resistance to the patronizing and debased anti-intellectualism propagated by many communist agitators as the strength of the British "autodidact" or self-taught working-class intellectual movement demonstrates.

Urban intelligentsia played a less important role in the Chinese revolution because of the continued domination of agriculture and the slower pace of industrialization and urbanization. It was not until the decades up to 1949 that a recognizable modern urban intelligentsia appeared in China, for example, the new breed of educated professionals in Shanghai who led organizational and ideological challenges to imperial, postimperial, and nationalistic governments. The relative weakness of this Chinese intelligentsia and changes in the communist state have meant that direct political challenges to government and party have been muted, and change has occurred through economic realities rather than intellectual endeavor.

Are Intellectuals on the Decline?

Some influential commentators in the United States, Britain, and elsewhere have argued that there has been a decline in intellectual life evidenced by the debased figure of the public intellectual and demise of the humanist ideal in higher education. Fears have been expressed that intellectuals, entrepreneurs, artists, and innovators are fleeing Western cities in the context of a modern global economy driven by intolerance, poor education, inequality, ineffectual government, and the allure of expanding developing economies. Of course, such arguments depend on the definition of intellectual adopted, and fears of intellectual decline have been expressed in various societies for centuries. It is argued that many public intellectuals are merely media commentators passing opinions on cultural and lifestyle issues beyond their original areas of expertise rather than making direct political interventions.

Knowledge-based institutions such as universities, especially in Europe, are now frequently viewed as tools of government economic intervention and motors for economic and social regeneration rather than autonomous bastions of learning, critical thought, and innovation. Despite the rapid expansion that has taken place in higher education, it is contended that there has been a decline in the quality of intellectual life and the educational experience offered in modern universities. This is due to excessive politically motivated and often contradictory governmental interference resulting in the erosion of academic autonomy, in student debt, and in the decline of the humanist ideal. Hence, although large quantities of academic work are being produced and universities are now frequently one of the largest provincial urban employers, a managerial instrumentalist and utilitarian ethos now dominates, enshrined in targets and public–private partnerships.

Can Intellectual Communities Be Revived or Created?

Governments have sought to revitalize and transform urban centers for political and economic reasons by implementing measures intended to foster the development of intellectual communities. Some support for this has come from considerable empirical work undertaken by economic geographers and others investigating concepts of the knowledge economy, learning regions, and the role of universities in fostering developmental strategies. Attempts have been made to replicate a formula or set of conditions under which urban intellectuals will thrive and help to inject vitality into local economies.

Interventions have taken various forms in different countries but have usually involved institutional subsidies or tax incentive schemes, partnerships between national and local government, local businesses, universities, and community groups. These attempts presuppose, to some extent, an interrelationship between the arts and sciences, and thriving artistic and intellectual communities have often been associated with economic success although, as studies of the knowledge economy and learning regions has shown, such a relationship is by no means certain. Societies experiencing economic or political decline have experienced an artistic renaissance.

The productiveness and originality of intellectuals and creative individuals is partly the result of their self-perception and status as a socially distinctive or marginal group with alternative values defined against dominant or majority culture. Hence, intellectual or artistic originality has often been associated with social distinctiveness or marginality as defined in terms of gender, religion, race, sexuality, or other characteristics. The homosexuality of Gertrude Stein, Alan Turing, Oscar Wilde, and Peter Tchaikovsky, for instance, is often regarded as a major factor in their creativity, casting them as partial outsiders struggling for identity and admittance. Similarly, when Chicago sociologists such as Robert Park and Everett Stonequist analyzed the strategies employed by immigrants such as Jews to preserve something of their individual culture, they found that integration into U.S. urban society was achieved through attaining excellence in special fields of endeavor.

Recent work on the knowledge economy, learning regions, the rise of a creative class, and patterns of economic growth provides some support for the idea that modern intellectuals are able to take advantage of the special qualities of modern urban living and that modern Western industrial economies depend for their success on creative originality. Intellectuals such as scientists, artists, entrepreneurs, and venture capitalists lead a bohemian lifestyle, deriving their identity from creativity. This has replaced the organizational and instrumental ethos that prevailed until the 1930s. Intellectuals are regionally differentiated; can be correlated with groups of bohemians, homosexuals, and other relatively distinctive categories; and while being regionally differentiated, in some estimates comprise 30 percent of the U.S. workforce.

Larger urban locations provide the necessary quasi-anonymity, sociability, and weaker social ties for stimulation and creative interplay and for the forging of original identities and the reinvention of the self. Intellectual groups capitalize on the irrational aspects of creativity, acting outside the norms of the wider society and following a distinctive lifestyle that includes ignoring normal working hours, dressing uniquely, and holding distinctive moral and aesthetic values.

Attempts have been made to replicate Silicon Valley in the context of the modern knowledge economy. At Wellington, New Zealand, for example, the growth of the film industry has attracted many innovators, lured by the city's technological infrastructure, the relatively low cost of labor and resources, and the quality of lifestyle. Other attempts have been made to replicate Silicon Valley by encouraging new economic spaces in other U.S. centers, such as Philadelphia and Atlanta, and also in Japan, parts of Germany, and some British towns such as Cambridge (called "Silicon Fen"). It is therefore possible that governments and local urban communities can meet the challenges of globalization by fostering the development of cities of knowledge, although the continued success of Silicon Valley has been the result of a complex nexus of factors difficult to replicate elsewhere.

The impersonal, irrational, quirky, contingent, and creative aspects of urban living encourage the interplay between arts and sciences on which creativity is founded. Sites of rationality cannot be neatly separated from sites of irrationality, with deliberate irrationality and emotionally founded distinctiveness being, in fact, often at the heart of intellectual originality. Urban centers can serve as forums for intellectuals where new ideas, behaviors, and identities are forged. Scientific, technological, and artistic creativity are intermixed, influencing each other through changing fads and fashions, which are also most rapid and transient in the relatively impersonal nexus of the urban melting pot. Far from trying to re-create the vast postwar technological military urban complexes of the cold war, this suggests we should be looking more to relatively informal coffeehouses, taverns, and clubs of the Enlightenment as the models for cities of knowledge.

Paul Elliott

See also Bohemian; Creative Class; Mumford, Lewis

Further Readings

Bender, T. 1987. *New York Intellect.* Baltimore: Johns Hopkins University Press.

Bourdieu, P. 1989. "The Corporatism of the Universal: The Role of Intellectuals in the Modern World. *Telos* 81:99–110.

Collini, S. 2006. *Absent Minds.* Oxford, UK: Oxford University Press.

Florida, R. 2002. *The Rise of the Creative Class.* New York: Basic Books.

Furedi, F. 2004. *Where Have All the Intellectuals Gone?* London: Continuum.

Harding, A., A. Scott, S. Laske, and C. Burtscher, eds. 2007. *Bright Satanic Mills: Universities, Regional Development, and the Knowledge Economy.* Burlington, VT; Aldershot, UK: Ashgate.

Melzer, A. M., J. Weinberger, and M. R. Zinman, eds. 2004. *The Public Intellectual: Between Philosophy and Politics.* Lanham, MD: Rowman & Littlefield.

Michael, J. 2003. *Anxious Intellects: Academic Professionals, Public Intellectuals, and Enlightenment Values.* Durham, NC: Duke University Press.

O'Mara, M. P. 2004. *Cities of Knowledge.* Princeton, NJ: Princeton University Press.

Posner, R. 2001. *Public Intellectuals: A Study of Decline.* Cambridge, MA: Harvard University Press.

Rose, J. 2001. *The Intellectual Life of the British Working Classes.* New Haven, CT: Yale University Press.

ISARD, WALTER

The founder of the field of regional science and its most prominent scholar in industrial location theory and methods of regional analysis, Walter Isard (1919–) established an interdisciplinary movement of regional and urban research in North America, Europe, and Asia. Through his determined leadership and insistent persuasion, Isard encouraged economists, geographers, sociologists, and urban, regional, and transportation planners to construct theories of urban and regional phenomena and to apply methods of analysis to the emerging policy issues of the middle and late twentieth century.

Isard's research contributions, while large and diverse, tend toward imaginative syntheses of current and earlier research, as contrasted with wholly new theory and methods. His interests in the location of regional and urban activities, formed during his graduate studies, led to his first major book, *Location and Space-Economy* (1956), which drew on the location theories expounded earlier by German economists and geographers. Next, he initiated research on the economic and social consequences of atomic power and industrial complexes and intensified his research on methods of regional and urban analysis, including population and migration projection methods, regional economic and social accounts, industrial location and complex analysis, interregional and regional interindustry models, interregional linear programming, and gravity, potential, and spatial interaction models. This comprehensive exposition appeared as his second, jointly authored major book, *Methods of Regional Analysis* (1960), later thoroughly updated as *Methods of Interregional and Regional Analysis* (1998). Isard's unique contribution to these two works were the chapters on "channels of synthesis," which demonstrated diagrammatically how the diverse methods of analysis described previously could be applied in a systematic, integrated manner.

During the 1960s, Isard turned to more theoretical pursuits related to individual behavior and decision making, as well as general equilibrium theory for a system of regions, presented in his third, jointly authored major book, *General Theory* (1969). Concurrently, he and his students undertook ecologic–economic-oriented studies as well as a major interindustry analysis of the Philadelphia region. Later, he coauthored a book on the theory of spatial dynamics and optimal space–time development.

Isard was born in 1919 in Philadelphia to immigrant parents. By 1939, he graduated with distinction from Temple University and entered Harvard University as a graduate student in its Economics Department. There, he developed a research interest in building construction, transportation development, the location of economic activities, and the cycles of growth and stagnation that characterized the 1920 to 1940 period. From 1941 to 1942, he studied economics at the University of Chicago, where his interest in mathematics was rekindled. As a Social Science Research Council predoctoral fellow, from 1942 to 1943, he was affiliated with the National Planning Resources Board. There, he completed his doctoral dissertation. Subsequently, he served in the Civilian Public Service as a conscientious objector; during the night hours at the state mental hospital where he was assigned, he translated into English the works of the German location theorists, including the works of August Lösch, Andreas Predöhl, and others.

During the postwar years as a Social Science Research Council postdoctoral fellow, 1946 to 1948, Isard accelerated his studies of industrial location theory and later joined W. W. Leontief's interindustry research project at Harvard. Simultaneously, he honed his teaching skills at various part-time appointments, offering the first course on location theory and regional development ever taught at Harvard's Economics Department. In 1948, at the age of 29, Isard initiated meetings of leading economists, geographers, sociologists, and demographers on interdisciplinary regional research. These efforts found a welcoming audience among participants of annual disciplinary conferences and continued intensively throughout the next six years. In December 1954 at the meetings of the allied social science associations in Detroit, he organized a conference program of 25 papers; at the business meeting, 60 scholars endorsed the idea of forming a separate association named the Regional Science Association (RSA).

Having launched the field of regional science, Isard served as associate professor of regional economics and director of the Section of Urban and Regional Studies at M.I.T. In 1956, he accepted a professorship in the Economics Department of the University of Pennsylvania and formed a graduate group in regional science. Two years later, he founded the Regional Science Department and the *Journal of*

Regional Science. In 1960, the first PhD in Regional Science was awarded to William Alonso for his seminal study of urban location and land use.

Isard then expanded his horizons to Europe and Asia. In 1960, he visited many research centers in Europe where he organized sections of the RSA. The first European Congress was held in 1961. Sections of the RSA were subsequently established in many countries throughout Europe and Asia as well as North America. During the mid-1960s, regional science summer institutes were held at the University of California at Berkeley, and, in 1970, the first European Summer Institute took place in Karlsruhe, Germany. Subsequently, summer institutes were held in Europe every two years. International conferences are now held every year in North America and Europe and every second year in the Pacific region. In 1989, the Regional Science Association was reorganized and its name modified to the Regional Science Association International (http://www.regionalscience.org).

In 1978, the RSA established its founder's medal in honor of Walter Isard. The following year, Isard moved to Cornell University as professor of economics, and six years later, he was elected to the National Academy of Sciences. He continued to teach until his recent retirement from active research. Over the decades, Isard received six honorary degrees, as follows: Poznan Academy of Economics, Poland (1976); Erasmus University of Rotterdam, the Netherlands (1978); the University of Karlsruhe, Germany (1979); Umeå University, Sweden (1980); the University of Illinois at Urbana-Champaign (1982); and Binghamton University (1997).

Throughout his career, Isard also pursued policy interests related to conflict management and resolution, disarmament, and peace science. He founded the Peace Research Society, later renamed the Peace Science Society, and the graduate group in peace science at the University of Pennsylvania. Several of his books, which number more than 20, as well as many of his 300 published papers, concern topics in peace science.

Isard's accomplishments are more related to interregional constructs and relationships than intraurban ones. The general focus concerns systems of cities and regions; even so, some of his thinking pertains to interactions among urban communities and neighborhoods. In fostering and developing the RSA and various journals on regional science, he welcomed contributions at any scale of region: neighborhood, city, economic region, country, and the world. His orientation was generally theoretical and methodological. Policy issues, such as regional development and environmental management, seemed to interest him more for their modeling challenges than their policy content.

David Boyce

See also Location Theory; Regional Planning; Transportation

Further Readings

Boyce, D. 2004. "A Short History of the Field of Regional Science." *Papers in Regional Science* 83:31–57.

Isard, W. 1956. *Location and Space-Economy, A General Theory Relating to Industrial Location, Market Areas, Land Use, Trade, and Urban Structure.* New York: The Technology Press of Massachusetts Institute of Technology and John Wiley.

———. 2003. *History of Regional Science and the Regional Science Association International: The Beginnings and Early History.* Berlin: Springer.

Isard, W., I. J. Azis, M. P. Drennan, R. E. Miller, S. Saltzman, and E. Thorbecke. 1998. *Methods of Interregional and Regional Analysis.* Brookfield, VT: Ashgate.

Isard, W., in association with D. F. Bramhall, G. A. P. Carrothers, J. H. Cumberland, L. N. Moses, D. O. Price, and E. W. Schooler. 1960. *Methods of Regional Analysis: An Introduction to Regional Science.* New York: The Technology Press of Massachusetts Institute of Technology and John Wiley.

Isard, W., in association with T. E. Smith, P. Isard, T. H. Tung, and M. Dacey. 1969. *General Theory: Social, Political, Economic, and Regional: with Particular Reference to Decision-making Analysis.* Cambridge: MIT Press.

ISLAMIC CITY

The term *madinah* by and large refers to the primordial Islamic city—the city of the Prophet Muhammad, established circa AD 622 to 632. Abu Nasr al-Farabi's (ca. 870–950) famous work, *The Virtuous City,* takes inspiration from the constitution of the city of the Prophet, al-Farabi notes that the linguistic term *madinah* denotes legal, ethical, social, political, and religious knowledge, transforming and transcending the contributions of mere human experience. The suggestion here is that the term *madinah* also embraces the idea of authority, submission, obedience, conformity, and consensus—the nature of the Islamic City.

Because the madinah also represents the cumulative experience of successive generations of urban dwellers, it offered a solid foundation for Ibn Khaldun (ca. 1332–1406) to reflect critically and to rethink the relationship between the interdependent conditions of urban existence. Writing on the subject of urbanism, Ibn Khaldun notes that *umran* (culture, habitat, milieu) is "the cumulative social heritage of a group [of people] as objectified in institutions and conventionalized activities in a particular time and place." In an attempt to provide an acute analysis of urban spaces in the Islamic city, the issue in contention here is twofold: (1), understanding how the representation of law (*shari'a*), order, and habitat are embodied in the appearance and fabric of the madinah; (2) in relation to hermeneutics, understanding how the topography of the Islamic city is linked as a text for reading various scales of space and the cultural landscape (*kulturlandschaft*) in relationship to urbanism.

This argument is particularly apt to the madinah of the Maghrib (North Africa) for three specific reasons: (1) knowledge of the mapping out of the city came with the first wave of Arab conquerors in the seventh century AD; (2) the establishment of the Maliki *madhhab* (school of law) in the Maghrib, ninth century AD, which led to the infusion of ideas and inhabitants from the Citadel of Faith; (3) as a result of the *reconquesta*, a fresh wave of émigrés (mostly Jews and Muslims) were forced to immigrate to the cities of the Maghrib in diaspora from Spain (*al-Andalus*) in the fourteenth and fifteenth centuries AD. The reconquesta altered the urban demographics of the madinah immensely, and it also influenced land use and the complexities of urbanism.

The Islamic City as a Legal Concept

The study of urbanism as it relates to the study of law is a relatively new concept. Karl Llewellyn's 1940 essay, *On the Good, the True, and the Beautiful in Law*, formulated a critique on the affinity between law and habitat in view of the fact that the city embodies a particular sense of urbanism, and building ordinances are a means of sustaining particular modes of dwelling. Undoubtedly, much has been written about the urban features of cities in the Muslim world up to the present day. Mohammed Arkun's essay "Islam, Urbanism, and Human Existence Today," highlights a number of lingering misconceptions about Islamic law as it relates to the fabric of the madinah. Arkun argues that the correspondence between law, the relative dimensions of habitat, the spatial equilibrium of the madinah, and the setting out of theoretical principles has guided the Islamic city up to the present day. Historical texts, which depict Muslim cities in North Africa, offer very similar interpretations about law and habitat, especially the treatment of public and private space.

Islamic Law (*shari'a*) has substantive meaning for the study of urbanism in the madinah or the premodern Islamic city, with reference to the efficacy of building ordinances (*ahkam al-bunyan*). The shari'a is a commonly accepted means of adjudication in habitat disputes; it is therefore a reasonable criterion for the ordering of habitat, which forms the corpus of building ordinances. Like zoning conventions, the ahkam al-bunyan allows action but also limits illegal actions. Because the principles and praxis of the shari'a is a normative practice for settling habitat conflicts, one of the goals of ahkam al-bunyan is to address spatial equilibrium. Above all, the difficulties of excluding the shari'a from the study of the madinah has been intensely debated. The problem includes two opposite worldviews, which imply antithetical models of habitat: One personified a landscape under Muslim law, the other personified a radically different concept of space whose roots predate the rise of Islam but that is clearly transformed by Muslim political rule. In all likelihood, the contrasting modulation of shari'a land-use ordinances contains more features than many historians would care to record or mention; furthermore, linguistic and historical evidence indicates the professional role of the jurist-consult, the specialist known as the *mufti*. It also implies a surprisingly sophisticated cadre of legal scholars, who could settle any environmental problem that confronted them. Clearly, by the fifteenth century AD, Maliki law was highly developed and enjoying much success among the urban population as well as in local towns and villages in the North Africa.

Speaking mostly about cities in North Africa, Brunschvig's 1947 "Urbanisme medieval et droit musulman" notes how Maliki law was applied in cases relating to roads, walls, rebuilding, and problems relating to water, neighborly relations, and the location of business like tanneries, forges, stables, the origination or the abolition of easements, and legal procedures in general. In his view, the defining element of the Islamic city is a typology with its own identity based on legal traditions, intimately associated with the shari'a. Apart from being sympathetic to Brunschvig's argument, Titus Burckhardt also refers to urban rules and building ordinances, which emerge from the tradition (*sunnah*) of the Prophet and customary law (*urf*).

This explains why the shari'a is needed to adjudicate disputes in building proximity, spatial organization, and the configuration of a dwelling, to safeguard the rights of people, and to prevent harm or reciprocal harm. Legal judgment applies to these situations, and it may well affect the way we critique the habitat conditions in the madinah. The madinah remains important, given the constantly shifting patterns and the construing of the word of law; the concept involves a considerable number of mental images that exist only in authority/power representations. The concept of the madinah informs our understanding of the underlying structure of urbanism. Finally, it enables us to refer to the pattern of language by the precise semantic properties.

Also useful for comparison is Ibn Khaldun, the fifteenth-century North African scholar, statesman, historian, and jurist, who provided a number of descriptive markers that characterize the Muslim city. In the *Muqaddimah: An Introduction to History*, Ibn Khaldun examined

several theoretical and practical concepts of the Muslim city. The text of the *Muqaddimah* is extraordinary for the way in which Ibn Khaldun modulates the interpretation of history and the dichotomies of urban life. A number of literary images emerge in juxtaposition: exegesis, economics, ethnicity, law, demography, and air and water pollution.

Because the image of the madinah is problematic, the meaning made possible by a hermeneutic reading lay emphasis on the ethos of the madinah accounting for the operative shari'a system. Furthermore, there remains an excess of physical evidence available for research, for that reason, historiography remains an open debate. The Muslim world includes a wide assortment of

Islamic city Tunisia, cobblestone street 1860–1900

Source: Copyright © Library of Congress.

Muslim cities. However, the existence of legal rulings and judgments in Maliki law can ultimately be traced to the exegesis of the sacred text, the Qur'an.

The Topos of the Islamic City

In summary, the topos of the Islamic city consists of a two primary tropes: a strong sense of affection (*topophilia*) for a place and a sense of aversion (*topophobia*). As a mode of dwelling, *topophilia* means that competing disputes can be resolved through mutual regard for one another in order to maintain mutual affection. *Topophilia* also means a social homogeneity, as evidenced in the topography of a landscape, is both figurative and communicative. The house is a private retreat or a mode of private dwelling; public gathering exists in the city in the congregational mosque. Bringing together public gathering and private dwelling, the madinah embodies a habitat, a physical expression, and the physical nature of a place and context. Although the character of the ground of a habitat varies, its space is what enables it to play its role in uniting a community of human beings, and the order of the space gives them identity and fellowship, hence the basis for a city.

The madinah Fes evolved in the ninth century AD as a magnificent example of urbanism and social hierarchy. The topos of Fes is a matrix of linear spaces immediately accessible (streets) and spaces conceived out of an empty central area (mosque courtyard, house, dwelling), both determining the laws of juxtaposition and organization. The courtyards are designed to isolate, to ensure the intimacy of the inside as opposed to the outside. These types of enclosures are antonymic, meaning the enclosure presents an opposition in its function to the order that brought it about in the first place. The opposition is materialized through the juxtaposition of inside as opposed to the outside defined by blind perimeter walls.

Apart from being a place of human habitation, the topos embodies political authority, religious knowledge, and collective memory. It is therefore possible to speak of the madinah in terms of the idiom power/knowledge. The well-known maxim, *I am the city of knowledge (Ana madinat al-Ilm)*, embodies topography, landscape, and meaning. Fes is a luminous example of collective memory, which

is associated with a pious primogenitor, Idris II, who is entombed within the precincts of the city.

We are told that when the city was fully inhabited, Idrıs II ascended the *minbar* and addressed the people of the city. He prayed for their sanctity, their prosperity, and the protection of the city. The collective influences of natural springs that provide fresh water to the inhabitants of Fes have a pervasive effect on the site. In the collective memory, it is impossible to ignore the power of Idris's words: He speaks with the language of incarnation, *verba concepta*. Idrıs II repeats the archetypal *du'a* (heavenly supplication) of Abraham for Makkah, the Prophet's du'a at the time of entering Madinah, and Uqba's du'a at the time of the founding of Qayrawan. Idrıs II also prayed for knowledge and sacred law. In the city of Fes, two significant monuments are associated with knowledge and sacred law: the Qarawiyyin (university) mosque and the sepulcher mosque of Idris II.

Many historians tell us that the city of Qayrawan was founded by Uqba b. Nafi's, and he sanctified the site with a du'a. Uqba's charisma is evident from the site of the mosque, which bears his eponym. It explains the importance of the city as a place embodied with ritual prayer, knowledge, and the enactment of sacred law.

Several conclusions can be drawn from the foregoing remarks. First, the Islamic city is a landscape immersed in knowledge and power. Second, the topos bears a relationship between language and landscape. It is possible that the extravagant claims associated with various indigenous narratives attached to the mapping out of settlements in the Islamic cities in North Africa may have encouraged some historians to ignore these claims and to adhere strictly to a list of chronological events. But extant physical evidence points to the narrative, inasmuch as it is a proviso that is naturally suggested by time and place. Habitat narratives are connected with custom and vernacular traditions, which are a source of collective memory and therefore cannot be easily ignored. The choice of a site and how that site is visually composed or how the building process becomes part of a shared human experience are among the reasons why the urbanism of the city has accepted a particular type of building activity or how a peculiar settlement pattern has evolved.

The madinah, it would seem, is well understood; scholars in history, cultural anthropology, architecture, urbanism, and geography have been devoted to the study of the features of the Islamic city. Cognizant of the fact that social, religious, and cultural traditions associated with urbanism or *umran* are often misunderstood, we reiterate that the meaning and use of domestic and public space and property ownership posit a wide spatiotemporal experience. The Islamic city stands in striking contrast to the polis or the Platonic city as in Plato's *Republic,* St. Augustine's *The City of God (De Civitate Dei)*, or More's *Utopia.*

In sum, three distinct accounts bid to explain the notion of the Islamic city. These are mentioned by Ibn Khaldūn, who used the terms, private ownership (*mulk*), tribal kinship, and solidarity (*asabiyah*). When Ibn Khaldūn says, "man is *madani* by nature," he is suggesting that his lifestyle depends on an urban culture and organization. This sheds light on the idea conceived by al-Farabi as well; authority, submission, obedience, conformity, and consensus govern the internal workings of the Islamic city, where spatial transparency can be achieved only by tacit agreement. This usage is legitimate because it presupposes a true social contract and implies that coercion does not exist where virtue is paramount. Al-Farabi's virtuous city is governed by the shari'a of the Qur'an, which exercises control over human behavior and serves as an apparatus to allow the society to exercise its freedom.

It should be noted that the notion of a collective social environment refers to the idea of culture as it is used in modern sociology and anthropology. Culture in this sense has an overriding influence on people's views and the things that people do on a daily basis, or whether the immediate community matters to society at large. Finally, as an idea, the term *madinah* relates to an ordered landscape as a semiotic space of dwelling, a discursive model, and legal practice. In other words, the Islamic city is not a grammar of objects or perceptions, which do not add up; it also characterizes an epistemic configuration of habitat in terms of Muslim conventions of political and religious authority.

Akel Ismail Kahera

See also Cairo, Egypt; *Caravanserai;* Damascus, Syria

Further Readings

Abu-Lughod, Janet. 1987. "The Islamic City—Historic Myth, Islamic Essence, and Contemporary Relevance." *International Journal of Middle East Studies* 19:155–76.

Al-Farabi. 1985. *On the Perfect State: Mabadi ara ahl al-Madinah al-Fadila.* Translated by Richard Walzer. Oxford, UK: Clarendon Press.

Arkun, Mohammed. 1983. "Islam, Urbanism, and Human Existence Today." P. 39 in *Architecture and Community Building in the Islamic World Today,* edited by Renata Hold and Darl Rastorfer. New York: Aperture.

Brunschvig, R. 1947. "Urbanisme medieval et droit musulman." *Revue des Etudes Islamiques* 15:127–55.

Burckhardt, Titus. 1980. "Fez." Pp. 166–76 in *The Islamic City,* edited by R. B. Serjeant. Paris: UNESCO.

Ibn Khaldun, 1967. *The Muqaddimah: An Introduction to History.* Translated by Franz Rosenthal. Princeton, NJ: Princeton University Press.

Kojiro, N. 1989. "Ibn Khaldun's Image of City." In *Proceedings of the International Conference on Urbanism in Islam,* edited by Y. Takeshi. Tokyo: The Middle Eastern Culture Center—University of Tokyo.

Madhi, M. 1964. *Ibn Khaldun's Philosophy of History.* Chicago: University of Chicago Press.

Masashi Haneda and Toru Miura, eds. 1994. *Islamic Urban Studies.* London: Kegan Paul.

ISTANBUL, TURKEY

Istanbul, previously known as Byzantium and later as Constantinople, can be described as an early modern city of the period 1500 to 1800. It was comparable with other great cities of western and central Europe during that time. This account of early modern Istanbul intends to show the city's urban features that belonged to the era. For much of the period Istanbul was one the most densely populated cities in Europe. It numbered probably 60,000 inhabitants in 1477. These people had been forcibly brought to the city from different areas of the Ottoman Empire following the Ottoman conquest in 1453. There were Muslims and non-Muslims, including Greeks, Armenians, Jews, and Gypsies. By the 1600s Istanbul had more than 300,000 inhabitants. The city's economic growth and prosperity attracted the people. Many also had left their hometowns or provinces because of the civil wars in Anatolia in those years. There was a continuous flow of immigrants to Istanbul. The population reached to over half a million in the seventeenth and eighteenth centuries, and it continued to grow thereafter. The first census of 1885 recorded 875,000 individuals living in the city.

Urban Development

In the sixteenth century, the walled city of Istanbul was administratively divided into 13 districts that contained varying numbers of quarters. These districts were identified by Friday mosques, the largest mosques of the district and where Friday noon prayer was held. Friday mosques were substituted for quarter mosques over the years, and new Friday mosques were founded within the existing districts. But the number of districts remained unchanged, at least until the end of the sixteenth century. The three succeeding volumes of Istanbul *vakif* (pious endowment) registers of 1546, 1578, and 1596 show the development pattern over the 50 years. The first volume records 219 quarters and 244 mosques in the city in 1546. Each quarter had at least one mosque and some had two or more. The number of quarters rose with the number of mosques to 227 with 254 mosques in 1578, and 230 with 256 mosques in 1596.

The rise in the number of quarters occurred in two ways in this period: First was the appearance of a new quarter under the name of an existing mosque that was the second mosque of an existing quarter. Second was the development of a new quarter in association with a newly constructed mosque. In the latter, the new mosque generated the urban development in its surroundings, and this was normally experienced in less densely built-up areas. In the areas where the quarters could not expand, new buildings had to be fitted into the existing urban fabric. Some buildings had to be pulled down to make room for the new developments. And the quarters became denser.

Urban Production and Consumption

It was not easy to supply the city with a population approaching half a million. Istanbul had become a center of consumption but relied heavily on imports. The Ottoman authorities tried to impose controls on the system of supply, giving priority to the walled city over the other places.

According to the regulations, various foodstuffs shipped to the city were to be unloaded in specific quays on the shore of Tahtakale. They were taken to some authorized depots inside the walls to be taxed and priced, and then to be distributed to wholesalers, producer-retailers, or both. For instance, many foodstuffs were brought to the Balkapan Han (literally Honey-Depot Inn), where they were to be distributed to grocers. And thus, groceries were concentrated on the area. However, often dealers smuggled goods outside markets to sell them at higher prices. Probably for this purpose, many possessed storehouses and shops in this area. As a result, the shoreline area had become highly congested. In 1579, the construction of new shops in the Tahtakale area outside the wall was prohibited.

The district of Unkapani, the other end of the busy shoreline area, was authorized as the unloading point for grain. It possessed the Grain/Flour Depot on the shore outside the wall near the quay for grain. Grain sent by ship and land was to be brought to the Grain/Flour Depot to be taxed and priced before it was distributed to millers and bakers. However, it was difficult to monitor the system of grain supply throughout the early modern era. Because grain was in short supply and its price was fixed, opportunist merchants emerged who intended to make money in trading grain. They either sold it on the way or hoarded it in their storehouses along the shore outside the wall to export it at a higher price. This caused a shortage and price rise in the city. And in this case, the authorities usually issued many decrees addressed to the authorities of supplying villages and towns to send grain immediately from their reserve.

The Grain/Flour Depot, giving its name to the district, seems to have dominated the occupations of the area. For example, grain merchants took up lodgings and shops on the shore, probably not to risk missing cargoes entering the city. Inside the wall, there were many mills and baker's shops. They were conveniently located close to their suppliers. However, mills and baker's shops were also scattered in the city. They were the two important links in the process of bread making, and thus they were established accordingly. Bakers were dependent on millers for supplies of freshly ground flour, and for this reason, most of them built their own mills, which were attached to the back of their

An apartment building in current-day Istanbul.

Source: Jill Buyan.

shops. This was also what the authorities preferred to maintain. Apparently, if there was a baker's shop in the neighborhood, there was most likely a mill nearby.

It was possible in those years to follow the whole process of bread production, from the arrival of grain cargoes at the city ports to the loaves of bread on the dinner table of Ottoman households. On a more local level, residents could hear their work noises or breathe the fumes coming out of their chimneys. The neighbors were familiar with the regular sounds of the process, when the next-door bakers started the day or if they finished early or the millers' busy time at work throughout the year. However, living next to one of the flour mills, most of which were operated by horse or mule power in Istanbul, was not

always very pleasant, even in the standard of the early modern era. Sometimes the neighbors complained about the noise and smoke or any pollution caused by the activities of these establishments in the neighborhood.

However, heavy industrial occupations were generally pushed outside the city walls, away from the neighborhood life. For example, the district of Edirnekapi housed the livestock market just beyond the city gate of the area, and thus it had become the center for some dependent establishments related to the meat supply. It possessed slaughterhouses even though it also had neighborhoods inside the wall. Candle and soap makers used animal fat in their production, and thus many workshops of candle and soap makers were located in this area near their suppliers. A part of Yedikule, marking the other end of the city on the coast of the Sea of Marmara outside the wall, had developed into a suburb of the tanning industry, most probably because of the convenience of water and large open space required for the tanning process. This area also possessed slaughterhouses, and workshops of candle and soap makers.

Neighborhoods

As in other cities of the Ottoman realms, the city quarter, *mahalle,* had administrative and fiscal meanings in Istanbul. It appears in official documents under the name of their local mosque. This system had been gradually introduced after the conquest, and in the sixteenth century, it was a normal practice in Istanbul, the walled city. However, this was not widely experienced in Galata, situated on the north bank of the Golden Horn, which was inhabited mainly by non-Muslims and foreigners. Many quarters of Galata bore names of ethnoreligious groups or congregations and churches of the area.

In those years, people were also officially identified by the quarter in which they were residents. This was important because in any dispute related to administrative, fiscal, or criminal matters they could be traced by the quarter of residence. In 1578, the authorities wanted to separate one quarter from another, probably to make it more controllable. For mainly security reasons, they said, they ordered the city inhabitants to construct the quarter gates at the entrance of each main street. But this project was not feasible and had to be abandoned. Apparently, Istanbul was then overpopulated, and it was very difficult to promote public security in the city. Newcomers, particularly bachelors, were blamed. In 1579, those who were unable to show a warrant in the city were to be deported, including those who had already managed to stay for five years.

Throughout the early modern era, the city's neighborhood was also socially defined in the minds of local inhabitants. Its boundaries were drawn by the familiarity and common practices. The locals could establish neighborly contacts among themselves, shopping in the same grocery or baker's shop and socializing in the coffeehouse or public bath of the area. The neighborhood was also a source of social and economic supports. For example, the male and female members of the

neighborhood would raise funds to cover the dome of their mosque with lead or to construct a public bath or a public fountain of the area. They sometimes shared the responsibility for tax payments and helped poor or needy people.

Public Places

The main public places in the neighborhood were the mosque, public bath, and the local market, with one or two grocery, butcher's, and baker's shops, and probably the street. Here, residents of the neighborhood came together not only for prayer meetings or special sermons but also for neighborly socializing activities. There were also public drinking and eating establishments, such as *boza*-houses (alehouses) and *başhanes* (cook shops specializing in sheep's head). These public houses provided complementary venues for public socializing. Taverns (*meyhanes*), by contrast, stayed outside the neighborhood's public life because the construction of taverns within the walls was not normally permitted. And those that had been built were often ordered to be closed down by the complaints of Muslim inhabitants of the area.

The public and private socializing began to change in the city by the arrival of coffeehouses in the 1550s. The first coffeehouses were opened in the Tahtakale area, which was the center for international and local trade. By the 1600s, the number of coffeehouses grew in these commercial areas and accelerated thereafter. Their popularity probably increased by the spread of the habit of tobacco smoking in the city during these years. Some earlier coffeehouses were converted from older boza-houses, but new ones were also built. Many neighborhoods acquired these new public drinking houses. They were built near the mosque and the public bath of the neighborhood, near communal residences. They attracted both wealthy and poor inhabitants of the area except for women. Women experienced public sociability as separate from men and usually in the public bath of the neighborhood. They sometimes spent the whole day there, conversing and drinking coffee.

However, as elsewhere in the early modern world, these public drinking houses were associated with a wide range of criminal activities, from prostitution to urban violence in the city. The authorities often issued decrees ordering the wholesale closure of coffeehouses, boza-houses, and taverns. They tried to control them, especially during the politically critical years. In the neighborhood, the inhabitants also often had problems with the presence of these establishments. There are cases where the locals played an active role in the closure of coffeehouses. But people continued to build them in the city, even in the years they were banned.

Urban Houses

In sixteenth-century Istanbul, rich and poor shared the same social and physical environment. Their houses were of different sizes and standards, but they were neighbors. It was not unusual for modest houses to be built against the outer walls of a palace or highly privileged houses in the noisiest area of the neighborhood. However, the analysis of three succeeding volumes of Istanbul *vakif*-registers of 1546, 1578, and 1596 has shown that the characteristics of houses and their future development varied according to their particular locations in the city. In predominantly commercial areas, some lived in their shops or workshops. For instance, there were many bakers living in their mills or bakeries, and many grocers and gardeners lodging in their shops and working areas; almost all of them were recent immigrants who had left their families in their hometowns.

At the neighborhood center were rows of one-room apartments. These were communal residences usually built by wealthier individuals in proximity to larger establishments. They were constructed against the walls of a mosque, a public bath, or a dervish lodge or above shops. Each apartment was almost the size of a street shop. Few contained individually used reception rooms, stables, and toilets. These row-apartment buildings (known as bachelors' rooms) generally accommodated working bachelor immigrants and poorer families who probably could not afford private houses in the city. Some rows housed Jewish lodgers exclusively; these were known as Jewish rooms and later Jewish houses, *Yahudhanes*. Some bore names of the occupations of their residents, such as fishermen's rooms and jewelers' rooms. They accommodated Christian and Muslim tenants of the same occupation. Many of these rows of one-room apartments developed through the construction of new apartment units in addition to old ones over the period of time.

However, in sixteenth-century Istanbul, the majority lived in simple houses of one or two rooms. These were generally two-story dwellings incorporated into larger related structures. They had no private kitchen or bath. The residents had to share the basic facilities with the neighbors. Some used the fireplaces in a shared courtyard for cooking or water from a shared well. Few occupied large houses with several rooms, private kitchen and bath, and gardens or courtyards. And these houses usually contained reception rooms (for male visitors only), coffee rooms, rooms for only servants or staff, and some stables and storage areas.

As the city grew and new inhabitants were added to the numbers, the older dwellings experienced some alterations and redevelopment. Some larger houses, depending on where they were sited, were converted into tenement blocks through subdivision, whereas others acquired new construction. The houses built in the commercial area of the neighborhood usually possessed shops on the street front. Those that had room for such development acquired them later. It was also often the case that the houses built on the main roads were turned into rows of one-room apartments associated with commercial units over the years. All these developments were to be supervised through the Organization of Imperial Architects. However, the control mechanism does not seem to have been effective enough to prevent illegal developments in early modern Istanbul. For example, the construction of any buildings against the city walls inside and outside was not permitted, and those built had to be pulled down. However, this was a common continuing practice, especially in the congested areas alongside the Golden Horn. In addition, although there were restrictions, people extended their properties through the construction of veranda-like structures, encroaching directly on the street.

Of note is the importance of neighborhood in the city's urban social and economic organizations across the early modern period. The neighborhood housed diverse social, religious, and ethnic groups even though some neighborhoods were dominated by a particular group. People lived and worked in the same area and they got together around neighborhood-based socioreligious and commercial foundations. Several occupations and productions also took place within the neighborhood next to residential life. Unlike our present time, they were parts of the urban environment in the early modern era.

Selma Akyazıcı Özkoçak

See also Bazaar; Damascus, Syria; Islamic City

Further Readings

Akyazıcı Özkoçak, S. 1998. "The Urban Development of Ottoman Istanbul in the Sixteenth Century." PhD thesis, School of Oriental and African Studies, University of London.

Eldem, E., D. Goffman, and B. Masters, eds. 1999. *The Ottoman City between East and West: Aleppo, Izmir and Istanbul*. New York: Cambridge University Press.

İnalcık, H. 1991. "Istanbul." Pp. 224–48 in *Encyclopedia of Islam*, edited by C. E. Bosworth. 2nd ed., Vol. 5. Leiden, the Netherlands: Brill.

Mantran, R. 1962. *Istanbul dans la seconde moitie du XVIIe siècle*. Paris: Librairie Adrien Maisonneuve.

J

JACKSON, KENNETH T.

Kenneth T. Jackson, one of the most prominent U.S. urban historians, has strongly influenced the agenda of the field and also made active collaborative and institutional contributions. His work covers the broad sweep of U.S. urban history and more specific topics, especially New York City, where he is Jacques Barzun Professor of History and the Social Sciences at Columbia University. Throughout his career, Jackson has shown an ongoing concern with linking the processes of urban organization and form with larger historical questions.

Born in 1939, Jackson earned his PhD from the University of Chicago in 1966 and a year later established his interest in the conflicts between social ideologies and urban life in his first book, *The Ku Klux Klan in the City, 1915–1930* (1967). His most widely read work remains *Crabgrass Frontier: The Suburbanization of the United States* (1985). The book addresses belief systems and public policies that contributed to the rise of the suburbs, along with the built and spatial forms that resulted. Jackson argues that the dominance of suburbia in the United States can be attributed to a constellation of causes ranging from the ideological to the economic. He especially sees economic forces working together to make suburban housing less expensive in the United States than elsewhere, with four factors being dominant: inexpensive transportation; abundant, cheap land; government subsidies for loans and infrastructure; and low-cost construction methods. In the years since its publication, this broad interpretive synthesis has encouraged much subsequent scholarship and remains foundational for the study of urban history.

In addition to scholarly monographs and articles, Jackson has made numerous collaborative contributions to the field and worked to promote organizational and institutional development. His work with photographer Camilo Jose Vergara resulted in several exhibitions and the book *Silent Cities: The Evolution of the American Cemetery* (1989). Among his many editorships, particularly notable for urban history is the monumental *Encyclopedia of New York City* (1995). More recently, *Robert Moses and the Modern City: The Transformation of New York* (2007), coedited by Hilary Ballon, calls for a reevaluation of that long-maligned city builder.

Institutionally, Jackson has contributed actively to urban history and U.S. history generally. Beginning in the mid-1960s, he played a major role in the Columbia University Seminar on the City, an important forum for discussion and scholarship. He has also headed several professional organizations, notably the Urban History Association and the Organization of American Historians, and he is currently president of the New York Historical Society and director of the Lehman Center for American History. Finally, Jackson's many documentary and media appearances have helped bring urban history to a wide and diverse audience.

Robert Buerglener

See also New York City, New York; Suburbanization; Urban History

411

Further Readings

Jackson, Kenneth T. and David S. Dunbar. 2002. *Empire City: New York through the Centuries*. New York: Columbia University Press.

Jackson, Kenneth T., John B. Manbeck, and Citizens Committee for New York City. 2004. *The Neighborhoods of Brooklyn*. New Haven, CT: Yale University Press.

Jackson, Kenneth T. and Stanley K. Schultz. 1972. *Cities in American History*. New York: Knopf.

JACOBS, JANE

Jane Jacobs (1916–2006) is among the most influential writers on cities in the twentieth century, both in the academic and popular spheres. Many of her most powerful ideas can be found in her first book, *The Death and Life of Great American Cities,* published in 1961. She argued powerfully against urban renewal projects of the mid-twentieth century and was a proponent of preserving the social and cultural life of neighborhoods. Jacobs was also an activist who played a pivotal role in protecting areas like New York City's West Village and SoHo from a variety of threats, paving the way for their eventual designation as historic preservation districts. Jacobs's goal was not simply preserving a neighborhood's buildings but rather sustaining the mix of people and activities that made up a vibrant community. She played a similar role in Toronto, Canada, after moving there to protest the Vietnam War.

Early Years

Born into a prosperous Scranton, Pennsylvania, household, Jacobs nevertheless observed the tenuous economic conditions faced by the miners in that anthracite coal region and the poor Appalachian farmers she encountered while accompanying her aunt on Presbyterian missionary work in North Carolina. These exposures—combined with the onset of the Great Depression as Jacobs was entering her teens—implanted in her a lifelong concern with the forces of community growth and decay. Her formal education in Scranton's public schools was unremarkable, and she recalled secretly reading books of her own choosing under her classroom desk. Her intellectual curiosity, however, led her to a long life of bucking academic authorities.

Although she never obtained a degree beyond a high school diploma, a six-month course in business stenography armed Jacobs by age 20 to follow her sister to New York City and obtain work as a secretary. At the same time, she began selling articles as a freelance writer on urban life to publications such as *Vogue* and the *Sunday Herald Tribune.*

Following two years of continuing education courses at Columbia University, Jacobs joined the New York branch of the Roosevelt administration's Office of War Information. She continued after 1945 in the State Department's Overseas Information Agency, essentially producing propaganda pieces about the United States for publication abroad. Her wartime writings included an appeal for federal action to aid rusting industrial centers like Scranton. In 1952, she left the State Department in the wake of a series of McCarthy-era interrogations about her labor activity in the United Public Workers of America.

During the 1930s and 1940s, Jacobs lived first in Brooklyn, then near Washington Square in Greenwich Village. She married architect Robert Hyde Jacobs, and in 1947, the couple purchased a converted candy store at 555 Hudson Street in the West Village neighborhood, where they had three children.

Writing About Cities

After leaving the State Department in 1952, Jacobs worked as an associate editor at *Architectural Forum*. Her work there brought her into contact with influential ideas and individuals during the high-water mark of government-funded urban renewal programs. She soon became skeptical about these large-scale redevelopment projects. An encounter with William Kirk of the Union Settlement in East Harlem alerted her to the social shortcomings of new high-rise public housing projects, which replaced the traditional street pattern with superblocks. Meeting renowned Philadelphia city planner Edmund Bacon, Jacobs was struck by his abstract, aesthetic preoccupation with modernization and his insensitivity to the vitality in older (even impoverished) neighborhoods.

Jacobs first expressed her criticisms publicly when her boss, Douglas Haskell, offered her the opportunity to speak at a 1956 Harvard University conference on urban design. Seizing the offensive, Jacobs challenged the assumptions of an audience composed of some of the most influential proponents of modernist urbanism, including Jose Luis Sert, Jacqueline Tyrwhitt, and Lewis Mumford. Mumford encouraged her to obtain a wider audience for her ideas, and soon thereafter, *Fortune* editor William H. Whyte, Jr., commissioned her to write for his magazine. In an April 1958 article, "Downtown Is for People," Jacobs suggested that planners, architects, and businessmen were working "at cross-purposes to the city" in ways that deadened all local flavor and vitality.

Jacobs's *Fortune* article was packed with enough ideas to fill a book, which is what she set about doing next, courtesy of a grant from the Rockefeller Foundation. The 1961 publication of Jacobs's first book, *The Death and Life of Great American Cities*, sparked a firestorm of debate about the means and ends of the urban renewal program and of city planning.

The success of that book enabled Jacobs to devote herself to writing for the next four decades. Two subsequent books—*The Economy of Cities* (1969) and *Cities and the Wealth of Nations* (1984)—explored first the economic and then the geopolitical functioning of cities. Together with *Death and Life*, these constituted a trilogy elaborating Jacobs's analysis of urban life. She also wrote works delving into ethics (*Systems of Survival: A Dialogue on the Moral Foundations of Commerce and Politics*, 1992), ecology (*The Nature of Economies*, 2000), and broad social criticism (*Dark Age Ahead*, 2004).

Activism in New York City

Beginning in the mid-1950s, Jacobs joined a number of public debates in the Greenwich Village neighborhood where she lived. In 1958, the community successfully opposed a proposal by Robert Moses to bisect Washington Square with a sunken traffic artery. She discussed some of those experiences in *Death and Life*, and her observations from these engagements formed the basis for her ideas about the nature of politics and power in cities.

Jacobs's most intense political battles came in response to the New York City Planning Commission's designation of her West Village neighborhood as blighted and the target of a 14-block urban renewal scheme. Leading a citizens' Committee to Save the West Village, Jacobs cultivated allies including Tammany leader Carmine DeSapio as well as Democratic reformer Ed Koch and the Republican U.S. Representative John Lindsay. Sustained publicity, as well as political and legal pressure, induced Mayor Robert Wagner to withdraw the proposal by early 1962. Later that same year, Jacobs became the chair of a committee to fight a proposed expressway across lower Manhattan. Once again, she proved herself a strategically and tactically effective leader, publicly articulating the case against the highway plan and speaking forcefully at government hearings.

In the mid-1960s, she devoted sustained energies, ideas, and organizing resources to bringing affordable housing to the West Village. The West Village Association, a community organization Jacobs cofounded, involved residents in the design and development of subsidized apartments that stood in stark contrast to other housing projects (both public and private). The envisioned West Village Houses would have entailed no demolition or tenant relocation, the buildings would have been oriented toward the street rather than on superblocks, and the architecture would have harmonized with the existing neighborhood.

To the association's frustration, the erection of the West Village Houses was stymied for nearly a decade by resistance from city officials, so the completed buildings fell short of the original projections for mixed use and amenities. More important over the long term, Jacobs was unable to find a suitable response to the erosion of affordable housing that was undermining the neighborhood she adored.

Relocation to Toronto

Beginning in 1965, Jacobs became an outspoken critic of the Vietnam War, contributing her name to high-profile protests, including a 1967 sit-in at New York's Whitehall Street Induction Center, where she was arrested along with pediatrician Benjamin Spock, writer Susan Sontag, and others. Jacobs's opposition to U.S. foreign policies was so intense that she cited it as the primary factor in the decision to move her entire family—including two draft-age sons—to Canada in 1968.

Settling into the university area of Toronto known as the Annex, Jacobs was immediately confronted by a plan to route an expressway through her new neighborhood. Joining with influential University of Toronto professor Marshall McLuhan, Jacobs lent her voice and her experience to a campaign that successfully defeated the Spadina expressway proposal in favor of mass transit.

Beyond Toronto highway opposition, Jacobs supported a broad civic reform initiative. Jacobs actively endorsed candidates such as radical neighborhood organizer John Sewell, who was elected to the city council after campaigning against slum clearance and overdevelopment. By the time this ideologically diffuse movement gained control of the mayoralty in 1974, reformers of all political stripes valued Jacobs's counsel, particularly on questions of urban development.

Jacobs's association with the reform administrations gave her influence over a variety of policies and projects. The most significant was the redevelopment of a 45-acre former industrial zone near downtown Toronto into a mixed-use residential area dubbed the St. Lawrence neighborhood. Conceived and built between 1974 and 1979, the initiative produced 3,500 new units and represented (according to designer Alan Littlewood) "the most complete expression of Jane Jacobs' ideas in concrete form."

In 1979, the Canadian Broadcasting Corporation commissioned Jacobs to deliver its Massey Lectures, a series of five radio addresses on the topic of Canadian cities and sovereignty association, which she later expanded and published as *The Question of Separatism: Quebec and the Struggle over Separation* (1980). Stepping into the center of the contentious debates around Canada's bicultural history, Jacobs encouraged the country to eschew emotional nationalisms, acknowledge the distinct needs of the Toronto- versus Montreal-centered economies, and conceive a step-by-step "model for peaceful separation." This position followed from Jacobs's opposition to the centralization of power but also resonated with broader trends of political devolution to subnational cultural regions like Catalonia in Spain (devolved in 1979).

As a founding board member of Energy Probe, Jacobs advocated deregulation in the energy sector and was particularly critical of the Ontario province's nuclear power plants. After the turn of the century, Jacobs brought together the mayors of Canada's five largest cities to press the provincial and national governments for more pro-urban policies.

Ideas and Influence

Many of Jacobs's most powerful ideas can be found *The Death and Life of Great American Cities*. The most immediately controversial—and ultimately the most effective—aspects of *Death and Life* centered on her trenchant critique of the urban renewal policies being applied in U.S. cities and of the erroneous assumptions and goals that underlay the attitudes of planners and policymakers. The latter included a set of influences dating back at least to the City Beautiful movement's emphasis on monumentality at the turn of the twentieth century, followed by the functionally segregated urbanism of Le Corbusier and other modernists at mid-century—all of whom she assailed as fundamentally anti-urban.

Jacobs articulated her critique not on aesthetic grounds but on the basis of her observations about how cities work, as well as why many recent interventions produced failures. *Death and Life* analyzed the dynamics of the public sphere in the most basic spaces of community interaction: parks, squares, sidewalks. One of the most renowned passages is an hour-by-hour account of "the intricate sidewalk ballet," which unfolded outside the window of her Hudson Street home on a typical day. With this memorable example, and others, she sought to point out the underappreciated strengths and social functions inherent in the traditional urban block form. In consequence, a "classic Jane Jacobs neighborhood" is one displaying a wide variety of lively activities throughout the day and night.

Jacobs then explored the structural underpinnings of such vitality. She identified four generators or conditions for healthy urban neighborhoods: First, they needed to host a mix of uses, thereby embracing the diversity that comes with various activities. Second, they should possess buildings of various ages, types, and conditions to incubate the broadest set of uses. Third, neighborhoods should exhibit a quite dense concentration of people in order to achieve a critical mass of activity. Finally, streets should be divided into relatively short blocks to maximize opportunities for choice and serendipity at their many intersections.

Notably, each of the characteristics stood in diametric opposition to basic tenets of modern planning and urban renewal, which included a preference for superblocks, lower densities with more open space, the replacement of older areas with new redevelopments, and the increasing segregation of various functions (e.g., housing, work, leisure, and transportation). Jacobs challenged a wide range of assumptions about how cities work, noting, for example, that parks were not an absolute good—nor was bigger necessarily better. Instead, vast open spaces, not easily traversed or monitored, could function as "border vacuums," deadening uses in their vicinity.

Generally, Jacobs provided lessons for urban social scientists as far away as Germany. In the United States, her influence is particularly evident in the work of Richard Sennett (*The Uses of Disorder: Personal Identity & City Life*, 1970). William H. Whyte continued to emphasize Jacobsean concerns in his Street Life Project (*The Social Life of Small Urban Spaces*, 1980). Jacobs's argument for having more activity—and hence more eyes—on the street was developed further in critiques of crime-ridden high-rise housing projects, where layouts prevented community self-policing, particularly Oscar Newman's "defensible space." Jacobs's general concept of unrecognized services that issue from community patterns prefigures political scientist Robert Putnam's exploration of civic community and social capital, as well as Richard Florida's writings on the creative class in cities. Nobel laureate economist Robert Lucas has suggested that she deserved a Nobel Prize for what he termed the "Jane Jacobs' externalities," that is, the effect of cities in catalyzing human innovation.

Jacobs concluded her first book with an extended meditation on what "kind of problem a city is"— namely a system of "organized complexity." She regularly compared urban systems to complex ecosystems with myriad niches and invoked organic metaphors. Her characterization of the gradually emergent, unpredictable patterns of urban society anticipated the later enthusiasm for chaos theory and other dynamics that are neither linear nor random. Her late writings turned to urban environmental questions, and she ultimately saw much promise in "bio-mimicry."

Jacobs delved deeper into the question of cities as dynamic, generative entities, particularly as engines of economic development. She held urban centers to be the necessary locus for nearly all of the most important developments in human civilization, even agriculture. In her view, cities were indispensable, constantly evolving sites of social organization, where innovation could be brought to bear in regional and eventually international markets. Her emphasis on the role of cities in a global context paved the way for later studies by sociologist Saskia Sassen, geographer Peter Hall, and economists Robert Lucas and Edward Glaeser.

Jacobs has directly influenced many important thinkers with particular relevance to urban studies: Robert Caro cited Jacobs as a primary inspiration for his devastating biographical attack on a master of urban renewal, *The Power Broker: Robert Moses and the Fall of New York* (1974). For Marshall Berman, Jacobs's vision was the apotheosis of urban democracy as expressed through an unruly "modernism of the streets," which he explored at length in *All That Is Solid Melts into Air: The Experience of Modernity* (1982).

More broadly, her reaffirmation of the traditional urban streetscape became a touchstone for architects, planners, and preservationists rejecting various aspects of modernist urbanism. Although urban professionals initially greeted Jacobs's first book with great hostility, by 1974, New York City Planning Commission Chair John Zuccotti claimed, "We are all neo-Jacobeans." In the 1990s, the new urbanism movement invoked Jacobs as a foundation for pedestrian- and community-oriented suburban developments like Seaside and Celebration, both in Florida.

Aside from the ire of planners directly stung by her critiques, Jacobs work engendered sustained criticism as well. Those on the political Left viewed her recommendations as insufficient responses to large-scale capitalist forces. Indeed, Jacobs often advocated entrepreneurship, innovation, and other self-help as the solution for "unslumming" economically depressed areas, while she attacked large-scale government programs, including not only urban renewal but also the Tennessee Valley Authority. Although never willing to label herself politically or ideologically, Jacobs harbored lifelong suspicions of power and authority.

Throughout her life, she remained a gradualist, opposed to cataclysmic change and tyrannical forces—whether public or private. She retained confidence in the inherent ability of healthy communities to be self-correcting in the face of a various dangers, and dedicated her writings and activism to ensuring the vigorous civic life she thought necessary to do so.

Christopher Klemek

See also Neighborhood Revitalization; New Urbanism; Public Realm; Urban Life; Urban Planning; Urban Village

Further Readings

Allen, Max, ed. 1997. *Ideas That Matter: The Worlds of Jane Jacobs*. Owen Sound, ON, Canada: Ginger Press.
Fishman, Robert. 1996. "The Mumford–Jacobs Debate." *Planning History Studies* 10:1–2.
Jane Jacobs tribute issues in the following journals: *City & Community* 5:3 (September 2006); *Journal of the Society of Architectural Historians* 66:1 (March 2007).
Klemek, Christopher. 2007. "Placing Jane Jacobs within the Transatlantic Urban Conversation." *Journal of the American Planning Association* 73:1.
———. 2008. "Jane Jacobs and the Fall of the Urban Renewal Order in New York and Toronto." *Journal of Urban History* 34:2.

JOURNEY TO WORK

The concept of journey to work normally refers to journeys from the residence to the workplace, usually also including the return from the workplace to the home. *Commute* is often used as a synonym. Often, journeys to work include stops on the way, for example, at kindergartens, coffee shops, kiosks, or grocery stores. In the United States, less than half of the journeys to work are nonstop trips between home and workplace.

In spite of a rapid increase in leisure travel, journeys to work still make up a major proportion of travel in urban areas on weekdays. Among workforce participants in the United States, work tours accounted for 45 percent of the travel time on weekdays and 42 percent of weekday traveling distance in 2001. In Europe, higher proportions of daily traveling distances are often reported; for instance, among workforce participants in the Copenhagen Metropolitan Area, commuting accounts for about two thirds of the distance traveled within the region on weekdays and nearly half the weekly traveling distance. Across nations, there is a general tendency for longer journeys to work among men than among women.

Although increasing use of flextime work has leveled out the morning and afternoon traffic peaks somewhat, journeys to work are still characterized by a higher temporal concentration than other traveling purposes. The capacity of urban expressways and public transit services are used to the highest extent in the peak periods, and changes in journey to work patterns are therefore important to congestion levels as well as revenues for transit companies. This has led to a strong focus on journeys to work in transport planning and research. These journeys have considerable social, economic, and local environmental implications associated with their nonoptional character and their temporal and spatial concentration. They are also important to overall energy use and emission levels. Journeys to work probably make up a higher proportion of actual travel time and distance than reported in many trip-based travel surveys, which often fail to take into account the role of the daily commute as the fixed and basic trip onto which other trip purposes, for example, grocery shopping, may be hitched.

Commuting Distances

Following general trends toward higher mobility, commuting distances have increased over time. This applies both to the journeys made by urban residents to workplaces within the same city and intercity commuting. In particular, the latter trips have become longer and more frequent as the friction of distance has been reduced through motorway construction and new high-speed rail connections, leading to a functional integration of increasingly large regions.

In countries like the United States and Denmark, one-way commuting distances are on average about 18 kilometers (11 miles). In comparison, on the affluent Chinese southeastern coast, where car ownership rates are still low but rapidly rising, urban workers travel on average less than one third of that distance to reach their workplace.

In most countries, the proportion traveling to the workplace by car is increasing. This also applies to societies where car ownership and usage has for a long time been high. In the United States, car commuting has risen from a share of about 85 percent in 1980 to 93 percent in 2001. Transit and nonmotorized modes now account for less than 4 percent each (although with higher rates of transit ridership in New York and other cities along the northeastern U.S. coast). In some European countries with gross domestic product on a par with the United States or above, commutes by public transport and nonmotorized modes account for relatively high proportions, in particular in the larger cities. For instance, in the Copenhagen Metropolitan Area, the proportions of journeys to work by car, public transit, and walk/bike are approximately 60 percent, 10 percent, and 30 percent, respectively, and these shares have changed only modestly during the recent decade.

The above-mentioned differences illustrate that traveling distances and modes for journeys to work are not merely a function of affluence levels. Neither can variations in travel behavior between countries or regions at similar levels of affluence be explained solely by cultural differences. A considerable body of research indicates that journeys to work can be influenced through transport policy measures and land use policies.

Duration of Travel

Evidence from a number of urban areas has shown that journeys to work are on average considerably shorter among inner-city residents than among their outer-area counterparts. This follows both from the generally higher concentration of workplaces in the inner than in the outer areas of most cities and from the fact that the distance to a randomly chosen address within an urban area will usually be longer from a peripheral than from a centrally located residence.

Checking for demographic, socioeconomic, and attitudinal differences, outer-area residents of the Copenhagen Metropolitan Area travel on average three times as long to reach their workplace as their inner-city counterparts do. The proportion of car commuters is more than 80 percent among residents living more that 28 kilometers (17 miles) from downtown Copenhagen, compared to

35 percent among those living less than six kilometers (about four miles) from the city center. Conversely, more than half of the latter respondents travel by bike or by foot to their workplace, compared to only 10 percent among those living in the outer suburbs. The implication of these findings, which are in line with results from studies in several other European cities, is that in-fill residential development—in particular in inner-city areas—will contribute to reduced commuting distances, a reduced share of car commuters, and an increased proportion of journeys to work by nonmotorized modes. In contrast, urban sprawl contributes to increase commuting distance and automobile usage for journeys to work.

The influence of residential location on the time spent on commuting is less clear. Some American studies have found shorter travel times for journeys to work among suburbanites than among inner-city dwellers, mainly due to more freely flowing car traffic on the roads in the outer areas. On the other hand, according to several European studies, lower average traveling speeds among inner-city residents (due to higher shares of nonmotorized travel and less freely flowing motorized traffic) are offset by shorter commuting distances. As a result, average commuting times are similar, or even somewhat shorter among residents living close to the city center than among their outer-area counterparts.

The proportion of white-collar workers commuting by car is usually lower if the workplace is located close to the city center than if it is located at the outskirts of the city. The accessibility by public transport is normally highest in the central parts of a city. In addition, congestion and scarcity of parking space in downtown areas may cause a number of potential car commuters to leave their car in the garage at home. In Oslo, Norway, and in Copenhagen, the proportion of car commuters is typically less than 25 percent at downtown workplaces, compared to 50 percent to 85 percent among employees at outer-area offices, depending on whether or not the job site is located close to a commuter train station. Similar results have been reported from other Scandinavian cities, with the most pronounced differences in modal shares between center and periphery typically found in the largest cities. For blue-collar workers, the difference in travel modes between centrally and peripherally located jobs is generally much smaller.

These results support the Dutch so-called ABC principle for workplace location, according to which workplaces (apart from local service facilities) attracting a high number of employees or visitors per area unit should be located in areas easily accessible by public and nonmotorized transport but less easily accessible by car. Blue-collar workplaces, which often generate considerable goods transport, should be located in areas with high accessibility for trucks.

Transport Infrastructure

Commuting travel patterns are also influenced by the provision of transport infrastructure. Although the phenomenon of induced traffic has been heavily disputed, there is growing evidence that road capacity increases in congested urban areas tend to attract more drivers to the new, less congested roads, thus making improved traveling speeds a short-lived relief. Conversely, faster and more frequent public transport improves the competitive power of the transit mode and can make some previous car travelers leave their car in the garage. Empirical studies in Oslo and Copenhagen show that the choices of travel modes among a considerable proportion of commuters is influenced by the ratio of door-to-door travel times between car and transit (and also between car and bike). Building larger urban expressways is thus a counterproductive way of dealing with congestion in situations where transport policy goals aim at curbing the growth in car commuting. In the United Kingdom, national transport authorities have since the late 1990s acknowledged these mechanisms.

In the United States, campaigns for carpooling have been an important policy measure to limit peak-period car travel in congested urban regions. In spite of this, the proportion of car commuters driving alone increased between 1990 and 2001. Among the 20 percent or so of car commuters who did not travel alone, three out of four traveled with members of the same household.

Many transport researchers have pointed to road pricing as a powerful instrument to reduce congestion in urban areas. Fear of negative voter response has prevented most governments from implementing such schemes. A few examples still exist, including Singapore's tolls introduced in 1975 and toll rings introduced in the 1990s around four Norwegian cities. In London, a toll ring established in 2003 around the inner city has reduced the number of cars and minicabs crossing the cordon by 35 percent to 40 percent while improving traffic flows within the affected area. In Stockholm, Sweden, an experiment that included a toll ring around the inner city improved transit services, and increased park-and-ride facilities were carried out in 2005/2006. This package of policy measures resulted in a reduction of car traffic across the toll ring by 20 percent to 25 percent, considerably less congestion on the arterial roads and in the downtown area, reduced air pollution in the inner city, and a gradually increasing public support of the policy measures.

Petter Næss

See also Streetcars; Suburbanization; Subway; Transportation; Urban Planning

Further Readings

McGuckin, N. and N. Srinivasan. 2005. "The Journey-to-Work in the Context of Daily Travel." Paper for the Census Data for Transportation Planning Conference, Federal Highway Administration, Washington, DC.

Næss, P. 2006. *Urban Structure Matters: Residential Location, Car Dependence, and Travel Behavior.* London: Routledge.

Noland R. B. and L. L. Lem. 2002. "A Review of the Evidence for Induced Travel and Changes in Transportation and Environmental Policy in the U.S. and the U.K." *Transportation Research Part D* 7:1–26.

K

KAMPUNG

Kampung, the Malay word for "village," refers to a small rural settlement but may also denote a separate urban community, neighborhood, or subdivision of a town. In Indonesia, the term is used to refer specifically to urban neighborhoods in contrast to rural *desa.* In Malaysia, however, it refers to predominantly (but not exclusively) Malay, rural settlements. The kampung often conjures up the idea of a strong sense of community, anchored on a moral discourse of egalitarian solidarity, mutual aid among neighbors, and strong family and kinship ties. It also symbolizes home and the locus of Malay identity. At the same time, the term is also used to signify "backwardness": People who are deemed to have behaved in an uncivilized manner are often called *kampungan* (villagelike). Both nostalgic and derogatory narratives locate the kampung as a site outside of, or marginal to, urban modernity.

As the main settlement form predating colonial urban planning in parts of Southeast Asia, kampungs were characterized by a distinct socioeconomic class stratification, which was exacerbated by the extension of colonial and postcolonial state bureaucracies from the early twentieth century. Although kampung livelihoods are primarily dependent on agriculture, there has been a shift in recent decades to a more diversified occupation structure and sources of income, with some kampungs becoming commuter villages characterized by a constant flow of people between the kampung and the nearby town.

In Malaysia in the 1990s, the government's call to produce "new" Malays—entrepreneurial individuals able to compete in a capitalist world economy—prescribed "urbanizing" the Malays and rescuing them from the entrapments of a "backward" kampung mentality. At the same time, the kampung remains the site of temporary return and reconnection with kin and a sense of Malayness. In practice, however, the rural–urban divide is fast dissolving, as urbanism as a cultural force—transmitted through mass media, education, and people movements—becomes pervasive in rural areas. Kampung dwellers today negotiate everyday lives in an overwhelmingly urban world. The reworking of rural spaces into urban ones is central to understandings of urbanism in many parts of Southeast Asia, as encapsulated in the concept of the *desa-kota* (literally "countryside city") region to describe the imagined and material space between urban center and rural periphery.

In Singapore where urbanization has almost completely erased the kampung landscape from the city-state, the notion of kampung living continues to be remembered as an idyllic place characterized by a relaxed pace of life and communitarian cooperation, in contradistinction to the stresses and strains of urban life. The timeless quality of kampung life associated with childhood innocence, social cohesion, spontaneous interaction, and the simple life functions as an immanent critique of the urban present.

Brenda S. A. Yeoh

See also Asian Cities; *Banlieue*; Community; *Favela*

419

Further Readings

Chua, Beng-Huat. 1995. "That Imagined Space: Nostalgia for Kampungs." Pp. 222–41 in *Portraits of Places: History, Community and Identity in Singapore,* edited by B. S. A. Yeoh and L. Kong. Singapore: Times Editions.

Thompson, Eric C. 2004. "Rural Villages as Socially Urban Spaces in Malaysia." *Urban Studies* 41(12):2357–76.

KOLKATA (CALCUTTA), INDIA

Kolkata, formerly known as Calcutta, is one of the world's most populous cities, with more than 13 million people inhabiting a metropolitan agglomeration that stretches outward from an urban core to envelop an expansive peri-urban hinterland, according to the Census of India in 2001. Known in popular discourse as the "black hole," Kolkata is seen to embody the stereotypes of third world megacities: crushing poverty, filth and disease, jostling masses, slums, and underdevelopment. In this imagination, Kolkata is also rescued by saintly figures, such as Mother Teresa and her tireless work for the city's beggars, lepers, and orphans, and it is thus also the "City of Joy," where compassion and humanity emerge from misery.

Colonial Calcutta

The appellation "black hole" refers to an alleged incident in 1756 when British prisoners suffocated to death in a small dungeon of the Nawab of Bengal. Indeed, Kolkata traces its origins to colonial battles. The city's official history begins in 1690 with British trade and settlement. As British mercantilist interests were transformed into colonial rule and military occupation, so Calcutta was declared, in 1772, capital of British India. And thus it remained until 1911, when a growing nationalist insurgency pressed the British to move the capital to the newly constructed and thus more easily controlled city of New Delhi. In 2001, Calcutta was renamed Kolkata, after one of the three tiny villages that dotted the land when British traders arrived, a renaming that was part of a more widespread move to reclaim Indian cities from their colonial legacies.

Colonial Calcutta, like many other colonial cities, was divided into two distinct areas—the British "White Town" and the Indian "Black Town." As the British White Town was known for its monuments of government and commerce and open spaces of leisure, so the Indian Black Town was known for its claustrophobic poverty. But in colonial Calcutta, these classic colonial distinctions between White and Other were more complex and ambiguous. By the early nineteenth century, Calcutta was witnessing a "Bengal Renaissance," with a flourishing Indian elite, increasingly fluent in English and more broadly in Western liberal philosophies. This was also a landowning elite that invested heavily in the White Town such that by the mid-nineteenth century, much of British Calcutta, the so-called city of palaces, was owned by Indians though occupied exclusively by Europeans (except for their Indian servants). The homes of rich Indians themselves in North Calcutta, the erstwhile Black Town, were often lavish compounds, indicating the lines of class and caste that cut through racial formations and calling into question the image of homogenous Indian poverty and shantytown life.

Colonial Calcutta was an economy built on the manufacture of, and trade in, key commodities, such as jute and paper. Postcolonial Calcutta was to witness the collapse of these industries and a steady deindustrialization of its economic base. At the moment of independence, in 1947, Calcutta and Bombay were the premier economic centers of India. Indeed, Calcutta bravely absorbed large numbers of Bengali "refugees," rendered stateless by the partition that accompanied independence. But by the 1970s, Bombay had cemented its prosperity while Calcutta was in the throes of capital flight and soaring unemployment. In the last decades of the twentieth century, Calcutta persisted primarily as an informalized economy: a city of day laborers, informal vendors, and domestic servants. This informalization was hastened by continuing migration from a vast rural hinterland of poverty—the wretched stretches of Bihar and Orissa and the villages of West Bengal where a communist government had promised but not fully delivered on land reforms and redistribution. The informal city found spatial expression in a landscape of slums, squatter settlements, and pavement dwellings, each governed by different forms of regulation, negotiation, and political barter, but all signs of the hollowing out of the city's formal economy.

Modern-Day Kolkata

Urban Renewal Under the New Communists

Kolkata is the capital of the state of West Bengal, which is ruled by the world's longest-running, democratically elected communist government, the Left Front, which has been in power since 1977. As the twentieth century ended, the Left Front adopted a new economic policy meant to liberalize the West Bengal economy and attract global investment, primarily in the sectors of real estate and high technology, to Calcutta. With this New Communism came new imperatives for urban renewal and redevelopment. Informal vendors who had long occupied the city's sidewalks were rapidly evicted; the peri-urban fringes of the city, inhabited by squatters and sharecroppers, were now earmarked for suburban subdivisions and new townships. The New Communists had rather obvious ambitions to place Calcutta on the map of globalization.

The eviction of informal vendors, in 1996, from the sidewalks of Calcutta happened under the banner of a municipal drive with an Orwellian title: Operation Sunshine. It was an eviction conducted to reclaim the *bhadralok* city, the gentlemanly city of order and discipline. However, the term *bhadralok* has deep roots in the cultural politics of the region. It refers to a Bengali urban intelligentsia that emerged in the crucible of colonialism, formed by English education and yet shaped by opposition to colonialism, a genteel and refined elite that stands in opposition to the poor and the proletariat but that is also the heart and soul of Bengali leftism. According to Dipesh Chakrabarty, the bhadralok are the bearers of a distinctive "Bengali modern" and the inhabitants of a bourgeois public sphere, including one that is being revived through the practices of New Communism.

Ethnic Division of Economic and Political Power

The bourgeois public sphere of Kolkata warrants closer scrutiny. A distinctive feature of Kolkata's elite structure is an ethnic disjuncture between economic and political power. In broad terms, while political power is held by the Bengali bhadralok, economic power is vested in the Marwaris, an ethnic group with roots in the state of Rajasthan. The Marwaris are not a new presence in Kolkata. Important traders during the nineteenth century, the Marwaris were to become industrialists in the twentieth century, establishing pan-Indian dominance in key industrial sectors. However, they were to rarely participate in the political life of Kolkata. In the colonial city, representative rule was introduced to the Calcutta Municipal Corporation in 1875. The Bengali bhadralok took up this form of rule. Today, Kolkata is governed by a mayor-in-council system with the Kolkata Municipal Corporation as an apex body and the Kolkata Metropolitan Development Authority as a regional authority. The Bengali dominance of the municipal corporation and regional authority has continued in uninterrupted fashion. The split between economic and political power also continues, with political institutions dominated by the Bengali bhadralok and economic life dominated by Marwari industrialists and merchants. It has been argued that Kolkata Marwaris draw upon the idioms of lineage, kinship, and community rather than on the imaginary of a bourgeois public sphere. Kolkata's cultural and political life—cinema, art, theater—then is animated by a distinctive Bengali radicalism, at once socialist and bourgeois, at once nationalist and modern.

The Bengali Middle Class

There is more to the bhadralok city than its public guise. The making and remaking of the Bengali (sub)urban middle class is a story not only of urban renewal and peri-urban frontiers but also a story of domestic labor. In Kolkata's informalized economy, domestic servants, mainly poor women, are a prominent feature. Raka Ray has pointed out that just as European colonialists had to negotiate the spatiality of their Calcutta homes and spatial proximity of their Indian servants, so today's middle class has to make itself in relation to the domestic subaltern. But it is also here that political life in Kolkata far exceeds the bourgeois public sphere. Through a rich repertoire of contestations and entitlements, the rural–urban poor claim space, services, livelihood, and voice. This "political society" stands in contrast to bourgeois "civil society," wrote Partha Chatterjee, and signals the ways in which the formal and governed realm of the "public" becomes a domain of quasi-claims and paralegal practices: the *pablik* (an interlingual term that captures how the original English word is pronounced in colloquial Bengali). There are historical traces of this pablik domain in colonial Calcutta, in the rowdy practices and critical narratives of poor women as they produced a popular culture of the streets that challenged the city of elite parlors.

Today, on the edges of Kolkata, new suburbs and townships are being imagined and implemented by a New Communism. The expansion of the bhadralok city seems endless. This urban frontier seems to have replaced the deindustrializing impulse of the twentieth century. But, in 2006, the edges of Kolkata were to witness a new type of political drama. As the state government sought to establish a special economic zone at Singur, to house a global factory for automobiles, so the long simmering controversy over the displacement of sharecroppers and squatters exploded. The Singur discontent spread and at Nandigram, peasants blocked entry to their village and resisted the implementation of a special economic zone. Had New Calcutta reached its limits? Or was the bhadralok city also always the informal city, the city of subalterns?

Ananya Roy

See also Asian Cities

Further Readings

Banerjee, S. 1989. *The Parlour and the Street: Elite and Popular Culture in Nineteenth Century Calcutta.* Calcutta, India: Seagull Press.

Chakrabarty, D. 2000. *Habitations of Modernity: Essays in the Wake of Subaltern Studies.* Chicago: University of Chicago Press.

Chatterjee, P. 2004. *The Politics of the Governed: Reflections on Popular Politics in Most of the World.* New York: Columbia University Press.

Chattopadhyay, S. 2005. *Representing Calcutta: Modernity, Nationalism, and the Colonial Uncanny.* New York: Routledge.

Hardgrove, A. 2004. *Community and Public Culture: The Marwaris in Calcutta, 1897–1997.* New York: Columbia University Press.

Kaviraj, S. 1997. "Filth and the Public Sphere: Concepts and Practices about Space in Calcutta." *Public Culture* 10(1):83–113.

Lapierre, D. 1985. *City of Joy.* New York: Warner Books.

Marshall, P. J. 2000. "The White Town of Calcutta under the Rule of the East India Company." *Modern Asian Studies* 34(2):307–31.

Ray, Rajat. 1979. *Urban Roots of Indian Nationalism: Pressure Groups and Conflict of Interests in Calcutta City Politics, 1875–1939.* New Delhi, India: Vikas.

Ray, Raka. 2000. "Masculinity, Femininity and Servitude: Domestic Workers in Calcutta in the Late Twentieth Century." *Feminist Studies* 26(3):691.

Roy, A. 2003. *City Requiem, Calcutta: Gender and the Politics of Poverty.* Minneapolis: University of Minnesota Press.

Sinha, P. 1990. "Calcutta and the Currents of History, 1690–1912." In *Calcutta: The Living City,* edited by S. Chaudhuri. New York: Oxford University Press.

KRACAUER, SIEGFRIED

A trained architect, the German–Jewish cultural critic Siegfried Kracauer (born in Frankfurt am Main in 1889, died in New York City in 1966) quickly gave up his profession in the early 1920s to devote himself to philosophical and sociological studies. First as a journalist and editor with the *Frankfurter Zeitung* and then as a film and cultural theorist, he was an original and prolific writer who explored the quotidian experiences, popular culture, and mass entertainments of the modern metropolis. Influenced by Marxism, psychoanalysis, and the sociology of his former professor in Berlin, Georg Simmel, and closely associated with the Critical Theory of the Frankfurt Institute for Social Research (the Frankfurt School), Kracauer came to develop a highly critical and frequently pessimistic vision of contemporary urban life as indelibly marked by a sense of spiritual homelessness, inner emptiness, and the diminished sensitivities of the present-day individual subject.

Writing the Urban Experience in Frankfurt and Berlin

Between 1921 and 1933, Kracauer wrote nearly 2,000 contributions to the *Frankfurter Zeitung* dealing with the widest possible array of subject matter drawn from the everyday lifeworld of Frankfurt and Berlin; articles relating particular (sometimes uncanny) experiences in the city's streets and squares; curious encounters with eccentric figures; visits to various bars, cafés, and restaurants; discussions of metropolitan architecture, planning, and design; numerous film and literary reviews; reports on contemporary exhibitions, shows, and premieres; and, additionally, occasional communiqués from other cities, Paris in particular.

For Kracauer, these miniature texts were of greater and more enduring significance than mere commonplace journalism. In true modernist fashion, and like his contemporaries Walter Benjamin and Ernst Bloch, Kracauer eschewed any systematic, totalizing account of the modern cityscape. Instead, he and they recognized the potential of textual fragments for authentically capturing and representing the disparate, fractured reality of mundane metropolitan existence. For Kracauer, in particular, the seemingly innocuous "surface manifestations" of the cityscape were nothing other than traces, hieroglyphs, or dream images that, once recovered and deciphered by the critical theorist, could render the metropolis momentarily legible.

Many years later Kracauer selected a number of these fragments for inclusion in two collections: *Das Ornament der Masse* (1963, translated as *The Mass Ornament,* 1995) and *Strassen in Berlin und Anderswo* (1964). These textual mosaics, or montages, repeatedly foreground the superficial and transient features of the urban environment. Shunning the planned and permanent architectural fabric of the city, for example, Kracauer is fascinated by the spontaneous figures and serendipitous formations fleetingly composed by the crowds and traffic in motion on the urban street. He is irresistibly drawn to the intricate play of memory, to the ephemeral glimpsed en passant, to the instantaneous and improvised. Indeed, "improvisation" understood as a freedom of flow between forms, as an effortless process of emergence and disappearance, as intentionless, endless unfolding, becomes the key concept in his writings. Improvisation, be it as a writer, a musician, an acrobat or dancer, be it as a *flâneur* in the city, is a kind of idiosyncratic and utopian mode of creative composition

in contrast to the strictly calculated and controlled routines choreographed by the culture industry and exemplified by the machine-like precision and repetition of the Tiller Girls dance troupe, the mass ornament par excellence.

Writing the Urban Ethnography

Kracauer's journalistic writings came together in a slightly different form during the Weimar Republic. Originally serialized in the *Frankfurter Zeitung,* his 1929 "ethnography" of the emergent and increasingly dominant class of white-collar workers in Berlin, *Die Angestellten* (The Salaried Masses: Duty and Distraction in Weimar Germany) constitutes a pioneering study of the terra incognita of the contemporary urban petite bourgeoisie. Drawing on a wealth of diverse documentary sources, interviews, and observations, Kracauer's study presents the thoroughly rationalized and routinized lifeworld of office employees as blighted by spiritual homelessness and boredom, impoverished by inner meaninglessness and existential isolation, abject feelings for which the distracting products of the city's rapidly expanding culture industry were peddled as compensation and consolation. In response to this crisis, the alienated modern individual, like the Tiller Girl, desperately sought integration into the wider social group, longed for a sense of purpose and belonging, all too happily fell into step, be it dancing, be it marching. Kracauer's eclectic ethnography presents a timely series of images of an urban petite bourgeoisie soon to swap its white collars for brown shirts.

Writing the Paris Cityscape

On the advice of the *Frankfurter Zeitung,* on February 28, 1933, the day after the Reichstag fire, Kracauer left Berlin for exile in Paris. There he began work on, and in 1937 published, *Jacques Offenbach and the Paris of His Time,* a "societal biography" (*Gesellschaftsbiographie*), which, instead of foregrounding the life of an individual like conventional biographies, took the experiences of the famous composer as a lens with which to view the socioeconomic, cultural, and political life of Parisians during the Second Empire. In tracing the fluctuating popularity of Offenbach's witty operettas and musical comedies, Kracauer's study provides a panoramic and critical representation of the prevailing cityscape from which these frivolous works drew their inspiration and in which they found acclaim: boulevards peopled by bohemians and journalists; the world exhibitions; the salons of fashionable society; the courtesans and the demi-monde; and the court of Napoleon III, with its imperial pomp and ceremony. Contemporaneous with Benjamin's planned but unwritten Arcades Project, Kracauer similarly sought to disenchant Paris, capital of the nineteenth century, as a locus of phantasmagoria, dreams, and chimeras. As itself an absurd "operetta world," the Second Empire found perfect expression in, and was subject to critical debunking by, Offenbach's seemingly innocent musical enchantments. Laced with unmistakable references to the brutality of dictatorships and their phony spell of "joy and glamour," Kracauer's study constitutes an exemplary reading of the metropolitan life of the recent past through one of its "surface," cultural phenomena.

Writing a Theory of Film

Kracauer escaped German-occupied France in 1941 and spent the rest of his life in New York City. There he wrote and published the two major (and much misunderstood and maligned) studies of film and cinema for which he is best known in Anglo-American scholarship: *From Caligari to Hitler: A Psychological History of the German Film* (1947) and *Theory of Film: The Redemption of Physical Reality* (1960). These are of particular relevance for urban studies for two reasons. First, as part of his "psychological history" of Weimar films as reflections or premonitions of deep-seated authoritarian predispositions and inclinations, Kracauer discusses in some detail the "street film" as a particular and popular genre during the 1920s. These films, typically portraying the doomed romantic rebellion of youth against the restrictions and cozy comforts of the bourgeois familial home, presented apparently contrasting messages. Films like *Die Strasse* (1923) served as warnings to the unwary as to the dangers of the metropolitan street as a site of vice, corruption, and brutality, whereas later variations on the theme, like *Die Freudlose Gasse* (1925) and *Asphalt*

(1929), sentimentally contrasted the impoverished integrity of a lowly but genuine life among social outcasts with the arrant hypocrisy and crass conventions of middle-class domesticity. The city as threatening chaos; the city as romantic escape—for Kracauer both of these clichéd images played their part in preparing the German public for what was to come.

Most significantly in the *Caligari* book, Kracauer begins to identify and sketch some key correspondences between the cinematic medium itself and the urban environment. These find much fuller development in, indeed become central to, his subsequent attempt to delineate a more general theory of film per se. For Kracauer, film has a special elective affinity with the city. The movie camera finds its most appropriate subject matter in the perpetual mobility, fluidity, transience, and happenstance of metropolitan existence. Film has a particular penchant for the "flow of life" on the urban street. Put another way: The city is itself cinematic. Indeed, Kracauer argues, in its ability to penetrate and record with unprecedented felicity everyday street life, film promises to reawaken our jaded senses to that which surrounds us. Film captures and focuses our attention on what is usually perceived in a state of weary distraction and indifference. In so doing, film images facilitate a new recognition and vital appreciation of our everyday environment. Redeemed by film, the city is restored to us. Film thereby becomes, for Kracauer, the very medium by means of which modern urbanites can overcome the rationalized and routinized existence of the big city. Film offers a home for the spiritually homeless.

Kracauer's varied writings on the theme of the city offer a kaleidoscopic, critical, and ultimately redemptive vision of the modern metropolis and popular urban culture.

Graeme Gilloch

See also Benjamin, Walter; Cinematic Urbanism; *Flâneur;* Paris, France; Simmel, Georg

Further Readings

Frisby, David. 1988. *Fragments of Modernity: Theories of Modernity in the Work of Simmel, Kracauer and Benjamin.* Cambridge: MIT Press.

Kracauer, Siegfried. 1995. *The Mass Ornament: Weimar Essays*. Cambridge MA: Harvard University Press.

———. 1998. *The Salaried Masses: Duty and Distraction in Weimar Germany*. London: Verso.

———. 2002. *Jacques Offenbach and the Paris of His Time*. New York: Zone.

Reeh, Henrik. 2004. *Ornaments of the Metropolis: Siegfried Kracauer and Modern Urban Culture*. Cambridge: MIT Press.

Ward, Janet. 2001. *Weimar Surfaces: Urban Visual Culture in 1920s Germany*. Berkeley: University of California Press.

L

LAGOS, NIGERIA

The modern city of Lagos developed from a fishing settlement originally founded in the fifteenth century by the Awori-Yoruba. Although it ceased to be the capital of Nigeria in 1991, Lagos remains the commercial, industrial, and political nerve center, and it was a critical factor in the development of the country, as this entry discusses.

Early Incursions

The intrusion of the Benin kingdom from the seventeenth century marked the first major external stimulus that shaped the fortunes of a community that rapidly developed into a melting pot of African and European elements. The abolition of the transatlantic slave trade and the establishment of British rule, two major developments of the first half of the nineteenth century, shaped the later development of the settlement. Declared a colony in 1861, it soon acquired the trappings of an outpost of Victorian Britain. Modern architecture, new food and dress styles, newspapers, the British legal and political system, formal schools, and Christian evangelization became the hallmarks of an emergent colonial city. As the seat of the nascent British administration, the missionary gateway to a hinterland wracked by the Yoruba civil wars and an increasingly important outlet for the (postslavery) forest produce of the hinterland, Lagos attracted voluntary and forced migrants from various communities in its hinterland.

Steady population growth was aided by an influx of returnee ex-slaves and their descendants from Brazil, Cuba, and Freetown (in Sierra Leone), founded in 1792 by the British to resettle former slaves. Many of the returnees, who still retained emotional ties to their Yoruba homeland, found refuge in Lagos. The émigrés brought various skills and cultural practices to an emerging city that welcomed and rapidly absorbed them. Lagos thus became the staging post for the expansion of British rule and values into the hinterland. Whereas the returnees from Brazil and Cuba were mainly artisans, those from Sierra Leone were essentially clerical in orientation. They became cultural intermediaries between the British and their indigenous counterparts and were, indeed, the purveyors of the British "civilizing mission." It was through them that Lagos pioneered the development of Western formal and technical education, along with a new urban lifestyle. The Brazilians, on the other hand, introduced and popularized the now famous Brazilian architecture that still adorns the Portuguese/Brazilian quarter in the city.

British Rule

By the end of the nineteenth century, Lagos had become the capital of the Lagos colony and the chief port of Nigeria. The imposition of British rule in the Yoruba hinterland was formalized in an agreement of 1893. This facilitated the introduction of modern economic, legal, and political systems that underpinned the expanding British administration. The British law and order regime, complete with the road and rail transport infrastructure, fostered the development of produce exports. Primary produce and imports were channeled through the Lagos port, which became Nigeria's dominant seaport outlet beginning in the 1890s. By that date, Lagos had earned the sobriquet of the Liverpool of West Africa.

During the twentieth century, Lagos became the hub of Nigeria's politics, economy, and society following administrative amalgamations carried out by the British in 1906 and 1914. Urban amenities and an expanding colonial economy enhanced the urban status of Lagos and linked it more effectively to a widening hinterland. As expected, leading European firms established their head offices in Lagos, and the major shipping lines offered regular services between Lagos and European metropolitan centers.

The presence of European traders, missionaries, and colonial officials, as well as Western-educated Africans, gave the city a cosmopolitan character. Indeed, with the possible exception of Freetown, Lagos was the most Westernized settlement in West Africa during the twentieth century. This was reflected in the city's fashions, tastes, and institutions. The legal system was essentially British, with the supreme court and lower courts operating in the city. The twentieth century witnessed a blend of architectural styles, although the Brazilian was dominant until the 1950s. In Lagos, corrugated iron roofing sheets began to displace the thatched roofs that had been dominant in indigenous parts of the metropolis. Commercial booms of 1906 through 1914 and 1918 through 1920 fostered conspicuous consumption and an ostentatious lifestyle that continue to characterize Lagos city life.

Residential segregation has been noticeable in Lagos since the nineteenth century, when European settlers established exclusive settlements on Lagos Island. By the 1920s, there was a distinct spatial segregation based on race in Lagos. The Macgregor canal separated the densely populated African town from the low-density European settlements and offices in the western parts of Lagos Island. The major European settlement at Ikoyi, east of the indigenous quarter, took off from the 1920s and subsequently developed into a status symbol that the Nigerian elite inherited from the 1950s. It is instructive that even in the African quarter, the émigrés from Sierra Leone and Brazil also developed their exclusive residential areas, at Olowogbowo and Popo Aguda, respectively.

The acquisition of a Western education, especially by the more clerical Sierra Leoneans, produced the first crop of African lawyers, medical doctors, missionaries, teachers, traders, and journalists in Lagos. Among such prominent Lagosians were Sapara Williams, R. B. Blaize, Sir Kitoyi Ajasa, Candido da Rocha, S. H. Pearse, J. H. Doherty, the Jacksons, the Macaulays, Eric Moore, and Dr. Orisadipe Obasa. The new African elite copied the marriage and social lifestyles of the British, which made them cultural hybrids. Yet, they were the pioneer African anticolonial nationalists although their principal aim was to seek accommodation in a system that discriminated against them regardless of their qualifications. Hence, most of them embraced cultural nationalism, a precursor of the anticolonial movement of the 1930s and 1940s. This African elite, however, had more in common with its members than with the indigenous Africans of Lagos. This was reflected not only in their residential segregation but also in their practice of marrying within their social class.

The indigenous Africans of Lagos were not totally eclipsed, although the *Oba* (king) and the traditional political order had been completely sidelined in the administration of the colony. Still, a good number of them embraced the colonial order, especially the commercial opportunities it provided. This response produced indigenous entrepreneurs such as Braimah Igbo, a prominent kolanut trader; W. A. Dawodu, the pioneer automobile entrepreneur in Nigeria; Karimu Kotun, a successful businessman who served as an agent for British firms in Liverpool and Manchester, and D. C. (Daniel Conrad) Taiwo, who came from lowly origins to accumulate wealth through the trade of palm oil and urban land holdings (Taiwo Olowo). The institution of the Obaship gradually assumed some political significance with the deposition and later reinstatement of Eshugbayi Eleko in the 1920s and 1930s.

The Contemporary City

Land is a scarce and highly valued commodity in Lagos. This is buttressed by the large number and protractedness of litigation over land in Lagos since the colonial period. The *Lewis v. Bankole* case, decided by the Supreme Court of Nigeria in 1912, affirmed the right of inheritance of property by female descendants. The Amodu Tijani landmark judgment by the Privy Council in London in 1921 upheld indigenous land rights in Lagos against the claims of the British colonial administration. Land speculation is rife, especially by indigenous Lagosians (*omo onile*), who continue to fuel violent crises in the community. This has contributed to the rise of the "area boys" (delinquent youth) in the downtown sections of the city.

Poor urban planning and waste management have been the bane of Lagos and its suburbs since the early twentieth century. The outbreak of bubonic plague in the 1920s and 1930s necessitated slum clearance on Lagos Island and the creation of new settlements at Yaba and Ebute Metta on the mainland. Government policies have failed to check unregulated urban and suburban development in Lagos, and poor waste management remains a great threat.

A long-standing feature of Lagos is the inadequacy of urban facilities in the face of a massive population increase down to the twenty-first century. With the massive increase in the population from 73,766 in 1911 to 655,246 in 1963 and more than 12 million by 2005, the gap between demand for and supply of water, electricity, and municipal transport facilities has become unbridgeable. Various government interventions, especially during the petroleum boom years of the 1970s, have failed to keep pace with demand in the face of the sharp decline in the value of the national currency, official corruption, and poor maintenance culture. A 2006 initiative by the federal government, the Lagos Mega City Project, is still unfolding.

Lagos has played a pioneering role in Nigerian political, social, and economic development. The first political parties (Peoples Union, 1908; Nigerian National Democratic Party, 1923) and the first pan-Nigerian political parties (Lagos/ Nigerian Youth Movement, 1934; the National Council of Nigeria and Cameroon, later known as the National Council of Nigerian Citizens, 1944) were established there. With a vibrant press, multiethnic population, and educational facilities, Lagos has been the hotbed of ethnic, cultural, and anticolonial nationalism. It was the birthplace of radical labor unionism, anchored on the agitation for higher cost of living allowances in the 1940s.

Lagos is also the entertainment capital of Nigeria with a large number of hotels and recreation centers. In music and social lifestyle, Lagos typifies the Nigerian urban milieu, a meeting point of various cultures and a theater of intense interpersonal and intergroup relations.

Ayodeji Olukoju

See also Colonial City

Further Readings

Gandy, Mathew. 2006. "Planning, Anti-planning and the Infrastructure Crisis Facing Metropolitan Lagos." *Urban Studies* 43(2):371–96.

Mann, Christine. 2007. *Slavery and the Birth of an African City: Lagos, 1760–1900.* Bloomington: Indiana University Press.

Packer, George. 2006. "The Megacity: Lagos Becomes an Urban Test Case." *The New Yorker,* November 13, pp. 62–75.

Salome, Abdou Maliq. 2004. *For the City Yet to Come: Changing African Life in Four Cities.* Durham, NC: Duke University Press.

Tijani, Hakeem Ibikunle. 2006. *Nigeria's Urban History: Past and Present.* Lanham, MD: University Press of America.

LAND DEVELOPMENT

Land development is a process of land use change most often initiated by the private sector, managed by the public sector, and subject to intense social conflict as existing and future interests collide. This is almost always true, regardless of the place of land development—whether in an urban neighborhood or at the city's edge. Urban land development can alter the character of neighborhoods through gentrification or revitalization; urban fringe development can lead to air and water pollution and declines in adjoining urban area viability while also providing for safe, affordable housing.

The land development process in the United States occurs in a highly decentralized system of governance and public finance. Authority for land development is a state government responsibility, but most states pass this authority to their local governments. Funds for public services are raised locally, and the types of services to be provided (schools, police, fire, etc.) are locally determined. The primary revenue source for services is the local property tax.

Pressures for land development originate from two sources that reinforce each other. First, in a system of decentralized governance and finance, local governments are compelled to continually grow physically and fiscally in response to ever-rising public services costs. Local officials have two choices—raise property taxes on existing landowners or generate more economic value from land. Encouraging land development is one easy way to generate more value. So, land intensification—whether in the form of urban gentrification or agricultural land conversion—increases the land's market value and thus the taxes that the land provides to local governments. Therefore, local officials are predisposed to pursue land development because such development allows for the continued provision of local services, and perhaps an increase in services, without having to increase tax burdens on existing owners.

A second source of land development pressure is the mismatch between the different logics of individual and social decision making about land. An individual landowner can achieve significant personal benefits by selling land for a more intensive use. Yet, the accumulation of a set of logical individual decisions can become socially illogical; for example, the inability of long-standing, elderly residents to live in a neighborhood because of increased assessed values or the loss of agricultural land and environmental resources. In short, local government wants land to be developed to generate more tax revenue, and some owners can want to intensify land use, but the result can be a loss for society.

Governments have experimented with a diverse set of tools to manage this process, including zoning, property tax relief, transfer of development rights, and support for nonprofit land and community development organizations. In selected places, these approaches have reshaped the geographic form of land development. Still, pressure on land continues.

Land development is not just about dollars and cents, but rather about the relationship of landownership to fundamental rights in a democratic market society. It is wrapped in complex historical and legal baggage that makes it difficult to address and resolve.

Harvey M. Jacobs

See also Developer: Environmental Policy: Growth Management; Real Estate; Sustainable Development; Urban Planning

Further Readings

Daniels, Tom and Deborah Bowers. 1997. *Holding Our Ground: Protecting America's Farms and Farmland.* Covelo, CA: Island Press.

Ely, James W., Jr. 1992. *The Guardian of Every Other Right: A Constitutional History of Property Rights.* New York: Oxford University Press.

Jacobs, Harvey M., ed. 1998. *Who Owns America? Social Conflict over Property Rights.* Madison: University of Wisconsin Press.

Logan, John R. and Harvey L. Molotch. 1987. *Urban Fortunes: The Political Economy of Place.* Berkeley: University of California Press.

LANDSCAPE ARCHITECTURE

Landscape architecture is broadly defined as the profession concerned with careful stewardship, wise planning, and artful design of natural and cultural environments. First use of the term as a professional title is often credited to Frederick Law Olmsted and Calvert Vaux in the 1850s, describing their role in the planning and design of Central Park in New York City. Drawing on traditions in agriculture, landscape gardening, architecture, and design, the professional title grew in popularity among early practitioners responding to public health, open space, and recreation needs in rapidly developing urban environments, culminating in the formation of professional degree programs and a professional association in the United States by the close of the nineteenth century.

Although rural environments and natural reserves have historically been important areas of work for landscape architects, the majority of work and accompanying discourse in the field has evolved in response to urbanization and has resulted in great diversity among the work of landscape architects today. Landscape architects are involved in the design and planning of large landscapes, such as watersheds and community-wide plans; many large urban spaces such as parks, recreation facilities, plazas, and streets; and many small spaces such as monuments and residential gardens. This work in urban environments has revealed significant ecological and social challenges that characterize the field.

Urban Ecological Challenges

The stewardship, planning, and design of natural environments by landscape architects requires an understanding of landscape structure, that is, the patterns of land form, plant, and animal species found to be existing within a region, as well as landscape function, the natural processes that shape these patterns. Urban development often dramatically alters landscape structure by displacing native vegetation and sensitive animal species, as well as landscape features such as wetlands, streams, or hillsides. Although it has long been common practice to preserve some existing landscape structure in urbanizing areas through the development of parks and open space reserves, these remnants often degrade in quality over time due to changes in the function of these landscapes. Key natural processes, such as the migration of plant and animal species, hydrology, carbon and nutrient cycling, and ecological disturbances such as flooding and fire, are typically suppressed or radically altered in terms of frequency, extent, and diminished beneficial impact.

The alteration of landscape structure and function affects the ecological integrity of open spaces as well as the quality of the overall urban environment. Some native species may become locally extinct due to insufficient or isolated habitat. Others may thrive due to their adaptability to urban conditions or the reduction of their predators or competitors. Alterations in natural processes, such as hydrology, may result in insufficient quantity to meet human demand, as well degradation of water quality due to chemicals, fertilizers, and sediments common to urban environments. Suppression of ecological disturbances such as flooding and fire may result in less

frequent, but more intense events that threaten life and property.

Current landscape architecture practice favors a variety of approaches designed to sustain the urban ecosystem over an extended period of time. A primary approach is the establishment of ecological networks, an assemblage of connected open space, often along streams and other hydrologic systems, to facilitate species migration and preserve natural hydrologic processes. Native plant species are often advocated for designs to provide wildlife habitat, reduce water usage, and prevent the use of exotic species that may be invasive to surrounding ecosystems. Efforts are made to capture and filter storm water runoff using wetland plants and microorganisms to enhance water quality, and some open spaces are designed to flood as a storm water management strategy. Efforts are made to reduce energy consumption of projects, both in terms of daily operations and maintenance, to reduce greenhouse gas emissions associated with development.

Ecological networks and sustainable processes are most effectively achieved if these concepts are integrated into the initial planning of urban environments, but landscape architecture has long been concerned with the reestablishment of ecologically beneficial landscape structure and function in existing cities, a sector of practice that has enjoyed renewed interest in recent years. These approaches often rely on the regenerative qualities of natural processes, which if supported possess the potential to restore landscape structure as well as address soil, water, and air pollution. Although the restored ecosystem is not identical to the native ecosystem displaced by urban development, it has the potential to be ecologically beneficial while also supportive of the surrounding urban community.

Urban Social Challenges for Landscape Architecture

As stewards, planners, and designers of the cultural environment, landscape architects are concerned with the broad range of social issues that impact community life, with particular attention paid to impacts from the physical environment. Work may include the design of large spaces to support community activities and smaller spaces for small groups and individuals. Such work often draws on environmental psychology and behavioral research in the creation of spaces that are comfortable and attractive for human activity. When working in existing communities, landscape architects typically strive to integrate their work into the fabric of the community in ways that respect and enhance cultural values and local sense of place.

Often serving as the technical experts in the real estate development or redevelopment process, landscape architects can enhance community life by supporting community investment through planning and design. However, this traditional role is inadequate in addressing the needs of communities lacking investment or communities whose interests are not served by redevelopment efforts. In such situations, community-based design has emerged as a small but critical tradition within the field of landscape architecture.

Advancing social justice is a fundamental concern of community-based designers, primarily through responses to inequities that disadvantage communities. As with the broader environmental justice movement that emerged in the 1960s, early community-based design efforts responded to environmental negatives that disproportionately affected disadvantaged communities, such as pollution and locally unwanted land uses. Design and planning efforts either eliminated or ameliorated the adverse impacts of these negatives. More recent efforts in landscape architecture have broadened the justice framework to address the distribution of environmental positives, such as access to recreation, open space, safe community spaces, and opportunities to experience natural areas. The influence of both negative and positive environmental factors on perceptions of justice have led some to conclude that ecological sustainability should be advanced in landscape architecture as a social justice issue: Disadvantaged communities are disproportionately affected by the adverse impacts of unsustainable practices in society, so strategies that promote ecological sustainability in urban environments also have the potential to promote social justice, if consciously recognized and addressed by practitioners.

Community-based design differs fundamentally from more traditional practice models of landscape architecture. Due to its focus on justice, the work often closely resembles community organizing, as the process of inclusion, participation, and empowerment

of local communities becomes as important as the resulting plan or design. This contrasts sharply with more traditional perspectives of the landscape architect as a highly trained technical expert who may engage local communities for input, but owns, analyzes, and synthesizes the information in developing external solutions or recommendations. Such diversity of viewpoints on the role of landscape architects in the stewardship, planning, and design processes illustrates another dimension of the diversity of landscape architectural work. For this reason, many scholars argue that professional identity stems as much from shared training, shared processes, and shared values in response to ecological and social challenges as it does from the outcomes or products of the work itself.

Kyle D. Brown

See also Parks; Renaissance City; Sustainable Development

Further Readings

Cantor, Steven L., ed. 1996. *Contemporary Trends in Landscape Architecture.* New York: Wiley.

Corner, James, ed. 1999. *Recovering Landscape: Essays in Contemporary Landscape Architecture.* Princeton, NJ: Princeton University Press.

Crewe, Katherine and Ann Forsyth. 2003. "LandSCAPES: A Typology of Approaches to Landscape Architecture." *Landscape Journal* 22(1):37–53.

Hester, Randolph T. 2006. *Design for Ecological Democracy.* Cambridge: MIT Press.

Pregill, Philip and Nancy Volkman. 1999. *Landscapes in History.* New York: Wiley.

Rotenberg, Robert. 1995. *Landscape and Power in Vienna.* Baltimore: Johns Hopkins University Press.

Swaffield, Simon R., ed. 2002. *Theory in Landscape Architecture: A Reader.* Philadelphia: University of Pennsylvania Press.

Treib, Mark, ed. 1994. *Modern Landscape Architecture: A Critical Review.* Cambridge: MIT Press.

LANDSCAPES OF POWER

Sharon Zukin's 1991 book, *Landscapes of Power,* developed an argument that the creative destruction inherent to capitalism also remakes the places in which people live, work, consume, and recreate. The term has been adopted by geographers, sociologists, urban studies, historians, anthropologists, and political scientists and is present in many different debates about economics and geography since the publication of Zukin's book. Because the term is about the dynamic relationship between economics, politics, culture, and space, it can be used to support a variety of arguments. This entry looks at the key arguments in Zukin and later adoptions to other areas of study.

Key Principles

Following in the tradition of the historian Karl Polanyi, who described the emergence of capitalism in *The Great Transformation,* Zukin outlines how deindustrialization and the shift to a postindustrial economy in the United States has changed five different locales.

The conception of landscapes of power includes the thesis that market forces and attachments to place have become ever more antagonistic. Zukin explores this thesis in a number of different regards. She examines how deindustrialization has meant that towns developed in relationship to particular industries are particularly vulnerable to changes in the economy. For instance, Detroit has become one of the most intensive concentrations of poverty in the United States as the domestic auto industry has lost its economic viability. Attachment to a particular place can be an economic disadvantage if workers do not want to relocate to follow economic opportunities, or if the economic opportunities available in a given locale do not match their skills. Douglas Rae has pointed out in his examination of New Haven, Connecticut, that the economy changes much more quickly than the infrastructure that is built to support it; therefore, we can see a gap between how quickly the market and the landscapes that support it can change.

This theme is also explored in recent work on globalization and place. The globalization of the economy has detached production from particular locations due to the reduced costs of transport. No longer do products need to be made near the spaces where materials are found, nor is it necessary that objects be made in proximity to where they will be sold or consumed. For this reason, economic production becomes less bound by geography.

Just as the concept of creative destruction encompasses the demise of some forms of market behavior and the birth of new ones, so the concept of landscapes of power argues that market forces end up destroying some landscapes while giving rise to new ones. The analysis explains both degenerative and generative changes in the built environment through reference to shifts in economic production. Deindustrialization has hollowed out former company towns such as Gary, Indiana, and Detroit, Michigan, but it has also spawned new developments such as those catering to retired workers in moderate climates.

Zukin also describes how landscapes of power can lose their particular characteristics as another example of the antagonism between the market and locality. For instance, malls around the country have the same stores, restaurants, and recreational opportunities. The economies of scale offer a competitive advantage over competed distinctive local establishments. On the other hand, divergence in the landscape is also evident. Zukin points to the growing disparity of economic opportunity in the United States between coastal regions and the interior as a result of shifts in the market. Evolving market arrangements do not entirely remake the landscape, however, and different layers of economic history are evident in many different locations, as, for example, the luxury loft apartments that have become common in abandoned warehouse space, showing how the economics of intensive capital can redefine—and recycle—the spaces of industrial production.

Another central element in the concept of landscapes of power is that economics reshapes all spaces of living, not just spaces of production. Deindustrialization has created the phenomenon of highly segregated spatial arrangements: Spaces of habitation are distinct from those of production, and places of consumption or leisure are segregated yet again. We move between distinctive environments to work, live, and play. Even those spaces that are designated as spaces of leisure are a result of market forces. Zukin's book considers how both Detroit and Disneyworld can be understood in relationship to the economics of deindustrialization in the United States.

Last, Zukin discusses how cultural forms can simultaneously oppose and reflect the rules of the market economy; for example, how spaces of alternative artistic production attract the forces of gentrification, as evident in Lower Manhattan. Landscapes of power include cultural forces that contest the values of capitalism, as well as providing spaces that allow people to escape the pressures of being a productive member of a late-capitalist economy. The concept unites what seem to be ever more disparate elements of the landscape, showing how they all reflect a singular economic system.

Impact in Other Areas

The literature on the emergence of global cities often adopts Zukin's framework as a model. While the original concept was articulated in relationship to deindustrialization, similar arguments have been made in terms of the globalization of the economy and the emergence of regional centers of the global economy, what are called global cities or world cities. Saskia Sassen, a sociologist, points out that the structures of the global economy have created distinctive labor patterns in these urban centers. There is also an increasing convergence of the labor patterns, consumption habits, and the built environments of these global cities, despite their distinctive histories and vastly different locations and cultures. Whereas cities such as New York, Tokyo, and Paris may be converging landscapes, the distinction between these global cities and cities that do not play a central role in the global economy is growing. For example, the patterns of living, working, and consuming are becoming more similar in London and Paris, but there is a greater difference between Paris and Lyon than there was 40 years ago because of the different roles these cities play in a globalized economy.

Recent work on the cultures of consumption, tourism, and leisure have also drawn heavily on the idea that even spaces designated as alternatives to economic production reflect market forces. For example, eco-tourism allows spaces that have fallen outside of the circuit of economic production to attract global capital. As spaces become more homogenized through transnational global investment, cities have discovered that developing more authentic depictions of their historical culture increases their economic viability by attracting tourism. Urbanism itself has become a major lifestyle attraction in many inner-city neighborhoods as it is redefined as a sophisticated, multicultural, and elite form of culture that is promoted by dense living space.

Keally McBride

See also Deindustrialization; Global City; Loft Living; Shopping

Further Readings

Abu-Lughod, J. L. 1999. *New York, Los Angeles, Chicago: America's Global Cities*. Minneapolis: University of Minnesota Press.

Brenner, Neil and Roger Keil, eds. 2006. *The Global Cities Reader*. London: Routledge.

McBride, Keally. 2005. *Collective Dreams: Political Imagination and Community*. University Park: Pennsylvania State University Press.

Polanyi, Karl. 2001. *The Great Transformation: The Political and Economic Origins of Our Time*. Boston: Beacon.

Rae, Douglas. 2003. *City: Urbanism and Its End*. New Haven, CT: Yale University Press.

Sassen, Saskia. 2000. *The Global City: New York, London, and Tokyo*. Princeton, NJ: Princeton University Press.

Sorkin, Michael, ed. 1992. *Variations on a Theme Park: The New American City and the End of Public Space*. New York: Hill and Wang.

Zukin, Sharon. 1991. *Landscapes of Power: From Detroit to Disneyworld*. Berkeley: University of California Press.

LAND TRUSTS

In the United States, land trusts are a form of social ownership of land. Typically, nonprofit organizations own land in trust through either a conservation land trust or a community land trust. The two types of land trusts are different from each other in origin, use, and intent. Conservation land trusts are nonprofit organizations that conserve land in perpetuity for natural, recreational, scenic, historic, and productive uses. Community land trusts are nonprofit organizations that typically own land to provide a perpetually affordable stock of housing for low- and moderate-income households; however, other uses are possible.

There are more than 1,500 conservation land trusts in the United States. Conservation land trusts either own land or are the recipients of conservation easements. Landowners sell or donate land to a land trust for stewardship. Alternatively, landowners may keep ownership of the land and donate or sell the conservation easements. These easements are legally binding agreements between landowners and the land trust or a government agency, which permanently limit the use of the land. For example, a landowner might donate a conservation easement that would permit the owner to continue to grow crops but restrict the building of additional structures. Future owners would also be bound by these restrictions. Donors of conservation easements typically receive a deduction on income taxes as well as estate tax benefits when the land is passed to heirs. In addition, 12 states have state tax credits for conservation easements. Some local governments assess land with conservation easements at below market rate, thus reducing the landowner's property tax bill. There is great variation in the use of conservation easements by land trusts due to variation in local capacity to select critical lands (e.g., those with greatest ecological value), enforce easements, maintain records, and manage the lands, among other issues.

The community land trust mechanism has roots in nineteenth-century England and Ireland, Ebenezer Howard's Garden City movement, and the Gandhian *Gramdan* (village gift) movement of the 1950s. The first community land trust in the United States was New Communities, Inc., established in rural Georgia in 1968 by the civil rights movement as a response to the displacement of black farmers in the rural South. Today, there are more than 150 community land trusts across the United States in rural, urban, and suburban settings. Most community land trusts are small organizations stewarding as few as a dozen units of housing. The largest of them stewards more than 2,000 units of housing. A new trend is the interest of municipal governments in sponsoring community land trusts, often to build and manage affordable housing created under inclusionary zoning.

Typically, a community land trust is governed by a tripartite board of directors, where one third represents the interests of leaseholders, one third represents the interests of residents from the community, and one third represents the public interest (e.g., public officials or funders). The leaseholder and community representatives to the board are elected from the trust membership, which includes leaseholders as well as community residents.

The ground lease is the legal document that governs the relationship between the homeowner and the community land trust. The trust establishes a resale formula that governs the sale of the house from one leaseholder to the next. Although the house passes from one owner to another, the land continues to be owned by the trust. The resale formula balances the goals of the organization and the interests of the current and future low- and moderate-income homeowners.

Rosalind Greenstein

See also Environmental Policy; Land Development; Sustainable Development

Further Readings

Burlington Associates (http://www.burlingtonassociates.com).

Community Land Trusts (UK) (http://www.communitylandtrust.org.uk).

Conservation Land Trusts (http://www.lta.org).

National Community Land Trust Network (http://www.cltnetwork.org).

Pidot, Jeff. 2005. *Reinventing Conservation Easements. A Critical Examination and Ideas for Reform.* Cambridge, MA: Lincoln Institute of Land Policy.

LAS VEGAS, NEVADA

Las Vegas, Nevada, represents a singularly fascinating subject within the field of urban studies. This is not so much because of its history in terms of urban development—which is nevertheless rich and illuminating—but more because of its *historiography*, in that its locus and meaning within scholarly discourse have changed dramatically and controversially within the past 50 years. As a place, Las Vegas continues to stimulate debate as globalized economics, social deprivation, and climate change begin to have a powerful impact on its future development.

There are, of course, other sites in the continental United States where gambling is legalized or where the focus of the urban environment is toward leisure and recreation. Atlantic City, New Jersey; Reno, Nevada; and Tunica, Mississippi, for example, as well as many state- or federal-sanctioned casinos on tribal lands and riverboats across the United States, play host to gambling and other forms of gaming. Compared with other places associated with gambling in the world, however, Las Vegas has attracted more attention, developed more innovatively, and courted more controversy. This entry begins with a historical review and then looks at key issues related to urban studies.

Historical Background

Gambling was first legalized in Nevada in 1896 and at that time was focused along Fremont Street in Las Vegas, adjacent to the railroad station. Gambling was then banned in 1911, and licenses were granted again only in 1931, a move intended to help Nevada, a state notable for its lack of industry, minimal agriculture, and depleted mines, survive the Great Depression. Las Vegas also got by thanks to the patronage of many of the 5,000 workers building the nearby Hoover Dam, and the so-called maverick state later came through World War II by an injection of federal government resources.

Robert E. Parker describes how Las Vegas then entered the "mob phase" of its history, marked by the opening of Bugsy Siegel's Flamingo casino in 1946, which paved the way for casinos along the Strip becoming ever more lavish and extravagant in their vision and their execution. The corporate phase began after 1967, when reclusive entrepreneur Howard Hughes began to buy up casinos on the Las Vegas Strip, starting with the Desert Inn, where he had been living. Hughes's investment in Las Vegas is thought to have helped the town throw off its associations with organized crime and move from being seen as the ultimate Sin City to a typical all-American city. As a result, perceptions of the Strip have now been upgraded with its renaming as Las Vegas Boulevard, and casino ownership has become increasingly monopolized by companies such as Harrah's, MGM Mirage, and Station Casinos: The big operators reputedly now own more than 60 percent of casino real estate.

By the 1990s, Las Vegas casinos had become enormous resort complexes, attracting a wide variety of international clientele, enticing them with spectacular events such as volcanoes erupting, fountains dancing, pirate ships sinking, and spectacular urban collages of New York, Venice, and Paris. Las Vegas's earlier incarnation as a Strip development where giant signs made up the skyline, where there were no buildings to speak of, has been replaced by an avenue of striking and substantial structures, where the architecture itself is the sign. The smaller and older casinos located in the former downtown area of Las Vegas along Fremont Street were suffering a loss of patronage due to the success of the megacasinos on the Strip and conceived a plan designed by architect Jon Jerde to attract customers back to this location. Jerde's branded Fremont Street Experience is an event space that consists of a high-tech vaulted canopy running the length of the now pedestrian street, and it is fitted with millions of programmable LED lights. Sound and light shows are programmed throughout the day, featuring aspects of American and local history, race car driving, and aliens; the space also hosts the town's New Year's Eve party, with fireworks relayed on the display system at 9 p.m., so as to be televised live at midnight on East Coast television screens.

So much for some brief Las Vegas facts and developmental timeline: As countless websites attest, elaborated chronology functions as a proxy for Las Vegas's identity and status, superficially legitimizing its contribution to urban history through a series of sensational build costs, insurance payouts, and visitor and land-take figures over the years. It still has the highest hotel room inventory of any city in the world. Richard Florida, writing in *Cities and the Creative Class*, notes, however, that Las Vegas might have ranked first for population growth and third in terms of job growth between 1990 and 2000, but in terms of per capita income growth, it came in 294th out of the 315 U.S. metropolitan areas surveyed. Las Vegas's population is 58 percent service class, and the city is unusual in its lack of interest

Las Vegas at night, from the top of the Luxor hotel on the Strip.

Source: Erin Monacelli.

in attracting the creative class that other cities across the world have found essential to sustain economic growth. Despite Las Vegas's proven viability to date as an economic force, many of its less attractive statistics are usually played down, and the reality of a city of low-paid workers working antisocial hours is masked, along with issues to do with the precarious situation regarding air pollution, energy consumption, water supply, underage and compulsive gambling, lack of affordable housing, male homelessness, degradation of the desert environment, and underinvestment in community benefits.

Urban Theory Research

The scholarly community has of late been turning its attention toward addressing these pressing topical issues and, in the process, reflecting on the role of Las Vegas within urban theory. Academic assessment of Las Vegas has in fact been continuous ever since the publication in 1972 of *Learning from Las Vegas* (LFLV) by Robert Venturi, Denise Scott Brown, and Steve Izenour. Their book was reputedly inspired by reading an essay by Tom Wolfe, quirkily titled "Las Vegas (What?) Las Vegas (Can't hear you! Too noisy) Las Vegas!!!" in which, according to Douglass and Raento, Wolfe "captures the essence of the city's postwar reinvention of itself and its metamorphosis into a true gaming destination."

The Original Study

LFLV is the culmination of the fieldwork of a group of architecture students from Yale University and contains essays, diagrams, and analysis of Las Vegas as they found it at the end of the 1960s. Their interest was in understanding how a commercial strip was organized, how it worked spatially and temporally, and where its popular appeal lay. By their account, it is clear than in 1972, Las Vegas was already embarking on an amelioration of its tawdry urban environment, and LFLV is thus not unlike Walter Benjamin's work on the Paris arcades, capturing an era that was in danger of being replaced by a new incarnation.

Sarfatti Larson reminds us that LFLV represented "a shocking comparison of private and public spaces in eighteenth-century Rome with the Las Vegas strip." Albert Pope, author of *Ladders*, qualifies arguments expressed within LFLV favoring chaotic urban form by suggesting that the authors overlooked a significant contradiction: Both the Strip and Fremont Street were in fact ordered around a linear armature, and despite the messy vitality of the discrete pieces of Las Vegas's urban form, this linearity served to unify and regulate the city's development.

Whatever reading is applied, there is no doubt that LFLV showed that as a place Las Vegas required a different mode of inquiry regarding how its urban landscape functioned compared to other twentieth-century places. A 2004 book on *Design-based Planning for Communities* goes as far as to suggest that *Learning from Las Vegas* represents "an important event in the demolition of modernist urban theory, it created room for the development of new ways of thinking about urbanism in America." Jon Goodbun allows an even more direct influence, establishing the place rather than the book about the place as the instrument of change: "Las Vegas represents the rejection of modernism."

Paradigm or Pariah

It is profoundly fascinating that Las Vegas could, as an object of study, have been responsible for prompting a wholesale shift within planning and urban design, a shift that has since given rise to Traditional Neighborhood Development (TND), Transit-Oriented Development (TOD), and other new urbanist concepts, especially given the lack of focus on public transportation in Las Vegas (the monorail system is still only partially built). Las Vegas is often held up simultaneously as a paradigm and a pariah in urban design terms. Reyner Banham registered how "so much has been written about that city as an image of fear, loathing,

bad taste, depravity, cultural emptiness and all the rest that the simple truth behind it can no longer be seen . . . [namely] a true oasis." Hal Rothman argues that Las Vegas is now in the process of switching from pariah to paradigm, in the sense that Las Vegas is no longer exceptional in the American urban landscape but wholly consistent with other places functioning as tourist destinations.

The Dutch architect Rem Koolhaas, who was a student at the time LFLV came out, and was taken with its premise, instigated a second look at the city with a bunch of East Coast students, this time from Harvard University. Koolhaas claims in his book, *Project on the City*, that "Las Vegas is one of the few cities to become paradigmatic twice in thirty years: from a city at the point of becoming virtual in 1972, to an almost irrevocably substantial condition in 2000."

In terms of benchmarking current practice, Las Vegas thus represents a changeable and problematic irritant to urban theorists, one that was consequently either belittled or ignored. Writing in the *Architectural Review* in 1962, Lewis Mumford saw Las Vegas as an example of "roadtown," and as such was an "anti-city," constituting an "incoherent and purposeless urbanoid nonentity, which dribbles over the devastated landscape." From the later vantage point of 1993, Alan Hess explains that "Las Vegas was largely incomprehensible to eastern architecture critics, but being ignored allowed it time to gestate as a city before it was noticed at all." Hess claimed that "Las Vegas is not an ideal urban model, but it is well worth considering as American urbanism gropes towards a new definition and a new form," especially given that most American cities are in a state of adolescence. At that time, the urban village concept was only just "emerging from the primal suburban soup," where by contrast, the Las Vegas Strip, although "no older than many such suburbs, has been changing and remodelling since . . . 1941."

The case for ignoring Las Vegas did not end with the publication of LFLV, however: witness the fact that despite Fredric Jameson declaring *Learning from Las Vegas* to be *the* canonical text of postmodernism, Nan Ellin, for example, in *Postmodern Urbanism*, does not discuss Las Vegas once, yet her book evolves an entire narrative about the relationship between cities and postmodern urban design theory. One is left to assume that, in her view, Las Vegas lies outside realms of deliberate strategic, design-centered urban development and is therefore not noteworthy.

Nevertheless, as a product of postmodern urbanism, the typology of the Urban Entertainment District (UED), which Las Vegas amply exemplifies, has generated a broad spectrum of unique selling propositions, which now extend from slot machines and video poker all the way up to fine dining (4 of the 17 five-star restaurants in the entire United States are on the Strip), haute couture (Caesar's Forum, at $1,300 per square foot for leased space, is the world's greatest concentration of luxury retail outlets), and upmarket art collections. Shopping now ranks first with visitors, above gambling, as the reason they come to the city.

Social and Cultural Studies

Studies of Las Vegas as an urban phenomenon have not been restricted to architectural theory and urban geography. Las Vegas also looms large within film studies, sociology, tourism and leisure studies, and critical theory. Within this multidisciplinary landscape, debate has tended to focus on the real/fake distinction, where Las Vegas is seen to offer a pertinent and challenging configuration. Judd and Fainstein suggest that "Las Vegas explicitly advertises itself as a fake neon city. . . . But tourists do not always want to be humored or amused. Instead they often seek immersion in the daily, ordinary, authentic life of a culture or place that is not their own." Hal Rothman's take is more nuanced: "It's not that people can't tell the difference [between authentic and inauthentic in Las Vegas]—they can. But in a culture without a dominant set of premises or culturally agreed upon values . . . it's hard to communicate why conventional authenticity is better."

Mark Gottdiener, coauthor of *Las Vegas: The Social Production of an All-American City* and author of *The Theming of America*, has examined the relationship between values and their communication via theming. He regards authenticity in Las Vegas as having to do with being overendowed with signification and meaning to produce an intensely specialized pleasure zone. Gottdiener also shows how this becomes part of a bigger process, where the stakes are raised for iconic skylines and buildings-as-brands. As such, the strong visual and iconic appeal of Las Vegas becomes normalized and contiguous with urban development agendas elsewhere, and Las Vegas consequently takes its place in the global order of things, as part of the global pecking order of other Guggenheim museums, other Dolce and Gabbana stores, other Hard Rock cafés.

Never far from debates about authenticity is the specter of Disneyfication and the privatization of public space. George Ritzer's take on Disneyfication regards it as a handmaiden to capitalism, capable of producing and sustaining markets with strong, infantilized, predictable, and controlling imagery. Las Vegas may have strayed into the market of family entertainment but never fully embraced it for fear of alienating its core customer base. Family-oriented elements are evident in Las Vegas, and the general ambience has become more daytime, more televisual, and consequently rehabilitated as a result. Ritzer sees the greatest similarity between Disney and Las Vegas in the notion of a *total institution*, defined by Erving Goffman as "places of residence and work, where large numbers of like situated individuals, cut off from the wider society for an appreciable period of time, together lead an enclosed, formally administered round of life." As a total institution, Las Vegas gathers and isolates those who come with hopes of winning but an underlying acceptance that they will lose money in the interests of enjoyment.

Writing his *Scenes in America Deserta* in 1982, Reyner Banham claimed that Las Vegas avoids the question of "How could they have made a place like that?" Today one could also claim that Vegas ducks the question "Do people actually live here?" There is an obvious disconnect between Las Vegas the UED and Las Vegas as an entire settlement. This leads one to question if in fact Las Vegas is a city at all—or conversely, is it what all cities are in the process of becoming?

Looking Ahead

Banham suggests that above all else, Las Vegas represents "the impermanence of man in the desert." It remains to be seen whether the quality of impermanence is to be realized: Will Las Vegas at some point be abandoned due to rising surface temperatures, the scarcity of land, and the prohibitive cost of oil? Or will it survive?

To date, there has been little emphasis on conservation or preservation of Las Vegas's ephemeral architecture, for either cultural or ecological reasons. As one of the most isolated cities in the United States, located in possibly the least hospitable part of the country, Las Vegas nevertheless seems to be responding to environmental pressures: The new 61-acre Union Park development on a brownfield site claims to herald a new era of green design, with a fully master-planned, Leadership in Environmental Design–certified, high-density, mixed-use, sustainability-centered urban village. Is it smart, however, to cater to the demand for dense urban lifestyles in a part of the United States where the prospects of supplying water and hence land suitable for development are diminishing? If it is to survive, Las Vegas will need to become an exemplar for low-impact development, as Edward McMahon, director of the Urban Land Institute, speculates: "Living in a desert has always been a challenge, but the realities of geography and global warming are going to force Las Vegas to go green or suffer the consequences."

The consequences include falling land values and the prospect of rising unemployment and social security claimants leading to a situation potentially where Sun Belt cities could come to eclipse Rust Belt cities in terms of their relative unviability, in which case Las Vegas would become more than just an extended boneyard of abandoned neon signage. Other places in history such as Fatehpur Sikri, Prypiat, and Thebes have suffered the same fate due to ecological or political reasons: In the future, it is not inconceivable that the main tourist motivation for visiting Las Vegas may be to experience a museum of historic twentieth century artifacts on an urban scale. Conservation and preservation will become the new thematic content of Las Vegas, the ghost town. Its very existence has perhaps been one long hundred-year gamble, for as Baudrillard says in *America,* "gambling itself is a desert form, inhuman, uncultured, initiatory, a challenge to the natural economy of value, a crazed activity on the fringes of exchange."

Sarah Chaplin

See also Cinematic Urbanism; Gottdiener, Mark; Tourism; Urban Planning; Urban Semiotics

Further Readings

Banham, Reyner. 1989. *Scenes in America Deserta.* Cambridge: MIT Press.

Baudrillard, Jean. 1989. *America.* New York: Verso.

Douglass, William, and Pauliina Raento. 2004. "The Tradition of Invention: Conceiving Las Vegas." *Annals of Tourism Research* 30(1): 7–23.

Earley, Pete. 2001. *Super Casino: Inside the "New" Las Vegas.* New York: Bantam.

Ellin, Nan. 1999. *Postmodern Urbanism.* Princeton, NJ: Princeton Architectural Press.

Florida, Richard. 2003. *Cities and the Creative Class.* New York: Basic Books.

Fox, William L. 2005. *In the Desert of Desire.* Reno: University of Nevada Press.

Franci, Giovanna and Federico Zignani. 2005. *Dreaming of Italy: Las Vegas and the Virtual Grand Tour.* Reno: University of Nevada Press.

Gottdiener, Mark. 2001. *The Theming of America.* Boulder, CO: Westview Press.

Gottdiener, Mark, Claudia Collins, and David Dickens. 2000. *Las Vegas: The Social Production of an All-American City.* Malden, MA: Wiley-Blackwell.

Hess, Alan. 1959. *Viva Las Vegas: After-hours Architecture.* San Francisco: Chronicle Books.

Judd, D. and S. Fainstein. 1999. *The Tourist City.* New Haven, CT: Yale University Press.

Land, Barbara and Myrick Land. 2004. *A Short History of Las Vegas.* Reno: University of Nevada Press.

Rattenbury, Kester, Robert Venturi, and Denise Scott Brown. 2008. *Learning from Las Vegas: SuperCrit 2.* London: Routledge.

Rothman, Hal. 2003. *Neon Metropolis: How Las Vegas Started the Twenty-first Century.* New York: Routledge.

Rothman, Hal and Mike Davis, eds. 2002. *The Grit beneath the Glitter: Tales from the Real Las Vegas.* Berkeley: University of California Press.

Schumacher, Geoff. 2004. *Sun, Sin, and Suburbia: An Essential History of Modern Las Vegas.* Las Vegas, NV: Stephens Press.

Venturi, Robert, Denise Scott Brown, and Steve Izenour. 1972. *Learning from Las Vegas.* Cambridge: MIT Press.

LAWN

A lawn is defined by four characteristics: It is composed only of grass species; it is subject to weed and pest control; it is subject to practices aimed at maintaining its green color; and it is regularly mowed to ensure an acceptable length. Although many authors

A well-maintained lawn in front of a home in a suburb of Detroit, Michigan.

Source: Karen Wiley.

include parks, golf courses, and playing fields within the broad rubric of the lawn, the term is most often associated with the green spaces that border private dwellings. Despite its commonplace presence in most North American and some European cities, the lawn generates considerable dialogue concerning its social and cultural symbolism as well as its role in urban ecological processes.

History

There is some evidence that manicured grassed landscapes made their first appearance in ancient China. A form of lawn is also associated with English and French elites of the sixteenth to eighteenth centuries. However, a more prosaic dating of the urban lawn places it with the growing middle class in the late-nineteenth-century cities. Rapid growth of industrial cities and concern for urban morals fueled the emergence of a pastoral idyll. And, whereas a complete removal from the city was impossible for many families, middle-class rural desires were manifest as a suburban, single detached home surrounded by private green space.

These desires depended on the convergence of a number of factors. First, the emergence of commuter travel and later the automobile allowed urban dwellers the necessary mobility to move to

suburban homes. Second, the adoption of the eight-hour workday and the five-day workweek meant that people had adequate time for lawn work. Finally, and contemporaneously, the development of technologies such as lawn mowers, irrigation devices (hoses and sprinklers), pesticides, and herbicides, as well as the identification of appropriate grass plants, offered homeowners the means through which lawns could be created and maintained.

Early-twentieth-century advertisers sought to convince homeowners of the moral, aesthetic, and social virtues of owning a lawn. However, in the 1930s, these same advertisers shifted strategies. That is, instead of persuading homeowners of the lawn's appropriateness, new advertisements offered consumers better means to care for a lawn. The implication is that by this time, most consumers were convinced of the appropriateness of the lawn and now needed to be disciplined to care of it. A post–World War II climate conducive to consumerism and the advent of mass suburban development fixed the lawn in discourses surrounding home and property ownership, public presentation, industriousness, gender, the nuclear family, and good citizenship. In North America, in particular, yard after yard of unfenced turf bespoke democracy.

Although it is impossible to fix the degree to which lawn covers the Earth's surface, there are some data that illustrate its extent. For example, 2008 estimates suggest that the lawn is North America's largest agricultural crop and that it covers nearly 2 percent of the continental United States. Furthermore, lawn maintenance has become big business. The production of lawn equipment and lawn products produce commodity chains that touch every continent except Antarctica. Global estimates in the early 2000s for lawn-related expenditure range between $22 billion and $35 billion annually. This amount includes the increasing use of professional lawn care companies that range from small (less than $50,000 in sales per year) to large (more than $1 million in sales per year). Estimates suggest that in 2008, more than 80,000 lawn and landscaping companies operated in the United States alone.

The Lawn as Sociocultural Landscape

Apologists make a number of claims concerning the benefits of a well-groomed lawn. First, many commentators contend that a uniform covering of turf is aesthetically pleasing. This has immediate benefits; it creates a good impression of the homeowner and adds significant value to any home. Second, proponents contend that a good lawn can be therapeutic. It offers urban residents opportunity to engage with nature on their home fronts. Moreover, both working on the lawn and relaxing on it afterward are good therapy for relieving the stresses of everyday life. A lawn also provides a good space for exercise and a soft, resistant space on which children can play safely next to their homes. Third, a neighborhood of good lawns is conducive to good citizenship. Lawns, proponents argue, function as detriment to litter and to crime. A SULIS report, for example, suggests that the social and material problems of inner cities may be combated with lawns and other forms of landscaping.

Despite these claims, the lawn lies at the interstices of numerous social divides. Scholars have historically associated suburban movements with white middle-class pioneers. Wishing to leave behind the perceived ugliness, disorderliness, and material and moral pollution of the city, these people sought refuge in the new suburbs. Central to this move was the desire to keep particular sets of values safe from undesirable people and obnoxious nuisances. At once reacting to and entrenching this demand, many developers enacted covenants that restricted habitation in subdivisions based on race, ethnicity, religion, and/or class. Although civil rights legislation has rendered most of these restrictions unlawful, scholarship suggests that they continue, but in the guise of discriminatory lending practices and real estate steering. The upshot is, a suburban home surrounded by a verdant lawn remains a landscape simultaneously raced and classed. Moreover, research suggests that these White, middle-class desires are reemerging in gated and otherwise closed communities. Upkeep of the lawn is often an initial clue of the homeowner's willingness to internalize the values implicit in these communities.

Like other markers of suburban conformity, the appearance of well-kept lawn continues to signify the gendered division of domestic labor. Inside work belongs to women; it is moral work based on family care. Where associated with outdoor work, women are limited to the gardens that fringe the lawn. Outside work belongs to men; it is also moral work but based on public performance and good citizenship. Furthermore, advertisers have targeted audiences along familiar gender roles; advertisements aimed at women tended to emphasize appearances and home care whereas those aimed at men emphasize mechanics and engineering. The reproduction of the lawn, then, is a key element in the reproduction of particular values centered on a nuclear family. Such roles continue seemingly unabated. Indeed, scholars have found that children as young as two or three years old identified yard work as appropriately masculine.

The lawn also points to a number of contradictions with which its owners must engage. First, the lawn is an important feature of discourses of the individual and privacy. Indeed, in many cases, the lawn marks the initial transition from public to private space. Yet, the autonomy of private green space is far from complete. That is, with its close association with good citizenship, public mindedness, and suitable aesthetics, the lawn is difficult to disavow. In many cities across North America, for example, it has been transformed from a sociocultural could or should to a legal must. By the mid twentieth century, officials in many North American cities codified regulations for the upkeep of lawns through bylaws; homeowners with unkempt lawns face fines and may have their lawns cut for them.

It is worth noting that this process is often complaint driven. This suggests neighbors augment formal laws with informal community standards. Scholars suggest that this kind of enforcement is based on the lawn's role in maintaining a veneer of conformity in an age of increasing anxiety over cultural and social difference. This conformity is manifest in the lawn's appearance and its ritualized care regimens. Deviance can be socially costly. Lawn dissidents are marked as uncooperative, lazy, and morally inept. Worse, lawn owners see these qualities as contagious. Neighbors may associate a single lawn dissident with lower property values, diminished local community standards, and moral and material pollution.

Second, the lawn represents an ecological dilemma. Although many lawn keepers are aware of the potential dangers of repeated applications of herbicides, pesticides, and fertilizers, they continue to apply them. This points to a complicated relationship among the needs of the lawn itself, the exigencies of capitalist production, and the social, cultural, political, and economic contexts of individual lawn owners. Lawn product manufacturers and lawn care companies have a stake in maintaining and strengthening markets in the face of environmental lobbies and competition. To that end, they work to continue to convince consumers that inputs are necessary for a good lawn and, therefore, for good families and communities. But in so doing, they also download the risk of using these products to consumers who have at least some knowledge of commensurate environmental and personal risk.

There are two strands of such risk. First, consumers become responsible for their own decisions regarding chemical use. Despite knowing something of the hazards of chemical application, many homeowners seem unwilling to change behaviors. This is may be explained by a second strand of risk. That is, consumers are also well aware of the financial (fines and falling real estate values) and socioeconomic (fall out with neighbors) costs of deviance.

The Lawn as Ecology

The lawn, because of its ubiquity and density in urban spaces, is at the center of intense debates over its ecological implications. Lawn critics suggest that the lawn and its related maintenance have a number of negative environmental consequences. First, critics suggest that the propagation of monoculture crops of introduced species erases local flora and fauna and thereby overcomes the ecological diversity of local areas. This leads to concerns over air, soil, and water quality as well as environmental health generally.

Second, critics maintain lawn care practice is environmentally deleterious. Some authors point to the vast amount of fossil fuels that lawn equipment consumes. The U.S. Environmental Protection Agency (EPA), for example, contends that in the United States alone, lawn owners consume 800 million gallons of gasoline annually to power lawn mowers. EPA also states that Americans use about 7 billion gallons of water per day for lawn and garden use.

Third, critics also point to the pollution that is produced through the operation of powered lawn care equipment and the application of chemicals; both are important sources of air, water, and soil pollution. By extension, several authors point to potential links between the use of gas-powered lawn equipment and chemicals and reproductive complications, neurological problems, and certain kinds of cancer. Children who play on treated lawns are at particular risk.

In answer to these allegations, lawn proponents claim that turf is an environmental asset. First, a healthy lawn makes positive contributions to the atmosphere. A lawn can play a large role in cooling urban environments. It also serves to generate oxygen as well as to sequester carbon dioxide. In fact, research suggests that the carbon dioxide output from a gas-powered mower is more than offset by the lawn's ability to use it. The conclusion is that homeowners who carefully manage their lawns do more for the environment than those who do not.

Second, proponents contend that a lawn can improve local water and soil quality. A healthy lawn should trap dust and pollutants. Constant microbial activity in the lawn breaks them down into harmless components before they can dissipate into the wider soil and water systems. The lawn also contains storm runoff and minimizes potential damage caused by erosion. Finally, the annual cycle of growth and decay contributes organic material to the soil, thereby contributing to its health.

Both sets of arguments lie at the heart of a mass of material that describes how the lawn might become even more environmentally sustainable. Indeed, a 2008 Internet search for key words *lawn* and *environment* generated nearly 30 million hits. Most of these outline environmentally friendly lawn care advice. Few, however, question whether or not there might be alternatives to the lawn. Lawn equipment and chemical companies and lawn care companies also contribute to the debate. In response to the stresses of another wave of environmental concern, most companies will make claims to using safe products and processes. But they have also become active lobbyists that attempt to thwart bans on chemicals, restrictions on noise, and/or other threats to the lawn. In the end, consumers must contend with a barrage of information with a dizzying variety of research outcomes provided by both environmental advocates and corporations.

Pressure to seek safer alternatives, however, continues to mount. Whereas most North American cities employ a weed inspector to uphold lawn standards, many cities have begun to ban pesticides and other chemical inputs, monitor water use, and issue noise restrictions. Lawn dissenters are becoming more common and much more active. Some have adopted "Freedom Lawns" (whereupon no chemicals are applied) or xeriscaped yards (use of only drought-resistant plants). Still others are pushing further. Advocacy groups encourage the use of private greenspace for growing food or rebuilding local environments. However, Robbins argues that the widespread acceptance of these alternatives will not be easily achieved. Enforcement of deeds, covenants, and weed laws limit what any individual may accomplish in particular neighborhoods.

At present, the lawn remains a seemingly permanent fixture in North American and some European urban landscapes. In fact, as more suburban homes are built, the lawn continues to expand its reach. Currently, it is the fastest-growing landscape in North America. Thus, despite emerging evidence that the lawn has serious ecological implications, many homeowners seem to have internalized the values it represents. However, although various apparatus help maintain the lawn as appropriate for private green space, an increasing number of people are searching for alternatives to swards of managed turf.

Michael Ripmeester

See also Environmental Policy; Gated Community; Gendered Space; Real Estate; Redlining; Racialization; Restrictive Covenant

Further Readings

Blomley, Nicholas. 2005. "The Borrowed View: Privacy, Propriety, and the Entanglements of Property." *Law and Social Inquiry* 30:617–61.

Borman, F. H. et al. 1993. *Redesigning the American Lawn: A Search for Environmental Harmony.* New Haven, CT: Yale University Press.

Christians, Nick and Ashton Richie. 2002. *Scotts Lawns: Your Guide to a Beautiful Yard.* Des Moines, IA: Meredith Books.

Feagan, Rob and Michael Ripmeester. 2001. "Reading Private Green Space: Competing Geographic Identities at the Level of the Lawn." *Philosophy & Geography* 4:79–95.

Jenkins, Virginia Scott. 1994. *The Lawn: A History of an American Obsession.* Washington, DC: Smithsonian Institution Press.

The Lawn Institute. 2008. "Environment." Retrieved November 2, 2008 (http://www.thelawninstitute.org/environment).

Robbins, Paul. 2007. *Lawn People: How Grasses, Weeds, and Chemicals Make Us Who We Are.* Philadelphia: Temple University Press.

Sahu, Ranajit (Ron). n.d. "Technical Assessment of the Carbon Sequestration Potential of Managed Turfgrass in the United States." Retrieved November 1, 2008 (http://www.opei.org/carbonreport/FullCarbonReport.pdf).

Steinberg, Ted. 2006. *American Green: The Obsessive Quest for the Perfect Lawn.* New York: W. W. Norton.

University of Minnesota. "Environmental Benefits of a Healthy, Sustainable Lawn" (SULIS series). Retrieved November 3, 2008 (http://www.sustland.umn.edu/maint/benefits.htm).

LE CORBUSIER

Le Corbusier was one of the most influential yet controversial architect–planners of the twentieth century, as well as being a prolific writer, painter, sculptor, and poet. He occupies a troubled place in architectural scholarship. Some cannot forgive him his arrogance and political opportunism. Others see a designer of genius and a polemically brilliant writer.

Early Years

Born Charles-Édouard Jeanneret in Switzerland in 1887, he seemed destined for a career in watch-case engraving before developing an interest in architecture. The first house he built was the Villa Fallet (1907), which reflected his hometown vernacular with its steep roof and ornamented façade. Between 1908 and 1911, however, Jeanneret was apprenticed to Auguste Perret and Peter Behrens, early pioneers of reinforced concrete construction and industrial design.

He traveled extensively around Europe and the near East, where the Hagia Sophia and Parthenon had a profound effect on him. It was also around this time that he read the works of the Viennese architect Adolf Loos, in particular *Ornament and Crime* (1908). These influences inspired Jeanneret to devise an architectural style that eschewed decoration and combined the latest building technologies with the monumentality of ancient architecture.

During World War I, Jeanneret attempted to patent a new housing prototype for postwar reconstruction. The Dom-Ino had six columns, a staircase, and three slabs for the ground, first floor, and roof. This design encapsulated the theory that would characterize his architectural work in the 1920s, the *Five Points of a New Architecture* (1926): *pilotis,* open plan, free façade, strip windows, roof garden.

Moving to Paris in 1917, Jeanneret met the painter Amédée Ozenfant, and together, they published *Après le Cubisme* (1918), the founding manifesto of the Purist movement. Their Purist still lifes had interlocking forms spread calmly across the canvas, often in gentle pastel colors, unlike the swirling, fragmented forms of Cubist still lifes. This pictorial orderliness was part of a more general return to order that Ozenfant and Jeanneret hoped to see in Europe after the upheavals of the war.

Architecture and town planning were part of the plan and these were discussed in the Purist journal, *L'Esprit Nouveau.* Le Corbusier was invented as a pseudonym for Jeanneret when writing about these topics, but soon the name stuck, and his articles were collected into books that define the Modern movement, including *Vers une Architecture* (1923) and *Urbanisme* (1924).

A Theory of Architecture

Vers une Architecture outlined Le Corbusier's theory of architecture as the sculptural arrangement of volumes under light, which he derived from his analysis of the Parthenon. It discussed also the architectural promenade, where the complexities of space are revealed as one passes through them in a carefully orchestrated sequence. These principles were put into practice in a series of elegant homes, including the Villa La Roche-Jeanneret (Paris, 1925) and the Villa Savoye (Poissy, 1929).

Urbanisme introduced Le Corbusier's theory of town planning. It focused on his designs for the Ville Contemporaine, exhibited at the Salon d'Automne of 1922. The centerpiece of this "city for two million inhabitants" was a transport hub complete with airport and surrounded by 24 skyscrapers, each of them 60 stories high, clad in glass and cruciform in plan. Further out were residential blocks arranged according to set-back and perimeter-block patterns. Each residence was soundproof and had a double-height living room and an internal garden, and each block enjoyed catering and cleaning services as well as allotments and sports facilities. The buildings were to be lifted up on pilotis, and the different grades of vehicular traffic were segregated, some running underground. This allowed the entire ground surface of the city to be cultivated into a vast park.

Le Corbusier observed later that this centralized design was flawed as it could not grow but only be duplicated. He remedied this in the 1930s with proposals for linear cities such as the Ville Radieuse: the different zones—commercial, industrial, residential—were arranged in linear bands that could be extended indefinitely. Even so, the central tenets of Le Corbusier's urbanism were contained in the Ville Contemporaine, not least his commitment to social engineering. Run by the managerial elite in the skyscrapers, the city would defuse revolutionary tendencies in the working classes by giving them better homes and the leisure time and facilities to cultivate body and mind.

The question of how to implement such grand plans seemed to resolve itself fortuitously around this time. In 1927, Le Corbusier submitted his competition entry for the League of Nations building. He appeared to have won, but his designs were later dismissed on the technicality that they were reproductions rather than original drawings. Le Corbusier and others saw this as a conspiracy, and the following year they formed the Congrès Internationaux d'Architecture Moderne (CIAM). CIAM became the official body of modern architecture and planning and included influential figures such as Hannes Meyer, Gerrit Rietveld, El Lissitzky and Josep Lluís Sert.

Members would gather for conferences to thrash out design policy, and although there was never perfect consensus, there was considerable agreement. CIAM delegates lobbied successfully to get their principles adopted in the building and land-use legislation of governments around the world, as well as in the educational curricula of the schools of architecture and planning. The reductionist tendencies of CIAM are represented best in *The Athens Charter* of 1943, where the city was presented as a simple puzzle with just four functions: dwelling, working, circulation, and recreation.

In addition to CIAM, Le Corbusier courted others whom he thought had the power and finances to implement his plans. He was scornful of the parliamentary infighting of France between the wars and believed the remedy was to adopt nonparliamentary means. This found an echo in the Redressement Français, a technocratic organization formed in 1925 that campaigned for society and the economy to be reorganized according to scientific principles and managed by experts.

But Le Corbusier was attracted to antiparliamentary movements more generally, such as the French fascist movement, Les Faisceau, and the paramilitary leagues that toppled the Radical government in the riots of February 1934. Working in Vichy during German occupation in 1941 to 1942, Le Corbusier lobbied Marshal Philippe Pétain to sanction his plans to redevelop Algiers, and imagined a postwar France that would see him crowned The Lawgiver with a mandate to remold the built fabric of the empire.

Le Corbusier was frustrated in these ambitions and after the war he appears to have given up on politics, and this is when he completed some of his most important work.

Masterpieces

The Unité d'habitation (Marseilles, 1952) was an opportunity for Le Corbusier to put his ideas on high-rise living into practice. The double-height apartments and amenities like shops, a gym, and school recall the mid-1920s, but they were presented here in a bold new sculptural style that became known as Brutalism. The concrete was untreated and retains imprints from the wooden forms, and deeply cut *brise-soleil* transform the exterior into a play of light and shade. This new expressiveness reached its zenith in the Chapel of Notre Dame du Haut at Ronchamp (1954), a building of wild exuberance, symbolism, and color.

The largest work undertaken by Le Corbusier was the city of Chandigarh, commissioned as a new capital for the Punjab after Indian independence and partition in 1947. The original design team was headed by the American military engineer Albert Mayer and the Polish architect Matthew Nowicki. The project stalled, however, and Le Corbusier was contracted to head a new team that included the civil engineer Pierre Jeanneret and the English architect–planners Maxwell Fry and Jane Drew. They arrived in India in 1951 with a mandate to implement the original plans, and while they kept certain ideas, such as neighborhood units and a capitol complex of government buildings, they straightened out the Garden City layout with a CIAM gridiron and increased the overall scale.

The residential sectors reflected the socioeconomic status of the residents. Luxurious homes for government officials are in the topmost sectors, space and amenities getting squeezed as one proceeds literally down. Sector 17 is the city center, with a cinema, banks, restaurants, and shops. Running the length of the city is a park containing fitness trails, fountains, and a museum. Le Corbusier divided traffic into seven different types—*les sept voies*—and provided routes for each, motorized traffic being privileged over foot and cycle paths. But he concentrated most attention on the buildings of the capitol complex, including the Palace of Assembly (1962), High Court (1956), and Secretariat (1958). These buildings are monumental in scale and sculptural in impact, the Secretariat being 250 meters long while the Palace of Assembly looks like a combination of industrial furnace and astronomical observatory.

Chandigarh suffered many problems, and Le Corbusier is often blamed. The scale made walking and cycling difficult, and relatively few early residents could afford cars. The commercial rents were too expensive for many shopkeepers, and there was little provision for markets and street vendors. Also, the house rents were too expensive for the very people who built and serviced the city, leading to the growth of squatter settlements that were periodically bulldozed by the authorities. But the question of blame is moot: Chandigarh was consistent with Jawaharlal Nehru's vision of a modern, technological India.

Le Corbusier died of a heart attack while swimming in 1965, leaving several major projects incomplete.

Simon Richards

See also Architecture; Brasília, Brazil; Sert, Josep Lluís; Urban Planning

Further Readings

Curtis, William 1992. *Le Corbusier: Ideas and Forms.* London: Phaidon Press.

Le Corbusier. 1998. *Essential Le Corbusier: L'Esprit Nouveau Articles.* London: Architectural Press.

McLeod, Mary. 1983. "'Architecture or Revolution': Taylorism, Technocracy, and Social Change." *Art Journal* 43(2):132–47.

Mumford, Eric. 2000. *The CIAM Discourse on Urbanism.* Cambridge: MIT Press.

Raeburn, Michael and Victoria Wilson, eds. 1987. *Le Corbusier: Architect of the Century.* London: Arts Council of Great Britain.

Richards, Simon. 2003. *Le Corbusier and the Concept of Self.* New Haven, CT: Yale University Press.

LEFEBVRE, HENRI

Henri Lefebvre (1901–1991) was one of the most original Marxist theorists to think with Marx beyond Marx about the changes taking place in the capitalist mode of production since his death in 1883, and especially since the first decade of the twentieth century when Lefebvre dates the emergence of modern capitalism, *modernity*. He had the good fortune of living a long, intellectually productive life in a century of political disasters that drove most intellectuals on the Left to despair or worse.

Lefebvre took the position that Marx's critical analysis of early capitalism was necessary but not sufficient for fully understanding modern capitalism. Lefebvre appropriated, in a critical manner, the concepts of some of the most important social theorists of the twentieth century in his analysis of modernity to fill in the gaps in Marx's analysis. He made a remarkable number of substantive contributions to the field of sociology in his critical analysis of this mutation: his reconceptualization of dialectical method; his analysis of new forms of alienation; the concepts of everyday life; the urban, difference, social space, modernity, reproduction of the relations of production as *the* structural process in modernity; and the reinvention of the meaning and the possibilities for social revolution.

This entry discusses urban sociology from the perspective of Henri Lefebvre's critical analysis of modern society, as well as discussing the possibilities for social change: the urban revolution and the revolution in everyday life. It explicates his critical concepts and then discusses recent events in light of the possibilities that Lefebvre envisioned in his writing on urban issues.

Critical Concepts

His dialectical method of conceptual analysis begins with the emergence of a concept and the attempt to grasp a new relation, a new aspect of reality in the historical process of becoming. This is the *retrojective* moment in his dialectical method.

Everydayness

According to Lefebvre, every historical form of preindustrial society has a daily life but no everydayness. Preindustrial daily life is structured by natural cycles—day and night, weeks, months, seasons, and lifecycles—and framed by religious meanings and the predominance of use values. For Marx, daily life in early capitalism was the working day organized on the production site.

For Lefebvre, everyday life emerges in the writings of early-twentieth-century novels like James Joyce's *Ulysses*. The center of daily life shifts from the working day to private life, the household, and urban social space. Everyday life is a modern experience that emerges with two additional relations, the urban and differences that he analyzes in the dialectical triad: the everyday/the urban/differences. Everyday life is lived experience, a potential moment for self-creation (a concept borrowed from Nietzsche). Everyday life is a residuum: a moment of history, what is left over after working activities are extracted, humble actions that are repeated daily and taken for granted, the positive moment, and potential power of daily life.

For Lefebvre, everyday life is the social structure of modernity, a mediator between particulars and the social totality, a level and foundation of the social totality. Like the classical working class, the new working classes reproduce the structure of neocapitalism voluntarily through their daily activities. But humans do not live by work alone; daily life provides meanings for the productive activities of working people, although in its present state, it is an alienated experience. According to Lefebvre, it is only when people can no longer live their everyday lives that the possibilities for change in social forms and social structures become imminent or concrete.

The Urban

The urban is another form that detaches itself from its content of encounters, assemblies, and simultaneity. It has been structured according to industrial, commodity, and bureaucratic logics. It is organized in ways to facilitate the movement of products and people, reflecting the logic of the technical division of labor. It is a place where the realization of surplus value and capital accumulation is accomplished. It is divided into levels: the global/the mixed/the private. It polarizes between those who manipulate this form—urban managers, and those who possess the active content—the inhabitants.

The urban develops and is generalized throughout the world, creating an urban world. While only one third of the world population was urbanized at the time that Lefebvre did most of his work on urban topics, more than one half of the world population is now living in urban areas. Moreover, urbanization casts its shadow across the countryside dissolving in the process the urban/rural opposition—the urbanization of the countryside.

Difference

Difference is another important concept that Lefebvre linked to the process of urbanization and the urban revolution. Difference is another form that becomes detached from its content, particularities. This leads to a polarization between those who manipulate the form—the technocrats—and those who possess the contents, differential groups. Urbanization has a differential logic; it creates a world of differences. Like urban sociologists at the University of Chicago in the early twentieth century, Lefebvre argues that one of the most unique qualities of the urban is all of the differences that are evident there.

While most American urban sociologists analyzed these differences in terms of subcultures or minority groups and natural ecological processes, Lefebvre used this concept to emphasize relations of inequality (of relations of domination and subordination) and thought about them in terms of political, economic, and cultural processes. In the struggles that take place in urban social space, differential groups affirm their difference against the process of homogenization. They assert their right to participate in the decision-making centers, against fragmentation and marginalization, and they claim their right to equality in difference against the process of creating hierarchy. According to Lefebvre, differential groups have no existence as groups until they appropriate a space of their own.

Space and the Worldwide

The reproduction of the relations of production creates new relations: space and the worldwide. Space is organized through the following dialectical sequence: homogenization/fragmentation/hierarchization. This process creates an abstract space that complements the abstract quality of alienated labor and the abstract time of everydayness. Capitalists increasingly invest their wealth in space, including industrial, commercial, agricultural, residential, and leisure spaces—even cosmic spaces. This allows capital to accumulate beyond the crisis tendency in the industrial sector, although this second circuit is also subject to crises of falling profits, overproduction, and depreciation, which is quite evident in the 2008 crisis in the real estate sector in the United States and across the globe.

According to Lefebvre, we move from the production of things in space in the nineteenth century to the production of space and things in space in the twentieth century. It sets in motion a conflict between the technocratic producers of this abstract space and the users who want to appropriate space as differential space, as lived space. The reproduction of the social relations of production becomes the central process, the total social phenomenon of modernity. However, there is no logic of reproduction; there is only a class strategy. Structures are not stable, eternal; structures are always destructuring, undermined by internal contradictions, and always require efforts to reproduce or change them.

When these production relations are reproduced, so are the relations of bureaucratic domination for the state and the domination of the technocrats as a class—the state/society relation. Crises in modernity are more political than economic in their origins in contrast with nineteenth-century capitalism. Failure to reproduce these relations usually creates a crisis, a destructuration, followed potentially by a regime change. Furthermore, it sets in motion the following dialectical sequence: history/space/worldliness. The production of space leads to the gradual dissolution of the state, the end of history (of the state), and either a worldwide urban society or the destruction of the human species (and possibly all of the other species). I will now turn to Lefebvre's analysis of the changes that have transformed the capitalist mode of production into modern capitalism, modernity, and to the state mode of production.

Perspectives on Events

In the modernization of French capitalism, the reproduction of capitalist relations of production were accompanied by a new process, urbanization, and new relations: the urban, the everyday, and differences (although this second process and these new relations were not perceived or understood). Lefebvre saw some virtual possibilities for the creation of new forms of time and space as well as an urban society where the problems of urbanization would predominate over the problems of industrialization. Modernity was slowly emerging in France, as the commoditization and the bureaucratization of everyday life was becoming much deeper, more alienating, and all the more pervasive.

The late 1960s provided another moment in Lefebvre's development. Once again capitalism was going through a political and then an economic crisis. Different groups (i.e., racial and ethnic groups, students, youth, women, homosexuals, peasants, and people in developing countries across the world) were contesting bureaucratic state authorities and the Western model of modernization, and later the Eastern model, in their struggles for self-determination and national liberation. The events in May 1968 in Paris became, in his eyes and analysis, the opening salvo in the urban revolution. The revolution in everyday life will become the metamorphosis of daily life into moments of presence, a permanent urban festival.

A Social Revolution

With the creation of modernity, many of the historical tasks of the working-class revolution have been accomplished, especially the growth of productive forces and rising standards of living. Lefebvre proposes a different path for social revolution: Revolution in everyday life and urban revolution will complement and extend the proletarian revolution, all directed toward generalized self-management and emancipation from class exploitation and bureaucratic domination at work, in public life, and in private life. This process will lead to the creation of an urban society that is likely to be a long historical process because changes in everyday life are slow in temporality. Lefebvre argues that the failure of revolutionary movements in Russia, China, and Cuba was in part a failure to produce new production and property relations to replace or displace the commodity form as well as new forms of time and space. For Lefebvre, we must shift from an obsession with economic growth to the development of social relations in far more depth and complexity.

Lefebvre's concepts of modernity and the urban society allow us to get beyond the dismal debate about postmodern or postindustrial societies. His concept of urban society is far more precise than the premature notion of a postindustrial society. While industrial work is shrinking in Western societies, industry is wandering off and flourishing in developing nations across the globe, which are tightly linked to the metropolitan centers through global commodity chains. The two processes are tightly linked, and one of the objectives of an urban revolution would be to subordinate industrialization to urbanization. Postmodern society is simply too vague. Does it mark a break from or a continuity with modernity? Lefebvre sees this as a form of hypercriticism that leads only to nihilism and perhaps a fatal nostalgia for the past. Lefebvre returns us to thinking about different possibilities, and perhaps the choice for us is between a worldwide urban society and the collapse of modernity, which some might call postmodern society.

A New Role for the State

The modernization of post–World War II capitalism proceeded with the entry of technology, knowledge, advertising, bureaucracy, a new class (the technocrats), and an interventionist state, with all of these elements creating a form of capitalist planning. This new form of capitalist planning would rival the centralized planning in the socialist bloc, with military procurement in particular requiring a lot of coordination among the state, research and development institutes, defense corporations, and financial capital. The state was coming to dominate society as a whole, whether in the East or the West.

The age of political economy would gradually transform the capitalist mode of production into the state mode of production. But this new strategy did not solve or dissolve the old contradictions of capitalism; it attenuated the old contradictions and added new contradictions related to the process of urbanization: center/periphery, segregation/integration. At the same time, there was a dissolution of essential relations: class relations, social relations in everyday life between the sexes, between age groups, and within communities.

The Worldwide

For Lefebvre an urban society was a virtual possibility, veiled by the way it was developing in modernity under the ideology of urbanism. The urbanization process was also producing a new social relation, space that would become generalized at the global level. Abstract space was detached from its content, living space, and became polarized as well between the technocrats and the inhabitants. Furthermore, the production of space would create a new relation—the worldwide, with space becoming militarized.

The worldwide was also detached from its content worldliness, and a polarization ensued between the technocrats and the global proletariat. Simultaneously, the creation of the worldwide was also leading to the dissolution of the nation and the states that organized these national territories. Multinational corporations and new global institutions were limiting the capacity of nation-states to organize their societies and economies. Again, the urban was the terrain of struggle between the local order of daily life and the global order of multinational corporations and nation-states.

The new strategy had two levels: the urban and the global, with the reproduction of the relations of production in play on both levels. Lefebvre analyzed this movement on the global level in terms of the following sequence: history/space/worldliness. In the process of the production of space, a new mode of production was emerging: the state mode of production.

These new processes, relations, and structures have produced the world we live in today without abolishing the contradictions along the way (although attenuating some of them, especially the old contradictions). The objectives of the urban revolution are dual: to fully subordinate industrialization to urbanization and to subordinate the global to the urban. Lefebvre's proposal for a counterstrategy involves the following:

1. Linking differential groups to groups in the centers that have broken from the ideology of economic growth, a new global proletariat defined as groups without legal claims on wealth. On the local level, opposition must create urban assemblies with the differences brought together in affirmation and in relations based on reciprocity and mutual respect. This would require institutionalizing the right to be different as an extension of citizenship rights. These new forms of urban democracy would need to be mediated to urban centers across the world.

2. A reorientation of economic growth to social needs and qualitative development in the urban (and in the everyday) with use values dominating exchange values. Urban rights would also include: rights to education, health care, leisure, housing, time for self-creation, the creation of community and qualified places for the realization of moments of lived time, and the creation of the city as a work of art.

3. Going beyond representative democracy to direct democracy: (a) the end of bureaucracy and the withering away of all states with the reappropriation of their legitimate administrative and security functions in new forms of self-management generalized across work, public life, and private life and (b) The right to participate—to be present—in decision making must be institutionalized as a new citizenship right.

This worldwide urban society will be the end of history—the end of the history of the state. This creation will become the meaning of the end of history; time will be liberated from the pseudo-cyclical time of modernity to become lived time in the lived space of the worldwide urban society.

With the worst economic crisis since the Great Depression currently in play, the question about how to distribute the social surplus is on the political agenda: Do we continue to invest in the military sector and pursue global domination, or do we invest it in unmet social needs in the world-wide urban? Do we give tacit consent to the authoritarian politics of the neoconservatives in both political parties in the United States, or do we change direction to create new forms of concrete democracy?

Michael T. Ryan

See also Gottdiener, Mark; Los Angeles School of Urban Studies; Marxism and the City; Social Production of Space; Social Space; Urban Space

Further Readings

Elden, S. 2004. *Understanding Henri Lefebvre.* London: Continuum.

Elden, S., E. Lebas, and E. Kofman, eds. 2003. *Henri Lefebvre.* London: Continuum.

Gottdiener, M. 1993. "Henri Lefebvre and the Production of Space." *Sociological Theory* 11(1):129–34.

———. 2000. "Lefebvre and the Bias of Academic Urbanism." *City* 4(1):93–101.

Kofman, F. and E. Lebas. 1996. "Introduction: Lost in Transposition: Time, Space, and the City." Pp. 3–60 in *Writings on Cities*, by Henri Lefebvre. Oxford, UK: Blackwell.

Lefebvre, H. 1968. *The Sociology of Marx.* New York: Pantheon Books.

———.1969. *The Explosion: Marxism and the French Upheaval.* New York: Monthly Review Press.

———. 1976. *The Survival of Capitalism.* London: Allison and Busby.

———. 1988. "Toward a Leftist Cultural Politics." Pp. 75–88 in *Marxism and the Interpretation of Culture.* Urbana: University of Illinois Press.

———. 1991. *Critique of Everyday Life*, Vol. 1. 2nd ed. London: Verso.

———. 1991. *The Production of Space.* Oxford, UK: Blackwell.

———. 1996. *Writings on Cities.* Oxford, UK: Blackwell.

———. 2002. *Critique of Everyday Life*, Vol. 2. London: Verso.

———. 2003. *Key Writings.* New York: Continuum.

———. 2003. *The Urban Revolution.* Minneapolis: University of Minnesota Press.

———. 2005. *Critique of Everyday Life*, Vol. 3. London: Verso.

Ross, K. 1997. "Lefebvre on the Situationists: An Interview." *October* 79:69–83.

Shields, R. 1999. *Lefebvre, Love, and Struggle.* London: Routledge.

LOCAL GOVERNMENT

A local government is any subnational territorial unit of the national state or government; the unit is formally responsible for administrative and policy functions related to the delivery of a range of public services. Where local government also includes elected offices, such as mayors or councils, it performs the political function of the representation of local interests.

Local governments are typically defined by geographic territory and range from the largest spatial units, such as regions or provinces, to cities, rural areas, and counties and villages. In many intergovernmental systems, local government refers to both meso (provinces, regions, or states) and municipal (urban and rural) levels. Local governments are here considered primarily at the latter level, also often referred to as "general purpose" local governments. "Special purpose" local governments (special districts responsible for the management of one or a few services) have become an increasingly important type. In a few cases, local governments can be established on ethnic or another nongeographical basis. Despite this variety, many issues are common to all types of local government.

Historical Development

The formation of modern nation-states offers distinct insights crucial to understanding local government in the modern world. Premodern medieval Europe was characterized by the existence of self-governing cities possessing municipal autonomy and ruled by urban oligarchies. During this period, central monarchs and parliaments were forced to partner with these local governments to govern regions and cities so as to secure the resources necessary for war making and state making. However, the development of modern national states depended crucially on the elimination of municipal autonomy in favor of centralizing state bureaucracies and power holders, transforming the state system from indirect to direct rule.

Between the late seventeenth century in absolutist France and mid-nineteenth-century reforms in England, most European states transformed varied forms of urban governments from autonomous units to professional, bureaucratic agents of the central government, and with that came the centralization of important public sector functions such as taxation and conscription. Ancillary to these goals were functions such as maintaining public order, providing housing, and organizing urban food supply, as well as the concession of power to local representative bodies.

Out of this process emerged modern national state systems and their expansion into social and economic policy. The new regime after the French revolution of 1789 represents an extreme case of the subordination or tutelage of local government as an instrument of centralized rule. All modern local governments are a legacy of this historical transformation. Most contemporary non-Western state systems are also modeled on one or the other version of European intergovernmental state systems.

Types of Local Government

The types of local government can be analyzed principally in terms of two variables related to the form of political regime: (1) power sharing, the type and degree of division of power, and (2) the degree of decentralization. Local governments also vary widely in their structure as well as their functions and services.

Almost all regimes, whether majority rule or consensus based, divide power to some degree between central and noncentral levels. In principle, the degree of autonomy of local government is highest in federal systems, which allocate constitutionally guaranteed powers to subnational units. In contrast, unitary states reserve final authority to central governments. A dramatic recent example of the exercise of central authority over local governments in a unitary state was the abolishing of the elected Greater London Council by Prime Minister Margaret Thatcher of the United Kingdom in 1985; it was reinstated in 2000.

Significant country-specific differences exist even within each of these categories. For example, although the United States is a federal state system, it provides constitutional autonomy only to the (50) states, whereas city governments are considered "creatures of the state" (this is known as Dillon's Rule after a U.S. Supreme Court case in 1868). This power relationship was illustrated most dramatically in the 1970s when the state of New York temporarily replaced the city council of New York City with a special board to manage the city's budget directly.

The design of local government autonomy is based on one of two principles. The *ultra vires* principle restricts municipal competencies to those explicitly granted them by central government. The principle of *general competence* permits local government authority in all areas except those explicitly restricted by central government law.

Decentralization is the process of transferring responsibilities from central to local government, often a combination of fiscal, political, or administrative functions. Decentralization often, although not always, corresponds to local governments getting a bigger share of total public-sector expenditures and revenues and greater local financial autonomy from central government. In the last three decades, many countries, including many unitary systems, have undertaken experiments to decentralize authority and administrative functions. From this perspective, the federal–unitary distinction appears less salient than the de facto degree of local autonomy.

Therefore, at the most generic level, all local government systems can be classified along two axes: (1) high/low degree of constitutional autonomy (fiscal, political, administrative) and (2) wide/ narrow range of functional responsibilities and services delivered. Although a majority of countries fall into either the unitary–centralized and federal–decentralized cells of the typology, other combinations also exist. For example, the Scandinavian countries and Japan are unitary and decentralized, whereas India is both federal and highly centralized.

Structures of local government can vary between two poles, stressing either the political or administrative aspects of governance. In the United States, for example, urban local government can be legally either mayor–council or council–manager in form, although in practice most cities are a mix of these two models. In the United Kingdom, the 2000 local government law permitted localities to choose from three distinct structures, with or without a directly elected mayor. Only a minority of countries permit local choice over the organizational shape of local government. The majority of local governments, particularly in the developing world, are highly constrained and controlled by central government, both in form and in content.

Most municipalities are responsible for basic maintenance of the streets and parks, for sanitation and solid waste management, and often for local traffic management and policing. Local governments typically are also responsible for urban land-use planning. More expanded functions include infrastructural development and construction (such as roads and sewerage systems). Some large municipalities may be responsible for social services such as health care and education and even welfare policies.

Economic Aspects

Local government (sometimes referred to as *fiscal federalism*) is studied extensively in the economic literature from the point of view of the efficient spatial allocation of public goods in an intergovernmental system. The principles of accountability to the full range of interests and intensity of needs in the community and responsiveness to the heterogeneous and time-varying needs in the local community underlie justifications for decentralizing functions from central to local governments. Decentralization is justified where preferences for a given public good meet the following criteria: (1) they are heterogeneous, (2) there are few jurisdictional spillovers or externalities, (3) there are few economies of scale, and (4) central government has less access to information about local preferences than local government. If these conditions are not met, then decentralizing to local governments is inefficient. Furthermore, if the sociocultural conditions necessary for democratic citizenship (such as education or the presence of plural local political

and associational life) are absent at the local level, then decentralization to local governments is unlikely to advance democratic accountability. Thus, the consensus in the field is that there cannot be any a presumption that decentralization will represent the interests of the poor more equitably or that it will necessarily improve the efficiency of public service delivery.

Democratic Aspects

A venerable assumption is that local government is a crucial arena in which individuals and groups can learn the arts of cooperative, participatory democratic governance. This is because local governments are responsible for issues of immediate concern to most people and operate at a scale accessible to ordinary people. For example, when conflicts arise over local government plans for physical urban development (such as urban renewal or road construction) that threaten local communities, democratic participation is a way for residents to express their (potentially conflicting) views on local matters.

In *Democracy in America,* published in 1835, Alexis de Tocqueville advanced the founding statement of this assumption: "Town-meetings are to liberty what primary schools are to science; they bring it within the people's reach, they teach men how to use and how to enjoy it. A nation may establish a system of free government, but without the spirit of municipal institutions it cannot have the spirit of liberty." This claim was echoed famously by J. S. Mill in 1859 and 1861; he saw local government as an arena in which citizens were educated in the habits and dispositions necessary for the exercise of free democratic government. This tradition continues to inform advocates of grassroots democracy.

History, however, has treated both the quantitative and qualitative aspects of this claim harshly: Rather than being an arena of vibrant and extensive political participation, local government today is less vibrant than national politics in terms of political activity, participation, and interest. Voter turnout rates, for example, are generally lower in local as opposed to national elections. Scholars have identified two main reasons why local politics is less appealing than national politics: (1) there are fewer institutional mechanisms at the local level to motivate participation, such as competitive political parties or media; and (2) local politics lacks the dramatic and emotive matters of high consequence, such as war and nationalism as well as charismatic politicians. Furthermore, in many cases, small-scale political institutions are equally if not more likely to encourage parochial self-interested behavior rather than cooperative and cosmopolitan attitudes and behaviors. Local jurisdictions of local government are often vulnerable to "state capture" by local elites, who then advance policies that are not responsive to the full range of interests in the local community.

In sum, historical experience shows that de Tocqueville's and Mill's equation of localism with greater democratic control is misleading: The premise that tackling a democratic deficit necessarily implies greater political decentralization to municipalities is not a priori sustainable. The objective of deepening democratic governance at all levels of government is not necessarily incompatible with greater central government control and even a diminished political role for lower levels of government. The unit of analysis for democratic institutions is primarily the intergovernmental system as a whole rather than local or central levels taken independently.

Paradigms in the Study of Local Government

Given its decentralized and federal structure and prominent cities, the United States has the most extensive theoretical debates over the nature of local government. These debates, which focus on issues including community power, comparative historical and political sociology, and urban regime theory, have influenced debates in other countries to greater or lesser extents.

The debate over community power has contrasted three paradigms, seeking to account for the nature of political power in local urban settings. Elite power theorists claim that local governments are dominated by social and economic elites and that politics and policy are shaped in accordance with elite interests, thereby marginalizing the interests of ethnic and racial minorities and the poor. In contrast, pluralists, such as Robert Dahl in his famous study of local politics in the city of New Haven, Connecticut (United States),

claim that in fact local government is an arena of competing political, economic, and social groups, which combine to shape the policy decisions of the local government. The different arenas of power do not accumulate into a single elite. Radical critics advance the idea that not all pertinent issues are permitted to reach the arena of pluralist bargaining between groups. Local elites and masses are subject to ideological biases against raising certain issues for debate (such as significant income redistribution in a capitalist system). These taboo issues are thus kept off the agenda, either as a result of conscious design or unconscious or ideological biases.

In an influential synthesis, Paul Peterson reversed the established causality between politics and policy: He argued that it was more fruitful to view the types of local politics (elitist, pluralist, or radical) as resulting from the nature of the policy tasks required of local governments (economic growth, allocation of economically neutral public services within the city, and redistribution, respectively). Where cities are forced to compete for economic resources (a situation particularly characterizing the United States but less so in other settings such as France or the United Kingdom), city politics is highly constrained.

Another influential strand in the study of local government draws on comparative historical and political sociology. Ira Katznelson's *City Trenches* demonstrated that different local government systems and the different political and sociospatial contexts in which they are embedded have played an important role in shaping local social movements as well as determining the boundaries of what local government can do.

Over the last two decades, urban regime theory has dominated the American political science and urban studies literature on local government. It seeks to develop a classification of local governments in terms of the relationships that local government has with the private sector and local civil society. Different types of relationship and influence lead to different types of urban regime. However, it is unclear to what extent this paradigm represents an advance over earlier debates; moreover, its applicability outside the U.S. context has been questioned. This paradigm should not be confused with debates over regime change. In post-communist Eastern Europe, for example, local governments often played important roles in the transition from communist to democratic capitalist regimes.

Future Trends

Scholars of local government in the Western developed countries point to three key trends that will shape local government in the near future: specialization, urbanization, and globalization.

The role of local governments as unique providers of services that cannot be provided by the private sector, quasi-public organizations, and nongovernmental organizations is increasingly called into question. Neoliberal emphasis on economic growth has resulted in diverse approaches, including public–private partnerships and contractual agreements between central, regional, and local government levels as well as nongovernmental organizations, and to greater competition between localities. Local government is becoming one element of an increasingly complex and diverse array of intergovernmental systems rather than an autonomous unit of governance. Whether local governments will take on a new leadership role in this broader coalition of actors is unclear.

Large metropolitan regions are increasingly becoming important units of local government. Metropolitan local governments will face the challenges of coordinating numerous and fragmented subunits.

This trend poses new challenges and potential new opportunities for local governments. In the Western countries in particular, many local governments find themselves having to contend with economic competitiveness to attract capital and labor; emerging claims and conflicts over specifically local citizenship rights resulting from multicultural populations; and the emerging international role of local governments in conflict resolution and human rights initiatives. In 2008, for example, the first International Conference on City Diplomacy convened mayors and international local government associations to advance the role of local governments as key players in negotiations over social and ethnic conflict in divided and conflict-ridden cities.

The key questions facing local government is the extent to which they can be a unique authoritative arena of governance and whether the principle of legitimacy of local government in the eyes of citizens, residents, and consumers will be primarily (1) administrative and economic performance or (2) democratic accountability and greater participation in decision making.

Kian Tajbakhsh

See also Citizenship; Community; Metropolitan Governance; Urban Politics

Further Readings

Bardhan, Pranab and Dilip Mookherjee. 2006. *Decentralization and Local Governance in Developing Countries: A Comparative Perspective.* Cambridge: MIT Press.

Caro, Robert. 1976. *The Power Broker: Robert Moses and the Fall of New York.* New York: Vintage.

Dahl, Robert. 1961. *Who Governs?* New Haven, CT: Yale University Press.

Katznelson, Ira. 1982. *City Trenches.* Chicago: University of Chicago Press.

Peterson, Paul. 1981. *City Limits.* Chicago: University of Chicago Press.

Pierre, Jon. 2005. "Comparative Urban Governance: Uncovering Complex Causalities." *Urban Affairs Review* 40(4):446–62.

Regulski, Jerzy. 2003. *Local Government Reform in Poland: An Insider's Story.* Budapest, Hungary: Local Government and Public Service Reform Initiative, OSI.

Rose, Lawrence and Bas Denters. 2005. *Comparing Local Governance: Trends and Developments.* Basingstoke, UK: Palgrave Macmillan.

Tilly, Charles. 1993. *Coercion, Capital, and European States: AD 990–1992.* Oxford, UK: Blackwell.

LOCATION THEORY

Location theory focuses on the geography of economic activity with particular attention to industry. Four industrial categories are used: primary (agriculture, mining, and fishing), secondary (manufacturing of goods), tertiary (services), and quaternary (information).

In relation to the primary industry, Johann Heinrich von Thünen developed a theory of agricultural location in his 1826 work, *Der Isolierte*

Staat (The Isolated State). He investigated the relationship between the distance from a market and the pattern of land use by hypothesizing an isolated area located in a homogeneous environmental plain. A single city served as the market and was surrounded by farmland. Von Thünen assumed that farmers attempt to maximize profit, or economic rent, with the determining factor being transportation costs. He also assumed that transportation costs rise with the distance from the market and that the fertility of the soil is equal across the area. Because transportation costs also increase as the weight of the specific farm product itself increases, the resultant geography is a series of concentric circles with a different crop planted in each circle.

Location theory exists for secondary industries as well, specifically goods production or manufacturing. In 1909, Alfred Weber developed the notion of a location triangle in his book, *Über den Standort der Industrien* (Theory of the Location of Industries). The location triangle is made up of three fixed locations: a market and two raw material sources. Weber sought to determine the optimum location of firms, given the requirement that they minimize transportation costs within the triangle. He assumed that production costs are the same everywhere. Thus, transport costs will control the choice of location. They are a function of the weight of the raw materials and the commodity being produced and the distances between the location of raw material sources, the market, and the firm. The optimum location is the center of gravity of the triangle as determined by transportation costs. To this, Weber added labor costs and the economies of agglomeration (i.e., the spatial concentration of firms). Minimizing transportation costs and labor costs and maximizing agglomeration economies results in an ideal location, one that minimizes total production costs.

A third major contribution to location theory is the central place theory developed by Walter Christaller in 1933. The main function of a central place is to supply goods and services to the surrounding population and to do so by minimizing the travel costs of the population in the surrounding region. The determining factor in its location is the threshold; that is, the smallest market or trade area that is needed to bring a new firm, service provider, or city into existence and keep it functioning. Once a threshold has been established, the central place will expand its economic activities by adding higher-order goods that have larger market areas. This will continue until the range—the maximum distance that consumers will travel to buy these services or goods—is reached.

Competitive forces will enable some places to have a greater proportion of higher-order goods—and thus more residents—than others, and this will lead to a hierarchy of places of different size. In this way, Christaller explained how settlements and places (or cities) are located in relation to one another and the number, distance between, and size of settlements within a region.

Since these earlier formulations, location theory has moved away from its emphasis on transportation costs and markets. Emphasis has shifted to agglomeration economies, access to educated labor, quality of life issues, information, and the availability of government subsidies. As economies have become less dominated by agriculture and natural resource extraction and less reliant on heavy manufacturing, location theorists have focused more on the location of light manufacturing, retail services, and a variety of businesses for which transportation costs are less important than highly skilled workers, complementary industries, and telecommunications technologies. Nevertheless, the issue remains where to locate one's business and, thus, what factors have to be taken into account.

Eun Jin Jung

See also Fujita, Masahisa; Lösch, August; Urban Economics; Urban Geography

Further Readings

Chisholm, M. 1962. *Rural Settlement and Land Use: An Essay in Location.* London: Hutchinson University Library.

Christaller, W. 1966. *Central Places in Southern Germany.* Translated by C. W. Baskin. Englewood Cliffs, NJ: Prentice Hall.

Lösch, A. 1952. *The Economics of Location.* Translated by W. H. Woglom. New Haven, CT: Yale University Press.

Smith, D. M. 1981. *Industrial Location: An Economic Geographical Analysis.* New York: Wiley.

Weber, A. 1929. *Theory of the Location of Industries.* Translated by C. J. Friedrich. Chicago: University of Chicago Press.

Loft Living

Loft living began in the 1970s in the United States as an informal way for artists and others to take old manufacturing spaces in the centers of cities and transform them into unconventional studios and residences. These spaces had been partly abandoned—at least, by the building owners—and, with the transfer of factory work to low-wage regions of the world as well as the obsolescence of multistory factory buildings, they became available at low rents to those who used their "sweat equity" (or own labor) to modernize and renovate them.

Within a few years, favorable media coverage and changes in local laws enabled the property market in living lofts to expand beyond artists communities and beyond cultural capitals like New York and London. Many cities encouraged both the creation of special artists' districts and new residential construction, which were in turn associated with center-city revival. Although loft living sparked a new style of chic home décor and generated new uses for old manufacturing districts, it raised serious questions about this type of gentrification: specifically, where future manufacturing would take place and whether loft neighborhoods ultimately benefited cultural consumers more than cultural producers.

Loft Living in New York City

New York, with its continually replenished stock of artists and a declining number of small manufacturers, offers an archetypal history of lofts. The city had been a trading center since the days of the Dutch colony in the seventeenth century, a center of crafts production as a British colony before the American Revolution, and a media and fashion center from the era after the Civil War. From the mid-nineteenth through the early twentieth century, waves of immigrants filled the streets and tenements, working in the factories and buying the products—especially clothing—that were now ready made. Many New Yorkers worked in garment factories, usually located in multistory buildings with open floors, high ceilings, structural weight-bearing columns, and cast iron facades. These floors were called lofts, after the spaces where sail makers plied their craft. Other New Yorkers worked in similar spaces in the printing industry, producing newspapers and magazines from hot type, making silk screen prints for artists and advertisements, and creating posters and sheet music for Broadway or Tin Pan Alley.

As workplaces, loft buildings were an integral part of the city's two main cultural industries—fashion and printing—from the 1860s. They filled a large part of lower Manhattan, stretching from north of the Wall Street financial district to midtown near Times Square. Lofts were located as well along the docks in Brooklyn and Queens—in warehouses, sugar refineries, and other specialized industrial buildings.

After World War II, the city's industries suffered structural decline. Garment manufacturers gradually shifted production to lower-wage towns in New Jersey, outside the urban core. Printers confronted technological improvements that replaced human workers with machines and eventually with computers. Losing readers to television and facing rising costs, most of the city's daily newspapers folded. By the late 1960s, employment in the garment and printing industries was steadily falling, and loft building owners refused to modernize their properties if they couldn't demand higher rents. At the same time, a vision of the city as a service rather than a manufacturing center made industry seem less desirable. Under these conditions, loft buildings seemed to be obsolete.

But, as in other postwar cities, private real-estate developers did not rush to create new districts in the historic core. Besides the mammoth building of the World Trade Center, New York City and state tried to goad developers into action by planning new infrastructure—a cross-Manhattan expressway along Broome Street, which would demolish a large number of late nineteenth-century loft buildings; a sports stadium nearby; apartment houses for the middle class so they could walk to work in Wall Street—but these plans aroused unexpectedly strong community protest.

Led by Jane Jacobs and other urbanists and activists, New Yorkers demonstrated at city planning hearings. They demanded an end to highway construction that tore neighborhoods apart, to new construction that erased structures with historical memory and character and put banal, homogeneous buildings in their place, and, most important, to the high-handed governmental action carried out by the appointed official, Robert Moses, who had torn down housing and built highways, bridges, parks, and public housing projects without consulting neighborhood groups. This popular backlash to the mode of urban renewal practiced during the 1950s and 1960s made it politically impossible to tear down loft districts. It also led to an unprecedented appreciation of their historic and aesthetic character, a point that was argued by a new social movement for historic preservation.

The future of Lower Manhattan's loft districts remained cloudy while many manufacturing tenants continued to downsize or move out of the city. Artists began to fill the gap, following the example of the abstract expressionists of the previous generation, who had begun to live and work in lofts during the 1940s and 1950s. Although they lacked standard residential amenities like heat, kitchens and bathrooms, and hot water, lofts were relatively cheap. They provided a large amount of floor space—usually from 1,500 to 5,000 square feet—and large windows with lots of natural light. The absence of residential neighbors permitted artists to fabricate work with noisy metal welding and smelly paints and dyes. Although younger artists did not yet form a concentration in specific neighborhoods, they made their live–work spaces in lofts more visible by staging performances, exhibitions, and concerts and by gradually opening up galleries in them.

In the late 1960s, several galleries and performance spaces opened in SoHo—a loft area south of Houston Street that prior to this point had no particular neighborhood name or character apart from manufacturing. At the same time, a private

An example of a modern loft in Manhattan, New York City

Source: Jennifer Herr.

foundation that wanted to support artists' housing gave a grant to the leader of the Fluxists, an avant-garde artists' group, to buy and renovate a loft building in the center of the district. This concentration of artists' lofts in SoHo marked the beginning of a widely recognized trend of loft living and its identification with an artistic way of life.

Shaping the Housing Market

At first, loft living was illegal in New York City because it violated the zoning laws, which restricted the use of space in industrial districts to manufacturing, as well as the building code, which required residences to meet specific conditions that did not apply to other kinds of structures. Lobbying by artists and their supporters, however, resulted in their getting a special status: If the Department of Cultural Affairs certified them as artists, they were allowed to live in lofts. To alert the fire department of their presence, an artist-in-residence sign was posted on the building's exterior.

During the 1970s, a series of laws protected the artists' right to live in SoHo and also permitted residence in adjacent loft areas of TriBeCa (the Triangle Below Canal Street) and NoHo (north of Houston Street), which slowly shifted from manufacturing to arts-related uses and residence. After the New York City Council established a Landmarks Preservation Commission in 1965, SoHo received a historic district designation for the loft buildings' cast iron facades, and this legal status confirmed the district's special aesthetic qualities. Equally important, preserving relatively short but dense structures prevented big developers from moving into the area, modernizing buildings, and turning lofts into standard apartments. All of these laws tended to establish living lofts as special spaces—legal for residence, aesthetically distinguished, and outside the mainstream of consumer culture.

These points were emphasized by increasing media coverage that featured photos and descriptions of artists' lofts. The media dramatized how artists individualized their lofts' décor, and, when richer people moved into them, articles dwelt on their expensive appliances, "industrial chic" aesthetic, and impressive modern art collections. Lofts did in fact offer large spaces at cheaper prices than apartments in the most expensive areas of the city. But it was their aesthetic distinction—and promise of an artful style of life—that made them into an influential cultural model.

Rising rents and sale prices soon made loft living more expensive—too expensive for either artists or manufacturers—and attracted the interest of big real-estate developers. With legalization of residential use, banks granted mortgages and construction loans to buy loft buildings as well as individual loft units. As a result, demand for loft living increased. Residents began to outnumber manufacturers in loft districts, and developers converted many buildings to standard apartments—although with the appeal of exposed structural components (columns, pipes, ducts, brick walls), concrete or old wooden floors, and open floor plans.

Loft Living Spreads Through the Heartland

Since the 1970s, with the further reduction of manufacturing in many cities in the United States, Canada, and Europe, loft living has become a popular housing style from Los Angeles to London and Montreal. The appeal always begins with artists and an artistic way of life—marketed as an opportunity to create your own living space in a structure whose gracious proportions are not possible in most housing built after World War II. The spread of loft living is also related to the revitalization of many downtowns, supporting their concentration of cultural amenities and raising their tax base. Whereas in cities such as Chicago or Minneapolis, loft living attracts wealthy empty nesters from the suburbs, in Austin, Texas, or Portland, Oregon, it appeals to young artists and other cultural producers who cannot afford more expensive downtown houses and do not want to live in the suburbs. Yet elements of loft living—exposed structure, large windows, open floor plans—have also been incorporated into new suburban developments, where denser buildings satisfy both potential residents and local laws that want less sprawl and more sense of community. Without the grit of an industrial past, loft living becomes just another model of townhouse design. In the old nineteenth-century buildings, however, loft living still offers a sense of authenticity.

Sharon Zukin

See also Back-to-the-City Movement; Downtown Revitalization; Gentrification; Housing; Sustainable Development

Further Readings

Podmore, Julie. 1998. "(Re)reading the 'Loft Living' Habitus in Montreal's Inner City." *International Journal of Urban & Regional Research* 22:283–302.

Wolfe, Mark R. 1999. "The Wired Loft: Lifestyle Innovation Diffusion and Industrial Networking in the Rise of San Francisco's Multimedia Gulch." *Urban Affairs Review* 34:707–28.

Zukin, Sharon. 1989. *Loft Living: Culture and Capital in Urban Change*. 2nd ed. New Brunswick, NJ: Rutgers University Press.

LONDON, UNITED KINGDOM

London has a long and fascinating history as Britain's capital city. Over the last 20 years, London has experienced a period of considerable, if very uneven, prosperity, largely as a result of its dominance in financial and business services and the large number of highly paid jobs this has generated. This has had major implications for house prices and housing affordability. The impact of the 2008 financial crisis is as yet unknown. This entry begins with a historical overview and then looks at issues directly related to housing.

Historical Background

Beginning as the Roman origins Londinium, London grew through its Norman and medieval periods up until the Great Fire of London in 1666, which destroyed much of the original city of half-timbered buildings. Subsequently, it grew and developed toward the West End, the center of the court and the royal palaces. By 1750, it was the biggest city in Europe, with a population of half a million.

A more significant growth spurt, however, came in the nineteenth century, when in the course of a hundred years, its population grew from 1 million to 6.5 million. This was the period when much of Georgian and Victorian London, with its distinctive terraced housing, was built. This period also saw the creation of areas of slum housing with poor families living one to a room. During the late nineteenth century, the City of London (the historic center of the city and a separate political entity) began to emerge as a major financial center, servicing both the needs of empire and capital investment worldwide.

London's most rapid physical expansion, however, was in the interwar period from 1919 to 1939, when its area doubled as suburban semidetached housing spread out, aided by the new subway system. Inner London, the former London County Council (LCC) area, is primarily nineteenth century in origin, whereas outer London is largely a twentieth-century creation. After World War II, the creation of the green belt limited the outward expansion of London, although some development jumped this barrier; the London region now extends into a commuting zone 30 miles or more beyond. The City and the East End of London around the docks suffered major bomb damage in World War II, with large areas of housing being destroyed. Miraculously, St. Paul's Cathedral, Christopher Wren's great masterpiece, survived intact, although many of his other City churches were destroyed.

A Global Financial Center

The contemporary economy, social structure, and housing market of London need to be seen in the context of its role as one of the world's leading global cities. London, along with New York, has been one of the two major centers of global finance since the deregulation of the late 1980s. Tokyo, which was also a major global financial center until the Japanese bubble economy collapsed in the early 1990s, has slipped back. The dominance of financial and business services in the London economy has been an important key to understanding the changing nature of the city over this period, and the global financial crisis of 2008, which hit London hard, is likely to have an equally important effect over the next few years.

The collapse or takeover of a number of major investment banks such as Bear Sterns, Lehman Brothers, and Merrill Lynch will inevitably have a big impact on employment in both London and New York, as will the partial nationalization of some of the major clearing banks and the collapse of some hedge funds, many of which are based in London. The effects in terms of earnings, spending, and house prices will be considerable, and it is likely that London's economy will suffer disproportionately from the financial crisis and subsequent recession, given its reliance on financial services. Although the financial crisis of 2008 is not the first one, it may prove to be the most severe in terms of its long-term repercussions.

An Economy Transformed

The key to understanding the magnitude of the transformation of London's economy over the last 40 years can be seen in the reversal in the importance of manufacturing industry and financial and business services. In 1961, manufacturing accounted for almost a third of total employment, and financial and business services for about 10 percent. By 2001, the proportions had been reversed; manufacturing employment now accounts for only 7 percent of jobs.

Another rapidly growing sector has been that of the cultural and creative industries, including film, music, publishing, theater, museums, art galleries, fashion, and digital arts, which has rapidly expanded the city's labor force. This dramatic shift in industrial structure, which has been paralleled in New York, Paris, and other global cities, has had important implications for the structure of occupations, for earnings and incomes, and for housing, gentrification, and the office and commercial property markets and people's lives.

Class Structure

The decline of manufacturing industry and the growth of financial and business services have led to a major shift in the occupational class structure of London, with a long-term decline in the size and proportion of traditional working-class jobs and a major increase in the size and proportion of middle-class, white-collar office jobs. Hamnett and colleagues have argued that this points to the professionalization of the occupational class structure of London, rather than to class polarization as defined by Sassen. A number of commentators have countered that this overlooks the growth of the low-wage, immigrant labor force of London, not all of whom are included in the official statistics.

There is no doubt that London has witnessed a dramatic increase in both immigration and the size and proportion of its ethnic minority population in recent decades. Immigration, both legal and undocumented, has grown rapidly, from both Eastern Europe and from a number of African countries. This has been a major factor in the growth of the population of Greater London to 7.5 million in the 20 years ending in 2007, reversing the long-standing loss of population from London. From 2001 to 2007, London's population grew by a net 500,000 from documented international migration. London accounts for a third to a half of net inward overseas migration to the United Kingdom.

In addition, the ethnic minority population of London has increased from about 3 percent in 1961 to 29 percent in 2001 and 34 percent in inner London. In three boroughs, the ethnic minority population now exceeds 50 percent, and there are a number of others where it exceeds 40 percent. In addition, London as a whole has seen a small fall in the size of its White population from 1991 to 2001; in some boroughs, this has exceeded 10 percent. To what extent this reflects replacement by ethnic minorities or an active process of White flight is impossible to say.

Thus, London has changed from an overwhelmingly monoethnic, White-dominated city to a multiethnic city with similarities to New York. The ethnic minority population of London has not been confined to the inner city, however, and 53 percent of minority groups now live in outer London. In the case of some Asian groups, in particular, a process of suburbanization has been accompanied by the growth of homeownership, although other, less economically successful, groups have become more strongly represented in social housing and privately rented housing.

The changes in ethnic composition have also had implications for educational attainment, which has long been seen as a major problem in London, with average attainment below that for England and Wales as a whole. There are large differences in attainment between the inner boroughs and the more affluent suburban boroughs, as well as large differences between ethnic groups. Indian and Chinese pupils have the highest levels of attainment, with Whites following and Black Caribbean and Bangladeshi pupils at the bottom. These differences are partly related to social class, but culture and home background also play a part. A key issue is the high proportion of pupils in some boroughs who do not have English as a first language, as this holds back both teaching and learning.

One of the major impacts of the growth of financial and business services has been the growth of high-earning and high-income individuals and households and large increases in the level of earnings and incomes for these groups. At the other end of the spectrum, low-earning and low-income groups have seen much smaller increases, if any, in real incomes. This has led to a sharp increase in the extent of earning and income inequality between the top 10 percent to 20 percent and the rest. In this respect, London's experience is broadly similar to that found in other major global cities, which have become both more affluent and much more unequal in income distribution over the last 20 to 30 years. There is a major difference between growing inequality and social polarization, however.

The Housing Market

The growth of a large affluent middle class has had a major impact on the housing market in terms of demand and prices. As the supply of housing is broadly fixed in the short and medium term, the impact of increased effective demand for housing in more attractive areas of London has had the effect of pushing up house prices across the board and generating major problems of housing affordability, which have been intensified by the large number of wealthy overseas buyers who bought investment property in London during the last 10 years. Average property prices in London in 2007 were in excess of 10 times average earnings. The house price slump of 2008 to 2009 is likely to reduce the problem of housing affordability.

The growth of the middle class has also had a major role in propelling the process of gentrification: a term first introduced by Ruth Glass in 1964 to describe the interaction of social class and housing changes in inner London. Large parts of inner London have now experienced some degree of gentrification as the process has spread outward from the original core areas. The gentrification process has taken a variety of different forms, ranging from the classic renovation of single-family houses to the conversion of houses into apartments; new build gentrification, particularly in Docklands and along the river and canals; and recently, loft conversions of former industrial/warehouse buildings, offices, and public buildings into luxury apartments. Many of these processes have introduced a new middle-class resident population into former working-class or run-down or derelict areas as well as the recolonization of areas

formerly built for the middle classes in the eighteenth or nineteenth centuries but later abandoned.

Gentrification is only one of the processes that have transformed the housing market of London in the last 40 years, however. In 1961, more than 60 percent of households in inner London still rented privately, and social housing and homeownership were both relatively small (each under 20 percent). During the 1960s and 1970s, large areas of poor-quality private rented housing were compulsorily acquired and demolished, and the areas were then redeveloped as large social housing estates, some but not all in the form of highrise tower blocks. As this sector expanded with the simultaneous growth of homeownership, a process of tenure social polarization began to occur in which social housing began to see a growing concentration of the economically inactive, unemployed, low-skill, and low-income workers, and some ethnic minority groups. This process of social residualization has persisted and intensified, and social housing in London today, as in Britain in general, has become linked with the less economically successful, the deprived, the socially excluded, and some ethnic minority groups.

This process has been intensified by the numerical success of the Conservative "right to buy" legislation introduced in 1980, which led to large numbers of council housing tenants buying their home from the council. Although this was beneficial to the tenants concerned, it had the effect of significantly reducing the size of the sector. In addition, the Conservatives also cut the money available for new construction significantly and directed funding to the housing association sector. As a result, the council sector has shrunk dramatically from its high-water mark in 1981, when it accounted for 42 percent of households in inner London, to 25 percent in 2001. A series of other policy measures, including the large-scale voluntary transfers of council homes, have also effectively forced many councils to dispose of their holdings to other social landlords.

The 10 years from the late 1990s to 2007 have also seen another major change in the structure of London's housing—the revival of renting from private landlords. This sector had declined continuously from the 1950s to the early 1990s, largely as a result of rent controls and security of tenure, which meant that many landlords sold when a property became vacant and others sold to the tenants. The introduction of assured tenancies from the late 1980s has led to a major resurgence of private landlordism or buy-to-let, although this appears to have hit problems in the wake of the financial, house price, and mortgage crisis of 2008. One indirect indicator of high prices and rents in London has been the high level of housing benefits paid in the city to subsidize rental costs for low-income groups. The inner London boroughs have taken a very disproportionate share of national housing benefit payments, although these effectively subsidize private landlords.

The result of all these changes is that London has seen a major shift in its housing tenure structure over the last 40 years, first with the decline of the private renting and the growth of both council housing and homeownership; after 1981, with the decline of council housing and the growth of other social landlords; and in the last 10 years with the resurgence of private renting. Overall, however, London now has a much higher level of ownership and a much lower level of private renting than it had in the 1960s.

East London's Growth

One of the important changes in the physical structure of London has been the growth of the office sector, the expansion of the City of London, and the development of a number of major new office developments, particularly the construction of Canary Wharf in the former docklands area of East London. Canary Wharf has become one of the largest commercial regeneration projects in Europe and now houses many of the world's leading banks and financial companies. As such, it has played a key role in terms of the provision of modern office space to enable London to compete successfully with other global financial centers. The success of Canary Wharf was assisted by construction of the Jubilee line underground extension, which provided direct access from central London, and by the development of London City airport, which provides easy access to European cities.

Other developments include Paddington Basin and King's Cross railway stations; the Stratford area of East London is undergoing major redevelopment in preparation for the 2012 Olympics. The planned Crossrail scheme, which is designed to link Heathrow Airport and Paddington to East London, will have big implications in terms of improving public transport and accessibility in London.

One of the major changes in planning policy in London in recent years has been the plan to focus more housing and other development in East London, particularly in the Thames Gateway. It is intended to build large numbers of new houses in this sector of London and to help shift the growth focus away from west London, but the recession of 2008 to 2009 has led to a sharp cyclical fall in both housing and office demand and construction, which may not recover for some time.

Important political developments in London were governed at the metropolitan level by the Greater London Council until 1986, when it and the other Labour party–controlled metropolitan councils were abolished by Thatcher's Conservative government. London survived with no metropolitan government until the formation of the Greater London Authority in 2000. The Labor party mayor until 2008 was Ken Livingstone, and he backed more high-rise office development to reinforce London's dominance as a leading European financial center, combined with an affordable housing policy, which required new housing developments to provide up to 50 percent of units as affordable housing, He also introduced the congestion charge for all vehicles entering central London, put more investment into bus services and public transport, and supported the London Development Agency. In the mayoral election in 2008, he was replaced by Conservative Boris Johnston. What the implications of this will be are uncertain, although the new mayor is committed to retaining London's leading role as a financial center.

Conclusion

London has experienced a period of considerable, if very uneven prosperity over the last 20 years, largely as a result of its dominance in financial and business services and the large number of highly paid jobs this has generated. This has had major implications for house prices and housing affordability. The financial crisis raises questions regarding the continuing viability of Sassen's global city thesis, which was predicated on the centrality of financial and business services. Although it is likely that London will retain its global city status, it is possible that the dominance of banking and finance may prove to be London's Achilles heel, at least in the short term; this could result in a major economic downturn with consequent impacts on people's lives. What the implications are for Sassen's polarization thesis remains to be seen.

While the impact of the financial crisis and recession will increase unemployment, it is unclear whether this will affect the highly skilled and high-paid groups more than the low-skilled groups. If it does, it could lead to a slowing or reversal of the growth of the middle classes and of immigration. What is very likely is that job losses and income cutbacks in the high-income sectors of banking and law will reduce earnings and income inequalities and increase housing affordability, at least in the short to medium term. Only time will tell whether London and New York will recover their global position or whether there will be a permanent shift in economic and financial power toward Southeast Asia.

Chris Hamnett

See also Gentrification; Globalization; Housing; Social Housing; World City

Further Readings

Atkinson, R. 2000. "Measuring Gentrification and Displacement in Greater London." *Urban Studies* 37(1):149–66.

Beaverstock, J. V., R. G. Smith, and P. J. Taylor. 1996. "The Global Capacity of a World City: A Relational Study of London." In *Globalisation Theory and Practice*, edited by E. Kofman and G. Youngs. London: Cassell.

Buck, N., I. Gordon, P. Hall, M. Harloe, and M. Kleinmann. 2002. *Working Capital: Life and Labour in Contemporary London*. London, Routledge.

Butler, T., C. Hamnett, and M. Ramsden. 2008. "Inward and Upward: Marking Out Social Class Change in London, 1981–2001." *Urban Studies* 45(1):67–88.

Davidson, M. and L. Lees. 2005. "New-Build 'Gentrification' and London's Riverside Renaissance." *Environment and Planning A* 37:1165–90.

Girouard, Mark. 1985. *Cities and People: A Social and Architectural History*. New Haven, CT: Yale University Press.

Greater London Authority. 2002. *Creativity: London's Core Business*. London: Author.

———. 2008. *London: A Cultural Audit*. London: Author.

Hall, P. 2007. *London Voices, London Lives: Tales from a Working Capital*. London: Routledge.

Hamnett, C. 2003. "Gentrification and the Middle-Class Remaking of Inner London, 1961–2001." *Urban Studies* 40(12):2401–26.

———. 2003. *Unequal City: London in the Global Arena*. London: Routledge.

Hamnett, C. and D. Whitelegg. 2007. "Loft Conversion and Gentrification in London: From Industrial to Post-industrial Land Use." *Environment and Planning A* 39(1):106–24.

Hebbert, M. 1998. *London: More by Fortune Than Design*. London: Wiley.

Newman, P. and I. Smith. 2000. "Cultural Production, Place, and Politics on the South Bank of the Thames." *International Journal of Urban and Regional Research* 24(1):9–24.

Sassen, S. 2001. *The Global City: New York, London, and Tokyo*. Princeton, NJ: Princeton University Press.

Thrift, N. 1994. "On the Social and Cultural Determinants of International Financial Centres: The Case of the City of London." In *Money, Power, and Space*, edited by S. Corbridge, N. Thrift, and R. Martin. Oxford, UK: Blackwell.

LOS ANGELES, CALIFORNIA

In the field of urban studies, Los Angeles is a key reference case for the analysis of contemporary urban restructuring. The followers of the Los Angeles School of Urban Studies ascribe to Los Angeles a paradigmatic status among postmodern urban regions. Los Angeles exemplifies a new model of urbanism, which, in contrast to the teachings of the Chicago School of Urbanism of the 1920s, is no longer organized around a central urban core or a central business district (CBD). Instead, its polycentric settlement pattern is best characterized as "dense sprawl." Less than 1 of 10 jobs and even fewer of the housing units in the region are located downtown. But even without an equivalent to midtown or downtown Manhattan, at 6,000 inhabitants per square mile, the Los Angeles urban area is the densest metropolitan region in the United States.

The greater Los Angeles area, also called "the Southland," extends over 400 square miles. Los

Angeles is the second-largest city in the United States and the largest city in the state of California. It is home to 3.8 million people, while Los Angeles County has about 10 million inhabitants. The surrounding five-county region has 17.6 million inhabitants and is expected to grow to about 25 million to 30 million people over the next decades.

Urban Development

Los Angeles's rapid ascent over the last century to an economic powerhouse and a leading world city is surprising, given its unfavorable environmental conditions compared to its regional competitors. The Los Angeles River carries a trickle of water during the dry summer months, hampering agricultural development. The proximity to the San Andreas Fault line makes the region prone to earthquakes. The San Gabriel and Santa Monica mountains provide natural barriers to freight shipping, while the geography of the ports is less ideal than other stretches of the coast. Also, because of its geographic location in a basin surrounded by water and mountains, Los Angeles is prone to smog, a situation further exacerbated by the region's excessive reliance on automobiles as the main means of transportation. So, early on, all signs pointed to San Francisco, Seattle, or San Diego as more likely candidates for the leading West Coast trade hub.

Working in favor of Los Angeles, however, was the unrelenting boosterism of its political and civic elites during the early twentieth century. These elites included such key figures as the water baron Walter Mulholland (prominently featured in the classic film *Chinatown*), the *Los Angeles Times* publisher and investor Harry Chandler, and the railroad and real estate tycoon Henry Huntington. The pleasant climatic conditions in the Land of Sunshine further encouraged the relocation of the entertainment industry, particularly the motion picture industry, from the East Coast in the 1920s.

But Los Angeles was a late bloomer compared to other leading American cities. Founded in 1777 in the viceroy-ruled territory of the Spanish Empire under the name of El Pueblo de Nuestra Señora la Reina de los Ángeles del Río de Porciúncula, the area had 650 residents in 1820. The economic development of the region rapidly accelerated only with the arrival of the Southern Pacific Railroad in 1876, the discovery of oil in 1892, and the completion of a much needed water aqueduct in 1913. Between 1890 and 1930, Los Angeles's increasingly diverse population grew from 50,400 to 1,200,000. The old Mexican ranchos were quickly replaced by citrus groves and endless subdivisions of single-family detached homes.

In contrast to classical industrial cities, where explosive growth during the mid- and late nineteenth century translated into extremely high inner-city population densities, urban growth in Los Angeles took a horizontal pattern right from the start. As early as 1930, population densities in downtown Los Angeles were less than three times higher than in surrounding suburbs, compared to a ratio of 30:1 in San Francisco and 26:1 in New York. Yet, contrary to common belief, the most crucial factor for this spread-out pattern was not the advent of the private automobile but rather the development of an extensive interurban passenger railway system. By the early 1910s, Henry Huntington's famous Pacific Electric Red Car Line had more than 1,000 miles of track and extended far into the surrounding counties. Even during their heyday, however, these passenger railway operations were never profitable by themselves. Rather, Huntington and others used them as loss leaders to encourage the real estate development of outlying suburban and exurban land. When the bulk of these parcels had been developed in the 1920s, the first Red Car lines were converted to cheaper buses.

In the next decades, buses and above all private cars began to dominate the regional transportation system. Despite a temporary boost in ridership during World War II, when gasoline shortages hampered further motorization, what was once the world's most extensive interurban rail system increasingly fell into disrepair; the last Red Car ran in 1961. However, contrary to a popular urban myth, the fate of electric rail in Los Angeles (and elsewhere) was not determined by General Motors, Firestone, Standard Oil, and other auto industry giants that bought up trolley lines across the nation and replaced them with buses. The so-called GM scandal merely accelerated a decline already in progress due to financial and structural problems of the trolley industry.

Also, influential urban planners advocated for "magic motorways" as the modern solution to southern California's urban congestion problems. Following the successful completion of the Arroyo Seco Parkway from downtown Los Angeles to Pasadena in 1940, the California Department of Public Works (now Caltrans) constructed a dense network of freeways in the coming decades, thus establishing the public image of Los Angeles as a sprawling, centerless sea of single-family homes, big-box stores, and low-rise office complexes connected by an endless number of fast-moving freeways.

After another half century of almost continuous population and economic growth in the region, this image has all but reversed itself. Motorization has increased to an astonishing rate of one car for every 1.8 people—the highest in the world—and traffic on the magic motorways is now crawling along at an average speed of 13 miles per hour for much of the day (which, ironically, is equal to the average speed of the Red Cars during their heyday). Due to growing political and neighborhood opposition, less than two thirds of the freeway miles originally proposed in the 1954 master plan have been built, with gaps particularly in affluent communities such as Beverly Hills and South Pasadena.

Meanwhile, Los Angeles continues to grow and become denser, with new multistory and high-rise living, working, and entertainment complexes going up all across the region. The mounting negative consequences of the region's sprawled settlement pattern have made Los Angeles, and southern California more generally, a hotbed for new urbanism ideas and practices such as transit-oriented, mixed-use development and smart growth.

Economic Development

Despite its strong and famous service sector industries, such as movie production, Los Angeles is by no means a postindustrial city. In fact, Los Angeles is the largest manufacturing center in the United States, with manufacturing accounting for almost 12 percent of all employment in the region (down from about 18 percent in 1990). From the 1920s onward, the motion picture and aerospace industries have provided important economic boosts to the region, complemented by other entertainment and media industries, oil, technology, fashion, and tourism as well as banking and finance. World War II concentrated military industries in the

region and thus brought an enormous economic and employment boon and a near doubling of the regional population. The end of the cold war and the subsequent collapse of the defense industry threw the region into recession in the early 1990s, but the military-industrial complex still plays an important role in the regional economy. Meanwhile, the world-famous Los Angeles district of Hollywood is synonymous with the world of movies and stars, leading to a unique clustering of film-related businesses and creative industries.

Los Angeles is also one of the world's most important trade gateways. The Long Beach/Los Angeles port complex ranks fifth in the world in container traffic and accounts for one third of all waterborne container traffic in the United States. By 2020, this already impressive volume is expected to double. Meanwhile, the Los Angeles International Airport (LAX) handles more "origin and destination" (as opposed to through-transit) passengers than any other airport in the world and is the world's sixth busiest in cargo traffic.

Politics and Governance

Local public life and politics in the immigrant city of Los Angeles have been fraught with class and racial tensions. Los Angeles has always been a stronghold of progressive, social, and labor movements, where artists frequently joined political radicals and working-class communities in reform struggles against big business. Progressives won important victories in the 1920s and 1930s, but in the 1940s, the political landscape became dominated by anti-Left, racist, and anti-Semitic sentiments. In 1947, foreshadowing what became known as McCarthyism in the 1950s, U.S. Congressman J. Parnell Thomas held secret hearings on the alleged communist infiltration of the Hollywood entertainment industry. The tides turned again with the advent of the civil rights movement, but deep racial and economic divides continued to strain the city's socioeconomic fabric as new groups of immigrants sought a place in Los Angeles's hodge-podge of cultures and ethnicities.

Los Angeles was the most segregated city in the United States during the 1960s. The African American neighborhood of Watts experienced five days of race rioting in 1965, primarily triggered by years of police brutality and harassment. In 1992, riots were sparked across the city after the acquittal of four white police officers who had been caught on videotape beating Rodney King, an African American, subsequent to a high-speed pursuit. The underlying racial animosities fueling the Rodney King uprising were different than during the Watts riots, however, as many historically black neighborhoods in south-central Los Angeles were turning increasingly Latino. Economic prospects for African Americans grew dimmer throughout the 1980s as unionized Black workers in downtown Los Angeles lost their jobs to Latino immigrants who were ready to work for substandard wages and African American–owned liquor and grocery stores were taken over by Asian immigrants.

In 1973, the Democrat Tom Bradley became the first Black mayor to be elected in a large U.S. city with a White majority. He governed Los Angeles for 20 years, contributing to the city's transformation into a multicultural world city. After Bradley's retirement, the businessman Richard Riordan became the city's first Republican mayor in more than 30 years. His administration was overshadowed by public controversy over the massive cost overruns and construction mismanagement related to the construction of Los Angeles's first modern-day heavy rail subway line, the Red Line.

Transit politics in Los Angeles have always been closely linked to complex ethnic and class struggles. In most other cities of the world, a federally subsidized rail project would have been hailed by a majority of residents as a much-needed project, but in Los Angeles, both the predominantly White residents on the affluent West Side and the poorer African American and Latino residents in South, Central, and East Los Angeles strongly objected to the Red Line. While the former group largely preferred car-oriented to transit-oriented solutions, the latter argued that a diversion of scarce funds from the overcrowded and underfinanced buses, which carried the vast majority of transit passengers and almost exclusively served transit-dependent people of color, to expensive new rail projects targeted at more affluent residents was racially and spatially discriminatory.

The Bus Riders Union (BRU), a civil rights advocacy group organized by the L.A. Labor/Community Strategy Center, brought a class action lawsuit against the Los Angeles County Metropolitan Transit Authority (MTA/Metro) in 1996 and successfully forced the authority into a 10-year consent decree designed to support bus operations and reduce bus overcrowding. The BRU consent decree has received nationwide attention as a key success story of the environmental justice movement.

In 2001, Riordan was succeeded by James Hahn, the son of the late Kenneth Hahn, who served on the Los Angeles County Board of Supervisors for 40 years from 1952 to 1992. Then, in a closely watched race, incumbent Hahn lost the 2005 mayoral race to Antonio Villaraigosa, who became the city's first Latino mayor since 1872. At the time Villaraigosa took office, Los Angeles was 48 percent Hispanic, 31 percent White, 11 percent Asian, and 10 percent Black. Villaraigosa arrived in office with strong credentials as a labor and community advocate, and he stepped onto the national political scene as a charismatic and progressive urban leader who vowed to put environmental and working-class community issues at the forefront of his local agenda.

However, many of the city's most pressing problems, such as environmental degradation, traffic congestion, unaffordable land and housing prices, and substandard public services, including poor educational and medical facilities, can be effectively addressed only at the regional or state level. Unfortunately, regional governance in the Greater Los Angeles area has always been extremely fragmented. Los Angeles County is a hodgepodge of 88 incorporated cities and many additional unincorporated areas, and the larger region has more than 180 individual municipalities.

Los Angeles's Urban Renaissance

Los Angeles is currently well on its way to defying most of its historical stereotypes. Downtown is undergoing a major urban renaissance. Apart from new museums and entertainment and sports centers, thousands of new residential loft and condominium apartments have been created since the city council passed an adaptive reuse ordinance in 1999, encouraging the conversion of vacant office and commercial buildings. Several spectacular mixed-used urban redevelopment megaprojects are in the advanced planning and early construction stages.

The future of the large industrial district around downtown is uncertain. Between 2005 and 2007,

New development in Los Angeles is transforming formerly run-down and neglected parts of the city into an entertainment, business, and residential hub.

Source: Tracy Buyan.

the downtown residential population jumped more than 20 percent to almost 40,000 residents. Most of the new development is taking place around the Staples entertainment center and in the Bunker Hill central business district core.

Bunker Hill has been an urban renewal area since the 1950s, when a massive slum clearance project replaced run-down historic Victorian residences with modern office towers. However, because of the city's high taxes, congestion, and economic recession, the vacancy rate for downtown commercial real estate was more than 20 percent by the 1990s. Commonly known by the name of Skid Row, the district immediately to the east of Bunker Hill is still home to several thousand homeless people living in cardboard boxes and tents. The gentrification of downtown Los Angeles now threatens the transient and low-income populations in this area with displacement, once again demonstrating how the politics and economics of urban growth divide Los Angeles into winners and losers.

Deike Peters

See also Davis, Mike; Los Angeles School of Urban Studies; Soja, Edward W.; Urban Geography; Urban Theory

Further Readings

Bottles, Scott. 1987. *Los Angeles and the Automobile: The Making of the Modern City.* Los Angeles: University of California Press.

Davis, Mike. 2006. *City of Quartz: Excavating the Future in Los Angeles.* Updated edition. New York: Verso.

Erie, Steve. 2004. *Globalizing L.A. Trade, Infrastructure, and Regional Development.* Stanford, CA: Stanford University Press.

Fulton, William. 1997. *The Reluctant Metropolis: The Politics of Urban Growth in Los Angeles.* Point Arena, CA: Solano Press Books.

Gottlieb, Robert, Mark Vallianatos, Regina M. Freer, and Peter Dreier. 2005. *The Next Los Angeles: The Struggle for a Livable City.* Los Angeles: University of California Press.

Hise, Greg and William Deverell, eds. 2005. *Land of Sunshine: The Environmental History of Metropolitan Los Angeles.* Pittsburgh, PA: University of Pittsburgh Press.

Los Angeles School of Urban Studies

In the early 1980s, urban researchers at the University of California, Los Angeles (UCLA) and the University of Southern California (USC) began to study urban restructuring processes through a series of detailed cases studies on the Los Angeles region. Much of the research in urban geography and sociology up to that time had focused on East Coast industrial cities and was largely informed by models developed by Chicago School scholars in the first half of the twentieth century. However, rather than finding a city with concentric zones ordered by a dominant center, Los Angeles researchers found a fragmented urban region with a center that was too weak to impose order on all the different parts.

These researchers believed that they had identified new patterns of urbanization and drew on a wide body of theoretical work (from Marxism to postmodernism) to understand them. Moreover, many suggested that although underlying urbanization processes were not unique to Los Angeles, they developed in Los Angeles earliest and with the greatest intensity. Although what could be called the Los Angeles School of Urban Studies (LA School) is far from a perfectly cohesive community of scholars, the scholars who compose it tend to be unified in the belief that several key urbanization processes are restructuring cities in entirely new ways and that these processes have intersected in particularly intense ways in Los Angeles, making it the paradigmatic city of the twenty-first century.

The Post-Fordist Turn

The LA School has its roots in urban economic geography, drawing from broad theoretical traditions including structural Marxism, neoclassical economics, and the Regulation School. Edward W. Soja draws from the Marxist-inspired work of David Harvey to argue that a central response to capitalist economic crises has been to reconcentrate certain aspects of capital and labor in certain cities while dispersing others across space. In Los Angeles and other global regions, this has resulted in a process of "extensification" whereby corporations have sought out inexpensive and unorganized sources of labor throughout the developing world. This has led to the deindustrialization of major urban areas in the advanced north.

Concomitantly, key functions (e.g., managerial, finance, and innovation) have been concentrated in several prominent regions in advanced capitalist

countries, resulting in profound changes in the physical form (central business districts, science parks, new consumption complexes, etc.) and class structures of these regions. Different processes combined in particularly intense ways in the 1970s and 1980s to restructure the economic logic of Los Angeles.

These researchers also drew insights from the Regulation School to argue that as large industrial plants underwent a process of deindustrialization, those industries that remained in urban regions like Los Angeles were likely to be organized according to post-Fordist principles. They suggested that firms were embracing new models of organizing the production process that centered on more flexible production systems, where small and medium-size firms were linked to one another in clusters of transaction-intensive networks. These changes improved the abilities of firms to reduce uncertainties; respond to new information, trends, and competitors; contain labor costs; and maximize innovation capacities.

The principal examples of these agglomeration economics in the Los Angeles region are Orange County's technology industry, Hollywood's entertainment industry, downtown Los Angeles's craft industry, and the Wilshire Corridor's financial and insurance industries.

The Polycentric City Region

These economic processes contributed to unleashing important changes in the sociospatial forms of urban regions in general and Los Angeles in particular. These processes transformed the concentrically centered cities identified by the Chicago School into sprawled, multinodal, and polycentric city regions. Early economic elites in Los Angeles laid the foundations for a sprawling and low-density metropolitan region with a loosely defined and increasingly inconsequential downtown. Changes in the economic structure beginning in the 1970s transformed this low-density and flat city into a polynucleated one.

The transition to a post-Fordist urban economy triggered important changes in the spatial structure of the region as activities in the most dynamic economic sectors clustered into different business and industrial districts throughout the metropolitan region. It must be stressed that the multicentered urban region is not the result of chaotic and anar-chic processes but rather reflects the spatial logic of post-Fordist capitalism in which small and medi-um-size firms agglomerate in distinct economic districts throughout urban regions. These new urban centers are distinctive from traditional resi-dential suburbs because they are relatively autono-mous poles that combine work, residential, leisure, and consumption activities.

New Modes of Stratification

Changes in the class structure intersected with rapid changes in race and ethnicity to produce a new system of social stratification in Los Angeles. In terms of the changing class structure, several Los Angeles scholars asserted a causal link between new patterns in urban restructuring and new inequalities. They maintained that globalization, labor-saving technologies, and plant closings com-bined to rid Los Angeles's economic landscape of Fordist manufacturers, resulting in the loss of 70,000 middle-income jobs between 1978 and 1983. As the supply of middle-income manufac-turing jobs declined, intense growth in other sec-tors of the economy (high technology, craft, finance) contributed to the expansion of jobs at both the top and bottom ends of the occupational structure and relatively weak growth of mid-level jobs. In addition to this, rapid growth at the top end of the occupational structure fueled growth at the bottom end by creating new demands for labor-intensive services (e.g., personal services, restaurants, hotels). These trends in the regional labor market combined to generate a highly polar-ized occupational and income structure.

Further contributing to the region's changing system of social stratification was the rapid increase of its non-White population. Los Angeles was one of America's most homogenous large cit-ies up until the 1940s. Three large waves of migrants changed the face of the urban region. First, African Americans moved to Los Angeles in the 1940s. After the late 1960s, antidiscrimina-tory hiring policies and expanded university opportunities created a sustainable Black middle class. At the same time, deindustrialization closed off a major source of employment for low- and semiskilled members of the Black community.

These two processes bifurcated the Black commu-nity along class and geographical lines.

Second, the Hart-Celler Act of 1965 eliminated strict immigration quotas and introduced new visa requirements based on labor market needs and family ties. Significant numbers of Asian profes-sionals were granted visas and were later able to sponsor their relatives. In addition to these profes-sionals, Los Angeles also attracted a flow of refugees from Southeast Asia. The economic endowments of a large proportion of Asian migrants (skills, entrepreneurial know-how, capital) distin-guished them from traditional working-class immigrants and facilitated their integration into the region's middle and upper-middle classes.

Third, the end of the temporary migrant pro-gram in 1962 prompted many Mexican migrants to settle in the United States, with social networks to their home communities enabling the migration of hundreds of thousands of Mexicans to Los Angeles. The region also experienced an important increase in El Salvadoran and Guatemalan refu-gees in the 1980s. Latino migrants have largely been low-skilled and have occupied labor market niches that offer little hope for upward economic mobility. Thus, dramatic changes in the region's occupational structure have intersected with a remarkable increase in immigration to produce a particularly new social division of labor. These changes have made the region a paradigmatic case for understanding the implications of this new system of social stratification.

Governing the Fragmented Metropolis

Los Angeles researchers have also highlighted the particularly weak and fragmented character of the region's governance institutions, with many of them placing the blame for this on the Lakewood Plan. The Lakewood Plan allowed residents of unincorporated areas to exercise municipal powers—zoning powers were particularly useful for limiting the access of low-income residents to middle-class areas—without incurring high taxes for service and administrative costs. This formula of municipal governance pro-vided the framework for 60 new municipalities formed between 1940 and the 1970s, further shat-tering the already fragmented metropolis.

Middle-class suburban areas were undergirded by a dense network of homeowners associations

(HOAs), which provided residents with a ready-made social infrastructure to mobilize against perceived threats to their interests (e.g., rising property values, low taxes, and racial homogeneity). In a series of mobilizations to limit property taxes, roll back school integration, and secede from the city of Los Angeles, these residents have played a central role in further fragmenting the region.

In terms of social policy, urban officials throughout the 1980s and 1990s cut social expenditures while redoubling spending in policing. What remained of a local welfare apparatus was scaled back dramatically during the 1980s, the result of a massive reduction in revenue to cities and counties (limits on property taxes and cutbacks in federal aid to large cities) and the policy choices of neoliberal city and county officials. As crime rates rose and the homeless population soared, a new culture of fear drove middle-class residents to embrace law and order policies (e.g., police repression, strict sentencing guidelines) and private security measures (e.g., surveillance, private security forces, gated communities, urban design and architecture). Widespread popularity of these measures resulted in the transformation of the urban landscape, with security technologies and instruments carving up the region into thousands of fortified zones ranging in scale from privately guarded homes to gated communities. Following from this, Mike Davis observed in 1990 that

> The old liberal paradigm of social control, attempting to balance repression with reform, has long been superseded by a rhetoric of social warfare that calculates the interests of the urban poor and the middle classes as a zero-sum game. In cities like Los Angeles, on the bad edge of postmodernity, one observes an unprecedented tendency to merge urban design, architecture and the police apparatus into a single, comprehensive security effort. (p. 224)

Postmodern Urbanism as a Way of Life?

Edward Soja and Michael Dear, two founders of the Los Angeles School, have also sought to understand the relation between new patterns of urbanization and the consciousness of urban residents. They have asserted that the particular features found in contemporary urban regions have

fueled a new postmodern urban consciousness. Southern California's fragmented and decentered character has blurred the real and imagined boundaries that once underpinned modernist categories for knowing the world.

The deconstruction of modernist precepts has resulted in greater conceptual instability, with signs and information no longer rooted in underlying truths and realities. For Soja, this presents both constraints and opportunities for new progressive politics. On the one hand, urban elites have stepped into this knowledge vacuum by combining and sanitizing cultural markers in the production of new spaces of mass consumption. Los Angeles's *City Walk* serves as an example of such a space, with entrepreneurs repackaging and representing urbanity to residents in a tightly controlled environment. As residents of the region isolate themselves in their guarded enclaves, encounters with urbanity are increasingly shaped through these types of spaces, transforming these idealized simulations of city life into a (hyper) reality.

At the same time, Soja maintains that the weakening of universalizing and essential political truths has provided ideological openings for establishing new hybrid alliances across traditional political divides (ideological, racial, class, spatial). In such a context, actors can form common alliances around pragmatic issues that bind them together, with internal differences often viewed as assets in the common struggle for social justice. Whereas modernist epistemologies based on universalizing truths made the development of alliances across traditional political and ideological divides difficult, more relativized and reflexive postmodern ways of thinking make these types of alliances more feasible.

The work of the LA School has proven to be very influential in national and international urban scholarship, with many researchers having adopted its central propositions. Nevertheless, the LA School has come under criticism from several well-known urban scholars. Some suggest that the "new" processes highlighted by the LA School are not so much *new* empirical realities but the application of *new* theories (largely developed by non–LA School scholars) to existing urban realities, revealing processes that classical urban theories had failed to uncover. The power of these new urban theories justifies a shift away from the

Chicago School model, but LA School researchers do not possess intellectual ownership over them. The label *new urban sociology* is seen as a more accurate reflection of the new theoretical developments in urban studies.

Others have questioned Los Angeles's status as the paradigmatic city of the twenty-first century and suggest that other cities are equally or more deserving of this title. The last type of criticism has targeted the politics of the LA School, with scholars from the Left and the Right attacking its ideological underpinnings and the political implications of its arguments. In spite of the merit of some of these criticisms, the individual scholars of the LA School have made important contributions to their respective areas of specialization (e.g., urban and regional economics, sociology and immigration, urban politics, postmodern urban theory) while collectively illustrating how these different strands can all come together to shape the form, function, and fate of a single urban region.

Walter J. Nicholls

See also Chicago School of Urban Sociology; Davis, Mike; Los Angeles, California; Soja, Edward W.; Urban Geography; Urban Sociology; Urban Theory

Further Readings

Davis, Mike. 1990. *City of Quartz: Excavating the Future in Los Angeles*. New York: Verso.

Dear, M., ed. 2002. *From Chicago to LA: Making Sense of Urban Theory*. London: Sage.

Scott, A. 1988. *Metropolis: From the Division of Labor to Urban Form*. Berkeley: University of California Press.

Soja, E. 2000. *Postmetropolis: Critical Studies of Cities and Regions*. Oxford, UK: Blackwell.

Waldinger, R. and M. Bozorgmehr, eds. 1996. *Ethnic Los Angeles*. New York: Russell Sage Foundation.

LÖSCH, AUGUST

Together with Johann Heinrich von Thünen (1780–1850), Wilhelm Launhardt (1832–1918), and Alfred Weber (1868–1958), August Lösch (1906–1945) is regarded as one of the early creators of spatial economic theory. His most important work, *Die räumliche Ordnung der Wirtschaft* (The Spatial Order of the Economy), translated into English 1954 under the slightly misleading title. *The Economics of Location*, became internationally recognized as an important theoretical base for the newly developing discipline of regional science.

Biographical Background

Lösch was born on October 15, 1906, in the small town of Öhringen in southwestern Germany. Two years later, the family moved to Heidenheim, where the young man passed *Abitur*, the German version of the high school final, in 1925. After an apprenticeship with a local industrial firm, he began his studies at the University of Tübingen. "A royal feeling," he writes, in youthful idealism, in his diary in July 1927, "to be free for all that is noble and true. To be on your own in research and in life!"

He continued his studies at the University of Freiburg and moved on to Bonn in 1930. There, he met professors Arthur Spiethoff and Joseph Schumpeter, who admitted him to his seminar and to a special philosophical–sociological workshop. Lösch received his doctorate in 1932, based on a thesis on the question, "What to Think about the Fall in Birthrate," an earlier version of which had already won a prize in 1931. He used the prize money to publish the manuscript under the original German title of *Was ist vom Geburtenrückgang zu halten?*

During the following years, Lösch concentrated his research on the interrelationships between the development paths of population and the economy. This interest continued into his first visit to the United States, where he went in the fall of 1934 on a one-year Rockefeller fellowship. After his return to Bonn, Lösch passed habilitation—in the German tradition, the prerequisite for a university career—in 1936 based on the manuscript of his new book on population waves and business cycles, *Bevölkerungswellen und Wechsellagen*.

In this book, he analyzes the differing impacts of population growth on the business cycle in economies dominated by the agricultural or industrial sectors. In the former case, a close relationship between demographic and economic variables can be clearly shown, but the interaction is not as strict in the latter. Here, the political frame conditions for technological and economic development are more important.

In 1936, Lösch's Rockefeller fellowship was extended for another year. During his U.S. visit, he met again with Schumpeter, who had moved to Harvard and who received him "like a father." In Schumpeter's seminar, he met old friends like Wolfgang Stolper—whom he knew from Schumpeter's seminar in Bonn—and made new ones—like Edgar M. Hoover, Jr., then Schumpeter's assistant. Deeply impressed by the diversity of the country, where he traveled rather extensively during his second visit, and by the spirit of freedom in America, Lösch began research on the topic of economic regions.

In 1933, after *Machtergreifung* by the Nazi party, Lösch wrote in his diary: "I will walk upright through these hopeless times." Many of his friends decided to leave Germany for good, and his birthrate book had been indexed by the German authorities in 1936. Nevertheless, he returned to his home country in 1937. "What would become of Germany, if all of us were leaving?" he asked.

During the following years, he worked in Heidenheim and Bonn as a freelance scientist on the manuscript of *Spatial Order*, which he completed in the fall of 1939. In 1940, the year when the first edition of this book was published, he entered the Kiel Institute for World Economics, where he worked as a coresearcher and later as the leader of a research group. Under the protection of the Kiel Institute, he wrote in a letter to a friend, "I could avoid to fight for Hitler."

His gratitude to the institute did not prevent Lösch from criticizing its policies. In his diary, he complained that the institute director forced on him "totally useless" reports, thus deliberately keeping him from productive work on his currency plan.

The currency plan that Lösch worked on during the last years of World War II and of his life dealt with developing a currency system that would, after the end of the war, help reintegrate the world economy. The first part of the concept is based on the assumption that a single world currency exists. The transfer system then works in relation to distance and the distribution of activities in space. Introducing partial currencies and thus approaching reality again, the point of view of the spatial distribution of activities is dominant in explaining the impact of price-level movements and price fluctuations on the rates of exchange.

In October 1944, after heavy air raids by allied forces on the city of Kiel, Lösch and his research group were evacuated to the small town of Ratzeburg. Here, weakened from exhaustion and the lack of medical attention, he died from an attack of scarlet fever on May 30, 1945. He did not complete his currency theory. The fragment was published posthumously in Weltwirtschaftliches Archiv 1949.

Intellectual Legacy

Lösch's *Economics of Location* is a book with many facets and is easy neither to read nor to understand. Lösch subdivides it into four parts: I. Location, II. Economic Areas, III. Trade, and IV. Examples. While the explorations elaborated in these four parts are closely interrelated, the most important and revolutionary concepts are developed in Part II.

Here, Lösch starts from the following set of assumptions: Economic activity takes place on an unlimited homogeneous plane where the population—equipped with equal preferences and

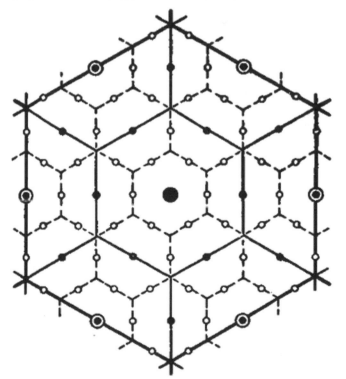

Lösch's Ideal Central-Place Hierarchy

Source: Lösch, A. 1954. *The Economics of Location.* Translated by W. H. Woglom and W. F. Stolper. New Haven, CT: Yale University Press.

Incomes—is settled in equidistant locations. Economic decisions are based on rational behavior and the possibility of free market entry. Production functions are independent from geographical location; however, the existence of economies of scale and agglomeration economies favor spatial clustering. The market area of the single producer is geographically extended until the price at market location becomes equal to the sum of factory price and product-specific linear transport costs, so that profits disappear—because factory prices are equal to average production costs. Most important, for each finished product, each location on the plane is supplied by exactly one production location.

Starting from the market area for a single producer and moving on to nets of markets for producers of competing products, Lösch describes, "for the various classes of commodities," nets of equilateral "hexagons, close-meshed and wide-meshed ones which, to begin with, we can throw across our plane at random." However, considering the existence of agglomeration economies, the nets are to be rearranged "in such a way that all of them have in common at least one center." Thus, a central city evolves, as shown in the figure on the previous page.

Then, the various market nets are rotated around the central city in such a way that the highest number of market locations coincide with each other. Thus, a sectoral pattern of densely and loosely clustered locations comes into existence: a Löschian economic area.

Next, moving away from the strict conditions of spatial homogeneity, the market areas have to be redetermined for differing conditions of the geographic distribution of consumers. Also to be considered is that production and demand functions for identical products may differ as a result of divergent impacts from natural or behavioral factors or political conditions. Finally, systems of market nets as derived from these redefined production and demand functions have to be introduced for different products, and the various market nets, again, have to be overlaid to form economic areas.

Whatever the detailed conditions, Lösch finds that "the honeycomb is the most advantageous form of economic areas," where the advantage benefits the totality of consumers, whereas for the single producer the circular market area would be most opportune.

On April 21, 1971, the first August Lösch Days were held by the City of Heidenheim, for more than three decades a series of biannual events. August Lösch in memoriam, as well as theoretical and practical problems of spatial structure and development have been discussed; the August Lösch prize for outstanding publications in regional science, written in German or—after a change of the constitution—in English, has been awarded. Most recently, commemorating the centenary of Lösch's birthday in October 2006, the event was held at the Kiel Institute for World Economics.

In 1982, the first August Lösch Ring of Regional Science, to be conferred on no more than six living persons of undisputed international renown in the field, was offered to Wolfgang F. Stolper. Further awardees are Leo H. Klaassen (1984), Torsten Hägerstrand (1986), Walter Isard (1988), Kazimierz Dziewonski (1992), Martin J. Beckmann (1998), and Herbert Giersch (2000).

Rolf Funck

See also Location Theory; Urban Economics; Urban Geography

Further Readings

Blum, Ulrich, Rolf H. Funck, Jan S. Kowalski, Antoni Kuklinski, and Werner Rothengatter, eds., with editorial assistant Guido von Thadden. 2007. *Space—Structure—Economy: A Tribute to August Lösch*. Baden Baden, Germany: Nomos.

Lösch, A. 1938. "The Nature of Economic Regions." *Southern Economic Journal* 5(1):71–78.

———. 1954. *The Economics of Location*. Translated by W. H. Woglom and W. F. Stolper. New Haven, CT: Yale University Press.

Stolper, W. F. 1954. August Lösch in Memoriam (Introduction). Pp vii–viii in *The Economics of Location*, by August Lösch. New Haven, CT: Yale University Press.

LYNCH, KEVIN

Kevin Lynch (1918–1984) was a professor of city planning at the Massachusetts Institute of

Technology, where he taught for more than 30 years. By all reckoning, he was a leading thinker in the field of city planning and design. His work inspired many researchers, practitioners, and students in his field and influenced academic thinking and writing in areas outside planning. His name is most commonly associated with his seminal work, *The Image of the City*. First published in 1960, the book has gone through multiple printings. It has been translated into many different languages and is widely read and consulted in academic work and practice.

Image Studies

In contrast to the prevalent Beaux-Arts and modernist traditions of city design, Lynch was committed to defining a new practice of design that would be informed by the human experiences of the built environment. By asking people to draw maps of their cities, and to tell what came to their mind first when they thought of their city, or to describe what the experience of the city meant to them and how that affected their sense of well being, Lynch demonstrated how it is possible to construct a collective or consensus image of the city. This "public image"—as he preferred to call it—consists of a collection of the physical features of the city that consistently appear in individual mental maps of the city: certain streets, significant buildings, functional districts, important public spaces, concentration and intensity of activities, major streets and roads commonly traveled, natural elements like rivers and hills, and so on. He suggested that such frequently mentioned elements shown in individual maps or included in the aggregated public image can be categorized as districts, edges, landmarks, nodes, and paths, although the respondents may not consciously use such rubrics. These concepts, however, are now routinely used in the practice of urban design.

Lynch argued further that some cities are more "imageable" than others, and this depends on the legibility of the urban form. What makes a city more or less legible? It is a function of three things, he proposed: identity, structure, and meaning. Cities that have buildings and natural features with strong identities, street patterns that are easy to comprehend, and other form elements that have functional and symbolic meanings are

likely to be more imageable than cities lacking such attributes.

Considered a seminal work, *The Image of the City* inspired both practice and pedagogy of city planning and design, on the one hand, and scholarly research on the other. Many urban design projects in U.S. cities to this day begin with an imageability study in an effort to understand how the form of a city is perceived by lay citizens and whether that conforms to the planners' own understanding and intuitions of the significant features of the city. But his theoretical insights about imageability—that is, identity, structure, and meaning, which would seem to have more relevance to city design policies—did not seem to take deep roots in the world of practice. Instead, the taxonomy he proposed for describing city image—districts, edges, landmarks, nodes, and paths—became a popular methodological tool for analyzing the visual form of cities.

The contribution of the image studies toward the formulation of urban design policies and guidelines, however, has been uneven, and Lynch himself expressed some disappointment in retrospect. Nevertheless, the methodology has become a popular pedagogic tool in many urban design studios. It is a common practice for instructors to ask students to do a "Lynch map" of the city or neighborhood they are studying. This methodology has proved an effective learning exercise in making the students aware of the visual form of the physical city.

In academia, Lynch's work inspired a whole new research paradigm that made human–environment relations and interactions integral to urban design. It paved the way for a host of cognitive mapping studies—a term that was taken from the title of an earlier article by psychologist Edward Tolman in 1948—by environmental psychologists, geographers, sociologists, and planning academics. Lynch himself never used the term, nor is he believed to have been aware of Tolman's work. Nevertheless, the gaggle of research that followed covered a broad spectrum of inquiry.

Many of these studies explored the differences in the images or mental maps—a term favored by geographers—of the same urban area by age, stage of life cycle, class, gender, location, and even occupation. Others examined the styles of representation and the developmental aspects of mental maps. Some of these studies included cross-cultural comparison. Collectively these studies confirmed Lynch's earlier findings, vindicated the methodology, and advanced additional insights.

Other Works

Although *The Image of the City* has almost exclusively defined Lynch's reputation worldwide and outside the field of planning, it is but a small part of his published work, which includes eight other volumes containing more than 3,000 printed pages. The 1962 volume titled *Site Planning*, his second publication, came out soon after the first, to be followed by two other updated and expanded editions in 1971 and 1984, the last edition coauthored with Gary Hack. Collectively, these three editions remain a scholarly treatise that combines principles and good practices of site planning with relevant theories from allied fields.

In the 1960s, Lynch coauthored another important book, *The View from the Road*, with Donald Appleyard and Jack Myer. Written against the backdrop of planning and construction of the inner-city links of the interstate highway system, this book documented, analyzed, and simulated the visual experience of high-speed travel through the newly constructed and proposed urban freeways. In the 1970s, several other publications followed in quick succession—the second edition of *Site Planning* (1971), *What Time Is This Place?* (1972), *Managing the Sense of the Region* (1976), and *Growing Up in Cities* (1977), the last one edited from the contributions of several authors. The last three addressed different aspects of city design: The volume *What Time Is This Place?* is a treatise on time, especially how time embeds in space, the resulting implications for growth, change, and decay in urban form and space, and what these mean for historic preservation. *Managing the Sense of the Region* (1976) focused on questions of environmental quality, livability, and sustainability at the regional and metropolitan scale and the possibilities for managing the sensory quality at a regional scale. Finally, *Growing Up in Cities*, a 1977 study sponsored by UNESCO, reported on a comparative study of the life experiences of adolescent children in urban settings in four different countries—Argentina, Australia, Poland, and Mexico—with a specific focus on the human consequences of the built environment.

In the 1980s, he published perhaps the most important book of his career, *A Theory of Good City Form* (1981), or *Good City Form* (in later editions). This was followed by a significant and enhanced edition of *Site Planning* (1984) coauthored with Gary Hack. Another volume, *Wasting Away* (1990), came much later and posthumously, under the editorship of Michael Southworth. This was a remarkable book that focused on the waste and inefficiency in modern consumer societies and the impact of waste on nature and environment. Translated into Spanish and Italian, the content of this volume has proved quite prescient today in the context of the global environmental crisis. Finally, another volume, titled *City Sense and City Design* (1990), edited by Tridib Banerjee and Michael Southworth, assembles all of his published journal articles and book chapters, along with other previously unpublished works and projects that defined his career profile. These nine volumes then define, more or less exhaustively, his professional and scholarly accomplishments in city planning and design.

A New Perspective

Arguably, the work of Kevin Lynch represents a distinct and new way of thinking about the design and planning of the built environment at an urban scale. When he began his academic career in the late 1950s, ideas of large-scale design of cities were dominated by the classical civic design traditions and large-scale landscape design, followed by influences of architecture and planning of the modernist era. The legacy of these traditions was profoundly deterministic and based on the belief that design of the environment can determine behavior and, if done right, improve the social and physical well-being of the users and their quality of life. The incipient field of urban design that found its identity in the interstitial spaces between architecture, landscape architecture, and planning continued this tradition in urban redevelopment and other large public works projects in the 1950s and 1960s.

Lynch distanced himself from the nascent field of urban design and preferred to use the term *city design* to define the scope and possibilities of the design of the large-scale built environment. His contribution was particularly significant at this time because the tradition of design at the large scale was very much under attack and discredited by the social scientists engaged in studies of contemporary urban problems and the attendant planning and policy response. Social scientists saw the deterministic approach of designers as megalomaniacal and what they had to offer as not particularly relevant for addressing the fundamental issues of social welfare and collective well-being. At best, the design concerns were relegated to a lower priority.

Lynch's approach to city design began with a conversation with community clients about how they organize and represent their experiences of the everyday built environment. In this approach, the design response was to be informed by the perceptions, values, and expectations of the public, not professional predilections. It was an argument that design matters in a fundamental way and not just as a window dressing. Furthermore, this was essentially a bottom-up approach, not the top-down authoritarian design of the earlier tradition of grand design and visionary aesthetics. In Lynch's approach, the role of the designer is to help people achieve their desired environment, one that fulfills their immediate needs and offers flexibility for change and adaptation. His scenario of city design would involve participation from the users of the environment in the design and future control of their urban space. In this view, the designer serves as a facilitator and technical expert, perhaps requiring a few minimal master strokes here and there, as Lynch's own practice and projects often reflected.

While championing this new approach, Lynch also advanced many normative positions in his writings. He was particularly interested in exploring future scenarios for change—possible utopias and dystopias (which he called *cacotopias*) of human society.

Thus, a career that began with a passion to understand the visual and perceived form of the city evolved into a distinct philosophy of city design. Lynch's earlier and renowned work, *The Image of the City,* helped restore the place of city design in public policy, and his subsequent research, writings, practice, and teaching reflected a new approach to design that emphasized human purposes and consequences of the built environment,

as well as possibilities of city design that engaged the public in the process.

The philosophical formulations of this approach culminated in *A Theory of Good City Form.* The theory was profoundly normative and explored the questions of what constitutes good city form and what might be its performance characteristics. Lynch searched for answers to these questions in the historical models of ideal city, examined them analytically and empirically in contemporary research, and explored them in speculative scenarios. Many of these writings were published in journal articles or book chapters. In *A Theory of Good City Form,* Lynch argued that a normative theory is necessary to identify the performance characteristics of good city form. He proposed five basic dimensions of performance—vitality, sense, fit, access, and control—and two meta-dimensions described as efficiency and justice. The first dimension, vitality, is the requirement of the form to sustain life, health, and biological functions of the inhabitants. Sense has to do with the perception and cognition of the environment and includes much of the imageability requirements he advanced earlier. The dimension of fit refers to the degree of congruence between the environmental form and the customary, desired, or expected behaviors of the users of the environment. Access is the dimension that defines availability of amenities, conveniences, and opportunities within the environmental form and the aggregate efficiency and equity in the distribution of such resources. The dimension of control refers to matters of rights, responsibilities, and ownership of common space, as well as the ability of the inhabitants to change and transform such spaces. Finally, the two meta-dimensions of efficiency and justice, according to Lynch, refer to the balancing act between minimizing cost while maximizing distributive justice and equity in the organization of resources in space.

One could reinterpret these criteria today in the form of a synthesis of John Rawls's 1971 original theory of justice and Amartya Sen's 1999 treatise on human capability as the basis for development as freedom. While Lynch was aware of and cited Rawls's work, it was not possible for him to anticipate Sen's work, much of which postdated his book. It is fair to assume that his emphasis on the justness of the city form was supported by the works of Rawls, which he discussed. The apparent convergence of Lynch's normative philosophy of good city form and Sen's moral theory of human functioning, capability, and freedom remains an area of future scholarly explorations.

Practice of City Design

While making such theoretical, if normative contributions to our understanding of the human purposes and consequences of urban form, Lynch was also engaged in the practice of city design throughout his career. He began his career as a city planner in Greensboro, North Carolina, before he was recruited by MIT to join the faculty of city planning. During his academic career, he never lost touch with practice and as a scholar-practitioner always combined pedagogy with research and clinical experiences. He often tried to apply his normative views in practice, while drawing from his practice in his teaching and writings.

Some of the more notable examples of his projects include a plan for Boston's waterfront development, a campus plan in Cleveland, a development scheme for the Rio Salado corridor in Phoenix, a plan for the future development of the San Diego metropolitan region (with Donald Appleyard), and a conservation plan for Martha's Vineyard. Lynch's projects were often collaborative and participatory but never deterministic or definitive. He often emphasized the process that can accommodate change and, rather than proposing a concrete scheme, almost always preferred broad guidelines, design rules, and illustrative possibilities.

Lynch had his share of detractors. While appreciating his intellectual contributions, social scientists found his work lacking rigor—they questioned the size and selection of samples for *The Image of the City*, for example—and full of assertions or speculations. Others found his writing imprecise and containing ambiguities and contradictions. Practitioners found his writings too visionary or unrealistic. Because Lynch never offered concrete images of the good city form he advocated, many found his work inspiring but difficult to translate into practice. His work did not lead to the kind of paradigms—new urbanism, for example—on which practitioners often rely.

Biographical Background

Lynch was born in Chicago, and grew up in the northern part of the city near the shores of Lake Michigan. He attended the progressive Francis Parker School where the curriculum was influenced by John Dewey's philosophy of learning by doing. His early years were influenced by major world events—the Spanish War, the Great Depression, and the rise of communism. In high school, he developed an interest in architecture and went to Yale to pursue this interest. Soon, he was disillusioned by the rigid Beaux-Arts tradition of Yale's architecture program. He was intrigued by Frank Lloyd Wright's work and contacted Wright about the possibility of studying architecture with him.

With encouragement from Wright, Lynch left Yale and joined Taliesin in Wisconsin. As Wright chose to move to Arizona, Lynch, along with other apprentices, accompanied him. He did not stay there too long, however, finding Wright's authoritarian style stifling. He went on to study biology at Rensselaer Polytechnic Institute in New York. In 1941, he married Anne Borders and soon was inducted by the U.S. Army and sent to the South Pacific, Japan, and the Philippines as a member of the Army Corps of Engineers.

After he came back, he went to MIT under the G.I. Bill and finished a bachelor's degree in city planning in 1947. He joined the MIT planning faculty in 1948 and began his early explorations on the visual form and images of the city with Gyorgy Kepes, a renowned expert on visual arts, and a colleague at MIT. A study grant from the Ford Foundation gave him the opportunity to spend a year in Italy, based mainly in Florence. His *flânerie* in European cities—not unlike Walter Benjamin's wanderings in Paris—was inspirational for him and helped him to conceptualize his seminal work, *The Image of the City*. After retiring from MIT in 1978 he became fully engaged in practice with the Cambridge, Massachusetts–based firm of Carr Lynch Associates, and he remained active in writing and practice until his unexpected death in 1984.

His students remember him as a kind, supportive, and affectionate mentor who always tried to inspire his students to explore new ideas and branch out to do original thinking. He appreciated creativity, unconventional views, and even wit and humor in student proposals. Many of his writings and projects involved collaborations with his students.

The legacy of Kevin Lynch continues to inspire architects, landscape architects, planners, and urban designers even though he never offered a concrete paradigm for one to follow. His approach was one based on many important influences—from arts and aesthetics to pragmatism, naturalism, and social change—and represents a unique blend of values and norms that remains an important anchor point of urban design theory and practice.

Tridib Banerjee

See also Environmental Design; Urban Design; Urban Planning

Further Readings

Banerjee, Tridib and Michael Southworth. 1993. "Kevin Lynch: His Life and Work." Pp. 439–68 in *The American Planner: Biographies and Recollections*, edited by Donald Krueckberg. New Brunswick, NJ: Center for Urban Policy Research.

Evans, Gary W. 1980. "Environmental Cognition." *Psychological Bulletin* 88:259–87.

Jameson, Frederic. 1991. *Postmodernism, or the Cultural Logic of Late Capitalism*. Durham, NC: Duke University Press.

Lynch, Kevin. 1984. "Reconsidering *The Image of the City*." In *Cities of the Mind*, edited by Lloyd Rodwin and Robert Hollister. New York: Plenum.

Rawls, John. 1971. *A Theory of Justice*. Cambridge, MA: Belknap Press of Harvard University Press.

Sen, Amartya. 1999. *Development as Freedom*. New York: Knopf.

Southworth, Michael. 1989. "Theory and Practice of Contemporary Urban Design: A Review of Urban Design Plans in the United States." *Town Planning Review* 60:4.

Tolman, Edward. 1948. "Cognitive Maps in Rats and Men." *The Psychological Review* 55(4):189–208.

M

MANCHESTER, UNITED KINGDOM

Manchester is a city of almost half a million people (441,200 in 2001) located in the northwest of England; 1 of the 10 boroughs of Greater Manchester, which constitute the third-largest conurbation in the United Kingdom (2,547,700). As a regional center, however, Manchester has long claimed to punch above its weight in terms of economic reach and cultural influence. In the last 30 years, this has taken the form of a highly visible regeneration of the city center. The re-imag(in)ing of Manchester as a postindustrial success story takes diverse strands of Manchester life and weaves them into a coherent strategy. In recent times, the name of Manchester has achieved its fame through, for example, the vibrancy of its music scene, the global reach of both its football teams (Manchester City and United), and its hosting of the 2002 Commonwealth Games. It has sought its fortune through a distinctive model of urban regeneration that pins its hopes on the commercial success of leisure and consumption and an urban politics bowed by the apparent exigencies of interurban competition.

Industrial Period

The history of Manchester is often told as a story of revolutionary change. Its emergence as the world's first industrial city was dizzyingly rapid and presaged an unprecedented scale and scope of social and economic change. In the mid-sixteenth century, Manchester was a relatively prosperous market town with a population of a few thousand. By 1773, the population was 43,000; by 1801, it was 80,000; and by 1851, well over 300,000. From a proto-industrial base including textiles and clock making, Manchester rose to become the central node in the dense network of southeast Lancashire cotton towns that served as cradle and crucible of the Industrial Revolution. The legacy of this industrial urbanization continues to dominate the city's built environment, labor market, social problems, civic pride, and political myths.

Between 1760 and 1850, Manchester was propelled from provincial center to the world city of an international cotton industry. The root causes of the city's success have been subject to much debate, with some emphasizing geographical advantages such as a damp climate suitable for spinning or proximity to coalfields. More intriguingly, the growth of urbanized labor, new forms of production, and the stimulation of enterprise generated what Peter Hall calls "the world's first innovative milieu." This set the scene for innovators such as Kay, Hargreaves, Arkwright, and Crompton to drive a decisive shift from domestic to factory production. By 1780, Manchester had become famous as a boomtown and an emerging symbol of all that was best and worst in the new age. By the 1840s, Manchester dominated contemporary reflections on the factory system and the state of England, showcasing the best and worst of capitalist urbanization. The details of this social geography are remarkable, from the extensive middle-class suburbs to the dense, dirty, and diseased working-class dwellings described by Friedrich Engels in 1844 or Elizabeth Gaskell's realist novel *Mary Barton* in 1848.

The stereotype of a self-made Cottonopolis has much truth to it but requires qualification. Manchester had its share of "dark satanic mills," but the city center's economy included commercial and service functions as well as factories, warehouses, and weavers. Likewise, for all of its bristling independence, Manchester's history is one of complex and changing interdependencies with cities like Bombay, Alexandria, and New Orleans, which provided the raw cotton to stock Manchester's warehouses and make yarn and cloth in mill towns like Oldham. Also notable is the industrial, if not political cooperation with Liverpool, which by the late eighteenth century had displaced London as England's major cotton port.

From the 1840s, the image of King Cotton dominated, and yet industrialization was underpinned by social revolutions in commercial and political culture as well as revolutions in technology, transport, and engineering. Manchester's strong tradition of political radicalism is a remarkable fusion of nineteenth-century liberalism and industrial socialism stretching from Chartism to the Anti-Corn Law League and the Cooperative Movement. Gradually, the cotton industry was faced with growing foreign competition (e.g., from India after 1914), but Manchester prospered well beyond the collapse of Britain's colonial and industrial hegemony. Particularly significant in this was the diversification of the manufacturing base: the opening of the Manchester Ship Canal in 1894, the parallel growth of the port, and the influx of (largely American) foreign capital to the world's first industrial park in the neighboring borough of Trafford.

After 1945, Manchester developed a series of grand city and urban plans and embarked on an intense period of slum clearance and public housing provision. This period of hope and stability gave way to the inner-city problem and urban policy responses of the late 1960s, with Manchester largely out of step with national modernization strategies. As late as 1971, Greater Manchester boasted a balance of 532,000 manufacturing and 577,000 service-sector jobs, but a series of increasingly severe waves of deindustrialization and decentralization saw a violent restructuring of the manufacturing base. The relative decline of Britain's

urban core was reflected in Greater Manchester, where 135,285 jobs were lost from 1971 to 1997 (12 percent of the workforce), two-thirds of them in Manchester itself. Manufacturing employment declined from a position of parity with services in 1971 to 283,000 by 1989. Although the service sector grew, it never compensated for the decline of full-time male industrial employment. By the end of the century, nearly 80 percent of jobs were in services, some in high-value sectors like finance, but many more casual and low wage. This devaluing was mirrored by counterurbanization and a concomitant decline in the quality of built environment and urban services.

Contemporary Renewal

Politically, the last three decades are best understood as a series of attempts to come to terms with this sequence of decline and renew Manchester's sense of purpose and progress, along with its urban fabric and population. The crisis of Manchester's political settlement was hastened in 1979 by the rise of a national Conservative government increasingly hostile to all forms of municipal socialism. The decisive period coincides with Graham Stringer's leadership of the city council (1984–1996) and struggle to rethink ideological defeat in terms of the pragmatism of the new urban left.

The emergence of Manchester as an entrepreneurial city is superficially encapsulated in the change of council slogan in 1987 from "Defending jobs and improving services" to "Make it happen." While the substance of this shift was vague, Manchester readily became a leading example of a new entrepreneurial mode of urban development, characterized by a civic boosterism that sought above all else to attract capital and people as sources of urban renewal. In lieu of a novel democratic response to globalization, the Manchester "growth machine" was galvanized through the strategic leadership of the city elite and council executive, while the governance of the new growth agenda was broadened to a partnership of public and private sector groups.

In adopting these tendencies toward urban entrepreneurialism, Manchester was far from unique, let alone self-determining, but it demonstrated an ability to adapt national policy to local demands for change, winning successive rounds of discretionary urban funding. The Central Manchester Development Corporation (1988–1996), with its renovation of the derelict canal sides of Castlefield, has become a case study of postindustrial regeneration as notable as London's Docklands. Indeed the whole idea of a Manchester model of regeneration has some force, even if much of it can be traced to the form of central government funding and the examples of cities like Barcelona. The 1990s saw an orthodoxy of partnership-led regeneration, from the redevelopment of the deprived residential area of Hulme to the successful bid to stage the 2002 Commonwealth Games and the ambitious strategic vision of City Pride, which aimed to remake the city as an outstanding European regional capital.

In the wake of the Irish Republican Army terrorist bombing of the city center in June 1996, the city elite mobilized around an unprecedented opportunity to redesign and redevelop the heart of the city center. The aftermath energized yet another version of partnership working in the guise of the Manchester Millennium, and yet the nature of the crisis generated diverse debate about how Manchester should be rebuilt and for whom. Although the basic tenets of urban entrepreneurialism remained, the crisis coincided with a period of change locally and nationally as the new Labor government of 1997 prioritized social concerns more explicitly. The decade since has seen a substantial revitalization of the retail core, along with significant projects in East Manchester and beyond.

But as Manchester has evolved from globalizer to globalized, the city has borne a paradoxical combination of economic decline and political revival, social ruin and cultural renaissance. Typical of many similar cities, Manchester has nevertheless attempted to make the process its own. One final example glosses this story. The 1819 Peterloo massacre was one of the defining moments of the early industrial period: Troops wielding sabers charged a crowd of 60,000, who had gathered to listen to Henry Hunt speak on behalf of parliamentary reform, causing 15 deaths and hundreds of injuries. The Free Trade Hall was built on the site, first in timber, then in brick, then finally in 1843 in stone, as a monument both to a particular idea of political economy and to the city's spirit of pragmatic individualism. Today, the building's shell houses a luxury and award-winning hotel adjacent to all the glittering prizes of city center renewal.

Adam Holden

See also Deindustrialization; Downtown Revitalization; Growth Machine; Local Government; Marxism and the City; Public–Private Partnerships; Regime Theory; Urban Politics

Further Readings

Briggs, A. 1963. "Manchester: Symbol of a New Age." In *Victorian Cities*. London: Pelican Books.

Engels, F. 1987. *The Condition of the Working Class in England*. London: Penguin.

Hall, P. 1998. "The First Industrial City: Manchester 1760–1830." Pp. 310–47 in *Cities in Civilization*. London: Weidenfeld & Nicholson.

Haslam, D. 1999. *Manchester, England: The Story of a Pop Cult City*. London: Fourth Estate.

Kidd, A. 1993. *Manchester*. Keele, Staffordshire, UK: Keele University Press, Ryburn Press.

Messenger, G. 1985. *Manchester in the Victorian Age: The Half-known City*. Manchester, UK: Manchester University Press.

Peck, J. and K. Ward, eds. 2002. *City of Revolution: Restructuring Manchester*. Manchester, UK: Manchester University Press.

Quilley, S. 1998. "Manchester First, from Municipal Socialism to the Entrepreneurial City." *International Journal of Urban and Regional Research* 24:601–21.

Williams, G. 2003. *The Enterprising City Centre: Manchester's Development Strategy*. London: Spon.

MANILA, PHILIPPINES

Metro Manila is the national capital region of the Philippines. In 2007, the Economics and Statistics Office of the National Statistical Coordination Board reported that it generates 33 percent of the country's gross domestic product (GDP). It has more than 11.5 million residents, which is 13 percent of the country's total population. This entry traces Metro Manila's colonial and historical past and its integration into the world trading system during the Spanish and American periods. It elaborates on a number of socioeconomic gains and environmental conditions that are associated with its present-day urbanization and spatial development.

Historical Background

Maynila was referred to as the Muslim Kingdom of Luzon on the eastern shores of Manila Bay before the fourteenth century. Accounts of dynamic trading activities in Maynila had caught the interest of Spanish conquistadores in the middle of the sixteenth century. They attempted to vanquish it on many occasions; on May 19, 1571, with the help of native warriors, they colonized Maynila. The colonizers had built on the banks of the Pasig River the fortified city of *Intramuros,* which literally means "inside the walls." Here the colonial city of Manila was established.

The chronicled monopoly of Spain on the production, manufacture, and trade of tobacco was based in Manila. From 1565 to 1815, the colonizers incorporated Manila into the commercially secluded galleon trade between Manila, Acapulco, and cities on the Iberian Peninsula. The galleon trade ended in 1815; its conclusion opened up Manila's ports to foreign shipping vessels and incorporated it into the emerging global economy.

According to Maria Serena Diokno and Ramon Villegas, the American and British merchants and shippers were behind the expansion of foreign trade opportunities in the Philippines at the turn of the nineteenth century. They propelled the development of the sugar, hemp, coffee, and silk industries. Manila became more economically competitive in 1889 with its street electrification and transport system improvement programs. The construction of the Manila–Dagupan rail line facilitated the transport of raw materials from peripheral areas in provinces north of the city. The installation of communication and telegraphic lines in Manila functionally linked it to Shanghai, Hong Kong, and Singapore.

The United States invaded Manila in 1898. Under the terms of the Treaty of Paris, Spain sold the Philippines to the Americans for $20 million. It was a flawed transaction because at the time of the sale, the Spaniards had already been defeated by the revolutionary Filipinos. From 1899 to 1903, the Americans thwarted the revolutionary movements of the Filipinos. The Americans made Manila its seat of colonial government and established the American-controlled Philippine Assembly in July of 1901.

Architect Daniel H. Burnham and Pierce Anderson drew the physical development plan for Manila in 1905. Burnham took into account the City Beautiful planning concepts, American imperialist interests, tropical climatic conditions, and some Philippine traditions. Burnham's plans provided a walkable city with a gridiron pattern, roads and streets that followed land contours, waterfronts and waterways, and government buildings that were facing each other in large open spaces. Architect William E. Parsons carefully executed Burnham's plans. Parson built spacious buildings, such as the Philippine General Hospital, with broad and deep archways and shaded porches that connected the cool and naturally lit building interiors; the designs derived inspirations from Spanish and Philippine traditions.

The American buildings housed the imperialist government, which further integrated Manila into the emerging global economy. Although Manila was devastated by World War II, the general outlines of Burnham's physical plan of Manila and Parsons's American–Spanish and Philippine-inspired building architecture became the standard for the development of the postwar Philippines.

From the 1950s to 1970s, Filipinos from different parts of the country migrated en masse to Manila. The suburbs of Manila had problems with the provision, maintenance, and deterioration of utilities and infrastructures. In 1976, President Ferdinand Marcos created Metro Manila. The Metropolitan Manila Commission (MMC) was created to manage the metropolis's physical infrastructure development. In 1986, President Corazon Aquino changed MMC to Metropolitan Manila Authority (MMA). In 1995, the MMA was renamed the Metropolitan Manila Development Authority (MMDA), which maintains and develops Metro Manila's garbage disposal and its traffic, flood, and sewage infrastructure systems, in coordination with officials of the Pasig River Rehabilitation Commission (PRRC) and the Department of Public Works and Highways (DPWH).

Contemporary Manila

Geographic Transformations and Ecological Ills

Metro Manila's land area is about 15 square miles or 38 square kilometers. It is bounded by the provinces of Bulacan, Rizal, and Cavite and the Laguna

Lake and Manila Bay. Its elevation ranges from less than 1 meter to 70 meters above the mean sea level. It has a tropical monsoon climate. Its dry season runs from November to May and its wet season from June to October. The average daily temperature ranges from 20° C to 38° C, and humidity is high year-round. The southwest monsoon and about six typhoons bring in a lot of moisture and cause floods in the city's low-lying parts during the rainy season.

Metro Manila's major rivers, such as Pasig, Marikina, Paranaque-Zapote, Malabon-Tullahan-Tenejeros, and San Juan, flow toward Manila Bay. The lack of environmental pollution control and abatement systems on waste generation and disposal among industries and households has led to the transformation of the river systems into massive sewage and industrial-effluent storage areas.

Population Growth and Competition

In 1903, the capital region contained 4 percent of the country's population (328,939 out of 7.6 million). As of 2007, Metro Manila's residents make up 13 percent of the 88.5 million Filipinos. Metro Manila covers only .21 percent of the country's total land area of 300,000 square kilometers. In 2007, the capital region's average population density of 18,166 people per square kilometer is way above the country's 295 people per square kilometer.

Job-seeking Filipinos who migrate each year from other regions have contributed to the fast urbanization of Metro Manila. Filipinos consider Metro Manila the center of job opportunities. The saturation of the labor market with qualified workers gives employers leeway to hire the most qualified and offer lower wages and fewer employment benefits. Decent living spaces are unaffordable to low-wage, underemployed, and unemployed migrants. Millions reside in living spaces without sewerage facilities, such as shanties built on pavements of side streets, open areas beside railways, and covered spaces under concrete bridges. Shacks are built in between tombs of public cemeteries and on top of putrid garbage dumps. Population density in squatter colonies, with multistory shacks or "shanty-condominiums," may number eight people per square meter. A recent trend, however, is the increasing number of houses on stilts in the

mouths of river systems and along the shallow waters of Manila Bay and Laguna Lake. The constricted roads in the settlements' drier portions are impassable to fire trucks. They lack sanitation infrastructure, institutional sources of potable water, and systematic collection of solid wastes.

Concentration of Wealth and Sociopolitical Privileges

Another trend in Metro Manila is the increasing exclusivity of affluent enclaves. The postwar central business district (CBD) of Makati occupies only 15 percent of the total land area of Makati City, but this includes some three million square meters of prime office spaces, which house half of the nation's international and domestic commercial activities. The income from licensing business activities and payment of real property taxes in the Makati CBD greatly contributes to the fiscal revenue of Makati City. The Makati CBD is where the national headquarters or offices of almost 40 percent of the top 1,000 corporations in the Philippines are based. To maintain their comparative advantage over other cities and financial centers in Metro Manila, the city revenues are spent by local government officials to further improve its world-class physical infrastructures and utilities.

Adjacent to the Makati CBD are the wealthiest neighborhoods in the country, where access by outsiders is greatly restricted by the uniformed and highly trained providers of security services. Among them are Forbes Park, Dasmariñas Village, Magallanes, and other gated neighborhoods. The wealthy families who reside in these enclaves comprise part of 20 percent of the country's population, and they control 97 percent of the country's GDP. Similar economic and sociopolitical conditions are found in other major financial districts of the country that are adjacent to high-class residential subdivisions.

Muslim Enclaves

The district of Quiapo, Manila, has always been the home of the Muslims, even before the advent of Spanish colonization. The spatial markers of the district include the Quiapo Islamic Center, DVD stores with signs using Arabic scripts, and women who don traditional Muslim headdresses and clothes. Every day, more than 30,000 Muslim Filipinos congregate in its trading places. The Muslim Filipino enclave in the district is expanding steadily. This can be attributed to the intensifying war and conflict in Mindanao and the national government's neglect, in terms of development, of the Autonomous Region of Muslim Mindanao. About 120,000 Muslim Filipinos were forced to migrate in Metro Manila. Muslim Filipinos have judged that the capital region is a safer place to live. The health facilities and educational opportunities in Metro Manila are a hundred times better and more accessible. Moreover, their children are not exposed to injuries and deaths due to perennial exchanges of gunfire.

Spatial Markers of Urbanization

The assigning of Manila as the seat of the colonial government and nucleus of trading activities of Spain, and consequently that of the United States, put in place the infrastructure and spatial characteristics that attract the influx of people in its urban spaces. The centrality of Manila led to siphoning of financial resources toward the city. The privileging of Manila also means marginalization of other places, such as the Autonomous Region of Muslim Mindanao.

Financial institutions congregate in central places where good physical and economic infrastructures abound. This is evident in the Makati CBD. Profits from extracting resources and other commercial activities from all parts of the nation are siphoned to this enclave. This condition leads to the increasing attractiveness of the city as a migration destination for the poor. However, poor migrants to Metro Manila are unable to get decent homes. They end up competing for small living spaces with appalling living conditions. Political privileging of spaces operates at different scales, and they imprint diverse economic benefits and spatial markers.

Some suggest that the concentration of infrastructure, energy, utilities, economic opportunities, information, and people in the metropolis will lead to the formation of Mega Manila—an area that will incorporate the adjacent towns and cities in the central Luzon region in the northern part of the metropolis and the Calabarzon and Mimaropa regions in the southern portion of Metro Manila.

Such a Mega Manila would contain nearly half of the country's population.

Further urbanization of Metro Manila does not mean development for the Philippines. The social and spatial transformations that urbanization brings result in impacts on diverse human groups, and the gains and ills of urbanization are experienced differently by those who occupy diverse places with differing spatial markers. If Metro Manila becomes more urbanized, leading to the formation of Mega Manila, the implications for the future are both promising and grim.

Doracie B. Zoleta-Nantes

See also Capital City; City Beautiful Movement; *Favela*

Further Readings

Agoncillo, Teodoro A. 1990. *History of the Filipino People.* Quezon City, the Philippines: Garotech.

Binay, Jejomar C. 2006. *Makati: A City for the People.* Makati, the Philippines: FCA Printhouse.

Diokno, Maria Serena and Ramon Villegas. 1998. "The End of the Galleon Trade." In *Kasaysayan: The Story of the Filipino People,* Vol. 4. Hong Kong: Asia Publishing Company.

Hines, Thomas S. 1972. "The Imperial Façade: Daniel H. Burnham and American Architectural Planning in the Philippines."*Pacific Historical Review* 41(1):33–53.

Hutchison, Ray. 2002. "Manila." Pp. 131–38 in *Encyclopedia of Urban Cultures: Cities and Cultures around the World,* edited by Melvin Ember and Carol R. Ember. Danbury, CT: Grolier.

National Statistical Coordination Board, National Statistics Office. 2008. *Population Figures and Gross Regional Domestic Product at Current Prices of the Philippines.* Philippines: National Statistical Coordination Board, National Statistics Office.

Salita, Domingo C. 1974. *Geography and Natural Resources of the Philippines.* Quezon City: University of the Philippines Press.

Marxism and the City

To clarify the contribution of Marxism to urban studies and to identify the contours of this theoretical approach, it is necessary to begin with the original work of Marx and Engels, before dealing with the more complex issue of how subsequent developments in urban theory and Marxism have overlapped and intertwined. For Marxists, modern cities are capitalist cities, not merely "cities in a capitalist society," and they are shaped in key respects by the dynamics of capitalist accumulation.

The most important characteristic of the capitalist production process, Marx argued, is the exclusion of the majority of workers from ownership of the means of production, with the result that workers are compelled to sell their labor power in order to survive. Unlike other commodities, labor power has a number of specific attributes, including its capacity to create new products. Under capitalism, when a worker sells his or her labor power, he or she does not receive the full value of the goods produced, and the resulting surplus is appropriated by the owner of the means of production. This mechanism of economic exploitation lies at the heart of capitalism and is linked to the Marxist analysis of social class and economic crisis.

In contemporary society, the labor process is highly fragmented, involving cognitive and material transformations that are carried out by a large number of workers with different skills and roles, and the complex division of labor that results is associated with changing social and spatial forms. Within this context, Marx confronts the specificity of the capitalist city, arguing that the distinction between city and countryside is a constitutive element of the capitalist division of labor.

The competitive nature of the accumulation process gives rise to a dynamic of continuous investment in the means of production and the transformation of production processes. The specificity of urban areas rests with the ways in which they bring together labor, capital, and land to form a dynamic and spatially uneven configuration of productive resources. The approach developed by Marx and Engels explains the historical development of urban areas by referring to the transformations generated by capitalist relations of production in agriculture and manufacturing. Agriculture is theorized in terms of primitive accumulation—the expropriation and enclosure of common lands—which led to the exclusion of agricultural laborers from the means of agricultural production, while manufacturing entailed a rapid expansion in the demand for labor in the industrial centers.

The concentration of large numbers of laborers in industrial cities gave rise, according to Marx and Engels, to a series of contradictions in the countryside (summarized by the notion of declining soil fertility) and the city (the impoverishment of the working class, segregation, and environmental degradation). In *The Condition of the Working Class in England,* Engels emphasizes the spatial form that this assumes, observing that, in each large city, it is possible to find one or more slums where the working class is concentrated. Nevertheless, rapid increases in productivity associated with mechanization and competitive development generated not only poverty, but also fantastic concentrations of wealth, which fed the expansionary logic of capitalism.

In Marxist theory, therefore, the capitalist relations of production are the chief driving force behind spatial and social organization in urban areas. Its commitment to "grand theory"—producing an integrated account of capitalist society as a structured whole—has been strongly criticized, particularly by postmodernist writers, while others have accused Marxist theory of subordinating gender differences, cultural influences, and issues of ethnic or gender identity to social class divisions. Marxists have responded by referring to the need for a comprehensive theory as a guide to political practice, simultaneously arguing that historical materialism can provide a nonreductionist account of cultural forms and social outcomes.

Cities also present unique characteristics that are not reducible to their position within the international division of labor. Marxists attribute these to the role and form of the state, to historically sedimented patterns of settlement, and to cultural and aesthetic ideals regarding the organization of urban space, while arguing for a class-based and materialist understanding of these phenomena.

During the late 1920s and throughout the 1930s, Walter Benjamin, a German Marxist, provided an important contribution to the development of Marxist ideas about the capitalist city. In the course of his arcades project, Benjamin gathered an enormous quantity of material on city life in nineteenth-century Paris, focusing on the city's roofed outdoor arcades and exploring the rationalization and commodification of urban space alongside the sensory experiences provided by Parisian street life. Later Marxists, such as Henri Lefebvre and David Harvey, took up Benjamin's invitation to develop a culturally rich and dynamic reading of the economic, political, and aesthetic aspects of the expansion of new forms of consumption within the space of the city.

Postwar Marxism and the Capitalist City

The wave of students' and workers' struggles that erupted in the advanced capitalist countries during the late 1960s and early 1970s had a far-reaching impact on urban studies. A new generation of geographers, urbanists, and sociologists, radicalized by their contact with these movements, looked to Marxism for the theoretical tools to explain the transformations that were taking place. This engagement led to a number of accounts of spatiality and scale, taking Marx's analysis of the accumulation and circulation of capital as a point of departure. The resulting theories, while remaining relatively abstract, played a key role in shifting debates within urban studies away from the evolutionist and functionalist theories that previously dominated this field.

Marxists study cities in terms of concentrations and flows of people, commodities, capital, means of production, and information. Two aspects—the relative stability that inheres within particular urban configurations, as well as the contradictions, tensions, and dynamics that they manifest—are deemed essential to providing a satisfactory theoretical account. In the following paragraphs, we will provide a brief overview of three distinct elements of Marxist theory in relation to the city, namely the concentration of capital, the role of the secondary circuit, and the role of the capitalist state.

The Marxist theory of accumulation, as outlined above, implies that regional structure emerges spontaneously from the accumulation process, along with increasing quantities of capital that cannot be invested profitably within the regional system. The Marxist theory of uneven development is based on this insight: that the competitive, profit-seeking behavior of individual capitalists gives rise to a systemic tendency toward overaccumulation and crisis. Contemporary Marxists argue that these crisis tendencies can be temporarily offset by a range of strategies—diverting surplus capital toward the financial and property markets, investing in the

social and physical infrastructure, exporting capital to new locations—although the result is to further intensify the initial contradictions.

Second, Marxist urban scholars have drawn attention to the importance of the secondary circuit of capital accumulation, which relates to the commodification of land and the extraction of monopoly rents. The diversion of capital from the productive sector to this sphere, it is argued, has the potential to generate substantial short-term profits, while setting in motion a complex set of processes that include the accentuation of scarcity in housing markets, the generation of speculative property "bubbles," and the displacement of profitability problems to the financial sector. These phenomena have been studied in relation to the emergence of the neoliberal city, gentrification processes, and the expulsion of poor residents from central areas.

These considerations regarding the relationship between capital accumulation and physical space, which have made a decisive contribution to urban studies, have also brought about a considerable renewal within Marxist thought. David Harvey has been at the center of this debate, developing the concept of the *spatiotemporal fix*, which describes the (temporary) displacement of crisis tendencies within a given region, at a specific time, either into the future or toward other regions, as capital engages in the "creative destruction" of urban landscape and space.

Third, Marxists argue that accumulation strategies increasingly depend on the role of the state as a vehicle for fixing productive resources and infrastructure in specific locations. The state plays an important role in coordinating urban labor markets, organizing private and collective consumption, elaborating strategies for infrastructural investment, and defusing resistance to exploitation. The development of the transport infrastructure is particularly central, as the construction of canals, railways, motorways, airports, and, increasingly, information, communication, and technology networks, is a key factor in explaining the historical development of urban space. Because of the scale of investment required to construct these infrastructures and the length of time required to recover the initial investments, the state typically plays a key financial role. Although Marxist scholars have, on occasion, lapsed into functionalist accounts of the state, attempts have been made to overcome this limit by focusing on the role of competition between rival blocks of capital located in different regions to establish an indirect link between state decision making and capital accumulation.

Although contemporary urbanization in eastern Asia appears to conform to the classical relationship between industrial growth and rural–urban migration described by Marx and Engels, in many other third world cities, the dynamics of urbanization have become increasingly detached from processes of economic development. The American Marxist, Mike Davis, attributes this to the effects of the debt crisis of the late 1970s and the structural adjustment programs that were implemented during the 1980s. The effect of these programs, together with the deregulation of international trade, was to render peasant families particularly vulnerable to the effects of drought, inflation, sickness, and civil war, giving rise to an exodus of surplus labor from rural areas. As a result, the number of people living in slums exceeded 1 billion in 2005, leading Davis to conclude that the principal role of these areas is to provide a dumping ground for an excess population that has little chance of being drawn into the primary circuit of global capital.

Arguably, the main contribution of Marxist theory to the study of cities is its capacity to explore changes in work, the built environment, and everyday urban life through the categories of political economy. This entails uncovering the ordering principles underlying patterns of accumulation and investment, as well as the ways in which capitalist social relationships are embedded in the fabric of urban society. But Marxists also emphasize the role of resistance to exploitation and oppression, viewing this as an active force in shaping cities.

In recent years, attempts have been made to extend Marx's concept of primitive accumulation to a range of ongoing processes involving the appropriation of assets that are bound by collective property rights or produced outside the capitalist economic system. Relevant examples include the privatization of public resources, the commodification of new forms of labor power, the suppression of alternative forms of production and consumption, the appropriation of assets using military force, and the extraction of rents via the "debt trap" or using patents and intellectual property rights. Many urban social movements, in the advanced capitalist countries as well as in the developing world, arise in response to this form of accumulation by dispossession. Marxists seek to explore the determinants of this process and to link these individual struggles in a generalized critique of capitalism that is rooted in the working class.

Jonathan Pratschke

See also Benjamin, Walter; Capitalist City; Castells, Manuel; Davis, Mike; Divided Cities; Harvey, David; Lefebvre, Henri; Right to the City; Uneven Development

Further Readings

Benjamin, W. 1999. *The Arcades Project.* Edited and translated by H. Eiland and K. McLaughlin. Cambridge, MA: Harvard University Press.

Castells, M. 1977. *The Urban Question: A Marxist Approach.* London: Edward Arnold.

Davis, M. 2006. *Planet of Slums.* London: Verso.

Engels, F. [1845] 1993. *The Condition of the Working Class in England.* Oxford, UK: Oxford University Press.

Gotham, Kevin Fox. 2006. "The Secondary Circuit of Capital Reconsidered: Globalization and the U.S. Real Estate Sector." *American Journal of Sociology* 112(1):231–75.

Harvey, D. 2001. *Spaces of Capital: Toward a Critical Geography.* New York: Routledge.

———. 2005. *Toward a Theory of Uneven Geographical Development.* New York: Routledge.

Katznelson, I. 1992. *Marxism and the City.* Oxford, UK: Oxford University Press.

Lefebvre, H. [1974] 1991. *The Production of Space.* Oxford, UK: Blackwell.

Lojkine, J. 1977. *Le Marxisme, l'État et la Question Urbaine.* Paris: Presses Universitaires de France.

Merrifield, A. 2002. *Metromarxism: A Marxist Tale of the City.* New York: Routledge.

Tabb, W. and L. Sawers. 1978. *Marxism and the Metropolis: New Perspectives in Urban Political Economy.* New York: Oxford University Press.

MEDIEVAL TOWN DESIGN

Most of the towns and cities of Europe owe their origins and early development to the period between the ninth and fourteenth centuries AD. This time of population growth and commercialism saw the expansion of older existing urban centers, especially those of Roman antecedence, as well as the foundation of new towns established sometimes on greenfield sites, virgin land that had not been under the plow, and sometimes by being grafted onto existing preurban settlement nuclei. These twin processes of urbanization affected the whole of medieval Europe, but as is typical with this period, contemporaries wrote down relatively little about who was involved in shaping these new urban landscapes and how they went about their work. Instead, the main indication that these changes were taking place lies in the physical forms and layouts of these towns and cities, which in many cases have survived through to the present day to be analyzed by geographers and archaeologists. This question of how urban landscapes were formed in the Middle Ages has led modern scholars to look for evidence of town planning and urban design in the morphology of medieval urban landscapes. In those rare cases where contemporaries do refer to planning and design processes, historians have been able to piece together from documentary records something of those individuals and groups that were involved and how they went about their work. The results of these modern historical studies, together with the work of urban morphologists, enables us to see now a little more clearly how urban landscapes were designed and planned in the Middle Ages.

Medieval Urban Design in Modern Urban Discourse

As well as the relative paucity of information to tell us about how medieval urban landscapes were formed, a further issue that has complicated the subject somewhat is the way that medieval towns and cities are represented in modern urban discourse. Textbooks on urbanism, for example, still widely refer to the uncontrolled or unplanned growth of most towns and cities of the medieval period, drawing a false distinction between planned and organic growth-type towns. Both are preconceptions that are overly simplistic and unhelpful in trying to understand urbanism in the Middle Ages. In part, these misunderstandings may be traced back to the start of the twentieth century and a battle drawn between planners and architects working in Europe who used the medieval town to make cases for their own particular aesthetic or for formulating design ideas for new urban forms. Le Corbusier in particular had great distain for the medieval period and its urbanism, and in his polemical works such as *Urbanisme* (published in 1924), he sought to paint a picture of the medieval city as barbaric and haphazard in its development and spatial organization. Those at the time who countered Le Corbusier's modernism by arguing for a picturesque approach to architecture and planning (such as Camillo Sitte and Raymond Unwin) likewise drew attention to the medieval forms of towns and cities, but while they were seeking inspiration in them for their new urban designs, all the same, like the modernists they too depicted medieval urban development to be on the whole unplanned and organic.

In the mid-twentieth century, urban studies began to reveal a more complicated picture, and medieval town planning gained acceptance as a historical reality. Much of this research focused on new towns of the Middle Ages, especially those towns that appeared to have been planted on greenfield sites by entrepreneurial landlords. In Europe, these studies tended to concern particular groups of such new towns, notably the *bastides* of southwest France, which attracted the attention especially of scholars in France. These towns have also fascinated British historians, notably T. F. Tout in the 1920s and M. W. Beresford in the 1960s. The latter in particular wrote his book, *New Towns of the Middle Ages,* as a comparative study of "town plantation" in England, Wales, and Gascony. He made claims that founding new towns was characteristic especially of the period between the eleventh and thirteenth centuries and that the process was led by enthusiastic lords seeking to populate and commercialize their lands.

Beresford's *New Towns* remains the standard work on the subject in English, despite its 1967 publication date. Even so, he still characterized medieval towns and cities according to the bipartite model differentiating between irregular and organic-growth towns, on the one hand, and regular, planned towns on the other. Toward the end of the twentieth century, more detailed studies of medieval urban forms, notably by geographers such as M. R. G. Conzen and T. R. Slater, as well as historians such as D. Friedman and A. Randolph, have revealed the complexity of these urban design and planning processes and finally begun to shatter the myth that urban landscapes in the Middle Ages grew spontaneously and were rarely planned.

Aspects of Urban Design in the Middle Ages

The formation of new urban landscapes in the Middle Ages involved a wide variety of different agents, as well as a long and negotiated decision-making processes. One part of this involved what we would understand to be design: that is, working out beforehand what an urban landscape was to look like. But more broadly, designing was a phase in a lengthier planning process that required a series of related stages including finding suitable sites for urban development, consulting between local landholders, working out property parcel sizes and street patterns, and laying out on the ground the plan elements that were required. Only after all this had been completed could townspeople come to take up residence. The whole process was thus carefully orchestrated and controlled by the different parties involved—it was certainly no free-for-all and not at all a spontaneous activity.

The final stage in the process in the case of founding a new town would come with granting legal privileges. These privileges were usually set out in a charter marking the town's foundation and were typically awarded by the local lord who had initiated the process. Even where the newly formed urban landscape was an addition to an already existing town or village, a grant of privileges might be made to likewise encourage newcomers to take up residence as townspeople. This entire process of creating new urban landscapes thus proceeded through a series of discrete stages, each involving different individuals and groups, which may be summarized diagrammatically (see Figure 1).

Of this process, the design stage is unfortunately one of the least visible in documentary records, yet from morphological evidence, it clearly did take place. A case in point is the town of Grenade-sur-Garonne, a bastide in southwest France founded in the 1290s that has a precise geometrical layout (Figure 2). This surely must have been designed before construction, but by whom is not clear.

Some contemporary sources help to illuminate this design stage of the planning process. For example, a parchment plan of Talamone, Italy, is likely to have been drawn for the purposes of deciding the shape and contents of the new town at the time of its foundation, to set out its plan, and to allocate properties. This plan is a unique manuscript, although there are also cases of architectural drawings—of elevations for

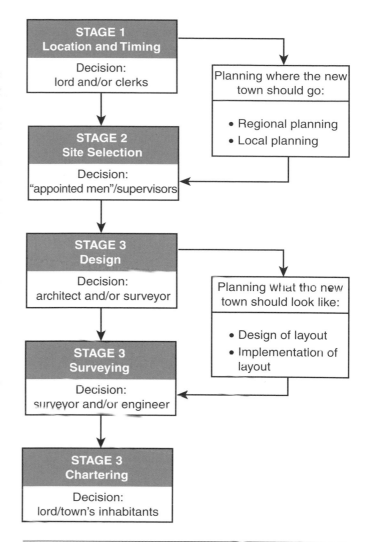

Figure 1   Flowchart Showing Stages in the Formation of a Medieval New Town

cathedrals and other important buildings, for example—that similarly show designs being worked out before work began. Again, however, it is rare to find accounts of who drew up these designs and guided this stage of the process, although through meticulous study of the records kept by the Florentine city government in the thirteenth and fourteenth centuries, David Friedman is able to show how committees were formed to help in the design of certain new towns being established in the territory around Florence. The individuals concerned with this often had experience of other building projects and design work.

The towns they designed were, in some cases such as Terranuova, highly geometrical in form, suggesting that some knowledge of geometry and its application in design work was important to the individuals employed on these projects and to their

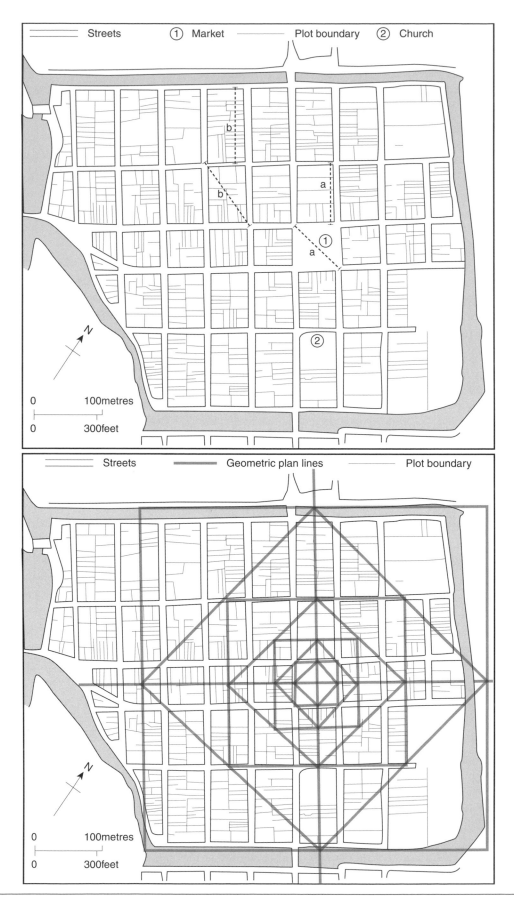

Figure 2 The Geometrical Design of Grenade-sur-Garonne (France)

idea of how to create a new town. Indeed, there are treatises called practical geometries surviving from the Middle Ages that seem to have been written with this purpose in mind and that often contained advice on how to use geometry to design towns and help in solving surveying problems.

Surveying and laying out a new urban landscape on the ground presumably followed on from the design stage. Again, however, this is somewhat difficult to discern from surviving written accounts, and the possibility has to be that, in the Middle Ages, an urban designer and surveyor were in some cases the same person, responsible for working on both. One thing is clear, however: Design was an important aspect of the formation of urban landscapes in Europe throughout the Middle Ages, and studying it as one part of a broader process of urbanization exposes the false distinction often drawn between planned and unplanned towns that has persistently dogged our modern understanding and appreciation of urbanism in medieval Europe.

Keith D. Lilley

See also City Planning; Florence, Italy; Historic Cities; Le Corbusier; Renaissance City; Urban Design; Urban Geography; Urban History; Urban Morphology; Urban Planning

Further Readings

Beresford, Maurice W. 1967. *New Towns of the Middle Ages: Town Plantation in England, Wales, and Gascony*. London: Lutterworth Press.

Friedman, David. 1988. *Florentine New Towns: Urban Design in the Later Middle Ages*. New York: MIT Press.

Kostof, Spiro. 1991. *The City Shaped: Urban Patterns and Meanings through History*. London: Thames and Hudson.

Lilley, Keith D. 2002. *Urban Life in the Middle Ages, 1000–1450*. London: Palgrave.

Lilley, Keith D., Christopher D. Lloyd, and Steven Trick. 2005. *Mapping Medieval Townscapes: A Digital Atlas of the New Towns of Edward I* [online]. Archaeology Data Service, University of York, UK. Retrieved January 12, 2009 (http://ads.ahds.ac.uk/catalogue/specColl/atlas_ahrb_2005).

Lilley, Keith D., Christopher D. Lloyd, and Steven Trick. 2007. "Designs and Designers of Medieval 'New Towns' in Wales." *Antiquity* 81:279–93.

Randolph, Adrian. 1995. "The Bastides of Southwest France." *The Art Bulletin* 77:290–307.

Slater, Terry R. 1987. "Ideal and Reality in English Episcopal Medieval Town Planning." *Transactions of the Institute of British Geographers, New Series* 12:191–220.

MEDITERRANEAN CITIES

South European and Middle Eastern cities, addressed as Mediterranean cities, are represented as a space between Orient and Occident, embedded in history of the *longue duree*, but "lagging behind" the European city and closely conditioned by the sea. These discourses do not always do justice to their cosmopolitan diversity or their uniqueness. The Mediterranean "sea in the midst of land" used to be a bridge, always punctuated by great cities: In antiquity, the city-state emerged here; in Roman times, the unifying sea, *Mare Nostrum* bridged urban civilizations; and during the Renaissance, Italian city-states rose to hegemony as a series of metropolitan leaders. Then, with the emergence of nation-states, the Mediterranean Sea turned from a bridge to a border, and the Industrial Revolution marginalized southern Europe and fragmented the Mediterranean region, so that scholarly definitions became necessary.

European Union (EU) cooperation programs usually define it through the nation-states with Mediterranean coasts, departing from Braudel's 1972 definition through the limit of the olive and palm trees. The latter delimitation included a lot of Portugal but excluded most of France from the Mediterranean. Besides ports and larger island towns, for purposes of this entry, Mediterranean cities will be cities by the sea and major inland cities of south Europe and north Africa in the limits set by Braudel.

The Mediterranean as a Bridge: Cities From Antiquity to the Renaissance

The Mediterranean was the cradle of Europe, according to a mythical narrative placing its epicenter on the island of Crete to the south of Hellas. Even before the period of written history, civilizations around the Mediterranean were distinctively urban. There were only a few rural monuments in the Minoan civilization, and that was also true of all Aegean civilizations, including the Cycladic and the Mycenian ones. Towns were animated by the sea as ports of trade and centers of weaving and other crafts, until the city-state emerged: the Greek *polis*, then the Latin *urbs* and *civitas*.

Miletus had earlier developed much of Greek civilization and scientific wisdom, but the most impressive early Mediterranean city was Athens in the fifth century BC, which has been a riddle for the density and excellence of intellectual, political, and cultural development in a mere century. In ancient Athens, a citizen, *politis,* was the resident of the city, *polis,* which developed a political culture of democracy, contrasting with earlier but also later periods of the same and other city-states. Renaissance Venice and Florence were enlightened tyrannies or paternalistic societies.

After the classical period, the Macedonian Empire constituted the first pan-Mediterranean empire; it transformed spatialities from city-states and their colonies to empires and their capital cities and introduced multicultural imaginations through interaction with the Orient after the wars, which also shifted the identities of conquerors. Alexander the Great expanded Hellas into Asia and created a Europe with an Oriental thrust, mapping from the Nile to the Indus, and the opposite spatiality of Rome, which soon would face to the West and return to the Mediterranean. Alexander introduced and in fact built capital cities, after living through a functional differentiation among three Macedonian ones: Pella was the main capital, political–administrative seat, and birthplace of the kings; Vergina was the economic–cultural capital; and Dion was the religious one. The seven Alexandrias (named after Alexander the Great), from the Nile through the Persian Gulf to the junction of the Acesines and Indus rivers, were also capital cities in their respective regions. However, the impressive Macedonian Empire was fragmented after Alexander's death at 32 in 322 BC.

As the Roman Empire rose to hegemony, the boundaries of Europe shifted from east to west toward the Mediterranean shores. The Roman Empire had its own capital cities besides the main one of Rome, most notably Constantinople, Cordoba, and Alexandria of Egypt. Although walled borders emerged, like Roman lime, the Hadrian wall in Britain, or that between the Rhine and Danube rivers, there were usually no boundaries. Nevertheless, allegiance to Caesar and later the king or rulers used to divide populations.

City walls were analogous to today's national boundaries before the partitioning of the world into nation-states. In the Roman Empire, they were ritually built, as indicated in examples from Arezzo in Tuscany to Purlebridge in Durham between first century BC and third century AD: A plough driven by a couple of black and white oxen dug the ditch at the perimeter where the city would be built. This

was consecrated by rituals of protection. The city often had a patron god—something still found today—and walls symbolized its status as state and bounded cultural identities, citizenship, migration, and social exclusion of "the other."

With the fall of the Roman Empire, cities declined and Europe went through a prolonged period of ruralization. The eastern Mediterranean hosted the birth of a new religion at the turn of the first millennium AD in Bethlehem, Jerusalem, Caesarea, Canah, and other towns of Palestine and Israel between Galilee and Sinai, on the west of the Dead Sea and River Jordan. Further to the north, on the Bosphorus, Constantinople was built during 325 to 330 AD, and by the fifth century, it had risen to be the cosmopolitan capital of Christianity named as *the* City, *Polis,* in discourse and geographical imaginations. It rose to hegemony in the eastern Mediterranean, while in the west, the Middle Ages were preparing the surprise: Since the eleventh century, as culture was reborn (Renaissance), the city-state reemerged in Italy.

Various historians have pointed to different reasons for this sudden and excellent development of a network of cities: Henri Pirenne has stressed commerce; Karl Marx has analyzed transformation from feudal relationships; Max Weber has introduced administration and governance; and Fernand Braudel has admired sea routes and material cultures.

A golden period of Italian city-states followed. During the ninth and tenth centuries, commerce with the East was rudimentary and centered especially in Amalfi, a tiny Italian walled port with colonies all over the Mediterranean. A series of war events and commerce with the East brought other cities to hegemony, alternating cosmopolitan metropolitan leaders: Venice, Florence, then Genoa in the west and Constantinople in the east. Land use and landscapes of these preindustrial cities were first systematized by Sjoberg in 1960 as structured with elite residences in the center and the proletariat outside the walls. This was contested by later urban historians, who pointed to the complexity of guild neighborhoods in the past, and by geographers who argued that there are no preindustrial cities at present. The piazza, the town square, unlike the ancient *agora,* was a place to stroll and watch rather than participate. It was encircled by small niches among colonnades (*stoa*) for congregation of different population groups, eavesdropping into the private lives of others, according to Pierro della Francesca.

The most prominent historian of the Mediterranean-as-a-bridge, communicating cultural interaction and technological interconnection, was Fernand Braudel. He was writing in the first decades after World War II, partly reacting to the conventional contrast between Christian and Muslim cultures, as were anthropologists simultaneously working in Africa and constructing a view about a unified Mediterranean. During a later period, however, they were all criticized by scholars who considered the Mediterranean as fragmented or as a sort of political counterreference (us versus them) of the "advanced" northern Europe.

In fact, the center of Europe would abandon the Mediterranean after the fifteenth century: The sea became a border and Europe was redefined vis-à-vis the others, the outsiders, after the defeat of the Moors and the Spanish *Reconquista* by 1492. This very year Columbus embarked for America, bringing Spanish and Portuguese ports driving the explorations to hegemony. A new reality emerged around the urban Mediterranean. The shift to the north, away from Africa, followed by half a century the fall of Constantinople and Ottoman occupation of the eastern Mediterranean in 1453. The region was divided into Orient and Occident for about four centuries after that, and this divide became as rigid as the north/south one in the fragmented Mediterranean.

Postcolonial and Modern Cities in the Divided Mediterranean

During the next centuries, all cities of southern Europe were marginalized and surpassed by northern ports in Belgium and Holland (Bruges, Antwerp, Amsterdam), and then London. The remarkable Industrial Revolution pushed the Mediterranean down from core to peripheral status in the global economy in a slow process of decline from the seventeenth to twentieth centuries. The celebrated Industrial Revolution—the factory, the railroad, the capitalist economy—did not take root in the south. Mediterranean civilizations crystallized instead around the urban-oriented cultures, which sought dignity in geographical imaginations of the city as a space for citizenship, synonymous with civilization (*polis/politismos*).

Urbanism has largely accounted for fast urbanization waves irrespective of late industrialization. A process of urbanization without industrialization, or rather, urbanization—triggered by poverty and insecurity in the countryside, informal work opportunities in the cities, the memory of the radiant city-states and the quest for the cultural identity of the urban citizen—made Mediterranean cities among the largest in the world. In 2006, population exceeded 10 million in Cairo (15.8) and Istanbul (11.6); 5 million in Madrid and Alexandria; close to 4 million in Algiers, Casablanca, and Milan; and 3 million in Barcelona, Athens, Rome, and Naples.

While divisions continued to be emphasized, scholars also saw Mediterranean unity by reference to either ease of communications or common physical features and ecologies. Geographers and urbanists who have analyzed the Mediterranean during the twentieth century consider the sea as a single entity (or a bridge) only within the orbit of environmental studies. EU cooperation programs did not have much success or duration and hardly touched the cities. They have tackled diplomacy and politics, or economy, considering peripherality and underdevelopment, but they mostly dealt with the environment, desertification, water pollution, and energy sources.

There are also tourism cooperation projects. Although tourism differs radically among Mediterranean regions and cities, especially after September 11, 2001, the tourist gaze is inspired by memories from the period when the Mediterranean was a bridge among cosmopolitan cities and captured by cultural hybridity. Arabian ruins are protected in both Africa and the Iberian Peninsula, contributing to Andalusian cultural identities; antiquity is recycled in Greek and Italian Christian churches, which are often built with stones and columns from ancient temples. Although secular and speculative building has since surrounded Mediterranean sacred spaces and ruins, it has never eradicated their presence or attractiveness to residents as well as global tourists.

Speculation includes illegal building and squatting, which constitutes a massive urban social movement. Precarious but popular owner occupation in illegal self-built shacks ensures that poverty does not automatically lead to homelessness; shacks may improve as the family income grows into more solid popular housing, sprawling onto cheap suburban land. In this and other ways, modernity has been diluted in informal modes of living and working.

Popular suburbs also surround postcolonial Mediterranean cities in North Africa, which animate Orientalism and the division between secular or European and Islamic cultures. Middle Eastern cities, from Morocco to Iran and from Turkey to Sudan, have incorporated social control or divine law rather than economic rationale in the city-building process. Medina, the Arabic name for the old city, is extended into the Rabad, that is, its later suburbs, while the Kasbah, attached to the Medina, has long served as a refuge in case of defeat. The Medina is built according to various schools of law, among which the Maliki is the most influential in Morocco and Algeria and the Hanafi is predominant in Tunisia and Libya. The urban building language consists of relatively few elements: a mosque foremost, then a main street and a governor's residence. The bazaar or the herb and spice market constitutes the public sphere of meeting and exchange. Space is sharply gendered (men/women, exterior/interior, public/private), women are not allowed into coffee houses and halls of many mosques, and clothing regulations make them "invisible," as we know from recent tensions since the appearance of veiled women in European public places. Segregation principles in Islamic cities are different from European ones because each *mahalla* houses people of a common ethnic or socioeconomic background under the administration of a mukhtar. Segregation has often been sealed in gated communities guarded at night, not only in the colonial but also in the postcolonial period. Ghettoes and migrant quarters in European cities are only pale parallels of *mahallas*.

Postcolonial Middle Eastern cities constitute material evidence of the Mediterranean as a border that hardened with war caused by foreign intervention and civil war. As the cold war walls are being demolished, such as the one in Gorizia between Italy and Slovenia, walled borders are erected in the southeastern Mediterranean. The one erected by the Israelis on the West Bank is the longest and the most notorious—next to the "green line" in Nicosia, Cyprus, yet another divided Mediterranean city. Postcolonial cityscapes of the holy cities themselves, such as Jerusalem, Bethlehem, Canah, but also Ramalla and Beirut, witness the rigidity and violence of ethnic divisions. The post–cold war epoch poses cultures and cultural identities as the main dimensions of social exclusion, fragmentation, and conflict. In 1997, Huntington published a widely read theory of the clash of civilizations, which has been criticized but endures, gaining relevance from the events of September 11, 2001. In that work, the Mediterranean springs to the foreground as a border between Islamic and Asiatic cultures, on the one hand, and the Western secular culture on the other. However, this border is often deconstructed by European Union cooperation programs, is ignored by tourist cruises, and is trespassed by migrants—usually illegal, floating to small European ports as boat people. Against theories to the contrary, the elements bring multicultural orientations to cities and symbolic borders, animating interaction of cultures in the broader Mediterranean.

A Theory for the Mediterranean City?

If there is a theory for the modern Mediterranean city, which will not exclude postcolonial Islamic social control rather than economic rationale in the Arabian medina (city), it has to do with the interplay of sacred and secular in everyday life, with a patron saint for each city and religious rituals on Easter, Ramadan, saints' feast days, and other occasions; with the attraction of the city, rather than pastoral utopias, and the strong cultural heritage of urbanism; with massive urbanization waves, which are not caused by industrialization but by rural poverty and insecurity, combined with opportunities in the city and the culture of urbanism.

Flows into Mediterranean cities in general consist of refugees, migrants, and illegal migrants from the south and the east; global tourism attracted by landscapes that are theaters of memory and contain conspicuous monuments of world heritage; and of residential tourism by north–south migrants lining the Mediterranean shores beyond cities, especially since the Maastricht treaty, which allowed property purchases within the EU. Spreading from the south of France to Italy and Spain, this urban sprawl is changing the face of Costa Blanca from Barcelona to Alicante, via Benidorm, while in Hellas (Greece), it is now approaching post-Olympic Attica. Finally, Mediterranean city theory has to include spontaneity of socioeconomic restructuring, with the informal economy and housing creating a postmodern collage in the urban landscape and society, before the label was even used in art and academic discourse.

At the level of Mediterranean cityscapes, recurring patterns and structures in postcolonial and south European cities are as follows: (1) the inverse-Burgess spatial pattern, with the affluent classes in the center and the poor on the periphery, undergoing constant gentrification in the center, on the one hand, and spontaneous urban development and popular suburbanization on the other, with less planning than in other world regions; (2) a compact cityscape with tall buildings, narrow streets, small open squares, suburbs quite close to the center, and problems of consequent environmental pollution; (3) social class and ethnic group segregation, vertical as well as horizontal, and (4) mixed land use (horizontally and vertically) rather than zoning of residence and economic activity, as well as bazaars, street markets, and kiosks that house the informal economy within a postmodern collage. In combination, informal work and informal housing or semisquatting challenge public top-down policy, solving problems of unemployment and homelessness by putting all the burden on the family.

Spontaneous popular settlements are now much rarer in the Mediterranean and have been finally controlled in southern Europe except Lisbon (but this is rarely defined as a Mediterranean city). After EU accession (1981 for Hellas, 1986 for Iberian countries) and especially in the postsocialist era, forces of diversification between the north and the south of the Mediterranean speeded up. In the latter, postcolonial cities are often shaken by violence. Cities of Mediterranean Europe are divided between poverty and vulnerability, on the one hand, especially as migrants and refugees keep arriving, and urban entrepreneurialism on the other: a new period of urban competition, which brings about the commodification of the city (or city marketing) for global tourism and transnational capital. In the new modes of urban regulation, neoliberal strategies for visibility through the attraction of international megaevents become a priority, as exemplified in Spain in 1992 with the triple success in Barcelona, Madrid, and Seville. The cultural economy of cities has risen in a smooth transition for the Mediterranean, which has not experienced much of an Industrial Revolution. Southern Europe slides easily from spontaneous urbanization to urban entrepreneurialism, postmodernism, and urban competition, and even influencing the latter to "Mediterraneanize" their landscapes.

Throughout the last century of Mediterranean history, the city has been stamped by cultures of urbanism and by informality or by the concept of spontaneity, coined by Antonio Gramsci, an intellectual of the south, as important for Mediterranean city theory as Antonio Negri. The two intellectuals see the southern metropolis in different ways and illuminate its current transformation. Earlier class structures are by immigrants and interest groups comprising residents, commuters, business people, and also global tourists as neoliberal globalization further reduces the role of the welfare state and as weak or occasional planning in urban design and restoration create environmental problems and vulnerability in a vast diversity of Mediterranean cities among three "continents."

Lila Leontidou

See also Athens, Greece; Colonial City; Islamic City; Istanbul, Turkey; Medieval Town Design; Piazza; Rome, Italy; Urban Design

Further Readings

Afouxenidis, A. 2006. "Urban Social Movements in Southern European Cities: Reflections on Toni Negri's 'The Mass and the Metropolis.'" *City: Analysis of Urban Trends, Culture, Theory, Policy, Action* 10(3).

Apostolopoulos Y., P. Loukissas, and L. Leontidou, eds. 2001. *Mediterranean Tourism: Facets of Socioeconomic Development and Cultural Change.* London: Routledge.

Benevolo, L. 1993. *The European City.* Oxford, UK: Blackwell.

Blake, G. H. and R. I. Lawless, eds. 1980. *The Changing Middle Eastern City.* London: Croom Helm.

Bourdieu, P. 1979. *Algeria 1960.* Cambridge, UK: Cambridge University Press.

Cowan, A., ed. 2001. *Mediterranean Urban Culture 1400–1700.* Exeter, UK: University of Exeter Press.

Garcia, S. 1993. "Local Economic Policies and Social Citizenship in Spanish Cities." *Antipode* 25(2):191–205.

Grenon, M. and M. Batisse. 1989. *Futures for the Mediterranean Basin: The Blue Plan.* Oxford, UK: Oxford University Press.

Hakim, B. S. 1986. *Arabic-Islamic Cities: Building and Planning Principles.* London: KPI Ltd.

Herzfeld, M. 1987. *Anthropology through the Looking-glass: Critical Ethnography on the Margins of Europe.* Cambridge, UK: Cambridge University Press.

Horden, P. and N. Purcell. 2000. *The Corrupting Sea: A Study of Mediterranean History.* Oxford, UK: Blackwell.

Jones, Emrys. 1990. *Metropolis: The World's Great Cities.* Oxford, UK: Oxford University Press.

Kazepov, Y., ed. 2005. *Cities of Europe: Changing Contexts, Local Arrangements, and the Challenge to Urban Cohesion.* Oxford, UK: Blackwell.

King, R., P. De Mas, and J. M. Beck, eds. 2001. *Geography, Environment, and Development in the Mediterranean.* Brighton, UK: Sussex Academic Press.

Korsholm Nielsen, H. C. and J. Skovgaard-Petersen, eds. 2001. *Middle Eastern Cities 1900–1950: Public Places and Public Spheres in Transformation.* Aarhus, Denmark: Aarhus University Press.

Leontidou, L. 1990. *The Mediterranean City in Transition: Social Change and Urban Development.* Cambridge, UK: Cambridge University Press.

———. 1993. "Postmodernism and the City: Mediterranean Versions." *Urban Studies* 30(6):949–65.

———. 2004. "The Boundaries of Europe: Deconstructing Three Regional Narratives." *Identities—Global Studies in Culture and Power* 11(4):593–617.

Leontidou, L. and E. Marmaras. 2001. "From Tourists to Migrants: International Residential Tourism and the 'Littoralization' of Europe." Pp. 257–67 in *Mediterranean Tourism: Facets of Socio-economic Development and Cultural Change*, edited by Y. Apostolopoulos, P. Loukissas, and L. Leontidou. London: Routledge.

Martinotti, G. 1993. *Metropoli: La nuova morfologia sociale della citta.* Bologna: Il Mulino.

Said, E. 1978. *Orientalism.* London: Pantheon Books.

Toynbee, A., ed. 1967. *Cities of Destiny.* London: Thames and Hudson.

MEGACITY

See Megalopolis; Urbanization

MEGALOPOLIS

Many academics have coined terms for their phenomenon of study, but few have been successful. But Jean Gottmann's proposal for *megalopolis* to refer to a string of closely interconnected metropolises was logical and inspired and has become part of the language. The term is derived from Greek and means simply "very large city." A group of ancient Greeks planned to construct a large city of this name on the Peloponnese Peninsula; only a small city of Megalopolis still exists. The best contemporary treatment of Megalopolis is a 1998 report by Birdsall and Florin, *The Megalapolitan Region,* which was prepared for the U.S. State Department and is available online.

Gottmann (1915–1994) was a French geographer who for 20 years studied the northeastern United States and published his seminal work in 1961. *Megalopolis* was a massive (more than 800 pages) undertaking, characterized by detailed scholarship and amazing insight; it traces the evolution of the 500-mile-long "main street" of what was then US 1 to the interconnected promise of I-95. Part 1 argues the dynamic role of these core cities in the economic and cultural making and control of the nation, the "economic hinge" of innovation—including suburbs as early as 1850. The bases for the development of the megalopolis include its close position to then-dominant Europe, a diverse coast penetrated by many quality harbors with access to the interior, and a topography providing local water power for industry. New York, a situational geographer would point out, was destined for preeminence because of its superior access across the Appalachians to the interior of the country.

Part 2 concentrates on the structure of population and land use, especially in the suburban fringe, noting the long-standing but now faster-growing penetration of urban uses into the country—that is, sprawl—again long before other parts of the country noticed. Perhaps there was a greater expectation that close-in agriculture would survive than has proven possible. The beginnings of urban decay and of renewal are treated, with a plea for rehabilitation instead of renewal—finally successful in the 1980s and 1990s.

Part 3 details patterns of economic structure and change; the chapter on the white-collar revolution outlining the restructuring to higher-level activities is probably the most important and prophetic analysis in the book, already in 1960 predicting the basic remaking of American society, with the megalopolis leading the way. Part 4, "Neighbors in Megalopolis," recognizes the diversity and segregation of the population along ethnic, racial, religious, and class lines, as well as the high level of inequality that characterizes creative cities; and finally, it notes the difficulty of coordinating planning

Table 1   Population in Megalopolitan Urbanized Areas (millions)

Year	Population	Area	Density	Year	Population	Area	Density
1950	24.5	3283	7315	1980	34.4	8390	4100
1960	29.4	5348	5285	1990	36.6	10185	3590
1970	34.0	7006	4768	2000	42.4	13490	3155

Note: Area in square miles.

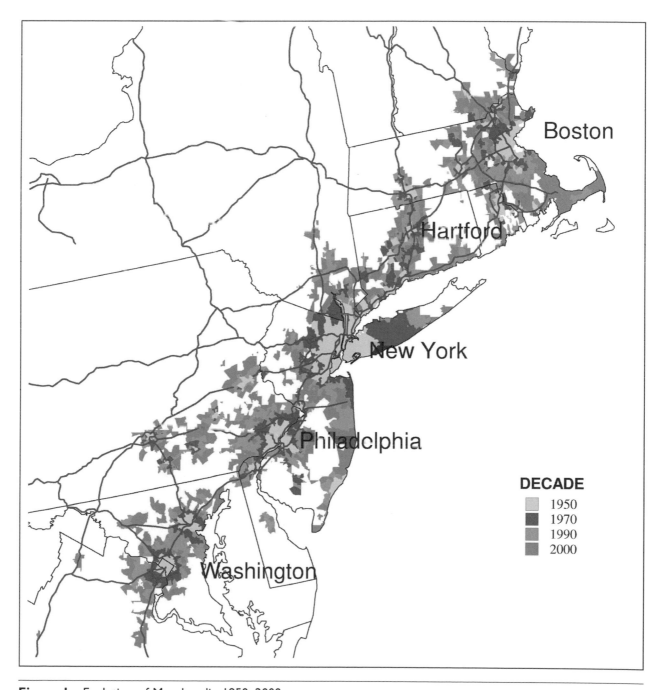

Figure 1   Evolution of Megalopolis, 1950–2000

Source: Map created by author, update of classic map by Browning (1974).

across utter jurisdictional complexity. In sum, the essence of the megalopolis is its intense "urbanness," its high level of investment in transport and communication, and its capacity for renewal to maintain world economic and cultural preeminence.

Gottmann later compared the U.S. megalopolis to other world megalopolitan systems and still later, in 1987, revisited *Megalopolis* in *Megalopolis Revisited 25 Years Later*. He was able to see the validation of his restructuring prediction and the incubator role of the megalopolis, and especially of New York. Yet, he notes as well the pace of deconcentration within the megalopolis.

For urban and population geographers, a wonderful and valuable map was produced by Clyde Browning, in the University of North Carolina *Studies in Geography,* called "Population and Urbanized Area Growth in Megalopolis, 1950–1970." This was both a quality representation of the megalopolis and an updating of its expansion through 1970. Browning's 1974 map was quite a large and detailed representation of the megalopolis, tracing its expansion to 1960 and to 1970. The monograph text was a thorough empirical and theoretical discussion of the magnitude and nature of change. Browning provides an overview of urbanized areas and of the megalopolis, and a statistical and graphic summary of the 1950-to-1970 change, noting that most cores had not coalesced and that the wider metropolitan region defined by Gottmann was still less than 20 percent urban territory. (See Figure 1 for an update of Browning's map.)

Megalopolis was further updated to 2000. The megalopolis now extends from Fredericksburg, south of Washington, D.C., to Portsmouth and Dover-Rochester, New Hampshire, and into southern Maine. The updated map depicts the further expansion of the nation's largest conurbation, whose constituent parts housed 24.5 million people in 1950 and 42.4 million in 2000, with an additional 8 million in exurban surroundings, in all housing one sixth of the U.S. population.

From Table 1, we can see that the population of the megalopolis has not quite doubled, but the total area has quadrupled, as mean densities have fallen from 7,315 to 3,155 people per square mile.

Consider the first (1950) and last (2000) stages. In 1950, the megalopolis was actually a string of pearls, with Washington, Baltimore, Wilmington, Philadelphia, Trenton, New York, Bridgeport–New Haven, Hartford, Springfield, Providence, Worcester and Boston, Lowell and Lawrence—all distinct places, separated by some rural territory. These were the core urban places arising in the colonial period, exhibiting an extraordinary linearity, based partly on physical character (the head of navigation at the fall line) and partly on the situation, sea or river ports and early industrial centers, convenient for trade with Europe.

By 1970, Wilmington-Philadelphia-Trenton were merged, as were Boston-Lowell-Lawrence, but perhaps surprising to many, no others, although there had been very significant suburbanization, especially around New York and Washington, D.C. New urbanized areas included Vineland, Danbury, Fitchburg, and Nashua.

By 2000, a continuous urban settlement structure for megalopolis was almost realized, with a smaller Washington-Baltimore-Aberdeen to the south, a giant Wilmington to Springfield and Norwich in the center, with links to formerly independent places like Atlantic City, Allentown, Lancaster, York, Harrisburg, and Poughkeepsie and a northern area from Providence and Barnstable through Boston to Manchester, Portsmouth, and Dover-Rochester. New outlying urbanized areas, not yet quite connected, include Fredericksburg, Dover, Wildwood, Frederick, and Kingston. The map graphically captures the massive urban diffusion from early cores, the gradual coalescence of these expanding cores, and the rise of and reaching out to satellite places.

Forces for Change in Megalopolis, 1950–2000

The second half of the twentieth century was an era of continuing metropolitan expansion in the United States. It is useful to summarize briefly the forces that produced these patterns of settlement change, even though this has been the subject of countless studies in several disciplines.

In the case of the megalopolis the underlying set of cores has been established for a century or more. The settlement processes that have dominated in the last 50 years included (1) sheer economic and demographic growth, (2) physical decentralization in the form of suburbanization, (3) extension of metropolitan commuting fields and the physical coalescence of formerly physically separate areas, (4) rise of or restructuring and reaching out to formerly distant satellites, and (5) restructuring and revitalization of high-level metropolitan cores.

1950–1970: The Rise of the Suburbs

Suburban growth was pervasive over most of what is now the megalopolis, fueled by the high fertility and natural increase of the baby boom, as the nation reacted to losses from World War II, and by very large domestic rural to urban migration. Almost all industrial sectors and types of cities grew, as part of postwar recovery—even the older industrial sectors and cities. Metropolitan growth reflected the dominance of both increasing returns to scale and to agglomeration and the proliferation of new products and services. But this growth was spatially expansive, via burgeoning new suburbs, mainly because of sheer population growth. The period was also one of large-scale in-migration of Blacks fleeing the more discriminatory South, which in turn precipitated large-scale White flight to the suburbs.

1970–1990

Megalopolis grew more slowly in population during this period, especially 1970 to 1985, than in the preceding or the following periods, despite continuing suburban growth, because of often declining absolute populations, and often, employment, in the dense, older central city cores. Indeed, the 1970s were rare years of more rapid nonmetropolitan than large metropolitan growth nationally, as the giant cities were beset by racial tension, large-scale White flight to the suburbs, and the decline of traditional industries, including manufacturing and transportation. But the megalopolis did continue to grow in area—from 7,000 to more than 10,000 square miles, up 45 percent, even as population growth was a mere 7 percent, as suburbanization continued and densities fell from 4,768 to 3,590 people per square mile.

Suburban downtowns, termed "edge cities," arose to challenge central city dominance. Yet, it proved premature to write off the old centers. Especially after 1980, the cities fought back, not by the unsuccessful urban renewal of the earlier period but by deliberate investment in attracting higher-class people and jobs.

1990–2000

Even before 1990, much of the megalopolis experienced a revitalization and resurgence of growth, with a hefty growth of 12 percent in the 1990s alone. Gottmann outlined the dimensions of this new urbanism in his 1985 book, *Megalopolis Revisited*. The larger downtowns and nearby historic areas were gentrified, as middle- and upper-class households reclaimed parts of the core. Economic restructuring, as presaged by Gottmann, led to massively increased service employment; business services and finance preferred central high-rise venues. Core populations rose, in part from the attraction of young, later, or not-marrying professionals and of empty-nesters. But growth was vibrant in the ever lengthening far suburban fringe as well, far exceeding in absolute population and jobs the revitalization of the cores, with continuing industrial, commercial, and residential expansion. Much of the growth could be termed low-density exurban sprawl, but where smart-growth urban planning came into vogue, some of the growth was concentrated in older, formerly independent satellite towns and cities, now incorporated into the megalopolitan web.

Megalopolis Around the World

The ingenuity of the term and the obvious functional reality and importance of interconnected sets of large cities inevitably led to the proclaiming of similar urban systems around the world. There is a degree of subjectivity in the definition and delineation of other megalopolises, depending on whether the conception is closer to a rather continuous conurbation of urban settlement or to a more loosely related set of metropolitan areas. Gottman's conception was of large urban centers functionally related by interaction of people and products, and the overlapping commuting fields of these urban cores, which he demonstrated for the Boston to Washington corridor. Equivalent data may or may not exist for other countries and may or may not have been applied consistently; and there is uncertainty about a lower threshold for reaching "mega" status. In the United States, the strongest contenders are the Milwaukee-Chicago-Detroit-Pittsburgh corridor (ChiPitts), greater Los Angeles–San Diego–Tijuana, and perhaps the San Francisco–San Jose–Sacramento urban region and Peninsular Florida. Others are more conjectural or incipient than real (e.g., Charlotte-Raleigh).

Outside the United States, the earliest recognized and the world's largest megalopolis is surely the Tokyo-Nagoya-Osaka corridor, with up to 80 million people. Other reasonable contenders are the urban regions centered on London, São Paulo–Rio de Janeiro, Beijing-Tianjin-Tangshan, the Pearl River Delta (Hong Kong–Guangzhou), and the Tangtze

River delta (greater Shanghai). Note that this excludes many of the world's largest cities, which are not part of a system of cities, for example, Mexico City, Mumbai, Kolkata, Jakarta, Bangkok, Delhi, Seoul, and Buenos Aires. Similarly functionally related city regions, but of smaller size, are, for example, Randstad (Netherlands-Belgium) and Rhine-Ruhr, Toronto, and Taipei. But if they see themselves as megalopolises, why not? Neil Pierce, in his 2008 opinion piece "The Megalopolis Century," clearly prefers a looser conception; he says that "more than 200 million people, two-thirds of the U.S. population already live in 10 megalapolitan regions."

Conclusion

It is reasonable to conclude, with Gottmann, that Megalopolis remains the main street of America, despite the much faster rate and amount of growth in the metropolitan South and West. California may well be the trend setter of the nation in many ways, but Megalopolis remains the control center of our information economy and the innovator of urban settlement change; it has proven remarkably adaptable in maintaining its preeminence. The area defined as megalopolis housed 42.4 million people in 2000. The exurban area surrounding megalopolis, with high levels of commuting to megalopolitan jobs, housed at least 8 million more people—a microcosm of incredible variance in settlement from utterly rural to the highest density—and land and site values. This amazing conurbation remains the most spectacular and powerful settlement complex and human imprint on the landscape.

Richard Morrill

See also Metropolitan; Metropolitan Governance; Sprawl; Suburbanization; Urban Geography; Urban Planning

Further Readings

Batty, M. 2001. "Polynculeated Urban Landscapes." *Urban Studies* 38:635–55.
Birdsall, S. and J. Florin. 1998. "The Megalopolis." Chapter 4 in *An Outline of American Geography: Regional Landscapes of the United States.* Washington, DC: U.S. Information Agency.
Browning, C. 1974. *Population and Urbanized Area Growth of Megalopolis, 1950–1970.* Studies in Geography No. 7. Chapel Hill: University of North Carolina.
Dunn, E. 1983. *The Development of the U.S. Urban System.* Baltimore: Johns Hopkins University Press.
Gottman, J. 1961. *Megalopolis, the Urbanized Northeastern Seaboard of the United States.* New York: Twentieth Century Fund.
———. 1976. "Megalopolitan Systems around the World." *Ekistics* (243):109–13.
———. 1987. *Megalopolis Revisited: 25 Years Later.* Baltimore: University of Maryland, Institute for Urban Studies.
Morrill, R. 2006. "Classic Map Revisited." *Professional Geographer* 58:155–60.
Pierce, N. 2005. "The Megalopolis Century." *Seattle Times*, July 25.
Regional Plan Association. 1967. *The Region's Growth.* New York: Author.

METROPOLIS

Eighty years after its premiere in Berlin on January 14, 1927, Austrian director Fritz Lang's *Metropolis* remains among the most powerful visions of urban modernity and the most famous German film in the history of cinema. It dramatically represented how the conflicts—economic, political, social, familial, psychosexual, architectural, and spiritual—of technological society dominate the prospects for life in the city. Already in its title, an English language word, it suggests a universal urban condition. Depicting the harshly routinized existence of city dwellers earlier analyzed by German sociologist Georg Simmel, *Metropolis* proposed the city as a productive but highly alienating machine.

Prior to Lang's film, which he claimed (falsely) was inspired by his vision of New York's bright lights during a visit in 1924 to promote his *The Nibelungen,* the city had rarely been represented in cinema as physically overwhelming. Dark alleys, criminal gangs, and moral corruption were the principal threats faced by most protagonists in silent movies. By contrast, *Metropolis* revealed the city as second nature, a human creation ultimately more inscrutable and dangerous than first nature, an idea telegraphically conveyed by advertising posters for the film in which masses of skyscrapers resemble mountain ranges. It suggested that the physical disparity between the increasingly vertical and machine-driven built environment and individual human beings resulted in feelings of anxiety and the sense that one had lost effective control over one's destiny.

Controlling Lang's futuristic city, located in the penthouse of a towering office building, is the cold and ruthlessly calculating industrialist Joh Fredersen (played by Alfred Abel). His son Freder Fredersen (Gustav Froelich) leads a life of indolent pleasure until he encounters the teacher, Maria (Brigite Helm), who one day ascends to his pleasure garden with a group of ragged children.

Metropolis depicts a vertically stratified society, and far below the surface of the Earth, its workers live and tend the Moloch-like turbines that keep it running. Maria preaches a gospel of love to them in an underground catacomb, which leads the threatened Fredersen Senior to approach the inventor Rotwang (Rudolf Klein-Rogge). He creates a robot replica of Maria, who incites the workers to destroy the machines and flood their underground city. Eventually, Fredersen and the machine foreman Groth reconcile themselves on the steps of a Gothic cathedral, according to the slogan "The mediator between head and hands must be the heart."

Evoking contemporaneous sources, such as the anti-urban philosophy of Oswald Spengler expounded in his book, *The Decline of the West*; Weimar architect Bruno Taut's notion of the tall building as "crown of the city"; and playwright Georg Kaiser's drama of an industrial accident *Gas*, *Metropolis* is rife with visual symbolism and intellectual references. Its skyscrapers freely cite modern architectural styles then advanced by Ludwig Mies van der Rohe and Erich Mendelssohn, while the stylized choreography with which its armies of black-clad workers move owed much to expressionist theater and seem to exemplify Siegfried Kracauer's notion of the crowd as "mass ornament." Novelist and screenplay author Thea von Harbou, then Lang's wife, wrote the treacly story that was the basis for Lang's visually haunting images, clearly indebted to the classic 1919 expressionist film *The Cabinet of Dr. Caligari*.

Metropolis spent over one and a half years in production, exceeded its budget by more than three times, and involved the use of 36,000 extras for its elaborate mob scenes. Intended to compete with large-scale Hollywood productions, the film is infused with German attitudes toward American urban civilization, most evidently in its valorization of skyscrapers, which epitomized what many contemporaneous observers regarded as the American fetishism of technology and mass production.

The splitting of the character of Maria and her re-creation as a robotic clone also finds a parallel in the debates about the arrival of the financially and sexually independent "new woman" in large cities such as Berlin. Despite a gala premiere in a Berlin movie house decorated with metallic silver paint and attended by elite cultural and political figures, Lang's film was a financial flop and received generally poor reviews at the time.

Critics complained that it contained too many ideas, was wildly contradictory, and was marred by an unconvincing happy ending that sidestepped its narrative of class struggle. Young Spanish film director Luis Buñuel was among the first to praise its compelling and original presentation of architecture and the city, a key influence on the development of the science fiction genre and later films such as 1982's *Blade Runner*. *Metropolis* is referenced in cultural products of varied sorts, including the 1973 novel *Gravity's Rainbow*, and it has been reset to music by Giorgio Moroder. More than a quarter of the footage shown when the film was first released has been lost, and the 1996 restoration by historian Enno Patalas now constitutes the most complete version available.

Released six years before National Socialist Adolf Hitler was elected chancellor of Germany, Lang's film is today frequently interpreted as an allegory of the social instability and political convulsions that brought the first German experiment with democracy during the Weimar Republic to an end in 1933.

Exiled film critic Sigfried Kracauer was among the first to develop this argument in his book, *From Caligari to Hitler: A Psychological History of the German Film*. As a summation of complex attitudes toward modernity, modernization, Americanism, and urbanization prevalent in Germany at the time, *Metropolis* remains without equal. Despite its frequent inconsistencies and lapses of logic, it has attained the status of a period classic studied alongside the work of master German political, social, and cultural theorists such as Max Weber, Georg Lukács, Walter Benjamin, and Ernst Jünger. Its visceral depiction of the rhythms of labor, workings of giant machines, and a dystopian urban environment have retained their force with the passage of time.

Edward Dimendberg

See also City and Film; Simmel, Georg

Further Readings

Eisner, Lotte. 1973. *The Haunted Screen*. Berkeley: University of California Press.

Elsaesser, Thomas. 2000. *Metropolis*. London: British Film Institute.

Kaes, Anton. 1994. "Metropolis, City, Cinema, Modernity." In *Expressionist Utopias: Paradise + Metropolis + Architectural Fantasy*, edited by Timothy O. Benson. Los Angeles: Los Angeles County Museum of Art.

Kaes, Anton, Martin Jay, and Edward Dimendberg, eds. 1994. *The Weimar Republic Sourcebook*. Berkeley: University of California Press.

Kracauer, Siegfried. 1947. *From Caligari to Hitler: A Psychological Study of the German Film*. Princeton, NJ: Princeton University Press.

Minden, Michael and Holger Bachmann, eds. 2000. *Fritz Lang's* Metropolis: *Cinematic Visions of Technology and Fear*. Rochester, NY: Camden House.

Neumann, Dietrich, ed. 1996. *Film Architecture from Metropolis to Blade Runner*. Munich: Prestel.

Patalas, Enno. 2001. *Metropolis in/aus Truemmern. Eine Filmgeschichte*. Berlin: Bertz + Fischer.

von Harbou, Thea. 1926. *Metropolis*. Rockville, MD: Sense of Wonder Press.

METROPOLITAN

Metropolitan generally refers to a city and the surrounding urbanized area. The term originates in ancient Greece, where a city that had established colonies in other lands was known as a *metropolis* (*meter* "mother" + *polis* "city"; literally the mother city, a city that had offspring). In the Middle Ages, the metropolitan was the seat of the archbishop, with jurisdiction over a specified patriarchal canonical territory. By the nineteenth century, the term *metropolitan* was commonly used in naming new municipal services such as the Metropolitan Police (in London) and civic institutions such as the Metropolitan Museum of Art, although the original meaning of the term (a city with colonial territories) has remained in use in France. In the last century, *metropolitan* was used to signify the growing urban populations in cities around the world, while the shortened *metro-* came to signify modern as well as cosmopolitan features of urban life.

Religious Organization

The Metropolitan was the title given to the bishop of the Christian church in the capital city or metropolis (mother city) of civil provinces in the Roman Empire, first appearing in documents at the Council of Nicea, convened by the Emperor Constantine in AD 325. As the church expanded, following the organizational patterns of the civil government, ecclesiastical provinces (the diocese) were established under the jurisdiction of bishops. This system of administration and control has remained unchanged in the modern Catholic, Orthodox, and Anglican churches. Some metropolitans were also granted the title of archbishop, and the archbishops of Canterbury and York have the three titles of Metropolitan, Archbishop, and primate of the Church of England. In ecclesiastical language of the present day, the term identifies church structures associated with the metropolis: the metropolitan church, metropolitan chapter, and the like.

Definitions

Blake McKelvey describes how American cities mushroomed in the early 1900s, taking on a new shape, new civic responsibilities, and new interrelationships: Larger cities were encircling neighboring towns, establishing new lines of communication, and exploring new sources of social and political power. The cities were rapidly expanding because of immigration, and the increasing urban populations spilled over the city boundaries; manufacturing moved to the suburban fringe because of overcrowded rail lines in the city. In 1910, the U.S. Bureau of the Census sought to capture the dynamic growth of urban areas by introducing a new term, the *metropolitan district*, for those urban areas with a population of 200,000 people, including a central city with a population of at least 100,000. In 1910, there were 15 such metropolitan areas. In 1930, the definition was extended down to include urban areas with a population of 200,000 but with cities of 50,000 or more people, and in 1940, there were 140 recognized metropolitan districts.

New definitions for metropolitan areas were issued in 1949 (for the 1950 census) using a county-based definition for the "standard metropolitan area" (SMA), and later definitions have evolved to *standard metropolitan statistical area* (SMSA), *metropolitan statistical area* (MSA), *metropolitan area* (MA), *metropolitan statistical areas* (MSAs), and *consolidated metropolitan statistical areas* (CMSAs) to capture the complexity of ever-expanding metropolitan regions. In each instance, the underlying concept, according to the Metropolitan Area Standards Review Committee of the U.S. Office of Management and the Budget, is that of "a large population nucleus and adjacent communities that have a high degree of integration with that nucleus." In 2007, nearly 85 percent of the U.S. population lived in metropolitan areas.

Metropolitan areas are used to define urban population concentrations in other countries as well. In Canada, *census metropolitan areas* (CMAs) are defined as having a total population of at least 100,000 people and an urban core of at least 50,000; this included 33 large metropolitan areas in the 2006 census. In India, by contrast, the Census Commission defines a metropolitan city as having a population of more than 4 million people; these cities include Mumbai, Delhi, Chennai, Kolkata, Bengaluru, Hyderabad, Surat, Ahmedabad, and Pune. *Metropolitan* is currently used to refer to a large identifiable area of continuous urbanization, including one or more large urban centers, and in time, this meaning has come to overlap with that of *megalopolis,* first used by Jean Gottman to describe the urban agglomeration of urban and urbanizing communities that stretched from Boston (on the north), through New York and Philadelphia, to Washington, D.C. (on the south).

Metropolitan Initiatives

Rapid urban growth in the last century has created problems in the planning and provision of public services in many countries. Cities alone cannot manage important urban problems in employment, housing, and social welfare because they often are spread across dozens of politically independent municipalities. In the urban studies literature of the 1970s, this would be described as the balkanization of the suburbs. Efforts have been made to create metropolitan service districts and even regional governments.

In Canada, a consolidated governing structure was established for the Toronto metropolitan area in 1952, which originally included 13 municipalities and a 25-member elected Council of Metropolitan Toronto (currently 35 members from six municipalities); it has established common property tax assessments and tax rates for regional issues including mass transit, housing, schools, water supply, and sewage disposal. Metropolitan governance has also been attempted in the United States with the merger of city and county government (Miami-Dade County in 1957, Nashville-Davidson County in 1963, and other cities mostly in the south) although with less comprehensive powers than in Toronto.

Metropolitan governmental structures are more common in Europe; in Germany, most large cities (including Frankfurt, Stuttgart, Munich, and Dresden) are consolidated city-county governments, and in England six "metropolitan counties" were created in 1974 (Greater Manchester, Merseyside, South Yorkshire, Tyne and Wear, West Midlands, and West Yorkshire) with joint boards for specific governing functions.

In other regions as well, metropolitan planning agencies and governance structures are used. The Tokyo metropolitan government was formed in 1943, with a publicly elected governor and metropolitan assembly; it includes 23 special wards, each with its own elected governing body. In the Philippines, Metro Manila includes the city and 16 surrounding cities and municipalities, each with its own local government; the Metropolitan Manila Development Authority (MMDA) operates as a regional governing body with its main headquarters in Makati City.

Other Uses of Metropolitan

While *metropolitan* has a specific genesis (from the Greek) and specific meanings (in both secular and nonsecular organizational structure), it has also been used in more generic fashion to refer to things urban and, especially, to those things that encompass the larger urban area. In London, the consolidation of essential services such as sanitation, water supply, street paving and lighting, relief of the poor, and maintenance of the peace were managed by the vestries of 90-odd parishes or precincts until establishment of the Metropolitan Board of Works; the establishment of the Metropolitan Police dates from the same period. In Paris, the subway system, opened in 1900, was called the Paris Metropolitan, shortened to Metro.

Metropolitan has also come to take on other meanings derived from the city and urban life, in this case referencing the cultural life of the city. The *Metropolitan Magazine*, published in Great Britain from 1833 through 1850, was intended for a cosmopolitan audience, with travel narratives and literature from around the world; a magazine of the same title appeared in New York from 1903 to 1911, and another with the shortened title *Metropolitan* was published from 1895 to 1925. Metropolitan has also been used as branding for products, including things as disparate as the Nash/Hudson Metropolitan automobile, produced from 1954 to 1962, and the New York Metropolitans baseball team (most often shortened to the New York Mets). In more recent years, the term *metrosexual* has come into use, derived from Mark Simpson's descriptions in *The Independent*: "Metrosexual Man, the single young man with a high disposable income, living or working in the city (because that's where all the best shops are), is perhaps the most promising consumer market of the decade."

In most of these examples, metropolitan refers to a larger urban region, to institutions that serve the urban region, or to cultural attributes associated with urban areas. One additional use, however, remains true to the original meaning of the mother city and colonies, and that is the French designation of Metropolitan France. This dates from the colonial period, when France was called the *metropole*, the mother city to the various territories and colonies where French was spoken (there was a similar usage by other European colonial powers). The term metropole is used to distinguish France from the overseas territories; the term Metropolitan France includes mainland France and Corsica.

Ray Hutchison

See also Megalopolis; Metropolitan Governance; Metropolitan Region; Suburbanization; Urban Agglomeration; Urban Politics

Further Readings

Gottman, Jean and Robert A. Harper, eds. 1990. *Since Megalopolis: The Urban Writings of Jean Gottman*. Baltimore: Johns Hopkins University Press.

McKelvey, Blake. 1968. *The Emergence of Metropolitan America, 1915–1966*. New Brunswick, NJ: Rutgers University Press.

Simpson, Mark. 1994. "Here Come the Mirror Men." *The Independent*, November 15.

METROPOLITAN GOVERNANCE

Metropolitan governance refers to a two-fold process of consolidating a new political space at the metropolitan scale, which involves intrametropolitan conflicts as well as political transformation through new governing instruments and interest-mediation mechanisms, and consolidating the metropolis as a collective actor in intergovernmental relations, global markets, and international politics. In brief, it entails profound transformations of the role of the city in the political process.

The debate around metropolitan governance is not new. At the turn of the twentieth century, a reform movement in the United States pushed for redefining urban politics, among other ways, by consolidating municipalities to counter a political fragmentation that was seen as fostering inequity, inefficiencies, and failures in the democratic system. In the post–World War II period, public choice theorists proposed instead that political fragmentation was a necessary condition for liberty, efficiency, and democracy. Charles Tiebout privileged the individual right to "vote with one's feet" when dissatisfied with the tax service package offered in a municipality. The ability for people to "shop" their residential location and to choose their neighbors was thought to produce more efficiency in delivering services and more democracy.

On the other hand, early reformers such as Chester Maxey trusted bureaucratic planning more than the aggregation of individual decisions. Planning was viewed as the most efficient means to effective service delivery and the most democratic solution, given that consolidation and tax sharing permitted a more uniform and equitable governance system throughout the metropolitan region.

The resurgence of interest in metropolitan governance in the 1990s came hand in hand with debates on the political effects of global economic restructuring. *New regionalism* is a label that conveys two meanings. First, effective metropolitan governance does not necessarily require municipal consolidation; it may be better to think in terms of a shift from governmental reform to new governance mechanisms. The notion of political territory is thereby replaced by a more fluid concept of political space. Second, the increasing importance of city-regions as collective actors in the global market and within national intergovernmental relations is a sign of a profound transformation of the political process under the ideological pressure of neoliberalism; that is, the ideological push toward fiscal austerity and the decentralization of governmental programs.

New Forms of Governance

New Political Space

Political territory is commonly understood as the container-like area within which politics unfolds. However, urban phenomena can hardly be conceived as restricted to territorial boundaries; urban politics may be better understood within a multicentered logic of horizontal relations that go beyond the hierarchical and territorial conception of governments. Metropolitan governance, in other words, recasts traditional definitions of the urban political process by insisting on open, overlapping, and fluid conceptions of the space of urban politics and focusing on networks, project-based decision making (rather than rational comprehensive planning), and the collaboration of state and nonstate actors. This constitutes the new political space.

In this context, difficulties of regulation and coordination caused by the unpredictability and chaos of urban life in sprawling and growing metropolitan areas are addressed by transforming the way decisions are made and legitimated, the way conflicting interests are mediated, and the way policies and programs are implemented and evaluated. These approaches replace institutional and territorial reforms such as the establishment of metropolitan two-tier governments.

Decision-Making and Legitimation Mechanisms

In the old debate, metropolitan governance meant consolidating municipalities and creating new governmental structures at a larger scale to ease the coordination of municipal decision making. Elected representatives would be compelled to work together by integrating municipal bureaucracies and pooling resources. In Toronto, for instance, the Municipality of Metropolitan Toronto was created in 1953 to equip the metropolitan area with adequate institutional capacity to face the challenges of rapid (sub)urbanization. This territorial reform was legitimated by the broad acceptance of rational and comprehensive planning and the belief that, in the modern world, a bigger city deserved a bigger governmental structure. Only in that way could it efficiently construct urban infrastructure such as freeways or suburban housing developments.

In the new debate, metropolitan governance mostly means inventing decision-making mechanisms that are not necessarily based on voting and comprehensive planning. Investing in megaprojects such as waterfront revitalization, airport expansion, or commercial street renaissance on an ad hoc basis provides leaders with more visibility and fame. Strategic planning still exists, but compliance mechanisms are more voluntary. The regional plan is often an opportunity to legitimate project-based decisions through controlled visionary exercises where well-known public and private leaders as well as selected citizens are called to imagine the future of the metropolitan area. Public consultations are also used to legitimate decisions that may or may not have been taken by elected representatives. In short, decision making mostly takes place in a debating or a bargaining mode between public and private actors, often leading to public–private partnerships for urban development. This networked, project-based logic of coordination and regulation is more prized than the traditional logic of representative democracy.

Legitimacy in this context comes from sources other than elections. Decisions that resonate with people's everyday practices and with their understandings will more easily be seen as legitimate. This implies more than one model of metropolitan governance, with governance arrangements varying according to the power dynamics and political culture of specific places. For instance, in Montreal, the government has chosen to create new metropolitan institutions (as in the old days) while incorporating practices of the new days (e.g., visioning exercises, performance measures, public–private partnerships, public consultations). In contrast, Toronto followed the lead of economic and other civil society leaders in constructing a metropolitan political space based on networks and specific projects such as the 2008 Olympic bid. These different trajectories can be explained by different configurations of actors and political cultures. Economic actors are more powerful in Toronto than Montreal, for instance, while the history of Montreal has led to a more social democratic state where, by comparison to Toronto, governmental structures are more trusted.

Despite these variations, metropolitan governance today is generally associated with a shared belief in the need for and the virtues of international competitiveness. Most citizens, elected representatives, bureaucrats, and civic leaders have internalized the idea that working together on a metropolitan scale will increase competitiveness in global markets and produce prosperity and happiness. This belief is at the core of the legitimation strategies for metropolitan governance reforms. This is not to say, that no one is contesting this idea. The problem for critics, however, is that transformation in interest-mediation mechanisms have made it more difficult for them to be heard.

Interest-Mediation Mechanisms

Traditionally, political parties, periodic elections, and corporate organizations such as trade unions or boards of trade were the main mechanisms to arbitrate between conflicting interests. Critical voices could thus be heard in an organized fashion. With the transformations under way since the 1980s, points of access to the decision-making process have multiplied at the same time as they have weakened. On the one hand, public consultations, the use of mainstream media channels, the creation of information hotlines by public agencies, and high-visibility urban projects have made urban politics more present in people's daily lives. On the other hand, the channels through which citizens can influence decision making depend more and more on personal networks. Unelected actors make important decisions outside of democratic accountability mechanisms, and access to these decision makers depends on personal networks. To counter these back-corridor decision-making practices, alternative forms of activism such as demonstrations and social justice work have become an integral part of the political life of metropolitan areas.

Policy Implementation and Evaluation

The consolidation–fragmentation debate was centered on the quest for the most effective and equitable service delivery system at the least cost for taxpayers. Programs were considered successful if residents were satisfied. The recent metropolitan governance debate is largely shaped by international transfers of knowledge on best practices, accompanied by ever more sophisticated performance measures and ranking schemes such as, for instance, Richard Florida's controversial Creative Index, which measures the proportion of educated, artistic, high-technology, and foreign-born population in cities to assess their potential for innovation and economic growth. In addition, authoritative auditing instruments based on legal contracts, norms, accounting categories, and new surveillance technologies aim to control how grant money is spent and how employees work.

City-Regions as Collective Actors

Internally, metropolitan governance refers to a profound transformation of the political process in terms of the multinodal and networked spatial configuration of political exchanges and the emergence of new decision-making, legitimating, interest-mediation, and evaluation mechanisms. Externally, metropolitan governance means the constitution of the city-region as a collective actor on global markets and in international governmental relations.

Seeing the city-region as a collective actor with the capacity to coordinate interests and actors and to represent the city externally implies a sense of common purpose rather than internal conflict. This may give the impression of a depoliticized region where there is a strong agreement on governing priorities. This apparent consensus, however, is usually the result of political struggles between interest-based strategizing practices. In Toronto, for example, the role of coalitions such as the Toronto City Summit Alliance, led by the Board of Trade, United Way, and union leaders, in fostering a common identity for the city-region is central. The dominant role of transnational capital within this coalition, created in 2002, is linked with its interest in making Toronto more competitive and amenable to global business. It also symbolizes the development of new strategies to influence the political process. While transnational banks, finance, trade, and multinational corporations have traditionally not been very involved in metropolitan politics in Toronto, preferring lobbying strategies at the national level, there has been a rescaling of their political activities toward metropolitan politics. They have become the most visible leaders of metropolitan governance in Toronto.

This is just one illustration of why it is important to consider both the internal and external aspects of metropolitan governance. The projected unity of a metropolitan area often hides power relations between actors within the metropolitan region. Simultaneously, the new debate on metropolitan governance has to be understood in relation to wider economic and state restructuring processes influenced by neoliberalism. Indeed, metropolitan governance also refers to the increasing importance of city-regions as collective actors in national and international intergovernmental relations.

Traditionally, in many Anglo-Saxon countries, municipal and metropolitan governments were considered service providers more than full-fledged, legitimate governments with legislative and executive powers. Increasingly, however, metropolitan areas play a significant political role on the national and international scenes, thus rebalancing their administrative and political functions. Toronto has become a central player in what has come to be known as the New Deal for Cities and Communities in Canada. This new political agenda gives more powers and monies to municipalities. Without the influence of coalitions such as the Toronto City Summit Alliance and the mayor of Toronto, this new Canadian urban agenda may have been less prominent. It has been pivotal in redefining immigrant settlement policies, infrastructure funding, and day care services. Similarly, metropolitan regions as collective actors are more and more present in international politics, whether through international cooperation programs, free trade agreements, or peace building. For example, the Canadian Department of Foreign Affairs and Trade has been active in leading an international agenda to give metropolitan areas a more prominent role in conflict resolution programs in countries devastated by war.

But the role of metropolitan governance in broader restructuring processes cannot be described simply as increasingly proactive. City-regions have also suffered the effects of the transformation of the welfare state. In many ways, the new debate on metropolitan governance demonstrates efforts to cope with the consequences of reforms whereby national and subnational levels of government have made local authorities responsible for the provision of social services. These fiscal and administrative forms of decentralization have had serious consequences for the fiscal health of municipalities, as well as the quality of services. The solution has

generally been twofold. In the case of Toronto, for instance, it was decided in 1997 to amalgamate six local municipalities with the Municipality of Metropolitan Toronto. The amalgamation included providing more resources to local authorities so that they could absorb the cost of welfare benefits. The second aspect of the solution has been to cut services while outsourcing them to the private sector. Metropolitan governance is not new, but these (upward, downward, and outward) rescaling processes have recast the terms of the debate.

Metropolitan governance has become a constitutive element of state restructuring and neoliberalization processes. The consequences of these metropolitan reforms on the political process are immense. They affect mechanisms of decision making and legitimation, interest-mediation, and policy implementation and evaluation.

Julie-Anne Boudreau

See also Governance; Metropolitan; Metropolitan Region; New Regionalism; Regional Governance

Further Readings

Brenner, Neil. 2004. *New State Spaces: Urban Governance and the Rescaling of Statehood.* Oxford, UK: Oxford University Press.

Florida, Richard. 2005. *The Flight of the Creative Class: The New Global Competition for Talent.* New York: HarperBusiness.

Maxey, Chester C. 1922. "The Political Integration of Metropolitan Communities." *National Municipal Review* 11(8):229–53.

Molotch, Harvey L. 1976. "The City as a Growth Machine: Towards a Political Economy of Place." *American Journal of Sociology* 82:309–30.

Orfield, Gary. 2002. *American Metropolitics: The New Suburban Realities.* Washington, DC: Brookings Institution Press.

Tiebout, Charles M. 1956. "A Pure Theory of Local Expenditures." *The Journal of Political Economy* 64(5):416–24.

METROPOLITAN REGION

The notion of metropolitan region refers to a collection of territories considered interdependent, some located in the central areas and others on the urban fringe. It is also identified with a plan to constitute a coherent territorial structure operating across several spatial scales. Yet, metropolitan territorial coherence is contradicted by the emergence of peripheral spaces, including "edge" and "edgeless" cities, which deny the predominant role of the center. However, the metropolitan region, a territory experienced as a functional construct by some but an abstraction by others, suffers from a lack of political recognition in most countries.

Scholarship in the area of urban studies views the metropolitan region, first and foremost, as the product of a process of an urban area's expansion. Thus, it is a territorial entity in perpetual reconfiguration with undetermined boundaries and lacking a well-defined political structure. In contrast, it is simpler to define the city, which remains a product of theoreticians and national statistical offices, than the metropolitan region. Nonetheless, metropolitan region refers increasingly to a social entity that calls on a regional identity and sense of belonging to a vaster territory beyond the neighborhood or municipality.

Thinking Metropolitan: The Theoretical Debates

The question of the legitimacy of the metropolitan region is part of a long-standing debate about size. A number of scholars of democracy, from Socrates to the political scientist Robert Dahl, have considered what the ideal size of the polity (in the democratic sense of the term) should be, however, the overwhelming growth of urbanization in the course of the twentieth century has shifted the debate from the size of the polity to that of the city. Discussion now focuses on the minimal population threshold for new urban forms, whether the city in the strict sense, the metropolitan region, or the megalopolis.

Size remains the lowest common denominator when we seek an objective and universal way to define types of urban areas. This is particularly the case for studies comparing metropolitan regions, which attempt to convey the complexity of urbanization. This process is impossible to capture empirically. Recognition of the significance of the metropolis must be found elsewhere; specifically, in the study of relationships among the activities within the metropolitan area. Interdependencies

between the central city and its hinterland lead us to reexamine our understanding of the metropolitan region from a historical perspective and in terms of the current challenges of metropolitanization.

A more fundamental debate exists between two conceptions of metropolitan space, one based on mobility characteristics, with commuting as an indicator of regional structural coherence, and the other focused on the ecology of social areas and, most recently, on the polarization of socially segregated areas. The goal is to describe an expanded urban area with interdependent parts. The theory of ecological expansion that was developed in the wake of the Chicago School's first publications is drawn on to understand the meaning of the idea of metropolitan community. This refers to a territory composed of a center along with socially differentiated social areas and suburbs that depend on the center. These intrametropolitan territories are connected, notably by daily commuter journeys, but also through residential trajectories following the invasion–succession model. This theory of metropolitan expansion supposes that the urban area grows to the extent that costs and commuting time decrease, on one hand, and households gain increased capacity for residential choice, on the other. It seeks to determine the limits of the metropolis and its structure, defined as the principal axes ensuring interrelations between the center and the periphery.

In this way, the metropolitan region is defined as a space of flows, specifically in terms of the level of commuting between residential areas and central places. The pattern of these flows is a function of the distance to be covered, accessibility to places, and the structure of economic locations. Residential choices are due to personal preferences as much as to cost rationality and travel times. This space of flows might also be structured by social forces that condition relationships between different parts of metropolises. In regional science, the attraction of different activity centers are considered as masses that differentially generate flows, their direction, and their spatial range. Spatial interactions arise from the structure of economic locations and the effect of the attraction of one sector for another as a function of size and distance. These interactions define the region's edge by indicating where the flows sharply dissipate.

Emerging metropolitan forms have been influenced by the decentralization of commercial activities, manufacturers, and, more recently, high technology. The debate is therefore about the general tendency of the phenomenon of decentralization and concentration of activities and employment in suburban centers. Is the pattern of contemporary metropolis polycentric or dispersed?

The question is whether suburban spaces are dependent or autonomous vis-à-vis the center. The recognition of a polynuclear metropolitan pattern based on the premise of territorial fragmentation and decentralization of urban activities and jobs shifting toward suburban centers—whether edge cities, technoburbs, or technopolises—affects the cohesion of metropolitan space. The dispersal of activities and jobs erases the boundaries of the metropolitan region, leading to the emergence of "edgeless" cities. *Exopolis* has been proposed to signify the end of the center's domination and of territorial cohesion. From this standpoint, the question of the centralized or multinuclear metropolitan region arises and whether it would not be replaced by a decentered metropolis. Nonetheless, postmodern urbanism claims that the periphery dominates the center and that the metropolitan region lacks precise boundaries. It is a collection of units, disconnected and closed in on themselves.

Postmodern urbanism offers an interpretation of metropolitan morphology based on the phenomena of decentralization and spatial fragmentation. Individual movements, their trajectories through life, and their daily travels are determined by preestablished frames of reference. The trajectories come to life with daily journeys constrained by distance and available modes of transport, yet also reflecting a real capacity for autonomy and freedom. These journeys form bundles or domains where social interactions, governed by rules, ritual, and conflicts, are exercised. From the perspective of time-geography, the metropolitan region is a structure articulated by the trajectories that individuals move through during their everyday lives.

The gravity and ecological models have, each in their own way, influenced the statistical definition of metropolitan regions. For a dozen years, now, the Organisation for Economic Co-operation and Development (OECD) has statistically delineated metropolitan regions and thus produced an institutional architecture as well as public policies on

urban space. Thus, the great majority of member countries (with the exceptions of Korea, Spain, Japan, Mexico, and Turkey, which have no official definition of metropolitan areas) use commuting conditions (with variations in methods of calculation) to assess metropolitan space. However, this interest in the metropolitan scale in most countries is recent. Canada and the United States have had official definitions for almost 60 years, whereas for other countries, such as Spain or Belgium, metropolitan statistics are relatively novel. The absence or presence of a statistical definition reveals the degree of political interest in the notion of metropolitan region and the efforts of recognition at work in different countries.

Thinking Metropolitan: Political Usage

The ambiguity in definition and the transformation of the concept following its political usage are not unique to discussions about the metropolitan region. However, the particularity of the conflict relates to the political nature of the term and has been exacerbated by globalization and the reorganization of the state. The metropolitan region might well be added to the political agenda as an ideal place for enhancing national economic competitiveness. This can be seen especially in the notion of the city-region.

Thus, the term metropolitan region is not politically neutral. It belongs to a body of discourse on the need to harmonize the functional territory (i.e., the metropolitan region) and the political territory. Therefore, it is a question of imposing a convincing definition of the metropolitan region with the goal of legitimizing an extended perimeter in which urban cohesion can exist, renewing our understanding of living together, and fostering public policy. Borders have always been sources of power. This is why the notion of metropolitan region refers back to a territory of interactions. The validity of political boundaries is always implicit. Basically, the political territory and the lived territory should be one and the same.

The transition from theory to politics is revealed in the importance of census taking and the efforts to define the metropolitan region statistically. From the perspective of size, for example, one of the factors pushing the Québec government in the early twentieth century to merge municipalities in part of the Montréal region was the threat of seeing the Québec metropolis move from its status as the second Canadian metropolis to fourth place in terms of population. Municipal mergers in Ontario in the 1990s allowed for the demographic enlargement of Toronto. Ottawa acted similarly and was poised to become the third-largest municipality in Canada. These concerns also affected the debate on municipal mergers in Montréal.

From a statistical perspective, a number of cases demonstrate how the definition of metropolitan region, even statistically, remains a matter of political controversy. In the United States, defining metropolitan statistical areas is useful for researchers and encourages elected local officials to recognize their membership in a larger entity. The critical importance of current debates in the United States, as elsewhere, bears witness to the political utility of statistically capturing metropolitan regions. For example, Israel's Central Bureau of Statistics does not define metropolitan space in Jerusalem due to political sensitivities unique to that region of the world.

However, the transfer of theory to the political world is strongly criticized around the use of the term *city-region*, which derives from metropolitan region. While the latter seeks to emphasize functional relations uniting cities and their peripheries, it currently refers to the functionality of metropolitan regions as understood in terms of creativity, innovation, and competitiveness of a global economy. This approach reifies metropolitan regions as key actors in a nation's economic health to the detriment of poorer areas of a country. The redistributive role of the state in building territorial equity is neglected. The attempt of political authorities to establish objective criteria for city-regions is suspect, particularly in Great Britain but also elsewhere in the world. If the pedagogical merits of the metropolitan region are expressed with the goal of preventing local officials from turning their backs on the central city, the search for legitimacy at the metropolitan level instead benefits certain metropolitan regions to the detriment of less favored territories. The metropolitan region is a contentious notion.

Laurence Bherer and Gilles Sénécal

See also Chicago School of Urban Sociology; Edge City; Exopolis; Journey to Work; Los Angeles School of Urban Studies; Metropolitan Governance; New Regionalism; Urban Geography; Urban Politics

Further Readings

Berry, B. J. L., P. G. Gohen, and H. Goldstein. 1969. *Metropolitan Region Definition: A Reevaluation of Concept and Statistical Practice.* Washington, DC: U.S. Bureau of Census.

Cervero, R. 1989. *America's Suburban Centers: The Land-use Transportation Link.* Boston: Unwin Hyman.

Garreau, J. 1991. *Edge City: Life on the New Frontier.* New York: Doubleday.

Jonas, E. G. and K. Ward. 2007. "Introduction to a Debate on City-regions: New Geographies of Governance, Democracy, and Social Reproduction." *International Journal of Urban and Regional Research* 31(1):169–78.

Lang, R. E. 2003. *Edgeless Cities, Exploring the Elusive Metropolis.* Washington, DC: Brookings Institution Press.

McKenzie, R. 1933. *The Metropolitan Community.* New York: McGraw-Hill.

Organisation for Economic Co-operation and Development. 2002. *Redefining Territories: The Functional Regions.* Paris: OECD.

Soja, E. W. 2000. "Exopolis: The Restructuring Urban Form." Pp. 233–63 in *Postmetropolis, Critical Studies of Cities and Regions.* Oxford, UK: Blackwell.

Mexico City, Mexico

Mexico City is the capital of the United States of Mexico; it is the country's largest urban center, the largest city in Latin America, and the third-largest megacity in the world. Mexico City generally refers to the whole metropolitan area, which not only covers the Federal District (*Distrito Federal,* or D.F.), but also parts of the states of Mexico and Hidalgo. At the beginning of this century, its metropolitan area stretched over an area of 5,122.86 square kilometers (about 2,000 square miles), of which the Federal District accounted for 28.6 percent, and in 2005, Mexico City had a population of 19,331,365, equivalent to almost 20 percent of the national population. The city sits at an altitude of approximately 2,250 meters and is located within a closed basin, which has resulted in a number of ongoing environmental challenges, particularly relating to water and pollution management.

Mexico City is a vibrant, modern city with a rich heritage, yet it is also one of stark contrasts, with opulent districts to the south and west of the city standing in stark contrast to the vast tracts of poverty concentrated toward the north and east, where many settlements lack even basic services. The larger of these municipalities, such as Nezahualcoyotl, have populations of a similar size to many important cities in Mexico. Today, while outlying areas of the city continue to grow, the central areas have been steadily losing population. In fact, the Population Council (*Consejo de la Poblacion,* Conapo) insists that the city has become a net population exporter. While throughout its history the city has traditionally been a symbol of the centralization of power, in recent years, decentralization policies have gone some way to reducing the country's heavy economic and political reliance on the capital city, and much heavy industry has been relocated, signifying a major shift in the city's economy toward the service and financial sectors.

History of the City

The ancient city of Tenochtitlan was founded by the Aztecs in AD 1325, and despite being built on a small flood-prone island, within a few centuries, it would become the capital of the powerful Aztec empire and the political, economic, and religious center of Mesoamerica. When the Spanish arrived in 1519, they found a thriving city at the center of what was at that time probably the largest and most densely populated urban area in the world. The Spanish conquest of the city in 1521 left much of Tenochtitlan destroyed, and on these ruins, the Spanish chose to build the capital of the viceroyalty of New Spain. In 1524, the municipality of Mexico City was established, known as *México Tenustitlán,* and officially known as *Ciudad de México* from 1585. The city soon became the most important in the Americas. Gradually, the dried lake bed was built on, such that by the seventeenth century, the city was a substantial agglomeration of houses, public buildings, and churches.

Mexico gained independence from Spain in 1821, after an 11-year civil war, and in 1824, the nation became a federal republic. In the 1840s, the capital was invaded and occupied by U.S. troops, which culminated in Mexico being obliged to cede a large amount of its northern territory to the United States. From 1865 to 1867, Emperor Maximilian I headed a brief monarchy, after which

the 35-year dictatorship of Porfirio Diaz saw (on the positive side) significant improvements to the infrastructure and left a notably French mark on the architecture of the city. Popular discontent with Diaz led to the Mexican Revolution, which began in 1910. The postrevolutionary government prioritized the capital as the core of the country, and particularly from the 1940s onward, the city began to stabilize and prosper.

In 1968, Mexico City hosted the Olympic Games, which left some lasting positive legacies for the city, such as the metro system. However, the event was marred by the massacre of hundreds of students a few days before the games began, following months of political unrest and protests.

On September 19, 1985, an earthquake measuring 8.1 on the Richter scale devastated the city, leaving between 10,000 and 30,000 people dead and 50,000 to 90,000 homeless and causing untold physical damage: In three minutes, 100,000 homes were destroyed, and $4 billion of damage was caused. A strong aftershock measuring 7.5 struck 36 hours later causing further damage and widespread panic. As a result of the quake, and the fact that buildings such as the Torre Latinoamericana (which had in-built technology to withstand tremors) survived the earthquake, seismic technologies, particularly for large constructions, have since been prioritized (the Torre Mayor, for example, is built to withstand an 8.5 earthquake). In addition, there is now an early warning system in place, which sends alerts to Mexico City via sensors in the coastal subduction zone off the coast of Guerrero State.

Geography and Environment

The city is located within central Mexico on an ancient lake bed in a basin measuring abut 9,600 square kilometers, surrounded by mountains. In 2005, the Metropolitan Zone of Mexico City (*Zona Metropolitana de la Ciudad de Mexico*) was formally established as constituting the 16 delegations of the Federal District, plus 40 municipalities from Mexico state and one from Hidalgo state. The traditional center of the city is the *Zocalo,* or main square, now officially called the *Plaza de la Constitución,* housing the Metropolitan Cathedral and the National Palace, which is built on the ruins of the ancient Aztec emperor's palace.

The Conservation Zone

Peripheral urbanization is placing extreme pressure on the immediate environment of the city and even jeopardizes its sustainable future growth. Although peripheral expansion of the city is numerically greatest in the northern and eastern regions of the metropolitan area, expansion to the south of the city has particularly significant environmental impacts. There is a large conservation area to the south of the Federal District, which is a vital environmental resource for a city so burdened with environmental problems, but which is threatened by illegal settlement. It has been estimated that between 1967 and 1995, urban sprawl in the southern periphery of the metropolitan area grew from 1,427 hectares to 11,896 hectares, which has implied a loss of 10,469 hectares of conservation land. This is in spite of government programs established to protect the conservation zone.

During the early twentieth century, the wealthy elite began gradually to move from the center toward the southern and western zones of the city, a process that continued throughout the century.

The island location of the original city meant that its expansion had depended on the Aztecs creating artificial land masses traversed by a system of canals. While the expansion of the city under such difficult conditions led to the development of very advanced water treatment and sanitation systems, a range of environmental difficulties inherent to the relatively inhospitable terrain have plagued the city as it has developed and grown. The decimation of the city of Tenochtitlan by the Spanish included the destruction of much of the original infrastructure, which had been designed to prevent flooding. From the colonial period onward, poor land management and consequent frequent flooding, together with demands for expansion, made it necessary to gradually drain the basin, such that present-day Mexico City is built on top of much of the ancient lake bed.

The construction of a deep drainage system and the drying out of the ancient lake beds meant that the subsoil, which had been strengthened by groundwater, became too weak to support the city above it, and between 1910 and 1987, the city center sank by about nine meters. The weakness also proved catastrophic during the earthquake of 1985. In addition, a lack of water continues to present a major problem for the city.

Another serious environmental concern is air pollution, whereby geographic and climatic factors hamper the dispersion of high levels of industrial and vehicle pollution. Yet, a reduction in heavy industry in Mexico City in recent years (itself in fact partly a result of government incentives to relocate away from the city), together with local and federal government action to reduce levels of pollution, have certainly had some effect.

Urban Planning and Administration

At the beginning of the 1970s, a shift toward metropolitan expansion emerged as a new form of urban growth in Mexico, which particularly affected Mexico City. There was a massive rural–urban migration flow, with about 3 million migrants moving to Mexico City in the 1960s. This translated into an annual growth rate of 5.7 percent, which was an historic high at this time.

As the city has grown, it has absorbed many old towns within its limits, particularly in the postrevolution period from the 1920s. This process continues to the present day, with more outlying towns becoming absorbed into the sprawl of the city. These ancient centers serve to provide the surrounding population with an alternative to the city center, in terms of supplying services, affordable goods, and informal employment opportunities. Thus, the growth of the city has been decentralized to some extent, which has reduced the population's reliance on the city center, making the city more efficient in meeting people's basic needs. Indeed, toward the end of the 1970s, support and development of these alternative centers became an intentional part of urban planning. Among the middle classes, this has meant that the city center—once the preferred shopping district—is losing out to an increasing number of suburban shopping centers, further challenging the relevance of the city center.

Santa Fe

The modernizing ambitions of the controversial President Salinas (1988–1994) are nowhere more evident than in the ostentatious Santa Fe financial development, located away from the center in the west of the city. Planned during his presidency and during a time of great economic optimism in Mexico, it was to be a world-class, ultra-modern business, residential, and commercial district. Although the economic crisis of the mid-1990s put plans on hold, the development was revived in 2000, and today it hosts many major multinational corporations including Nokia, Sony, General Electric, and the Ford Motor Company, along with key Mexican companies such as Televisa and Grupo Bimbo and three universities and colleges. However, it has been a controversial development from the outset and has arguably fallen short of expectations. Its location has meant displacement and disruption for the low-income population of Pueblo de Santa Fe, particularly those who lived near and around the rubbish dump on which the new development was constructed: This poor community has been totally dispossessed. Furthermore, in terms of the development itself, it has been criticized for being extremely car-centric, yet lacking sufficient access roads, as being both isolated and isolating by design, and as lacking commercial success.

Despite positive aspects of this growth in terms of localized urban management, the fact that the city has now spread over three different states means that it has been increasingly difficult to manage and plan a city so administratively divided. Moreover, systematic urban planning was nonexistent until the 1970s, with restrictions on urban growth and land use determination being dictated by individual policies or politicians. Since then, plans for national urban development have largely been concerned with decentralization and the creation of development poles away from Mexico City. Despite continuing administrative challenges, developments in urban planning over this period have been largely positive in terms of decentralization, a plurality of political parties, and governments willing to experiment. This in fact has been reflected by national government policy, such as the decentralist New Federalism introduced by the Zedillo government (1994–2000), which has given greater autonomy to individual states.

At a national level, perhaps the most important political change in recent years in Mexico has been the ousting of the long-ruling PRI in the presidential elections of 2000, which was the culmination of a series of state-level victories for rival parties since 1989. In terms of the political administration of Mexico City, a hugely significant development was the reform in 1997 of the anomalous law that allowed the residing government to choose the governor of Mexico City, rather than its people as was the case in other Mexican cities. Since they were given the right to vote for their governor, the people of Mexico City have elected the left-wing PRD party in every election. As of 2000, each of the delegations in Mexico City is headed by an elected representative. While still nascent, it can be said that a more pluralistic democratic political system both in Mexico City and the country as a whole has developed in recent years.

Economy

Despite the emergence of regional economic hubs, Mexico City remains the country's most economically important center and the wealthiest urban agglomeration in Latin America. Today, the city relies less on traditional industry and more on the service and commercial sectors, accounting for about 45 percent of the country's commercial activity. Financial services are also concentrated here, with all the main banks, the country's stock exchange, and the central bank, the Bank of Mexico, all being located in the city. At the beginning of the 1980s, the city absorbed more than a fifth of national labor power.

An import substitution industrialization strategy was implemented in Mexico in the 1940s, creating conditions of stability and prosperity that made Mexico City the most important industrial center in the country. In the second half of the twentieth century, heavy industry began to be relocated away from the city, although some plants still remain in the northern district. The most important industries are chemicals, plastics, cement, and textiles, although light industry is becoming increasingly important.

Although over recent decades Mexico (and particularly Mexico City) has been hit by a series of economic crises, not least the devaluation of the peso and subsequent financial-sector crisis in 1994 to 1995, the economy has proved surprisingly resilient and has continued to grow.

In Mexico, the informal sector accounted for 12.1 percent of GDP in 2006. An estimated 11.5 million people work in this sector, which is equivalent to 27.2 percent of the country's economically active population. This parallel economy takes place in public space, through the sale of goods and services, and has become a dynamic and essential practice among the most disadvantaged sections of the population and an alternative supply system for the general population. Thousands of products and services are offered both in a flexible (such as mobile vendors, street markets, car washing) and fixed (such as eateries) way. Although local and municipal authorities are responsible for regulating this activity through issuing permits to street vendors and receiving associated levies, this has led to some degree of collusion between the authorities and vendor representatives, who then exert pressure on the authorities to allow commerce in the most lucrative sites. Whether this sector is seen as one of entrepreneurial flair or pure necessity, it supplies a huge demand among the low-income population of Mexico City for low-cost goods.

Population

Demographic change in twentieth-century Mexico City can be divided into three main periods. From 1900 to 1940, the city was recovering from the upheavals of the revolution and trying to modernize and establish a firm base for economic growth and lasting social peace. From 1940 to 1970, the city experienced a phenomenal growth rate, due largely to economic and industrial expansion, with growth rates in each decade exceeding 5 percent. As such, the population of the metropolitan area grew from 1,644,921 in 1940, to 8,623,157 in 1970. The maximum population concentration was reached in 1980, when 19.4 percent of all Mexicans lived in the capital. This figure has slowly reduced to 18.8 percent in 1990 and to 18.4 percent in 2000.

After a decade of transition in the 1970s when the birthrate began to fall (the last phase of the demographic transition) and migration began to reverse, the final two decades of the twentieth century saw a reduction in population growth to near natural levels. In the 1980s, the city's growth rate at 1.67 percent fell below the national rate of 2.02 percent. It has remained below the national level ever since, marking the start of demographic stabilization.

An interesting aspect of migration to Mexico City is that throughout the twentieth century, it was predominantly women who moved to the city, suggesting improved job prospects for women in the capital compared to other regions. This leveled off slightly in the 1990s, perhaps due to increased demand for female labor in the *maquilas* in the north of the country.

Overall rates of human development in Mexico are relatively high, with a global human Development Index (HDI) ranking of 57, which classifies it as a country with high human development. Nevertheless, there are significant subnational and subregional differences and inequalities. There are marked differences in poverty between urban and rural areas. For example, the urban population unable to meet the basic food needs of their family stood at 11.4 percent in 2002, compared to 38.4 percent of the rural population. Indeed, Mexico City, despite its vast inequalities, has on average the highest HDI of all regions of the country, highest average incomes, highest levels of gender equity, and unsurprisingly also scores highest in the education and health indices. Furthermore, the delegation of Benito Juarez in the Federal District has the highest HDI of any municipality in Mexico (0.91); if it were to be compared to national HDIs, it would be similar to Italy or Hong Kong. The lowest HDI is in Metlatónoc, Guerrero State (0.38), a similar level of development to Malawi or Angola. There are also marked differences within the metropolitan zone. Financial crisis and structural adjustment policies during the 1980s led to a decrease in earnings among the poor and an increase in extreme poverty: The proportion of the population considered to be in extreme poverty as a proportion of the total poor population increased from 37.1 percent in 1984 to 53.9 percent in 1992, which even then was still lower than the national average of 66 percent in 1992.

Adrian Guillermo Aguilar and Ailsa Winton

See also City Planning; Deindustrialization; Globalization; Growth Management; Metropolitan Governance; Social Exclusion; Sprawl; Sustainable Development; Urban Planning

Further Readings

Aguilar, Adrian Guillermo. 2000. "Localización Geográfica de La Cuenca de México." Pp. 31–38 *La Ciudad de México en el fin del Segundo milenio*, edited by Gustavo Garza. Mexico City: Gobierno del Distrito Federal/El Colegio de México.

Carrillo-Rivera, J. J., A. Cardona, R. Huizar-Alvarez, M. Perevochtchikova, and E. Graniel. 2008. "Response of the Interaction between Groundwater and Other Components of the Environment in Mexico." *Environmental Geology* 55(2):303–19.

Colliers International. 2007. "Mexico City Market Overview, Offices 2006–2007." Boston: Colliers International.

Damián, Araceli. 2000. "Pobreza Urbana." Pp. 297–302 in *La Ciudad de México en el fin del Segundo milenio*, edited by Gustavo Garza. Mexico City: Gobierno del Distrito Federal/El Colegio de México.

Ezcurra, Exequiel, Mariso Mazari, Irene Pisanty, and Adrian Guillermo Aguilar. 2006. *La Cuenca de México*. Mexico City: Fondo de Cultura Económica.

Islas Rivera, Victor. 2000. "Red Vial." Pp. 362–70 in *La Ciudad de México en el fin del Segundo milenio*, edited by Gustavo Garza. Mexico City: Gobierno del Distrito Federal/El Colegio de México.

Negrete Salas, María Eugenia. 2000. "Dinámica Demográfica." Pp. 247–55 in *La Ciudad de México en el fin del Segundo milenio*, edited by Gustavo Garza. Mexico City: Gobierno del Distrito Federal/El Colegio de México.

Pacheco Gómez Muñoz, María Edith. 2004. *Ciudad de México, heterogénea y desigual: un estudio sobre el mercado de trabajo*. Mexico City: El Colegio de Mexico.

UNDP. 2003. *Informe sobre Desarrollo Humano México 2002*. Mexico City: Mundi-Prensa.

———. 2005. *Informe sobre Desarrollo Social y Humano México 2004*. Mexico City: Mundi-Prensa.

———. 2007. *Human Development Report 2007/8*. Basingstoke, UK: Palgrave Macmillan.

Ward, Peter M. 2004. *México Megaciudad: Desarrollo y Política, 1970–2000*. Mexico City: Grupo Angel Porrua/El Colegio Mexiquense.

MOSCOW, RUSSIAN FEDERATION

Moscow is the capital of the Russian Federation. With more than 10 million inhabitants living within the incorporated area of the city, Moscow is one of the ten most populous cities of the world and the most populous city in Europe. It is one of the two (with St. Petersburg) "cities of federal importance," cities that are separate subjects of Russian Federation; it is administratively separate from the Moscow Region (*Oblast'*). The history of Moscow spans more than eight centuries of growth from a tiny trade settlement to the capital of a world superpower throughout much of the twentieth century. At one time an iconic socialist city, on the verge of the third millennium, Moscow is still going through rapid transformation.

Moscow Before 1917

The region of Moscow was inhabited at least since Neolithic times. In the eleventh century, the region was populated by several Slavic ethnic groups, prominently *Viatichi* and *Krivichi*. The first record of Moscow (as *Moscov*) in church chronicles is dated 1174. *Moscov* was mentioned as an outpost in the domain of Suzdal Prince Yuri Dolgoruki, who is popularly held to be the founder of the city. However, archaeological research shows that a small fortified settlement already existed at the inflow of the Neglinnaya River into the Moskva River. It specialized in trade and handicrafts and enjoyed merchant connections extending at least as far as Kiev (at that time the center of *Kyivan Rus*).

The political position of the Moscow Principality strengthened during the thirteenth through fifteenth centuries. By the fourteenth century, Moscow emerged as the center of the Grand Duchy (*Knyazhestvo*) of Moscow. In the late fifteenth century, Moscow became the capital of the centralized Russian state. Its symbolic status was crystallized under the reign of Tsar Ivan the Terrible (1547–1584), the first tsar of the Tsardom of Russia. In the sixteenth and seventeenth centuries, three fortification lines were constructed, the *Kitai-Gorod* (Trade City, the ancient territory of Moscow), the *Belyi Gorod* (White City, named after the white plastering of intricate fortifications roughly corresponding to contemporary Boulevard Ring roads), and the *Zemlyanoi Gorod* (Earth City, an earthen rampart that later became the Garden Ring roads). These fortifications essentially created the Moscow center region and its structure as we know it today.

Despite the decision of Tsar Peter I the Great to move the capital to the newly established Saint Petersburg in 1712, Moscow retained its importance and continued its growth. A modern education system started to focus on Moscow in the late seventeenth century. In 1755, the Decree of Empress Elizabeth established Moscow State University. In 1812, when Napoleon's army entered the city, Moscow suffered a devastating fire. French forces held Moscow for less than 40 days and were routed to leave the smoldering ruin of city buildings that had been mostly wooden. Moscow was swiftly rebuilt, and the fire opened the way for the first massively implemented urban planning effort.

The Scotsman William Hastie developed the first postfire plan in 1813, but it was rejected and a more feasible project plan was approved in 1817, written by the Commission for the Construction of Moscow led by famed architect Osip Bove. The plan was largely implemented under Moscow Governor-General Fyodor Rostopchin. Landmark developments included dismantling the obsolete Earth City and White City fortifications as well as many other defensive structures and constructing several prominent buildings such as the *Manezh* (Riding Arena) near the Kremlin.

Socialist Moscow

By the end of the nineteenth century, Moscow converted from a center for nobility and merchants to a capitalist manufacturing city specializing in light industry, prominently textiles and machinery. It was the key locus of revolutionary events during 1905 liberal revolution and during the 1917 socialist revolution that created the Soviet Union.

After the October revolution, the country was torn by civil war. Threats of foreign interventions led to returning the capital to Moscow in 1918. Yet, the newly installed Soviet authorities took seriously the question of urban planning in Moscow. The city was to become the capital of new communist world. Throughout the twentieth century, the governance of Moscow, formally in the hands of Moscow Soviets, was directly controlled by the party; its general secretaries personally approved major planning decisions.

Early Soviet planning was heavily influenced by European utopian thinking, notably by Ebenezer Howard's garden cities. Moscow's symbolic landscape was massively altered by eradicating all references to monarchy, religion, and capitalism in street names and architectural landmarks. Nevertheless, limited conservation efforts prevented the proposed destruction of several landmarks (notably churches of the Kremlin complex).

The new economic policy of the twenties prompted a quick boom of Moscow's population. At this time, modernism and constructivism became important trends in architecture and planning, fused with communist ideology. A lasting modernist imprint on Moscow is the *Tsentrosoyuz* building (1929–1936), designed by Le Corbusier.

Gradual abandonment of the new economic policy and setting on the course of industrialization and collectivization in late 1920s brought new planning policy for Moscow. The building that then dominated the Moscow skyline, the Cathedral of Christ the Savior on Sparrow (Lenin) Hills, was blown up in 1931. It was to be replaced with a monumental Palace of Soviets, but that was never completed beyond a foundation pit; in 1960, that pit became a heated open-air swimming pool. Several other landmarks were also destroyed.

In 1935, the Central Committee of the Communist Party adopted the new master plan of Moscow. The construction of a subway (*Metropoliten,* or *Metro*) commenced in 1931, and in 1935, the first line was opened. Metro was the symbol of Soviet achievements and a project for the entire country. Despite the close approach of German forces in 1941 and 1942, Moscow was not occupied, and, thanks to an advanced air defense, it suffered relatively little direct damage.

Among notable postwar developments are seven high-rise buildings (the *Vysotkas,* including the Moscow University main building at Sparrow Hills), designed in "Stalin classicism" style and vaguely reminiscent of the Empire State Building. All commenced in 1947 to celebrate the 800th anniversary of the city; they were to establish the new urban skyline.

However, behind the apparent progress, there was an immense dualism: Showcase projects were grossly incapable of improving living conditions of the majority of population. Many residents (principally workers at the new factories) inhabited wooden bunkhouses and barracks, suffering from overpopulation and lack of sanitation. Under Secretary Nikita Khrushchev, a massive housing construction program was launched. The *khrushchevkas,* cheap standardized concrete panel housing (with a projected service life of 25 to 30 years), brought long-awaited relief to bunkhouse dwellers throughout the Soviet Union. In Moscow they constituted the bulk of residential units built in between 1960 and 1985. A typical two-room single-family flat had 45 square meters. For many people, this was a significant improvement in living conditions. Other important developments include the *MKAD*. Constructed in 1961, the outer circular highway has formally designated the administrative boundary of Moscow.

A new 20-year master plan was adopted in 1971 under Secretary Leonid Brezhnev to incorporate a target population of 8 million (with about 7 million in 1970) and with a goal of improving living conditions, particularly living space per capita, removing dirty industry, and implementing stricter zoning policies. In 1980, Moscow hosted the Summer Olympics, and the Moscow Soviet executed a redevelopment program. Events of the late 1980s made the master plan for the most part impracticable, and Olympic construction essentially remained the last Moscow reconstruction before 1991.

Soviet Moscow endured the radical sweeping away of the old social and cultural fabric of the city and an immense population increase. State-led development and forced imposition of artificially created symbolic landscape were coupled with destruction of old local communities, including the erasure of whole districts of the old city. Formation of new localities was strongly discouraged in favor of allegiance to the Communist Party. Nevertheless, the core of old Moscow as well as the radial pattern of development survived and, in 1991, entered the new epoch.

Moscow After Socialism

Moscow was the locus of many events surrounding the fall of the Soviet Union and the beginning of post-Soviet Russia. The current system of Moscow governance came into being in 1993. The legislative branch is the elected Moscow *Duma* (parliament). The Moscow government is the executive branch. Since 2004, the mayor of Moscow is no longer elected but nominated by the president of the Russian Federation for appointment by the Moscow Duma. Following the short tenure (1991–1992) of Gavriil Kh. Popov, Yuri M. Luzhkov was appointed the city mayor in 1992 and still held the post in 2009. The present city consists of ten

wards (*Administrativnye Okruga*, AO). Each is divided into several districts (*Rayons*). In 1991, Zelenograd, a city of 200,000 people established in between 1958 and 1962 as a center of microelectronic research and industry, was incorporated into Moscow as the 10th *Okrug*, becoming an exclave.

In the 1990s, the profile of Moscow has drastically shifted. Widespread industrial decline coincided with booming growth of the service economy, particularly financial and business services linked to Russia's natural resource exports. A showcase development is the Moscow City, a cluster of state-of-the-art skyscrapers in the center of Moscow near the White House. It is planned to become one of the largest business centers in the world. While employment and wages in science and high technology industry plummeted in the 1990s, higher education swelled, with hundreds of establishments providing education in newly popular professions such as economics, law, and finance.

Acute polarization in lifestyle and income between Moscow and the rest of Russia and abolishment of official residence restrictions (replaced by a semilegal registration system) led to further population increases. Official statistics indicate that, between 1990 and 2006, the population grew from slightly less than 9 million to 10.5 million people. Moscow traditionally was home to significant populations of ethnic Belarusians, Ukrainians, and Jews as well as Armenians, Georgians, and many other ethnic groups. The recent inflow of guest workers of non-Slavic origin (including migrants from ethnic regions of Russia and from ex-Soviet countries of Central Asia) has increased ethnic diversity and led to growing tension and recent outbreaks of hate crimes and ethnic violence. It is likely that ethnic enclaves will eventually form on the fringes of the city. However, no reliable data are available on the real size of newly immigrant population and its ethnic constitution. According to some estimates, the metropolis may actually house more than 14 million people.

A number of terrorist acts occurred between 1999 and 2004 (notably the Chechen separatist fighters taking hostages in a theater in 2000). These added to the usual list of security threats such as crime, ethnic violence, and civil unrest. Security measures were tightened in response, to the extent that in the late 2000s, special police forces were routinely deployed for patrolling important public places, subway, and transportation hubs.

Tripling of the Moscow population and incorporation of a very large territory into the city radius between 1930 and 1990 led to the continuation of a radial–concentric pattern of development coupled with incoherence of landscape and structure of the city districts. The established central city region inside the three- to five-kilometer (about two- to three-mile) radius from the Kremlin (the old Earth City radius and its surroundings populated in the eighteenth century) with its dense symbolic pattern became the meeting point of radial developments along major traffic ways. The outer central radius became crystallized in the late 1990s to early 2000s with the construction of the Third Circular Road. The area between the fringes of the central city and the *MKAD* was mostly built up throughout the twentieth century in a patchy pattern of planned districts and zones interspersed with stripes of marginal and sparsely developed land outside planned areas. In recent years, the differences in regulation and taxation between Moscow and the Moscow region led to proliferation of large trade complexes just outside the administrative boundaries. These include several large malls (frequently housing international retail chain outlets such as IKEA and Auchan). A new stage of housing construction put modern flat complexes in place of dilapidated *khrushchevkas*. However, real estate inside MKAD is often bought for investment and left uninhabited while displaced residents are forced to move to newly incorporated areas outside MKAD with insufficient transport connections and lack of amenities.

Moscow houses nine major railroad terminals, three international airports, and a domestic airport. The railroad carries relatively few daily intracity passengers, and mostly serves commuters from the Moscow region. Mass transit services in Moscow are predominantly publicly owned and include streetcars, buses, and trolleybuses (although several private companies offer bus services to complement regular routes). The cornerstone of Moscow mass transit is the subway. Currently transporting up to 9 million passengers per day, the subway since its inception has been the focal point of transport planning. Gradually, mass transit became geared to transporting passengers to the nearest subway station. Traffic jams skyrocketed after 2000 because of growing private car ownership and lack of planning for car traffic, virtually stalling all mass transit services except the subway.

Separation of Moscow and the rest of Russia grew throughout Soviet times and, owing to polarization of living standards and to the popular perception of Moscow as a culturally separate (globalized) place, continued after 1991. It was given further impetus with the recent strengthening of governmental vertical power. The city is separated internally, as well, with the historic center being symbolically in opposition to the greater part of Moscow territory; this indicates a Russian-doll reproduction of center–periphery patterns of spatial organization on different levels of Russian society.

Postsocialist Moscow, Global Moscow, Capitalist Moscow?

The rapid decline of traditional industry and expansion of business services, the retail economy, and education in the 1990s and 2000s was not followed by the rise of a real information economy. Quantitative expansion of education services was accompanied by a drastic reduction in their quality. While state power was in decline in 1990, the urban governance system under the all-powerful mayor crystallized in a machine-type coalition of business, administration, and shadow economy. In the 2000s, state power returned to manifest itself in ever-present policing of urban space and shrinking of public political freedoms. The real estate market suffers from lack of stable legal practices and the prevalence of shadow and criminal activities as well as the failure of the mortgage system. Paralysis of the overburdened transportation system leads to an increase in everyday stress for ordinary inhabitants of the city. The reverse side of boomtown increasingly reveals itself as a playground of negative consequences of the postsocialist transition and urban globalization processes.

Moscow is capable of both impressing and confusing an urban researcher. Foundations of the current spatial structure of the radial city were laid in the very beginning of Moscow's history. This structure has been repeated and consolidated ever since. Radial expansion from the central trading district toward the outer residential areas, coupled with the absence of major natural obstacles, tempts one to see the classical Chicago concentric model virtually imprinted into the rings and radii of Moscow landscapes. Yet Moscow defies traditional models and concepts such as the all too widespread labels of global, world, capitalist, or post-socialist. Their hasty application to Moscow reveals their weaknesses and limitations.

Overpopulation, traffic collapse, growing ethnic and civil tensions, precarious management and governance, mounting pollution, and ecological strain—these are only some challenges that Moscow has for its citizens and authorities. Before 1991, Moscow was one of the key sites of the great socialist experiment. After 1991, it underwent an experiment in forced construction of capitalism. In the coming years, it will likely remain an immense laboratory where important processes and pressing urban problems could be observed in their ongoing development. Hence, it will also be of lasting interest to urban research.

Nikita A. Kharlamov

See also Global City; Subway; Tenement; Urban Planning

Further Readings

Chase, William J. 1987. *Workers, Society, and the Soviet State: Labor and Life in Moscow, 1918–1929.* Urbana: University of Illinois Press.

Colton, Timothy J. 1995. *Moscow: Governing the Socialist Metropolis.* Cambridge, MA: The Belknap Press of Harvard University Press.

Dmitrieva, Marina. 2006. "Moscow Architecture between Stalinism and Modernism." *International Review of Sociology—Revue Internationale de Sociologie* 16(2):427–50.

Gritsai, Olga. 2004. "Global Business Services in Moscow: Patterns of Involvement." *Urban Studies* 41(10):2001–24.

O'Loughlin, John and Vladimir Kolossov, eds. 2002. "Moscow as an Emerging World City." Special issue. *Eurasian Geography and Economics* 43(3).

Paperny, Vladimir. 2002. *Architecture in the Age of Stalin: Culture Two.* Translated by John Hill and Roann Barris. Cambridge, UK: Cambridge University Press.

MOSES, ROBERT

Robert Moses (1888–1981) was one of the most influential figures involved in the planning and construction of urban infrastructure in the twentieth century. He has been both celebrated for his accomplishments—the completion of public works on a scale unrivaled by any other public official in American history—and sometimes vilified for the manner in which he achieved them. Most notably, among the projects that he oversaw were three enormous initiatives that changed the face of New York City: an extensive metropolitan network of highways and bridges that adapted the nation's largest city to the automobile age; dozens of public housing and urban renewal projects throughout the city; and new parks and recreational facilities in all five boroughs, including numerous public swimming pools, playgrounds, and the fairgrounds in Queens used for two world's fairs. Over his 50-year career as a public official, he earned a national reputation, such that he and his staff were sought after as consultants and expert advisers by many other cities across the United States.

Moses was not an architect or an engineer, nor was he formally trained as an urban planner, and all of his projects were designed and planned by others, but he is nevertheless widely regarded as the single individual most responsible for the shaping of modern New York City. This was a result of his remarkable ability to gather power, take advantage of ever changing funding streams, and cut through bureaucratic red tape to complete public works projects that others could only imagine.

Early Years

Born in 1888 in New Haven as the son of a department store owner, Moses had a comfortable middle-class upbringing. When he was nine years old, his family moved to Manhattan, where he attended private school before returning to New Haven to attend Yale as a 16-year-old in 1905. When he graduated in 1909, he was one of only five Jews in his class. An avid reader and reportedly brilliant student, he continued his education, first at Oxford and then at Columbia University, where he was awarded a PhD in political science in 1914. In England and New York, Moses investigated the inner workings of public bureaucracies, writing a dissertation on *The Civil Service of Great Britain*, while also completing a detailed assessment of New York City's civil service system for the Municipal Research Bureau, a nonprofit reform organization. This work led to a job in the administration of incoming New York Governor Al Smith in 1919, the first of the dozens of appointed positions in state and local government that Moses eventually held.

His civil service reform efforts failed to achieve any notable results. Governor Smith recognized Moses talents, however, and after reelection in 1922 made him a key member of the administration. At this point, Moses first got involved with large-scale public works. Smith relied on Moses' expert knowledge of government bureaucracies to loosen the rusty cogs of government and produce a visible and tangible record of accomplishment, starting with parks projects. Moses used his arcane expertise to draft legislation creating two new agencies, the Long Island State Park Commission and the State Council of Parks. Smith's electoral mandate ensured passage, and Moses was installed as chair of both entities. As he would do often over the course of his career, Moses paid careful attention to all the details of the enabling statutes to assure that these new agencies would be as flexible, durable, and powerful as possible.

Moses first big public works project was Jones Beach State Park, a brand-new public recreational facility, which opened to the public in 1930. As head of the Long Island State Park Commission, he used state funds to convert swampy, sparsely settled, and inaccessible dunes on the south shore of Long Island into elaborate bathhouses, fountains, monuments, and long pristine stretches of sandy beach, laced with landscaped paths and served by acres of new parking lots.

At the same time, to provide public access to the remotely located facility, Moses began work on a network of parkways spanning Long Island. The first of these were the Southern State Parkway (1927), the Wantagh State Parkway (1929), Ocean Parkway (1930), the beginnings of the Northern State Parkway (1930), and the Meadowbrook State Parkway (1934). These parkways, which earned Moses nationwide acclaim, were the product of his blend of ambition and pragmatism. They were *park*ways because he had not been put in charge of highways or roads, which were tightly controlled by the engineers at the State Highway Department and the federal Bureau of Public Roads. Instead, he had carefully written his commission's enabling statute to include the authority to build paths and access roads within parks. So, to build motorways throughout Long Island, he created ribbonlike parks with landscaped roads within them (i.e., parkways).

The idea was first demonstrated in nearby Westchester County, where the first modern American parkway, the Bronx River Parkway, had opened to great acclaim and public accolades in 1924. Heralded as a harbinger of a future where automobiles would enable the urban masses to drive through the countryside and escape the overcrowded city, the Bronx River Parkway invited duplication. Moses quickly stepped in, not only because he recognized the transformative social force of such transportation corridors, but also because he recognized that this type of project would garner the public and political support that civil service reform never had. In a pattern repeated often in his career, Moses adapted his activities to available funding streams, even while borrowing state-of-the-art planning and design ideas, like the modern parkway, that had been innovated or advanced by others.

As an opportunistic builder of public works, Moses was in the right place at the right time, partially by design but also somewhat by random chance. The unprecedented public spending initiatives of the New Deal coincided with the success of his first parks and parkway projects. His new reputation as a man who could get things done could not have come at a better time.

New York and the New Deal

In 1933, he was put in charge of New York's Emergency Public Works Commission and in 1934 incoming Mayor Fiorello La Guardia appointed him City Parks Commissioner. In these new roles, Moses used federal work-relief grants, alongside state and city park funds, to go on a massive citywide building spree: public swimming pools, new sports and recreation fields, and hundreds of new playgrounds throughout the five boroughs. He extended the network of Long Island parkways, completing the Interborough Parkway (now known as the Jackie Robinson Parkway) in 1934, the Grand Central Parkway in 1936, and both the Belt Parkway and the Long Island Expressway in 1940.

Furthermore, his highway-building activities were no longer limited to Long Island. In Manhattan, he oversaw the completion of the last stages of the West Side Highway and spearheaded the West Side Improvement Project. This latter project included an extensive relandscaping of Riverside Park as well as the construction of the Henry Hudson Parkway, which upon its completion in 1937 extended along the Hudson River waterfront for seven miles before weaving through the Bronx to the city line. In suburban Westchester County, he helped to supervise the Saw Mill Parkway in 1935 and the Hutchinson River Parkway in 1941. To knit all of these routes together, Moses oversaw a number of crucial bridge projects, including the Triborough Bridge and the Henry Hudson Memorial Bridge, both of which opened in 1936, and the Bronx-Whitestone Bridge, which he brought to completion in 1939.

Moses drew extensively on New Deal grants and available state funds, and on many of these projects, he also installed toll booths to bring in additional money. This enabled him to borrow against these revenues, either to complete underfunded projects or to fund subsequent initiatives. The biggest such revenue generator, by far, was the Triborough Bridge, the keystone of Moses' growing empire. Moses was able to use the toll revenues from the Triborough Bridge Authority, combined with the revenue streams flowing into his other bridge and parkway authorities, to continue building, even after the end of the Depression-era work-relief programs. This strategy, using public benefit corporations to build and perpetuate his power, was—like his earlier emulation of the innovations of the Bronx River Parkway—modeled after the Port of New York Authority run by Austin Tobin, which had established precedents that Moses would adapt to his own purposes. Similarly, the Triborough Bridge itself had also been conceived, initiated, and approved by others before Moses completed the job. Construction had proceeded haltingly and had finally stopped altogether at the onset of the Depression, but Moses' opportunistic administrative and resource-gathering skills rescued the endeavor.

A few years later, Moses expanded his reach even further. When the NYC Tunnel Authority ran out of money part way through the construction of the Queens-Midtown Tunnel in 1938, he rescued the project, completed it by 1940, and took over the controlling agency, eventually merging it with Triborough to form the Triborough Bridge and Tunnel Authority, his main base of operations for the next quarter century.

Moses' Depression-era reach extended well beyond parks and parkways. In 1936, because of his proven track record of successfully pushing projects through to completion, Mayor LaGuardia put him in charge of the newly created New York City World's Fair Commission. To prepare for the fair, which would be held in 1939, Moses oversaw the construction of the Flushing Meadows Park on a waterfront site in Queens formerly occupied by ash dumps. In addition, he supervised the construction of new access highways and parking lots and the erection of the exhibit buildings—including GM's famous Futurama and the iconic Perisphere building, which housed the Democracity display, both of which presented fairgoers with visions of cities of the future not unlike the one Moses was trying to build for New York, far-flung and expansive, yet held together by a web of highways and bridges. In Moses' vision, and in the World's Fair exhibits, there was an underlying assumption that everyone would be dependent on private automobiles for transportation.

Postwar Power

After the end of World War II, Americans did, in fact, increasingly turn to automobiles for routine transportation, not just for recreational excursions. As a consequence, toll revenues steadily increased on Moses' bridges and parkways, fueling the growth, stability, and reach of his empire. For certain, he was no longer dependent on park funds, as he had been when he started. So, his highways no longer emphasized the carefully landscaped borders and medians of his earlier *park*ways, instead becoming more like *express*ways—less scenic, wider, and more efficient. After 1956, when federal interstate highway grants began to flow freely, Moses abandoned parkway design aesthetic entirely.

This gradual transition can be seen by comparing his earlier parkways to the highway projects he worked on in the postwar era, including the Van Wyck Expressway (1950), the Sprain Brook Parkway (1953), the Prospect Expressway (1955), the Major Degan Expressway (1956–1961), the New England Thruway (1958), the Cross Bronx Expressway (1963), the Whitestone Expressway (1963), and the Staten Island Expressway (1964). His overall approach did not change, however, and even while the design of his highway projects shifted to adapt to the constraints and objectives of state and federal grant programs, he nevertheless continued to expand his own independent revenue base by building toll bridges, including the Throgs

Neck Bridge (1961) and the Verrazano Narrows Bridge (1962).

With steadily growing funding from toll collections, Moses became less and less dependent on the political support of mayors and governors. In fact, they soon became dependent on him and his stellar public works record, his flush bank accounts, and his easy access to the capital markets that arose from the ever-growing stream of toll revenues. Furthermore, they discovered that they could not control him. His various official positions were for staggered, overlapping, or even perpetual terms, and he was in charge of so many different agencies that he had made himself indispensable. In fact, his list of positions actually lengthened as politicians continued to ask for his help on a widening array of tasks. In 1946, he took on three important new posts. He was asked to chair the Mayor's Committee for a Permanent World Capital and was centrally involved in the process that eventually brought the United Nations to its current site in New York. He was also appointed to the newly created position of City Construction Coordinator and designated the chair of the Emergency Committee on Housing.

Moses' next wholesale citywide initiatives, slum clearance and urban renewal, serve as another example of his shrewd and opportunistic approach to public works. He seemed to be at his best in situations that called for someone to rapidly and efficiently draw down federal and state funds for ambitious undertakings. To alleviate the postwar housing shortage and poor conditions in many urban neighborhoods, the federal government was prepared to devote enormous sums to the twin goals of slum clearance and public housing construction. Yet again, Moses was the right man at the right place and time. His repertoire expanded to encompass this new activity under the auspices of the Slum Clearance Committee, which he chaired on its creation in 1949.

Moses knew that a key to success in this endeavor would be preparation. Accordingly, he tried to anticipate each successive federal initiative so that he could be ready and waiting with turnkey plans and applications. Ultimately, he would oversee numerous low- and middle-income housing projects throughout the city as well as huge redevelopment efforts for educational and civic institutions. Best-known among these are the New York Coliseum, which was completed in 1956 and has since been replaced by the Time Warner Center at Columbus Circle, and the Lincoln Center for the Performing Arts, which opened in 1962. The largest performing arts complex in the world, Lincoln Center provided new and modern state-of-the-art facilities for the New York Philharmonic, the New York City Ballet, the New York City Opera, the Metropolitan Opera, the Public Library for the Performing Arts, and the Juilliard School.

Moses' activities had the greatest impact in the New York City metropolitan area, but his power also reached across the farthest corners of the state. In 1935, he arranged for the construction of two bridges connecting Grand Island to the mainland near Buffalo. He was also responsible for the Thousand Islands Bridge to Canada, near Massena, which opened in 1938. Later, as chair of the New York State Power Authority, he presided over the financing and construction of a hydroelectric power dam on the St. Lawrence and Niagara rivers in 1958 and 1961, respectively. In both instances, he simultaneously created new state parks, and the scenic parkway he built at the Niagara site is now known as Robert Moses Parkway.

Declining Years

In the late nineteen fifties and early sixties, even as his power was extending into these new areas and his responsibilities grew to encompass an ever-larger range of public works activities, Moses ran into a series of setbacks that eventually led to his ouster. Granted, he had experienced occasional defeats earlier in his career, interspersed among his many high-profile successes. The most visible of these were his failed run for governor in 1934 and his attempt to build a Brooklyn-Battery Bridge in the forties. The later defeats, however, were more frequent and more damaging. This was partially because some of his later initiatives were inherently more controversial, but it was also a consequence of his imperious manner. As his power and activities expanded, he demonstrated little patience or sympathy for those who opposed his projects, nor for those who would attempt to supervise him. From the grassroots to the backrooms at City Hall and the State House, opposition to Moses was quietly growing.

The newspapers first turned a consistently critical eye toward Moses' projects when a crowd of stroller-pushing Manhattan housewives blocked a team of his bulldozers on their way to build a new parking lot in Central Park in 1956. This was followed in 1959 by another public relations disaster when he tried to prevent Joseph Papp from offering free Shakespeare performances in city parks. That same year, he was ensnared in ongoing scandals involving contractors and developers working on his slum clearance projects. Moses himself was never implicated in the improprieties, but the bad publicity tarnished his reputation nonetheless.

To make matters worse, his next round of major highway projects ran into stiff and well-organized opposition. He urged the construction of two huge cross-Manhattan Expressways that had been on the drawing boards since the twenties, one through midtown and one across lower Manhattan. His latest bridge project, an enormous effort to cross Long Island Sound, also faced powerful resistance. Each of these proposals carried the prospect of considerable disruption. The expressway projects in particular seemed to threaten the urban fabric of Manhattan, the heart of the metropolis. The resultant stream of bad publicity and public outcry provided an opportunity for elected politicians to chip away at Moses' power.

Gradually, he was forced to give up his many positions. In 1960, he relinquished most of his New York City positions in exchange for a seven-year contract as head of the 1964 World's Fair. The 1939 site in Queens would be reused for this return engagement, but Moses took charge of the extensive renovation and expansion of many of the park and highway facilities in the area, as well as the construction of Shea Stadium (1962). At the state level, Governor Nelson Rockefeller began to reclaim power from Moses starting in 1962, appointing new officials to take Moses' seats on state agencies, one by one. Finally, in 1968, Rockefeller merged the Triborough Bridge and Tunnel Authority into the newly formed Metropolitan Transportation Authority and in so doing removed Robert Moses from power altogether.

Moses died in 1981 in West Islip, Long Island.

Owen D. Gutfreund

See also Jacobs, Jane; New York City, New York; New York World's Fair, 1939; Parks; Public Authorities; Transportation; Urban Planning

Further Readings

Ballon, Hilary and Kenneth T. Jackson, eds. 2007. *Robert Moses and the Modern City: The Transformation of New York.* New York: W. W. Norton.
Caro, Robert A. 1974. *The Power Broker: Robert Moses and the Fall of New York.* New York: Random House.
Krieg, Joann P., ed. 1989. *Robert Moses: Single-minded Genius.* Hempstead, NY: Long Island Studies Institute.
Moses, Robert. 1970. *Public Works: A Dangerous Trade.* New York: McGraw-Hill.

MOTEL

See Hotel, Motel

MULTICULTURAL CITIES

At the beginning of the third millennium, more than half of the global population lives in cities. In addition, the United Nations reports that 3 percent of the global population lives outside of their country of birth. That is, 191 million people worldwide are classified as migrants. Patterns of international migration, economic integration, and globalization are said to fuel cultural diversity within urban centers. The ramifications of these processes, which are by no means new phenomena, unfold at the local level, meaning that neighborhoods and urban communities are transformed by the social, cultural, and economic diversity of their new arrivals. This richness also poses dilemmas and challenges. Examining what multicultural cities implicate, then, is central to urban social scientists. The multicultural city as a unit of social scientific study, however, is not without its limitations. These will be discussed first. Next, some cities that narrate themselves as multicultural will be described. Last, integration as a means of multicultural urban production will be reviewed.

Concepts in Multicultural Cities

In the social sciences, multicultural cities are conceptualized in a couple of ways. Multicultural cities that follow melting-pot models develop policies that target homogeneity. It has been said that this is a common model in the United States. Multicultural cities that follow mosaic models target the preservation of pluralism and difference. This has been a model that Canada has made famous. The latter is sometimes said to be preferable because it allows individuals and groups to retain and practice their identity. These models are somewhat problematic, however, as it is observed and experienced in some cities with a long history of immigration, such as Toronto, that classification is impossible and futile, if not implicitly or explicitly racist. A demographic and descriptive meaning of multicultural refers to the coexistence of a heterogeneity of cultures within a specified area. As Vince Marotta has noted, too, demographic–descriptive meanings raise some curious questions about multicultural cities in general. At what point is a city multicultural? How many supposed cultures must be present before a city can appropriately label itself as such? Are there any homogeneous cities in the world at all?

Central to the concept of multiculturalism is the notion of difference. All models of multicultural cities require a categorization of difference at some level. Marotta also observed that the demographic meaning of multiculturalism posits difference along a problematic continuum spanning from heterogeneity toward homogeneity. Kanishka Goonewardena and Stefan Kipfer have noted the hybridity or creolization of Torontonians, and the resulting nonexisting plurality. Plurality cannot exist if members of so-called ethnic groups do not replicate their cultural norms. Zygmunt Bauman has also written extensively on the liquid character of modern cities. The category of culture, then, is a myth, similar to the mythical categories of sex and gender as discussed by poststructuralist Judith Butler. From a radical poststructural stance, then, the multicultural city is nothing more than a social construction.

All of the objectives of a multicultural city are about confrontations with, and attempts to resolve, otherness. This interaction among others is also what Marotta noted as the difference between what he calls multiethnic (having a lot of different ethnic groups) and multicultural (having some appreciable level of interaction among these groups). As socially constructed as the category of other may ultimately be, it may still be a useful tool in identifying social disparities and locating conflict, as well as resolutions and fusions, among various identity groups.

The Multicultural Narrative

Labeling a city is also ultimately an urban narrative. It involves capturing a snapshot representation of any given urban space, at any given point in time, and describing it, interpreting it, and attaching values to it: a café latte to go; a lecture given by a second-generation Tamil professor; perogies in Thai sauce for lunch; a workshop with fellow students, none of whom speak English with their parents; a subway home to Little Greece for a break; and a relaxing evening with a friend over a Heineken or a piña colada at an Asian-techno dance club. This might be one such personal narrative in a multicultural city. This particular one is a story of consumption.

An infinite number of trajectories can be dreamed up or experienced in a multicultural city. In light of globalization and transnationalization of economies and peoples, city administrations around the world—particularly in countries of the capitalist democratic tradition—promote and celebrate their social diversity. At official city home pages and in tourist guides, the demographic multicultural narrative is often marketed as an attractive feature of the city. Goonewardena and Kipfer, however, argue that such metanarratives are dangerous. They are—especially in the consumption and commodification suggested by the narratives above—top-down identification processes.

Enter the words "multicultural city" into the Google search engine and information about Toronto is the first link to appear. Also easy to find are New York, Los Angeles, Sydney, London, and Amsterdam as among the most multicultural cities in the world. By visiting the official web pages of these cities, one can easily get a picture of their demographics. The categories used in this section are those chosen by the respective city administrations.

In the Greater Toronto area, a population of more than 5.5 million speaks more than 140 languages.

More than 30 percent speak a language other than English or French at home. After English, the five most common languages are Chinese (Cantonese or Mandarin), Italian, Punjabi, Tagalog, and Portuguese. Five percent have no knowledge of the official Canadian languages, French or English. Forty-seven percent report themselves as members of a visible minority. More than half of Toronto's residents were born outside of Canada. Twenty percent of Canada's immigrants have settled in Toronto, and between 2001 and 2006, about 55,000 new immigrants were received annually.

Sydney, a city of 4.3 million, celebrates its cultural diversity and declares that multiculturalism is one of the main factors contributing to the city's social, cultural, and economic success. Most commonly, newcomers immigrated from the United Kingdom. Others came from China, New Zealand, Indonesia, South Korea, Thailand, Hong Kong, Malaysia, and Vietnam. In 2006, Mandarin was the second most common language after English, followed by Cantonese, Indonesian, Korean, Greek, Russian, Spanish, and Vietnamese.

More than 300 languages are spoken in London, and migrants are reported to have originated from more than 160 countries. In 2005, the Greater London Authority reported census findings to affirm that the city had become more diverse in recent years. In 2001, the percentage of Whites had declined to 71.2 percent from 79.8 percent in 1991. The remaining 28.8 percent included Blacks, Chinese, Asians, and people of mixed race. The Oxford Economic Ltd. reported that the foreign-born population increased by 546,000 from 1991 to 2001. At the time of the 2001 census, London's population was 24.8 percent foreign born. More than half of the population is Christian, but London is also home to 40 Hindu temples, 25 Sikh temples, and more than 150 mosques.

On continental Europe, Amsterdam and Berlin are two cities that celebrate their diversity. Amsterdam is home to residents representing more than 170 nationalities, and 45 percent of its residents are classified as belonging to ethnic minorities The classifications were Surinam, Antillean, Turkish, Moroccan, other non-Western foreigners; Western foreigners; and native Dutch. Of Berlin's 3.4 million people, 13.7 percent carry a non-German passport. The most common country of origin is Turkey, followed by Poland, Serbia, and Montenegro. In total, 80 nationalities are represented in Berlin.

Turning to American examples, Los Angeles and New York stand out. Los Angeles, an enormous city with an estimated population nearing 10 million, is 46.5 percent Hispanic, 29.7 percent White/non-Hispanic, 10.9 percent African American, 9.9 percent Asian, 2.4 percent multiracial, 0.2 percent American Indian, 0.2 percent other, and 0.1 percent Pacific Islander. Of New York's 8 million residents, 36 percent are foreign born. Those born in South or Central America numbered more than 1.5 million. The second-largest group was those born in Asia. They numbered 687,000.

There are some immediate observations that one might have to these demographics. First, direct comparison is difficult because of the different data sets collected by each city. Some city administrations use "foreign born" to identify immigrants. These overlook second-, third-, fourth-, or fifth-generation immigrants. Some city administrations measure their population according to citizenship. This classification overlooks the already naturalized. Some use language. Some use religion. Some use the rather dubious classification of skin color.

Second, simple statistical diversity reveals little about the interactive character of the city. Is there segregation? Are there social disparities? If so, along what demarcations does this fragmentation occur? Although it celebrates its diversity, for example, Los Angeles has had the worst race riots in American history. The various communities are also geographically isolated and segregated. Optimistic liberal demographic narratives, then, can easily overlook real existing social disparities, which emerge, according to Goonewardena and Kipfer, through bottom-up social struggle and self-identification. Multicultural urban formations cannot merely refer to a static composition of identities collected within a certain territory. Rather it needs to call to mind the transformatory and shifting condition of urban spaces where interactions transpire between and across differences.

Integration as a Means of Multicultural Urban Production

In 2005, the Berliner Senate concluded the document titled *Encouraging Diversity—Strengthening Cohesion,* which was written as a guideline for integration policy for Berlin. In practice, integration is the mechanism through which multicultural cities are produced, which is reached when no systematic differences can be identified along distribution of social position, status, and resources (e.g., money, appearance, occupation, living standards). That is, when everyone is not necessarily the same but equal. It is perhaps overly idealistic and simplistic to believe that this is possible, but if this goal is ever to be met, certain objectives need to be addressed in policy and in social praxis. Among other things, there must be (1) a general acceptance of newcomers and encouragement of their participation and upward mobility, (2) recognition of multiple citizenships, (3) the possibility of public communication in a variety of languages, (4) the acceptance of alternate codes of attire, and (5) a political means of participation that is conscious of difference. Most cities that promote themselves as multicultural address at least some of the aforementioned factors. All still have many obstacles to overcome.

Segregated Communities

The acceptance of difference and co-presence of newcomers is a goal of just about all of the cities mentioned. How this plays out, however, is varied. The formation of ghettos or the presence/absence of xenophobic practices may be indicators of general acceptance of newcomers. In Los Angeles, the various groups are concentrated into particular corners of the city and constitute African American ghettos, Latino and Mexican barrios, and middle- and upper-class Anglo-Saxon gated communities. This extreme segregation is not conducive to exchange and enrichment through diversity and difference.

In Berlin, newcomers are overrepresented in the neighborhoods of Kreuzberg, Neuköln, and Wedding. Toronto is also divided up into a variety of neighborhoods, such as Little India, Little Italy, Little Portugal, or Chinatown. In the cases of Berlin and Toronto, however, the respective neighborhoods are well connected to and serviced by the wider city. Residence in these neighborhoods is a result of neither economic nor violent pressure. These areas do not, therefore, constitute ghettos in the social science sense. In Berlin, certain districts, on the other hand, are viewed as dangerous to people with darker skin color. Violent crimes committed

by neo-Nazis became commonplace enough that some were willing to publish warnings to prospective visitors.

During the summer of 2006, Germany was host to the World Cup. Shortly before it began, the Africarat in Berlin circulated 10,000 flyers that warned of no-go areas in Berlin. This sparked massive public debate. Yet despite recognition of the problem in the public discourse that newcomers felt unsafe in some areas, in 2006, Berliner citizens voted members of the National Democratic Party of Germany—seen by some as the direct successor to Adolf Hitler's National Socialist German Worker's Party—into four district parliaments across the city. Obviously, such currents are not favorable to diversity and equality.

Citizenship and Language

Recognition of multiple citizenships is essential so that immigrants can maintain economic as well as social transnational ties. This issue, however, is also handled differently among the various nations. Newcomers may retain multiple citizenships in the United States, Canada, Australia, and Britain. About 85 percent of Toronto's population retains Canadian citizenship. Newcomers to Amsterdam, in contrast, must renounce former citizenships to obtain Dutch citizenship. Former passports must also be renounced when applying for German citizenship—unless the former nationality was within the European Union. Children born in Germany, who have one German parent, are also permitted to keep the nationalities of both parents. Germany actively campaigns for the German passport and urges landed residents to assume citizenship. Despite its efforts, however, rates of naturalization have not increased. As a result, German politicians have begun reviewing the laws governing immigration and looking for ways that might ease the process.

To overcome language barriers, the city of Toronto has a language service hotline that is ready to translate more than 150 languages. Public documents and notices are published by the city administration in 10 languages. Street signs are written in different alphabets. The city administrations for London, New York, and Sydney also offer translations in various languages. Los Angeles offers Spanish, Cantonese, or

Mandarin translation services for council meetings. To acquire these services, the Los Angeles Council and Public Services must be contacted at least 72 hours in advance.

Dress Codes

There are two strategies of dealing with codes of attire. The first is a strategy that adopts acceptance of a diversity of appearances. The second strategy demands a condition of neutrality. Sikh men, for example, have been confronted with this problem and have fought to be able to wear a turban and carry a *kirpan* (a ceremonial sword)—symbols of their Sikh faith—in schools and in the workplace. In Canada and England, this attire is permitted. Employers and schools must align their dress codes to accommodate the religious freedom of their workers. Thus, Canadian Mounted Police of the Sikh faith may wear a turban in place of the traditional broad-rimmed cap, and Sikh school boys may carry a kirpan to school despite the regulations of some schools to ban weapons. In the United States, Sikhs have been fighting for this right on a case by case basis. Between 2001 and 2007, there were more than 20 successful court cases—including one in Los Angeles and four in New York City—in which Sikh men won the right to wear their religious symbols.

In Germany, dress codes are governed at the state level. Berlin, a city-state, has taken the route of the second strategy. Wearing religious symbols in workplaces where neutral clothing is demanded, such as in civil services and schools, is not permitted. This applies to Christian crosses, Jewish yarmulkes, Muslim tschadors or hijabs, or Sikh turbans and kirpans—all of which are prohibited.

Models of political discourse are perhaps one of the hottest topics facing multicultural cities today. They are discussed widely in twentieth-century political theory. A famous debate between Jürgen Habermas and Nancy Fraser illustrates two essential poles to the discussion. Habermas argued that one open public sphere in which all members participate on equal footing was the ideal political forum. Fraser, in response, argued that this was impossible. For a variety of reasons, women—or others in general—could not expect to compete on an equal basis. The outcome would be that alternative discourse would inevitably be drowned out by so-called common interest topics. To account for difference, then, Fraser argued for alternative public spheres. These were forums targeted for specific groups, who could then meet in an exclusive sphere to discuss their ideas and develop their counterdiscourse, which could later be brought back to a common wider forum. Habermas and Fraser then represent two models of participation: the melting-pot public forum and the plurality of forums.

In practical terms, the Province of Ontario in Canada in 2006 overturned the use of shari`ah law as a form of family arbitration. It was decided that it would not be acceptable because the code of ethics existing under shari`ah law would undermine Canadian Muslim women. Muslim women who did not have the means to hire a lawyer would have little choice but to turn to a Muslim-based tribunal, which would disadvantage them. Their access to the equal treatment of individuals guaranteed under the Canadian constitution was thereby severely hindered. This decision immediately called into the question the legitimacy of Roman Catholic, Jewish, and Aboriginal arbitration, which too were rendered legally unbinding.

The openness to, and recognition of, diversity and self-proclaimed difference is most certainly a positive response to increased urbanization and international migration. It is more, however, than the self-image of a city as spatial agglomeration of articulated social segments, as suggested by demographic multiculturalism. On a conceptual level, careful thought needs to be given to the consequences of classification and essentialization of individuals and social groups into mythical categories of otherness, and to the risk of getting caught in the liberal–pluralist trap that the commodification of culture ensures. Multiculturalism addresses a nonstatic, dynamic interplay of differences through time. On a practical level, integration as a mechanism of building multicultural spaces is a very complex process. Measures must carefully address social, political, and economic needs of residents, as well as compensate for, and respond to, social spatial and temporal urban transformations. It will remain a constant project for residents of multicultural cities, therefore, to keep up with social changes and to promote and encourage social diversity, inclusion, and equality.

Constance Carr

See also Berlin, Germany; Creative Class; Cultural Heritage; Ethnic Enclave; Ethnic Entrepreneurship; Ghetto; Global City; Globalization; Racialization; Urban Culture; World City

Further Readings

Bauman, Zygmunt. 2007. *Liquid Times: Living in an Age of Uncertainty.* Cambridge, UK: Polity Press.

Butler, Judith. 2006. *Gender Trouble.* New York: Routledge.

Commissioner for Integration and Migration of the Senate of Berlin. 2005. *Encouraging Diversity—Strengthening Cohesion: Integration Policy in Berlin.* Berlin: Commissioner for Integration and Migration of the Senate of Berlin.

Fraser, N. 1993. "Rethinking the Public Sphere: A Contribution to the Critique of Actually Existing Democracy." In *The Phantom Public Sphere,* edited by Bruce Robbins. Minneapolis: University of Minnesota Press.

Goonewardena, Kanishka and Stefan Kipfer. 2004. "Creole City: Culture, Class, and Capital in Toronto." Pp. 224–29 in *Contested Metropolis,* edited by Raffaele Paloscia. Basel, Switzerland: Birkhauser.

Greater London Authority, Data Management and Analysis Group. 2005. *London—the World in a City.* London: Greater London Authority.

Habermas, Jürgen. 1989. *The Structural Transformation of the Public Sphere: An Inquiry into a Category of Bourgeois Society.* Cambridge: MIT Press.

Marotta, Vince. 2007. "Multicultural and Multiethnic Cities in Australia." Pp. 41–62 in *Ethnic Landscapes in an Urban World,* edited by Ray Hutchison and Jerome Krase. Amsterdam: Elsevier.

Oxford Economics Ltd. 2007. *London's Place in the U.K. Economy, 2007–2008.* London: City of London.

MUMBAI (BOMBAY), INDIA

Mumbai, formerly known as Bombay, is an island city located on India's west coast; with a population of 18 million people, it is one of the largest cities in the world. Mumbai is responsible for more than half of India's foreign trade, has become a center for the country's global dealings in financial and producer services, and constitutes 40 percent of the state's annual direct central revenue. Since India's economic liberalization reforms in 1985 and 1991, Mumbai's economy, particularly the southwest area of Nariman Point, has increasingly globalized.

Mumbai occupies a key site in the Indian modern economic and cultural imagination. The city has often been described as inevitably cosmopolitan, given its economic and cultural diversity, drawing Hindus, Muslims, Parsis, Christians, Sikhs, Jains, and others. The city is home to Bollywood, the Hindi film industry, which produces more films than any other film industry in the world, films that combine dancing, simple melodies, and extravagant spectacles with narratives of everyday life. Mumbai has a varied cultural life beyond Bollywood, evidenced, for example, in its large Marathi or Gujarati literary history.

Historically, Mumbai has been a focus for global trade around the Arabian Sea and beyond, owing in large part to its endowment with one of the largest natural harbors in South Asia. Originally a collection of seven fishing islands, Mumbai was established as a Portuguese outpost in the early sixteenth century and was passed to the British crown in 1662 as part of a marriage dowry. From the mid-nineteenth century, it was transformed into a booming industrial city, especially in textiles. The city's first textile mill was established in the 1850s; and when the U.S. Civil War cut off cotton imports from America, Bombay became Britain's principal cotton supplier.

The colonial city was split between a walled fort to the south, well supplied with housing and infrastructures, and a neglected native town. The city's geographical extent advanced through massive programs of land reclamation from the sea. By the 1860s, it had been established as one of the leading ports and manufacturing centers of the British Empire, and south Bombay had assembled much of its famous Bombay Gothic British–Indian architecture, most notably the spectacular train station, Victoria Terminus.

Contemporary Mumbai is the capital of the state of Maharashtra, the state with the highest-ranking per capita income in India; it constitutes 20 percent of the state's GDP. Despite the city's generally impressive economic statistics, there was a drop from 7 percent to 2.4 percent in the city's GDP per annum between 1994 and 2002. Often referred to as India's maximum city, Mumbai is the country's most unequal city. More than half of the city's population lives in informal settlements of varying infrastructure, income, economy, ethnicity, and religion, squeezed into whatever space can be found, from bridges and railways to pavements and shantytowns.

The growth in informal settlements reflects both the spectacular and ongoing rise in real estate prices during the 1990s, driven by the city's economic growth and orchestrated through an often corrupt coalition of the state, builders, developers, and the city's infamous underworld, along with the inadequacy of the state's social housing commitment. Most people in informal settlements lack security of tenure, live in poor-quality housing vulnerable to monsoon rains, suffer from frequent bouts of state or private demolition, lack access to sufficient and clean water and sanitation facilities, and live in highly polluted environments vulnerable to illness and disease. Given that there is often a weak relationship between income and access to basic services and infrastructures in Mumbai's informal settlements, it is unlikely that economic growth itself could be a solution to these issues.

If Mumbai is often described as India's most modern city, this discourse has taken a new turn with the emergence of a new managerial and technical elite associated with the growth of global financial services in particular parts of the city. Radjani Mazumdar charted the increasing escape of Mumbai's urban elite from the "city of debris" to the "city of spectacle"—that is, from the city of informal settlements, dense neighborhoods, street hawkers, traffic congestion, construction debris, and refuse to the city of elite design and consumption of high-end housing, entertainment, shopping, and associated service industries. Despite a bitter union struggle, the mills have all but closed.

In this context, recent years have witnessed intense debates around the transformation of public space. Two recent controversial rulings by the Supreme Court are instructive: one would transform two-thirds of the vacant mill lands in the center of the city not into social housing as many had hoped but into shopping malls and corporate entertainment; and a second allows the redevelopment of 19,000 of Mumbai's dilapidated buildings—often *chawls,* the traditional double-story 100-square-foot tenements used to house mill workers—which many commentators worry will create more elite housing enclaves with little public space.

Much recent research on Mumbai focuses on the nature and effects of economic liberalization and deindustrialization and the breakdown of class-based affiliations—these followed, in particular, the 1982 textile strike—and their replacement with collective identity rooted in ethnic and religious chauvinism. The idea of the city as cosmopolitan is a constant feature in narratives of its recent decline. Most discussions of cosmopolitanism in Mumbai focus on communal tension, tolerance, and violence, and a range of commentators have remarked on a decline of the cosmopolitan city, marking as a watershed the communal riots and bombings that occurred in the early 1990s.

This is due in particular to the mass riots that took place in late 1992 and early 1993, which followed the destruction of the Babri Masjid in Ayodhya in north India by Hindu extremists. The events spurred existing local tensions, resulting in the worst riots in the city's history: 900 people were killed and the psychosocial geography of the city was drastically altered. The riots were followed by 13 bomb blasts on March 12, 1993, the most destructive bomb explosions in Indian history, which killed more than 250 and left 700 injured. The bombs targeted key political and economic structures in the city, including the stock exchange and the political headquarters of the Hindu extremist party, the Shiv Sena (Shivaji's Army), and were widely interpreted as retaliation by Muslim gangs in response to the riots.

Tensions between Mumbai's different groups were, of course, present in the city before these riots. In 1984, the city witnessed the first major communal riots since independence. In many of these cases, the Shiv Sena played a crucial mobilizing role. One of the most xenophobic regional parties in India, the zenith of the Sena movement arrived when the party made it into power at both the city and state level in Maharashtra in 1995. During its time in state government, the party renamed Bombay as Mumbai. This renaming should not be viewed as a straightforward effort to shake off a British colonial heritage; it is an active attempt to reinscribe the space of the city as Hindu, to the exclusion, in particular, of Muslims.

In recent years, a mass program of demolition of informal settlements has been driven not just by ethnicity, but by politico–corporate Mumbai's self-declared trajectory to become the next

Shanghai by 2013. As part of this, an estimated 90,000 huts were torn down during the winter of 2004 and 2005, leaving some 350,000 people homeless and without alternative accommodation. This agenda is caught up with a variety of processes in the city, including a current effort to demolish Dharavi, one of Asia's largest slums, and construct a world-class cultural, knowledge, business, and health center in its place; the proliferation of securitized and high-end shopping malls, gated communities, and gentrified neighborhoods; the growth of Special Economic Zones (SEZs); and even a new town—*Maha Mumbai*—planned and built by the huge infrastructure firm Reliance Energy—explicitly aimed at imitating rival global locations like Dubai's Jebel Ali and the SEZ phenomenon in China.

If urban conflict has been one focus of research on Mumbai, narratives of violence resurfaced following bombings on July 11, 2006, when 200 people were killed and more than 700 injured when seven bombs exploded within the space of 11 minutes during rush hour on the city's commuter rail network, the busiest domestic rail system in the world. The police claimed the bombings were carried out by Lashkar-e-Toiba and Students Islamic Movement of India, both Islamist militant organizations banned in India. Lashkar have also been blamed for the street terrorism of November 2008, in which at least 173 people were killed. However, events have shown that in the face of violence or crisis, Mumbaikers often exhibit generosity and a determined spirit. After the bombings, people scrambled to assist the emergency services in treating victims and transporting them to hospitals. Within hours, the wreckage had been cleared, and the railway system was up and running again.

Mumbai has seen similar responses to adversity from its citizenry. For example, when the 2005 monsoon floods killed more than 1,000 people, predominantly in informal settlements, and left thousands stranded in floods that covered one-third of the city's surface and that reached almost five meters in depth in low-lying areas, there was no looting, theft, or violence but rather an outpouring of spontaneous acts of kindness and generosity. While state authorities were in disarray and largely abdicated responsibility, media reports were full of stories of slum dwellers rescuing those stranded in cars, offering *chai* and biscuits and in many cases a room to sleep in.

Colin McFarlane

See also Colonial City; Global City; Kolkata (Calcutta), India

Further Readings

D'Monte, D. 2002. *Ripping the Fabric: The Decline of Mumbai and Its Mills*. New Delhi: Oxford University Press.

Hansen, T. B. 2001. *Wages of Violence: Naming and Identity in Postcolonial Bombay*. Princeton, NJ: Princeton University Press.

Mazumdar, R. 2007. *Bombay Cinema: An Archive of the City*. Minneapolis: University of Minnesota Press.

Mehta, S. 2004. *Maximum City: Bombay Lost and Found*. London: Review.

Patel, S. and J. Masselos, eds. 2003. *Bombay and Mumbai: The City in Transition*. Oxford, UK: Oxford University Press.

Patel, Sujata and Alice Thorner, eds. 1995. *Bombay: Metaphor for Modern India*. Oxford, UK: Oxford University Press.

———. 1995. *Bombay: Mosaic of Modern Culture*. Oxford, UK: Oxford University Press.

Pinto, R. and N. Fernandes, eds. 2003. *Bombay, meri jaan*. New Delhi: Penguin.

Zaidi, H. S. 2003. *Black Friday: The True Story of the Bombay Bomb Blasts*. New Delhi: Penguin.

MUMFORD, LEWIS

Lewis Mumford (1895–1990) is widely recognized as a major American intellectual, who, despite his self-definition as a "generalist," is known primarily as an authority on technology, architecture, and urbanism and secondarily as a scholar of American culture. Yet, he remains a somewhat misunderstood figure in the twenty-first century, especially regarding cities. He was the most committed American disciple of both Patrick Geddes and Ebenezer Howard, advocating consistently for the creation of interconnected garden cities within a regional framework. Especially in later years, Mumford was labeled anti-urban, but more correctly, he was antimetropolitan in the manner of

Howard. Cities must reach a critical mass before they could sustain a viable culture, he argued; however, if too large, they would choke on their own successes.

Early Years

Mumford was born in 1895 in Queens County, New York. His mother, a widow, had become pregnant unexpectedly, and she raised her young son on Manhattan's Upper West Side. What could have been a solitary childhood was happily relieved by the close bond Mumford forged with his stepgrandfather, who introduced him to the teeming metropolis. Mumford attended the prestigious Stuyvesant High School, but his academic record was mixed.

Lacking the credentials to gain admission to a traditional college or university, he enrolled at the City College of New York's evening program in fall of 1912. He toyed with the idea of pursuing an advanced degree in philosophy, but when he transferred to the more formally organized day program, he foundered academically once again. After being diagnosed with incipient tuberculosis, he withdrew from City College altogether; as a result, he would never earn his baccalaureate degree.

Although Mumford was already something of an autodidact, what truly saved him from spiraling into an unfocused adulthood was his reading of *Evolution*, a book cowritten by Patrick Geddes and J. Arthur Thomson and published in 1911. Mumford immediately grasped the implications of Geddes's essential thesis: that humankind's cultural evolution was akin to its biological evolution and that the former could be subjected to as careful a scientific scrutiny as the latter. The investigative tool that Geddes proffered was the regional survey, a sociocultural study of a region and its myriad inhabitants. Mesmerized, Mumford devoured other books by Geddes, and in the process, he determined to model his own career path after Geddes: not to become a specialist in one discipline, but rather, to embrace all disciplines. The city, as the summation of all of man's intellectual and practical activities, would become for Mumford, as it had already for Geddes, the subject around which he organized his myriad interests.

Not long after encountering Geddes's writings, Mumford read Ebenezer Howard's seminal planning treatise, *Garden Cities of To-morrow*. That Howard's Garden City neatly complemented Geddes's regionalism became almost immediately apparent to Mumford. With pen and notepad in hand, Mumford began to comb the city of his youth with his eyes freshly attuned to sights ranging from geological formations to real estate development patterns. The next several years proved to be a period of intensive urban study for Mumford, interrupted only briefly by a stateside tour of duty with the U.S. Navy near the end of World War I.

Mumford recognized the need to earn a living, especially after his 1921 marriage to Sophia Wittenberg, and thus, he began expanding his notes into published essays, articles, book reviews, and, eventually, books. As a freelance writer and critic, he explored such topics as architecture, literature, sociology, and politics in such publications as the *Journal of the American Institute of Architects*, the *Dial*, and the *New Republic*. In the early 1930s, Mumford began his long tenure as the *New Yorker*'s art and architecture critic, a position that permitted him to continue his regional surveys while earning a substantial income. As an architecture critic, he disavowed romantic revivalism while embracing such progressive currents as the organicism of Frank Lloyd Wright and the functionalism of various European modernists.

Writings and Advocacy

Two interrelated themes predominated in Mumford's early writings: the role of utopian ideals in the reconstruction of post–World War I society and the rediscovery of America's pre-1900 cultural roots as a means of reinvigorating creativity in the present. The first theme found a receptive audience via the publication of Mumford's first book, *The Story of Utopias* (1922). The first part of the book surveyed utopian writings from antiquity to the present, while the second part examined what Mumford called "collective utopias," essentially the social, political, and economic constraints that reified class boundaries. One might have expected Mumford to conclude his book with a call to Marxist revolution, but he instead imparted gentler prescriptions derived from Geddes's regional survey and Howard's Garden City. Mumford defined this new world order by the ancient Greek term *Eutopia*, roughly translated as "the good place," and he urged his readers to strive toward this goal when converting ideas into practice.

Although *The Story of Utopias* garnered positive notices, Mumford felt compelled to break free of Geddes's ideological hold in his next several books by exploring a new theme: America's cultural heritage. *Sticks and Stones* (1924) examined America's past from an architectural perspective and *The Golden Day* (1926) from a literary angle. *Herman Melville* (1929), a biography of the well-known author, and the *Brown Decades* (1931) amplified and corrected many of the observations contained in the earlier works. In all four books, Mumford presented evidence of a significant cultural efflorescence led by a distinguished group of writers, architects, artists, and other creative types in the mid-to-late nineteenth century. Moreover, in Mumford's view, some key figures—notably Alfred Stieglitz and Frank Lloyd Wright—had effectively bridged the nineteenth and twentieth centuries. These were the exemplars that Mumford challenged his contemporaries to emulate.

Even as Mumford's profile as a writer and critic rose significantly during the 1920s, so did his profile as a housing and community advocate. In 1923, he became a founding member of the Regional Planning Association of America. The association's membership was small and based largely in the New York metropolitan area but included some of the most progressive minds of the era: architects Clarence Stein, Frederick Ackerman, and Henry Wright; editor Charles Harris Whitaker; and conservationist Benton MacKaye. Mumford served as the association's secretary and general spokesman. Due in part to his influence, the association broadly embraced both Geddes's regional survey and Howard's Garden City. Geddes's imprint may be seen on the association's most famous project, the Appalachian Trail, a public–private wilderness easement along the mountainous areas of the eastern United States, which was conceived by MacKaye.

Howard's imprint may be seen in the association's focus on solving the nation's affordable housing shortage in the years following World War I. Toward this end, the association formed a subsidiary, the City Housing Corporation, to undertake the development of two planned communities: Sunnyside Gardens (1924–1928) in the New York City borough of Queens and Radburn (1928–1932) in northern New Jersey. Mumford and his wife moved to Sunnyside Gardens following the birth of their son, Geddes, in 1925; 11 years later, they made the rural village of Amenia in upstate New York their permanent home.

As the association's spokesman, Mumford wrote numerous articles and essays extolling its regionalist ideals. In May 1925, Mumford edited a special graphic issue of *The Survey* that featured essays on regional planning by many of the association's members; notably, it was Mumford's introductory essay, titled "Planning the Fourth Migration," that set the issue's ideological tenor. What he deemed the first migration was the pioneers' westward journey across North America. The second migration saw the clustering of settlers from farms into industrial towns, while the third migration saw an even greater movement of people from smaller towns into major cities. In Mumford's view, the fourth migration would reverse this flow. Improvements in transportation, communication, and the electrical power grid would negate the magnetic pull of the metropolis, making it possible for Americans to enjoy the benefits of big city life in smaller towns and even in the primeval wilderness. Mumford was essentially updating Howard's rationale for the Garden City, but advancing it to its logical conclusion: Evolving technology might make the Garden City itself obsolete. Six years later, he coauthored an influential article with Benton MacKaye on the "townless highway," in which Radburn's separation of traffic would be extended into the countryside via limited access highways to link similarly planned towns.

Master Works

By the early 1930s, Mumford was ready for new intellectual challenges. Eutopia, the overarching theme of his first book, returned to the forefront of his writings, and it would ultimately define the rest of his career. His next major project was a four-volume study of Western civilization known as *The Renewal of Life*. The series's expansive scope owed a great intellectual debt to Geddes, with the first volume, *Technics and Civilization* (1934), corresponding to Geddes's sociocultural category of work; the second, *The Culture of Cities* (1938), to his category of place; and the third and fourth, *The Condition of Man* (1944) and *The Conduct of Life* (1951), to his category of folk. On a more profound level, the project's core thesis was predicated on what Geddes's termed insurgency, a word that has, of course, unpleasant associations with war, but which Geddes used to describe a life force in the throes of renewing itself.

Of the books in the series, *The Culture of Cities* earned Mumford particular acclaim. *Time* magazine placed Mumford on its cover, and *Life* magazine ran a multipage photographic spread on the book. Invitations to consult on city and regional plans soon followed: Honolulu and Portland and the Pacific Northwest region in 1938, and London in 1943 and 1945, all resulting in significant essays. Mumford was not content to rest on his laurels, however. He became more politically active, writing two books that urged American involvement in World War II: *Men Must Act* (1939) and *Faith for Living* (1940). Outraged by the Allied bombings of Hiroshima and Nagasaki in August 1945, Mumford penned an article in March 1946 for the *Saturday Review of Literature* titled "Gentlemen, You are Mad!" becoming one of the first American intellectuals to warn of the perils of the nuclear age.

In 1945, he collected the Honolulu and London essays, along with several others, in an anthology titled *City Development*. The following year, he wrote a new introduction to *Garden Cities of Tomorrow,* re-presenting Howard's vision just as the British parliament passed enabling legislation for the construction of garden-city-style satellites known as the "new towns." Yet, when Mumford visited several of the new towns in person in 1953, he was disappointed by their general sprawl. Lansbury, a redeveloped, more compact neighborhood in East London, proved more to his liking. Other major cities, including Rotterdam, Marseilles, Rome, Athens, Philadelphia, and New York, endured his critical scrutiny during the 1950s.

Still, as Mumford aged, his relationship with cities in general changed. Although he would live intermittently in New York and other major cities, he became more an urban visitor than an urban resident. He was also slow to recognize how rapidly cities were being transformed, directly on the ground by the automobile and indirectly from the sky by the airplane, but once he did so, he sounded the alarm repeatedly. Subsequently, he would also rue the dismantling of the nation's passenger railroad system. Ironically, the man who had embraced

and had urged the mastery of technology in the 1920s and 1930s became in later years rather confounded by it. The regional surveyor slowly evolved into the regional oracle, quick to make solemn pronouncements on planning mishaps, but reluctant to give practical planning advice based on firsthand experience.

Mumford's disconnection with the modern city became glaringly apparent when, in 1962, he wrote a scathing review of Jane Jacobs's *Death and Life of Great America Cities* (1961). To Jacobs, the ideal neighborhood evolved over time, with a variety of functions, buildings, and residents, as represented by her own city block. Her essential thesis was, in fact, rather similar to Geddes's line of thinking a half century earlier, but Mumford failed to see this connection. Jacobs's book turned the planning profession upside down, paving the way to a more pluralistic—even postmodern—approach to revitalizing America's cities in the decades to come.

Nevertheless, the 1950s and 1960s proved to be extraordinarily productive for Mumford as a writer. He updated and revised several of his earlier books on American culture, and he collected many of his previously published articles and essays on architecture, planning, and other subjects into convenient anthologies. His most pressing concern, however, was the pall cast over modern civilization by the nuclear arms race and the cold war. *The Transformations of Man* (1956) was his attempt to condense the message of *The Renewal of Life* into a single, more accessible volume, but he recognized quickly that the original message would need to be expanded and bolstered for a new generation of readers.

The City in History (1961), arguably Mumford's most famous book, began as a revision of *The Culture of Cities.* Although the core chapters of the book remained essentially intact, Mumford bracketed them with wholly new sections on prehistoric and ancient cities and a new, rather pessimistic conclusion colored by the impending prospect of nuclear annihilation. Dire as its pronouncements were, *The City in History* was a critical and popular success, garnering Mumford the coveted National Book Award for Nonfiction in 1962. Mumford's last major work, the two-volume *Myth of the Machine* (1967, 1970), revisited the thesis of *Technics and Civilization* but posited an even bleaker world outlook in which scientific and military leaders were conspiring to bring civilization to its untimely end. In his view, Eutopia, the good place, would inevitably be bested by Utopia, the perfect place. Still, Mumford did not relinquish his faith in the ability of humankind to renew itself.

Were Mumford alive today, he would undoubtedly be in the forefront of the sustainability and green movements, advocating cleaner power, organic farming, and wilderness protection. To his small, somewhat isolated farmhouse, he would likely have welcomed the Internet and the television satellite, even as he would likely have cursed the superabundance of misinformation they sometimes deliver. Last, he would almost certainly be urging his readers to learn from their collective past while taking control of their present and future: to let shared human values guide their hopes and dreams rather than the machine and its empty materialistic promises.

Robert Wojtowicz

See also Geddes, Patrick; Intellectuals; Utopia

Further Readings

Miller, Donald L. 1989. *Lewis Mumford: A Life.* New York: Weidenfeld and Nicolson.

Mumford, Lewis. 1938. *The Renewal of Life.* Vol. 2, *The Culture of Cities.* New York: Harcourt, Brace.

———. 1945. *City Development: Studies in Disintegration and Renewal.* New York: Harcourt, Brace.

———. 1961. *The City in History: Its Origins, Its Transformations, and Its Prospects.* New York: Harcourt, Brace and World.

———. 1982. *Sketches from Life: The Autobiography of Lewis Mumford, The Early Years.* New York: Dial Press.

Wojtowicz, Robert. 1996. *Lewis Mumford and American Modernism: Eutopian Theories for Architecture and Urban Planning.* Cambridge, UK: Cambridge University Press.

MUSEUMS

The museum has been bound up with the emergence of urban civic cultures over the last two centuries. This entry looks at the emergence of the civic, metropolitan, and postmodern museum complexes, with the latter in the context of urban renewal initiatives, and examines how museums are embedded in cities and what urban cultures they support. It draws in the wider development of museum and preserved districts—as in the museum-ification of parts of cities. It connects the changing ways the world is presented in museums with our understandings of the world and the museum as a technology of cultural governance in the city.

The Birth of the Civic Museum

The modern civic museum emerged in the late eighteenth through nineteenth centuries. It emerged with the democratization of preservation from royal collections and princely *studiolo, wunderkamera* and cabinets of curiosities and their replacement with public collections. Key moments are often pointed to in different nations, be it Hans Sloane's donations initiating the British Museum in 1754; the purchase of the Angerstine collection of painting in 1824 to start London's National Gallery; James Smithson's bequest to found the Smithsonian in Washington, D.C., in 1854; or the postrevolutionary opening of royal collections using the former palace of the Louvre in Paris. Museums became vehicles for public education and civic improvement. We might determine two phases here, opening the collections and then developing the museum as an architectural form to house them. In terms of the latter, the nineteenth century is marked by the creation of built forms deemed able to carry through a civic mission.

Museums are technologies for producing social effects, tools of governance that as Tony Bennett argues operate in registers that are both civic and epistemological. That is, museums organize objects to be viewed and at the same time they organize the viewing public. Where formerly the intended viewer saw through the eyes of the monarch and the museum thus encoded royal power, civic arrangements created the viewer as the urban public. Museums helped create a sense of shared views on the world and knowledge about the world. They worked to categorize and order the world, positioning object and self in the rapidly changing world of the modern city. Museum displays deployed categorizations and classifications of objects in ways that appeared to convey universal secular truths. The typologies

The British Museum in London houses both national and world art and antiquities from ancient to modern times.

Source: Rachel Buyan.

and classifications made cultures and histories legible to the public.

Thus, the Louvre offered a survey of the development of art, categorized by periods and schools that it served to define, leading to the pinnacle of then contemporary (French) art. In the British Museum, the classification of ethnological artifacts served to help support the idea of races, peoples, and their evolutions and relationships. The national story becomes sublated into the great chain of being, where the march of civilization takes us ineluctably toward the pinnacle represented in the current city. The epistemology of the disembodied, depersonalized gaze of visual knowledge was transformed into physical form, where rooms and buildings spatialized categories and set material objects out as visual proof of the logic behind the museum.

This became a form of cultural governance inscribing identities through viewing positions—as a national public—and also a technology for mass instruction, where the democratic use of objects was intended to inculcate civic virtues via civic rituals. Thus, the visiting of galleries and museums became both an expression of civic belonging and a means of inculcating it.

As well as their internal organization, one can chart the ornamental exterior of museums as secular temples to learning and the celebration of national virtues. Over the nineteenth century, the hegemony of the neoclassical portico and form set the museum up as a shrine but to secular values of state and nation. Its pretensions to universal knowledge are symbolized by the debate between universal classical forms, exemplifying values of order through symmetry and geometry, and competing national built forms, such as mock Gothic in Britain, seen as celebrating the specific history of the nation. The entwining of universal and national values can be seen, for instance, in the British Museum's main south entrance which is a neoclassical frontage whose pediment by Sir Richard Westmacott interprets the Progress of Civilisation; within the entrance are memorials to staff who gave their lives in two world wars.

Metropolitan Museums

If museums individually used their internal spaces to discipline objects and make them useful for social narratives, then cumulatively they formed part of what Bennett called the emerging exhibitionary complex in the modern city. Thus, alongside zoos, world fairs, arcades, and department stores, museums are an arena for displaying objects to the public. They thus become a means for appealing to and managing urban attention as spectacles of modernity. They also framed the world as something to be seen and, more fundamentally, as something that could be seen—treating, in Mitchell's phrase, the world as exhibition.

The connection can be exemplified in the construction of Albertopolis as a complex of museums, knowledge establishments, and exhibitionary spaces in South Kensington in London. It is named after its inspiration, Prince Albert, who was the patron of the first Great Exhibition in 1851. When the exhibition closed, permanent exhibitions were built on the site, including the Science Museum and the Victoria and Albert Museum. Driver and Gilbert suggest this forms one point of what became an imperial display triangle anchored on Kensington, Whitehall, and Trafalgar Square creating a symbolically charged zone in the city. They formed part of a self-consciously imperial metropole. Promotional campaigns in the early twentieth century advertised the ability to take the underground to see all of the empire—botanical specimens at Kew, colonial embassies around the Strand, through to the Victoria and Albert museum with the reconstructed Gwalior Gate from India framing its oriental exhibitions entrance and the Imperial Institute offering "all the empire under one roof" in South Kensington.

Museums and collections created a sense of metropolitan centrality. They became technologies of global knowledge and power and centers of representation and calculation for the world. Artifacts and specimens were relocated from peripheral and exotic locations around the planet and placed together in these metropolitan centers, through networks of exchange and collection among artifacts and knowledge.

Postmodern Museums and Museumized Cities

Recently, there has been a shift away from the ideals of the civic museum with its implied educative goals and national or imperial subjects. Instead, museums have become connected to audiences by providing entertainment and emotional encounters—with reconstructions and dioramas and a profusion of new forms designed to attend to the demands of a more variegated public. The public addressed is no longer a singular mass audience but one splintered by age, taste, cultural identity, and so forth, with more specialist museums catering to different fractions. There has been significant new investment and formation of museums. Major initiatives now often speak not to a national mission but a global art and celebrity culture.

Brands of museums such as the Guggenheim have emerged, which can be coupled with spectacular architectural forms to offer hallmark developments in urban regeneration. The most celebrated example is the Guggenheim in Bilbao, which has transformed the image of a deindustrializing steel town into one of a cultural and tourist center through a globally iconic museum—whose architectural form is as potent in image as its contents. The museum's much emulated interlocking planes and curves speak of anything but a temple to civic ritual. Moreover, the location in a regional capital rather than a national one speaks to the ability of regional elites to use new institutions to renegotiate their political relations and the urban cultural hierarchy.

Museum developments have become part of a calculus over the value of culture as a means of economic redevelopment. Examples of parts of cities being refashioned from derelict industrial quarters and uses into museums and heritage centers are plentiful. In the United States, for instance,

Monterey, California, refashioned former canneries and docksides to resemble the cannery row depicted in Steinbeck's novel—the depiction the indignant city council at the time of publication had dismissed as almost entirely fallacious and misleading in its portrayal of the seedy side of life. In Lowell, Massachusetts, textile mills were refashioned as art spaces. In Britain, the Albert Docks in Liverpool became a restored complex hosting the art gallery Tate North; the Baltic Flour Mill in Gateshead became an art gallery; and the former Quays at Salford, just outside Manchester, now host the Lowry museum and the Imperial War Museum North. Or districts may be conserved as museum spaces themselves as in Australia where a derelict former working-class harbor district in Sydney is redeveloped to contain "the Rocks" or in Singapore, where the *godowns* and shophouses along the river are preserved as bars, restaurants, and clubs.

The museum developments often form state-led initiatives, which are intended to attract visitors while anchoring cultural quarters for media industries and the creative class. Salford Quays, for instance, is now the planned location for much of the BBC's production work. But such initiatives blur from specific museums being created to more general preservation districts, with mixtures of public and private control. From new museums in the city to the city as museum, all speak to the public through the market—as techniques of governance, they sell leisure experiences and urban environments as commodities rather than media of civic improvement.

Mike Crang

See also Bilbao, Spain; Creative Class; Cultural Heritage; Heritage City; Historic Cities; London, United Kingdom; Manchester, United Kingdom; Singapore

Further Readings

Bennett, T. 2004. *Pasts beyond Memory: Evolution, Museums, Colonialism, Museum Meanings*. London: Routledge.

———. 2005. "Civic Laboratories: Museums, Cultural Objecthood, and the Governance of the Social." *Cultural Studies* 19(5):521–47.

Driver, F. and D. Gilbert. 1998. "Heart of Empire? Landscape, Space, and Performance in Imperial London." *Environment & Planning D: Society and Space* 16:11–28.

Duncan, C. 1991. "Art Museums and the Ritual of Citizenship." Pp. 88–103 in *Exhibiting Cultures: The Politics and Poetics of Museum Display*, edited by I. Karp and S. Lavine. Washington, DC: Smithsonian Press.

Duncan, C. and A. Wallach. 1980. "The Universal Survey Museum." *Art History* 3(4):448–69.

Gilbert, D. and F. Driver. 2000. "Capital and Empire: Geographies of Imperial London." *GeoJournal* 51:3–32.

Hetherington, K. 2006. "Museum." *Theory, Culture, & Society* 23(2–3):597–603.

McNeill, D. 2000. "Mcguggenisation? National Identity and Globalisation in the Basque Country." *Political Geography* 19(4):473–94.

Mitchell, W. J. T. 1994. *Landscape and Power*. Chicago: University of Chicago Press.

Plaza, B. 2000. "Evaluating the Influence of a Large Cultural Artifact in the Attraction of Tourism: The Guggenheim Museum Bilbao Case." *Urban Affairs Review* 36:264–74.

Prior, N. 2002. *Museums and Modernity: Art Galleries and the Making of Modern Culture*. Oxford, UK: Berg.